# THE CIA WORLD FACTBOOK

## VOLUME 3

### FULL-SIZE
### 2019 EDITION

Portugal ~ Zimbabwe, Appendices

Central Intelligence Agency

**The CIA World Factbook Volume 3: Full-Size 2019 Edition**

**Giant Format, 600+ Pages: The #1 Global Reference, Complete & Unabridged - Vol. 3 of 3, Portugal ~ Zimbabwe, Appendices**

**Central Intelligence Agency**

This edition first published 2019 by Carlile Intelligence Library. "Carlile Intelligence Library" and its associated logos and devices are trademarks. Carlile Intelligence Library is an imprint of Carlile Media (a division of Creadyne Developments LLC). The appearance of U.S. Government visual information does not imply or constitute U.S. Government endorsement. This book is published for information purposes only.

New material copyright © 2019 Carlile Media. **All rights reserved.**

**Published in the United States of America.**

ISBN-13: 978-1-79299-741-9
ISBN-10: 1792997418

WWW.CARLILE.MEDIA

# TABLE OF CONTENTS

PORTUGAL :: 1

PUERTO RICO :: 9

QATAR :: 15

ROMANIA :: 22

RUSSIA :: 30

RWANDA :: 40

SAINT BARTHELMY :: 47

SAINT HELENA :: 50

SAINT KITTS AND NEVIS :: 56

SAINT LUCIA :: 62

SAINT MARTIN :: 68

SAINT PIERRE AND MIQUELON :: 71

SAINT VINCENT AND THE GRENADINES :: 76

SAMOA :: 83

SAN MARINO :: 89

SAO TOME AND PRINCIPE :: 94

SAUDI ARABIA :: 101

SENEGAL :: 109

SERBIA :: 117

SEYCHELLES :: 125

SIERRA LEONE :: 132

SINGAPORE :: 139

SINT MAAARTEN :: 146

SLOVAKIA :: 150

SLOVENIA :: 157

SOLOMON ISLANDS :: 165

SOMALIA :: 171

SOUTH AFRICA :: 179

SOUTH GEORGIA AND SOUTH SANDWICH ISLANDS :: 188

SOUTH SUDAN :: 190

SOUTHERN OCEAN :: 197

SPAIN :: 199

SPRATLY ISLANDS :: 208

SRI LANKA :: 210

SUDAN :: 218

SURINAME :: 226

SVALBARD :: 233

SWEDEN :: 236

SWITZERLAND :: 243

SYRIA :: 251

TAIWAN :: 260

TAJIKISTAN :: 267

TANZANIA :: 274

THAILAND :: 283

TIMOR-LESTE :: 292

TOGO :: 299

TOKELAU :: 306

TONGA :: 310

TRINIDAD AND TOBAGO :: 316

TUNISIA :: 323

TURKEY :: 331

TURKMENISTAN :: 340

TURKS AND CAICOS ISLANDS :: 347

TUVALU :: 352

UGANDA :: 357

UKRAINE :: 365

UNITED ARAB EMIRATES :: 374

UNITED KINGDOM :: 381

UNITED STATES :: 390

UNITED STATES PACIFIC ISLAND WILDLIFE REFUGES :: 400

URUGUAY :: 404

UZBEKISTAN :: 412

VANUATU :: 420

VENEZUALA :: 427

VIETNAM :: 436

VIRGIN ISLANDS :: 444

WAKE ISLAND :: 449

WALLIS AND FUTUNA :: 451

WEST BANK :: 455

WESTERN SAHARA :: 461

YEMEN :: 466

ZAMBIA :: 474

ZIMBABWE :: 481

APPENDIX A :: ABBREVIATIONS :: 489

APPENDIX B :: INTERNATIONAL ORGANIZATIONS AND GROUPS :: 502

APPENDIX C :: SELECTED ENVIRONMENTAL AGREEMENTS :: 539

APPENDIX D :: CROSS-REFERENCE LIST OF COUNTRY DATA CODES :: 549

APPENDIX E :: CROSS-REFERENCE LIST OF HYDROGRAPHIC DATA CODES :: 559

APPENDIX F :: CROSS-REFERENCE LIST OF GEOGRAPHIC NAMES :: 560

# APPENDIX G :: WEIGHTS AND MEASURES :: 608

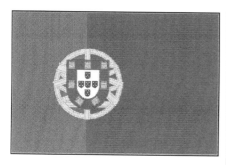

# EUROPE :: PORTUGAL

## INTRODUCTION :: PORTUGAL

### BACKGROUND:

Following its heyday as a global maritime power during the 15th and 16th centuries, Portugal lost much of its wealth and status with the destruction of Lisbon in a 1755 earthquake, occupation during the Napoleonic Wars, and the independence of Brazil, its wealthiest colony, in 1822. A 1910 revolution deposed the monarchy; for most of the next six decades, repressive governments ran the country. In 1974, a left-wing military coup installed broad democratic reforms. The following year, Portugal granted independence to all of its African colonies. Portugal is a founding member of NATO and entered the EC (now the EU) in 1986.

## GEOGRAPHY :: PORTUGAL

### LOCATION:
Southwestern Europe, bordering the North Atlantic Ocean, west of Spain

### GEOGRAPHIC COORDINATES:
39 30 N, 8 00 W

### MAP REFERENCES:
Europe

### AREA:
total: 92,090 sq km

land: 91,470 sq km

water: 620 sq km

note: includes Azores and Madeira Islands

country comparison to the world: 112

### AREA - COMPARATIVE:
slightly smaller than Virginia

### LAND BOUNDARIES:
total: 1,224 km

border countries (1): Spain 1224 km

### COASTLINE:
1,793 km

### MARITIME CLAIMS:
territorial sea: 12 nm

exclusive economic zone: 200 nm

contiguous zone: 24 nm

continental shelf: 200-m depth or to the depth of exploitation

### CLIMATE:
maritime temperate; cool and rainy in north, warmer and drier in south

### TERRAIN:
the west-flowing Tagus River divides the country: the north is mountainous toward the interior, while the south is characterized by rolling plains

### ELEVATION:
mean elevation: 372 m

elevation extremes: 0 m lowest point: Atlantic Ocean

2351 highest point: Ponta do Pico (Pico or Pico Alto) on Ilha do Pico in the Azores

### NATURAL RESOURCES:
fish, forests (cork), iron ore, copper, zinc, tin, tungsten, silver, gold,

uranium, marble, clay, gypsum, salt, arable land, hydropower

## LAND USE:

**agricultural land:** 39.7% (2011 est.)

**arable land:** 11.9% (2011 est.) / **permanent crops:** 7.8% (2011 est.) / **permanent pasture:** 20% (2011 est.)

**forest:** 37.8% (2011 est.)

**other:** 22.5% (2011 est.)

## IRRIGATED LAND:

5,400 sq km (2012)

## POPULATION DISTRIBUTION:

concentrations are primarily along or near the Atlantic coast; both Lisbon and the second largest city, Porto, are coastal cities

## NATURAL HAZARDS:

Azores subject to severe earthquakes

**volcanism:** limited volcanic activity in the Azores Islands; Fayal or Faial (1,043 m) last erupted in 1958; most volcanoes have not erupted in centuries; historically active volcanoes include Agua de Pau, Furnas, Pico, Picos Volcanic System, San Jorge, Sete Cidades, and Terceira

## ENVIRONMENT - CURRENT ISSUES:

soil erosion; air pollution caused by industrial and vehicle emissions; water pollution, especially in urban centers and coastal areas

## ENVIRONMENT - INTERNATIONAL AGREEMENTS:

**party to:** Air Pollution, Biodiversity, Climate Change, Climate Change-Kyoto Protocol, Desertification, Endangered Species, Hazardous Wastes, Law of the Sea, Marine Dumping, Marine Life Conservation, Ozone Layer Protection, Ship Pollution, Tropical Timber 83, Tropical Timber 94, Wetlands, Whaling

**signed, but not ratified:** Air Pollution-Persistent Organic Pollutants, Air Pollution-Volatile Organic Compounds, Environmental Modification

## GEOGRAPHY - NOTE:

Azores and Madeira Islands occupy strategic locations along western sea approaches to Strait of Gibraltar

# PEOPLE AND SOCIETY :: PORTUGAL

## POPULATION:

10,355,493 (July 2018 est.)

**country comparison to the world:** 87

## NATIONALITY:

**noun:** Portuguese (singular and plural)

**adjective:** Portuguese

## ETHNIC GROUPS:

white homogeneous Mediterranean population; citizens of black African descent who immigrated to mainland during decolonization number less than 100,000; since 1990, Eastern Europeans have migrated to Portugal

## LANGUAGES:

Portuguese (official), Mirandese (official, but locally used)

## RELIGIONS:

Roman Catholic 81%, other Christian 3.3%, other (includes Jewish, Muslim, other) 0.6%, none 6.8%, unspecified 8.3% (2011 est.)

**note:** represents population 15 years of age and older

## AGE STRUCTURE:

**0-14 years:** 14.01% (male 743,277 /female 707,437)

**15-24 years:** 10.89% (male 580,709 /female 546,908)

**25-54 years:** 42.04% (male 2,143,735 /female 2,209,736)

**55-64 years:** 12.8% (male 605,113 /female 720,192)

**65 years and over:** 20.26% (male 838,606 /female 1,259,780) (2018 est.)

## DEPENDENCY RATIOS:

**total dependency ratio:** 53.4 (2015 est.)

**youth dependency ratio:** 21.6 (2015 est.)

**elderly dependency ratio:** 31.8 (2015 est.)

**potential support ratio:** 3.1 (2015 est.)

## MEDIAN AGE:

**total:** 43.7 years

**male:** 41.8 years

**female:** 45.6 years (2018 est.)

**country comparison to the world:** 17

## POPULATION GROWTH RATE:

-0.27% (2018 est.)

**country comparison to the world:** 216

## BIRTH RATE:

8.2 births/1,000 population (2018 est.)

**country comparison to the world:** 220

## DEATH RATE:

10.6 deaths/1,000 population (2018 est.)

**country comparison to the world:** 25

## NET MIGRATION RATE:

2.5 migrant(s)/1,000 population (2017 est.)

**country comparison to the world:** 37

## POPULATION DISTRIBUTION:

concentrations are primarily along or near the Atlantic coast; both Lisbon and the second largest city, Porto, are coastal cities

## URBANIZATION:

**urban population:** 65.2% of total population (2018)

**rate of urbanization:** 0.47% annual rate of change (2015-20 est.)

## MAJOR URBAN AREAS - POPULATION:

2.927 million LISBON (capital), 1.307 million Porto (2018)

## SEX RATIO:

**at birth:** 1.07 male(s)/female (2017 est.)

**0-14 years:** 1.09 male(s)/female (2017 est.)

**15-24 years:** 1.13 male(s)/female (2017 est.)

**25-54 years:** 1.03 male(s)/female (2017 est.)

**55-64 years:** 0.88 male(s)/female (2017 est.)

**65 years and over:** 0.69 male(s)/female (2017 est.)

**total population:** 0.96 male(s)/female (2017 est.)

## MOTHER'S MEAN AGE AT FIRST BIRTH:

30.2 years (2015 est.)

## MATERNAL MORTALITY RATE:

10 deaths/100,000 live births (2015 est.)

**country comparison to the world:** 149

## INFANT MORTALITY RATE:

**total:** 2.6 deaths/1,000 live births (2018 est.)

**male:** 3 deaths/1,000 live births (2018 est.)

**female:** 2.2 deaths/1,000 live births (2018 est.)

**country comparison to the world:** 215

## LIFE EXPECTANCY AT BIRTH:

**total population:** 80.9 years (2018 est.)

**male:** 77.7 years (2018 est.)

**female:** 84.2 years (2018 est.)

country comparison to the world: 38

**TOTAL FERTILITY RATE:**

1.39 children born/woman (2018 est.)

country comparison to the world: 213

**CONTRACEPTIVE PREVALENCE RATE:**

73.9% (2014)

**HEALTH EXPENDITURES:**

9.5% of GDP (2014)

country comparison to the world: 31

**PHYSICIANS DENSITY:**

4.43 physicians/1,000 population (2014)

**HOSPITAL BED DENSITY:**

3.4 beds/1,000 population (2013)

**DRINKING WATER SOURCE:**

improved:

urban: 100% of population (2015 est.)
rural: 100% of population (2015 est.)
total: 100% of population (2015 est.)

unimproved:

urban: 0% of population (2015 est.)
rural: 0% of population (2015 est.)
total: 0% of population (2015 est.)

**SANITATION FACILITY ACCESS:**

improved:

urban: 99.6% of population (2015 est.)
rural: 99.8% of population (2015 est.)
total: 99.7% of population (2015 est.)

unimproved:

urban: 0.4% of population (2015 est.)
rural: 0.2% of population (2015 est.)
total: 0.3% of population (2015 est.)

**HIV/AIDS - ADULT PREVALENCE RATE:**

0.6% (2017 est.)

country comparison to the world: 61

**HIV/AIDS - PEOPLE LIVING WITH HIV/AIDS:**

40,000 (2017 est.)

country comparison to the world: 66

**HIV/AIDS - DEATHS:**

<500 (2017 est.)

**OBESITY - ADULT PREVALENCE RATE:**

20.8% (2016)

country comparison to the world: 95

**EDUCATION EXPENDITURES:**

5.1% of GDP (2014)

country comparison to the world: 70

**LITERACY:**

definition: age 15 and over can read and write (2015 est.)

total population: 95.7% (2015 est.)

male: 97.1% (2015 est.)

female: 94.4% (2015 est.)

**SCHOOL LIFE EXPECTANCY (PRIMARY TO TERTIARY EDUCATION):**

total: 17 years (2014)

male: 17 years (2014)

female: 17 years (2014)

**UNEMPLOYMENT, YOUTH AGES 15-24:**

total: 23.9% (2017 est.)

male: 22.4% (2017 est.)

female: 25.5% (2017 est.)

country comparison to the world: 51

## GOVERNMENT :: PORTUGAL

**COUNTRY NAME:**

conventional long form: Portuguese Republic

conventional short form: Portugal

local long form: Republica Portuguesa

local short form: Portugal

etymology: name derives from the Roman designation "Portus Cale" meaning "Port of Cale"; Cale was an ancient Celtic town and port in present-day northern Portugal

**GOVERNMENT TYPE:**

semi-presidential republic

**CAPITAL:**

name: Lisbon

geographic coordinates: 38 43 N, 9 08 W

time difference: UTC 0 (5 hours ahead of Washington, DC, during Standard Time)

daylight saving time: +1hr, begins last Sunday in March; ends last Sunday in October

note: Portugal has two time zones, including the Azores (UTC-1)

**ADMINISTRATIVE DIVISIONS:**

18 districts (distritos, singular - distrito) and 2 autonomous regions* (regioes autonomas, singular - regiao autonoma); Aveiro, Acores (Azores)*, Beja, Braga, Braganca, Castelo Branco, Coimbra, Evora, Faro, Guarda, Leiria, Lisboa (Lisbon), Madeira*, Portalegre, Porto, Santarem, Setubal, Viana do Castelo, Vila Real, Viseu

**INDEPENDENCE:**

1143 (Kingdom of Portugal recognized);1 December 1640 (independence reestablished following 60-years of Spanish rule);5 October 1910 (republic proclaimed)

**NATIONAL HOLIDAY:**

Portugal Day (Dia de Portugal), 10 June (1580); note - also called Camoes Day, the day that revered national poet Luis DE CAMOES (1524-80) died

**CONSTITUTION:**

history: several previous; latest adopted 2 April 1976, effective 25 April 1976 (2016)

amendments: proposed by the Assembly of the Republic; adoption requires two-thirds majority vote of Assembly members; amended several times, last in 2005 (2016)

**LEGAL SYSTEM:**

civil law system; Constitutional Court review of legislative acts

**INTERNATIONAL LAW ORGANIZATION PARTICIPATION:**

accepts compulsory ICJ jurisdiction with reservations; accepts ICCt jurisdiction

**CITIZENSHIP:**

citizenship by birth: no

citizenship by descent only: at least one parent must be a citizen of Portugal

dual citizenship recognized: yes

residency requirement for naturalization: 10 years; 6 years if from a Portuguese-speaking country

**SUFFRAGE:**

18 years of age; universal

**EXECUTIVE BRANCH:**

chief of state: President Marcelo REBELO DE SOUSA (since 9 March 2016)

head of government: Prime Minister Antonio Luis Santos da COSTA (since 24 November 2015)

cabinet: Council of Ministers appointed by the president on the recommendation of the prime minister

elections/appointments: president directly elected by absolute majority popular vote in 2 rounds if needed for a 5-year term (eligible for a second term); election last held on 24 January

2016 (next to be held in January 2021); following legislative elections the leader of the majority party or majority coalition is usually appointed prime minister by the president

**election results:** Marcelo REBELO DE SOUSA elected president in the first round; percent of vote - Marcelo REBELO DE SOUSA (PSD) 52%, Antonio Sampaio da NOVA (independent) 22.9%, Marisa MATISA (BE) 10.1%, Maria de BELEM (independent) 4.2%, other 10.8%

**note:** there is also a Council of State that acts as a consultative body to the president

## LEGISLATIVE BRANCH:

**description:** unicameral Assembly of the Republic or Assembleia da Republica (230 seats; 226 members directly elected in multi-seat constituencies by proportional representation vote and 4 members - 2 each in 2 constituencies representing Portuguese living abroad - directly elected by proportional representation vote; members serve 4-year terms)

**elections:** last held on 4 October 2015 (next to be held by October 2019)

**election results:** percent of vote by party - PaF 36.9%, PS 32.3%, B.E. 10.2%, CDU 8.3%, PPD/PSD (Azores and Madeira) 1.5%, PAN 1.4%, other 9.4%; seats by party - PaF 102, PS 86, B.E. 19, CDU 17, PPD/PSD (Azores and Madeira) 5, PAN 1; composition - men 158, women 72, percent of women 31.3%

## JUDICIAL BRANCH:

**highest courts:** Supreme Court or Supremo Tribunal de Justica (consists of 12 justices); Constitutional Court or Tribunal Constitucional (consists of 13 judges)

**judge selection and term of office:** Supreme Court justices nominated by the president and appointed by the Assembly of the Republic; judges appointed for life; Constitutional Court judges - 10 elected by the Assembly and 3 elected by the other Constitutional Court judges; judges elected for 6-year non-renewable terms

**subordinate courts:** Supreme Administrative Court (Supremo Tribunal Administrativo); Audit Court (Tribunal de Contas); appellate, district, and municipal courts

## POLITICAL PARTIES AND LEADERS:

Democratic and Social Center/Popular Party or CDS-PP [Assuncao CRISTAS]
Ecologist Party "The Greens" or PEV [Heloisa APOLONiA]
People_Animals_Nature Party or PAN [Andre SILVA]
Portuguese Communist Party or PCP [Jeronimo DE SOUSA]
Social Democratic Party or PPD/SD [Rui RIO]
Socialist Party or PS [Antonio COSTA]
The Left Bloc or BE or o Bloco [Catarina MARTINS]
Unitary Democratic Coalition or CDU [Jeronimo DE SOUSA] (includes PCP and PEV)

## INTERNATIONAL ORGANIZATION PARTICIPATION:

ADB (nonregional member), AfDB (nonregional member), Australia Group, BIS, CD, CE, CERN, CPLP, EAPC, EBRD, ECB, EIB, EMU, ESA, EU, FAO, FATF, IADB, IAEA, IBRD, ICAO, ICC (national committees), ICCt, ICRM, IDA, IEA, IFAD, IFC, IFRCS, IHO, ILO, IMF, IMO, IMSO, Interpol, IOC, IOM, IPU, ISO, ITSO, ITU, ITUC (NGOs), LAIA (observer), MIGA, MINUSMA, NATO, NEA, NSG, OAS (observer), OECD, OPCW, OSCE, Pacific Alliance (observer), Paris Club (associate), PCA, Schengen Convention, SELEC (observer), UN, UNCTAD, UNESCO, UNHCR, UNIDO, Union Latina, UNWTO, UPU, WCO, WFTU (NGOs), WHO, WIPO, WMO, WTO, ZC

## DIPLOMATIC REPRESENTATION IN THE US:

**chief of mission:** Ambassador Domingos Teixeira de Abreu FEZAS VITAL (since 28 January 2016)

**chancery:** 2012 Massachusetts Avenue NW, Washington, DC 20036

**telephone:** [1] (202) 328-8610

**FAX:** [1] (202) 462-3726

**consulate(s) general:** Boston, New York, San Francisco

**consulate(s):** New Bedford (MA), Newark (NJ), Providence (RI)

## DIPLOMATIC REPRESENTATION FROM THE US:

**chief of mission:** Ambassador George E. GLASS (since 25 August 2017)

**embassy:** Avenida das Forcas Armadas, 1600-081 Lisbon

**mailing address:** Apartado 43033, 1601-301 Lisboa; PSC 83, APO AE 09726

**telephone:** [351] (21) 727-3300

**FAX:** [351] (21) 726-9109

**consulate(s):** Ponta Delgada (Azores)

## FLAG DESCRIPTION:

two vertical bands of green (hoist side, two-fifths) and red (three-fifths) with the national coat of arms (armillary sphere and Portuguese shield) centered on the dividing line; explanations for the color meanings are ambiguous, but a popular interpretation has green symbolizing hope and red the blood of those defending the nation

## NATIONAL SYMBOL(S):

armillary sphere (a spherical astrolabe modeling objects in the sky and representing the Republic); national colors: red, green

## NATIONAL ANTHEM:

**name:** "A Portugesa" (The Song of the Portuguese)

**lyrics/music:** Henrique LOPES DE MENDOCA/Alfredo KEIL

**note:** adopted 1910; "A Portuguesa" was originally written to protest the Portuguese monarchy's acquiescence to the 1890 British ultimatum forcing Portugal to give up areas of Africa; the lyrics refer to the "insult" that resulted from the event

# ECONOMY :: PORTUGAL

## ECONOMY - OVERVIEW:

Portugal has become a diversified and increasingly service-based economy since joining the European Community - the EU's predecessor - in 1986. Over the following two decades, successive governments privatized many state-controlled firms and liberalized key areas of the economy, including the financial and telecommunications sectors. The country joined the Economic and Monetary Union in 1999 and began circulating the euro on 1 January 2002 along with 11 other EU members.

The economy grew by more than the EU average for much of the 1990s, but the rate of growth slowed in 2001-08. After the global financial crisis in 2008, Portugal's economy contracted in 2009 and fell into recession from 2011 to 2013, as the government implemented spending cuts and tax increases to comply with conditions of an EU-IMF financial rescue package, signed in May 2011. Portugal successfully exited its EU-IMF program in May 2014, and its economic recovery gained traction in 2015 because of strong exports and a rebound in private consumption. GDP growth accelerated in 2016, and probably reached 2.5 % in 2017.

Unemployment remained high, at 9.7% in 2017, but has improved steadily since peaking at 18% in 2013.

The center-left minority Socialist government has unwound some unpopular austerity measures while managing to remain within most EU fiscal targets. The budget deficit fell from 11.2% of GDP in 2010 to 1.8% in 2017, the country's lowest since democracy was restored in 1974, and surpassing the EU and IMF projections of 3%. Portugal exited the EU's excessive deficit procedure in mid-2017.

## GDP (PURCHASING POWER PARITY):

$314.1 billion (2017 est.)

$305.9 billion (2016 est.)

$301 billion (2015 est.)

note: data are in 2017 dollars

country comparison to the world: 55

## GDP (OFFICIAL EXCHANGE RATE):

$218 billion (2017 est.) (2017 est.)

## GDP - REAL GROWTH RATE:

2.7% (2017 est.)

1.6% (2016 est.)

1.8% (2015 est.)

country comparison to the world: 126

## GDP - PER CAPITA (PPP):

$30,500 (2017 est.)

$29,600 (2016 est.)

$29,100 (2015 est.)

note: data are in 2017 dollars

country comparison to the world: 67

## GROSS NATIONAL SAVING:

16.8% of GDP (2017 est.)

16.1% of GDP (2016 est.)

15.9% of GDP (2015 est.)

country comparison to the world: 124

## GDP - COMPOSITION, BY END USE:

household consumption: 65.1% (2017 est.)

government consumption: 17.6% (2017 est.)

investment in fixed capital: 16.2% (2017 est.)

investment in inventories: 0.1% (2017 est.)

exports of goods and services: 43.1% (2017 est.)

imports of goods and services: -42.1% (2017 est.)

## GDP - COMPOSITION, BY SECTOR OF ORIGIN:

agriculture: 2.2% (2017 est.)

industry: 22.1% (2017 est.)

services: 75.7% (2017 est.)

## AGRICULTURE - PRODUCTS:

grain, potatoes, tomatoes, olives, grapes; sheep, cattle, goats, pigs, poultry, dairy products; fish

## INDUSTRIES:

textiles, clothing, footwear, wood and cork, paper and pulp, chemicals, fuels and lubricants, automobiles and auto parts, base metals, minerals, porcelain and ceramics, glassware, technology, telecommunications; dairy products, wine, other foodstuffs; ship construction and refurbishment; tourism, plastics, financial services, optics

## INDUSTRIAL PRODUCTION GROWTH RATE:

3.5% (2017 est.)

country comparison to the world: 89

## LABOR FORCE:

5.233 million (2017 est.)

country comparison to the world: 80

## LABOR FORCE - BY OCCUPATION:

agriculture: 8.6%

industry: 23.9%

services: 67.5% (2014 est.)

## UNEMPLOYMENT RATE:

8.9% (2017 est.)

11.1% (2016 est.)

country comparison to the world: 127

## POPULATION BELOW POVERTY LINE:

19% (2015 est.)

## HOUSEHOLD INCOME OR CONSUMPTION BY PERCENTAGE SHARE:

lowest 10%: 25.9% (2015 est.)

highest 10%: 25.9% (2015 est.)

## DISTRIBUTION OF FAMILY INCOME - GINI INDEX:

33.9 (2015 est.)

34 (2014 est.)

country comparison to the world: 108

## BUDGET:

revenues: 93.55 billion (2017 est.)

expenditures: 100 billion (2017 est.)

## TAXES AND OTHER REVENUES:

42.9% (of GDP) (2017 est.)

country comparison to the world: 29

## BUDGET SURPLUS (+) OR DEFICIT (-):

-3% (of GDP) (2017 est.)

country comparison to the world: 134

## PUBLIC DEBT:

125.7% of GDP (2017 est.)

129.9% of GDP (2016 est.)

note: data cover general government debt and include debt instruments issued (or owned) by government entities other than the treasury; the data include treasury debt held by foreign entities; the data include debt issued by subnational entities, as well as intragovernmental debt; intragovernmental debt consists of treasury borrowings from surpluses in the social funds, such as for retirement, medical care, and unemployment; debt instruments for the social funds are not sold at public auctions

country comparison to the world: 9

## FISCAL YEAR:

calendar year

## INFLATION RATE (CONSUMER PRICES):

1.6% (2017 est.)

0.6% (2016 est.)

country comparison to the world: 91

## CENTRAL BANK DISCOUNT RATE:

0% (2016)

0.05% (2015)

note: this is the European Central Bank's rate on the marginal lending facility, which offers overnight credit to banks in the euro area

country comparison to the world: 159

## COMMERCIAL BANK PRIME LENDING RATE:

3.21% (31 December 2017 est.)

3.77% (31 December 2016 est.)

country comparison to the world: 171

## STOCK OF NARROW MONEY:

$106.8 billion (31 December 2017 est.)

$81.15 billion (31 December 2016 est.)

note: see entry for the European Union for money supply for the entire euro area; the European Central Bank (ECB) controls monetary policy for the 18 members of the Economic and Monetary Union (EMU); individual members of the EMU do not control the quantity of money circulating within their own borders

country comparison to the world: 38

## STOCK OF BROAD MONEY:

$106.8 billion (31 December 2017 est.)

$81.15 billion (31 December 2016 est.)

country comparison to the world: 38

**STOCK OF DOMESTIC CREDIT:**

$356.8 billion (31 December 2017 est.)

$311.6 billion (31 December 2016 est.)

country comparison to the world: 32

**MARKET VALUE OF PUBLICLY TRADED SHARES:**

$59.84 billion (31 December 2015 est.)

$57.77 billion (31 December 2014 est.)

$79.18 billion (31 December 2013 est.)

country comparison to the world: 47

**CURRENT ACCOUNT BALANCE:**

$993 million (2017 est.)

$1.218 billion (2016 est.)

country comparison to the world: 49

**EXPORTS:**

$61 billion (2017 est.)

$54.76 billion (2016 est.)

country comparison to the world: 47

**EXPORTS - PARTNERS:**

Spain 25.2%, France 12.5%, Germany 11.3%, UK 6.6%, US 5.2%, Netherlands 4% (2017)

**EXPORTS - COMMODITIES:**

agricultural products, foodstuffs, wine, oil products, chemical products, plastics and rubber, hides, leather, wood and cork, wood pulp and paper, textile materials, clothing, footwear, machinery and tools, base metals

**IMPORTS:**

$74.73 billion (2017 est.)

$64.98 billion (2016 est.)

country comparison to the world: 45

**IMPORTS - COMMODITIES:**

agricultural products, chemical products, vehicles and other transport material, optical and precision instruments, computer accessories and parts, semiconductors and related devices, oil products, base metals, food products, textile materials

**IMPORTS - PARTNERS:**

Spain 32%, Germany 13.7%, France 7.4%, Italy 5.5%, Netherlands 5.4% (2017)

**RESERVES OF FOREIGN EXCHANGE AND GOLD:**

$26.11 billion (31 December 2017 est.)

$19.4 billion (31 December 2015 est.)

country comparison to the world: 55

**DEBT - EXTERNAL:**

$449 billion (31 March 2016 est.)

$447 billion (31 March 2015 est.)

country comparison to the world: 27

**STOCK OF DIRECT FOREIGN INVESTMENT - AT HOME:**

$185.7 billion (31 December 2017 est.)

$147.1 billion (31 December 2016 est.)

country comparison to the world: 33

**STOCK OF DIRECT FOREIGN INVESTMENT - ABROAD:**

$103.1 billion (31 December 2017 est.)

$84.73 billion (31 December 2016 est.)

country comparison to the world: 34

**EXCHANGE RATES:**

euros (EUR) per US dollar -

0.885 (2017 est.)

0.903 (2016 est.)

0.9214 (2015 est.)

0.7525 (2014 est.)

0.7634 (2013 est.)

## ENERGY :: PORTUGAL

**ELECTRICITY ACCESS:**

electrification - total population: 100% (2016)

**ELECTRICITY - PRODUCTION:**

56.9 billion kWh (2016 est.)

country comparison to the world: 51

**ELECTRICITY - CONSUMPTION:**

46.94 billion kWh (2016 est.)

country comparison to the world: 52

**ELECTRICITY - EXPORTS:**

9.701 billion kWh (2016 est.)

country comparison to the world: 21

**ELECTRICITY - IMPORTS:**

4.616 billion kWh (2016 est.)

country comparison to the world: 40

**ELECTRICITY - INSTALLED GENERATING CAPACITY:**

20.56 million kW (2016 est.)

country comparison to the world: 43

**ELECTRICITY - FROM FOSSIL FUELS:**

41% of total installed capacity (2016 est.)

country comparison to the world: 168

**ELECTRICITY - FROM NUCLEAR FUELS:**

0% of total installed capacity (2017 est.)

country comparison to the world: 167

**ELECTRICITY - FROM HYDROELECTRIC PLANTS:**

25% of total installed capacity (2017 est.)

country comparison to the world: 78

**ELECTRICITY - FROM OTHER RENEWABLE SOURCES:**

35% of total installed capacity (2017 est.)

country comparison to the world: 10

**CRUDE OIL - PRODUCTION:**

0 bbl/day (2017 est.)

country comparison to the world: 186

**CRUDE OIL - EXPORTS:**

0 bbl/day (2017 est.)

country comparison to the world: 180

**CRUDE OIL - IMPORTS:**

285,200 bbl/day (2017 est.)

country comparison to the world: 26

**CRUDE OIL - PROVED RESERVES:**

0 bbl (1 January 2018 est.)

country comparison to the world: 182

**REFINED PETROLEUM PRODUCTS - PRODUCTION:**

323,000 bbl/day (2017 est.)

country comparison to the world: 39

**REFINED PETROLEUM PRODUCTS - CONSUMPTION:**

247,200 bbl/day (2017 est.)

country comparison to the world: 51

**REFINED PETROLEUM PRODUCTS - EXPORTS:**

143,500 bbl/day (2017 est.)

country comparison to the world: 36

**REFINED PETROLEUM PRODUCTS - IMPORTS:**

78,700 bbl/day (2017 est.)

country comparison to the world: 64

**NATURAL GAS - PRODUCTION:**

0 cu m (2017 est.)

country comparison to the world: 184

**NATURAL GAS - CONSUMPTION:**

6.258 billion cu m (2017 est.)

country comparison to the world: 54

**NATURAL GAS - EXPORTS:**

0 cu m (2017 est.)

country comparison to the world: 169

**NATURAL GAS - IMPORTS:**

6.541 billion cu m (2017 est.)

country comparison to the world: 30

**NATURAL GAS - PROVED RESERVES:**

0 cu m (1 January 2014 est.)

country comparison to the world: 182

**CARBON DIOXIDE EMISSIONS FROM CONSUMPTION OF ENERGY:**

54.97 million Mt (2017 est.)

country comparison to the world: 57

# COMMUNICATIONS :: PORTUGAL

## TELEPHONES - FIXED LINES:

total subscriptions: 4,831,022 (2017 est.)

subscriptions per 100 inhabitants: 45 (2017 est.)

country comparison to the world: 29

## TELEPHONES - MOBILE CELLULAR:

total subscriptions: 11,764,106 (2017 est.)

subscriptions per 100 inhabitants: 109 (2017 est.)

country comparison to the world: 78

## TELEPHONE SYSTEM:

general assessment: Portugal's telephone system has a state-of-the-art network with broadband, high-speed capabilities (2015)

domestic: integrated network of coaxial cables, open-wire, microwave radio relay, and domestic satellite earth stations (2015)

international: country code - 351; a combination of submarine cables provide connectivity to Europe, North and East Africa, South Africa, the Middle East, Asia, and the US; satellite earth stations - 3 Intelsat (2 Atlantic Ocean and 1 Indian Ocean), NA Eutelsat; tropospheric scatter to Azores (2015)

## BROADCAST MEDIA:

Radio e Televisao de Portugal (RTP), the publicly owned TV broadcaster, operates 4 domestic channels and external service channels to Africa; overall, roughly 40 domestic TV stations; viewers have widespread access to international broadcasters with more than half of all households connected to multi-channel cable or satellite TV systems; publicly owned radio operates 3 national networks and provides regional and external services; several privately owned national radio stations and some 300 regional and local commercial radio stations (2014)

## INTERNET COUNTRY CODE:

.pt

## INTERNET USERS:

total: 7,629,560 (July 2016 est.)

percent of population: 70.4% (July 2016 est.)

country comparison to the world: 56

## BROADBAND - FIXED SUBSCRIPTIONS:

total: 3,574,047 (2017 est.)

subscriptions per 100 inhabitants: 33 (2017 est.)

country comparison to the world: 34

# TRANSPORTATION :: PORTUGAL

## NATIONAL AIR TRANSPORT SYSTEM:

number of registered air carriers: 12 (2015)

inventory of registered aircraft operated by air carriers: 122 (2015)

annual passenger traffic on registered air carriers: 12,635,233 (2015)

annual freight traffic on registered air carriers: 343,971,094 mt-km (2015)

## CIVIL AIRCRAFT REGISTRATION COUNTRY CODE PREFIX:

CR, CS (2016)

## AIRPORTS:

64 (2013)

country comparison to the world: 77

## AIRPORTS - WITH PAVED RUNWAYS:

total: 43 (2017)

over 3,047 m: 5 (2017)

2,438 to 3,047 m: 7 (2017)

1,524 to 2,437 m: 8 (2017)

914 to 1,523 m: 15 (2017)

under 914 m: 8 (2017)

## AIRPORTS - WITH UNPAVED RUNWAYS:

total: 21 (2013)

914 to 1,523 m: 1 (2013)

under 914 m: 20 (2013)

## PIPELINES:

1344 km gas, 11 km oil, 188 km refined products (2013)

## RAILWAYS:

total: 3,075 km (2014)

narrow gauge: 108.1 km 1.000-m gauge (2014)

broad gauge: 2,439 km 1.668-m gauge (1,633.4 km electrified) (2014)

other: 528 km (gauge unspecified) (2014)

country comparison to the world: 60

## ROADWAYS:

total: 82,900 km (2008)

paved: 71,294 km (includes 2,613 km of expressways) (2008)

unpaved: 11,606 km (2008)

country comparison to the world: 60

## WATERWAYS:

210 km (on Douro River from Porto) (2011)

country comparison to the world: 95

## MERCHANT MARINE:

total: 466 (2017)

by type: bulk carrier 52, container ship 165, general cargo 57, oil tanker 7, other 185 (2017)

country comparison to the world: 41

## PORTS AND TERMINALS:

major seaport(s): Leixoes, Lisbon, Setubal, Sines

container port(s) (TEUs): Sines (1,513,083) (2016)

LNG terminal(s) (import): Sines

# MILITARY AND SECURITY :: PORTUGAL

## MILITARY EXPENDITURES:

1.84% of GDP (2016)

1.79% of GDP (2015)

1.79% of GDP (2014)

country comparison to the world: 60

## MILITARY BRANCHES:

Portuguese Army (Exercito Portuguesa), Portuguese Navy (Marinha Portuguesa; includes Marine Corps), Portuguese Air Force (Forca Aerea Portuguesa, FAP) (2013)

## MILITARY SERVICE AGE AND OBLIGATION:

18-30 years of age for voluntary military service; no compulsory military service, but conscription possible if insufficient volunteers available; women serve in the armed forces, on naval ships since 1993, but are prohibited from serving in some combatant specialties; reserve obligation to age 35 (2012)

# TRANSNATIONAL ISSUES :: PORTUGAL

## DISPUTES - INTERNATIONAL:

Portugal does not recognize Spanish sovereignty over the territory of Olivenza based on a difference of interpretation of the 1815 Congress of Vienna and the 1801 Treaty of Badajoz

**REFUGEES AND INTERNALLY DISPLACED PERSONS:**

stateless persons: 14 (2017)

**ILLICIT DRUGS:**

seizing record amounts of Latin American cocaine destined for Europe; a European gateway for Southwest Asian heroin; transshipment point for hashish from North Africa to Europe; consumer of Southwest Asian heroin

# CENTRAL AMERICA :: PUERTO RICO

## INTRODUCTION :: PUERTO RICO

### BACKGROUND:

Populated for centuries by aboriginal peoples, the island was claimed by the Spanish Crown in 1493 following Christopher COLUMBUS' second voyage to the Americas. In 1898, after 400 years of colonial rule that saw the indigenous population nearly exterminated and African slave labor introduced, Puerto Rico was ceded to the US as a result of the Spanish-American War. Puerto Ricans were granted US citizenship in 1917. Popularly elected governors have served since 1948. In 1952, a constitution was enacted providing for internal self-government. In plebiscites held in 1967, 1993, and 1998, voters chose not to alter the existing political status with the US, but the results of a 2012 vote left open the possibility of American statehood. Economic recession on the island has led to a net population loss since about 2005, as large numbers of residents moved to the US mainland. The trend has accelerated since 2010; in 2014, Puerto Rico experienced a net population loss to the mainland of 64,000, more than double the net loss of 26,000 in 2010. Hurricane Maria struck the island on 20 September 2017 causing catastrophic damage, including destruction of the electrical grid that had been cripled by Hurricane Irma just two weeks before. It was the worst storm to hit the island in eight decades, and damage is estimated in the tens of billions of dollars.

## GEOGRAPHY :: PUERTO RICO

### LOCATION:
Caribbean, island between the Caribbean Sea and the North Atlantic Ocean, east of the Dominican Republic

### GEOGRAPHIC COORDINATES:
18 15 N, 66 30 W

### MAP REFERENCES:
Central America and the Caribbean

### AREA:
total: 9,104 sq km

land: 8,959 sq km

water: 145 sq km

country comparison to the world: 171

### AREA - COMPARATIVE:
slightly less than three times the size of Rhode Island

### LAND BOUNDARIES:
0 km

### COASTLINE:
501 km

### MARITIME CLAIMS:
territorial sea: 12 nm

exclusive economic zone: 200 nm

### CLIMATE:
tropical marine, mild; little seasonal temperature variation

### TERRAIN:
mostly mountains with coastal plain in north; precipitous mountains to the sea on west coast; sandy beaches along most coastal areas

### ELEVATION:
mean elevation: 261 m

elevation extremes: 0 m lowest point: Caribbean Sea

1338 highest point: Cerro de Punta

### NATURAL RESOURCES:
some copper and nickel; potential for onshore and offshore oil

### LAND USE:
agricultural land: 22% (2011 est.)

arable land: 6.6% (2011 est.) / permanent crops: 5.6% (2011 est.) / permanent pasture: 9.8% (2011 est.)

forest: 63.2% (2011 est.)

other: 14.8% (2011 est.)

### IRRIGATED LAND:
220 sq km (2012)

### POPULATION DISTRIBUTION:
population clusters tend to be found along the coast, the largest of these is found in and around San Juan; an exception to this is a sizeable population located in the interior of the island immediately south of the capital around Caguas; most of the interior, particularly in the western half of the island, is dominated by the Cordillera Central mountains, where population density is low

### NATURAL HAZARDS:
periodic droughts; hurricanes

### ENVIRONMENT - CURRENT ISSUES:
soil erosion; occasional droughts cause water shortages; industrial pollution

### GEOGRAPHY - NOTE:
important location along the Mona Passage - a key shipping lane to the Panama Canal; San Juan is one of the biggest and best natural harbors in the Caribbean; many small rivers and high central mountains ensure land is well watered; south coast relatively dry; fertile coastal plain belt in north

## PEOPLE AND SOCIETY :: PUERTO RICO

### POPULATION:
3,294,626 (July 2018 est.)

country comparison to the world: 134

### NATIONALITY:
noun: Puerto Rican(s) (US citizens)

adjective: Puerto Rican

### ETHNIC GROUPS:
white 75.8%, black/African American 12.4%, other 8.5% (includes American Indian, Alaskan Native, Native Hawaiian, other Pacific Islander, and others), mixed 3.3% (2010 est.)

note: 99% of the population is Latino

### LANGUAGES:
Spanish, English

### RELIGIONS:
Roman Catholic 85%, Protestant and other 15%

### AGE STRUCTURE:
0-14 years: 15.25% (male 256,866 /female 245,518)

15-24 years: 13.39% (male 224,434 /female 216,664)

25-54 years: 37.99% (male 595,818 /female 655,890)

55-64 years: 13.14% (male 198,577 /female 234,490)

65 years and over: 20.23% (male 286,630 /female 379,739) (2018 est.)

### DEPENDENCY RATIOS:
total dependency ratio: 49.6 (2015 est.)

youth dependency ratio: 27.9 (2015 est.)

elderly dependency ratio: 21.7 (2015 est.)

potential support ratio: 4.6 (2015 est.)

### MEDIAN AGE:
total: 42.2 years

male: 40.2 years

female: 43.9 years (2018 est.)

country comparison to the world: 34

### POPULATION GROWTH RATE:
-1.7% (2018 est.)

country comparison to the world: 232

### BIRTH RATE:
8 births/1,000 population (2018 est.)

country comparison to the world: 222

### DEATH RATE:
8.9 deaths/1,000 population (2018 est.)

country comparison to the world: 65

### NET MIGRATION RATE:
-16.9 migrant(s)/1,000 population (2017 est.)

country comparison to the world: 217

### POPULATION DISTRIBUTION:
population clusters tend to be found along the coast, the largest of these is found in and around San Juan; an exception to this is a sizeable population located in the interior of the island immediately south of the capital around Caguas; most of the interior, particularly in the western half of the island, is dominated by the Cordillera Central mountains, where population density is low

### URBANIZATION:
urban population: 93.6% of total population (2018)

rate of urbanization: -0.14% annual rate of change (2015-20 est.)

### MAJOR URBAN AREAS - POPULATION:
2.454 million SAN JUAN (capital) (2018)

### SEX RATIO:
at birth: 1.02 male(s)/female (2017 est.)

0-14 years: 1.04 male(s)/female (2017 est.)

15-24 years: 1.05 male(s)/female (2017 est.)

25-54 years: 0.92 male(s)/female (2017 est.)

55-64 years: 0.83 male(s)/female (2017 est.)

65 years and over: 0.76 male(s)/female (2017 est.)

total population: 0.91 male(s)/female (2017 est.)

### MATERNAL MORTALITY RATE:
14 deaths/100,000 live births (2015 est.)

country comparison to the world: 138

### INFANT MORTALITY RATE:
total: 6.3 deaths/1,000 live births (2018 est.)

male: 6.9 deaths/1,000 live births (2018 est.)

female: 5.6 deaths/1,000 live births (2018 est.)

country comparison to the world: 165

### LIFE EXPECTANCY AT BIRTH:
total population: 81 years (2018 est.)

male: 77.7 years (2018 est.)

female: 84.5 years (2018 est.)

country comparison to the world: 36

### TOTAL FERTILITY RATE:
1.21 children born/woman (2018 est.)

country comparison to the world: 220

### DRINKING WATER SOURCE:
improved:

urban: 93.6% of population (2001 est.)

rural: 93.6% of population (2001 est.)

total: 93.6% of population (2001 est.)

unimproved:

urban: 6.4% of population (2001 est.)

rural: 6.4% of population (2001 est.)

total: 6.4% of population (2001 est.)

### SANITATION FACILITY ACCESS:
improved:

urban: 99.3% of population (2015 est.)

rural: 99.3% of population (2015 est.)

total: 99.3% of population (2015 est.)

unimproved:

urban: 0.7% of population (2015 est.)

rural: 0.7% of population (2015 est.)

total: 0.7% of population (2015 est.)

### HIV/AIDS - ADULT PREVALENCE RATE:
NA

### HIV/AIDS - PEOPLE LIVING WITH HIV/AIDS:
NA

### HIV/AIDS - DEATHS:
NA

### MAJOR INFECTIOUS DISEASES:
note: active local transmission of Zika virus by Aedes species mosquitoes has been identified in this country (as of August 2016); it poses an important risk (a large number of cases possible) among US citizens if bitten by an infective mosquito; other less common ways to get Zika are through sex, via blood transfusion, or during pregnancy, in which the pregnant woman passes Zika virus to her fetus

### EDUCATION EXPENDITURES:
6% of GDP (2014)

country comparison to the world: 36

### LITERACY:
definition: age 15 and over can read and write (2015 est.)

total population: 93.3% (2015 est.)

male: 92.8% (2015 est.)

female: 93.8% (2015 est.)

### SCHOOL LIFE EXPECTANCY (PRIMARY TO TERTIARY EDUCATION):
total: 14 years (2014)

male: 13 years (2014)

female: 15 years (2014)

**UNEMPLOYMENT, YOUTH AGES 15-24:**

total: 26.6% (2012 est.)

male: 28.9% (2012 est.)

female: 23.1% (2012 est.)

country comparison to the world: 43

## GOVERNMENT :: PUERTO RICO

**COUNTRY NAME:**

conventional long form: Commonwealth of Puerto Rico

conventional short form: Puerto Rico

abbreviation: PR

etymology: Christopher COLUMBUS named the island San Juan Bautista (Saint John the Baptist) and the capital city and main port Cuidad de Puerto Rico (Rich Port City); over time, however, the names were shortened and transposed and the island came to be called Puerto Rico and its capital San Juan

**DEPENDENCY STATUS:**

unincorporated organized territory of the US; policy relations between Puerto Rico and the US conducted under the jurisdiction of the Office of the President

**GOVERNMENT TYPE:**

presidential democracy; a self-governing commonwealth in political association with the US

**CAPITAL:**

name: San Juan

geographic coordinates: 18 28 N, 66 07 W

time difference: UTC-4 (1 hour ahead of Washington, DC, during Standard Time)

**ADMINISTRATIVE DIVISIONS:**

none (territory of the US with commonwealth status); there are no first-order administrative divisions as defined by the US Government, but there are 78 municipalities (municipios, singular - municipio) at the second order; Adjuntas, Aguada, Aguadilla, Aguas Buenas, Aibonito, Anasco, Arecibo, Arroyo, Barceloneta, Barranquitas, Bayamon, Cabo Rojo, Caguas, Camuy, Canovanas, Carolina, Catano, Cayey, Ceiba, Ciales, Cidra, Coamo, Comerio, Corozal, Culebra, Dorado, Fajardo, Florida, Guanica, Guayama, Guayanilla, Guaynabo, Gurabo, Hatillo, Hormigueros, Humacao, Isabela, Jayuya, Juana Diaz, Juncos, Lajas, Lares, Las Marias, Las Piedras, Loiza, Luquillo, Manati, Maricao, Maunabo, Mayaguez, Moca, Morovis, Naguabo, Naranjito, Orocovis, Patillas, Penuelas, Ponce, Quebradillas, Rincon, Rio Grande, Sabana Grande, Salinas, San German, San Juan, San Lorenzo, San Sebastian, Santa Isabel, Toa Alta, Toa Baja, Trujillo Alto, Utuado, Vega Alta, Vega Baja, Vieques, Villalba, Yabucoa, Yauco

**INDEPENDENCE:**

none (territory of the US with commonwealth status)

**NATIONAL HOLIDAY:**

US Independence Day, 4 July (1776)Puerto Rico Constitution Day, 25 July (1952)

**CONSTITUTION:**

history: previous 1900 (Organic Act, or Foraker Act); latest ratified by referendum 3 March 1952, approved 3 July 1952, effective 25 July 1952 (2018)

amendments: proposed by a concurrent resolution of at least two-thirds majority by the total Legislative Assembly membership; approval requires at least two-thirds majority vote by the membership of both houses and approval by a majority of voters in a special referendum; if passed by at least three-fourths Assembly vote, the referendum can be held concurrently with the next general election; constitutional articles such as the republican form of government or the bill of rights cannot be amended; amended 1952 (2018)

**LEGAL SYSTEM:**

civil law system based on the Spanish civil code and within the framework of the US federal system

**CITIZENSHIP:**

see United States

**SUFFRAGE:**

18 years of age; universal; note - island residents are US citizens but do not vote in US presidential elections

**EXECUTIVE BRANCH:**

chief of state: President Donald J. TRUMP (since 20 January 2017); Vice President Michael R. PENCE (since 20 January 2017)

head of government: Governor Ricardo ROSSELLO (since 2 January 2017)

cabinet: Cabinet appointed by governor with the consent of the Legislative Assembly

elections/appointments: president and vice president indirectly elected on the same ballot by an Electoral College of 'electors' chosen from each state; president and vice president serve a 4-year term (eligible for a second term); under the US Constitution, residents of Puerto Rico do not vote in elections for US president and vice president; however, they may vote in Democratic and Republican party presidential primary elections; governor directly elected by simple majority popular vote for a 4-year term (no term limits); election last held on 8 November 2016 (next to be held in November 2020)

election results: Ricardo ROSSELLO elected governor; percent of vote - Ricardo ROSSELLO (PNP) 41.8%, David BERNIER (PPD) 38.9%, Alexandra LUGARO (independent) 11.1%, Manuel CIDRE (independent) 5.7%

**LEGISLATIVE BRANCH:**

description: bicameral Legislative Assembly or Asamblea Legislativa consists of:
Senate or Senado (30 seats; 16 members directly elected in 8 2-seat constituencies by simple majority vote and 14 at-large members directly elected by simple majority vote to serve 4-year terms)
House of Representatives or Camara de Representantes (51 seats; members directly elected in single-seat constituencies by simple majority vote to serve 4-year terms)

elections:
Senate - last held on 8 November 2016 (next to be held on 3 November 2020)
House of Representatives - last held on 8 November 2016 (next to be held on 3 November 2020)

election results:
Senate - percent of vote by party - NA; seats by party - PNP 21, PPD 7, PIP 1, Independent 1
House of Representatives - percent of vote by party - NA; seats by party - PNP 34, PPD 16, PIP 1

note: Puerto Rico directly elects 1 member by simple majority vote to serve a 4-year term as a commissioner to the US House of Representatives; the commissioner can vote when serving on a committee and when the House meets as the Committee of the Whole House but not when legislation is submitted for a 'full floor' House vote; election of commissioner last held on 8 November 2016 (next to be held on 6 November 2018)

**JUDICIAL BRANCH:**

**highest courts:** Supreme Court (consists of the chief justice and 8 associate justices)

**judge selection and term of office:** justices appointed by the governor and confirmed by majority Senate vote; judges serve until compulsory retirement at age 70

**subordinate courts:** Court of Appeals; First Instance Court comprised of superior and municipal courts

## POLITICAL PARTIES AND LEADERS:

National Democratic Party [Charlie RODRIGUEZ]
National Republican Party of Puerto Rico [Jenniffer GONZALEZ]
New Progressive Party or PNP [Ricardo ROSSELLO] (pro-US statehood)
Popular Democratic Party or PPD [Alejandro GARCIA Padillo] (pro-commonwealth)
Puerto Rican Independence Party or PIP [Ruben BERRIOS Martinez] (pro-independence)

## INTERNATIONAL ORGANIZATION PARTICIPATION:

AOSIS (observer), Caricom (observer), Interpol (subbureau), IOC, UNWTO (associate), UPU, WFTU (NGOs)

## DIPLOMATIC REPRESENTATION IN THE US:

none (territory of the US)

## DIPLOMATIC REPRESENTATION FROM THE US:

none (territory of the US with commonwealth status)

## FLAG DESCRIPTION:

five equal horizontal bands of red (top, center, and bottom) alternating with white; a blue isosceles triangle based on the hoist side bears a large, white, five-pointed star in the center; the white star symbolizes Puerto Rico; the three sides of the triangle signify the executive, legislative and judicial parts of the government; blue stands for the sky and the coastal waters; red symbolizes the blood shed by warriors, while white represents liberty, victory, and peace

**note:** design initially influenced by the US flag, but similar to the Cuban flag, with the colors of the bands and triangle reversed

## NATIONAL SYMBOL(S):

Puerto Rican spindalis (bird), coqui (frog); national colors: red, white, blue

## NATIONAL ANTHEM:

**name:** "La Borinquena" (The Puerto Rican)

**lyrics/music:** Manuel Fernandez JUNCOS/Felix Astol ARTES

**note:** music adopted 1952, lyrics adopted 1977; the local anthem's name is a reference to the indigenous name of the island, Borinquen; the music was originally composed as a dance in 1867 and gained popularity in the early 20th century; there is some evidence that the music was written by Francisco RAMIREZ; as a commonwealth of the US, "The Star-Spangled Banner" is official (see United States)

# ECONOMY :: PUERTO RICO

## ECONOMY - OVERVIEW:

Puerto Rico had one of the most dynamic economies in the Caribbean region until 2006; however, growth has been negative for each of the last 11 years. The downturn coincided with the phaseout of tax preferences that had led US firms to invest heavily in the Commonwealth since the 1950s, and a steep rise in the price of oil, which generates most of the island's electricity.

Diminished job opportunities prompted a sharp rise in outmigration, as many Puerto Ricans sought jobs on the US mainland. Unemployment reached 16% in 2011, but declined to 11.5% in December 2017. US minimum wage laws apply in Puerto Rico, hampering job expansion. Per capita income is about two-thirds that of the US mainland.

The industrial sector greatly exceeds agriculture as the locus of economic activity and income. Tourism has traditionally been an important source of income with estimated arrivals of more than 3.6 million tourists in 2008. Puerto Rico's merchandise trade surplus is exceptionally strong, with exports nearly 50% greater than imports, and its current account surplus about 10% of GDP.

Closing the budget deficit while restoring economic growth and employment remain the central concerns of the government. The gap between revenues and expenditures amounted to 0.6% of GDP in 2016, although analysts believe that not all expenditures have been accounted for in the budget and a better accounting of costs would yield an overall deficit of roughly 5% of GDP. Public debt remained steady at 92.5% of GDP in 2017, about $17,000 per person, or nearly three times the per capita debt of the State of Connecticut, the highest in the US. Much of that debt was issued by state-run schools and public corporations, including water and electric utilities. In June 2015, Governor Alejandro GARCIA Padilla announced that the island could not pay back at least $73 billion in debt and that it would seek a deal with its creditors.

Hurricane Maria hit Puerto Rico square on in September 2017, causing electrical power outages to 90% of the territory, as well as extensive loss of housing and infrastructure and contamination of potable water. Despite massive efforts, more than 40% of the territory remained without electricity as of yearend 2017. As a result of the destruction, many Puerto Ricans have emigrated to the US mainland.

## GDP (PURCHASING POWER PARITY):

$130 billion (2017 est.)
$133.1 billion (2016 est.)
$134.9 billion (2015 est.)

**note:** data are in 2017 dollars

**country comparison to the world:** 81

## GDP (OFFICIAL EXCHANGE RATE):

$104.2 billion (2017 est.) (2017 est.)

## GDP - REAL GROWTH RATE:

-2.4% (2017 est.)
-1.3% (2016 est.)
-1% (2015 est.)

**country comparison to the world:** 207

## GDP - PER CAPITA (PPP):

$39,400 (2017 est.)
$39,000 (2016 est.)
$38,800 (2015 est.)

**note:** data are in 2017 dollars

**country comparison to the world:** 47

## GDP - COMPOSITION, BY END USE:

**household consumption:** 87.7% (2017 est.)

**government consumption:** 12.2% (2017 est.)

**investment in fixed capital:** 11.7% (2017 est.)

**investment in inventories:** 0.5% (2017 est.)

exports of goods and services: 117.8% (2017 est.)

imports of goods and services: -129.8% (2017 est.)

## GDP - COMPOSITION, BY SECTOR OF ORIGIN:

agriculture: 0.8% (2017 est.)

industry: 50.1% (2017 est.)

services: 49.1% (2017 est.)

## AGRICULTURE - PRODUCTS:

sugarcane, coffee, pineapples, plantains, bananas; livestock products, chickens

## INDUSTRIES:

pharmaceuticals, electronics, apparel, food products, tourism

## INDUSTRIAL PRODUCTION GROWTH RATE:

-2.1% (2017 est.)

country comparison to the world: 184

## LABOR FORCE:

1.139 million (December 2014 est.)

country comparison to the world: 142

## LABOR FORCE - BY OCCUPATION:

agriculture: 2.1%

industry: 19%

services: 79% (2005 est.)

## UNEMPLOYMENT RATE:

10.8% (2017 est.)

11.8% (2016 est.)

country comparison to the world: 146

## POPULATION BELOW POVERTY LINE:

NA

## HOUSEHOLD INCOME OR CONSUMPTION BY PERCENTAGE SHARE:

lowest 10%: NA

highest 10%: NA

## BUDGET:

revenues: 9.268 billion (2017 est.)

expenditures: 9.974 billion (2017 est.)

## TAXES AND OTHER REVENUES:

8.9% (of GDP) (2017 est.)

country comparison to the world: 217

## BUDGET SURPLUS (+) OR DEFICIT (-):

-0.7% (of GDP) (2017 est.)

country comparison to the world: 68

## PUBLIC DEBT:

51.6% of GDP (2017 est.)

50.1% of GDP (2016 est.)

country comparison to the world: 97

## FISCAL YEAR:

1 July - 30 June

## INFLATION RATE (CONSUMER PRICES):

1.8% (2017 est.)

-0.3% (2016 est.)

country comparison to the world: 95

## COMMERCIAL BANK PRIME LENDING RATE:

5% (31 December 2017 est.)

4% (31 December 2016 est.)

country comparison to the world: 151

## MARKET VALUE OF PUBLICLY TRADED SHARES:

NA

## CURRENT ACCOUNT BALANCE:

$0 (2017 est.)

$0 (2016 est.)

country comparison to the world: 66

## EXPORTS:

$73.17 billion (2017 est.)

$73.2 billion (2016 est.)

country comparison to the world: 41

## EXPORTS - COMMODITIES:

chemicals, electronics, apparel, canned tuna, rum, beverage concentrates, medical equipment

## IMPORTS:

$49.01 billion (2017 est.)

$48.86 billion (2016 est.)

country comparison to the world: 54

## IMPORTS - COMMODITIES:

chemicals, machinery and equipment, clothing, food, fish, petroleum products

## DEBT - EXTERNAL:

$56.82 billion (31 December 2010 est.)

$52.98 billion (31 December 2009 est.)

country comparison to the world: 61

## EXCHANGE RATES:

the US dollar is used

# ENERGY :: PUERTO RICO

## ELECTRICITY ACCESS:

population without electricity: 357,805 (2012)

electrification - total population: 91% (2012)

electrification - urban areas: 91% (2012)

electrification - rural areas: 80% (2012)

## ELECTRICITY - PRODUCTION:

20.95 billion kWh (2016 est.)

country comparison to the world: 75

## ELECTRICITY - CONSUMPTION:

19.48 billion kWh (2016 est.)

country comparison to the world: 72

## ELECTRICITY - EXPORTS:

0 kWh (2016 est.)

country comparison to the world: 185

## ELECTRICITY - IMPORTS:

0 kWh (2016 est.)

country comparison to the world: 187

## ELECTRICITY - INSTALLED GENERATING CAPACITY:

6.294 million kW (2016 est.)

country comparison to the world: 76

## ELECTRICITY - FROM FOSSIL FUELS:

94% of total installed capacity (2016 est.)

country comparison to the world: 47

## ELECTRICITY - FROM NUCLEAR FUELS:

0% of total installed capacity (2017 est.)

country comparison to the world: 168

## ELECTRICITY - FROM HYDROELECTRIC PLANTS:

2% of total installed capacity (2017 est.)

country comparison to the world: 142

## ELECTRICITY - FROM OTHER RENEWABLE SOURCES:

4% of total installed capacity (2017 est.)

country comparison to the world: 117

## CRUDE OIL - PRODUCTION:

0 bbl/day (2017 est.)

country comparison to the world: 187

## CRUDE OIL - EXPORTS:

0 bbl/day (2015 est.)

country comparison to the world: 181

## CRUDE OIL - IMPORTS:

0 bbl/day (2015 est.)

country comparison to the world: 182

## CRUDE OIL - PROVED RESERVES:

0 bbl (1 January 2018 est.)

country comparison to the world: 183

## REFINED PETROLEUM PRODUCTS - PRODUCTION:

0 bbl/day (2015 est.)

country comparison to the world: 190

**REFINED PETROLEUM PRODUCTS - CONSUMPTION:**

98,000 bbl/day (2016 est.)

country comparison to the world: 81

**REFINED PETROLEUM PRODUCTS - EXPORTS:**

18,420 bbl/day (2015 est.)

country comparison to the world: 70

**REFINED PETROLEUM PRODUCTS - IMPORTS:**

127,100 bbl/day (2015 est.)

country comparison to the world: 46

**NATURAL GAS - PRODUCTION:**

0 cu m (2017 est.)

country comparison to the world: 185

**NATURAL GAS - CONSUMPTION:**

1.303 billion cu m (2017 est.)

country comparison to the world: 86

**NATURAL GAS - EXPORTS:**

0 cu m (2017 est.)

country comparison to the world: 170

**NATURAL GAS - IMPORTS:**

1.303 billion cu m (2017 est.)

country comparison to the world: 57

**NATURAL GAS - PROVED RESERVES:**

0 cu m (1 January 2014 est.)

country comparison to the world: 183

**CARBON DIOXIDE EMISSIONS FROM CONSUMPTION OF ENERGY:**

19.85 million Mt (2017 est.)

country comparison to the world: 87

# COMMUNICATIONS :: PUERTO RICO

**TELEPHONES - FIXED LINES:**

total subscriptions: 783,739 (2017 est.)

subscriptions per 100 inhabitants: 23 (2017 est.)

country comparison to the world: 81

**TELEPHONES - MOBILE CELLULAR:**

total subscriptions: 3,389,402 (2017 est.)

subscriptions per 100 inhabitants: 101 (2017 est.)

country comparison to the world: 137

**TELEPHONE SYSTEM:**

general assessment: modern system integrated with that of the US by high-capacity submarine cable and Intelsat with high-speed data capability (2016)

domestic: digital telephone system; mobile-cellular services (2016)

international: country code - 1-787, 939; submarine cables provide connectivity to the US, Caribbean, Central and South America; satellite earth station - 1 Intelsat (2016)

**BROADCAST MEDIA:**

more than 30 TV stations operating; cable TV subscription services are available; roughly 125 radio stations (2007)

**INTERNET COUNTRY CODE:**

.pr

**INTERNET USERS:**

total: 2,873,895 (July 2016 est.)

percent of population: 80.3% (July 2016 est.)

country comparison to the world: 98

**BROADBAND - FIXED SUBSCRIPTIONS:**

total: 660,100 (2017 est.)

subscriptions per 100 inhabitants: 20 (2017 est.)

country comparison to the world: 76

# TRANSPORTATION :: PUERTO RICO

**AIRPORTS:**

29 (2013)

country comparison to the world: 119

**AIRPORTS - WITH PAVED RUNWAYS:**

total: 17 (2017)

over 3,047 m: 2 (2017)

2,438 to 3,047 m: 1 (2017)

1,524 to 2,437 m: 2 (2017)

914 to 1,523 m: 7 (2017)

under 914 m: 5 (2017)

**AIRPORTS - WITH UNPAVED RUNWAYS:**

total: 12 (2013)

1,524 to 2,437 m: 1 (2013)

914 to 1,523 m: 1 (2013)

under 914 m: 10 (2013)

**ROADWAYS:**

total: 26,862 km (includes 454 km of expressways) (2012)

country comparison to the world: 100

**PORTS AND TERMINALS:**

major seaport(s): Ensenada Honda, Mayaguez, Playa de Guayanilla, Playa de Ponce, San Juan

container port(s) (TEUs): San Juan (1,210,503) (2015)

LNG terminal(s) (import): Guayanilla Bay

# MILITARY AND SECURITY :: PUERTO RICO

**MILITARY BRANCHES:**

no regular indigenous military forces; paramilitary National Guard, Police Force

**MILITARY - NOTE:**

defense is the responsibility of the US

# TRANSNATIONAL ISSUES :: PUERTO RICO

**DISPUTES - INTERNATIONAL:**

increasing numbers of illegal migrants from the Dominican Republic cross the Mona Passage to Puerto Rico each year looking for work

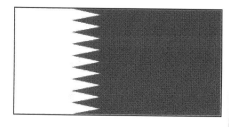

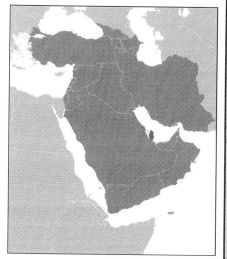

# MIDDLE EAST :: QATAR

## INTRODUCTION :: QATAR

**BACKGROUND:**

Ruled by the Al Thani family since the mid-1800s, Qatar within the last 60 years transformed itself from a poor British protectorate noted mainly for pearling into an independent state with significant oil and natural gas revenues. The continuous siphoning off of petroleum revenue through the mid-1990s by Qatari amirs permanently residing in Europe had stunted Qatar's economic growth. Former amir HAMAD bin Khalifa Al Thani, who overthrew his father in a bloodless coup in 1995, ushered in wide-sweeping political and media reforms, unprecedented economic investment, and a growing Qatari regional leadership role, in part through the creation of the pan-Arab satellite news network Al-Jazeera and Qatar's mediation of some regional conflicts. In the 2000s, Qatar resolved its longstanding border disputes with both Bahrain and Saudi Arabia and by 2007 had attained the highest per capita income in the world. Qatar did not experience domestic unrest or violence like that seen in other Near Eastern and North African countries in 2010-11, due in part to its immense wealth. In mid-2013, HAMAD peacefully abdicated, transferring power to his son, the current Amir TAMIM bin Hamad. TAMIM remains popular with the Qatari public, having prioritized improving the domestic welfare of Qataris, including establishing advanced healthcare and education systems and expanding the country's infrastructure in anticipation of Doha's hosting of the 2022 World Cup.

Recently, Qatar's relationships with its neighbors have been tense at times. Following the outbreak of regional unrest in 2011, Doha prided itself on its support for many popular revolutions, particularly in Libya and Syria. This stance was to the detriment of Qatar's relations with Bahrain, Saudi Arabia, and the United Arab Emirates (UAE), which temporarily recalled their respective ambassadors from Doha in March 2014. TAMIM later oversaw a warming of Qatar's relations with Bahrain, Saudi Arabia, and the UAE in November 2014 following Kuwaiti mediation and signing of the Riyadh Agreement. In June 2017, however, the Quartet — Bahrain, Egypt, Saudi Arabia, and the UAE — cut diplomatic and economic ties with Qatar in response to alleged violations of the agreement.

## GEOGRAPHY :: QATAR

**LOCATION:**

Middle East, peninsula bordering the Persian Gulf and Saudi Arabia

**GEOGRAPHIC COORDINATES:**

25 30 N, 51 15 E

**MAP REFERENCES:**

Middle East

**AREA:**

total: 11,586 sq km

land: 11,586 sq km

water: 0 sq km

country comparison to the world: 165

**AREA - COMPARATIVE:**

almost twice the size of Delaware; slightly smaller than Connecticut

**LAND BOUNDARIES:**

total: 87 km

border countries (1): Saudi Arabia 87 km

**COASTLINE:**

563 km

**MARITIME CLAIMS:**

territorial sea: 12 nm

exclusive economic zone: as determined by bilateral agreements or the median line

contiguous zone: 24 nm

**CLIMATE:**

arid; mild, pleasant winters; very hot, humid summers

**TERRAIN:**

mostly flat and barren desert

**ELEVATION:**

mean elevation: 28 m

elevation extremes: 0 m lowest point: Persian Gulf

103 highest point: Tuwayyir al Hamir

**NATURAL RESOURCES:**

petroleum, fish, natural gas

**LAND USE:**

agricultural land: 5.6% (2011 est.)

arable land: 1.1% (2011 est.) / permanent crops: 0.2% (2011 est.) / permanent pasture: 4.3% (2011 est.)

forest: 0% (2011 est.)

other: 94.4% (2011 est.)

**IRRIGATED LAND:**

130 sq km (2012)

**POPULATION DISTRIBUTION:**

most of the population is clustered in or around the capital of Doha on the eastern side of the peninsula

**NATURAL HAZARDS:**

haze, dust storms, sandstorms common

**ENVIRONMENT - CURRENT ISSUES:**

air, land, and water pollution are significant environmental issues; limited natural freshwater resources are increasing dependence on large-scale desalination facilities; other issues include conservation of oil supplies and preservation of the natural wildlife heritage

**ENVIRONMENT - INTERNATIONAL AGREEMENTS:**

party to: Biodiversity, Climate Change, Climate Change-Kyoto Protocol, Desertification, Endangered Species, Hazardous Wastes, Law of the Sea, Ozone Layer Protection, Ship Pollution

signed, but not ratified: none of the selected agreements

**GEOGRAPHY - NOTE:**

the peninsula occupies a strategic location in the central Persian Gulf near major petroleum deposits

## PEOPLE AND SOCIETY :: QATAR

**POPULATION:**

2,363,569 (July 2018 est.)

country comparison to the world: 143

**NATIONALITY:**

noun: Qatari(s)

adjective: Qatari

**ETHNIC GROUPS:**

non-Qatari 88.4%, Qatari 11.6% (2015 est.)

**LANGUAGES:**

Arabic (official), English commonly used as a second language

**RELIGIONS:**

Muslim 67.7%, Christian 13.8%, Hindu 13.8%, Buddhist 3.1%, folk religion (2010 est.)

**AGE STRUCTURE:**

0-14 years: 12.7% (male 151,888 /female 148,186)

15-24 years: 12.12% (male 205,242 /female 81,297)

25-54 years: 70.67% (male 1,391,192 /female 279,256)

55-64 years: 3.44% (male 62,683 /female 18,731)

65 years and over: 1.06% (male 16,295 /female 8,799) (2018 est.)

**DEPENDENCY RATIOS:**

total dependency ratio: 17.5 (2015 est.)

youth dependency ratio: 16.3 (2015 est.)

elderly dependency ratio: 1.3 (2015 est.)

potential support ratio: 78.1 (2015 est.)

**MEDIAN AGE:**

total: 33.4 years

male: 34.6 years

female: 28.2 years (2018 est.)

country comparison to the world: 95

**POPULATION GROWTH RATE:**

1.95% (2018 est.)

country comparison to the world: 50

**BIRTH RATE:**

9.5 births/1,000 population (2018 est.)

country comparison to the world: 200

**DEATH RATE:**

1.6 deaths/1,000 population (2018 est.)

country comparison to the world: 226

**NET MIGRATION RATE:**

14.6 migrant(s)/1,000 population (2017 est.)

country comparison to the world: 3

**POPULATION DISTRIBUTION:**

most of the population is clustered in or around the capital of Doha on the eastern side of the peninsula

**URBANIZATION:**

urban population: 99.1% of total population (2018)

rate of urbanization: 2.41% annual rate of change (2015-20 est.)

**MAJOR URBAN AREAS - POPULATION:**

633,000 DOHA (capital) (2018)

**SEX RATIO:**

at birth: 1.02 male(s)/female (2017 est.)

0-14 years: 1.03 male(s)/female (2017 est.)

15-24 years: 2.64 male(s)/female (2017 est.)

25-54 years: 4.91 male(s)/female (2017 est.)

55-64 years: 3.38 male(s)/female (2017 est.)

65 years and over: 1.71 male(s)/female (2017 est.)

total population: 3.41 male(s)/female (2017 est.)

**MATERNAL MORTALITY RATE:**

13 deaths/100,000 live births (2015 est.)

country comparison to the world: 140

**INFANT MORTALITY RATE:**

total: 6 deaths/1,000 live births (2018 est.)

male: 6.3 deaths/1,000 live births (2018 est.)

female: 5.7 deaths/1,000 live births (2018 est.)

country comparison to the world: 166

**LIFE EXPECTANCY AT BIRTH:**

total population: 79 years (2018 est.)

male: 76.9 years (2018 est.)

female: 81.2 years (2018 est.)

country comparison to the world: 53

**TOTAL FERTILITY RATE:**

1.89 children born/woman (2018 est.)

country comparison to the world: 136

**CONTRACEPTIVE PREVALENCE RATE:**

37.5% (2012)

**HEALTH EXPENDITURES:**

2.2% of GDP (2014)

country comparison to the world: 189

**PHYSICIANS DENSITY:**

1.96 physicians/1,000 population (2014)

**HOSPITAL BED DENSITY:**

1.2 beds/1,000 population (2014)

**DRINKING WATER SOURCE:**

improved:

urban: 100% of population

rural: 100% of population

total: 100% of population

unimproved:

urban: 0% of population

rural: 0% of population

total: 0% of population (2015 est.)

**SANITATION FACILITY ACCESS:**

improved:

urban: 98% of population (2015 est.)

rural: 98% of population (2015 est.)

total: 98% of population (2015 est.)

unimproved:

urban: 2% of population (2015 est.)

rural: 2% of population (2015 est.)

total: 2% of population (2015 est.)

**HIV/AIDS - ADULT PREVALENCE RATE:**

0.1% (2017 est.)

country comparison to the world: 118

**HIV/AIDS - PEOPLE LIVING WITH HIV/AIDS:**

<500 (2017 est.)

**HIV/AIDS - DEATHS:**

<100 (2017 est.)

**OBESITY - ADULT PREVALENCE RATE:**

35.1% (2016)

country comparison to the world: 15

**EDUCATION EXPENDITURES:**

3.6% of GDP (2014)

country comparison to the world: 125

**LITERACY:**

definition: age 15 and over can read and write (2015 est.)

total population: 97.3% (2015 est.)

male: 97.4% (2015 est.)

female: 96.8% (2015 est.)

**SCHOOL LIFE EXPECTANCY (PRIMARY TO TERTIARY EDUCATION):**

total: 13 years (2011)

male: 13 years (2011)

female: 14 years (2011)

**UNEMPLOYMENT, YOUTH AGES 15-24:**

total: 0.5% (2016 est.)

male: 0.2% (2016 est.)

female: 2.1% (2016 est.)

country comparison to the world: 174

## GOVERNMENT :: QATAR

**COUNTRY NAME:**

conventional long form: State of Qatar

conventional short form: Qatar

local long form: Dawlat Qatar

local short form: Qatar

etymology: the origin of the name is uncertain, but it dates back at least 2,000 years since a term "Catharrei" was used to describe the inhabitants of the peninsula by Pliny the Elder (1st century A.D.), and a "Catara" peninsula is depicted on a map by Ptolemy (2nd century A.D.)

note: closest approximation of the native pronunciation is gattar or cottar

**GOVERNMENT TYPE:**

absolute monarchy

**CAPITAL:**

name: Doha

geographic coordinates: 25 17 N, 51 32 E

time difference: UTC+3 (8 hours ahead of Washington, DC, during Standard Time)

**ADMINISTRATIVE DIVISIONS:**

8 municipalities (baladiyat, singular - baladiyah); Ad Dawhah, Al Khawr wa adh Dhakhirah, Al Wakrah, Ar Rayyan, Ash Shamal, Ash Shihaniyah, Az Za'ayin, Umm Salal

**INDEPENDENCE:**

3 September 1971 (from the UK)

**NATIONAL HOLIDAY:**

National Day, 18 December (1878), anniversary of Al Thani family accession to the throne; Independence Day, 3 September (1971)

**CONSTITUTION:**

history: previous 1972 (provisional); latest drafted 2 July 2002, approved by referendum 29 April 2003, endorsed 8 June 2004, effective 9 June 2005 (2016)

amendments: proposed by the emir or by one-third of Advisory Council members; passage requires two-thirds majority vote of Advisory Council members and approval and promulgation by the emir; articles pertaining to the rule of state and its inheritance, functions of the emir, and citizen rights and liberties cannot be amended (2016)

**LEGAL SYSTEM:**

mixed legal system of civil law and Islamic law (in family and personal matters)

**INTERNATIONAL LAW ORGANIZATION PARTICIPATION:**

has not submitted an ICJ jurisdiction declaration; non-party state to the ICCt

**CITIZENSHIP:**

citizenship by birth: no

citizenship by descent only: the father must be a citizen of Qatar

dual citizenship recognized: no

residency requirement for naturalization: 20 years; 15 years if an Arab national

**SUFFRAGE:**

18 years of age; universal

**EXECUTIVE BRANCH:**

chief of state: Amir TAMIM bin Hamad Al Thani (since 25 June 2013)

head of government: Prime Minister ABDALLAH bin Nasir bin Khalifa Al Thani (since 26 June 2013); Deputy Prime Minister and Minister of State for Defense Affairs Khalid bin Mohamed al-Thani (since 14 November 2017); Deputy Prime Minister and Minister of Foreign Affairs Mohamed bin Abdulrahman Al Thani (since 14 November 2017)

**cabinet:** Council of Ministers appointed by the amir

**elections/appointments:** the monarchy is hereditary; prime minister and deputy prime minister appointed by the amir

## LEGISLATIVE BRANCH:

**description:** unicameral Advisory Council or Majlis al-Shura (45 seats; 30 members directly elected by popular vote for 4-year re-electable terms and 15 appointed by the monarch to serve until resignation or until relieved

**elections:** last on 17 June 2016 (term extended to 2019)

**election results:** NA; composition - men 41, women 4, percent of women 8.9%

## JUDICIAL BRANCH:

**highest courts:** Supreme Court or Court of Cassation (consists of the court president and several judges); Supreme Constitutional Court (consists of the chief justice and 6 members)

**judge selection and term of office:** Supreme Court judges nominated by the Supreme Judiciary Council, a 9-member independent body consisting of judiciary heads appointed by the Amir; judges appointed for 3-year renewable terms; Supreme Constitutional Court members nominated by the Supreme Judiciary Council and appointed by the monarch; term of appointment NA

**subordinate courts:** Courts of Appeal; Administrative Court; courts of first instance; sharia courts; Courts of Justice; Qatar International Court and Dispute Resolution Center, established in 2009, provides dispute resolution services for institutions and bodies in Qatar, as well as internationally

## POLITICAL PARTIES AND LEADERS:

political parties are banned

## INTERNATIONAL ORGANIZATION PARTICIPATION:

ABEDA, AFESD, AMF, CAEU, CD, CICA (observer), EITI (implementing country), FAO, G-77, GCC, IAEA, IBRD, ICAO, ICC (national committees), ICRM, IDA, IDB, IFAD, IFC, IFRCS, IHO, ILO, IMF, IMO, IMSO, Interpol, IOC, IOM (observer), IPU, ISO, ITSO, ITU, LAS, MIGA, NAM, OAPEC, OAS (observer), OIC, OIF, OPCW, OPEC, PCA, UN, UNCTAD, UNESCO, UNIDO, UNIFIL, UNWTO, UPU, WCO, WHO, WIPO, WMO, WTO

## DIPLOMATIC REPRESENTATION IN THE US:

**chief of mission:** Ambassador MISHAL bin Hamad bin Muhammad Al Thani (since 24 April 2017)

**chancery:** 2555 M Street NW, Washington, DC 20037

**telephone:** [1] (202) 274-1600

**FAX:** [1] (202) 237-0682

**consulate(s) general:** Houston, Los Angeles

## DIPLOMATIC REPRESENTATION FROM THE US:

**chief of mission:** Ambassador (vacant); Charge d'Affaires Ryan GLIHA (since 30 November 2017)

**embassy:** 22 February Street, Al Luqta District, Doha

**mailing address:** P. O. Box 2399, Doha

**telephone:** [974] 4496-6000

**FAX:** [974] 4488-4298

## FLAG DESCRIPTION:

maroon with a broad white serrated band (nine white points) on the hoist side; maroon represents the blood shed in Qatari wars, white stands for peace; the nine-pointed serrated edge signifies Qatar as the ninth member of the "reconciled emirates" in the wake of the Qatari-British treaty of 1916

**note:** the other eight emirates are the seven that compose the UAE and Bahrain; according to some sources, the dominant color was formerly red, but this darkened to maroon upon exposure to the sun and the new shade was eventually adopted

## NATIONAL SYMBOL(S):

a maroon field surmounted by a white serrated band with nine white points; national colors: maroon, white

## NATIONAL ANTHEM:

**name:** "Al-Salam Al-Amiri" (The Amiri Salute)

**lyrics/music:** Sheikh MUBARAK bin Saif al-Thani/Abdul Aziz Nasser OBAIDAN

**note:** adopted 1996; anthem first performed that year at a meeting of the Gulf Cooperative Council hosted by Qatar

# ECONOMY :: QATAR

## ECONOMY - OVERVIEW:

Qatar's oil and natural gas resources are the country's main economic engine and government revenue source, driving Qatar's high economic growth and per capita income levels, robust state spending on public entitlements, and booming construction spending, particularly as Qatar prepares to host the World Cup in 2022. Although the government has maintained high capital spending levels for ongoing infrastructure projects, low oil and natural gas prices in recent years have led the Qatari Government to tighten some spending to help stem its budget deficit.

Qatar's reliance on oil and natural gas is likely to persist for the foreseeable future. Proved natural gas reserves exceed 25 trillion cubic meters - 13% of the world total and, among countries, third largest in the world. Proved oil reserves exceed 25 billion barrels, allowing production to continue at current levels for about 56 years. Despite the dominance of oil and natural gas, Qatar has made significant gains in strengthening non-oil sectors, such as manufacturing, construction, and financial services, leading non-oil GDP to steadily rise in recent years to just over half the total.

Following trade restriction imposed by Saudi Arabia, the UAE, Bahrain, and Egypt in 2017, Qatar established new trade routes with other countries to maintain access to imports.

## GDP (PURCHASING POWER PARITY):

$339.5 billion (2017 est.)

$334.2 billion (2016 est.)

$327.3 billion (2015 est.)

note: data are in 2017 dollars

**country comparison to the world:** 52

## GDP (OFFICIAL EXCHANGE RATE):

$166.9 billion (2017 est.) (2017 est.)

## GDP - REAL GROWTH RATE:

1.6% (2017 est.)

2.1% (2016 est.)

3.7% (2015 est.)

**country comparison to the world:** 169

## GDP - PER CAPITA (PPP):

$124,100 (2017 est.)

$127,700 (2016 est.)

$134,200 (2015 est.)

note: data are in 2017 dollars

country comparison to the world: 2

## GROSS NATIONAL SAVING:

50.2% of GDP (2017 est.)

42.4% of GDP (2016 est.)

47.4% of GDP (2015 est.)

country comparison to the world: 1

## GDP - COMPOSITION, BY END USE:

household consumption: 24.6% (2017 est.)

government consumption: 17% (2017 est.)

investment in fixed capital: 43.1% (2017 est.)

investment in inventories: 1.5% (2017 est.)

exports of goods and services: 51% (2017 est.)

imports of goods and services: -37.3% (2017 est.)

## GDP - COMPOSITION, BY SECTOR OF ORIGIN:

agriculture: 0.2% (2017 est.)

industry: 50.3% (2017 est.)

services: 49.5% (2017 est.)

## AGRICULTURE - PRODUCTS:

fruits, vegetables; poultry, dairy products, beef; fish

## INDUSTRIES:

liquefied natural gas, crude oil production and refining, ammonia, fertilizer, petrochemicals, steel reinforcing bars, cement, commercial ship repair

## INDUSTRIAL PRODUCTION GROWTH RATE:

3% (2017 est.)

country comparison to the world: 105

## LABOR FORCE:

1.953 million (2017 est.)

country comparison to the world: 126

## UNEMPLOYMENT RATE:

8.9% (2017 est.)

11.1% (2016 est.)

country comparison to the world: 128

## POPULATION BELOW POVERTY LINE:

NA

## HOUSEHOLD INCOME OR CONSUMPTION BY PERCENTAGE SHARE:

lowest 10%: 35.9% (2007)

highest 10%: 35.9% (2007)

## DISTRIBUTION OF FAMILY INCOME - GINI INDEX:

41.1 (2007)

country comparison to the world: 58

## BUDGET:

revenues: 44.1 billion (2017 est.)

expenditures: 53.82 billion (2017 est.)

## TAXES AND OTHER REVENUES:

26.4% (of GDP) (2017 est.)

country comparison to the world: 112

## BUDGET SURPLUS (+) OR DEFICIT (-):

-5.8% (of GDP) (2017 est.)

country comparison to the world: 179

## PUBLIC DEBT:

53.8% of GDP (2017 est.)

46.7% of GDP (2016 est.)

country comparison to the world: 88

## FISCAL YEAR:

1 April - 31 March

## INFLATION RATE (CONSUMER PRICES):

0.4% (2017 est.)

2.7% (2016 est.)

country comparison to the world: 25

## CENTRAL BANK DISCOUNT RATE:

5% (16 March 2017)

4.5% (31 December 2012)

country comparison to the world: 82

## COMMERCIAL BANK PRIME LENDING RATE:

4.95% (31 December 2017 est.)

4.51% (31 December 2016 est.)

country comparison to the world: 152

## STOCK OF NARROW MONEY:

$34.71 billion (31 December 2017 est.)

$36.14 billion (31 December 2016 est.)

country comparison to the world: 59

## STOCK OF BROAD MONEY:

$34.71 billion (31 December 2017 est.)

$36.14 billion (31 December 2016 est.)

country comparison to the world: 59

## STOCK OF DOMESTIC CREDIT:

$246.7 billion (31 December 2017 est.)

$224.2 billion (31 December 2016 est.)

country comparison to the world: 42

## MARKET VALUE OF PUBLICLY TRADED SHARES:

$142.6 billion (31 December 2015 est.)

$185.9 billion (31 December 2014 est.)

$152.6 billion (31 December 2013 est.)

country comparison to the world: 38

## CURRENT ACCOUNT BALANCE:

$6.426 billion (2017 est.)

-$8.27 billion (2016 est.)

country comparison to the world: 27

## EXPORTS:

$67.5 billion (2017 est.)

$57.25 billion (2016 est.)

country comparison to the world: 44

## EXPORTS - PARTNERS:

Japan 17.3%, South Korea 16%, India 12.6%, China 11.2%, Singapore 8.2%, UAE 6.4% (2017)

## EXPORTS - COMMODITIES:

liquefied natural gas (LNG), petroleum products, fertilizers, steel

## IMPORTS:

$30.77 billion (2017 est.)

$31.93 billion (2016 est.)

country comparison to the world: 68

## IMPORTS - COMMODITIES:

machinery and transport equipment, food, chemicals

## IMPORTS - PARTNERS:

China 10.9%, US 8.9%, UAE 8.5%, Germany 8.1%, UK 5.5%, India 5.4%, Japan 5.3%, Italy 4.3% (2017)

## RESERVES OF FOREIGN EXCHANGE AND GOLD:

$15.01 billion (31 December 2017 est.)

$31.89 billion (31 December 2016 est.)

country comparison to the world: 68

## DEBT - EXTERNAL:

$167.8 billion (31 December 2017 est.)

$157.9 billion (31 December 2016 est.)

country comparison to the world: 39

## STOCK OF DIRECT FOREIGN INVESTMENT - AT HOME:

$36.29 billion (31 December 2017 est.)

$35.31 billion (31 December 2016 est.)

country comparison to the world: 66

## STOCK OF DIRECT FOREIGN INVESTMENT - ABROAD:

$59.33 billion (31 December 2017 est.)

$57.63 billion (31 December 2016 est.)

country comparison to the world: 39

## EXCHANGE RATES:

Qatari rials (QAR) per US dollar -

3.64 (2017 est.)

3.64 (2016 est.)

3.64 (2015 est.)

3.64 (2014 est.)
3.64 (2013 est.)

## ENERGY :: QATAR

**ELECTRICITY ACCESS:**

population without electricity: 45,165 (2012)

electrification - total population: 98% (2012)

electrification - urban areas: 98% (2012)

electrification - rural areas: 93% (2012)

**ELECTRICITY - PRODUCTION:**

39.78 billion kWh (2016 est.)

country comparison to the world: 58

**ELECTRICITY - CONSUMPTION:**

37.24 billion kWh (2016 est.)

country comparison to the world: 58

**ELECTRICITY - EXPORTS:**

0 kWh (2016 est.)

country comparison to the world: 186

**ELECTRICITY - IMPORTS:**

0 kWh (2016 est.)

country comparison to the world: 188

**ELECTRICITY - INSTALLED GENERATING CAPACITY:**

8.796 million kW (2016 est.)

country comparison to the world: 66

**ELECTRICITY - FROM FOSSIL FUELS:**

100% of total installed capacity (2016 est.)

country comparison to the world: 15

**ELECTRICITY - FROM NUCLEAR FUELS:**

0% of total installed capacity (2017 est.)

country comparison to the world: 169

**ELECTRICITY - FROM HYDROELECTRIC PLANTS:**

0% of total installed capacity (2017 est.)

country comparison to the world: 193

**ELECTRICITY - FROM OTHER RENEWABLE SOURCES:**

1% of total installed capacity (2017 est.)

country comparison to the world: 163

**CRUDE OIL - PRODUCTION:**

1.5 million bbl/day (2017 est.)

country comparison to the world: 17

**CRUDE OIL - EXPORTS:**

1.15 million bbl/day (2015 est.)

country comparison to the world: 13

**CRUDE OIL - IMPORTS:**

0 bbl/day (2015 est.)

country comparison to the world: 183

**CRUDE OIL - PROVED RESERVES:**

25.24 billion bbl (1 January 2018 est.)

country comparison to the world: 13

**REFINED PETROLEUM PRODUCTS - PRODUCTION:**

273,800 bbl/day (2015 est.)

country comparison to the world: 46

**REFINED PETROLEUM PRODUCTS - CONSUMPTION:**

277,000 bbl/day (2016 est.)

country comparison to the world: 45

**REFINED PETROLEUM PRODUCTS - EXPORTS:**

485,000 bbl/day (2015 est.)

country comparison to the world: 18

**REFINED PETROLEUM PRODUCTS - IMPORTS:**

12,300 bbl/day (2015 est.)

country comparison to the world: 143

**NATURAL GAS - PRODUCTION:**

166.4 billion cu m (2017 est.)

country comparison to the world: 4

**NATURAL GAS - CONSUMPTION:**

39.9 billion cu m (2017 est.)

country comparison to the world: 26

**NATURAL GAS - EXPORTS:**

126.5 billion cu m (2017 est.)

country comparison to the world: 2

**NATURAL GAS - IMPORTS:**

0 cu m (2017 est.)

country comparison to the world: 176

**NATURAL GAS - PROVED RESERVES:**

24.07 trillion cu m (1 January 2018 est.)

country comparison to the world: 3

**CARBON DIOXIDE EMISSIONS FROM CONSUMPTION OF ENERGY:**

114.2 million Mt (2017 est.)

country comparison to the world: 40

## COMMUNICATIONS :: QATAR

**TELEPHONES - FIXED LINES:**

total subscriptions: 440,909 (2017 est.)

subscriptions per 100 inhabitants: 19 (2017 est.)

country comparison to the world: 100

**TELEPHONES - MOBILE CELLULAR:**

total subscriptions: 3,913,809 (2017 est.)

subscriptions per 100 inhabitants: 169 (2017 est.)

country comparison to the world: 128

**TELEPHONE SYSTEM:**

general assessment: modern system centered in Doha (2016)

domestic: combined fixed-line and mobile-cellular telephone subscribership exceeds 175 telephones per 100 persons (2016)

international: country code - 974; landing point for the Fiber-Optic Link Around the Globe (FLAG) submarine cable network that provides links to Asia, Middle East, Europe, and the US; tropospheric scatter to Bahrain; microwave radio relay to Saudi Arabia and the UAE; satellite earth stations - 2 Intelsat (1 Atlantic Ocean and 1 Indian Ocean) and 1 Arabsat (2016)

**BROADCAST MEDIA:**

TV and radio broadcast licensing and access to local media markets are state controlled; home of the satellite TV channel Al-Jazeera, which was originally owned and financed by the Qatari government but has evolved to independent corporate status; Al-Jazeera claims editorial independence in broadcasting; local radio transmissions include state, private, and international broadcasters on FM frequencies in Doha; in August 2013, Qatar's satellite company Es'hailSat launched its first communications satellite Es'hail 1 (manufactured in the US), which entered commercial service in December 2013 to provide improved television broadcasting capability and expand availability of voice and Internet; Es'hailSat expects to launch its second satellite in 2018 (2014)

**INTERNET COUNTRY CODE:**

.qa

**INTERNET USERS:**

total: 2,129,360 (July 2016 est.)

percent of population: 94.3% (July 2016 est.)

country comparison to the world: 110

**BROADBAND - FIXED SUBSCRIPTIONS:**

total: 256,094 (2017 est.)

subscriptions per 100 inhabitants: 11 (2017 est.)

country comparison to the world: 101

## TRANSPORTATION :: QATAR

### NATIONAL AIR TRANSPORT SYSTEM:
number of registered air carriers: 2 (2015)

inventory of registered aircraft operated by air carriers: 199 (2015)

annual passenger traffic on registered air carriers: 25,263,224 (2015)

annual freight traffic on registered air carriers: 7,563,307,390 mt-km (2015)

### CIVIL AIRCRAFT REGISTRATION COUNTRY CODE PREFIX:
A7 (2016)

### AIRPORTS:
6 (2013)

country comparison to the world: 174

### AIRPORTS - WITH PAVED RUNWAYS:
total: 4 (2017)

over 3,047 m: 3 (2017)

1,524 to 2,437 m: 1 (2017)

### AIRPORTS - WITH UNPAVED RUNWAYS:
total: 2 (2013)

914 to 1,523 m: 1 (2013)

under 914 m: 1 (2013)

### HELIPORTS:
1 (2013)

### PIPELINES:
288 km condensate, 221 km condensate/gas, 2383 km gas, 90 km liquid petroleum gas, 745 km oil, 103 km refined products (2013)

### ROADWAYS:
total: 9,830 km (2010)

country comparison to the world: 136

### MERCHANT MARINE:
total: 143 (2017)

by type: bulk carrier 8, container ship 6, general cargo 5, oil tanker 6, other 118 (2017)

country comparison to the world: 75

### PORTS AND TERMINALS:
major seaport(s): Doha, Musay'id, Ra's Laffan

LNG terminal(s) (export): Ras Laffan

## MILITARY AND SECURITY :: QATAR

### MILITARY BRANCHES:
Qatari Emiri Land Force (QELF), Qatari Emiri Navy (QEN), Qatari Emiri Air Force (QEAF) (2013)

### MILITARY SERVICE AGE AND OBLIGATION:
conscription for males aged 18-35; 4-month general obligation, 3 months for graduates (2014)

## TERRORISM :: QATAR

### TERRORIST GROUPS - FOREIGN BASED:
**HAMAS:**
aim(s): continue engagement with the Qatari Government
area(s) of operation: maintains a limited office in Doha (April 2018)

## TRANSNATIONAL ISSUES :: QATAR

### DISPUTES - INTERNATIONAL:
none

### REFUGEES AND INTERNALLY DISPLACED PERSONS:
stateless persons: 1,200 (2017)

### TRAFFICKING IN PERSONS:
current situation: Qatar is a destination country for men, women, and children subjected to forced labor, and, to a much lesser extent, forced prostitution; the predominantly foreign workforce migrates to Qatar legally for low- and semi-skilled work but often experiences situations of forced labor, including debt bondage, delayed or nonpayment of salaries, confiscation of passports, abuse, hazardous working conditions, and squalid living arrangements; foreign female domestic workers are particularly vulnerable to trafficking because of their isolation in private homes and lack of protection under Qatari labor laws; some women who migrate for work are also forced into prostitution

tier rating: Tier 2 Watch List – Qatar does not fully comply with the minimum standards for the elimination of trafficking; however, it is making significant efforts to do so; the government investigated 11 trafficking cases but did not prosecute or convict any offenders, including exploitative employers and recruitment agencies; the primary solution for resolving labor violations was to transfer a worker's sponsorship to a new employer with minimal effort to investigate whether a forced labor violation had occurred; authorities increased their efforts to protect some trafficking victims, although many victims of forced labor, particularly domestic workers, remained unidentified and unprotected and were sometimes punished for immigration violations or running away from an employer or sponsor; authorities visited worksites throughout the country to meet and educate workers and employers on trafficking regulations, but the government failed to abolish or reform the sponsorship system, perpetuating Qatar's forced labor problem (2015)

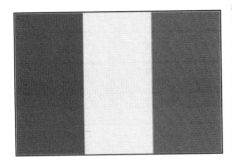

# EUROPE :: ROMANIA

## INTRODUCTION :: ROMANIA

### BACKGROUND:

The principalities of Wallachia and Moldavia - for centuries under the suzerainty of the Turkish Ottoman Empire - secured their autonomy in 1856; they were de facto linked in 1859 and formally united in 1862 under the new name of Romania. The country gained recognition of its independence in 1878. It joined the Allied Powers in World War I and acquired new territories - most notably Transylvania - following the conflict. In 1940, Romania allied with the Axis powers and participated in the 1941 German invasion of the USSR. Three years later, overrun by the Soviets, Romania signed an armistice. The post-war Soviet occupation led to the formation of a communist "people's republic" in 1947 and the abdication of the king. The decades-long rule of dictator Nicolae CEAUSESCU, who took power in 1965, and his Securitate police state became increasingly oppressive and draconian through the 1980s. CEAUSESCU was overthrown and executed in late 1989. Former communists dominated the government until 1996 when they were swept from power. Romania joined NATO in 2004 and the EU in 2007.

## GEOGRAPHY :: ROMANIA

### LOCATION:
Southeastern Europe, bordering the Black Sea, between Bulgaria and Ukraine

### GEOGRAPHIC COORDINATES:
46 00 N, 25 00 E

### MAP REFERENCES:
Europe

### AREA:
total: 238,391 sq km

land: 229,891 sq km

water: 8,500 sq km

country comparison to the world: 84

### AREA - COMPARATIVE:
twice the size of Pennsylvania; slightly smaller than Oregon

### LAND BOUNDARIES:
total: 2,844 km

border countries (5): Bulgaria 605 km, Hungary 424 km, Moldova 683 km, Serbia 531 km, Ukraine 601 km

### COASTLINE:
225 km

### MARITIME CLAIMS:
territorial sea: 12 nm

exclusive economic zone: 200 nm

contiguous zone: 24 nm

continental shelf: 200-m depth or to the depth of exploitation

### CLIMATE:
temperate; cold, cloudy winters with frequent snow and fog; sunny summers with frequent showers and thunderstorms

### TERRAIN:
central Transylvanian Basin is separated from the Moldavian Plateau on the east by the Eastern Carpathian Mountains and separated from the Walachian Plain on the south by the Transylvanian Alps

### ELEVATION:
mean elevation: 414 m

elevation extremes: 0 m lowest point: Black Sea

2544 highest point: Moldoveanu

### NATURAL RESOURCES:
petroleum (reserves declining), timber, natural gas, coal, iron ore, salt, arable land, hydropower

### LAND USE:
agricultural land: 60.7% (2011 est.)

arable land: 39.1% (2011 est.) / permanent crops: 1.9% (2011 est.) / permanent pasture: 19.7% (2011 est.)

forest: 28.7% (2011 est.)

other: 10.6% (2011 est.)

### IRRIGATED LAND:
31,490 sq km (2012)

### POPULATION DISTRIBUTION:
urbanization is not particularly high, and a fairly even population distribution can be found throughout most of the country, with urban areas attracting larger and denser populations; Hungarians, the country's largest minority, have a particularly strong presence in eastern Transylvania

### NATURAL HAZARDS:
earthquakes, most severe in south and southwest; geologic structure and climate promote landslides

### ENVIRONMENT - CURRENT ISSUES:
soil erosion, degradation, and desertification; water pollution; air pollution in south from industrial effluents; contamination of Danube delta wetlands

### ENVIRONMENT - INTERNATIONAL AGREEMENTS:

party to: Air Pollution, Air Pollution-Persistent Organic Pollutants, Antarctic-Environmental Protocol, Antarctic Treaty, Biodiversity, Climate Change, Climate Change-Kyoto Protocol, Desertification, Endangered Species, Environmental Modification, Hazardous Wastes, Law of the Sea, Ozone Layer Protection, Ship Pollution, Wetlands

signed, but not ratified: none of the selected agreements

### GEOGRAPHY - NOTE:

controls the most easily traversable land route between the Balkans, Moldova, and Ukraine; the Carpathian Mountains dominate the center of the country, while the Danube River forms much of the southern boundary with Serbia and Bulgaria

# PEOPLE AND SOCIETY :: ROMANIA

### POPULATION:
21,457,116 (July 2018 est.)

country comparison to the world: 58

### NATIONALITY:
noun: Romanian(s)

adjective: Romanian

### ETHNIC GROUPS:
Romanian 83.4%, Hungarian 6.1%, Romani 3.1%, Ukrainian 0.3%, German 0.2%, other 0.7%, unspecified 6.1% (2011 est.)

note: Romani populations are usually underestimated in official statistics and may represent 5–11% of Romania's population

### LANGUAGES:
Romanian (official) 85.4%, Hungarian 6.3%, Romani 1.2%, other 1%, unspecified 6.1% (2011 est.)

### RELIGIONS:
Eastern Orthodox (including all sub-denominations) 81.9%, Protestant (various denominations including Reformed and Pentecostal) 6.4%, Roman Catholic 4.3%, other (includes Muslim) 0.9%, none or atheist 0.2%, unspecified 6.3% (2011 est.)

### AGE STRUCTURE:
0-14 years: 14.31% (male 1,576,621 /female 1,493,082)

15-24 years: 10.45% (male 1,151,312 /female 1,091,956)

25-54 years: 46.11% (male 5,010,272 /female 4,883,090)

55-64 years: 12.37% (male 1,244,669 /female 1,409,854)

65 years and over: 16.76% (male 1,454,320 /female 2,141,940) (2018 est.)

### DEPENDENCY RATIOS:
total dependency ratio: 48 (2015 est.)

youth dependency ratio: 22.8 (2015 est.)

elderly dependency ratio: 25.2 (2015 est.)

potential support ratio: 4 (2015 est.)

### MEDIAN AGE:
total: 41.6 years

male: 40.2 years

female: 43 years (2018 est.)

country comparison to the world: 38

### POPULATION GROWTH RATE:
-0.35% (2018 est.)

country comparison to the world: 219

### BIRTH RATE:
8.7 births/1,000 population (2018 est.)

country comparison to the world: 211

### DEATH RATE:
12 deaths/1,000 population (2018 est.)

country comparison to the world: 17

### NET MIGRATION RATE:
-0.2 migrant(s)/1,000 population (2017 est.)

country comparison to the world: 112

### POPULATION DISTRIBUTION:
urbanization is not particularly high, and a fairly even population distribution can be found throughout most of the country, with urban areas attracting larger and denser populations; Hungarians, the country's largest minority, have a particularly strong presence in eastern Transylvania

### URBANIZATION:
urban population: 54% of total population (2018)

rate of urbanization: -0.38% annual rate of change (2015-20 est.)

### MAJOR URBAN AREAS - POPULATION:
1.821 million BUCHAREST (capital) (2018)

### SEX RATIO:
at birth: 1.06 male(s)/female (2017 est.)

0-14 years: 1.06 male(s)/female (2017 est.)

15-24 years: 1.05 male(s)/female (2017 est.)

25-54 years: 1.02 male(s)/female (2017 est.)

55-64 years: 0.88 male(s)/female (2017 est.)

65 years and over: 0.68 male(s)/female (2017 est.)

total population: 0.95 male(s)/female (2017 est.)

### MOTHER'S MEAN AGE AT FIRST BIRTH:
26.7 years (2014 est.)

### MATERNAL MORTALITY RATE:
31 deaths/100,000 live births (2015 est.)

country comparison to the world: 112

### INFANT MORTALITY RATE:
total: 9.2 deaths/1,000 live births (2018 est.)

male: 10.4 deaths/1,000 live births (2018 est.)

female: 7.8 deaths/1,000 live births (2018 est.)

country comparison to the world: 143

### LIFE EXPECTANCY AT BIRTH:
total population: 75.6 years (2018 est.)

male: 72.1 years (2018 est.)

female: 79.2 years (2018 est.)

country comparison to the world: 106

### TOTAL FERTILITY RATE:
1.36 children born/woman (2018 est.)

country comparison to the world: 215

### HEALTH EXPENDITURES:
5.6% of GDP (2014)

country comparison to the world: 121

### PHYSICIANS DENSITY:
2.67 physicians/1,000 population (2013)

### HOSPITAL BED DENSITY:
6.3 beds/1,000 population (2013)

### DRINKING WATER SOURCE:
improved:

urban: 100% of population (2015 est.)

rural: 100% of population (2015 est.)

total: 100% of population (2015 est.)

unimproved:

urban: 0% of population (2015 est.)

rural: 0% of population (2015 est.)

total: 0% of population (2015 est.)

## SANITATION FACILITY ACCESS:

**improved:**

urban: 92.2% of population (2015 est.)

rural: 63.3% of population (2015 est.)

total: 79.1% of population (2015 est.)

**unimproved:**

urban: 7.8% of population (2015 est.)

rural: 36.7% of population (2015 est.)

total: 20.9% of population (2015 est.)

## HIV/AIDS - ADULT PREVALENCE RATE:

0.1% (2017 est.)

country comparison to the world: 119

## HIV/AIDS - PEOPLE LIVING WITH HIV/AIDS:

16,000 (2017 est.)

country comparison to the world: 86

## HIV/AIDS - DEATHS:

<200 (2017 est.)

## OBESITY - ADULT PREVALENCE RATE:

22.5% (2016)

country comparison to the world: 75

## EDUCATION EXPENDITURES:

3.1% of GDP (2014)

country comparison to the world: 141

## LITERACY:

definition: age 15 and over can read and write (2015 est.)

total population: 98.8% (2015 est.)

male: 99.1% (2015 est.)

female: 98.5% (2015 est.)

## SCHOOL LIFE EXPECTANCY (PRIMARY TO TERTIARY EDUCATION):

total: 15 years (2015)

male: 15 years (2015)

female: 15 years (2015)

## UNEMPLOYMENT, YOUTH AGES 15-24:

total: 20.6% (2016 est.)

male: 19.9% (2016 est.)

female: 21.8% (2016 est.)

country comparison to the world: 62

# GOVERNMENT :: ROMANIA

## COUNTRY NAME:

conventional long form: none

conventional short form: Romania

local long form: none

local short form: Romania

former: Kingdom of Romania, Romanian People's Republic, Socialist Republic of Romania

etymology: the name derives from the Latin "Romanus" meaning "citizen of Rome" and was used to stress the common ancient heritage of Romania's three main regions - Moldavia, Transylvania, and Wallachia - during their gradual unification between the mid-19th century and early 20th century

## GOVERNMENT TYPE:

semi-presidential republic

## CAPITAL:

name: Bucharest

geographic coordinates: 44 26 N, 26 06 E

time difference: UTC+2 (7 hours ahead of Washington, DC, during Standard Time)

daylight saving time: +1hr, begins last Sunday in March; ends last Sunday in October

## ADMINISTRATIVE DIVISIONS:

41 counties (judete, singular - judet) and 1 municipality* (municipiu); Alba, Arad, Arges, Bacau, Bihor, Bistrita-Nasaud, Botosani, Braila, Brasov, Bucuresti (Bucharest)*, Buzau, Calarasi, Caras-Severin, Cluj, Constanta, Covasna, Dambovita, Dolj, Galati, Gorj, Giurgiu, Harghita, Hunedoara, Ialomita, Iasi, Ilfov, Maramures, Mehedinti, Mures, Neamt, Olt, Prahova, Salaj, Satu Mare, Sibiu, Suceava, Teleorman, Timis, Tulcea, Vaslui, Valcea, Vrancea

## INDEPENDENCE:

9 May 1877 (independence proclaimed from the Ottoman Empire;13 July 1878 (independence recognized by the Treaty of Berlin);26 March 1881 (kingdom proclaimed);30 December 1947 (republic proclaimed)

## NATIONAL HOLIDAY:

Unification Day (unification of Romania and Transylvania), 1 December (1918)

## CONSTITUTION:

history: several previous; latest adopted 21 November 1991, approved by referendum and effective 8 December 1991 (2016)

amendments: initiated by the president of Romania through a proposal by the government, by at least one-fourths of deputies or senators in Parliament, or by petition of eligible voters representing at least half of Romania's counties; passage requires at least two-thirds majority vote by both chambers or – if mediation is required - by three-fourths majority vote in a joint session, followed by approval in a referendum; articles including those on national sovereignty, form of government, political pluralism, and fundamental rights and freedoms cannot be amended; amended 2003 (2016)

## LEGAL SYSTEM:

civil law system

## INTERNATIONAL LAW ORGANIZATION PARTICIPATION:

accepts compulsory ICJ jurisdiction with reservations; accepts ICCt jurisdiction

## CITIZENSHIP:

citizenship by birth: no

citizenship by descent only: at least one parent must be a citizen of Romania

dual citizenship recognized: yes

residency requirement for naturalization: 5 years

## SUFFRAGE:

18 years of age; universal

## EXECUTIVE BRANCH:

chief of state: President Klaus Werner IOHANNIS (since 21 December 2014)

head of government: Prime Minister Viorica DANCILA (since 29 January 2018); Deputy Prime Ministers Gratiela GAVRILESCU (since 29 June 2017), Paul STANESCU (17 October 2017), Viorel STEFAN (since 29 January 2018), Ana BIRCHALL (since 29 January 2018); note - DANCILA is Romania's first woman prime minister

cabinet: Council of Ministers appointed by the prime minister

elections/appointments: president directly elected by absolute majority popular vote in 2 rounds if needed for a 5-year term (eligible for a second term); election last held on 2 November 2014 with a runoff on 16 November 2014 (next to be held in November 2019); prime minister appointed by the president with consent of Parliament

election results: Klaus IOHANNIS elected president in second round; percent of vote - Klaus IOHANNIS (PNL) 54.4%, Victor PONTA (PSD)

45.6%; Viorica DANCILA approved as prime minister 282-136

## LEGISLATIVE BRANCH:

**description:** bicameral Parliament or Parliament consists of:
Senate or Senat (136 seats; members directly elected in single- and multi-seat constituencies - including 2 seats for diaspora - by party-list, proportional representation vote; members serve 4-year terms)
Chamber of Deputies or Camera Deputatilor (329 seats; members directly elected in single- and multi-seat constituencies - including 4 seats for diaspora - by party-list, proportional representation vote; members serve 4-year terms)

**elections:**
Senate - last held on 11 December 2016 (next to be held by December 2020)
Chamber of Deputies - last held on 11 December 2016 (next to be held by December 2020)

**election results:**
Senate - percent of vote by party - PSD 45.7%, PNL 20.4%, USR 8.9%, UDMR 6.2%, ALDE 6%, PMP 5.7%, other 7.1%; seats by party - PSD 67, PNL 30, USR 13, UDMR 9, ALDE 9, PMP 8; composition - men 116, women 20, percent of women 14.7%
Chamber of Deputies - percent of vote by party - PSD 45.5%, PNL 20%, USR 8.9%, UDMR 6.2%, ALDE 5.6%, PMP 5.4%, other 8.4%; seats by party - PSD 154, PNL 69, USR 30, UDMR 21, ALDE 20, PMP 18, minorities 17; composition men 261, women 68, percent of women 20.7%; note - total Parliament percent of women 20.7%

## JUDICIAL BRANCH:

**highest courts:** High Court of Cassation and Justice (consists of 111 judges organized into civil, penal, commercial, contentious administrative and fiscal business, and joint sections); Supreme Constitutional Court (consists of 9 members)

**judge selection and term of office:** High Court of Cassation and Justice judges appointed by the president upon nomination by the Superior Council of Magistracy, a 19-member body of judges, prosecutors, and law specialists; judges appointed for 6-year renewable terms; Constitutional Court members - 6 elected by Parliament and 3 appointed by the president; members serve 9-year, nonrenewable terms

**subordinate courts:** Courts of Appeal; regional tribunals; first instance courts; military and arbitration courts

## POLITICAL PARTIES AND LEADERS:

Christian-Democratic National Peasants' Party or PNT-CD [Aurelian PAVELESCU]
Democratic Union of Hungarians in Romania or UDMR [Hunor KELEMEN]
Civic Hungarian Party [Zsolt BIRO]
Ecologist Party of Romania or PER [Danut POP]
Greater Romania Party or PRM [Adrian POPESCU]
M10 Party [Ioana CONSTANTIN]
National Liberal Party or PNL [Ludovic ORBAN]
New Romania Party or PNR [Sebastian POPESCU]
Our Romania Alliance [Marian MUNTEANU]
Party of the Alliance of Liberals and Democrats or ALDE [Calin POPESCU TARICEANU]
Popular Movement Party or PMP [Traian BASESCU]
Romanian Social Party or PSRo [Mircea GEOANA]
Save Romania Union Party or Partidul USR [Dan BARNA]
Social Democratic Party or PSD [Liviu DRAGNEA]
United Romania Party or PRU [Robert BUGA]

## INTERNATIONAL ORGANIZATION PARTICIPATION:

Australia Group, BIS, BSEC, CBSS (observer), CD, CE, CEI, EAPC, EBRD, ECB, EIB, ESA, EU, FAO, G-9, IAEA, IBRD, ICAO, ICC (national committees), ICCt, ICRM, IDA, IFAD, IFC, IFRCS, IHO, ILO, IMF, IMO, IMSO, Interpol, IOC, IOM, IPU, ISO, ITSO, ITU, ITUC (NGOs), LAIA (observer), MIGA, MONUSCO, NATO, NSG, OAS (observer), OIF, OPCW, OSCE, PCA, SELEC, UN, UNCTAD, UNESCO, UNHCR, UNIDO, Union Latina, UNMIL, UNMISS, UNOCI, UNWTO, UPU, WCO, WFTU (NGOs), WHO, WIPO, WMO, WTO, ZC

## DIPLOMATIC REPRESENTATION IN THE US:

**chief of mission:** Ambassador George Cristian MAIOR (since 17 September 2015)

**chancery:** 1607 23rd Street NW, Washington, DC 20008

**telephone:** [1] (202) 332-4846, 4848, 4851, 4852

**FAX:** [1] (202) 232-4748

**consulate(s) general:** Chicago, Los Angeles, New York

## DIPLOMATIC REPRESENTATION FROM THE US:

**chief of mission:** Ambassador Hans G. KLEMM (since 21 September 2015)

**embassy:** 4-6, Dr. Liviu Librescu Blvd., District 1, Bucharest, 015118

**mailing address:** American Embassy Bucharest, US Department of State, 5260 Bucharest Place, Washington, DC 20521-5260 (pouch)

**telephone:** [40] (21) 200-3300

**FAX:** [40] (21) 200-3442

## FLAG DESCRIPTION:

three equal vertical bands of cobalt blue (hoist side), chrome yellow, and vermilion red; modeled after the flag of France, the colors are those of the principalities of Walachia (red and yellow) and Moldavia (red and blue), which united in 1862 to form Romania; the national coat of arms that used to be centered in the yellow band has been removed

**note:** now similar to the flag of Chad, whose blue band is darker; also resembles the flags of Andorra and Moldova

## NATIONAL SYMBOL(S):

golden eagle; national colors: blue, yellow, red

## NATIONAL ANTHEM:

**name:** "Desteapta-te romane!" (Wake up, Romanian!)

**lyrics/music:** Andrei MURESIANU/Anton PANN

**note:** adopted 1990; the anthem was written during the 1848 Revolution

# ECONOMY :: ROMANIA

## ECONOMY - OVERVIEW:

Romania, which joined the EU on 1 January 2007, began the transition from communism in 1989 with a largely obsolete industrial base and a pattern of output unsuited to the country's needs. Romania's macroeconomic gains have only recently started to spur creation of a middle class and to address Romania's widespread poverty. Corruption and red tape continue to permeate the business environment.

In the aftermath of the global financial crisis, Romania signed a $26 billion emergency assistance package from the IMF, the EU, and other international lenders, but GDP contracted until 2011. In March 2011, Romania and the IMF/EU/World Bank signed a 24-month precautionary standby agreement, worth $6.6 billion, to promote fiscal discipline, encourage progress on structural reforms, and strengthen financial sector stability; no funds were drawn. In September 2013, Romanian authorities and the IMF/EU agreed to a follow-on standby agreement, worth $5.4 billion, to continue with reforms. This agreement expired in September 2015, and no funds were drawn. Progress on structural reforms has been uneven, and the economy still is vulnerable to external shocks.

Economic growth rebounded in the 2013-17 period, driven by strong industrial exports, excellent agricultural harvests, and, more recently, expansionary fiscal policies in 2016-2017 that nearly quadrupled Bucharest's annual fiscal deficit, from +0.8% of GDP in 2015 to -3% of GDP in 2016 and an estimated -3.4% in 2017. Industry outperformed other sectors of the economy in 2017. Exports remained an engine of economic growth, led by trade with the EU, which accounts for roughly 70% of Romania trade. Domestic demand was the major driver, due to tax cuts and large wage increases that began last year and are set to continue in 2018.

An aging population, emigration of skilled labor, significant tax evasion, insufficient health care, and an aggressive loosening of the fiscal package compromise Romania's long-term growth and economic stability and are the economy's top vulnerabilities.

**GDP (PURCHASING POWER PARITY):**

$483.4 billion (2017 est.)

$452 billion (2016 est.)

$431.2 billion (2015 est.)

note: data are in 2017 dollars

country comparison to the world: 41

**GDP (OFFICIAL EXCHANGE RATE):**

$211.9 billion (2017 est.) (2017 est.)

**GDP - REAL GROWTH RATE:**

6.9% (2017 est.)

4.8% (2016 est.)

3.9% (2015 est.)

country comparison to the world: 23

**GDP - PER CAPITA (PPP):**

$24,600 (2017 est.)

$22,900 (2016 est.)

$21,700 (2015 est.)

note: data are in 2017 dollars

country comparison to the world: 83

**GROSS NATIONAL SAVING:**

21.1% of GDP (2017 est.)

21.7% of GDP (2016 est.)

23.9% of GDP (2015 est.)

country comparison to the world: 87

**GDP - COMPOSITION, BY END USE:**

household consumption: 70% (2017 est.)

government consumption: 7.7% (2017 est.)

investment in fixed capital: 22.6% (2017 est.)

investment in inventories: 1.9% (2017 est.)

exports of goods and services: 41.4% (2017 est.)

imports of goods and services: -43.6% (2017 est.)

**GDP - COMPOSITION, BY SECTOR OF ORIGIN:**

agriculture: 4.2% (2017 est.)

industry: 33.2% (2017 est.)

services: 62.6% (2017 est.)

**AGRICULTURE - PRODUCTS:**

wheat, corn, barley, sugar beets, sunflower seed, potatoes, grapes; eggs, sheep

**INDUSTRIES:**

electric machinery and equipment, auto assembly, textiles and footwear, light machinery, metallurgy, chemicals, food processing, petroleum refining, mining, timber, construction materials

**INDUSTRIAL PRODUCTION GROWTH RATE:**

5.5% (2017 est.)

country comparison to the world: 50

**LABOR FORCE:**

8.951 million (2017 est.)

country comparison to the world: 54

**LABOR FORCE - BY OCCUPATION:**

agriculture: 28.3%

industry: 28.9%

services: 42.8% (2014)

**UNEMPLOYMENT RATE:**

4.9% (2017 est.)

5.9% (2016 est.)

country comparison to the world: 71

**POPULATION BELOW POVERTY LINE:**

22.4% (2012 est.)

**HOUSEHOLD INCOME OR CONSUMPTION BY PERCENTAGE SHARE:**

lowest 10%: 7.6% (2014 est.)

highest 10%: 7.6% (2014 est.)

**DISTRIBUTION OF FAMILY INCOME - GINI INDEX:**

27.3 (2012)

28.2 (2010)

country comparison to the world: 143

**BUDGET:**

revenues: 62.14 billion (2017 est.)

expenditures: 68.13 billion (2017 est.)

**TAXES AND OTHER REVENUES:**

29.3% (of GDP) (2017 est.)

country comparison to the world: 84

**BUDGET SURPLUS (+) OR DEFICIT (-):**

-2.8% (of GDP) (2017 est.)

country comparison to the world: 125

**PUBLIC DEBT:**

36.8% of GDP (2017 est.)

38.8% of GDP (2016 est.)

note: defined by the EU's Maastricht Treaty as consolidated general government gross debt at nominal value, outstanding at the end of the year in the following categories of government liabilities: currency and deposits, securities other than shares excluding financial derivatives, and loans; general government sector comprises the subsectors: central government, state government, local government, and social security funds

country comparison to the world: 145

**FISCAL YEAR:**

calendar year

**INFLATION RATE (CONSUMER PRICES):**

1.3% (2017 est.)

-1.6% (2016 est.)

country comparison to the world: 71

**CENTRAL BANK DISCOUNT RATE:**

1.75% (31 December 2017)

1.75% (31 December 2016)

country comparison to the world: 125

**COMMERCIAL BANK PRIME LENDING RATE:**

5.57% (31 December 2017 est.)

5.71% (31 December 2016 est.)

country comparison to the world: 132

**STOCK OF NARROW MONEY:**

$54.13 billion (31 December 2017 est.)

$41.82 billion (31 December 2016 est.)

country comparison to the world: 52

**STOCK OF BROAD MONEY:**

$54.13 billion (31 December 2017 est.)

$41.82 billion (31 December 2016 est.)

country comparison to the world: 52

**STOCK OF DOMESTIC CREDIT:**

$72.54 billion (31 December 2017 est.)

$60.3 billion (31 December 2016 est.)

country comparison to the world: 59

**MARKET VALUE OF PUBLICLY TRADED SHARES:**

$42.24 billion (31 December 2017 est.)

$34.06 billion (31 December 2016 est.)

$42.59 billion (31 December 2013 est.)

country comparison to the world: 55

**CURRENT ACCOUNT BALANCE:**

-$7.114 billion (2017 est.)

-$3.93 billion (2016 est.)

country comparison to the world: 188

**EXPORTS:**

$64.58 billion (2017 est.)

$57.72 billion (2016 est.)

country comparison to the world: 45

**EXPORTS - PARTNERS:**

Germany 23%, Italy 11.2%, France 6.8%, Hungary 4.7%, UK 4.1% (2017)

**EXPORTS - COMMODITIES:**

machinery and equipment, other manufactured goods, agricultural products and foodstuffs, metals and metal products, chemicals, minerals and fuels, raw materials

**IMPORTS:**

$78.12 billion (2017 est.)

$68 billion (2016 est.)

country comparison to the world: 43

**IMPORTS - COMMODITIES:**

machinery and equipment, other manufactured goods, chemicals, agricultural products and foodstuffs, fuels and minerals, metals and metal products, raw materials

**IMPORTS - PARTNERS:**

Germany 20%, Italy 10%, Hungary 7.5%, Poland 5.5%, France 5.3%, China 5%, Netherlands 4% (2017)

**RESERVES OF FOREIGN EXCHANGE AND GOLD:**

$44.43 billion (31 December 2017 est.)

$40 billion (31 December 2016 est.)

country comparison to the world: 43

**DEBT - EXTERNAL:**

$95.97 billion (31 December 2017 est.)

$93.71 billion (31 December 2016 est.)

country comparison to the world: 49

**STOCK OF DIRECT FOREIGN INVESTMENT - AT HOME:**

$94 billion (31 December 2017 est.)

$76.93 billion (31 December 2016 est.)

country comparison to the world: 47

**STOCK OF DIRECT FOREIGN INVESTMENT - ABROAD:**

$6.822 billion (31 December 2017 est.)

$5.963 billion (31 December 2016 est.)

country comparison to the world: 70

**EXCHANGE RATES:**

lei (RON) per US dollar -

4.077 (2017 est.)

4.0592 (2016 est.)

4.0592 (2015 est.)

4.0057 (2014 est.)

3.3492 (2013 est.)

## ENERGY :: ROMANIA

**ELECTRICITY ACCESS:**

electrification - total population: 100% (2016)

**ELECTRICITY - PRODUCTION:**

61.78 billion kWh (2016 est.)

country comparison to the world: 47

**ELECTRICITY - CONSUMPTION:**

49.64 billion kWh (2016 est.)

country comparison to the world: 49

**ELECTRICITY - EXPORTS:**

11.22 billion kWh (2015 est.)

country comparison to the world: 18

**ELECTRICITY - IMPORTS:**

4.177 billion kWh (2016 est.)

country comparison to the world: 45

**ELECTRICITY - INSTALLED GENERATING CAPACITY:**

23.94 million kW (2016 est.)

country comparison to the world: 38

**ELECTRICITY - FROM FOSSIL FUELS:**

47% of total installed capacity (2016 est.)

country comparison to the world: 156

**ELECTRICITY - FROM NUCLEAR FUELS:**

6% of total installed capacity (2017 est.)

country comparison to the world: 20

**ELECTRICITY - FROM HYDROELECTRIC PLANTS:**

29% of total installed capacity (2017 est.)

country comparison to the world: 70

**ELECTRICITY - FROM OTHER RENEWABLE SOURCES:**

19% of total installed capacity (2017 est.)

country comparison to the world: 45

**CRUDE OIL - PRODUCTION:**

73,740 bbl/day (2017 est.)

country comparison to the world: 47

**CRUDE OIL - EXPORTS:**

2,076 bbl/day (2015 est.)

country comparison to the world: 70

**CRUDE OIL - IMPORTS:**

145,300 bbl/day (2015 est.)

country comparison to the world: 38

**CRUDE OIL - PROVED RESERVES:**

600 million bbl (1 January 2018 est.)

country comparison to the world: 42

**REFINED PETROLEUM PRODUCTS - PRODUCTION:**

232,600 bbl/day (2015 est.)

country comparison to the world: 47

**REFINED PETROLEUM PRODUCTS - CONSUMPTION:**

198,000 bbl/day (2016 est.)

country comparison to the world: 58

**REFINED PETROLEUM PRODUCTS - EXPORTS:**

103,000 bbl/day (2015 est.)

country comparison to the world: 44

**REFINED PETROLEUM PRODUCTS - IMPORTS:**

49,420 bbl/day (2015 est.)

country comparison to the world: 81

**NATURAL GAS - PRODUCTION:**

10.87 billion cu m (2017 est.)

country comparison to the world: 40

**NATURAL GAS - CONSUMPTION:**

11.58 billion cu m (2017 est.)

country comparison to the world: 45

**NATURAL GAS - EXPORTS:**

22.65 million cu m (2017 est.)

country comparison to the world: 53

**NATURAL GAS - IMPORTS:**

1.218 billion cu m (2017 est.)

country comparison to the world: 59

**NATURAL GAS - PROVED RESERVES:**

105.5 billion cu m (1 January 2018 est.)

country comparison to the world: 50

**CARBON DIOXIDE EMISSIONS FROM CONSUMPTION OF ENERGY:**

72.07 million Mt (2017 est.)

country comparison to the world: 50

## COMMUNICATIONS :: ROMANIA

**TELEPHONES - FIXED LINES:**

total subscriptions: 3.89 million (2017 est.)

subscriptions per 100 inhabitants: 18 (2017 est.)

country comparison to the world: 35

**TELEPHONES - MOBILE CELLULAR:**

total subscriptions: 22.55 million (2017 est.)

subscriptions per 100 inhabitants: 105 (2017 est.)

country comparison to the world: 54

**TELEPHONE SYSTEM:**

general assessment: the telecommunications sector is being expanded and modernized; domestic and international service improving rapidly, especially mobile-cellular services (2016)

domestic: fixed-line teledensity is about 20 telephones per 100 persons; mobile market served by five mobile network operators; mobile-cellular teledensity over 105 telephones per 100 persons (2016)

international: country code - 40; the Black Sea Fiber-Optic Cable System provides connectivity to Bulgaria and Turkey; satellite earth stations - 10; digital, international, direct-dial exchanges operate in Bucharest (2016)

**BROADCAST MEDIA:**

a mixture of public and private TV stations; there are 7 public TV stations (2 national, 5 regional) using terrestrial broadcasting and 187 private TV stations (out of which 171 offer local coverage) using terrestrial broadcasting, plus 11 public TV stations using satellite broadcasting and 86 private TV stations using satellite broadcasting; state-owned public radio broadcaster operates 4 national networks and regional and local stations, having in total 20 public radio stations by terrestrial broadcasting plus 4 public radio stations by satellite broadcasting; there are 502 operational private radio stations using terrestrial broadcasting and 26 private radio stations using satellite broadcasting (2014)

**INTERNET COUNTRY CODE:**

.ro

**INTERNET USERS:**

total: 12,852,696 (July 2016 est.)

percent of population: 59.5% (July 2016 est.)

country comparison to the world: 44

**BROADBAND - FIXED SUBSCRIPTIONS:**

total: 4.78 million (2017 est.)

subscriptions per 100 inhabitants: 22 (2017 est.)

country comparison to the world: 29

## TRANSPORTATION :: ROMANIA

**NATIONAL AIR TRANSPORT SYSTEM:**

number of registered air carriers: 5 (2015)

inventory of registered aircraft operated by air carriers: 51 (2015)

annual passenger traffic on registered air carriers: 3,636,642 (2015)

annual freight traffic on registered air carriers: 4,691,280 mt-km (2015)

**CIVIL AIRCRAFT REGISTRATION COUNTRY CODE PREFIX:**

YR (2016)

**AIRPORTS:**

45 (2013)

country comparison to the world: 95

**AIRPORTS - WITH PAVED RUNWAYS:**

total: 26 (2017)

over 3,047 m: 4 (2017)

2,438 to 3,047 m: 10 (2017)

1,524 to 2,437 m: 11 (2017)

under 914 m: 1 (2017)

**AIRPORTS - WITH UNPAVED RUNWAYS:**

total: 19 (2013)

914 to 1,523 m: 5 (2013)

under 914 m: 14 (2013)

**HELIPORTS:**

2 (2013)

**PIPELINES:**

3726 km gas, 2451 km oil (2013)

**RAILWAYS:**

total: 11,268 km (2014)

standard gauge: 10,781 km 1.435-m gauge (3,292 km electrified) (2014)

narrow gauge: 427 km 0.760-m gauge (2014)

broad gauge: 60 km 1.524-m gauge (2014)

country comparison to the world: 23

**ROADWAYS:**

total: 84,185 km (2012)

paved: 49,873 km (includes 337 km of expressways) (2012)

unpaved: 34,312 km (2012)

country comparison to the world: 58

**WATERWAYS:**

1,731 km (includes 1,075 km on the Danube River, 524 km on secondary branches, and 132 km on canals) (2010)

country comparison to the world: 45

**MERCHANT MARINE:**

total: 114 (2017)

by type: general cargo 13, oil tanker 7, other 94 (2017)

country comparison to the world: 79

**PORTS AND TERMINALS:**

major seaport(s): Constanta, Midia

river port(s): Braila, Galati (Galatz), Mancanului (Giurgiu), Tulcea (Danube River)

## MILITARY AND SECURITY :: ROMANIA

**MILITARY EXPENDITURES:**

1.42% of GDP (2016)

1.45% of GDP (2015)

1.35% of GDP (2014)

country comparison to the world: 82

**MILITARY BRANCHES:**

Ground Forces, Navy, Air Force (2016)

**MILITARY SERVICE AGE AND OBLIGATION:**

conscription ended 2006; 18 years of age for male and female voluntary service; all military inductees (including women) contract for an initial 5-year term of service, with subsequent successive 3-year terms until age 36 (2015)

## TRANSNATIONAL ISSUES :: ROMANIA

**DISPUTES - INTERNATIONAL:**

the ICJ ruled largely in favor of Romania in its dispute submitted in 2004 over Ukrainian-administered

Zmiyinyy/Serpilor (Snake) Island and Black Sea maritime boundary delimitationRomania opposes Ukraine's reopening of a navigation canal from the Danube border through Ukraine to the Black Sea

**REFUGEES AND INTERNALLY DISPLACED PERSONS:**

stateless persons: 238 (2017)

**ILLICIT DRUGS:**

major transshipment point for Southwest Asian heroin transiting the Balkan route and small amounts of Latin American cocaine bound for Western Europe; although not a significant financial center, role as a narcotics conduit leaves it vulnerable to laundering, which occurs via the banking system, currency exchange houses, and casinos

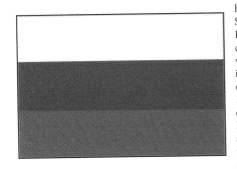

# CENTRAL ASIA :: RUSSIA

## INTRODUCTION :: RUSSIA

### BACKGROUND:

Founded in the 12th century, the Principality of Muscovy was able to emerge from over 200 years of Mongol domination (13th-15th centuries) and to gradually conquer and absorb surrounding principalities. In the early 17th century, a new ROMANOV Dynasty continued this policy of expansion across Siberia to the Pacific. Under PETER I (ruled 1682-1725), hegemony was extended to the Baltic Sea and the country was renamed the Russian Empire. During the 19th century, more territorial acquisitions were made in Europe and Asia. Defeat in the Russo-Japanese War of 1904-05 contributed to the Revolution of 1905, which resulted in the formation of a parliament and other reforms. Devastating defeats and food shortages in World War I led to widespread rioting in the major cities of the Russian Empire and to the overthrow in 1917 of the ROMANOV Dynasty. The communists under Vladimir LENIN seized power soon after and formed the USSR. The brutal rule of Iosif STALIN (1928-53) strengthened communist rule and Russian dominance of the Soviet Union at a cost of tens of millions of lives. After defeating Germany in World War II as part of an alliance with the US (1939-1945), the USSR expanded its territory and influence in Eastern Europe and emerged as a global power. The USSR was the principal adversary of the US during the Cold War (1947-1991). The Soviet economy and society stagnated in the decades following Stalin's rule, until General Secretary Mikhail GORBACHEV (1985-91) introduced glasnost (openness) and perestroika (restructuring) in an attempt to modernize communism, but his initiatives inadvertently released forces that by December 1991 led to the dissolution of the USSR into Russia and 14 other independent states.

Following economic and political turmoil during President Boris YELTSIN's term (1991-99), Russia shifted toward a centralized authoritarian state under President Vladimir PUTIN (2000-2008, 2012-present) in which the regime seeks to legitimize its rule through managed elections, populist appeals, a foreign policy focused on enhancing the country's geopolitical influence, and commodity-based economic growth. Russia faces a largely subdued rebel movement in Chechnya and some other surrounding regions, although violence still occurs throughout the North Caucasus.

## GEOGRAPHY :: RUSSIA

### LOCATION:
North Asia bordering the Arctic Ocean, extending from Europe (the portion west of the Urals) to the North Pacific Ocean

### GEOGRAPHIC COORDINATES:
60 00 N, 100 00 E

### MAP REFERENCES:
Asia

### AREA:
total: 17,098,242 sq km

land: 16,377,742 sq km

water: 720,500 sq km

country comparison to the world: 1

### AREA - COMPARATIVE:
approximately 1.8 times the size of the US

### LAND BOUNDARIES:
total: 22,408 km

border countries (15): Azerbaijan 338 km, Belarus 1312 km, China (southeast) 4133 km, China (south) 46 km, Estonia 324 km, Finland 1309 km, Georgia 894 km, Kazakhstan 7644 km, North Korea 18 km, Latvia 332 km, Lithuania (Kaliningrad Oblast) 261 km, Mongolia 3452 km, Norway 191 km, Poland (Kaliningrad Oblast) 210 km, Ukraine 1944 km

### COASTLINE:
37,653 km

### MARITIME CLAIMS:
territorial sea: 12 nm

exclusive economic zone: 200 nm

contiguous zone: 24 nm

continental shelf: 200-m depth or to the depth of exploitation

### CLIMATE:
ranges from steppes in the south through humid continental in much of European Russia; subarctic in Siberia to tundra climate in the polar north; winters vary from cool along Black Sea coast to frigid in Siberia; summers vary from warm in the steppes to cool along Arctic coast

### TERRAIN:
broad plain with low hills west of Urals; vast coniferous forest and tundra in Siberia; uplands and mountains along southern border regions

### ELEVATION:
mean elevation: 600 m

elevation extremes: -28 m lowest point: Caspian Sea

5642 highest point: Gora El'brus (highest point in Europe)

### NATURAL RESOURCES:

wide natural resource base including major deposits of oil, natural gas, coal, and many strategic minerals, bauxite, reserves of rare earth elements, timber, note, formidable obstacles of climate, terrain, and distance hinder exploitation of natural resources

### LAND USE:

agricultural land: 13.1% (2011 est.)

arable land: 7.3% (2011 est.) / permanent crops: 0.1% (2011 est.) / permanent pasture: 5.7% (2011 est.)

forest: 49.4% (2011 est.)

other: 37.5% (2011 est.)

### IRRIGATED LAND:

43,000 sq km (2012)

### POPULATION DISTRIBUTION:

population is heavily concentrated in the westernmost fifth of the country extending from the Baltic Sea, south to the Caspian Sea, and eastward parallel to the Kazakh border; elsewhere, sizeable pockets are isolated and generally found in the south

### NATURAL HAZARDS:

permafrost over much of Siberia is a major impediment to development; volcanic activity in the Kuril Islands; volcanoes and earthquakes on the Kamchatka Peninsula; spring floods and summer/autumn forest fires throughout Siberia and parts of European Russia

volcanism: significant volcanic activity on the Kamchatka Peninsula and Kuril Islands; the peninsula alone is home to some 29 historically active volcanoes, with dozens more in the Kuril Islands; Kliuchevskoi (4,835 m), which erupted in 2007 and 2010, is Kamchatka's most active volcano; Avachinsky and Koryaksky volcanoes, which pose a threat to the city of Petropavlovsk-Kamchatsky, have been deemed Decade Volcanoes by the International Association of Volcanology and Chemistry of the Earth's Interior, worthy of study due to their explosive history and close proximity to human populations; other notable historically active volcanoes include Bezymianny, Chikurachki, Ebeko, Gorely, Grozny, Karymsky, Ketoi, Kronotsky, Ksudach, Medvezhia, Mutnovsky, Sarychev Peak, Shiveluch, Tiatia, Tolbachik, and Zheltovsky; see note 2 under "Geography - note"

### ENVIRONMENT - CURRENT ISSUES:

air pollution from heavy industry, emissions of coal-fired electric plants, and transportation in major cities; industrial, municipal, and agricultural pollution of inland waterways and seacoasts; deforestation; soil erosion; soil contamination from improper application of agricultural chemicals; nuclear waste disposal; scattered areas of sometimes intense radioactive contamination; groundwater contamination from toxic waste; urban solid waste management; abandoned stocks of obsolete pesticides

### ENVIRONMENT - INTERNATIONAL AGREEMENTS:

party to: Air Pollution, Air Pollution-Nitrogen Oxides, Air Pollution-Sulfur 85, Antarctic-Environmental Protocol, Antarctic-Marine Living Resources, Antarctic Seals, Antarctic Treaty, Biodiversity, Climate Change, Climate Change-Kyoto Protocol, Desertification, Endangered Species, Environmental Modification, Hazardous Wastes, Law of the Sea, Marine Dumping, Ozone Layer Protection, Ship Pollution, Tropical Timber 83, Wetlands, Whaling

signed, but not ratified: Air Pollution-Sulfur 94

### GEOGRAPHY - NOTE:

note 1: largest country in the world in terms of area but unfavorably located in relation to major sea lanes of the world; despite its size, much of the country lacks proper soils and climates (either too cold or too dry) for agriculture

note 2: Russia's far east, particularly the Kamchatka Peninsula, lies along the Ring of Fire, a belt of active volcanoes and earthquake epicenters bordering the Pacific Ocean; up to 90% of the world's earthquakes and some 75% of the world's volcanoes occur within the Ring of Fire

note 3: Mount El'brus is Europe's tallest peak; Lake Baikal, the deepest lake in the world, is estimated to hold one fifth of the world's fresh surface water

note 4: Kaliningrad oblast is an exclave annexed from Germany following World War II (it was formerly part of East Prussia); its capital city of Kaliningrad - formerly Koenigsberg - is the only Baltic port in Russia that remains ice free in the winter

# PEOPLE AND SOCIETY :: RUSSIA

### POPULATION:

142,122,776 (July 2018 est.)

country comparison to the world: 9

### NATIONALITY:

noun: Russian(s)

adjective: Russian

### ETHNIC GROUPS:

Russian 77.7%, Tatar 3.7%, Ukrainian 1.4%, Bashkir 1.1%, Chuvash 1%, Chechen 1%, other 10.2%, unspecified 3.9% (2010 est.)

note: nearly 200 national and/or ethnic groups are represented in Russia's 2010 census

### LANGUAGES:

Russian (official) 85.7%, Tatar 3.2%, Chechen 1%, other 10.1% (2010 est.)

note: data represent native language spoken

### RELIGIONS:

Russian Orthodox 15-20%, Muslim 10-15%, other Christian 2% (2006 est.)

note: estimates are of practicing worshipers; Russia has large populations of non-practicing believers and non-believers, a legacy of over seven decades of official atheism under Soviet rule; Russia officially recognizes Orthodox Christianity, Islam, Judaism, and Buddhism as the country's traditional religions

### AGE STRUCTURE:

0-14 years: 17.21% (male 12,566,314 /female 11,896,416)

15-24 years: 9.41% (male 6,840,759 /female 6,530,991)

25-54 years: 44.21% (male 30,868,831 /female 31,960,407)

55-64 years: 14.51% (male 8,907,031 /female 11,709,921)

65 years and over: 14.66% (male 6,565,308 /female 14,276,798) (2018 est.)

### DEPENDENCY RATIOS:

total dependency ratio: 43.5 (2015 est.)

youth dependency ratio: 24.2 (2015 est.)

elderly dependency ratio: 19.4 (2015 est.)

potential support ratio: 5.2 (2015 est.)

### MEDIAN AGE:

total: 39.8 years

male: 36.9 years

female: 42.7 years (2018 est.)

country comparison to the world: 52

**POPULATION GROWTH RATE:**

-0.11% (2018 est.)

country comparison to the world: 205

**BIRTH RATE:**

10.7 births/1,000 population (2018 est.)

country comparison to the world: 184

**DEATH RATE:**

13.4 deaths/1,000 population (2018 est.)

country comparison to the world: 8

**NET MIGRATION RATE:**

1.7 migrant(s)/1,000 population (2017 est.)

country comparison to the world: 52

**POPULATION DISTRIBUTION:**

population is heavily concentrated in the westernmost fifth of the country extending from the Baltic Sea, south to the Caspian Sea, and eastward parallel to the Kazakh border; elsewhere, sizeable pockets are isolated and generally found in the south

**URBANIZATION:**

urban population: 74.4% of total population (2018)

rate of urbanization: 0.18% annual rate of change (2015-20 est.)

**MAJOR URBAN AREAS - POPULATION:**

12.41 million MOSCOW (capital), 5.383 million Saint Petersburg, 1.636 million Novosibirsk, 1.482 million Yekaterinburg, 1.264 million Nizhniy Novgorod, 1.164 million Samara (2018)

**SEX RATIO:**

at birth: 1.06 male(s)/female (2017 est.)

0-14 years: 1.06 male(s)/female (2017 est.)

15-24 years: 1.05 male(s)/female (2017 est.)

25-54 years: 0.96 male(s)/female (2017 est.)

55-64 years: 0.75 male(s)/female (2017 est.)

65 years and over: 0.45 male(s)/female (2017 est.)

total population: 0.86 male(s)/female (2017 est.)

**MOTHER'S MEAN AGE AT FIRST BIRTH:**

24.6 years (2009 est.)

**MATERNAL MORTALITY RATE:**

25 deaths/100,000 live births (2015 est.)

country comparison to the world: 124

**INFANT MORTALITY RATE:**

total: 6.7 deaths/1,000 live births (2018 est.)

male: 7.5 deaths/1,000 live births (2018 est.)

female: 5.8 deaths/1,000 live births (2018 est.)

country comparison to the world: 162

**LIFE EXPECTANCY AT BIRTH:**

total population: 71.3 years (2018 est.)

male: 65.6 years (2018 est.)

female: 77.3 years (2018 est.)

country comparison to the world: 155

**TOTAL FERTILITY RATE:**

1.61 children born/woman (2018 est.)

country comparison to the world: 179

**CONTRACEPTIVE PREVALENCE RATE:**

68% (2011)

note: percent of women aged 15-44

**HEALTH EXPENDITURES:**

7.1% of GDP (2014)

country comparison to the world: 79

**PHYSICIANS DENSITY:**

3.98 physicians/1,000 population (2015)

**HOSPITAL BED DENSITY:**

8.2 beds/1,000 population (2013)

**DRINKING WATER SOURCE:**

improved:

urban: 98.9% of population

rural: 91.2% of population

total: 96.9% of population

unimproved:

urban: 1.1% of population

rural: 8.8% of population

total: 3.1% of population (2015 est.)

**SANITATION FACILITY ACCESS:**

improved:

urban: 77% of population (2015 est.)

rural: 58.7% of population (2015 est.)

total: 72.2% of population (2015 est.)

unimproved:

urban: 23% of population (2015 est.)

rural: 41.3% of population (2015 est.)

total: 27.8% of population (2015 est.)

**HIV/AIDS - ADULT PREVALENCE RATE:**

1.2% (2017 est.)

country comparison to the world: 40

**HIV/AIDS - PEOPLE LIVING WITH HIV/AIDS:**

1 million (2017 est.)

country comparison to the world: 11

**HIV/AIDS - DEATHS:**

NA

**MAJOR INFECTIOUS DISEASES:**

degree of risk: intermediate (2016)

food or waterborne diseases: bacterial diarrhea (2016)

vectorborne diseases: tickborne encephalitis (2016)

**OBESITY - ADULT PREVALENCE RATE:**

23.1% (2016)

country comparison to the world: 70

**EDUCATION EXPENDITURES:**

3.8% of GDP (2012)

country comparison to the world: 120

**LITERACY:**

definition: age 15 and over can read and write (2015 est.)

total population: 99.7% (2015 est.)

male: 99.7% (2015 est.)

female: 99.6% (2015 est.)

**SCHOOL LIFE EXPECTANCY (PRIMARY TO TERTIARY EDUCATION):**

total: 15 years (2014)

male: 15 years (2014)

female: 15 years (2014)

**UNEMPLOYMENT, YOUTH AGES 15-24:**

total: 16.1% (2015 est.)

male: 15.4% (2015 est.)

female: 17% (2015 est.)

country comparison to the world: 83

# GOVERNMENT :: RUSSIA

**COUNTRY NAME:**

conventional long form: Russian Federation

conventional short form: Russia

local long form: Rossiyskaya Federatsiya

local short form: Rossiya

**former:** Russian Empire, Russian Soviet Federative Socialist Republic

**etymology:** Russian lands were generally referred to as Muscovy until PETER I officially declared the Russian Empire in 1721; the new name sought to invoke the patrimony of the medieval eastern European Rus state centered on Kyiv in present-day Ukraine; the Rus were a Varangian (eastern Viking) elite that imposed their rule and eventually their name on their Slavic subjects

## GOVERNMENT TYPE:
semi-presidential federation

## CAPITAL:
**name:** Moscow

**geographic coordinates:** 55 45 N, 37 36 E

**time difference:** UTC+3 (8 hours ahead of Washington, DC, during Standard Time)

**note:** Russia has 11 time zones, the largest number of contiguous time zones of any country in the world; in 2014, two time zones were added and DST dropped

## ADMINISTRATIVE DIVISIONS:
46 provinces (oblasti, singular - oblast), 21 republics (respubliki, singular - respublika), 4 autonomous okrugs (avtonomnyye okrugi, singular - avtonomnyy okrug), 9 krays (kraya, singular - kray), 2 federal cities (goroda, singular - gorod), and 1 autonomous oblast (avtonomnaya oblast')

**oblasts:** Amur (Blagoveshchensk), Arkhangel'sk, Astrakhan', Belgorod, Bryansk, Chelyabinsk, Irkutsk, Ivanovo, Kaliningrad, Kaluga, Kemerovo, Kirov, Kostroma, Kurgan, Kursk, Leningrad, Lipetsk, Magadan, Moscow, Murmansk, Nizhniy Novgorod, Novgorod, Novosibirsk, Omsk, Orenburg, Orel, Penza, Pskov, Rostov, Ryazan', Sakhalin (Yuzhno-Sakhalinsk), Samara, Saratov, Smolensk, Sverdlovsk (Yekaterinburg), Tambov, Tomsk, Tula, Tver', Tyumen', Ul'yanovsk, Vladimir, Volgograd, Vologda, Voronezh, Yaroslavl';

**republics:** Adygeya (Maykop), Altay (Gorno-Altaysk), Bashkortostan (Ufa), Buryatiya (Ulan-Ude), Chechnya (Groznyy), Chuvashiya (Cheboksary), Dagestan (Makhachkala), Ingushetiya (Magas), Kabardino-Balkariya (Nal'chik), Kalmykiya (Elista), Karachayevo-Cherkesiya (Cherkessk), Kareliya (Petrozavodsk), Khakasiya (Abakan), Komi (Syktyvkar), Mariy-El (Yoshkar-Ola), Mordoviya (Saransk), North Ossetia (Vladikavkaz), Sakha [Yakutiya] (Yakutsk), Tatarstan (Kazan'), Tyva (Kyzyl), Udmurtiya (Izhevsk);

**autonomous okrugs:** Chukotka (Anadyr'), Khanty-Mansi-Yugra (Khanty-Mansiysk), Nenets (Nar'yan-Mar), Yamalo-Nenets (Salekhard);

**krays:** Altay (Barnaul), Kamchatka (Petropavlovsk-Kamchatskiy), Khabarovsk, Krasnodar, Krasnoyarsk, Perm', Primorskiy [Maritime] (Vladivostok), Stavropol', Zabaykal'sk [Transbaikal] (Chita);

**federal cities:** Moscow [Moskva], Saint Petersburg [Sankt-Peterburg];

**autonomous oblast:** Yevreyskaya [Jewish] (Birobidzhan)

**note:** administrative divisions have the same names as their administrative centers (exceptions have the administrative center name following in parentheses)

**note:** the United States does not recognize Russia's annexation of Ukraine's Autonomous Republic of Crimea and the municipality of Sevastopol, nor their redesignation as the "Republic of Crimea" and the "Federal City of Sevastopol"

## INDEPENDENCE:
25 December 1991 (from the Soviet Union; Russian SFSR renamed Russian Federation); notable earlier dates: 1157 (Principality of Vladimir-Suzdal created); 16 January 1547 (Tsardom of Muscovy established); 22 October 1721 (Russian Empire proclaimed); 30 December 1922 (Soviet Union established)

## NATIONAL HOLIDAY:
Russia Day, 12 June (1990); note - commemorates the adoption of the Declaration of State Sovereignty of the Russian Soviet Federative Socialist Republic (RSFSR)

## CONSTITUTION:
**history:** several previous (during Russian Empire and Soviet era); latest drafted 12 July 1993, adopted by referendum 12 December 1993, effective 25 December 1993 (2017)

**amendments:** proposed by the president of the Russian Federation, by either house of the Federal Assembly, by the government of the Russian Federation, or by legislative (representative) bodies of the Federation's constituent entities; proposals to amend the government's constitutional system, human and civil rights and freedoms, and procedures for amending or drafting a new constitution require formation of a Constitutional Assembly; passage of such amendments requires two-thirds majority vote of its total membership; passage in a referendum requires participation of an absolute majority of eligible voters and an absolute majority of valid votes; approval of proposed amendments to the government structure, authorities, and procedures requires approval by the legislative bodies of at least two-thirds of the Russian Federation's constituent entities; amended 2008, 2014 (2017)

## LEGAL SYSTEM:
civil law system; judicial review of legislative acts

## INTERNATIONAL LAW ORGANIZATION PARTICIPATION:
has not submitted an ICJ jurisdiction declaration; non-party state to the ICCt

## CITIZENSHIP:
**citizenship by birth:** no

**citizenship by descent only:** at least one parent must be a citizen of Russia

**dual citizenship recognized:** yes

**residency requirement for naturalization:** 3-5 years

## SUFFRAGE:
18 years of age; universal

## EXECUTIVE BRANCH:
**chief of state:** President Vladimir Vladimirovich PUTIN (since 7 May 2012)

**head of government:** Premier Dmitriy Anatolyevich MEDVEDEV (since 8 May 2012); First Deputy Premier Anton Germanovich SILUANOV (since 18 May 2018); Deputy Premiers Maksim Alekseyevich AKIMOV (since 18 May 2018), Yuriy Ivanovich BORISOV (since 18 May 2018), Konstantin Anatolyevich CHUYCHENKO (since 18 May 2018), Tatyana Alekseyevna GOLIKOVA (since 18 May 2018), Olga Yuryevna GOLODETS (since 21 May 2012), Aleksey Vasilevich GORDEYEV (since 18 May 2018), Dmitriy Nikolayevich KOZAK (since 14 October 2008), Vitaliy Leontyevich MUTKO (since 19 October 2016); Yuriy Petrovich TRUTNEV (since 31 August 2013)

**cabinet:** the "Government" is composed of the premier, his deputies, and ministers, all appointed by the president; the premier is also confirmed by the Duma

**elections/appointments:** president directly elected by absolute majority popular vote in 2 rounds if needed for a 6-year term (eligible for a second term); election last held on 18 March 2018 (next to be held in March 2024); note - term length extended to 6 years from 4 years in late 2008, effective after the 2012 election; there is no vice president; premier appointed by the president with the approval of the Duma

**election results:** Vladimir PUTIN reelected president; percent of vote - Vladimir PUTIN (independent) 77.5%, Pavel GRUDININ (CPRF) 11.9%, Vladimir ZHIRINOVSKIY (LDPR) 5.7%, other 5.8%; Dmitriy MEDVEDEV (United Russia) reapproved as premier by Duma on 8 May 2018; vote - 374 to 56

**note:** there is also a Presidential Administration that provides staff and policy support to the president, drafts presidential decrees, and coordinates policy among government agencies; a Security Council also reports directly to the president

## LEGISLATIVE BRANCH:

**description:** bicameral Federal Assembly or Federalnoye Sobraniye consists of:
Federation Council or Sovet Federatsii (170 seats; 2 members in each of the 83 federal administrative units (see note below) - oblasts, krays, republics, autonomous okrugs and oblasts, and federal cities of Moscow and Saint Petersburg - appointed by the top executive and legislative officials; members serve 4-year terms)
State Duma or Gosudarstvennaya Duma (450 seats (see note below); as of February 2014, the electoral system reverted to a mixed electoral system for the 2016 election, in which one-half of the members are directly elected by simple majority vote and one-half directly elected by proportional representation vote; members serve 5-year terms)

**elections:**
State Duma - last held on 18 September 2016 (next to be held in fall 2021)

**election results:**
State Duma - United Russia 54.2%, CPRF 13.3%, LDPR 13.1%, A Just Russia 6.2%, Rodina 1.5%, CP 0.2%, other minor parties 11.5%; seats by party - United Russia 343, CPRF 42, LDPR 39, A Just Russia 23, Rodina 1, CP 1, independent 1; seats by party as of December 2018 - United Russia 341, CPRF 43, LDPR 39, A Just Russia 23, independent 2, vacant 2

**note:** the State Duma now includes 3 representatives from the "Republic of Crimea," while the Federation Council includes 2 each from the "Republic of Crimea" and the "Federal City of Sevastopol," both regions that Russia occupied and attempted to annex from Ukraine and that the US does not recognize as part of Russia

## JUDICIAL BRANCH:

**highest courts:** Supreme Court of the Russian Federation (consists of 170 members organized into the Judicial Panel for Civil Affairs, the Judicial Panel for Criminal Affairs, and the Military Panel); Constitutional Court (consists of 19 members); note - in February 2014, Russia's Superior Court of Arbitration was abolished and its former authorities transferred to the Supreme Court, which in addition to being the country's highest judicial authority for appeals, civil, criminal, administrative, and military cases, and the disciplinary judicial board now has jurisdiction over economic disputes

**judge selection and term of office:** all members of Russia's 3 highest courts nominated by the president and appointed by the Federation Council (the upper house of the legislature); members of all 3 courts appointed for life

**subordinate courts:** Higher Arbitration Court; regional (kray) and provincial (oblast) courts; Moscow and St. Petersburg city courts; autonomous province and district courts; note - the 21 Russian Republics have court systems specified by their own constitutions

## POLITICAL PARTIES AND LEADERS:

A Just Russia [Sergey MIRONOV]
Civic Platform or CP [Rifat SHAYKHUTDINOV]
Communist Party of the Russian Federation or CPRF [Gennadiy ZYUGANOV]
Liberal Democratic Party of Russia or LDPR [Vladimir ZHIRINOVSKIY]
Rodina [Aleksei ZHURAVLYOV]
United Russia [Dmitriy MEDVEDEV]

**note:** 64 political parties are registered with Russia's Ministry of Justice (as of September 2018), but only four parties maintain representation in Russia's national legislature

## INTERNATIONAL ORGANIZATION PARTICIPATION:

APEC, Arctic Council, ARF, ASEAN (dialogue partner), BIS, BRICS, BSEC, CBSS, CD, CE, CERN (observer), CICA, CIS, CSTO, EAEC, EAEU, EAPC, EAS, EBRD, FAO, FATF, G-20, GCTU, IAEA, IBRD, ICAO, ICC (national committees), ICRM, IDA, IFAD, IFC, IFRCS, IHO, ILO, IMF, IMO, IMSO, Interpol, IOC, IOM (observer), IPU, ISO, ITSO, ITU, ITUC (NGOs), LAIA (observer), MIGA, MINURSO, MONUSCO, NEA, NSG, OAS (observer), OIC (observer), OPCW, OSCE, Paris Club, PCA, PFP, SCO, UN, UNCTAD, UNESCO, UNHCR, UNIDO, UNISFA, UNMIL, UNMISS, UNOCI, UN Security Council (permanent), UNTSO, UNWTO, UPU, WCO, WFTU (NGOs), WHO, WIPO, WMO, WTO, ZC

## DIPLOMATIC REPRESENTATION IN THE US:

**chief of mission:** Ambassador Anatoliy Ivanovich ANTONOV (since 8 September 2017)

**chancery:** 2650 Wisconsin Avenue NW, Washington, DC 20007

**telephone:** [1] (202) 298-5700, 5701, 5704, 5708

**FAX:** [1] (202) 298-5735

**consulate(s) general:** Houston, New York, Seattle

## DIPLOMATIC REPRESENTATION FROM THE US:

**chief of mission:** Ambassador Jon HUNTSMAN (since 3 October 2017)

**embassy:** Bolshoy Deviatinskiy Pereulok No. 8, 121099 Moscow

**mailing address:** PSC-77, APO AE 09721

**telephone:** [7] (495) 728-5000

**FAX:** [7] (495) 728-5090

**consulate(s) general:** Saint Petersburg, Vladivostok, Yekaterinburg

## FLAG DESCRIPTION:

three equal horizontal bands of white (top), blue, and red

**note:** the colors may have been based on those of the Dutch flag; despite many popular interpretations, there is no official meaning assigned to the colors of the Russian flag; this flag inspired several other Slav countries to adopt horizontal tricolors of the same colors but in different arrangements, and so red, blue, and white became the Pan-Slav colors

**NATIONAL SYMBOL(S):**

bear, double-headed eagle; national colors: white, blue, red

**NATIONAL ANTHEM:**

name: "Gimn Rossiyskoy Federatsii" (National Anthem of the Russian Federation)

lyrics/music: Sergey Vladimirovich MIKHALKOV/Aleksandr Vasilyevich ALEKSANDROV

note: in 2000, Russia adopted the tune of the anthem of the former Soviet Union (composed in 1939); the lyrics, also adopted in 2000, were written by the same person who authored the Soviet lyrics in 1943

## ECONOMY :: RUSSIA

### ECONOMY - OVERVIEW:

Russia has undergone significant changes since the collapse of the Soviet Union, moving from a centrally planned economy towards a more market-based system. Both economic growth and reform have stalled in recent years, however, and Russia remains a predominantly statist economy with a high concentration of wealth in officials' hands. Economic reforms in the 1990s privatized most industry, with notable exceptions in the energy, transportation, banking, and defense-related sectors. The protection of property rights is still weak, and the state continues to interfere in the free operation of the private sector.

Russia is one of the world's leading producers of oil and natural gas, and is also a top exporter of metals such as steel and primary aluminum. Russia is heavily dependent on the movement of world commodity prices as reliance on commodity exports makes it vulnerable to boom and bust cycles that follow the volatile swings in global prices. The economy, which had averaged 7% growth during the 1998-2008 period as oil prices rose rapidly, has seen diminishing growth rates since then due to the exhaustion of Russia's commodity-based growth model.

A combination of falling oil prices, international sanctions, and structural limitations pushed Russia into a deep recession in 2015, with GDP falling by close to 2.8%. The downturn continued through 2016, with GDP contracting another 0.2%, but was reversed in 2017 as world demand picked up. Government support for import substitution has increased recently in an effort to diversify the economy away from extractive industries.

### GDP (PURCHASING POWER PARITY):

$4.016 trillion (2017 est.)

$3.955 trillion (2016 est.)

$3.963 trillion (2015 est.)

note: data are in 2017 dollars

country comparison to the world: 6

### GDP (OFFICIAL EXCHANGE RATE):

$1.578 trillion (2017 est.) (2017 est.)

### GDP - REAL GROWTH RATE:

1.5% (2017 est.)

-0.2% (2016 est.)

-2.5% (2015 est.)

country comparison to the world: 173

### GDP - PER CAPITA (PPP):

$27,900 (2017 est.)

$27,500 (2016 est.)

$27,500 (2015 est.)

note: data are in 2017 dollars

country comparison to the world: 74

### GROSS NATIONAL SAVING:

26.5% of GDP (2017 est.)

25.9% of GDP (2016 est.)

26.8% of GDP (2015 est.)

country comparison to the world: 48

### GDP - COMPOSITION, BY END USE:

household consumption: 52.4% (2017 est.)

government consumption: 18% (2017 est.)

investment in fixed capital: 21.6% (2017 est.)

investment in inventories: 2.3% (2017 est.)

exports of goods and services: 26.2% (2017 est.)

imports of goods and services: -20.6% (2017 est.)

### GDP - COMPOSITION, BY SECTOR OF ORIGIN:

agriculture: 4.7% (2017 est.)

industry: 32.4% (2017 est.)

services: 62.3% (2017 est.)

### AGRICULTURE - PRODUCTS:

grain, sugar beets, sunflower seeds, vegetables, fruits; beef, milk

### INDUSTRIES:

complete range of mining and extractive industries producing coal, oil, gas, chemicals, and metals; all forms of machine building from rolling mills to high-performance aircraft and space vehicles; defense industries (including radar, missile production, advanced electronic components), shipbuilding; road and rail transportation equipment; communications equipment; agricultural machinery, tractors, and construction equipment; electric power generating and transmitting equipment; medical and scientific instruments; consumer durables, textiles, foodstuffs, handicrafts

### INDUSTRIAL PRODUCTION GROWTH RATE:

-1% (2017 est.)

country comparison to the world: 177

### LABOR FORCE:

76.53 million (2017 est.)

country comparison to the world: 6

### LABOR FORCE - BY OCCUPATION:

agriculture: 9.4%

industry: 27.6%

services: 63% (2016 est.)

### UNEMPLOYMENT RATE:

5.2% (2017 est.)

5.5% (2016 est.)

country comparison to the world: 77

### POPULATION BELOW POVERTY LINE:

13.3% (2015 est.)

### HOUSEHOLD INCOME OR CONSUMPTION BY PERCENTAGE SHARE:

lowest 10%: 32.2% (2012 est.)

highest 10%: 32.2% (2012 est.)

### DISTRIBUTION OF FAMILY INCOME - GINI INDEX:

41.2 (2015)

41.9 (2013)

country comparison to the world: 57

### BUDGET:

revenues: 258.6 billion (2017 est.)

expenditures: 281.4 billion (2017 est.)

### TAXES AND OTHER REVENUES:

16.4% (of GDP) (2017 est.)

country comparison to the world: 181

**BUDGET SURPLUS (+) OR DEFICIT (-):**

-1.4% (of GDP) (2017 est.)

country comparison to the world: 88

**PUBLIC DEBT:**

15.5% of GDP (2017 est.)

16.1% of GDP (2016 est.)

note: data cover general government debt and include debt instruments issued (or owned) by government entities other than the treasury; the data include treasury debt held by foreign entities; the data include debt issued by subnational entities, as well as intragovernmental debt; intragovernmental debt consists of treasury borrowings from surpluses in the social funds, such as for retirement, medical care, and unemployment, debt instruments for the social funds are not sold at public auctions

country comparison to the world: 194

**FISCAL YEAR:**

calendar year

**INFLATION RATE (CONSUMER PRICES):**

3.7% (2017 est.)

7.1% (2016 est.)

country comparison to the world: 149

**CENTRAL BANK DISCOUNT RATE:**

10% (31 December 2016 est.)

11% (3 August 2015)

note: this is the so-called refinancing rate, but in Russia banks do not get refinancing at this rate; this is a reference rate used primarily for fiscal purposes

country comparison to the world: 23

**COMMERCIAL BANK PRIME LENDING RATE:**

10.55% (31 December 2017 est.)

12.59% (31 December 2016 est.)

country comparison to the world: 80

**STOCK OF NARROW MONEY:**

$255.2 billion (31 December 2017 est.)

$195.9 billion (31 December 2016 est.)

country comparison to the world: 21

**STOCK OF BROAD MONEY:**

$255.2 billion (31 December 2017 est.)

$195.9 billion (31 December 2016 est.)

country comparison to the world: 21

**STOCK OF DOMESTIC CREDIT:**

$940.4 billion (31 December 2017 est.)

$827.3 billion (31 December 2016 est.)

country comparison to the world: 16

**MARKET VALUE OF PUBLICLY TRADED SHARES:**

$635.9 billion (31 December 2016 est.)

$393.2 billion (31 December 2015 est.)

$385.9 billion (31 December 2014 est.)

country comparison to the world: 19

**CURRENT ACCOUNT BALANCE:**

$35.44 billion (2017 est.)

$24.4 billion (2016 est.)

country comparison to the world: 11

**EXPORTS:**

$353 billion (2017 est.)

$281.9 billion (2016 est.)

country comparison to the world: 14

**EXPORTS - PARTNERS:**

China 10.9%, Netherlands 10%, Germany 7.1%, Belarus 5.1%, Turkey 4.9% (2017)

**EXPORTS - COMMODITIES:**

petroleum and petroleum products, natural gas, metals, wood and wood products, chemicals, and a wide variety of civilian and military manufactures

**IMPORTS:**

$238 billion (2017 est.)

$191.6 billion (2016 est.)

country comparison to the world: 20

**IMPORTS - COMMODITIES:**

machinery, vehicles, pharmaceutical products, plastic, semi-finished metal products, meat, fruits and nuts, optical and medical instruments, iron, steel

**IMPORTS - PARTNERS:**

China 21.2%, Germany 10.7%, US 5.6%, Belarus 5%, Italy 4.5%, France 4.2% (2017)

**RESERVES OF FOREIGN EXCHANGE AND GOLD:**

$432.7 billion (31 December 2017 est.)

$377.7 billion (31 December 2016 est.)

country comparison to the world: 6

**DEBT - EXTERNAL:**

$539.6 billion (31 December 2017 est.)

$434.8 billion (31 December 2016 est.)

country comparison to the world: 22

**STOCK OF DIRECT FOREIGN INVESTMENT - AT HOME:**

$535.2 billion (31 December 2017 est.)

$461.7 billion (31 December 2016 est.)

country comparison to the world: 18

**STOCK OF DIRECT FOREIGN INVESTMENT - ABROAD:**

$470.9 billion (31 December 2017 est.)

$418 billion (31 December 2016 est.)

country comparison to the world: 18

**EXCHANGE RATES:**

Russian rubles (RUB) per US dollar -

58.39 (2017 est.)

67.056 (2016 est.)

67.056 (2015 est.)

60.938 (2014 est.)

38.378 (2013 est.)

## ENERGY :: RUSSIA

**ELECTRICITY ACCESS:**

electrification - total population: 100% (2016)

**ELECTRICITY - PRODUCTION:**

1.031 trillion kWh (2016 est.)

country comparison to the world: 4

**ELECTRICITY - CONSUMPTION:**

909.6 billion kWh (2016 est.)

country comparison to the world: 5

**ELECTRICITY - EXPORTS:**

13.13 billion kWh (2016 est.)

country comparison to the world: 14

**ELECTRICITY - IMPORTS:**

3.194 billion kWh (2016 est.)

country comparison to the world: 48

**ELECTRICITY - INSTALLED GENERATING CAPACITY:**

244.9 million kW (2016 est.)

country comparison to the world: 5

**ELECTRICITY - FROM FOSSIL FUELS:**

68% of total installed capacity (2016 est.)

country comparison to the world: 115

**ELECTRICITY - FROM NUCLEAR FUELS:**

11% of total installed capacity (2017 est.)

country comparison to the world: 13

**ELECTRICITY - FROM HYDROELECTRIC PLANTS:**

21% of total installed capacity (2017 est.)

country comparison to the world: 86

**ELECTRICITY - FROM OTHER RENEWABLE SOURCES:**

1% of total installed capacity (2017 est.)

country comparison to the world: 164

**CRUDE OIL - PRODUCTION:**

10.58 million bbl/day (2017 est.)

country comparison to the world: 1
**CRUDE OIL - EXPORTS:**
4.921 million bbl/day (2015 est.)

country comparison to the world: 2
**CRUDE OIL - IMPORTS:**
76,220 bbl/day (2015 est.)

country comparison to the world: 48
**CRUDE OIL - PROVED RESERVES:**
80 billion bbl (1 January 2018 est.)

country comparison to the world: 8
**REFINED PETROLEUM PRODUCTS - PRODUCTION:**
6.076 million bbl/day (2015 est.)

country comparison to the world: 3
**REFINED PETROLEUM PRODUCTS - CONSUMPTION:**
3.65 million bbl/day (2016 est.)

country comparison to the world: 5
**REFINED PETROLEUM PRODUCTS - EXPORTS:**
2.671 million bbl/day (2015 est.)

country comparison to the world: 2
**REFINED PETROLEUM PRODUCTS - IMPORTS:**
41,920 bbl/day (2015 est.)

country comparison to the world: 88
**NATURAL GAS - PRODUCTION:**
665.6 billion cu m (2017 est.)

country comparison to the world: 2
**NATURAL GAS - CONSUMPTION:**
467.5 billion cu m (2017 est.)

country comparison to the world: 2
**NATURAL GAS - EXPORTS:**
210.2 billion cu m (2017 est.)

country comparison to the world: 1
**NATURAL GAS - IMPORTS:**
15.77 billion cu m (2017 est.)

country comparison to the world: 19
**NATURAL GAS - PROVED RESERVES:**
47.8 trillion cu m (1 January 2018 est.)

country comparison to the world: 1
**CARBON DIOXIDE EMISSIONS FROM CONSUMPTION OF ENERGY:**
1.847 billion Mt (2017 est.)

country comparison to the world: 4

## COMMUNICATIONS :: RUSSIA

**TELEPHONES - FIXED LINES:**
total subscriptions: 31,190,855 (2017 est.)

subscriptions per 100 inhabitants: 22 (2017 est.)

country comparison to the world: 8
**TELEPHONES - MOBILE CELLULAR:**
total subscriptions: 227,341,873 (2017 est.)

subscriptions per 100 inhabitants: 160 (2017 est.)

country comparison to the world: 6
**TELEPHONE SYSTEM:**
general assessment: telecom sector impacted by sanctions related to the annexations in Ukraine; mobile market dominaed by four major operators; the estimated number of mobile subscribers jumped from fewer than 1 million in 1998 to 255 million in 2016; fixed-line service has improved but a large demand remains (2016)

domestic: cross-country digital trunk lines run from Saint Petersburg to Khabarovsk, and from Moscow to Novorossiysk; the telephone systems in 60 regional capitals have modern digital infrastructures; cellular services, both analog and digital, are available in many areas; in rural areas, telephone services are still outdated, inadequate, and low-density (2016)

international: country code - 7; connected internationally by undersea fiber-optic cables; satellite earth stations provide access to Intelsat, Intersputnik, Eutelsat, Inmarsat, and Orbita systems (2016)

**BROADCAST MEDIA:**
13 national TV stations with the federal government owning 1 and holding a controlling interest in a second; state-owned Gazprom maintains a controlling interest in 2 of the national channels; government-affiliated Bank Rossiya owns controlling interest in a fourth and fifth, while a sixth national channel is owned by the Moscow city administration; the Russian Orthodox Church and the Russian military, respectively, own 2 additional national channels; roughly 3,300 national, regional, and local TV stations with over two-thirds completely or partially controlled by the federal or local governments; satellite TV services are available; 2 state-run national radio networks with a third majority-owned by Gazprom; roughly 2,400 public and commercial radio stations (2016)

**INTERNET COUNTRY CODE:**
.ru; note - Russia also has responsibility for a legacy domain ".su" that was allocated to the Soviet Union and is being phased out

**INTERNET USERS:**
total: 108,772,470 (July 2016 est.)

percent of population: 76.4% (July 2016 est.)

country comparison to the world: 6
**BROADBAND - FIXED SUBSCRIPTIONS:**
total: 30,872,788 (2017 est.)

subscriptions per 100 inhabitants: 22 (2017 est.)

country comparison to the world: 5

## TRANSPORTATION :: RUSSIA

**NATIONAL AIR TRANSPORT SYSTEM:**
number of registered air carriers: 32 (2015)

inventory of registered aircraft operated by air carriers: 661 (2015)

annual passenger traffic on registered air carriers: 76,846,126 (2015)

annual freight traffic on registered air carriers: 4,761,047,070 mt-km (2015)

**CIVIL AIRCRAFT REGISTRATION COUNTRY CODE PREFIX:**
RA (2016)

**AIRPORTS:**
1,218 (2013)

country comparison to the world: 5
**AIRPORTS - WITH PAVED RUNWAYS:**
total: 594 (2017)

over 3,047 m: 54 (2017)

2,438 to 3,047 m: 197 (2017)

1,524 to 2,437 m: 123 (2017)

914 to 1,523 m: 95 (2017)

under 914 m: 125 (2017)

**AIRPORTS - WITH UNPAVED RUNWAYS:**
total: 624 (2013)

over 3,047 m: 4 (2013)

2,438 to 3,047 m: 13 (2013)

1,524 to 2,437 m: 69 (2013)

914 to 1,523 m: 81 (2013)

under 914 m: 457 (2013)

**HELIPORTS:**
49 (2013)

**PIPELINES:**

177700 km gas, 54800 km oil, 19300 km refined products (2016)

### RAILWAYS:

**total:** 87,157 km (2014)

**narrow gauge:** 957 km 1.067-m gauge (on Sakhalin Island) (2014)

**broad gauge:** 86,200 km 1.520-m gauge (40,300 km electrified) (2014)

**note:** an additional 30,000 km of non-common carrier lines serve industries

**country comparison to the world:** 3

### ROADWAYS:

**total:** 1,283,387 km (2012)

**paved:** 927,721 km (includes 39,143 km of expressways) (2012)

**unpaved:** 355,666 km (2012)

**country comparison to the world:** 5

### WATERWAYS:

102,000 km (including 48,000 km with guaranteed depth; the 72,000-km system in European Russia links Baltic Sea, White Sea, Caspian Sea, Sea of Azov, and Black Sea) (2009)

**country comparison to the world:** 2

### MERCHANT MARINE:

**total:** 2,572 (2017)

**by type:** bulk carrier 16, container ship 13, general cargo 874, oil tanker 411, other 1258 (2017)

**country comparison to the world:** 10

### PORTS AND TERMINALS:

**major seaport(s):** Kaliningrad, Nakhodka, Novorossiysk, Primorsk, Vostochnyy

**oil terminal(s):** Kavkaz oil terminal

**container port(s) (TEUs):** Saint Petersburg (1,457,800) (2016)

**LNG terminal(s) (export):** Sakhalin Island

**river port(s):** Saint Petersburg (Neva River)

# MILITARY AND SECURITY :: RUSSIA

### MILITARY EXPENDITURES:

4.24% of GDP (2017)

5.4% of GDP (2016)

4.86% of GDP (2015)

4.1% of GDP (2014)

3.96% of GDP (2013)

**country comparison to the world:** 12

### MILITARY BRANCHES:

Ground Troops (Sukhoputnyye Voyskia, SV), Navy (Voyenno-Morskoy Flot, VMF), Aerospace Forces (Vozdushno-Kosmicheskiye Sily, VKS); Airborne Troops (Vozdushno-Desantnyye Voyska, VDV) and Missile Troops of Strategic Purpose (Raketnyye Voyska Strategicheskogo Naznacheniya, RVSN) referred to commonly as Strategic Rocket Forces, are independent "combat arms," not subordinate to any of the three branches (2017)

### MILITARY SERVICE AGE AND OBLIGATION:

18-27 years of age for compulsory or voluntary military service; males are registered for the draft at 17 years of age; 1-year service obligation (conscripts can only be sent to combat zones after 6 months of training); reserve obligation for non-officers to age 50; enrollment in military schools from the age of 16, cadets classified as members of the armed forces (2018)

**note:** from 2016 to 2018, Russian officials assessed that about 76-79% of draft age males were sufficiently fit for military service

# TERRORISM :: RUSSIA

### TERRORIST GROUPS - HOME BASED:

**The Caucasus Emirate (Imarat Kavkaz, IK):**
**aim(s):** establish an Islamic caliphate and end Moscow's rule in the majority-Muslim North Caucasus region
**area(s) of operation:** the North Caucasus, primarily Chechnya, Dagestan, Ingushetiya, Kabardino-Balkaria, and Karachay-Cherkessia
**note:** most IK members switched allegiance to ISIS in 2015 (April 2018)

### TERRORIST GROUPS - FOREIGN BASED:

**Aum Shinrikyo (AUM):**
**aim(s):** attract new members seeking religious guidance and exhibiting a willingness to financially support the organization
**area(s) of operation:** between 1,500 and 30,000 AUM members live across Russia; recruitment efforts have intensified in recent years (April 2018)

**Islamic State of Iraq and ash-Sham-Caucasus (ISIS-Caucasus):**
**aim(s):** implement its strict interpretation of sharia in Dagestan, Chechnya, Ingushetia, and Kabardino-Balkariya; retaliate for Russian involvement in the Syria conflict
**area(s) of operation:** operational in the Russian North Caucasus, where the branch is known as Wilayat Kavkaz; recruits mainly from Central Asian migrant populations across Russia for domestic operations (April 2018)

# TRANSNATIONAL ISSUES :: RUSSIA

### DISPUTES - INTERNATIONAL:

Russia remains concerned about the smuggling of poppy derivatives from Afghanistan through Central Asian countriesChina and Russia have demarcated the once disputed islands at the Amur and Ussuri confluence and in the Argun River in accordance with the 2004 Agreement, ending their centuries-long border disputesthe sovereignty dispute over the islands of Etorofu, Kunashiri, Shikotan, and the Habomai group, known in Japan as the "Northern Territories" and in Russia as the "Southern Kurils," occupied by the Soviet Union in 1945, now administered by Russia, and claimed by Japan, remains the primary sticking point to signing a peace treaty formally ending World War II hostilitiesRussia's military support and subsequent recognition of Abkhazia and South Ossetia independence in 2008 continue to sour relations with GeorgiaAzerbaijan, Kazakhstan, and Russia ratified Caspian seabed delimitation treaties based on equidistance, while Iran continues to insist on a one-fifth slice of the seaNorway and Russia signed a comprehensive maritime boundary agreement in 2010various groups in Finland advocate restoration of Karelia (Kareliya) and other areas ceded to the Soviet Union following World War II but the Finnish Government asserts no territorial demandsRussia and Estonia signed a technical border agreement in May 2005, but Russia recalled its signature in June 2005 after the Estonian parliament added to its domestic ratification act a historical preamble referencing the Soviet occupation and Estonia's pre-war borders under the 1920 Treaty of TartuRussia contends that the preamble allows Estonia to make territorial claims on Russia in the future, while Estonian officials deny that the preamble has any legal impact on the treaty textRussia demands better treatment of the Russian-speaking population in Estonia and Latvia; Russia remains involved in the conflict in eastern Ukraine while also occupying Ukraine's territory of Crimea

Lithuania and Russia committed to demarcating their boundary in 2006 in accordance with the land and maritime treaty ratified by Russia in May 2003 and by Lithuania in 1999Lithuania operates a simplified transit regime for Russian nationals traveling from the Kaliningrad coastal exclave into Russia, while still conforming, as an EU member state with an EU external border, where strict Schengen border rules applypreparations for the demarcation delimitation of land boundary with Ukraine have commencedthe dispute over the boundary between Russia and Ukraine through the Kerch Strait and Sea of Azov is suspended due to the occupation of Crimea by RussiaKazakhstan and Russia boundary delimitation was ratified on November 2005 and field demarcation should commence in 2007Russian Duma has not yet ratified 1990 Bering Sea Maritime Boundary Agreement with the USDenmark (Greenland) and Norway have made submissions to the Commission on the Limits of the Continental Shelf (CLCS) and Russia is collecting additional data to augment its 2001 CLCS submission

## REFUGEES AND INTERNALLY DISPLACED PERSONS:

**refugees (country of origin):** 427,240 (Ukraine) (2017) note - estimate represents asylum applicants since the beginning of the Ukraine crisis in 2014 to September 2017

**IDPs:** 19,000 (armed conflict, human rights violations, generalized violence in North Caucasus, particularly Chechnya and North Ossetia) (2017)

**stateless persons:** 82,148 (2017); note - Russia's stateless population consists of Roma, Meskhetian Turks, and ex-Soviet citizens from the former republics; between 2003 and 2010 more than 600,000 stateless people were naturalized; most Meskhetian Turks, followers of Islam with origins in Georgia, fled or were evacuated from Uzbekistan after a 1989 pogrom and have lived in Russia for more than the required five-year residency period; they continue to be denied registration for citizenship and basic rights by local Krasnodar Krai authorities on the grounds that they are temporary illegal migrants

## TRAFFICKING IN PERSONS:

**current situation:** Russia is a source, transit, and destination country for men, women, and children who are subjected to forced labor and sex trafficking; with millions of foreign workers, forced labor is Russia's predominant human trafficking problem and sometimes involves organized crime syndicates; workers from Russia, other European countries, Central Asia, and East and Southeast Asia, including North Korea and Vietnam, are subjected to forced labor in the construction, manufacturing, agricultural, textile, grocery store, maritime, and domestic service industries, as well as in forced begging, waste sorting, and street sweeping; women and children from Europe, Southeast Asia, Africa, and Central Asia are subject to sex trafficking in Russia; Russian women and children are victims of sex trafficking domestically and in Northeast Asia, Europe, Central Asia, Africa, the US, and the Middle East

**tier rating:** Tier 3 - Russia does not fully comply with the minimum standards for the elimination of trafficking and is not making a significant effort to do so; prosecutions of trafficking offenders remained low in comparison to the scope of Russia's trafficking problem; the government did not develop or employ a formal system for identifying trafficking victims or referring them to protective services, although authorities reportedly assisted a limited number of victims on an ad hoc basis; foreign victims, the largest group in Russia, were not entitled to state-provided rehabilitative services and were routinely detained and deported; the government has not reported investigating reports of slave-like conditions among North Korean workers in Russia; authorities have made no effort to reduce the demand for forced labor or to develop public awareness of forced labor or sex trafficking (2015)

## ILLICIT DRUGS:

limited cultivation of illicit cannabis and opium poppy and producer of methamphetamine, mostly for domestic consumption; government has active illicit crop eradication program; used as transshipment point for Asian opiates, cannabis, and Latin American cocaine bound for growing domestic markets, to a lesser extent Western and Central Europe, and occasionally to the US; major source of heroin precursor chemicals; corruption and organized crime are key concerns; major consumer of opiates

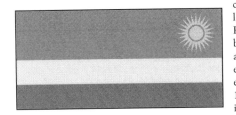

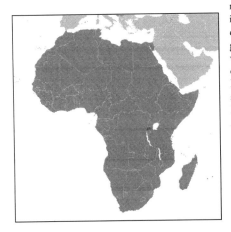

# AFRICA :: RWANDA

## INTRODUCTION :: RWANDA

### BACKGROUND:

In 1959, three years before independence from Belgium, the majority ethnic group, the Hutus, overthrew the ruling Tutsi king. Over the next several years, thousands of Tutsis were killed, and some 150,000 driven into exile in neighboring countries. The children of these exiles later formed a rebel group, the Rwandan Patriotic Front (RPF), and began a civil war in 1990. The war, along with several political and economic upheavals, exacerbated ethnic tensions, culminating in April 1994 in a state-orchestrated genocide, in which Rwandans killed up to a million of their fellow citizens, including approximately three-quarters of the Tutsi population. The genocide ended later that same year when the predominantly Tutsi RPF, operating out of Uganda and northern Rwanda, defeated the national army and Hutu militias, and established an RPF-led government of national unity. Approximately 2 million Hutu refugees - many fearing Tutsi retribution - fled to neighboring Burundi, Tanzania, Uganda, and former Zaire. Since then, most of the refugees have returned to Rwanda, but several thousand remained in the neighboring Democratic Republic of the Congo (DRC, the former Zaire) and formed an extremist insurgency bent on retaking Rwanda, much as the RPF did in 1990. Rwanda held its first local elections in 1999 and its first post-genocide presidential and legislative elections in 2003. Rwanda in 2009 staged a joint military operation with the Congolese Army in DRC to rout out the Hutu extremist insurgency there, and Kigali and Kinshasa restored diplomatic relations. Rwanda also joined the Commonwealth in late 2009. President Paul KAGAME won the presidential election in August 2017 after changing the constitution in 2016 to allow him to run for a third term.

## GEOGRAPHY :: RWANDA

### LOCATION:
Central Africa, east of the Democratic Republic of the Congo, north of Burundi

### GEOGRAPHIC COORDINATES:
2 00 S, 30 00 E

### MAP REFERENCES:
Africa

### AREA:
total: 26,338 sq km
land: 24,668 sq km
water: 1,670 sq km
country comparison to the world: 149

### AREA - COMPARATIVE:
slightly smaller than Maryland

### LAND BOUNDARIES:
total: 930 km
border countries (4): Burundi 315 km, Democratic Republic of the Congo 221 km, Tanzania 222 km, Uganda 172 km

### COASTLINE:
0 km (landlocked)

### MARITIME CLAIMS:
none (landlocked)

### CLIMATE:
temperate; two rainy seasons (February to April, November to January); mild in mountains with frost and snow possible

### TERRAIN:
mostly grassy uplands and hills; relief is mountainous with altitude declining from west to east

### ELEVATION:
mean elevation: 1,598 m
elevation extremes: 950 m lowest point: Rusizi River
4519 highest point: Volcan Karisimbi

### NATURAL RESOURCES:
gold, cassiterite (tin ore), wolframite (tungsten ore), methane, hydropower, arable land

### LAND USE:
agricultural land: 74.5% (2011 est.)
arable land: 47% (2011 est.) / permanent crops: 10.1% (2011 est.) / permanent pasture: 17.4% (2011 est.)
forest: 18% (2011 est.)
other: 7.5% (2011 est.)

### IRRIGATED LAND:
96 sq km (2012)

### POPULATION DISTRIBUTION:
one of Africa's most densely populated countries; large concentrations tend to be in the central regions and along the shore of Lake Kivu in the west

### NATURAL HAZARDS:
periodic droughts; the volcanic Virunga Mountains are in the northwest along the border with Democratic Republic of the Congo

volcanism: Visoke (3,711 m), located on the border with the Democratic Republic of the Congo, is the country's only historically active volcano

### ENVIRONMENT - CURRENT ISSUES:

deforestation results from uncontrolled cutting of trees for fuel; overgrazing; land degradation; soil erosion; a decline in soil fertility (soil exhaustion); wetland degradation and loss of biodiversity; widespread poaching

### ENVIRONMENT - INTERNATIONAL AGREEMENTS:

party to: Biodiversity, Climate Change, Climate Change-Kyoto Protocol, Desertification, Endangered Species, Hazardous Wastes, Ozone Layer Protection, Wetlands

signed, but not ratified: Law of the Sea

### GEOGRAPHY - NOTE:

landlocked; most of the country is savanna grassland with the population predominantly rural

# PEOPLE AND SOCIETY :: RWANDA

### POPULATION:

12,187,400 (July 2018 est.)

note: estimates for this country explicitly take into account the effects of excess mortality due to AIDS; this can result in lower life expectancy, higher infant mortality, higher death rates, lower population growth rates, and changes in the distribution of population by age and sex than would otherwise be expected

country comparison to the world: 74

### NATIONALITY:

noun: Rwandan(s)

adjective: Rwandan

### ETHNIC GROUPS:

Hutu, Tutsi, Twa (Pygmy)

### LANGUAGES:

Kinyarwanda (official, universal Bantu vernacular) 93.2%, French (official) (2002 est.)

### RELIGIONS:

Protestant 49.5% (includes Adventist 11.8% and other Protestant 37.7%), Roman Catholic 43.7%, Muslim 2%, other 0.9% (includes Jehovah's Witness), none 2.5%, unspecified 1.3% (2012 est.)

### DEMOGRAPHIC PROFILE:

Rwanda's fertility rate declined sharply during the last decade, as a result of the government's commitment to family planning, the increased use of contraceptives, and a downward trend in ideal family size. Increases in educational attainment, particularly among girls, and exposure to social media also contributed to the reduction in the birth rate. The average number of births per woman decreased from a 5.6 in 2005 to 4.5 in 2016. Despite these significant strides in reducing fertility, Rwanda's birth rate remains very high and will continue to for an extended period of time because of its large population entering reproductive age. Because Rwanda is one of the most densely populated countries in Africa, its persistent high population growth and increasingly small agricultural landholdings will put additional strain on families' ability to raise foodstuffs and access potable water. These conditions will also hinder the government's efforts to reduce poverty and prevent environmental degradation.

The UNHCR recommended that effective 30 June 2013 countries invoke a cessation of refugee status for those Rwandans who fled their homeland between 1959 and 1998, including the 1994 genocide, on the grounds that the conditions that drove them to seek protection abroad no longer exist. The UNHCR's decision is controversial because many Rwandan refugees still fear persecution if they return home, concerns that are supported by the number of Rwandans granted asylum since 1998 and by the number exempted from the cessation. Rwandan refugees can still seek an exemption or local integration, but host countries are anxious to send the refugees back to Rwanda and are likely to avoid options that enable them to stay. Conversely, Rwanda itself hosts almost 160,000 refugees as of 2017; virtually all of them fleeing conflict in neighboring Burundi and the Democratic Republic of the Congo.

### AGE STRUCTURE:

0-14 years: 40.98% (male 2,521,169 /female 2,473,055)

15-24 years: 19.45% (male 1,187,249 /female 1,183,278)

25-54 years: 32.93% (male 1,903,087 /female 2,109,839)

55-64 years: 4.15% (male 225,273 /female 280,545)

65 years and over: 2.49% (male 120,952 /female 182,953) (2018 est.)

### DEPENDENCY RATIOS:

total dependency ratio: 77.3 (2015 est.)

youth dependency ratio: 72.4 (2015 est.)

elderly dependency ratio: 5 (2015 est.)

potential support ratio: 20.1 (2015 est.)

### MEDIAN AGE:

total: 19.2 years

male: 18.5 years

female: 20 years (2018 est.)

country comparison to the world: 200

### POPULATION GROWTH RATE:

2.3% (2018 est.)

country comparison to the world: 34

### BIRTH RATE:

29.8 births/1,000 population (2018 est.)

country comparison to the world: 39

### DEATH RATE:

6.3 deaths/1,000 population (2018 est.)

country comparison to the world: 154

### NET MIGRATION RATE:

0.2 migrant(s)/1,000 population (2017 est.)

country comparison to the world: 68

### POPULATION DISTRIBUTION:

one of Africa's most densely populated countries; large concentrations tend to be in the central regions and along the shore of Lake Kivu in the west

### URBANIZATION:

urban population: 17.2% of total population (2018)

rate of urbanization: 2.86% annual rate of change (2015-20 est.)

### MAJOR URBAN AREAS - POPULATION:

1.058 million KIGALI (capital) (2018)

### SEX RATIO:

at birth: 1.03 male(s)/female (2017 est.)

0-14 years: 1.02 male(s)/female (2017 est.)

15-24 years: 1 male(s)/female (2017 est.)

25-54 years: 1 male(s)/female (2017 est.)

55-64 years: 0.88 male(s)/female (2017 est.)

65 years and over: 0.7 male(s)/female (2017 est.)

total population: 1 male(s)/female (2017 est.)

### MOTHER'S MEAN AGE AT FIRST BIRTH:

23 years (2014/15 est.)

note: median age at first birth among women 25-29

**MATERNAL MORTALITY RATE:**

290 deaths/100,000 live births (2015 est.)

country comparison to the world: 43

**INFANT MORTALITY RATE:**

total: 29.1 deaths/1,000 live births (2018 est.)

male: 32 deaths/1,000 live births (2018 est.)

female: 26.2 deaths/1,000 live births (2018 est.)

country comparison to the world: 64

**LIFE EXPECTANCY AT BIRTH:**

total population: 64.5 years (2018 est.)

male: 62.6 years (2018 est.)

female: 66.5 years (2018 est.)

country comparison to the world: 188

**TOTAL FERTILITY RATE:**

3.75 children born/woman (2018 est.)

country comparison to the world: 41

**CONTRACEPTIVE PREVALENCE RATE:**

53.2% (2014/15)

**HEALTH EXPENDITURES:**

7.5% of GDP (2014)

country comparison to the world: 67

**PHYSICIANS DENSITY:**

0.06 physicians/1,000 population (2015)

**DRINKING WATER SOURCE:**

improved:

urban: 86.6% of population

rural: 71.9% of population

total: 76.1% of population

unimproved:

urban: 13.4% of population

rural: 28.1% of population

total: 23.9% of population (2015 est.)

**SANITATION FACILITY ACCESS:**

improved:

urban: 58.5% of population (2015 est.)

rural: 62.9% of population (2015 est.)

total: 61.6% of population (2015 est.)

unimproved:

urban: 41.5% of population (2015 est.)

rural: 37.1% of population (2015 est.)

total: 38.4% of population (2015 est.)

**HIV/AIDS - ADULT PREVALENCE RATE:**

2.7% (2017 est.)

country comparison to the world: 21

**HIV/AIDS - PEOPLE LIVING WITH HIV/AIDS:**

220,000 (2017 est.)

country comparison to the world: 27

**HIV/AIDS - DEATHS:**

3,100 (2017 est.)

country comparison to the world: 39

**MAJOR INFECTIOUS DISEASES:**

degree of risk: very high (2016)

food or waterborne diseases: bacterial diarrhea, hepatitis A, and typhoid fever (2016)

vectorborne diseases: malaria and dengue fever (2016)

animal contact diseases: rabies (2016)

**OBESITY - ADULT PREVALENCE RATE:**

5.8% (2016)

country comparison to the world: 174

**CHILDREN UNDER THE AGE OF 5 YEARS UNDERWEIGHT:**

8.1% (2015)

country comparison to the world: 70

**EDUCATION EXPENDITURES:**

3.5% of GDP (2016)

country comparison to the world: 130

**LITERACY:**

definition: age 15 and over can read and write (2015 est.)

total population: 70.5% (2015 est.)

male: 73.2% (2015 est.)

female: 68% (2015 est.)

**SCHOOL LIFE EXPECTANCY (PRIMARY TO TERTIARY EDUCATION):**

total: 11 years (2013)

male: 11 years (2013)

female: 11 years (2013)

**UNEMPLOYMENT, YOUTH AGES 15-24:**

total: 1.9% (2014 est.)

male: 1.4% (2014 est.)

female: 2.5% (2014 est.)

country comparison to the world: 167

## GOVERNMENT :: RWANDA

**COUNTRY NAME:**

conventional long form: Republic of Rwanda

conventional short form: Rwanda

local long form: Republika y'u Rwanda

local short form: Rwanda

former: Ruanda, German East Africa

etymology: the name translates as "domain" in the native Kinyarwanda language

**GOVERNMENT TYPE:**

presidential republic

**CAPITAL:**

name: Kigali

geographic coordinates: 1 57 S, 30 03 E

time difference: UTC+2 (7 hours ahead of Washington, DC, during Standard Time)

**ADMINISTRATIVE DIVISIONS:**

4 provinces (in French - provinces, singular - province; in Kinyarwanda - intara for singular and plural) and 1 city* (in French - ville; in Kinyarwanda - umujyi); Est (Eastern), Kigali*, Nord (Northern), Ouest (Western), Sud (Southern)

**INDEPENDENCE:**

1 July 1962 (from Belgium-administered UN trusteeship)

**NATIONAL HOLIDAY:**

Independence Day, 1 July (1962)

**CONSTITUTION:**

history: several previous; latest adopted by referendum 26 May 2003, effective 4 June 2003 (2017)

amendments: proposed by the president of the republic (with Council of Ministers approval) or by two-thirds majority support of both houses of Parliament; passage requires at least three-quarters majority vote in both houses; changes to constitutional articles on national sovereignty, the presidential term, the form and system of government, and political pluralism also require approval in a referendum; amended 2008, 2010, 2015 (2017)

**LEGAL SYSTEM:**

mixed legal system of civil law, based on German and Belgian models, and customary law; judicial review of legislative acts in the Supreme Court

**INTERNATIONAL LAW ORGANIZATION PARTICIPATION:**

has not submitted an ICJ jurisdiction declaration; non-party state to the ICCt

**CITIZENSHIP:**

citizenship by birth: no

citizenship by descent only: the father must be a citizen of Rwanda; if the father is stateless or unknown, the mother must be a citizen

dual citizenship recognized: no

residency requirement for naturalization: 10 years

**SUFFRAGE:**

18 years of age; universal

**EXECUTIVE BRANCH:**

chief of state: President Paul KAGAME (since 22 April 2000)

head of government: Prime Minister Edouard NGIRENTE (since 30 August 2017)

cabinet: Council of Ministers appointed by the president

elections/appointments: president directly elected by simple majority vote for a 5-year term (eligible for a second term); note - a constitutional amendment approved in December 2016 reduced the presidential term from 7 to 5 years but included an exception that allowed President KAGAME to serve another 7-year term in 2017, potentially followed by two additional 5-year terms; election last held on 4 August 2017 (next to be held in August 2024); prime minister appointed by the president

election results: Paul KAGAME reelected president; Paul KAGAME (RPF) 98.8%, Philippe MPAYIMANA (independent) 0.7%, Frank HABINEZA (DGPR) 0.5%

**LEGISLATIVE BRANCH:**

description: bicameral Parliament consists of:
Senate or Senat (26 seats; 12 members indirectly elected by local councils, 8 appointed by the president, 4 appointed by the Political Organizations Forum - a body of registered political parties, and 2 selected by institutions of higher learning; members serve 8-year terms) Chamber of Deputies or Chambre des Deputes (80 seats; 53 members directly elected by proportional representation vote, 24 women selected by special interest groups, and 3 selected by youth and disability organizations; members serve 5-year terms)

elections:
Senate - last held on 26-27 September 2011 (next to be held in 2019)
Chamber of Deputies - last held on 16-18 September 2013 (next to be held on 3 September 2018)

election results:
Chamber of Deputies - percent of vote by party - Rwandan Patriotic Front Coalition 76.2%, PSD 13%, PL 9.3%, other 1.5%; seats by party - Rwandan Patriotic Front Coalition 41, PSD 7, PL 5, 27 indirectly elected members

**JUDICIAL BRANCH:**

highest courts: Supreme Court (consists of the chief and deputy chief justices and 15 judges; normally organized into 3-judge panels); High Court (consists of the court president, vice president, and a minimum of 24 judges and organized into 5 chambers

judge selection and term of office: High Court of the Republic; commercial courts including the High Commercial Court; intermediate courts; primary courts; and military specialized courts

subordinate courts: High Court of the Republic; commercial courts including the High Commercial Court; intermediate courts; primary courts; and military specialized courts

note: Supreme Court judges nominated by the president after consultation with the Cabinet and the Superior Council of the Judiciary or SCJ (a 27-member body of judges, other judicial officials, and legal professionals) and approved by the Senate; chief and deputy chief justices appointed for 8-year nonrenewable terms; tenure of judges NA; High Court president and vice president appointed by the president of the republic upon approval by the Senate; judges appointed by the Supreme Court chief justice upon approval of the SCJ; judge tenure NA

**POLITICAL PARTIES AND LEADERS:**

Democratic Green Party of Rwanda or DGPR [Frank HABINEZA]
Liberal Party or PL [Donatille MUKABALISA]
Party for Progress and Concord or PPC [Dr. Alivera MUKABARAMBA]
Party Imberakuri or PS-Imberakuri [Christine MUKABUNANI]
Rwandan Patriotic Front or RPF [Paul KAGAME]
Rwandan Patriotic Front Coalition (includes RPF, PPC) [Paul KAGAME]
Social Democratic Party or PSD [Vincent BIRUTA]

**INTERNATIONAL ORGANIZATION PARTICIPATION:**

ACP, AfDB, AU, C, CEPGL, COMESA, EAC, EADB, FAO, G-77, IAEA, IBRD, ICAO, ICRM, IDA, IFAD, IFC, IFRCS, ILO, IMF, Interpol, IOC, IOM, IPU, ISO, ITSO, ITU, ITUC (NGOs), MIGA, MINUSMA, NAM, OIF, OPCW, PCA, UN, UNAMID, UNCTAD, UNESCO, UNHCR, UNIDO, UNISFA, UNMISS, UNWTO, UPU, WCO, WHO, WIPO, WMO, WTO

**DIPLOMATIC REPRESENTATION IN THE US:**

chief of mission: Ambassador Mathilde MUKANTABANA (since 18 July 2013)

chancery: 1875 Connecticut Avenue, NW, Suite 418, Washington, DC, 20009

telephone: [1] (202) 232-2882

FAX: [1] (202) 232-4544

**DIPLOMATIC REPRESENTATION FROM THE US:**

chief of mission: Ambassador Peter H. VROOMAN (since 5 April 2018)

embassy: 2657 Avenue de la Gendarmerie, Kigali

mailing address: B.P. 28, Kigali

telephone: [250] 252 596-400

FAX: [250] 252 580 325

**FLAG DESCRIPTION:**

three horizontal bands of sky blue (top, double width), yellow, and green, with a golden sun with 24 rays near the fly end of the blue band; blue represents happiness and peace, yellow economic development and mineral wealth, green hope of prosperity and natural resources; the sun symbolizes unity, as well as enlightenment and transparency from ignorance

**NATIONAL SYMBOL(S):**

traditional woven basket with peaked lid; national colors: blue, yellow, green

**NATIONAL ANTHEM:**

name: "Rwanda nziza" (Rwanda, Our Beautiful Country)

lyrics/music: Faustin MURIGO/Jean-Bosco HASHAKAIMANA

note: adopted 2001

# ECONOMY :: RWANDA

**ECONOMY - OVERVIEW:**

Rwanda is a rural, agrarian country with agriculture accounting for about 63% of export earnings, and with some mineral and agro-processing.

Population density is high but, with the exception of the capital Kigali, is not concentrated in large cities – its 12 million people are spread out on a small amount of land (smaller than the state of Maryland). Tourism, minerals, coffee, and tea are Rwanda's main sources of foreign exchange. Despite Rwanda's fertile ecosystem, food production often does not keep pace with demand, requiring food imports. Energy shortages, instability in neighboring states, and lack of adequate transportation linkages to other countries continue to handicap private sector growth.

The 1994 genocide decimated Rwanda's fragile economic base, severely impoverished the population, particularly women, and temporarily stalled the country's ability to attract private and external investment. However, Rwanda has made substantial progress in stabilizing and rehabilitating its economy well beyond pre-1994 levels. GDP has rebounded with an average annual growth of 6%-8% since 2003 and inflation has been reduced to single digits. In 2015, 39% of the population lived below the poverty line, according to government statistics, compared to 57% in 2006.

The government has embraced an expansionary fiscal policy to reduce poverty by improving education, infrastructure, and foreign and domestic investment. Rwanda consistently ranks well for ease of doing business and transparency.

The Rwandan Government is seeking to become a regional leader in information and communication technologies and aims to reach middle-income status by 2020 by leveraging the service industry. In 2012, Rwanda completed the first modern Special Economic Zone (SEZ) in Kigali. The SEZ seeks to attract investment in all sectors, but specifically in agribusiness, information and communications, trade and logistics, mining, and construction. In 2016, the government launched an online system to give investors information about public land and its suitability for agricultural development.

**GDP (PURCHASING POWER PARITY):**

$24.68 billion (2017 est.)

$23.26 billion (2016 est.)

$21.94 billion (2015 est.)

note: data are in 2017 dollars

country comparison to the world: 142

**GDP (OFFICIAL EXCHANGE RATE):**

$9.136 billion (2017 est.) (2017 est.)

**GDP - REAL GROWTH RATE:**

6.1% (2017 est.)

6% (2016 est.)

8.9% (2015 est.)

country comparison to the world: 33

**GDP - PER CAPITA (PPP):**

$2,100 (2017 est.)

$2,000 (2016 est.)

$1,900 (2015 est.)

note: data are in 2017 dollars

country comparison to the world: 208

**GROSS NATIONAL SAVING:**

12.5% of GDP (2017 est.)

6.1% of GDP (2016 est.)

7.5% of GDP (2015 est.)

country comparison to the world: 147

**GDP - COMPOSITION, BY END USE:**

household consumption: 75.9% (2017 est.)

government consumption: 15.2% (2017 est.)

investment in fixed capital: 22.9% (2017 est.)

investment in inventories: 0.5% (2017 est.)

exports of goods and services: 18.2% (2017 est.)

imports of goods and services: -32.8% (2017 est.)

**GDP - COMPOSITION, BY SECTOR OF ORIGIN:**

agriculture: 30.9% (2017 est.)

industry: 17.6% (2017 est.)

services: 51.5% (2017 est.)

**AGRICULTURE - PRODUCTS:**

coffee, tea, pyrethrum (insecticide made from chrysanthemums), bananas, beans, sorghum, potatoes; livestock

**INDUSTRIES:**

cement, agricultural products, small-scale beverages, soap, furniture, shoes, plastic goods, textiles, cigarettes

**INDUSTRIAL PRODUCTION GROWTH RATE:**

4.2% (2017 est.)

country comparison to the world: 72

**LABOR FORCE:**

6.227 million (2017 est.)

country comparison to the world: 72

**LABOR FORCE - BY OCCUPATION:**

agriculture: 75.3%

industry: 6.7%

services: 18% (2012 est.)

**UNEMPLOYMENT RATE:**

2.7% (2014 est.)

country comparison to the world: 29

**POPULATION BELOW POVERTY LINE:**

39.1% (2015 est.)

**HOUSEHOLD INCOME OR CONSUMPTION BY PERCENTAGE SHARE:**

lowest 10%: 43.2% (2011 est.)

highest 10%: 43.2% (2011 est.)

**DISTRIBUTION OF FAMILY INCOME - GINI INDEX:**

50.4 (2013 est.)

51.3 (2010 est.)

country comparison to the world: 17

**BUDGET:**

revenues: 1.943 billion (2017 est.)

expenditures: 2.337 billion (2017 est.)

**TAXES AND OTHER REVENUES:**

21.3% (of GDP) (2017 est.)

country comparison to the world: 142

**BUDGET SURPLUS (+) OR DEFICIT (-):**

-4.3% (of GDP) (2017 est.)

country comparison to the world: 162

**PUBLIC DEBT:**

40.5% of GDP (2017 est.)

37.3% of GDP (2016 est.)

country comparison to the world: 125

**FISCAL YEAR:**

calendar year

**INFLATION RATE (CONSUMER PRICES):**

4.8% (2017 est.)

5.7% (2016 est.)

country comparison to the world: 170

**CENTRAL BANK DISCOUNT RATE:**

7.75% (31 December 2010)

11.25% (31 December 2008)

country comparison to the world: 40

**COMMERCIAL BANK PRIME LENDING RATE:**

17.17% (31 December 2017 est.)

17.29% (31 December 2016 est.)

country comparison to the world: 26

**STOCK OF NARROW MONEY:**

$963.9 million (31 December 2017 est.)

$895 million (31 December 2016 est.)

country comparison to the world: 159

**STOCK OF BROAD MONEY:**

$963.9 million (31 December 2017 est.)

$895 million (31 December 2016 est.)

country comparison to the world: 164

**STOCK OF DOMESTIC CREDIT:**

$1.861 billion (31 December 2017 est.)

$1.614 billion (31 December 2016 est.)

country comparison to the world: 154

**MARKET VALUE OF PUBLICLY TRADED SHARES:**

NA

**CURRENT ACCOUNT BALANCE:**

-$622 million (2017 est.)

-$1.336 billion (2016 est.)

country comparison to the world: 124

**EXPORTS:**

$1.05 billion (2017 est.)

$745 million (2016 est.)

country comparison to the world: 158

**EXPORTS - PARTNERS:**

UAE 38.3%, Kenya 15.1%, Switzerland 9.9%, Democratic Republic of the Congo 9.5%, US 4.9%, Singapore 4.5% (2017)

**EXPORTS - COMMODITIES:**

coffee, tea, hides, tin ore

**IMPORTS:**

$1.922 billion (2017 est.)

$2.036 billion (2016 est.)

country comparison to the world: 167

**IMPORTS - COMMODITIES:**

foodstuffs, machinery and equipment, steel, petroleum products, cement and construction material

**IMPORTS - PARTNERS:**

China 20.4%, Uganda 11%, India 7.2%, Kenya 7.1%, Tanzania 5.3%, UAE 5.1% (2017)

**RESERVES OF FOREIGN EXCHANGE AND GOLD:**

$997.6 million (31 December 2017 est.)

$1.104 billion (31 December 2016 est.)

country comparison to the world: 132

**DEBT - EXTERNAL:**

$3.258 billion (31 December 2017 est.)

$2.611 billion (31 December 2016 est.)

country comparison to the world: 141

**STOCK OF DIRECT FOREIGN INVESTMENT - AT HOME:**

$2.378 billion (31 December 2017 est.)

$2.072 billion (31 December 2016 est.)

country comparison to the world: 117

**STOCK OF DIRECT FOREIGN INVESTMENT - ABROAD:**

$113.2 million (31 December 2017 est.)

$26.8 million (31 December 2016 est.)

country comparison to the world: 111

**EXCHANGE RATES:**

Rwandan francs (RWF) per US dollar -

839.1 (2017 est.)

787.25 (2016 est.)

787.25 (2015 est.)

720.54 (2014 est.)

680.95 (2013 est.)

## ENERGY :: RWANDA

**ELECTRICITY ACCESS:**

population without electricity: 9.3 million (2013)

electrification - total population: 21% (2013)

electrification - urban areas: 67% (2013)

electrification - rural areas: 5% (2013)

**ELECTRICITY - PRODUCTION:**

525 million kWh (2016 est.)

country comparison to the world: 164

**ELECTRICITY - CONSUMPTION:**

527.3 million kWh (2016 est.)

country comparison to the world: 169

**ELECTRICITY - EXPORTS:**

4 million kWh (2015 est.)

country comparison to the world: 92

**ELECTRICITY - IMPORTS:**

42 million kWh (2016 est.)

country comparison to the world: 108

**ELECTRICITY - INSTALLED GENERATING CAPACITY:**

191,000 kW (2016 est.)

country comparison to the world: 166

**ELECTRICITY - FROM FOSSIL FUELS:**

42% of total installed capacity (2016 est.)

country comparison to the world: 164

**ELECTRICITY - FROM NUCLEAR FUELS:**

0% of total installed capacity (2017 est.)

country comparison to the world: 170

**ELECTRICITY - FROM HYDROELECTRIC PLANTS:**

51% of total installed capacity (2017 est.)

country comparison to the world: 37

**ELECTRICITY - FROM OTHER RENEWABLE SOURCES:**

7% of total installed capacity (2017 est.)

country comparison to the world: 96

**CRUDE OIL - PRODUCTION:**

0 bbl/day (2017 est.)

country comparison to the world: 188

**CRUDE OIL - EXPORTS:**

0 bbl/day (2015 est.)

country comparison to the world: 182

**CRUDE OIL - IMPORTS:**

0 bbl/day (2015 est.)

country comparison to the world: 184

**CRUDE OIL - PROVED RESERVES:**

0 bbl (1 January 2018 est.)

country comparison to the world: 184

**REFINED PETROLEUM PRODUCTS - PRODUCTION:**

0 bbl/day (2015 est.)

country comparison to the world: 191

**REFINED PETROLEUM PRODUCTS - CONSUMPTION:**

6,700 bbl/day (2016 est.)

country comparison to the world: 167

**REFINED PETROLEUM PRODUCTS - EXPORTS:**

0 bbl/day (2015 est.)

country comparison to the world: 192

**REFINED PETROLEUM PRODUCTS - IMPORTS:**

6,628 bbl/day (2015 est.)

country comparison to the world: 162

**NATURAL GAS - PRODUCTION:**

0 cu m (2017 est.)

country comparison to the world: 186

**NATURAL GAS - CONSUMPTION:**

0 cu m (2017 est.)

country comparison to the world: 188

**NATURAL GAS - EXPORTS:**

0 cu m (2017 est.)

country comparison to the world: 171

**NATURAL GAS - IMPORTS:**

0 cu m (2017 est.)

country comparison to the world: 177

**NATURAL GAS - PROVED RESERVES:**

56.63 billion cu m (1 January 2018 est.)

country comparison to the world: 61

**CARBON DIOXIDE EMISSIONS FROM CONSUMPTION OF ENERGY:**

985,600 Mt (2017 est.)

country comparison to the world: 169

# COMMUNICATIONS :: RWANDA

**TELEPHONES - FIXED LINES:**

total subscriptions: 12,333 (2017 est.)

subscriptions per 100 inhabitants: less than 1 (December 2017 est.) (2017 est.)

country comparison to the world: 191

**TELEPHONES - MOBILE CELLULAR:**

total subscriptions: 8,819,217 (2017 est.)

subscriptions per 100 inhabitants: 74 (2017 est.)

country comparison to the world: 89

**TELEPHONE SYSTEM:**

general assessment: small, inadequate telephone system primarily serves business, education, and government (2017)

domestic: the capital, Kigali, is connected to provincial centers by microwave radio relay and, recently, by cellular telephone service; much of the network depends on wire and HF radiotelephone; combined fixed-line and mobile-cellular telephone density has increased and now exceeds 70 telephones per 100 persons (2017)

international: country code - 250; international connections employ microwave radio relay to neighboring countries and satellite communications to more distant countries; satellite earth stations - 1 Intelsat (Indian Ocean) in Kigali (includes telex and telefax service) (2017)

**BROADCAST MEDIA:**

13 TV stations; 35 radio stations registered, including international broadcasters, government owns most popular TV and radio stations; regional satellite-based TV services available (2016)

**INTERNET COUNTRY CODE:**

.rw

**INTERNET USERS:**

total: 3,724,678 (Dec 2017 est.)

percent of population: 29.8% (Dec 2017 est.)

country comparison to the world: 90

**BROADBAND - FIXED SUBSCRIPTIONS:**

total: 21,780 (2017 est.)

subscriptions per 100 inhabitants: less than 1 (2017 est.)

country comparison to the world: 150

# TRANSPORTATION :: RWANDA

**NATIONAL AIR TRANSPORT SYSTEM:**

number of registered air carriers: 1 (2015)

inventory of registered aircraft operated by air carriers: 9 (2015)

annual passenger traffic on registered air carriers: 645,815 (2015)

annual freight traffic on registered air carriers: 21,382,897 mt-km (2015)

**CIVIL AIRCRAFT REGISTRATION COUNTRY CODE PREFIX:**

9XR (2016)

**AIRPORTS:**

7 (2013)

country comparison to the world: 170

**AIRPORTS - WITH PAVED RUNWAYS:**

total: 4 (2017)

over 3,047 m: 1 (2017)

914 to 1,523 m: 2 (2017)

under 914 m: 1 (2017)

**AIRPORTS - WITH UNPAVED RUNWAYS:**

total: 3 (2013)

914 to 1,523 m: 2 (2013)

under 914 m: 1 (2013)

**ROADWAYS:**

total: 4,700 km (2012)

paved: 1,207 km (2012)

unpaved: 3,493 km (2012)

country comparison to the world: 152

**WATERWAYS:**

(Lac Kivu navigable by shallow-draft barges and native craft) (2011)

**PORTS AND TERMINALS:**

lake port(s): Cyangugu, Gisenyi, Kibuye (Lake Kivu)

# MILITARY AND SECURITY :: RWANDA

**MILITARY EXPENDITURES:**

1.21% of GDP (2016)

1.25% of GDP (2015)

1.13% of GDP (2014)

1.08% of GDP (2013)

1.09% of GDP (2012)

country comparison to the world: 98

**MILITARY BRANCHES:**

Rwanda Defense Force (RDF): Rwanda Army (Rwanda Land Force), Rwanda Air Force (Force Aerienne Rwandaise, FAR) (2013)

**MILITARY SERVICE AGE AND OBLIGATION:**

18 years of age for voluntary military service; no conscription; Rwandan citizenship is required, as is a 9th-grade education for enlisted recruits and an A-level certificate for officer candidates; enlistment is either as contract (5-years, renewable twice) or career; retirement (for officers and senior NCOs) after 20 years of service or at 40-60 years of age (2012)

# TRANSNATIONAL ISSUES :: RWANDA

**DISPUTES - INTERNATIONAL:**

Burundi and Rwanda dispute two sq km (0.8 sq mi) of Sabanerwa, a farmed area in the Rukurazi Valley where the Akanyaru/Kanyaru River shifted its course southward after heavy rains in 1965fighting among ethnic groups - loosely associated political rebels, armed gangs, and various government forces in Great Lakes region transcending the boundaries of Burundi, Democratic Republic of the Congo (DROC), Rwanda, and Uganda - abated substantially from a decade ago due largely to UN peacekeeping, international mediation, and efforts by local governments to create civil societiesnonetheless, 57,000 Rwandan refugees still reside in 21 African states, including Zambia, Gabon, and 20,000 who fled to Burundi in 2005 and 2006 to escape drought and recriminations from traditional courts investigating the 1994 massaresthe 2005 DROC and Rwanda border verification mechanism to stem rebel actions on both sides of the border remains in place

**REFUGEES AND INTERNALLY DISPLACED PERSONS:**

refugees (country of origin): 80,755 (Democratic Republic of the Congo), 69,089 (Burundi) (2018)

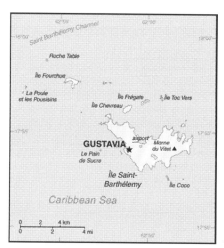

# CENTRAL AMERICA :: SAINT BARTHELEMY

## INTRODUCTION :: SAINT BARTHELEMY

### BACKGROUND:

Discovered in 1493 by Christopher COLUMBUS who named it for his brother Bartolomeo, Saint Barthelemy was first settled by the French in 1648. In 1784, the French sold the island to Sweden, which renamed the largest town Gustavia, after the Swedish King GUSTAV III, and made it a free port; the island prospered as a trade and supply center during the colonial wars of the 18th century. France repurchased the island in 1877 and took control the following year. It was placed under the administration of Guadeloupe. Saint Barthelemy retained its free port status along with various Swedish appellations such as Swedish street and town names, and the three-crown symbol on the coat of arms. In 2003, the islanders voted to secede from Guadeloupe, and in 2007, the island became a French overseas collectivity. In 2012, it became an overseas territory of the EU, allowing it to exert local control over the permanent and temporary immigration of foreign workers including non-French European citizens.

## GEOGRAPHY :: SAINT BARTHELEMY

### LOCATION:
Caribbean, island between the Caribbean Sea and the North Atlantic Ocean; located in the Leeward Islands (northern) group; Saint Barthelemy lies east of the US Virgin Islands

### GEOGRAPHIC COORDINATES:
17 90 N, 62 85 W

### MAP REFERENCES:
Central America and the Caribbean

### AREA:
total: 25 sq km

land: 25 sq km

water: negligible

country comparison to the world: 239

### AREA - COMPARATIVE:
less than one-eighth the size of Washington, DC

### LAND BOUNDARIES:
0 km

### CLIMATE:
tropical, with practically no variation in temperature; has two seasons (dry and humid)

### TERRAIN:
hilly, almost completely surrounded by shallow-water reefs, with plentiful beaches

### ELEVATION:
0 m lowest point: Caribbean Ocean

286 highest point: Morne du Vitet

### NATURAL RESOURCES:
few natural resources; beaches foster tourism

### POPULATION DISTRIBUTION:
most of the populace concentrated in and around the capital of Gustavia, but scattered settlements exist around the island periphery

### ENVIRONMENT - CURRENT ISSUES:
land-based pollution; urbanization; with no natural rivers or streams, fresh water is in short supply, especially in summer, and is provided by the desalination of sea water, the collection of rain water, or imported via water tanker; overfishing

### GEOGRAPHY - NOTE:
a 1,200-hectare marine nature reserve, the Reserve Naturelle, is made up of five zones around the island that form a network to protect the island's coral reefs, seagrass, and endangered marine species

## PEOPLE AND SOCIETY :: SAINT BARTHELEMY

### POPULATION:
7,160 (July 2018 est.)

country comparison to the world: 226

### ETHNIC GROUPS:
other white, Creole (mulatto), black, Guadeloupe Mestizo (French-East Asia)

### LANGUAGES:
French (primary), English

### RELIGIONS:
Roman Catholic, Protestant, Jehovah's Witnesses

### AGE STRUCTURE:
0-14 years: 15.96% (male 587 /female 556)

15-24 years: 7.26% (male 272 /female 248)

25-54 years: 43.13% (male 1,682 /female 1,406)

55-64 years: 16.13% (male 621 /female 534)

65 years and over: 17.51% (male 631 /female 623) (2018 est.)

### MEDIAN AGE:
total: 44.7 years

male: 44.6 years

female: 44.7 years (2018 est.)

**country comparison to the world:** 9

## POPULATION DISTRIBUTION:

most of the populace concentrated in and around the capital of Gustavia, but scattered settlements exist around the island periphery

## SEX RATIO:

**at birth:** 1.06 male(s)/female (2017 est.)

**0-14 years:** 1.06 male(s)/female (2017 est.)

**15-24 years:** 1.1 male(s)/female (2017 est.)

**25-54 years:** 1.19 male(s)/female (2017 est.)

**55-64 years:** 1.19 male(s)/female (2017 est.)

**65 years and over:** 1 male(s)/female (2017 est.)

**total population:** 1.13 male(s)/female (2017 est.)

## MAJOR INFECTIOUS DISEASES:

**note:** active local transmission of Zika virus by Aedes species mosquitoes has been identified in this country (as of August 2016); it poses an important risk (a large number of cases possible) among US citizens if bitten by an infective mosquito; other less common ways to get Zika are through sex, via blood transfusion, or during pregnancy, in which the pregnant woman passes Zika virus to her fetus

# GOVERNMENT :: SAINT BARTHELEMY

## COUNTRY NAME:

**conventional long form:** Overseas Collectivity of Saint Barthelemy

**conventional short form:** Saint Barthelemy

**local long form:** Collectivite d'outre mer de Saint-Barthelemy

**local short form:** Saint-Barthelemy

**abbreviation:** Saint-Barth (French); St. Barts or St. Barths (English)

**etymology:** explorer Christopher COLUMBUS named the island in honor of his brother Bartolomeo's namesake saint in 1493

## DEPENDENCY STATUS:

overseas collectivity of France

## GOVERNMENT TYPE:

parliamentary democracy (Territorial Council); overseas collectivity of France

## CAPITAL:

**name:** Gustavia

**geographic coordinates:** 17 53 N, 62 51 W

**time difference:** UTC-4 (1 hour ahead of Washington, DC, during Standard Time)

## INDEPENDENCE:

none (overseas collectivity of France)

## NATIONAL HOLIDAY:

Fete de la Federation, 14 July (1790); note - local holiday is St. Barthelemy Day, 24 August (1572)

## CONSTITUTION:

**history:** 4 October 1958 (French Constitution) (2018)

**amendments:** amendment procedures of France's constitution apply (2018)

## LEGAL SYSTEM:

French civil law

## CITIZENSHIP:

see France

## SUFFRAGE:

18 years of age, universal

## EXECUTIVE BRANCH:

**chief of state:** President Emmanuel MACRON (since 14 May 2017), represented by Prefect Anne LAUBIES (since 8 June 2015)

**head of government:** President of Territorial Council Bruno MAGRAS (since 16 July 2007)

**cabinet:** Executive Council elected by the Territorial Council; note - there is also an advisory, economic, social, and cultural council

**elections/appointments:** French president directly elected by absolute majority popular vote in 2 rounds if needed for a 5-year term (eligible for a second term); prefect appointed by the French president on the advice of French Ministry of Interior; president of Territorial Council indirectly elected by its members for a 5-year term; election last held on 2 April 2017 (next to be held in 2022)

**election results:** Bruno MAGRAS (SBA) reelected president; Territorial Council vote - NA

## LEGISLATIVE BRANCH:

**description:** unicameral Territorial Council (19 seats; members elected by absolute majority vote in the first round vote and proportional representation vote in the second round; members serve 5-year terms) Saint Barthelemy indirectly elects 1 senator to the French Senate by an electoral college for a 6-year term and directly elects 1 deputy (shared with Saint Martin) to the French National Assembly

**elections:** Territorial Council - last held on 19 March 2017 (next to be held in 2022) French Senate - election last held in September 2014 (next to be held not later than September 2017) French National Assembly - election last held on 11 and 18 June 2017 (next to be held by June 2022)

**election results:** Territorial Council - percent of vote by party - SBA 53.7%, United for Saint Barth 20.6%, Saint Barth Essential 18.1%, All for Saint Barth 7.7%; seats by party - SBA 14, United for Saint Barth 2, Saint Barth Essential 2, All for Saint Barth 1 French Senate - percent of vote by party NA; seats by party UMP 1 French National Assembly - percent of vote by party NA; seats by party UMP 1

## POLITICAL PARTIES AND LEADERS:

All for Saint Barth (Tous pour Saint-Barth) [Bettina COINTRE]
Saint Barth Essential (Saint-Barth Autrement) [Marie-Helene BERNIER]
Saint Barth First! (Saint-Barth d'Abord!) or SBA [Bruno MAGRAS]
Saint Barth United (Unis pour Saint-Barthelemy) [Xavier LEDEE]

## INTERNATIONAL ORGANIZATION PARTICIPATION:

UPU

## DIPLOMATIC REPRESENTATION IN THE US:

none (overseas collectivity of France)

## DIPLOMATIC REPRESENTATION FROM THE US:

none (overseas collectivity of France)

## FLAG DESCRIPTION:

the flag of France is used

## NATIONAL SYMBOL(S):

pelican

## NATIONAL ANTHEM:

**name:** "L'Hymne a St. Barthelemy" (Hymn to St. Barthelemy)

**lyrics/music:** Isabelle Massart DERAVIN/Michael VALENTI

**note:** local anthem in use since 1999; as a collectivity of France, "La Marseillaise" is official (see France)

## ECONOMY :: SAINT BARTHELEMY

### ECONOMY - OVERVIEW:
The economy of Saint Barthelemy is based upon high-end tourism and duty-free luxury commerce, serving visitors primarily from North America. The luxury hotels and villas host 70,000 visitors each year with another 130,000 arriving by boat. The relative isolation and high cost of living inhibits mass tourism. The construction and public sectors also enjoy significant investment in support of tourism. With limited fresh water resources, all food must be imported, as must all energy resources and most manufactured goods. The tourism sector creates a strong employment demand and attracts labor from Brazil and Portugal. The country's currency is the euro.

### EXCHANGE RATES:
2013 est.)

0.885 (2017 est.)

0.903 (2016 est.)

0.9214 (2015 est.)

0.885 (2014 est.)

## COMMUNICATIONS :: SAINT BARTHELEMY

### TELEPHONE SYSTEM:
**general assessment:** fully integrated access (2008)

**domestic:** direct dial capability with both fixed and wireless systems (2008)

**international:** country code - 590; undersea fiber-optic cable provides voice and data connectivity to Puerto Rico and Guadeloupe (2008)

### BROADCAST MEDIA:
no local TV broadcasters; 3 FM radio channels (2 via repeater)

### INTERNET COUNTRY CODE:
.bl; note - .gp, the Internet country code for Guadeloupe, and .fr, the Internet country code for France, might also be encountered

## TRANSPORTATION :: SAINT BARTHELEMY

### AIRPORTS:
1 (2013)

**country comparison to the world:** 234

### AIRPORTS - WITH PAVED RUNWAYS:
**total:** 1 (2017)

**under 914 m:** 1 (2017)

### PORTS AND TERMINALS:
**major seaport(s):** Gustavia

### TRANSPORTATION - NOTE:
nearest airport for international flights is Princess Juliana International Airport (SXM) located on Sint Maarten

## MILITARY AND SECURITY :: SAINT BARTHELEMY

### MILITARY - NOTE:
defense is the responsibility of France

# AFRICA :: SAINT HELENA, ASCENSION, AND TRISTAN DA CUNHA

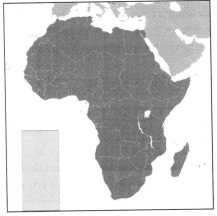

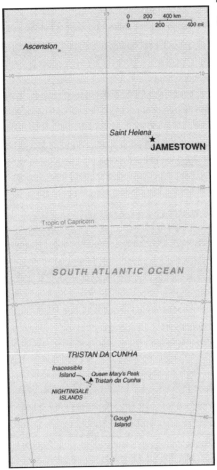

## INTRODUCTION :: SAINT HELENA, ASCENSION, AND TRISTAN DA CUNHA

### BACKGROUND:

Saint Helena is a British Overseas Territory consisting of Saint Helena and Ascension Islands, and the island group of Tristan da Cunha.

**Saint Helena:** Uninhabited when first discovered by the Portuguese in 1502, Saint Helena was garrisoned by the British during the 17th century. It acquired fame as the place of Napoleon BONAPARTE's exile from 1815 until his death in 1821, but its importance as a port of call declined after the opening of the Suez Canal in 1869. During the Anglo-Boer War in South Africa, several thousand Boer prisoners were confined on the island between 1900 and 1903.;

Saint Helena is one of the most remote populated places in the world. The British Government committed to building an airport on Saint Helena in 2005. After more than a decade of delays and construction, a commercial air service to South Africa via Namibia was inaugurated in October of 2017. The weekly service to Saint Helena from Johannesburg via Windhoek in Namibia takes just over six hours (including the refueling stop in Windhoek) and replaces the mail ship that had made a five-day journey to the island every three weeks.;

**Ascension Island:** This barren and uninhabited island was discovered and named by the Portuguese in 1503. The British garrisoned the island in 1815 to prevent a rescue of Napoleon from Saint Helena. It served as a provisioning station for the Royal Navy's West Africa Squadron on anti-slavery patrol. The island remained under Admiralty control until 1922, when it became a dependency of Saint Helena. During World War II, the UK permitted the US to construct an airfield on Ascension in support of transatlantic flights to Africa and anti-submarine operations in the South Atlantic. In the 1960s the island became an important space tracking station for the US. In 1982, Ascension was an essential staging area for British forces during the Falklands War. It remains a critical refueling point in the air-bridge from the UK to the South Atlantic.;

The island hosts one of four dedicated ground antennas that assist in the operation of the Global Positioning System (GPS) navigation system (the others are on Diego Garcia (British Indian Ocean Territory), Kwajalein (Marshall Islands), and at Cape Canaveral, Florida (US)). NASA and the US Air Force also operate a Meter-Class Autonomous Telescope (MCAT) on Ascension as part of the deep space surveillance system for tracking orbital debris, which can be a hazard to spacecraft and astronauts.

**Tristan da Cunha:** The island group consists of Tristan da Cunha, Nightingale, Inaccessible, and Gough Islands. Tristan da Cunha, named after its Portuguese discoverer (1506), was garrisoned by the British in 1816 to prevent any attempt to rescue Napoleon from Saint Helena. Gough and Inaccessible Islands have been designated World Heritage Sites. South Africa leases a site for a meteorological station on Gough Island.

## GEOGRAPHY :: SAINT HELENA, ASCENSION, AND TRISTAN DA CUNHA

### LOCATION:

islands in the South Atlantic Ocean, about midway between South America and Africa; Ascension Island lies 1,300 km (800 mi) northwest of Saint Helena; Tristan da Cunha lies 4,300 km (2,700 mi) southwest of Saint Helena

### GEOGRAPHIC COORDINATES:

Saint Helena: 15 57 S, 5 42 W;

Ascension Island: 7 57 S, 14 22 W;

Tristan da Cunha island group: 37 15 S, 12 30 W

## MAP REFERENCES:
Africa

## AREA:
**total:** 394 sq km

**land:** 122 sq km Saint Helena Island

**water:** 0 sq km

88 Ascension Island 184 Tristan da Cunha island group (includes Tristan (98 sq km), Inaccessible, Nightingale, and Gough islands)

**country comparison to the world:** 204

## AREA - COMPARATIVE:
slightly more than twice the size of Washington, DC

## LAND BOUNDARIES:
0 km

## COASTLINE:
**Saint Helena:** 60 km
**Ascension Island:** NA
**Tristan da Cunha (island only):** 34 km

## MARITIME CLAIMS:
**territorial sea:** 12 nm

**exclusive fishing zone:** 200 nm

## CLIMATE:
**Saint Helena:** tropical marine; mild, tempered by trade winds;

**Ascension Island:** tropical marine; mild, semi-arid;

**Tristan da Cunha:** temperate marine; mild, tempered by trade winds (tends to be cooler than Saint Helena)

## TERRAIN:
the islands of this group are of volcanic origin associated with the Atlantic Mid-Ocean Ridge

**Saint Helena:** rugged, volcanic; small scattered plateaus and plains;

**Ascension:** surface covered by lava flows and cinder cones of 44 dormant volcanoes; terrain rises to the east;

**Tristan da Cunha:** sheer cliffs line the coastline of the nearly circular island; the flanks of the central volcanic peak are deeply dissected; narrow coastal plain lies between The Peak and the coastal cliffs

## ELEVATION:
0 m lowest point: Atlantic Ocean 2060 highest point: Queen Mary's Peak on Tristan da Cunha 859 Green Mountain on Ascension Island 818 Mount Actaeon on Saint Helena Island

## NATURAL RESOURCES:
fish, lobster

## LAND USE:
**agricultural land:** 30.8% (2011 est.)

**arable land:** 10.3% (2011 est.) / **permanent crops:** 0% (2011 est.) / **permanent pasture:** 20.5% (2011 est.)

**forest:** 5.1% (2011 est.)

**other:** 64.1% (2011 est.)

## IRRIGATED LAND:
0 sq km (2012)

## POPULATION DISTRIBUTION:
Saint Helena - population is concentrated in and around the capital Jamestown in the northwest, with another significant cluster in the interior Longwood area; Ascension - largest settlement, and location of most of the population, is Georgetown; Tristan da Cunha - most of the nearly 300 inhabitants live in the northern coastal town of Edinburgh of the Seven Seas

## NATURAL HAZARDS:
active volcanism on Tristan da Cunha

**volcanism:** the island volcanoes of Tristan da Cunha (2,060 m) and Nightingale Island (365 m) experience volcanic activity; Tristan da Cunha erupted in 1962 and Nightingale in 2004

## ENVIRONMENT - CURRENT ISSUES:
development threatens unique biota on Saint Helena

## GEOGRAPHY - NOTE:
Saint Helena harbors at least 40 species of plants unknown elsewhere in the world; Ascension is a breeding ground for sea turtles and sooty terns; Queen Mary's Peak on Tristan da Cunha is the highest island mountain in the South Atlantic and a prominent landmark on the sea lanes around southern Africa

# PEOPLE AND SOCIETY :: SAINT HELENA, ASCENSION, AND TRISTAN DA CUNHA

## POPULATION:
7,841 (July 2018 est.)

**note:** Saint Helena's statistical agency estimated the enumerated national population (including Ascension Island and Tristan da Cuhna) to be 5,901 in 2016, according to the 2016 census; only Saint Helena, Ascension, and Tristan da Cunha islands are inhabited, none of the other nearby islands/islets are

**country comparison to the world:** 225

## NATIONALITY:
**noun:** Saint Helenian(s)

**adjective:** Saint Helenian

**note:** referred to locally as "Saints"

## ETHNIC GROUPS:
African descent 50%, white 25%, Chinese 25%

## LANGUAGES:
English

## RELIGIONS:
Protestant 75.9% (includes Anglican 68.9, Baptist 2.1%, Seventh Day Adventist 1.8%, Salvation Army 1.7%, New Apostolic 1.4%), Jehovah's Witness 4.1%, Roman Catholic 1.2%, other 2.5% (includes Baha'i), unspecified 0.8%, none 6.1%, no response 9.4% (2016 est.)

**note:** data represent Saint Helena only

## DEMOGRAPHIC PROFILE:
The vast majority of the population of Saint Helena, Ascension, and Tristan da Cunha live on Saint Helena. Ascension has no indigenous or permanent residents and is inhabited only by persons contracted to work on the island (mainly with the UK and US military or in the space and communications industries) or their dependents, while Tristan da Cunha – the main island in a small archipelago – has fewer than 300 residents. The population of Saint Helena consists of the descendants of 17th century British sailors and settlers from the East India Company, African slaves, and indentured servants and laborers from India, Indonesia, and China. Most of the population of Ascension are Saint Helenians, Britons, and Americans, while that of Tristan da Cunha descends from shipwrecked sailors and Saint Helenians.

Change in Saint Helena's population size is driven by net outward migration. Since the 1980s, Saint Helena's population steadily has shrunk and aged as the birth rate has decreased and many working-age residents left for better opportunities elsewhere. The restoration of British citizenship in 2002 accelerated family emigration; from 1998 to 2008 alone, population declined by about 20%.

In the last few years, population has experienced some temporary growth, as foreigners and returning Saint Helenians, have come to build an international airport, but numbers are beginning to fade as the project reaches completion and workers depart. In the long term, once the airport is fully operational, increased access to the remote island has the potential to boost tourism and fishing, provide more jobs for Saint Helenians domestically, and could encourage some ex-patriots to return home. In the meantime, however, Saint Helena, Ascension, and Tristan da Cunha have to contend with the needs of an aging population. The elderly population of the islands has risen from an estimated 9.4% in 1998 to 20.4% in 2016.

### AGE STRUCTURE:

**0-14 years:** 15.69% (male 627 /female 603)

**15-24 years:** 12.21% (male 487 /female 470)

**25-54 years:** 43.59% (male 1,695 /female 1,723)

**55-64 years:** 12.86% (male 512 /female 496)

**65 years and over:** 15.66% (male 627 /female 601) (2018 est.)

### MEDIAN AGE:

**total:** 42.4 years

**male:** 42.4 years

**female:** 42.4 years (2018 est.)

**country comparison to the world:** 32

### POPULATION GROWTH RATE:

0.14% (2018 est.)

**country comparison to the world:** 185

### BIRTH RATE:

9.4 births/1,000 population (2018 est.)

**country comparison to the world:** 201

### DEATH RATE:

8 deaths/1,000 population (2018 est.)

**country comparison to the world:** 91

### NET MIGRATION RATE:

0 migrant(s)/1,000 population (2017 est.)

**country comparison to the world:** 96

### POPULATION DISTRIBUTION:

Saint Helena - population is concentrated in and around the capital Jamestown in the northwest, with another significant cluster in the interior Longwood area; Ascension - largest settlement, and location of most of the population, is Georgetown; Tristan da Cunha - most of the nearly 300 inhabitants live in the northern coastal town of Edinburgh of the Seven Seas

### URBANIZATION:

**urban population:** 39.8% of total population (2018)

**rate of urbanization:** 0.73% annual rate of change (2015-20 est.)

### MAJOR URBAN AREAS - POPULATION:

1,000 JAMESTOWN (capital) (2018)

### SEX RATIO:

**at birth:** 1.06 male(s)/female (2017 est.)

**0-14 years:** 1.04 male(s)/female (2017 est.)

**15-24 years:** 1.05 male(s)/female (2017 est.)

**25-54 years:** 0.98 male(s)/female (2017 est.)

**55-64 years:** 1.09 male(s)/female (2017 est.)

**65 years and over:** 1.04 male(s)/female (2017 est.)

**total population:** 1.02 male(s)/female (2017 est.)

### INFANT MORTALITY RATE:

**total:** 12.8 deaths/1,000 live births (2018 est.)

**male:** 15.1 deaths/1,000 live births (2018 est.)

**female:** 10.4 deaths/1,000 live births (2018 est.)

**country comparison to the world:** 106

### LIFE EXPECTANCY AT BIRTH:

**total population:** 79.8 years (2018 est.)

**male:** 76.8 years (2018 est.)

**female:** 82.9 years (2018 est.)

**country comparison to the world:** 47

### TOTAL FERTILITY RATE:

1.59 children born/woman (2018 est.)

**country comparison to the world:** 184

### HIV/AIDS - ADULT PREVALENCE RATE:

NA

### HIV/AIDS - PEOPLE LIVING WITH HIV/AIDS:

NA

### HIV/AIDS - DEATHS:

NA

## GOVERNMENT :: SAINT HELENA, ASCENSION, AND TRISTAN DA CUNHA

### COUNTRY NAME:

**conventional long form:** Saint Helena, Ascension, and Tristan da Cunha

**conventional short form:** none

**etymology:** Saint Helena was discovered in 1502 by Galician navigator Joao da NOVA, sailing in the service of the Kingdom of Portugal, who named it "Santa Helena"; Ascension was named in 1503 by Portuguese navigator Afonso de ALBUQUERQUE who sighted the island on the Feast Day of the Ascension; Tristan da Cunha was discovered in 1506 by Portuguese explorer Tristao da CUNHA who christened the main island after himself (the name was subsequently anglicized)

### DEPENDENCY STATUS:

overseas territory of the UK

### GOVERNMENT TYPE:

parliamentary democracy (Legislative Council); limited self-governing overseas territory of the UK

### CAPITAL:

**name:** Jamestown

**geographic coordinates:** 15 56 S, 5 43 W

**time difference:** UTC 0 (5 hours ahead of Washington, DC, during Standard Time)

### ADMINISTRATIVE DIVISIONS:

3 administrative areas; Ascension, Saint Helena, Tristan da Cunha

### INDEPENDENCE:

none (overseas territory of the UK)

### NATIONAL HOLIDAY:

Birthday of Queen ELIZABETH II, third Monday in April (1926)

### CONSTITUTION:

several previous; latest effective 1 September 2009 (St Helena, Ascension and Tristan da Cunha Constitution Order, 2009) (2018)

### LEGAL SYSTEM:

English common law and local statutes

### CITIZENSHIP:

see United Kingdom

### SUFFRAGE:

18 years of age

## EXECUTIVE BRANCH:

**chief of state:** Queen ELIZABETH II (since 6 February 1952)

**head of government:** Governor Lisa PHILLIPS (since 25 April 2016)

**cabinet:** Executive Council consists of the governor, 3 ex-officio officers, and 5 elected members of the Legislative Council

**elections/appointments:** none; the monarchy is hereditary; governor appointed by the monarch

**note:** the constitution order provides for an administrator for Ascension and Tristan da Cunha appointed by the governor

## LEGISLATIVE BRANCH:

**description:** unicameral Legislative Council (17 seats including the speaker and deputy speaker; 12 members directly elected in a single countrywide constituency by simple majority vote and 3 ex-officio members - the chief secretary, financial secretary, and attorney general; members serve 4-year terms)

**elections:** last held on 26 July 2017 (next to be held in 2021)

**election results:** percent of vote - NA; seats by party - independent 12

**note:** the Constitution Order provides for separate Island Councils for both Ascension and Tristan da Cunha

## JUDICIAL BRANCH:

**highest courts:** Court of Appeal (consists of the court president and 2 justices); Supreme Court (consists of the chief justice - a non-resident - and NA judges); note - appeals beyond the Court of Appeal are heard by the Judicial Committee of the Privy Council (in London)

**judge selection and term of office:** Court of Appeal and Supreme Court justices appointed by the governor acting upon the instructions from a secretary of state acting on behalf of Queen ELIZABETH II; justices of both courts appointed until retirement at age 70 but terms can be extended

**subordinate courts:** Magistrate's Court; Small Claims Court; Juvenile Court

## POLITICAL PARTIES AND LEADERS:

none

## INTERNATIONAL ORGANIZATION PARTICIPATION:

UPU

## DIPLOMATIC REPRESENTATION IN THE US:

none (overseas territory of the UK)

## DIPLOMATIC REPRESENTATION FROM THE US:

none (overseas territory of the UK)

## FLAG DESCRIPTION:

blue with the flag of the UK in the upper hoist-side quadrant and the Saint Helenian shield centered on the outer half of the flag; the upper third of the shield depicts a white plover (wire bird) on a yellow field; the remainder of the shield depicts a rocky coastline on the left, offshore is a three-masted sailing ship with sails furled but flying an English flag

## NATIONAL SYMBOL(S):

Saint Helena plover (bird)

## NATIONAL ANTHEM:

**note:** as a territory of the UK, "God Save the Queen" is official (see United Kingdom)

# ECONOMY :: SAINT HELENA, ASCENSION, AND TRISTAN DA CUNHA

## ECONOMY - OVERVIEW:

The economy depends largely on financial assistance from the UK, which amounted to about $27 million in FY06/07 or more than twice the level of annual budgetary revenues. The local population earns income from fishing, raising livestock, and sales of handicrafts. Because there are few jobs, 25% of the work force has left to seek employment on Ascension Island, on the Falklands, and in the UK.

## GDP (PURCHASING POWER PARITY):

$31.1 million (FY09/10 est.)

country comparison to the world: 227

## GDP (OFFICIAL EXCHANGE RATE):

NA

## GDP - REAL GROWTH RATE:

NA

## GDP - PER CAPITA (PPP):

$7,800 (FY09/10 est.)

country comparison to the world: 153

## GDP - COMPOSITION, BY SECTOR OF ORIGIN:

agriculture: NA

industry: NA

services: NA

## AGRICULTURE - PRODUCTS:

coffee, corn, potatoes, vegetables; fish, lobster; livestock; timber

## INDUSTRIES:

construction, crafts (furniture, lacework, fancy woodwork), fishing, collectible postage stamps

## INDUSTRIAL PRODUCTION GROWTH RATE:

NA

## LABOR FORCE:

2,486 (1998 est.)

country comparison to the world: 226

## LABOR FORCE - BY OCCUPATION:

agriculture: 6%

industry: 48%

services: 46% (1987 est.)

## UNEMPLOYMENT RATE:

14% (1998 est.)

country comparison to the world: 169

## POPULATION BELOW POVERTY LINE:

NA

## HOUSEHOLD INCOME OR CONSUMPTION BY PERCENTAGE SHARE:

lowest 10%: NA

highest 10%: NA

## BUDGET:

revenues: 8.427 million (FY06/07 est.)

expenditures: 20.7 million (FY06/07 est.)

**note:** revenue data reflect only locally raised revenues; the budget deficit is resolved by grant aid from the UK

## FISCAL YEAR:

1 April - 31 March

## INFLATION RATE (CONSUMER PRICES):

4% (2012 est.)

country comparison to the world: 156

## EXPORTS:

$19 million (2004 est.)

country comparison to the world: 211

## EXPORTS - COMMODITIES:

fish (frozen, canned, and salt-dried skipjack, tuna), coffee, handicrafts

## IMPORTS:

$20.53 million (2010 est.)

country comparison to the world: 221

## IMPORTS - COMMODITIES:

food, beverages, tobacco, fuel oils, animal feed, building materials, motor vehicles and parts, machinery and parts

**DEBT - EXTERNAL:**

NA

**STOCK OF DIRECT FOREIGN INVESTMENT - AT HOME:**

(31 December 2009 est.)

**EXCHANGE RATES:**

Saint Helenian pounds (SHP) per US dollar -

0.7836 (2017 est.)

0.6542 (2016 est.)

0.6542 (2015)

0.607 (2014 est.)

0.6391 (2013 est.)

## ENERGY :: SAINT HELENA, ASCENSION, AND TRISTAN DA CUNHA

**ELECTRICITY - PRODUCTION:**

7 million kWh (2016 est.)

country comparison to the world: 215

**ELECTRICITY - CONSUMPTION:**

6.51 million kWh (2016 est.)

country comparison to the world: 214

**ELECTRICITY - EXPORTS:**

0 kWh (2016 est.)

country comparison to the world: 187

**ELECTRICITY - IMPORTS:**

0 kWh (2016 est.)

country comparison to the world: 189

**ELECTRICITY - INSTALLED GENERATING CAPACITY:**

8,000 kW (2016 est.)

country comparison to the world: 210

**ELECTRICITY - FROM FOSSIL FUELS:**

100% of total installed capacity (2016 est.)

country comparison to the world: 16

**ELECTRICITY - FROM NUCLEAR FUELS:**

0% of total installed capacity (2017 est.)

country comparison to the world: 171

**ELECTRICITY - FROM HYDROELECTRIC PLANTS:**

0% of total installed capacity (2017 est.)

country comparison to the world: 194

**ELECTRICITY - FROM OTHER RENEWABLE SOURCES:**

0% of total installed capacity (2017 est.)

country comparison to the world: 205

**CRUDE OIL - PRODUCTION:**

0 bbl/day (2017 est.)

country comparison to the world: 189

**CRUDE OIL - EXPORTS:**

0 bbl/day (2015 est.)

country comparison to the world: 183

**CRUDE OIL - IMPORTS:**

0 bbl/day (2015 est.)

country comparison to the world: 185

**CRUDE OIL - PROVED RESERVES:**

0 bbl (1 January 2018 est.)

country comparison to the world: 185

**REFINED PETROLEUM PRODUCTS - PRODUCTION:**

0 bbl/day (2015 est.)

country comparison to the world: 192

**REFINED PETROLEUM PRODUCTS - CONSUMPTION:**

70 bbl/day (2016 est.)

country comparison to the world: 214

**REFINED PETROLEUM PRODUCTS - EXPORTS:**

0 bbl/day (2015 est.)

country comparison to the world: 193

**REFINED PETROLEUM PRODUCTS - IMPORTS:**

65 bbl/day (2015 est.)

country comparison to the world: 210

**NATURAL GAS - PRODUCTION:**

0 cu m (2017 est.)

country comparison to the world: 187

**NATURAL GAS - CONSUMPTION:**

0 cu m (2017 est.)

country comparison to the world: 189

**NATURAL GAS - EXPORTS:**

0 cu m (2017 est.)

country comparison to the world: 172

**NATURAL GAS - IMPORTS:**

0 cu m (2017 est.)

country comparison to the world: 178

**NATURAL GAS - PROVED RESERVES:**

0 cu m (1 January 2014 est.)

country comparison to the world: 184

**CARBON DIOXIDE EMISSIONS FROM CONSUMPTION OF ENERGY:**

10,650 Mt (2017 est.)

country comparison to the world: 212

## COMMUNICATIONS :: SAINT HELENA, ASCENSION, AND TRISTAN DA CUNHA

**TELEPHONES - FIXED LINES:**

total subscriptions: 576 (July 2016 est.)

subscriptions per 100 inhabitants: 35 (July 2016 est.)

country comparison to the world: 217

**TELEPHONES - MOBILE CELLULAR:**

total subscriptions: 3,018 (July 2016 est.)

subscriptions per 100 inhabitants: 39 (July 2016 est.)

country comparison to the world: 216

**TELEPHONE SYSTEM:**

general assessment: can communicate worldwide (2010)

domestic: automatic digital network (2010)

international: country code (Saint Helena) - 290, (Ascension Island) - 247; international direct dialing; satellite voice and data communications; satellite earth stations - 5 (Ascension Island - 4, Saint Helena - 1) (2010)

**BROADCAST MEDIA:**

Saint Helena has no local TV station; 2 local radio stations, one of which is relayed to Ascension Island; satellite TV stations rebroadcast terrestrially; Ascension Island has no local TV station but has 1 local radio station and receives relays of broadcasts from 1 radio station on Saint Helena; broadcasts from the British Forces Broadcasting Service (BFBS) are available, as well as TV services for the US military; Tristan da Cunha has 1 local radio station and receives BFBS TV and radio broadcasts (2007)

**INTERNET COUNTRY CODE:**

.sh; note - Ascension Island assigned .ac

**INTERNET USERS:**

total: 1,800 (July 2016 est.)

percent of population: 23.1% (July 2016 est.)

country comparison to the world: 221

**BROADBAND - FIXED SUBSCRIPTIONS:**

total: 1,347 (2017 est.)

subscriptions per 100 inhabitants: 17 (2017 est.)

country comparison to the world: 188

**COMMUNICATIONS - NOTE:**

Ascension Island hosts one of four dedicated ground antennas that assist in the operation of the Global Positioning System (GPS) navigation system (the others are on Diego Garcia (British Indian Ocean Territory), Kwajalein (Marshall Islands), and at Cape Canaveral, Florida (US)); South Africa maintains a meteorological station on Gough Island in the Tristan da Cunha archipelago

## TRANSPORTATION :: SAINT HELENA, ASCENSION, AND TRISTAN DA CUNHA

**CIVIL AIRCRAFT REGISTRATION COUNTRY CODE PREFIX:**

VQ-H (2016)

**AIRPORTS:**

2 (2015)

country comparison to the world: 203

**AIRPORTS - WITH PAVED RUNWAYS:**

total: 2 (2017)

over 3,047 m: 1 Ascension Island - Wideawake Field (ASI) (2017)

1,524 to 2,437 m: 1 Saint Helena (HLE); (2017)

note - weekly commercial air service to South Africa via Namibia commenced on 14 October 2017

**ROADWAYS:**

total: 198 km (Saint Helena 138 km, Ascension 40 km, Tristan da Cunha 20 km) (2002)

paved: 168 km (Saint Helena 118 km, Ascension 40 km, Tristan da Cunha 10 km) (2002)

unpaved: 30 km (Saint Helena 20 km, Tristan da Cunha 10 km) (2002)

country comparison to the world: 211

**PORTS AND TERMINALS:**

major seaport(s): Saint Helena

Saint Helena: Jamestown

Ascension Island: Georgetown

Tristan da Cunha: Calshot Harbor (Edinburgh)

**TRANSPORTATION - NOTE:**

the new airport on Saint Helena opened for limited operations in July 2016, and the first commercial flight took place on 14 October 2017, marking the start of weekly air service between Saint Helena and South Africa via Namibia; the military airport on Ascension Island is closed to civilian traffic; there is no air connection to Tristan da Cunha and very limited sea connections making it one of the most isolated communities on the planet

## MILITARY AND SECURITY :: SAINT HELENA, ASCENSION, AND TRISTAN DA CUNHA

**MILITARY - NOTE:**

defense is the responsibility of the UK

## TRANSNATIONAL ISSUES :: SAINT HELENA, ASCENSION, AND TRISTAN DA CUNHA

**DISPUTES - INTERNATIONAL:**

none

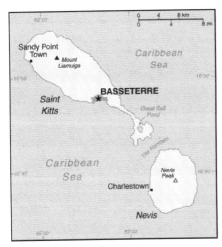

# CENTRAL AMERICA :: SAINT KITTS AND NEVIS

## INTRODUCTION :: SAINT KITTS AND NEVIS

### BACKGROUND:

Carib Indians occupied the islands of the West Indies for hundreds of years before the British began settlement in 1623. In 1967, the island territory of Saint Christopher-Nevis-Anguilla became an associated state of the UK with full internal autonomy. The island of Anguilla rebelled and was allowed to secede in 1971. The remaining islands achieved independence in 1983 as Saint Kitts and Nevis. In 1998, a referendum on Nevis to separate from Saint Kitts fell short of the two-thirds majority vote needed. Nevis continues in its efforts to separate from Saint Kitts.

## GEOGRAPHY :: SAINT KITTS AND NEVIS

### LOCATION:
Caribbean, islands in the Caribbean Sea, about one-third of the way from Puerto Rico to Trinidad and Tobago

### GEOGRAPHIC COORDINATES:
17 20 N, 62 45 W

### MAP REFERENCES:
Central America and the Caribbean

### AREA:
total: 261 sq km (Saint Kitts 168 sq km; Nevis 93 sq km)

land: 261 sq km

water: 0 sq km

country comparison to the world: 212

### AREA - COMPARATIVE:
1.5 times the size of Washington, DC

### LAND BOUNDARIES:
0 km

### COASTLINE:
135 km

### MARITIME CLAIMS:
territorial sea: 12 nm

exclusive economic zone: 200 nm

contiguous zone: 24 nm

continental shelf: 200 nm or to the edge of the continental margin

### CLIMATE:
tropical, tempered by constant sea breezes; little seasonal temperature variation; rainy season (May to November)

### TERRAIN:
volcanic with mountainous interiors

### ELEVATION:
0 m lowest point: Caribbean Sea

1156 highest point: Mount Liamuiga

### NATURAL RESOURCES:
arable land

### LAND USE:
agricultural land: 23.1% (2011 est.)

arable land: 19.2% (2011 est.) / permanent crops: 0.4% (2011 est.) / permanent pasture: 3.5% (2011 est.)

forest: 42.3% (2011 est.)

other: 34.6% (2011 est.)

### IRRIGATED LAND:
8 sq km (2012)

### POPULATION DISTRIBUTION:
population clusters are found in the small towns located on the periphery of both islands

### NATURAL HAZARDS:
hurricanes (July to October)

volcanism: Mount Liamuiga (1,156 m) on Saint Kitts, and Nevis Peak (985 m) on Nevis, are both volcanoes that are part of the volcanic island arc of the Lesser Antilles, which extends from Saba in the north to Grenada in the south

### ENVIRONMENT - CURRENT ISSUES:
deforestation; soil erosion and silting affects marine life on coral reefs; water pollution from uncontrolled dumping of sewage

### ENVIRONMENT - INTERNATIONAL AGREEMENTS:
party to: Biodiversity, Climate Change, Climate Change-Kyoto Protocol, Desertification, Endangered Species, Hazardous Wastes, Law of the Sea, Marine Dumping, Ozone Layer Protection, Ship Pollution, Whaling

signed, but not ratified: none of the selected agreements

### GEOGRAPHY - NOTE:
smallest country in the Americas and Western Hemisphere; with coastlines in the shape of a baseball bat and ball, the two volcanic islands are separated by a 3-km-wide channel called The Narrows; on the southern tip of long, baseball bat-shaped Saint Kitts lies the Great Salt Pond; Nevis Peak sits in the center of its almost circular namesake island and its ball shape complements that of its sister island

## PEOPLE AND SOCIETY :: SAINT KITTS AND NEVIS

### POPULATION:
53,094 (July 2018 est.)

country comparison to the world: 208

### NATIONALITY:

**noun:** Kittitian(s), Nevisian(s)

**adjective:** Kittitian, Nevisian

### ETHNIC GROUPS:

African origin 92.5%, mixed 3%, white 2.1%, East Indian 1.5%, other .6%, unspecified .3% (2001 est.)

### LANGUAGES:

English (official)

### RELIGIONS:

Protestant 74.4% (includes Anglican 20.6%, Methodist 19.1%, Pentecostal 8.2%, Church of God 6.8%, Moravian 5.5%, Baptist 4.8%, Seventh Day Adventist 4.7%, Evangelical 2.6%, Brethern 1.8%, other .3%), Roman Catholic 6.7%, Rastafarian 1.7%, Jehovah's Witness 1.3%, other 7.6%, none 5.2%, unspecified 3.2% (2001 est.)

### AGE STRUCTURE:

**0-14 years:** 20.09% (male 5,354 /female 5,311)

**15-24 years:** 14.28% (male 3,645 /female 3,936)

**25-54 years:** 44.25% (male 12,059 /female 11,437)

**55-64 years:** 12.35% (male 3,274 /female 3,283)

**65 years and over:** 9.03% (male 2,236 /female 2,559) (2018 est.)

### MEDIAN AGE:

**total:** 35.5 years

**male:** 35.7 years

**female:** 35.3 years (2018 est.)

**country comparison to the world:** 79

### POPULATION GROWTH RATE:

0.7% (2018 est.)

**country comparison to the world:** 142

### BIRTH RATE:

13 births/1,000 population (2018 est.)

**country comparison to the world:** 148

### DEATH RATE:

7.2 deaths/1,000 population (2018 est.)

**country comparison to the world:** 124

### NET MIGRATION RATE:

1.2 migrant(s)/1,000 population (2017 est.)

**country comparison to the world:** 55

### POPULATION DISTRIBUTION:

population clusters are found in the small towns located on the periphery of both islands

### URBANIZATION:

**urban population:** 30.8% of total population (2018)

**rate of urbanization:** 0.92% annual rate of change (2015-20 est.)

### MAJOR URBAN AREAS - POPULATION:

14,000 BASSETERRE (capital) (2018)

### SEX RATIO:

**at birth:** 1.03 male(s)/female (2017 est.)

**0-14 years:** 1.01 male(s)/female (2017 est.)

**15-24 years:** 0.94 male(s)/female (2017 est.)

**25-54 years:** 1.05 male(s)/female (2017 est.)

**55-64 years:** 1 male(s)/female (2017 est.)

**65 years and over:** 0.83 male(s)/female (2017 est.)

**total population:** 1 male(s)/female (2017 est.)

### INFANT MORTALITY RATE:

**total:** 8.2 deaths/1,000 live births (2018 est.)

**male:** 5.8 deaths/1,000 live births (2018 est.)

**female:** 10.6 deaths/1,000 live births (2018 est.)

**country comparison to the world:** 149

### LIFE EXPECTANCY AT BIRTH:

**total population:** 76.2 years (2018 est.)

**male:** 73.7 years (2018 est.)

**female:** 78.7 years (2018 est.)

**country comparison to the world:** 92

### TOTAL FERTILITY RATE:

1.77 children born/woman (2018 est.)

**country comparison to the world:** 157

### HEALTH EXPENDITURES:

5.1% of GDP (2014)

**country comparison to the world:** 137

### HOSPITAL BED DENSITY:

4.8 beds/1,000 population (2012)

### DRINKING WATER SOURCE:

**improved:**

urban: 98.3% of population (2015 est.)

rural: 98.3% of population (2015 est.)

total: 98.3% of population (2015 est.)

**unimproved:**

urban: 1.7% of population (2015 est.)

rural: 1.7% of population (2015 est.)

total: 1.7% of population (2015 est.)

### SANITATION FACILITY ACCESS:

**improved:**

urban: 87.3% of population (2007 est.)

rural: 87.3% of population (2007 est.)

total: 87.3% of population (2007 est.)

**unimproved:**

urban: 12.7% of population (2007 est.)

rural: 12.7% of population (2007 est.)

total: 12.7% of population (2007 est.)

### HIV/AIDS - ADULT PREVALENCE RATE:

NA

### HIV/AIDS - PEOPLE LIVING WITH HIV/AIDS:

NA

### HIV/AIDS - DEATHS:

NA

### OBESITY - ADULT PREVALENCE RATE:

22.9% (2016)

**country comparison to the world:** 71

### EDUCATION EXPENDITURES:

2.8% of GDP (2015)

**country comparison to the world:** 157

### SCHOOL LIFE EXPECTANCY (PRIMARY TO TERTIARY EDUCATION):

**total:** 14 years (2015)

**male:** 13 years (2015)

**female:** 16 years (2015)

## GOVERNMENT :: SAINT KITTS AND NEVIS

### COUNTRY NAME:

**conventional long form:** Federation of Saint Kitts and Nevis

**conventional short form:** Saint Kitts and Nevis

**former:** Federation of Saint Christopher and Nevis

**etymology:** Saint Kitts was, and still is, referred to as Saint Christopher and this name was well established by the 17th century (although who first applied the name is unclear); in the 17th century a common nickname for Christopher was Kit or Kitt, so the island began to be referred to as "Saint Kitt's Island" or just "Saint Kitts"; Nevis is derived from the original

Spanish name "Nuestra Senora de las Nieves" (Our Lady of the Snows) and refers to the white halo of clouds that generally wreathes Nevis Peak

note: Nevis is pronounced neevis

## GOVERNMENT TYPE:
federal parliamentary democracy (National Assembly) under a constitutional monarchy; a Commonwealth realm

## CAPITAL:
name: Basseterre

geographic coordinates: 17 18 N, 62 43 W

time difference: UTC-4 (1 hour ahead of Washington, DC, during Standard Time)

## ADMINISTRATIVE DIVISIONS:
14 parishes; Christ Church Nichola Town, Saint Anne Sandy Point, Saint George Basseterre, Saint George Gingerland, Saint James Windward, Saint John Capesterre, Saint John Figtree, Saint Mary Cayon, Saint Paul Capesterre, Saint Paul Charlestown, Saint Peter Basseterre, Saint Thomas Lowland, Saint Thomas Middle Island, Trinity Palmetto Point

## INDEPENDENCE:
19 September 1983 (from the UK)

## NATIONAL HOLIDAY:
Independence Day, 19 September (1983)

## CONSTITUTION:
history: several previous (preindependence); latest presented 22 June 1983, effective 23 June 1983 (2018)

amendments: proposed by the National Assembly; passage requires approval by at least two-thirds majority of the total Assembly membership and assent to by the governor general; amendments to constitutional provisions such as the sovereignty of the federation, fundamental rights and freedoms, the judiciary, and the Nevis Island Assembly also require approval in a referendum by at least two-thirds of the votes cast in Saint Kitts and in Nevis (2018)

## LEGAL SYSTEM:
English common law

## INTERNATIONAL LAW ORGANIZATION PARTICIPATION:
has not submitted an ICJ jurisdiction declaration; accepts ICCt jurisdiction

## CITIZENSHIP:
citizenship by birth: yes

citizenship by descent only: yes

dual citizenship recognized: yes

residency requirement for naturalization: 14 years

## SUFFRAGE:
18 years of age; universal

## EXECUTIVE BRANCH:
chief of state: Queen ELIZABETH II (since 6 February 1952); represented by Governor General Samuel W.T. SEATON (since 2 September 2015); note - SEATON was acting Governor General from 20 May to 2 September 2015

head of government: Prime Minister Timothy HARRIS (since 18 February 2015); Deputy Prime Minister Shawn RICHARDS (since 22 February 2015)

cabinet: Cabinet appointed by governor general in consultation with prime minister

elections/appointments: the monarchy is hereditary; governor general appointed by the monarch; following legislative elections, the leader of the majority party or majority coalition usually appointed prime minister by governor general; deputy prime minister appointed by governor general

## LEGISLATIVE BRANCH:
description: unicameral National Assembly (14 seats; 11 members directly elected in single-seat constituencies by simple majority vote and 3 appointed by the governor general; members serve 5-year terms)

elections: last held on 16 February 2015 (next to be held by 2020)

election results: percent of vote by party - SKNLP 39.3%, PAM 27.9% CCM 13.0% NRP 10.8%, PLP 9.0%; seats by party - PAM 4, SKNLP 3, CCM 2, NRP 1, PLP 1

## JUDICIAL BRANCH:
highest courts: the Eastern Caribbean Supreme Court (ECSC) is the superior court of the Organization of Eastern Caribbean States; the ECSC - headquartered on St. Lucia - consists of the Court of Appeal - headed by the chief justice and 4 judges - and the High Court with 18 judges; the Court of Appeal is itinerant, travelling to member states on a schedule to hear appeals from the High Court and subordinate courts; High Court judges reside at the member states with 2 assigned to Saint Kitts and Nevis; note - the ECSC in 2003 replaced the Judicial Committee of the Privy Council in London as the final court of appeal on Saint Kitts and Nevis; Saint Kitts and Nevis is also a member of the Caribbean Court of Justice

judge selection and term of office: chief justice of Eastern Caribbean Supreme Court appointed by Her Majesty, Queen ELIZABETH II; other justices and judges appointed by the Judicial and Legal Services Commission, an independent body of judicial officials; Court of Appeal justices appointed for life with mandatory retirement at age 65; High Court judges appointed for life with mandatory retirement at age 62

subordinate courts: magistrates' courts

## POLITICAL PARTIES AND LEADERS:
Concerned Citizens Movement or CCM [Mark BRANTLEY]
Nevis Reformation Party or NRP [Joseph PARRY]
People's Action Movement or PAM [Shawn RICHARDS]
People's Labour Party or PLP [Dr. Timothy HARRIS]
Saint Kitts and Nevis Labor Party or SKNLP [Dr. Denzil DOUGLAS]

## INTERNATIONAL ORGANIZATION PARTICIPATION:
ACP, AOSIS, C, Caricom, CDB, CELAC, FAO, G-77, IBRD, ICAO, ICCt, ICRM, IDA, IFAD, IFC, IFRCS, ILO, IMF, IMO, Interpol, IOC, ITU, MIGA, OAS, OECS, OPANAL, OPCW, Petrocaribe, UN, UNCTAD, UNESCO, UNIDO, UPU, WHO, WIPO, WTO

## DIPLOMATIC REPRESENTATION IN THE US:
chief of mission: Ambassador Dr. Thelma Patricia PHILLIP-BROWNE (since 28 January 2016)

chancery: 3216 New Mexico Avenue NW, Washington, DC 20016

telephone: [1] (202) 686-2636

FAX: [1] (202) 686-5740

consulate(s) general: Los Angeles, New York

## DIPLOMATIC REPRESENTATION FROM THE US:
the US does not have an embassy in Saint Kitts and Nevis; the US Ambassador to Barbados is accredited to Saint Kitts and Nevis

## FLAG DESCRIPTION:
divided diagonally from the lower hoist side by a broad black band

bearing two white, five-pointed stars; the black band is edged in yellow; the upper triangle is green, the lower triangle is red; green signifies the island's fertility, red symbolizes the struggles of the people from slavery, yellow denotes year-round sunshine, and black represents the African heritage of the people; the white stars stand for the islands of Saint Kitts and Nevis, but can also express hope and liberty, or independence and optimism

**NATIONAL SYMBOL(S):**

brown pelican, royal poinciana (flamboyant) tree; national colors: green, yellow, red, black, white

**NATIONAL ANTHEM:**

name: Oh Land of Beauty!

lyrics/music: Kenrick Anderson GEORGES

note: adopted 1983

## ECONOMY :: SAINT KITTS AND NEVIS

### ECONOMY - OVERVIEW:

The economy of Saint Kitts and Nevis depends on tourism; since the 1970s, tourism has replaced sugar as the economy's traditional mainstay. Roughly 200,000 tourists visited the islands in 2009, but reduced tourism arrivals and foreign investment led to an economic contraction in the 2009-2013 period, and the economy returned to growth only in 2014. Like other tourist destinations in the Caribbean, Saint Kitts and Nevis is vulnerable to damage from natural disasters and shifts in tourism demand.

Following the 2005 harvest, the government closed the sugar industry after several decades of losses. To compensate for lost jobs, the government has embarked on a program to diversify the agricultural sector and to stimulate other sectors of the economy, such as export-oriented manufacturing and offshore banking. The government has made notable progress in reducing its public debt, from 154% of GDP in 2011 to 83% in 2013, although it still faces one of the highest levels in the world, largely attributable to public enterprise losses. Saint Kitts and Nevis is among other countries in the Caribbean that supplement their economic activity through economic citizenship programs, whereby foreigners can obtain citizenship from Saint Kitts and Nevis by investing there.

### GDP (PURCHASING POWER PARITY):

$1.55 billion (2017 est.)

$1.518 billion (2016 est.)

$1.476 billion (2015 est.)

note: data are in 2017 dollars

country comparison to the world: 199

### GDP (OFFICIAL EXCHANGE RATE):

$964 million (2017 est.) (2017 est.)

### GDP - REAL GROWTH RATE:

2.1% (2017 est.)

2.9% (2016 est.)

2.7% (2015 est.)

country comparison to the world: 147

### GDP - PER CAPITA (PPP):

$28,200 (2017 est.)

$27,600 (2016 est.)

$27,300 (2015 est.)

note: data are in 2017 dollars

country comparison to the world: 73

### GROSS NATIONAL SAVING:

19.9% of GDP (2017 est.)

19.3% of GDP (2016 est.)

15.4% of GDP (2015 est.)

country comparison to the world: 98

### GDP - COMPOSITION, BY END USE:

household consumption: 41.4% (2017 est.)

government consumption: 25.9% (2017 est.)

investment in fixed capital: 30.8% (2017 est.)

investment in inventories: 0% (2017 est.)

exports of goods and services: 62.5% (2017 est.)

imports of goods and services: -60.4% (2017 est.)

### GDP - COMPOSITION, BY SECTOR OF ORIGIN:

agriculture: 1.1% (2017 est.)

industry: 30% (2017 est.)

services: 68.9% (2017 est.)

### AGRICULTURE - PRODUCTS:

sugarcane, rice, yams, vegetables, bananas; fish

### INDUSTRIES:

tourism, cotton, salt, copra, clothing, footwear, beverages

### INDUSTRIAL PRODUCTION GROWTH RATE:

5% (2017 est.)

country comparison to the world: 56

### LABOR FORCE:

18,170 (June 1995 est.)

country comparison to the world: 212

### UNEMPLOYMENT RATE:

4.5% (1997)

country comparison to the world: 65

### POPULATION BELOW POVERTY LINE:

NA

### HOUSEHOLD INCOME OR CONSUMPTION BY PERCENTAGE SHARE:

lowest 10%: NA

highest 10%: NA

### BUDGET:

revenues: 307 million (2017 est.)

expenditures: 291.1 million (2017 est.)

### TAXES AND OTHER REVENUES:

31.9% (of GDP) (2017 est.)

country comparison to the world: 70

### BUDGET SURPLUS (+) OR DEFICIT (-):

1.7% (of GDP) (2017 est.)

country comparison to the world: 18

### PUBLIC DEBT:

62.9% of GDP (2017 est.)

61.5% of GDP (2016 est.)

country comparison to the world: 67

### FISCAL YEAR:

calendar year

### INFLATION RATE (CONSUMER PRICES):

0% (2017 est.)

-0.3% (2016 est.)

country comparison to the world: 12

### CENTRAL BANK DISCOUNT RATE:

6.5% (31 December 2009)

6.5% (31 December 2008)

country comparison to the world: 62

### COMMERCIAL BANK PRIME LENDING RATE:

9.09% (31 December 2017 est.)

9.23% (31 December 2016 est.)

country comparison to the world: 93

### STOCK OF NARROW MONEY:

$196.1 million (31 December 2017 est.)

$210.1 million (31 December 2016 est.)

country comparison to the world: 184

**STOCK OF BROAD MONEY:**

$196.1 million (31 December 2017 est.)

$210.1 million (31 December 2016 est.)

country comparison to the world: 187

**STOCK OF DOMESTIC CREDIT:**

$721.5 million (31 December 2017 est.)

$704.8 million (31 December 2016 est.)

country comparison to the world: 171

**MARKET VALUE OF PUBLICLY TRADED SHARES:**

$598.4 million (31 December 2011)

$623.9 million (2010 est.)

country comparison to the world: 111

**CURRENT ACCOUNT BALANCE:**

-$97 million (2017 est.)

-$102 million (2016 est.)

country comparison to the world: 85

**EXPORTS:**

$57.4 million (2017 est.)

$53.9 million (2016 est.)

country comparison to the world: 202

**EXPORTS - PARTNERS:**

US 49.6%, Poland 15.2%, Turkey 11.6% (2016)

**EXPORTS - COMMODITIES:**

machinery, food, electronics, beverages, tobacco

**IMPORTS:**

$335.3 million (2017 est.)

$307.9 million (2016 est.)

country comparison to the world: 201

**IMPORTS - COMMODITIES:**

machinery, manufactures, food, fuels

**IMPORTS - PARTNERS:**

US 56.8%, Trinidad and Tobago 6.8%, Cyprus 6.2%, Japan 4% (2016)

**RESERVES OF FOREIGN EXCHANGE AND GOLD:**

$365.1 million (31 December 2017 est.)

$320.5 million (31 December 2016 est.)

country comparison to the world: 162

**DEBT - EXTERNAL:**

$201.8 million (31 December 2017 est.)

$187.9 million (31 December 2016 est.)

country comparison to the world: 187

**EXCHANGE RATES:**

East Caribbean dollars (XCD) per US dollar -

2.7 (2017 est.)

2.7 (2016 est.)

2.7 (2015 est.)

2.7 (2014 est.)

2.7 (2013 est.)

## ENERGY :: SAINT KITTS AND NEVIS

**ELECTRICITY ACCESS:**

population without electricity: 5,232 (2012)

electrification - total population: 91% (2012)

electrification - urban areas: 100% (2012)

electrification - rural areas: 80% (2012)

**ELECTRICITY - PRODUCTION:**

208 million kWh (2016 est.)

country comparison to the world: 191

**ELECTRICITY - CONSUMPTION:**

193.4 million kWh (2016 est.)

country comparison to the world: 193

**ELECTRICITY - EXPORTS:**

0 kWh (2016 est.)

country comparison to the world: 188

**ELECTRICITY - IMPORTS:**

0 kWh (2016 est.)

country comparison to the world: 190

**ELECTRICITY - INSTALLED GENERATING CAPACITY:**

64,200 kW (2016 est.)

country comparison to the world: 187

**ELECTRICITY - FROM FOSSIL FUELS:**

94% of total installed capacity (2016 est.)

country comparison to the world: 48

**ELECTRICITY - FROM NUCLEAR FUELS:**

0% of total installed capacity (2017 est.)

country comparison to the world: 172

**ELECTRICITY - FROM HYDROELECTRIC PLANTS:**

0% of total installed capacity (2017 est.)

country comparison to the world: 195

**ELECTRICITY - FROM OTHER RENEWABLE SOURCES:**

6% of total installed capacity (2017 est.)

country comparison to the world: 102

**CRUDE OIL - PRODUCTION:**

0 bbl/day (2017 est.)

country comparison to the world: 190

**CRUDE OIL - EXPORTS:**

0 bbl/day (2015 est.)

country comparison to the world: 184

**CRUDE OIL - IMPORTS:**

0 bbl/day (2015 est.)

country comparison to the world: 186

**CRUDE OIL - PROVED RESERVES:**

0 bbl (1 January 2018 est.)

country comparison to the world: 186

**REFINED PETROLEUM PRODUCTS - PRODUCTION:**

0 bbl/day (2015 est.)

country comparison to the world: 193

**REFINED PETROLEUM PRODUCTS - CONSUMPTION:**

1,700 bbl/day (2016 est.)

country comparison to the world: 196

**REFINED PETROLEUM PRODUCTS - EXPORTS:**

0 bbl/day (2015 est.)

country comparison to the world: 194

**REFINED PETROLEUM PRODUCTS - IMPORTS:**

1,743 bbl/day (2015 est.)

country comparison to the world: 192

**NATURAL GAS - PRODUCTION:**

0 cu m (2017 est.)

country comparison to the world: 188

**NATURAL GAS - CONSUMPTION:**

0 cu m (2017 est.)

country comparison to the world: 190

**NATURAL GAS - EXPORTS:**

0 cu m (2017 est.)

country comparison to the world: 173

**NATURAL GAS - IMPORTS:**

0 cu m (2017 est.)

country comparison to the world: 179

**NATURAL GAS - PROVED RESERVES:**

0 cu m (1 January 2014 est.)

country comparison to the world: 185

**CARBON DIOXIDE EMISSIONS FROM CONSUMPTION OF ENERGY:**

248,100 Mt (2017 est.)

country comparison to the world: 195

## COMMUNICATIONS :: SAINT KITTS AND NEVIS

**TELEPHONES - FIXED LINES:**

total subscriptions: 17,293 (2017 est.)

subscriptions per 100 inhabitants: 33 (2017 est.)

country comparison to the world: 182

**TELEPHONES - MOBILE CELLULAR:**

total subscriptions: 76,878 (2017 est.)

subscriptions per 100 inhabitants: 146 (2017 est.)

country comparison to the world: 196

**TELEPHONE SYSTEM:**

general assessment: good interisland and international connections (2016)

domestic: interisland links via ECFS; construction of enhanced wireless infrastructure launched in November 2004; fixed-line teledensity about 32 per 100 persons; mobile-cellular teledensity is roughly 140 per 100 persons (2016)

international: country code - 1-869; connected internationally by the East ECFS and Southern Caribbean Fiber submarine cables (2016)

**BROADCAST MEDIA:**

the government operates a national TV network that broadcasts on 2 channels; cable subscription services provide access to local and international channels; the government operates a national radio network; a mix of government-owned and privately owned broadcasters operate roughly 15 radio stations (2007)

**INTERNET COUNTRY CODE:**

.kn

**INTERNET USERS:**

total: 39,000 (July 2016 est.)

percent of population: 75.7% (July 2016 est.)

country comparison to the world: 200

**BROADBAND - FIXED SUBSCRIPTIONS:**

total: 16,400 (2017 est.)

subscriptions per 100 inhabitants: 31 (2017 est.)

country comparison to the world: 158

## TRANSPORTATION :: SAINT KITTS AND NEVIS

**CIVIL AIRCRAFT REGISTRATION COUNTRY CODE PREFIX:**

V4 (2016)

**AIRPORTS:**

2 (2013)

country comparison to the world: 204

**AIRPORTS - WITH PAVED RUNWAYS:**

total: 2 (2017)

1,524 to 2,437 m: 1 (2017)

914 to 1,523 m: 1 (2017)

**RAILWAYS:**

total: 50 km (2008)

narrow gauge: 50 km 0.762-m gauge on Saint Kitts for tourists (2008)

country comparison to the world: 132

**ROADWAYS:**

total: 383 km (2002)

paved: 163 km (2002)

unpaved: 220 km (2002)

country comparison to the world: 202

**MERCHANT MARINE:**

total: 274 (2017)

by type: bulk carrier 6, container ship 5, general cargo 58, oil tanker 60, other 145 (2017)

country comparison to the world: 56

**PORTS AND TERMINALS:**

major seaport(s): Basseterre, Charlestown

## MILITARY AND SECURITY :: SAINT KITTS AND NEVIS

**MILITARY BRANCHES:**

Ministry of Foreign Affairs, National Security, Labour, Immigration, and Social Security: Royal Saint Kitts and Nevis Defense Force (includes Coast Guard), Royal Saint Kitts and Nevis Police Force (2013)

**MILITARY SERVICE AGE AND OBLIGATION:**

18 years of age for voluntary military service; no conscription (2012)

## TRANSNATIONAL ISSUES :: SAINT KITTS AND NEVIS

**DISPUTES - INTERNATIONAL:**

joins other Caribbean states to counter Venezuela's claim that Aves Island sustains human habitation, a criterion under UN Convention on the Law of the Sea, which permits Venezuela to extend its EEZ/continental shelf over a large portion of the eastern Caribbean Sea

**ILLICIT DRUGS:**

transshipment point for South American drugs destined for the US and Europe; some money-laundering activity

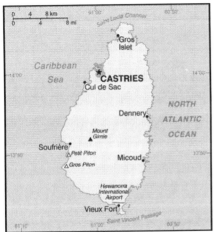

# CENTRAL AMERICA :: SAINT LUCIA

## INTRODUCTION :: SAINT LUCIA

### BACKGROUND:

The island, with its fine natural harbor at Castries, was contested between England and France throughout the 17th and early 18th centuries (changing possession 14 times); it was finally ceded to the UK in 1814. Even after the abolition of slavery on its plantations in 1834, Saint Lucia remained an agricultural island, dedicated to producing tropical commodity crops. Self-government was granted in 1967 and independence in 1979.

## GEOGRAPHY :: SAINT LUCIA

### LOCATION:
Caribbean, island between the Caribbean Sea and North Atlantic Ocean, north of Trinidad and Tobago

### GEOGRAPHIC COORDINATES:
13 53 N, 60 58 W

### MAP REFERENCES:
Central America and the Caribbean

### AREA:
total: 616 sq km
land: 606 sq km
water: 10 sq km
country comparison to the world: 193

### AREA - COMPARATIVE:
three and a half times the size of Washington, DC

### LAND BOUNDARIES:
0 km

### COASTLINE:
158 km

### MARITIME CLAIMS:
territorial sea: 12 nm
exclusive economic zone: 200 nm
contiguous zone: 24 nm
continental shelf: 200 nm or to the edge of the continental margin

### CLIMATE:
tropical, moderated by northeast trade winds; dry season January to April, rainy season May to August

### TERRAIN:
volcanic and mountainous with broad, fertile valleys

### ELEVATION:
0 m lowest point: Caribbean Sea
948 highest point: Mount Gimie

### NATURAL RESOURCES:
forests, sandy beaches, minerals (pumice), mineral springs, geothermal potential

### LAND USE:
agricultural land: 17.4% (2011 est.)
arable land: 4.9% (2011 est.) / permanent crops: 11.5% (2011 est.) / permanent pasture: 1% (2011 est.)
forest: 77% (2011 est.)
other: 5.6% (2011 est.)

### IRRIGATED LAND:
30 sq km (2012)

### POPULATION DISTRIBUTION:
most of the population is found on the periphery of the island, with a larger concentration in the north around the capital of Castries

### NATURAL HAZARDS:
hurricanes

volcanism: Mount Gimie (948 m), also known as Qualibou, is a caldera on the west of the island; the iconic twin pyramidal peaks of Gros Piton (771 m) and Petit Piton (743 m) are lava dome remnants associated with the Soufriere volcano; there have been no historical magmatic eruptions, but a minor steam eruption in 1766 spread a thin layer of ash over a wide area; Saint Lucia is part of the volcanic island arc of the Lesser Antilles that extends from Saba in the north to Grenada in the south

### ENVIRONMENT - CURRENT ISSUES:
deforestation; soil erosion, particularly in the northern region

### ENVIRONMENT - INTERNATIONAL AGREEMENTS:
party to: Biodiversity, Climate Change, Climate Change-Kyoto Protocol, Desertification, Endangered Species, Environmental Modification, Hazardous Wastes, Law of the Sea, Marine Dumping, Ozone Layer Protection, Ship Pollution, Wetlands, Whaling
signed, but not ratified: none of the selected agreements

### GEOGRAPHY - NOTE:
the twin Pitons (Gros Piton and Petit Piton), striking cone-shaped peaks south of Soufriere, are one of the scenic natural highlights of the Caribbean

## PEOPLE AND SOCIETY :: SAINT LUCIA

### POPULATION:
165,510 (July 2018 est.)
country comparison to the world: 187

### NATIONALITY:
noun: Saint Lucian(s)
adjective: Saint Lucian

### ETHNIC GROUPS:

black/African descent 85.3%, mixed 10.9%, East Indian 2.2%, other 1.6%, unspecified 0.1% (2010 est.)

## LANGUAGES:
English (official), French patois

## RELIGIONS:
Roman Catholic 61.5%, Protestant 25.5% (includes Seventh Day Adventist 10.4%, Pentecostal 8.9%, Baptist 2.2%, Anglican 1.6%, Church of God 1.5%, other Protestant 0.9%), other Christian 3.4% (includes Evangelical 2.3% and Jehovah's Witness 1.1%), Rastafarian 1.9%, other 0.4%, none 5.9%, unspecified 1.4% (2010 est.)

## AGE STRUCTURE:
**0-14 years:** 19.77% (male 16,840/female 15,874)

**15-24 years:** 14.79% (male 12,419/female 12,060)

**25-54 years:** 42.93% (male 34,228/female 36,818)

**55-64 years:** 10.41% (male 7,944/female 9,284)

**65 years and over:** 12.11% (male 9,086/female 10,957) (2018 est.)

## DEPENDENCY RATIOS:
**total dependency ratio:** 41.1 (2015 est.)

**youth dependency ratio:** 27.9 (2015 est.)

**elderly dependency ratio:** 13.3 (2015 est.)

**potential support ratio:** 7.5 (2015 est.)

## MEDIAN AGE:
**total:** 35.5 years

**male:** 34.3 years

**female:** 36.6 years (2018 est.)

**country comparison to the world:** 80

## POPULATION GROWTH RATE:
0.31% (2018 est.)

**country comparison to the world:** 168

## BIRTH RATE:
13.1 births/1,000 population (2018 est.)

**country comparison to the world:** 146

## DEATH RATE:
7.8 deaths/1,000 population (2018 est.)

**country comparison to the world:** 98

## NET MIGRATION RATE:
-2.5 migrant(s)/1,000 population (2017 est.)

**country comparison to the world:** 170

## POPULATION DISTRIBUTION:
most of the population is found on the periphery of the island, with a larger concentration in the north around the capital of Castries

## URBANIZATION:
**urban population:** 18.7% of total population (2018)

**rate of urbanization:** 0.8% annual rate of change (2015-20 est.)

## MAJOR URBAN AREAS - POPULATION:
22,000 CASTRIES (capital) (2018)

## SEX RATIO:
**at birth:** 1.06 male(s)/female (2017 est.)

**0-14 years:** 1.06 male(s)/female (2017 est.)

**15-24 years:** 1.03 male(s)/female (2017 est.)

**25-54 years:** 0.93 male(s)/female (2017 est.)

**55-64 years:** 0.86 male(s)/female (2017 est.)

**65 years and over:** 0.83 male(s)/female (2017 est.)

**total population:** 0.95 male(s)/female (2017 est.)

## MATERNAL MORTALITY RATE:
48 deaths/100,000 live births (2015 est.)

**country comparison to the world:** 97

## INFANT MORTALITY RATE:
**total:** 10.6 deaths/1,000 live births (2018 est.)

**male:** 10.2 deaths/1,000 live births (2018 est.)

**female:** 11 deaths/1,000 live births (2018 est.)

**country comparison to the world:** 129

## LIFE EXPECTANCY AT BIRTH:
**total population:** 78.1 years (2018 est.)

**male:** 75.4 years (2018 est.)

**female:** 81 years (2018 est.)

**country comparison to the world:** 64

## TOTAL FERTILITY RATE:
1.74 children born/woman (2018 est.)

**country comparison to the world:** 164

## CONTRACEPTIVE PREVALENCE RATE:
55.5% (2011/12)

## HEALTH EXPENDITURES:
6.7% of GDP (2014)

**country comparison to the world:** 89

## PHYSICIANS DENSITY:
0.1 physicians/1,000 population (2009)

## HOSPITAL BED DENSITY:
1.3 beds/1,000 population (2013)

## DRINKING WATER SOURCE:
**improved:**

urban: 99.5% of population (2015 est.)

rural: 95.6% of population (2015 est.)

total: 96.3% of population (2015 est.)

**unimproved:**

urban: 0.5% of population (2015 est.)

rural: 4.4% of population (2015 est.)

total: 3.7% of population (2015 est.)

## SANITATION FACILITY ACCESS:
**improved:**

urban: 84.7% of population (2015 est.)

rural: 91.9% of population (2015 est.)

total: 90.5% of population (2015 est.)

**unimproved:**

urban: 15.3% of population (2015 est.)

rural: 8.1% of population (2015 est.)

total: 9.5% of population (2015 est.)

## HIV/AIDS - ADULT PREVALENCE RATE:
NA

## HIV/AIDS - PEOPLE LIVING WITH HIV/AIDS:
NA

## HIV/AIDS - DEATHS:
NA

## MAJOR INFECTIOUS DISEASES:
**note:** active local transmission of Zika virus by Aedes species mosquitoes has been identified in this country (as of August 2016); it poses an important risk (a large number of cases possible) among US citizens if bitten by an infective mosquito; other less common ways to get Zika are through sex, via blood transfusion, or during pregnancy, in which the pregnant woman passes Zika virus to her fetus

## OBESITY - ADULT PREVALENCE RATE:
19.7% (2016)

**country comparison to the world:** 111

## CHILDREN UNDER THE AGE OF 5 YEARS UNDERWEIGHT:
2.8% (2012)

country comparison to the world: 104
**EDUCATION EXPENDITURES:**
5.7% of GDP (2016)
country comparison to the world: 45
**UNEMPLOYMENT, YOUTH AGES 15-24:**
total: 46.2% (2016 est.)
male: 42.6% (2016 est.)
female: 51% (2016 est.)
country comparison to the world: 9

# GOVERNMENT :: SAINT LUCIA

**COUNTRY NAME:**
conventional long form: none
conventional short form: Saint Lucia
etymology: named after Saint LUCY of Syracuse by French sailors who were shipwrecked on the island on 13 December 1502, the saint's feast day
note: pronounced saynt-looshya

**GOVERNMENT TYPE:**
parliamentary democracy (Parliament) under a constitutional monarchy; a Commonwealth realm

**CAPITAL:**
name: Castries
geographic coordinates: 14 00 N, 61 00 W
time difference: UTC-4 (1 hour ahead of Washington, DC, during Standard Time)

**ADMINISTRATIVE DIVISIONS:**
10 districts; Anse-la-Raye, Canaries, Castries, Choiseul, Dennery, Gros-Islet, Laborie, Micoud, Soufriere, Vieux-Fort

**INDEPENDENCE:**
22 February 1979 (from the UK)

**NATIONAL HOLIDAY:**
Independence Day, 22 February (1979)

**CONSTITUTION:**
history: previous 1958, 1960 (preindependence); latest presented 20 December 1978, effective 22 February 1979 (2018)
amendments: proposed by Parliament; passage requires at least two-thirds majority by the House of Assembly membership in the final reading and assent to by the governor general; passage of amendments to various constitutional sections such as those on fundamental rights and freedoms, government finances, the judiciary, and procedures for amending the constitution, require at least three-quarters majority vote by the House and assent to by the governor general; passage of amendments approved by the House but rejected by the Senate require a majority of votes cast in a referendum (2018)

**LEGAL SYSTEM:**
English common law

**INTERNATIONAL LAW ORGANIZATION PARTICIPATION:**
has not submitted an ICJ jurisdiction declaration; accepts ICCt jurisdiction

**CITIZENSHIP:**
citizenship by birth: yes
citizenship by descent only: at least one parent must be a citizen of Saint Lucia
dual citizenship recognized: yes
residency requirement for naturalization: 8 years

**SUFFRAGE:**
18 years of age; universal

**EXECUTIVE BRANCH:**
chief of state: Queen ELIZABETH II (since 6 February 1952); represented by Governor General Neville CENAC (since 12 January 2018)
head of government: Prime Minister Allen CHASTANET (since 7 June 2016)
cabinet: Cabinet appointed by the governor general on the advice of the prime minister
elections/appointments: the monarchy is hereditary; governor general appointed by the monarch; following legislative elections, the leader of the majority party or majority coalition usually appointed prime minister by governor general; deputy prime minister appointed by governor general

**LEGISLATIVE BRANCH:**
description: bicameral Parliament consists of:
Senate (11 seats; 6 members appointed on the advice of the prime minister, 3 on the advice of the leader of the opposition, and 2 upon consultation with religious, economic, and social groups; members serve 5-year terms)
House of Assembly (17 seats; members directly elected in single-seat constituencies by simple majority vote to serve 5-year terms)
elections:
House of Assembly - last held on 6 June 2016 (next to be held in 2021)
election results:
House of Assembly - percent of vote by party - UWP 54.8%, SLP 44.1%, other 1.1%; seats by party - UWP 11, SLP 6

**JUDICIAL BRANCH:**
highest courts: the Eastern Caribbean Supreme Court (ECSC) is the superior court of the Organization of Eastern Caribbean States; the ECSC - headquartered on St. Lucia - consists of the Court of Appeal - headed by the chief justice and 4 judges - and the High Court with 18 judges; the Court of Appeal is itinerant, travelling to member states on a schedule to hears appeals from the High Court and subordinate courts; High Court judges reside at the member states with 4 on Saint Lucia; Saint Lucia is a member of the Caribbean Court of Justice
judge selection and term of office: chief justice of Eastern Caribbean Supreme Court appointed by Her Majesty, Queen ELIZABETH II; other justices and judges appointed by the Judicial and Legal Services Commission, an independent body of judicial officials; Court of Appeal justices appointed for life with mandatory retirement at age 65; High Court judges appointed for life with mandatory retirement at age 62
subordinate courts: magistrate's court

**POLITICAL PARTIES AND LEADERS:**
Lucian People's Movement or LPM [Therold PRUDENT]
Saint Lucia Labor Party or SLP [Philip J. PIERRE]
United Workers Party or UWP [Allen CHASTANET]

**INTERNATIONAL ORGANIZATION PARTICIPATION:**
ACP, AOSIS, C, Caricom, CD, CDB, CELAC, FAO, G-77, IBRD, ICAO, ICCt, ICRM, IDA, IFAD, IFC, IFRCS, ILO, IMF, IMO, Interpol, IOC, ISO, ITU, ITUC (NGOs), MIGA, NAM, OAS, OECS, OIF, OPANAL, OPCW, Petrocaribe, UN, UNCTAD, UNESCO, UNIDO, UPU, WCO, WFTU (NGOs), WHO, WIPO, WMO, WTO

**DIPLOMATIC REPRESENTATION IN THE US:**
chief of mission: Ambassador Anton Edsel EDMUNDS (since 8 September 2017)
chancery: 1628 K Street, NW, Suite 1250, Washington, DC 20006

telephone: [1] (202) 364-6792 through 6795

FAX: [1] (202) 364-6723

consulate(s) general: New York

**DIPLOMATIC REPRESENTATION FROM THE US:**

the US does not have an embassy in Saint Lucia; the US Ambassador to Barbados is accredited to Saint Lucia

**FLAG DESCRIPTION:**

cerulean blue with a gold isosceles triangle below a black arrowhead; the upper edges of the arrowhead have a white border; the blue color represents the sky and sea, gold stands for sunshine and prosperity, and white and black the racial composition of the island (with the latter being dominant); the two major triangles invoke the twin Pitons (Gros Piton and Petit Piton), cone-shaped volcanic plugs that are a symbol of the island

**NATIONAL SYMBOL(S):**

twin pitons (volcanic peaks), Saint Lucia parrot; national colors: cerulean blue, gold, black, white

**NATIONAL ANTHEM:**

name: Sons and Daughters of St. Lucia

lyrics/music: Charles JESSE/Leton Felix THOMAS

note: adopted 1967

## ECONOMY :: SAINT LUCIA

**ECONOMY - OVERVIEW:**

The island nation has been able to attract foreign business and investment, especially in its offshore banking and tourism industries. Tourism is Saint Lucia's main source of jobs and income - accounting for 65% of GDP - and the island's main source of foreign exchange earnings. The manufacturing sector is the most diverse in the Eastern Caribbean area. Crops such as bananas, mangos, and avocados continue to be grown for export, but St. Lucia's once solid banana industry has been devastated by strong competition.

Saint Lucia is vulnerable to a variety of external shocks, including volatile tourism receipts, natural disasters, and dependence on foreign oil. Furthermore, high public debt - 77% of GDP in 2012 - and high debt servicing obligations constrain the CHASTANET administration's ability to respond to adverse external shocks.

St. Lucia has experienced anemic growth since the onset of the global financial crisis in 2008, largely because of a slowdown in tourism - airlines cut back on their routes to St. Lucia in 2012. Also, St. Lucia introduced a value added tax in 2012 of 15%, becoming the last country in the Eastern Caribbean to do so. In 2013, the government introduced a National Competitiveness and Productivity Council to address St. Lucia's high public wages and lack of productivity.

**GDP (PURCHASING POWER PARITY):**

$2.542 billion (2017 est.)

$2.469 billion (2016 est.)

$2.388 billion (2015 est.)

note: data are in 2017 dollars

country comparison to the world: 191

**GDP (OFFICIAL EXCHANGE RATE):**

$1.686 billion (2017 est.) (2017 est.)

**GDP - REAL GROWTH RATE:**

3% (2017 est.)

3.4% (2016 est.)

-0.9% (2015 est.)

country comparison to the world: 115

**GDP - PER CAPITA (PPP):**

$14,400 (2017 est.)

$14,200 (2016 est.)

$13,800 (2015 est.)

note: data are in 2017 dollars

country comparison to the world: 117

**GROSS NATIONAL SAVING:**

19.4% of GDP (2017 est.)

15.5% of GDP (2016 est.)

24.3% of GDP (2015 est.)

country comparison to the world: 102

**GDP - COMPOSITION, BY END USE:**

household consumption: 66.1% (2017 est.)

government consumption: 11.2% (2017 est.)

investment in fixed capital: 16.9% (2017 est.)

investment in inventories: 0.1% (2017 est.)

exports of goods and services: 62.7% (2017 est.)

imports of goods and services: -56.9% (2017 est.)

**GDP - COMPOSITION, BY SECTOR OF ORIGIN:**

agriculture: 2.9% (2017 est.)

industry: 14.2% (2017 est.)

services: 82.8% (2017 est.)

**AGRICULTURE - PRODUCTS:**

bananas, coconuts, vegetables, citrus, root crops, cocoa

**INDUSTRIES:**

tourism; clothing, assembly of electronic components, beverages, corrugated cardboard boxes, lime processing, coconut processing

**INDUSTRIAL PRODUCTION GROWTH RATE:**

6% (2017 est.)

country comparison to the world: 42

**LABOR FORCE:**

79,700 (2012 est.)

country comparison to the world: 183

**LABOR FORCE - BY OCCUPATION:**

agriculture: 21.7%

industry: 24.7%

services: 53.6% (2002 est.)

**UNEMPLOYMENT RATE:**

20% (2003 est.)

country comparison to the world: 186

**POPULATION BELOW POVERTY LINE:**

NA

**HOUSEHOLD INCOME OR CONSUMPTION BY PERCENTAGE SHARE:**

lowest 10%: NA

highest 10%: NA

**BUDGET:**

revenues: 398.2 million (2017 est.)

expenditures: 392.8 million (2017 est.)

**TAXES AND OTHER REVENUES:**

23.6% (of GDP) (2017 est.)

country comparison to the world: 125

**BUDGET SURPLUS (+) OR DEFICIT (-):**

0.3% (of GDP) (2017 est.)

country comparison to the world: 41

**PUBLIC DEBT:**

70.7% of GDP (2017 est.)

69.2% of GDP (2016 est.)

country comparison to the world: 49

**FISCAL YEAR:**

1 April - 31 March

**INFLATION RATE (CONSUMER PRICES):**

0.1% (2017 est.)

-3.1% (2016 est.)

country comparison to the world: 15

**CENTRAL BANK DISCOUNT RATE:**

6.5% (31 December 2010)

6.5% (31 December 2009)

country comparison to the world: 63

**COMMERCIAL BANK PRIME LENDING RATE:**

8.34% (31 December 2017 est.)

8.47% (31 December 2016 est.)

country comparison to the world: 100

**STOCK OF NARROW MONEY:**

$334.2 million (31 December 2017 est.)

$318.4 million (31 December 2016 est.)

country comparison to the world: 180

**STOCK OF BROAD MONEY:**

$334.2 million (31 December 2017 est.)

$318.4 million (31 December 2016 est.)

country comparison to the world: 183

**STOCK OF DOMESTIC CREDIT:**

$1.267 billion (31 December 2017 est.)

$1.297 billion (31 December 2016 est.)

country comparison to the world: 164

**CURRENT ACCOUNT BALANCE:**

$21 million (2017 est.)

-$31 million (2016 est.)

country comparison to the world: 61

**EXPORTS:**

$185.1 million (2017 est.)

$188.2 million (2016 est.)

country comparison to the world: 191

**EXPORTS - PARTNERS:**

US 67.6%, UK 5.9%, Trinidad and Tobago 5.5% (2017)

**EXPORTS - COMMODITIES:**

bananas 41%, clothing, cocoa, avocados, mangoes, coconut oil (2010 est.)

**IMPORTS:**

$600 million (2017 est.)

$575.9 million (2016 est.)

country comparison to the world: 195

**IMPORTS - COMMODITIES:**

food, manufactured goods, machinery and transportation equipment, chemicals, fuels

**IMPORTS - PARTNERS:**

US 53.3%, Trinidad and Tobago 10.8% (2017)

**RESERVES OF FOREIGN EXCHANGE AND GOLD:**

$321.8 million (31 December 2017 est.)

$320.7 million (31 December 2016 est.)

country comparison to the world: 166

**DEBT - EXTERNAL:**

$570.6 million (31 December 2017 est.)

$529 million (31 December 2015 est.)

country comparison to the world: 176

**EXCHANGE RATES:**

East Caribbean dollars (XCD) per US dollar -

2.7 (2017 est.)

2.7 (2016 est.)

2.7 (2015 est.)

2.7 (2014 est.)

2.7 (2013 est.)

## ENERGY :: SAINT LUCIA

**ELECTRICITY ACCESS:**

population without electricity: 16,446 (2012)

electrification - total population: 91% (2012)

electrification - urban areas: 100% (2012)

electrification - rural areas: 80% (2012)

**ELECTRICITY - PRODUCTION:**

369 million kWh (2016 est.)

country comparison to the world: 174

**ELECTRICITY - CONSUMPTION:**

343.2 million kWh (2016 est.)

country comparison to the world: 181

**ELECTRICITY - EXPORTS:**

0 kWh (2016 est.)

country comparison to the world: 189

**ELECTRICITY - IMPORTS:**

0 kWh (2016 est.)

country comparison to the world: 191

**ELECTRICITY - INSTALLED GENERATING CAPACITY:**

89,000 kW (2016 est.)

country comparison to the world: 180

**ELECTRICITY - FROM FOSSIL FUELS:**

99% of total installed capacity (2016 est.)

country comparison to the world: 25

**ELECTRICITY - FROM NUCLEAR FUELS:**

0% of total installed capacity (2017 est.)

country comparison to the world: 173

**ELECTRICITY - FROM HYDROELECTRIC PLANTS:**

0% of total installed capacity (2017 est.)

country comparison to the world: 196

**ELECTRICITY - FROM OTHER RENEWABLE SOURCES:**

1% of total installed capacity (2017 est.)

country comparison to the world: 165

**CRUDE OIL - PRODUCTION:**

0 bbl/day (2017 est.)

country comparison to the world: 191

**CRUDE OIL - EXPORTS:**

0 bbl/day (2015 est.)

country comparison to the world: 185

**CRUDE OIL - IMPORTS:**

0 bbl/day (2015 est.)

country comparison to the world: 187

**CRUDE OIL - PROVED RESERVES:**

0 bbl (1 January 2018 est.)

country comparison to the world: 187

**REFINED PETROLEUM PRODUCTS - PRODUCTION:**

0 bbl/day (2015 est.)

country comparison to the world: 194

**REFINED PETROLEUM PRODUCTS - CONSUMPTION:**

3,100 bbl/day (2016 est.)

country comparison to the world: 187

**REFINED PETROLEUM PRODUCTS - EXPORTS:**

0 bbl/day (2015 est.)

country comparison to the world: 195

**REFINED PETROLEUM PRODUCTS - IMPORTS:**

3,113 bbl/day (2015 est.)

country comparison to the world: 184

**NATURAL GAS - PRODUCTION:**

0 cu m (2017 est.)

country comparison to the world: 189

**NATURAL GAS - CONSUMPTION:**

0 cu m (2017 est.)

country comparison to the world: 191

**NATURAL GAS - EXPORTS:**

0 cu m (2017 est.)

country comparison to the world: 174

**NATURAL GAS - IMPORTS:**

0 cu m (2017 est.)

country comparison to the world: 180

**NATURAL GAS - PROVED RESERVES:**

0 cu m (1 January 2014 est.)

country comparison to the world: 186

**CARBON DIOXIDE EMISSIONS FROM CONSUMPTION OF ENERGY:**

437,900 Mt (2017 est.)

country comparison to the world: 186

## COMMUNICATIONS :: SAINT LUCIA

**TELEPHONES - FIXED LINES:**

total subscriptions: 35,014 (2017 est.)

subscriptions per 100 inhabitants: 21 (2017 est.)

country comparison to the world: 166

**TELEPHONES - MOBILE CELLULAR:**

total subscriptions: 176,694 (2017 est.)

subscriptions per 100 inhabitants: 107 (2017 est.)

country comparison to the world: 184

**TELEPHONE SYSTEM:**

general assessment: an adequate system that is automatically switched (2016)

domestic: fixed-line teledensity is 20 per 100 persons and mobile-cellular teledensity is roughly 105 per 100 persons (2016)

international: country code - 1-758; the East Caribbean Fiber System and Southern Caribbean Fiber submarine cables, along with Intelsat from Martinique, carry calls internationally; direct microwave radio relay link with Martinique and Saint Vincent and the Grenadines; tropospheric scatter to Barbados (2016)

**BROADCAST MEDIA:**

3 privately owned TV stations; 1 public TV station operating on a cable network; multi-channel cable TV service available; a mix of state-owned and privately owned broadcasters operate nearly 25 radio stations including repeater transmission stations (2007)

**INTERNET COUNTRY CODE:**

.lc

**INTERNET USERS:**

total: 86,000 (July 2016 est.)

percent of population: 52.4% (July 2016 est.)

country comparison to the world: 178

**BROADBAND - FIXED SUBSCRIPTIONS:**

total: 31,781 (2017 est.)

subscriptions per 100 inhabitants: 19 (2017 est.)

country comparison to the world: 139

## TRANSPORTATION :: SAINT LUCIA

**CIVIL AIRCRAFT REGISTRATION COUNTRY CODE PREFIX:**

J6 (2016)

**AIRPORTS:**

2 (2013)

country comparison to the world: 205

**AIRPORTS - WITH PAVED RUNWAYS:**

total: 2 (2017)

2,438 to 3,047 m: 1 (2017)

1,524 to 2,437 m: 1 (2017)

**ROADWAYS:**

total: 1,210 km (2011)

paved: 847 km (2011)

unpaved: 363 km (2011)

country comparison to the world: 181

**PORTS AND TERMINALS:**

major seaport(s): Castries, Cul-de-Sac, Vieux-Fort

## MILITARY AND SECURITY :: SAINT LUCIA

**MILITARY BRANCHES:**

no regular military forces; Royal Saint Lucia Police Force (includes Special Service Unit, Marine Unit) (2012)

**MILITARY SERVICE AGE AND OBLIGATION:**

18 years of age for voluntary security service; no national army (2012)

## TRANSNATIONAL ISSUES :: SAINT LUCIA

**DISPUTES - INTERNATIONAL:**

joins other Caribbean states to counter Venezuela's claim that Aves Island sustains human habitation, a criterion under UN Convention on the Law of the Sea, which permits Venezuela to extend its EEZ/continental shelf over a large portion of the eastern Caribbean Sea

**ILLICIT DRUGS:**

transit point for South American drugs destined for the US and Europe

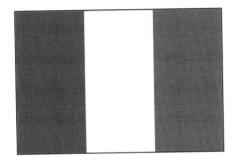

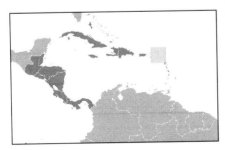

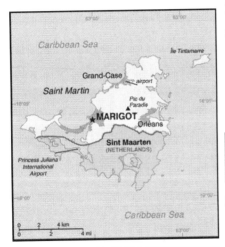

# CENTRAL AMERICA :: SAINT MARTIN

## INTRODUCTION :: SAINT MARTIN

### BACKGROUND:

Although sighted by Christopher COLUMBUS in 1493 and claimed for Spain, it was the Dutch who occupied the island in 1631 and set about exploiting its salt deposits. The Spanish retook the island in 1633, but continued to be harassed by the Dutch. The Spanish finally relinquished Saint Martin to the French and Dutch, who divided it between themselves in 1648. Friction between the two sides caused the border to frequently fluctuate over the next two centuries, with the French eventually holding the greater portion of the island (about 57%). The cultivation of sugar cane introduced African slavery to the island in the late 18th century; the practice was not abolished until 1848. The island became a free port in 1939; the tourism industry was dramatically expanded during the 1970s and 1980s. In 2003, the populace of Saint Martin voted to secede from Guadeloupe and in 2007, the northern portion of the island became a French overseas collectivity. In 2010, the southern Dutch portion of the island became the independent nation of Sint Maarten within the Kingdom of the Netherlands. On 6 September 2017, Hurricane Irma passed over the island of Saint Martin causing extensive damage to roads, communications, electrical power, and housing; the UN estimated that 90% of the buildings were damaged or destroyed.

## GEOGRAPHY :: SAINT MARTIN

### LOCATION:
Caribbean, located in the Leeward Islands (northern) group; French part of the island of Saint Martin in the Caribbean Sea; Saint Martin lies east of the US Virgin Islands

### GEOGRAPHIC COORDINATES:
18 05 N, 63 57 W

### MAP REFERENCES:
Central America and the Caribbean

### AREA:
total: 54.4 sq km
land: 54.4 sq km
water: negligible
country comparison to the world: 231

### AREA - COMPARATIVE:
more than one-third the size of Washington, DC

### LAND BOUNDARIES:
total: 16 km
border countries (1): Sint Maarten 16 km

### COASTLINE:
58.9 km (for entire island)

### CLIMATE:
temperature averages 27-29 degrees Celsius all year long; low humidity, gentle trade winds, brief, intense rain showers; hurricane season stretches from July to November

### ELEVATION:
0 m lowest point: Caribbean Ocean
424 highest point: Pic du Paradis

### NATURAL RESOURCES:
salt

### POPULATION DISTRIBUTION:
most of the population is found along the coast, with a largest concentrations around the capital Marigot, Orleans, and Grand-Case

### NATURAL HAZARDS:
subject to hurricanes from July to November

### ENVIRONMENT - CURRENT ISSUES:
excessive population pressure (increasing settlement); waste management; salinity intrusions into the main land of the island; fresh water supply is dependent on desalination of sea water; over exploitation of marine resources (reef fisheries, coral and shell); indiscriminate anchoring of boats damages coral reefs,causing underwater pollution and changes the sediment dynamics of Saint Martin's Island

### GEOGRAPHY - NOTE:
the southern border is shared with Sint Maarten, a country within the Kingdom of the Netherlands; together, these two entities make up the smallest landmass in the world shared by two self-governing states

## PEOPLE AND SOCIETY :: SAINT MARTIN

### POPULATION:
32,284 (July 2018 est.)
country comparison to the world: 216

### ETHNIC GROUPS:
other Creole (mulatto), black, Guadeloupe Mestizo (French-East Asia), white, East Indian

### LANGUAGES:
French (official), English, Dutch, French Patois, Spanish, Papiamento (dialect of Netherlands Antilles)

**RELIGIONS:**

Roman Catholic, Jehovah's Witness, Protestant, Hindu

**AGE STRUCTURE:**

**0-14 years:** 26.05% (male 4,184/female 4,225)

**15-24 years:** 10.29% (male 1,638/female 1,685)

**25-54 years:** 46.52% (male 7,181/female 7,836)

**55-64 years:** 8.76% (male 1,317/female 1,511)

**65 years and over:** 8.38% (male 1,195/female 1,512) (2018 est.)

**MEDIAN AGE:**

**total:** 32.8 years

**male:** 31.9 years

**female:** 33.7 years (2018 est.)

**country comparison to the world:** 97

**POPULATION DISTRIBUTION:**

most of the population is found along the coast, with a largest concentrations around the capital Marigot, Orleans, and Grand-Case

**SEX RATIO:**

**at birth:** 1.03 male(s)/female (2017 est.)

**0-14 years:** 0.99 male(s)/female (2017 est.)

**15-24 years:** 0.99 male(s)/female (2017 est.)

**25-54 years:** 0.91 male(s)/female (2017 est.)

**55-64 years:** 0.87 male(s)/female (2017 est.)

**65 years and over:** 0.81 male(s)/female (2017 est.)

**total population:** 0.93 male(s)/female (2017 est.)

**MAJOR INFECTIOUS DISEASES:**

**note:** active local transmission of Zika virus by Aedes species mosquitoes has been identified in this country (as of August 2016); it poses an important risk (a large number of cases possible) among US citizens if bitten by an infective mosquito; other less common ways to get Zika are through sex, via blood transfusion, or during pregnancy, in which the pregnant woman passes Zika virus to her fetus

## GOVERNMENT :: SAINT MARTIN

**COUNTRY NAME:**

**conventional long form:** Overseas Collectivity of Saint Martin

**conventional short form:** Saint Martin

**local long form:** Collectivite d'outre mer de Saint-Martin

**local short form:** Saint-Martin

**etymology:** explorer Christopher COLUMBUS named the island after Saint MARTIN of Tours because the 11 November 1493 day of discovery was the saint's feast day

**DEPENDENCY STATUS:**

overseas collectivity of France

**note:** the only French overseas collectivity that is part of the EU

**GOVERNMENT TYPE:**

parliamentary democracy (Territorial Council); overseas collectivity of France

**CAPITAL:**

**name:** Marigot

**geographic coordinates:** 18 04 N, 63 05 W

**time difference:** UTC-4 (1 hour ahead of Washington, DC, during Standard Time)

**INDEPENDENCE:**

none (overseas collectivity of France)

**NATIONAL HOLIDAY:**

Fete de la Federation, 14 July (1790); note - local holiday is Schoelcher Day (Slavery Abolition Day) 12 July (1848)

**CONSTITUTION:**

**history:** 4 October 1958 (French Constitution) (2018)

**amendments:** amendment procedures of France's constitution apply (2018)

**LEGAL SYSTEM:**

French civil law

**CITIZENSHIP:**

see France

**SUFFRAGE:**

18 years of age, universal

**EXECUTIVE BRANCH:**

**chief of state:** President Emmanuel MACRON (since 14 May 2017); represented by Prefect Anne LAUBIES (since 8 June 2015)

**head of government:** President of Territorial Council Daniel GIBBS (since 2 April 2017); First Vice President Valerie DAMASEAU (since 2 April 2017)

**cabinet:** Executive Council; note - there is also an advisory economic, social, and cultural council

**elections/appointments:** French president directly elected by absolute majority popular vote in 2 rounds if needed for a 5-year term (eligible for a second term); prefect appointed by French president on the advice of French Ministry of Interior; president of Territorial Council elected by its members for a 5-year term; election last held on 26 March 2017

**election results:** Daniel GIBBS (TDG) elected president; Territorial Council vote - 18 votes, 4 blank, 1 invalid

**LEGISLATIVE BRANCH:**

**description:** unicameral Territorial Council (23 seats; members directly elected by absolute majority vote in 2 rounds if needed to serve 5-year terms); Saint Martin elects 1 member to the French Senate and one member (shared with Saint Barthelemy) to the French National Assembly

**elections:** Territorial Council - last held on 18 and 25 March 2017 (next to be held in March 2022)

**election results:** Territorial Council - percent of vote by party (first round) - TDG 49.1%, MJP 13.7%, MVP 12.3%, HOPE 8.7%, Continuons pour Saint-Martin 6.5%, other 9.7%; seats by party - NA; percent of vote by party (second round) - TDG 64.3%, MJP 24.2%, MVP 11.5.5%; seats by party - TDG 18, MJP 4, MVP 1

French Senate - held on 28 September 2014 (next to be held not later than September 2020) French National Assembly - last held on 11 and 18 June 2017 (next to be held by June 2022) French Senate - 1 seat: UMP 1 French National Assembly - 1 seat: UMP 1

**POLITICAL PARTIES AND LEADERS:**

Continuons pour St. Martin [Aline HANSON]
En marche vers le progres or MVP [Alain RICHARDSON]
Gereration Hope or HOPE [Jules CHARVILLE]
Movement for Justice and Prosperity or MJP [Louis MUSSINGTON]
New Direction [Jeanne VANTERPOOL]
Rally Responsibility Success (Rassemblement Responsabilite Reussite or RRR [Alain RICHARDSON]
Team Daniel Gibbs 2017 or TDG [Daniel GIBBS]
Union for Progress (Union Pour le Progres or UPP) [Louis-Constant FLEMING]; affiliated with UMP

**INTERNATIONAL ORGANIZATION PARTICIPATION:**

UPU

**DIPLOMATIC REPRESENTATION IN THE US:**

none (overseas collectivity of France)

**DIPLOMATIC REPRESENTATION FROM THE US:**

none (overseas collectivity of France)

**FLAG DESCRIPTION:**

the flag of France is used

**NATIONAL SYMBOL(S):**

brown pelican

**NATIONAL ANTHEM:**

name: O Sweet Saint Martin's Land

lyrics/music: Gerard KEMPS

note: the song, written in 1958, is used as an unofficial anthem for the entire island (both French and Dutch sides); as a collectivity of France, in addition to the local anthem, "La Marseillaise" remains official on the French side (see France); as a constituent part of the Kingdom of the Netherlands, in addition to the local anthem, "Het Wilhelmus" remains official on the Dutch side (see Netherlands)

# ECONOMY :: SAINT MARTIN

**ECONOMY - OVERVIEW:**

The economy of Saint Martin centers on tourism with 85% of the labor force engaged in this sector. Over one million visitors come to the island each year with most arriving through the Princess Juliana International Airport in Sint Maarten. The financial sector is also important to Saint Martin's economy as it facilitates financial mediation for its thriving tourism sector. No significant agriculture and limited local fishing means that almost all food must be imported. Energy resources and manufactured goods are also imported, primarily from Mexico and the US. Saint Martin is reported to have one of the highest per capita income in the Caribbean. As with the rest of the Caribbean, Saint Martin's financial sector is having to deal with losing correspondent banking relationships.

In September 2017, Hurricane Irma destroyed 95% of the French side of Saint Martin. Along the coastline of Marigot, the nerve center of the economy, the storm wiped out restaurants, shops, banks and open-air markets impacting more than 36,000 inhabitants.

**GDP (PURCHASING POWER PARITY):**

$561.5 million (2005 est.)

country comparison to the world: 212

**GDP (OFFICIAL EXCHANGE RATE):**

$561.5 million (2005 est.)

**GDP - PER CAPITA (PPP):**

$19,300 (2005 est.)

country comparison to the world: 92

**GDP - COMPOSITION, BY SECTOR OF ORIGIN:**

agriculture: 1% (2000)

industry: 15% (2000)

services: 84% (2000)

**INDUSTRIES:**

tourism, light industry and manufacturing, heavy industry

**LABOR FORCE:**

17,300 (2008 est.)

country comparison to the world: 214

**LABOR FORCE - BY OCCUPATION:**

85 directly or indirectly employed in tourist industry

**IMPORTS - COMMODITIES:**

crude petroleum, food, manufactured items

**EXCHANGE RATES:**

euros (EUR) per US dollar -

0.885 (2017 est.)

0.903 (2016 est.)

0.9214 (2015 est.)

0.885 (2014 est.)

0.7634 (2013 est.)

# ENERGY :: SAINT MARTIN

**ELECTRICITY ACCESS:**

population without electricity: 3,194 (2012)

electrification - total population: 91% (2012)

electrification - urban areas: 100% (2012)

electrification - rural areas: 80% (2012)

# COMMUNICATIONS :: SAINT MARTIN

**TELEPHONE SYSTEM:**

general assessment: fully integrated access (2009)

domestic: direct dial capability with both fixed and wireless systems (2009)

international: country code - 590; undersea fiber-optic cable provides voice and data connectivity to Puerto Rico and Guadeloupe (2009)

**BROADCAST MEDIA:**

1 local TV station; access to about 20 radio stations, including RFO Guadeloupe radio broadcasts via repeater (2008)

**INTERNET COUNTRY CODE:**

.mf; note - .gp, the Internet country code for Guadeloupe, and .fr, the Internet country code for France, might also be encountered

**INTERNET USERS:**

total: 1,100 (July 2016 est.)

percent of population: 3.5% (July 2016 est.)

country comparison to the world: 222

# TRANSPORTATION :: SAINT MARTIN

**AIRPORTS:**

1 (2013)

country comparison to the world: 235

**AIRPORTS - WITH PAVED RUNWAYS:**

total: 1 (2017)

914 to 1,523 m: 1 (2017)

**TRANSPORTATION - NOTE:**

nearest airport for international flights is Princess Juliana International Airport (SXM) located on Sint Maarten

# MILITARY AND SECURITY :: SAINT MARTIN

**MILITARY - NOTE:**

defense is the responsibility of France

# NORTH AMERICA :: SAINT PIERRE AND MIQUELON

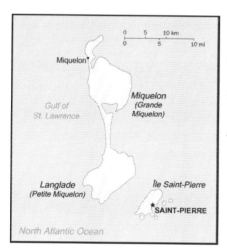

## INTRODUCTION :: SAINT PIERRE AND MIQUELON

### BACKGROUND:
First settled by the French in the early 17th century, the islands represent the sole remaining vestige of France's once vast North American possessions. They attained the status of an overseas collectivity in 2003.

## GEOGRAPHY :: SAINT PIERRE AND MIQUELON

### LOCATION:
Northern North America, islands in the North Atlantic Ocean, south of Newfoundland (Canada)

### GEOGRAPHIC COORDINATES:
46 50 N, 56 20 W

### MAP REFERENCES:
North America

### AREA:
total: 242 sq km

land: 242 sq km

water: 0 sq km

note: includes eight small islands in the Saint Pierre and the Miquelon groups

country comparison to the world: 214

### AREA - COMPARATIVE:
one and half times the size of Washington, DC

### LAND BOUNDARIES:
0 km

### COASTLINE:
120 km

### MARITIME CLAIMS:
territorial sea: 12 nm

exclusive economic zone: 200 nm

### CLIMATE:
cold and wet, with considerable mist and fog; spring and autumn are often windy

### TERRAIN:
mostly barren rock

### ELEVATION:
0 m lowest point: Atlantic Ocean

240 highest point: Morne de la Grande Montagne

### NATURAL RESOURCES:
fish, deepwater ports

### LAND USE:
agricultural land: 8.7% (2011 est.)

arable land: 8.7% (2011 est.) / permanent crops: 0% (2011 est.) / permanent pasture: 0% (2011 est.)

forest: 12.5% (2011 est.)

other: 78.8% (2011 est.)

### IRRIGATED LAND:
0 sq km (2012)

### POPULATION DISTRIBUTION:
most of the population is found on Saint Pierre Island; a small settlement is located on the north end of Miquelon Island

### NATURAL HAZARDS:
persistent fog throughout the year can be a maritime hazard

### ENVIRONMENT - CURRENT ISSUES:
overfishing; recent test drilling for oil in waters around Saint Pierre and Miquelon may bring future development that would impact the environment

### GEOGRAPHY - NOTE:
vegetation scanty; the islands are actually part of the northern Appalachians along with Newfoundland

## PEOPLE AND SOCIETY :: SAINT PIERRE AND MIQUELON

### POPULATION:
5,471 (July 2018 est.)

country comparison to the world: 227

### NATIONALITY:
noun: Frenchman(men), Frenchwoman(women)

adjective: French

**ETHNIC GROUPS:**

Basques and Bretons (French fishermen)

**LANGUAGES:**

French (official)

**RELIGIONS:**

Roman Catholic 99%, other 1%

**AGE STRUCTURE:**

0-14 years: 14.88% (male 420 /female 394)

15-24 years: 8.99% (male 255 /female 237)

25-54 years: 41.44% (male 1,109 /female 1,158)

55-64 years: 13.69% (male 389 /female 360)

65 years and over: 21% (male 489 /female 660) (2018 est.)

**MEDIAN AGE:**

total: 47.2 years

male: 46.7 years

female: 47.7 years (2018 est.)

country comparison to the world: 4

**POPULATION GROWTH RATE:**

-1.13% (2018 est.)

country comparison to the world: 229

**BIRTH RATE:**

7 births/1,000 population (2018 est.)

country comparison to the world: 225

**DEATH RATE:**

10.2 deaths/1,000 population (2018 est.)

country comparison to the world: 32

**NET MIGRATION RATE:**

-8 migrant(s)/1,000 population (2017 est.)

country comparison to the world: 206

**POPULATION DISTRIBUTION:**

most of the population is found on Saint Pierre Island; a small settlement is located on the north end of Miquelon Island

**URBANIZATION:**

urban population: 90.2% of total population (2018)

rate of urbanization: 0.36% annual rate of change (2015-20 est.)

**MAJOR URBAN AREAS - POPULATION:**

6,000 SAINT-PIERRE (capital) (2018)

**SEX RATIO:**

at birth: 1.11 male(s)/female (2017 est.)

0-14 years: 1.06 male(s)/female (2017 est.)

15-24 years: 1.08 male(s)/female (2017 est.)

25-54 years: 0.97 male(s)/female (2017 est.)

55-64 years: 1.1 male(s)/female (2017 est.)

65 years and over: 0.72 male(s)/female (2017 est.)

total population: 0.95 male(s)/female (2017 est.)

**INFANT MORTALITY RATE:**

total: 6.4 deaths/1,000 live births (2018 est.)

male: 7.4 deaths/1,000 live births (2018 est.)

female: 5.3 deaths/1,000 live births (2018 est.)

country comparison to the world: 164

**LIFE EXPECTANCY AT BIRTH:**

total population: 80.7 years (2018 est.)

male: 78.4 years (2018 est.)

female: 83.2 years (2018 est.)

country comparison to the world: 41

**TOTAL FERTILITY RATE:**

1.57 children born/woman (2018 est.)

country comparison to the world: 188

**HIV/AIDS - ADULT PREVALENCE RATE:**

NA

**HIV/AIDS - PEOPLE LIVING WITH HIV/AIDS:**

NA

**HIV/AIDS - DEATHS:**

NA

## GOVERNMENT :: SAINT PIERRE AND MIQUELON

**COUNTRY NAME:**

conventional long form: Territorial Collectivity of Saint Pierre and Miquelon

conventional short form: Saint Pierre and Miquelon

local long form: Departement de Saint-Pierre et Miquelon

local short form: Saint-Pierre et Miquelon

etymology: Saint-Pierre is named after Saint PETER, the patron saint of fishermen; Miquelon may be a corruption of the Basque name Mikelon

**DEPENDENCY STATUS:**

overseas collectivity of France

**GOVERNMENT TYPE:**

parliamentary democracy (Territorial Council); overseas collectivity of France

**CAPITAL:**

name: Saint-Pierre

geographic coordinates: 46 46 N, 56 11 W

time difference: UTC-3 (2 hours ahead of Washington, DC, during Standard Time)

daylight saving time: +1hr, begins second Sunday in March; ends first Sunday in November

**ADMINISTRATIVE DIVISIONS:**

none (territorial overseas collectivity of France); note - there are no first-order administrative divisions as defined by the US Government, but there are 2 communes at the second order - Saint Pierre, Miquelon

**INDEPENDENCE:**

none (overseas collectivity collectivity of France; has been under French control since 1763)

**NATIONAL HOLIDAY:**

Fete de la Federation, 14 July (1790)

**CONSTITUTION:**

history: 4 October 1958 (French Constitution) (2018)

amendments: amendment procedures of France's constitution apply (2018)

**LEGAL SYSTEM:**

French civil law

**CITIZENSHIP:**

see France

**SUFFRAGE:**

18 years of age; universal

**EXECUTIVE BRANCH:**

chief of state: President Emmanuel MACRON (since 14 May 2017); represented by Prefect Thierry DEVIMEUX (since 17 January 2018)

head of government: President of Territorial Council Stephane LENORMAND (since 24 October 2017)

cabinet: Le Cabinet du Prefet

elections/appointments: French president directly elected by absolute majority popular vote in 2 rounds if needed for a 5-year term (eligible for a second term); election last held on 23 April and 6 May 2017 (next to be held in 2022); prefect appointed by French president on the advice of French Ministry of Interior

## LEGISLATIVE BRANCH:

**description:** unicameral Territorial Council or Conseil Territorial (19 seats - Saint Pierre 15, Miquelon 4; members directly elected in single-seat constituencies by absolute majority vote in 2 rounds if needed to serve 6-year terms);
Saint Pierre and Miquelon indirectly elects 1 senator to the French Senate by an electoral college to serve a 6-year term and directly elects 1 deputy to the French National Assembly by absolute majority vote to serve a 5-year term

**elections:** Territorial Council - last held on 19 March 2017 (next to be held in March 2023)
French Senate - last held on 28 September 2014 (next to be held no later than September 2020)
French National Assembly - last held on 17 June 2012 (next to be held by June 2017)

**election results:** Territorial Council - percent of vote by party - AD 70.2%, Cap sur l'Avenir 29.8%; seats by party - AD 17, Cap sur l'Avenir 2
French Senate - percent of vote by party - NA; seats by party - AD 1 (affiliated with UMP)
French National Assembly - percent of vote by party - NA; seats by party - Ensemble pour l'Avenir 1 (affiliated with PRG)

## JUDICIAL BRANCH:

**highest courts:** Superior Tribunal of Appeals or Tribunal Superieur d'Appel (composition NA)

**judge selection and term of office:** judge selection and tenure NA

**subordinate courts:** NA

## POLITICAL PARTIES AND LEADERS:

Archipelago Tomorrow or AD (affiliated with UMP)
Cap sur l'Avenir [Annick GIRARDIN] (affiliated with Left Radical Party)
Togerther for the Future (Ensemble pour l'Avenir) (affiliated with PRG)SPM ensemble

## INTERNATIONAL ORGANIZATION PARTICIPATION:

UPU, WFTU (NGOs)

## DIPLOMATIC REPRESENTATION IN THE US:

none (territorial overseas collectivity of France)

## DIPLOMATIC REPRESENTATION FROM THE US:

none (territorial overseas collectivity of France)

## FLAG DESCRIPTION:

a yellow three-masted sailing ship facing the hoist side rides on a blue background with scattered, white, wavy lines under the ship; a continuous black-over-white wavy line divides the ship from the white wavy lines; on the hoist side, a vertical band is divided into three parts: the top part (called ikkurina) is red with a green diagonal cross extending to the corners overlaid by a white cross dividing the rectangle into four sections; the middle part has a white background with an ermine pattern; the third part has a red background with two stylized yellow lions outlined in black, one above the other; these three heraldic arms represent settlement by colonists from the Basque Country (top), Brittany, and Normandy; the blue on the main portion of the flag symbolizes the Atlantic Ocean and the stylized ship represents the Grande Hermine in which Jacques Cartier "discovered" the islands in 1536

**note:** the flag of France used for official occasions

## NATIONAL SYMBOL(S):

16th-century sailing ship

## NATIONAL ANTHEM:

**note:** as a collectivity of France, "La Marseillaise" is official (see France)

# ECONOMY :: SAINT PIERRE AND MIQUELON

## ECONOMY - OVERVIEW:

The inhabitants have traditionally earned their livelihood by fishing and by servicing fishing fleets operating off the coast of Newfoundland. The economy has been declining, however, because of disputes with Canada over fishing quotas and a steady decline in the number of ships stopping at Saint Pierre. The services sector accounted for 86% of GDP in 2010, the last year data is available for. Government employment accounts for than 46% of the GDP, and 78% of the population is working age.

The government hopes an expansion of tourism will boost economic prospects. Fish farming, crab fishing, and agriculture are being developed to diversify the local economy. Recent test drilling for oil may pave the way for development of the energy sector. Trade is the second largest sector in terms of value added created, where it contributes significantly to economic activity. The extractive industries and energy sector is the third largest sector of activity in the archipelago, attributable in part to the construction of a new thermal power plant in 2015.

## GDP (PURCHASING POWER PARITY):

$261.3 million (2015 est.)

$215.3 million (2006 est.)

**note:** supplemented by annual payments from France of about $60 million

**country comparison to the world:** 218

## GDP (OFFICIAL EXCHANGE RATE):

$261.3 million (2015 est.) (2015 est.)

## GDP - REAL GROWTH RATE:

NA

## GDP - PER CAPITA (PPP):

$46,200 (2006 est.)

$34,900 (2005)

**country comparison to the world:** 36

## GDP - COMPOSITION, BY SECTOR OF ORIGIN:

**agriculture:** 2% (2006 est.)

**industry:** 15% (2006 est.)

**services:** 83% (2006 est.)

## AGRICULTURE - PRODUCTS:

vegetables; poultry, cattle, sheep, pigs; fish

## INDUSTRIES:

fish processing and supply base for fishing fleets; tourism

## INDUSTRIAL PRODUCTION GROWTH RATE:

NA

## LABOR FORCE:

4,429 (2015)

**country comparison to the world:** 224

## LABOR FORCE - BY OCCUPATION:

**agriculture:** 18%

**industry:** 41%

**services:** 41% (1996 est.)

## UNEMPLOYMENT RATE:

8.7% (2015 est.)

9.9% (2008 est.)

**country comparison to the world:** 125

## POPULATION BELOW POVERTY LINE:

NA

**HOUSEHOLD INCOME OR CONSUMPTION BY PERCENTAGE SHARE:**

lowest 10%: NA

highest 10%: NA

**BUDGET:**

revenues: 70 million (1996 est.)

expenditures: 60 million (1996 est.)

**TAXES AND OTHER REVENUES:**

26.8% (of GDP) (1996 est.)

country comparison to the world: 104

**BUDGET SURPLUS (+) OR DEFICIT (-):**

3.8% (of GDP) (1996 est.)

country comparison to the world: 10

**FISCAL YEAR:**

calendar year

**INFLATION RATE (CONSUMER PRICES):**

1.5% (2015)

4.5% (2010)

country comparison to the world: 85

**EXPORTS:**

$6.641 million (2010 est.)

$5.5 million (2005 est.)

country comparison to the world: 217

**EXPORTS - COMMODITIES:**

fish and fish products, soybeans, animal feed, mollusks and crustaceans, fox and mink pelts

**IMPORTS:**

$95.35 million (2010 est.)

$68.2 million (2005 est.)

country comparison to the world: 216

**IMPORTS - COMMODITIES:**

meat, clothing, fuel, electrical equipment, machinery, building materials

**DEBT - EXTERNAL:**

NA

**EXCHANGE RATES:**

euros (EUR) per US dollar -

0.885 (2017 est.)

0.903 (2016 est.)

0.9214 (2015 est.)

0.885 (2014 est.)

0.7634 (2013 est.)

## ENERGY :: SAINT PIERRE AND MIQUELON

**ELECTRICITY - PRODUCTION:**

46 million kWh (2016 est.)

country comparison to the world: 206

**ELECTRICITY - CONSUMPTION:**

42.78 million kWh (2016 est.)

country comparison to the world: 206

**ELECTRICITY - EXPORTS:**

0 kWh (2016 est.)

country comparison to the world: 190

**ELECTRICITY - IMPORTS:**

0 kWh (2016 est.)

country comparison to the world: 192

**ELECTRICITY - INSTALLED GENERATING CAPACITY:**

27,600 kW (2016 est.)

country comparison to the world: 202

**ELECTRICITY - FROM FOSSIL FUELS:**

96% of total installed capacity (2016 est.)

country comparison to the world: 42

**ELECTRICITY - FROM NUCLEAR FUELS:**

0% of total installed capacity (2017 est.)

country comparison to the world: 174

**ELECTRICITY - FROM HYDROELECTRIC PLANTS:**

0% of total installed capacity (2017 est.)

country comparison to the world: 197

**ELECTRICITY - FROM OTHER RENEWABLE SOURCES:**

4% of total installed capacity (2017 est.)

country comparison to the world: 118

**CRUDE OIL - PRODUCTION:**

0 bbl/day (2017 est.)

country comparison to the world: 192

**CRUDE OIL - EXPORTS:**

0 bbl/day (2015 est.)

country comparison to the world: 186

**CRUDE OIL - IMPORTS:**

0 bbl/day (2015 est.)

country comparison to the world: 188

**CRUDE OIL - PROVED RESERVES:**

0 bbl (1 January 2018 est.)

country comparison to the world: 188

**REFINED PETROLEUM PRODUCTS - PRODUCTION:**

0 bbl/day (2015 est.)

country comparison to the world: 195

**REFINED PETROLEUM PRODUCTS - CONSUMPTION:**

660 bbl/day (2016 est.)

country comparison to the world: 208

**REFINED PETROLEUM PRODUCTS - EXPORTS:**

0 bbl/day (2015 est.)

country comparison to the world: 196

**REFINED PETROLEUM PRODUCTS - IMPORTS:**

650 bbl/day (2015 est.)

country comparison to the world: 204

**NATURAL GAS - PRODUCTION:**

0 cu m (2017 est.)

country comparison to the world: 190

**NATURAL GAS - CONSUMPTION:**

0 cu m (2017 est.)

country comparison to the world: 192

**NATURAL GAS - EXPORTS:**

0 cu m (2017 est.)

country comparison to the world: 175

**NATURAL GAS - IMPORTS:**

0 cu m (2017 est.)

country comparison to the world: 181

**NATURAL GAS - PROVED RESERVES:**

0 cu m (1 January 2014 est.)

country comparison to the world: 187

**CARBON DIOXIDE EMISSIONS FROM CONSUMPTION OF ENERGY:**

100,200 Mt (2017 est.)

country comparison to the world: 206

## COMMUNICATIONS :: SAINT PIERRE AND MIQUELON

**TELEPHONES - FIXED LINES:**

total subscriptions: 4,800 (July 2016 est.)

subscriptions per 100 inhabitants: 80 (July 2016 est.)

country comparison to the world: 206

**TELEPHONE SYSTEM:**

general assessment: adequate

international: country code - 508; radiotelephone communication with most countries in the world; satellite earth station - 1 in French domestic satellite system

**BROADCAST MEDIA:**

2 TV stations with a third repeater station, all part of the French Overseas Network; radio stations on St. Pierre and on Miquelon are part of the French Overseas Network (2007)

**INTERNET COUNTRY CODE:**

.pm

**INTERNET USERS:**

total: 4,500 (July 2016 est.)

percent of population: 79.5% (July 2016 est.)

country comparison to the world: 216

## TRANSPORTATION :: SAINT PIERRE AND MIQUELON

**AIRPORTS:**
2 (2013)

country comparison to the world: 206

**AIRPORTS - WITH PAVED RUNWAYS:**

total: 2 (2017)

1,524 to 2,437 m: 1 (2017)

914 to 1,523 m: 1 (2017)

**ROADWAYS:**

total: 117 km (2009)

paved: 80 km (2009)

unpaved: 37 km (2009)

country comparison to the world: 215

**PORTS AND TERMINALS:**

major seaport(s): Saint-Pierre

## MILITARY AND SECURITY :: SAINT PIERRE AND MIQUELON

**MILITARY - NOTE:**
defense is the responsibility of France

## TRANSNATIONAL ISSUES :: SAINT PIERRE AND MIQUELON

**DISPUTES - INTERNATIONAL:**
none

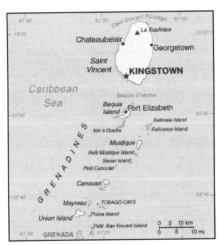

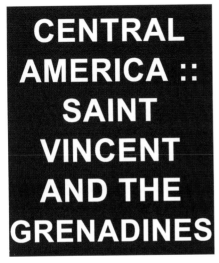

## INTRODUCTION :: SAINT VINCENT AND THE GRENADINES

### BACKGROUND:
Resistance by native Caribs prevented colonization on Saint Vincent until 1719. Disputed between France and the UK for most of the 18th century, the island was ceded to the latter in 1783. Between 1960 and 1962, Saint Vincent and the Grenadines was a separate administrative unit of the Federation of the West Indies. Autonomy was granted in 1969 and independence in 1979.

## GEOGRAPHY :: SAINT VINCENT AND THE GRENADINES

### LOCATION:
Caribbean, islands between the Caribbean Sea and North Atlantic Ocean, north of Trinidad and Tobago

### GEOGRAPHIC COORDINATES:
13 15 N, 61 12 W

### MAP REFERENCES:
Central America and the Caribbean

### AREA:
total: 389 sq km (Saint Vincent 344 sq km)

land: 389 sq km

water: 0 sq km

country comparison to the world: 205

### AREA - COMPARATIVE:
twice the size of Washington, DC

### LAND BOUNDARIES:
0 km

### COASTLINE:
84 km

### MARITIME CLAIMS:
territorial sea: 12 nm

exclusive economic zone: 200 nm

contiguous zone: 24 nm

continental shelf: 200 nm

### CLIMATE:
tropical; little seasonal temperature variation; rainy season (May to November)

### TERRAIN:
volcanic, mountainous

### ELEVATION:
0 m lowest point: Caribbean Sea

1234 highest point: La Soufriere

### NATURAL RESOURCES:
hydropower, arable land

### LAND USE:
agricultural land: 25.6% (2011 est.)

arable land: 12.8% (2011 est.) / permanent crops: 7.7% (2011 est.) / permanent pasture: 5.1% (2011 est.)

forest: 68.7% (2011 est.)

other: 5.7% (2011 est.)

### IRRIGATED LAND:
10 sq km (2012)

### POPULATION DISTRIBUTION:
most of the population is concentrated in and around the capital of Kingstown

### NATURAL HAZARDS:
hurricanes; La Soufriere volcano on the island of Saint Vincent is a constant threat

volcanism: La Soufriere (1,234 m) on the island of Saint Vincent last erupted in 1979; the island of Saint Vincent is part of the volcanic island arc of the Lesser Antilles that extends from Saba in the north to Grenada in the south

### ENVIRONMENT - CURRENT ISSUES:
pollution of coastal waters and shorelines from discharges by pleasure yachts and other effluents; in some areas, pollution is severe enough to make swimming prohibitive; poor land use planning; deforestation; watershed management and squatter settlement control

### ENVIRONMENT - INTERNATIONAL AGREEMENTS:
party to: Biodiversity, Climate Change, Climate Change-Kyoto Protocol, Desertification, Endangered Species, Environmental Modification, Hazardous Wastes, Law of the Sea, Marine Dumping, Ozone Layer Protection, Ship Pollution, Whaling

signed, but not ratified: none of the selected agreements

### GEOGRAPHY - NOTE:
the administration of the islands of the Grenadines group is divided between Saint Vincent and the Grenadines and Grenada; Saint Vincent and the Grenadines is comprised of 32 islands and cays

# PEOPLE AND SOCIETY :: SAINT VINCENT AND THE GRENADINES

### POPULATION:
101,844 (July 2018 est.)

country comparison to the world: 195

### NATIONALITY:
noun: Saint Vincentian(s) or Vincentian(s)

adjective: Saint Vincentian or Vincentian

### ETHNIC GROUPS:
African/black 72.8%, mixed 20%, Carib 3.6%, East Indian 1.4%, European 4%, other 1.5%, unspecified 0.6% (2001 est.)

### LANGUAGES:
English, Vincentian Creole English, French patois

### RELIGIONS:
Protestant 70.6% (Anglican 17.8%, Pentecostal 17.6%, Methodist 10.8%, Seventh Day Adventist 10.2%, Baptist 10%, Church of God 2.5%, Brethren 1.3%, Salvation Army .3%, Presbyterian/Congregational .1%), Roman Catholic 7.5%, Evangelical 2.8%, Rastafarian 1.5%, Jehovah's Witness 0.6%, other 6.7%, none 8.8%, unspecified 1.5% (2001 est.)

### AGE STRUCTURE:
0-14 years: 20.87% (male 10,725 /female 10,534)

15-24 years: 15.58% (male 8,003 /female 7,865)

25-54 years: 42.7% (male 22,567 /female 20,924)

55-64 years: 11.03% (male 5,792 /female 5,437)

65 years and over: 9.82% (male 4,715 /female 5,282) (2018 est.)

### DEPENDENCY RATIOS:
total dependency ratio: 46.8 (2015 est.)

youth dependency ratio: 36 (2015 est.)

elderly dependency ratio: 10.8 (2015 est.)

potential support ratio: 9.3 (2015 est.)

### MEDIAN AGE:
total: 34.2 years

male: 34.3 years

female: 34 years (2018 est.)

country comparison to the world: 87

### POPULATION GROWTH RATE:
-0.23% (2018 est.)

country comparison to the world: 209

### BIRTH RATE:
13 births/1,000 population (2018 est.)

country comparison to the world: 149

### DEATH RATE:
7.4 deaths/1,000 population (2018 est.)

country comparison to the world: 117

### NET MIGRATION RATE:
-8.4 migrant(s)/1,000 population (2017 est.)

country comparison to the world: 208

### POPULATION DISTRIBUTION:
most of the population is concentrated in and around the capital of Kingstown

### URBANIZATION:
urban population: 52.2% of total population (2018)

rate of urbanization: 1.03% annual rate of change (2015-20 est.)

### MAJOR URBAN AREAS - POPULATION:
27,000 KINGSTOWN (capital) (2018)

### SEX RATIO:
at birth: 1.03 male(s)/female (2017 est.)

0-14 years: 1.02 male(s)/female (2017 est.)

15-24 years: 1.02 male(s)/female (2017 est.)

25-54 years: 1.08 male(s)/female (2017 est.)

55-64 years: 1.06 male(s)/female (2017 est.)

65 years and over: 0.87 male(s)/female (2017 est.)

total population: 1.03 male(s)/female (2017 est.)

### MATERNAL MORTALITY RATE:
45 deaths/100,000 live births (2015 est.)

country comparison to the world: 99

### INFANT MORTALITY RATE:
total: 11.7 deaths/1,000 live births (2018 est.)

male: 12.7 deaths/1,000 live births (2018 est.)

female: 10.6 deaths/1,000 live births (2018 est.)

country comparison to the world: 122

### LIFE EXPECTANCY AT BIRTH:
total population: 75.8 years (2018 est.)

male: 73.7 years (2018 est.)

female: 77.9 years (2018 est.)

country comparison to the world: 101

### TOTAL FERTILITY RATE:
1.78 children born/woman (2018 est.)

country comparison to the world: 154

### HEALTH EXPENDITURES:
8.6% of GDP (2014)

country comparison to the world: 46

### HOSPITAL BED DENSITY:
2.6 beds/1,000 population (2014)

### DRINKING WATER SOURCE:
improved:

urban: 95.1% of population (2015 est.)

rural: 95.1% of population (2015 est.)

total: 95.1% of population (2015 est.)

unimproved:

urban: 4.9% of population (2015 est.)

rural: 4.9% of population (2015 est.)

total: 4.9% of population (2015 est.)

### SANITATION FACILITY ACCESS:
improved:

urban: 76.1% of population (2007 est.)

rural: 76.1% of population (2007 est.)

total: 76.1% of population (2007 est.)

unimproved:

urban: 23.9% of population (2007 est.)

rural: 23.9% of population (2007 est.)

total: 23.9% of population (2007 est.)

### HIV/AIDS - ADULT PREVALENCE RATE:
NA

### HIV/AIDS - PEOPLE LIVING WITH HIV/AIDS:
NA

### HIV/AIDS - DEATHS:
NA

### MAJOR INFECTIOUS DISEASES:
note: active local transmission of Zika virus by Aedes species mosquitoes has been identified in this country (as of August 2016); it poses an important risk (a large number of cases possible) among US citizens if bitten by an infective mosquito; other less common ways to get Zika are through sex, via blood transfusion, or during pregnancy, in which the pregnant woman passes Zika virus to her fetus

**OBESITY - ADULT PREVALENCE RATE:**

23.7% (2016)

country comparison to the world: 64

**EDUCATION EXPENDITURES:**

5.8% of GDP (2016)

country comparison to the world: 42

**UNEMPLOYMENT, YOUTH AGES 15-24:**

total: 33.8% (2008 est.)

male: 27.8% (2008 est.)

female: 41.4% (2008 est.)

country comparison to the world: 25

# GOVERNMENT :: SAINT VINCENT AND THE GRENADINES

**COUNTRY NAME:**

conventional long form: none

conventional short form: Saint Vincent and the Grenadines

etymology: Saint Vincent was named by explorer Christopher COLUMBUS after Saint VINCENT of Saragossa because the 22 January 1498 day of discovery was the saint's feast day

**GOVERNMENT TYPE:**

parliamentary democracy (House of Assembly) under a constitutional monarchy; a Commonwealth realm

**CAPITAL:**

name: Kingstown

geographic coordinates: 13 08 N, 61 13 W

time difference: UTC-4 (1 hour ahead of Washington, DC, during Standard Time)

**ADMINISTRATIVE DIVISIONS:**

6 parishes; Charlotte, Grenadines, Saint Andrew, Saint David, Saint George, Saint Patrick

**INDEPENDENCE:**

27 October 1979 (from the UK)

**NATIONAL HOLIDAY:**

Independence Day, 27 October (1979)

**CONSTITUTION:**

history: previous 1969, 1975; latest drafted 26 July 1979, effective 27 October 1979 (The Saint Vincent Constitution Order 1979) (2018)

amendments: proposed by the House of Assembly; passage requires at least two-thirds majority vote of the Assembly membership and assent to by the governor general; passage of amendments to constitutional sections on fundamental rights and freedoms, citizen protections, various government functions and authorities, and constitutional amendment procedures requires approval by the Assembly membership, approval in a referendum of at least two-thirds of the votes cast, and assent to by governor general (2018)

**LEGAL SYSTEM:**

English common law

**INTERNATIONAL LAW ORGANIZATION PARTICIPATION:**

has not submitted an ICJ jurisdiction declaration; accepts ICCt jurisdiction

**CITIZENSHIP:**

citizenship by birth: yes

citizenship by descent only: at least one parent must be a citizen of Saint Vincent and the Grenadines

dual citizenship recognized: yes

residency requirement for naturalization: 7 years

**SUFFRAGE:**

18 years of age; universal

**EXECUTIVE BRANCH:**

chief of state: Queen ELIZABETH II (since 6 February 1952); represented by Governor General Sir Frederick Nathaniel BALLANTYNE (since 2 September 2002)

head of government: Prime Minister Ralph E. GONSALVES (since 29 March 2001)

cabinet: Cabinet appointed by the governor general on the advice of the prime minister

elections/appointments: the monarchy is hereditary; governor general appointed by the monarch; following legislative elections, the leader of the majority party usually appointed prime minister by the governor general; deputy prime minister appointed by the governor general on the advice of the prime minister

**LEGISLATIVE BRANCH:**

description: unicameral House of Assembly (23 seats; 15 representatives directly elected in single-seat constituencies by simple majority vote, 6 senators appointed by the governor general, and 2 ex officio members - the speaker of the house and the attorney general; members serve 5-year terms)

elections: last held on 9 December 2015 (next to be held in 2020)

election results: percent of vote by party - ULP 52.3%, NDP 47.4%, other 0.3%; seats by party - ULP 8, NDP 7

**JUDICIAL BRANCH:**

highest courts: the Eastern Caribbean Supreme Court (ECSC) is the superior court of the Organization of Eastern Caribbean States; the ECSC - headquartered on St. Lucia - consists of the Court of Appeal - headed by the chief justice and 4 judges - and the High Court with 18 judges; the Court of Appeal is itinerant, travelling to member states on a schedule to hear appeals from the High Court and subordinate courts; High Court judges reside at the member states with 2 assigned to Saint Vincent and the Grenadines; note - Saint Vincent and the Grenadines is also a member of the Caribbean Court of Justice

judge selection and term of office: chief justice of Eastern Caribbean Supreme Court appointed by Her Majesty, Queen ELIZABETH II; other justices and judges appointed by the Judicial and Legal Services Commission, an independent body of judicial officials; Court of Appeal justices appointed for life with mandatory retirement at age 65; High Court judges appointed for life with mandatory retirement at age 62

subordinate courts: magistrates' courts

**POLITICAL PARTIES AND LEADERS:**

Democratic Republican Party or DRP [Anesia BAPTISTE]
New Democratic Party or NDP [Godwin L. FRIDAY]
Unity Labor Party or ULP [Dr. Ralph GONSALVES] (formed in 1994 by the coalition of Saint Vincent Labor Party or SVLP and the Movement for National Unity or MNU)
SVG Green Party or SVGP [Ivan O'NEAL]

**INTERNATIONAL ORGANIZATION PARTICIPATION:**

ACP, AOSIS, C, Caricom, CDB, CELAC, FAO, G-77, IBRD, ICAO, ICCt, ICRM, IDA, IFAD, IFRCS, ILO, IMF, IMO, Interpol, IOC, IOM, ISO (subscriber), ITU, MIGA, NAM, OAS, OECS, OPANAL, OPCW, Petrocaribe, UN, UNCTAD, UNESCO, UNIDO, UPU, WFTU (NGOs), WHO, WIPO, WTO

**DIPLOMATIC REPRESENTATION IN THE US:**

chief of mission: Ambassador Lou-Anne Gaylene GILCHRIST (since 18 January 2017) chancery: 1627 K Street, NW, Suite 1202, Washington, DC 20006

telephone: [1] (202) 364-6730

FAX: [1] (202) 364-6730

consulate(s) general: New York

**DIPLOMATIC REPRESENTATION FROM THE US:**

the US does not have an embassy in Saint Vincent and the Grenadines; the US Ambassador to Barbados is accredited to Saint Vincent and the Grenadines

**FLAG DESCRIPTION:**

three vertical bands of blue (hoist side), gold (double width), and green; the gold band bears three green diamonds arranged in a V pattern, which stands for Vincent; the diamonds recall the islands as "the Gems of the Antilles" and are set slightly lowered in the gold band to reflect the nation's position in the Antilles; blue conveys the colors of a tropical sky and crystal waters, yellow signifies the golden Grenadine sands, and green represents lush vegetation

**NATIONAL SYMBOL(S):**

Saint Vincent parrot; national colors: blue, gold, green

**NATIONAL ANTHEM:**

name: St. Vincent! Land So Beautiful!

lyrics/music: Phyllis Joyce MCCLEAN PUNNETT/Joel Bertram MIGUEL

note: adopted 1967

## ECONOMY :: SAINT VINCENT AND THE GRENADINES

**ECONOMY - OVERVIEW:**

Success of the economy hinges upon seasonal variations in agriculture, tourism, and construction activity, as well as remittances. Much of the workforce is employed in banana production and tourism. Saint Vincent and the Grenadines is home to a small offshore banking sector and continues to fully adopt international regulatory standards.

This lower-middle-income country remains vulnerable to natural and external shocks. The economy has shown some signs of recovery due to increased tourist arrivals, falling oil prices and renewed growth in the construction sector. The much anticipated international airport opened in early 2017 with hopes for increased airlift and tourism activity. The government's ability to invest in social programs and respond to external shocks is constrained by its high public debt burden, which was 67% of GDP at the end of 2013.

**GDP (PURCHASING POWER PARITY):**

$1.265 billion (2017 est.)

$1.256 billion (2016 est.)

$1.246 billion (2015 est.)

note: data are in 2017 dollars

country comparison to the world: 202

**GDP (OFFICIAL EXCHANGE RATE):**

$785 million (2017 est.) (2017 est.)

**GDP - REAL GROWTH RATE:**

0.7% (2017 est.)

0.8% (2016 est.)

0.8% (2015 est.)

country comparison to the world: 190

**GDP - PER CAPITA (PPP):**

$11,500 (2017 est.)

$11,400 (2016 est.)

$11,300 (2015 est.)

note: data are in 2017 dollars

country comparison to the world: 133

**GROSS NATIONAL SAVING:**

12.1% of GDP (2017 est.)

10.3% of GDP (2016 est.)

10.4% of GDP (2015 est.)

country comparison to the world: 148

**GDP - COMPOSITION, BY END USE:**

household consumption: 87.3% (2017 est.)

government consumption: 16.6% (2017 est.)

investment in fixed capital: 10.8% (2017 est.)

investment in inventories: -0.2% (2017 est.)

exports of goods and services: 37.1% (2017 est.)

imports of goods and services: -51.7% (2017 est.)

**GDP - COMPOSITION, BY SECTOR OF ORIGIN:**

agriculture: 7.1% (2017 est.)

industry: 17.4% (2017 est.)

services: 75.5% (2017 est.)

**AGRICULTURE - PRODUCTS:**

bananas, coconuts, sweet potatoes, spices; small numbers of cattle, sheep, pigs, goats; fish

**INDUSTRIES:**

tourism; food processing, cement, furniture, clothing, starch

**INDUSTRIAL PRODUCTION GROWTH RATE:**

2.5% (2017 est.)

country comparison to the world: 118

**LABOR FORCE:**

57,520 (2007 est.)

country comparison to the world: 188

**LABOR FORCE - BY OCCUPATION:**

agriculture: 26%

industry: 17%

services: 57% (1980 est.)

**UNEMPLOYMENT RATE:**

18.8% (2008 est.)

country comparison to the world: 182

**POPULATION BELOW POVERTY LINE:**

NA

**HOUSEHOLD INCOME OR CONSUMPTION BY PERCENTAGE SHARE:**

lowest 10%: NA

highest 10%: NA

**BUDGET:**

revenues: 225.2 million (2017 est.)

expenditures: 230 million (2017 est.)

**TAXES AND OTHER REVENUES:**

28.7% (of GDP) (2017 est.)

country comparison to the world: 93

**BUDGET SURPLUS (+) OR DEFICIT (-):**

-0.6% (of GDP) (2017 est.)

country comparison to the world: 66

**PUBLIC DEBT:**

73.8% of GDP (2017 est.)

82.8% of GDP (2016 est.)

country comparison to the world: 42

**FISCAL YEAR:**

calendar year

**INFLATION RATE (CONSUMER PRICES):**

2.2% (2017 est.)

-0.2% (2016 est.)

country comparison to the world: 115

**CENTRAL BANK DISCOUNT RATE:**

6.5% (31 December 2010)

6.5% (31 December 2009)

country comparison to the world: 64

**COMMERCIAL BANK PRIME LENDING RATE:**

8.75% (31 December 2017 est.)

9.12% (31 December 2016 est.)

country comparison to the world: 96

**STOCK OF NARROW MONEY:**

$190.6 million (31 December 2017 est.)

$177.7 million (31 December 2016 est.)

country comparison to the world: 185

**STOCK OF BROAD MONEY:**

$190.6 million (31 December 2017 est.)

$177.7 million (31 December 2016 est.)

country comparison to the world: 188

**STOCK OF DOMESTIC CREDIT:**

$443 million (31 December 2017 est.)

$424.6 million (31 December 2016 est.)

country comparison to the world: 179

**CURRENT ACCOUNT BALANCE:**

-$116 million (2017 est.)

-$122 million (2016 est.)

country comparison to the world: 89

**EXPORTS:**

$48.6 million (2017 est.)

$47.3 million (2016 est.)

country comparison to the world: 203

**EXPORTS - PARTNERS:**

Jordan 40.7%, France 12.5%, Barbados 7%, St. Lucia 6.8%, Antigua and Barbuda 5.7%, US 5.5%, Trinidad and Tobago 4.7% (2017)

**EXPORTS - COMMODITIES:**

bananas, eddoes and dasheen (taro), arrowroot starch; tennis racquets

**IMPORTS:**

$295.9 million (2017 est.)

$294.6 million (2016 est.)

country comparison to the world: 204

**IMPORTS - COMMODITIES:**

foodstuffs, machinery and equipment, chemicals and fertilizers, minerals and fuels

**IMPORTS - PARTNERS:**

US 36.8%, Trinidad and Tobago 19.1%, UK 7%, China 5.8% (2017)

**RESERVES OF FOREIGN EXCHANGE AND GOLD:**

$182.1 million (31 December 2017 est.)

$192.3 million (31 December 2016 est.)

country comparison to the world: 178

**DEBT - EXTERNAL:**

$362.2 million (31 December 2017 est.)

$330.8 million (31 December 2016 est.)

country comparison to the world: 183

**STOCK OF DIRECT FOREIGN INVESTMENT - AT HOME:**

(31 December 2009 est.)

**EXCHANGE RATES:**

East Caribbean dollars (XCD) per US dollar -

2.7 (2017 est.)

2.7 (2016 est.)

2.7 (2015 est.)

2.7 (2014 est.)

2.7 (2013 est.)

## ENERGY :: SAINT VINCENT AND THE GRENADINES

**ELECTRICITY ACCESS:**

population without electricity: 25,587 (2012)

electrification - total population: 76% (2012)

electrification - urban areas: 100% (2012)

electrification - rural areas: 32% (2012)

**ELECTRICITY - PRODUCTION:**

157 million kWh (2016 est.)

country comparison to the world: 196

**ELECTRICITY - CONSUMPTION:**

146 million kWh (2016 est.)

country comparison to the world: 198

**ELECTRICITY - EXPORTS:**

0 kWh (2016 est.)

country comparison to the world: 191

**ELECTRICITY - IMPORTS:**

0 kWh (2016 est.)

country comparison to the world: 193

**ELECTRICITY - INSTALLED GENERATING CAPACITY:**

54,000 kW (2016 est.)

country comparison to the world: 189

**ELECTRICITY - FROM FOSSIL FUELS:**

85% of total installed capacity (2016 est.)

country comparison to the world: 72

**ELECTRICITY - FROM NUCLEAR FUELS:**

0% of total installed capacity (2017 est.)

country comparison to the world: 175

**ELECTRICITY - FROM HYDROELECTRIC PLANTS:**

13% of total installed capacity (2017 est.)

country comparison to the world: 110

**ELECTRICITY - FROM OTHER RENEWABLE SOURCES:**

2% of total installed capacity (2017 est.)

country comparison to the world: 143

**CRUDE OIL - PRODUCTION:**

0 bbl/day (2017 est.)

country comparison to the world: 193

**CRUDE OIL - EXPORTS:**

0 bbl/day (2015 est.)

country comparison to the world: 187

**CRUDE OIL - IMPORTS:**

0 bbl/day (2015 est.)

country comparison to the world: 189

**CRUDE OIL - PROVED RESERVES:**

0 bbl (1 January 2018 est.)

country comparison to the world: 189

**REFINED PETROLEUM PRODUCTS - PRODUCTION:**

0 bbl/day (2015 est.)

country comparison to the world: 196

**REFINED PETROLEUM PRODUCTS - CONSUMPTION:**

1,620 bbl/day (2016 est.)

country comparison to the world: 198

**REFINED PETROLEUM PRODUCTS - EXPORTS:**

0 bbl/day (2015 est.)

country comparison to the world: 197

**REFINED PETROLEUM PRODUCTS - IMPORTS:**

1,621 bbl/day (2015 est.)

country comparison to the world: 194

**NATURAL GAS - PRODUCTION:**

0 cu m (2017 est.)

country comparison to the world: 191

**NATURAL GAS - CONSUMPTION:**

0 cu m (2017 est.)

country comparison to the world: 193

**NATURAL GAS - EXPORTS:**

0 cu m (2017 est.)

country comparison to the world: 176

**NATURAL GAS - IMPORTS:**

0 cu m (2017 est.)

country comparison to the world: 182

**NATURAL GAS - PROVED RESERVES:**

0 cu m (1 January 2014 est.)

country comparison to the world: 188

**CARBON DIOXIDE EMISSIONS FROM CONSUMPTION OF ENERGY:**

226,800 Mt (2017 est.)

country comparison to the world: 197

## COMMUNICATIONS :: SAINT VINCENT AND THE GRENADINES

**TELEPHONES - FIXED LINES:**

total subscriptions: 20,111 (2017 est.)

subscriptions per 100 inhabitants: 20 (2017 est.)

country comparison to the world: 178

**TELEPHONES - MOBILE CELLULAR:**

total subscriptions: 116,161 (2017 est.)

subscriptions per 100 inhabitants: 114 (2017 est.)

country comparison to the world: 190

**TELEPHONE SYSTEM:**

general assessment: adequate islandwide, fully automatic telephone system (2016)

domestic: fixed-line teledensity exceeds 19 per 100 persons and mobile-cellular teledensity is about 103 per 100 persons (2016)

international: country code - 1-784; the East Caribbean Fiber System and Southern Caribbean Fiber submarine cables carry international calls; connectivity also provided by VHF/UHF radiotelephone from Saint Vincent to Barbados; SHF radiotelephone to Grenada and Saint Lucia; access to Intelsat earth station in Martinique through Saint Lucia (2016)

**BROADCAST MEDIA:**

St. Vincent and the Grenadines Broadcasting Corporation operates 1 TV station and 5 repeater stations that provide near total coverage to the multi-island state; multi-channel cable TV service available; a partially government-funded national radio service broadcasts on 1 station and has 2 repeater stations; about a dozen privately owned radio stations and repeater stations (2007)

**INTERNET COUNTRY CODE:**

.vc

**INTERNET USERS:**

total: 53,000 (July 2016 est.)

percent of population: 51.8% (July 2016 est.)

country comparison to the world: 192

**BROADBAND - FIXED SUBSCRIPTIONS:**

total: 24,507 (2017 est.)

subscriptions per 100 inhabitants: 24 (2017 est.)

country comparison to the world: 146

## TRANSPORTATION :: SAINT VINCENT AND THE GRENADINES

**NATIONAL AIR TRANSPORT SYSTEM:**

number of registered air carriers: 2 (2015)

inventory of registered aircraft operated by air carriers: 11 (2015)

**CIVIL AIRCRAFT REGISTRATION COUNTRY CODE PREFIX:**

J8 (2016)

**AIRPORTS:**

6 (2013)

country comparison to the world: 175

**AIRPORTS - WITH PAVED RUNWAYS:**

total: 5 (2017)

1,524 to 2,437 m: 1 (2017)

914 to 1,523 m: 3 (2017)

under 914 m: 1 (2017)

**AIRPORTS - WITH UNPAVED RUNWAYS:**

total: 1 (2013)

under 914 m: 1 (2013)

**ROADWAYS:**

total: 829 km (2003)

paved: 580 km (2003)

unpaved: 249 km (2003)

country comparison to the world: 189

**MERCHANT MARINE:**

total: 882 (2017)

by type: bulk carrier 22, container ship 12, general cargo 198, oil tanker 17, other 633 (2017)

country comparison to the world: 26

**PORTS AND TERMINALS:**

major seaport(s): Kingstown

## MILITARY AND SECURITY :: SAINT VINCENT AND THE GRENADINES

**MILITARY BRANCHES:**

no regular military forces; Royal Saint Vincent and the Grenadines Police Force (RSVPF) (2013)

## TRANSNATIONAL ISSUES :: SAINT VINCENT AND THE GRENADINES

**DISPUTES - INTERNATIONAL:**

joins other Caribbean states to counter Venezuela's claim that Aves Island sustains human habitation, a criterion under UN Convention on the Law of the Sea, which permits Venezuela to extend its EEZ/continental shelf over a large portion of the eastern Caribbean Sea

**TRAFFICKING IN PERSONS:**

current situation: Saint Vincent and the Grenadines is a source, transit, and destination country for men, women, and children subjected to forced labor and sex trafficking; some children under 18 are pressured to engage in sex acts in exchange for money or gifts; foreign workers may experience forced labor and are particularly vulnerable when employed by small, foreign-owned companies; adults and children are vulnerable to forced labor domestically, especially in the agriculture sector

tier rating: Tier 2 Watch List – Saint Vincent and the Grenadines does not fully comply with the minimum standards for the elimination of trafficking; however, it is making significant efforts to do so; the government for the first time acknowledged a trafficking problem, launched an anti-trafficking public awareness campaign, and conducted anti-trafficking training for law enforcement, immigration, and labor officials; in 2014, authorities initiated three trafficking investigations, two of which were ultimately determined not to be trafficking cases, and did not prosecute or convict any trafficking offenders; the government did not identify or refer any potential trafficking victims to care (2015)

**ILLICIT DRUGS:**

transshipment point for South American drugs destined for the US

and Europe; small-scale cannabis
cultivation

# AUSTRALIA - OCEANIA :: SAMOA

## INTRODUCTION :: SAMOA

### BACKGROUND:

New Zealand occupied the German protectorate of Western Samoa at the outbreak of World War I in 1914. It continued to administer the islands as a mandate and then as a trust territory until 1962, when the islands became the first Polynesian nation to reestablish independence in the 20th century. The country dropped the "Western" from its name in 1997.

## GEOGRAPHY :: SAMOA

### LOCATION:
Oceania, group of islands in the South Pacific Ocean, about halfway between Hawaii and New Zealand

### GEOGRAPHIC COORDINATES:
13 35 S, 172 20 W

### MAP REFERENCES:
Oceania

### AREA:
total: 2,831 sq km

land: 2,821 sq km

water: 10 sq km

country comparison to the world: 178

### AREA - COMPARATIVE:
slightly smaller than Rhode Island

### LAND BOUNDARIES:
0 km

### COASTLINE:
403 km

### MARITIME CLAIMS:
territorial sea: 12 nm

exclusive economic zone: 200 nm

contiguous zone: 24 nm

### CLIMATE:
tropical; rainy season (November to April), dry season (May to October)

### TERRAIN:
two main islands (Savaii, Upolu) and several smaller islands and uninhabited islets; narrow coastal plain with volcanic, rugged mountains in interior

### ELEVATION:
0 m lowest point: Pacific Ocean

1857 highest point: Mount Silisili

### NATURAL RESOURCES:
hardwood forests, fish, hydropower

### LAND USE:
agricultural land: 12.4% (2011 est.)

arable land: 2.8% (2011 est.) / permanent crops: 7.8% (2011 est.) / permanent pasture: 1.8% (2011 est.)

forest: 60.4% (2011 est.)

other: 27.2% (2011 est.)

### IRRIGATED LAND:
0 sq km (2012)

### POPULATION DISTRIBUTION:
about three-quarters of the population lives on the island of Upolu

### NATURAL HAZARDS:
occasional cyclones; active volcanism

volcanism: Savai'I Island (1,858 m), which last erupted in 1911, is historically active

### ENVIRONMENT - CURRENT ISSUES:
soil erosion, deforestation, invasive species, overfishing

### ENVIRONMENT - INTERNATIONAL AGREEMENTS:
party to: Biodiversity, Climate Change, Climate Change-Kyoto Protocol, Desertification, Hazardous Wastes, Law of the Sea, Ozone Layer Protection, Ship Pollution, Wetlands

signed, but not ratified: none of the selected agreements

### GEOGRAPHY - NOTE:
occupies an almost central position within Polynesia

## PEOPLE AND SOCIETY :: SAMOA

### POPULATION:
201,316 (July 2018 est.)

country comparison to the world: 185

### NATIONALITY:
noun: Samoan(s)

adjective: Samoan

### ETHNIC GROUPS:
Samoan 96%, Samoan/New Zealander 2%, other 1.9% (2011 est.)

note: data represent the population by country of citizenship

### LANGUAGES:
Samoan (Polynesian) (official) 91.1%, Somoan/English 6.7%, English (official) 0.5%, other 0.2%, unspecified 1.6% (2006 est.)

### RELIGIONS:
Protestant 52.6% (Congregationalist 29%, Methodist 12.4%, Assembly of God 6.8%, Seventh Day Adventist 4.4%), Roman Catholic 18.8%, Mormon 16.9%, Worship Centre 2.8%, other Christian 6.3%, other Protestant 2.4%, other 2.4% (includes Baha'i, Muslim), none 0.2% (2016 est.)

### AGE STRUCTURE:
0-14 years: 30.67% (male 31,862 /female 29,875)

15-24 years: 19.76% (male 20,413/female 19,357)

25-54 years: 36.68% (male 37,944/female 35,893)

55-64 years: 7.05% (male 7,223/female 6,973)

65 years and over: 5.85% (male 5,126/female 6,650) (2018 est.)

## DEPENDENCY RATIOS:

total dependency ratio: 74.2 (2015 est.)

youth dependency ratio: 64.9 (2015 est.)

elderly dependency ratio: 9.3 (2015 est.)

potential support ratio: 10.8 (2015 est.)

## MEDIAN AGE:

total: 24.8 years

male: 24.5 years

female: 25.1 years (2018 est.)

country comparison to the world: 159

## POPULATION GROWTH RATE:

0.61% (2018 est.)

country comparison to the world: 147

## BIRTH RATE:

20.2 births/1,000 population (2018 est.)

country comparison to the world: 77

## DEATH RATE:

5.4 deaths/1,000 population (2018 est.)

country comparison to the world: 181

## NET MIGRATION RATE:

-9.1 migrant(s)/1,000 population (2017 est.)

country comparison to the world: 210

## POPULATION DISTRIBUTION:

about three-quarters of the population lives on the island of Upolu

## URBANIZATION:

urban population: 18.2% of total population (2018)

rate of urbanization: -0.47% annual rate of change (2015-20 est.)

## MAJOR URBAN AREAS - POPULATION:

36,000 APIA (capital) (2018)

## SEX RATIO:

at birth: 1.05 male(s)/female (2017 est.)

0-14 years: 1.07 male(s)/female (2017 est.)

15-24 years: 1.05 male(s)/female (2017 est.)

25-54 years: 1.07 male(s)/female (2017 est.)

55-64 years: 1.04 male(s)/female (2017 est.)

65 years and over: 0.77 male(s)/female (2017 est.)

total population: 1.04 male(s)/female (2017 est.)

## MOTHER'S MEAN AGE AT FIRST BIRTH:

23.6 years (2009 est.)

note: median age at first birth among women 25-29

## MATERNAL MORTALITY RATE:

51 deaths/100,000 live births (2015 est.)

country comparison to the world: 95

## INFANT MORTALITY RATE:

total: 18 deaths/1,000 live births (2018 est.)

male: 21.6 deaths/1,000 live births (2018 est.)

female: 14.2 deaths/1,000 live births (2018 est.)

country comparison to the world: 87

## LIFE EXPECTANCY AT BIRTH:

total population: 74.2 years (2018 est.)

male: 71.3 years (2018 est.)

female: 77.3 years (2018 est.)

country comparison to the world: 129

## TOTAL FERTILITY RATE:

2.64 children born/woman (2018 est.)

country comparison to the world: 67

## CONTRACEPTIVE PREVALENCE RATE:

26.9% (2014)

## HEALTH EXPENDITURES:

7.2% of GDP (2014)

country comparison to the world: 77

## PHYSICIANS DENSITY:

0.34 physicians/1,000 population (2010)

## DRINKING WATER SOURCE:

improved:

urban: 97.5% of population

rural: 99.3% of population

total: 99% of population

unimproved:

urban: 2.5% of population

rural: 0.7% of population

total: 1% of population (2015 est.)

## SANITATION FACILITY ACCESS:

improved:

urban: 93.3% of population (2015 est.)

rural: 91.1% of population (2015 est.)

total: 91.5% of population (2015 est.)

unimproved:

urban: 6.7% of population (2015 est.)

rural: 8.9% of population (2015 est.)

total: 8.5% of population (2015 est.)

## HIV/AIDS - ADULT PREVALENCE RATE:

NA

## HIV/AIDS - PEOPLE LIVING WITH HIV/AIDS:

NA

## HIV/AIDS - DEATHS:

NA

## MAJOR INFECTIOUS DISEASES:

note: active local transmission of Zika virus by Aedes species mosquitoes has been identified in this country (as of August 2016); it poses an important risk (a large number of cases possible) among US citizens if bitten by an infective mosquito; other less common ways to get Zika are through sex, via blood transfusion, or during pregnancy, in which the pregnant woman passes Zika virus to her fetus

## OBESITY - ADULT PREVALENCE RATE:

47.3% (2016)

country comparison to the world: 8

## CHILDREN UNDER THE AGE OF 5 YEARS UNDERWEIGHT:

2.7% (2014)

country comparison to the world: 105

## EDUCATION EXPENDITURES:

4.1% of GDP (2016)

country comparison to the world: 108

## LITERACY:

definition: age 15 and over can read and write (2015 est.)

total population: 99% (2015 est.)

male: 99.1% (2015 est.)

female: 98.8% (2015 est.)

## UNEMPLOYMENT, YOUTH AGES 15-24:

total: 19.1% (2014 est.)

male: 15.6% (2014 est.)

female: 25.3% (2014 est.)

country comparison to the world: 68

# GOVERNMENT :: SAMOA

**COUNTRY NAME:**

*conventional long form:* Independent State of Samoa

*conventional short form:* Samoa

*local long form:* Malo Sa'oloto Tuto'atasi o Samoa

*local short form:* Samoa

*former:* Western Samoa

*etymology:* the name "Samoa" is composed of two parts, "sa" meaning sacred and "moa" meaning center, so the name can mean Holy Center; alternatively, it can mean "place of the sacred moa bird" of Polynesian mythology

**GOVERNMENT TYPE:**

parliamentary republic

**CAPITAL:**

*name:* Apia

*geographic coordinates:* 13 49 S, 171 46 W

*time difference:* UTC+13 (18 hours ahead of Washington, DC, during Standard Time)

*daylight saving time:* +1hr, begins last Sunday in September; ends first Sunday in April

**ADMINISTRATIVE DIVISIONS:**

11 districts; A'ana, Aiga-i-le-Tai, Atua, Fa'asaleleaga, Gaga'emauga, Gagaifomauga, Palauli, Satupa'itea, Tuamasaga, Va'a-o-Fonoti, Vaisigano

**INDEPENDENCE:**

1 January 1962 (from New Zealand-administered UN trusteeship)

**NATIONAL HOLIDAY:**

Independence Day Celebration, 1 June (1962); note - 1 January 1962 is the date of independence from the New Zealand-administered UN trusteeship, but it is observed in June

**CONSTITUTION:**

*history:* several previous (preindependence); latest 1 January 1962 (2017)

*amendments:* proposed as an act by the Legislative Assembly; passage requires at least two-thirds majority vote by the Assembly membership in the third reading - provided at least 90 days have elapsed since the second reading, and assent to by the chief of state; passage of amendments affecting constitutional articles on customary land or constitutional amendment procedures also requires at least two-thirds majority approval in a referendum; amended several times, last in 2015 (2017)

**LEGAL SYSTEM:**

mixed legal system of English common law and customary law; judicial review of legislative acts with respect to fundamental rights of the citizen

**INTERNATIONAL LAW ORGANIZATION PARTICIPATION:**

has not submitted an ICJ jurisdiction declaration; accepts ICCt jurisdiction

**CITIZENSHIP:**

*citizenship by birth:* no

*citizenship by descent only:* at least one parent must be a citizen of Samoa

*dual citizenship recognized:* no

*residency requirement for naturalization:* 5 years

**SUFFRAGE:**

21 years of age; universal

**EXECUTIVE BRANCH:**

*chief of state:* TUIMALEALI'IFANO Va'aletoa Sualauvi II (since 21 July 2017)

*head of government:* Prime Minister TUILA'EPA Lupesoliai Sailele Malielegaoi (since 23 November 1998); Deputy Prime Minister FIAME Naomi Mata'afa (since 2016)

*cabinet:* Cabinet appointed by the chief of state on the prime minister's advice

*elections/appointments:* chief of state indirectly elected by the Legislative Assembly to serve a 5-year term (no term limits); election last held on 4 July 2017 (next to be held in 2022); following legislative elections, the leader of the majority party usually appointed prime minister by the chief of state, approved by the Legislative Assembly

*election results:* TUIMALEALI'IFANO Va'aletoa Sualauvi unanimously elected by the Legislative Assembly on 5 July 2017

**LEGISLATIVE BRANCH:**

*description:* unicameral Legislative Assembly or Fono (50 seats for 2016-2021 term); members from 49 single-seat constituencies directly elected by simple majority vote and 1 seat for a woman, added for the 2016 election to meet the mandated 10% representation of women in the Assembly; members serve 5-year terms)

*elections:* election last held on 4 March 2016 (next election to be held no later than March 2021)

*election results:* percent of vote by party - HRPP 89.8%, Tautua Samoa 4.1%, independent 6.1%; seats by party – initial election results - HRPP 44, Tautua Samoa 2, independents 3; post-election party affiliation – HRPP 47, (informal) opposition 3; composition - men 45, women 5, percent of women 10%

**JUDICIAL BRANCH:**

*highest courts:* Court of Appeal (consists of the chief justice and 2 Supreme Court judges and meets once or twice a year); Supreme Court (consists of the chief justice and several judges)

*judge selection and term of office:* chief justice appointed by the head of state upon the advice of the prime minister; other Supreme Court judges appointed by the Judicial Service Commission, a 3-member body chaired by the chief justice and includes the attorney general and an appointee of the Minister of Justice; judges normally appointed until retirement at age 68

*subordinate courts:* District Court; Magistrates' Courts; Land and Titles Courts; village fono or village chief councils

**POLITICAL PARTIES AND LEADERS:**

Human Rights Protection Party or HRPP [TUILA'EPA Sailele Malielegaoi]

**INTERNATIONAL ORGANIZATION PARTICIPATION:**

ACP, ADB, AOSIS, C, FAO, G-77, IBRD, ICAO, ICCt, ICRM, IDA, IFAD, IFC, IFRCS, ILO, IMF, IMO, Interpol, IOC, IPU, ITU, ITUC (NGOs), MIGA, OPCW, PIF, Sparteca, SPC, UN, UNCTAD, UNESCO, UNIDO, UPU, WCO, WHO, WIPO, WMO, WTO

**DIPLOMATIC REPRESENTATION IN THE US:**

*chief of mission:* Ambassador Aliioaiga Feturi ELISAIA (since 4 December 2003)

*chancery:* 800 Second Avenue, Suite 400J, New York, NY 10017

*telephone:* [1] (212) 599-6196 through 6197

*FAX:* [1] (212) 599-0797

*consulate(s) general:* Pago Pago (American Samoa)

### DIPLOMATIC REPRESENTATION FROM THE US:

**chief of mission:** the US Ambassador to New Zealand is accredited to Samoa

**embassy:** Accident Corporation Building, 5th Floor, Matafele, Apia

**mailing address:** P. O. Box 3430, Matafele, Apia

**telephone:** [685] 21-631 (2018)

**FAX:** [685] 22-030 (2018)

### FLAG DESCRIPTION:

red with a blue rectangle in the upper hoist-side quadrant bearing five white, five-pointed stars representing the Southern Cross constellation; red stands for courage, blue represents freedom, and white signifies purity

**note:** similar to the flag of Taiwan

### NATIONAL SYMBOL(S):

Southern Cross constellation (five, five-pointed stars); national colors: red, white, blue

### NATIONAL ANTHEM:

**name:** "O le Fu'a o le Sa'olotoga o Samoa" (The Banner of Freedom)

**lyrics/music:** Sauni Liga KURESA

**note:** adopted 1962; also known as "Samoa Tula'i" (Samoa Arise)

## ECONOMY :: SAMOA

### ECONOMY - OVERVIEW:

The economy of Samoa has traditionally been dependent on development aid, family remittances from overseas, tourism, agriculture, and fishing. It has a nominal GDP of $844 million. Agriculture, including fishing, furnishes 90% of exports, featuring fish, coconut oil, nonu products, and taro. The manufacturing sector mainly processes agricultural products. Industry accounts for nearly 22% of GDP while employing less than 6% of the work force. The service sector accounts for nearly two-thirds of GDP and employs approximately 50% of the labor force. Tourism is an expanding sector accounting for 25% of GDP; 132,000 tourists visited the islands in 2013.

The country is vulnerable to devastating storms. In September 2009, an earthquake and the resulting tsunami severely damaged Samoa and nearby American Samoa, disrupting transportation and power generation, and resulting in about 200 deaths. In December 2012, extensive flooding and wind damage from Tropical Cyclone Evan killed four people, displaced over 6,000, and damaged or destroyed an estimated 1,500 homes on Samoa's Upolu Island.

The Samoan Government has called for deregulation of the country's financial sector, encouragement of investment, and continued fiscal discipline, while at the same time protecting the environment. Foreign reserves are relatively healthy and inflation is low, but external debt is approximately 45% of GDP. Samoa became the 155th member of the WTO in May 2012, and graduated from least developed country status in January 2014.

### GDP (PURCHASING POWER PARITY):

$1.137 billion (2017 est.)

$1.11 billion (2016 est.)

$1.036 billion (2015 est.)

**note:** data are in 2017 dollars

**country comparison to the world:** 204

### GDP (OFFICIAL EXCHANGE RATE):

$841 million (2017 est.) (2017 est.)

### GDP - REAL GROWTH RATE:

2.5% (2017 est.)

7.1% (2016 est.)

1.6% (2015 est.)

**country comparison to the world:** 133

### GDP - PER CAPITA (PPP):

$5,700 (2017 est.)

$5,700 (2016 est.)

$5,300 (2015 est.)

**note:** data are in 2017 dollars

**country comparison to the world:** 169

### GDP - COMPOSITION, BY END USE:

**household consumption:** NA

**government consumption:** NA

**investment in fixed capital:** NA

**investment in inventories:** NA

**exports of goods and services:** 27.2% (2015 est.)

**imports of goods and services:** -50.5% (2015 est.)

### GDP - COMPOSITION, BY SECTOR OF ORIGIN:

**agriculture:** 10.4% (2017 est.)

**industry:** 23.6% (2017 est.)

**services:** 66% (2017 est.)

### AGRICULTURE - PRODUCTS:

coconuts, nonu, bananas, taro, yams, coffee, cocoa

### INDUSTRIES:

food processing, building materials, auto parts

### INDUSTRIAL PRODUCTION GROWTH RATE:

-1.8% (2017 est.)

**country comparison to the world:** 180

### LABOR FORCE:

50,700 (2016 est.)

**country comparison to the world:** 192

### LABOR FORCE - BY OCCUPATION:

**agriculture:** 65%

**industry:** 6%

**services:** 29% (2015 est.)

### UNEMPLOYMENT RATE:

5.2% (2017 est.)

5.5% (2016 est.)

NA

**country comparison to the world:** 78

### POPULATION BELOW POVERTY LINE:

NA

### HOUSEHOLD INCOME OR CONSUMPTION BY PERCENTAGE SHARE:

**lowest 10%:** NA

**highest 10%:** NA

### BUDGET:

**revenues:** 237.3 million (2017 est.)

**expenditures:** 276.8 million (2017 est.)

### TAXES AND OTHER REVENUES:

28.2% (of GDP) (2017 est.)

**country comparison to the world:** 95

### BUDGET SURPLUS (+) OR DEFICIT (-):

-4.7% (of GDP) (2017 est.)

**country comparison to the world:** 166

### PUBLIC DEBT:

49.1% of GDP (2017 est.)

52.6% of GDP (2016 est.)

**country comparison to the world:** 103

### FISCAL YEAR:

June 1 - May 31

### INFLATION RATE (CONSUMER PRICES):

1.3% (2017 est.)

0.1% (2016 est.)

**country comparison to the world:** 72

### COMMERCIAL BANK PRIME LENDING RATE:

8.76% (31 December 2017 est.)

9.09% (31 December 2016 est.)

country comparison to the world: 95
**STOCK OF NARROW MONEY:**
$147 million (31 December 2017 est.)
$131.7 million (31 December 2016 est.)
country comparison to the world: 186
**STOCK OF BROAD MONEY:**
$147 million (31 December 2017 est.)
$131.7 million (31 December 2016 est.)
country comparison to the world: 191
**STOCK OF DOMESTIC CREDIT:**
$404.3 million (31 December 2017 est.)
$389.5 million (31 December 2016 est.)
country comparison to the world: 181
**MARKET VALUE OF PUBLICLY TRADED SHARES:**
NA
**CURRENT ACCOUNT BALANCE:**
-$19 million (2017 est.)
-$37 million (2016 est.)
country comparison to the world: 72
**EXPORTS:**
$27.5 million (2014 est.)
country comparison to the world: 207
**EXPORTS - PARTNERS:**
Australia 22.9%, NZ 22.8%, American Samoa 22.1%, Afghanistan 14.9%, US 5.9% (2017)
**EXPORTS - COMMODITIES:**
fish, coconut oil and cream, nonu, copra, taro, automotive parts, garments, beer
**IMPORTS:**
$89.29 billion (2018 est.)
$312.6 million (2016 est.)
country comparison to the world: 41
**IMPORTS - COMMODITIES:**
machinery and equipment, industrial supplies, foodstuffs
**IMPORTS - PARTNERS:**
NZ 22%, Singapore 20.7%, US 12.5%, China 10.1%, Australia 8.6%, Fiji 5.2% (2017)
**RESERVES OF FOREIGN EXCHANGE AND GOLD:**
$133 million (31 December 2017 est.)
$122.5 million (31 December 2015 est.)
country comparison to the world: 180
**DEBT - EXTERNAL:**
$447.2 million (31 December 2013 est.)
country comparison to the world: 180
**EXCHANGE RATES:**
tala (SAT) per US dollar -
2.566 (2017 est.)
2.565 (2016 est.)
2.565 (2015 est.)
2.5609 (2014 est.)
2.3318 (2013 est.)

## ENERGY :: SAMOA

**ELECTRICITY ACCESS:**
population without electricity: 10,942 (2012)
electrification - total population: 94% (2012)
electrification - urban areas: 100% (2012)
electrification - rural areas: 93% (2012)
**ELECTRICITY - PRODUCTION:**
132 million kWh (2016 est.)
country comparison to the world: 197
**ELECTRICITY - CONSUMPTION:**
122.8 million kWh (2016 est.)
country comparison to the world: 199
**ELECTRICITY - EXPORTS:**
0 kWh (2016 est.)
country comparison to the world: 192
**ELECTRICITY - IMPORTS:**
0 kWh (2016 est.)
country comparison to the world: 194
**ELECTRICITY - INSTALLED GENERATING CAPACITY:**
45,000 kW (2016 est.)
country comparison to the world: 194
**ELECTRICITY - FROM FOSSIL FUELS:**
48% of total installed capacity (2016 est.)
country comparison to the world: 155
**ELECTRICITY - FROM NUCLEAR FUELS:**
0% of total installed capacity (2017 est.)
country comparison to the world: 176
**ELECTRICITY - FROM HYDROELECTRIC PLANTS:**
23% of total installed capacity (2017 est.)
country comparison to the world: 85
**ELECTRICITY - FROM OTHER RENEWABLE SOURCES:**
29% of total installed capacity (2017 est.)
country comparison to the world: 20
**CRUDE OIL - PRODUCTION:**
0 bbl/day (2017 est.)
country comparison to the world: 194
**CRUDE OIL - EXPORTS:**
0 bbl/day (2015 est.)
country comparison to the world: 188
**CRUDE OIL - IMPORTS:**
0 bbl/day (2015 est.)
country comparison to the world: 190
**CRUDE OIL - PROVED RESERVES:**
0 bbl (1 January 2018 est.)
country comparison to the world: 190
**REFINED PETROLEUM PRODUCTS - PRODUCTION:**
0 bbl/day (2017 est.)
country comparison to the world: 197
**REFINED PETROLEUM PRODUCTS - CONSUMPTION:**
2,400 bbl/day (2016 est.)
country comparison to the world: 191
**REFINED PETROLEUM PRODUCTS - EXPORTS:**
0 bbl/day (2015 est.)
country comparison to the world: 198
**REFINED PETROLEUM PRODUCTS - IMPORTS:**
2,363 bbl/day (2015 est.)
country comparison to the world: 187
**NATURAL GAS - PRODUCTION:**
0 cu m (2017 est.)
country comparison to the world: 192
**NATURAL GAS - CONSUMPTION:**
0 cu m (2017 est.)
country comparison to the world: 194
**NATURAL GAS - EXPORTS:**
0 cu m (2017 est.)
country comparison to the world: 177
**NATURAL GAS - IMPORTS:**
0 cu m (2017 est.)
country comparison to the world: 183
**NATURAL GAS - PROVED RESERVES:**
0 cu m (1 January 2014 est.)
country comparison to the world: 189
**CARBON DIOXIDE EMISSIONS FROM CONSUMPTION OF ENERGY:**
341,100 Mt (2017 est.)
country comparison to the world: 191

# COMMUNICATIONS :: SAMOA

**TELEPHONES - FIXED LINES:**

total subscriptions: 8,454 (2017 est.)

subscriptions per 100 inhabitants: 4 (2017 est.)

country comparison to the world: 197

**TELEPHONES - MOBILE CELLULAR:**

total subscriptions: 124,211 (2017 est.)

subscriptions per 100 inhabitants: 62 (2017 est.)

country comparison to the world: 188

**TELEPHONE SYSTEM:**

general assessment: most households have at least one mobile phone; all businesses in the greater Apia area have access to broadband and Wi-Fi, which is reasonably reliable and fast, but relatively expensive; in rural Upolu and on Savaii Island there is limited availability of high-speed Internet and Wi-Fi; Samoa recently completed the installation of a National Broadband Highway that will provide fiber optic data services and 4G LTE cellular data speeds to the entire country; 4G LTE data speeds are operative and commercially available to limited areas; 4G Internet accessibility from cellular devices is currently available nationwide (2017)

domestic: combined fixed-line and mobile-cellular teledensity roughly 70 telephones per 100 persons (2016)

international: country code - 685; satellite earth station - 1 Intelsat (Pacific Ocean) (2015)

**BROADCAST MEDIA:**

state-owned TV station privatized in 2008; 4 privately owned television broadcast stations; about a half-dozen privately owned radio stations and one state-owned radio station; TV and radio broadcasts of several stations from American Samoa are available (2009)

**INTERNET COUNTRY CODE:**

.ws

**INTERNET USERS:**

total: 58,508 (July 2016 est.)

percent of population: 29.4% (July 2016 est.)

country comparison to the world: 188

**BROADBAND - FIXED SUBSCRIPTIONS:**

total: 1,692 (2017 est.)

subscriptions per 100 inhabitants: 1 (2017 est.)

country comparison to the world: 184

# TRANSPORTATION :: SAMOA

**NATIONAL AIR TRANSPORT SYSTEM:**

number of registered air carriers: 1 (2015)

inventory of registered aircraft operated by air carriers: 1 (2015)

annual passenger traffic on registered air carriers: 270,908 (2015)

annual freight traffic on registered air carriers: 0 mt-km (2015)

**CIVIL AIRCRAFT REGISTRATION COUNTRY CODE PREFIX:**

5W (2016)

**AIRPORTS:**

4 (2013)

country comparison to the world: 188

**AIRPORTS - WITH PAVED RUNWAYS:**

total: 1 (2017)

2,438 to 3,047 m: 1 (2017)

**AIRPORTS - WITH UNPAVED RUNWAYS:**

total: 3 (2013)

under 914 m: 3 (2013)

**ROADWAYS:**

total: 1,200 km (2017)

paved: 1,105 km (2017)

unpaved: 95 km (2017)

country comparison to the world: 182

**MERCHANT MARINE:**

total: 10 (2017)

by type: general cargo 4, other 6 (2017)

country comparison to the world: 148

**PORTS AND TERMINALS:**

major seaport(s): Apia

# MILITARY AND SECURITY :: SAMOA

**MILITARY BRANCHES:**

no regular military forces; Samoa Police Force

**MILITARY - NOTE:**

Samoa has no formal defense structure or regular armed forces; informal defense ties exist with NZ, which is required to consider any Samoan request for assistance under the 1962 Treaty of Friendship

# TRANSNATIONAL ISSUES :: SAMOA

**DISPUTES - INTERNATIONAL:**

none

# EUROPE :: SAN MARINO

## INTRODUCTION :: SAN MARINO

**BACKGROUND:**

Geographically the third smallest state in Europe (after the Holy See and Monaco), San Marino also claims to be the world's oldest republic. According to tradition, it was founded by a Christian stonemason named MARINUS in A.D. 301. San Marino's foreign policy is aligned with that of the EU, although it is not a member; social and political trends in the republic track closely with those of its larger neighbor, Italy.

## GEOGRAPHY :: SAN MARINO

**LOCATION:**

Southern Europe, an enclave in central Italy

**GEOGRAPHIC COORDINATES:**

43 46 N, 12 25 E

**MAP REFERENCES:**

Europe

**AREA:**

total: 61 sq km

land: 61 sq km

water: 0 sq km

country comparison to the world: 229

**AREA - COMPARATIVE:**

about one-third the size of Washington, DC

**LAND BOUNDARIES:**

total: 37 km

border countries (1): Italy 37 km

**COASTLINE:**

0 km (landlocked)

**MARITIME CLAIMS:**

none (landlocked)

**CLIMATE:**

Mediterranean; mild to cool winters; warm, sunny summers

**TERRAIN:**

rugged mountains

**ELEVATION:**

55 m lowest point: Torrente Ausa

739 highest point: Monte Titano

**NATURAL RESOURCES:**

building stone

**LAND USE:**

agricultural land: 16.7% (2011 est.)

arable land: 16.7% (2011 est.) / permanent crops: 0% (2011 est.) / permanent pasture: 0% (2011 est.)

forest: 0% (2011 est.)

other: 83.3% (2011 est.)

**IRRIGATED LAND:**

0 sq km (2012)

**NATURAL HAZARDS:**

occasional earthquakes

**ENVIRONMENT - CURRENT ISSUES:**

air pollution; urbanization decreasing rural farmlands; water shortage

**ENVIRONMENT - INTERNATIONAL AGREEMENTS:**

party to: Biodiversity, Climate Change, Desertification, Whaling

signed, but not ratified: Air Pollution

**GEOGRAPHY - NOTE:**

landlocked; an enclave of (completely surrounded by) Italy; smallest independent state in Europe after the Holy See and Monaco; dominated by the Apennine Mountains

## PEOPLE AND SOCIETY :: SAN MARINO

**POPULATION:**

33,779 (July 2018 est.)

country comparison to the world: 215

**NATIONALITY:**

noun: Sammarinese (singular and plural)

adjective: Sammarinese

**ETHNIC GROUPS:**

Sammarinese, Italian

**LANGUAGES:**

Italian

**RELIGIONS:**

Roman Catholic

**AGE STRUCTURE:**

0-14 years: 15.04% (male 2,687 /female 2,392)

15-24 years: 11.59% (male 2,046 /female 1,869)

25-54 years: 40.23% (male 6,391 /female 7,198)

55-64 years: 13.35% (male 2,215 /female 2,294)

65 years and over: 19.8% (male 3,006 /female 3,681) (2018 est.)

**MEDIAN AGE:**

total: 44.7 years

male: 43.5 years

female: 45.7 years (2018 est.)

country comparison to the world: 10
**POPULATION GROWTH RATE:**

0.7% (2018 est.)

country comparison to the world: 143
**BIRTH RATE:**

8.6 births/1,000 population (2018 est.)

country comparison to the world: 214
**DEATH RATE:**

8.8 deaths/1,000 population (2018 est.)

country comparison to the world: 70
**NET MIGRATION RATE:**

7.5 migrant(s)/1,000 population (2017 est.)

country comparison to the world: 14
**URBANIZATION:**

urban population: 97.2% of total population (2018)

rate of urbanization: 0.67% annual rate of change (2015-20 est.)

**MAJOR URBAN AREAS - POPULATION:**

4,000 SAN MARINO (2018)

**SEX RATIO:**

at birth: 1.09 male(s)/female (2017 est.)

0-14 years: 1.14 male(s)/female (2017 est.)

15-24 years: 1.06 male(s)/female (2017 est.)

25-54 years: 0.89 male(s)/female (2017 est.)

55-64 years: 0.99 male(s)/female (2017 est.)

65 years and over: 0.81 male(s)/female (2017 est.)

total population: 0.94 male(s)/female (2017 est.)

**INFANT MORTALITY RATE:**

total: 4.3 deaths/1,000 live births (2018 est.)

male: 4.5 deaths/1,000 live births (2018 est.)

female: 4.1 deaths/1,000 live births (2018 est.)

country comparison to the world: 185
**LIFE EXPECTANCY AT BIRTH:**

total population: 83.4 years (2018 est.)

male: 80.8 years (2018 est.)

female: 86.2 years (2018 est.)

country comparison to the world: 5
**TOTAL FERTILITY RATE:**

1.51 children born/woman (2018 est.)

country comparison to the world: 195
**HEALTH EXPENDITURES:**

6.1% of GDP (2014)

country comparison to the world: 104
**PHYSICIANS DENSITY:**

6.36 physicians/1,000 population (2014)

**HOSPITAL BED DENSITY:**

3.8 beds/1,000 population (2012)

**HIV/AIDS - ADULT PREVALENCE RATE:**

NA

**HIV/AIDS - PEOPLE LIVING WITH HIV/AIDS:**

NA

**HIV/AIDS - DEATHS:**

NA

**EDUCATION EXPENDITURES:**

2.4% of GDP (2011)

country comparison to the world: 167
**SCHOOL LIFE EXPECTANCY (PRIMARY TO TERTIARY EDUCATION):**

total: 15 years (2012)

male: 15 years (2012)

female: 16 years (2012)

**UNEMPLOYMENT, YOUTH AGES 15-24:**

total: 27.4% (2016 est.)

male: 21.4% (2016 est.)

female: 36% (2016 est.)

country comparison to the world: 41

## GOVERNMENT :: SAN MARINO

**COUNTRY NAME:**

conventional long form: Republic of San Marino

conventional short form: San Marino

local long form: Repubblica di San Marino

local short form: San Marino

etymology: named after Saint MARINUS, the traditional founder of the country

**GOVERNMENT TYPE:**

parliamentary republic

**CAPITAL:**

name: San Marino (city)

geographic coordinates: 43 56 N, 12 25 E

time difference: UTC+1 (6 hours ahead of Washington, DC, during Standard Time)

daylight saving time: +1hr, begins last Sunday in March; ends last Sunday in October

**ADMINISTRATIVE DIVISIONS:**

9 municipalities (castelli, singular - castello); Acquaviva, Borgo Maggiore, Chiesanuova, Domagnano, Faetano, Fiorentino, Montegiardino, San Marino Citta, Serravalle

**INDEPENDENCE:**

3 September 301 (traditional founding date)

**NATIONAL HOLIDAY:**

Founding of the Republic (or Feast of Saint Marinus), 3 September (A.D. 301)

**CONSTITUTION:**

history: consists of several legislative instruments, chief among them the Statutes (Leges Statuti) of 1600 and the Declaration of Citizen Rights of 1974 (2016)

amendments: proposed by the Great and General Council; passage requires two-thirds majority Council vote; Council passage by absolute majority vote also requires passage in a referendum; Declaration of Civil Rights amended several times, last in 2012 (2016)

**LEGAL SYSTEM:**

civil law system with Italian civil law influences

**INTERNATIONAL LAW ORGANIZATION PARTICIPATION:**

has not submitted an ICJ jurisdiction declaration; accepts ICCt jurisdiction

**CITIZENSHIP:**

citizenship by birth: no

citizenship by descent only: at least one parent must be a citizen of San Marino

dual citizenship recognized: no

residency requirement for naturalization: 30 years

**SUFFRAGE:**

18 years of age; universal

**EXECUTIVE BRANCH:**

chief of state: co-chiefs of state Captain Regent Stefano PALMIERI and Captain Regent Matteo CIACCI (for the period 1 April 2018 - 1 October 2018)

head of government: Secretary of State for Foreign and Political Affairs

Nicola RENZI (since 27 December 2016)

**cabinet:** Congress of State elected by the Grand and General Council

**elections/appointments:** co-chiefs of state (captains regent) indirectly elected by the Grand and General Council for a single 6-month term; election last held in March 2018 (next to be held in September 2018); secretary of state for foreign and political affairs indirectly elected by the Grand and General Council for a single 5-year term; election last held on 4 December 2016 (next to be held by November 2021)

**election results:** Stefano PALMIERI (RF) and Matteo CIACCI (Civic 10) elected captains regent; percent of Grand and General Council vote - NA; Pasquale VALENTINI (PDCS) elected secretary of state for foreign and political affairs; percent of Grand and General Council vote - NA

**note:** the captains regent preside over meetings of the Grand and General Council and its cabinet (Congress of State), which has 9 other members who are selected by the Grand and General Council; assisting the captains regent are 9 secretaries of state; the secretary of state for Foreign Affairs has some prime ministerial roles

## LEGISLATIVE BRANCH:

**description:** unicameral Grand and General Council or Consiglio Grande e Generale (60 seats; members directly elected in single- and multi-seat constituencies by proportional representation vote in 2 rounds if needed; members serve 5-year terms)

**elections:** last held on 20 November 2016 with a runoff held on 4 December 2016 (next to be held by November 2021)

**election results:** percent of vote by party/coalition in the first round - San Marino First 41.7% (PDCS 24.5%, PS 7.7%, PSD 7.2%, other 2.3%), Adesso.sm 31.4% (SSD 12.1%, RF 9.6%, Civic 10 9.3%, other .4%), Democracy in Action 23.2% (RETE Movement 18.3%, Democratic Movement-San Marino Together 4.5%, other .4%), other 3.7%; percent of vote by coalition in the second round - Adesso.sm 57.9%, San Marino First 42.1%; seats by party - Adesso.sm 35 (SSD 14, RF 11, Civic 10 10), San Marino First 10 (PDCS 10, PS 3, PSD 3), Democracy in Action 9 (RETE Movement 8, Democratic Movement-San Marino Together 1); composition - men 46, women 14, percent of women 23.3%

**note** - because no coalition won a majority in the first round, a runoff was held between the two coalitions that had received the greatest percent of the vote, San Marino First and Adesso.sm; Adesso.sm won the runoff, and the seats were reallocated

## JUDICIAL BRANCH:

**highest courts:** Council of Twelve or Consiglio dei XII (consists of 12 members); note - the College of Guarantors for the Constitutionality and General Norms functions as San Marino's constitutional court

**judge selection and term of office:** judges elected by the Grand and General Council from among its own to serve 5-year terms

**subordinate courts:** first instance and first appeal criminal, administrative, and civil courts; Court for the Trust and Trustee Relations; justices of the peace or conciliatory judges

## POLITICAL PARTIES AND LEADERS:

San Marino Common Good (includes Sammarinese Christian Democratic Party or PDCS [Marco GATTI], We Sammarinese or NS [Marco ARZILLI], Party of Socialists and Democrats or PSD [Paride ANDREOLI], Popular Alliance or AP [Gabriele GATTI]) Entente for the Country (Intesa per il Paese; includes Socialist Party or PS [Alessandro BEVITORI], Union for the Republic or UPR [Marco PODESCHI])
Active Citizenship (includes Civic 10 [Mateo CIACCI], United Left or SU [Gastone PASOLINI], Future Republic [Mario VENTURINI])

## INTERNATIONAL ORGANIZATION PARTICIPATION:

CE, FAO, IAEA, IBRD, ICAO, ICC (NGOs), ICCt, ICRM, IDA, IFRCS, ILO, IMF, IMO, Interpol, IOC, IOM (observer), IPU, ITU, ITUC (NGOs), LAIA (observer), OPCW, OSCE, Schengen Convention (de facto member), UN, UNCTAD, UNESCO, Union Latina, UNWTO, UPU, WHO, WIPO

## DIPLOMATIC REPRESENTATION IN THE US:

**chief of mission:** Ambassador Damiano BELEFFI (since 21 July 2017)

**chancery:** 1711 N Street NW, 2nd floor, Washington, DC 20036

**telephone:** [1] (202) 250-1535

**FAX:** [1] (202) 223-2748

## DIPLOMATIC REPRESENTATION FROM THE US:

the US does not have an embassy in San Marino; the US Ambassador to Italy is accredited to San Marino

## FLAG DESCRIPTION:

two equal horizontal bands of white (top) and light blue with the national coat of arms superimposed in the center; the main colors derive from the shield of the coat of arms, which features three white towers on three peaks on a blue field; the towers represent three castles built on San Marino's highest feature, Mount Titano: Guaita, Cesta, and Montale; the coat of arms is flanked by a wreath, below a crown and above a scroll bearing the word LIBERTAS (Liberty); the white and blue colors are also said to stand for peace and liberty respectively

## NATIONAL SYMBOL(S):

three peaks each displaying a tower; national colors: white, blue

## NATIONAL ANTHEM:

**name:** "Inno Nazionale della Repubblica" (National Anthem of the Republic)

**lyrics/music:** no lyrics/Federico CONSOLO

**note:** adopted 1894; the music for the lyric-less anthem is based on a 10th century chorale piece

# ECONOMY :: SAN MARINO

## ECONOMY - OVERVIEW:

San Marino's economy relies heavily on tourism, banking, and the manufacture and export of ceramics, clothing, fabrics, furniture, paints, spirits, tiles, and wine. The manufacturing and financial sectors account for more than half of San Marino's GDP. The per capita level of output and standard of living are comparable to those of the most prosperous regions of Italy.

San Marino's economy contracted considerably in the years since 2008, largely due to weakened demand from Italy - which accounts for nearly 90% of its export market - and financial sector consolidation. Difficulties in the banking sector, the global economic downturn, and the sizable decline in tax revenues all contributed to negative real GDP growth. The government adopted measures to counter the downturn, including subsidized credit to businesses and is seeking to shift its growth model away from a reliance on bank and tax secrecy. San Marino does not issue public debt securities; when necessary, it finances deficits by drawing down central bank deposits.

The economy benefits from foreign investment due to its relatively low corporate taxes and low taxes on interest earnings. The income tax rate is also very low, about one-third the average EU level. San Marino continues to work towards harmonizing its fiscal laws with EU and international standards. In September 2009, the OECD removed San Marino from its list of tax havens that have yet to fully adopt global tax standards, and in 2010 San Marino signed Tax Information Exchange Agreements with most major countries. In 2013, the San Marino Government signed a Double Taxation Agreement with Italy, but a referendum on EU membership failed to reach the quorum needed to bring it to a vote.

**GDP (PURCHASING POWER PARITY):**

$2.064 billion (2017 est.)

$2.026 billion (2016 est.)

$1.983 billion (2015 est.)

note: data are in 2017 dollars

country comparison to the world: 195

**GDP (OFFICIAL EXCHANGE RATE):**

$1.643 billion (2017 est.) (2017 est.)

**GDP - REAL GROWTH RATE:**

1.9% (2017 est.)

2.2% (2016 est.)

0.6% (2015 est.)

country comparison to the world: 157

**GDP - PER CAPITA (PPP):**

$59,000 (2017 est.)

$59,600 (2016 est.)

$58,300 (2015 est.)

note: data are in 2017 dollars

country comparison to the world: 20

**GDP - COMPOSITION, BY END USE:**

household consumption: NA (2011 est.)

government consumption: NA (2011 est.)

investment in fixed capital: NA (2011 est.)

investment in inventories: NA (2011 est.)

exports of goods and services: 176.6% (2011)

imports of goods and services: -153.3% (2011)

**GDP - COMPOSITION, BY SECTOR OF ORIGIN:**

agriculture: 0.1% (2009)

industry: 39.2% (2009)

services: 60.7% (2009)

**AGRICULTURE - PRODUCTS:**

wheat, grapes, corn, olives; cattle, pigs, horses, beef, cheese, hides

**INDUSTRIES:**

tourism, banking, textiles, electronics, ceramics, cement, wine

**INDUSTRIAL PRODUCTION GROWTH RATE:**

-1.1% (2012 est.)

country comparison to the world: 178

**LABOR FORCE:**

21,960 (September 2013 est.)

country comparison to the world: 211

**LABOR FORCE - BY OCCUPATION:**

agriculture: 0.2%

industry: 33.5%

services: 66.3% (September 2013 est.)

**UNEMPLOYMENT RATE:**

8.1% (2017 est.)

8.6% (2016 est.)

country comparison to the world: 118

**POPULATION BELOW POVERTY LINE:**

NA

**HOUSEHOLD INCOME OR CONSUMPTION BY PERCENTAGE SHARE:**

lowest 10%: NA

highest 10%: NA

**BUDGET:**

revenues: 667.7 million (2011 est.)

expenditures: 715.3 million (2011 est.)

**TAXES AND OTHER REVENUES:**

40.6% (of GDP) (2011 est.)

country comparison to the world: 36

**BUDGET SURPLUS (+) OR DEFICIT (-):**

-2.9% (of GDP) (2011 est.)

country comparison to the world: 129

**PUBLIC DEBT:**

24.1% of GDP (2017 est.)

22.5% of GDP (2016 est.)

country comparison to the world: 180

**FISCAL YEAR:**

calendar year

**INFLATION RATE (CONSUMER PRICES):**

1% (2017 est.)

0.6% (2016 est.)

country comparison to the world: 53

**COMMERCIAL BANK PRIME LENDING RATE:**

5.92% (31 December 2011 est.)

5.38% (31 December 2010 est.)

country comparison to the world: 127

**STOCK OF NARROW MONEY:**

$1.326 billion (31 December 2007)

country comparison to the world: 147

**STOCK OF BROAD MONEY:**

$4.584 billion (31 December 2007)

country comparison to the world: 113

**STOCK OF DOMESTIC CREDIT:**

$8.822 billion (30 September 2010)

$8.008 billion (31 December 2009)

country comparison to the world: 112

**MARKET VALUE OF PUBLICLY TRADED SHARES:**

NA

**CURRENT ACCOUNT BALANCE:**

$0 (2017 est.)

$0 (2016 est.)

country comparison to the world: 67

**EXPORTS:**

$3.827 billion (2011 est.)

$2.576 billion (2010 est.)

country comparison to the world: 120

**EXPORTS - COMMODITIES:**

building stone, lime, wood, chestnuts, wheat, wine, baked goods, hides, ceramics

**IMPORTS:**

$2.551 billion (2011 est.)

$2.132 billion (2010 est.)

country comparison to the world: 157

**IMPORTS - COMMODITIES:**

wide variety of consumer manufactures, food, energy

**RESERVES OF FOREIGN EXCHANGE AND GOLD:**

$392 million (2014 est.)

$539.3 million (2013 est.)

country comparison to the world: 161

**DEBT - EXTERNAL:**

NA

**EXCHANGE RATES:**

euros (EUR) per US dollar -

0.885 (2017 est.)

0.903 (2016 est.)

0.9214 (2015 est.)

0.885 (2014 est.)

0.7634 (2013 est.)

## ENERGY :: SAN MARINO

**ELECTRICITY ACCESS:**

electrification - total population: 100% (2016)

## COMMUNICATIONS :: SAN MARINO

**TELEPHONES - FIXED LINES:**

total subscriptions: 15,800 (2017 est.)

subscriptions per 100 inhabitants: 47 (2017 est.)

country comparison to the world: 188

**TELEPHONES - MOBILE CELLULAR:**

total subscriptions: 38,000 (2017 est.)

subscriptions per 100 inhabitants: 113 (2017 est.)

country comparison to the world: 205

**TELEPHONE SYSTEM:**

general assessment: automatic telephone system completely integrated into Italian system (2016)

domestic: combined fixed-line and mobile-cellular teledensity over 155 telephones per 100 persons (2016)

international: country code - 378; connected to Italian international network (2016)

**BROADCAST MEDIA:**

state-owned public broadcaster operates 1 TV station and 3 radio stations; receives radio and TV broadcasts from Italy (2012)

**INTERNET COUNTRY CODE:**

.sm

**INTERNET USERS:**

total: 17,200 (July 2016 est.)

percent of population: 52.6% (July 2016 est.)

country comparison to the world: 206

**BROADBAND - FIXED SUBSCRIPTIONS:**

total: 12,500 (2017 est.)

subscriptions per 100 inhabitants: 37 (2017 est.)

country comparison to the world: 166

## TRANSPORTATION :: SAN MARINO

**CIVIL AIRCRAFT REGISTRATION COUNTRY CODE PREFIX:**

T7 (2016)

**ROADWAYS:**

total: 292 km (2006)

paved: 292 km (2006)

country comparison to the world: 207

## MILITARY AND SECURITY :: SAN MARINO

**MILITARY BRANCHES:**

no regular military forces; voluntary Military Corps (Corpi Militari) performs ceremonial duties and limited police support functions (2010)

**MILITARY SERVICE AGE AND OBLIGATION:**

18 is the legal minimum age for voluntary military service; no conscription; government has the authority to call up all San Marino citizens from 16-60 years of age to service in the military (2012)

**MILITARY - NOTE:**

defense is the responsibility of Italy

## TRANSNATIONAL ISSUES :: SAN MARINO

**DISPUTES - INTERNATIONAL:**

none

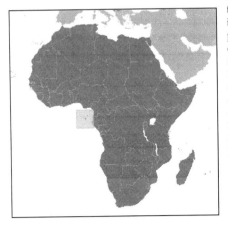

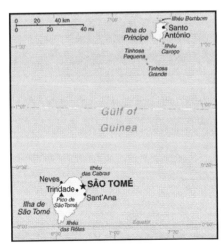

# AFRICA :: SAO TOME AND PRINCIPE

## INTRODUCTION :: SAO TOME AND PRINCIPE

**BACKGROUND:**

Discovered and claimed by Portugal in the late 15th century, the islands' sugar-based economy gave way to coffee and cocoa in the 19th century - all grown with African plantation slave labor, a form of which lingered into the 20th century. While independence was achieved in 1975, democratic reforms were not instituted until the late 1980s. The country held its first free elections in 1991, but frequent internal wrangling between the various political parties precipitated repeated changes in leadership and four failed, non-violent coup attempts in 1995, 1998, 2003, and 2009. In 2012, three opposition parties combined in a no confidence vote to bring down the majority government of former Prime Minister Patrice TROVOADA, but in 2014, legislative elections returned him to the office. President Evaristo CARVALHO, of the same political party as Prime Minister TROVOADA, was elected in September 2016, marking a rare instance in which the positions of president and prime minister are held by the same party. New oil discoveries in the Gulf of Guinea may attract increased attention to the small island nation.

## GEOGRAPHY :: SAO TOME AND PRINCIPE

**LOCATION:**

Central Africa, islands in the Gulf of Guinea, just north of the Equator, west of Gabon

**GEOGRAPHIC COORDINATES:**

1 00 N, 7 00 E

**MAP REFERENCES:**

Africa

**AREA:**

total: 964 sq km

land: 964 sq km

water: 0 sq km

country comparison to the world: 185

**AREA - COMPARATIVE:**

more than five times the size of Washington, DC

**LAND BOUNDARIES:**

0 km

**COASTLINE:**

209 km

**MARITIME CLAIMS:**

territorial sea: 12 nm

exclusive economic zone: 200 nm measured from claimed archipelagic baselines

**CLIMATE:**

tropical; hot, humid; one rainy season (October to May)

**TERRAIN:**

volcanic, mountainous

**ELEVATION:**

0 m lowest point: Atlantic Ocean

2024 highest point: Pico de Sao Tome

**NATURAL RESOURCES:**

fish, hydropower

**LAND USE:**

agricultural land: 50.7% (2011 est.)

arable land: 9.1% (2011 est.) / permanent crops: 40.6% (2011 est.) / permanent pasture: 1% (2011 est.)

forest: 28.1% (2011 est.)

other: 21.2% (2011 est.)

**IRRIGATED LAND:**

100 sq km (2012)

**POPULATION DISTRIBUTION:**

Sao Tome, the capital city, has roughly a quarter of the nation's population; Santo Antonio is the largest town on Principe; the northern areas of both islands have the highest population densities

**NATURAL HAZARDS:**

flooding

**ENVIRONMENT - CURRENT ISSUES:**

deforestation and illegal logging; soil erosion and exhaustion; inadequate sewage treatment in cities; biodiversity preservation

**ENVIRONMENT - INTERNATIONAL AGREEMENTS:**

party to: Biodiversity, Climate Change, Climate Change-Kyoto Protocol, Desertification, Endangered Species, Environmental Modification, Hazardous Wastes, Law of the Sea, Ozone Layer Protection, Ship Pollution, Wetlands

signed, but not ratified: none of the selected agreements

**GEOGRAPHY - NOTE:**

the smallest country in Africa; the two main islands form part of a chain of extinct volcanoes and both are mountainous

# PEOPLE AND SOCIETY :: SAO TOME AND PRINCIPE

## POPULATION:
204,454 (July 2018 est.)

country comparison to the world: 184

## NATIONALITY:
noun: Sao Tomean(s)

adjective: Sao Tomean

## ETHNIC GROUPS:
mestico, angolares (descendants of Angolan slaves), forros (descendants of freed slaves), servicais (contract laborers from Angola, Mozambique, and Cabo Verde), tongas (children of servicais born on the islands), Europeans (primarily Portuguese), Asians (mostly Chinese)

## LANGUAGES:
Portuguese 98.4% (official), Forro 36.2%, Cabo Verdian 8.5%, French 6.8%, Angolar 6.6%, English 4.9%, Lunguie 1%, other (including sign language) 2.4% (2012 est.)

note: shares sum to more than 100% because some respondents gave more than one answer on the census

## RELIGIONS:
Catholic 55.7%, Adventist 4.1%, Assembly of God 3.4%, New Apostolic 2.9%, Mana 2.3%, Universal Kingdom of God 2%, Jehovah's Witness 1.2%, other 6.2%, none 21.2%, unspecified 1% (2012 est.)

## DEMOGRAPHIC PROFILE:
Sao Tome and Principe's youthful age structure – more than 60% of the population is under the age of 25 – and high fertility rate ensure future population growth. Although Sao Tome has a net negative international migration rate, emigration is not a sufficient safety valve to reduce already high levels of unemployment and poverty. While literacy and primary school attendance have improved in recent years, Sao Tome still struggles to improve its educational quality and to increase its secondary school completion rate. Despite some improvements in education and access to healthcare, Sao Tome and Principe has much to do to decrease its high poverty rate, create jobs, and increase its economic growth.

The population of Sao Tome and Principe descends primarily from the islands' colonial Portuguese settlers, who first arrived in the late 15th century, and the much larger number of African slaves brought in for sugar production and the slave trade. For about 100 years after the abolition of slavery in 1876, the population was further shaped by the widespread use of imported unskilled contract laborers from Portugal's other African colonies, who worked on coffee and cocoa plantations. In the first decades after abolition, most workers were brought from Angola under a system similar to slavery. While Angolan laborers were technically free, they were forced or coerced into long contracts that were automatically renewed and extended to their children. Other contract workers from Mozambique and famine-stricken Cape Verde first arrived in the early 20th century under short-term contracts and had the option of repatriation, although some chose to remain in Sao Tome and Principe.

Today's Sao Tomean population consists of mesticos (creole descendants of the European immigrants and African slaves that first inhabited the islands), forros (descendants of freed African slaves), angolares (descendants of runaway African slaves that formed a community in the south of Sao Tome Island and today are fishermen), servicais (contract laborers from Angola, Mozambique, and Cape Verde), tongas (locally born children of contract laborers), and lesser numbers of Europeans and Asians.

## AGE STRUCTURE:
**0-14 years:** 41.2% (male 42,825/female 41,403)

**15-24 years:** 21.01% (male 21,767/female 21,188)

**25-54 years:** 31.03% (male 31,218/female 32,229)

**55-64 years:** 3.93% (male 3,708/female 4,332)

**65 years and over:** 2.83% (male 2,545/female 3,239) (2018 est.)

## DEPENDENCY RATIOS:
total dependency ratio: 86.7 (2015 est.)

youth dependency ratio: 81.1 (2015 est.)

elderly dependency ratio: 5.6 (2015 est.)

potential support ratio: 17.8 (2015 est.)

## MEDIAN AGE:
total: 18.7 years

male: 18.3 years

female: 19.1 years (2018 est.)

country comparison to the world: 207

## POPULATION GROWTH RATE:
1.66% (2018 est.)

country comparison to the world: 62

## BIRTH RATE:
31.5 births/1,000 population (2018 est.)

country comparison to the world: 32

## DEATH RATE:
6.7 deaths/1,000 population (2018 est.)

country comparison to the world: 138

## NET MIGRATION RATE:
-8.3 migrant(s)/1,000 population (2017 est.)

country comparison to the world: 207

## POPULATION DISTRIBUTION:
Sao Tome, the capital city, has roughly a quarter of the nation's population; Santo Antonio is the largest town on Principe; the northern areas of both islands have the highest population densities

## URBANIZATION:
urban population: 72.8% of total population (2018)

rate of urbanization: 3.33% annual rate of change (2015-20 est.)

## MAJOR URBAN AREAS - POPULATION:
80,000 SAO TOME (capital) (2018)

## SEX RATIO:
at birth: 1.03 male(s)/female (2017 est.)

0-14 years: 1.03 male(s)/female (2017 est.)

15-24 years: 1.03 male(s)/female (2017 est.)

25-54 years: 0.96 male(s)/female (2017 est.)

55-64 years: 0.84 male(s)/female (2017 est.)

65 years and over: 0.81 male(s)/female (2017 est.)

total population: 1 male(s)/female (2017 est.)

## MOTHER'S MEAN AGE AT FIRST BIRTH:
19.4 years (2008/09 est.)

note: median age at first birth among women 25-29

## MATERNAL MORTALITY RATE:

156 deaths/100,000 live births (2015 est.)

country comparison to the world: 58

**INFANT MORTALITY RATE:**

total: 44.1 deaths/1,000 live births (2018 est.)

male: 46 deaths/1,000 live births (2018 est.)

female: 42.1 deaths/1,000 live births (2018 est.)

country comparison to the world: 41

**LIFE EXPECTANCY AT BIRTH:**

total population: 65.7 years (2018 est.)

male: 64.3 years (2018 est.)

female: 67.1 years (2018 est.)

country comparison to the world: 179

**TOTAL FERTILITY RATE:**

4.11 children born/woman (2018 est.)

country comparison to the world: 31

**CONTRACEPTIVE PREVALENCE RATE:**

40.6% (2014)

**HEALTH EXPENDITURES:**

8.4% of GDP (2014)

country comparison to the world: 49

**HOSPITAL BED DENSITY:**

2.9 beds/1,000 population (2011)

**DRINKING WATER SOURCE:**

improved:

urban: 98.9% of population (2015 est.)

rural: 93.6% of population (2015 est.)

total: 97.1% of population (2015 est.)

unimproved:

urban: 1.1% of population (2015 est.)

rural: 6.4% of population (2015 est.)

total: 2.9% of population (2015 est.)

**SANITATION FACILITY ACCESS:**

improved:

urban: 40.8% of population (2015 est.)

rural: 23.3% of population (2015 est.)

total: 34.7% of population (2015 est.)

unimproved:

urban: 59.2% of population (2015 est.)

rural: 76.7% of population (2015 est.)

total: 65.3% of population (2015 est.)

**HIV/AIDS - ADULT PREVALENCE RATE:**

NA

**HIV/AIDS - PEOPLE LIVING WITH HIV/AIDS:**

NA

**HIV/AIDS - DEATHS:**

NA

**MAJOR INFECTIOUS DISEASES:**

degree of risk: high (2016)

food or waterborne diseases: bacterial diarrhea, hepatitis A, and typhoid fever (2016)

vectorborne diseases: malaria and dengue fever (2016)

water contact diseases: schistosomiasis (2016)

**OBESITY - ADULT PREVALENCE RATE:**

12.4% (2016)

country comparison to the world: 133

**CHILDREN UNDER THE AGE OF 5 YEARS UNDERWEIGHT:**

8.8% (2014)

country comparison to the world: 66

**EDUCATION EXPENDITURES:**

3.7% of GDP (2014)

country comparison to the world: 122

**LITERACY:**

definition: age 15 and over can read and write (2015 est.)

total population: 74.9% (2015 est.)

male: 81.8% (2015 est.)

female: 68.4% (2015 est.)

**SCHOOL LIFE EXPECTANCY (PRIMARY TO TERTIARY EDUCATION):**

total: 13 years (2015)

male: 13 years (2015)

female: 13 years (2015)

**UNEMPLOYMENT, YOUTH AGES 15-24:**

total: 20.8% (2012 est.)

male: NA (2012 est.)

female: NA (2012 est.)

country comparison to the world: 60

## GOVERNMENT :: SAO TOME AND PRINCIPE

**COUNTRY NAME:**

conventional long form: Democratic Republic of Sao Tome and Principe

conventional short form: Sao Tome and Principe

local long form: Republica Democratica de Sao Tome e Principe

local short form: Sao Tome e Principe

etymology: Sao Tome was named after Saint THOMAS the Apostle by the Portuguese who discovered the island on 21 December 1470 (or 1471), the saint's feast day; Principe is a shortening of the original Portuguese name of "Ilha do Principe" (Isle of the Prince) referring to the Prince of Portugal to whom duties on the island's sugar crop were paid

**GOVERNMENT TYPE:**

semi-presidential republic

**CAPITAL:**

name: Sao Tome

geographic coordinates: 0 20 N, 6 44 E

time difference: UTC 0 (5 hours ahead of Washington, DC, during Standard Time)

**ADMINISTRATIVE DIVISIONS:**

6 districts (distritos, singular - distrito), 1 autonomous region* (regiao autonoma); Agua Grande, Cantagalo, Caue, Lemba, Lobata, Me-Zochi, Principe*

**INDEPENDENCE:**

12 July 1975 (from Portugal)

**NATIONAL HOLIDAY:**

Independence Day, 12 July (1975)

**CONSTITUTION:**

history: approved 5 November 1975 (2017)

amendments: proposed by the National Assembly; passage requires two-thirds majority vote by the Assembly; the Assembly can propose to the president of the republic that an amendment be submitted to a referendum; revised several times, last in 2006 (2017)

**LEGAL SYSTEM:**

mixed legal system of civil law based on the Portuguese model and customary law

**INTERNATIONAL LAW ORGANIZATION PARTICIPATION:**

has not submitted an ICJ jurisdiction declaration; non-party state to the ICCt

**CITIZENSHIP:**

citizenship by birth: no

citizenship by descent only: at least one parent must be a citizen of Sao Tome and Principe

**dual citizenship recognized:** no

**residency requirement for naturalization:** 5 years

## SUFFRAGE:

18 years of age; universal

## EXECUTIVE BRANCH:

**chief of state:** President Evaristo CARVALHO (since 3 September 2016)

**head of government:** Prime Minister Jorge Bom JESUS (since 3 December 2018)

**cabinet:** Council of Ministers proposed by the prime minister, appointed by the president

**elections/appointments:** president directly elected by absolute majority popular vote in 2 rounds if needed for a 5-year term (eligible for a second term); election last held on 7 July 2016 and 7 August 2016 (next to be held in July 2021); prime minister chosen by the National Assembly and approved by the president

**election results:** Evaristo CARVALHO elected president; percent of vote - Evaristo CARVALHO (ADI) 49.8%, Manuel Pinto DA COSTA (independent) 24.8%, Maria DAS NEVES (MLSTP-PSD) 24.1%; note - first round results for CARVALHO were revised downward from just over 50%, prompting the 7 August runoff; however, on 1 August 2016 DA COSTA withdrew from the runoff, citing voting irregularities, and CARVALHO was declared the winner

## LEGISLATIVE BRANCH:

**description:** unicameral National Assembly or Assembleia Nacional (55 seats; members directly elected in multi-seat constituencies by closed party-list proportional representation vote to serve 4-year terms)

**elections:** last held on 7 October 2018 (next to be held in October 2022)

**election results:** percent of vote by party - ADI 41.8%, MLSTP/PSD 40.3%, PCD-GR 9.5%, MCISTP 2.1%, other 6.3%; seats by party - ADI 25, MLSTP-PSD 23, PCD-MDFM-UDD 5, MCISTP 2

## JUDICIAL BRANCH:

**highest courts:** Supreme Court or Supremo Tribunal Justica (consists of 5 judges); Constitutional Court or Tribunal Constitucional (consists of 5 judges, 3 of whom are from the Supreme Court)

**judge selection and term of office:** Supreme Court judges appointed by the National Assembly; judge tenure NA; Constitutional Court judges nominated by the president of the republic and elected by the National Assembly for 5-year terms

**subordinate courts:** Court of First Instance; Audit Court

## POLITICAL PARTIES AND LEADERS:

Force for Democratic Change Movement or MDFM [Fradique Bandeira Melo DE MENEZES]
Independent Democratic Action or ADI [Patrice TROVOADA]
Movement for the Liberation of Sao Tome and Principe-Social Democratic Party or MLSTP-PSD [Aurelio MARTINS]
Party for Democratic Convergence-Reflection Group or PCD-GR [Leonel Mario D'ALVA]
other small parties

## INTERNATIONAL ORGANIZATION PARTICIPATION:

ACP, AfDB, AOSIS, AU, CD, CEMAC, CPLP, EITI (candidate country), FAO, G-77, IBRD, ICAO, ICRM, IDA, IFAD, IFC, IFRCS, ILO, IMF, IMO, Interpol, IOC, IOM (observer), IPU, ITU, ITUC (NGOs), MIGA, NAM, OIF, OPCW, PCA, UN, UNCTAD, UNESCO, UNIDO, Union Latina, UNWTO, UPU, WCO, WHO, WIPO, WMO, WTO (observer)

## DIPLOMATIC REPRESENTATION IN THE US:

**chief of mission:** Ambassador Carlos Filomeno Azevedo Agostinho das NEVES (since 3 December 2013)

**chancery:** 675 Third Avenue, Suite 1807, New York, NY 10017

**telephone:** [1] (212) 651-8116

**FAX:** [1] (212) 651-8117

## DIPLOMATIC REPRESENTATION FROM THE US:

the US does not have an embassy in Sao Tome and Principe; the US Ambassador to Gabon is accredited to Sao Tome and Principe on a nonresident basis

## FLAG DESCRIPTION:

three horizontal bands of green (top), yellow (double width), and green with two black five-pointed stars placed side by side in the center of the yellow band and a red isosceles triangle based on the hoist side; green stands for the country's rich vegetation, red recalls the struggle for independence, and yellow represents cocoa, one of the country's main agricultural products; the two stars symbolize the two main islands

**note:** uses the popular Pan-African colors of Ethiopia

## NATIONAL SYMBOL(S):

palm tree; national colors: green, yellow, red, black

## NATIONAL ANTHEM:

**name:** "Independencia total" (Total Independence)

**lyrics/music:** Alda Neves DA GRACA do Espirito Santo/Manuel dos Santos Barreto de Sousa e ALMEIDA

**note:** adopted 1975

# ECONOMY :: SAO TOME AND PRINCIPE

## ECONOMY - OVERVIEW:

The economy of São Tomé and Príncipe is small, based mainly on agricultural production, and, since independence in 1975, increasingly dependent on the export of cocoa beans. Cocoa production has substantially declined in recent years because of drought and mismanagement. Sao Tome depends heavily on imports of food, fuels, most manufactured goods, and consumer goods, and changes in commodity prices affect the country's inflation rate. Maintaining control of inflation, fiscal discipline, and increasing flows of foreign direct investment into the nascent oil sector are major economic problems facing the country. In recent years the government has attempted to reduce price controls and subsidies. In 2017, several business-related laws were enacted that aim to improve the business climate.

São Tomé and Príncipe has had difficulty servicing its external debt and has relied heavily on concessional aid and debt rescheduling. In April 2011, the country completed a Threshold Country Program with The Millennium Challenge Corporation to help increase tax revenues, reform customs, and improve the business environment. In 2016, Sao Tome and Portugal signed a five-year cooperation agreement worth approximately $64 million, some of which will be provided as loans. In 2017, China and São Tomé signed a mutual cooperation agreement in areas such as infrastructure, health, and agriculture worth approximately $146 million over five years.

Considerable potential exists for development of tourism, and the government has taken steps to expand tourist facilities in recent years. Potential also exists for the development of petroleum resources in São Tomé and Príncipe's territorial waters in the oil-rich Gulf of Guinea, some of which are being jointly developed in a 60-40 split with Nigeria, but production is at least several years off.

Volatile aid and investment inflows have limited growth, and poverty remains high. Restrictedded capacity at the main port increases the periodic risk of shortages of consumer goods. Contract enforcement in the country's judicial system is difficult. The IMF in late 2016 expressed concern about vulnerabilities in the country's banking sector, although the country plans some austerity measures in line with IMF recommendations under their three year extended credit facility. Deforestation, coastal erosion, poor waste management, and misuse of natural resources also are challenging issues.

**GDP (PURCHASING POWER PARITY):**

$686 million (2017 est.)

$660.4 million (2016 est.)

$633.9 million (2015 est.)

note: data are in 2017 dollars

country comparison to the world: 208

**GDP (OFFICIAL EXCHANGE RATE):**

$393 million (2017 est.) (2017 est.)

**GDP - REAL GROWTH RATE:**

3.9% (2017 est.)

4.2% (2016 est.)

3.8% (2015 est.)

country comparison to the world: 83

**GDP - PER CAPITA (PPP):**

$3,200 (2017 est.)

$3,200 (2016 est.)

$3,100 (2015 est.)

note: data are in 2017 dollars

country comparison to the world: 191

**GROSS NATIONAL SAVING:**

18.7% of GDP (2017 est.)

21% of GDP (2016 est.)

19.3% of GDP (2015 est.)

country comparison to the world: 107

**GDP - COMPOSITION, BY END USE:**

household consumption: 81.4% (2017 est.)

government consumption: 17.6% (2017 est.)

investment in fixed capital: 33.4% (2017 est.)

investment in inventories: 0% (2017 est.)

exports of goods and services: 7.9% (2017 est.)

imports of goods and services: -40.4% (2017 est.)

**GDP - COMPOSITION, BY SECTOR OF ORIGIN:**

agriculture: 11.8% (2017 est.)

industry: 14.8% (2017 est.)

services: 73.4% (2017 est.)

**AGRICULTURE - PRODUCTS:**

cocoa, coconuts, palm kernels, copra, cinnamon, pepper, coffee, bananas, papayas, beans; poultry; fish

**INDUSTRIES:**

light construction, textiles, soap, beer, fish processing, timber

**INDUSTRIAL PRODUCTION GROWTH RATE:**

5% (2017 est.)

country comparison to the world: 57

**LABOR FORCE:**

72,600 (2017 est.)

country comparison to the world: 186

**LABOR FORCE - BY OCCUPATION:**

agriculture: 26.1%

industry: 21.4%

services: 52.5% (2014 est.)

**UNEMPLOYMENT RATE:**

12.2% (2017 est.)

12.6% (2016 est.)

country comparison to the world: 163

**POPULATION BELOW POVERTY LINE:**

66.2% (2009 est.)

**HOUSEHOLD INCOME OR CONSUMPTION BY PERCENTAGE SHARE:**

lowest 10%: NA

highest 10%: NA

**DISTRIBUTION OF FAMILY INCOME - GINI INDEX:**

30.8 (2010 est.)

32.1 (2000 est.)

country comparison to the world: 129

**BUDGET:**

revenues: 103 million (2017 est.)

expenditures: 112.4 million (2017 est.)

**TAXES AND OTHER REVENUES:**

26.2% (of GDP) (2017 est.)

country comparison to the world: 114

**BUDGET SURPLUS (+) OR DEFICIT (-):**

-2.4% (of GDP) (2017 est.)

country comparison to the world: 113

**PUBLIC DEBT:**

88.4% of GDP (2017 est.)

93.1% of GDP (2016 est.)

country comparison to the world: 27

**FISCAL YEAR:**

calendar year

**INFLATION RATE (CONSUMER PRICES):**

5.7% (2017 est.)

5.4% (2016 est.)

country comparison to the world: 182

**CENTRAL BANK DISCOUNT RATE:**

16% (31 December 2009)

28% (31 December 2008)

country comparison to the world: 11

**COMMERCIAL BANK PRIME LENDING RATE:**

19.61% (31 December 2017 est.)

19.59% (31 December 2016 est.)

country comparison to the world: 15

**STOCK OF NARROW MONEY:**

$75.38 million (31 December 2017 est.)

$64.95 million (31 December 2016 est.)

country comparison to the world: 189

**STOCK OF BROAD MONEY:**

$75.38 million (31 December 2017 est.)

$64.95 million (31 December 2016 est.)

country comparison to the world: 194

**STOCK OF DOMESTIC CREDIT:**

$96.03 million (31 December 2017 est.)

$73.35 million (31 December 2016 est.)

country comparison to the world: 188

**MARKET VALUE OF PUBLICLY TRADED SHARES:**

NA

**CURRENT ACCOUNT BALANCE:**

-$32 million (2017 est.)

-$23 million (2016 est.)

country comparison to the world: 76

**EXPORTS:**

$15.6 million (2017 est.)

$9.31 million (2016 est.)

country comparison to the world: 215

**EXPORTS - PARTNERS:**

Guyana 43.7%, Germany 23.6%, Portugal 6%, Netherlands 5.5%, Poland 4.4% (2017)

**EXPORTS - COMMODITIES:**

cocoa 68%, copra, coffee, palm oil (2010 est.)

**IMPORTS:**

$127.7 million (2017 est.)

$119.1 million (2016 est.)

country comparison to the world: 212

**IMPORTS - COMMODITIES:**

machinery and electrical equipment, food products, petroleum products

**IMPORTS - PARTNERS:**

Portugal 54.7%, Angola 16.5%, China 5.6% (2017)

**RESERVES OF FOREIGN EXCHANGE AND GOLD:**

$58.95 million (31 December 2017 est.)

$61.5 million (31 December 2016 est.)

country comparison to the world: 185

**DEBT - EXTERNAL:**

$292.9 million (31 December 2017 est.)

$308.5 million (31 December 2016 est.)

country comparison to the world: 185

**STOCK OF DIRECT FOREIGN INVESTMENT - AT HOME:**

$469.5 million (31 December 2017 est.)

$430.3 million (31 December 2016 est.)

country comparison to the world: 130

**STOCK OF DIRECT FOREIGN INVESTMENT - ABROAD:**

$3.98 million (31 December 2017 est.)

$2.2 million (31 December 2016 est.)

country comparison to the world: 117

**EXCHANGE RATES:**

dobras (STD) per US dollar -

22,689 (2017 est.)

21,797 (2016 est.)

22,149 (2015 est.)

22,091 (2014 est.)

18,466 (2013 est.)

# ENERGY :: SAO TOME AND PRINCIPE

**ELECTRICITY ACCESS:**

population without electricity: 100,000 (2013)

electrification - total population: 59% (2013)

electrification - urban areas: 70% (2013)

electrification - rural areas: 40% (2013)

**ELECTRICITY - PRODUCTION:**

66 million kWh (2016 est.)

country comparison to the world: 203

**ELECTRICITY - CONSUMPTION:**

61.38 million kWh (2016 est.)

country comparison to the world: 203

**ELECTRICITY - EXPORTS:**

0 kWh (2016)

country comparison to the world: 193

**ELECTRICITY - IMPORTS:**

0 kWh (2016 est.)

country comparison to the world: 195

**ELECTRICITY - INSTALLED GENERATING CAPACITY:**

18,100 kW (2016 est.)

country comparison to the world: 205

**ELECTRICITY - FROM FOSSIL FUELS:**

88% of total installed capacity (2016 est.)

country comparison to the world: 60

**ELECTRICITY - FROM NUCLEAR FUELS:**

0% of total installed capacity (2017 est.)

country comparison to the world: 177

**ELECTRICITY - FROM HYDROELECTRIC PLANTS:**

11% of total installed capacity (2017 est.)

country comparison to the world: 115

**ELECTRICITY - FROM OTHER RENEWABLE SOURCES:**

1% of total installed capacity (2017 est.)

country comparison to the world: 166

**CRUDE OIL - PRODUCTION:**

0 bbl/day (2017 est.)

country comparison to the world: 195

**CRUDE OIL - EXPORTS:**

0 bbl/day (2015 est.)

country comparison to the world: 189

**CRUDE OIL - IMPORTS:**

0 bbl/day (2015 est.)

country comparison to the world: 191

**CRUDE OIL - PROVED RESERVES:**

0 bbl (1 January 2018)

country comparison to the world: 191

**REFINED PETROLEUM PRODUCTS - PRODUCTION:**

0 bbl/day (2017 est.)

country comparison to the world: 198

**REFINED PETROLEUM PRODUCTS - CONSUMPTION:**

1,000 bbl/day (2016 est.)

country comparison to the world: 206

**REFINED PETROLEUM PRODUCTS - EXPORTS:**

0 bbl/day (2015 est.)

country comparison to the world: 199

**REFINED PETROLEUM PRODUCTS - IMPORTS:**

1,027 bbl/day (2015 est.)

country comparison to the world: 202

**NATURAL GAS - PRODUCTION:**

0 cu m (2017 est.)

country comparison to the world: 193

**NATURAL GAS - CONSUMPTION:**

0 cu m (2017 est.)

country comparison to the world: 195

**NATURAL GAS - EXPORTS:**

0 cu m (2017 est.)

country comparison to the world: 178

**NATURAL GAS - IMPORTS:**

0 cu m (2017 est.)

country comparison to the world: 184

**NATURAL GAS - PROVED RESERVES:**

0 cu m (1 January 2014 est.)

country comparison to the world: 190

**CARBON DIOXIDE EMISSIONS FROM CONSUMPTION OF ENERGY:**

148,100 Mt (2017 est.)

country comparison to the world: 204

# COMMUNICATIONS :: SAO TOME AND PRINCIPE

**TELEPHONES - FIXED LINES:**

total subscriptions: 5,569 (2017 est.)

subscriptions per 100 inhabitants: 3 (2017 est.)

country comparison to the world: 205

**TELEPHONES - MOBILE CELLULAR:**

total subscriptions: 173,646 (2017 est.)

subscriptions per 100 inhabitants: 86 (2017 est.)

country comparison to the world: 185

## TELEPHONE SYSTEM:

general assessment: local telephone network of adequate quality with most lines connected to digital switches (2016)

domestic: combined fixed-line and mobile-cellular teledensity roughly 70 telephones per 100 persons (2016)

international: country code - 239; satellite earth station - 1 Intelsat (Atlantic Ocean) (2016)

## BROADCAST MEDIA:

1 government-owned TV station; 1 government-owned radio station; 3 independent local radio stations authorized in 2005 with 2 operating at the end of 2006; transmissions of multiple international broadcasters are available (2007)

## INTERNET COUNTRY CODE:

.st

## INTERNET USERS:

total: 50,000 (July 2016 est.)

percent of population: 25.8% (July 2016 est.)

country comparison to the world: 194

## BROADBAND - FIXED SUBSCRIPTIONS:

total: 1,479 (2017 est.)

subscriptions per 100 inhabitants: 1 (2017 est.)

country comparison to the world: 187

# TRANSPORTATION :: SAO TOME AND PRINCIPE

## NATIONAL AIR TRANSPORT SYSTEM:

number of registered air carriers: 1 (2015)

inventory of registered aircraft operated by air carriers: 1 (2015)

annual passenger traffic on registered air carriers: 50,716 (2015)

annual freight traffic on registered air carriers: 0 mt-km (2015)

## CIVIL AIRCRAFT REGISTRATION COUNTRY CODE PREFIX:

S9 (2016)

## AIRPORTS:

2 (2013)

country comparison to the world: 207

## AIRPORTS - WITH PAVED RUNWAYS:

total: 2 (2017)

1,524 to 2,437 m: 1 (2017)

914 to 1,523 m: 1 (2017)

## ROADWAYS:

total: 320 km (2000)

paved: 218 km (2000)

unpaved: 102 km (2000)

country comparison to the world: 206

## MERCHANT MARINE:

total: 16 (2017)

by type: general cargo 12, other 4 (2017)

country comparison to the world: 144

## PORTS AND TERMINALS:

major seaport(s): Sao Tome

# MILITARY AND SECURITY :: SAO TOME AND PRINCIPE

## MILITARY BRANCHES:

Armed Forces of Sao Tome and Principe (Forcas Armadas de Sao Tome e Principe, FASTP): Army, Coast Guard of Sao Tome e Principe (Guarda Costeira de Sao Tome e Principe, GCSTP; also called "Navy"), Presidential Guard, National Guard (2015)

## MILITARY SERVICE AGE AND OBLIGATION:

18 is the legal minimum age for compulsory military service; 17 is the legal minimum age for voluntary service (2012)

## MILITARY - NOTE:

Sao Tome and Principe's army is a tiny force with almost no resources at its disposal and would be wholly ineffective operating unilaterally; infantry equipment is considered simple to operate and maintain but may require refurbishment or replacement after 25 years in tropical climates; poor pay, working conditions, and alleged nepotism in the promotion of officers have been problems in the past, as reflected in the 1995 and 2003 coups; these issues are being addressed with foreign assistance aimed at improving the army and its focus on realistic security concerns; command is exercised from the president, through the Minister of Defense, to the Chief of the Armed Forces (infantry, technical issues) and the Chief of the General Staff (logistics, administration, finances) (2012)

# TRANSNATIONAL ISSUES :: SAO TOME AND PRINCIPE

## DISPUTES - INTERNATIONAL:

none

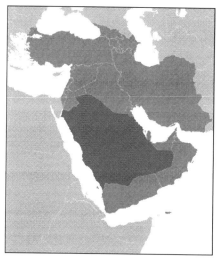

# INTRODUCTION :: SAUDI ARABIA

## BACKGROUND:

Saudi Arabia is the birthplace of Islam and home to Islam's two holiest shrines in Mecca and Medina. The king's official title is the Custodian of the Two Holy Mosques. The modern Saudi state was founded in 1932 by ABD AL-AZIZ bin Abd al-Rahman Al SAUD (Ibn Saud) after a 30-year campaign to unify most of the Arabian Peninsula. One of his male descendants rules the country today, as required by the country's 1992 Basic Law. Following Iraq's invasion of Kuwait in 1990, Saudi Arabia accepted the Kuwaiti royal family and 400,000 refugees while allowing Western and Arab troops to deploy on its soil for the liberation of Kuwait the following year. The continuing presence of foreign troops on Saudi soil after the liberation of Kuwait became a source of tension between the royal family and the public until all operational US troops left the country in 2003. Major terrorist attacks in May and November 2003 spurred a strong ongoing campaign against domestic terrorism and extremism.

From 2005 to 2015, King ABDALLAH incrementally modernized the Kingdom. Driven by personal ideology and political pragmatism, he introduced a series of social and economic initiatives, including expanding employment and social opportunities for women, attracting foreign investment, increasing the role of the private sector in the economy, and discouraging businesses from hiring foreign workers. Saudi Arabia saw some protests during the 2011 Arab Spring but not the level of bloodshed seen in protests elsewhere in the region. Shia Muslims in the Eastern Province protested primarily against the detention of political prisoners, endemic discrimination, and Bahraini and Saudi Government actions in Bahrain. Riyadh took a cautious but firm approach by arresting some protesters but releasing most of them quickly and by using its state-sponsored clerics to counter political and Islamist activism.

The government held its first-ever elections in 2005 and 2011, when Saudis went to the polls to elect municipal councilors. In December 2015, women were allowed to vote and stand as candidates for the first time in municipal council elections, with 19 women winning seats. King SALMAN bin Abd al-Aziz Al Saud ascended to the throne in 2015 and placed the first next-generation prince, MUHAMMAD BIN NAIF bin Abd al-Aziz Al Saud, in the line of succession as Crown Prince. He designated his son, MUHAMMAD BIN SALMAN bin Abd al-Aziz Al Saud, as the Deputy Crown Prince. In March 2015, Saudi Arabia led a coalition of 10 countries in a military campaign to restore the legitimate government of Yemen, which had been ousted by Huthi forces allied with former president ALI ABDULLAH al-Salih. The war in Yemen has drawn international criticism for civilian casualties and its effect on the country's dire humanitarian situation. In December 2015, then Deputy Crown Prince MUHAMMAD BIN SALMAN announced Saudi Arabia would lead a 34-nation Islamic Coalition to fight terrorism (it has since grown to 41 nations). In May 2017, Saudi Arabia inaugurated the Global Center for Combatting Extremist Ideology (also known as "Etidal") as part of its ongoing efforts to counter violent extremism. In June 2017, King SALMAN elevated MUHAMMAD BIN SALMAN to Crown Prince. In September 2017, King SALMAN issued a royal decree recognizing the right of Saudi women to drive beginning in June 2018.

The country remains a leading producer of oil and natural gas and holds about 16% of the world's proven oil reserves as of 2015. The government continues to pursue economic reform and diversification, particularly since Saudi Arabia's accession to the WTO in 2005, and promotes foreign investment in the Kingdom. In April 2016, the Saudi government announced a broad set of socio-economic reforms, known as Vision 2030. Low global oil prices throughout 2015 and 2016 significantly lowered Saudi Arabia's governmental revenue. In response, the government cut subsidies on water, electricity, and gasoline; reduced government employee compensation packages; and announced limited new land taxes. In coordination with OPEC and some key non-OPEC countries, Saudi Arabia agreed cut oil output in early 2017 to regulate supply and help elevate global prices.

# GEOGRAPHY :: SAUDI ARABIA

**LOCATION:**
Middle East, bordering the Persian Gulf and the Red Sea, north of Yemen

**GEOGRAPHIC COORDINATES:**
25 00 N, 45 00 E

**MAP REFERENCES:**
Middle East

**AREA:**
total: 2,149,690 sq km
land: 2,149,690 sq km
water: 0 sq km
country comparison to the world: 14

**AREA - COMPARATIVE:**
slightly more than one-fifth the size of the US

**LAND BOUNDARIES:**
total: 4,272 km
border countries (7): Iraq 811 km, Jordan 731 km, Kuwait 221 km, Oman 658 km, Qatar 87 km, UAE 457 km, Yemen 1307 km

**COASTLINE:**
2,640 km

**MARITIME CLAIMS:**
territorial sea: 12 nm
contiguous zone: 18 nm
continental shelf: not specified

**CLIMATE:**
harsh, dry desert with great temperature extremes

**TERRAIN:**
mostly sandy desert

**ELEVATION:**
mean elevation: 665 m
elevation extremes: 0 m lowest point: Persian Gulf
3133 highest point: Jabal Sawda'

**NATURAL RESOURCES:**
petroleum, natural gas, iron ore, gold, copper

**LAND USE:**
agricultural land: 80.7% (2011 est.)
arable land: 1.5% (2011 est.) / permanent crops: 0.1% (2011 est.) / permanent pasture: 79.1% (2011 est.)
forest: 0.5% (2011 est.)
other: 18.8% (2011 est.)

**IRRIGATED LAND:**
16,200 sq km (2012)

**POPULATION DISTRIBUTION:**
historically a population that was mostly nomadic or semi-nomadic, the Saudi population has become more settled since petroleum was discovered in the 1930s; most of the economic activities - and with it the country's population - is concentrated in a wide area across the middle of the peninsula, from Ad Dammam in the east, through Riyadh in the interior, to Mecca-Medina in the west near the Red Sea

**NATURAL HAZARDS:**
frequent sand and dust storms

volcanism: despite many volcanic formations, there has been little activity in the past few centuries; volcanoes include Harrat Rahat, Harrat Khaybar, Harrat Lunayyir, and Jabal Yar

**ENVIRONMENT - CURRENT ISSUES:**
desertification; depletion of underground water resources; the lack of perennial rivers or permanent water bodies has prompted the development of extensive seawater desalination facilities; coastal pollution from oil spills; air pollution; waste management

**ENVIRONMENT - INTERNATIONAL AGREEMENTS:**
party to: Biodiversity, Climate Change, Climate Change-Kyoto Protocol, Desertification, Endangered Species, Hazardous Wastes, Law of the Sea, Marine Dumping, Ozone Layer Protection, Ship Pollution
signed, but not ratified: none of the selected agreements

**GEOGRAPHY - NOTE:**
Saudi Arabia is the largest country in the world without a river; extensive coastlines on the Persian Gulf and Red Sea provide great leverage on shipping (especially crude oil) through the Persian Gulf and Suez Canal

# PEOPLE AND SOCIETY :: SAUDI ARABIA

**POPULATION:**
33,091,113 (July 2017 est.) (July 2018 est.)
note: immigrants make up 37% of the total population, according to UN data (2017)
country comparison to the world: 41

**NATIONALITY:**
noun: Saudi(s)
adjective: Saudi or Saudi Arabian

**ETHNIC GROUPS:**
Arab 90%, Afro-Asian 10%

**LANGUAGES:**
Arabic (official)

**RELIGIONS:**
Muslim (official; citizens are 85-90% Sunni and 10-15% Shia), other (includes Eastern Orthodox, Protestant, Roman Catholic, Jewish, Hindu, Buddhist, and Sikh) (2012 est.)

note: despite having a large expatriate community of various faiths (more than 30% of the population), most forms of public religious expression inconsistent with the government-sanctioned interpretation of Sunni Islam are restricted; non-Muslims are not allowed to have Saudi citizenship and non-Muslim places of worship are not permitted (2013)

**AGE STRUCTURE:**
0-14 years: 25.74% (male 4,348,227 /female 4,170,944)
15-24 years: 15.58% (male 2,707,229 /female 2,447,519)
25-54 years: 49.88% (male 9,951,080 /female 6,554,525)
55-64 years: 5.48% (male 1,112,743 /female 700,553)
65 years and over: 3.32% (male 586,606 /female 511,687) (2018 est.)

**DEPENDENCY RATIOS:**
total dependency ratio: 40.9 (2015 est.)
youth dependency ratio: 36.6 (2015 est.)
elderly dependency ratio: 4.3 (2015 est.)
potential support ratio: 23.2 (2015 est.)

**MEDIAN AGE:**
total: 29.9 years
male: 32.1 years
female: 27.2 years (2018 est.)
country comparison to the world: 120

**POPULATION GROWTH RATE:**
1.63% (2018 est.)
country comparison to the world: 64

**BIRTH RATE:**
15.6 births/1,000 population (2018 est.)

country comparison to the world: 116

**DEATH RATE:**

3.3 deaths/1,000 population (2018 est.)

country comparison to the world: 220

**NET MIGRATION RATE:**

-0.5 migrant(s)/1,000 population (2017 est.)

country comparison to the world: 126

**POPULATION DISTRIBUTION:**

historically a population that was mostly nomadic or semi-nomadic, the Saudi population has become more settled since petroleum was discovered in the 1930s; most of the economic activities - and with it the country's population - is concentrated in a wide area across the middle of the peninsula, from Ad Dammam in the east, through Riyadh in the interior, to Mecca-Medina in the west near the Red Sea

**URBANIZATION:**

urban population: 83.8% of total population (2018)

rate of urbanization: 2.17% annual rate of change (2015-20 est.)

**MAJOR URBAN AREAS - POPULATION:**

6.907 million RIYADH (capital), 4.433 million Jeddah, 1.967 million Mecca, 1.43 million Medina, 1.197 million Ad Dammam (2018)

**SEX RATIO:**

at birth: 1.05 male(s)/female (2017 est.)

0-14 years: 1.05 male(s)/female (2017 est.)

15-24 years: 1.15 male(s)/female (2017 est.)

25-54 years: 1.31 male(s)/female (2017 est.)

55-64 years: 1.21 male(s)/female (2017 est.)

65 years and over: 1.05 male(s)/female (2017 est.)

total population: 1.19 male(s)/female (2017 est.)

**MATERNAL MORTALITY RATE:**

12 deaths/100,000 live births (2015 est.)

country comparison to the world: 142

**INFANT MORTALITY RATE:**

total: 12.1 deaths/1,000 live births (2018 est.)

male: 13 deaths/1,000 live births (2018 est.)

female: 11.1 deaths/1,000 live births (2018 est.)

country comparison to the world: 113

**LIFE EXPECTANCY AT BIRTH:**

total population: 75.7 years (2018 est.)

male: 74.2 years (2018 est.)

female: 77.3 years (2018 est.)

country comparison to the world: 104

**TOTAL FERTILITY RATE:**

2.04 children born/woman (2018 est.)

country comparison to the world: 111

**CONTRACEPTIVE PREVALENCE RATE:**

24.6% (2016)

**HEALTH EXPENDITURES:**

4.7% of GDP (2014)

country comparison to the world: 152

**PHYSICIANS DENSITY:**

2.57 physicians/1,000 population (2014)

**HOSPITAL BED DENSITY:**

2.7 beds/1,000 population (2014)

**DRINKING WATER SOURCE:**

improved:

urban: 97% of population (2015 est.)

rural: 97% of population (2015 est.)

total: 97% of population (2015 est.)

unimproved:

rural: 3% of population (2015 est.)

total: 3% of population (2015 est.)

**SANITATION FACILITY ACCESS:**

improved:

urban: 100% of population (2015 est.)

rural: 100% of population (2015 est.)

total: 100% of population (2015 est.)

unimproved:

urban: 0% of population (2015 est.)

rural: 0% of population (2015 est.)

total: 0% of population (2015 est.)

**HIV/AIDS - ADULT PREVALENCE RATE:**

<.1% (2016 est.)

**HIV/AIDS - PEOPLE LIVING WITH HIV/AIDS:**

8,200 (2016 est.)

country comparison to the world: 105

**HIV/AIDS - DEATHS:**

<500 (2016 est.)

**OBESITY - ADULT PREVALENCE RATE:**

35.4% (2016)

country comparison to the world: 14

**EDUCATION EXPENDITURES:**

5.1% of GDP (2008)

country comparison to the world: 71

**LITERACY:**

definition: age 15 and over can read and write (2015 est.)

total population: 94.7% (2015 est.)

male: 97% (2015 est.)

female: 91.1% (2015 est.)

**SCHOOL LIFE EXPECTANCY (PRIMARY TO TERTIARY EDUCATION):**

total: 16 years (2014)

male: 17 years (2014)

female: 15 years (2014)

**UNEMPLOYMENT, YOUTH AGES 15-24:**

total: 24.2% (2016 est.)

male: 17.4% (2016 est.)

female: 46.3% (2016 est.)

country comparison to the world: 49

# GOVERNMENT :: SAUDI ARABIA

**COUNTRY NAME:**

conventional long form: Kingdom of Saudi Arabia

conventional short form: Saudi Arabia

local long form: Al Mamlakah al Arabiyah as Suudiyah

local short form: Al Arabiyah as Suudiyah

etymology: named after the ruling dynasty of the country, the House of Saud; the name "Arabia" can be traced back many centuries B.C., the ancient Egyptians referred to the region as "Ar Rabi"

**GOVERNMENT TYPE:**

absolute monarchy

**CAPITAL:**

name: Riyadh

geographic coordinates: 24 39 N, 46 42 E

time difference: UTC+3 (8 hours ahead of Washington, DC, during Standard Time)

**ADMINISTRATIVE DIVISIONS:**

13 regions (manatiq, singular - mintaqah); Al Bahah, Al Hudud ash Shamaliyah (Northern Border), Al

Jawf, Al Madinah al Munawwarah (Medina), Al Qasim, Ar Riyad (Riyadh), Ash Sharqiyah (Eastern), 'Asir, Ha'il, Jazan, Makkah al Mukarramah (Mecca), Najran, Tabuk

## INDEPENDENCE:
23 September 1932 (unification of the kingdom)

## NATIONAL HOLIDAY:
Saudi National Day (Unification of the Kingdom), 23 September (1932)

## CONSTITUTION:
**history:** 1 March 1992 - Basic Law of Government, issued by royal decree, serves as the constitutional framework and is based on the Qur'an and the life and traditions of the Prophet Muhammad (2016)

**amendments:** proposed by the king directly or proposed to the king by the Consultative Assembly or by the Council of Ministers; passage by the king through royal decree; Basic Law amended many times, last in 2005 (2016)

## LEGAL SYSTEM:
Islamic (sharia) legal system with some elements of Egyptian, French, and customary law; note - several secular codes have been introduced; commercial disputes handled by special committees

## INTERNATIONAL LAW ORGANIZATION PARTICIPATION:
has not submitted an ICJ jurisdiction declaration; non-party state to the ICCt

## CITIZENSHIP:
**citizenship by birth:** no

**citizenship by descent only:** the father must be a citizen of Saudi Arabia; a child born out of wedlock in Saudi Arabia to a Saudi mother and unknown father

**dual citizenship recognized:** no

**residency requirement for naturalization:** 5 years

## SUFFRAGE:
18 years of age; restricted to males; universal for municipal elections

## EXECUTIVE BRANCH:
**chief of state:** King and Prime Minister SALMAN bin Abd al-Aziz Al Saud (since 23 January 2015); Crown Prince MUHAMMAD BIN SALMAN bin Abd al-Aziz Al Saud (born 31 August 1985); note - the monarch is both chief of state and head of government

**head of government:** King and Prime Minister SALMAN bin Abd al-Aziz Al Saud (since 23 January 2015); Crown Prince MUHAMMAD BIN SALMAN bin Abd al-Aziz Al Saud (born 31 August 1985)

**cabinet:** Council of Ministers appointed by the monarch every 4 years and includes many royal family members

**elections/appointments:** none; the monarchy is hereditary; an Allegiance Council created by royal decree in October 2006 established a committee of Saudi princes for a voice in selecting future Saudi kings

## LEGISLATIVE BRANCH:
**description:** unicameral Consultative Council or Majlis al-Shura (150 seats; members appointed by the monarch to serve 4-year terms); note - in early 2013, the monarch granted women 30 seats on the Council

note: composition as of 2013 - men 121, women 30, percent of women 19.9%

## JUDICIAL BRANCH:
**highest courts:** High Court (consists of the court chief and is organized into circuits with 3-judge panels, except for the criminal circuit, which has a 5-judge panel for cases involving major punishments)

**judge selection and term of office:** High Court chief and chiefs of the High Court Circuits appointed by royal decree following the recommendation of the Supreme Judiciary Council, a 10-member body of high-level judges and other judicial heads; new judges and assistant judges serve 1- and 2-year probations, respectively, before permanent assignment

**subordinate courts:** Court of Appeals; Specialized Criminal Court, first-degree courts composed of general, criminal, personal status, and commercial courts; Labor Court; a hierarchy of administrative courts

## POLITICAL PARTIES AND LEADERS:
none

## INTERNATIONAL ORGANIZATION PARTICIPATION:
ABEDA, AfDB (nonregional member), AFESD, AMF, BIS, CAEU, CP, FAO, G-20, G-77, GCC, IAEA, IBRD, ICAO, ICC (national committees), ICRM, IDA, IDB, IFAD, IFC, IFRCS, IHO, ILO, IMF, IMO, IMSO, Interpol, IOC, IOM (observer), IPU, ISO, ITSO, ITU, LAS, MIGA, NAM, OAPEC, OAS (observer), OIC, OPCW, OPEC, PCA, UN, UNCTAD, UNESCO, UNIDO, UNRWA, UNWTO, UPU, WCO, WFTU (NGOs), WHO, WIPO, WMO, WTO

## DIPLOMATIC REPRESENTATION IN THE US:
**chief of mission:** Ambassador Khalid bin Salman bin Abdulaziz AL SAUD (since 21 July 2017)

**chancery:** 601 New Hampshire Avenue NW, Washington, DC 20037

**telephone:** [1] (202) 342-3800

**FAX:** [1] (202) 944-5983

**consulate(s) general:** Houston, Los Angeles, New York

## DIPLOMATIC REPRESENTATION FROM THE US:
**chief of mission:** Ambassador (vacant); Charge d'Affaires Christopher HENZEL (since 9 January 2017)

**embassy:** P.O. Box 94309, Riyadh 4693

**mailing address:** American Embassy, Unit 61307, APO AE 09803-1307; International Mail: P. O. Box 94309, Riyadh 11693

**telephone:** [966] (11) 488-3800

**FAX:** [966] (11) 488-7360

**consulate(s) general:** Dhahran, Jiddah (Jeddah)

## FLAG DESCRIPTION:
green, a traditional color in Islamic flags, with the Shahada or Muslim creed in large white Arabic script (translated as "There is no god but God; Muhammad is the Messenger of God") above a white horizontal saber (the tip points to the hoist side); design dates to the early twentieth century and is closely associated with the Al Saud family, which established the kingdom in 1932; the flag is manufactured with differing obverse and reverse sides so that the Shahada reads - and the sword points - correctly from right to left on both sides

**note:** the only national flag to display an inscription as its principal design; one of only three national flags that differ on their obverse and reverse sides - the others are Moldova and Paraguay

## NATIONAL SYMBOL(S):
palm tree surmounting two crossed swords; national colors: green, white

## NATIONAL ANTHEM:

name: "Aash Al Maleek" (Long Live Our Beloved King)

lyrics/music: Ibrahim KHAFAJI/Abdul Rahman al-KHATEEB

note: music adopted 1947, lyrics adopted 1984

## ECONOMY :: SAUDI ARABIA

### ECONOMY - OVERVIEW:

Saudi Arabia has an oil-based economy with strong government controls over major economic activities. It possesses about 16% of the world's proven petroleum reserves, ranks as the largest exporter of petroleum, and plays a leading role in OPEC. The petroleum sector accounts for roughly 87% of budget revenues, 42% of GDP, and 90% of export earnings.

Saudi Arabia is encouraging the growth of the private sector in order to diversify its economy and to employ more Saudi nationals. Approximately 6 million foreign workers play an important role in the Saudi economy, particularly in the oil and service sectors; at the same time, however, Riyadh is struggling to reduce unemployment among its own nationals. Saudi officials are particularly focused on employing its large youth population.

In 2017, the Kingdom incurred a budget deficit estimated at 8.3% of GDP, which was financed by bond sales and drawing down reserves. Although the Kingdom can finance high deficits for several years by drawing down its considerable foreign assets or by borrowing, it has cut capital spending and reduced subsidies on electricity, water, and petroleum products and recently introduced a value-added tax of 5%. In January 2016, Crown Prince and Deputy Prime Minister MUHAMMAD BIN SALMAN announced that Saudi Arabia intends to list shares of its state-owned petroleum company, ARAMCO - another move to increase revenue and outside investment. The government has also looked at privatization and diversification of the economy more closely in the wake of a diminished oil market. Historically, Saudi Arabia has focused diversification efforts on power generation, telecommunications, natural gas exploration, and petrochemical sectors. More recently, the government has approached investors about expanding the role of the private sector in the health care, education and tourism industries. While Saudi Arabia has emphasized their goals of diversification for some time, current low oil prices may force the government to make more drastic changes ahead of their long-run timeline.

### GDP (PURCHASING POWER PARITY):

$1.775 trillion (2017 est.)

$1.79 trillion (2016 est.)

$1.761 trillion (2015 est.)

note: data are in 2017 dollars

country comparison to the world: 16

### GDP (OFFICIAL EXCHANGE RATE):

$686.7 billion (2017 est.) (2017 est.)

### GDP - REAL GROWTH RATE:

-0.9% (2017 est.)

1.7% (2016 est.)

4.1% (2015 est.)

country comparison to the world: 202

### GDP - PER CAPITA (PPP):

$54,500 (2017 est.)

$56,400 (2016 est.)

$56,800 (2015 est.)

note: data are in 2017 dollars

country comparison to the world: 22

### GROSS NATIONAL SAVING:

30.1% of GDP (2017 est.)

27.2% of GDP (2016 est.)

26.5% of GDP (2015 est.)

country comparison to the world: 32

### GDP - COMPOSITION, BY END USE:

household consumption: 41.3% (2017 est.)

government consumption: 24.5% (2017 est.)

investment in fixed capital: 23.2% (2017 est.)

investment in inventories: 4.7% (2017 est.)

exports of goods and services: 34.8% (2017 est.)

imports of goods and services: -28.6% (2017 est.)

### GDP - COMPOSITION, BY SECTOR OF ORIGIN:

agriculture: 2.6% (2017 est.)

industry: 44.2% (2017 est.)

services: 53.2% (2017 est.)

### AGRICULTURE - PRODUCTS:

wheat, barley, tomatoes, melons, dates, citrus; mutton, chickens, eggs, milk

### INDUSTRIES:

crude oil production, petroleum refining, basic petrochemicals, ammonia, industrial gases, sodium hydroxide (caustic soda), cement, fertilizer, plastics, metals, commercial ship repair, commercial aircraft repair, construction

### INDUSTRIAL PRODUCTION GROWTH RATE:

-2.4% (2017 est.)

country comparison to the world: 186

### LABOR FORCE:

13.8 million (2017 est.)

note: comprised of 3.1 million Saudis and 10.7 million non-Saudis

country comparison to the world: 42

### LABOR FORCE - BY OCCUPATION:

agriculture: 6.7%

industry: 21.4%

services: 71.9% (2005 est.)

### UNEMPLOYMENT RATE:

6% (2017 est.)

5.6% (2016 est.)

note: data are for total population; unemployment among Saudi nationals is more than double

country comparison to the world: 92

### POPULATION BELOW POVERTY LINE:

NA

### HOUSEHOLD INCOME OR CONSUMPTION BY PERCENTAGE SHARE:

lowest 10%: NA

highest 10%: NA

### DISTRIBUTION OF FAMILY INCOME - GINI INDEX:

45.9 (2013 est.)

country comparison to the world: 37

### BUDGET:

revenues: 181 billion (2017 est.)

expenditures: 241.8 billion (2017 est.)

### TAXES AND OTHER REVENUES:

26.4% (of GDP) (2017 est.)

country comparison to the world: 113

### BUDGET SURPLUS (+) OR DEFICIT (-):

-8.9% (of GDP) (2017 est.)

country comparison to the world: 204

### PUBLIC DEBT:

17.2% of GDP (2017 est.)

13.1% of GDP (2016 est.)

country comparison to the world: 193

**FISCAL YEAR:**

calendar year

**INFLATION RATE (CONSUMER PRICES):**

-0.9% (2017 est.)

2% (2016 est.)

country comparison to the world: 3

**CENTRAL BANK DISCOUNT RATE:**

2.5% (31 December 2008)

country comparison to the world: 115

**COMMERCIAL BANK PRIME LENDING RATE:**

8.3% (31 December 2017 est.)

7.1% (31 December 2016 est.)

country comparison to the world: 102

**STOCK OF NARROW MONEY:**

$312.6 billion (31 December 2017 est.)

$305.2 billion (31 December 2016 est.)

country comparison to the world: 15

**STOCK OF BROAD MONEY:**

$312.6 billion (31 December 2017 est.)

$305.2 billion (31 December 2016 est.)

country comparison to the world: 15

**STOCK OF DOMESTIC CREDIT:**

$267.1 billion (31 December 2017 est.)

$219.7 billion (31 December 2016 est.)

country comparison to the world: 40

**MARKET VALUE OF PUBLICLY TRADED SHARES:**

$421.1 billion (31 December 2015 est.)

$483.1 billion (31 December 2014 est.)

$467.4 billion (31 December 2013 est.)

country comparison to the world: 23

**CURRENT ACCOUNT BALANCE:**

$15.23 billion (2017 est.)

-$23.87 billion (2016 est.)

country comparison to the world: 19

**EXPORTS:**

$221.1 billion (2017 est.)

$183.6 billion (2016 est.)

country comparison to the world: 24

**EXPORTS - PARTNERS:**

Japan 12.2%, China 11.7%, South Korea 9%, India 8.9%, US 8.3%, UAE 6.7%, Singapore 4.2% (2017)

**EXPORTS - COMMODITIES:**

petroleum and petroleum products 90% (2012 est.)

**IMPORTS:**

$119.3 billion (2017 est.)

$127.8 billion (2016 est.)

country comparison to the world: 33

**IMPORTS - COMMODITIES:**

machinery and equipment, foodstuffs, chemicals, motor vehicles, textiles

**IMPORTS - PARTNERS:**

China 15.4%, US 13.6%, UAE 6.5%, Germany 5.8%, Japan 4.1%, India 4.1%, South Korea 4% (2017)

**RESERVES OF FOREIGN EXCHANGE AND GOLD:**

$496.4 billion (31 December 2017 est.)

$535.8 billion (31 December 2016 est.)

country comparison to the world: 4

**DEBT - EXTERNAL:**

$205.1 billion (31 December 2017 est.)

$189.3 billion (31 December 2016 est.)

country comparison to the world: 36

**STOCK OF DIRECT FOREIGN INVESTMENT - AT HOME:**

$264.6 billion (31 December 2017 est.)

$258.1 billion (31 December 2016 est.)

country comparison to the world: 24

**STOCK OF DIRECT FOREIGN INVESTMENT - ABROAD:**

$56.09 billion (31 December 2017 est.)

$46.45 billion (31 December 2016 est.)

country comparison to the world: 41

**EXCHANGE RATES:**

Saudi riyals (SAR) per US dollar -

3.75 (2017 est.)

3.75 (2016 est.)

3.75 (2015 est.)

3.75 (2014 est.)

3.75 (2013 est.)

## ENERGY :: SAUDI ARABIA

**ELECTRICITY ACCESS:**

population without electricity: 200,000 (2013)

electrification - total population: 98% (2013)

electrification - urban areas: 99% (2013)

electrification - rural areas: 93% (2013)

**ELECTRICITY - PRODUCTION:**

324.1 billion kWh (2016 est.)

country comparison to the world: 11

**ELECTRICITY - CONSUMPTION:**

296.2 billion kWh (2016 est.)

country comparison to the world: 12

**ELECTRICITY - EXPORTS:**

0 kWh (2016 est.)

country comparison to the world: 194

**ELECTRICITY - IMPORTS:**

0 kWh (2016 est.)

country comparison to the world: 196

**ELECTRICITY - INSTALLED GENERATING CAPACITY:**

82.94 million kW (2016 est.)

country comparison to the world: 14

**ELECTRICITY - FROM FOSSIL FUELS:**

100% of total installed capacity (2016 est.)

country comparison to the world: 17

**ELECTRICITY - FROM NUCLEAR FUELS:**

0% of total installed capacity (2017 est.)

country comparison to the world: 178

**ELECTRICITY - FROM HYDROELECTRIC PLANTS:**

0% of total installed capacity (2017 est.)

country comparison to the world: 198

**ELECTRICITY - FROM OTHER RENEWABLE SOURCES:**

0% of total installed capacity (2017 est.)

country comparison to the world: 206

**CRUDE OIL - PRODUCTION:**

10.13 million bbl/day (2017 est.)

country comparison to the world: 2

**CRUDE OIL - EXPORTS:**

7.341 million bbl/day (2015 est.)

country comparison to the world: 1

**CRUDE OIL - IMPORTS:**

0 bbl/day (2015 est.)

country comparison to the world: 192

**CRUDE OIL - PROVED RESERVES:**

266.2 billion bbl (1 January 2018 est.)

country comparison to the world: 2

**REFINED PETROLEUM PRODUCTS - PRODUCTION:**

2.476 million bbl/day (2015 est.)

country comparison to the world: 8

**REFINED PETROLEUM PRODUCTS - CONSUMPTION:**

3.287 million bbl/day (2016 est.)

country comparison to the world: 6

**REFINED PETROLEUM PRODUCTS - EXPORTS:**

1.784 million bbl/day (2015 est.)

country comparison to the world: 5
**REFINED PETROLEUM PRODUCTS - IMPORTS:**
609,600 bbl/day (2015 est.)

country comparison to the world: 13
**NATURAL GAS - PRODUCTION:**
109.3 billion cu m (2017 est.)

country comparison to the world: 8
**NATURAL GAS - CONSUMPTION:**
109.3 billion cu m (2017 est.)

country comparison to the world: 7
**NATURAL GAS - EXPORTS:**
0 cu m (2017 est.)

country comparison to the world: 179
**NATURAL GAS - IMPORTS:**
0 cu m (2017 est.)

country comparison to the world: 185
**NATURAL GAS - PROVED RESERVES:**
8.619 trillion cu m (1 January 2018 est.)

country comparison to the world: 4
**CARBON DIOXIDE EMISSIONS FROM CONSUMPTION OF ENERGY:**
657.1 million Mt (2017 est.)

country comparison to the world: 8

## COMMUNICATIONS :: SAUDI ARABIA

**TELEPHONES - FIXED LINES:**
total subscriptions: 3,619,352 (2017 est.)
subscriptions per 100 inhabitants: 13 (2017 est.)
country comparison to the world: 40

**TELEPHONES - MOBILE CELLULAR:**
total subscriptions: 40,210,965 (2017 est.)
subscriptions per 100 inhabitants: 141 (2017 est.)
country comparison to the world: 35

**TELEPHONE SYSTEM:**
general assessment: modern system including a combination of extensive microwave radio relays, coaxial cables, and fiber-optic cables (2016)
domestic: mobile-cellular subscribership has been increasing rapidly (2016)
international: country code - 966; landing point for the international submarine cable Fiber-Optic Link Around the Globe (FLAG) and for both the SEA-ME-WE-3 and SEA-ME-WE-4 submarine cable networks providing connectivity to Asia, Middle East, Europe, and US; microwave radio relay to Bahrain, Jordan, Kuwait, Qatar, UAE, Yemen, and Sudan; coaxial cable to Kuwait and Jordan; satellite earth stations - 5 Intelsat (3 Atlantic Ocean and 2 Indian Ocean), 1 Arabsat, and 1 Inmarsat (Indian Ocean region) (2016)

**BROADCAST MEDIA:**
broadcast media are state-controlled; state-run TV operates 4 networks; Saudi Arabia is a major market for pan-Arab satellite TV broadcasters; state-run radio operates several networks; multiple international broadcasters are available (2007)

**INTERNET COUNTRY CODE:**
.sa

**INTERNET USERS:**
total: 20,768,456 (July 2016 est.)
percent of population: 73.8% (July 2016 est.)
country comparison to the world: 31

**BROADBAND - FIXED SUBSCRIPTIONS:**
total: 2,498,692 (2017 est.)
subscriptions per 100 inhabitants: 9 (2017 est.)
country comparison to the world: 47

## TRANSPORTATION :: SAUDI ARABIA

**NATIONAL AIR TRANSPORT SYSTEM:**
number of registered air carriers: 12 (2015)
inventory of registered aircraft operated by air carriers: 214 (2015)
annual passenger traffic on registered air carriers: 32,778,827 (2015)
annual freight traffic on registered air carriers: 1,783,086,000 mt-km (2015)

**CIVIL AIRCRAFT REGISTRATION COUNTRY CODE PREFIX:**
HZ (2016)

**AIRPORTS:**
214 (2013)
country comparison to the world: 26

**AIRPORTS - WITH PAVED RUNWAYS:**
total: 82 (2017)
over 3,047 m: 33 (2017)
2,438 to 3,047 m: 16 (2017)
1,524 to 2,437 m: 27 (2017)
914 to 1,523 m: 2 (2017)
under 914 m: 4 (2017)

**AIRPORTS - WITH UNPAVED RUNWAYS:**
total: 132 (2013)
2,438 to 3,047 m: 7 (2013)
1,524 to 2,437 m: 72 (2013)
914 to 1,523 m: 37 (2013)
under 914 m: 16 (2013)

**HELIPORTS:**
10 (2013)

**PIPELINES:**
209 km condensate, 2940 km gas, 1183 km liquid petroleum gas, 5117 km oil, 1151 km refined products (2013)

**RAILWAYS:**
total: 5,410 km (2016)
standard gauge: 5,410 km 1.435-m gauge (with branch lines and sidings) (2016)
country comparison to the world: 36

**ROADWAYS:**
total: 221,372 km (2006)
paved: 47,529 km (includes 3,891 km of expressways) (2006)
unpaved: 173,843 km (2006)
country comparison to the world: 23

**MERCHANT MARINE:**
total: 357 (2017)
by type: bulk carrier 5, container ship 1, general cargo 19, oil tanker 31, other 301 (2017)
country comparison to the world: 48

**PORTS AND TERMINALS:**
major seaport(s): Ad Dammam, Al Jubayl, Jeddah, King Abdulla, Yanbu'
container port(s) (TEUs): Ad Dammam (1,785,000), Jeddah (3,956,856), King Abdulla (1,402,225) (2016)

## MILITARY AND SECURITY :: SAUDI ARABIA

**MILITARY EXPENDITURES:**
9.85% of GDP (2016)
13.33% of GDP (2015)
10.68% of GDP (2014)
country comparison to the world: 3

**MILITARY BRANCHES:**
Ministry of Defense: Royal Saudi Land Forces, Royal Saudi Naval Forces (includes Marine Forces and Special Forces), Royal Saudi Air Force (Al-

Quwwat al-Jawwiya al-Malakiya as-Sa'udiya), Royal Saudi Air Defense Forces, Royal Saudi Strategic Rocket Forces, Ministry of the National Guard (SANG) (2015)

**MILITARY SERVICE AGE AND OBLIGATION:**

17 is the legal minimum age for voluntary military service; no conscription (2012)

## TERRORISM :: SAUDI ARABIA

**TERRORIST GROUPS - FOREIGN BASED:**

al-Qa'ida (AQ):
aim(s): oppose the Saudi Islamic monarchy due to its cooperation with the US and the West, particularly US military bases in the Kingdom; eradicate US and Western influence and presence from Saudi Arabia
area(s) of operation: maintains familial connections but lacks a persistent operational presence; probably retains some supporters in the country who could facilitate future operations (April 2018)

al-Qa'ida in the Arabian Peninsula (AQAP):
aim(s): ultimately overthrow the Saudi Islamic monarchy; eradicate US and Western influence and presence from Yemen and the rest of the Arabian Peninsula
area(s) of operation: maintains familial connections but lacks an operational presence inside Saudi Arabia; operates widely in neighboring Yemen (April 2018)

Islamic State of Iraq and ash-Sham (ISIS)-Saudi Arabia:
aim(s): replace the Saudi Islamic monarchy with an Islamic state applying ISIS's strict interpretation of Sharia; target minority Shia Muslims, Saudi security personnel, and their interests
area(s) of operation: maintains a recruitment presence; conducts deadly strikes against Saudi security personnel and bombs Shia Muslim mosques, markets, and other places where Shia Muslims gather (April 2018)

## TRANSNATIONAL ISSUES :: SAUDI ARABIA

**DISPUTES - INTERNATIONAL:**

Saudi Arabia has reinforced its concrete-filled security barrier along sections of the now fully demarcated border with Yemen to stem illegal cross-border activitiesKuwait and Saudi Arabia continue discussions on a maritime boundary with IranSaudi Arabia claims Egyptian-administered islands of Tiran and Sanafir

**REFUGEES AND INTERNALLY DISPLACED PERSONS:**

refugees (country of origin): 30,000 (Yemen) (2017)

stateless persons: 70,000 (2017); note - thousands of biduns (stateless Arabs) are descendants of nomadic tribes who were not officially registered when national borders were established, while others migrated to Saudi Arabia in search of jobs; some have temporary identification cards that must be renewed every five years, but their rights remain restricted; most Palestinians have only legal resident status; some naturalized Yemenis were made stateless after being stripped of their passports when Yemen backed Iraq in its invasion of Kuwait in 1990; Saudi women cannot pass their citizenship on to their children, so if they marry a non-national, their children risk statelessness

**TRAFFICKING IN PERSONS:**

current situation: Saudi Arabia is a destination country for men and women subjected to forced labor and, to a lesser extent, forced prostitution; men and women from South and East Asia, the Middle East, and Africa who voluntarily travel to Saudi Arabia as domestic servants or low-skilled laborers subsequently face conditions of involuntary servitude, including nonpayment and withholding of passports; some migrant workers are forced to work indefinitely beyond the term of their contract because their employers will not grant them a required exit visa; female domestic workers are particularly vulnerable because of their isolation in private homes; women, primarily from Asian and African countries, are believed to be forced into prostitution in Saudi Arabia, while other foreign women were reportedly kidnapped and forced into prostitution after running away from abusive employers; children from South Asia, East Africa, and Yemen are subjected to forced labor as beggars and street vendors in Saudi Arabia, facilitated by criminal gangs

tier rating: Tier 2 Watch List - Saudi Arabia does not fully comply with the minimum standards for the elimination of trafficking; however, it is making significant efforts to do so; government officials and high-level religious leaders demonstrated greater political will to combat trafficking and publically acknowledged the problem – specifically forced labor; the government reported increased numbers of prosecutions and convictions of trafficking offenders; however, it did not proactively investigate and prosecute employers for potential labor trafficking crimes following their withholding of workers' wages and passports, which are illegal; authorities did not systematically use formal criteria to proactively identify victims, resulting in some unidentified victims being arrested, detained, deported, and sometimes prosecuted; more victims were identified and referred to protective services in 2014 than the previous year, but victims of sex trafficking and male trafficking victims were not provided with shelter and remained vulnerable to punishment (2015)

**ILLICIT DRUGS:**

regularly enforces the death penalty for drug traffickers, with foreigners being convicted and executed disproportionately; improving anti-money-laundering legislation and enforcement

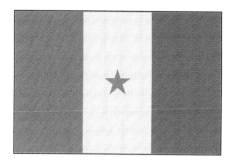

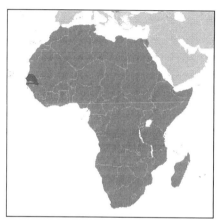

# AFRICA :: SENEGAL

## INTRODUCTION :: SENEGAL

### BACKGROUND:

The French colonies of Senegal and French Sudan were merged in 1959 and granted independence in 1960 as the Mali Federation. The union broke up after only a few months. Senegal joined with The Gambia to form the nominal confederation of Senegambia in 1982. The envisaged integration of the two countries was never implemented, and the union was dissolved in 1989. The Movement of Democratic Forces in the Casamance has led a low-level separatist insurgency in southern Senegal since the 1980s. Several peace deals have failed to resolve the conflict, but an unofficial cease-fire has remained largely in effect since 2012. Senegal remains one of the most stable democracies in Africa and has a long history of participating in international peacekeeping and regional mediation. Senegal was ruled by a Socialist Party for 40 years until Abdoulaye WADE was elected president in 2000. He was reelected in 2007 and during his two terms amended Senegal's constitution over a dozen times to increase executive power and weaken the opposition. His decision to run for a third presidential term sparked a large public backlash that led to his defeat in a March 2012 runoff with Macky SALL, whose term runs until 2019. A 2016 constitutional referendum reduced the term to five years with a maximum of two consecutive terms for future presidents.

## GEOGRAPHY :: SENEGAL

### LOCATION:
Western Africa, bordering the North Atlantic Ocean, between Guinea-Bissau and Mauritania

### GEOGRAPHIC COORDINATES:
14 00 N, 14 00 W

### MAP REFERENCES:
Africa

### AREA:
total: 196,722 sq km

land: 192,530 sq km

water: 4,192 sq km

country comparison to the world: 89

### AREA - COMPARATIVE:
slightly smaller than South Dakota

### LAND BOUNDARIES:
total: 2,684 km

border countries (5): The Gambia 749 km, Guinea 363 km, Guinea-Bissau 341 km, Mali 489 km, Mauritania 742 km

### COASTLINE:
531 km

### MARITIME CLAIMS:
territorial sea: 12 nm

exclusive economic zone: 200 nm

contiguous zone: 24 nm

continental shelf: 200 nm or to the edge of the continental margin

### CLIMATE:
tropical; hot, humid; rainy season (May to November) has strong southeast winds; dry season (December to April) dominated by hot, dry, harmattan wind

### TERRAIN:
generally low, rolling, plains rising to foothills in southeast

### ELEVATION:
mean elevation: 69 m

elevation extremes: 0 m lowest point: Atlantic Ocean

648 highest point: unnamed elevation 2.8 km southeast of Nepen Diaka

### NATURAL RESOURCES:
fish, phosphates, iron ore

### LAND USE:
agricultural land: 46.8% (2011 est.)

arable land: 17.4% (2011 est.) / permanent crops: 0.3% (2011 est.) / permanent pasture: 29.1% (2011 est.)

forest: 43.8% (2011 est.)

other: 9.4% (2011 est.)

### IRRIGATED LAND:
1,200 sq km (2012)

### POPULATION DISTRIBUTION:
the population is concentrated in the west, with Dakar anchoring a well-defined core area; approximately 70% of the population is rural

### NATURAL HAZARDS:
lowlands seasonally flooded; periodic droughts

### ENVIRONMENT - CURRENT ISSUES:
deforestation; overgrazing; soil erosion; desertification; periodic droughts; seasonal flooding; overfishing; weak environmental protective laws; wildlife populations threatened by poaching

### ENVIRONMENT - INTERNATIONAL AGREEMENTS:
party to: Biodiversity, Climate Change, Climate Change-Kyoto Protocol, Desertification, Endangered

Species, Hazardous Wastes, Law of the Sea, Marine Life Conservation, Ozone Layer Protection, Ship Pollution, Wetlands, Whaling

**signed, but not ratified:** none of the selected agreements

### GEOGRAPHY - NOTE:
westernmost country on the African continent; The Gambia is almost an enclave within Senegal

# PEOPLE AND SOCIETY :: SENEGAL

### POPULATION:
15,020,945 (July 2018 est.)

**country comparison to the world:** 72

### NATIONALITY:
**noun:** Senegalese (singular and plural)

**adjective:** Senegalese

### ETHNIC GROUPS:
Wolof 37.1%, Pular 26.2%, Serer 17%, Mandinka 5.6%, Jola 4.5%, Soninke 1.4%, other 8.3% (includes Europeans and persons of Lebanese descent) (2017 est.)

### LANGUAGES:
French (official), Wolof, Pular, Jola, Mandinka, Serer, Soninke

### RELIGIONS:
Muslim 95.9% (most adhere to one of the four main Sufi brotherhoods), Christian 4.1% (mostly Roman Catholic) (2016 est.)

### DEMOGRAPHIC PROFILE:
Senegal has a large and growing youth population but has not been successful in developing its potential human capital. Senegal's high total fertility rate of almost 4.5 children per woman continues to bolster the country's large youth cohort – more than 60% of the population is under the age of 25. Fertility remains high because of the continued desire for large families, the low use of family planning, and early childbearing. Because of the country's high illiteracy rate (more than 40%), high unemployment (even among university graduates), and widespread poverty, Senegalese youths face dim prospects; women are especially disadvantaged.

Senegal historically was a destination country for economic migrants, but in recent years West African migrants more often use Senegal as a transit point to North Africa – and sometimes illegally onward to Europe. The country also has been host to several thousand black Mauritanian refugees since they were expelled from their homeland during its 1989 border conflict with Senegal. The country's economic crisis in the 1970s stimulated emigration; departures accelerated in the 1990s. Destinations shifted from neighboring countries, which were experiencing economic decline, civil wars, and increasing xenophobia, to Libya and Mauritania because of their booming oil industries and to developed countries (most notably former colonial ruler France, as well as Italy and Spain). The latter became attractive in the 1990s because of job opportunities and their periodic regularization programs (legalizing the status of illegal migrants).

Additionally, about 16,000 Senegalese refugees still remain in The Gambia and Guinea-Bissau as a result of more than 30 years of fighting between government forces and rebel separatists in southern Senegal's Casamance region.

### AGE STRUCTURE:
**0-14 years:** 41.15% (male 3,106,942 /female 3,074,740)

**15-24 years:** 20.33% (male 1,521,868 /female 1,531,484)

**25-54 years:** 31.45% (male 2,176,052 /female 2,547,566)

**55-64 years:** 4.05% (male 261,682 /female 347,374)

**65 years and over:** 3.02% (male 200,079 /female 253,158) (2018 est.)

### DEPENDENCY RATIOS:
**total dependency ratio:** 85.4 (2015 est.)

**youth dependency ratio:** 79.8 (2015 est.)

**elderly dependency ratio:** 5.6 (2015 est.)

**potential support ratio:** 18 (2015 est.)

### MEDIAN AGE:
**total:** 19 years

**male:** 18.1 years

**female:** 19.9 years (2018 est.)

**country comparison to the world:** 205

### POPULATION GROWTH RATE:
2.36% (2018 est.)

**country comparison to the world:** 30

### BIRTH RATE:
32.9 births/1,000 population (2018 est.)

**country comparison to the world:** 27

### DEATH RATE:
7.9 deaths/1,000 population (2018 est.)

**country comparison to the world:** 94

### NET MIGRATION RATE:
-1.5 migrant(s)/1,000 population (2017 est.)

**country comparison to the world:** 149

### POPULATION DISTRIBUTION:
the population is concentrated in the west, with Dakar anchoring a well-defined core area; approximately 70% of the population is rural

### URBANIZATION:
**urban population:** 47.2% of total population (2018)

**rate of urbanization:** 3.73% annual rate of change (2015-20 est.)

### MAJOR URBAN AREAS - POPULATION:
2.978 million DAKAR (capital) (2018)

### SEX RATIO:
**at birth:** 1.02 male(s)/female (2017 est.)

**0-14 years:** 1.01 male(s)/female (2017 est.)

**15-24 years:** 0.99 male(s)/female (2017 est.)

**25-54 years:** 0.85 male(s)/female (2017 est.)

**55-64 years:** 0.76 male(s)/female (2017 est.)

**65 years and over:** 0.82 male(s)/female (2017 est.)

**total population:** 0.94 male(s)/female (2017 est.)

### MOTHER'S MEAN AGE AT FIRST BIRTH:
21.9 years (2017 est.)

**note:** median age at first birth among women 25-29

### MATERNAL MORTALITY RATE:
315 deaths/100,000 live births (2015 est.)

**country comparison to the world:** 40

### INFANT MORTALITY RATE:
**total:** 48 deaths/1,000 live births (2018 est.)

**male:** 53.7 deaths/1,000 live births (2018 est.)

**female:** 42.1 deaths/1,000 live births (2018 est.)

**country comparison to the world:** 32

### LIFE EXPECTANCY AT BIRTH:

total population: 62.5 years (2018 est.)

male: 60.4 years (2018 est.)

female: 64.7 years (2018 est.)

country comparison to the world: 199

**TOTAL FERTILITY RATE:**

4.2 children born/woman (2018 est.)

country comparison to the world: 30

**CONTRACEPTIVE PREVALENCE RATE:**

25.1% (2016)

**HEALTH EXPENDITURES:**

4.7% of GDP (2014)

country comparison to the world: 153

**PHYSICIANS DENSITY:**

0.07 physicians/1,000 population (2016)

**HOSPITAL BED DENSITY:**

0.3 beds/1,000 population (2008)

**DRINKING WATER SOURCE:**

improved:

urban: 92.9% of population (2015 est.)

rural: 67.3% of population (2015 est.)

total: 78.5% of population (2015 est.)

unimproved:

urban: 7.1% of population (2015 est.)

rural: 32.7% of population (2015 est.)

total: 21.5% of population (2015 est.)

**SANITATION FACILITY ACCESS:**

improved:

urban: 65.4% of population (2015 est.)

rural: 33.8% of population (2015 est.)

total: 47.6% of population (2015 est.)

unimproved:

urban: 34.6% of population (2015 est.)

rural: 66.2% of population (2015 est.)

total: 52.4% of population (2015 est.)

**HIV/AIDS - ADULT PREVALENCE RATE:**

0.4% (2017 est.)

country comparison to the world: 76

**HIV/AIDS - PEOPLE LIVING WITH HIV/AIDS:**

43,000 (2017 est.)

country comparison to the world: 63

**HIV/AIDS - DEATHS:**

2,100 (2017 est.)

country comparison to the world: 49

**MAJOR INFECTIOUS DISEASES:**

degree of risk: very high (2016)

food or waterborne diseases: bacterial and protozoal diarrhea, hepatitis A, and typhoid fever (2016)

vectorborne diseases: malaria and dengue fever (2016)

water contact diseases: schistosomiasis (2016)

animal contact diseases: rabies (2016)

respiratory diseases: meningococcal meningitis (2016)

**OBESITY - ADULT PREVALENCE RATE:**

8.8% (2016)

country comparison to the world: 146

**CHILDREN UNDER THE AGE OF 5 YEARS UNDERWEIGHT:**

13.5% (2016)

country comparison to the world: 49

**EDUCATION EXPENDITURES:**

7.1% of GDP (2015)

country comparison to the world: 21

**LITERACY:**

definition: age 15 and over can read and write (2015 est.)

total population: 57.7% (2015 est.)

male: 69.7% (2015 est.)

female: 46.6% (2015 est.)

**SCHOOL LIFE EXPECTANCY (PRIMARY TO TERTIARY EDUCATION):**

total: 9 years (2015)

male: 9 years (2015)

female: 9 years (2015)

**UNEMPLOYMENT, YOUTH AGES 15-24:**

total: 5.3% (2015 est.)

male: 5.2% (2015 est.)

female: 5.5% (2015 est.)

country comparison to the world: 154

## GOVERNMENT :: SENEGAL

**COUNTRY NAME:**

conventional long form: Republic of Senegal

conventional short form: Senegal

local long form: Republique du Senegal

local short form: Senegal

former: Senegambia (along with The Gambia), Mali Federation

etymology: named for the Senegal River that forms the northern border of the country; many theories exist for the origin of the river name; perhaps the most widely cited derives the name from "Azenegue," the Portuguese appellation for the Berber Zenaga people who lived north of the river

**GOVERNMENT TYPE:**

presidential republic

**CAPITAL:**

name: Dakar

geographic coordinates: 14 44 N, 17 38 W

time difference: UTC 0 (5 hours ahead of Washington, DC, during Standard Time)

**ADMINISTRATIVE DIVISIONS:**

14 regions (regions, singular - region); Dakar, Diourbel, Fatick, Kaffrine, Kaolack, Kedougou, Kolda, Louga, Matam, Saint-Louis, Sedhiou, Tambacounda, Thies, Ziguinchor

**INDEPENDENCE:**

4 April 1960 (from France); note - complete independence achieved upon dissolution of federation with Mali on 20 August 1960

**NATIONAL HOLIDAY:**

Independence Day, 4 April (1960)

**CONSTITUTION:**

history: previous 1959 (preindependence), 1963; latest adopted by referendum 7 January 2001, promulgated 22 January 2001 (2017)

amendments: proposed by the president of the republic, by the prime minister through the president, or by the National Assembly; passage requires Assembly approval and approval in a referendum; the president can bypass a referendum and submit an amendment directly to the Assembly, which requires at least three-fifths majority vote; the republican form of government is not amendable; amended several times, last in 2016 (2017)

**LEGAL SYSTEM:**

civil law system based on French law; judicial review of legislative acts in Constitutional Court

**INTERNATIONAL LAW ORGANIZATION PARTICIPATION:**

accepts compulsory ICJ jurisdiction with reservations; accepts ICCt jurisdiction

**CITIZENSHIP:**

citizenship by birth: no

citizenship by descent only: at least one parent must be a citizen of Senegal

dual citizenship recognized: no, but Senegalese citizens do not automatically lose their citizenship if they acquire citizenship in another state

residency requirement for naturalization: 5 years

**SUFFRAGE:**

18 years of age; universal

**EXECUTIVE BRANCH:**

chief of state: President Macky SALL (since 2 April 2012)

head of government: Prime Minister Mohammed Abdallah Boun DIONNE (since 4 July 2014)

cabinet: Council of Ministers appointed by the prime minister in consultation with the president

elections/appointments: president directly elected by absolute majority popular vote in 2 rounds if needed for a 7-year term (eligible for a second consecutive term); election last held on 26 February 2012 with a runoff on 25 March 2012 (next to be held on 24 February 2019); prime minister appointed by the president

election results: Macky SALL elected president in second round; percent of vote - Macky SALL (APR) 65.8%, Abdoulaye WADE (PDS) 34.2%

**LEGISLATIVE BRANCH:**

description: unicameral National Assembly or Assemblee Nationale (165 seats; 105 members including 15 representing Senegalese diaspora directly elected by plurality vote in single- and multi-seat constituencies and 60 members directly elected by proportional representation vote in single- and multi-seat constituencies)

elections: National Assembly - last held on 2 July 2017 (next to be held in July 2022)

election results: National Assembly results - percent of vote by party/coalition - BBK 49.5%, CGWS 16.7%, MTS 11.7%, PUR 4.7%, CP-Kaddu Askan Wi 2%, other 15.4%; seats by party/coalition - BBY 125, CGWS 19, MTS 7, PUR 3, CP-Kaddu Askan Wi 2, other 9

**JUDICIAL BRANCH:**

highest courts: Supreme Court or Cour Supreme (consists of the president and 12 judges and organized into civil and commercial, criminal, administrative, and social chambers); Constitutional Council or Conseil Constitutionel (consists of 7 members including the court president, vice president, and 5 judges)

judge selection and term of office: Supreme Court judges' appointed by the president of the republic upon recommendation of the Higher Council of the Judiciary, a body chaired by the president; judge tenure NA; Constitutional Council members appointed - 5 by the president and 2 by the National Assembly speaker to serve 6-year terms with the renewal of 2 members every 2 years

subordinate courts: High Court of Justice (for crimes of high treason by the president); Courts of Appeal; Court of Auditors; assize courts; regional and district courts; Labor Court; note - in early 2013, the Extraordinary African Chambers were established by agreement of the African Union and the Government of Senegal to try cases of high-level officials involved in crimes committed in Chad during the period 1982-1990

**POLITICAL PARTIES AND LEADERS:**

Alliance for the Republic-Yakaar or APR-Yakaar [Macky SALL]
Alliance of Forces of Progress or AFP [Moustapha NIASSE]
And-Jef/African Party for Democracy and Socialism or AJ/PADS [Mamadou DIOP Decriox]
And-Jef/African Party for Democracy and Socialism or AJ/PADS-A [Landing SAVANE]
Benno Bokk Yakaar or BBY (United in Hope) [Macky SALL] (coalition includes AFP, APR, LD-MPT, PIT, PS, UNP)
Bokk Gis Gis coalition [Pape DIOP]
Citizen Movement for National Reform or MCRN-Bes Du Nakk [Mansour Sy DJAMIL]
Democratic League-Labor Party Movement or LD-MPT [Mamadou NDOYE]
Front for Socialism and Democracy/Benno Jubel or FSD/BJ [Cheikh Abdoulaye Bamba DIEYE]
Gainde Centrist Bloc or BGC [Jean-Paul DIAS]
Grand Party or GP [Malick GAKOU]
Independence and Labor Party or PIT [Magatte THIAM]
Manko Taxawu Senegaal or MTS [Khalifa SALL] (coalition includes BGC, Du Nakk, FSD/BJ, GP, MCRN/Bes, Rewmi)
National Union for the People or UNP [Souleymane Ndene NDIAYE]
Party for Truth and Development or PVD [Cheikh Ahmadou Kara MBAKE]
Party of Unity and Rally or PUR [El Hadji SALL]
Patriotic Convergence Kaddu Askan Wi or CP-Kaddu Askan Wi [Abdoulaye BALDE]
Reform Party or PR [Abdourahim AGNE]
Rewmi Party [Idrissa SECK]
Senegalese Democratic Party or PDS [Abdoulaye WADE]
Socialist Party or PS [Ousmane Tanor DIENG]
Tekki Movement [Mamadou Lamine DIALLO]
Union for Democratic Renewal or URD [Djibo Leyti KA]
Winning Coalition Wattu Senegal or CGWS [Abdoulaye WADE] (includes AJ/PADS, AJ/PADS-A, Bokk Gis Gis, PDS, Tekki Movement)

**INTERNATIONAL ORGANIZATION PARTICIPATION:**

ACP, AfDB, AU, CD, CPLP (associate), ECOWAS, EITI (candidate country), FAO, FZ, G-15, G-77, IAEA, IBRD, ICAO, ICC (national committees), ICCt, ICRM, IDA, IDB, IFAD, IFC, IFRCS, ILO, IMF, IMO, IMSO, Interpol, IOC, IOM, IPU, ISO, ITSO, ITU, ITUC (NGOs), MIGA, MINUSMA, MONUSCO, NAM, OIC, OIF, OPCW, PCA, UN, UNAMID, UNCTAD, UNESCO, UNHCR, UNIDO, UNMIL, UNMISS, UNOCI, UNWTO, UPU, WADB (regional), WAEMU, WCO, WFTU (NGOs), WHO, WIPO, WMO, WTO

**DIPLOMATIC REPRESENTATION IN THE US:**

chief of mission: Ambassador Momar DIOP (since 22 June 2018)

chancery: 2215 M Street, NW, Washington, DC 20007

telephone: [1] (202) 234-0540

FAX: [1] (202) 629-2961

consulate(s) general: Houston, New York

**DIPLOMATIC REPRESENTATION FROM THE US:**

chief of mission: ambassador Tulinabo S. MUSHINGI (since August 2017); note - also accredited to Guinea-Bissau

embassy: Route des Almadies, Dakar

mailing address: B.P. 49, Dakar

telephone: [221] 33-879-4000

FAX: [221] 33-822-2991

**FLAG DESCRIPTION:**

three equal vertical bands of green (hoist side), yellow, and red with a small green five-pointed star centered in the yellow band; green represents Islam, progress, and hope; yellow signifies natural wealth and progress; red symbolizes sacrifice and determination; the star denotes unity and hope

**note:** uses the popular Pan-African colors of Ethiopia; the colors from left to right are the same as those of neighboring Mali and the reverse of those on the flag of neighboring Guinea

### NATIONAL SYMBOL(S):

lion; national colors: green, yellow, red

### NATIONAL ANTHEM:

**name:** "Pincez Tous vos Koras, Frappez les Balafons" (Pluck Your Koras, Strike the Balafons)

**lyrics/music:** Leopold Sedar SENGHOR/Herbert PEPPER

**note:** adopted 1960; lyrics written by Leopold Sedar SENGHOR, Senegal's first president; the anthem sometimes played incorporating the Koras (harp-like stringed instruments) and Balafons (types of xylophones) mentioned in the title

## ECONOMY :: SENEGAL

### ECONOMY - OVERVIEW:

Senegal's economy is driven by mining, construction, tourism, fisheries and agriculture, which are the primary sources of employment in rural areas. The country's key export industries include phosphate mining, fertilizer production, agricultural products and commercial fishing and Senegal is also working on oil exploration projects. It relies heavily on donor assistance, remittances and foreign direct investment. Senegal reached a growth rate of 7% in 2017, due in part to strong performance in agriculture despite erratic rainfall.

President Macky SALL, who was elected in March 2012 under a reformist policy agenda, inherited an economy with high energy costs, a challenging business environment, and a culture of overspending. President SALL unveiled an ambitious economic plan, the Emerging Senegal Plan (ESP), which aims to implement priority economic reforms and investment projects to increase economic growth while preserving macroeconomic stability and debt sustainability. Bureaucratic bottlenecks and a challenging business climate are among the perennial challenges that may slow the implementation of this plan.

Senegal receives technical support from the IMF under a Policy Support Instrument (PSI) to assist with implementation of the ESP. The PSI implementation continues to be satisfactory as concluded by the IMF's fifth review in December 2017. Financial markets have signaled confidence in Senegal through successful Eurobond issuances in 2014, 2017, and 2018.

The government is focusing on 19 projects under the ESP to continue The government's goal under the ESP is structural transformation of the economy. Key projects include the Thiès-Touba Highway, the new international airport opened in December 2017, and upgrades to energy infrastructure. The cost of electricity is a chief constraint for Senegal's development. Electricity prices in Senegal are among the highest in the world. Power Africa, a US presidential initiative led by USAID, supports Senegal's plans to improve reliability and increase generating capacity.

### GDP (PURCHASING POWER PARITY):

$54.8 billion (2017 est.)

$51.15 billion (2016 est.)

$48.15 billion (2015 est.)

**note:** data are in 2017 dollars

**country comparison to the world:** 107

### GDP (OFFICIAL EXCHANGE RATE):

$21.11 billion (2017 est.) (2017 est.)

### GDP - REAL GROWTH RATE:

7.2% (2017 est.)

6.2% (2016 est.)

6.4% (2015 est.)

**country comparison to the world:** 18

### GDP - PER CAPITA (PPP):

$3,500 (2017 est.)

$3,300 (2016 est.)

$3,200 (2015 est.)

**note:** data are in 2017 dollars

**country comparison to the world:** 188

### GROSS NATIONAL SAVING:

21.2% of GDP (2017 est.)

21.3% of GDP (2016 est.)

20.4% of GDP (2015 est.)

**country comparison to the world:** 86

### GDP - COMPOSITION, BY END USE:

**household consumption:** 71.9% (2017 est.)

**government consumption:** 15.2% (2017 est.)

**investment in fixed capital:** 25.1% (2017 est.)

**investment in inventories:** 3.4% (2017 est.)

**exports of goods and services:** 27% (2017 est.)

**imports of goods and services:** -42.8% (2017 est.)

### GDP - COMPOSITION, BY SECTOR OF ORIGIN:

**agriculture:** 16.9% (2017 est.)

**industry:** 24.3% (2017 est.)

**services:** 58.8% (2017 est.)

### AGRICULTURE - PRODUCTS:

peanuts, millet, corn, sorghum, rice, cotton, tomatoes, green vegetables; cattle, poultry, pigs; fish

### INDUSTRIES:

agricultural and fish processing, phosphate mining, fertilizer production, petroleum refining, zircon, and gold mining, construction materials, ship construction and repair

### INDUSTRIAL PRODUCTION GROWTH RATE:

7.7% (2017 est.)

**country comparison to the world:** 26

### LABOR FORCE:

6.966 million (2017 est.)

**country comparison to the world:** 67

### LABOR FORCE - BY OCCUPATION:

**agriculture:** 77.5%

**industry:** 22.5%

**industry and services:** 22.5% (2007 est.)

### UNEMPLOYMENT RATE:

48% (2007 est.)

**country comparison to the world:** 216

### POPULATION BELOW POVERTY LINE:

46.7% (2011 est.)

### HOUSEHOLD INCOME OR CONSUMPTION BY PERCENTAGE SHARE:

**lowest 10%:** 31.1% (2011)

**highest 10%:** 31.1% (2011)

### DISTRIBUTION OF FAMILY INCOME - GINI INDEX:

40.3 (2011)

country comparison to the world: 63

**BUDGET:**

revenues: 4.139 billion (2017 est.)

expenditures: 4.9 billion (2017 est.)

**TAXES AND OTHER REVENUES:**

19.6% (of GDP) (2017 est.)

country comparison to the world: 155

**BUDGET SURPLUS (+) OR DEFICIT (-):**

-3.6% (of GDP) (2017 est.)

country comparison to the world: 151

**PUBLIC DEBT:**

48.3% of GDP (2017 est.)

47.8% of GDP (2016 est.)

country comparison to the world: 108

**FISCAL YEAR:**

calendar year

**INFLATION RATE (CONSUMER PRICES):**

1.3% (2017 est.)

0.8% (2016 est.)

country comparison to the world: 73

**CENTRAL BANK DISCOUNT RATE:**

0.25% (31 December 2010)

4.25% (31 December 2009)

country comparison to the world: 140

**COMMERCIAL BANK PRIME LENDING RATE:**

5.4% (31 December 2017 est.)

5.3% (31 December 2016 est.)

country comparison to the world: 138

**STOCK OF NARROW MONEY:**

$5.944 billion (31 December 2017 est.)

$4.689 billion (31 December 2016 est.)

country comparison to the world: 97

**STOCK OF BROAD MONEY:**

$5.944 billion (31 December 2017 est.)

$4.689 billion (31 December 2016 est.)

country comparison to the world: 99

**STOCK OF DOMESTIC CREDIT:**

$6.695 billion (31 December 2017 est.)

$5.219 billion (31 December 2016 est.)

country comparison to the world: 121

**MARKET VALUE OF PUBLICLY TRADED SHARES:**

NA

**CURRENT ACCOUNT BALANCE:**

-$1.547 billion (2017 est.)

-$769 million (2016 est.)

country comparison to the world: 157

**EXPORTS:**

$2.362 billion (2017 est.)

$2.498 billion (2016 est.)

country comparison to the world: 134

**EXPORTS - PARTNERS:**

Mali 14.8%, Switzerland 11.4%, India 6%, Cote dIvoire 5.3%, UAE 5.1%, Gambia, The 4.2%, Spain 4.1% (2017)

**EXPORTS - COMMODITIES:**

fish, groundnuts (peanuts), petroleum products, phosphates, cotton

**IMPORTS:**

$5.217 billion (2017 est.)

$4.966 billion (2016 est.)

country comparison to the world: 125

**IMPORTS - COMMODITIES:**

food and beverages, capital goods, fuels

**IMPORTS - PARTNERS:**

France 16.3%, China 10.4%, Nigeria 8%, India 7.2%, Netherlands 4.8%, Spain 4.2% (2017)

**RESERVES OF FOREIGN EXCHANGE AND GOLD:**

$1.827 billion (31 December 2017 est.)

$116.9 million (31 December 2016 est.)

country comparison to the world: 122

**DEBT - EXTERNAL:**

$8.571 billion (31 December 2017 est.)

$6.327 billion (31 December 2016 est.)

country comparison to the world: 119

**EXCHANGE RATES:**

Communaute Financiere Africaine francs (XOF) per US dollar -

617.4 (2017 est.)

593.01 (2016 est.)

593.01 (2015 est.)

591.45 (2014 est.)

494.42 (2013 est.)

## ENERGY :: SENEGAL

**ELECTRICITY ACCESS:**

population without electricity: 6.4 million (2013)

electrification - total population: 55% (2013)

electrification - urban areas: 90% (2013)

electrification - rural areas: 28% (2013)

**ELECTRICITY - PRODUCTION:**

4.167 billion kWh (2016 est.)

country comparison to the world: 126

**ELECTRICITY - CONSUMPTION:**

3.497 billion kWh (2016 est.)

country comparison to the world: 133

**ELECTRICITY - EXPORTS:**

0 kWh (2016 est.)

country comparison to the world: 195

**ELECTRICITY - IMPORTS:**

0 kWh (2016 est.)

country comparison to the world: 197

**ELECTRICITY - INSTALLED GENERATING CAPACITY:**

977,000 kW (2016 est.)

country comparison to the world: 129

**ELECTRICITY - FROM FOSSIL FUELS:**

82% of total installed capacity (2016 est.)

country comparison to the world: 79

**ELECTRICITY - FROM NUCLEAR FUELS:**

0% of total installed capacity (2017 est.)

country comparison to the world: 179

**ELECTRICITY - FROM HYDROELECTRIC PLANTS:**

7% of total installed capacity (2017 est.)

country comparison to the world: 127

**ELECTRICITY - FROM OTHER RENEWABLE SOURCES:**

11% of total installed capacity (2017 est.)

country comparison to the world: 80

**CRUDE OIL - PRODUCTION:**

0 bbl/day (2017 est.)

country comparison to the world: 196

**CRUDE OIL - EXPORTS:**

0 bbl/day (2015 est.)

country comparison to the world: 190

**CRUDE OIL - IMPORTS:**

17,880 bbl/day (2015 est.)

country comparison to the world: 65

**CRUDE OIL - PROVED RESERVES:**

0 bbl (1 January 2018 est.)

country comparison to the world: 192

**REFINED PETROLEUM PRODUCTS - PRODUCTION:**

17,590 bbl/day (2015 est.)

country comparison to the world: 90

**REFINED PETROLEUM PRODUCTS - CONSUMPTION:**

48,000 bbl/day (2016 est.)

country comparison to the world: 107

**REFINED PETROLEUM PRODUCTS - EXPORTS:**

4,063 bbl/day (2015 est.)

country comparison to the world: 94

**REFINED PETROLEUM PRODUCTS - IMPORTS:**

32,050 bbl/day (2015 est.)

country comparison to the world: 98

**NATURAL GAS - PRODUCTION:**

59.46 million cu m (2017 est.)

country comparison to the world: 85

**NATURAL GAS - CONSUMPTION:**

59.46 million cu m (2017 est.)

country comparison to the world: 111

**NATURAL GAS - EXPORTS:**

0 cu m (2017 est.)

country comparison to the world: 180

**NATURAL GAS - IMPORTS:**

0 cu m (2017 est.)

country comparison to the world: 186

**NATURAL GAS - PROVED RESERVES:**

0 cu m (1 January 2012 est.)

country comparison to the world: 191

**CARBON DIOXIDE EMISSIONS FROM CONSUMPTION OF ENERGY:**

8.644 million Mt (2017 est.)

country comparison to the world: 113

## COMMUNICATIONS :: SENEGAL

**TELEPHONES - FIXED LINES:**

total subscriptions: 290,636 (2017 est.)

subscriptions per 100 inhabitants: 2 (2017 est.)

country comparison to the world: 115

**TELEPHONES - MOBILE CELLULAR:**

total subscriptions: 15,758,366 (2017 est.)

subscriptions per 100 inhabitants: 107 (2017 est.)

country comparison to the world: 64

**TELEPHONE SYSTEM:**

general assessment: good system with microwave radio relay, coaxial cable and fiber-optic cable in trunk system (2017)

domestic: generally reliable urban system with a fiber-optic network; about two-thirds of all fixed-line connections are in Dakar; mobile-cellular service is steadily displacing fixed-line service, even in urban areas (2017)

international: country code - 221; the ACE fiber-optic cable connects Senegal to Europe, the SAT-3/WASC provides fiber-optic connectivity to Europe and Asia, and Atlantis-2 provides connectivity to South America; satellite earth station - 1 Intelsat (Atlantic Ocean) (2017)

**BROADCAST MEDIA:**

state-run Radiodiffusion Television Senegalaise (RTS) broadcasts TV programs from five cities in Senegal; in most regions of the country, viewers can receive TV programming from at least 7 private broadcasters; a wide range of independent TV programming is available via satellite; RTS operates a national radio network and a number of regional FM stations; at least 7 community radio stations and 18 private-broadcast radio stations are available; transmissions of at least 5 international broadcasters are accessible on FM in Dakar (2017)

**INTERNET COUNTRY CODE:**

.sn

**INTERNET USERS:**

total: 3,675,209 (July 2016 est.)

percent of population: 25.7% (July 2016 est.)

country comparison to the world: 91

**BROADBAND - FIXED SUBSCRIPTIONS:**

total: 111,795 (2017 est.)

subscriptions per 100 inhabitants: 1 (2017 est.)

country comparison to the world: 119

## TRANSPORTATION :: SENEGAL

**NATIONAL AIR TRANSPORT SYSTEM:**

annual passenger traffic on registered air carriers: 115,355 (2015)

annual freight traffic on registered air carriers: 3,095,523 mt-km (2015)

**CIVIL AIRCRAFT REGISTRATION COUNTRY CODE PREFIX:**

6V (2016)

**AIRPORTS:**

20 (2013)

country comparison to the world: 136

**AIRPORTS - WITH PAVED RUNWAYS:**

total: 9 (2017)

over 3,047 m: 2 (2017)

1,524 to 2,437 m: 6 (2017)

914 to 1,523 m: 1 (2017)

**AIRPORTS - WITH UNPAVED RUNWAYS:**

total: 11 (2013)

1,524 to 2,437 m: 7 (2013)

914 to 1,523 m: 3 (2013)

under 914 m: 1 (2013)

**PIPELINES:**

43 km gas, 8 km refined products (2017)

**RAILWAYS:**

total: 906 km (713 km operational in 2017) (2017)

narrow gauge: 906 km 1.000-m gauge (2017)

country comparison to the world: 94

**ROADWAYS:**

total: 16,496 km (2017)

paved: 5,957 km (includes 72 km of expressways) (2017)

unpaved: 10,539 km (2017)

country comparison to the world: 121

**WATERWAYS:**

1,000 km (primarily on the Senegal, Saloum, and Casamance Rivers) (2012)

country comparison to the world: 63

**MERCHANT MARINE:**

total: 26 (2017)

by type: general cargo 3, oil tanker 1, other 22 (2017)

country comparison to the world: 133

**PORTS AND TERMINALS:**

major seaport(s): Dakar

## MILITARY AND SECURITY :: SENEGAL

**MILITARY EXPENDITURES:**

1.89% of GDP (2017 est.)

1.73% of GDP (2016)

1.58% of GDP (2015)

country comparison to the world: 54

**MILITARY BRANCHES:**

Senegalese Armed Forces: Army, Senegalese National Navy (Marine Senegalaise, MNS), Senegalese Air Force (Armee de l'Air du Senegal) (2017)

**MILITARY SERVICE AGE AND OBLIGATION:**

18 years of age for voluntary military service; 20 years of age for selective conscript service; 2-year service

# TRANSNATIONAL ISSUES :: SENEGAL

**DISPUTES - INTERNATIONAL:** obligation; women have been accepted into military service since 2008 (2013)

cross-border trafficking in persons, timber, wildlife, and cannabis; rebels from the Movement of Democratic Forces in the Casamance find refuge in Guinea-Bissau

**REFUGEES AND INTERNALLY DISPLACED PERSONS:**

refugees (country of origin): 13,779 (Mauritania) (2018)

IDPs: 22,000 (clashes between government troops and separatists in Casamance region) (2017)

**ILLICIT DRUGS:**

transshipment point for Southwest and Southeast Asian heroin and South American cocaine moving to Europe and North America; illicit cultivator of cannabis

# EUROPE :: SERBIA

## INTRODUCTION :: SERBIA

### BACKGROUND:

The Kingdom of Serbs, Croats, and Slovenes was formed in 1918; its name was changed to Yugoslavia in 1929. Communist Partisans resisted the Axis occupation and division of Yugoslavia from 1941 to 1945 and fought nationalist opponents and collaborators as well. The military and political movement headed by Josip Broz "TITO" (Partisans) took full control of Yugoslavia when their domestic rivals and the occupiers were defeated in 1945. Although communists, TITO and his successors (Tito died in 1980) managed to steer their own path between the Warsaw Pact nations and the West for the next four and a half decades. In 1989, Slobodan MILOSEVIC became president of the Republic of Serbia and his ultranationalist calls for Serbian domination led to the violent breakup of Yugoslavia along ethnic lines. In 1991, Croatia, Slovenia, and Macedonia declared independence, followed by Bosnia in 1992. The remaining republics of Serbia and Montenegro declared a new Federal Republic of Yugoslavia (FRY) in April 1992 and under MILOSEVIC's leadership, Serbia led various military campaigns to unite ethnic Serbs in neighboring republics into a "Greater Serbia." These actions ultimately failed and, after international intervention, led to the signing of the Dayton Peace Accords in 1995.

MILOSEVIC retained control over Serbia and eventually became president of the FRY in 1997. In 1998, an ethnic Albanian insurgency in the formerly autonomous Serbian province of Kosovo provoked a Serbian counterinsurgency campaign that resulted in massacres and massive expulsions of ethnic Albanians living in Kosovo. The MILOSEVIC government's rejection of a proposed international settlement led to NATO's bombing of Serbia in the spring of 1999. Serbian military and police forces withdrew from Kosovo in June 1999, and the UN Security Council authorized an interim UN administration and a NATO-led security force in Kosovo. FRY elections in late 2000 led to the ouster of MILOSEVIC and the installation of democratic government. In 2003, the FRY became the State Union of Serbia and Montenegro, a loose federation of the two republics. Widespread violence predominantly targeting ethnic Serbs in Kosovo in March 2004 led to more intense calls to address Kosovo's status, and the UN began facilitating status talks in 2006. In June 2006, Montenegro seceded from the federation and declared itself an independent nation. Serbia subsequently gave notice that it was the successor state to the union of Serbia and Montenegro.

In February 2008, after nearly two years of inconclusive negotiations, Kosovo declared itself independent of Serbia - an action Serbia refuses to recognize. At Serbia's request, the UN General Assembly (UNGA) in October 2008 sought an advisory opinion from the International Court of Justice (ICJ) on whether Kosovo's unilateral declaration of independence was in accordance with international law. In a ruling considered unfavorable to Serbia, the ICJ issued an advisory opinion in July 2010 stating that international law did not prohibit declarations of independence. In late 2010, Serbia agreed to an EU-drafted UNGA Resolution acknowledging the ICJ's decision and calling for a new round of talks between Serbia and Kosovo, this time on practical issues rather than Kosovo's status. Serbia and Kosovo signed the first agreement of principles governing the normalization of relations between the two countries in April 2013 and are in the process of implementing its provisions. In 2015, Serbia and Kosovo reached four additional agreements within the EU-led Brussels Dialogue framework. These included agreements on the Community of Serb-Majority Municipalities; telecommunications; energy production and distribution; and freedom of movement. President Aleksandar VUCIC has promoted an ambitious goal of Serbia joining the EU by 2025. Under his leadership as prime minister, in January 2014 Serbia opened formal negotiations for accession. The EU's Western Balkans Strategy, released in February 2018, outlines the steps that Serbia needs to take to complete the accession process in a 2025 perspective.

## GEOGRAPHY :: SERBIA

**LOCATION:**

Southeastern Europe, between Macedonia and Hungary

**GEOGRAPHIC COORDINATES:**

44 00 N, 21 00 E

**MAP REFERENCES:**

Europe

**AREA:**

total: 77,474 sq km

land: 77,474 sq km

water: 0 sq km

country comparison to the world: 118

**AREA - COMPARATIVE:**

slightly smaller than South Carolina

**LAND BOUNDARIES:**

total: 2,322 km

border countries (8): Bosnia and Herzegovina 345 km, Bulgaria 344 km, Croatia 314 km, Hungary 164 km, Kosovo 366 km, Macedonia 101 km, Montenegro 157 km, Romania 531 km

**COASTLINE:**

0 km (landlocked)

**MARITIME CLAIMS:**

none (landlocked)

**CLIMATE:**

in the north, continental climate (cold winters and hot, humid summers with well-distributed rainfall); in other parts, continental and Mediterranean climate (relatively cold winters with heavy snowfall and hot, dry summers and autumns)

**TERRAIN:**

extremely varied; to the north, rich fertile plains; to the east, limestone ranges and basins; to the southeast, ancient mountains and hills

**ELEVATION:**

mean elevation: 442 m

elevation extremes: 35 m lowest point: Danube and Timok Rivers

2169 highest point: Midzor

**NATURAL RESOURCES:**

oil, gas, coal, iron ore, copper, zinc, antimony, chromite, gold, silver, magnesium, pyrite, limestone, marble, salt, arable land

**LAND USE:**

agricultural land: 57.9% (2011 est.)

arable land: 37.7% (2011 est.) / permanent crops: 3.4% (2011 est.) / permanent pasture: 16.8% (2011 est.)

forest: 31.6% (2011 est.)

other: 10.5% (2011 est.)

**IRRIGATED LAND:**

950 sq km (2012)

**POPULATION DISTRIBUTION:**

a fairly even distribution throughout most of the country, with urban areas attracting larger and denser populations

**NATURAL HAZARDS:**

destructive earthquakes

**ENVIRONMENT - CURRENT ISSUES:**

air pollution around Belgrade and other industrial cities; water pollution from industrial wastes dumped into the Sava which flows into the Danube; inadequate management of domestic, industrial, and hazardous waste

**ENVIRONMENT - INTERNATIONAL AGREEMENTS:**

party to: Air Pollution, Biodiversity, Climate Change, Climate Change-Kyoto Protocol, Desertification, Endangered Species, Hazardous Wastes, Law of the Sea, Marine Dumping, Marine Life Conservation, Ozone Layer Protection, Ship Pollution, Wetlands

signed, but not ratified: none of the selected agreements

**GEOGRAPHY - NOTE:**

landlocked; controls one of the major land routes from Western Europe to Turkey and the Near East

# PEOPLE AND SOCIETY :: SERBIA

**POPULATION:**

7,078,110 (July 2018 est.)

note: does not include the population of Kosovo

country comparison to the world: 103

**NATIONALITY:**

noun: Serb(s)

adjective: Serbian

**ETHNIC GROUPS:**

Serb 83.3%, Hungarian 3.5%, Romani 2.1%, Bosniak 2%, other 5.7%, undeclared or unknown 3.4% (2011 est.)

note: most ethnic Albanians boycotted the 2011 census; Romani populations are usually underestimated in official statistics and may represent 5–11% of Serbia's population

**LANGUAGES:**

Serbian (official) 88.1%, Hungarian 3.4%, Bosnian 1.9%, Romani 1.4%, other 3.4%, undeclared or unknown 1.8% (2011 est.)

note: Serbian, Hungarian, Slovak, Romanian, Croatian, and Ruthenian (Rusyn) are official in the Autonomous Province of Vojvodina; most ethnic Albanians boycotted the 2011 census

**RELIGIONS:**

Orthodox 84.6%, Catholic 5%, Muslim 3.1%, Protestant 1%, atheist 1.1%, other 0.8% (includes agnostics, other Christians, Eastern religionists, Jewish), undeclared or unknown 4.5% (2011 est.)

note: most ethnic Albanians boycotted the 2011 census

**AGE STRUCTURE:**

0-14 years: 14.35% (male 523,473 /female 492,339)

15-24 years: 11.19% (male 408,379 /female 383,385)

25-54 years: 41.27% (male 1,475,243 /female 1,445,935)

55-64 years: 14.21% (male 485,849 /female 520,126)

65 years and over: 18.98% (male 557,307 /female 786,074) (2018 est.)

**DEPENDENCY RATIOS:**

total dependency ratio: 49.2 (2015 est.)

youth dependency ratio: 24.9 (2015 est.)

elderly dependency ratio: 24.3 (2015 est.)

potential support ratio: 4.1 (2015 est.)

note: data include Kosovo

**MEDIAN AGE:**

total: 42.8 years

male: 41.2 years

female: 44.5 years (2018 est.)

country comparison to the world: 24

**POPULATION GROWTH RATE:**

-0.47% (2018 est.)

country comparison to the world: 220

**BIRTH RATE:**

8.9 births/1,000 population (2018 est.)

country comparison to the world: 207

**DEATH RATE:**

13.6 deaths/1,000 population (2018 est.)

country comparison to the world: 7

**NET MIGRATION RATE:**

0 migrant(s)/1,000 population (2017 est.)

country comparison to the world: 97

**POPULATION DISTRIBUTION:**

a fairly even distribution throughout most of the country, with urban areas attracting larger and denser populations

**URBANIZATION:**

urban population: 56.1% of total population (2018)

rate of urbanization: -0.07% annual rate of change (2015-20 est.)

note: data include Kosovo

**MAJOR URBAN AREAS - POPULATION:**

1.389 million BELGRADE (capital) (2018)

**SEX RATIO:**

at birth: 1.06 male(s)/female (2017 est.)

0-14 years: 1.06 male(s)/female (2017 est.)

15-24 years: 1.06 male(s)/female (2017 est.)

25-54 years: 1.02 male(s)/female (2017 est.)

55-64 years: 0.93 male(s)/female (2017 est.)

65 years and over: 0.7 male(s)/female (2017 est.)

total population: 0.95 male(s)/female (2017 est.)

**MOTHER'S MEAN AGE AT FIRST BIRTH:**

27.9 years (2014 est.)

note: data do not cover Kosovo or Metohija

**MATERNAL MORTALITY RATE:**

17 deaths/100,000 live births (2015 est.)

country comparison to the world: 133

**INFANT MORTALITY RATE:**

total: 5.7 deaths/1,000 live births (2018 est.)

male: 6.6 deaths/1,000 live births (2018 est.)

female: 4.8 deaths/1,000 live births (2018 est.)

country comparison to the world: 169

**LIFE EXPECTANCY AT BIRTH:**

total population: 75.9 years (2018 est.)

male: 73 years (2018 est.)

female: 79 years (2018 est.)

country comparison to the world: 98

**TOTAL FERTILITY RATE:**

1.44 children born/woman (2018 est.)

country comparison to the world: 208

**CONTRACEPTIVE PREVALENCE RATE:**

58.4% (2014)

**HEALTH EXPENDITURES:**

10.4% of GDP (2014)

country comparison to the world: 21

**PHYSICIANS DENSITY:**

2.46 physicians/1,000 population (2014)

**HOSPITAL BED DENSITY:**

5.7 beds/1,000 population (2012)

**DRINKING WATER SOURCE:**

improved:

urban: 99.4% of population

rural: 98.9% of population

total: 99.2% of population

unimproved:

urban: 0.6% of population

rural: 1.1% of population

total: 0.8% of population (2015 est.)

**SANITATION FACILITY ACCESS:**

improved:

urban: 98.2% of population (2015 est.)

rural: 94.2% of population (2015 est.)

total: 96.4% of population (2015 est.)

unimproved:

urban: 1.8% of population (2015 est.)

rural: 5.8% of population (2015 est.)

total: 3.6% of population (2015 est.)

**HIV/AIDS - ADULT PREVALENCE RATE:**

<.1% (2017 est.)

**HIV/AIDS - PEOPLE LIVING WITH HIV/AIDS:**

2,700 (2017 est.)

country comparison to the world: 128

**HIV/AIDS - DEATHS:**

<100 (2017 est.)

**MAJOR INFECTIOUS DISEASES:**

degree of risk: intermediate (2016)

food or waterborne diseases: bacterial diarrhea (2016)

**OBESITY - ADULT PREVALENCE RATE:**

21.5% (2016)

country comparison to the world: 88

**CHILDREN UNDER THE AGE OF 5 YEARS UNDERWEIGHT:**

1.8% (2014)

country comparison to the world: 114

**EDUCATION EXPENDITURES:**

4% of GDP (2015)

country comparison to the world: 112

**LITERACY:**

definition: age 15 and over can read and write (2016 est.)

total population: 98.8% (2016 est.)

male: 99.5% (2016 est.)

female: 98.2% (2016 est.)

**SCHOOL LIFE EXPECTANCY (PRIMARY TO TERTIARY EDUCATION):**

total: 15 years (2015)

male: 14 years (2015)

female: 15 years (2015)

**UNEMPLOYMENT, YOUTH AGES 15-24:**

total: 34.9% (2016 est.)

male: 32.2% (2016 est.)

female: 39.5% (2016 est.)

country comparison to the world: 22

## GOVERNMENT :: SERBIA

**COUNTRY NAME:**

conventional long form: Republic of Serbia

conventional short form: Serbia

local long form: Republika Srbija

local short form: Srbija

former: People's Republic of Serbia, Socialist Republic of Serbia

etymology: the origin of the name is uncertain, but seems to be related to the name of the West Slavic Sorbs who reside in the Lusatian region in present-day eastern Germany; by tradition, the Serbs migrated from that region to the Balkans in about the 6th century A.D.

**GOVERNMENT TYPE:**

parliamentary republic

**CAPITAL:**

name: Belgrade (Beograd)

geographic coordinates: 44 50 N, 20 30 E

time difference: UTC+1 (6 hours ahead of Washington, DC, during Standard Time)

daylight saving time: +1hr, begins last Sunday in March; ends last Sunday in October

**ADMINISTRATIVE DIVISIONS:**

119 municipalities (opstine, singular - opstina) and 26 cities (gradovi, singular - grad)

municipalities: Ada*, Aleksandrovac, Aleksinac, Alibunar*, Apatin*, Arandelovac, Arilje, Babusnica, Bac*,

Backa Palanka*, Backa Topola*, Backi Petrovac*, Bajina Basta, Batocina, Becej*, Bela Crkva*, Bela Palanka, Beocin*, Blace, Bogatic, Bojnik, Boljevac, Bor, Bosilegrad, Brus, Bujanovac, Cajetina, Cicevac, Coka*, Crna Trava, Cuprija, Despotovac, Dimitrov, Doljevac, Gadzin Han, Golubac, Gornji Milanovac, Indija*, Irig*, Ivanjica, Kanjiza*, Kladovo, Knic, Knjazevac, Koceljeva, Kosjeric, Kovacica*, Kovin*, Krupanj, Kucevo, Kula*, Kursumlija, Lajkovac, Lapovo, Lebane, Ljig, Ljubovija, Lucani, Majdanpek, Mali Idos*, Mali Zvornik, Malo Crnice, Medveda, Merosina, Mionica, Negotin, Nova Crnja*, Nova Varos, Novi Becej*, Novi Knezevac*, Odzaci*, Opovo*, Osecina, Paracin, Pecinci*, Petrovac na Mlavi, Plandiste*, Pozega, Presevo, Priboj, Prijepolje, Prokuplje, Raca, Raska, Razanj, Rekovac, Ruma*, Secanj*, Senta*, Sid*, Sjenica, Smederevska Palanka, Sokobanja, Srbobran*, Sremski Karlovci*, Stara Pazova*, Surdulica, Svilajnac, Svrljig, Temerin*, Titel*, Topola, Trgoviste, Trstenik, Tutin, Ub, Varvarin, Velika Plana, Veliko Gradiste, Vladicin Han, Vladimirci, Vlasotince, Vrbas*, Vrnjacka Banja, Zabalj*, Zabari, Zagubica, Zitiste*, Zitorada;

**cities:** Beograd, Cacak, Jagodina, Kikinda*, Kragujevac, Kraljevo, Krusevac, Leskovac, Loznica, Nis, Novi Pazar, Novi Sad*, Pancevo*, Pirot, Pozarevac, Sabac, Smederevo, Sombor*, Sremska Mitrovica*, Subotica*, Uzice, Valjevo, Vranje, Vrsac*, Zajecar, Zrenjanin*

**note:** the northern 37 municipalities and 8 cities - about 28% of Serbia's area - compose the Autonomous Province of Vojvodina and are indicated with *

## INDEPENDENCE:

5 June 2006 (from the State Union of Serbia and Montenegro); notable earlier dates: 1217 (Serbian Kingdom established); 16 April 1346 (Serbian Empire established); 13 July 1878 (Congress of Berlin recognizes Serbian independence); 1 December 1918 (Kingdom of Serbs, Croats, and Slovenes (Yugoslavia) established)

## NATIONAL HOLIDAY:

National Day (Statehood Day), 15 February (1835), the day the first constitution of the country was adopted

## CONSTITUTION:

**history:** many previous; latest adopted 30 September 2006, approved by referendum 28-29 October 2006, effective 8 November 2006 (2016)

**amendments:** proposed by at least one-third of deputies in the National Assembly, by the president of the republic, by the government, or by petition of at least 150,000 voters; passage of proposals and draft amendments each requires at least two-thirds majority vote in the Assembly; amendments to constitutional articles including the preamble, constitutional principles, and human and minority rights and freedoms also require passage by simple majority vote in a referendum (2016)

## LEGAL SYSTEM:

civil law system

## INTERNATIONAL LAW ORGANIZATION PARTICIPATION:

has not submitted an ICJ jurisdiction declaration; accepts ICCt jurisdiction

## CITIZENSHIP:

**citizenship by birth:** no

**citizenship by descent only:** at least one parent must be a citizen of Serbia

**dual citizenship recognized:** yes

**residency requirement for naturalization:** 3 years

## SUFFRAGE:

18 years of age, 16 if employed; universal

## EXECUTIVE BRANCH:

**chief of state:** President Aleksandar VUCIC (since 31 May 2017)

**head of government:** Prime Minister Ana BRNABIC (since 29 June 2017)

**cabinet:** Cabinet elected by the National Assembly

**elections/appointments:** president directly elected by absolute majority popular vote in 2 rounds if needed for a 5-year term (eligible for a second term); election last held on 2 April 2017 (next to be held in 2022); prime minister elected by the National Assembly

**election results:** Aleksandar VUCIC elected president in the first round; percent of vote - Aleksandar VUCIC (SNS) 55.1%, Sasa JANKOVIC (independent) 16.4%, Luka MAKSIMOVIC (independent) 9.4%, Vuk JEREMIC (independent) 5.7%, Vojislav SESELJ (SRS) 4.5%, Bosko OBRADOVIC (Dveri) 2.3%, other 5.0%, invalid/blank 1.6%

## LEGISLATIVE BRANCH:

**description:** unicameral National Assembly or Narodna Skupstina (250 seats; members directly elected by party list proportional representation vote in a single nationwide constituency to serve 4-year terms)

**elections:** last held on 24 April 2016 (next to be held by April 2020)

**election results:** percent of vote by party/coalition - Serbia is Winning 48.3%, SPS-JS-ZS-KP 11.0%, SRS 8.1%, For a Just Serbia 6.0%, DJB 6.0%, Alliance for a Better Serbia 5.0%, Dveri-DSS 5.0%, SVM 1.5%, other 9.1%; seats by party/coalition Serbia is Winning 131, SPS-JS-ZS-KP 29, SRS 22, For a Just Serbia 16, DJB 16, Alliance for a Better Serbia 13, Dveri-DSS 13, SVM 4, other 6; composition - men 165, women 85, percent of women 34%

**note:** seats by party, as of May 2018 - SNS 89, SRS 22, SPS 20, DS 12, SDPS 10, PUPS 9, Dveri 6, JS 6, LDP 4, SDS 4, SVM 4, other 34, independent 30; composition - men 164, women 86, percent of women 34.4%

## JUDICIAL BRANCH:

**highest courts:** Supreme Court of Cassation (consists of 36 judges, including the court president); Constitutional Court (consists of 15 judges, including the court president and vice president)

**judge selection and term of office:** Supreme Court justices proposed by the High Judicial Council (HJC), an 11-member independent body of which 8 are judges elected by the National Assembly and 3 ex-officio members; justices appointed by the National Assembly; Constitutional Court judges elected - 5 each by the National Assembly, the president, and the Supreme Court of Cassation; initial appointment of Supreme Court judges by the HJC is 3 years and beyond that period tenure is permament; Constitutional Court judges elected for 9-year terms

**subordinate courts:** basic courts, higher courts, appellate courts; courts of special jurisdiction include the Administrative Court, commercial courts, and misdemeanor courts

## POLITICAL PARTIES AND LEADERS:

Alliance for a Better Serbia (electoral coalition including LDP, LSV, SDS)
Alliance of Vojvodina Hungarians or SVM [Istvan PASZTOR]
Bosniak Democratic Union of Sandzak or BDZS [Jahja FEHRATOVIC]
Communist Party or KP [Josip Joska

BROZ]
Democratic Party or DS [Zoran LUTOVAC]
Democratic Party of Serbia or DSS [Milos JOVANOVIC]
Dveri [Bosko OBRADOVIC]
Enough is Enough or DJB [Branislav MIHAJLOVIC]
For a Just Serbia (electoral coalition including DS, NS, DSVH, VVS)
Greens of Serbia or ZS [Ivan KARIC]
League of Social Democrats of Vojvodina or LSV [Nenad CANAK]
Liberal Democratic Party or LDP [Cedomir JOVANOVIC]
Movement of Socialists or PS [Aleksandar VULIN]
New Party or NOVA [Zoran ZIVKOVIC]
New Serbia or NS [Velimir ILIC]
Party for Democratic Action or PDD [Riza HALIMI]
Party of Democratic Action of the Sandzak or SDA [Sulejman UGLJANIN]
Party of United Pensioners of Serbia or PUPS [Milan KRKOBABIC]
People's Party or NARODNA [Vuk JEREMIC]
Serbia is Winning (electoral coalition including NDSS, NS, PS, PSS, PUPS, SDPS, SNP, SNS, SPO)
Serbian People's Party or SNP [Nenad POPOVIC]
Serbian Progressive Party or SNS [Aleksandar VUCIC]
Serbian Radical Party or SRS [Vojislav SESELJ]
Serbian Renewal Movement or SPO [Vuk DRASKOVIC]
Social Democratic Party or SDS [Boris TADIC]
Social Democratic Party of Serbia or SDPS [Rasim LJAJIC]
Socialist Party of Serbia or SPS [Ivica DACIC]
Strength of Serbia or PSS [Bogoljub KARIC]
Together for Serbia or ZZS [Dusan PETROVIC]
United Serbia or JS [Dragan MARKOVIC]

**note:** Serbia has more than 110 registered political parties and citizens' associations

## INTERNATIONAL ORGANIZATION PARTICIPATION:

BIS, BSEC, CD, CE, CEI, EAPC, EBRD, EU (candidate country), FAO, G-9, IAEA, IBRD, ICAO, ICC (national committees), ICCt, ICRM, IDA, IFC, IFRCS, IHO, ILO, IMF, IMO, IMSO, Interpol, IOC, IOM, IPU, ISO, ITSO, ITU, ITUC (NGOs), MIGA, MONUSCO, NAM (observer), NSG, OAS (observer), OIF (observer), OPCW, OSCE, PCA, PFP, SELEC, UN, UNCTAD, UNESCO, UNFICYP, UNHCR, UNIDO, UNIFIL, UNMIL, UNOCI, UNTSO, UNWTO, UPU, WCO, WHO, WIPO, WMO, WTO (observer)

## DIPLOMATIC REPRESENTATION IN THE US:

**chief of mission:** Ambassador Djerdj MATKOVIC (since 23 February 2015)

**chancery:** 2233 Wisconsin Ave NW #410, Washington, DC 20007

**telephone:** [1] (202) 332-0333

**FAX:** [1] (202) 332-3933

**consulate(s) general:** Chicago, New York

## DIPLOMATIC REPRESENTATION FROM THE US:

**chief of mission:** Ambassador Kyle SCOTT (since 5 February 2016)

**embassy:** 92 Bulevar kneza Aleksandra Karadjordjevica, 11040 Belgrade, Serbia

**mailing address:** 5070 Belgrade Place, Washington, DC 20521-5070

**telephone:** [381] (11) 706-4000

**FAX:** [381] (11) 706-4005

## FLAG DESCRIPTION:

three equal horizontal stripes of red (top), blue, and white - the Pan-Slav colors representing freedom and revolutionary ideals; charged with the coat of arms of Serbia shifted slightly to the hoist side; the principal field of the coat of arms represents the Serbian state and displays a white two-headed eagle on a red shield; a smaller red shield on the eagle represents the Serbian nation, and is divided into four quarters by a white cross; interpretations vary as to the meaning and origin of the white, curved symbols resembling firesteels (fire strikers) or Cyrillic "C's" in each quarter; a royal crown surmounts the coat of arms

**note:** the Pan-Slav colors were inspired by the 19th-century flag of Russia

## NATIONAL SYMBOL(S):

white double-headed eagle; national colors: red, blue, white

## NATIONAL ANTHEM:

**name:** "Boze pravde" (God of Justice)

**lyrics/music:** Jovan DORDEVIC/Davorin JENKO

**note:** adopted 1904; song originally written as part of a play in 1872 and has been used as an anthem by the Serbian people throughout the 20th and 21st centuries

# ECONOMY :: SERBIA

## ECONOMY - OVERVIEW:

Serbia has a transitional economy largely dominated by market forces, but the state sector remains significant in certain areas. The economy relies on manufacturing and exports, driven largely by foreign investment. MILOSEVIC-era mismanagement of the economy, an extended period of international economic sanctions, civil war, and the damage to Yugoslavia's infrastructure and industry during the NATO airstrikes in 1999 left the economy worse off than it was in 1990. In 2015, Serbia's GDP was 27.5% below where it was in 1989.

After former Federal Yugoslav President MILOSEVIC was ousted in September 2000, the Democratic Opposition of Serbia (DOS) coalition government implemented stabilization measures and embarked on a market reform program. Serbia renewed its membership in the IMF in December 2000 and rejoined the World Bank and the European Bank for Reconstruction and Development. Serbia has made progress in trade liberalization and enterprise restructuring and privatization, but many large enterprises - including the power utilities, telecommunications company, natural gas company, and others - remain state-owned. Serbia has made some progress towards EU membership, gaining candidate status in March 2012. In January 2014, Serbia's EU accession talks officially opened and, as of December 2017, Serbia had opened 12 negotiating chapters including one on foreign trade. Serbia's negotiations with the WTO are advanced, with the country's complete ban on the trade and cultivation of agricultural biotechnology products representing the primary remaining obstacle to accession. Serbia maintains a three-year Stand-by Arrangement with the IMF worth approximately $1.3 billion that is scheduled to end in February 2018. The government has shown progress implementing economic reforms, such as fiscal consolidation, privatization, and reducing public spending.

Unemployment in Serbia, while relatively low (16% in 2017) compared with its Balkan neighbors, remains significantly above the European average. Serbia is slowly implementing structural economic reforms needed to ensure the country's long-term prosperity. Serbia reduced its budget deficit to 1.7% of GDP and its public debt to 71% of GDP in 2017. Public debt had more than doubled between 2008 and 2015. Serbia's concerns about inflation and exchange-rate stability preclude the use of expansionary monetary policy.

Major economic challenges ahead include: stagnant household incomes; the need for private sector job creation; structural reforms of state-owned companies; strategic public sector reforms; and the need for new foreign direct investment. Other serious longer-term challenges include an inefficient judicial system, high levels of corruption, and an aging population. Factors favorable to Serbia's economic growth include the economic reforms it is undergoing as part of its EU accession process and IMF agreement, its strategic location, a relatively inexpensive and skilled labor force, and free trade agreements with the EU, Russia, Turkey, and countries that are members of the Central European Free Trade Agreement.

**GDP (PURCHASING POWER PARITY):**

$105.7 billion (2017 est.)

$103.8 billion (2016 est.)

$101 billion (2015 est.)

note: data are in 2017 dollars

country comparison to the world: 82

**GDP (OFFICIAL EXCHANGE RATE):**

$41.43 billion (2017 est.) (2017 est.)

**GDP - REAL GROWTH RATE:**

1.9% (2017 est.)

2.8% (2016 est.)

0.8% (2015 est.)

country comparison to the world: 158

**GDP - PER CAPITA (PPP):**

$15,100 (2017 est.)

$14,700 (2016 est.)

$14,200 (2015 est.)

note: data are in 2017 dollars

country comparison to the world: 111

**GROSS NATIONAL SAVING:**

15.3% of GDP (2017 est.)

16% of GDP (2016 est.)

14.1% of GDP (2015 est.)

country comparison to the world: 134

**GDP - COMPOSITION, BY END USE:**

household consumption: 78.2% (2017 est.)

government consumption: 10.1% (2017 est.)

investment in fixed capital: 18.5% (2017 est.)

investment in inventories: 2% (2017 est.)

exports of goods and services: 52.5% (2017 est.)

imports of goods and services: -61.3% (2017 est.)

**GDP - COMPOSITION, BY SECTOR OF ORIGIN:**

agriculture: 9.8% (2017 est.)

industry: 41.1% (2017 est.)

services: 49.1% (2017 est.)

**AGRICULTURE - PRODUCTS:**

wheat, maize, sunflower, sugar beets, grapes/wine, fruits (raspberries, apples, sour cherries), vegetables (tomatoes, peppers, potatoes), beef, pork, and meat products, milk and dairy products

**INDUSTRIES:**

automobiles, base metals, furniture, food processing, machinery, chemicals, sugar, tires, clothes, pharmaceuticals

**INDUSTRIAL PRODUCTION GROWTH RATE:**

3.9% (2017 est.)

country comparison to the world: 78

**LABOR FORCE:**

2.92 million (2017 est.)

country comparison to the world: 106

**LABOR FORCE - BY OCCUPATION:**

agriculture: 19.4%

industry: 24.5%

services: 56.1% (2017 est.)

**UNEMPLOYMENT RATE:**

14.1% (2017 est.)

15.9% (2016 est.)

country comparison to the world: 170

**POPULATION BELOW POVERTY LINE:**

8.9% (2014 est.)

**HOUSEHOLD INCOME OR CONSUMPTION BY PERCENTAGE SHARE:**

lowest 10%: 2.2% (2011)

highest 10%: 23.8% (2011)

**DISTRIBUTION OF FAMILY INCOME - GINI INDEX:**

38.7 (2014 est.)

28.2 (2008 est.)

country comparison to the world: 76

**BUDGET:**

revenues: 17.69 billion (2017 est.)

expenditures: 17.59 billion (2017 est.)

note: data include both central government and local goverment budgets

**TAXES AND OTHER REVENUES:**

42.7% (of GDP) (2017 est.)

country comparison to the world: 30

**BUDGET SURPLUS (+) OR DEFICIT (-):**

0.2% (of GDP) (2017 est.)

country comparison to the world: 43

**PUBLIC DEBT:**

62.5% of GDP (2017 est.)

73.1% of GDP (2016 est.)

country comparison to the world: 70

**INFLATION RATE (CONSUMER PRICES):**

3.1% (2017 est.)

1.1% (2016 est.)

country comparison to the world: 133

**CENTRAL BANK DISCOUNT RATE:**

3.5% (9 October 2017)

4% (31 December 2016)

country comparison to the world: 103

**COMMERCIAL BANK PRIME LENDING RATE:**

8.2% (31 December 2017 est.)

8.45% (31 December 2016 est.)

country comparison to the world: 105

**STOCK OF NARROW MONEY:**

$6.756 billion (31 December 2017 est.)

$5.189 billion (31 December 2016 est.)

country comparison to the world: 93

**STOCK OF BROAD MONEY:**

$6.756 billion (31 December 2017 est.)

$5.189 billion (31 December 2016 est.)

country comparison to the world: 96

**STOCK OF DOMESTIC CREDIT:**

$24.42 billion (31 December 2017 est.)

$20.22 billion (31 December 2016 est.)

country comparison to the world: 87

**MARKET VALUE OF PUBLICLY TRADED SHARES:**

$5.064 billion (31 December 2016 est.)

$5.841 billion (31 December 2015 est.)

$4.525 billion (31 December 2014 est.)

country comparison to the world: 83
**CURRENT ACCOUNT BALANCE:**
-$2.354 billion (2017 est.)
-$1.189 billion (2016 est.)
country comparison to the world: 170
**EXPORTS:**
$15.92 billion (2017 est.)
$13.99 billion (2016 est.)
country comparison to the world: 75
**EXPORTS - PARTNERS:**
Italy 13.5%, Germany 12.8%, Bosnia and Herzegovina 8.2%, Russia 6%, Romania 4.9% (2017)
**EXPORTS - COMMODITIES:**
automobiles, iron and steel, rubber, clothes, wheat, fruit and vegetables, nonferrous metals, electric appliances, metal products, weapons and ammunition
**IMPORTS:**
$20.44 billion (2017 est.)
$17.63 billion (2016 est.)
country comparison to the world: 77
**IMPORTS - COMMODITIES:**
machinery and transport equipment, fuels and lubricants, manufactured goods, chemicals, food and live animals, raw materials
**IMPORTS - PARTNERS:**
Germany 12.7%, Italy 10%, China 8.2%, Russia 7.3%, Hungary 4.9%, Poland 4.1% (2017)
**RESERVES OF FOREIGN EXCHANGE AND GOLD:**
$11.91 billion (31 December 2017 est.)
$10.76 billion (31 December 2016 est.)
country comparison to the world: 70
**DEBT - EXTERNAL:**
$29.5 billion (31 December 2017 est.)
$30.38 billion (31 December 2016 est.)
country comparison to the world: 81
**STOCK OF DIRECT FOREIGN INVESTMENT - AT HOME:**
$41.52 billion (31 December 2016 est.)
$11.95 billion (31 December 2015 est.)
country comparison to the world: 63
**STOCK OF DIRECT FOREIGN INVESTMENT - ABROAD:**
NA
**EXCHANGE RATES:**
Serbian dinars (RSD) per US dollar -
112.4 (2017 est.)
111.278 (2016 est.)
111.278 (2015 est.)
108.811 (2014 est.)
88.405 (2013 est.)

## ENERGY :: SERBIA

**ELECTRICITY ACCESS:**
electrification - total population: 100% (2016)
**ELECTRICITY - PRODUCTION:**
36.54 billion kWh (2016 est.)
country comparison to the world: 59
**ELECTRICITY - CONSUMPTION:**
29.81 billion kWh (2016 est.)
country comparison to the world: 62
**ELECTRICITY - EXPORTS:**
6.428 billion kWh (2016 est.)
country comparison to the world: 29
**ELECTRICITY - IMPORTS:**
5.068 billion kWh (2016 est.)
country comparison to the world: 38
**ELECTRICITY - INSTALLED GENERATING CAPACITY:**
7.342 million kW (2016 est.)
country comparison to the world: 73
**ELECTRICITY - FROM FOSSIL FUELS:**
65% of total installed capacity (2016 est.)
country comparison to the world: 119
**ELECTRICITY - FROM NUCLEAR FUELS:**
0% of total installed capacity (2017 est.)
country comparison to the world: 180
**ELECTRICITY - FROM HYDROELECTRIC PLANTS:**
35% of total installed capacity (2017 est.)
country comparison to the world: 61
**ELECTRICITY - FROM OTHER RENEWABLE SOURCES:**
1% of total installed capacity (2017 est.)
country comparison to the world: 167
**CRUDE OIL - PRODUCTION:**
18,740 bbl/day (2017 est.)
country comparison to the world: 66
**CRUDE OIL - EXPORTS:**
123 bbl/day (2015 est.)
country comparison to the world: 81
**CRUDE OIL - IMPORTS:**
40,980 bbl/day (2015 est.)
country comparison to the world: 56
**CRUDE OIL - PROVED RESERVES:**
77.5 million bbl (1 January 2018 est.)
country comparison to the world: 73
**REFINED PETROLEUM PRODUCTS - PRODUCTION:**
74,350 bbl/day (2015 est.)
country comparison to the world: 71
**REFINED PETROLEUM PRODUCTS - CONSUMPTION:**
74,000 bbl/day (2016 est.)
country comparison to the world: 90
**REFINED PETROLEUM PRODUCTS - EXPORTS:**
15,750 bbl/day (2015 est.)
country comparison to the world: 73
**REFINED PETROLEUM PRODUCTS - IMPORTS:**
18,720 bbl/day (2015 est.)
country comparison to the world: 126
**NATURAL GAS - PRODUCTION:**
509.7 million cu m (2017 est.)
country comparison to the world: 71
**NATURAL GAS - CONSUMPTION:**
2.718 billion cu m (2017 est.)
country comparison to the world: 75
**NATURAL GAS - EXPORTS:**
0 cu m (2017 est.)
country comparison to the world: 181
**NATURAL GAS - IMPORTS:**
2.01 billion cu m (2017 est.)
country comparison to the world: 52
**NATURAL GAS - PROVED RESERVES:**
48.14 billion cu m (1 January 2018 est.)
country comparison to the world: 63
**CARBON DIOXIDE EMISSIONS FROM CONSUMPTION OF ENERGY:**
50.21 million Mt (2017 est.)
country comparison to the world: 60

## COMMUNICATIONS :: SERBIA

**TELEPHONES - FIXED LINES:**
total subscriptions: 2,609,592 (2017 est.)
subscriptions per 100 inhabitants: 37 (2017 est.)
country comparison to the world: 52
**TELEPHONES - MOBILE CELLULAR:**
total subscriptions: 8,626,903 (2017 est.)
subscriptions per 100 inhabitants: 121 (2017 est.)
country comparison to the world: 94

## TELEPHONE SYSTEM:

**general assessment:** replacements of, and upgrades to, telecommunications equipment damaged during the 1999 war resulted in a modern digitalized telecommunications system (2016)

**domestic:** wireless service, available through multiple providers with national coverage, is growing very rapidly; best telecommunications services are centered in urban centers; 4G/LTE mobile network launched in March 2015 (2016)

**international:** country code - 381 (2016)

## INTERNET COUNTRY CODE:

.rs

## INTERNET USERS:

**total:** 4,790,488 (July 2016 est.)

**percent of population:** 67.1% (July 2016 est.)

**country comparison to the world:** 78

## BROADBAND - FIXED SUBSCRIPTIONS:

**total:** 1,474,970 (2017 est.)

**subscriptions per 100 inhabitants:** 21 (2017 est.)

**country comparison to the world:** 60

# TRANSPORTATION :: SERBIA

## NATIONAL AIR TRANSPORT SYSTEM:

**number of registered air carriers:** 2 (2015)

**inventory of registered aircraft operated by air carriers:** 21 (2015)

**annual passenger traffic on registered air carriers:** 2,424,886 (2015)

**annual freight traffic on registered air carriers:** 2.748 million mt-km (2015)

## CIVIL AIRCRAFT REGISTRATION COUNTRY CODE PREFIX:

YU (2016)

## AIRPORTS:

26 (2013)

**country comparison to the world:** 126

## AIRPORTS - WITH PAVED RUNWAYS:

**total:** 10 (2017)

**over 3,047 m:** 2 (2017)

**2,438 to 3,047 m:** 3 (2017)

**1,524 to 2,437 m:** 3 (2017)

**914 to 1,523 m:** 2 (2017)

## AIRPORTS - WITH UNPAVED RUNWAYS:

**total:** 16 (2013)

**1,524 to 2,437 m:** 1 (2013)

**914 to 1,523 m:** 10 (2013)

**under 914 m:** 5 (2013)

## HELIPORTS:

2 (2012)

## PIPELINES:

1936 km gas, 413 km oil

## RAILWAYS:

**total:** 3,809 km (2015)

**standard gauge:** 3,809 km 1.435-m gauge (3,526 km one-track lines and 283 km double-track lines) out of which 1,279 km electrified (1,000 km one-track lines and 279 km double-track lines) (2015)

**country comparison to the world:** 50

## ROADWAYS:

**total:** 44,248 km (2016)

**paved:** 28,000 km (16,162 km state roads, out of which 741 km highways) (2016)

**unpaved:** 16,248 km (2016)

**country comparison to the world:** 82

## WATERWAYS:

587 km (primarily on the Danube and Sava Rivers) (2009)

**country comparison to the world:** 80

## PORTS AND TERMINALS:

**river port(s):** Belgrade (Danube)

# MILITARY AND SECURITY :: SERBIA

## MILITARY EXPENDITURES:

1.34% of GDP (2017 est.)

1.25% of GDP (2016)

1.41% of GDP (2015)

**country comparison to the world:** 86

## MILITARY BRANCHES:

Serbian Armed Forces (Vojska Srbije, VS): Land Forces (includes Riverine Component, consisting of a river flotilla on the Danube), Air and Air Defense Forces (2016)

## MILITARY SERVICE AGE AND OBLIGATION:

18 years of age for voluntary military service; conscription abolished December 2010; reserve obligation to age 60 for men and age 50 for women (2013)

# TRANSNATIONAL ISSUES :: SERBIA

## DISPUTES - INTERNATIONAL:

Serbia protests the US, and other states', recognition of Kosovo's declaration of its status as a sovereign and independent state-ethnic Serbian municipalities living in Kosovo along the northern border challenge final status of Kosovo-Serbia boundary-several thousand NATO-led Kosovo Force peacekeepers under UN Interim Administration Mission in Kosovo authority continue to keep the peace within Kosovo between the ethnic Albanian majority and the Serb minority in Kosovo-Serbia delimited about half of the boundary with Bosnia and Herzegovina, but sections along the Drina River remain in dispute-Serbia and Croatia have an unresolved border dispute along the Danube river and numerous other unresolved bilateral issues dating back to the conflicts in the 1990s

## REFUGEES AND INTERNALLY DISPLACED PERSONS:

**refugees (country of origin):** 20,346 (Croatia), 9,081 (Bosnia and Herzegovina) (2016)

**IDPs:** 199,584 (most are Kosovar Serbs, some are Roma, Ashkalis, and Egyptian (RAE); some RAE IDPs are unregistered) (2018)

**stateless persons:** 2,155 (includes stateless persons in Kosovo) (2017)

**note:** 685,921 estimated refugee and migrant arrivals (January 2015-November 2018); Serbia is predominantly a transit country and hosts an estimated 3,975 migrants and asylum seekers as of the end of June 2018

## ILLICIT DRUGS:

transshipment point for Southwest Asian heroin moving to Western Europe on the Balkan route; economy vulnerable to money laundering

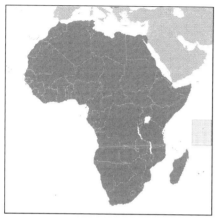

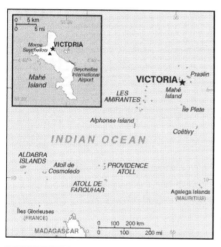

# AFRICA :: SEYCHELLES

## INTRODUCTION :: SEYCHELLES

### BACKGROUND:

A lengthy struggle between France and Great Britain for the islands ended in 1814, when they were ceded to the latter. During colonial rule, a plantation-based economy developed that relied on imported labor, primarily from European colonies in Africa. Independence came in 1976. Single-party rule was brought to a close with a new constitution and free elections in 1993. President France-Albert RENE, who had served since 1977, was reelected in 2001, but stepped down in 2004. Vice President James Alix MICHEL took over the presidency and in 2006 was elected to a new five-year term; he was reelected in 2011 and again in 2015. In 2016, James MICHEL resigned and handed over the presidency to his Vice-President Danny FAURE.

## GEOGRAPHY :: SEYCHELLES

### LOCATION:
archipelago in the Indian Ocean, northeast of Madagascar

### GEOGRAPHIC COORDINATES:
4 35 S, 55 40 E

### MAP REFERENCES:
Africa

### AREA:
total: 455 sq km
land: 455 sq km
water: 0 sq km
country comparison to the world: 199

### AREA - COMPARATIVE:
2.5 times the size of Washington, DC

### LAND BOUNDARIES:
0 km

### COASTLINE:
491 km

### MARITIME CLAIMS:
territorial sea: 12 nm
exclusive economic zone: 200 nm
contiguous zone: 24 nm
continental shelf: 200 nm or to the edge of the continental margin

### CLIMATE:
tropical marine; humid; cooler season during southeast monsoon (late May to September); warmer season during northwest monsoon (March to May)

### TERRAIN:
Mahe Group is volcanic with a narrow coastal strip and rocky, hilly interior; others are coral, flat, elevated reefs

### ELEVATION:
0 m lowest point: Indian Ocean
905 highest point: Morne Seychellois

### NATURAL RESOURCES:
fish, coconuts (copra), cinnamon trees

### LAND USE:
agricultural land: 6.5% (2011 est.)
arable land: 2.2% (2011 est.) / permanent crops: 4.3% (2011 est.) / permanent pasture: 0% (2011 est.)
forest: 88.5% (2011 est.)
other: 5% (2011 est.)

### IRRIGATED LAND:
3 sq km (2012)

### POPULATION DISTRIBUTION:
more than three-quarters of the population lives on the main island of Mahe; Praslin contains less than 10%; a smaller percent on La Digue and the outer islands

### NATURAL HAZARDS:
lies outside the cyclone belt, so severe storms are rare; occasional short droughts

### ENVIRONMENT - CURRENT ISSUES:
water supply depends on catchments to collect rainwater; water pollution; biodiversity maintainance

### ENVIRONMENT - INTERNATIONAL AGREEMENTS:
party to: Biodiversity, Climate Change, Climate Change-Kyoto Protocol, Desertification, Endangered Species, Hazardous Wastes, Law of the Sea, Marine Dumping, Ozone Layer Protection, Ship Pollution, Wetlands
signed, but not ratified: none of the selected agreements

### GEOGRAPHY - NOTE:
smallest African country; the constitution of the Republic of Seychelles lists 155 islands: 42 granitic and 113 coralline; by far the largest island is Mahe, which is home to about 90% of the population and the site of the capital city of Victoria

## PEOPLE AND SOCIETY :: SEYCHELLES

### POPULATION:
94,633 (July 2018 est.)
country comparison to the world: 198

### NATIONALITY:
noun: Seychellois (singular and plural)
adjective: Seychellois

### ETHNIC GROUPS:

predominantly black; mixed French, African, Indian, Chinese, and Arab

**LANGUAGES:**

Seychellois Creole (official) 89.1%, English (official) 5.1%, French (official) 0.7%, other 3.8%, unspecified 1.4% (2010 est.)

**RELIGIONS:**

Roman Catholic 76.2%, Protestant 10.5% (Anglican 6.1%, Pentecostal Assembly 1.5%, Seventh Day Adventist 1.2%, other Protestant 1.7), other Christian 2.4%, Hindu 2.4%, Muslim 1.6%, other non-Christian 1.1%, unspecified 4.8%, none 0.9% (2010 est.)

**DEMOGRAPHIC PROFILE:**

Seychelles has no indigenous population and was first permanently settled by a small group of French planters, African slaves, and South Indians in 1770. Seychelles' modern population is composed of the descendants of French and later British settlers, Africans, and Indian, Chinese, and Middle Eastern traders and is concentrated on three of its 155 islands – the vast majority on Mahe and lesser numbers on Praslin and La Digue. Seychelles' population grew rapidly during the second half of the 20th century, largely due to natural increase, but the pace has slowed because of fertility decline. The total fertility rate dropped sharply from 4.0 children per woman in 1980 to 1.9 in 2015, mainly as a result of a family planning program, free education and health care, and increased female labor force participation. Life expectancy has increased steadily, but women on average live 9 years longer than men, a difference that is higher than that typical of developed countries.

The combination of reduced fertility and increased longevity has resulted in an aging population, which will put pressure on the government's provision of pensions and health care. Seychelles' sustained investment in social welfare services, such as free primary health care and education up to the post-secondary level, have enabled the country to achieve a high human development index score – among the highest in Africa. Despite some of its health and education indicators being nearly on par with Western countries, Seychelles has a high level of income inequality.

An increasing number of migrant workers – mainly young men – have been coming to Seychelles in recent years to work in the construction and tourism industries. As of 2011, foreign workers made up nearly a quarter of the workforce. Indians are the largest non-Seychellois population – representing half of the country's foreigners – followed by Malagasy.

**AGE STRUCTURE:**

**0-14 years:** 19.52% (male 9,482/female 8,989)

**15-24 years:** 12.96% (male 6,461/female 5,806)

**25-54 years:** 49.29% (male 24,841/female 21,800)

**55-64 years:** 10.44% (male 5,008/female 4,870)

**65 years and over:** 7.79% (male 2,974/female 4,402) (2018 est.)

**DEPENDENCY RATIOS:**

**total dependency ratio:** 42.8 (2015 est.)

**youth dependency ratio:** 31 (2015 est.)

**elderly dependency ratio:** 11.7 (2015 est.)

**potential support ratio:** 8.5 (2015 est.)

**MEDIAN AGE:**

**total:** 35.8 years

**male:** 35.3 years

**female:** 36.5 years (2018 est.)

**country comparison to the world:** 76

**POPULATION GROWTH RATE:**

0.74% (2018 est.)

**country comparison to the world:** 136

**BIRTH RATE:**

13.4 births/1,000 population (2018 est.)

**country comparison to the world:** 142

**DEATH RATE:**

7 deaths/1,000 population (2018 est.)

**country comparison to the world:** 130

**NET MIGRATION RATE:**

1 migrant(s)/1,000 population (2017 est.)

**country comparison to the world:** 57

**POPULATION DISTRIBUTION:**

more than three-quarters of the population lives on the main island of Mahe; Praslin contains less than 10%; a smaller percent on La Digue and the outer islands

**URBANIZATION:**

**urban population:** 56.7% of total population (2018)

**rate of urbanization:** 1.26% annual rate of change (2015-20 est.)

**MAJOR URBAN AREAS - POPULATION:**

28,000 VICTORIA (capital) (2018)

**SEX RATIO:**

**at birth:** 1.03 male(s)/female (2017 est.)

**0-14 years:** 1.05 male(s)/female (2017 est.)

**15-24 years:** 1.1 male(s)/female (2017 est.)

**25-54 years:** 1.12 male(s)/female (2017 est.)

**55-64 years:** 1.06 male(s)/female (2017 est.)

**65 years and over:** 0.64 male(s)/female (2017 est.)

**total population:** 1.06 male(s)/female (2017 est.)

**INFANT MORTALITY RATE:**

**total:** 9.7 deaths/1,000 live births (2018 est.)

**male:** 12.1 deaths/1,000 live births (2018 est.)

**female:** 7.2 deaths/1,000 live births (2018 est.)

**country comparison to the world:** 136

**LIFE EXPECTANCY AT BIRTH:**

**total population:** 75.2 years (2018 est.)

**male:** 70.7 years (2018 est.)

**female:** 79.8 years (2018 est.)

**country comparison to the world:** 111

**TOTAL FERTILITY RATE:**

1.85 children born/woman (2018 est.)

**country comparison to the world:** 144

**HEALTH EXPENDITURES:**

3.4% of GDP (2014)

**country comparison to the world:** 176

**PHYSICIANS DENSITY:**

0.98 physicians/1,000 population (2012)

**HOSPITAL BED DENSITY:**

3.6 beds/1,000 population (2011)

**DRINKING WATER SOURCE:**

**improved:**

urban: 95.7% of population

rural: 95.7% of population

total: 95.7% of population

**unimproved:**

urban: 4.3% of population

rural: 4.3% of population

total: 4.3% of population (2015 est.)

**SANITATION FACILITY ACCESS:**

**improved:**

urban: 98.4% of population (2015 est.)

rural: 98.4% of population (2015 est.)

total: 98.4% of population (2015 est.)

**unimproved:**

urban: 1.6% of population (2015 est.)

rural: 1.6% of population (2015 est.)

total: 1.6% of population (2015 est.)

## HIV/AIDS - ADULT PREVALENCE RATE:

NA

## HIV/AIDS - PEOPLE LIVING WITH HIV/AIDS:

NA

## HIV/AIDS - DEATHS:

NA

## OBESITY - ADULT PREVALENCE RATE:

14% (2016)

country comparison to the world: 130

## CHILDREN UNDER THE AGE OF 5 YEARS UNDERWEIGHT:

3.6% (2012)

country comparison to the world: 91

## EDUCATION EXPENDITURES:

3.6% of GDP (2011)

country comparison to the world: 126

## LITERACY:

definition: age 15 and over can read and write (2012 est.)

total population: 91.8% (2012 est.)

male: 91.4% (2012 est.)

female: 92.3% (2012 est.)

## SCHOOL LIFE EXPECTANCY (PRIMARY TO TERTIARY EDUCATION):

total: 14 years (2015)

male: 13 years (2015)

female: 15 years (2015)

## UNEMPLOYMENT, YOUTH AGES 15-24:

total: 14% (2015 est.)

male: 12.1% (2015 est.)

female: 16.2% (2015 est.)

country comparison to the world: 94

# GOVERNMENT :: SEYCHELLES

## COUNTRY NAME:

conventional long form: Republic of Seychelles

conventional short form: Seychelles

local long form: Republic of Seychelles

local short form: Seychelles

etymology: named by French Captain Corneille Nicholas MORPHEY after Jean Moreau de SECHELLES, the finance minister of France, in 1756

## GOVERNMENT TYPE:

presidential republic

## CAPITAL:

name: Victoria

geographic coordinates: 4 37 S, 55 27 E

time difference: UTC+4 (9 hours ahead of Washington, DC, during Standard Time)

## ADMINISTRATIVE DIVISIONS:

25 administrative districts; Anse aux Pins, Anse Boileau, Anse Etoile, Anse Royale, Au Cap, Baie Lazare, Baie Sainte Anne, Beau Vallon, Bel Air, Bel Ombre, Cascade, Glacis, Grand Anse Mahe, Grand Anse Praslin, Inner Islands, La Riviere Anglaise, Les Mamalles, Mont Buxton, Mont Fleuri, Plaisance, Pointe Larue, Port Glaud, Roche Caiman, Saint Louis, Takamaka

## INDEPENDENCE:

29 June 1976 (from the UK)

## NATIONAL HOLIDAY:

Constitution Day, 18 June (1993)Independence Day (National Day), 29 June (1976)

## CONSTITUTION:

history: previous 1970, 1979; latest drafted May 1993, approved by referendum 18 June 1993, effective 23 June 1993 (2017)

amendments: proposed by the National Assembly; passage requires at least two-thirds majority vote by the National Assembly; passage of amendments affecting the country's sovereignty, symbols and languages, the supremacy of the constitution, fundamental rights and freedoms, amendment procedures, and dissolution of the Assembly also requires approval by at least 60% of voters in a referendum; amended several times, last in 2017 (2017)

## LEGAL SYSTEM:

mixed legal system of English common law, French civil law, and customary law

## INTERNATIONAL LAW ORGANIZATION PARTICIPATION:

has not submitted an ICJ jurisdiction declaration; accepts ICCt jurisdiction

## CITIZENSHIP:

citizenship by birth: no

citizenship by descent only: at least one parent must be a citizen of the Seychelles

dual citizenship recognized: no

residency requirement for naturalization: 5 years

## SUFFRAGE:

18 years of age; universal

## EXECUTIVE BRANCH:

chief of state: President Danny FAURE (since 16 October 2016); Vice President Vincent MERITON (since 28 October 2016); note - James Alix MICHEL resigned the presidency effective 16 October 2016; the president is both chief of state and head of government

head of government: President Danny FAURE (since 16 October 2016); Vice President Vincent MERITON (since 28 October 2016); note - James Alix MICHEL resigned the presidency effective 16 October 2016

cabinet: Council of Ministers appointed by the president

elections/appointments: president directly elected by absolute majority popular vote in 2 rounds if needed for a 5-year term (eligible for 1 additional term); election last held on 3-5 December 2015 with runoff a on 16-18 December 2015 (next to be held in December 2020)

election results: President James Alix MICHEL reelected president in second round; percent of vote - James Alix MICHEL (PL) 50.2%, Wavel RAMKALAWAN (SNP) 49.8%

## LEGISLATIVE BRANCH:

description: unicameral National Assembly or Assemblee Nationale (up to 35 seats - the Assembly elected in September 2016 has 33 members; 25 members directly elected in single-seat constituencies by simple majority vote and up to 10 members elected by proportional representation vote; members serve 5-year terms)

elections: last held on 8-10 September 2016 (next to be held in 2021); note - the National Assembly was dissolved in July 2011 resulting in early elections

**election results:** percent of vote by party - LDS 49.6%, PL 49.2%, other 1.2%; seats by party - LDS 19, PL 14; composition - men 26, women 7, percent of women 21.2%

## JUDICIAL BRANCH:

**highest courts:** Seychelles Court of Appeal (consists of the court president and 4 justices); Supreme Court of Seychelles (consists of the chief justice and 9 puisne judges); Constitutional Court (consists of 3 Supreme Court judges)

**judge selection and term of office:** all judges appointed by the president of the republic upon the recommendation of the Constitutional Appointments Authority, a 3-member body, with 1 member appointed by the president of the republic, 1 by the opposition leader in the National Assembly, and 1 by the other 2 appointees; judges appointed until retirement at age 70

**subordinate courts:** Magistrates' Courts of Seychelles; Family Tribunal for issues such as domestic violence, child custody, and maintenance; Employment Tribunal for labor-related disputes

## POLITICAL PARTIES AND LEADERS:

Lafors Demokratik Seselwa or LSD (Martin AGLAE)
People's Party (Parti Lepep) or PL [James Alix MICHEL] (formerly SPPF)
Seselwa (Seychelles) United Party or SUP [Robert ERNESTA] (formerly the New Democratic Party or NDP)
Seychelles National Party or SNP [Wavel RAMKALAWAN] (formerly the United Opposition or UO)
Seychelles Party for Social Justice and Democracy or SPSD
Seychelles Patriotic Movement or SPM [Regis FRANCOURT]
Seychelloise Alliance (Lalyans Seselwa) [Patrick PILLAY]
Seychellois Democratic Alliance (Linyon Demokratik Seselwa) or LDS [Roger MANCIENNE] (includes SNP, Seychelloise Alliance, SPSD, SUP)

## INTERNATIONAL ORGANIZATION PARTICIPATION:

ACP, AfDB, AOSIS, AU, C, CD, COMESA, EITI (candidate country), FAO, G-77, IAEA, IBRD, ICAO, ICC (NGOs), ICCt, ICRM, IDA, IFAD, IFC, IFRCS, ILO, IMF, IMO, InOC, Interpol, IOC, IOM, IPU, ISO (correspondent), ITU, MIGA, NAM, OIF, OPCW, SADC, UN, UNCTAD, UNESCO, UNIDO, UNWTO, UPU, WCO, WHO, WIPO, WMO, WTO (observer)

## DIPLOMATIC REPRESENTATION IN THE US:

**chief of mission:** Ambassador Ronald Jean JUMEAU (since 8 September 2017)

**chancery:** 800 Second Avenue, Suite 400C, New York, NY 10017

**telephone:** [1] (212) 972-1785

**FAX:** [1] (212) 972-1786

**consulate(s) general:** New York

## DIPLOMATIC REPRESENTATION FROM THE US:

the US does not have an embassy in Seychelles; the US Ambassador to Mauritius is accredited to Seychelles

## FLAG DESCRIPTION:

five oblique bands of blue (hoist side), yellow, red, white, and green (bottom) radiating from the bottom of the hoist side; the oblique bands are meant to symbolize a dynamic new country moving into the future; blue represents sky and sea, yellow the sun giving light and life, red the peoples' determination to work for the future in unity and love, white social justice and harmony, and green the land and natural environment

## NATIONAL SYMBOL(S):

coco de mer (sea coconut); national colors: blue, yellow, red, white, green

## NATIONAL ANTHEM:

**name:** "Koste Seselwa" (Seychellois Unite)

**lyrics/music:** David Francois Marc ANDRE and George Charles Robert PAYET

**note:** adopted 1996

# ECONOMY :: SEYCHELLES

## ECONOMY - OVERVIEW:

Since independence in 1976, per capita output in this Indian Ocean archipelago has expanded to roughly seven times the pre-independence, near-subsistence level, moving the island into the high income group of countries. Growth has been led by the tourist sector, which directly employs about 26% of the labor force and directly and indirectly accounts for more than 55% of GDP, and by tuna fishing. In recent years, the government has encouraged foreign investment to upgrade hotels and tourism industry services. At the same time, the government has moved to reduce the dependence on tourism by promoting the development of the offshore financial, information, and communication sectors, and renewable energy.

In 2008, having depleted its foreign exchange reserves, Seychelles defaulted on interest payments due on a $230 million Eurobond, requested assistance from the IMF, and immediately enacted a number of significant structural reforms, including liberalization of the exchange rate, reform of the public sector to include layoffs, and the sale of some state assets. In December 2013, the IMF declared that Seychelles had successfully transitioned to a market-based economy with full employment and a fiscal surplus. However, state-owned enterprises still play a prominent role in the economy. Effective 1 January 2017, Seychelles was no longer eligible for trade benefits under the US African Growth and Opportunities Act after having gained developed country status. Seychelles grew at 5% in 2017 because of a strong tourism sector and low commodity prices. The Seychellois Government met the IMF's performance criteria for 2017 but recognizes a need to make additional progress to reduce high income inequality, represented by a Gini coefficient of 46.8.

As a very small open economy dependent on tourism, Seychelles remains vulnerable to developments such as economic downturns in countries that supply tourists, natural disasters, and changes in local climatic conditions and ocean temperature. One of the main challenges facing the government is implementing strategies that will increase Seychelles' long-term resilience to climate change without weakening economic growth.

## GDP (PURCHASING POWER PARITY):

$2.75 billion (2017 est.)

$2.612 billion (2016 est.)

$2.499 billion (2015 est.)

**note:** data are in 2017 dollars

**country comparison to the world:** 190

## GDP (OFFICIAL EXCHANGE RATE):

$1.498 billion (2017 est.) (2017 est.)

## GDP - REAL GROWTH RATE:

5.3% (2017 est.)

4.5% (2016 est.)

4.9% (2015 est.)

country comparison to the world: 43

## GDP - PER CAPITA (PPP):

$29,300 (2017 est.)

$27,800 (2016 est.)

$26,900 (2015 est.)

note: data are in 2017 dollars

country comparison to the world: 70

## GROSS NATIONAL SAVING:

8.1% of GDP (2017 est.)

10.2% of GDP (2016 est.)

15.2% of GDP (2015 est.)

country comparison to the world: 169

## GDP - COMPOSITION, BY END USE:

household consumption: 52.7% (2017 est.)

government consumption: 34.4% (2017 est.)

investment in fixed capital: 26.7% (2017 est.)

investment in inventories: 0% (2017 est.)

exports of goods and services: 79.4% (2017 est.)

imports of goods and services: -93.2% (2017 est.)

## GDP - COMPOSITION, BY SECTOR OF ORIGIN:

agriculture: 2.5% (2017 est.)

industry: 13.8% (2017 est.)

services: 83.7% (2017 est.)

## AGRICULTURE - PRODUCTS:

coconuts, cinnamon, vanilla, sweet potatoes, cassava (manioc, tapioca), copra, bananas; tuna

## INDUSTRIES:

fishing, tourism, beverages

## INDUSTRIAL PRODUCTION GROWTH RATE:

2.3% (2017 est.)

country comparison to the world: 121

## LABOR FORCE:

47,210 (2017 est.)

country comparison to the world: 194

## LABOR FORCE - BY OCCUPATION:

agriculture: 3%

industry: 23%

services: 74% (2006)

## UNEMPLOYMENT RATE:

3% (2017 est.)

2.7% (2016 est.)

country comparison to the world: 37

## POPULATION BELOW POVERTY LINE:

39.3% (2013 est.)

## HOUSEHOLD INCOME OR CONSUMPTION BY PERCENTAGE SHARE:

lowest 10%: 15.4% (2007)

highest 10%: 15.4% (2007)

## DISTRIBUTION OF FAMILY INCOME - GINI INDEX:

46.8 (2013 est.)

country comparison to the world: 29

## BUDGET:

revenues: 593.4 million (2017 est.)

expenditures: 600.7 million (2017 est.)

## TAXES AND OTHER REVENUES:

39.6% (of GDP) (2017 est.)

country comparison to the world: 44

## BUDGET SURPLUS (+) OR DEFICIT (-):

-0.5% (of GDP) (2017 est.)

country comparison to the world: 63

## PUBLIC DEBT:

63.6% of GDP (2017 est.)

69.1% of GDP (2016 est.)

country comparison to the world: 65

## FISCAL YEAR:

calendar year

## INFLATION RATE (CONSUMER PRICES):

2.9% (2017 est.)

-1% (2016 est.)

country comparison to the world: 132

## CENTRAL BANK DISCOUNT RATE:

11.17% (31 December 2010)

country comparison to the world: 17

## COMMERCIAL BANK PRIME LENDING RATE:

12.24% (31 December 2017 est.)

12.36% (31 December 2016 est.)

country comparison to the world: 67

## STOCK OF NARROW MONEY:

$627.3 million (31 December 2017 est.)

$556.5 million (31 December 2016 est.)

country comparison to the world: 165

## STOCK OF BROAD MONEY:

$627.3 million (31 December 2017 est.)

$556.5 million (31 December 2016 est.)

country comparison to the world: 169

## STOCK OF DOMESTIC CREDIT:

$650.3 million (31 December 2017 est.)

$565.9 million (31 December 2016 est.)

country comparison to the world: 173

## MARKET VALUE OF PUBLICLY TRADED SHARES:

NA

## CURRENT ACCOUNT BALANCE:

-$307 million (2017 est.)

-$286 million (2016 est.)

country comparison to the world: 106

## EXPORTS:

$564.8 million (2017 est.)

$477.6 million (2016 est.)

country comparison to the world: 173

## EXPORTS - PARTNERS:

UAE 28.5%, France 24%, UK 13.8%, Italy 8.9%, Germany 4.6% (2017)

## EXPORTS - COMMODITIES:

canned tuna, frozen fish, petroleum products (reexports)

## IMPORTS:

$1.155 billion (2017 est.)

$991 million (2016 est.)

country comparison to the world: 179

## IMPORTS - COMMODITIES:

machinery and equipment, foodstuffs, petroleum products, chemicals, other manufactured goods

## IMPORTS - PARTNERS:

UAE 13.4%, France 9.4%, Spain 5.7%, South Africa 5% (2017)

## RESERVES OF FOREIGN EXCHANGE AND GOLD:

$545.2 million (31 December 2017 est.)

$523.5 million (31 December 2016 est.)

country comparison to the world: 149

## DEBT - EXTERNAL:

$2.559 billion (31 December 2017 est.)

$2.651 billion (31 December 2016 est.)

country comparison to the world: 148

## EXCHANGE RATES:

Seychelles rupees (SCR) per US dollar -

13.64 (2017 est.)

13.319 (2016 est.)

13.319 (2015 est.)

13.314 (2014 est.)

12.747 (2013 est.)

## ENERGY :: SEYCHELLES

**ELECTRICITY ACCESS:**

population without electricity: 2,795 (2012)

electrification - total population: 97% (2012)

electrification - urban areas: 97% (2012)

electrification - rural areas: 97% (2012)

**ELECTRICITY - PRODUCTION:**
350 million kWh (2016 est.)

country comparison to the world: 175

**ELECTRICITY - CONSUMPTION:**
325.5 million kWh (2016 est.)

country comparison to the world: 182

**ELECTRICITY - EXPORTS:**
0 kWh (2016 est.)

country comparison to the world: 196

**ELECTRICITY - IMPORTS:**
0 kWh (2016 est.)

country comparison to the world: 198

**ELECTRICITY - INSTALLED GENERATING CAPACITY:**
88,000 kW (2016 est.)

country comparison to the world: 181

**ELECTRICITY - FROM FOSSIL FUELS:**
91% of total installed capacity (2016 est.)

country comparison to the world: 56

**ELECTRICITY - FROM NUCLEAR FUELS:**
0% of total installed capacity (2017 est.)

country comparison to the world: 181

**ELECTRICITY - FROM HYDROELECTRIC PLANTS:**
0% of total installed capacity (2017 est.)

country comparison to the world: 199

**ELECTRICITY - FROM OTHER RENEWABLE SOURCES:**
9% of total installed capacity (2017 est.)

country comparison to the world: 83

**CRUDE OIL - PRODUCTION:**
0 bbl/day (2017 est.)

country comparison to the world: 197

**CRUDE OIL - EXPORTS:**
0 bbl/day (2015 est.)

country comparison to the world: 191

**CRUDE OIL - IMPORTS:**
0 bbl/day (2015 est.)

country comparison to the world: 193

**CRUDE OIL - PROVED RESERVES:**
0 bbl (1 January 2018 est.)

country comparison to the world: 193

**REFINED PETROLEUM PRODUCTS - PRODUCTION:**
0 bbl/day (2015 est.)

country comparison to the world: 199

**REFINED PETROLEUM PRODUCTS - CONSUMPTION:**
7,300 bbl/day (2016 est.)

country comparison to the world: 166

**REFINED PETROLEUM PRODUCTS - EXPORTS:**
0 bbl/day (2015 est.)

country comparison to the world: 200

**REFINED PETROLEUM PRODUCTS - IMPORTS:**
7,225 bbl/day (2015 est.)

country comparison to the world: 155

**NATURAL GAS - PRODUCTION:**
0 cu m (2017 est.)

country comparison to the world: 194

**NATURAL GAS - CONSUMPTION:**
0 cu m (2017 est.)

country comparison to the world: 196

**NATURAL GAS - EXPORTS:**
0 cu m (2017 est.)

country comparison to the world: 182

**NATURAL GAS - IMPORTS:**
0 cu m (2017 est.)

country comparison to the world: 187

**NATURAL GAS - PROVED RESERVES:**
0 cu m (1 January 2014 est.)

country comparison to the world: 192

**CARBON DIOXIDE EMISSIONS FROM CONSUMPTION OF ENERGY:**
1.15 million Mt (2017 est.)

country comparison to the world: 165

## COMMUNICATIONS :: SEYCHELLES

**TELEPHONES - FIXED LINES:**

total subscriptions: 19,652 (2017 est.)

subscriptions per 100 inhabitants: 21 (2017 est.)

country comparison to the world: 180

**TELEPHONES - MOBILE CELLULAR:**

total subscriptions: 167,282 (2017 est.)

subscriptions per 100 inhabitants: 178 (2017 est.)

country comparison to the world: 186

**TELEPHONE SYSTEM:**

general assessment: effective system (2016)

domestic: combined fixed-line and mobile-cellular teledensity is approximately 185 telephones per 100 persons; radiotelephone communications between islands in the archipelago (2016)

international: country code - 248; direct radiotelephone communications with adjacent island countries and African coastal countries; satellite earth station - 1 Intelsat (Indian Ocean) (2016)

**BROADCAST MEDIA:**

the government operates the only terrestrial TV station, which provides local programming and airs broadcasts from international services; multi-channel cable and satellite TV are available through 2 providers; the government operates 1 AM and 1 FM radio station; there is 1 privately operated radio station; transmissions of 2 international broadcasters are accessible in Victoria (2016)

**INTERNET COUNTRY CODE:**

.sc

**INTERNET USERS:**

total: 52,664 (July 2016 est.)

percent of population: 56.5% (July 2016 est.)

country comparison to the world: 193

**BROADBAND - FIXED SUBSCRIPTIONS:**

total: 15,221 (2017 est.)

subscriptions per 100 inhabitants: 16 (2017 est.)

country comparison to the world: 161

## TRANSPORTATION :: SEYCHELLES

**NATIONAL AIR TRANSPORT SYSTEM:**

number of registered air carriers: 1 (2015)

inventory of registered aircraft operated by air carriers: 3 (2015)

annual passenger traffic on registered air carriers: 497,496 (2015)

annual freight traffic on registered air carriers: 19,234,992 mt-km (2015)

**CIVIL AIRCRAFT REGISTRATION COUNTRY CODE PREFIX:**

S7 (2016)

**AIRPORTS:**

14 (2013)

country comparison to the world: 150

**AIRPORTS - WITH PAVED RUNWAYS:**

total: 7 (2017)

2,438 to 3,047 m: 1 (2017)

914 to 1,523 m: 5 (2017)

under 914 m: 1 (2017)

**AIRPORTS - WITH UNPAVED RUNWAYS:**

total: 7 (2013)

914 to 1,523 m: 2 (2013)

under 914 m: 5 (2013)

**HELIPORTS:**

1 (2013)

**ROADWAYS:**

total: 526 km (2015)

paved: 514 km (2015)

unpaved: 12 km (2015)

country comparison to the world: 196

**MERCHANT MARINE:**

total: 24 (2017)

by type: general cargo 4, oil tanker 6, other 14 (2017)

country comparison to the world: 134

**PORTS AND TERMINALS:**

major seaport(s): Victoria

## MILITARY AND SECURITY :: SEYCHELLES

**MILITARY EXPENDITURES:**

1.29% of GDP (2016)

1.21% of GDP (2015)

2.17% of GDP (2014)

country comparison to the world: 88

**MILITARY BRANCHES:**

Seychelles People's Defense Forces (SPDF): Army (includes infantry, Special Forces (Tazar)), Coast Guard (includes Naval Wing, Air Wing) (2015)

**MILITARY SERVICE AGE AND OBLIGATION:**

18 years of age for voluntary military service (younger with parental consent); no conscription (2012)

## TRANSNATIONAL ISSUES :: SEYCHELLES

**DISPUTES - INTERNATIONAL:**

Mauritius and Seychelles claim the Chagos Islands (UK-administered British Indian Ocean Territory)

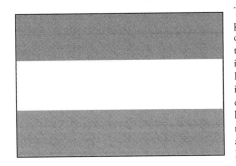

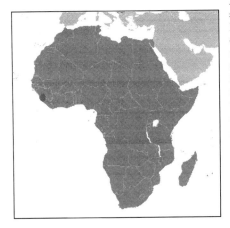

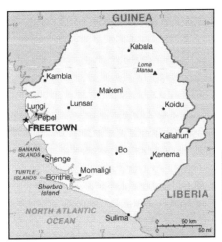

# AFRICA :: SIERRA LEONE

## INTRODUCTION :: SIERRA LEONE

### BACKGROUND:

The British set up a trading post near present-day Freetown in the 17th century. Originally the trade involved timber and ivory, but later it expanded into slaves. Following the American Revolution, a colony was established in 1787 and Sierra Leone became a destination for resettling black loyalists who had originally been resettled in Nova Scotia. After the abolition of the slave trade in 1807, British crews delivered thousands of Africans liberated from illegal slave ships to Sierra Leone, particularly Freetown. The colony gradually expanded inland during the course of the 19th century; independence was attained in 1961. Democracy is slowly being reestablished after the civil war (1991-2002) that resulted in tens of thousands of deaths and the displacement of more than 2 million people (about one third of the population). The military, which took over full responsibility for security following the departure of UN peacekeepers at the end of 2005, has developed as a guarantor of the country's stability; the armed forces remained on the sideline during the 2007 and 2012 national elections. In March 2014, the closure of the UN Integrated Peacebuilding Office in Sierra Leone marked the end of more than 15 years of peacekeeping and political operations in Sierra Leone. The government's stated priorities include furthering development - including recovering from the Ebola epidemic - creating jobs, and stamping out endemic corruption.

## GEOGRAPHY :: SIERRA LEONE

### LOCATION:
Western Africa, bordering the North Atlantic Ocean, between Guinea and Liberia

### GEOGRAPHIC COORDINATES:
8 30 N, 11 30 W

### MAP REFERENCES:
Africa

### AREA:
total: 71,740 sq km
land: 71,620 sq km
water: 120 sq km
country comparison to the world: 120

### AREA - COMPARATIVE:
slightly smaller than South Carolina

### LAND BOUNDARIES:
total: 1,093 km
border countries (2): Guinea 794 km, Liberia 299 km

### COASTLINE:
402 km

### MARITIME CLAIMS:
territorial sea: 12 nm
exclusive economic zone: 200 nm
contiguous zone: 24 nm
continental shelf: 200 nm

### CLIMATE:
tropical; hot, humid; summer rainy season (May to December); winter dry season (December to April)

### TERRAIN:
coastal belt of mangrove swamps, wooded hill country, upland plateau, mountains in east

### ELEVATION:
mean elevation: 279 m
elevation extremes: 0 m lowest point: Atlantic Ocean
1948 highest point: Loma Mansa (Bintimani)

### NATURAL RESOURCES:
diamonds, titanium ore, bauxite, iron ore, gold, chromite

### LAND USE:
agricultural land: 56.2% (2011 est.)
arable land: 23.4% (2011 est.) / permanent crops: 2.3% (2011 est.) / permanent pasture: 30.5% (2011 est.)
forest: 37.5% (2011 est.)
other: 6.3% (2011 est.)

### IRRIGATED LAND:
300 sq km (2012)

### POPULATION DISTRIBUTION:
population clusters are found in the lower elevations of the south and west; the northern third of the country is less populated

### NATURAL HAZARDS:
dry, sand-laden harmattan winds blow from the Sahara (December to February); sandstorms, dust storms

### ENVIRONMENT - CURRENT ISSUES:
rapid population growth pressuring the environment; overharvesting of timber, expansion of cattle grazing, and slash-and-burn agriculture have resulted in deforestation, soil exhaustion, and flooding; loss of

biodiversity; air pollution; water pollution; overfishing

**ENVIRONMENT - INTERNATIONAL AGREEMENTS:**

party to: Biodiversity, Climate Change, Climate Change-Kyoto Protocol, Desertification, Endangered Species, Hazardous Wastes, Law of the Sea, Marine Life Conservation, Ozone Layer Protection, Ship Pollution, Wetlands

signed, but not ratified: Environmental Modification

**GEOGRAPHY - NOTE:**

rainfall along the coast can reach 495 cm (195 inches) a year, making it one of the wettest places along coastal, western Africa

## PEOPLE AND SOCIETY :: SIERRA LEONE

**POPULATION:**

6,312,212 (July 2018 est.)

country comparison to the world: 108

**NATIONALITY:**

noun: Sierra Leonean(s)

adjective: Sierra Leonean

**ETHNIC GROUPS:**

Temne 35.5%, Mende 33.2%, Limba 6.4%, Kono 4.4%, Fullah 3.4%, Loko 2.9%, Koranko 2.8%, Sherbro 2.6%, Mandingo 2.4%, Creole 1.2% (descendants of freed Jamaican slaves who were settled in the Freetown area in the late-18th century; also known as Krio), other Sierra Leone 4.7%, other foreign 0.3% (includes refugees from Liberia's recent civil war, and small numbers of Europeans, Lebanese, Pakistanis, and Indians), unspecified 0.2% (2013 est.)

**LANGUAGES:**

English (official, regular use limited to literate minority), Mende (principal vernacular in the south), Temne (principal vernacular in the north), Krio (English-based Creole, spoken by the descendants of freed Jamaican slaves who were settled in the Freetown area, a lingua franca and a first language for 10% of the population but understood by 95%)

**RELIGIONS:**

Muslim 78.6%, Christian 20.8%, other 0.3%, unspecified 0.2% (2013 est.)

**DEMOGRAPHIC PROFILE:**

Sierra Leone's youthful and growing population is driven by its high total fertility rate (TFR) of almost 5 children per woman, which has declined little over the last two decades. Its elevated TFR is sustained by the continued desire for large families, the low level of contraceptive use, and the early start of childbearing. Despite its high TFR, Sierra Leone's population growth is somewhat tempered by high infant, child, and maternal mortality rates that are among the world's highest and are a result of poverty, a lack of potable water and sanitation, poor nutrition, limited access to quality health care services, and the prevalence of female genital cutting.

Sierra Leone's large youth cohort – about 60% of the population is under the age of 25 – continues to struggle with high levels of unemployment, which was one of the major causes of the country's 1991-2002 civil war and remains a threat to stability today. Its estimated 60% youth unemployment rate is attributed to high levels of illiteracy and unskilled labor, a lack of private sector jobs, and low pay.

Sierra Leone has been a source of and destination for refugees. Sierra Leone's civil war internally displaced as many as 2 million people, or almost half the population, and forced almost another half million to seek refuge in neighboring countries (370,000 Sierra Leoneans fled to Guinea and 120,000 to Liberia). The UNHCR has helped almost 180,000 Sierra Leoneans to return home, while more than 90,000 others have repatriated on their own. Of the more than 65,000 Liberians who took refuge in Sierra Leone during their country's civil war (1989-2003), about 50,000 have been voluntarily repatriated by the UNHCR and others have returned home independently. As of 2015, less than 1,000 Liberians still reside in Sierra Leone.

**AGE STRUCTURE:**

0-14 years: 41.71% (male 1,314,905 /female 1,317,921)

15-24 years: 18.6% (male 572,274 /female 602,105)

25-54 years: 32.23% (male 973,698 /female 1,060,688)

55-64 years: 3.7% (male 110,176 /female 123,268)

65 years and over: 3.76% (male 97,922 /female 139,255) (2018 est.)

**DEPENDENCY RATIOS:**

total dependency ratio: 82.6 (2015 est.)

youth dependency ratio: 78 (2015 est.)

elderly dependency ratio: 4.6 (2015 est.)

potential support ratio: 21.9 (2015 est.)

**MEDIAN AGE:**

total: 19.1 years

male: 18.4 years

female: 19.7 years (2018 est.)

country comparison to the world: 201

**POPULATION GROWTH RATE:**

2.4% (2018 est.)

country comparison to the world: 27

**BIRTH RATE:**

36 births/1,000 population (2018 est.)

country comparison to the world: 18

**DEATH RATE:**

10.2 deaths/1,000 population (2018 est.)

country comparison to the world: 33

**NET MIGRATION RATE:**

-2.1 migrant(s)/1,000 population (2017 est.)

country comparison to the world: 164

**POPULATION DISTRIBUTION:**

population clusters are found in the lower elevations of the south and west; the northern third of the country is less populated

**URBANIZATION:**

urban population: 42.1% of total population (2018)

rate of urbanization: 3.12% annual rate of change (2015-20 est.)

**MAJOR URBAN AREAS - POPULATION:**

1.136 million FREETOWN (capital) (2018)

**SEX RATIO:**

at birth: 1.02 male(s)/female (2017 est.)

0-14 years: 1 male(s)/female (2017 est.)

15-24 years: 0.94 male(s)/female (2017 est.)

25-54 years: 0.92 male(s)/female (2017 est.)

55-64 years: 0.86 male(s)/female (2017 est.)

65 years and over: 0.73 male(s)/female (2017 est.)

total population: 0.95 male(s)/female (2017 est.)

**MOTHER'S MEAN AGE AT FIRST BIRTH:**

19.2 years (2013 est.)

note: median age at first birth among women 25-29

**MATERNAL MORTALITY RATE:**

1,360 deaths/100,000 live births (2015 est.)

country comparison to the world: 1

**INFANT MORTALITY RATE:**

total: 66.7 deaths/1,000 live births (2018 est.)

male: 74.9 deaths/1,000 live births (2018 est.)

female: 58.3 deaths/1,000 live births (2018 est.)

country comparison to the world: 9

**LIFE EXPECTANCY AT BIRTH:**

total population: 59 years (2018 est.)

male: 56.4 years (2018 est.)

female: 61.7 years (2018 est.)

country comparison to the world: 212

**TOTAL FERTILITY RATE:**

4.69 children born/woman (2018 est.)

country comparison to the world: 21

**CONTRACEPTIVE PREVALENCE RATE:**

16.6% (2013)

**HEALTH EXPENDITURES:**

11.1% of GDP (2014)

country comparison to the world: 13

**PHYSICIANS DENSITY:**

0.02 physicians/1,000 population (2010)

**DRINKING WATER SOURCE:**

improved:

urban: 84.9% of population (2015 est.)

rural: 47.8% of population (2015 est.)

total: 62.6% of population (2015 est.)

unimproved:

urban: 15.1% of population (2015 est.)

rural: 52.2% of population (2015 est.)

total: 37.4% of population (2015 est.)

**SANITATION FACILITY ACCESS:**

improved:

urban: 22.8% of population (2015 est.)

rural: 6.9% of population (2015 est.)

total: 13.3% of population (2015 est.)

unimproved:

urban: 77.2% of population (2015 est.)

rural: 93.1% of population (2015 est.)

total: 86.7% of population (2015 est.)

**HIV/AIDS - ADULT PREVALENCE RATE:**

1.4% (2017 est.)

country comparison to the world: 35

**HIV/AIDS - PEOPLE LIVING WITH HIV/AIDS:**

61,000 (2017 est.)

country comparison to the world: 55

**HIV/AIDS - DEATHS:**

2,600 (2017 est.)

country comparison to the world: 43

**MAJOR INFECTIOUS DISEASES:**

degree of risk: very high (2016)

food or waterborne diseases: bacterial and protozoal diarrhea, hepatitis A, and typhoid fever (2016)

vectorborne diseases: malaria, dengue fever, and yellow fever (2016)

water contact diseases: schistosomiasis (2016)

animal contact diseases: rabies (2016)

aerosolized dust or soil contact diseases: Lassa fever (2016)

**OBESITY - ADULT PREVALENCE RATE:**

8.7% (2016)

country comparison to the world: 147

**CHILDREN UNDER THE AGE OF 5 YEARS UNDERWEIGHT:**

18.1% (2013)

country comparison to the world: 31

**EDUCATION EXPENDITURES:**

2.9% of GDP (2016)

country comparison to the world: 148

**LITERACY:**

definition: age 15 and over can read and write English, Mende, Temne, or Arabic (2015 est.)

total population: 48.1% (2015 est.)

male: 58.7% (2015 est.)

female: 37.7% (2015 est.)

**UNEMPLOYMENT, YOUTH AGES 15-24:**

total: 9.4% (2014 est.)

male: 14.8% (2014 est.)

female: 6.1% (2014 est.)

country comparison to the world: 130

# GOVERNMENT :: SIERRA LEONE

**COUNTRY NAME:**

conventional long form: Republic of Sierra Leone

conventional short form: Sierra Leone

local long form: Republic of Sierra Leone

local short form: Sierra Leone

etymology: the Portuguese explorer Pedro de SINTRA named the country "Serra Leoa" (Lion Mountains) for the impressive mountains he saw while sailing the West African coast in 1462

**GOVERNMENT TYPE:**

presidential republic

**CAPITAL:**

name: Freetown

geographic coordinates: 8 29 N, 13 14 W

time difference: UTC 0 (5 hours ahead of Washington, DC, during Standard Time)

**ADMINISTRATIVE DIVISIONS:**

4 provinces and 1 area*; Eastern, Northern, North Western, Southern, Western*

**INDEPENDENCE:**

27 April 1961 (from the UK)

**NATIONAL HOLIDAY:**

Independence Day, 27 April (1961)

**CONSTITUTION:**

history: several previous; latest effective 1 October 1991 (2017)

amendments: proposed by Parliament; passage of amendments requires at least two-thirds majority vote of Parliament in two successive readings and assent by the president of the republic; passage of amendments affecting fundamental rights and freedoms and many other constitutional sections also requires approval in a referendum with participation of at least one-half of qualified voters and at least two-thirds of votes cast; amended several times, last in 2013 (2017)

**LEGAL SYSTEM:**

mixed legal system of English common law and customary law

**INTERNATIONAL LAW ORGANIZATION PARTICIPATION:**

has not submitted an ICJ jurisdiction declaration; accepts ICCt jurisdiction

**CITIZENSHIP:**

*citizenship by birth:* no

*citizenship by descent only:* at least one parent or grandparent must be a citizen of Sierra Leone

*dual citizenship recognized:* yes

*residency requirement for naturalization:* 5 years

**SUFFRAGE:**

18 years of age; universal

**EXECUTIVE BRANCH:**

*chief of state:* President Julius Maada BIO (since 4 April 2018); Vice President Mohamed Juldeh JALLOH (since 4 April 2018) ; note - the president is both chief of state and head of government

*head of government:* President Julius Maada BIO (since 4 April 2018); Vice President Mohamed Juldeh JALLOH (since 4 April 2018)

*cabinet:* Ministers of State appointed by the president, approved by Parliament; the cabinet is responsible to the president

*elections/appointments:* president directly elected by absolute majority popular vote in 2 rounds if needed for a 5-year term (eligible for a second term); election last held on 4 April 2018 (next to be in March 2023)

*election results:* Julius Maada BIO elected president in second round; percent of vote - Julius Maada BIO (SLPP) 51.8%, Samura KAMARA (APC) 48.2%

**LEGISLATIVE BRANCH:**

*description:* unicameral Parliament (146 seats; 132 members directly elected in single-seat constituencies by simple majority vote and 14 seats filled in separate elections by non-partisan members of Parliament called "paramount chiefs;" members serve 5-year terms)

*elections:* last held on 7 March 2018 (next to be held in March 2023)

*election results:* percent of vote by party - n/a; seats by party - APC 68, SLPP 49, C4C 8, other 7

**JUDICIAL BRANCH:**

*highest courts:* Superior Court of Judicature (consists of the Supreme Court - at the apex - with the chief justice and 4 other judges, the Court of Appeal with the chief justice and 7 other judges, and the High Court of Justice with the chief justice and 9 other judges; note – the Judicature has jurisdiction in all civil, criminal, and constitutional matters

*judge selection and term of office:* Supreme Court chief justice and other judges of the Judicature appointed by the president on the advice of the Judicial and Legal Service Commission (a 7-member independent body of judges, presidential appointees, and the Commission chairman) and are subject to the approval of Parliament; all Judicature judges appointed until retirement at age 65

*subordinate courts:* magistrates' courts; District Appeals Court; local courts

**POLITICAL PARTIES AND LEADERS:**

All People's Congress or APC [Ernest Bai KOROMA]
Coalition for Change or C4C [Tamba R. SANDY]
Sierra Leone People's Party or SLPP [Dr. Prince HARDING]
numerous other parties

**INTERNATIONAL ORGANIZATION PARTICIPATION:**

ACP, AfDB, AU, C, ECOWAS, EITI (compliant country), FAO, G-77, IAEA, IBRD, ICAO, ICCt, ICRM, IDA, IDB, IFAD, IFC, IFRCS, IHO (pending member), ILO, IMF, IMO, Interpol, IOC, IOM, IPU, ISO (correspondent), ITU, ITUC (NGOs), MIGA, MINUSMA, NAM, OIC, OPCW, UN, UNAMID, UNCTAD, UNESCO, UNIDO, UNIFIL, UNISFA, UNWTO, UPU, WCO, WFTU (NGOs), WHO, WIPO, WMO, WTO

**DIPLOMATIC REPRESENTATION IN THE US:**

*chief of mission:* Ambassador Bockari Kortu STEVENS (since 4 April 2008)

*chancery:* 1701 19th Street NW, Washington, DC 20009

*telephone:* [1] (202) 939-9261 through 9263

*FAX:* [1] (202) 483-1793

**DIPLOMATIC REPRESENTATION FROM THE US:**

*chief of mission:* Ambassador Maria E. BREWER (since 20 December 2017)

*embassy:* Southridge-Hill Station, Freetown

*mailing address:* use embassy street address

*telephone:* [232] 99 105 000

*FAX:* [232] 99 515 355

**FLAG DESCRIPTION:**

three equal horizontal bands of light green (top), white, and light blue; green symbolizes agriculture, mountains, and natural resources, white represents unity and justice, and blue the sea and the natural harbor in Freetown

**NATIONAL SYMBOL(S):**

lion; national colors: green, white, blue

**NATIONAL ANTHEM:**

*name:* High We Exalt Thee, Realm of the Free

*lyrics/music:* Clifford Nelson FYLE/John Joseph AKA

*note:* adopted 1961

## ECONOMY :: SIERRA LEONE

**ECONOMY - OVERVIEW:**

Sierra Leone is extremely poor and nearly half of the working-age population engages in subsistence agriculture. The country possesses substantial mineral, agricultural, and fishery resources, but it is still recovering from a civil war that destroyed most institutions before ending in the early 2000s.

In recent years, economic growth has been driven by mining - particularly iron ore. The country's principal exports are iron ore, diamonds, and rutile, and the economy is vulnerable to fluctuations in international prices. Until 2014, the government had relied on external assistance to support its budget, but it was gradually becoming more independent. The Ebola outbreak of 2014 and 2015, combined with falling global commodities prices, caused a significant contraction of economic activity in all areas. While the World Health Organization declared an end to the Ebola outbreak in Sierra Leone in November 2015, low commodity prices in 2015-2016 contributed to the country's biggest fiscal shortfall since 2001. In 2017, increased iron ore exports, together with the end of the Ebola epidemic, supported a resumption of economic growth.

Continued economic growth will depend on rising commodities prices and increased efforts to diversify the sources of growth. Non-mining activities will remain constrained by inadequate infrastructure, such as power and roads, even though power sector projects may provide some additional electricity capacity in the near term. Pervasive corruption and undeveloped human capital will continue to deter foreign investors. Sustained international donor support in the near future will partially offset these fiscal constraints.

**GDP (PURCHASING POWER PARITY):**

$11.55 billion (2017 est.)

$11.14 billion (2016 est.)

$10.48 billion (2015 est.)

note: data are in 2017 dollars

country comparison to the world: 158

**GDP (OFFICIAL EXCHANGE RATE):**

$3.612 billion (2017 est.) (2017 est.)

**GDP - REAL GROWTH RATE:**

3.7% (2017 est.)

6.3% (2016 est.)

-20.5% (2015 est.)

country comparison to the world: 92

**GDP - PER CAPITA (PPP):**

$1,600 (2017 est.)

$1,500 (2016 est.)

$1,500 (2015 est.)

note: data are in 2017 dollars

country comparison to the world: 219

**GROSS NATIONAL SAVING:**

10% of GDP (2017 est.)

7.9% of GDP (2016 est.)

-5.9% of GDP (2015 est.)

country comparison to the world: 163

**GDP - COMPOSITION, BY END USE:**

household consumption: 97.9% (2017 est.)

government consumption: 12.1% (2017 est.)

investment in fixed capital: 18.1% (2017 est.)

investment in inventories: 0.4% (2017 est.)

exports of goods and services: 26.8% (2017 est.)

imports of goods and services: -55.3% (2017 est.)

**GDP - COMPOSITION, BY SECTOR OF ORIGIN:**

agriculture: 60.7% (2017 est.)

industry: 6.5% (2017 est.)

services: 32.9% (2017 est.)

**AGRICULTURE - PRODUCTS:**

rice, coffee, cocoa, palm kernels, palm oil, peanuts, cashews; poultry, cattle, sheep, pigs; fish

**INDUSTRIES:**

diamond mining; iron ore, rutile and bauxite mining; small-scale manufacturing (beverages, textiles, footwear)

**INDUSTRIAL PRODUCTION GROWTH RATE:**

15.5% (2017 est.)

country comparison to the world: 3

**LABOR FORCE:**

2.972 million (2017 est.)

country comparison to the world: 105

**LABOR FORCE - BY OCCUPATION:**

agriculture: 61.1%

industry: 5.5%

services: 33.4% (2014 est.)

**UNEMPLOYMENT RATE:**

15% (2017 est.)

17.2% (2016 est.)

country comparison to the world: 172

**POPULATION BELOW POVERTY LINE:**

70.2% (2004 est.)

**HOUSEHOLD INCOME OR CONSUMPTION BY PERCENTAGE SHARE:**

lowest 10%: 33.6% (2003)

highest 10%: 33.6% (2003)

**DISTRIBUTION OF FAMILY INCOME - GINI INDEX:**

34 (2011)

62.9 (1989)

country comparison to the world: 106

**BUDGET:**

revenues: 562 million (2017 est.)

expenditures: 846.4 million (2017 est.)

**TAXES AND OTHER REVENUES:**

15.6% (of GDP) (2017 est.)

country comparison to the world: 189

**BUDGET SURPLUS (+) OR DEFICIT (-):**

-7.9% (of GDP) (2017 est.)

country comparison to the world: 199

**PUBLIC DEBT:**

63.9% of GDP (2017 est.)

54.9% of GDP (2016 est.)

country comparison to the world: 63

**FISCAL YEAR:**

calendar year

**INFLATION RATE (CONSUMER PRICES):**

18.2% (2017 est.)

10.9% (2016 est.)

country comparison to the world: 215

**CENTRAL BANK DISCOUNT RATE:**

NA

**COMMERCIAL BANK PRIME LENDING RATE:**

17.92% (31 December 2017 est.)

18.04% (31 December 2016 est.)

country comparison to the world: 23

**STOCK OF NARROW MONEY:**

$387.4 million (31 December 2017 est.)

$381.8 million (31 December 2016 est.)

country comparison to the world: 177

**STOCK OF BROAD MONEY:**

$387.4 million (31 December 2017 est.)

$381.8 million (31 December 2016 est.)

country comparison to the world: 181

**STOCK OF DOMESTIC CREDIT:**

$572.6 million (31 December 2017 est.)

$527.6 million (31 December 2016 est.)

country comparison to the world: 174

**MARKET VALUE OF PUBLICLY TRADED SHARES:**

NA

**CURRENT ACCOUNT BALANCE:**

-$407 million (2017 est.)

-$88 million (2016 est.)

country comparison to the world: 113

**EXPORTS:**

$808.4 million (2017 est.)

$670 million (2016 est.)

country comparison to the world: 170

**EXPORTS - PARTNERS:**

Cote dIvoire 37.7%, Belgium 20.5%, US 15.7%, China 10.2%, Netherlands 6.1% (2017)

**EXPORTS - COMMODITIES:**

iron ore, diamonds, rutile, cocoa, coffee, fish

**IMPORTS:**

$1.107 billion (2017 est.)

$972.8 million (2016 est.)

country comparison to the world: 182

**IMPORTS - COMMODITIES:**

foodstuffs, machinery and equipment, fuels and lubricants, chemicals

**IMPORTS - PARTNERS:**

China 11.5%, US 9.2%, Belgium 8.8%, UAE 7.7%, India 7.4%, Turkey 5.2%, Senegal 5.1%, Netherlands 4.3% (2017)

**RESERVES OF FOREIGN EXCHANGE AND GOLD:**

$478 million (31 December 2017 est.)

$497.2 million (31 December 2016 est.)

country comparison to the world: 152

**DEBT - EXTERNAL:**

$1.615 billion (31 December 2017 est.)

$1.503 billion (31 December 2016 est.)

country comparison to the world: 159

**STOCK OF DIRECT FOREIGN INVESTMENT - AT HOME:**

$1.042 billion (31 December 2017 est.)

$1.832 billion (31 December 2016 est.)

country comparison to the world: 123

**STOCK OF DIRECT FOREIGN INVESTMENT - ABROAD:**

$56.8 billion (31 December 2017 est.)

$6.7 million (31 December 2014 est.)

country comparison to the world: 40

**EXCHANGE RATES:**

leones (SLL) per US dollar -

7,396.3 (2017 est.)

6,289.9 (2016 est.)

6,289.9 (2015 est.)

5,080.8 (2014 est.)

4,524.2 (2013 est.)

## ENERGY :: SIERRA LEONE

**ELECTRICITY ACCESS:**

population without electricity: 5.8 million (2013)

electrification - total population: 5% (2013)

electrification - urban areas: 11% (2013)

electrification - rural areas: 1% (2013)

**ELECTRICITY - PRODUCTION:**

300 million kWh (2016 est.)

country comparison to the world: 185

**ELECTRICITY - CONSUMPTION:**

279 million kWh (2016 est.)

country comparison to the world: 188

**ELECTRICITY - EXPORTS:**

0 kWh (2016 est.)

country comparison to the world: 197

**ELECTRICITY - IMPORTS:**

0 kWh (2016 est.)

country comparison to the world: 199

**ELECTRICITY - INSTALLED GENERATING CAPACITY:**

113,300 kW (2016 est.)

country comparison to the world: 179

**ELECTRICITY - FROM FOSSIL FUELS:**

23% of total installed capacity (2016 est.)

country comparison to the world: 194

**ELECTRICITY - FROM NUCLEAR FUELS:**

0% of total installed capacity (2017 est.)

country comparison to the world: 182

**ELECTRICITY - FROM HYDROELECTRIC PLANTS:**

51% of total installed capacity (2017 est.)

country comparison to the world: 38

**ELECTRICITY - FROM OTHER RENEWABLE SOURCES:**

26% of total installed capacity (2017 est.)

country comparison to the world: 27

**CRUDE OIL - PRODUCTION:**

0 bbl/day (2017 est.)

country comparison to the world: 198

**CRUDE OIL - EXPORTS:**

0 bbl/day (2015 est.)

country comparison to the world: 192

**CRUDE OIL - IMPORTS:**

0 bbl/day (2015 est.)

country comparison to the world: 194

**CRUDE OIL - PROVED RESERVES:**

0 bbl (1 January 2018 est.)

country comparison to the world: 194

**REFINED PETROLEUM PRODUCTS - PRODUCTION:**

0 bbl/day (2017 est.)

country comparison to the world: 200

**REFINED PETROLEUM PRODUCTS - CONSUMPTION:**

6,500 bbl/day (2016 est.)

country comparison to the world: 169

**REFINED PETROLEUM PRODUCTS - EXPORTS:**

0 bbl/day (2015 est.)

country comparison to the world: 201

**REFINED PETROLEUM PRODUCTS - IMPORTS:**

6,439 bbl/day (2015 est.)

country comparison to the world: 164

**NATURAL GAS - PRODUCTION:**

0 cu m (2017 est.)

country comparison to the world: 195

**NATURAL GAS - CONSUMPTION:**

0 cu m (2017 est.)

country comparison to the world: 197

**NATURAL GAS - EXPORTS:**

0 cu m (2017 est.)

country comparison to the world: 183

**NATURAL GAS - IMPORTS:**

0 cu m (2017 est.)

country comparison to the world: 188

**NATURAL GAS - PROVED RESERVES:**

0 cu m (1 January 2014 est.)

country comparison to the world: 193

**CARBON DIOXIDE EMISSIONS FROM CONSUMPTION OF ENERGY:**

984,800 Mt (2017 est.)

country comparison to the world: 170

## COMMUNICATIONS :: SIERRA LEONE

**TELEPHONES - FIXED LINES:**

total subscriptions: 17,000 (July 2016 est.)

subscriptions per 100 inhabitants: less than 1 (July 2016 est.)

country comparison to the world: 185

**TELEPHONES - MOBILE CELLULAR:**

total subscriptions: 6,279,270 (July 2016 est.)

subscriptions per 100 inhabitants: 102 (July 2016 est.)

country comparison to the world: 111

**TELEPHONE SYSTEM:**

general assessment: telephone service improving with the expansion of the mobile sector (2016)

domestic: the national microwave radio relay trunk system connects Freetown to Bo and Kenema; mobile-cellular service has grown rapidly from a small base, overcoming the deficiencies of the fixed-line sector (2016)

international: country code - 232; satellite earth station - 1 Intelsat (Atlantic Ocean) (2016)

**BROADCAST MEDIA:**

1 government-owned TV station; 3 private TV stations; a pay-TV service began operations in late 2007; 1 government-owned national radio station; about two-dozen private radio

stations primarily clustered in major cities; transmissions of several international broadcasters are available (2016)

**INTERNET COUNTRY CODE:**

.sl

**INTERNET USERS:**

total: 708,615 (July 2016 est.)

percent of population: 11.8% (July 2016 est.)

country comparison to the world: 142

## TRANSPORTATION :: SIERRA LEONE

**NATIONAL AIR TRANSPORT SYSTEM:**

annual passenger traffic on registered air carriers: 50,193 (2015)

annual freight traffic on registered air carriers: 0 mt-km (2015)

**CIVIL AIRCRAFT REGISTRATION COUNTRY CODE PREFIX:**

9L (2016)

**AIRPORTS:**

8 (2013)

country comparison to the world: 162

**AIRPORTS - WITH PAVED RUNWAYS:**

total: 1 (2017)

over 3,047 m: 1 (2017)

**AIRPORTS - WITH UNPAVED RUNWAYS:**

total: 7 (2013)

914 to 1,523 m: 7 (2013)

**HELIPORTS:**

2 (2013)

**ROADWAYS:**

total: 11,300 km (2002)

paved: 904 km (2002)

unpaved: 10,396 km (2002)

country comparison to the world: 133

**WATERWAYS:**

800 km (600 km navigable year-round) (2011)

country comparison to the world: 72

**MERCHANT MARINE:**

total: 451 (2017)

by type: bulk carrier 20, container ship 10, general cargo 252, oil tanker 59, other 110 (2017)

country comparison to the world: 42

**PORTS AND TERMINALS:**

major seaport(s): Freetown, Pepel, Sherbro Islands

## MILITARY AND SECURITY :: SIERRA LEONE

**MILITARY EXPENDITURES:**

0.81% of GDP (2016)

0.92% of GDP (2015)

0.97% of GDP (2014)

country comparison to the world: 131

**MILITARY BRANCHES:**

Republic of Sierra Leone Armed Forces (RSLAF): Army (includes Maritime Wing and Air Wing) (2013)

**MILITARY SERVICE AGE AND OBLIGATION:**

18 is the legal minimum age for voluntary military service (younger with parental consent); women are eligible to serve; no conscription; candidates must be HIV negative (2012)

## TRANSNATIONAL ISSUES :: SIERRA LEONE

**DISPUTES - INTERNATIONAL:**

Sierra Leone opposes Guinean troops' continued occupation of Yenga, a small village on the Makona River that serves as a border with Guinea; Guinea's forces came to Yenga in the mid-1990s to help the Sierra Leonean military to suppress rebels and to secure their common border but have remained there even after both countries signed a 2005 agreement acknowledging that Yenga belonged to Sierra Leone; in 2012, the two sides signed a declaration to demilitarize the area

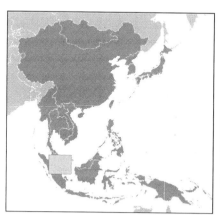

# EAST ASIA / SOUTHEAST ASIA :: SINGAPORE

## INTRODUCTION :: SINGAPORE

### BACKGROUND:
A Malay trading port known as Temasek existed on the island of Singapore by the 14th century. The settlement changed hands several times in the ensuing centuries and was eventually burned in the 17th century and fell into obscurity. The British founded Singapore as a trading colony on the site in 1819. It joined the Malaysian Federation in 1963 but was ousted two years later and became independent. Singapore subsequently became one of the world's most prosperous countries with strong international trading links (its port is one of the world's busiest in terms of tonnage handled) and with per capita GDP equal to that of the leading nations of Western Europe.

## GEOGRAPHY :: SINGAPORE

### LOCATION:
Southeastern Asia, islands between Malaysia and Indonesia

### GEOGRAPHIC COORDINATES:
1 22 N, 103 48 E

### MAP REFERENCES:
Southeast Asia

### AREA:
total: 719.2 sq km

land: 709.2 sq km

water: 10 sq km

country comparison to the world: 191

### AREA - COMPARATIVE:
slightly more than 3.5 times the size of Washington, DC

### LAND BOUNDARIES:
0 km

### COASTLINE:
193 km

### MARITIME CLAIMS:
territorial sea: 3 nm

exclusive fishing zone: within and beyond territorial sea, as defined in treaties and practice

### CLIMATE:
tropical; hot, humid, rainy; two distinct monsoon seasons - northeastern monsoon (December to March) and southwestern monsoon (June to September); inter-monsoon - frequent afternoon and early evening thunderstorms

### TERRAIN:
lowlying, gently undulating central plateau

### ELEVATION:
0 m lowest point: Singapore Strait

166 highest point: Bukit Timah

### NATURAL RESOURCES:
fish, deepwater ports

### LAND USE:
agricultural land: 1% (2011 est.)

arable land: 0.9% (2011 est.) / permanent crops: 0.1% (2011 est.) / permanent pasture: 0% (2011 est.)

forest: 3.3% (2011 est.)

other: 95.7% (2011 est.)

### IRRIGATED LAND:
0 sq km (2012)

### POPULATION DISTRIBUTION:
most of the urbanization is along the southern coast, with relatively dense population clusters found in the central areas

### NATURAL HAZARDS:
flash floods

### ENVIRONMENT - CURRENT ISSUES:
water pollution; industrial pollution; limited natural freshwater resources; limited land availability presents waste disposal problems; air pollution; deforestation; seasonal smoke/haze resulting from forest fires in Indonesia

### ENVIRONMENT - INTERNATIONAL AGREEMENTS:
party to: Biodiversity, Climate Change, Climate Change-Kyoto Protocol, Desertification, Endangered Species, Hazardous Wastes, Law of the Sea, Ozone Layer Protection, Ship Pollution

signed, but not ratified: none of the selected agreements

### GEOGRAPHY - NOTE:
focal point for Southeast Asian sea routes; consists of about 60 islands, by far the largest of which is Pulau Ujong; land reclamation has removed many former islands and created a number of new ones

## PEOPLE AND SOCIETY :: SINGAPORE

### POPULATION:
5,995,991 (July 2018 est.)

country comparison to the world: 112

### NATIONALITY:

noun: Singaporean(s)

adjective: Singapore

**ETHNIC GROUPS:**

Chinese 74.3%, Malay 13.4%, Indian 9%, other 3.2% (2017 est.)

note: individuals self-identify; the population is divided into four categories: Chinese, Malay (includes Malays and Indonesians), Indian (includes Indian, Pakistani, Bangladeshi, or Sri Lankan), and other ethnic groups (includes Eurasians, Caucasians, Japanese, Filipino, Vietnamese

**LANGUAGES:**

English (official) 36.9%, Mandarin (official) 34.9%, other Chinese dialects (includes Hokkien, Cantonese, Teochew) 12.2%, Malay (official) 10.7%, Tamil (official) 3.3%, other 2% (2015 est.)

note: data represent language most frequently spoken at home

**RELIGIONS:**

Buddhist 33.2%, Christian 18.8%, Muslim 14%, Taoist 10%, Hindu 5%, other 0.6%, none 18.5% (2015 est.)

**AGE STRUCTURE:**

0-14 years: 12.77% (male 391,714 /female 373,766)

15-24 years: 16.05% (male 473,012 /female 489,553)

25-54 years: 50.61% (male 1,476,528 /female 1,558,179)

55-64 years: 10.53% (male 316,001 /female 315,648)

65 years and over: 10.03% (male 274,863 /female 326,727) (2018 est.)

**DEPENDENCY RATIOS:**

total dependency ratio: 37.3 (2015 est.)

youth dependency ratio: 21.3 (2015 est.)

elderly dependency ratio: 16 (2015 est.)

potential support ratio: 6.2 (2015 est.)

**MEDIAN AGE:**

total: 34.9 years

male: 34.8 years

female: 35.1 years (2018 est.)

country comparison to the world: 84

**POPULATION GROWTH RATE:**

1.79% (2018 est.)

country comparison to the world: 58

**BIRTH RATE:**

8.7 births/1,000 population (2018 est.)

country comparison to the world: 212

**DEATH RATE:**

3.5 deaths/1,000 population (2018 est.)

country comparison to the world: 216

**NET MIGRATION RATE:**

13.1 migrant(s)/1,000 population (2017 est.)

country comparison to the world: 5

**POPULATION DISTRIBUTION:**

most of the urbanization is along the southern coast, with relatively dense population clusters found in the central areas

**URBANIZATION:**

urban population: 100% of total population (2018)

rate of urbanization: 1.39% annual rate of change (2015-20 est.)

**MAJOR URBAN AREAS - POPULATION:**

5.792 million SINGAPORE (capital) (2018)

**SEX RATIO:**

at birth: 1.07 male(s)/female (2017 est.)

0-14 years: 1.05 male(s)/female (2017 est.)

15-24 years: 0.97 male(s)/female (2017 est.)

25-54 years: 0.95 male(s)/female (2017 est.)

55-64 years: 1 male(s)/female (2017 est.)

65 years and over: 0.83 male(s)/female (2017 est.)

total population: 0.96 male(s)/female (2017 est.)

**MOTHER'S MEAN AGE AT FIRST BIRTH:**

30.5 years (2015 est.)

median age

**MATERNAL MORTALITY RATE:**

10 deaths/100,000 live births (2015 est.)

country comparison to the world: 150

**INFANT MORTALITY RATE:**

total: 2.3 deaths/1,000 live births (2018 est.)

male: 2.5 deaths/1,000 live births (2018 est.)

female: 2.1 deaths/1,000 live births (2018 est.)

country comparison to the world: 220

**LIFE EXPECTANCY AT BIRTH:**

total population: 85.5 years (2018 est.)

male: 82.8 years (2018 est.)

female: 88.3 years (2018 est.)

country comparison to the world: 3

**TOTAL FERTILITY RATE:**

0.84 children born/woman (2018 est.)

country comparison to the world: 224

**HEALTH EXPENDITURES:**

4.9% of GDP (2014)

country comparison to the world: 145

**PHYSICIANS DENSITY:**

2.28 physicians/1,000 population (2016)

**HOSPITAL BED DENSITY:**

2.4 beds/1,000 population (2015)

**DRINKING WATER SOURCE:**

improved:

urban: 100% of population

total: 100% of population

unimproved:

urban: 0% of population

total: 0% of population (2015 est.)

**SANITATION FACILITY ACCESS:**

improved:

urban: 100% of population (2015 est.)

total: 100% of population (2015 est.)

unimproved:

urban: 0% of population (2015 est.)

total: 0% of population (2015 est.)

**HIV/AIDS - ADULT PREVALENCE RATE:**

0.2% (2017 est.)

country comparison to the world: 103

**HIV/AIDS - PEOPLE LIVING WITH HIV/AIDS:**

7,600 (2017 est.)

country comparison to the world: 108

**HIV/AIDS - DEATHS:**

<100 (2017 est.)

**MAJOR INFECTIOUS DISEASES:**

note: active local transmission of Zika virus by Aedes species mosquitoes has been identified in this country (as of August 2016); it poses an important risk (a large number of cases possible) among US citizens if bitten by an infective mosquito; other less common ways to get Zika are through sex, via blood transfusion, or during pregnancy, in which the pregnant woman passes Zika virus to her fetus

**OBESITY - ADULT PREVALENCE RATE:**

6.1% (2016)

country comparison to the world: 171

**EDUCATION EXPENDITURES:**

2.9% of GDP (2013)

country comparison to the world: 149

**LITERACY:**

definition: age 15 and over can read and write (2016 est.)

total population: 97% (2016 est.)

male: 98.7% (2016 est.)

female: 95.4% (2016 est.)

**SCHOOL LIFE EXPECTANCY (PRIMARY TO TERTIARY EDUCATION):**

total: 13 years (2009)

male: 13 years (2009)

female: 13 years (2009)

**UNEMPLOYMENT, YOUTH AGES 15-24:**

total: 9.1% (2016 est.)

male: 6.2% (2016 est.)

female: 12.5% (2016 est.)

country comparison to the world: 132

## GOVERNMENT :: SINGAPORE

**COUNTRY NAME:**

conventional long form: Republic of Singapore

conventional short form: Singapore

local long form: Republic of Singapore

local short form: Singapore

etymology: name derives from the Sanskrit words "singa" (lion) and "pura" (city) to describe the city-state's leonine symbol

**GOVERNMENT TYPE:**

parliamentary republic

**CAPITAL:**

name: Singapore

geographic coordinates: 1 17 N, 103 51 E

time difference: UTC+8 (13 hours ahead of Washington, DC, during Standard Time)

**ADMINISTRATIVE DIVISIONS:**

none

**INDEPENDENCE:**

9 August 1965 (from Malaysian Federation)

**NATIONAL HOLIDAY:**

National Day, 9 August (1965)

**CONSTITUTION:**

history: several previous; latest adopted 22 December 1965 (2018)

amendments: proposed by Parliament; passage requires two-thirds majority vote in the second and third readings by the elected Parliament membership and assent by the president of the republic; passage of amendments affecting constitutional articles on fundamental liberties, the president, or constitutional amendment procedures also requires at least two-thirds majority vote in a referendum; amended many times, last in 2016 (2018)

**LEGAL SYSTEM:**

English common law

**INTERNATIONAL LAW ORGANIZATION PARTICIPATION:**

has not submitted an ICJ jurisdiction declaration; non-party state to the ICCt

**CITIZENSHIP:**

citizenship by birth: no

citizenship by descent only: at least one parent must be a citizen of Singapore

dual citizenship recognized: no

residency requirement for naturalization: 10 years

**SUFFRAGE:**

21 years of age; universal and compulsory

**EXECUTIVE BRANCH:**

chief of state: President HALIMAH Yacob (since 14 September 2017); note - President TAN's term ended on 31 August 2017; HALIMAH is Singapore's first female president; the head of the Council of Presidential Advisors, J.Y. PILLAY, served as acting president until HALIMAH was sworn in as president on 14 September 2017

head of government: Prime Minister LEE Hsien Loong (since 12 August 2004); Deputy Prime Ministers TEO Chee Hean (since 1 April 2009) and Tharman SHANMUGARATNAM (since 21 May 2011)

cabinet: Cabinet appointed by the president on the advice of the prime minister; Cabinet responsible to Parliament

elections/appointments: president directly elected by simple majority popular vote for a single 6-year term; election last held on 13 September 2017 (next to be held in 2023); following legislative elections, leader of majority party or majority coalition appointed prime minister by president; deputy prime ministers appointed by the president

election results: HALIMAH Yacob was declared president on 13 September 2017, being the only eligible candidate; Tony TAN Keng Yam elected president in the previous contested election on 27 August 2011; percent of vote - Tony TAN Keng Yam (independent) 35.2% , TAN Cheng Bock (independent) 34.9%, TAN Jee Say (independent) 25%, TAN Kin Lian (independent) 4.9%

**LEGISLATIVE BRANCH:**

description: unicameral Parliament (101 seats; 89 members directly elected by popular vote, up to 9 nominated by a parliamentary selection committee and appointed by the president, and up to 9 but currently 3 non-constituency members from opposition parties to ensure political diversity; members serve 5-year terms)

elections: last held on 11 September 2015 (next to be held in 2020)

election results: percent of vote by party - PAP 69.9%, WP 12.5%, other 17.6%; seats by party - PAP 83, WP 6; composition - men 77, women 24, percent of women 23.8%

**JUDICIAL BRANCH:**

highest courts: Supreme Court (although the number varies - as of Feb 2018 it had a total of 21 judges, 7 judicial commissioners, 4 senior judges, and 15 international judges; the court is organized into an upper tier Appeal Court and a lower tier High Court)

judge selection and term of office: judges appointed by the president from candidates recommended by the prime minister after consultation with the chief justice; judges usually serve until retirement at age 65 but can be extended

subordinate courts: district, magistrates', juvenile, family, community, and coroners' courts; small claims tribunals; employment claims tribunals

**POLITICAL PARTIES AND LEADERS:**

National Solidarity Party or NSP
People's Action Party or PAP [LEE Hsien Loong]
Singapore Democratic Party or SDP [Dr. CHEE Soon Juan]
Workers' Party or WP [Pritam SINGH]

**INTERNATIONAL ORGANIZATION PARTICIPATION:**

ADB, AOSIS, APEC, Arctic Council (observer), ARF, ASEAN, BIS, C, CP, EAS, FAO, FATF, G-77, IAEA, IBRD, ICAO, ICC (national committees), ICCt, ICRM, IDA, IFC, IFRCS, IHO, ILO, IMF, IMO, IMSO, Interpol, IOC, IPU, ISO, ITSO, ITU, ITUC (NGOs), MIGA, NAM, OPCW, Pacific Alliance (observer), PCA, UN, UNCTAD, UNESCO, UNHCR, UPU, WCO, WHO, WIPO, WMO, WTO

**DIPLOMATIC REPRESENTATION IN THE US:**

chief of mission: Ambassador Ashok Kumar MIRPURI (since 30 July 2012)

chancery: 3501 International Place NW, Washington, DC 20008

telephone: [1] (202) 537-3100

FAX: [1] (202) 537-0876

consulate(s) general: San Francisco

consulate(s): New York

**DIPLOMATIC REPRESENTATION FROM THE US:**

chief of mission: Ambassador (vacant); Charge d'Affaires Stephanie SYPTAK-RAMNATH (since 20 January 2017)

embassy: 27 Napier Road, Singapore 258508

mailing address: FPO AP 96507-0001

telephone: [65] 6476-9100

FAX: [65] 6476-9340

**FLAG DESCRIPTION:**

two equal horizontal bands of red (top) and white; near the hoist side of the red band, there is a vertical, white crescent (closed portion is toward the hoist side) partially enclosing five white five-pointed stars arranged in a circle; red denotes brotherhood and equality; white signifies purity and virtue; the waxing crescent moon symbolizes a young nation on the ascendancy; the five stars represent the nation's ideals of democracy, peace, progress, justice, and equality

**NATIONAL SYMBOL(S):**

lion, merlion (mythical half lion-half fish creature), orchid; national colors: red, white

**NATIONAL ANTHEM:**

name: "Majulah Singapura" (Onward Singapore)

lyrics/music: ZUBIR Said

note: adopted 1965; first performed in 1958 at the Victoria Theatre, the anthem is sung only in Malay

## ECONOMY :: SINGAPORE

**ECONOMY - OVERVIEW:**

Singapore has a highly developed and successful free-market economy. It enjoys an open and corruption-free environment, stable prices, and a per capita GDP higher than that of most developed countries. Unemployment is very low. The economy depends heavily on exports, particularly of electronics, petroleum products, chemicals, medical and optical devices, pharmaceuticals, and on Singapore's vibrant transportation, business, and financial services sectors.

The economy contracted 0.6% in 2009 as a result of the global financial crisis, but has continued to grow since 2010. Growth from 2012-2017 was slower than during the previous decade, a result of slowing structural growth - as Singapore reached high-income levels - and soft global demand for exports. Growth recovered to 3.6% in 2017 with a strengthening global economy.

The government is attempting to restructure Singapore's economy to reduce its dependence on foreign labor, raise productivity growth, and increase wages amid slowing labor force growth and an aging population. Singapore has attracted major investments in advanced manufacturing, pharmaceuticals, and medical technology production and will continue efforts to strengthen its position as Southeast Asia's leading financial and technology hub. Singapore is a signatory of the Comprehensive and Progressive Agreement for Trans-Pacific Partnership (CPTPP), and a party to the Regional Comprehensive Economic Partnership (RCEP) negotiations with nine other ASEAN members plus Australia, China, India, Japan, South Korea, and New Zealand. In 2015, Singapore formed, with the other ASEAN members, the ASEAN Economic Community.

**GDP (PURCHASING POWER PARITY):**

$528.1 billion (2017 est.)

$509.7 billion (2016 est.)

$497.8 billion (2015 est.)

note: data are in 2017 dollars

country comparison to the world: 38

**GDP (OFFICIAL EXCHANGE RATE):**

$323.9 billion (2017 est.) (2017 est.)

**GDP - REAL GROWTH RATE:**

3.6% (2017 est.)

2.4% (2016 est.)

2.2% (2015 est.)

country comparison to the world: 96

**GDP - PER CAPITA (PPP):**

$94,100 (2017 est.)

$90,900 (2016 est.)

$89,900 (2015 est.)

note: data are in 2017 dollars

country comparison to the world: 7

**GROSS NATIONAL SAVING:**

46.5% of GDP (2017 est.)

46% of GDP (2016 est.)

45.7% of GDP (2015 est.)

country comparison to the world: 5

**GDP - COMPOSITION, BY END USE:**

household consumption: 35.6% (2017 est.)

government consumption: 10.9% (2017 est.)

investment in fixed capital: 24.8% (2017 est.)

investment in inventories: 2.8% (2017 est.)

exports of goods and services: 173.3% (2017 est.)

imports of goods and services: -149.1% (2017 est.)

**GDP - COMPOSITION, BY SECTOR OF ORIGIN:**

agriculture: 0% (2017 est.)

industry: 24.8% (2017 est.)

services: 75.2% (2017 est.)

**AGRICULTURE - PRODUCTS:**

vegetables; poultry, eggs; fish, ornamental fish, orchids

**INDUSTRIES:**

electronics, chemicals, financial services, oil drilling equipment, petroleum refining, biomedical products, scientific instruments, telecommunication equipment, processed food and beverages, ship repair, offshore platform construction, entrepot trade

**INDUSTRIAL PRODUCTION GROWTH RATE:**

5.7% (2017 est.)

country comparison to the world: 46

**LABOR FORCE:**

3.657 million (2017 est.)

note: excludes non-residents

country comparison to the world: 99

**LABOR FORCE - BY OCCUPATION:**

agriculture: 0.7%

industry: 25.6%

services: 73.7% (2017)

note: excludes non-residents

**UNEMPLOYMENT RATE:**

2.2% (2017 est.)

2.1% (2016 est.)

country comparison to the world: 21

**POPULATION BELOW POVERTY LINE:**

NA

**HOUSEHOLD INCOME OR CONSUMPTION BY PERCENTAGE SHARE:**

lowest 10%: 27.5% (2017)

highest 10%: 27.5% (2017)

**DISTRIBUTION OF FAMILY INCOME - GINI INDEX:**

45.9 (2017)

45.8 (2016)

country comparison to the world: 38

**BUDGET:**

revenues: 50.85 billion (2017 est.)

expenditures: 51.87 billion (2017 est.)

note: expenditures include both operational and development expenditures

**TAXES AND OTHER REVENUES:**

15.7% (of GDP) (2017 est.)

country comparison to the world: 187

**BUDGET SURPLUS (+) OR DEFICIT (-):**

-0.3% (of GDP) (2017 est.)

country comparison to the world: 55

**PUBLIC DEBT:**

111.1% of GDP (2017 est.)

106.8% of GDP (2016 est.)

note: Singapore's public debt consists largely of Singapore Government Securities (SGS) issued to assist the Central Provident Fund (CPF), which administers Singapore's defined contribution pension fund; special issues of SGS are held by the CPF, and are non-tradable; the government has not borrowed to finance deficit expenditures since the 1980s; Singapore has no external public debt

country comparison to the world: 11

**FISCAL YEAR:**

1 April - 31 March

**INFLATION RATE (CONSUMER PRICES):**

0.6% (2017 est.)

-0.5% (2016 est.)

country comparison to the world: 33

**CENTRAL BANK DISCOUNT RATE:**

2.15% (2017 est.)

1.17% (2016 est.)

country comparison to the world: 118

**COMMERCIAL BANK PRIME LENDING RATE:**

5.28% (31 December 2017 est.)

5.35% (31 December 2016 est.)

country comparison to the world: 143

**STOCK OF NARROW MONEY:**

$137.4 billion (31 December 2017 est.)

$119.4 billion (31 December 2016 est.)

country comparison to the world: 31

**STOCK OF BROAD MONEY:**

$137.4 billion (31 December 2017 est.)

$119.4 billion (31 December 2016 est.)

country comparison to the world: 31

**STOCK OF DOMESTIC CREDIT:**

$471.2 billion (31 December 2017 est.)

$383.3 billion (31 December 2016 est.)

country comparison to the world: 27

**MARKET VALUE OF PUBLICLY TRADED SHARES:**

$809.4 billion (31 December 2017 est.)

$712.3 billion (31 December 2016 est.)

$696 billion (31 December 2015 est.)

country comparison to the world: 14

**CURRENT ACCOUNT BALANCE:**

$60.99 billion (2017 est.)

$58.85 billion (2016 est.)

country comparison to the world: 8

**EXPORTS:**

$396.8 billion (2017 est.)

$338 billion (2016 est.)

country comparison to the world: 13

**EXPORTS - PARTNERS:**

China 14.7%, Hong Kong 12.6%, Malaysia 10.8%, US 6.6%, Indonesia 5.8%, Japan 4.7%, South Korea 4.6%, Thailand 4% (2017)

**EXPORTS - COMMODITIES:**

machinery and equipment (including electronics and telecommunications), pharmaceuticals and other chemicals, refined petroleum products, foodstuffs and beverages

**IMPORTS:**

$312.1 billion (2017 est.)

$277.6 billion (2016 est.)

country comparison to the world: 16

**IMPORTS - COMMODITIES:**

machinery and equipment, mineral fuels, chemicals, foodstuffs, consumer goods

**IMPORTS - PARTNERS:**

China 13.9%, Malaysia 12%, US 10.7%, Japan 6.3%, South Korea 5% (2017)

**RESERVES OF FOREIGN EXCHANGE AND GOLD:**

$279.9 billion (31 December 2017 est.)

$271.8 billion (31 December 2016 est.)

country comparison to the world: 11

**DEBT - EXTERNAL:**

$566.1 billion (31 December 2017 est.)

$464.1 billion (30 September 2017 est.)

country comparison to the world: 20

**STOCK OF DIRECT FOREIGN INVESTMENT - AT HOME:**

$1.285 trillion (31 December 2017 est.)

$1.22 trillion (31 December 2016 est.)

country comparison to the world: 9

**STOCK OF DIRECT FOREIGN INVESTMENT - ABROAD:**

$841.4 billion (31 December 2017 est.)

$759.2 billion (31 December 2016 est.)

country comparison to the world: 13

**EXCHANGE RATES:**

Singapore dollars (SGD) per US dollar -

1.3 (2017 est.)

1.35 (2016 est.)

1.3815 (2015 est.)

1.3748 (2014 est.)

1.2671 (2013 est.)

## ENERGY :: SINGAPORE

**ELECTRICITY ACCESS:**

electrification - total population: 100% (2016)

**ELECTRICITY - PRODUCTION:**

48.66 billion kWh (2016 est.)

country comparison to the world: 55

**ELECTRICITY - CONSUMPTION:**

47.69 billion kWh (2016 est.)

country comparison to the world: 51

**ELECTRICITY - EXPORTS:**

0 kWh (2016 est.)

country comparison to the world: 198

**ELECTRICITY - IMPORTS:**

0 kWh (2016 est.)

country comparison to the world: 200

**ELECTRICITY - INSTALLED GENERATING CAPACITY:**

13.35 million kW (2016 est.)

country comparison to the world: 53

**ELECTRICITY - FROM FOSSIL FUELS:**

98% of total installed capacity (2016 est.)

country comparison to the world: 29

**ELECTRICITY - FROM NUCLEAR FUELS:**

0% of total installed capacity (2017 est.)

country comparison to the world: 183

**ELECTRICITY - FROM HYDROELECTRIC PLANTS:**

0% of total installed capacity (2017 est.)

country comparison to the world: 200

**ELECTRICITY - FROM OTHER RENEWABLE SOURCES:**

2% of total installed capacity (2017 est.)

country comparison to the world: 144

**CRUDE OIL - PRODUCTION:**

0 bbl/day (2017 est.)

country comparison to the world: 199

**CRUDE OIL - EXPORTS:**

14,780 bbl/day (2015 est.)

country comparison to the world: 54

**CRUDE OIL - IMPORTS:**

783,300 bbl/day (2015 est.)

country comparison to the world: 15

**CRUDE OIL - PROVED RESERVES:**

0 bbl (1 January 2018 est.)

country comparison to the world: 195

**REFINED PETROLEUM PRODUCTS - PRODUCTION:**

755,000 bbl/day (2015 est.)

country comparison to the world: 24

**REFINED PETROLEUM PRODUCTS - CONSUMPTION:**

1.322 million bbl/day (2016 est.)

country comparison to the world: 17

**REFINED PETROLEUM PRODUCTS - EXPORTS:**

1.82 million bbl/day (2015 est.)

country comparison to the world: 4

**REFINED PETROLEUM PRODUCTS - IMPORTS:**

2.335 million bbl/day (2015 est.)

country comparison to the world: 1

**NATURAL GAS - PRODUCTION:**

0 cu m (2017 est.)

country comparison to the world: 196

**NATURAL GAS - CONSUMPTION:**

12.97 billion cu m (2017 est.)

country comparison to the world: 44

**NATURAL GAS - EXPORTS:**

622.9 million cu m (2017 est.)

country comparison to the world: 41

**NATURAL GAS - IMPORTS:**

13.48 billion cu m (2017 est.)

country comparison to the world: 23

**NATURAL GAS - PROVED RESERVES:**

0 cu m (1 January 2017 est.)

country comparison to the world: 194

**CARBON DIOXIDE EMISSIONS FROM CONSUMPTION OF ENERGY:**

249.5 million Mt (2017 est.)

country comparison to the world: 27

# COMMUNICATIONS :: SINGAPORE

**TELEPHONES - FIXED LINES:**

total subscriptions: 1,983,100 (2017 est.)

subscriptions per 100 inhabitants: 34 (2017 est.)

country comparison to the world: 58

**TELEPHONES - MOBILE CELLULAR:**

total subscriptions: 8,462,800 (2017 est.)

subscriptions per 100 inhabitants: 144 (2017 est.)

country comparison to the world: 97

**TELEPHONE SYSTEM:**

general assessment: excellent service (2016)

domestic: excellent domestic facilities; combined fixed-line and mobile-cellular teledensity more than 180 telephones per 100 persons; multiple providers of high-speed Internet connectivity (2016)

international: country code - 65; numerous submarine cables provide links throughout Asia, Australia, the Middle East, Europe, and US; satellite earth stations - 4; supplemented by VSAT coverage (2016)

**BROADCAST MEDIA:**

state controls broadcast media; 7 domestic TV stations operated by MediaCorp which is wholly owned by a state investment company; broadcasts from Malaysian and Indonesian stations available; satellite dishes banned; multi-channel cable TV services available; a total of 18 domestic radio stations broadcasting, with MediaCorp operating 11, Singapore Press Holdings, also government-linked, another 5, and another 2 controlled by the Singapore Armed Forces Reservists Association; Malaysian and Indonesian radio stations are available as is BBC; a number of Internet service radio stations are also available

**INTERNET COUNTRY CODE:**

.sg

**INTERNET USERS:**

total: 4,683,200 (July 2016 est.)

percent of population: 81% (July 2016 est.)

country comparison to the world: 80

**BROADBAND - FIXED SUBSCRIPTIONS:**

total: 1,470,400 (2017 est.)

subscriptions per 100 inhabitants: 25 (2017 est.)

country comparison to the world: 61

# TRANSPORTATION :: SINGAPORE

**NATIONAL AIR TRANSPORT SYSTEM:**

number of registered air carriers: 5 (2015)

inventory of registered aircraft operated by air carriers: 197 (2015)

annual passenger traffic on registered air carriers: 33,290,544 (2015)

annual freight traffic on registered air carriers: 6,154,365,275 mt-km (2015)

**CIVIL AIRCRAFT REGISTRATION COUNTRY CODE PREFIX:**

9V (2016)

**AIRPORTS:**

9 (2013)

country comparison to the world: 159

**AIRPORTS - WITH PAVED RUNWAYS:**

total: 9 (2017)

over 3,047 m: 2 (2017)

2,438 to 3,047 m: 2 (2017)

1,524 to 2,437 m: 3 (2017)

914 to 1,523 m: 1 (2017)

under 914 m: 1 (2017)

## PIPELINES:

3220 km domestic gas (2014), 1122 km cross-border pipelines (2017), 8 km refined products (2013)

## ROADWAYS:

total: 3,496 km (2014)

paved: 3,496 km (includes 164 km of expressways) (2014)

country comparison to the world: 161

## MERCHANT MARINE:

total: 3,558 (2017)

by type: bulk carrier 592, container ship 504, general cargo 134, oil tanker 722, other 1606 (2017)

country comparison to the world: 6

## PORTS AND TERMINALS:

major seaport(s): Singapore

container port(s) (TEUs): Singapore (30,903,600) (2016)

LNG terminal(s) (import): Singapore

# MILITARY AND SECURITY :: SINGAPORE

## MILITARY EXPENDITURES:

3.35% of GDP (2016)

3.16% of GDP (2015)

3.11% of GDP (2014)

country comparison to the world: 24

## MILITARY BRANCHES:

Singapore Armed Forces: Army, Navy, Air Force (includes Air Defense) (2013)

## MILITARY SERVICE AGE AND OBLIGATION:

18-21 years of age for male compulsory military service; 16 1/2 years of age for volunteers; 2-year conscript service obligation, with a reserve obligation to age 40 (enlisted) or age 50 (officers) (2012)

## MARITIME THREATS:

the International Maritime Bureau reports the territorial and offshore waters in the South China Sea as high risk for piracy and armed robbery against ships; numerous commercial vessels have been attacked and hijacked both at anchor and while underway; hijacked vessels are often disguised and cargo diverted to ports in East Asia; crews have been murdered or cast adrift; the Singapore Straits saw four attacks against commercial vessels in 2017, a slight increase over the two attacks in 2016

# TERRORISM :: SINGAPORE

## TERRORIST GROUPS - FOREIGN BASED:

Islamic State of Iraq and ash-Sham (ISIS) network in Singapore:
aim(s): enhance its networks in Singapore; implement ISIS's strict interpretation of sharia
area(s) of operation: attacks in Bangladesh are staged in Singapore; operates under the name the Islamic State in Bangladesh (April 2018)

Jemaah Islamiyah (JI):
aim(s): enhance its networks in Singapore and, ultimately, overthrow the Singapore Government and establish a pan-Islamic state across Southeast Asia
area(s) of operation: maintains a presence (April 2018)

# TRANSNATIONAL ISSUES :: SINGAPORE

## DISPUTES - INTERNATIONAL:

disputes persist with Malaysia over each country's extensive land reclamation works, bridge construction, and maritime boundaries in the Johor and Singapore Straitsin 2008, ICJ awarded sovereignty of Pedra Branca (Pulau Batu Puteh/Horsburgh Island) to Singapore, and Middle Rocks to Malaysia, but did not rule on maritime regimes, boundaries, or disposition of South Ledgein 2017, Malaysia filed a challenge to the 2008 ruling and applied for ownership of South Ledge; piracy remains a problem in the Malacca Strait

## ILLICIT DRUGS:

drug abuse limited because of aggressive law enforcement efforts, including carrying out death sentences; as a transportation and financial services hub, Singapore is vulnerable, despite strict laws and enforcement, as a venue for money laundering

# CENTRAL AMERICA :: SINT MAARTEN

## INTRODUCTION :: SINT MAARTEN

### BACKGROUND:
Although sighted by Christopher COLUMBUS in 1493 and claimed for Spain, it was the Dutch who occupied the island in 1631 and began exploiting its salt deposits. The Spanish retook the island in 1633, but continued to be harassed by the Dutch. The Spanish finally relinquished the island of Saint Martin to the French and Dutch, who divided it amongst themselves in 1648. The establishment of cotton, tobacco, and sugar plantations dramatically expanded African slavery on the island in the 18th and 19th centuries; the practice was not abolished in the Dutch half until 1863. The island's economy declined until 1939 when it became a free port; the tourism industry was dramatically expanded beginning in the 1950s. In 1954, Sint Maarten and several other Dutch Caribbean possessions became part of the Kingdom of the Netherlands as the Netherlands Antilles. In a 2000 referendum, the citizens of Sint Maarten voted to become a self-governing country within the Kingdom of the Netherlands. The change in status became effective in October of 2010 with the dissolution of the Netherlands Antilles. On 6 September 2017, Hurricane Irma passed over the island of Saint Martin/Sint Maarten causing extensive damage to roads, communications, electrical power, and housing; the UN estimated that 90% of the buildings were damaged or destroyed. Princess Juliana International Airport was heavily damaged and forced to close to commercial air traffic for five weeks.

## GEOGRAPHY :: SINT MAARTEN

### LOCATION:
Caribbean, located in the Leeward Islands (northern) group; Dutch part of the island of Saint Martin in the Caribbean Sea; Sint Maarten lies east of the US Virgin Islands

### GEOGRAPHIC COORDINATES:
18 4 N, 63 4 W

### MAP REFERENCES:
Central America and the Caribbean

### AREA:
total: 34 sq km

land: 34 sq km

water: 0 sq km

note: Dutch part of the island of Saint Martin

country comparison to the world: 236

### AREA - COMPARATIVE:
one-fifth the size of Washington, DC

### LAND BOUNDARIES:
total: 16 km

border countries (1): Saint Martin (France) 16 km

### COASTLINE:
58.9 km (for entire island)

### MARITIME CLAIMS:
territorial sea: 12 nm

exclusive economic zone: 200 nm

### CLIMATE:
tropical marine climate, ameliorated by northeast trade winds, results in moderate temperatures; average rainfall of 150 cm/year; hurricane season stretches from July to November

### TERRAIN:
low, hilly terrain, volcanic origin

### ELEVATION:
mean elevation: NA

elevation extremes: 0 m lowest point: Caribbean Sea

383 highest point: Mount Flagstaff

### NATURAL RESOURCES:
fish, salt

### POPULATION DISTRIBUTION:
most populous areas are Lower Prince's Quarter (north of Philipsburg), followed closely by Cul de Sac

### NATURAL HAZARDS:
subject to hurricanes from July to November

### ENVIRONMENT - CURRENT ISSUES:
scarcity of potable water (increasing percentage provided by desalination); inadequate solid waste management; pollution from construction, chemical runoff, and sewage harms reefs

### GEOGRAPHY - NOTE:
the northern border is shared with the French overseas collectivity of Saint Martin; together, these two entities make up the smallest landmass in the world shared by two self-governing states

## PEOPLE AND SOCIETY :: SINT MAARTEN

### POPULATION:
42,677 (July 2018 est.)

country comparison to the world: 212

### LANGUAGES:

English (official) 67.5%, Spanish 12.9%, Creole 8.2%, Dutch (official) 4.2%, Papiamento (a Spanish-Portuguese-Dutch-English dialect) 2.2%, French 1.5%, other 3.5% (2001 census)

### RELIGIONS:

Protestant 41.9% (Pentecostal 14.7%, Methodist 10.0%, Seventh Day Adventist 6.6%, Baptist 4.7%, Anglican 3.1%, other Protestant 2.8%), Roman Catholic 33.1%, Hindu 5.2%, Christian 4.1%, Jehovah's Witness 1.7%, Evangelical 1.4%, Muslim/Jewish 1.1%, other 1.3% (includes Buddhist, Sikh, Rastafarian), none 7.9%, no response 2.4% (2011 est.)

### AGE STRUCTURE:

**0-14 years:** 18.5% (male 4,110 /female 3,785)

**15-24 years:** 14.19% (male 3,049 /female 3,009)

**25-54 years:** 40.93% (male 8,539 /female 8,930)

**55-64 years:** 16.52% (male 3,356 /female 3,694)

**65 years and over:** 9.85% (male 2,017 /female 2,188) (2018 est.)

### MEDIAN AGE:

**total:** 41.2 years

**male:** 39.8 years

**female:** 42.2 years (2018 est.)

**country comparison to the world:** 43

### POPULATION GROWTH RATE:

1.39% (2018 est.)

**country comparison to the world:** 80

### BIRTH RATE:

13.1 births/1,000 population (2018 est.)

**country comparison to the world:** 147

### DEATH RATE:

5.4 deaths/1,000 population (2018 est.)

**country comparison to the world:** 182

### NET MIGRATION RATE:

6.3 migrant(s)/1,000 population (2017 est.)

**country comparison to the world:** 15

### POPULATION DISTRIBUTION:

most populous areas are Lower Prince's Quarter (north of Philipsburg), followed closely by Cul de Sac

### URBANIZATION:

**urban population:** 100% of total population (2018)

**rate of urbanization:** 1.56% annual rate of change (2015-20 est.)

### MAJOR URBAN AREAS - POPULATION:

1327 PHILIPSBURG (capital) (2011)

### SEX RATIO:

**at birth:** 1.05 male(s)/female (2017 est.)

**0-14 years:** 1.09 male(s)/female (2017 est.)

**15-24 years:** 0.98 male(s)/female (2017 est.)

**25-54 years:** 0.95 male(s)/female (2017 est.)

**55-64 years:** 0.92 male(s)/female (2017 est.)

**65 years and over:** 0.92 male(s)/female (2017 est.)

**total population:** 0.98 male(s)/female (2017 est.)

### INFANT MORTALITY RATE:

**total:** 7.9 deaths/1,000 live births (2018 est.)

**male:** 8.6 deaths/1,000 live births (2018 est.)

**female:** 7.2 deaths/1,000 live births (2018 est.)

**country comparison to the world:** 152

### LIFE EXPECTANCY AT BIRTH:

**total population:** 78.5 years (2018 est.)

**male:** 76.1 years (2018 est.)

**female:** 80.9 years (2018 est.)

**country comparison to the world:** 62

### TOTAL FERTILITY RATE:

2.04 children born/woman (2018 est.)

**country comparison to the world:** 112

### HIV/AIDS - ADULT PREVALENCE RATE:

NA

### HIV/AIDS - PEOPLE LIVING WITH HIV/AIDS:

NA

### HIV/AIDS - DEATHS:

NA

### MAJOR INFECTIOUS DISEASES:

**note:** active local transmission of Zika virus by Aedes species mosquitoes has been identified in this country (as of August 2016); it poses an important risk (a large number of cases possible) among US citizens if bitten by an infective mosquito; other less common ways to get Zika are through sex, via blood transfusion, or during pregnancy, in which the pregnant woman passes Zika virus to her fetus

## GOVERNMENT :: SINT MAARTEN

### COUNTRY NAME:

**conventional long form:** none

**conventional short form:** Sint Maarten

**local long form:** Land Sint Maarten (Dutch); Country of Sint Maarten (English)

**local short form:** Sint Maarten (Dutch and English)

**former:** Netherlands Antilles; Curacao and Dependencies

**etymology:** explorer Christopher COLUMBUS named the island after Saint MARTIN of Tours because the 11 November 1493 day of discovery was the saint's feast day

### DEPENDENCY STATUS:

constituent country within the Kingdom of the Netherlands; full autonomy in internal affairs granted in 2010; Dutch Government responsible for defense and foreign affairs

### GOVERNMENT TYPE:

parliamentary democracy (Estates of Sint Maarten) under a constitutional monarchy

### CAPITAL:

**name:** Philipsburg

**geographic coordinates:** 18 1 N, 63 2 W

**time difference:** UTC-4 (1 hour ahead of Washington, DC, during Standard Time)

### ADMINISTRATIVE DIVISIONS:

none (part of the Kingdom of the Netherlands)

**note:** Sint Maarten is one of four constituent countries of the Kingdom of the Netherlands; the other three are the Netherlands, Aruba, and Curacao

### INDEPENDENCE:

none (part of the Kingdom of the Netherlands)

### NATIONAL HOLIDAY:

King's Day (birthday of King WILLEM-ALEXANDER), 27 April (1967); note - King's or Queen's Day are observed on the ruling monarch's birthday; celebrated on 26 April if 27 April is a Sunday

### CONSTITUTION:

previous 1947, 1955; latest adopted 21 July 2010, entered into force 10 October 2010 (regulates governance of

Sint Maarten but is subordinate to the Charter for the Kingdom of the Netherlands) (2018)

**LEGAL SYSTEM:**

based on Dutch civil law system with some English common law influence

**CITIZENSHIP:**

see the Netherlands

**SUFFRAGE:**

18 years of age; universal

**EXECUTIVE BRANCH:**

chief of state: King WILLEM-ALEXANDER of the Netherlands (since 30 April 2013); represented by Governor General Eugene HOLIDAY (since 10 October 2010)

head of government: Prime Minister Leona MARLIN-ROMEO (since 15 January 2018)

cabinet: Cabinet nominated by the prime minister and appointed by the governor-general

elections/appointments: the monarch is hereditary; governor general appointed by the monarch for a 6-year term; following parliamentary elections, the leader of the majority party usually elected prime minister by Parliament

**LEGISLATIVE BRANCH:**

description: unicameral parliament or Staten (15 seats; members directly elected by proportional representation vote to serve 4-year terms)

elections: last held 26 February 2018 (next to be held in 2022)

election results: percent of vote by party - UD 42.4%, NA 30.5%, US Party 13.2%, SMCP 8.7%; seats by party - UD 7, NA 5, US Party 2, SMCP 1

**JUDICIAL BRANCH:**

highest courts: Joint Court of Justice of Aruba, Curacao, Sint Maarten, and of Bonaire, Sint Eustatius and Saba or "Joint Court of Justice" (consists of the presiding judge, other members, and their substitutes); final appeals heard by the Supreme Court, in The Hague, Netherlands; note - prior to 2010, the Joint Court of Justice was the Common Court of Justice of the Netherlands Antilles and Aruba

judge selection and term of office: Joint Court judges appointed by the monarch for life

subordinate courts: Courts in First Instance

**POLITICAL PARTIES AND LEADERS:**

National Alliance or NA [William MARLIN]
Sint Maarten Christian Party or SMCP [Wycliffe SMITH]
United Democrats Party or UD [Theodore HEYLIGER]
United Sint Maarten Party or US Party [Frans RICHARDSON]

**INTERNATIONAL ORGANIZATION PARTICIPATION:**

Caricom (observer), ILO, Interpol, UNESCO (associate), UPU, WMO

**DIPLOMATIC REPRESENTATION IN THE US:**

none (represented by the Kingdom of the Netherlands)

**DIPLOMATIC REPRESENTATION FROM THE US:**

the US does not have an embassy in Sint Maarten; the Consul General to Curacao is accredited to Sint Maarten

**FLAG DESCRIPTION:**

two equal horizontal bands of red (top) and blue with a white isosceles triangle based on the hoist side; the center of the triangle displays the Sint Maarten coat of arms; the arms consist of an orange-bordered blue shield prominently displaying the white court house in Philipsburg, as well as a bouquet of yellow sage (the national flower) in the upper left, and the silhouette of a Dutch-French friendship monument in the upper right; the shield is surmounted by a yellow rising sun in front of which is a brown pelican in flight; a yellow scroll below the shield bears the motto: SEMPER PROGREDIENS (Always Progressing); the three main colors are identical to those on the Dutch flag

note: the flag somewhat resembles that of the Philippines but with the main red and blue bands reversed; the banner more closely evokes the wartime Philippine flag

**NATIONAL SYMBOL(S):**

brown pelican, yellow sage (flower); national colors: red, white, blue

**NATIONAL ANTHEM:**

name: O Sweet Saint Martin's Land

lyrics/music: Gerard KEMPS

note: the song, written in 1958, is used as an unofficial anthem for the entire island (both French and Dutch sides); as a collectivity of France, in addition to the local anthem, "La Marseillaise" is official on the French side (see France); as a constituent part of the Kingdom of the Netherlands, in addition to the local anthem, "Het Wilhelmus" is official on the Dutch side (see Netherlands)

# ECONOMY :: SINT MAARTEN

**ECONOMY - OVERVIEW:**

The economy of Sint Maarten centers around tourism with nearly four-fifths of the labor force engaged in this sector. Nearly 1.8 million visitors came to the island by cruise ship and roughly 500,000 visitors arrived through Princess Juliana International Airport in 2013. Cruise ships and yachts also call on Sint Maarten's numerous ports and harbors. Limited agriculture and local fishing means that almost all food must be imported. Energy resources and manufactured goods are also imported. Sint Maarten had the highest per capita income among the five islands that formerly comprised the Netherlands Antilles.

**GDP (PURCHASING POWER PARITY):**

$365.8 million (2014 est.)

$353.5 million (2013 est.)

$339.6 million (2012 est.)

note: data are in 2014 US dollars

country comparison to the world: 214

**GDP (OFFICIAL EXCHANGE RATE):**

$304.1 million (2014 est.)

**GDP - REAL GROWTH RATE:**

3.6% (2014 est.)

4.1% (2013 est.)

1.9% (2012 est.)

country comparison to the world: 97

**GDP - PER CAPITA (PPP):**

$66,800 (2014 est.)

$65,500 (2013 est.)

$63,900 (2012 est.)

note: data are in 2015 US dollars

country comparison to the world: 14

**GDP - COMPOSITION, BY SECTOR OF ORIGIN:**

agriculture: 0.4% (2008 est.)

industry: 18.3% (2008 est.)

services: 81.3% (2008 est.)

**AGRICULTURE - PRODUCTS:**

sugar

**INDUSTRIES:**

tourism, light industry

**LABOR FORCE:**

23,200 (2008 est.)

country comparison to the world: 210
**LABOR FORCE - BY OCCUPATION:**

agriculture: 1.1%

industry: 15.2%

services: 83.7% (2008 est.)

**UNEMPLOYMENT RATE:**

12% (2012 est.)

10.6% (2008 est.)

country comparison to the world: 160

**INFLATION RATE (CONSUMER PRICES):**

4% (2012 est.)

0.7% (2009 est.)

country comparison to the world: 157

**EXPORTS - COMMODITIES:**

sugar

**EXCHANGE RATES:**

Netherlands Antillean guilders (ANG) per US dollar -

1.79 (2017 est.)

1.79 (2016 est.)

1.79 (2015 est.)

1.79 (2014 est.)

1.79 (2013 est.)

## ENERGY :: SINT MAARTEN

**ELECTRICITY - PRODUCTION:**

304.3 million kWh (2008 est.)

country comparison to the world: 181

**CRUDE OIL - EXPORTS:**

0 bbl/day (2015 est.)

country comparison to the world: 193

**CRUDE OIL - IMPORTS:**

0 bbl/day (2015 est.)

country comparison to the world: 195

**REFINED PETROLEUM PRODUCTS - PRODUCTION:**

0 bbl/day (2015 est.)

country comparison to the world: 201

**REFINED PETROLEUM PRODUCTS - CONSUMPTION:**

10,600 bbl/day (2016 est.)

country comparison to the world: 161

**REFINED PETROLEUM PRODUCTS - EXPORTS:**

0 bbl/day (2015 est.)

country comparison to the world: 202

**REFINED PETROLEUM PRODUCTS - IMPORTS:**

10,440 bbl/day (2015 est.)

country comparison to the world: 148

## COMMUNICATIONS :: SINT MAARTEN

**TELEPHONE SYSTEM:**

general assessment: generally adequate facilities (2010)

domestic: extensive interisland microwave radio relay links (2010)

international: country code - 1-721; the Americas Region Caribbean Ring System (ARCOS-1) and the Americas-2 submarine cable systems provide connectivity to Central America, parts of South America, the Caribbean, and the U.S.; satellite earth stations - 2 Intelsat (Atlantic Ocean) (2010)

**INTERNET COUNTRY CODE:**

.sx; note - IANA has designated .sx for Sint Maarten, but has not yet assigned it to a sponsoring organization

## TRANSPORTATION :: SINT MAARTEN

**AIRPORTS:**

1 (2013)

country comparison to the world: 236

**AIRPORTS - WITH PAVED RUNWAYS:**

total: 1 (2017)

1,524 to 2,437 m: 1 (2017)

note: Princess Juliana International Airport (SXM) was severely damaged on 6 September 2017 by hurricane Irma, but resumed commercial operations on 10 October 2017

**ROADWAYS:**

total: 53 km

country comparison to the world: 219

**PORTS AND TERMINALS:**

major seaport(s): Philipsburg

oil terminal(s): Coles Bay oil terminal

## MILITARY AND SECURITY :: SINT MAARTEN

**MILITARY BRANCHES:**

no regular military forces (2012)

**MILITARY - NOTE:**

defense is the responsibility of the Kingdom of the Netherlands

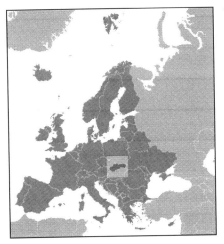

# EUROPE :: SLOVAKIA

## INTRODUCTION :: SLOVAKIA

### BACKGROUND:

Slovakia traces its roots to the 9th century state of Great Moravia. Subsequently, the Slovaks became part of the Hungarian Kingdom, where they remained for the next 1,000 years. Following the formation of the dual Austro-Hungarian monarchy in 1867, language and education policies favoring the use of Hungarian (Magyarization) resulted in a strengthening of Slovak nationalism and a cultivation of cultural ties with the closely related Czechs, who were under Austrian rule. After the dissolution of the Austro-Hungarian Empire at the close of World War I, the Slovaks joined the Czechs to form Czechoslovakia. During the interwar period, Slovak nationalist leaders pushed for autonomy within Czechoslovakia, and in 1939 Slovakia became an independent state allied with Nazi Germany. Following World War II, Czechoslovakia was reconstituted and came under communist rule within Soviet-dominated Eastern Europe. In 1968, an invasion by Warsaw Pact troops ended the efforts of the country's leaders to liberalize communist rule and create "socialism with a human face," ushering in a period of repression known as "normalization." The peaceful "Velvet Revolution" swept the Communist Party from power at the end of 1989 and inaugurated a return to democratic rule and a market economy. On 1 January 1993, the country underwent a nonviolent "velvet divorce" into its two national components, Slovakia and the Czech Republic. Slovakia joined both NATO and the EU in the spring of 2004 and the euro zone on 1 January 2009.

## GEOGRAPHY :: SLOVAKIA

### LOCATION:
Central Europe, south of Poland

### GEOGRAPHIC COORDINATES:
48 40 N, 19 30 E

### MAP REFERENCES:
Europe

### AREA:
total: 49,035 sq km

land: 48,105 sq km

water: 930 sq km

country comparison to the world: 131

### AREA - COMPARATIVE:
about one and a half times the size of Maryland; about twice the size of New Hampshire

### LAND BOUNDARIES:
total: 1,611 km

border countries (5): Austria 105 km, Czech Republic 241 km, Hungary 627 km, Poland 541 km, Ukraine 97 km

### COASTLINE:
0 km (landlocked)

### MARITIME CLAIMS:
none (landlocked)

### CLIMATE:
temperate; cool summers; cold, cloudy, humid winters

### TERRAIN:
rugged mountains in the central and northern part and lowlands in the south

### ELEVATION:
mean elevation: 458 m

elevation extremes: 94 m lowest point: Bodrok River

2655 highest point: Gerlachovsky Stit

### NATURAL RESOURCES:
lignite, small amounts of iron ore, copper and manganese ore; salt; arable land

### LAND USE:
agricultural land: 40.1% (2011 est.)

arable land: 28.9% (2011 est.) / permanent crops: 0.4% (2011 est.) / permanent pasture: 10.8% (2011 est.)

forest: 40.2% (2011 est.)

other: 19.7% (2011 est.)

### IRRIGATED LAND:
869 sq km (2012)

### POPULATION DISTRIBUTION:
a fairly even distribution throughout most of the country; slightly larger concentration in the west in proximity to the Czech border

### NATURAL HAZARDS:
flooding

### ENVIRONMENT - CURRENT ISSUES:
air pollution and acid rain present human health risks and damage forests; land erosion caused by agricultural and mining practices; water pollution

### ENVIRONMENT - INTERNATIONAL AGREEMENTS:
party to: Air Pollution, Air Pollution-Nitrogen Oxides, Air Pollution-Persistent Organic Pollutants, Air Pollution-Sulfur 85, Air Pollution-Sulfur 94, Air Pollution-Volatile Organic Compounds, Antarctic Treaty, Biodiversity, Climate Change, Climate Change-Kyoto Protocol, Desertification, Endangered Species, Environmental Modification, Hazardous Wastes, Law of the Sea, Ozone Layer Protection, Ship Pollution, Wetlands, Whaling

**signed, but not ratified:** none of the selected agreements

### GEOGRAPHY - NOTE:
landlocked; most of the country is rugged and mountainous; the Tatra Mountains in the north are interspersed with many scenic lakes and valleys

## PEOPLE AND SOCIETY :: SLOVAKIA

### POPULATION:
5,445,040 (July 2018 est.)

**country comparison to the world:** 118

### NATIONALITY:
**noun:** Slovak(s)

**adjective:** Slovak

### ETHNIC GROUPS:
Slovak 80.7%, Hungarian 8.5%, Romani 2%, other 1.8% (includes Czech, Ruthenian, Ukrainian, Russian, German, Polish), unspecified 7% (2011 est.)

**note:** data represent population by nationality; Romani populations are usually underestimated in official statistics and may represent 7-11% of Slovakia's population

### LANGUAGES:
Slovak (official) 78.6%, Hungarian 9.4%, Roma 2.3%, Ruthenian 1%, other or unspecified 8.8% (2011 est.)

### RELIGIONS:
Roman Catholic 62%, Protestant 8.2%, Greek Catholic 3.8%, other or unspecified 12.5%, none 13.4% (2011 est.)

### AGE STRUCTURE:
**0-14 years:** 15.2% (male 424,921/female 402,483)

**15-24 years:** 10.48% (male 293,573/female 277,041)

**25-54 years:** 45.04% (male 1,239,670/female 1,212,687)

**55-64 years:** 13.32% (male 345,114/female 380,077)

**65 years and over:** 15.97% (male 339,350/female 530,124) (2018 est.)

### DEPENDENCY RATIOS:
**total dependency ratio:** 41.5 (2015 est.)

**youth dependency ratio:** 21.6 (2015 est.)

**elderly dependency ratio:** 19.9 (2015 est.)

**potential support ratio:** 5 (2015 est.)

### MEDIAN AGE:
**total:** 41 years

**male:** 39.3 years

**female:** 42.7 years (2018 est.)

**country comparison to the world:** 46

### POPULATION GROWTH RATE:
-0.02% (2018 est.)

**country comparison to the world:** 197

### BIRTH RATE:
9.6 births/1,000 population (2018 est.)

**country comparison to the world:** 198

### DEATH RATE:
9.9 deaths/1,000 population (2018 est.)

**country comparison to the world:** 38

### NET MIGRATION RATE:
0.1 migrant(s)/1,000 population (2017 est.)

**country comparison to the world:** 69

### POPULATION DISTRIBUTION:
a fairly even distribution throughout most of the country; slightly larger concentration in the west in proximity to the Czech border

### URBANIZATION:
**urban population:** 53.7% of total population (2018)

**rate of urbanization:** 0% annual rate of change (2015-20 est.)

### MAJOR URBAN AREAS - POPULATION:
430,000 BRATISLAVA (capital) (2018)

### SEX RATIO:
**at birth:** 1.07 male(s)/female (2017 est.)

**0-14 years:** 1.05 male(s)/female (2017 est.)

**15-24 years:** 1.06 male(s)/female (2017 est.)

**25-54 years:** 1.02 male(s)/female (2017 est.)

**55-64 years:** 0.9 male(s)/female (2017 est.)

**65 years and over:** 0.62 male(s)/female (2017 est.)

**total population:** 0.94 male(s)/female (2017 est.)

### MOTHER'S MEAN AGE AT FIRST BIRTH:
27.6 years (2014 est.)

### MATERNAL MORTALITY RATE:
6 deaths/100,000 live births (2015 est.)

**country comparison to the world:** 168

### INFANT MORTALITY RATE:
**total:** 5 deaths/1,000 live births (2018 est.)

**male:** 5.7 deaths/1,000 live births (2018 est.)

**female:** 4.4 deaths/1,000 live births (2018 est.)

**country comparison to the world:** 176

### LIFE EXPECTANCY AT BIRTH:
**total population:** 77.4 years (2018 est.)

**male:** 73.9 years (2018 est.)

**female:** 81.2 years (2018 est.)

**country comparison to the world:** 74

### TOTAL FERTILITY RATE:
1.42 children born/woman (2018 est.)

**country comparison to the world:** 210

### HEALTH EXPENDITURES:
8.1% of GDP (2014)

**country comparison to the world:** 56

### PHYSICIANS DENSITY:
3.45 physicians/1,000 population (2015)

### HOSPITAL BED DENSITY:
5.8 beds/1,000 population (2015)

### DRINKING WATER SOURCE:
**improved:**

urban: 100% of population (2015 est.)

rural: 100% of population (2015 est.)

total: 100% of population (2015 est.)

**unimproved:**

urban: 0% of population (2015 est.)

rural: 0% of population (2015 est.)

total: 0% of population (2015 est.)

### SANITATION FACILITY ACCESS:
**improved:**

urban: 99.4% of population (2015 est.)

rural: 98.2% of population (2015 est.)

total: 98.8% of population (2015 est.)

**unimproved:**

urban: 0.6% of population (2015 est.)

rural: 1.8% of population (2015 est.)

total: 1.2% of population (2015 est.)

### HIV/AIDS - ADULT PREVALENCE RATE:
<.1% (2017 est.)

**HIV/AIDS - PEOPLE LIVING WITH HIV/AIDS:**

<1000 (2017 est.)

**HIV/AIDS - DEATHS:**

<100 (2017 est.)

**OBESITY - ADULT PREVALENCE RATE:**

20.5% (2016)

country comparison to the world: 98

**EDUCATION EXPENDITURES:**

4.6% of GDP (2015)

country comparison to the world: 90

**SCHOOL LIFE EXPECTANCY (PRIMARY TO TERTIARY EDUCATION):**

total: 15 years (2014)

male: 14 years (2014)

female: 16 years (2014)

**UNEMPLOYMENT, YOUTH AGES 15-24:**

total: 22.2% (2016 est.)

male: 19.8% (2016 est.)

female: 26.3% (2016 est.)

country comparison to the world: 54

# GOVERNMENT :: SLOVAKIA

**COUNTRY NAME:**

conventional long form: Slovak Republic

conventional short form: Slovakia

local long form: Slovenska republika

local short form: Slovensko

etymology: related to the Slavic autonym (self-designation) "Slovenin," a derivation from "slovo" (word), denoting "people who speak (the same language)" (i.e., people who understand each other)

**GOVERNMENT TYPE:**

parliamentary republic

**CAPITAL:**

name: Bratislava

geographic coordinates: 48 09 N, 17 07 E

time difference: UTC+1 (6 hours ahead of Washington, DC, during Standard Time)

daylight saving time: +1hr, begins last Sunday in March; ends last Sunday in October

**ADMINISTRATIVE DIVISIONS:**

8 regions (kraje, singular - kraj); Banskobystricky, Bratislavsky, Kosicky, Nitriansky, Presovsky, Trenciansky, Trnavsky, Zilinsky

**INDEPENDENCE:**

1 January 1993 (Czechoslovakia split into the Czech Republic and Slovakia)

**NATIONAL HOLIDAY:**

Constitution Day, 1 September (1992)

**CONSTITUTION:**

history: several previous (preindependence); latest passed by the National Council 1 September 1992, signed 3 September 1992, effective 1 October 1992 (2017)

amendments: proposed by the National Council; passage requires at least three-fifths majority vote of Council members; amended many times, last in 2017 (2017)

**LEGAL SYSTEM:**

civil law system based on Austro-Hungarian codes; note - legal code modified to comply with the obligations of Organization on Security and Cooperation in Europe

**INTERNATIONAL LAW ORGANIZATION PARTICIPATION:**

accepts compulsory ICJ jurisdiction with reservations; accepts ICCt jurisdiction

**CITIZENSHIP:**

citizenship by birth: no

citizenship by descent only: at least one parent must be a citizen of Slovakia

dual citizenship recognized: no

residency requirement for naturalization: 5 years

**SUFFRAGE:**

18 years of age; universal

**EXECUTIVE BRANCH:**

chief of state: President Andrej KISKA (since 15 June 2014)

head of government: Prime Minister Peter PELLIGRINI (since 22 March 2018); Deputy Prime Ministers Peter KAZIMIR (since 22 March 2018), Richard RASI (since 22 March 2018), Laszlo SOLYMOS (since 22 March 2018), Gabriela MATECNA (since 29 November 2017)

cabinet: Cabinet appointed by the president on the recommendation of the prime minister

elections/appointments: president directly elected by absolute majority popular vote in 2 rounds if needed for a 5-year term (eligible for a second term); election last held on 15 and 29 March 2014 (next to be held on 9 March 2019); following National Council elections (every 4 years), the leader of the majority party or majority coalition usually appointed prime minister by the president

election results: Andrej KISKA elected president in second round; percent of vote - Andrej KISKA (independent) 59.4%, Robert FICO (Smer-SD) 40.6%

**LEGISLATIVE BRANCH:**

description: unicameral National Council or Narodna Rada (150 seats; members directly elected in a single- and multi-seat constituencies by closed, party-list proportional representation vote; members serve 4-year terms)

elections: last held on 5 March 2016 (next to be held in March 2020)

election results: percent of vote by party - Smer-SD 28.3%, SaS 12.1%, OLaNO-NOVA 11%, SNS 8.6%, LSNS 8%, Sme-Rodina 6.6%, Most-Hid 6.5%, Siet 5.6%, other 13.3%; seats by party - Smer-SD 49, SaS 21, OLaNO-NOVA 19, SNS 15, LSNS 14, Sme-Rodina 11, Most-Hid 11, Siet 10; composition - men 120, women 30, percent of women 20%

**JUDICIAL BRANCH:**

highest courts: Supreme Court of the Slovak Republic (consists of the court president, vice president, and approximately 80 judges organized into criminal, civil, commercial, and administrative divisions with 3- and 5-judge panels); Constitutional Court of the Slovak Republic (consists of 13 judges organized into 3-judge panels)

judge selection and term of office: Supreme Court judge candidates nominated by the Judicial Council of the Slovak Republic, an 18-member self-governing body to include the Supreme Court chief justice and presidential, governmental, parliamentary, and judiciary appointees; judges appointed by the president for life subject to removal by the president at age 65; Constitutional Court judges nominated by the National Council of the Republic and appointed by the president; judges appointed for 12-year terms

subordinate courts: regional and district civil courts; Special Criminal Court; Higher Military Court; military district courts; Court of Audit;

**POLITICAL PARTIES AND LEADERS:**

Christian Democratic Movement or KDH [Alojz HLINA]
Bridge or Most-Hid [Bela BUGAR]
Direction-Social Democracy or Smer-SD [Robert FICO]
Freedom and Solidarity or SaS [Richard SULIK]
Kotleba-People's Party Our Slovakia or LSNS [Marian KOTLEBA]
Ordinary People and Independent Personalities - New Majority or OLaNO-NOVA [Igor MATOVIC]
Party of the Hungarian Coalition or SMK [Jozsef MENYHART]
Progressive Slovakia [Ivan STEFUNKO]
Slovak Conservative Party or SKS [Ivan ZUZULA] (formerly the SIET party)
Slovak National Party or SNS [Andrej DANKO]
Together or Spolu [Miroslav BEBLAVY]
We Are Family or Sme-Rodina [Boris KOLLAR]

**INTERNATIONAL ORGANIZATION PARTICIPATION:**

Australia Group, BIS, BSEC (observer), CBSS (observer), CD, CE, CEI, CERN, EAPC, EBRD, ECB, EIB, EMU, EU, FAO, IAEA, IBRD, ICAO, ICC (national committees), ICRM, IDA, IEA, IFC, IFRCS, ILO, IMF, IMO, IMSO, Interpol, IOC, IOM, IPU, ISO, ITU, ITUC (NGOs), MIGA, NATO, NEA, NSG, OAS (observer), OECD, OIF (observer), OPCW, OSCE, PCA, Schengen Convention, SELEC (observer), UN, UNCTAD, UNESCO, UNFICYP, UNIDO, UNTSO, UNWTO, UPU, WCO, WFTU (NGOs), WHO, WIPO, WMO, WTO, ZC

**DIPLOMATIC REPRESENTATION IN THE US:**

**chief of mission:** Ambassador Ivan KORCOK (since 17 September 2018)

**chancery:** 3523 International Court NW, Washington, DC 20008

**telephone:** [1] (202) 237-1054

**FAX:** [1] (202) 237-6438

**consulate(s) general:** Los Angeles, New York

**DIPLOMATIC REPRESENTATION FROM THE US:**

**chief of mission:** Ambassador Adam H. STERLING (since 31 August 2016)

**embassy:** Hviezdoslavovo Namestie 4, 81102 Bratislava

**mailing address:** P.O. Box 309, 814 99 Bratislava

**telephone:** [421] (2) 5443-3338

**FAX:** [421] (2) 5441-5148

**FLAG DESCRIPTION:**

three equal horizontal bands of white (top), blue, and red derive from the Pan-Slav colors; the Slovakian coat of arms (consisting of a red shield bordered in white and bearing a white double-barred cross of St. Cyril and St. Methodius surmounting three blue hills) is centered over the bands but offset slightly to the hoist side

**note:** the Pan-Slav colors were inspired by the 19th-century flag of Russia

**NATIONAL SYMBOL(S):**

double-barred cross (Cross of St. Cyril and St. Methodius) surmounting three peaks; national colors: white, blue, red

**NATIONAL ANTHEM:**

**name:** "Nad Tatrou sa blyska" (Lightning Over the Tatras)

**lyrics/music:** Janko MATUSKA/traditional

**note:** adopted 1993, in use since 1844; music based on the Slovak folk song "Kopala studienku"

## ECONOMY :: SLOVAKIA

**ECONOMY - OVERVIEW:**

Slovakia's economy suffered from a slow start in the first years after its separation from the Czech Republic in 1993, due to the country's authoritarian leadership and high levels of corruption, but economic reforms implemented after 1998 have placed Slovakia on a path of strong growth. With a population of 5.4 million, the Slovak Republic has a small, open economy driven mainly by automobile and electronics exports, which account for more than 80% of GDP. Slovakia joined the EU in 2004 and the euro zone in 2009. The country's banking sector is sound and predominantly foreign owned.

Slovakia has been a regional FDI champion for several years, attractive due to a relatively low-cost yet skilled labor force, and a favorable geographic location in the heart of Central Europe. Exports and investment have been key drivers of Slovakia's robust growth in recent years. The unemployment rate fell to historical lows in 2017, and rising wages fueled increased consumption, which played a more prominent role in 2017 GDP growth. A favorable outlook for the Eurozone suggests continued strong growth prospects for Slovakia during the next few years, although inflation is also expected to pick up.

Among the most pressing domestic issues potentially threatening the attractiveness of the Slovak market are shortages in the qualified labor force, persistent corruption issues, and an inadequate judiciary, as well as a slow transition to an innovation-based economy. The energy sector in particular is characterized by unpredictable regulatory oversight and high costs, in part driven by government interference in regulated tariffs. Moreover, the government's attempts to maintain low household energy prices could harm the profitability of domestic energy firms while undercutting energy efficiency initiatives.

**GDP (PURCHASING POWER PARITY):**

$179.7 billion (2017 est.)

$173.8 billion (2016 est.)

$168.2 billion (2015 est.)

**note:** data are in 2017 dollars

**country comparison to the world:** 69

**GDP (OFFICIAL EXCHANGE RATE):**

$95.96 billion (2017 est.) (2017 est.)

**GDP - REAL GROWTH RATE:**

3.4% (2017 est.)

3.3% (2016 est.)

3.9% (2015 est.)

**country comparison to the world:** 102

**GDP - PER CAPITA (PPP):**

$33,100 (2017 est.)

$32,000 (2016 est.)

$31,000 (2015 est.)

**note:** data are in 2017 dollars

**country comparison to the world:** 61

**GROSS NATIONAL SAVING:**

20.6% of GDP (2017 est.)

21.1% of GDP (2016 est.)

22.5% of GDP (2015 est.)

**country comparison to the world:** 92

**GDP - COMPOSITION, BY END USE:**

**household consumption:** 54.7% (2017 est.)

**government consumption:** 19.2% (2017 est.)

**investment in fixed capital:** 21.2% (2017 est.)

investment in inventories: 1.2% (2017 est.)

exports of goods and services: 96.3% (2017 est.)

imports of goods and services: -92.9% (2017 est.)

**GDP - COMPOSITION, BY SECTOR OF ORIGIN:**

agriculture: 3.8% (2017 est.)

industry: 35% (2017 est.)

services: 61.2% (2017 est.)

**AGRICULTURE - PRODUCTS:**

grains, potatoes, sugar beets, hops, fruit; pigs, cattle, poultry; forest products

**INDUSTRIES:**

automobiles; metal and metal products; electricity, gas, coke, oil, nuclear fuel; chemicals, synthetic fibers, wood and paper products; machinery; earthenware and ceramics; textiles; electrical and optical apparatus; rubber products; food and beverages; pharmaceutical

**INDUSTRIAL PRODUCTION GROWTH RATE:**

2.7% (2017 est.)

country comparison to the world: 114

**LABOR FORCE:**

2.758 million (2017 est.)

country comparison to the world: 110

**LABOR FORCE - BY OCCUPATION:**

agriculture: 3.9%

industry: 22.7%

services: 73.4% (2015)

**UNEMPLOYMENT RATE:**

8.1% (2017 est.)

9.7% (2016 est.)

country comparison to the world: 119

**POPULATION BELOW POVERTY LINE:**

12.3% (2015 est.)

**HOUSEHOLD INCOME OR CONSUMPTION BY PERCENTAGE SHARE:**

lowest 10%: 19.3% (2015 est.)

highest 10%: 19.3% (2015 est.)

**DISTRIBUTION OF FAMILY INCOME - GINI INDEX:**

23.7 (2015)

26.1 (2014)

country comparison to the world: 155

**BUDGET:**

revenues: 37.79 billion (2017 est.)

expenditures: 38.79 billion (2017 est.)

**TAXES AND OTHER REVENUES:**

39.4% (of GDP) (2017 est.)

country comparison to the world: 47

**BUDGET SURPLUS (+) OR DEFICIT (-):**

-1% (of GDP) (2017 est.)

country comparison to the world: 81

**PUBLIC DEBT:**

50.9% of GDP (2017 est.)

51.8% of GDP (2016 est.)

note: data cover general Government Gross Debt and include debt instruments issued (or owned) by Government entities, including sub-sectors of central, state, local government, and social security funds

country comparison to the world: 98

**FISCAL YEAR:**

calendar year

**INFLATION RATE (CONSUMER PRICES):**

1.3% (2017 est.)

-0.5% (2016 est.)

country comparison to the world: 74

**CENTRAL BANK DISCOUNT RATE:**

0% (31 December 2017 est.)

0% (31 December 2016 est.)

note: this is the European Central Bank's rate on the marginal lending facility, which offers overnight credit to banks from the euro area; Slovakia became a member of the Economic and Monetary Union (EMU) on 1 January 2009

country comparison to the world: 160

**COMMERCIAL BANK PRIME LENDING RATE:**

2.44% (31 December 2017 est.)

2.7% (31 December 2016 est.)

country comparison to the world: 182

**STOCK OF NARROW MONEY:**

$56.46 billion (31 December 2017 est.)

$45.63 billion (31 December 2016 est.)

note: see entry for the European Union for money supply for the entire euro area; the European Central Bank (ECB) controls monetary policy for the 18 members of the Economic and Monetary Union (EMU); individual members of the EMU do not control the quantity of money circulating within their own borders

country comparison to the world: 51

**STOCK OF BROAD MONEY:**

$56.46 billion (31 December 2017 est.)

$45.63 billion (31 December 2016 est.)

country comparison to the world: 51

**STOCK OF DOMESTIC CREDIT:**

$85.56 billion (31 December 2017 est.)

$70.84 billion (31 December 2016 est.)

country comparison to the world: 57

**MARKET VALUE OF PUBLICLY TRADED SHARES:**

$4.567 billion (31 December 2016 est.)

$4.634 billion (31 December 2015 est.)

$4.732 billion (31 December 2014 est.)

country comparison to the world: 86

**CURRENT ACCOUNT BALANCE:**

-$2.005 billion (2017 est.)

-$1.309 billion (2016 est.)

country comparison to the world: 164

**EXPORTS:**

$80.8 billion (2017 est.)

$75.53 billion (2016 est.)

country comparison to the world: 40

**EXPORTS - PARTNERS:**

Germany 20.7%, Czech Republic 11.6%, Poland 7.7%, France 6.3%, Italy 6.1%, UK 6%, Hungary 6%, Austria 6% (2017)

**EXPORTS - COMMODITIES:**

vehicles and related parts 27%, machinery and electrical equipment 20%, nuclear reactors and furnaces 12%, iron and steel 4%, mineral oils and fuels 5% (2015 est.)

**IMPORTS:**

$80.07 billion (2017 est.)

$72.51 billion (2016 est.)

country comparison to the world: 42

**IMPORTS - COMMODITIES:**

machinery and electrical equipment 20%, vehicles and related parts 14%, nuclear reactors and furnaces 12%, fuel and mineral oils 9% (2015 est.)

**IMPORTS - PARTNERS:**

Germany 19.1%, Czech Republic 16.3%, Austria 10.3%, Poland 6.5%, Hungary 6.4%, South Korea 4.5%, Russia 4.5%, France 4.3%, China 4.2% (2017)

**RESERVES OF FOREIGN EXCHANGE AND GOLD:**

$3.622 billion (31 December 2017 est.)

$2.892 billion (31 December 2016 est.)

country comparison to the world: 102

**DEBT - EXTERNAL:**

$75.04 billion (31 March 2016 est.)

$74.19 billion (31 March 2015 est.)

country comparison to the world: 58

**STOCK OF DIRECT FOREIGN INVESTMENT - AT HOME:**

$69.92 billion (31 December 2017 est.)

$54.03 billion (31 December 2016 est.)

country comparison to the world: 53

**STOCK OF DIRECT FOREIGN INVESTMENT - ABROAD:**

$21.29 billion (31 December 2017 est.)

$15.06 billion (31 December 2016 est.)

country comparison to the world: 51

**EXCHANGE RATES:**

euros (EUR) per US dollar -

0.885 (2017 est.)

0.903 (2016 est.)

0.9214 (2015 est.)

0.885 (2014 est.)

0.7634 (2013 est.)

## ENERGY :: SLOVAKIA

**ELECTRICITY ACCESS:**

electrification - total population: 100% (2016)

**ELECTRICITY - PRODUCTION:**

25.32 billion kWh (2016 est.)

country comparison to the world: 72

**ELECTRICITY - CONSUMPTION:**

26.64 billion kWh (2016 est.)

country comparison to the world: 66

**ELECTRICITY - EXPORTS:**

10.6 billion kWh (2016 est.)

country comparison to the world: 19

**ELECTRICITY - IMPORTS:**

13.25 billion kWh (2016 est.)

country comparison to the world: 19

**ELECTRICITY - INSTALLED GENERATING CAPACITY:**

7.644 million kW (2016 est.)

country comparison to the world: 72

**ELECTRICITY - FROM FOSSIL FUELS:**

36% of total installed capacity (2016 est.)

country comparison to the world: 176

**ELECTRICITY - FROM NUCLEAR FUELS:**

27% of total installed capacity (2017 est.)

country comparison to the world: 3

**ELECTRICITY - FROM HYDROELECTRIC PLANTS:**

24% of total installed capacity (2017 est.)

country comparison to the world: 81

**ELECTRICITY - FROM OTHER RENEWABLE SOURCES:**

13% of total installed capacity (2017 est.)

country comparison to the world: 70

**CRUDE OIL - PRODUCTION:**

200 bbl/day (2017 est.)

country comparison to the world: 95

**CRUDE OIL - EXPORTS:**

1,022 bbl/day (2017 est.)

country comparison to the world: 74

**CRUDE OIL - IMPORTS:**

111,200 bbl/day (2017 est.)

country comparison to the world: 42

**CRUDE OIL - PROVED RESERVES:**

9 million bbl (1 January 2018 est.)

country comparison to the world: 91

**REFINED PETROLEUM PRODUCTS - PRODUCTION:**

131,300 bbl/day (2017 est.)

country comparison to the world: 64

**REFINED PETROLEUM PRODUCTS - CONSUMPTION:**

85,880 bbl/day (2017 est.)

country comparison to the world: 85

**REFINED PETROLEUM PRODUCTS - EXPORTS:**

81,100 bbl/day (2017 est.)

country comparison to the world: 46

**REFINED PETROLEUM PRODUCTS - IMPORTS:**

38,340 bbl/day (2017 est.)

country comparison to the world: 91

**NATURAL GAS - PRODUCTION:**

104.8 million cu m (2017 est.)

country comparison to the world: 81

**NATURAL GAS - CONSUMPTION:**

4.672 billion cu m (2017 est.)

country comparison to the world: 62

**NATURAL GAS - EXPORTS:**

0 cu m (2017 est.)

country comparison to the world: 184

**NATURAL GAS - IMPORTS:**

4.984 billion cu m (2017 est.)

country comparison to the world: 37

**NATURAL GAS - PROVED RESERVES:**

14.16 billion cu m (1 January 2018 est.)

country comparison to the world: 75

**CARBON DIOXIDE EMISSIONS FROM CONSUMPTION OF ENERGY:**

34.86 million Mt (2017 est.)

country comparison to the world: 73

## COMMUNICATIONS :: SLOVAKIA

**TELEPHONES - FIXED LINES:**

total subscriptions: 758,842 (2017 est.)

subscriptions per 100 inhabitants: 14 (2017 est.)

country comparison to the world: 83

**TELEPHONES - MOBILE CELLULAR:**

total subscriptions: 7,117,753 (2017 est.)

subscriptions per 100 inhabitants: 131 (2017 est.)

country comparison to the world: 105

**TELEPHONE SYSTEM:**

general assessment: a modern telecommunications system that has expanded dramatically in recent years with the growth of cellular services (2017)

domestic: Slovak Telecom maintains a near monopoly on fixed-line service; four companies have a license to operate cellular networks and provide nationwide cellular services (cellular operators); a few other companies provide services but do not have their own networks (2017)

international: country code - 421; 3 international exchanges (1 in Bratislava and 2 in Banska Bystrica) are available; Slovakia is participating in several international telecommunications projects that will increase the availability of external services (2017)

**BROADCAST MEDIA:**

state-owned public broadcaster, Radio and Television of Slovakia (RTVS), operates 2 national TV stations and multiple national and regional radio networks; roughly 50 privately owned TV stations operating nationally, regionally, and locally; about 40% of households are connected to multi-channel cable or satellite TV; 32 privately owned radio stations (2016)

**INTERNET COUNTRY CODE:**

.sk

**INTERNET USERS:**

total: 4,382,558 (July 2016 est.)

percent of population: 80.5% (July 2016 est.)

country comparison to the world: 82

**BROADBAND - FIXED SUBSCRIPTIONS:**

total: 1,404,751 (2017 est.)

subscriptions per 100 inhabitants: 26 (2017 est.)

country comparison to the world: 62

## TRANSPORTATION :: SLOVAKIA

**NATIONAL AIR TRANSPORT SYSTEM:**

number of registered air carriers: 4 (2015)

inventory of registered aircraft operated by air carriers: 23 (2015)

annual passenger traffic on registered air carriers: 11,100 (2015)

annual freight traffic on registered air carriers: 0 mt-km (2015)

**CIVIL AIRCRAFT REGISTRATION COUNTRY CODE PREFIX:**

OM (2016)

**AIRPORTS:**

35 (2013)

country comparison to the world: 111

**AIRPORTS - WITH PAVED RUNWAYS:**

total: 21 (2013)

over 3,047 m: 2 (2013)

2,438 to 3,047 m: 2 (2013)

1,524 to 2,437 m: 3 (2013)

914 to 1,523 m: 3 (2013)

under 914 m: 11 (2013)

**AIRPORTS - WITH UNPAVED RUNWAYS:**

total: 14 (2013)

914 to 1,523 m: 9 (2013)

under 914 m: 5 (2013)

**HELIPORTS:**

1 (2013)

**PIPELINES:**

2270 km gas transmission pipelines, 6278 km high-pressure gas distribution pipelines, 27023 km mid- and low-pressure gas distribution pipelines (2016), 510 km oil (2015)

**RAILWAYS:**

total: 3,580 km (2016)

standard gauge: 3,435 km 1.435-m gauge (1,587 km electrified) (2016)

narrow gauge: 46 km 1.000-m or 0.750-m gauge (2016)

broad gauge: 99 km 1.520-m gauge (2016)

country comparison to the world: 54

**ROADWAYS:**

total: 56,926 km (includes local roads, national roads, and 464 km of highways) (2016)

country comparison to the world: 75

**WATERWAYS:**

172 km (on Danube River) (2012)

country comparison to the world: 99

**PORTS AND TERMINALS:**

river port(s): Bratislava, Komarno (Danube)

## MILITARY AND SECURITY :: SLOVAKIA

**MILITARY EXPENDITURES:**

1.16% of GDP (2017 est.)

1.13% of GDP (2016)

1.14% of GDP (2015)

country comparison to the world: 101

**MILITARY BRANCHES:**

Armed Forces of the Slovak Republic (Ozbrojene Sily Slovenskej Republiky): Land Forces (Pozemne Sily), Air Forces (Vzdusne Sily) (2010)

**MILITARY SERVICE AGE AND OBLIGATION:**

18-30 years of age for voluntary military service; conscription in peacetime suspended in 2006; women are eligible to serve (2012)

## TRANSNATIONAL ISSUES :: SLOVAKIA

**DISPUTES - INTERNATIONAL:**

bilateral government, legal, technical and economic working group negotiations continued between Slovakia and Hungary over Hungary's completion of its portion of the Gabcikovo-Nagymaros hydroelectric dam project along the Danubeas a member state that forms part of the EU's external border, Slovakia has implemented strict Schengen border rules

**REFUGEES AND INTERNALLY DISPLACED PERSONS:**

stateless persons: 1,523 (2017)

**ILLICIT DRUGS:**

transshipment point for Southwest Asian heroin bound for Western Europe; producer of synthetic drugs for regional market; consumer of ecstasy

# EUROPE :: SLOVENIA

## INTRODUCTION :: SLOVENIA

### BACKGROUND:

The Slovene lands were part of the Austro-Hungarian Empire until the latter's dissolution at the end of World War I. In 1918, the Slovenes joined the Serbs and Croats in forming a new multinational state, which was named Yugoslavia in 1929. After World War II, Slovenia became a republic of the renewed Yugoslavia, which though communist, distanced itself from Moscow's rule. Dissatisfied with the exercise of power by the majority Serbs, the Slovenes succeeded in establishing their independence in 1991 after a short 10-day war. Historical ties to Western Europe, a strong economy, and a stable democracy have assisted in Slovenia's transformation to a modern state. Slovenia acceded to both NATO and the EU in the spring of 2004; it joined the euro zone and the Schengen zone in 2007.

## GEOGRAPHY :: SLOVENIA

### LOCATION:
south Central Europe, Julian Alps between Austria and Croatia

### GEOGRAPHIC COORDINATES:
46 07 N, 14 49 E

### MAP REFERENCES:
Europe

### AREA:
total: 20,273 sq km

land: 20,151 sq km

water: 122 sq km

country comparison to the world: 155

### AREA - COMPARATIVE:
slightly smaller than New Jersey

### LAND BOUNDARIES:
total: 1,211 km

border countries (4): Austria 299 km, Croatia 600 km, Hungary 94 km, Italy 218 km

### COASTLINE:
46.6 km

### MARITIME CLAIMS:
territorial sea: 12 nm

### CLIMATE:
Mediterranean climate on the coast, continental climate with mild to hot summers and cold winters in the plateaus and valleys to the east

### TERRAIN:
a short southwestern coastal strip of Karst topography on the Adriatic; an alpine mountain region lies adjacent to Italy and Austria in the north; mixed mountains and valleys with numerous rivers to the east

### ELEVATION:
mean elevation: 492 m

elevation extremes: 0 m lowest point: Adriatic Sea

2864 highest point: Triglav

### NATURAL RESOURCES:
lignite, lead, zinc, building stone, hydropower, forests

### LAND USE:
agricultural land: 22.8% (2011 est.)

arable land: 8.4% (2011 est.) / permanent crops: 1.3% (2011 est.) / permanent pasture: 13.1% (2011 est.)

forest: 62.3% (2011 est.)

other: 14.9% (2011 est.)

### IRRIGATED LAND:
60 sq km (2012)

### POPULATION DISTRIBUTION:
a fairly even distribution throughout most of the country, with urban areas attracting larger and denser populations; pockets in the mountainous northwest exhibit less density than elsewhere

### NATURAL HAZARDS:
flooding; earthquakes

### ENVIRONMENT - CURRENT ISSUES:
air pollution from road traffic, domestic heating (wood buring), power generation, and industry; water pollution; biodiversity protection

### ENVIRONMENT - INTERNATIONAL AGREEMENTS:
party to: Air Pollution, Air Pollution-Nitrogen Oxides, Air Pollution-Persistent Organic Pollutants, Air Pollution-Sulfur 94, Biodiversity, Climate Change, Climate Change-Kyoto Protocol, Desertification, Endangered Species, Environmental Modification, Hazardous Wastes, Law of the Sea, Marine Dumping, Ozone Layer Protection, Ship Pollution, Wetlands, Whaling

signed, but not ratified: none of the selected agreements

### GEOGRAPHY - NOTE:
despite its small size, this eastern Alpine country controls some of Europe's major transit routes

## PEOPLE AND SOCIETY :: SLOVENIA

### POPULATION:
2,102,126 (July 2018 est.)

country comparison to the world: 147

**NATIONALITY:**

noun: Slovene(s)

adjective: Slovenian

**ETHNIC GROUPS:**

Slovene 83.1%, Serb 2%, Croat 1.8%, Bosniak 1.1%, other or unspecified 12% (2002 est.)

**LANGUAGES:**

Slovenian (official) 91.1%, Serbo-Croatian 4.5%, other or unspecified 4.4%, Italian (official, only in municipalities where Italian national communities reside), Hungarian (official, only in municipalities where Hungarian national communities reside) (2002 census)

**RELIGIONS:**

Catholic 57.8%, Muslim 2.4%, Orthodox 2.3%, other Christian 0.9%, unaffiliated 3.5%, other or unspecified 23%, none 10.1% (2002 census)

**AGE STRUCTURE:**

0-14 years: 14.8% (male 159,700 /female 151,351)

15-24 years: 9.1% (male 98,856 /female 92,407)

25-54 years: 41.71% (male 458,826 /female 417,875)

55-64 years: 14.26% (male 149,714 /female 150,045)

65 years and over: 20.14% (male 180,080 /female 243,272) (2018 est.)

**DEPENDENCY RATIOS:**

total dependency ratio: 48.7 (2015 est.)

youth dependency ratio: 21.9 (2015 est.)

elderly dependency ratio: 26.8 (2015 est.)

potential support ratio: 3.7 (2015 est.)

**MEDIAN AGE:**

total: 44.2 years

male: 42.7 years

female: 46 years (2018 est.)

country comparison to the world: 13

**POPULATION GROWTH RATE:**

0.03% (2018 est.)

country comparison to the world: 188

**BIRTH RATE:**

9.2 births/1,000 population (2018 est.)

country comparison to the world: 204

**DEATH RATE:**

9.9 deaths/1,000 population (2018 est.)

country comparison to the world: 39

**NET MIGRATION RATE:**

0.4 migrant(s)/1,000 population (2017 est.)

country comparison to the world: 64

**POPULATION DISTRIBUTION:**

a fairly even distribution throughout most of the country, with urban areas attracting larger and denser populations; pockets in the mountainous northwest exhibit less density than elsewhere

**URBANIZATION:**

urban population: 54.5% of total population (2018)

rate of urbanization: 0.56% annual rate of change (2015-20 est.)

**MAJOR URBAN AREAS - POPULATION:**

286,000 LJUBLJANA (capital) (2018)

**SEX RATIO:**

at birth: 1.07 male(s)/female (2017 est.)

0-14 years: 1.06 male(s)/female (2017 est.)

15-24 years: 1.05 male(s)/female (2017 est.)

25-54 years: 1.02 male(s)/female (2017 est.)

55-64 years: 0.97 male(s)/female (2017 est.)

65 years and over: 0.68 male(s)/female (2017 est.)

total population: 0.95 male(s)/female (2017 est.)

**MOTHER'S MEAN AGE AT FIRST BIRTH:**

29.1 years (2014 est.)

**MATERNAL MORTALITY RATE:**

9 deaths/100,000 live births (2015 est.)

country comparison to the world: 154

**INFANT MORTALITY RATE:**

total: 1.6 deaths/1,000 live births (2018 est.)

male: 1.7 deaths/1,000 live births (2018 est.)

female: 1.5 deaths/1,000 live births (2018 est.)

country comparison to the world: 224

**LIFE EXPECTANCY AT BIRTH:**

total population: 81.2 years (2018 est.)

male: 78.3 years (2018 est.)

female: 84.2 years (2018 est.)

country comparison to the world: 32

**TOTAL FERTILITY RATE:**

1.58 children born/woman (2018 est.)

country comparison to the world: 185

**HEALTH EXPENDITURES:**

9.2% of GDP (2014)

country comparison to the world: 37

**PHYSICIANS DENSITY:**

2.82 physicians/1,000 population (2015)

**HOSPITAL BED DENSITY:**

4.6 beds/1,000 population (2013)

**DRINKING WATER SOURCE:**

improved:

urban: 99.7% of population (2015 est.)

rural: 99.4% of population (2015 est.)

total: 99.5% of population (2015 est.)

unimproved:

urban: 0.3% of population (2015 est.)

rural: 0.6% of population (2015 est.)

total: 0.5% of population (2015 est.)

**SANITATION FACILITY ACCESS:**

improved:

urban: 99.1% of population (2015 est.)

rural: 99.1% of population (2015 est.)

total: 99.1% of population (2015 est.)

unimproved:

urban: 0.9% of population (2015 est.)

rural: 0.9% of population (2015 est.)

total: 0.9% of population (2015 est.)

**HIV/AIDS - ADULT PREVALENCE RATE:**

<.1% (2017 est.)

**HIV/AIDS - PEOPLE LIVING WITH HIV/AIDS:**

<1000 (2017 est.)

**HIV/AIDS - DEATHS:**

<100 (2017 est.)

**OBESITY - ADULT PREVALENCE RATE:**

20.2% (2016)

country comparison to the world: 104

**EDUCATION EXPENDITURES:**

5.3% of GDP (2014)

country comparison to the world: 62

**LITERACY:**

definition: NA (2015 est.)

**total population:** 99.7% (2015 est.)

**male:** 99.7% (2015 est.)

**female:** 99.7% (2015 est.)

## SCHOOL LIFE EXPECTANCY (PRIMARY TO TERTIARY EDUCATION):

**total:** 17 years (2014)

**male:** 17 years (2014)

**female:** 18 years (2014)

## UNEMPLOYMENT, YOUTH AGES 15-24:

**total:** 15.2% (2016 est.)

**male:** 15.6% (2016 est.)

**female:** 14.7% (2016 est.)

**country comparison to the world:** 89

# GOVERNMENT :: SLOVENIA

## COUNTRY NAME:

**conventional long form:** Republic of Slovenia

**conventional short form:** Slovenia

**local long form:** Republika Slovenija

**local short form:** Slovenija

**former:** People's Republic of Slovenia, Socialist Republic of Slovenia

**etymology:** related to the Slavic autonym (self-designation) "Slovenin," a derivation from "slovo" (word), denoting "people who speak (the same language)" (i.e., people who understand each other)

## GOVERNMENT TYPE:

parliamentary republic

## CAPITAL:

**name:** Ljubljana

**geographic coordinates:** 46 03 N, 14 31 E

**time difference:** UTC+1 (6 hours ahead of Washington, DC, during Standard Time)

**daylight saving time:** +1hr, begins last Sunday in March; ends last Sunday in October

## ADMINISTRATIVE DIVISIONS:

201 municipalities (obcine, singular - obcina) and 11 urban municipalities (mestne obcine, singular - mestna obcina)

**municipalities:** Ajdovscina, Ankaran, Apace, Beltinci, Benedikt, Bistrica ob Sotli, Bled, Bloke, Bohinj, Borovnica, Bovec, Braslovce, Brda, Brezice, Brezovica, Cankova, Cerklje na Gorenjskem, Cerknica, Cerkno, Cerkvenjak, Cirkulane, Crensovci, Crna na Koroskem, Crnomelj, Destrnik, Divaca, Dobje, Dobrepolje, Dobrna, Dobrova-Polhov Gradec, Dobrovnik/Dobronak, Dolenjske Toplice, Dol pri Ljubljani, Domzale, Dornava, Dravograd, Duplek, Gorenja Vas-Poljane, Gorisnica, Gorje, Gornja Radgona, Gornji Grad, Gornji Petrovci, Grad, Grosuplje, Hajdina, Hoce-Slivnica, Hodos, Horjul, Hrastnik, Hrpelje-Kozina, Idrija, Ig, Ilirska Bistrica, Ivancna Gorica, Izola/Isola, Jesenice, Jezersko, Jursinci, Kamnik, Kanal, Kidricevo, Kobarid, Kobilje, Kocevje, Komen, Komenda, Kosanjevica na Krki, Kostel, Kozje, Kranjska Gora, Krizevci, Krsko, Kungota, Kuzma, Lasko, Lenart, Lendava/Lendva, Litija, Ljubno, Ljutomer, Log-Dragomer, Logatec, Loska Dolina, Loski Potok, Lovrenc na Pohorju, Luce, Lukovica,;

Majsperk, Makole, Markovci, Medvode, Menges, Metlika, Mezica, Miklavz na Dravskem Polju, Miren-Kostanjevica, Mirna, Mirna Pec, Mislinja, Mokronog-Trebelno, Moravce, Moravske Toplice, Mozirje, Muta, Naklo, Nazarje, Odranci, Oplotnica, Ormoz, Osilnica, Pesnica, Piran/Pirano, Pivka, Podcetrtek, Podlehnik, Podvelka, Poljcane, Polzela, Postojna, Prebold, Preddvor, Prevalje, Puconci, Race-Fram, Radece, Radenci, Radlje ob Dravi, Radovljica, Ravne na Koroskem, Razkrizje, Recica ob Savinji, Rence-Vogrsko, Ribnica, Ribnica na Pohorju, Rogaska Slatina, Rogasovci, Rogatec, Ruse, Selnica ob Dravi, Semic, Sevnica, Sezana, Slovenska Bistrica, Slovenske Konjice, Sodrazica, Solcava, Sredisce ob Dravi, Starse, Straza, Sveta Ana, Sveta Trojica v Slovenskih Goricah, Sveti Andraz v Slovenskih Goricah, Sveti Jurij ob Scavnici, Sveti Jurij v Slovenskih Goricah, Sveti Tomaz, Salovci, Sempeter-Vrtojba, Sencur, Sentilj, Sentjernej, Sentjur, Sentrupert, Skocjan, Skofja Loka, Skofljica, Smarje pri Jelsah, Smarjeske Toplice, Smartno ob Paki, Smartno pri Litiji, Sostanj, Store, Tabor, Tisina, Tolmin, Trbovlje, Trebnje, Trnovska Vas, Trzic, Trzin, Turnisce, Velika Polana, Velike Lasce, Verzej, Videm, Vipava, Vitanje, Vodice, Vojnik, Vransko, Vrhnika, Vuzenica, Zagorje ob Savi, Zalec, Zavrc, Zelezniki, Zetale, Ziri, Zirovnica, Zrece, Zuzemberk;

**urban municipalities:** Celje, Koper-Capodistria, Kranj, Ljubljana, Maribor, Murska Sobota, Nova Gorica, Novo Mesto, Ptuj, Slovenj Gradec, Velenje

## INDEPENDENCE:

25 June 1991 (from Yugoslavia)

## NATIONAL HOLIDAY:

Independence Day/Statehood Day, 25 June (1991)

## CONSTITUTION:

**history:** previous 1974 (preindependence); latest passed by Parliament 23 December 1991 (2016)

**amendments:** proposed by at least 20 National Assembly members, by the government, or by petition of at least 30,000 voters; passage requires at least two-thirds majority vote by the Assembly; referendum required if agreed upon by at least 30 Assembly members; passage in a referendum requires participation of a majority of eligible voters and a simple majority of votes cast; amended several times, last in 2015 (2016)

## LEGAL SYSTEM:

civil law system

## INTERNATIONAL LAW ORGANIZATION PARTICIPATION:

has not submitted an ICJ jurisdiction declaration; accepts ICCt jurisdiction

## CITIZENSHIP:

**citizenship by birth:** no

**citizenship by descent only:** at least one parent must be a citizen of Slovenia; both parents if the child is born outside of Slovenia

**dual citizenship recognized:** yes, for select cases

**residency requirement for naturalization:** 10 years, the last 5 of which have been continuous

## SUFFRAGE:

18 years of age, 16 if employed; universal

## EXECUTIVE BRANCH:

**chief of state:** President Borut PAHOR (since 22 December 2012)

**head of government:** Prime Minister Marjan SAREC (since 13 September 2018); note - Miro CERAR resigned on 14 March 2018; an early parliamentary election was held on 3 June 2018, but President PAHOR did not nominate a new prime minister because no party had majority support in the parliament; parliament nominated and then approved Marjan SAREC as prime minister-designate on 17 August 2018

**cabinet:** Council of Ministers nominated by the prime minister, elected by the National Assembly

**elections/appointments:** president directly elected by absolute majority popular vote in 2 rounds if needed for a 5-year term (eligible for a second term); election last held on 22 October 2017 with a runoff on 12 November 2017 (next election to be held by November 2022); following National Assembly elections, the leader of the majority party or majority coalition usually nominated prime minister by the president and elected by the National Assembly

**election results:** Borut PAHOR is reelected president in second round; percent of vote in first round - Borut PAHOR (independent) 47.1%, Marjan SAREC (Marjan Sarec List) 25%, Romana TOMC (SDS) 13.7%, Ljudmila NOVAK (NSi) 7.2%, other 7%; percent of vote in second round - Borut PAHOR 52.9%, Marjan SAREC 47.1%; Marjan SAREC (LMS) elected prime minister; National Assembly vote - 55-31

## LEGISLATIVE BRANCH:

**description:** bicameral Parliament consists of:
National Council or Drzavni Svet (40 seats; members indirectly elected by an electoral college to serve 5-year terms); note - the Council is primarily an advisory body with limited legislative powers
National Assembly or Drzavni Zbor (90 seats; 88 members directly elected in single-seat constituencies by proportional representation vote and 2 directly elected in special constituencies for Italian and Hungarian minorities by simple majority vote; members serve 4-year terms)

**elections:**
National Council - last held on 22 November 2017 (next to be held in 2022)
National Assembly - last held on 3 June 2018 (next to be held in 2022)

**election results:**
National Council - percent of vote by party - NA; seats by party - NA; composition - men 36, women 4, percent of women 10%
National Assembly - percent of vote by party - SDS 24.9%, LMS 12.7%, SD 9.9%, SMC 9.8%, Levica 9.3%, NSi 7.1%, Stranka AB 5.1%, DeSUS 4.9%, SNS 4.2%, other 12.1%; seats by party - SDS 25, LMS 13, SD 10, SMC 10, Levica 9, NSi 7, Stranka AB 5, DeSUS 5, SNS 4, Italian and Hungarian minorities 2; composition - men 68, women 22, percent of women 24.4%; note - total Parliament percent of women 20%

## JUDICIAL BRANCH:

**highest courts:** Supreme Court (consists of the court president and 37 judges organized into civil, criminal, commercial, labor and social security, administrative, and registry departments); Constitutional Court (consists of the court president, vice president, and 7 judges)

**judge selection and term of office:** Supreme Court president and vice president appointed by the National Assembly upon the proposal of the Minister of Justice based on the opinions of the Judicial Council, an 11-member independent body elected by the National Assembly from proposals submitted by the president, attorneys, law universities, and sitting judges; other Supreme Court judges elected by the National Assembly from candidates proposed by the Judicial Council; Supreme Court judges appointed for life; Constitutional Court judges appointed by the National Assembly from nominations by the president of the republic; Constitutional Court president selected from among their own for a 3-year term; other judges elected for single 9-year terms

**subordinate courts:** county, district, regional, and high courts; specialized labor-related and social courts; Court of Audit; Administrative Court

## POLITICAL PARTIES AND LEADERS:

Democratic Party of Pensioners of Slovenia or DeSUS [Karl ERJAVEC]
List of Marjan Sarec or LMS [Marjan SAREC]
Modern Center Party or SMC [Miro CERAR]
New Slovenia or NSi [Matej TONIN]
Party of Alenka Bratusek or Stranka AB [Alenka BRATUSEK] (formerly Alliance of Social Liberal Democrats or ZSD and before that Alliance of Alenka Bratusek or ZaAB)
Slovenian Democratic Party or SDS [Janez JANSA]
Slovenian National Party or SNS [Zmago JELINCIC Plemeniti]
Social Democrats or SD [Dejan ZIDAN]
The Left or Levica [Luka MESEC] (successor to United Left or ZL)

## INTERNATIONAL ORGANIZATION PARTICIPATION:

Australia Group, BIS, CD, CE, CEI, EAPC, EBRD, ECB, EIB, EMU, ESA (cooperating state), EU, FAO, IADB, IAEA, IBRD, ICAO, ICC (national committees), ICCt, ICRM, IDA, IFC, IFRCS, IHO, ILO, IMF, IMO, Interpol, IOC, IOM, IPU, ISO, ITU, MIGA, NATO, NEA, NSG, OAS (observer), OECD, OIF (observer), OPCW, OSCE, PCA, Schengen Convention, SELEC, UN, UNCTAD, UNESCO, UNHCR, UNIDO, UNIFIL, UNTSO, UNWTO, UPU, WCO, WHO, WIPO, WMO, WTO, ZC

## DIPLOMATIC REPRESENTATION IN THE US:

**chief of mission:** Ambassador Stanislav VIDOVIC (since 21 July 2017)

**chancery:** 2410 California Street N.W., Washington, DC 20008

**telephone:** [1] (202) 386-6601

**FAX:** [1] (202) 386-6633

**consulate(s) general:** Cleveland (OH)

## DIPLOMATIC REPRESENTATION FROM THE US:

**chief of mission:** Ambassador (vacant); Charge d'Affaires Guatam RANA (since July 2018)

**embassy:** Presernova 31, 1000 Ljubljana

**mailing address:** American Embassy Ljubljana, US Department of State, 7140 Ljubljana Place, Washington, DC 20521-7140

**telephone:** [386] (1) 200-5500

**FAX:** [386] (1) 200-5555

## FLAG DESCRIPTION:

three equal horizontal bands of white (top), blue, and red, derive from the medieval coat of arms of the Duchy of Carniola; the Slovenian seal (a shield with the image of Triglav, Slovenia's highest peak, in white against a blue background at the center; beneath it are two wavy blue lines depicting seas and rivers, and above it are three six-pointed stars arranged in an inverted triangle, which are taken from the coat of arms of the Counts of Celje, the prominent Slovene dynastic house of the late 14th and early 15th centuries) appears in the upper hoist side of the flag centered on the white and blue bands

## NATIONAL SYMBOL(S):

Mount Triglav; national colors: white, blue, red

## NATIONAL ANTHEM:

**name:** "Zdravljica" (A Toast)

**lyrics/music:** France PRESEREN/Stanko PREMRL

**note:** adopted in 1989 while still part of Yugoslavia; originally written in 1848; the full poem, whose seventh verse is used as the anthem, speaks of pan-Slavic nationalism

## ECONOMY :: SLOVENIA

**ECONOMY - OVERVIEW:**

With excellent infrastructure, a well-educated work force, and a strategic location between the Balkans and Western Europe, Slovenia has one of the highest per capita GDPs in Central Europe, despite having suffered a protracted recession in the 2008-09 period in the wake of the global financial crisis. Slovenia became the first 2004 EU entrant to adopt the euro (on 1 January 2007) and has experienced a stable political and economic transition.

In March 2004, Slovenia became the first transition country to graduate from borrower status to donor partner at the World Bank. In 2007, Slovenia was invited to begin the process for joining the OECD; it became a member in 2012. From 2014 to 2016, export-led growth, fueled by demand in larger European markets, pushed annual GDP growth above 2.3%. Growth reached 5.0% in 2017 and is projected to near or reach 5% in 2018. What used to be stubbornly high unemployment fell below 5.5% in early 2018, driven by strong exports and increasing consumption that boosted labor demand. Continued fiscal consolidation through increased tax collection and social security contributions will likely result in a balanced government budget in 2019.

Prime Minister Cerar's government took office in September 2014, pledging to press ahead with commitments to privatize a select group of state-run companies, rationalize public spending, and further stabilize the banking sector. Efforts to privatize Slovenia's largely state-owned banking sector have largely stalled, however, amid concerns about an ongoing dispute over Yugoslav-era foreign currency deposits.

**GDP (PURCHASING POWER PARITY):**

$71.23 billion (2017 est.)

$67.84 billion (2016 est.)

$65.77 billion (2015 est.)

note: data are in 2017 dollars

country comparison to the world: 99

**GDP (OFFICIAL EXCHANGE RATE):**

$48.87 billion (2017 est.) (2017 est.)

**GDP - REAL GROWTH RATE:**

5% (2017 est.)

3.1% (2016 est.)

2.3% (2015 est.)

country comparison to the world: 51

**GDP - PER CAPITA (PPP):**

$34,500 (2017 est.)

$32,900 (2016 est.)

$31,900 (2015 est.)

note: data are in 2017 dollars

country comparison to the world: 58

**GROSS NATIONAL SAVING:**

26.4% of GDP (2017 est.)

24.2% of GDP (2016 est.)

23.9% of GDP (2015 est.)

country comparison to the world: 49

**GDP - COMPOSITION, BY END USE:**

household consumption: 52.6% (2017 est.)

government consumption: 18.2% (2017 est.)

investment in fixed capital: 18.4% (2017 est.)

investment in inventories: 1.1% (2017 est.)

exports of goods and services: 82.3% (2017 est.)

imports of goods and services: -72.6% (2017 est.)

**GDP - COMPOSITION, BY SECTOR OF ORIGIN:**

agriculture: 1.8% (2017 est.)

industry: 32.2% (2017 est.)

services: 65.9% (2017 est.)

**AGRICULTURE - PRODUCTS:**

hops, wheat, coffee, corn, apples, pears; cattle, sheep, poultry

**INDUSTRIES:**

ferrous metallurgy and aluminum products, lead and zinc smelting; electronics (including military electronics), trucks, automobiles, electric power equipment, wood products, textiles, chemicals, machine tools

**INDUSTRIAL PRODUCTION GROWTH RATE:**

8.6% (2017 est.)

country comparison to the world: 22

**LABOR FORCE:**

959,000 (2017 est.)

country comparison to the world: 145

**LABOR FORCE - BY OCCUPATION:**

agriculture: 5.5%

industry: 31.2%

services: 63.3% (2017 est.)

**UNEMPLOYMENT RATE:**

6.6% (2017 est.)

8% (2016 est.)

country comparison to the world: 98

**POPULATION BELOW POVERTY LINE:**

13.9% (2016 est.)

**HOUSEHOLD INCOME OR CONSUMPTION BY PERCENTAGE SHARE:**

lowest 10%: 20.1% (2016)

highest 10%: 20.1% (2016)

**DISTRIBUTION OF FAMILY INCOME - GINI INDEX:**

24.4 (2016)

24.5 (2015)

country comparison to the world: 154

**BUDGET:**

revenues: 21.07 billion (2017 est.)

expenditures: 21.06 billion (2017 est.)

**TAXES AND OTHER REVENUES:**

43.1% (of GDP) (2017 est.)

country comparison to the world: 28

**BUDGET SURPLUS (+) OR DEFICIT (-):**

0% (of GDP) (2017 est.)

country comparison to the world: 46

**PUBLIC DEBT:**

73.6% of GDP (2017 est.)

78.6% of GDP (2016 est.)

note: defined by the EU's Maastricht Treaty as consolidated general government gross debt at nominal value, outstanding at the end of the year in the following categories of government liabilities: currency and deposits, securities other than shares excluding financial derivatives, and loans; general government sector comprises the central, state, local government, and social security funds

country comparison to the world: 44

**FISCAL YEAR:**

calendar year

## INFLATION RATE (CONSUMER PRICES):

1.4% (2017 est.)

-0.1% (2016 est.)

country comparison to the world: 80

## CENTRAL BANK DISCOUNT RATE:

0% (31 December 2017)

0% (16 March 2016)

note: this is the European Central Bank's rate on the marginal lending facility, which offers overnight credit to banks in the euro area

country comparison to the world: 161

## COMMERCIAL BANK PRIME LENDING RATE:

2.59% (31 December 2017 est.)

2.81% (31 December 2016 est.)

country comparison to the world: 180

## STOCK OF NARROW MONEY:

$21.53 billion (31 December 2017 est.)

$16.54 billion (31 December 2016 est.)

note: see entry for the European Union for money supply for the entire euro area; the European Central Bank (ECB) controls monetary policy for the 18 members of the Economic and Monetary Union (EMU); individual members of the EMU do not control the quantity of money circulating within their own borders

country comparison to the world: 68

## STOCK OF BROAD MONEY:

$21.53 billion (31 December 2017 est.)

$16.54 billion (31 December 2016 est.)

country comparison to the world: 69

## STOCK OF DOMESTIC CREDIT:

$35.34 billion (31 December 2017 est.)

$30.23 billion (31 December 2016 est.)

country comparison to the world: 75

## MARKET VALUE OF PUBLICLY TRADED SHARES:

$6.328 billion (31 December 2017 est.)

$5.6 billion (31 December 2016 est.)

$5.94 billion (31 December 2015 est.)

country comparison to the world: 82

## CURRENT ACCOUNT BALANCE:

$3.475 billion (2017 est.)

$2.461 billion (2016 est.)

country comparison to the world: 33

## EXPORTS:

$32.14 billion (2017 est.)

$27.65 billion (2016 est.)

country comparison to the world: 63

## EXPORTS - PARTNERS:

Germany 18.9%, Italy 10.7%, Austria 7.4%, Croatia 7.1%, France 4.8%, Poland 4.2%, Hungary 4.2% (2017)

## EXPORTS - COMMODITIES:

manufactured goods, machinery and transport equipment, chemicals, food

## IMPORTS:

$30.38 billion (2017 est.)

$25.95 billion (2016 est.)

country comparison to the world: 69

## IMPORTS - COMMODITIES:

machinery and transport equipment, manufactured goods, chemicals, fuels and lubricants, food

## IMPORTS - PARTNERS:

Germany 16.5%, Italy 13.5%, Austria 9.3%, Turkey 5.8%, Croatia 4.8%, China 4.5% (2017)

## RESERVES OF FOREIGN EXCHANGE AND GOLD:

$889.9 million (31 December 2017 est.)

$853 million (31 December 2016 est.)

country comparison to the world: 135

## DEBT - EXTERNAL:

$46.3 billion (31 January 2017 est.)

$48.2 billion (31 January 2016 est.)

country comparison to the world: 69

## STOCK OF DIRECT FOREIGN INVESTMENT - AT HOME:

$19.23 billion (31 December 2017 est.)

$14.83 billion (31 December 2016 est.)

country comparison to the world: 80

## STOCK OF DIRECT FOREIGN INVESTMENT - ABROAD:

$9.914 billion (31 December 2017 est.)

$7.837 billion (31 December 2016 est.)

country comparison to the world: 66

## EXCHANGE RATES:

euros (EUR) per US dollar -

0.885 (2017 est.)

0.903 (2016 est.)

0.9214 (2015 est.)

0.885 (2014 est.)

0.7634 (2013 est.)

# ENERGY :: SLOVENIA

## ELECTRICITY ACCESS:

electrification - total population: 100% (2016)

## ELECTRICITY - PRODUCTION:

15.46 billion kWh (2016 est.)

country comparison to the world: 88

## ELECTRICITY - CONSUMPTION:

13.4 billion kWh (2016 est.)

country comparison to the world: 84

## ELECTRICITY - EXPORTS:

7.972 billion kWh (2017 est.)

country comparison to the world: 26

## ELECTRICITY - IMPORTS:

8.359 billion kWh (2016 est.)

country comparison to the world: 29

## ELECTRICITY - INSTALLED GENERATING CAPACITY:

3.536 million kW (2016 est.)

country comparison to the world: 95

## ELECTRICITY - FROM FOSSIL FUELS:

37% of total installed capacity (2016 est.)

country comparison to the world: 174

## ELECTRICITY - FROM NUCLEAR FUELS:

20% of total installed capacity (2017 est.)

country comparison to the world: 9

## ELECTRICITY - FROM HYDROELECTRIC PLANTS:

34% of total installed capacity (2017 est.)

country comparison to the world: 63

## ELECTRICITY - FROM OTHER RENEWABLE SOURCES:

9% of total installed capacity (2017 est.)

country comparison to the world: 84

## CRUDE OIL - PRODUCTION:

5 bbl/day (2017 est.)

country comparison to the world: 100

## CRUDE OIL - EXPORTS:

0 bbl/day (2017 est.)

country comparison to the world: 194

## CRUDE OIL - IMPORTS:

0 bbl/day (2017 est.)

country comparison to the world: 196

## CRUDE OIL - PROVED RESERVES:

0 bbl (1 January 2018 est.)

country comparison to the world: 196

## REFINED PETROLEUM PRODUCTS - PRODUCTION:

0 bbl/day (2017 est.)

country comparison to the world: 202

## REFINED PETROLEUM PRODUCTS - CONSUMPTION:

52,140 bbl/day (2017 est.)

country comparison to the world: 102

**REFINED PETROLEUM PRODUCTS - EXPORTS:**

29,350 bbl/day (2017 est.)

country comparison to the world: 63

**REFINED PETROLEUM PRODUCTS - IMPORTS:**

93,060 bbl/day (2017 est.)

country comparison to the world: 56

**NATURAL GAS - PRODUCTION:**

8 million cu m (2017 est.)

country comparison to the world: 94

**NATURAL GAS - CONSUMPTION:**

906.1 million cu m (2017 est.)

country comparison to the world: 94

**NATURAL GAS - EXPORTS:**

2.832 million cu m (2017 est.)

country comparison to the world: 55

**NATURAL GAS - IMPORTS:**

906.1 million cu m (2017 est.)

country comparison to the world: 62

**NATURAL GAS - PROVED RESERVES:**

NA cu m (2017 est.)

**CARBON DIOXIDE EMISSIONS FROM CONSUMPTION OF ENERGY:**

14.37 million Mt (2017 est.)

country comparison to the world: 94

# COMMUNICATIONS :: SLOVENIA

**TELEPHONES - FIXED LINES:**

total subscriptions: 717,235 (2017 est.)

subscriptions per 100 inhabitants: 36 (2017 est.)

country comparison to the world: 85

**TELEPHONES - MOBILE CELLULAR:**

total subscriptions: 2,443,172 (2017 est.)

subscriptions per 100 inhabitants: 124 (2017 est.)

country comparison to the world: 145

**TELEPHONE SYSTEM:**

general assessment: well-developed telecommunications infrastructure (2016)

domestic: combined fixed-line and mobile-cellular teledensity roughly 155 telephones per 100 persons (2016)

international: country code - 386 (2016)

**BROADCAST MEDIA:**

public TV broadcaster, Radiotelevizija Slovenija (RTV), operates a system of national and regional TV stations; 35 domestic commercial TV stations operating nationally, regionally, and locally; about 60% of households are connected to multi-channel cable TV; public radio broadcaster operates 3 national and 4 regional stations; more than 75 regional and local commercial and non-commercial radio stations (2017)

**INTERNET COUNTRY CODE:**

.si

**INTERNET USERS:**

total: 1,493,382 (July 2016 est.)

percent of population: 75.5% (July 2016 est.)

country comparison to the world: 121

**BROADBAND - FIXED SUBSCRIPTIONS:**

total: 601,821 (2017 est.)

subscriptions per 100 inhabitants: 31 (2017 est.)

country comparison to the world: 77

# TRANSPORTATION :: SLOVENIA

**NATIONAL AIR TRANSPORT SYSTEM:**

number of registered air carriers: 2 (2015)

inventory of registered aircraft operated by air carriers: 35 (2015)

annual passenger traffic on registered air carriers: 1,130,637 (2015)

annual freight traffic on registered air carriers: 1,349,442 mt-km (2015)

**CIVIL AIRCRAFT REGISTRATION COUNTRY CODE PREFIX:**

S5 (2016)

**AIRPORTS:**

16 (2013)

country comparison to the world: 144

**AIRPORTS - WITH PAVED RUNWAYS:**

total: 7 (2013)

over 3,047 m: 1 (2013)

2,438 to 3,047 m: 1 (2013)

1,524 to 2,437 m: 1 (2013)

914 to 1,523 m: 3 (2013)

under 914 m: 1 (2013)

**AIRPORTS - WITH UNPAVED RUNWAYS:**

total: 9 (2013)

1,524 to 2,437 m: 1 (2013)

914 to 1,523 m: 3 (2013)

under 914 m: 5 (2013)

**PIPELINES:**

1155 km gas, 5 km oil (2017)

**RAILWAYS:**

total: 1,229 km (2014)

standard gauge: 1,229 km 1.435-m gauge (503 km electrified) (2014)

country comparison to the world: 86

**ROADWAYS:**

total: 38,985 km (2012)

paved: 38,985 km (includes 769 km of expressways) (2012)

country comparison to the world: 91

**WATERWAYS:**

(some transport on the Drava River) (2012)

**MERCHANT MARINE:**

total: 7 (2017)

by type: other 7 (2017)

country comparison to the world: 158

**PORTS AND TERMINALS:**

major seaport(s): Koper

# MILITARY AND SECURITY :: SLOVENIA

**MILITARY EXPENDITURES:**

0.98% of GDP (2017)

0.92% of GDP (2016)

0.94% of GDP (2015)

country comparison to the world: 117

**MILITARY BRANCHES:**

Slovenian Armed Forces (Slovenska Vojska, SV): Forces Command (with ground units, naval element, air and air defense brigade); Administration for Civil Protection and Disaster Relief (ACPDR) (2013)

**MILITARY SERVICE AGE AND OBLIGATION:**

18-25 years of age for voluntary military service; conscription abolished in 2003 (2012)

# TRANSNATIONAL ISSUES :: SLOVENIA

**DISPUTES - INTERNATIONAL:**

since the breakup of Yugoslavia in the early 1990s, Croatia and Slovenia have each claimed sovereignty over Piranski Bay and four villages, and Slovenia has objected to Croatia's claim of an exclusive economic zone in the Adriatic Sea; in 2009, however Croatia and Slovenia signed a binding international arbitration agreement to define their disputed land and maritime borders, which led Slovenia to lift its objections to Croatia joining the EUas a member state that forms part of the EU's external border, Slovenia has implemented the strict Schengen border rules to curb illegal migration and commerce through southeastern Europe while encouraging close cross-border ties with Croatia; Slovenia continues to impose a hard border Schengen regime with Croatia, which joined the EU in 2013 but has not yet fulfilled Schengen requirements

## REFUGEES AND INTERNALLY DISPLACED PERSONS:

note: estimated refugee and migrant arrivals (January 2015-December 2016); migration through the Western Balkans has decreased significantly since March 2016; Slovenia is predominantly a transit country and hosts approximately 300 asylum seekers as of the end of June 2018

## ILLICIT DRUGS:

minor transit point for cocaine and Southwest Asian heroin bound for Western Europe, and for precursor chemicals

# AUSTRALIA - OCEANIA :: SOLOMON ISLANDS

## INTRODUCTION :: SOLOMON ISLANDS

### BACKGROUND:
The UK established a protectorate over the Solomon Islands in the 1890s. Some of the bitterest fighting of World War II occurred on this archipelago and the Guadalcanal Campaign (August 1942-February 1943) proved a turning point in the Pacific War, since after the operation the Japanese lost their strategic initiative and remained on the defensive until thier final defeat in 1945. Self-government for the Solomon Islands came in 1976 and independence two years later. Ethnic violence, government malfeasance, endemic crime, and a narrow economic base have undermined stability and civil society. In June 2003, then Prime Minister Sir Allan KEMAKEZA sought the assistance of Australia in reestablishing law and order; the following month, an Australian-led multinational force arrived to restore peace and disarm ethnic militias. The Regional Assistance Mission to the Solomon Islands (RAMSI) has generally been effective in restoring law and order and rebuilding government institutions.

## GEOGRAPHY :: SOLOMON ISLANDS

### LOCATION:
Oceania, group of islands in the South Pacific Ocean, east of Papua New Guinea

### GEOGRAPHIC COORDINATES:
8 00 S, 159 00 E

### MAP REFERENCES:
Oceania

### AREA:
total: 28,896 sq km

land: 27,986 sq km

water: 910 sq km

country comparison to the world: 144

### AREA - COMPARATIVE:
slightly smaller than Maryland

### LAND BOUNDARIES:
0 km

### COASTLINE:
5,313 km

### MARITIME CLAIMS:
territorial sea: 12 nm

exclusive economic zone: 200 nm

continental shelf: 200 nm

measured from claimed archipelagic baselines

### CLIMATE:
tropical monsoon; few temperature and weather extremes

### TERRAIN:
mostly rugged mountains with some low coral atolls

### ELEVATION:
0 m lowest point: Pacific Ocean

2335 highest point: Mount Popomanaseu

### NATURAL RESOURCES:
fish, forests, gold, bauxite, phosphates, lead, zinc, nickel

### LAND USE:
agricultural land: 3.9% (2011 est.)

arable land: 0.7% (2011 est.) / permanent crops: 2.9% (2011 est.) / permanent pasture: 0.3% (2011 est.)

forest: 78.9% (2011 est.)

other: 17.2% (2011 est.)

### IRRIGATED LAND:
0 sq km NA (2012)

### POPULATION DISTRIBUTION:
most of the population lives along the coastal regions; about one in five live in urban areas, and of these some two-thirds reside in Honiara, the largest town and chief port

### NATURAL HAZARDS:
tropical cyclones, but rarely destructive; geologically active region with frequent earthquakes, tremors, and volcanic activity; tsunamis

volcanism: Tinakula (851 m) has frequent eruption activity, while an eruption of Savo (485 m) could affect the capital Honiara on nearby Guadalcanal

### ENVIRONMENT - CURRENT ISSUES:
deforestation; soil erosion; many of the surrounding coral reefs are dead or dying; effects of climate change and rising sea levels

### ENVIRONMENT - INTERNATIONAL AGREEMENTS:
party to: Biodiversity, Climate Change, Climate Change-Kyoto Protocol, Desertification, Environmental Modification, Law of the Sea, Marine Dumping, Marine Life Conservation, Ozone Layer Protection, Whaling

signed, but not ratified: none of the selected agreements

### GEOGRAPHY - NOTE:
strategic location on sea routes between the South Pacific Ocean, the Solomon Sea, and the Coral Sea

## PEOPLE AND SOCIETY :: SOLOMON ISLANDS

### POPULATION:
660,121 (July 2018 est.)

country comparison to the world: 167

### NATIONALITY:

noun: Solomon Islander(s)

adjective: Solomon Islander

## ETHNIC GROUPS:

Melanesian 95.3%, Polynesian 3.1%, Micronesian 1.2%, other 0.3% (2009 est.)

## LANGUAGES:

Melanesian pidgin (in much of the country is lingua franca), English (official but spoken by only 1%-2% of the population), 120 indigenous languages

## RELIGIONS:

Protestant 73.4% (Church of Melanesia 31.9%, South Sea Evangelical 17.1%, Seventh Day Adventist 11.7%, United Church 10.1%, Christian Fellowship Church 2.5%), Roman Catholic 19.6%, other Christian 2.9%, other 4%, none 0.03%, unspecified 0.1% (2009 est.)

## AGE STRUCTURE:

0-14 years: 34.05% (male 115,734 /female 109,009)

15-24 years: 19.95% (male 67,794 /female 63,925)

25-54 years: 36.89% (male 123,930 /female 119,577)

55-64 years: 4.77% (male 16,112 /female 15,389)

65 years and over: 4.34% (male 13,515 /female 15,136) (2018 est.)

## DEPENDENCY RATIOS:

total dependency ratio: 75.4 (2015 est.)

youth dependency ratio: 69.4 (2015 est.)

elderly dependency ratio: 6 (2015 est.)

potential support ratio: 16.6 (2015 est.)

## MEDIAN AGE:

total: 22.8 years

male: 22.6 years

female: 23.1 years (2018 est.)

country comparison to the world: 178

## POPULATION GROWTH RATE:

1.9% (2018 est.)

country comparison to the world: 54

## BIRTH RATE:

24.5 births/1,000 population (2018 est.)

country comparison to the world: 51

## DEATH RATE:

3.8 deaths/1,000 population (2018 est.)

country comparison to the world: 213

## NET MIGRATION RATE:

-1.7 migrant(s)/1,000 population (2017 est.)

country comparison to the world: 152

## POPULATION DISTRIBUTION:

most of the population lives along the coastal regions; about one in five live in urban areas, and of these some two-thirds reside in Honiara, the largest town and chief port

## URBANIZATION:

urban population: 23.7% of total population (2018)

rate of urbanization: 3.91% annual rate of change (2015-20 est.)

## MAJOR URBAN AREAS - POPULATION:

82,000 HONIARA (capital) (2018)

## SEX RATIO:

at birth: 1.05 male(s)/female (2017 est.)

0-14 years: 1.06 male(s)/female (2017 est.)

15-24 years: 1.06 male(s)/female (2017 est.)

25-54 years: 1.04 male(s)/female (2017 est.)

55-64 years: 1.02 male(s)/female (2017 est.)

65 years and over: 0.92 male(s)/female (2017 est.)

total population: 1.04 male(s)/female (2017 est.)

## MOTHER'S MEAN AGE AT FIRST BIRTH:

22.6 years (2015 est.)

note: median age at first birth among women 25-29

## MATERNAL MORTALITY RATE:

114 deaths/100,000 live births (2015 est.)

country comparison to the world: 71

## INFANT MORTALITY RATE:

total: 14.3 deaths/1,000 live births (2018 est.)

male: 16.3 deaths/1,000 live births (2018 est.)

female: 12.2 deaths/1,000 live births (2018 est.)

country comparison to the world: 101

## LIFE EXPECTANCY AT BIRTH:

total population: 75.8 years (2018 est.)

male: 73.1 years (2018 est.)

female: 78.6 years (2018 est.)

country comparison to the world: 102

## TOTAL FERTILITY RATE:

3.09 children born/woman (2018 est.)

country comparison to the world: 50

## CONTRACEPTIVE PREVALENCE RATE:

29.3% (2015)

## HEALTH EXPENDITURES:

5.1% of GDP (2014)

country comparison to the world: 138

## PHYSICIANS DENSITY:

0.19 physicians/1,000 population (2013)

## HOSPITAL BED DENSITY:

1.4 beds/1,000 population (2012)

## DRINKING WATER SOURCE:

improved:

urban: 93.2% of population

rural: 77.2% of population

total: 80.8% of population

unimproved:

urban: 6.8% of population

rural: 22.8% of population

total: 19.2% of population (2015 est.)

## SANITATION FACILITY ACCESS:

improved:

urban: 81.4% of population (2015 est.)

rural: 15% of population (2015 est.)

total: 29.8% of population (2015 est.)

unimproved:

urban: 18.6% of population (2015 est.)

rural: 85% of population (2015 est.)

total: 70.2% of population (2015 est.)

## HIV/AIDS - ADULT PREVALENCE RATE:

NA

## HIV/AIDS - PEOPLE LIVING WITH HIV/AIDS:

NA

## HIV/AIDS - DEATHS:

NA

## OBESITY - ADULT PREVALENCE RATE:

22.5% (2016)

country comparison to the world: 76

## CHILDREN UNDER THE AGE OF 5 YEARS UNDERWEIGHT:

15.5% (2015)

**country comparison to the world:** 40

## EDUCATION EXPENDITURES:
10% of GDP (2010)

**country comparison to the world:** 5

## LITERACY:
**definition:** age 15 and over can read and write (2009 est.)

**total population:** 84.1% (2009 est.)

**male:** 88.9% (2009 est.)

**female:** 79.2% (2009 est.)

# GOVERNMENT :: SOLOMON ISLANDS

## COUNTRY NAME:
**conventional long form:** none

**conventional short form:** Solomon Islands

**local long form:** none

**local short form:** Solomon Islands

**former:** British Solomon Islands

**etymology:** Spanish explorer Alvaro de MENDANA named the isles in 1568 after the wealthy biblical King SOLOMON in the mistaken belief that the islands contained great riches

## GOVERNMENT TYPE:
parliamentary democracy (National Parliament) under a constitutional monarchy; a Commonwealth realm

## CAPITAL:
**name:** Honiara

**geographic coordinates:** 9 26 S, 159 57 E

**time difference:** UTC+11 (16 hours ahead of Washington, DC, during Standard Time)

## ADMINISTRATIVE DIVISIONS:
9 provinces and 1 city*; Central, Choiseul, Guadalcanal, Honiara*, Isabel, Makira and Ulawa, Malaita, Rennell and Bellona, Temotu, Western

## INDEPENDENCE:
7 July 1978 (from the UK)

## NATIONAL HOLIDAY:
Independence Day, 7 July (1978)

## CONSTITUTION:
**history:** adopted 31 May 1978, effective 7 July 1978; note - in late 2017, provincial leaders agreed to adopt a new federal constitution, and passage is expected in 2018 (2018)

**amendments:** proposed by the National Parliament; passage of constitutional sections including those on fundamental rights and freedoms, the legal system, Parliament, alteration of the constitution and the ombudsman requires three-fourths majority vote by Parliament and assent to by the governor-general; passage of other amendments requires two-thirds majority vote and assent to by the governor-general; amended several times, last in 2014 (2018)

## LEGAL SYSTEM:
mixed legal system of English common law and customary law

## INTERNATIONAL LAW ORGANIZATION PARTICIPATION:
has not submitted an ICJ jurisdiction declaration; non-party state to the ICCt

## CITIZENSHIP:
**citizenship by birth:** no

**citizenship by descent only:** at least one parent must be a citizen of the Solomon Islands

**dual citizenship recognized:** no

**residency requirement for naturalization:** 7 years

## SUFFRAGE:
21 years of age; universal

## EXECUTIVE BRANCH:
**chief of state:** Queen ELIZABETH II (since 6 February 1952); represented by Governor General Frank KABUI (since 7 July 2009)

**head of government:** Prime Minister Rick HOU (since 16 November 2017)

**cabinet:** Cabinet appointed by the governor general on the advice of the prime minister

**elections/appointments:** the monarchy is hereditary; governor general appointed by the monarch on the advice of the National Parliament for up to 5 years (eligible for a second term); following legislative elections, the leader of the majority party or majority coalition usually elected prime minister by the National Parliament; deputy prime minister appointed by the governor general on the advice of the prime minister from among members of the National Parliament

**election results:** Manasseh SOGAVARE (independent) defeated in no-confidence vote on 6 November 2017; Rick HOU elected prime minister on 15 November 2017

## LEGISLATIVE BRANCH:
**description:** unicameral National Parliament (50 seats; members directly elected in single-seat constituencies by simple majority vote to serve 4-year terms)

**elections:** last held on 19 November 2014 (next to be held in February or March 2019)

**election results:** percent of vote by party - UDP 10.7%, DAP 7.8%, PAP 4.4%, other 20.8%, independent 56.3%; seats by party - DAP 7, UDP 5, PAP 3, KPSI 1, SIPFP 1, SIPRA 1, independent 32; composition - men 49, women 1, percent of women 2%

## JUDICIAL BRANCH:
**highest courts:** Court of Appeal (consists of the court president, and ex officio members to include the High Court chief justice and its puisne judges); High Court (consists of the chief justice and puisne judges as prescribed by the National Parliament)

**judge selection and term of office:** Court of Appeal and High Court president, chief justices, and puisne judges appointed by the governor-general upon recommendation of the Judicial and Legal Service Commission, chaired by the chief justice to include 5 members, mostly judicial officials and legal professionals; all judges appointed until retirement at age 60

**subordinate courts:** Magistrates' Courts; Customary Land Appeal Court; local courts

## POLITICAL PARTIES AND LEADERS:
Democratic Alliance Party or DAP [Steve ABANA]
Kadere Party of Solomon Islands or KPSI [Peter BOYERS]
People's Alliance Party or PAP [Nathaniel WAENA]
Solomon Islands People First Party or SIPFP [Dr. Jimmie RODGERS]
Solomon Islands Party for Rural Advancement or SIPRA [Manasseh MAELANGA]
United Democratic Party or UDP [Sir Thomas Ko CHAN]

**note:** in general, Solomon Islands politics is characterized by fluid coalitions

## INTERNATIONAL ORGANIZATION PARTICIPATION:
ACP, ADB, AOSIS, C, EITI (candidate country), ESCAP, FAO, G-77, IBRD, ICAO, ICRM, IDA, IFAD, IFC, IFRCS, ILO, IMF, IMO, IOC, ITU, MIGA, OPCW, PIF, Sparteca, SPC, UN, UNCTAD, UNESCO, UPU, WFTU, WHO, WMO, WTO

**DIPLOMATIC REPRESENTATION IN THE US:**

chief of mission: Ambassador Robert SISILO (since 21 July 2017)

chancery: 800 Second Avenue, Suite 400L, New York, NY 10017

telephone: [1] (212) 599-6192, 6193

FAX: [1] (212) 661-8925

**DIPLOMATIC REPRESENTATION FROM THE US:**

the US does not have an embassy in the Solomon Islands; the US Ambassador to Papua New Guinea is accredited to the Solomon Islands

**FLAG DESCRIPTION:**

divided diagonally by a thin yellow stripe from the lower hoist-side corner; the upper triangle (hoist side) is blue with five white five-pointed stars arranged in an X pattern; the lower triangle is green; blue represents the ocean, green the land, and yellow sunshine; the five stars stand for the five main island groups of the Solomon Islands

**NATIONAL SYMBOL(S):**

national colors: blue, yellow, green, white

**NATIONAL ANTHEM:**

name: God Save Our Solomon Islands

lyrics/music: Panapasa BALEKANA and Matila BALEKANA/Panapasa BALEKANA

note: adopted 1978

## ECONOMY :: SOLOMON ISLANDS

**ECONOMY - OVERVIEW:**

The bulk of the population depends on agriculture, fishing, and forestry for at least part of its livelihood. Most manufactured goods and petroleum products must be imported. The islands are rich in undeveloped mineral resources such as lead, zinc, nickel, and gold. Prior to the arrival of The Regional Assistance Mission to the Solomon Islands (RAMSI), severe ethnic violence, the closure of key businesses, and an empty government treasury culminated in economic collapse. RAMSI's efforts, which concluded in Jun 2017, to restore law and order and economic stability have led to modest growth as the economy rebuilds.

**GDP (PURCHASING POWER PARITY):**

$1.33 billion (2017 est.)

$1.285 billion (2016 est.)

$1.242 billion (2015 est.)

note: data are in 2017 dollars

country comparison to the world: 200

**GDP (OFFICIAL EXCHANGE RATE):**

$1.298 billion (2017 est.) (2017 est.)

**GDP - REAL GROWTH RATE:**

3.5% (2017 est.)

3.5% (2016 est.)

2.5% (2015 est.)

country comparison to the world: 100

**GDP - PER CAPITA (PPP):**

$2,200 (2017 est.)

$2,100 (2016 est.)

$2,100 (2015 est.)

note: data are in 2017 dollars

country comparison to the world: 207

**GROSS NATIONAL SAVING:**

13.1% of GDP (2017 est.)

15.2% of GDP (2016 est.)

14.5% of GDP (2015 est.)

country comparison to the world: 145

**GDP - COMPOSITION, BY END USE:**

household consumption: NA

government consumption: NA

investment in fixed capital: NA

investment in inventories: NA

exports of goods and services: 25.8% (2011 est.)

imports of goods and services: -49.6% (2011 est.)

**GDP - COMPOSITION, BY SECTOR OF ORIGIN:**

agriculture: 34.3% (2017 est.)

industry: 7.6% (2017 est.)

services: 58.1% (2017 est.)

**AGRICULTURE - PRODUCTS:**

cocoa, coconuts, palm kernels, rice, fruit; cattle, pigs; fish; timber

**INDUSTRIES:**

fish (tuna), mining, timber

**INDUSTRIAL PRODUCTION GROWTH RATE:**

3.6% (2017 est.)

country comparison to the world: 83

**LABOR FORCE:**

202,500 (2007 est.)

country comparison to the world: 171

**LABOR FORCE - BY OCCUPATION:**

agriculture: 75%

industry: 5%

services: 20% (2000 est.)

**UNEMPLOYMENT RATE:**

NA

**POPULATION BELOW POVERTY LINE:**

NA

**HOUSEHOLD INCOME OR CONSUMPTION BY PERCENTAGE SHARE:**

lowest 10%: NA

highest 10%: NA

**BUDGET:**

revenues: 532.5 million (2017 est.)

expenditures: 570.5 million (2017 est.)

**TAXES AND OTHER REVENUES:**

41% (of GDP) (2017 est.)

country comparison to the world: 33

**BUDGET SURPLUS (+) OR DEFICIT (-):**

-2.9% (of GDP) (2017 est.)

country comparison to the world: 130

**PUBLIC DEBT:**

9.4% of GDP (2017 est.)

7.9% of GDP (2016 est.)

country comparison to the world: 198

**FISCAL YEAR:**

calendar year

**INFLATION RATE (CONSUMER PRICES):**

0.5% (2017 est.)

0.5% (2016 est.)

country comparison to the world: 29

**COMMERCIAL BANK PRIME LENDING RATE:**

10.7% (31 December 2017 est.)

10.1% (31 December 2016 est.)

country comparison to the world: 78

**STOCK OF NARROW MONEY:**

$499.8 million (31 December 2017 est.)

$429.5 million (31 December 2016 est.)

country comparison to the world: 170

**STOCK OF BROAD MONEY:**

$499.8 million (31 December 2017 est.)

$429.5 million (31 December 2016 est.)

country comparison to the world: 175

**STOCK OF DOMESTIC CREDIT:**

$152.6 million (31 December 2017 est.)

$149.6 million (31 December 2016 est.)

country comparison to the world: 186
**CURRENT ACCOUNT BALANCE:**

-$54 million (2017 est.)

-$49 million (2016 est.)

country comparison to the world: 81
**EXPORTS:**

$468.6 million (2017 est.)

$419.9 million (2016 est.)

country comparison to the world: 177
**EXPORTS - PARTNERS:**

China 64.5%, Italy 6.2%, Switzerland 4.6%, Philippines 4.4% (2017)

**EXPORTS - COMMODITIES:**

timber, fish, copra, palm oil, cocoa, coconut oil

**IMPORTS:**

$462.1 million (2017 est.)

$419.3 million (2016 est.)

country comparison to the world: 198
**IMPORTS - COMMODITIES:**

food, plant and equipment, manufactured goods, fuels, chemicals

**IMPORTS - PARTNERS:**

China 21.9%, Australia 19.6%, Singapore 10.7%, Vietnam 7.5%, NZ 6.2%, Papua New Guinea 5%, South Korea 4.7% (2017)

**RESERVES OF FOREIGN EXCHANGE AND GOLD:**

$0 (31 December 2017 est.)

$421 million (31 December 2016 est.)

country comparison to the world: 194
**DEBT - EXTERNAL:**

$757 million (31 December 2017 est.)

$643 million (31 December 2016 est.)

country comparison to the world: 172
**STOCK OF DIRECT FOREIGN INVESTMENT - AT HOME:**

$594.8 million (31 December 2017 est.)

$571.2 million (31 December 2016 est.)

country comparison to the world: 126
**STOCK OF DIRECT FOREIGN INVESTMENT - ABROAD:**

$59.2 million (31 December 2017 est.)

$50.1 million (31 December 2016 est.)

country comparison to the world: 114
**EXCHANGE RATES:**

Solomon Islands dollars (SBD) per US dollar -

7.9 (2017 est.)

7.94 (2016 est.)

7.94 (2015 est.)

7.9147 (2014 est.)

7.3754 (2013 est.)

## ENERGY :: SOLOMON ISLANDS

**ELECTRICITY ACCESS:**

population without electricity: 495,321 (2012)

electrification - total population: 23% (2012)

electrification - urban areas: 62% (2012)

electrification - rural areas: 13% (2012)

**ELECTRICITY - PRODUCTION:**

103 million kWh (2016 est.)

country comparison to the world: 200
**ELECTRICITY - CONSUMPTION:**

95.79 million kWh (2016 est.)

country comparison to the world: 202
**ELECTRICITY - EXPORTS:**

0 kWh (2016 est.)

country comparison to the world: 199
**ELECTRICITY - IMPORTS:**

0 kWh (2016 est.)

country comparison to the world: 201
**ELECTRICITY - INSTALLED GENERATING CAPACITY:**

38,000 kW (2016 est.)

country comparison to the world: 198
**ELECTRICITY - FROM FOSSIL FUELS:**

92% of total installed capacity (2016 est.)

country comparison to the world: 52
**ELECTRICITY - FROM NUCLEAR FUELS:**

0% of total installed capacity (2017 est.)

country comparison to the world: 184
**ELECTRICITY - FROM HYDROELECTRIC PLANTS:**

0% of total installed capacity (2017 est.)

country comparison to the world: 201
**ELECTRICITY - FROM OTHER RENEWABLE SOURCES:**

8% of total installed capacity (2017 est.)

country comparison to the world: 90
**CRUDE OIL - PRODUCTION:**

0 bbl/day (2017 est.)

country comparison to the world: 200
**CRUDE OIL - EXPORTS:**

0 bbl/day (2015 est.)

country comparison to the world: 195
**CRUDE OIL - IMPORTS:**

0 bbl/day (2015 est.)

country comparison to the world: 197
**CRUDE OIL - PROVED RESERVES:**

0 bbl (1 January 2018 est.)

country comparison to the world: 197
**REFINED PETROLEUM PRODUCTS - PRODUCTION:**

0 bbl/day (2015 est.)

country comparison to the world: 203
**REFINED PETROLEUM PRODUCTS - CONSUMPTION:**

1,600 bbl/day (2016 est.)

country comparison to the world: 199
**REFINED PETROLEUM PRODUCTS - EXPORTS:**

0 bbl/day (2015 est.)

country comparison to the world: 203
**REFINED PETROLEUM PRODUCTS - IMPORTS:**

1,577 bbl/day (2015 est.)

country comparison to the world: 195
**NATURAL GAS - PRODUCTION:**

0 cu m (2017 est.)

country comparison to the world: 197
**NATURAL GAS - CONSUMPTION:**

0 cu m (2017 est.)

country comparison to the world: 198
**NATURAL GAS - EXPORTS:**

0 cu m (2017 est.)

country comparison to the world: 185
**NATURAL GAS - IMPORTS:**

0 cu m (2017 est.)

country comparison to the world: 189
**NATURAL GAS - PROVED RESERVES:**

0 cu m (1 January 2014 est.)

country comparison to the world: 195
**CARBON DIOXIDE EMISSIONS FROM CONSUMPTION OF ENERGY:**

233,500 Mt (2017 est.)

country comparison to the world: 196

# COMMUNICATIONS :: SOLOMON ISLANDS

**TELEPHONES - FIXED LINES:**

total subscriptions: 7,405 (2017 est.)

subscriptions per 100 inhabitants: 1 (2017 est.)

country comparison to the world: 200

**TELEPHONES - MOBILE CELLULAR:**

total subscriptions: 465,331 (2017 est.)

subscriptions per 100 inhabitants: 72 (2017 est.)

country comparison to the world: 172

**TELEPHONE SYSTEM:**

domestic: mobile-cellular telephone density is about 65 per 100 persons (2016)

international: country code - 677; satellite earth station - 1 Intelsat (Pacific Ocean) (2016)

**BROADCAST MEDIA:**

Solomon Islands Broadcasting Corporation (SIBC) does not broadcast television; multi-channel pay-TV is available; SIBC operates 2 national radio stations and 2 provincial stations; there are 2 local commercial radio stations; Radio Australia is available via satellite feed (since 2009) (2018)

**INTERNET COUNTRY CODE:**

.sb

**INTERNET USERS:**

total: 69,859 (July 2016 est.)

percent of population: 11% (July 2016 est.)

country comparison to the world: 180

**BROADBAND - FIXED SUBSCRIPTIONS:**

total: 1,166 (2017 est.)

subscriptions per 100 inhabitants: less than 1 (2017 est.)

country comparison to the world: 189

# TRANSPORTATION :: SOLOMON ISLANDS

**NATIONAL AIR TRANSPORT SYSTEM:**

number of registered air carriers: 1 (2015)

inventory of registered aircraft operated by air carriers: 3 (2015)

annual passenger traffic on registered air carriers: 373,738 (2015)

annual freight traffic on registered air carriers: 3,691,584 mt-km (2015)

**CIVIL AIRCRAFT REGISTRATION COUNTRY CODE PREFIX:**

H4 (2016)

**AIRPORTS:**

36 (2013)

country comparison to the world: 110

**AIRPORTS - WITH PAVED RUNWAYS:**

total: 1 (2013)

1,524 to 2,437 m: 1 (2013)

**AIRPORTS - WITH UNPAVED RUNWAYS:**

total: 35 (2013)

1,524 to 2,437 m: 1 (2013)

914 to 1,523 m: 10 (2013)

under 914 m: 24 (2013)

**HELIPORTS:**

3 (2013)

**ROADWAYS:**

total: 1,390 km (2011)

paved: 34 km (2011)

unpaved: 1,356 km (2011)

note: includes 920 km of private plantation roads

country comparison to the world: 178

**MERCHANT MARINE:**

total: 22 (2017)

by type: general cargo 6, other 16 (2017)

country comparison to the world: 136

**PORTS AND TERMINALS:**

major seaport(s): Honiara, Malloco Bay, Viru Harbor, Tulaghi

# MILITARY AND SECURITY :: SOLOMON ISLANDS

**MILITARY BRANCHES:**

no regular military forces; Royal Solomon Islands Police Force (2013)

# TRANSNATIONAL ISSUES :: SOLOMON ISLANDS

**DISPUTES - INTERNATIONAL:**

from 2003 to 2017, the Regional Assistance Mission to Solomon Islands, consisting of police, military, and civilian advisors drawn from 15 countries, assisted in reestablishing and maintaining civil and political order while reinforcing regional stability and security

**TRAFFICKING IN PERSONS:**

current situation: the Solomon Islands is a source and destination country for local adults and children and Southeast Asian men and women subjected to forced labor and forced prostitution; women from China, Indonesia, Malaysia, and the Philippines are recruited for legitimate work and upon arrival are forced into prostitution; men from Indonesia and Malaysia recruited to work in the Solomon Islands' mining and logging industries may be subjected to forced labor; local children are forced into prostitution near foreign logging camps, on fishing vessels, at hotels, and entertainment venues; some local children are also sold by their parents for marriage to foreign workers or put up for "informal adoption" to pay off debts and then find themselves forced into domestic servitude or forced prostitution

tier rating: Tier 2 Watch List – the Solomon Islands does not fully comply with the minimum standards for the elimination of trafficking; however, it is making significant efforts to do so; in 2014, the Solomon Islands was granted a waiver from an otherwise required downgrade to Tier 3 because its government has a written plan that, if implemented, would constitute making significant efforts to bring itself into compliance with the minimum standards for the elimination of trafficking; the government gazetted implementing regulations for the 2012 immigration act prohibiting transnational trafficking, but the penalties are not sufficiently stringent because they allow the option of paying a fine; a new draft law to address these weaknesses awaits parliamentary review; no new trafficking investigations were conducted, even after labor inspections at logging and fishing companies, no existing cases led to prosecutions or convictions, and no funding was allocated for national anti-trafficking efforts; authorities did not identify or protect any victims and lack any procedures or shelters to do so; civil society and religious organizations provide most of the limited services available; a lack of understanding of the crime of trafficking remains a serious challenge (2015)

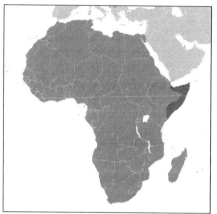

# AFRICA :: SOMALIA

## INTRODUCTION :: SOMALIA

### BACKGROUND:

Britain withdrew from British Somaliland in 1960 to allow its protectorate to join with Italian Somaliland and form the new nation of Somalia. In 1969, a coup headed by Mohamed SIAD Barre ushered in an authoritarian socialist rule characterized by the persecution, jailing, and torture of political opponents and dissidents. After the regime's collapse early in 1991, Somalia descended into turmoil, factional fighting, and anarchy. In May 1991, northern clans declared an independent Republic of Somaliland that now includes the administrative regions of Awdal, Woqooyi Galbeed, Togdheer, Sanaag, and Sool. Although not recognized by any government, this entity has maintained a stable existence and continues efforts to establish a constitutional democracy, including holding municipal, parliamentary, and presidential elections. The regions of Bari, Nugaal, and northern Mudug comprise a neighboring semi-autonomous state of Puntland, which has been self-governing since 1998 but does not aim at independence; it has also made strides toward reconstructing a legitimate, representative government but has suffered some civil strife. Puntland disputes its border with Somaliland as it also claims the regions of Sool and Sanaag, and portions of Togdheer. Beginning in 1993, a two-year UN humanitarian effort (primarily in south-central Somalia) was able to alleviate famine conditions, but when the UN withdrew in 1995, having suffered significant casualties, order still had not been restored.

In 2000, the Somalia National Peace Conference (SNPC) held in Djibouti resulted in the formation of an interim government, known as the Transitional National Government (TNG). When the TNG failed to establish adequate security or governing institutions, the Government of Kenya, under the auspices of the Intergovernmental Authority on Development (IGAD), led a subsequent peace process that concluded in October 2004 with the election of Abdullahi YUSUF Ahmed as President of a second interim government, known as the Transitional Federal Government (TFG) of the Somali Republic. The TFG included a 275-member parliamentary body, known as the Transitional Federal Parliament (TFP). President YUSUF resigned late in 2008 while UN-sponsored talks between the TFG and the opposition Alliance for the Re-Liberation of Somalia (ARS) were underway in Djibouti. In January 2009, following the creation of a TFG-ARS unity government, Ethiopian military forces, which had entered Somalia in December 2006 to support the TFG in the face of advances by the opposition Islamic Courts Union (ICU), withdrew from the country. The TFP was doubled in size to 550 seats with the addition of 200 ARS and 75 civil society members of parliament. The expanded parliament elected Sheikh SHARIF Sheikh Ahmed, the former ICU and ARS chairman as president in January 2009. The creation of the TFG was based on the Transitional Federal Charter (TFC), which outlined a five-year mandate leading to the establishment of a new Somali constitution and a transition to a representative government following national elections. In 2009, the TFP amended the TFC to extend TFG's mandate until 2011 and in 2011 Somali principals agreed to institute political transition by August 2012. The transition process ended in September 2012 when clan elders replaced the TFP by appointing 275 members to a new parliament who subsequently elected a new president.

## GEOGRAPHY :: SOMALIA

### LOCATION:
Eastern Africa, bordering the Gulf of Aden and the Indian Ocean, east of Ethiopia

### GEOGRAPHIC COORDINATES:
10 00 N, 49 00 E

### MAP REFERENCES:
Africa

### AREA:
total: 637,657 sq km

land: 627,337 sq km

water: 10,320 sq km

country comparison to the world: 45

### AREA - COMPARATIVE:
almost five times the size of Alabama; slightly smaller than Texas

### LAND BOUNDARIES:
total: 2,385 km

border countries (3): Djibouti 61 km, Ethiopia 1640 km, Kenya 684 km

### COASTLINE:
3,025 km

### MARITIME CLAIMS:
territorial sea: 200 nm

## CLIMATE:

principally desert; northeast monsoon (December to February), moderate temperatures in north and hot in south; southwest monsoon (May to October), torrid in the north and hot in the south, irregular rainfall, hot and humid periods (tangambili) between monsoons

## TERRAIN:

mostly flat to undulating plateau rising to hills in north

## ELEVATION:

mean elevation: 410 m

elevation extremes: 0 m lowest point: Indian Ocean

2416 highest point: Shimbiris

## NATURAL RESOURCES:

uranium and largely unexploited reserves of iron ore, tin, gypsum, bauxite, copper, salt, natural gas, likely oil reserves

## LAND USE:

agricultural land: 70.3% (2011 est.)

arable land: 1.8% (2011 est.) / permanent crops: 0% (2011 est.) / permanent pasture: 68.5% (2011 est.)

forest: 10.6% (2011 est.)

other: 19.1% (2011 est.)

## IRRIGATED LAND:

2,000 sq km (2012)

## POPULATION DISTRIBUTION:

distribution varies greatly throughout the country; least densely populated areas are in the northeast and central regions, as well as areas along the Kenyan border; most populated areas are in and around the cities of Mogadishu, Marka, Boorama, Hargeysa, and Baidoa

## NATURAL HAZARDS:

recurring droughts; frequent dust storms over eastern plains in summer; floods during rainy season

## ENVIRONMENT - CURRENT ISSUES:

water scarcity; contaminated water contributes to human health problems; improper waste disposal; deforestation; land degradation; overgrazing; soil erosion; desertification

## ENVIRONMENT - INTERNATIONAL AGREEMENTS:

party to: Biodiversity, Desertification, Endangered Species, Hazardous Wastes, Law of the Sea, Ozone Layer Protection

signed, but not ratified: none of the selected agreements

## GEOGRAPHY - NOTE:

strategic location on Horn of Africa along southern approaches to Bab el Mandeb and route through Red Sea and Suez Canal

# PEOPLE AND SOCIETY :: SOMALIA

## POPULATION:

11,259,029 (July 2018 est.)

note: this estimate was derived from an official census taken in 1975 by the Somali Government; population counting in Somalia is complicated by the large number of nomads and by refugee movements in response to famine and clan warfare

country comparison to the world: 81

## NATIONALITY:

noun: Somali(s)

adjective: Somali

## ETHNIC GROUPS:

Somali 85%, Bantu and other non-Somali 15% (including 30,000 Arabs)

## LANGUAGES:

Somali (official, according to the 2012 Transitional Federal Charter), Arabic (official, according to the 2012 Transitional Federal Charter), Italian, English

## RELIGIONS:

Sunni Muslim (Islam) (official, according to the 2012 Transitional Federal Charter)

## DEMOGRAPHIC PROFILE:

Somalia scores very low for most humanitarian indicators, suffering from poor governance, protracted internal conflict, underdevelopment, economic decline, poverty, social and gender inequality, and environmental degradation. Despite civil war and famine raising its mortality rate, Somalia's high fertility rate and large proportion of people of reproductive age maintain rapid population growth, with each generation being larger than the prior one. More than 60% of Somalia's population is younger than 25, and the fertility rate is among the world's highest at almost 6 children per woman – a rate that has decreased little since the 1970s.

A lack of educational and job opportunities is a major source of tension for Somalia's large youth cohort, making them vulnerable to recruitment by extremist and pirate groups. Somalia has one of the world's lowest primary school enrollment rates – just over 40% of children are in school – and one of world's highest youth unemployment rates. Life expectancy is low as a result of high infant and maternal mortality rates, the spread of preventable diseases, poor sanitation, chronic malnutrition, and inadequate health services.

During the two decades of conflict that followed the fall of the SIAD regime in 1991, hundreds of thousands of Somalis fled their homes. Today Somalia is the world's third highest source country for refugees, after Syria and Afghanistan. Insecurity, drought, floods, food shortages, and a lack of economic opportunities are the driving factors.

As of 2016, more than 1.1 million Somali refugees were hosted in the region, mainly in Kenya, Yemen, Egypt, Ethiopia, Djibouti, and Uganda, while more than 1.1 million Somalis were internally displaced. Since the implementation of a tripartite voluntary repatriation agreement among Kenya, Somalia, and the UNHCR in 2013, nearly 40,000 Somali refugees have returned home from Kenya's Dadaab refugee camp – still houses to approximately 260,000 Somalis. The flow sped up rapidly after the Kenyan Government in May 2016 announced its intention to close the camp, worsening security and humanitarian conditions in receiving communities in south-central Somalia. Despite the conflict in Yemen, thousands of Somalis and other refugees and asylum seekers from the Horn of Africa risk their lives crossing the Gulf of Aden to reach Yemen and beyond (often Saudi Arabia). Bossaso in Puntland overtook Obock, Djibouti, as the primary departure point in mid-2014.

## AGE STRUCTURE:

0-14 years: 42.87% (male 2,410,215 /female 2,416,629)

15-24 years: 19.35% (male 1,097,358 /female 1,081,762)

25-54 years: 31.23% (male 1,821,823 /female 1,694,873)

55-64 years: 4.35% (male 245,744 /female 243,893)

65 years and over: 2.19% (male 95,845 /female 150,887) (2018 est.)

## DEPENDENCY RATIOS:

total dependency ratio: 97.4 (2015 est.)

youth dependency ratio: 92.1 (2015 est.)

elderly dependency ratio: 5.3 (2015 est.)

potential support ratio: 18.8 (2015 est.)

### MEDIAN AGE:

total: 18.2 years

male: 18.4 years

female: 18 years (2018 est.)

country comparison to the world: 211

### POPULATION GROWTH RATE:

2.08% (2018 est.)

country comparison to the world: 45

### BIRTH RATE:

39.3 births/1,000 population (2018 est.)

country comparison to the world: 9

### DEATH RATE:

12.8 deaths/1,000 population (2018 est.)

country comparison to the world: 13

### NET MIGRATION RATE:

-6.5 migrant(s)/1,000 population (2017 est.)

country comparison to the world: 201

### POPULATION DISTRIBUTION:

distribution varies greatly throughout the country; least densely populated areas are in the northeast and central regions, as well as areas along the Kenyan border; most populated areas are in and around the cities of Mogadishu, Marka, Boorama, Hargeysa, and Baidoa

### URBANIZATION:

urban population: 45% of total population (2018)

rate of urbanization: 4.23% annual rate of change (2015-20 est.)

### MAJOR URBAN AREAS - POPULATION:

2.082 million MOGADISHU (capital) (2018)

### SEX RATIO:

at birth: 1.02 male(s)/female (2017 est.)

0-14 years: 1 male(s)/female (2017 est.)

15-24 years: 1.02 male(s)/female (2017 est.)

25-54 years: 1.07 male(s)/female (2017 est.)

55-64 years: 0.96 male(s)/female (2017 est.)

65 years and over: 0.64 male(s)/female (2017 est.)

total population: 1.01 male(s)/female (2017 est.)

### MATERNAL MORTALITY RATE:

732 deaths/100,000 live births (2015 est.)

country comparison to the world: 6

### INFANT MORTALITY RATE:

total: 93 deaths/1,000 live births (2018 est.)

male: 101.4 deaths/1,000 live births (2018 est.)

female: 84.3 deaths/1,000 live births (2018 est.)

country comparison to the world: 2

### LIFE EXPECTANCY AT BIRTH:

total population: 53.2 years (2018 est.)

male: 51 years (2018 est.)

female: 55.4 years (2018 est.)

country comparison to the world: 220

### TOTAL FERTILITY RATE:

5.7 children born/woman (2018 est.)

country comparison to the world: 6

### PHYSICIANS DENSITY:

0.03 physicians/1,000 population (2014)

### HOSPITAL BED DENSITY:

8.7 beds/1,000 population (2014)

### DRINKING WATER SOURCE:

improved:

urban: 69.6% of population (2011 est.)

rural: 8.8% of population (2011 est.)

total: 31.7% of population (2011 est.)

unimproved:

urban: 30.4% of population (2011 est.)

rural: 91.2% of population (2011 est.)

total: 68.3% of population (2011 est.)

### SANITATION FACILITY ACCESS:

improved:

urban: 52% of population (2011 est.)

rural: 6.3% of population (2011 est.)

total: 23.6% of population (2011 est.)

unimproved:

urban: 48% of population (2011 est.)

rural: 93.7% of population (2011 est.)

total: 76.4% of population (2011 est.)

### HIV/AIDS - ADULT PREVALENCE RATE:

0.1% (2017 est.)

country comparison to the world: 120

### HIV/AIDS - PEOPLE LIVING WITH HIV/AIDS:

11,000 (2017 est.)

country comparison to the world: 97

### HIV/AIDS - DEATHS:

<1000 (2017 est.)

### MAJOR INFECTIOUS DISEASES:

degree of risk: very high (2016)

food or waterborne diseases: bacterial and protozoal diarrhea, hepatitis A and E, and typhoid fever (2016)

vectorborne diseases: dengue fever, malaria, and Rift Valley fever (2016)

water contact diseases: schistosomiasis (2016)

animal contact diseases: rabies (2016)

### OBESITY - ADULT PREVALENCE RATE:

8.3% (2016)

country comparison to the world: 153

### CHILDREN UNDER THE AGE OF 5 YEARS UNDERWEIGHT:

23% (2009)

country comparison to the world: 23

### EDUCATION EXPENDITURES:

NA

## GOVERNMENT :: SOMALIA

### COUNTRY NAME:

conventional long form: Federal Republic of Somalia

conventional short form: Somalia

local long form: Jamhuuriyadda Federaalkaa Soomaaliya

local short form: Soomaaliya

former: Somali Republic, Somali Democratic Republic

etymology: "Land of the Somali" (ethnic group)

### GOVERNMENT TYPE:

federal parliamentary republic

### CAPITAL:

name: Mogadishu

geographic coordinates: 2 04 N, 45 20 E

**time difference:** UTC+3 (8 hours ahead of Washington, DC, during Standard Time)

## ADMINISTRATIVE DIVISIONS:

18 regions (plural - NA, singular - gobolka); Awdal, Bakool, Banaadir, Bari, Bay, Galguduud, Gedo, Hiiraan, Jubbada Dhexe (Middle Jubba), Jubbada Hoose (Lower Jubba), Mudug, Nugaal, Sanaag, Shabeellaha Dhexe (Middle Shabeelle), Shabeellaha Hoose (Lower Shabeelle), Sool, Togdheer, Woqooyi Galbeed

## INDEPENDENCE:

1 July 1960 (from a merger of British Somaliland that became independent from the UK on 26 June 1960 and Italian Somaliland that became independent from the Italian-administered UN trusteeship on 1 July 1960 to form the Somali Republic)

## NATIONAL HOLIDAY:

Foundation of the Somali Republic, 1 July (1960)note - 26 June (1960) in Somaliland

## CONSTITUTION:

**history:** previous 1961, 1979; latest drafted 12 June 2012, approved 1 August 2012 (provisional) (2017)

**amendments:** proposed by the federal government, by members of the state governments, the Federal Parliament, or by public petition; proposals require review by a joint committee of Parliament with inclusion of public comments and state legislatures' comments; passage requires at least two-thirds majority vote in both houses of Parliament and approval by a majority of votes cast in a referendum; constitutional clauses on Islamic principles, the federal system, human rights and freedoms, powers and authorities of the government branches, and inclusion of women in national institutions cannot be amended (2017)

## LEGAL SYSTEM:

mixed legal system of civil law, Islamic law, and customary law (referred to as Xeer)

## INTERNATIONAL LAW ORGANIZATION PARTICIPATION:

accepts compulsory ICJ jurisdiction with reservations; non-party state to the ICCt

## CITIZENSHIP:

**citizenship by birth:** no

**citizenship by descent only:** the father must be a citizen of Somalia

**dual citizenship recognized:** no

**residency requirement for naturalization:** 7 years

## SUFFRAGE:

18 years of age; universal

## EXECUTIVE BRANCH:

**chief of state:** President Mohamed ABDULLAHI Mohamed "Farmaajo" (since 8 February 2017)

**head of government:** Prime Minister Hassan Ali KHAYRE (since 1 March 2017)

**cabinet:** Cabinet appointed by the prime minister, approved by the House of the People

**elections/appointments:** president indirectly elected by the Federal Parliament by two-thirds majority vote in 2 rounds if needed for a single 4-year term; election last held on 8 February 2017 (previously scheduled for 30 September 2016 but postponed repeatedly); prime minister appointed by the president, approved by the House of the People

**election results:** Mohamed ABDULLAHI Mohamed "Farmaajo" elected president in second round; Federal Parliament second round vote - Mohamed ABDULLAHI Mohamed "Farmaajo" (TPP) 184, HASSAN SHEIKH Mohamud (PDP) 97, Sheikh SHARIF Sheikh Ahmed (ARS) 46

## LEGISLATIVE BRANCH:

**description:** bicameral Federal Parliament to consist of:
Upper House (54 seats; senators indirectly elected by state assemblies to serve 4-year terms)
House of the People (275 seats; members indirectly elected by regional delegates to serve 4-year terms)

**elections:**
Upper House - first held 10 October 2016 (next NA)
House of the People - first held 23 October - 10 November 2016 (next NA)

**election results:**
Upper House - NA
House of the People - NA

**note:** the inaugural House of the People was appointed in September 2012 by clan elders; in 2016 and 2017, the Federal Parliament became bicameral with elections scheduled for 10 October 2016 for the Upper House and 23 October to 10 November 2016 for the House of the People; while the elections were delayed, they were eventually held in most regions despite voting irregularities; on 27 December 2016, 41 Upper House senators and 242 House of the People members were sworn in

## JUDICIAL BRANCH:

**highest courts:** the provisional constitution stipulates the establishment of the Constitutional Court (consists of 5 judges including the chief judge and deputy chief judge); note - under the terms of the 2004 Transitional National Charter, a Supreme Court based in Mogadishu and an Appeal Court were established; yet most regions have reverted to local forms of conflict resolution, either secular, traditional Somali customary law, or sharia Islamic law

**judge selection and term of office:** judges appointed by the president upon proposal of the Judicial Service Commission, a 9-member judicial and administrative body; judge tenure NA

**subordinate courts:** federal courts; federal member state-level courts; military courts; sharia courts

## POLITICAL PARTIES AND LEADERS:

Cosmopolitan Democratic Party [Yarow Sharef ADEN]
Daljir Party or DP [Hassan MOALIM]
Democratic Green Party of Somalia or DGPS [Abdullahi Y. MAHAMOUD]
Democratic Party of Somalia or DPS [Maslah Mohamed SIAD]
Green Leaf for Democracy or GLED
Hiil Qaran
Justice and Communist Party [Mohamed NUR]
Justice and Development of Democracy and Self-Respectfulness Party or CAHDI [Abdirahman Abdigani IBRAHIM Bile]
Liberal Party of Somalia
National Unity Party (Xisbiga MIdnimo-Quaran) [Abdurahman BAADIYOW]
Peace and Development Party or PDP
Somali National Party or SNP [Mohammed Ameen Saeed AHMED]
Somali People's Party [Mahamud Hassan RAGE]
Somali Green Party (local chapter of Federation of Green Parties of Africa)
Tayo or TPP [Mohamed Abdullahi MOHAMED]
Tiir Party [Fadhil Sheik MOHAMUD]
United and Democratic Party [Salad Ali JELLE]
United Somali Parliamentarians
**inactive:** Alliance for the Reliberation of Somalia; reportedly inactive since 2009

## INTERNATIONAL ORGANIZATION PARTICIPATION:

ACP, AfDB, AFESD, AMF, AU, CAEU (candidate), FAO, G-77, IBRD, ICAO, ICRM, IDA, IDB, IFAD, IFC, IFRCS, IGAD, ILO, IMF, IMO, Interpol, IOC, IOM, IPU, ITSO, ITU, LAS, NAM, OIC, OPCW, OPCW (signatory), UN, UNCTAD, UNESCO, UNHCR, UNIDO, UPU, WFTU (NGOs), WHO, WIPO, WMO

## DIPLOMATIC REPRESENTATION IN THE US:

chief of mission: Ambassador (vacant); Charge d'Affaires Run Said KORSHEL (since 16 February 2018)

chancery: 425 East 61st Street, Suite 702, New York City, NY 10021

telephone: [1] (212) 688-9410, 688-5046

FAX: [1] (212) 759-0651

## DIPLOMATIC REPRESENTATION FROM THE US:

Ambassador Donald Y. YAMAMOTO (since 18 November 2018)

Note: the US Mission to Somalia operates out of the US Embassy in Nairobi, Kenya

## FLAG DESCRIPTION:

light blue with a large white five-pointed star in the center; the blue field was originally influenced by the flag of the UN but today is said to denote the sky and the neighboring Indian Ocean; the five points of the star represent the five regions in the horn of Africa that are inhabited by Somali people: the former British Somaliland and Italian Somaliland (which together make up Somalia), Djibouti, Ogaden (Ethiopia), and the North East Province (Kenya)

## NATIONAL SYMBOL(S):

leopard; national colors: blue, white

## NATIONAL ANTHEM:

name: "Qolobaa Calankeed" (Every Nation Has its own Flag)

lyrics/music: lyrics/music: Abdullahi QARSHE

note: adopted 2012; written in 1959

## GOVERNMENT - NOTE:

regional and local governing bodies continue to exist and control various areas of the country, including the self-declared Republic of Somaliland in northwestern Somalia

# ECONOMY :: SOMALIA

## ECONOMY - OVERVIEW:

Despite the lack of effective national governance, Somalia maintains an informal economy largely based on livestock, remittance/money transfer companies, and telecommunications. Somalia's government lacks the ability to collect domestic revenue and external debt – mostly in arrears – was estimated at about 77% of GDP in 2017.

Agriculture is the most important sector, with livestock normally accounting for about 40% of GDP and more than 50% of export earnings. Nomads and semi-pastoralists, who are dependent upon livestock for their livelihood, make up a large portion of the population. Economic activity is estimated to have increased by 2.4% in 2017 because of growth in the agriculture, construction and telecommunications sector. Somalia's small industrial sector, based on the processing of agricultural products, has largely been looted and the machinery sold as scrap metal.

In recent years, Somalia's capital city, Mogadishu, has witnessed the development of the city's first gas stations, supermarkets, and airline flights to Turkey since the collapse of central authority in 1991. Mogadishu's main market offers a variety of goods from food to electronic gadgets. Hotels continue to operate and are supported with private-security militias. Formalized economic growth has yet to expand outside of Mogadishu and a few regional capitals, and within the city, security concerns dominate business. Telecommunication firms provide wireless services in most major cities and offer the lowest international call rates on the continent. In the absence of a formal banking sector, money transfer/remittance services have sprouted throughout the country, handling up to $1.6 billion in remittances annually, although international concerns over the money transfers into Somalia continues to threaten these services' ability to operate in Western nations. In 2017, Somalia elected a new president and collected a record amount of foreign aid and investment, a positive sign for economic recovery.

## GDP (PURCHASING POWER PARITY):

$20.44 billion (2017 est.)

$19.98 billion (2016 est.)

$19.14 billion (2015 est.)

note: data are in 2016 US dollars

country comparison to the world: 148

## GDP (OFFICIAL EXCHANGE RATE):

$7.052 billion (2017 est.) (2017 est.)

## GDP - REAL GROWTH RATE:

2.3% (2017 est.)

4.4% (2016 est.)

3.9% (2015 est.)

country comparison to the world: 143

## GDP - PER CAPITA (PPP):

$NA (2017)

$NA (2016)

$NA (2015)

## GDP - COMPOSITION, BY END USE:

household consumption: 72.6% (2015 est.)

government consumption: 8.7% (2015 est.)

investment in fixed capital: 20% (2015 est.)

investment in inventories: 0.8% (2016 est.)

exports of goods and services: 0.3% (2015 est.)

imports of goods and services: -1.6% (2015 est.)

## GDP - COMPOSITION, BY SECTOR OF ORIGIN:

agriculture: 60.2% (2013 est.)

industry: 7.4% (2013 est.)

services: 32.5% (2013 est.)

## AGRICULTURE - PRODUCTS:

bananas, sorghum, corn, coconuts, rice, sugarcane, mangoes, sesame seeds, beans; cattle, sheep, goats; fish

## INDUSTRIES:

light industries, including sugar refining, textiles, wireless communication

## INDUSTRIAL PRODUCTION GROWTH RATE:

3.5% (2014 est.)

country comparison to the world: 90

## LABOR FORCE:

4.154 million (2016 est.)

country comparison to the world: 91

## LABOR FORCE - BY OCCUPATION:

agriculture: 71%

industry: 29%

industry and services: 29% (1975)

## UNEMPLOYMENT RATE:

NA

**POPULATION BELOW POVERTY LINE:**

NA

**HOUSEHOLD INCOME OR CONSUMPTION BY PERCENTAGE SHARE:**

lowest 10%: NA

highest 10%: NA

**BUDGET:**

revenues: 145.3 million (2014 est.)

expenditures: 151.1 million (2014 est.)

**TAXES AND OTHER REVENUES:**

2.1% (of GDP) (2014 est.)

country comparison to the world: 221

**BUDGET SURPLUS (+) OR DEFICIT (-):**

-0.1% (of GDP) (2014 est.)

country comparison to the world: 49

**PUBLIC DEBT:**

76.7% of GDP (2017 est.)

93% of GDP (2014 est.)

country comparison to the world: 39

**FISCAL YEAR:**

NA

**INFLATION RATE (CONSUMER PRICES):**

1.5% (2017 est.)

-71.1% (2016 est.)

country comparison to the world: 86

**CENTRAL BANK DISCOUNT RATE:**

NA

**COMMERCIAL BANK PRIME LENDING RATE:**

NA

**CURRENT ACCOUNT BALANCE:**

-$464 million (2017 est.)

-$427 million (2016 est.)

country comparison to the world: 116

**EXPORTS:**

$819 million (2014 est.)

$779 million (2013 est.)

country comparison to the world: 168

**EXPORTS - PARTNERS:**

Oman 31.7%, Saudi Arabia 18.7%, UAE 16.3%, Nigeria 5.1%, Yemen 4.8%, Pakistan 4% (2017)

**EXPORTS - COMMODITIES:**

livestock, bananas, hides, fish, charcoal, scrap metal

**IMPORTS:**

$94.43 billion (2018 est.)

$80.07 billion (2017 est.)

country comparison to the world: 38

**IMPORTS - COMMODITIES:**

manufactures, petroleum products, foodstuffs, construction materials, qat

**IMPORTS - PARTNERS:**

China 17.6%, India 17.2%, Ethiopia 10.5%, Oman 10.3%, Kenya 6.9%, Turkey 5.3%, Malaysia 4.1% (2017)

**RESERVES OF FOREIGN EXCHANGE AND GOLD:**

$30.45 million (2014 est.)

country comparison to the world: 189

**DEBT - EXTERNAL:**

$5.3 billion (31 December 2014 est.)

country comparison to the world: 131

**STOCK OF DIRECT FOREIGN INVESTMENT - AT HOME:**

NA

**EXCHANGE RATES:**

Somali shillings (SOS) per US dollar - 23,960 (2016 est.)

## ENERGY :: SOMALIA

**ELECTRICITY ACCESS:**

population without electricity: 8.9 million (2013)

electrification - total population: 15% (2013)

electrification - urban areas: 33% (2013)

electrification - rural areas: 4% (2013)

**ELECTRICITY - PRODUCTION:**

339 million kWh (2016 est.)

country comparison to the world: 176

**ELECTRICITY - CONSUMPTION:**

315.3 million kWh (2016 est.)

country comparison to the world: 183

**ELECTRICITY - EXPORTS:**

0 kWh (2016 est.)

country comparison to the world: 200

**ELECTRICITY - IMPORTS:**

0 kWh (2016 est.)

country comparison to the world: 202

**ELECTRICITY - INSTALLED GENERATING CAPACITY:**

85,000 kW (2016 est.)

country comparison to the world: 182

**ELECTRICITY - FROM FOSSIL FUELS:**

93% of total installed capacity (2016 est.)

country comparison to the world: 51

**ELECTRICITY - FROM NUCLEAR FUELS:**

0% of total installed capacity (2017 est.)

country comparison to the world: 185

**ELECTRICITY - FROM HYDROELECTRIC PLANTS:**

0% of total installed capacity (2017 est.)

country comparison to the world: 202

**ELECTRICITY - FROM OTHER RENEWABLE SOURCES:**

7% of total installed capacity (2017 est.)

country comparison to the world: 97

**CRUDE OIL - PRODUCTION:**

0 bbl/day (2017 est.)

country comparison to the world: 201

**CRUDE OIL - EXPORTS:**

0 bbl/day (2015 est.)

country comparison to the world: 196

**CRUDE OIL - IMPORTS:**

0 bbl/day (2015 est.)

country comparison to the world: 198

**CRUDE OIL - PROVED RESERVES:**

0 bbl (1 January 2018 est.)

country comparison to the world: 198

**REFINED PETROLEUM PRODUCTS - PRODUCTION:**

0 bbl/day (2015 est.)

country comparison to the world: 204

**REFINED PETROLEUM PRODUCTS - CONSUMPTION:**

5,600 bbl/day (2016 est.)

country comparison to the world: 174

**REFINED PETROLEUM PRODUCTS - EXPORTS:**

0 bbl/day (2015 est.)

country comparison to the world: 204

**REFINED PETROLEUM PRODUCTS - IMPORTS:**

5,590 bbl/day (2015 est.)

country comparison to the world: 167

**NATURAL GAS - PRODUCTION:**

0 cu m (2017 est.)

country comparison to the world: 198

**NATURAL GAS - CONSUMPTION:**

0 cu m (2017 est.)

country comparison to the world: 199

**NATURAL GAS - EXPORTS:**

0 cu m (2017 est.)

country comparison to the world: 186

**NATURAL GAS - IMPORTS:**

0 cu m (2017 est.)

country comparison to the world: 190

**NATURAL GAS - PROVED RESERVES:**

5.663 billion cu m (1 January 2018 est.)

country comparison to the world: 90

**CARBON DIOXIDE EMISSIONS FROM CONSUMPTION OF ENERGY:**

852,500 Mt (2017 est.)

country comparison to the world: 173

## COMMUNICATIONS :: SOMALIA

**TELEPHONES - FIXED LINES:**

total subscriptions: 48,000 (July 2016 est.)

subscriptions per 100 inhabitants: less than 1 (July 2016 est.)

country comparison to the world: 158

**TELEPHONES - MOBILE CELLULAR:**

total subscriptions: 6,653,040 (July 2016 est.)

subscriptions per 100 inhabitants: 60 (July 2016 est.)

country comparison to the world: 108

**TELEPHONE SYSTEM:**

general assessment: the public telecom system was almost completely destroyed or dismantled during the civil war; private companies offer limited local fixed-line service, and private wireless companies offer service in most major cities, while charging some of the lowest rates on the continent (2016)

domestic: seven networks compete for customers in the mobile sector; some of these mobile-service providers offer fixed-line and Internet services (2016)

international: country code - 252; Mogadishu is a landing point for the EASSy fiber-optic submarine cable system linking East Africa with Europe and North America; this connection ended the country's expensive satellite-dependent Internet access (2016)

**BROADCAST MEDIA:**

2 private TV stations rebroadcast Al-Jazeera and CNN; Somaliland has 1 government-operated TV station and Puntland has 1 private TV station; the transitional government operates Radio Mogadishu; 1 SW and roughly 10 private FM radio stations broadcast in Mogadishu; several radio stations operate in central and southern regions; Somaliland has 1 government-operated radio station; Puntland has roughly a half-dozen private radio stations; transmissions of at least 2 international broadcasters are available (2007)

**INTERNET COUNTRY CODE:**

.so

**INTERNET USERS:**

total: 203,366 (July 2016 est.)

percent of population: 1.9% (July 2016 est.)

country comparison to the world: 169

**BROADBAND - FIXED SUBSCRIPTIONS:**

total: 92,000 (2017 est.)

subscriptions per 100 inhabitants: 1 (2017 est.)

country comparison to the world: 121

## TRANSPORTATION :: SOMALIA

**NATIONAL AIR TRANSPORT SYSTEM:**

number of registered air carriers: 1 (2015)

inventory of registered aircraft operated by air carriers: 1 (2015)

annual passenger traffic on registered air carriers: 251,652 (2015)

annual freight traffic on registered air carriers: 0 mt-km (2015)

**CIVIL AIRCRAFT REGISTRATION COUNTRY CODE PREFIX:**

6O (2016)

**AIRPORTS:**

61 (2013)

country comparison to the world: 81

**AIRPORTS - WITH PAVED RUNWAYS:**

total: 6 (2013)

over 3,047 m: 4 (2013)

2,438 to 3,047 m: 1 (2013)

1,524 to 2,437 m: 1 (2013)

**AIRPORTS - WITH UNPAVED RUNWAYS:**

total: 55 (2013)

over 3,047 m: 1 (2013)

2,438 to 3,047 m: 5 (2013)

1,524 to 2,437 m: 20 (2013)

914 to 1,523 m: 23 (2013)

under 914 m: 6 (2013)

**ROADWAYS:**

total: 22,100 km (2000)

paved: 2,608 km (2000)

unpaved: 19,492 km (2000)

country comparison to the world: 106

**MERCHANT MARINE:**

total: 5 (2017)

by type: general cargo 2, other 3 (2017)

country comparison to the world: 163

**PORTS AND TERMINALS:**

major seaport(s): Berbera, Kismaayo

## MILITARY AND SECURITY :: SOMALIA

**MILITARY EXPENDITURES:**

0% of GDP (2016)

0% of GDP (2015)

0% of GDP (2014)

country comparison to the world: 155

**MILITARY BRANCHES:**

National Security Force (NSF): Somali National Army (2017)

**MILITARY SERVICE AGE AND OBLIGATION:**

18 is the legal minimum age for compulsory and voluntary military service (2012)

**MARITIME THREATS:**

the International Maritime Bureau continues to report the territorial and offshore waters in the Gulf of Aden and Indian Ocean as a region of significant risk for piracy and armed robbery against ships; during 2017, five vessels were attacked or hijacked compared with one in 2016; Operation Ocean Shield, the NATO naval task force established in 2009 to combat Somali piracy, concluded its operations in December 2016 as a result of the drop in reported incidents over the last few years; additional anti-piracy measures on the part of ship operators, including the use of on-board armed security teams, have reduced piracy incidents in that body of water; Somali pirates tend to be heavily armed with automatic weapons and rocket propelled grenades; the use of "mother ships" from which skiffs can be launched to attack vessels allows these pirates to extend the range of their operations hundreds of nautical miles offshore

## TERRORISM :: SOMALIA

**TERRORIST GROUPS - HOME BASED:**

**al-Shabaab:**
  **aim(s):** discredit and destabilize the Federal Government of Somalia and target any countries or entities that support Somalia's fight against al-Shabaab; establish Islamic rule across Somalia
  **area(s) of operation:** a core al-Qa'ida affiliate that maintains strongholds in rural areas in the south, where it controls a large swathe of the Lower and Middle Juba and Lower Shabelle regions; responsible for numerous high-profile bombings and shootings throughout Somalia and in the northeast in Puntland State (April 2018)

**Islamic State of Iraq and ash-Sham (ISIS) networks in Somalia:**
  **aim(s):** replace the Federal Government of Somalia with an Islamic state and implement ISIS's strict interpretation of Sharia; replace al-Shabaab as the dominant armed opposition to federal authority in Somalia
  **area(s) of operation:** directs operations, recruitment, and training from Puntland, the semiautonomous region in the northeast; conducts sporadic attacks against African Union and Somali Government personnel throughout the country (April 2018)

# TRANSNATIONAL ISSUES :: SOMALIA

## DISPUTES - INTERNATIONAL:

Ethiopian forces invaded southern Somalia and routed Islamist Courts from Mogadishu in January 2007"Somaliland" secessionists provide port facilities in Berbera to landlocked Ethiopia and have established commercial ties with other regional states"Puntland" and "Somaliland" "governments" seek international support in their secessionist aspirations and overlapping border claimsthe undemarcated former British administrative line has little meaning as a political separation to rival clans within Ethiopia's Ogaden and southern Somalia's Oromo regionKenya works hard to prevent the clan and militia fighting in Somalia from spreading south across the border, which has long been open to nomadic pastoralists

## REFUGEES AND INTERNALLY DISPLACED PERSONS:

  **refugees (country of origin):** 19,615 (Ethiopia) (refugees and asylum seekers), 12,125 (Yemen) (refugees and asylum seekers) (2018)

  **IDPs:** 2.1 million (civil war since 1988, clan-based competition for resources; 2011 famine; insecurity because of fighting between al-Shabaab and the Transitional Federal Government's allied forces) (2018)

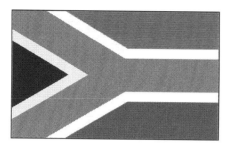
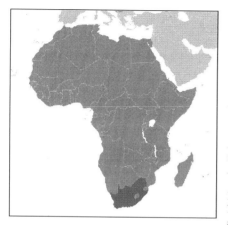

# AFRICA :: SOUTH AFRICA

## INTRODUCTION :: SOUTH AFRICA

### BACKGROUND:

South Africa is home to some of the world's oldest human fossils, and during the modern era the region was settled by Khoisan and Bantu peoples. Dutch traders landed at the southern tip of modern day South Africa in 1652 and established a stopover point on the spice route between the Netherlands and the Far East, founding the city of Cape Town. After the British seized the Cape of Good Hope area in 1806, many of the Dutch settlers (Afrikaners, called "Boers" (farmers) by the British) trekked north to found their own republics, Transvaal and Orange Free State. The discovery of diamonds (1867) and gold (1886) spurred wealth and immigration and intensified the subjugation of the native inhabitants. The Afrikaners resisted British encroachments but were defeated in the Second South African War (1899-1902); however, the British and the Afrikaners, ruled together beginning in 1910 under the Union of South Africa, which became a republic in 1961 after a whites-only referendum. In 1948, the Afrikaner-dominated National Party was voted into power and instituted a policy of apartheid - the separate development of the races - which favored the white minority at the expense of the black majority. The African National Congress (ANC) led the opposition to apartheid and many top ANC leaders, such as Nelson MANDELA, spent decades in South Africa's prisons. Internal protests and insurgency, as well as boycotts by some Western nations and institutions, led to the regime's eventual willingness to negotiate a peaceful transition to majority rule.

The first multi-racial elections in 1994 following the end of apartheid ushered in majority rule under an ANC-led government. South Africa has since struggled to address apartheid-era imbalances in decent housing, education, and health care. Jacob ZUMA became president in 2009 and was reelected in 2014, but was forced to resign in February 2018 after numerous corruption scandals and gains by opposition parties in municipal elections in 2016. His successor, Cyril RAMAPHOSA, has pledged to crack down on corruption and shore up state-owned enterprises, and is the ANC's likely candidate for May 2019 national elections.

## GEOGRAPHY :: SOUTH AFRICA

### LOCATION:

Southern Africa, at the southern tip of the continent of Africa

### GEOGRAPHIC COORDINATES:

29 00 S, 24 00 E

### MAP REFERENCES:

Africa

### AREA:

total: 1,219,090 sq km

land: 1,214,470 sq km

water: 4,620 sq km

note: includes Prince Edward Islands (Marion Island and Prince Edward Island)

country comparison to the world: 26

### AREA - COMPARATIVE:

slightly less than twice the size of Texas

### LAND BOUNDARIES:

total: 5,244 km

border countries (6): Botswana 1969 km, Lesotho 1106 km, Mozambique 496 km, Namibia 1005 km, Eswatini 438 km, Zimbabwe 230 km

### COASTLINE:

2,798 km

### MARITIME CLAIMS:

territorial sea: 12 nm

exclusive economic zone: 200 nm

contiguous zone: 24 nm

continental shelf: 200 nm or to edge of the continental margin

### CLIMATE:

mostly semiarid; subtropical along east coast; sunny days, cool nights

### TERRAIN:

vast interior plateau rimmed by rugged hills and narrow coastal plain

### ELEVATION:

mean elevation: 1,034 m

elevation extremes: 0 m lowest point: Atlantic Ocean

3408 highest point: Njesuthi

### NATURAL RESOURCES:

gold, chromium, antimony, coal, iron ore, manganese, nickel, phosphates, tin, rare earth elements, uranium, gem diamonds, platinum, copper, vanadium, salt, natural gas

### LAND USE:

agricultural land: 79.4% (2011 est.)

arable land: 9.9% (2011 est.) / permanent crops: 0.3% (2011 est.) / permanent pasture: 69.2% (2011 est.)

forest: 7.6% (2011 est.)

other: 13% (2011 est.)

**IRRIGATED LAND:**

16,700 sq km (2012)

**POPULATION DISTRIBUTION:**

the population concentrated along the southern and southeastern coast, and inland around Pretoria; the eastern half of the country is more densely populated than the west

**NATURAL HAZARDS:**

prolonged droughts

volcanism: the volcano forming Marion Island in the Prince Edward Islands, which last erupted in 2004, is South Africa's only active volcano

**ENVIRONMENT - CURRENT ISSUES:**

lack of important arterial rivers or lakes requires extensive water conservation and control measures; growth in water usage outpacing supply; pollution of rivers from agricultural runoff and urban discharge; air pollution resulting in acid rain; deforestation; soil erosion; land degradation; desertification; solid waste pollution

**ENVIRONMENT - INTERNATIONAL AGREEMENTS:**

party to: Antarctic-Environmental Protocol, Antarctic-Marine Living Resources, Antarctic Seals, Antarctic Treaty, Biodiversity, Climate Change, Climate Change-Kyoto Protocol, Desertification, Endangered Species, Hazardous Wastes, Law of the Sea, Marine Dumping, Marine Life Conservation, Ozone Layer Protection, Ship Pollution, Wetlands, Whaling

signed, but not ratified: none of the selected agreements

**GEOGRAPHY - NOTE:**

South Africa completely surrounds Lesotho and almost completely surrounds Eswatini

## PEOPLE AND SOCIETY :: SOUTH AFRICA

**POPULATION:**

55,380,210 (July 2018 est.)

note: estimates for this country explicitly take into account the effects of excess mortality due to AIDS; this can result in lower life expectancy, higher infant mortality, higher death rates, lower population growth rates, and changes in the distribution of population by age and sex than would otherwise be expected

country comparison to the world: 26

**NATIONALITY:**

noun: South African(s)

adjective: South African

**ETHNIC GROUPS:**

black African 80.9%, colored 8.8%, white 7.8%, Indian/Asian 2.5% (2018 est.)

note: colored is a term used in South Africa, including on the national census, for persons of mixed race ancestry

**LANGUAGES:**

isiZulu (official) 24.7%, isiXhosa (official) 15.6%, Afrikaans (official) 12.1%, Sepedi (official) 9.8%, Setswana (official) 8.9%, English (official) 8.4%, Sesotho (official) 8%, Xitsonga (official) 4%, siSwati (official) 2.6%, Tshivenda (official) 2.5%, isiNdebele (official) 1.6%, other (includes Khoi, Nama, and San languages) 1.9% (2017 est.)

note: data represent language spoken most often at home

**RELIGIONS:**

Christian 86%, ancestral, tribal, animist, or other traditional African religions 5.4%, Muslim 1.9%, other 1.5%, nothing in particular 5.2% (2015 est.)

**DEMOGRAPHIC PROFILE:**

South Africa's youthful population is gradually aging, as the country's total fertility rate (TFR) has declined dramatically from about 6 children per woman in the 1960s to roughly 2.2 in 2014. This pattern is similar to fertility trends in South Asia, the Middle East, and North Africa, and sets South Africa apart from the rest of sub-Saharan Africa, where the average TFR remains higher than other regions of the world. Today, South Africa's decreasing number of reproductive age women is having fewer children, as women increase their educational attainment, workforce participation, and use of family planning methods; delay marriage; and opt for smaller families.

As the proportion of working-age South Africans has grown relative to children and the elderly, South Africa has been unable to achieve a demographic dividend because persistent high unemployment and the prevalence of HIV/AIDs have created a larger-than-normal dependent population. HIV/AIDS was also responsible for South Africa's average life expectancy plunging to less than 43 years in 2008; it has rebounded to 63 years as of 2017. HIV/AIDS continues to be a serious public health threat, although awareness-raising campaigns and the wider availability of anti-retroviral drugs is stabilizing the number of new cases, enabling infected individuals to live longer, healthier lives, and reducing mother-child transmissions.

Migration to South Africa began in the second half of the 17th century when traders from the Dutch East India Company settled in the Cape and started using slaves from South and southeast Asia (mainly from India but also from present-day Indonesia, Bangladesh, Sri Lanka, and Malaysia) and southeast Africa (Madagascar and Mozambique) as farm laborers and, to a lesser extent, as domestic servants. The Indian subcontinent remained the Cape Colony's main source of slaves in the early 18th century, while slaves were increasingly obtained from southeast Africa in the latter part of the 18th century and into the 19th century under British rule.

After slavery was completely abolished in the British Empire in 1838, South Africa's colonists turned to temporary African migrants and indentured labor through agreements with India and later China, countries that were anxious to export workers to alleviate domestic poverty and overpopulation. Of the more than 150,000 indentured Indian laborers hired to work in Natal's sugar plantations between 1860 and 1911, most exercised the right as British subjects to remain permanently (a small number of Indian immigrants came freely as merchants). Because of growing resentment toward Indian workers, the 63,000 indentured Chinese workers who mined gold in Transvaal between 1904 and 1911 were under more restrictive contracts and generally were forced to return to their homeland.

In the late 19th century and nearly the entire 20th century, South Africa's then British colonies' and Dutch states' enforced selective immigration policies that welcomed "assimilable" white Europeans as permanent residents but excluded or restricted other immigrants. Following the Union of South Africa's passage of a law in 1913 prohibiting Asian and other non-white immigrants and its elimination of the indenture system in

1917, temporary African contract laborers from neighboring countries became the dominant source of labor in the burgeoning mining industries. Others worked in agriculture and smaller numbers in manufacturing, domestic service, transportation, and construction. Throughout the 20th century, at least 40% of South Africa's miners were foreigners; the numbers peaked at over 80% in the late 1960s. Mozambique, Lesotho, Botswana, and Eswatini were the primary sources of miners, and Malawi and Zimbabwe were periodic suppliers.

Under apartheid, a "two gates" migration policy focused on policing and deporting illegal migrants rather than on managing migration to meet South Africa's development needs. The exclusionary 1991 Aliens Control Act limited labor recruitment to the highly skilled as defined by the ruling white minority, while bilateral labor agreements provided exemptions that enabled the influential mining industry and, to a lesser extent, commercial farms, to hire temporary, low-paid workers from neighboring states. Illegal African migrants were often tacitly allowed to work for low pay in other sectors but were always under threat of deportation.

The abolishment of apartheid in 1994 led to the development of a new inclusive national identity and the strengthening of the country's restrictive immigration policy. Despite South Africa's protectionist approach to immigration, the downsizing and closing of mines, and rising unemployment, migrants from across the continent believed that the country held work opportunities. Fewer African labor migrants were issued temporary work permits and, instead, increasingly entered South Africa with visitors' permits or came illegally, which drove growth in cross-border trade and the informal job market. A new wave of Asian immigrants has also arrived over the last two decades, many operating small retail businesses.

In the post-apartheid period, increasing numbers of highly skilled white workers emigrated, citing dissatisfaction with the political situation, crime, poor services, and a reduced quality of life. The 2002 Immigration Act and later amendments were intended to facilitate the temporary migration of skilled foreign labor to fill labor shortages, but instead the legislation continues to create regulatory obstacles. Although the education system has improved and brain drain has slowed in the wake of the 2008 global financial crisis, South Africa continues to face skills shortages in several key sectors, such as health care and technology.

South Africa's stability and economic growth has acted as a magnet for refugees and asylum seekers from nearby countries, despite the prevalence of discrimination and xenophobic violence. Refugees have included an estimated 350,000 Mozambicans during its 1980s civil war and, more recently, several thousand Somalis, Congolese, and Ethiopians. Nearly all of the tens of thousands of Zimbabweans who have applied for asylum in South Africa have been categorized as economic migrants and denied refuge.

## AGE STRUCTURE:

**0-14 years:** 28.18% (male 7,815,651/female 7,793,261)

**15-24 years:** 17.24% (male 4,711,480/female 4,837,897)

**25-54 years:** 42.05% (male 11,782,848/female 11,503,831)

**55-64 years:** 6.71% (male 1,725,034/female 1,992,035)

**65 years and over:** 5.81% (male 1,351,991/female 1,866,182) (2018 est.)

## DEPENDENCY RATIOS:

**total dependency ratio:** 52.5 (2015 est.)

**youth dependency ratio:** 44.8 (2015 est.)

**elderly dependency ratio:** 7.7 (2015 est.)

**potential support ratio:** 12.9 (2015 est.)

## MEDIAN AGE:

**total:** 27.4 years

**male:** 27.2 years

**female:** 27.6 years (2018 est.)

**country comparison to the world:** 144

## POPULATION GROWTH RATE:

0.97% (2018 est.)

**country comparison to the world:** 114

## BIRTH RATE:

19.9 births/1,000 population (2018 est.)

**country comparison to the world:** 78

## DEATH RATE:

9.3 deaths/1,000 population (2018 est.)

**country comparison to the world:** 57

## NET MIGRATION RATE:

-0.9 migrant(s)/1,000 population (2017 est.)

**country comparison to the world:** 136

## POPULATION DISTRIBUTION:

the population concentrated along the southern and southeastern coast, and inland around Pretoria; the eastern half of the country is more densely populated than the west

## URBANIZATION:

**urban population:** 66.4% of total population (2018)

**rate of urbanization:** 1.97% annual rate of change (2015-20 est.)

## MAJOR URBAN AREAS - POPULATION:

9.227 million Johannesburg (includes Ekurhuleni), 4.43 million Cape Town (legislative capital), 3.134 million Durban, 2.378 million PRETORIA (capital), 1.231 million Port Elizabeth, 765,000 Vereeniging (2018)

## SEX RATIO:

**at birth:** 1.01 male(s)/female (2017 est.)

**0-14 years:** 1.01 male(s)/female (2017 est.)

**15-24 years:** 0.98 male(s)/female (2017 est.)

**25-54 years:** 1.02 male(s)/female (2017 est.)

**55-64 years:** 0.87 male(s)/female (2017 est.)

**65 years and over:** 0.73 male(s)/female (2017 est.)

**total population:** 0.98 male(s)/female (2017 est.)

## MATERNAL MORTALITY RATE:

138 deaths/100,000 live births (2015 est.)

**country comparison to the world:** 63

## INFANT MORTALITY RATE:

**total:** 29.9 deaths/1,000 live births (2018 est.)

**male:** 33.2 deaths/1,000 live births (2018 est.)

**female:** 26.5 deaths/1,000 live births (2018 est.)

**country comparison to the world:** 62

## LIFE EXPECTANCY AT BIRTH:

**total population:** 64.1 years (2018 est.)

**male:** 62.7 years (2018 est.)

female: 65.6 years (2018 est.)

country comparison to the world: 190

**TOTAL FERTILITY RATE:**

2.26 children born/woman (2018 est.)

country comparison to the world: 91

**CONTRACEPTIVE PREVALENCE RATE:**

54.6% (2016)

**HEALTH EXPENDITURES:**

8.8% of GDP (2014)

country comparison to the world: 44

**PHYSICIANS DENSITY:**

0.82 physicians/1,000 population (2016)

**DRINKING WATER SOURCE:**

improved:

urban: 99.6% of population (2015 est.)

rural: 81.4% of population (2015 est.)

total: 93.2% of population (2015 est.)

unimproved:

urban: 0.4% of population (2015 est.)

rural: 18.6% of population (2015 est.)

total: 6.8% of population (2015 est.)

**SANITATION FACILITY ACCESS:**

improved:

urban: 69.6% of population (2015 est.)

rural: 60.5% of population (2015 est.)

total: 66.4% of population (2015 est.)

unimproved:

urban: 30.4% of population (2015 est.)

rural: 39.5% of population (2015 est.)

total: 33.6% of population (2015 est.)

**HIV/AIDS - ADULT PREVALENCE RATE:**

18.8% (2017 est.)

country comparison to the world: 4

**HIV/AIDS - PEOPLE LIVING WITH HIV/AIDS:**

7.2 million (2016 est.)

country comparison to the world: 1

**HIV/AIDS - DEATHS:**

110,000 (2017 est.)

country comparison to the world: 2

**MAJOR INFECTIOUS DISEASES:**

degree of risk: intermediate (2016)

food or waterborne diseases: bacterial diarrhea, hepatitis A, and typhoid fever (2016)

water contact diseases: schistosomiasis (2016)

**OBESITY - ADULT PREVALENCE RATE:**

28.3% (2016)

country comparison to the world: 31

**CHILDREN UNDER THE AGE OF 5 YEARS UNDERWEIGHT:**

5.9% (2016)

country comparison to the world: 76

**EDUCATION EXPENDITURES:**

5.9% of GDP (2016)

country comparison to the world: 40

**LITERACY:**

definition: age 15 and over can read and write (2015 est.)

total population: 94.4% (2015 est.)

male: 95.4% (2015 est.)

female: 93.4% (2015 est.)

**SCHOOL LIFE EXPECTANCY (PRIMARY TO TERTIARY EDUCATION):**

total: 13 years (2012)

male: 12 years (2012)

female: 13 years (2012)

**UNEMPLOYMENT, YOUTH AGES 15-24:**

total: 53.5% (2017 est.)

male: 49.3% (2017 est.)

female: 58.7% (2017 est.)

country comparison to the world: 4

# GOVERNMENT :: SOUTH AFRICA

**COUNTRY NAME:**

conventional long form: Republic of South Africa

conventional short form: South Africa

former: Union of South Africa

abbreviation: RSA

etymology: self-descriptive name from the country's location on the continent; "Africa" is derived from the Roman designation of the area corresponding to present-day Tunisia "Africa terra," which meant "Land of the Afri" (the tribe resident in that area), but which eventually came to mean the entire continent

**GOVERNMENT TYPE:**

parliamentary republic

**CAPITAL:**

name: Pretoria (administrative capital); Cape Town (legislative capital); Bloemfontein (judicial capital)

geographic coordinates: 25 42 S, 28 13 E

time difference: UTC+2 (7 hours ahead of Washington, DC, during Standard Time)

**ADMINISTRATIVE DIVISIONS:**

9 provinces; Eastern Cape, Free State, Gauteng, KwaZulu-Natal, Limpopo, Mpumalanga, Northern Cape, North West, Western Cape

**INDEPENDENCE:**

31 May 1910 (Union of South Africa formed from four British colonies: Cape Colony, Natal, Transvaal, and Orange Free State);22 August 1934 (Status of the Union Act);31 May 1961 (republic declared);27 April 1994 (majority rule)

**NATIONAL HOLIDAY:**

Freedom Day, 27 April (1994)

**CONSTITUTION:**

history: several previous; latest drafted 8 May 1996, approved by Constitutional Court 4 December 1996, effective 4 February 1997 (2017)

amendments: proposed by the National Assembly of Parliament; passage of amendments affecting constitutional sections on human rights and freedoms, non-racism and non-sexism, supremacy of the constitution, suffrage, the multi-party system of democratic government, and amendment procedures requires at least 75% majority vote of the Assembly, approval by at least six of the nine provinces represented in the National Council of Provinces, and assent by the president of the republic; passage of amendments affecting the Bill of Rights, and those related to provincial boundaries, powers, and authorities requires at least two-thirds majority vote of the Assembly, approval by at least six of the nine provinces represented in the National Council, and assent by the president; amended many times, last in 2013 (2017)

**LEGAL SYSTEM:**

mixed legal system of Roman-Dutch civil law, English common law, and customary law

**INTERNATIONAL LAW ORGANIZATION PARTICIPATION:**

has not submitted an ICJ jurisdiction declaration; accepts ICCt jurisdiction

## CITIZENSHIP:

**citizenship by birth:** no

**citizenship by descent only:** at least one parent must be a citizen of South Africa

**dual citizenship recognized:** yes, but requires prior permission of the government

**residency requirement for naturalization:** 1 year

## SUFFRAGE:

18 years of age; universal

## EXECUTIVE BRANCH:

**chief of state:** President Matamela Cyril RAMAPHOSA (since 15 February 2018); Deputy President David MABUZA (26 February 2018); note - the president is both chief of state and head of government; Jacob ZUMA resigned the presidency on 14 February 2018

**head of government:** President Matamela Cyril RAMAPHOSA (since 15 February 2018); deputy president David MABUZA (26 February 2018)

**cabinet:** Cabinet appointed by the president

**elections/appointments:** president indirectly elected by the National Assembly for a 5-year term (eligible for a second term); election last held on 15 February 2018 to elect Cyril RAMAPHOSA as acting president to replace ZUMA for the remainder of his term (next to be held in May 2019)

**election results:** Matamela Cyril RAMAPHOSA (ANC) elected president by the National Assembly unopposed

## LEGISLATIVE BRANCH:

**description:** bicameral Parliament consists of:
National Council of Provinces (90 seats; 10-member delegations appointed by each of the 9 provincial legislatures to serve 5-year terms; note - the Council has special powers to protect regional interests, including safeguarding cultural and linguistic traditions among ethnic minorities)
National Assembly (400 seats; members directly elected in multi-seat constituencies by proportional representation vote to serve 5-year terms)

**elections:**
National Council of Provinces and National Assembly - last held on 7 May 2014 (next to be held in 2019)

**election results:**
National Council of Provinces - percent of vote by party - NA; seats by party - ANC 60, DA 20, EFF 7, IFP 1, NFP 1, UDM 1
National Assembly - percent of vote by party - ANC 62.2%, DA 22.2%, EFF 6.4%, IFP 2.4%, NFP 1.6%, UDM 1%, other 4.2%; seats by party - ANC 249, DA 89, EFF 25, IFP 10, NFP 6, UDM 4, other 17

## JUDICIAL BRANCH:

**highest courts:** Supreme Court of Appeals (consists of the court president, deputy president, and 21 judges); Constitutional Court (consists of the chief and deputy chief justices and 9 judges)

**judge selection and term of office:** Supreme Court of Appeals president and vice president appointed by the national president after consultation with the Judicial Services Commission (JSC), a 23-member body chaired by the chief justice and includes other judges and judicial executives, members of parliament, practicing lawyers and advocates, a teacher of law, and several members designated by the national president; other Supreme Court judges appointed by the national president on the advice of the JSC and hold office until discharged from active service by an Act of Parliament; Constitutional Court chief and deputy chief justices appointed by the national president after consultation with the JSC and with heads of the National Assembly; other Constitutional Court judges appointed by the national president after consultation with the chief justice and leaders of the National Assembly; Constitutional Court judges appointed for 12-year non-renewable terms or until age 70

**subordinate courts:** High Courts; Magistrates' Courts; labor courts; land claims courts

## POLITICAL PARTIES AND LEADERS:

African Christian Democratic Party or ACDP [Kenneth MESHOE]
African Independent Congress or AIC [Mandla GALO]
African National Congress or ANC [Cyril RAMAPHOSA]
African People's Convention or APC [Themba GODI]Agang SA [Mike TSHISHONGA]
Congress of the People or COPE [Mosiuoa LEKOTA]
Democratic Alliance or DA [Mmusi MAIMANE]
Economic Freedom Fighters or EFF [Julius Sello MALEMA]
Freedom Front Plus or FF+ [Pieter GROENEWALD]
Inkatha Freedom Party or IFP [Mangosuthu BUTHELEZI]
National Freedom Party or NFP [Zanele kaMAGWAZA-MSIBI]
Pan-Africanist Congress of Azania or PAC [Luthanado MBINDA]
United Christian Democratic Party or UCDP [Isaac Sipho MFUNDISI]
United Democratic Movement or UDM [Bantu HOLOMISA]

## INTERNATIONAL ORGANIZATION PARTICIPATION:

ACP, AfDB, AU, BIS, BRICS, C, CD, FAO, FATF, G-20, G-24, G-5, G-77, IAEA, IBRD, ICAO, ICC (national committees), ICCt, ICRM, IDA, IFAD, IFC, IFRCS, IHO, ILO, IMF, IMO, IMSO, Interpol, IOC, IOM, IPU, ISO, ITSO, ITU, ITUC (NGOs), MIGA, MONUSCO, NAM, NSG, OECD (enhanced engagement), OPCW, Paris Club (associate), PCA, SACU, SADC, UN, UNAMID, UNCTAD, UNESCO, UNHCR, UNIDO, UNITAR, UNWTO, UPU, WCO, WFTU (NGOs), WHO, WIPO, WMO, WTO, ZC

## DIPLOMATIC REPRESENTATION IN THE US:

**chief of mission:** Ambassador Mninwa Johannes MAHLANGU (since 23 February 2015)

**chancery:** 3051 Massachusetts Avenue NW, Washington, DC 20008

**telephone:** [1] (202) 232-4400

**FAX:** [1] (202) 265-1607

**consulate(s) general:** Chicago, Los Angeles, New York

## DIPLOMATIC REPRESENTATION FROM THE US:

**chief of mission:** Ambassador (vacant); Charge d'Affaires Jessica "Jessye" LAPENN (since 16 December 2016)

**embassy:** 877 Pretorius Street, Arcadia, Pretoria

**mailing address:** P.O. Box 9536, Pretoria 0001

**telephone:** [27] (12) 431-4000

**FAX:** [27] (12) 342-2299

**consulate(s) general:** Cape Town, Durban, Johannesburg

## FLAG DESCRIPTION:

two equal width horizontal bands of red (top) and blue separated by a central green band that splits into a horizontal Y, the arms of which end at the corners of the hoist side; the Y embraces a black isosceles triangle from which the arms are separated by narrow yellow bands; the red and blue bands are separated from the green band and its arms by narrow white stripes; the flag colors do not have any official symbolism, but the Y stands for the "convergence of diverse elements within South African society, taking the road ahead in unity"; black, yellow, and green are found on the flag of the African National Congress, while red, white, and blue are the colors in the flags of the Netherlands and the UK, whose settlers ruled South Africa during the colonial era

note: the South African flag is one of only two national flags to display six colors as part of its primary design, the other is South Sudan's

## NATIONAL SYMBOL(S):

springbok (antelope), king protea flower; national colors: red, green, blue, yellow, black, white

## NATIONAL ANTHEM:

name: National Anthem of South Africa

lyrics/music: Enoch SONTONGA and Cornelius Jacob LANGENHOVEN/Enoch SONTONGA and Marthinus LOURENS de Villiers

note: adopted 1994; a combination of "N'kosi Sikelel' iAfrica" (God Bless Africa) and "Die Stem van Suid Afrika" (The Call of South Africa), which were respectively the anthems of the non-white and white communities under apartheid; official lyrics contain a mixture of Xhosa, Zulu, Sesotho, Afrikaans, and English (i.e., the five most widely spoken of South Africa's 11 official languages); music incorporates the melody used in the Tanzanian and Zambian anthems

# ECONOMY :: SOUTH AFRICA

## ECONOMY - OVERVIEW:

South Africa is a middle-income emerging market with an abundant supply of natural resources; well-developed financial, legal, communications, energy, and transport sectors; and a stock exchange that is Africa's largest and among the top 20 in the world.

Economic growth has decelerated in recent years, slowing to an estimated 0.7% in 2017. Unemployment, poverty, and inequality - among the highest in the world - remain a challenge. Official unemployment is roughly 27% of the workforce, and runs significantly higher among black youth. Even though the country's modern infrastructure supports a relatively efficient distribution of goods to major urban centers throughout the region, unstable electricity supplies retard growth. Eskom, the state-run power company, is building three new power stations and is installing new power demand management programs to improve power grid reliability but has been plagued with accusations of mismanagement and corruption and faces an increasingly high debt burden.

South Africa's economic policy has focused on controlling inflation while empowering a broader economic base; however, the country faces structural constraints that also limit economic growth, such as skills shortages, declining global competitiveness, and frequent work stoppages due to strike action. The government faces growing pressure from urban constituencies to improve the delivery of basic services to low-income areas, to increase job growth, and to provide university level-education at affordable prices. Political infighting among South Africa's ruling party and the volatility of the rand risks economic growth. International investors are concerned about the country's long-term economic stability; in late 2016, most major international credit ratings agencies downgraded South Africa's international debt to junk bond status.

## GDP (PURCHASING POWER PARITY):

$767.2 billion (2017 est.)

$757.2 billion (2016 est.)

$752.9 billion (2015 est.)

note: data are in 2017 dollars

country comparison to the world: 30

## GDP (OFFICIAL EXCHANGE RATE):

$349.3 billion (2017 est.) (2017 est.)

## GDP - REAL GROWTH RATE:

1.3% (2017 est.)

0.6% (2016 est.)

1.3% (2015 est.)

country comparison to the world: 179

## GDP - PER CAPITA (PPP):

$13,600 (2017 est.)

$13,600 (2016 est.)

$13,800 (2015 est.)

note: data are in 2017 dollars

country comparison to the world: 118

## GROSS NATIONAL SAVING:

16.1% of GDP (2017 est.)

16.6% of GDP (2016 est.)

16.4% of GDP (2015 est.)

country comparison to the world: 128

## GDP - COMPOSITION, BY END USE:

household consumption: 59.4% (2017 est.)

government consumption: 20.9% (2017 est.)

investment in fixed capital: 18.7% (2017 est.)

investment in inventories: -0.1% (2017 est.)

exports of goods and services: 29.8% (2017 est.)

imports of goods and services: -28.4% (2017 est.)

## GDP - COMPOSITION, BY SECTOR OF ORIGIN:

agriculture: 2.8% (2017 est.)

industry: 29.7% (2017 est.)

services: 67.5% (2017 est.)

## AGRICULTURE - PRODUCTS:

corn, wheat, sugarcane, fruits, vegetables; beef, poultry, mutton, wool, dairy products

## INDUSTRIES:

mining (world's largest producer of platinum, gold, chromium), automobile assembly, metalworking, machinery, textiles, iron and steel, chemicals, fertilizer, foodstuffs, commercial ship repair

## INDUSTRIAL PRODUCTION GROWTH RATE:

1.2% (2017 est.)

country comparison to the world: 151

## LABOR FORCE:

22.19 million (2017 est.)

country comparison to the world: 29

## LABOR FORCE - BY OCCUPATION:

agriculture: 4.6%

industry: 23.5%

services: 71.9% (2014 est.)

## UNEMPLOYMENT RATE:

27.5% (2017 est.)

26.7% (2016 est.)

country comparison to the world: 200

## POPULATION BELOW POVERTY LINE:

16.6% (2016 est.)

## HOUSEHOLD INCOME OR CONSUMPTION BY PERCENTAGE SHARE:

lowest 10%: 51.3% (2011 est.)

highest 10%: 51.3% (2011 est.)

**DISTRIBUTION OF FAMILY INCOME - GINI INDEX:**

62.5 (2013 est.)

63.4 (2011 est.)

country comparison to the world: 2

**BUDGET:**

revenues: 92.86 billion (2017 est.)

expenditures: 108.3 billion (2017 est.)

**TAXES AND OTHER REVENUES:**

26.6% (of GDP) (2017 est.)

country comparison to the world: 107

**BUDGET SURPLUS (+) OR DEFICIT (-):**

-4.4% (of GDP) (2017 est.)

country comparison to the world: 163

**PUBLIC DEBT:**

53% of GDP (2017 est.)

51.6% of GDP (2016 est.)

country comparison to the world: 92

**FISCAL YEAR:**

1 April - 31 March

**INFLATION RATE (CONSUMER PRICES):**

5.3% (2017 est.)

6.3% (2016 est.)

country comparison to the world: 174

**CENTRAL BANK DISCOUNT RATE:**

5.75% (31 December 2014)

7% (31 December 2009)

country comparison to the world: 72

**COMMERCIAL BANK PRIME LENDING RATE:**

10.38% (31 December 2017 est.)

10.46% (31 December 2016 est.)

country comparison to the world: 83

**STOCK OF NARROW MONEY:**

$137.5 billion (31 December 2017 est.)

$117.3 billion (31 December 2016 est.)

country comparison to the world: 30

**STOCK OF BROAD MONEY:**

$137.5 billion (31 December 2017 est.)

$117.3 billion (31 December 2016 est.)

country comparison to the world: 30

**STOCK OF DOMESTIC CREDIT:**

$295.9 billion (31 December 2017 est.)

$244.8 billion (31 December 2016 est.)

country comparison to the world: 38

**MARKET VALUE OF PUBLICLY TRADED SHARES:**

$735.9 billion (31 December 2015 est.)

$933.9 billion (31 December 2014 est.)

$942.8 billion (31 December 2013 est.)

country comparison to the world: 16

**CURRENT ACCOUNT BALANCE:**

-$8.584 billion (2017 est.)

-$8.237 billion (2016 est.)

country comparison to the world: 189

**EXPORTS:**

$94.93 billion (2017 est.)

$75.16 billion (2016 est.)

country comparison to the world: 39

**EXPORTS - PARTNERS:**

China 9.5%, US 7.7%, Germany 7.1%, Japan 4.7%, India 4.6%, Botswana 4.3%, Namibia 4.1% (2017)

**EXPORTS - COMMODITIES:**

gold, diamonds, platinum, other metals and minerals, machinery and equipment

**IMPORTS:**

$89.36 billion (2017 est.)

$79.57 billion (2016 est.)

country comparison to the world: 40

**IMPORTS - COMMODITIES:**

machinery and equipment, chemicals, petroleum products, scientific instruments, foodstuffs

**IMPORTS - PARTNERS:**

China 18.3%, Germany 11.9%, US 6.6%, Saudi Arabia 4.7%, India 4.7% (2017)

**RESERVES OF FOREIGN EXCHANGE AND GOLD:**

$50.72 billion (31 December 2017 est.)

$47.23 billion (31 December 2016 est.)

country comparison to the world: 39

**DEBT - EXTERNAL:**

$156.3 billion (31 December 2017 est.)

$144.6 billion (31 December 2016 est.)

country comparison to the world: 41

**STOCK OF DIRECT FOREIGN INVESTMENT - AT HOME:**

$156.8 billion (31 December 2017 est.)

$136.8 billion (31 December 2016 est.)

country comparison to the world: 38

**STOCK OF DIRECT FOREIGN INVESTMENT - ABROAD:**

$270.3 billion (31 December 2017 est.)

$172.8 billion (31 December 2016 est.)

country comparison to the world: 24

**EXCHANGE RATES:**

rand (ZAR) per US dollar -

13.67 (2017 est.)

14.6924 (2016 est.)

14.6924 (2015 est.)

12.7581 (2014 est.)

10.8469 (2013 est.)

# ENERGY :: SOUTH AFRICA

**ELECTRICITY ACCESS:**

population without electricity: 7.7 million (2013)

electrification - total population: 85% (2013)

electrification - urban areas: 90% (2013)

electrification - rural areas: 77% (2013)

**ELECTRICITY - PRODUCTION:**

234.5 billion kWh (2016 est.)

country comparison to the world: 21

**ELECTRICITY - CONSUMPTION:**

207.1 billion kWh (2016 est.)

country comparison to the world: 21

**ELECTRICITY - EXPORTS:**

16.55 billion kWh (2016 est.)

country comparison to the world: 11

**ELECTRICITY - IMPORTS:**

10.56 billion kWh (2016 est.)

country comparison to the world: 24

**ELECTRICITY - INSTALLED GENERATING CAPACITY:**

50.02 million kW (2016 est.)

country comparison to the world: 21

**ELECTRICITY - FROM FOSSIL FUELS:**

85% of total installed capacity (2016 est.)

country comparison to the world: 73

**ELECTRICITY - FROM NUCLEAR FUELS:**

4% of total installed capacity (2017 est.)

country comparison to the world: 24

**ELECTRICITY - FROM HYDROELECTRIC PLANTS:**

1% of total installed capacity (2017 est.)

country comparison to the world: 150

**ELECTRICITY - FROM OTHER RENEWABLE SOURCES:**

10% of total installed capacity (2017 est.)

country comparison to the world: 81

**CRUDE OIL - PRODUCTION:**

2,000 bbl/day (2017 est.)

country comparison to the world: 89

**CRUDE OIL - EXPORTS:**

0 bbl/day (2015 est.)

country comparison to the world: 197

**CRUDE OIL - IMPORTS:**

404,000 bbl/day (2015 est.)

country comparison to the world: 22

**CRUDE OIL - PROVED RESERVES:**

15 million bbl (1 January 2018 est.)

country comparison to the world: 86

**REFINED PETROLEUM PRODUCTS - PRODUCTION:**

487,100 bbl/day (2015 est.)

country comparison to the world: 33

**REFINED PETROLEUM PRODUCTS - CONSUMPTION:**

621,000 bbl/day (2016 est.)

country comparison to the world: 32

**REFINED PETROLEUM PRODUCTS - EXPORTS:**

105,600 bbl/day (2015 est.)

country comparison to the world: 42

**REFINED PETROLEUM PRODUCTS - IMPORTS:**

195,200 bbl/day (2015 est.)

country comparison to the world: 34

**NATURAL GAS - PRODUCTION:**

906.1 million cu m (2017 est.)

country comparison to the world: 70

**NATURAL GAS - CONSUMPTION:**

5.069 billion cu m (2017 est.)

country comparison to the world: 60

**NATURAL GAS - EXPORTS:**

0 cu m (2017 est.)

country comparison to the world: 187

**NATURAL GAS - IMPORTS:**

4.162 billion cu m (2017 est.)

country comparison to the world: 39

**NATURAL GAS - PROVED RESERVES:**

0 cu m (1 January 2012 est.)

country comparison to the world: 196

**CARBON DIOXIDE EMISSIONS FROM CONSUMPTION OF ENERGY:**

572.3 million Mt (2017 est.)

country comparison to the world: 11

## COMMUNICATIONS :: SOUTH AFRICA

**TELEPHONES - FIXED LINES:**

total subscriptions: 3,629,141 (2017 est.)

subscriptions per 100 inhabitants: 7 (2017 est.)

country comparison to the world: 39

**TELEPHONES - MOBILE CELLULAR:**

total subscriptions: 91,878,275 (2017 est.)

subscriptions per 100 inhabitants: 168 (2017 est.)

country comparison to the world: 17

**TELEPHONE SYSTEM:**

general assessment: the system is the best-developed and most modern in Africa (2016)

domestic: combined fixed-line and mobile-cellular teledensity exceeds 145 telephones per 100 persons; consists of carrier-equipped open-wire lines, coaxial cables, microwave radio relay links, fiber-optic cable, radiotelephone communication stations, and wireless local loops; key centers are Bloemfontein, Cape Town, Durban, Johannesburg, Port Elizabeth, and Pretoria (2016)

international: country code - 27; the SAT-3/WASC and SAFE fiber-optic submarine cable systems connect South Africa to Europe and Asia; the EASSy fiber-optic cable system connects with Europe and North America; satellite earth stations - 3 Intelsat (1 Indian Ocean and 2 Atlantic Ocean) (2016)

**BROADCAST MEDIA:**

the South African Broadcasting Corporation (SABC) operates 4 TV stations, 3 are free-to-air and 1 is pay TV; e.tv, a private station, is accessible to more than half the population; multiple subscription TV services provide a mix of local and international channels; well-developed mix of public and private radio stations at the national, regional, and local levels; the SABC radio network, state-owned and controlled but nominally independent, operates 18 stations, one for each of the 11 official languages, 4 community stations, and 3 commercial stations; more than 100 community-based stations extend coverage to rural areas (2007)

**INTERNET COUNTRY CODE:**

.za

**INTERNET USERS:**

total: 29,322,380 (July 2016 est.)

percent of population: 54% (July 2016 est.)

country comparison to the world: 25

**BROADBAND - FIXED SUBSCRIPTIONS:**

total: 1,698,360 (2017 est.)

subscriptions per 100 inhabitants: 3 (2017 est.)

country comparison to the world: 57

## TRANSPORTATION :: SOUTH AFRICA

**NATIONAL AIR TRANSPORT SYSTEM:**

number of registered air carriers: 23 (2015)

inventory of registered aircraft operated by air carriers: 216 (2015)

annual passenger traffic on registered air carriers: 17,188,887 (2015)

annual freight traffic on registered air carriers: 885,277,991 mt-km (2015)

**CIVIL AIRCRAFT REGISTRATION COUNTRY CODE PREFIX:**

ZS (2016)

**AIRPORTS:**

566 (2013)

country comparison to the world: 11

**AIRPORTS - WITH PAVED RUNWAYS:**

total: 144 (2013)

over 3,047 m: 11 (2013)

2,438 to 3,047 m: 7 (2013)

1,524 to 2,437 m: 52 (2013)

914 to 1,523 m: 65 (2013)

under 914 m: 9 (2013)

**AIRPORTS - WITH UNPAVED RUNWAYS:**

total: 422 (2013)

2,438 to 3,047 m: 1 (2013)

1,524 to 2,437 m: 31 (2013)

914 to 1,523 m: 258 (2013)

under 914 m: 132 (2013)

**HELIPORTS:**

1 (2013)

**PIPELINES:**

94 km condensate, 1293 km gas, 992 km oil, 1460 km refined products (2013)

**RAILWAYS:**

total: 20,986 km (2014)

standard gauge: 80 km 1.435-m gauge (80 km electrified) (2014)

**narrow gauge:** 19,756 km 1.065-m gauge (8,271 km electrified) (2014)

**other:** 1,150 km (passenger rail, gauge unspecified, 1,115.5 km electrified) (2014)

**country comparison to the world:** 13

## ROADWAYS:

**total:** 747,014 km (2014)

**paved:** 158,952 km (2014)

**unpaved:** 588,062 km (2014)

**country comparison to the world:** 10

## MERCHANT MARINE:

**total:** 82 (2017)

**by type:** bulk carrier 2, general cargo 1, oil tanker 5, other 74 (2017)

**country comparison to the world:** 95

## PORTS AND TERMINALS:

**major seaport(s):** Cape Town, Durban, Port Elizabeth, Richards Bay, Saldanha Bay

**container port(s) (TEUs):** Durban (2,620,000) (2016)

**LNG terminal(s) (import):** Mossel Bay

# MILITARY AND SECURITY :: SOUTH AFRICA

## MILITARY EXPENDITURES:

1.07% of GDP (2016)

1.09% of GDP (2015)

1.11% of GDP (2014)

**country comparison to the world:** 109

## MILITARY BRANCHES:

South African National Defense Force (SANDF): South African Army, South African Navy (SAN), South African Air Force (SAAF), South African Military Health Services (2013)

## MILITARY SERVICE AGE AND OBLIGATION:

18 years of age for voluntary military service; women are eligible to serve in noncombat roles; 2-year service obligation (2012)

# TRANSNATIONAL ISSUES :: SOUTH AFRICA

## DISPUTES - INTERNATIONAL:

South Africa has placed military units to assist police operations along the border of Lesotho, Zimbabwe, and Mozambique to control smuggling, poaching, and illegal migrationthe governments of South Africa and Namibia have not signed or ratified the text of the 1994 Surveyor's General agreement placing the boundary in the middle of the Orange River

## REFUGEES AND INTERNALLY DISPLACED PERSONS:

**refugees (country of origin):** 28,695 (Somalia), 17,776 (Ethiopia), 5,394 (Republic of the Congo) (2016), 59,480 (Democratic Republic of the Congo) (2018) (refugees and asylum seekers) (2018)

## ILLICIT DRUGS:

transshipment center for heroin, hashish, and cocaine, as well as a major cultivator of marijuana in its own right; cocaine and heroin consumption on the rise; world's largest market for illicit methaqualone, usually imported illegally from India through various east African countries, but increasingly producing its own synthetic drugs for domestic consumption; attractive venue for money launderers given the increasing level of organized criminal and narcotics activity in the region and the size of the South African economy

# SOUTH AMERICA :: SOUTH GEORGIA AND SOUTH SANDWICH ISLANDS

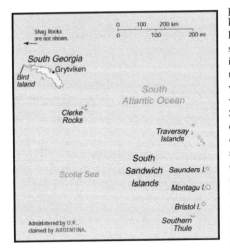

## INTRODUCTION :: SOUTH GEORGIA AND SOUTH SANDWICH ISLANDS

### BACKGROUND:

The islands, with large bird and seal populations, lie approximately 1,000 km east of the Falkland Islands and have been under British administration since 1908 - except for a brief period in 1982 when Argentina occupied them. Grytviken, on South Georgia, was a 19th and early 20th century whaling station. Famed explorer Ernest SHACKLETON stopped there in 1914 en route to his ill-fated attempt to cross Antarctica on foot. He returned some 20 months later with a few companions in a small boat and arranged a successful rescue for the rest of his crew, stranded off the Antarctic Peninsula. He died in 1922 on a subsequent expedition and is buried in Grytviken. Today, the station houses scientists from the British Antarctic Survey. Recognizing the importance of preserving the marine stocks in adjacent waters, the UK, in 1993, extended the exclusive fishing zone from 12 nm to 200 nm around each island.

## GEOGRAPHY :: SOUTH GEORGIA AND SOUTH SANDWICH ISLANDS

### LOCATION:

Southern South America, islands in the South Atlantic Ocean, east of the tip of South America

### GEOGRAPHIC COORDINATES:

54 30 S, 37 00 W

### MAP REFERENCES:

Antarctic Region

### AREA:

total: 3,903 sq km

land: 3,903 sq km

water: 0 sq km

note: includes Shag Rocks, Black Rock, Clerke Rocks, South Georgia Island, Bird Island, and the South Sandwich Islands, which consist of 11 islands

country comparison to the world: 177

### AREA - COMPARATIVE:

slightly larger than Rhode Island

### LAND BOUNDARIES:

0 km

### COASTLINE:

NA

### MARITIME CLAIMS:

territorial sea: 12 nm

exclusive fishing zone: 200 nm

### CLIMATE:

variable, with mostly westerly winds throughout the year interspersed with periods of calm; nearly all precipitation falls as snow

### TERRAIN:

most of the islands are rugged and mountainous rising steeply from the sea; South Georgia is largely barren with steep, glacier-covered mountains; the South Sandwich Islands are of volcanic origin with some active volcanoes

### ELEVATION:

0 m lowest point: Atlantic Ocean

2934 highest point: Mount Paget (South Georgia)

### NATURAL RESOURCES:

fish

### LAND USE:

agricultural land: 0% (2011 est.)

arable land: 0% (2011 est.) / permanent crops: 0% (2011 est.) / permanent pasture: 0% (2011 est.)

forest: 0% (2011 est.)

other: 100% (2011 est.)

### IRRIGATED LAND:

0 sq km (2011)

**NATURAL HAZARDS:**

the South Sandwich Islands have prevailing weather conditions that generally make them difficult to approach by ship; they are also subject to active volcanism

**ENVIRONMENT - CURRENT ISSUES:**

reindeer - introduced to the islands in the 20th century - devastated the native flora and bird species; some reindeer were translocated to the Falkland Islands in 2001, the rest were exterminated (2013-14); a parallel effort (2010-15) eradicated rats and mice that came to the islands as stowaways on ships as early as the late 18th century

**GEOGRAPHY - NOTE:**

the north coast of South Georgia has several large bays, which provide good anchorage

# PEOPLE AND SOCIETY :: SOUTH GEORGIA AND SOUTH SANDWICH ISLANDS

**POPULATION:**

no indigenous inhabitants

note: the small military garrison on South Georgia withdrew in March 2001, replaced by a permanent group of scientists of the British Antarctic Survey, which also has a biological station on Bird Island; the South Sandwich Islands are uninhabited

# GOVERNMENT :: SOUTH GEORGIA AND SOUTH SANDWICH ISLANDS

**COUNTRY NAME:**

conventional long form: South Georgia and the South Sandwich Islands

conventional short form: South Georgia and South Sandwich Islands

abbreviation: SGSSI

etymology: South Georgia was named "the Isle of Georgia" in 1775 by Captain James COOK in honor of British King GEORGE III; the explorer also discovered the Sandwich Islands Group that year, which he named "Sandwich Land" after John MONTAGU, the Earl of Sandwich and First Lord of the Admiralty; the word "South" was later added to distinguish these islands from the other Sandwich Islands, now known as the Hawaiian Islands

**DEPENDENCY STATUS:**

overseas territory of the UK, also claimed by Argentina; administered from the Falkland Islands by a commissioner, who is concurrently governor of the Falkland Islands, representing Queen ELIZABETH II

**LEGAL SYSTEM:**

the laws of the UK, where applicable, apply

**INTERNATIONAL ORGANIZATION PARTICIPATION:**

UPU

**DIPLOMATIC REPRESENTATION IN THE US:**

none (overseas territory of the UK, also claimed by Argentina)

**DIPLOMATIC REPRESENTATION FROM THE US:**

none (overseas territory of the UK, also claimed by Argentina)

**FLAG DESCRIPTION:**

blue with the flag of the UK in the upper hoist-side quadrant and the South Georgia and South Sandwich Islands coat of arms centered on the outer half of the flag; the coat of arms features a shield with a golden lion rampant, holding a torch; the shield is supported by a fur seal on the left and a Macaroni penguin on the right; a reindeer appears above the crest, and below the shield on a scroll is the motto LEO TERRAM PROPRIAM PROTEGAT (Let the Lion Protect its Own Land); the lion with the torch represents the UK and discovery; the background of the shield, blue and white estoiles, are found in the coat of arms of James Cook, discoverer of the islands; all the outer supporting animals represented are native to the islands

# ECONOMY :: SOUTH GEORGIA AND SOUTH SANDWICH ISLANDS

**ECONOMY - OVERVIEW:**

Some fishing takes place in adjacent waters. Harvesting finfish and krill are potential sources of income. The islands receive income from postage stamps produced in the UK, the sale of fishing licenses, and harbor and landing fees from tourist vessels. Tourism from specialized cruise ships is increasing rapidly.

# COMMUNICATIONS :: SOUTH GEORGIA AND SOUTH SANDWICH ISLANDS

# TRANSPORTATION :: SOUTH GEORGIA AND SOUTH SANDWICH ISLANDS

**PORTS AND TERMINALS:**

major seaport(s): Grytviken

# MILITARY AND SECURITY :: SOUTH GEORGIA AND SOUTH SANDWICH ISLANDS

**MILITARY - NOTE:**

defense is the responsibility of the UK

# TRANSNATIONAL ISSUES :: SOUTH GEORGIA AND SOUTH SANDWICH ISLANDS

**DISPUTES - INTERNATIONAL:**

Argentina, which claims the islands in its constitution and briefly occupied them by force in 1982, agreed in 1995 to no longer seek settlement by force

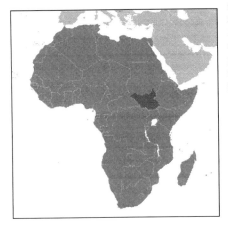

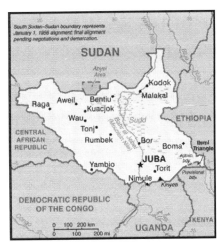

# AFRICA :: SOUTH SUDAN

## INTRODUCTION :: SOUTH SUDAN

### BACKGROUND:

Egypt attempted to colonize the region of southern Sudan by establishing the province of Equatoria in the 1870s. Islamic Mahdist revolutionaries overran the region in 1885, but in 1898 a British force was able to overthrow the Mahdist regime. An Anglo-Egyptian Sudan was established the following year with Equatoria being the southernmost of its eight provinces. The isolated region was largely left to itself over the following decades, but Christian missionaries converted much of the population and facilitated the spread of English. When Sudan gained its independence in 1956, it was with the understanding that the southerners would be able to participate fully in the political system. When the Arab Khartoum government reneged on its promises, a mutiny began that led to two prolonged periods of conflict (1955-1972 and 1983-2005) in which perhaps 2.5 million people died - mostly civilians - due to starvation and drought. Ongoing peace talks finally resulted in a Comprehensive Peace Agreement, signed in January 2005. As part of this agreement, the south was granted a six-year period of autonomy to be followed by a referendum on final status. The result of this referendum, held in January 2011, was a vote of 98% in favor of secession.

Since independence on 9 July 2011, South Sudan has struggled with good governance and nation building and has attempted to control opposition forces operating in its territory. Economic conditions have deteriorated since January 2012 when the government decided to shut down oil production following bilateral disagreements with Sudan. In December 2013, conflict between government and opposition forces killed tens of thousands and led to a dire humanitarian crisis with millions of South Sudanese displaced and food insecure. The warring parties signed a peace agreement in August 2015 that created a transitional government of national unity in April 2016. However, in July 2016, fighting broke out in Juba between the two principal signatories, plunging the country back into conflict.

## GEOGRAPHY :: SOUTH SUDAN

### LOCATION:

East-Central Africa; south of Sudan, north of Uganda and Kenya, west of Ethiopia

### GEOGRAPHIC COORDINATES:

8 00 N, 30 00 E

### MAP REFERENCES:

Africa

### AREA:

total: 644,329 sq km

land: NA

water: NA

country comparison to the world: 43

### AREA - COMPARATIVE:

more than four times the size of Georgia; slightly smaller than Texas

### LAND BOUNDARIES:

total: 6,018 km

border countries (6): Central African Republic 1055 km, Democratic Republic of the Congo 714 km, Ethiopia 1299 km, Kenya 317 km, Sudan 2158 km, Uganda 475 km

note: South Sudan-Sudan boundary represents 1 January 1956 alignment; final alignment pending negotiations and demarcation; final sovereignty status of Abyei Area pending negotiations between South Sudan and Sudan

### COASTLINE:

0 km (landlocked)

### MARITIME CLAIMS:

none (landlocked)

### CLIMATE:

hot with seasonal rainfall influenced by the annual shift of the Inter-Tropical Convergence Zone; rainfall heaviest in upland areas of the south and diminishes to the north

### TERRAIN:

plains in the north and center rise to southern highlands along the border with Uganda and Kenya; the White Nile, flowing north out of the uplands of Central Africa, is the major geographic feature of the country; The Sudd (a name derived from floating vegetation that hinders navigation) is a large swampy area of more than 100,000 sq km fed by the waters of the White Nile that dominates the center of the country

### ELEVATION:

381 m lowest point: White Nile

3187 highest point: Kinyeti

### NATURAL RESOURCES:

hydropower, fertile agricultural land, gold, diamonds, petroleum, hardwoods, limestone, iron ore, copper, chromium ore, zinc, tungsten, mica, silver

**LAND USE:**

agricultural land: 100%

arable land: 0% / permanent crops: 0% / permanent pasture: 100%

forest: 0%

other: 0%

**IRRIGATED LAND:**
1,000 sq km (2012)

**POPULATION DISTRIBUTION:**
clusters found in urban areas, particularly in the western interior and around the White Nile

**ENVIRONMENT - CURRENT ISSUES:**
water pollution; inadequate supplies of potable water; wildlife conservation and loss of biodiversity; deforestation; soil erosion; desertification; periodic drought

**GEOGRAPHY - NOTE:**
landlocked; The Sudd is a vast swamp in the north central region of South Sudan, formed by the White Nile, its size is variable but can reach some 15% of the country's total area during the rainy season; it is one of the world's largest wetlands

## PEOPLE AND SOCIETY :: SOUTH SUDAN

**POPULATION:**
10,204,581 (July 2018 est.)

country comparison to the world: 89

**NATIONALITY:**

noun: South Sudanese (singular and plural)

adjective: South Sudanese

**ETHNIC GROUPS:**
Dinka 35.8%, Nuer 15.6%, Shilluk, Azande, Bari, Kakwa, Kuku, Murle, Mandari, Didinga, Ndogo, Bviri, Lndi, Anuak, Bongo, Lango, Dungotona, Acholi, Baka, Fertit (2011 est.)

**LANGUAGES:**
English (official), Arabic (includes Juba and Sudanese variants), regional languages include Dinka, Nuer, Bari, Zande, Shilluk

**RELIGIONS:**
animist, Christian

**DEMOGRAPHIC PROFILE:**
South Sudan, independent from Sudan since July 2011 after decades of civil war, is one of the world's poorest countries and ranks among the lowest in many socioeconomic categories. Problems are exacerbated by ongoing tensions with Sudan over oil revenues and land borders, fighting between government forces and rebel groups, and inter-communal violence. Most of the population lives off of farming, while smaller numbers rely on animal husbandry; more than 80% of the populace lives in rural areas. The maternal mortality rate is among the world's highest for a variety of reasons, including a shortage of health care workers, facilities, and supplies; poor roads and a lack of transport; and cultural beliefs that prevent women from seeking obstetric care. Most women marry and start having children early, giving birth at home with the assistance of traditional birth attendants, who are unable to handle complications.

Educational attainment is extremely poor due to the lack of schools, qualified teachers, and materials. Less than a third of the population is literate (the rate is even lower among women), and half live below the poverty line. Teachers and students are also struggling with the switch from Arabic to English as the language of instruction. Many adults missed out on schooling because of warfare and displacement.

Almost 2 million South Sudanese have sought refuge in neighboring countries since the current conflict began in December 2013. Another 1.96 million South Sudanese are internally displaced as of August 2017. Despite South Sudan's instability and lack of infrastructure and social services, more than 240,000 people have fled to South Sudan to escape fighting in Sudan.

**AGE STRUCTURE:**

0-14 years: 42.3% (male 2,194,952 /female 2,121,990)

15-24 years: 20.94% (male 1,113,008 /female 1,023,954)

25-54 years: 30.45% (male 1,579,519 /female 1,528,165)

55-64 years: 3.82% (male 215,247 /female 174,078)

65 years and over: 2.49% (male 145,812 /female 107,856) (2018 est.)

**DEPENDENCY RATIOS:**

total dependency ratio: 83.7 (2015 est.)

youth dependency ratio: 77.3 (2015 est.)

elderly dependency ratio: 6.4 (2015 est.)

potential support ratio: 15.7 (2015 est.)

**MEDIAN AGE:**

total: 18.1 years

male: 18.4 years

female: 17.8 years (2018 est.)

country comparison to the world: 212

**POPULATION GROWTH RATE:**
-1.16% (2018 est.)

country comparison to the world: 230

**BIRTH RATE:**
36.9 births/1,000 population (2018 est.)

country comparison to the world: 15

**DEATH RATE:**
19.3 deaths/1,000 population (2018 est.)

country comparison to the world: 1

**NET MIGRATION RATE:**
10.6 migrant(s)/1,000 population (2017 est.)

country comparison to the world: 8

**POPULATION DISTRIBUTION:**
clusters found in urban areas, particularly in the western interior and around the White Nile

**URBANIZATION:**

urban population: 19.6% of total population (2018)

rate of urbanization: 4.1% annual rate of change (2015-20 est.)

**MAJOR URBAN AREAS - POPULATION:**
369,000 JUBA (capital) (2018)

**SEX RATIO:**

0-14 years: 1.04 male(s)/female

15-24 years: 1.11 male(s)/female

25-54 years: 0.94 male(s)/female

55-64 years: 1.16 male(s)/female

65 years and over: 1.32 male(s)/female

total population: 1.03 male(s)/female

**MATERNAL MORTALITY RATE:**
789 deaths/100,000 live births (2015 est.)

country comparison to the world: 5

**INFANT MORTALITY RATE:**

total: 90.4 deaths/1,000 live births (2018 est.)

male: 97.1 deaths/1,000 live births (2018 est.)

female: 83.5 deaths/1,000 live births (2018 est.)

country comparison to the world: 3

**TOTAL FERTILITY RATE:**

5.34 children born/woman (2018 est.)

country comparison to the world: 10

**CONTRACEPTIVE PREVALENCE RATE:**

4% (2010)

**HEALTH EXPENDITURES:**

2.7% of GDP (2014)

country comparison to the world: 185

**DRINKING WATER SOURCE:**

improved:

urban: 66.7% of population

rural: 56.9% of population

total: 58.7% of population

unimproved:

urban: 33.3% of population

rural: 43.1% of population

total: 41.3% of population (2015 est.)

**SANITATION FACILITY ACCESS:**

improved:

urban: 16.4% of population (2015 est.)

rural: 4.5% of population (2015 est.)

total: 6.7% of population (2015 est.)

unimproved:

urban: 83.6% of population (2015 est.)

rural: 95.5% of population (2015 est.)

total: 93.3% of population (2015 est.)

**HIV/AIDS - ADULT PREVALENCE RATE:**

2.4% (2017 est.)

country comparison to the world: 22

**HIV/AIDS - PEOPLE LIVING WITH HIV/AIDS:**

150,000 (2017 est.)

country comparison to the world: 34

**HIV/AIDS - DEATHS:**

12,000 (2017 est.)

country comparison to the world: 20

**MAJOR INFECTIOUS DISEASES:**

degree of risk: very high (2016)

food or waterborne diseases: bacterial and protozoal diarrhea, hepatitis A and E, and typhoid fever (2016)

vectorborne diseases: malaria, dengue fever, trypanosomiasis-Gambiense (African sleeping sickness) (2016)

water contact diseases: schistosomiasis (2016)

animal contact diseases: rabies (2016)

respiratory diseases: meningococcal meningitis (2016)

**OBESITY - ADULT PREVALENCE RATE:**

6.6% (2014)

country comparison to the world: 165

**CHILDREN UNDER THE AGE OF 5 YEARS UNDERWEIGHT:**

27.6% (2010)

country comparison to the world: 13

**EDUCATION EXPENDITURES:**

1.8% of GDP (2016)

country comparison to the world: 174

**LITERACY:**

definition: age 15 and over can read and write (2009 est.)

total population: 27% (2009 est.)

male: 40% (2009 est.)

female: 16% (2009 est.)

**UNEMPLOYMENT, YOUTH AGES 15-24:**

total: 18.5% (2008 est.)

male: 20% (2008 est.)

female: 17% (2008 est.)

country comparison to the world: 70

# GOVERNMENT :: SOUTH SUDAN

**COUNTRY NAME:**

conventional long form: Republic of South Sudan

conventional short form: South Sudan

etymology: self-descriptive name from the country's former position within Sudan prior to independence; the name "Sudan" derives from the Arabic "bilad-as-sudan" meaning "Land of the Black [peoples]"

**GOVERNMENT TYPE:**

presidential republic

**CAPITAL:**

name: Juba

geographic coordinates: 04 51 N, 31 37 E

time difference: UTC+3 (8 hours ahead of Washington, DC, during Standard Time)

**ADMINISTRATIVE DIVISIONS:**

10 states; Central Equatoria, Eastern Equatoria, Jonglei, Lakes, Northern Bahr el Ghazal, Unity, Upper Nile, Warrap, Western Bahr el Ghazal, Western Equatoria; note - in 2015, the creation of 28 new states was announced and in 2017 four additional, but these 32 states have not yet been vetted by the US Board on Geographic Names

**INDEPENDENCE:**

9 July 2011 (from Sudan)

**NATIONAL HOLIDAY:**

Independence Day, 9 July (2011)

**CONSTITUTION:**

history: previous 2005 (preindependence); latest signed 7 July 2011, effective 9 July 2011 (Transitional Constitution of the Republic of South Sudan, 2011) (2018)

amendments: proposed by the National Legislature or by the president of the republic; passage requires submission of the proposal to the Legislature at least one month prior to consideration, approval by at least two-thirds majority vote in both houses of the Legislature, and assent by the president; amended 2013, 2015, 2018 (2018)

**CITIZENSHIP:**

citizenship by birth: no

citizenship by descent only: at least one parent must be a citizen of South Sudan

dual citizenship recognized: yes

residency requirement for naturalization: 10 years

**SUFFRAGE:**

18 years of age; universal

**EXECUTIVE BRANCH:**

chief of state: President Salva KIIR Mayardit (since 9 July 2011); First Vice President Taban Deng GAI (since 26 July 2016); Second Vice President James Wani IGGA (since 26 April 2016); note - the president is both chief of state and head of government

head of government: President Salva KIIR Mayardit (since 9 July 2011); First Vice President Taban Deng GAI (since 26 July 2016); Second Vice President James Wani IGGA (since 26 April 2016)

cabinet: National Council of Ministers appointed by the president, approved by the Transitional National Legislative Assembly

elections/appointments: president directly elected by simple majority popular vote for a 4-year term (eligible for a second term); election last held on 11-15 April 2010 (next election scheduled for 2015 postponed to 2018 and again to 2021)

**election results:** Salva KIIR Mayardit elected president; percent of vote - Salva KIIR Mayardit (SPLM) 93%, Lam AKOL (SPLM-DC) 7%

## LEGISLATIVE BRANCH:

**description:** bicameral National Legislature consists of:
Council of States, established by presidential decree in August 2011 (50 seats; 20 former members of the Council of States and 30 appointed representatives)
Transitional National Legislative Assembly, established on 4 August 2016, in accordance with the August 2015 Agreement on the Resolution of the Conflict in the Republic of South Sudan (400 seats; 170 members elected in April 2010, 96 members of the former National Assembly, 66 members appointed after independence, and 68 members added as a result of the 2016 Agreement)

**elections:**
Council of States - established and members appointed 1 August 2011
National Legislative Assembly - last held 11-15 April 2010 but did not take office until July 2011; current parliamentary term extended until 2021)

**election results:**
Council of States - percent of vote by party - NA; seats by party - SPLM 20, unknown 30
National Legislative Assembly - percent of vote by party - NA; seats by party - SPLM 251, DCP 10, independent 6, unknown 65

## JUDICIAL BRANCH:

**highest courts:** Supreme Court of South Sudan (consists of the chief and deputy chief justices, 9 other justices and normally organized into panels of 3 justices except when sitting as a Constitutional panel of all 9 justices chaired by the chief justice)

**judge selection and term of office:** justices appointed by the president upon proposal of the Judicial Service Council, a 9-member judicial and administrative body; justice tenure set by the National Legislature

**subordinate courts:** national level - Courts of Appeal; High Courts; County Courts; state level - High Courts; County Courts; customary courts; other specialized courts and tribunals

## POLITICAL PARTIES AND LEADERS:

Democratic Change or DC [Onyoti Adigo NYIKWEC] (formerly Sudan People's Liberation Movement-Democratic Movement or SPLM-DC)Sudan People's Liberation Movement or SPLM [Salva KIIR Mayardit]Sudan People's Liberation Movement-In Opposition or SPLM-IO [Riek MACHAR Teny Dhurgon]

## INTERNATIONAL ORGANIZATION PARTICIPATION:

AU, FAO, G-77, IBRD, ICAO, ICRM, IDA, IFAD, IFC, IFRCS, ILO, IMF, Interpol, IOM, IPU, ITU, MIGA, UN, UNCTAD, UNESCO, UPU, WCO, WHO, WMO

## DIPLOMATIC REPRESENTATION IN THE US:

**chief of mission:** Ambassador Philip Jada NATANA (since 17 September 2018)

**chancery:** 1015 31st St., NW, Third Floor, Washington, DC, 20007

**telephone:** [1] (202) 293-7940

**FAX:** [1] (202) 293-7941

## DIPLOMATIC REPRESENTATION FROM THE US:

**chief of mission:** Ambassador Thomas HUSHEK (since 5 June 2018)

**embassy:** Kololo Road adjacent to the EU's compound, Juba

**telephone:** [211] 912-105-188

## FLAG DESCRIPTION:

three equal horizontal bands of black (top), red, and green; the red band is edged in white; a blue isosceles triangle based on the hoist side contains a gold, five-pointed star; black represents the people of South Sudan, red the blood shed in the struggle for freedom, green the verdant land, and blue the waters of the Nile; the gold star represents the unity of the states making up South Sudan

**note:** resembles the flag of Kenya; one of only two national flags to display six colors as part of its primary design, the other is South Africa's

## NATIONAL SYMBOL(S):

African fish eagle; national colors: red, green, blue, yellow, black, white

## NATIONAL ANTHEM:

**name:** South Sudan Oyee! (Hooray!)

**lyrics/music:** collective of 49 poets/Juba University students and teachers

**note:** adopted 2011; anthem selected in a national contest

# ECONOMY :: SOUTH SUDAN

## ECONOMY - OVERVIEW:

Industry and infrastructure in landlocked South Sudan are severely underdeveloped and poverty is widespread, following several decades of civil war with Sudan. Continued fighting within the new nation is disrupting what remains of the economy. The vast majority of the population is dependent on subsistence agriculture and humanitarian assistance. Property rights are insecure and price signals are weak, because markets are not well-organized.

South Sudan has little infrastructure – about 10,000 kilometers of roads, but just 2% of them paved. Electricity is produced mostly by costly diesel generators, and indoor plumbing and potable water are scarce, so less than 2% of the population has access to electricity. About 90% of consumed goods, capital, and services are imported from neighboring countries – mainly Uganda, Kenya and Sudan. Chinese investment plays a growing role in the infrastructure and energy sectors.

Nevertheless, South Sudan does have abundant natural resources. South Sudan holds one of the richest agricultural areas in Africa, with fertile soils and abundant water supplies. Currently the region supports 10-20 million head of cattle. At independence in 2011, South Sudan produced nearly three-fourths of former Sudan's total oil output of nearly a half million barrels per day. The Government of South Sudan relies on oil for the vast majority of its budget revenues, although oil production has fallen sharply since independence. South Sudan is one of the most oil-dependent countries in the world, with 98% of the government's annual operating budget and 80% of its gross domestic product (GDP) derived from oil. Oil is exported through a pipeline that runs to refineries and shipping facilities at Port Sudan on the Red Sea. The economy of South Sudan will remain linked to Sudan for some time, given the existing oil infrastructure. The outbreak of conflict in December 2013, combined with falling crude oil production and prices, meant that GDP fell significantly between 2014 and 2017. Since the second half of 2017 oil production has risen, and is currently about 130,000 barrels per day.

Poverty and food insecurity has risen due to displacement of people caused by the conflict. With famine spreading, 66% of the population in South Sudan is living on less than about $2 a day, up from 50.6% in 2009, according to the World Bank. About 80% of the population lives in rural areas, with agriculture, forestry and fishing providing the livelihood for a majority of the households. Much of rural sector activity is focused on low-input, low-output subsistence agriculture.

South Sudan is burdened by considerable debt because of increased military spending and high levels of government corruption. Economic mismanagement is prevalent. Civil servants, including police and the military, are not paid on time, creating incentives to engage in looting and banditry. South Sudan has received more than $11 billion in foreign aid since 2005, largely from the US, the UK, and the EU. Inflation peaked at over 800% per year in October 2016 but dropped to 118% in 2017. The government has funded its expenditures by borrowing from the central bank and foreign sources, using forward sales of oil as collateral. The central bank's decision to adopt a managed floating exchange rate regime in December 2015 triggered a 97% depreciation of the currency and spawned a growing black market.

Long-term challenges include rooting out public sector corruption, improving agricultural productivity, alleviating poverty and unemployment, improving fiscal transparency - particularly in regard to oil revenues, taming inflation, improving government revenues, and creating a rules-based business environment.

## GDP (PURCHASING POWER PARITY):

$20.01 billion (2017 est.)

$21.1 billion (2016 est.)

$24.52 billion (2015 est.)

note: data are in 2017 dollars

country comparison to the world: 149

## GDP (OFFICIAL EXCHANGE RATE):

$3.06 billion (2017 est.) (2017 est.)

## GDP - REAL GROWTH RATE:

-5.2% (2017 est.)

-13.9% (2016 est.)

-0.2% (2015 est.)

country comparison to the world: 218

## GDP - PER CAPITA (PPP):

$1,600 (2017 est.)

$1,700 (2016 est.)

$2,100 (2015 est.)

note: data are in 2017 dollars

country comparison to the world: 220

## GROSS NATIONAL SAVING:

3.6% of GDP (2017 est.)

18.7% of GDP (2016 est.)

7.4% of GDP (2015 est.)

country comparison to the world: 179

## GDP - COMPOSITION, BY END USE:

household consumption: 34.9% (2011 est.)

government consumption: 17.1% (2011 est.)

investment in fixed capital: 10.4% (2011 est.)

exports of goods and services: 64.9% (2011 est.)

imports of goods and services: -27.2% (2011 est.)

## AGRICULTURE - PRODUCTS:

sorghum, maize, rice, millet, wheat, gum arabic, sugarcane, mangoes, papayas, bananas, sweet potatoes, sunflower seeds, cotton, sesame seeds, cassava (manioc, tapioca), beans, peanuts; cattle, sheep

## POPULATION BELOW POVERTY LINE:

66% (2015 est.)

## DISTRIBUTION OF FAMILY INCOME - GINI INDEX:

46 (2010 est.)

country comparison to the world: 34

## BUDGET:

revenues: 259.6 million (FY2017/18 est.)

expenditures: 298.6 million (FY2017/18 est.)

## TAXES AND OTHER REVENUES:

8.5% (of GDP) (FY2017/18 est.)

country comparison to the world: 218

## BUDGET SURPLUS (+) OR DEFICIT (-):

-1.3% (of GDP) (FY2017/18 est.)

country comparison to the world: 87

## PUBLIC DEBT:

62.7% of GDP (2017 est.)

86.6% of GDP (2016 est.)

country comparison to the world: 69

## INFLATION RATE (CONSUMER PRICES):

187.9% (2017 est.)

379.8% (2016 est.)

country comparison to the world: 225

## COMMERCIAL BANK PRIME LENDING RATE:

13.38% (December 2017)

9.72% (December 2016)

country comparison to the world: 55

## STOCK OF NARROW MONEY:

$491.9 million (31 December 2017)

$409.1 million (31 December 2016)

country comparison to the world: 171

## STOCK OF BROAD MONEY:

$550.5 million (31 December 2017 est.)

$494.7 million (31 December 2016 est.)

country comparison to the world: 173

## CURRENT ACCOUNT BALANCE:

-$154 million (2017 est.)

$39 million (2016 est.)

country comparison to the world: 93

## EXPORTS:

$1.13 billion (2016 est.)

country comparison to the world: 156

## IMPORTS:

$3.795 billion (2016 est.)

$3.795 billion (2016 est.)

country comparison to the world: 141

## RESERVES OF FOREIGN EXCHANGE AND GOLD:

$73 million (31 December 2016 est.)

country comparison to the world: 184

## EXCHANGE RATES:

South Sudanese pounds (SSP) per US dollar -

0.885 (2017 est.)

0.903 (2016 est.)

0.9214 (2015 est.)

0.885 (2014 est.)

0.7634 (2013 est.)

# ENERGY :: SOUTH SUDAN

## ELECTRICITY ACCESS:

population without electricity: 11.2 million (2013)

electrification - total population: 1% (2013)

electrification - urban areas: 4% (2013)

electrification - rural areas: 0% (2013)

**ELECTRICITY - PRODUCTION:**

412.8 million kWh (2016 est.)

country comparison to the world: 169

**ELECTRICITY - CONSUMPTION:**

391.8 million kWh (2016 est.)

country comparison to the world: 175

**ELECTRICITY - EXPORTS:**

0 kWh (2016 est.)

country comparison to the world: 201

**ELECTRICITY - IMPORTS:**

0 kWh (2016 est.)

country comparison to the world: 203

**ELECTRICITY - INSTALLED GENERATING CAPACITY:**

80,400 kW (2016 est.)

country comparison to the world: 185

**ELECTRICITY - FROM FOSSIL FUELS:**

100% of total installed capacity (2016 est.)

country comparison to the world: 18

**ELECTRICITY - FROM NUCLEAR FUELS:**

0% of total installed capacity (2017 est.)

country comparison to the world: 186

**ELECTRICITY - FROM HYDROELECTRIC PLANTS:**

0% of total installed capacity (2017 est.)

country comparison to the world: 203

**ELECTRICITY - FROM OTHER RENEWABLE SOURCES:**

1% of total installed capacity (2017 est.)

country comparison to the world: 168

**CRUDE OIL - PRODUCTION:**

150,200 bbl/day (2017 est.)

country comparison to the world: 39

**CRUDE OIL - EXPORTS:**

147,300 bbl/day (2015 est.)

country comparison to the world: 32

**CRUDE OIL - IMPORTS:**

0 bbl/day (2015 est.)

country comparison to the world: 199

**CRUDE OIL - PROVED RESERVES:**

3.75 billion bbl (1 January 2017 est.)

country comparison to the world: 26

**REFINED PETROLEUM PRODUCTS - PRODUCTION:**

0 bbl/day (2017 est.)

country comparison to the world: 205

**REFINED PETROLEUM PRODUCTS - CONSUMPTION:**

8,000 bbl/day (2016 est.)

country comparison to the world: 165

**REFINED PETROLEUM PRODUCTS - EXPORTS:**

0 bbl/day (2015 est.)

country comparison to the world: 205

**REFINED PETROLEUM PRODUCTS - IMPORTS:**

7,160 bbl/day (2015 est.)

country comparison to the world: 157

**NATURAL GAS - PRODUCTION:**

0 cu m (2017 est.)

country comparison to the world: 199

**NATURAL GAS - CONSUMPTION:**

0 cu m (2017 est.)

country comparison to the world: 200

**NATURAL GAS - EXPORTS:**

0 cu m (2017 est.)

country comparison to the world: 188

**NATURAL GAS - IMPORTS:**

0 cu m (2017 est.)

country comparison to the world: 191

**NATURAL GAS - PROVED RESERVES:**

63.71 billion cu m (1 January 2016 est.)

country comparison to the world: 59

**CARBON DIOXIDE EMISSIONS FROM CONSUMPTION OF ENERGY:**

1.224 million Mt (2017 est.)

country comparison to the world: 163

## COMMUNICATIONS :: SOUTH SUDAN

**TELEPHONES - FIXED LINES:**

0 (2017 est.)

country comparison to the world: 221

**TELEPHONES - MOBILE CELLULAR:**

total subscriptions: 1,511,529 (2017 est.)

subscriptions per 100 inhabitants: 12 (2017 est.)

country comparison to the world: 154

**TELEPHONE SYSTEM:**

general assessment: one of the least developed telecommunications and Internet systems in the world; domestic mobile providers are waiting for a political settlement and the return of social stability in order to expand their networks; the few carriers in the market have reduced the areas in which they offer service, not expanded them; the government shut down the largest cellphone carrier, Vivacell, in March 2018, stranding 1.4 million customers over a disputed service fee arrangement (2017)

international: country code - 211 (2017)

**BROADCAST MEDIA:**

a single TV channel is controlled by the government; several private FM stations are operational, mostly sponsored by outside aid donors; some foreign radio broadcasts are available

**INTERNET COUNTRY CODE:**

.ss

**BROADBAND - FIXED SUBSCRIPTIONS:**

total: 150 (2017 est.)

subscriptions per 100 inhabitants: less than 1 (2017 est.)

country comparison to the world: 196

## TRANSPORTATION :: SOUTH SUDAN

**NATIONAL AIR TRANSPORT SYSTEM:**

annual freight traffic on registered air carriers: 0 mt-km

**CIVIL AIRCRAFT REGISTRATION COUNTRY CODE PREFIX:**

Z8 (2016)

**AIRPORTS:**

85 (2013)

country comparison to the world: 64

**AIRPORTS - WITH PAVED RUNWAYS:**

total: 3 (2013)

2,438 to 3,047 m: 1 (2013)

1,524 to 2,437 m: 2 (2013)

**AIRPORTS - WITH UNPAVED RUNWAYS:**

total: 82 (2013)

2,438 to 3,047 m: 1 (2013)

1,524 to 2,437 m: 12 (2013)

914 to 1,523 m: 35 (2013)

under 914 m: 34 (2013)

**HELIPORTS:**

1 (2013)

**RAILWAYS:**

total: 248 km (2018)

note: a narrow gauge, single-track railroad between Babonosa (Sudan) and Wau, the only existing rail system, was repaired in 2010 with $250 million in UN funds, but is not currently operational

**country comparison to the world:** 126
## ROADWAYS:
**total:** 7,000 km (2012)

**note:** most of the road network is unpaved and much of it is in disrepair; a 192-km paved road between the capital, Juba, and Nimule on the Ugandan border was constructed with USAID funds in 2012

**country comparison to the world:** 145
## WATERWAYS:
see entry for Sudan

# MILITARY AND SECURITY :: SOUTH SUDAN

## MILITARY EXPENDITURES:
10.93% of GDP (2015)

9.77% of GDP (2014)

7.41% of GDP (2013)

9.53% of GDP (2012)

5.91% of GDP (2011)

**country comparison to the world:** 2
## MILITARY BRANCHES:
South Sudan Defense Force (SSDF): ground force, navy, air force and air defense units (2017)

## MILITARY SERVICE AGE AND OBLIGATION:
18 is the legal minimum age for compulsory and voluntary military service; the Government of South Sudan signed agreements in March 2012 and August 2015 that included the demobilization of all child soldiers within the armed forces and opposition, but the recruitment of child soldiers by the warring parties continues; as of the end of 2017, UNICEF estimates that more than 19,000 child soldiers had been used in the country's civil war since it began in December 2013 (2017)

# TRANSNATIONAL ISSUES :: SOUTH SUDAN

## DISPUTES - INTERNATIONAL:
South Sudan-Sudan boundary represents 1 January 1956 alignment, final alignment pending negotiations and demarcationfinal sovereignty status of Abyei Area pending negotiations between South Sudan and Sudanperiodic violent skirmishes with South Sudanese residents over water and grazing rights persist among related pastoral populations along the border with the Central African Republicthe boundary that separates Kenya and South Sudan's sovereignty is unclear in the "Ilemi Triangle," which Kenya has administered since colonial times

## REFUGEES AND INTERNALLY DISPLACED PERSONS:
**refugees (country of origin):** 277,183 (Sudan) (refugees and asylum seekers), 15,432 (Democratic Republic of the Congo) (refugees and asylum seekers) (2018)

**IDPs:** 1.76 million (alleged coup attempt and ethnic conflict beginning in December 2013; information is lacking on those displaced in earlier years by: fighting in Abyei between the Sudanese Armed Forces and the Sudan People's Liberation Army (SPLA) in May 2011; clashes between the SPLA and dissident militia groups in South Sudan; inter-ethnic conflicts over resources and cattle; attacks from the Lord's Resistance Army; floods and drought) (2018)

## TRAFFICKING IN PERSONS:
**current situation:** South Sudan is a source and destination country for men, women, and children subjected to forced labor and sex trafficking; South Sudanese women and girls, particularly those who are internally displaced, orphaned, refugees, or from rural areas, are vulnerable to forced labor and sexual exploitation, often in urban centers; children may be victims of forced labor in construction, market vending, shoe shining, car washing, rock breaking, brick making, delivery cart pulling, and begging; girls are also forced into marriages and subsequently subjected to sexual slavery or domestic servitude; women and girls migrate willingly from Uganda, Kenya, Ethiopia, Eritrea, and the Democratic Republic of the Congo to South Sudan with the promise of legitimate jobs and are forced into the sex trade; inter-ethnic abductions and abductions by criminal groups continue, with abductees subsequently forced into domestic servitude, herding, or sex trafficking; in 2014, the recruitment and use of child soldiers increased significantly within government security forces and was also prevalent among opposition forces

**tier rating:** Tier 3 – South Sudan does not fully comply with the minimum standards for the elimination of trafficking and is not making significant efforts to do so; despite the government's formal recommitment to an action plan to eliminate the recruitment and use of child soldiers by 2016, the practice expanded during 2014, and the government did not hold any officers criminally responsible; government officials reportedly are complicit in trafficking offenses but these activities continue to go uninvestigated; authorities reportedly identified five trafficking victims but did not transfer them to care facilities; law enforcement continued to arrest and imprison individuals for prostitution, including trafficking victims; no known steps were taken to address the exploitation of South Sudanese nationals working abroad or foreign workers in South Sudan (2015)

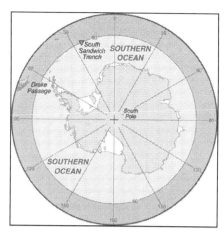

# OCEANS :: SOUTHERN OCEAN

## INTRODUCTION :: SOUTHERN OCEAN

### BACKGROUND:

A large body of recent oceanographic research has shown that the Antarctic Circumpolar Current (ACC), an ocean current that flows from west to east around Antarctica, plays a crucial role in global ocean circulation. The region where the cold waters of the ACC meet and mingle with the warmer waters of the north defines a distinct border - the Antarctic Convergence - which fluctuates with the seasons, but which encompasses a discrete body of water and a unique ecologic region. The Convergence concentrates nutrients, which promotes marine plant life, and which, in turn, allows for a greater abundance of animal life. In 2000, the International Hydrographic Organization delimited the waters within the Convergence as a fifth world ocean - the Southern Ocean - by combining the southern portions of the Atlantic Ocean, Indian Ocean, and Pacific Ocean. The Southern Ocean extends from the coast of Antarctica north to 60 degrees south latitude, which coincides with the Antarctic Treaty region and which approximates the extent of the Antarctic Convergence. As such, the Southern Ocean is now the fourth largest of the world's five oceans (after the Pacific Ocean, Atlantic Ocean, and Indian Ocean, but larger than the Arctic Ocean). It should be noted that inclusion of the Southern Ocean does not imply recognition of this feature as one of the world's primary oceans by the US Government.

## GEOGRAPHY :: SOUTHERN OCEAN

### LOCATION:

body of water between 60 degrees south latitude and Antarctica

### GEOGRAPHIC COORDINATES:

60 00 S, 90 00 E (nominally), but the Southern Ocean has the unique distinction of being a large circumpolar body of water totally encircling the continent of Antarctica; this ring of water lies between 60 degrees south latitude and the coast of Antarctica and encompasses 360 degrees of longitude

### MAP REFERENCES:

Antarctic Region

### AREA:

total: 20.327 million sq km

note: includes Amundsen Sea, Bellingshausen Sea, part of the Drake Passage, Ross Sea, a small part of the Scotia Sea, Weddell Sea, and other tributary water bodies

### AREA - COMPARATIVE:

slightly more than twice the size of the US

### COASTLINE:

17,968 km

### CLIMATE:

sea temperatures vary from about 10 degrees Celsius to -2 degrees Celsius; cyclonic storms travel eastward around the continent and frequently are intense because of the temperature contrast between ice and open ocean; the ocean area from about latitude 40 south to the Antarctic Circle has the strongest average winds found anywhere on Earth; in winter the ocean freezes outward to 65 degrees south latitude in the Pacific sector and 55 degrees south latitude in the Atlantic sector, lowering surface temperatures well below 0 degrees Celsius; at some coastal points intense persistent drainage winds from the interior keep the shoreline ice-free throughout the winter

### TERRAIN:

the Southern Ocean is 4,000 to 5,000-m deep over most of its extent with only limited areas of shallow water; the Antarctic continental shelf is generally narrow and unusually deep, its edge lying at depths of 400 to 800 m (the global mean is 133 m); the Antarctic icepack grows from an average minimum of 2.6 million sq km in March to about 18.8 million sq km in September, better than a sixfold increase in area

major surface currents: the cold, clockwise-flowing Antarctic Circumpolar Current (West Wind Drift; 21,000 km long) moves perpetually eastward around the continent and is the world's largest and strongest ocean current, transporting 130 million cubic meters of water per second - 100 times the flow of all the world's rivers; it is also the only current that flows all the way around the planet and connects the Atlantic, Pacific, and Indian Oceans; the cold Antarctic Coastal Current (East Wind Drift) is the southernmost current in the world, flowing westward and parallel to the Antarctic coastline

### ELEVATION:

elevation extremes: -7,235 m lowest point: southern end of the South Sandwich Trench

mean depth: -3,270 m

0 highest point: sea level

### NATURAL RESOURCES:

probable large oil and gas fields on the continental margin; manganese nodules, possible placer deposits, sand and gravel, fresh water as icebergs; squid, whales, and seals - none exploited; krill, fish

### NATURAL HAZARDS:

huge icebergs with drafts up to several hundred meters; smaller bergs and iceberg fragments; sea ice (generally 0.5 to 1 m thick) with sometimes dynamic short-term variations and with large annual and interannual variations; deep continental shelf floored by glacial deposits varying widely over short distances; high winds and large waves much of the year; ship icing, especially May-October; most of region is remote from sources of search and rescue

### ENVIRONMENT - CURRENT ISSUES:

changes to the ocean's physical, chemical, and biological systems have taken place because of climate change, ocean acidification, and commercial exploitation

## ENVIRONMENT - INTERNATIONAL AGREEMENTS:

the Southern Ocean is subject to all international agreements regarding the world's oceans; in addition, it is subject to these agreements specific to the Antarctic region: International Whaling Commission (prohibits commercial whaling south of 40 degrees south [south of 60 degrees south between 50 degrees and 130 degrees west]); Convention on the Conservation of Antarctic Seals (limits sealing); Convention on the Conservation of Antarctic Marine Living Resources (regulates fishing)

note: many nations (including the US) prohibit mineral resource exploration and exploitation south of the fluctuating Polar Front (Antarctic Convergence), which is in the middle of the Antarctic Circumpolar Current and serves as the dividing line between the cold polar surface waters to the south and the warmer waters to the north

## GEOGRAPHY - NOTE:

the major chokepoint is the Drake Passage between South America and Antarctica; the Polar Front (Antarctic Convergence) is the best natural definition of the northern extent of the Southern Ocean; it is a distinct region at the middle of the Antarctic Circumpolar Current that separates the cold polar surface waters to the south from the warmer waters to the north; the Front and the Current extend entirely around Antarctica, reaching south of 60 degrees south near New Zealand and near 48 degrees south in the far South Atlantic coinciding with the path of the maximum westerly winds

# GOVERNMENT :: SOUTHERN OCEAN

## COUNTRY NAME:

etymology: the International Hydrographic Organization (IHO) included the ocean and its definition as the waters south of 60 degrees south in its year 2000 revision, but this has not formally been adopted; the 2000 IHO definition, however, was circulated in a draft edition in 2002 and has acquired de facto usage by many nations and organizations, including the CIA

# ECONOMY :: SOUTHERN OCEAN

## ECONOMY - OVERVIEW:

Fisheries in 2013-14 landed 302,960 metric tons, of which 96% (291,370 tons-the highest reported catch since 1991) was krill and 4% (11,590 tons) Patagonian toothfish (also known as Chilean sea bass), compared to 15,330 tons in 2012-13 (estimated fishing from the area covered by the Convention of the Conservation of Antarctic Marine Living Resources, which extends slightly beyond the Southern Ocean area). International agreements were adopted in late 1999 to reduce illegal, unreported, and unregulated fishing, which in the 2000-01 season landed, by one estimate, 8,376 metric tons of Patagonian and Antarctic toothfish. In the 2014-15 Antarctic summer, 36,702 tourists visited the Southern Ocean, slightly lower than the 37,405 visitors in 2013-14 (estimates provided to the Antarctic Treaty by the International Association of Antarctica Tour Operators, and does not include passengers on overflights and those flying directly in and out of Antarctica).

# TRANSPORTATION :: SOUTHERN OCEAN

## PORTS AND TERMINALS:

major seaport(s): McMurdo, Palmer, and offshore anchorages in Antarctica

note: few ports or harbors exist on the southern side of the Southern Ocean; ice conditions limit use of most to short periods in midsummer; even then some cannot be entered without icebreaker escort; most Antarctic ports are operated by government research stations and, except in an emergency, are not open to commercial or private vessels

## TRANSPORTATION - NOTE:

Drake Passage offers alternative to transit through the Panama Canal

# TRANSNATIONAL ISSUES :: SOUTHERN OCEAN

## DISPUTES - INTERNATIONAL:

Antarctic Treaty defers claims (see Antarctica entry), but Argentina, Australia, Chile, France, NZ, Norway, and UK assert claims (some overlapping), including the continental shelf in the Southern Oceanseveral states have expressed an interest in extending those continental shelf claims under the UN Convention on the Law of the Sea to include undersea ridgesthe US and most other states do not recognize the land or maritime claims of other states and have made no claims themselves (the US and Russia have reserved the right to do so)no formal claims exist in the waters in the sector between 90 degrees west and 150 degrees west

# EUROPE :: SPAIN

## INTRODUCTION :: SPAIN

### BACKGROUND:

Spain's powerful world empire of the 16th and 17th centuries ultimately yielded command of the seas to England. Subsequent failure to embrace the mercantile and industrial revolutions caused the country to fall behind Britain, France, and Germany in economic and political power. Spain remained neutral in World War I and II but suffered through a devastating civil war (1936-39). A peaceful transition to democracy following the death of dictator Francisco FRANCO in 1975, and rapid economic modernization (Spain joined the EU in 1986) gave Spain a dynamic and rapidly growing economy and made it a global champion of freedom and human rights. More recently Spain has emerged from a severe economic recession that began in mid-2008, posting three straight years of GDP growth above the EU average. Unemployment has fallen, but remains high especially among youth. Spain is the Eurozone's fourth largest economy. In October 2017, the Catalan regional government conducted an illegal independence referendum and declared independence from Madrid. In response, the Spanish Government partially suspended Catalonia's autonomy and the international community has not recognized Catalonia's unilateral declaration of independence.

## GEOGRAPHY :: SPAIN

### LOCATION:

Southwestern Europe, bordering the Mediterranean Sea, North Atlantic Ocean, Bay of Biscay, and Pyrenees Mountains; southwest of France

### GEOGRAPHIC COORDINATES:

40 00 N, 4 00 W

### MAP REFERENCES:

Europe

### AREA:

**total:** 505,370 sq km

**land:** 498,980 sq km

**water:** 6,390 sq km

**note:** there are two autonomous cities - Ceuta and Melilla - and 17 autonomous communities including Balearic Islands and Canary Islands, and three small Spanish possessions off the coast of Morocco - Islas Chafarinas, Penon de Alhucemas, and Penon de Velez de la Gomera

country comparison to the world: 53

### AREA - COMPARATIVE:

almost five times the size of Kentucky; slightly more than twice the size of Oregon

### LAND BOUNDARIES:

**total:** 1,952.7 km

**border countries (6):** Andorra 63 km, France 646 km, Gibraltar 1.2 km, Portugal 1224 km, Morocco (Ceuta) 8 km, Morocco (Melilla) 10.5 km

**note:** an additional 75-meter border segment exists between Morocco and the Spanish exclave of Penon de Velez de la Gomera

### COASTLINE:

4,964 km

### MARITIME CLAIMS:

**territorial sea:** 12 nm

**exclusive economic zone:** 200 nm (applies only to the Atlantic Ocean)

**contiguous zone:** 24 nm

### CLIMATE:

temperate; clear, hot summers in interior, more moderate and cloudy along coast; cloudy, cold winters in interior, partly cloudy and cool along coast

### TERRAIN:

large, flat to dissected plateau surrounded by rugged hills; Pyrenees Mountains in north

### ELEVATION:

**mean elevation:** 660 m

**elevation extremes:** 0 m lowest point: Atlantic Ocean

3718 highest point: Pico de Teide (Tenerife) on Canary Islands

### NATURAL RESOURCES:

coal, lignite, iron ore, copper, lead, zinc, uranium, tungsten, mercury, pyrites, magnesite, fluorspar, gypsum, sepiolite, kaolin, potash, hydropower, arable land

### LAND USE:

**agricultural land:** 54.1% (2011 est.)

**arable land:** 24.9% (2011 est.) / **permanent crops:** 9.1% (2011 est.) / **permanent pasture:** 20.1% (2011 est.)

**forest:** 36.8% (2011 est.)

**other:** 9.1% (2011 est.)

### IRRIGATED LAND:

38,000 sq km (2012)

### POPULATION DISTRIBUTION:

with the notable exception of Madrid, Sevilla, and Zaragoza, the largest urban agglomerations are found along the Mediterranean and Atlantic coasts; numerous smaller cities are spread throughout the interior reflecting

Spain's agrarian heritage; dense settlement is found around the capital of Madrid, as well as the port city of Barcelona

### NATURAL HAZARDS:

periodic droughts, occasional flooding

**volcanism**: volcanic activity in the Canary Islands, located off Africa's northwest coast; Teide (3,715 m) has been deemed a Decade Volcano by the International Association of Volcanology and Chemistry of the Earth's Interior, worthy of study due to its explosive history and close proximity to human populations; La Palma (2,426 m), which last erupted in 1971, is the most active of the Canary Islands volcanoes; Lanzarote is the only other historically active volcano

### ENVIRONMENT - CURRENT ISSUES:

pollution of the Mediterranean Sea from raw sewage and effluents from the offshore production of oil and gas; water quality and quantity nationwide; air pollution; deforestation; desertification

### ENVIRONMENT - INTERNATIONAL AGREEMENTS:

**party to**: Air Pollution, Air Pollution-Nitrogen Oxides, Air Pollution-Sulfur 94, Air Pollution-Volatile Organic Compounds, Antarctic-Environmental Protocol, Antarctic-Marine Living Resources, Antarctic Treaty, Biodiversity, Climate Change, Climate Change-Kyoto Protocol, Desertification, Endangered Species, Environmental Modification, Hazardous Wastes, Law of the Sea, Marine Dumping, Marine Life Conservation, Ozone Layer Protection, Ship Pollution, Tropical Timber 83, Tropical Timber 94, Wetlands, Whaling

**signed, but not ratified**: Air Pollution-Persistent Organic Pollutants

### GEOGRAPHY - NOTE:

strategic location along approaches to Strait of Gibraltar; Spain controls a number of territories in northern Morocco including the enclaves of Ceuta and Melilla, and the islands of Penon de Velez de la Gomera, Penon de Alhucemas, and Islas Chafarinas

## PEOPLE AND SOCIETY :: SPAIN

### POPULATION:

49,331,076 (July 2018 est.)

country comparison to the world: 28

### NATIONALITY:

noun: Spaniard(s)

adjective: Spanish

### ETHNIC GROUPS:

Spanish 86.4%, Morocco 1.8%, Romania 1.3%, other 10.5% (2018 est.)

**note**: data represent population by country of birth

### LANGUAGES:

Castilian Spanish (official nationwide) 74%, Catalan (official in Catalonia, the Balearic Islands, and the Valencian Community (where it is known as Valencian)) 17%, Galician (official in Galicia) 7%, Basque (official in the Basque Country and in the Basque-speaking area of Navarre) 2%, Aranese (official in the northwest corner of Catalonia (Vall d'Aran) along with Catalan, <5,000 speakers)

**note**: Aragonese, Aranese Asturian, Basque, Calo, Catalan, Galician, and Valencian are recognized as regional languages under the European Charter for Regional or Minority Languages

### RELIGIONS:

Roman Catholic 70.2%, atheist 9.9%, other 2.6%, non-believer 15.1%, unspecified 2.1% (2016 est.)

### AGE STRUCTURE:

**0-14 years**: 15.29% (male 3,879,229 /female 3,664,016)

**15-24 years**: 9.65% (male 2,458,486 /female 2,299,523)

**25-54 years**: 44.54% (male 11,208,598 /female 10,762,651)

**55-64 years**: 12.38% (male 2,980,206 /female 3,125,949)

**65 years and over**: 18.15% (male 3,833,601 /female 5,118,817) (2018 est.)

### DEPENDENCY RATIOS:

**total dependency ratio**: 51 (2015 est.)

**youth dependency ratio**: 22.5 (2015 est.)

**elderly dependency ratio**: 28.5 (2015 est.)

**potential support ratio**: 3.5 (2015 est.)

### MEDIAN AGE:

**total**: 43.1 years

**male**: 41.9 years

**female**: 44.3 years (2018 est.)

country comparison to the world: 21

### POPULATION GROWTH RATE:

0.73% (2018 est.)

country comparison to the world: 137

### BIRTH RATE:

9 births/1,000 population (2018 est.)

country comparison to the world: 205

### DEATH RATE:

9.2 deaths/1,000 population (2018 est.)

country comparison to the world: 59

### NET MIGRATION RATE:

7.8 migrant(s)/1,000 population (2017 est.)

country comparison to the world: 13

### POPULATION DISTRIBUTION:

with the notable exception of Madrid, Sevilla, and Zaragoza, the largest urban agglomerations are found along the Mediterranean and Atlantic coasts; numerous smaller cities are spread throughout the interior reflecting Spain's agrarian heritage; dense settlement is found around the capital of Madrid, as well as the port city of Barcelona

### URBANIZATION:

**urban population**: 80.3% of total population (2018)

**rate of urbanization**: 0.33% annual rate of change (2015-20 est.)

**note**: data include Canary Islands, Ceuta, and Melilla

### MAJOR URBAN AREAS - POPULATION:

6.497 million MADRID (capital), 5.494 million Barcelona, 830,000 Valencia (2018)

### SEX RATIO:

**at birth**: 1.06 male(s)/female (2017 est.)

**0-14 years**: 1.06 male(s)/female (2017 est.)

**15-24 years**: 1.07 male(s)/female (2017 est.)

**25-54 years**: 1.04 male(s)/female (2017 est.)

**55-64 years**: 0.95 male(s)/female (2017 est.)

**65 years and over**: 0.74 male(s)/female (2017 est.)

**total population**: 0.98 male(s)/female (2017 est.)

### MOTHER'S MEAN AGE AT FIRST BIRTH:

30.7 years (2015 est.)

### MATERNAL MORTALITY RATE:

5 deaths/100,000 live births (2015 est.)

country comparison to the world: 173

### INFANT MORTALITY RATE:

total: 3.3 deaths/1,000 live births (2018 est.)

male: 3.6 deaths/1,000 live births (2018 est.)

female: 2.9 deaths/1,000 live births (2018 est.)

country comparison to the world: 207

**LIFE EXPECTANCY AT BIRTH:**

total population: 81.8 years (2018 est.)

male: 78.8 years (2018 est.)

female: 85 years (2018 est.)

country comparison to the world: 23

**TOTAL FERTILITY RATE:**

1.5 children born/woman (2018 est.)

country comparison to the world: 196

**CONTRACEPTIVE PREVALENCE RATE:**

70.9% (2016)

**HEALTH EXPENDITURES:**

9% of GDP (2014)

country comparison to the world: 41

**PHYSICIANS DENSITY:**

3.87 physicians/1,000 population (2015)

**HOSPITAL BED DENSITY:**

3 beds/1,000 population (2013)

**DRINKING WATER SOURCE:**

improved:

urban: 100% of population

rural: 100% of population

total: 100% of population

unimproved:

urban: 0% of population

rural: 0% of population

total: 0% of population (2015 est.)

**SANITATION FACILITY ACCESS:**

improved:

urban: 99.8% of population (2015 est.)

rural: 100% of population (2015 est.)

total: 99.9% of population (2015 est.)

unimproved:

urban: 0.2% of population (2015 est.)

rural: 0% of population (2015 est.)

total: 0.1% of population (2015 est.)

**HIV/AIDS - ADULT PREVALENCE RATE:**

0.4% (2017 est.)

country comparison to the world: 77

**HIV/AIDS - PEOPLE LIVING WITH HIV/AIDS:**

150,000 (2017 est.)

country comparison to the world: 35

**HIV/AIDS - DEATHS:**

NA

**OBESITY - ADULT PREVALENCE RATE:**

23.8% (2016)

country comparison to the world: 62

**EDUCATION EXPENDITURES:**

4.3% of GDP (2014)

country comparison to the world: 104

**LITERACY:**

definition: age 15 and over can read and write (2016 est.)

total population: 98.3% (2016 est.)

male: 98.8% (2016 est.)

female: 97.7% (2016 est.)

**SCHOOL LIFE EXPECTANCY (PRIMARY TO TERTIARY EDUCATION):**

total: 18 years (2015)

male: 18 years (2015)

female: 18 years (2015)

**UNEMPLOYMENT, YOUTH AGES 15-24:**

total: 38.6% (2017 est.)

male: 39.5% (2017 est.)

female: 37.4% (2017 est.)

country comparison to the world: 14

## GOVERNMENT :: SPAIN

**COUNTRY NAME:**

conventional long form: Kingdom of Spain

conventional short form: Spain

local long form: Reino de Espana

local short form: Espana

etymology: derivation of the name "Espana" is uncertain, but may come from the Phoenician term "span," related to the word "spy," meaning "to forge metals," so, "i-spn-ya" would mean "place where metals are forged"; the ancient Phoenicians long exploited the Iberian Peninsula for its mineral wealth

**GOVERNMENT TYPE:**

parliamentary constitutional monarchy

**CAPITAL:**

name: Madrid

geographic coordinates: 40 24 N, 3 41 W

time difference: UTC+1 (6 hours ahead of Washington, DC, during Standard Time)

daylight saving time: +1hr, begins last Sunday in March; ends last Sunday in October

note: Spain has two time zones, including the Canary Islands (UTC 0)

**ADMINISTRATIVE DIVISIONS:**

17 autonomous communities (comunidades autonomas, singular - comunidad autonoma) and 2 autonomous cities* (ciudades autonomas, singular - ciudad autonoma); Andalucia; Aragon; Asturias; Canarias (Canary Islands); Cantabria; Castilla-La Mancha; Castilla-Leon; Cataluna (Castilian), Catalunya (Catalan), Catalonha (Aranese) [Catalonia]; Ceuta*; Comunidad Valenciana (Castilian), Comunitat Valenciana (Valencian) [Valencian Community]; Extremadura; Galicia; Illes Baleares (Balearic Islands); La Rioja; Madrid; Melilla*; Murcia; Navarra (Castilian), Nafarroa (Basque) [Navarre]; Pais Vasco (Castilian), Euskadi (Basque) [Basque Country]

note: the autonomous cities of Ceuta and Melilla plus three small islands of Islas Chafarinas, Penon de Alhucemas, and Penon de Velez de la Gomera, administered directly by the Spanish central government, are all along the coast of Morocco and are collectively referred to as Places of Sovereignty (Plazas de Soberania)

**INDEPENDENCE:**

1492; the Iberian peninsula was characterized by a variety of independent kingdoms prior to the Muslim occupation that began in the early 8th century A.D. and lasted nearly seven centuries; the small Christian redoubts of the north began the reconquest almost immediately, culminating in the seizure of Granada in 1492; this event completed the unification of several kingdoms and is traditionally considered the forging of present-day Spain

**NATIONAL HOLIDAY:**

National Day (Hispanic Day), 12 October (1492); note - commemorates COLUMBUS' arrival in the Americas

**CONSTITUTION:**

history: previous 1812; latest approved by the General Courts 31 October 1978, passed by referendum 6

December 1978, signed by the king 27 December 1978, effective 29 December 1978 (2016)

**amendments:** proposed by the government, by the General Courts (the Congress or the Senate), or by the self-governing communities submitted through the government; passage requires three-fifths majority vote by both houses and passage by referendum if requested by one-tenth of members of either house; proposals disapproved by both houses are submitted to a joint committee, which submits an agreed upon text for another vote; passage requires two-thirds vote in Congress and simple majority vote in the Senate; amended 1992, 2007, 2011 (2016)

## LEGAL SYSTEM:

civil law system with regional variations

## INTERNATIONAL LAW ORGANIZATION PARTICIPATION:

accepts compulsory ICJ jurisdiction with reservations; accepts ICCt jurisdiction

## CITIZENSHIP:

**citizenship by birth:** no

**citizenship by descent only:** at least one parent must be a citizen of Spain

**dual citizenship recognized:** only with select Latin American countries

**residency requirement for naturalization:** 10 years for persons with no ties to Spain

## SUFFRAGE:

18 years of age; universal

## EXECUTIVE BRANCH:

**chief of state:** King FELIPE VI (since 19 June 2014); Heir Apparent Princess LEONOR, Princess of Asturias (daughter of the monarch, born 31 October 2005)

**head of government:** President of the Government (Prime Minister-equivalent) Pedro SANCHEZ Perez-Castejon (since 2 June 2018); Vice President (and Minister of the President's Office) Maria del Carmen CALVO Poyato (since 7 June 2018); note - Prime Minister RAJOY was ousted in a non-confidence vote on 1 June 2018

**cabinet:** Council of Ministers designated by the president

**elections/appointments:** the monarchy is hereditary; following legislative elections, the monarch usually proposes as president the leader of the party or coalition with the largest majority of seats, who is then indirectly elected by the Congress of Deputies; election last held on 26 June 2016 (next to be held in June 2020); vice president and Council of Ministers appointed by the president

**election results:** percent of National Assembly vote - NA

**note:** there is also a Council of State that is the supreme consultative organ of the government, but its recommendations are non-binding

## LEGISLATIVE BRANCH:

**description:** bicameral General Courts or Las Cortes Generales consists of: Senate or Senado (266 seats; 208 members directly elected in multi-seat constituencies by simple majority vote and 58 members indirectly elected by the legislatures of the autonomouse communities; members serve 4-year terms)
Congress of Deputies or Congreso de los Diputados (350 seats; 348 members directly elected in 50 multi-seat constituencies by proportional representation vote and 2 directly elected from the North African Ceuta and Melilla enclaves by simple majority vote; members serve 4-year terms or until the government is dissolved)

**elections:**
Senate - last held on 26 June 2016 (next to be held no later than June 2020)
Congress of Deputies - last held on 26 June 2016 (next to be held no later than June 2020)

**election results:**
Senate - percent of vote by party - NA; seats by party - PP 149, PSOE 62, Unidos Podemos 20, ERC 12, EAJ/PNV 6, other 17; composition - men 165, women 101, percent of women 38%
Congress of Deputies - percent of vote by party - PP 33%, PSOE 22.7%, Podemos 21.1%, C's 13%, ERC-CatSi 2.6%, EAJ/PNV 1.2%, other 6.4%; seats by party - PP 134, PSOE 84, Podemos 67, C's 32, ERC-CatSi 9, EAJ/PNV 5, other 19; composition - men 213, women 137, percent of women 38.6%

## JUDICIAL BRANCH:

**highest courts:** Supreme Court or Tribunal Supremo (consists of the court president and organized into the Civil Room with a president and 9 judges, the Penal Room with a president and 14 judges, the Administrative Room with a president and 32 judges, the Social Room with a president and 12 judges, and the Military Room with a president and 7 judges); Constitutional Court or Tribunal Constitucional de Espana (consists of 12 judges)

**judge selection and term of office:** Supreme Court judges appointed by the monarch from candidates proposed by the General Council of the Judiciary Power, a 20-member governing board chaired by the monarch that includes presidential appointees, and lawyers and jurists confirmed by the National Assembly; judges can serve until age 70; Constitutional Court judges nominated by the National Assembly, executive branch, and the General Council of the Judiciary, and appointed by the monarch for 9-year terms

**subordinate courts:** National High Court; High Courts of Justice (in each of the autonomous communities); provincial courts; courts of first instance

## POLITICAL PARTIES AND LEADERS:

Asturias Forum or FAC [Cristina COTO]
Basque Country Unite (Euskal Herria Bildu) or EH Bildu [Arnaldo OTEGI Mondragon] (coalition of 4 Basque pro-independence parties)
Basque Nationalist Party or PNV or EAJ [Andoni ORTUZAR]
Canarian Coalition or CC [Claudina MORALES Rodriguez] (coalition of 5 parties)
Canarian Nationalist Party or PNC [Juan Manuel GARCIA Ramos]
Catalan European Democratic Party or PDeCat [Artur MAS] (formerly Democratic Convergence of Catalonia)
Ciudadanos Party or C's [Albert RIVERA]
Compromis [Eric MORERA i Catala]
Galician Nationalist Bloc or BNG [Ana PONTON Mondelo]
Gomera Socialist Group or ASG [Casimiro CURBELO]
Initiative for Catalonia Greens or ICV [Joan HERRERA i Torres and Dolors CAMATS]
Unidos Podemos [Pablo IGLESIAS Turrion] (formerly Podemos IU; electoral coalition formed for May 2016 election)
Popular Party or PP [Pablo CASADO]
Republican Left of Catalonia or ERC [Oriol JUNQUERAS i Vies]
Spanish Socialist Workers Party or PSOE [Pedro SANCHEZ]
Union of People of Navarra or UPN [Javier ESPARZA]
Union, Progress and Democracy or

UPyD [Cristiano BROWN]
United Left or IU [Alberto GARZON] (coalition includes Communist Party of Spain or PCE and other small parties; ran as Popular Unity or UP in 2016 election)
Yes to the Future or Geroa Bai [Uxue BARKOS] (coalition include 4 Navarran parties)

### INTERNATIONAL ORGANIZATION PARTICIPATION:

ADB (nonregional member), AfDB (nonregional member), Arctic Council (observer), Australia Group, BCIE, BIS, CAN (observer), CBSS (observer), CD, CE, CERN, EAPC, EBRD, ECB, EIB, EITI (implementing country), EMU, ESA, EU, FAO, FATF, IADB, IAEA, IBRD, ICAO, ICC (national committees), ICCt, ICRM, IDA, IEA, IFAD, IFC, IFRCS, IHO, ILO, IMF, IMO, IMSO, Interpol, IOC, IOM, IPU, ISO, ITSO, ITU, ITUC (NGOs), LAIA (observer), MIGA, NATO, NEA, NSG, OAS (observer), OECD, OPCW, OSCE, Pacific Alliance (observer), Paris Club, PCA, PIF (partner), Schengen Convention, SELEC (observer), SICA (observer), UN, UNCTAD, UNESCO, UNHCR, UNIDO, UNIFIL, Union Latina, UNOCI, UNRWA, UNWTO, UPU, WCO, WHO, WIPO, WMO, WTO, ZC

### DIPLOMATIC REPRESENTATION IN THE US:

**chief of mission:** Ambassador Santiago CABANAS Ansorena (since 17 September 2018)

**chancery:** 2375 Pennsylvania Avenue NW, Washington, DC 20037

**telephone:** [1] (202) 452-0100, 728-2340

**FAX:** [1] (202) 833-5670

**consulate(s) general:** Boston, Chicago, Houston, Los Angeles, Miami, New York, San Francisco, San Juan (Puerto Rico)

**consulate(s):** Kansas City (MO)

### DIPLOMATIC REPRESENTATION FROM THE US:

**chief of mission:** Ambassador Richard BUCHAN (since December 2017) note - also accredited to Andorra

**embassy:** Serrano 75, 28006 Madrid

**mailing address:** PSC 61, APO AE 09642

**telephone:** [34] (91) 587-2200

**FAX:** [34] (91) 587-2303

**consulate(s) general:** Barcelona

### FLAG DESCRIPTION:

three horizontal bands of red (top), yellow (double width), and red with the national coat of arms on the hoist side of the yellow band; the coat of arms is quartered to display the emblems of the traditional kingdoms of Spain (clockwise from upper left, Castile, Leon, Navarre, and Aragon) while Granada is represented by the stylized pomegranate at the bottom of the shield; the arms are framed by two columns representing the Pillars of Hercules, which are the two promontories (Gibraltar and Ceuta) on either side of the eastern end of the Strait of Gibraltar; the red scroll across the two columns bears the imperial motto of "Plus Ultra" (further beyond) referring to Spanish lands beyond Europe; the triband arrangement with the center stripe twice the width of the outer dates to the 18th century

**note:** the red and yellow colors are related to those of the oldest Spanish kingdoms: Aragon, Castile, Leon, and Navarre

### NATIONAL SYMBOL(S):

Pillars of Hercules; national colors: red, yellow

### NATIONAL ANTHEM:

**name:** "Himno Nacional Espanol" (National Anthem of Spain)

**lyrics/music:** no lyrics/unknown

**note:** officially in use between 1770 and 1931, restored in 1939; the Spanish anthem is the first anthem to be officially adopted, but it has no lyrics; in the years prior to 1931 it became known as "Marcha Real" (The Royal March); it first appeared in a 1761 military bugle call book and was replaced by "Himno de Riego" in the years between 1931 and 1939; the long version of the anthem is used for the king, while the short version is used for the prince, prime minister, and occasions such as sporting events

## ECONOMY :: SPAIN

### ECONOMY - OVERVIEW:

After a prolonged recession that began in 2008 in the wake of the global financial crisis, Spain marked the fourth full year of positive economic growth in 2017, with economic activity surpassing its pre-crisis peak, largely because of increased private consumption. The financial crisis of 2008 broke 16 consecutive years of economic growth for Spain, leading to an economic contraction that lasted until late 2013. In that year, the government successfully shored up its struggling banking sector - heavily exposed to the collapse of Spain's real estate boom - with the help of an EU-funded restructuring and recapitalization program.

Until 2014, contraction in bank lending, fiscal austerity, and high unemployment constrained domestic consumption and investment. The unemployment rate rose from a low of about 8% in 2007 to more than 26% in 2013, but labor reforms prompted a modest reduction to 16.4% in 2017. High unemployment strained Spain's public finances, as spending on social benefits increased while tax revenues fell. Spain's budget deficit peaked at 11.4% of GDP in 2010, but Spain gradually reduced the deficit to about 3.3% of GDP in 2017. Public debt has increased substantially – from 60.1% of GDP in 2010 to nearly 96.7% in 2017.

Strong export growth helped bring Spain's current account into surplus in 2013 for the first time since 1986 and sustain Spain's economic growth. Increasing labor productivity and an internal devaluation resulting from moderating labor costs and lower inflation have improved Spain's export competitiveness and generated foreign investor interest in the economy, restoring FDI flows.

In 2017, the Spanish Government's minority status constrained its ability to implement controversial labor, pension, health care, tax, and education reforms. The European Commission expects the government to meet its 2017 budget deficit target and anticipates that expected economic growth in 2018 will help the government meet its deficit target. Spain's borrowing costs are dramatically lower since their peak in mid-2012, and increased economic activity has generated a modest level of inflation, at 2% in 2017.

### GDP (PURCHASING POWER PARITY):

$1.778 trillion (2017 est.)

$1.727 trillion (2016 est.)

$1.674 trillion (2015 est.)

**note:** data are in 2017 dollars

**country comparison to the world:** 15

### GDP (OFFICIAL EXCHANGE RATE):

$1.314 trillion (2017 est.) (2017 est.)

### GDP - REAL GROWTH RATE:

3% (2017 est.)

3.2% (2016 est.)

3.6% (2015 est.)

country comparison to the world: 116

**GDP - PER CAPITA (PPP):**

$38,400 (2017 est.)

$37,200 (2016 est.)

$36,100 (2015 est.)

note: data are in 2017 dollars

country comparison to the world: 49

**GROSS NATIONAL SAVING:**

23% of GDP (2017 est.)

22.4% of GDP (2016 est.)

21.5% of GDP (2015 est.)

country comparison to the world: 76

**GDP - COMPOSITION, BY END USE:**

household consumption: 57.7% (2017 est.)

government consumption: 18.5% (2017 est.)

investment in fixed capital: 20.6% (2017 est.)

investment in inventories: 0.6% (2017 est.)

exports of goods and services: 34.1% (2017 est.)

imports of goods and services: -31.4% (2017 est.)

**GDP - COMPOSITION, BY SECTOR OF ORIGIN:**

agriculture: 2.6% (2017 est.)

industry: 23.2% (2017 est.)

services: 74.2% (2017 est.)

**AGRICULTURE - PRODUCTS:**

grain, vegetables, olives, wine grapes, sugar beets, citrus; beef, pork, poultry, dairy products; fish

**INDUSTRIES:**

textiles and apparel (including footwear), food and beverages, metals and metal manufactures, chemicals, shipbuilding, automobiles, machine tools, tourism, clay and refractory products, footwear, pharmaceuticals, medical equipment

**INDUSTRIAL PRODUCTION GROWTH RATE:**

4% (2017 est.)

country comparison to the world: 76

**LABOR FORCE:**

22.75 million (2017 est.)

country comparison to the world: 27

**LABOR FORCE - BY OCCUPATION:**

agriculture: 4.2%

industry: 24%

services: 71.7% (2009)

**UNEMPLOYMENT RATE:**

17.2% (2017 est.)

19.6% (2016 est.)

country comparison to the world: 179

**POPULATION BELOW POVERTY LINE:**

21.1% (2012 est.)

**HOUSEHOLD INCOME OR CONSUMPTION BY PERCENTAGE SHARE:**

lowest 10%: 24% (2011)

highest 10%: 24% (2011)

**DISTRIBUTION OF FAMILY INCOME - GINI INDEX:**

35.9 (2012)

32 (2005)

country comparison to the world: 93

**BUDGET:**

revenues: 498.1 billion (2017 est.)

expenditures: 539 billion (2017 est.)

**TAXES AND OTHER REVENUES:**

37.9% (of GDP) (2017 est.)

country comparison to the world: 52

**BUDGET SURPLUS (+) OR DEFICIT (-):**

-3.1% (of GDP) (2017 est.)

country comparison to the world: 136

**PUBLIC DEBT:**

98.4% of GDP (2017 est.)

99% of GDP (2016 est.)

country comparison to the world: 18

**FISCAL YEAR:**

calendar year

**INFLATION RATE (CONSUMER PRICES):**

2% (2017 est.)

-0.2% (2016 est.)

country comparison to the world: 107

**CENTRAL BANK DISCOUNT RATE:**

0.05% (10 September 2014)

0.25% (13 November 2013)

note: this is the European Central Bank's rate on the marginal lending facility, which offers overnight credit to banks in the euro area

country comparison to the world: 146

**COMMERCIAL BANK PRIME LENDING RATE:**

2.03% (31 December 2017 est.)

2.19% (31 December 2016 est.)

country comparison to the world: 184

**STOCK OF NARROW MONEY:**

$1.088 trillion (31 December 2017 est.)

$841.6 billion (31 December 2016 est.)

note: see entry for the European Union for money supply for the entire euro area; the European Central Bank (ECB) controls monetary policy for the 18 members of the Economic and Monetary Union (EMU); individual members of the EMU do not control the quantity of money circulating within their own borders

country comparison to the world: 7

**STOCK OF BROAD MONEY:**

$1.088 trillion (31 December 2017 est.)

$841.6 billion (31 December 2016 est.)

country comparison to the world: 7

**STOCK OF DOMESTIC CREDIT:**

$2.491 trillion (31 December 2017 est.)

$2.21 trillion (31 December 2016 est.)

country comparison to the world: 10

**MARKET VALUE OF PUBLICLY TRADED SHARES:**

$787.2 billion (31 December 2015 est.)

$992.9 billion (31 December 2014 est.)

$1.117 trillion (31 December 2013 est.)

country comparison to the world: 15

**CURRENT ACCOUNT BALANCE:**

$24.74 billion (2017 est.)

$23.77 billion (2016 est.)

country comparison to the world: 15

**EXPORTS:**

$313.7 billion (2017 est.)

$280.5 billion (2016 est.)

country comparison to the world: 16

**EXPORTS - PARTNERS:**

France 15.1%, Germany 11.3%, Italy 7.8%, Portugal 7.1%, UK 6.9%, US 4.4% (2017)

**EXPORTS - COMMODITIES:**

machinery, motor vehicles; foodstuffs, pharmaceuticals, medicines, other consumer goods

**IMPORTS:**

$338.6 billion (2017 est.)

$300.2 billion (2016 est.)

country comparison to the world: 15

**IMPORTS - COMMODITIES:**

machinery and equipment, fuels, chemicals, semi-finished goods, foodstuffs, consumer goods, measuring and medical control instruments

**IMPORTS - PARTNERS:**

Germany 14.2%, France 11.9%, China 6.9%, Italy 6.8%, Netherlands 5.1%, UK 4% (2017)

**RESERVES OF FOREIGN EXCHANGE AND GOLD:**

$69.41 billion (31 December 2017 est.)

$63.14 billion (31 December 2016 est.)

country comparison to the world: 32

**DEBT - EXTERNAL:**

$2.094 trillion (31 December 2017 est.)

$1.963 trillion (31 March 2015 est.)

country comparison to the world: 10

**STOCK OF DIRECT FOREIGN INVESTMENT - AT HOME:**

$824.8 billion (31 December 2017 est.)

$739.7 billion (31 December 2016 est.)

country comparison to the world: 13

**STOCK OF DIRECT FOREIGN INVESTMENT - ABROAD:**

$776.8 billion (31 December 2017 est.)

$696.9 billion (31 December 2016 est.)

country comparison to the world: 14

**EXCHANGE RATES:**

euros (EUR) per US dollar -

0.885 (2017 est.)

0.903 (2016 est.)

0.9214 (2015 est.)

0.7525 (2014 est.)

0.7634 (2013 est.)

## ENERGY :: SPAIN

**ELECTRICITY ACCESS:**

electrification - total population: 100% (2016)

**ELECTRICITY - PRODUCTION:**

258.6 billion kWh (2016 est.)

country comparison to the world: 17

**ELECTRICITY - CONSUMPTION:**

239.5 billion kWh (2016 est.)

country comparison to the world: 15

**ELECTRICITY - EXPORTS:**

14.18 billion kWh (2016 est.)

country comparison to the world: 13

**ELECTRICITY - IMPORTS:**

21.85 billion kWh (2016 est.)

country comparison to the world: 9

**ELECTRICITY - INSTALLED GENERATING CAPACITY:**

105.9 million kW (2016 est.)

country comparison to the world: 12

**ELECTRICITY - FROM FOSSIL FUELS:**

47% of total installed capacity (2016 est.)

country comparison to the world: 157

**ELECTRICITY - FROM NUCLEAR FUELS:**

7% of total installed capacity (2017 est.)

country comparison to the world: 19

**ELECTRICITY - FROM HYDROELECTRIC PLANTS:**

14% of total installed capacity (2017 est.)

country comparison to the world: 108

**ELECTRICITY - FROM OTHER RENEWABLE SOURCES:**

32% of total installed capacity (2017 est.)

country comparison to the world: 15

**CRUDE OIL - PRODUCTION:**

2,252 bbl/day (2017 est.)

country comparison to the world: 85

**CRUDE OIL - EXPORTS:**

0 bbl/day (2017 est.)

country comparison to the world: 198

**CRUDE OIL - IMPORTS:**

1.325 million bbl/day (2017 est.)

country comparison to the world: 8

**CRUDE OIL - PROVED RESERVES:**

150 million bbl (1 January 2018 est.)

country comparison to the world: 62

**REFINED PETROLEUM PRODUCTS - PRODUCTION:**

1.361 million bbl/day (2017 est.)

country comparison to the world: 13

**REFINED PETROLEUM PRODUCTS - CONSUMPTION:**

1.296 million bbl/day (2017 est.)

country comparison to the world: 18

**REFINED PETROLEUM PRODUCTS - EXPORTS:**

562,400 bbl/day (2017 est.)

country comparison to the world: 16

**REFINED PETROLEUM PRODUCTS - IMPORTS:**

464,800 bbl/day (2017 est.)

country comparison to the world: 18

**NATURAL GAS - PRODUCTION:**

36.81 million cu m (2017 est.)

country comparison to the world: 87

**NATURAL GAS - CONSUMPTION:**

31.27 billion cu m (2017 est.)

country comparison to the world: 29

**NATURAL GAS - EXPORTS:**

2.888 billion cu m (2017 est.)

country comparison to the world: 36

**NATURAL GAS - IMPORTS:**

34.63 billion cu m (2017 est.)

country comparison to the world: 12

**NATURAL GAS - PROVED RESERVES:**

2.548 billion cu m (1 January 2018 est.)

country comparison to the world: 96

**CARBON DIOXIDE EMISSIONS FROM CONSUMPTION OF ENERGY:**

286.7 million Mt (2017 est.)

country comparison to the world: 25

## COMMUNICATIONS :: SPAIN

**TELEPHONES - FIXED LINES:**

total subscriptions: 19,680,973 (2017 est.)

subscriptions per 100 inhabitants: 40 (2017 est.)

country comparison to the world: 14

**TELEPHONES - MOBILE CELLULAR:**

total subscriptions: 52,484,655 (2017 est.)

subscriptions per 100 inhabitants: 107 (2017 est.)

country comparison to the world: 28

**TELEPHONE SYSTEM:**

general assessment: well-developed, modern facilities (2016)

domestic: combined fixed-line and mobile-cellular teledensity exceeds 145 telephones per 100 persons (2016)

international: country code - 34; submarine cables provide connectivity to Europe, Middle East, Asia, and US; satellite earth stations - 2 Intelsat (1 Atlantic Ocean and 1 Indian Ocean), NA Eutelsat; tropospheric scatter to adjacent countries (2016)

**BROADCAST MEDIA:**

a mixture of both publicly operated and privately owned TV and radio stations; overall, hundreds of TV channels are available including national, regional, local, public, and international channels; satellite and cable TV systems available; multiple national radio networks, a large number of regional radio networks, and a larger number of local radio stations; overall, hundreds of radio stations (2008)

**INTERNET COUNTRY CODE:**

.es

**INTERNET USERS:**

total: 39,123,384 (July 2016 est.)

percent of population: 80.6% (July 2016 est.)

country comparison to the world: 17

**BROADBAND - FIXED SUBSCRIPTIONS:**

total: 14,473,888 (2017 est.)

subscriptions per 100 inhabitants: 30 (2017 est.)

country comparison to the world: 13

## TRANSPORTATION :: SPAIN

**NATIONAL AIR TRANSPORT SYSTEM:**

number of registered air carriers: 20 (2015)

inventory of registered aircraft operated by air carriers: 414 (2015)

annual passenger traffic on registered air carriers: 60,809,228 (2015)

annual freight traffic on registered air carriers: 1,040,913,279 mt-km (2015)

**CIVIL AIRCRAFT REGISTRATION COUNTRY CODE PREFIX:**

EC (2016)

**AIRPORTS:**

150 (2013)

country comparison to the world: 38

**AIRPORTS - WITH PAVED RUNWAYS:**

total: 99 (2013)

over 3,047 m: 18 (2013)

2,438 to 3,047 m: 14 (2013)

1,524 to 2,437 m: 19 (2013)

914 to 1,523 m: 24 (2013)

under 914 m: 24 (2013)

**AIRPORTS - WITH UNPAVED RUNWAYS:**

total: 51 (2013)

1,524 to 2,437 m: 2 (2013)

914 to 1,523 m: 13 (2013)

under 914 m: 36 (2013)

**HELIPORTS:**

10 (2013)

**PIPELINES:**

10481 km gas, 616 km oil, 3461 km refined products (2013)

**RAILWAYS:**

total: 16,102 km (2014)

standard gauge: 2,312 km 1.435-m gauge (2,312 km electrified) (2014)

narrow gauge: 1,884.9 km 1.000-m gauge (807 km electrified) (2014)

broad gauge: 11,873 km 1.668-m gauge (6,488 km electrified) (2014)

28 0.914-m gauge (28 km electrified) 3.6 0.600-m gauge

country comparison to the world: 18

**ROADWAYS:**

total: 683,175 km (2011)

paved: 683,175 km (includes 16,205 km of expressways) (2011)

country comparison to the world: 11

**WATERWAYS:**

1,000 km (2012)

country comparison to the world: 64

**MERCHANT MARINE:**

total: 472 (2017)

by type: bulk carrier 1, general cargo 44, oil tanker 28, other 399 (2017)

country comparison to the world: 40

**PORTS AND TERMINALS:**

major seaport(s): Algeciras, Barcelona, Bilbao, Cartagena, Huelva, Tarragona, Valencia (all in Spain); Las Palmas, Santa Cruz de Tenerife (in the Canary Islands)

container port(s) (TEUs): Algeciras (4,761,428), Barcelona (2,236,960), Valencia (4,722,000) (2016)

LNG terminal(s) (import): Barcelona, Bilbao, Cartagena, Huelva, Mugardos, Sagunto

## MILITARY AND SECURITY :: SPAIN

**MILITARY EXPENDITURES:**

0.91% of GDP (2017)

1.21% of GDP (2016)

1.18% of GDP (2015)

country comparison to the world: 122

**MILITARY BRANCHES:**

Spanish Armed Forces: Army (Ejercito de Tierra), Spanish Navy (Armada Espanola, AE, includes Marine Corps), Spanish Air Force (Ejercito del Aire Espanola, EdA) (2013)

**MILITARY SERVICE AGE AND OBLIGATION:**

18-26 years of age for voluntary military service by a Spanish citizen or legal immigrant, 2-3 year obligation; women allowed to serve in all SAF branches, including combat units; no conscription, but Spanish Government retains right to mobilize citizens 19-25 years of age in a national emergency; mandatory retirement of non-NCO enlisted personnel at age 45 or 58, depending on service length (2013)

## TERRORISM :: SPAIN

**TERRORIST GROUPS - HOME BASED:**

Basque Fatherland and Liberty (ETA):
aim(s): establish an independent Basque homeland in northern Spain and southwestern France based on Marxist principles
area(s) of operation: headquartered in northern Spain, reportedly disarmed in 2017 (April 2018)

## TRANSNATIONAL ISSUES :: SPAIN

**DISPUTES - INTERNATIONAL:**

in 2002, Gibraltar residents voted overwhelmingly by referendum to reject any "shared sovereignty" arrangement; the Government of Gibraltar insists on equal participation in talks between the UK and Spain; Spain disapproves of UK plans to grant Gibraltar greater autonomyafter voters in the UK chose to leave the EU in a June 2016 referendum, Spain again proposed shared sovereignty of Gibraltar; UK officials rejected Spain's joint sovereignty proposalMorocco protests Spain's control over the coastal enclaves of Ceuta, Melilla, and the islands of Penon de Velez de la Gomera, Penon de Alhucemas, and Islas Chafarinas, and surrounding waters; both countries claim Isla Perejil (Leila Island)Morocco serves as the primary launching site of illegal migration into Spain from North AfricaPortugal does not recognize Spanish sovereignty over the territory of Olivenza based on a difference of interpretation of the 1815 Congress of Vienna and the 1801 Treaty of Badajoz

**REFUGEES AND INTERNALLY DISPLACED PERSONS:**

refugees (country of origin): 8,205 (Afghanistan) (2016), 29,603 (Venezuela) (economic and political crisis; includes Venezuelans who have claimed asylum or have received alternative legal stay), 9,260 (Ukraine)

(2018) note - estimate represents asylum applicants since the beginning of the Ukraine crisis in 2014 to September 2017

**stateless persons:** 1,596 (2017)

**note:** 120,198 estimated refugee and migrant arrivals (January 2015-December 2018); 28,707 migrant arrivals in 2017

## ILLICIT DRUGS:

despite rigorous law enforcement efforts, North African, Latin American, Galician, and other European traffickers take advantage of Spain's long coastline to land large shipments of cocaine and hashish for distribution to the European market; consumer for Latin American cocaine and North African hashish; destination and minor transshipment point for Southwest Asian heroin; money-laundering site for Colombian narcotics trafficking organizations and organized crime

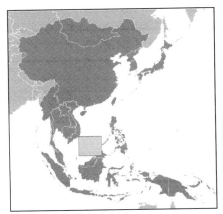

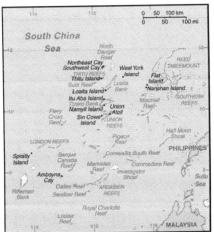

# EAST ASIA / SOUTHEAST ASIA :: SPRATLY ISLANDS

## INTRODUCTION :: SPRATLY ISLANDS

### BACKGROUND:
The Spratly Islands consist of more than 100 small islands or reefs surrounded by rich fishing grounds - and potentially by gas and oil deposits. They are claimed in their entirety by China, Taiwan, and Vietnam, while portions are claimed by Malaysia and the Philippines. About 45 islands are occupied by relatively small numbers of military forces from China, Malaysia, the Philippines, Taiwan, and Vietnam. Since 1985 Brunei has claimed a continental shelf that overlaps a southern reef but has not made any formal claim to the reef. Brunei claims an exclusive economic zone over this area.

## GEOGRAPHY :: SPRATLY ISLANDS

### LOCATION:
Southeastern Asia, group of reefs and islands in the South China Sea, about two-thirds of the way from southern Vietnam to the southern Philippines

### GEOGRAPHIC COORDINATES:
8 38 N, 111 55 E

### MAP REFERENCES:
Southeast Asia

### AREA:
**total:** 5 sq km less than

**land:** 5 sq km less than

**water:** 0 sq km

**note:** includes 100 or so islets, coral reefs, and sea mounts scattered over an area of nearly 410,000 sq km (158,000 sq mi) of the central South China Sea

**country comparison to the world:** 251

### AREA - COMPARATIVE:
land area is about seven times the size of the National Mall in Washington, DC

### LAND BOUNDARIES:
0 km

### COASTLINE:
926 km

### MARITIME CLAIMS:
NA

### CLIMATE:
tropical

### TERRAIN:
small, flat islands, islets, cays, and reefs

### ELEVATION:
0 m lowest point: South China Sea

6 highest point: unnamed location on Southwest Cay

### NATURAL RESOURCES:
fish, guano, undetermined oil and natural gas potential

### LAND USE:
**agricultural land:** 0% (2011 est.)

**arable land:** 0% (2011 est.) / **permanent crops:** 0% (2011 est.) / **permanent pasture:** 0% (2011 est.)

**forest:** 0% (2011 est.)

**other:** 100% (2011 est.)

### NATURAL HAZARDS:
typhoons; numerous reefs and shoals pose a serious maritime hazard

### ENVIRONMENT - CURRENT ISSUES:
China's use of dredged sand and coral to build artificial islands harms reef systems; illegal fishing practices indiscriminately harvest endangered species, including sea turtles and giant clams

### GEOGRAPHY - NOTE:
strategically located near several primary shipping lanes in the central South China Sea; includes numerous small islands, atolls, shoals, and coral reefs

## PEOPLE AND SOCIETY :: SPRATLY ISLANDS

### POPULATION:
no indigenous inhabitants

**note:** there are scattered garrisons occupied by military personnel of several claimant states

## GOVERNMENT :: SPRATLY ISLANDS

### COUNTRY NAME:
**conventional long form:** none

**conventional short form:** Spratly Islands

**etymology:** named after a British whaling captain Richard SPRATLY, who sighted Spratly Island in 1843; the name of the island eventually passed to the entire archipelago

## ECONOMY :: SPRATLY ISLANDS

### ECONOMY - OVERVIEW:
Economic activity is limited to commercial fishing. The proximity to nearby oil- and gas-producing sedimentary basins indicate potential oil and gas deposits, but the region is largely unexplored. No reliable estimates of potential reserves are

available. Commercial exploitation has yet to be developed.

## TRANSPORTATION :: SPRATLY ISLANDS

### AIRPORTS:
4 (2013)

country comparison to the world: 189

### AIRPORTS - WITH PAVED RUNWAYS:
total: 3 (2013)

914 to 1,523 m: 2 (2013)

under 914 m: 1 (2013)

### AIRPORTS - WITH UNPAVED RUNWAYS:
total: 1 (2013)

914 to 1,523 m: 1 (2013)

### HELIPORTS:
3 (2013)

### PORTS AND TERMINALS:
none; offshore anchorage only

## MILITARY AND SECURITY :: SPRATLY ISLANDS

### MILITARY - NOTE:
Spratly Islands consist of more than 100 small islands or reefs of which about 45 are claimed and occupied by China, Malaysia, the Philippines, Taiwan, and Vietnam

## TRANSNATIONAL ISSUES :: SPRATLY ISLANDS

### DISPUTES - INTERNATIONAL:
all of the Spratly Islands are claimed by China (including Taiwan) and Vietnamparts of them are claimed by Brunei, Malaysia and the Philippinesdespite no public territorial claim to Louisa Reef, Brunei implicitly lays claim by including it within the natural prolongation of its continental shelf and basis for a seabed median with Vietnamclaimants in November 2002 signed the "Declaration on the Conduct of Parties in the South China Sea," which has eased tensions but falls short of a legally binding "code of conduct"in March 2005, the national oil companies of China, the Philippines, and Vietnam signed a joint accord to conduct marine seismic activities in the Spratly Islands

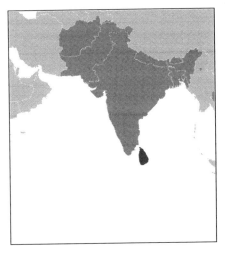

# SOUTH ASIA :: SRI LANKA

## INTRODUCTION :: SRI LANKA

### BACKGROUND:

The first Sinhalese arrived in Sri Lanka late in the 6th century B.C., probably from northern India. Buddhism was introduced circa 250 B.C., and the first kingdoms developed at the cities of Anuradhapura (from circa 200 B.C. to circa A.D. 1000) and Polonnaruwa (from about 1070 to 1200). In the 14th century, a south Indian dynasty established a Tamil kingdom in northern Sri Lanka. The Portuguese controlled the coastal areas of the island in the 16th century followed by the Dutch in the 17th century. The island was ceded to the British in 1796, became a crown colony in 1802, and was formally united under British rule by 1815. As Ceylon, it became independent in 1948; its name was changed to Sri Lanka in 1972. Prevailing tensions between the Sinhalese majority and Tamil separatists erupted into war in July 1983. Fighting between the government and Liberation Tigers of Tamil Eelam (LTTE) continued for over a quarter century. Although Norway brokered peace negotiations that led to a ceasefire in 2002, the fighting slowly resumed and was again in full force by 2006. The government defeated the LTTE in May 2009.

During the post-conflict years under President Mahinda RAJAPAKSA, the government enacted an ambitious program of infrastructure development projects, many of which were financed by loans from the Government of China. In 2015, a new coalition government headed by President Maithripala SIRISENA of the Sri Lanka Freedom Party and Prime Minister Ranil WICKREMESINGHE of the United National Party came to power with pledges to advance economic, governance, anti-corruption, reconciliation, justice, and accountability reforms. The government co-sponsored UN Human Rights Council resolutions articulating many of these commitments in 2015 and 2017, though progress on implementation has been uneven. Parliamentary discussions have yet to resolve differences on constitutional revision. Impunity for human rights violations and corruption remains a problem. According to government sources, 891,125 conflict-era internally displaced persons had resettled by October 2017.

## GEOGRAPHY :: SRI LANKA

### LOCATION:
Southern Asia, island in the Indian Ocean, south of India

### GEOGRAPHIC COORDINATES:
7 00 N, 81 00 E

### MAP REFERENCES:
Asia

### AREA:
total: 65,610 sq km
land: 64,630 sq km
water: 980 sq km
country comparison to the world: 123

### AREA - COMPARATIVE:
slightly larger than West Virginia

### LAND BOUNDARIES:
0 km

### COASTLINE:
1,340 km

### MARITIME CLAIMS:
territorial sea: 12 nm
exclusive economic zone: 200 nm
contiguous zone: 24 nm
continental shelf: 200 nm or to the edge of the continental margin

### CLIMATE:
tropical monsoon; northeast monsoon (December to March); southwest monsoon (June to October)

### TERRAIN:
mostly low, flat to rolling plain; mountains in south-central interior

### ELEVATION:
mean elevation: 228 m
elevation extremes: 0 m lowest point: Indian Ocean
2524 highest point: Pidurutalagala

### NATURAL RESOURCES:
limestone, graphite, mineral sands, gems, phosphates, clay, hydropower, arable land

### LAND USE:
agricultural land: 43.5% (2011 est.)
arable land: 20.7% (2011 est.) / permanent crops: 15.8% (2011 est.) / permanent pasture: 7% (2011 est.)
forest: 29.4% (2011 est.)
other: 27.1% (2011 est.)

### IRRIGATED LAND:
5,700 sq km (2012)

### POPULATION DISTRIBUTION:

the population is primarily concentrated within a broad wet zone in the southwest, urban centers along the eastern coast, and on the Jaffna Peninsula in the north

### NATURAL HAZARDS:
occasional cyclones and tornadoes

### ENVIRONMENT - CURRENT ISSUES:
deforestation; soil erosion; wildlife populations threatened by poaching and urbanization; coastal degradation from mining activities and increased pollution; coral reef destruction; freshwater resources being polluted by industrial wastes and sewage runoff; waste disposal; air pollution in Colombo

### ENVIRONMENT - INTERNATIONAL AGREEMENTS:
party to: Biodiversity, Climate Change, Climate Change-Kyoto Protocol, Desertification, Endangered Species, Environmental Modification, Hazardous Wastes, Law of the Sea, Ozone Layer Protection, Ship Pollution, Wetlands

signed, but not ratified: Marine Life Conservation

### GEOGRAPHY - NOTE:
strategic location near major Indian Ocean sea lanes; Adam's Bridge is a chain of limestone shoals between the southeastern coast of India and the northwestern coast of Sri Lanka; geological evidence suggests that this 50-km long Bridge once connected India and Sri Lanka; ancient records seem to indicate that a foot passage was possible between the two land masses until the 15th century when the land bridge broke up in a cyclone

## PEOPLE AND SOCIETY :: SRI LANKA

### POPULATION:
22,576,592 (July 2018 est.)

country comparison to the world: 57

### NATIONALITY:
noun: Sri Lankan(s)

adjective: Sri Lankan

### ETHNIC GROUPS:
Sinhalese 74.9%, Sri Lankan Tamil 11.2%, Sri Lankan Moors 9.2%, Indian Tamil 4.2%, other 0.5% (2012 est.)

### LANGUAGES:
Sinhala (official and national language) 87%, Tamil (official and national language) 28.5%, English 23.8% (2012 est.)

note: data represent main languages spoken by the population aged 10 years and older; shares sum to more than 100% because some respondents gave more than one answer on the census; English is commonly used in government and is referred to as the "link language" in the constitution

### RELIGIONS:
Buddhist (official) 70.2%, Hindu 12.6%, Muslim 9.7%, Roman Catholic 6.1%, other Christian 1.3%, other 0.05% (2012 est.)

### AGE STRUCTURE:
0-14 years: 23.75% (male 2,734,114 /female 2,627,695)

15-24 years: 14.6% (male 1,677,547 /female 1,618,922)

25-54 years: 41.46% (male 4,596,388 /female 4,762,913)

55-64 years: 10.22% (male 1,067,258 /female 1,239,204)

65 years and over: 9.98% (male 951,213 /female 1,301,338) (2018 est.)

### DEPENDENCY RATIOS:
total dependency ratio: 51.2 (2015 est.)

youth dependency ratio: 37.2 (2015 est.)

elderly dependency ratio: 14.1 (2015 est.)

potential support ratio: 7.1 (2015 est.)

### MEDIAN AGE:
total: 33.1 years

male: 31.8 years

female: 34.4 years (2018 est.)

country comparison to the world: 96

### POPULATION GROWTH RATE:
0.73% (2018 est.)

country comparison to the world: 138

### BIRTH RATE:
14.8 births/1,000 population (2018 est.)

country comparison to the world: 129

### DEATH RATE:
6.3 deaths/1,000 population (2018 est.)

country comparison to the world: 155

### NET MIGRATION RATE:
-1.3 migrant(s)/1,000 population (2017 est.)

country comparison to the world: 146

### POPULATION DISTRIBUTION:
the population is primarily concentrated within a broad wet zone in the southwest, urban centers along the eastern coast, and on the Jaffna Peninsula in the north

### URBANIZATION:
urban population: 18.5% of total population (2018)

rate of urbanization: 0.85% annual rate of change (2015-20 est.)

### MAJOR URBAN AREAS - POPULATION:
600,000 COLOMBO (capital), 103,000 Sri Jayewardenepura Kotte (legislative capital) (2018)

### SEX RATIO:
at birth: 1.04 male(s)/female (2017 est.)

0-14 years: 1.04 male(s)/female (2017 est.)

15-24 years: 1.03 male(s)/female (2017 est.)

25-54 years: 0.96 male(s)/female (2017 est.)

55-64 years: 0.86 male(s)/female (2017 est.)

65 years and over: 0.74 male(s)/female (2017 est.)

total population: 0.96 male(s)/female (2017 est.)

### MOTHER'S MEAN AGE AT FIRST BIRTH:
25.6 years (2016 est.)

note: median age at first birth among women 30-34

### MATERNAL MORTALITY RATE:
30 deaths/100,000 live births (2015 est.)

country comparison to the world: 114

### INFANT MORTALITY RATE:
total: 8.2 deaths/1,000 live births (2018 est.)

male: 9.1 deaths/1,000 live births (2018 est.)

female: 7.3 deaths/1,000 live births (2018 est.)

country comparison to the world: 150

### LIFE EXPECTANCY AT BIRTH:
total population: 77.1 years (2018 est.)

male: 73.7 years (2018 est.)

female: 80.8 years (2018 est.)

country comparison to the world: 80

### TOTAL FERTILITY RATE:
2.05 children born/woman (2018 est.)

country comparison to the world: 109

## CONTRACEPTIVE PREVALENCE RATE:
61.7% (2016)

## HEALTH EXPENDITURES:
3.5% of GDP (2014)

country comparison to the world: 173

## PHYSICIANS DENSITY:
0.88 physicians/1,000 population (2015)

## HOSPITAL BED DENSITY:
3.6 beds/1,000 population (2012)

## DRINKING WATER SOURCE:
**improved:**

urban: 98.5% of population

rural: 95% of population

total: 95.6% of population

**unimproved:**

urban: 1.5% of population

rural: 5% of population

total: 4.4% of population (2015 est.)

## SANITATION FACILITY ACCESS:
**improved:**

urban: 88.1% of population (2015 est.)

rural: 96.7% of population (2015 est.)

total: 95.1% of population (2015 est.)

**unimproved:**

urban: 11.9% of population (2015 est.)

rural: 3.3% of population (2015 est.)

total: 4.9% of population (2015 est.)

## HIV/AIDS - ADULT PREVALENCE RATE:
<.1% (2017 est.)

## HIV/AIDS - PEOPLE LIVING WITH HIV/AIDS:
3,500 (2017 est.)

country comparison to the world: 120

## HIV/AIDS - DEATHS:
<500 (2017 est.)

## MAJOR INFECTIOUS DISEASES:
**degree of risk:** high (2016)

**food or waterborne diseases:** bacterial diarrhea and hepatitis A (2016)

**vectorborne diseases:** dengue fever (2016)

**water contact diseases:** leptospirosis (2016)

**animal contact diseases:** rabies (2016)

## OBESITY - ADULT PREVALENCE RATE:
5.2% (2016)

country comparison to the world: 182

## CHILDREN UNDER THE AGE OF 5 YEARS UNDERWEIGHT:
20.5% (2016)

country comparison to the world: 25

## EDUCATION EXPENDITURES:
3.5% of GDP (2016)

country comparison to the world: 131

## LITERACY:
**definition:** age 15 and over can read and write (2015 est.)

**total population:** 92.6% (2015 est.)

**male:** 93.6% (2015 est.)

**female:** 91.7% (2015 est.)

## SCHOOL LIFE EXPECTANCY (PRIMARY TO TERTIARY EDUCATION):
**total:** 14 years (2013)

**male:** 14 years (2013)

**female:** 14 years (2013)

## UNEMPLOYMENT, YOUTH AGES 15-24:
**total:** 21.6% (2016 est.)

**male:** 17.1% (2016 est.)

**female:** 29.2% (2016 est.)

country comparison to the world: 57

# GOVERNMENT :: SRI LANKA

## COUNTRY NAME:
**conventional long form:** Democratic Socialist Republic of Sri Lanka

**conventional short form:** Sri Lanka

**local long form:** Shri Lanka Prajatantrika Samajavadi Janarajaya/Ilankai Jananayaka Choshalichak Kutiyarachu

**local short form:** Shri Lanka/Ilankai

**former:** Serendib, Ceylon

**etymology:** the name means "resplendent island" in Sanskrit

## GOVERNMENT TYPE:
presidential republic

## CAPITAL:
**name:** Colombo (commercial capital); Sri Jayewardenepura Kotte (legislative capital)

**geographic coordinates:** 6 55 N, 79 50 E

**time difference:** UTC+5.5 (10.5 hours ahead of Washington, DC, during Standard Time)

## ADMINISTRATIVE DIVISIONS:
9 provinces; Central, Eastern, North Central, Northern, North Western, Sabaragamuwa, Southern, Uva, Western

## INDEPENDENCE:
4 February 1948 (from the UK)

## NATIONAL HOLIDAY:
Independence Day (National Day), 4 February (1948)

## CONSTITUTION:
**history:** several previous; latest adopted 16 August 1978, certified 31 August 1978 (2018)

**amendments:** proposed by Parliament; passage requires at least two-thirds majority vote of its total membership, certification by the president of the republic or the Parliament speaker, and approval in a referendum by absolute majority of valid votes; amended many times, last in 2015; note - deliberatons by a constitutional assembly tasked with revising the constitution in March 2016 had stalled by August 2018 (2018)

## LEGAL SYSTEM:
mixed legal system of Roman-Dutch civil law, English common law, Jaffna Tamil customary law, and Muslim personal law

## INTERNATIONAL LAW ORGANIZATION PARTICIPATION:
has not submitted an ICJ jurisdiction declaration; non-party state to the ICCt

## CITIZENSHIP:
**citizenship by birth:** no

**citizenship by descent only:** at least one parent must be a citizen of Sri Lanka

**dual citizenship recognized:** no, except in cases where the government rules it is to the benefit of Sri Lanka

**residency requirement for naturalization:** 7 years

## SUFFRAGE:
18 years of age; universal

## EXECUTIVE BRANCH:
**chief of state:** President Maithripala SIRISENA (since 9 January 2015); note - the president is both chief of state and head of government; Ranil WICKREMESINGHE (since 9 January 2015) holds the title of prime minister

**head of government:** President Maithripala SIRISENA (since 9 January 2015)

**cabinet:** Cabinet appointed by the president in consultation with the prime minister

**elections/appointments:** president directly elected by preferential majority popular vote for a 5-year term (eligible for a second term); election last held on 8 January 2015 (next to be held by January 2020)

**election results:** Maithripala SIRISENA elected president; percent of vote - Maithripala SIRISENA (SLFP) 51.3%, Mahinda RAJAPAKSA (SLFP) 47.6%, other 1.1%

## LEGISLATIVE BRANCH:

**description:** unicameral Parliament (225 seats; 196 members directly elected in multi-seat constituencies by proportional representation vote using a preferential method in which voters select 3 candidates in order of preference; remaining 29 seats allocated to other political parties and groups in proportion to share of national vote; members serve 5-year terms)

**elections:** last held on 17 August 2015 (next to be held on 5 January 2019 following the dissolution of Parliament by President SIRISENA on 9 November 2018)

**election results:** percent of vote by coalition/party - UNFGG 45.7%, UPFA 42.4%, JVP 4.9%, TNA 4.6%, SLMC 0.4%, EPDP 0.3% other 1.7%; seats by coalition/party UNFGG 106, UPFA 95, TNA 16, JVP 6, SLMC 1, EPDP 1; composition - men 214, women 11, percent of women 4.9%

## JUDICIAL BRANCH:

**highest courts:** Supreme Court of the Republic (consists of the chief justice and 9 justices); note - the court has exclusive jurisdiction to review legislation

**judge selection and term of office:** chief justice nominated by the Constitutional Council (CC), a 9-member high-level advisory body, and appointed by the president; other justices nominated by the CC and appointed by the president on the advice of the chief justice; all justices can serve until age 65

**subordinate courts:** Court of Appeals; High Courts; Magistrates' Courts; municipal and primary courts

## POLITICAL PARTIES AND LEADERS:

Eelam People's Democratic Party or EPDP [Douglas DEVANANDA]
Eelam People's Revolutionary Liberation Front [Suresh PREMACHANDRAN]
Janatha Vimukthi Peramuna or JVP [Anura Kumara DISSANAYAKE]
Jathika Hela Urumaya or JHU [Karunarathna PARANAWITHANA and Ven Hadigalle WIMALASARA THERO]Sri Lanka Freedom Party or SLFP [Maithripala SIRISENA]
Sri Lanka Muslim Congress or SLMC [Rauff HAKEEM]
Sri Lanka Podujana Peramuna or SLPP [G. L. PEIRIS]
Tamil National Alliance or TNA [Rajavarothiam SAMPANTHAN] (alliance includes Illankai Tamil Arasu Kachchi [Mavai SENATHIRAJAH], People's Liberation Organisation of Tamil Eelam [D. SIDDARTHAN], Tamil Eelam Liberation Organization [Selvam ADAIKALANATHAN])
United National Front for Good Governance or UNFGG [Ranil WICKREMESINGHE] (coalition includes JHU, UNP)
United National Party or UNP [Ranil WICKREMESINGHE]
United People's Freedom Alliance or UPFA [Maithripala SIRISENA] (coalition includes SLFP)

## INTERNATIONAL ORGANIZATION PARTICIPATION:

ABEDA, ADB, ARF, BIMSTEC, C, CD, CICA (observer), CP, FAO, G-11, G-15, G-24, G-77, IAEA, IBRD, ICAO, ICC (national committees), ICRM, IDA, IFAD, IFC, IFRCS, IHO, ILO, IMF, IMO, IMSO, Interpol, IOC, IOM, IPU, ISO, ITSO, ITU, ITUC (NGOs), MIGA, MINURSO, MINUSTAH, MONUSCO, NAM, OAS (observer), OPCW, PCA, SAARC, SACEP, SCO (dialogue member), UN, UNCTAD, UNESCO, UNIDO, UNIFIL, UNISFA, UNMISS, UNWTO, UPU, WCO, WFTU (NGOs), WHO, WIPO, WMO, WTO

## DIPLOMATIC REPRESENTATION IN THE US:

**chief of mission:** Ambassador (vacant); Charge d'Affaires Priyanga WICKRAMASINGHE (since 27 October 2017)

**chancery:** 3025 Whitehaven Street NW, Washington, DC 20008

**telephone:** [1] (202) 483-4025 through 4028

**FAX:** [1] (202) 232-7181

**consulate(s) general:** Los Angeles, New York

## DIPLOMATIC REPRESENTATION FROM THE US:

**chief of mission:** Ambassador Alaina B. TEPLITZ (since 1 November 2018); note - also accredited to Maldives

**embassy:** 210 Galle Road, Colombo 3

**mailing address:** P. O. Box 106, Colombo

**telephone:** [94] (11) 249-8500

**FAX:** [94] (11) 243-7345

## FLAG DESCRIPTION:

yellow with two panels; the smaller hoist-side panel has two equal vertical bands of green (hoist side) and orange; the other larger panel depicts a yellow lion holding a sword on a maroon rectangular field that also displays a yellow bo leaf in each corner; the yellow field appears as a border around the entire flag and extends between the two panels; the lion represents Sinhalese ethnicity, the strength of the nation, and bravery; the sword demonstrates the sovereignty of the nation; the four bo leaves - symbolizing Buddhism and its influence on the country - stand for the four virtues of kindness, friendliness, happiness, and equanimity; orange signifies Sri Lankan Tamils, green Sri Lankan Moors, and maroon the Sinhalese majority; yellow denotes other ethnic groups; also referred to as the Lion Flag

## NATIONAL SYMBOL(S):

lion, water lily; national colors: maroon, yellow

## NATIONAL ANTHEM:

**name:** "Sri Lanka Matha" (Mother Sri Lanka)

**lyrics/music:** Ananda SAMARKONE

**note:** adopted 1951

# ECONOMY :: SRI LANKA

## ECONOMY - OVERVIEW:

Sri Lanka is attempting to sustain economic growth while maintaining macroeconomic stability under the IMF program it began in 2016. The government's high debt payments and bloated civil service, which have contributed to historically high budget deficits, remain a concern. Government debt is about 79% of GDP and remains among the highest of the emerging markets. In the coming years, Sri Lanka will need to balance its elevated debt repayment schedule with its need to maintain adequate foreign exchange reserves.

In May 2016, Sri Lanka regained its preferential trade status under the European Union's Generalized System of Preferences Plus, enabling many of its firms to export products, including its top export garments, tax free to the EU. In 2017, Parliament passed a new Inland Revenue Act in an effort to increase tax collection and broaden the tax base in response to recommendations made under its IMF program. In November 2017, the Financial Action Task Force on money laundering and terrorist financing listed Sri Lanka as non-compliant, but reported subsequently that Sri Lanka had made good progress in implementing an action plan to address deficiencies.

Tourism has experienced strong growth in the years since the resolution of the government's 26-year conflict with the Liberation Tigers of Tamil Eelam. In 2017, the government promulgated plans to transform the country into a knowledge-based, export-oriented Indian Ocean hub by 2025.

**GDP (PURCHASING POWER PARITY):**

$275.8 billion (2017 est.)

$267 billion (2016 est.)

$255.6 billion (2015 est.)

note: data are in 2017 dollars

country comparison to the world: 61

**GDP (OFFICIAL EXCHANGE RATE):**

$87.35 billion (2017 est.) (2017 est.)

**GDP - REAL GROWTH RATE:**

3.3% (2017 est.)

4.5% (2016 est.)

5% (2015 est.)

country comparison to the world: 106

**GDP - PER CAPITA (PPP):**

$12,900 (2017 est.)

$12,600 (2016 est.)

$12,200 (2015 est.)

note: data are in 2017 dollars

country comparison to the world: 121

**GROSS NATIONAL SAVING:**

33.8% of GDP (2017 est.)

32.8% of GDP (2016 est.)

28.8% of GDP (2015 est.)

country comparison to the world: 20

**GDP - COMPOSITION, BY END USE:**

household consumption: 62% (2017 est.)

government consumption: 8.5% (2017 est.)

investment in fixed capital: 26.3% (2017 est.)

investment in inventories: 10.2% (2017 est.)

exports of goods and services: 21.9% (2017 est.)

imports of goods and services: -29.1% (2017 est.)

**GDP - COMPOSITION, BY SECTOR OF ORIGIN:**

agriculture: 7.8% (2017 est.)

industry: 30.5% (2017 est.)

services: 61.7% (2017 est.)

**AGRICULTURE - PRODUCTS:**

rice, sugarcane, grains, pulses, oilseed, spices, vegetables, fruit, tea, rubber, coconuts; milk, eggs, hides, beef; fish

**INDUSTRIES:**

processing of rubber, tea, coconuts, tobacco and other agricultural commodities; telecommunications, insurance, banking; tourism, shipping; clothing, textiles; cement, petroleum refining, information technology services, construction

**INDUSTRIAL PRODUCTION GROWTH RATE:**

4.6% (2017 est.)

country comparison to the world: 64

**LABOR FORCE:**

8.937 million (2017 est.)

country comparison to the world: 55

**LABOR FORCE - BY OCCUPATION:**

agriculture: 27%

industry: 26%

services: 47% (31 December 2016)

**UNEMPLOYMENT RATE:**

4.4% (2017 est.)

4.4% (2016 est.)

country comparison to the world: 59

**POPULATION BELOW POVERTY LINE:**

6.7% (2012 est.)

**HOUSEHOLD INCOME OR CONSUMPTION BY PERCENTAGE SHARE:**

lowest 10%: 32.2% (2012 est.)

highest 10%: 32.2% (2012 est.)

**DISTRIBUTION OF FAMILY INCOME - GINI INDEX:**

39.2 (2012 est.)

46 (1995)

country comparison to the world: 73

**BUDGET:**

revenues: 12.07 billion (2017 est.)

expenditures: 16.88 billion (2017 est.)

**TAXES AND OTHER REVENUES:**

13.8% (of GDP) (2017 est.)

country comparison to the world: 204

**BUDGET SURPLUS (+) OR DEFICIT (-):**

-5.5% (of GDP) (2017 est.)

country comparison to the world: 174

**PUBLIC DEBT:**

79.1% of GDP (2017 est.)

79.6% of GDP (2016 est.)

note: covers central government debt and excludes debt instruments directly owned by government entities other than the treasury (e.g. commercial bank borrowings of a government corporation); the data includes treasury debt held by foreign entities as well as intragovernmental debt; intragovernmental debt consists of treasury borrowings from surpluses in the social funds, such as for retirement; sub-national entities are usually not permitted to sell debt instruments

country comparison to the world: 35

**FISCAL YEAR:**

calendar year

**INFLATION RATE (CONSUMER PRICES):**

6.5% (2017 est.)

4% (2016 est.)

country comparison to the world: 190

**CENTRAL BANK DISCOUNT RATE:**

7.25% (30 November 2017)

6% (31 December 2015)

country comparison to the world: 45

**COMMERCIAL BANK PRIME LENDING RATE:**

11.6% (31 December 2017 est.)

10.49% (31 December 2016 est.)

country comparison to the world: 68

**STOCK OF NARROW MONEY:**

$5.19 billion (31 December 2017 est.)

$5.184 billion (31 December 2016 est.)

country comparison to the world: 101

**STOCK OF BROAD MONEY:**

$5.19 billion (31 December 2017 est.)

$5.184 billion (31 December 2016 est.)

country comparison to the world: 104

**STOCK OF DOMESTIC CREDIT:**

$53.53 billion (31 December 2017 est.)

$46.21 billion (31 December 2016 est.)

country comparison to the world: 65

**MARKET VALUE OF PUBLICLY TRADED SHARES:**

$18.9 billion (30 September 2017 est.)

$23.67 billion (31 December 2014 est.)

$18.81 billion (31 December 2013 est.)

country comparison to the world: 65

**CURRENT ACCOUNT BALANCE:**

-$2.31 billion (2017 est.)

-$1.743 billion (2016 est.)

country comparison to the world: 169

**EXPORTS:**

$11.36 billion (2017 est.)

$10.31 billion (2016 est.)

country comparison to the world: 89

**EXPORTS - PARTNERS:**

US 24.6%, UK 9%, India 5.8%, Singapore 4.5%, Germany 4.3%, Italy 4.3% (2017)

**EXPORTS - COMMODITIES:**

textiles and apparel, tea and spices; rubber manufactures; precious stones; coconut products, fish

**IMPORTS:**

$20.98 billion (2017 est.)

$19.18 billion (2016 est.)

country comparison to the world: 74

**IMPORTS - COMMODITIES:**

petroleum, textiles, machinery and transportation equipment, building materials, mineral products, foodstuffs

**IMPORTS - PARTNERS:**

India 22%, China 19.9%, Singapore 6.9%, UAE 5.7%, Japan 4.9% (2017)

**RESERVES OF FOREIGN EXCHANGE AND GOLD:**

$7.959 billion (31 December 2017 est.)

$6.019 billion (31 December 2016 est.)

country comparison to the world: 78

**DEBT - EXTERNAL:**

$51.72 billion (31 December 2017 est.)

$45.26 billion (31 December 2016 est.)

country comparison to the world: 64

**STOCK OF DIRECT FOREIGN INVESTMENT - AT HOME:**

$NA (31 December 2016)

**STOCK OF DIRECT FOREIGN INVESTMENT - ABROAD:**

NA

**EXCHANGE RATES:**

Sri Lankan rupees (LKR) per US dollar -

154.1 (2017 est.)

145.58 (2016 est.)

145.58 (2015 est.)

135.86 (2014 est.)

130.57 (2013 est.)

## ENERGY :: SRI LANKA

**ELECTRICITY ACCESS:**

population without electricity: 1,334,100 (2013)

electrification - total population: 94% (2013)

electrification - urban areas: 99% (2013)

electrification - rural areas: 93% (2013)

**ELECTRICITY - PRODUCTION:**

13.66 billion kWh (2016 est.)

country comparison to the world: 90

**ELECTRICITY - CONSUMPTION:**

12.67 billion kWh (2016 est.)

country comparison to the world: 86

**ELECTRICITY - EXPORTS:**

0 kWh (2016 est.)

country comparison to the world: 202

**ELECTRICITY - IMPORTS:**

0 kWh (2016 est.)

country comparison to the world: 204

**ELECTRICITY - INSTALLED GENERATING CAPACITY:**

3.998 million kW (2016 est.)

country comparison to the world: 89

**ELECTRICITY - FROM FOSSIL FUELS:**

52% of total installed capacity (2016 est.)

country comparison to the world: 146

**ELECTRICITY - FROM NUCLEAR FUELS:**

0% of total installed capacity (2017 est.)

country comparison to the world: 187

**ELECTRICITY - FROM HYDROELECTRIC PLANTS:**

42% of total installed capacity (2017 est.)

country comparison to the world: 49

**ELECTRICITY - FROM OTHER RENEWABLE SOURCES:**

6% of total installed capacity (2017 est.)

country comparison to the world: 103

**CRUDE OIL - PRODUCTION:**

0 bbl/day (2017 est.)

country comparison to the world: 202

**CRUDE OIL - EXPORTS:**

0 bbl/day (2015 est.)

country comparison to the world: 199

**CRUDE OIL - IMPORTS:**

33,540 bbl/day (2015 est.)

country comparison to the world: 60

**CRUDE OIL - PROVED RESERVES:**

0 bbl (1 January 2018 est.)

country comparison to the world: 199

**REFINED PETROLEUM PRODUCTS - PRODUCTION:**

34,210 bbl/day (2017 est.)

country comparison to the world: 84

**REFINED PETROLEUM PRODUCTS - CONSUMPTION:**

116,000 bbl/day (2016 est.)

country comparison to the world: 74

**REFINED PETROLEUM PRODUCTS - EXPORTS:**

3,871 bbl/day (2015 est.)

country comparison to the world: 96

**REFINED PETROLEUM PRODUCTS - IMPORTS:**

66,280 bbl/day (2015 est.)

country comparison to the world: 70

**NATURAL GAS - PRODUCTION:**

0 cu m (2017 est.)

country comparison to the world: 200

**NATURAL GAS - CONSUMPTION:**

0 cu m (2017 est.)

country comparison to the world: 201

**NATURAL GAS - EXPORTS:**

0 cu m (2017 est.)

country comparison to the world: 189

**NATURAL GAS - IMPORTS:**

0 cu m (2017 est.)

country comparison to the world: 192

**NATURAL GAS - PROVED RESERVES:**

0 cu m (1 January 2014 est.)

country comparison to the world: 197

**CARBON DIOXIDE EMISSIONS FROM CONSUMPTION OF ENERGY:**

25.19 million Mt (2017 est.)

country comparison to the world: 80

## COMMUNICATIONS :: SRI LANKA

**TELEPHONES - FIXED LINES:**

total subscriptions: 2,603,178 (2017 est.)

subscriptions per 100 inhabitants: 12 (2017 est.)

country comparison to the world: 53

**TELEPHONES - MOBILE CELLULAR:**

total subscriptions: 28,199,083 (2017 est.)

subscriptions per 100 inhabitants: 126 (2017 est.)

country comparison to the world: 46

**TELEPHONE SYSTEM:**

general assessment: telephone services have improved significantly and are available in most parts of the country (2018)

domestic: national trunk network consists of digital microwave radio relay and fiber-optic links; fixed wireless local loops have been installed; competition is strong in mobile cellular systems and mobile cellular subscribership is increasing (2018)

international: country code - 94; the SEA-ME-WE-3, SEA-ME-WE-4, SEA-ME-WE-5, FLAG, and the Bay of Bengal Gateway submarine cables provide connectivity to Asia, Australia, Middle East, Europe, US; satellite earth stations - 2 Intelsat (Indian Ocean) (2018)

**BROADCAST MEDIA:**

government operates 5 TV channels and 19 radio channels; multi-channel satellite and cable TV subscription services available; 25 private TV stations and about 43 radio stations; 6 non-profit TV stations and 4 radio stations (2017)

**INTERNET COUNTRY CODE:**

.lk

**INTERNET USERS:**

total: 7,126,540 (July 2016 est.)

percent of population: 32.1% (July 2016 est.)

country comparison to the world: 60

**BROADBAND - FIXED SUBSCRIPTIONS:**

total: 1,220,504 (2017 est.)

subscriptions per 100 inhabitants: 5 (2017 est.)

country comparison to the world: 67

# TRANSPORTATION :: SRI LANKA

**NATIONAL AIR TRANSPORT SYSTEM:**

number of registered air carriers: 3 (2015)

inventory of registered aircraft operated by air carriers: 25 (2015)

annual passenger traffic on registered air carriers: 4,911,730 (2015)

annual freight traffic on registered air carriers: 381,381,300 mt-km (2015)

**CIVIL AIRCRAFT REGISTRATION COUNTRY CODE PREFIX:**

4R (2016)

**AIRPORTS:**

19 (2013)

country comparison to the world: 138

**AIRPORTS - WITH PAVED RUNWAYS:**

total: 15 (2013)

over 3,047 m: 2 (2013)

1,524 to 2,437 m: 6 (2013)

914 to 1,523 m: 7 (2013)

**AIRPORTS - WITH UNPAVED RUNWAYS:**

total: 4 (2013)

914 to 1,523 m: 1 (2013)

under 914 m: 3 (2013)

**HELIPORTS:**

1 (2013)

**PIPELINES:**

7 km refined products

**RAILWAYS:**

total: 1,562 km (2016)

broad gauge: 1,562 km 1.676-m gauge (2016)

country comparison to the world: 82

**ROADWAYS:**

total: 114,093 km (2010)

paved: 16,977 km (2010)

unpaved: 97,116 km (2010)

country comparison to the world: 42

**WATERWAYS:**

160 km (primarily on rivers in southwest) (2012)

country comparison to the world: 100

**MERCHANT MARINE:**

total: 82 (2017)

by type: bulk carrier 8, container ship 1, general cargo 9, oil tanker 10, other 54 (2017)

country comparison to the world: 96

**PORTS AND TERMINALS:**

major seaport(s): Colombo

container port(s) (TEUs): Colombo (5,734,923) (2016)

# MILITARY AND SECURITY :: SRI LANKA

**MILITARY EXPENDITURES:**

2.14% of GDP (2017)

2.44% of GDP (2016)

2.55% of GDP (2015)

2.41% of GDP (2014)

2.15% of GDP (2013)

country comparison to the world: 49

**MILITARY BRANCHES:**

Sri Lanka Army, Sri Lanka Navy (includes Marine Corps), Sri Lanka Air Force, Sri Lanka Coast Guard (2016)

**MILITARY SERVICE AGE AND OBLIGATION:**

18-22 years of age for voluntary military service; no conscription; 12-year service obligation (2018)

# TERRORISM :: SRI LANKA

**TERRORIST GROUPS - HOME BASED:**

Liberation Tigers of Tamil Eelam (LTTE):
aim(s): revive the movement to establish a Tamil homeland
area(s) of operation: presence is primarily in the east where members occasionally plot attacks (April 2018)

# TRANSNATIONAL ISSUES :: SRI LANKA

**DISPUTES - INTERNATIONAL:**

none

**REFUGEES AND INTERNALLY DISPLACED PERSONS:**

IDPs: 42,000 (civil war; more than half displaced prior to 2008; many of the more than 480,000 IDPs registered as returnees have not reached durable solutions) (2017)

**TRAFFICKING IN PERSONS:**

current situation: Sri Lanka is primarily a source and, to a lesser extent, a destination country for men, women, and children subjected to forced labor and sex trafficking; some Sri Lankan adults and children who migrate willingly to the Middle East,

Southeast Asia, and Afghanistan to work in the construction, garment, and domestic service sectors are subsequently subjected to forced labor or debt bondage (incurred through high recruitment fees or money advances); some Sri Lankan women are forced into prostitution in Jordan, Maldives, Malaysia, Singapore, and other countries; within Sri Lanka, women and children are subjected to sex trafficking, and children are also forced to beg and work in the agriculture, fireworks, and fish-drying industries; a small number of women from Asia, Central Asia, Europe, and the Middle East have been forced into prostitution in Sri Lanka in recent years

**tier rating:** Tier 2 Watch List – Sri Lanka does not fully comply with the minimum standards for the elimination of trafficking; however, it is making significant efforts to do so; in 2014, Sri Lanka was granted a waiver from an otherwise required downgrade to Tier 3 because its government has a written plan that, if implemented, would constitute making significant efforts to bring itself into compliance with the minimum standards for the elimination of trafficking; law enforcement continues to demonstrate a lack of understanding of trafficking crimes and inadequate investigations, relying on trafficking cases to be prosecuted under the procurement statute rather than the trafficking statute, which carries more stringent penalties; authorities convicted only one offender under the procurement statute, a decrease from 2013; the government approved guidelines for the identification of victims and their referral to protective services but failed to ensure that victims were not jailed and charged for crimes committed as a direct result of being trafficked; no government employees were investigated or prosecuted, despite allegations of complicity (2015)

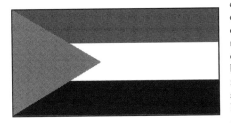

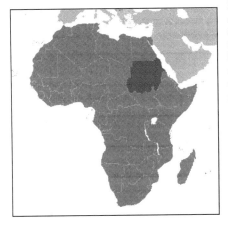

# AFRICA :: SUDAN

## INTRODUCTION :: SUDAN

### BACKGROUND:

Military regimes favoring Islamic-oriented governments have dominated national politics since independence from Anglo-Egyptian co-rule in 1956. Sudan was embroiled in two prolonged civil wars during most of the remainder of the 20th century. These conflicts were rooted in northern economic, political, and social domination of largely non-Muslim, non-Arab southern Sudanese. The first civil war ended in 1972 but another broke out in 1983. Peace talks gained momentum in 2002-04 with the signing of several accords. The final North/South Comprehensive Peace Agreement (CPA), signed in January 2005, granted the southern rebels autonomy for six years followed by a referendum on independence for Southern Sudan. The referendum was held in January 2011 and indicated overwhelming support for independence. South Sudan became independent on 9 July 2011. Sudan and South Sudan have yet to fully implement security and economic agreements signed in September 2012 relating to the normalization of relations between the two countries. The final disposition of the contested Abyei region has also to be decided.

Following South Sudan's independence, conflict broke out between the government and the Sudan People's Liberation Movement-North in Southern Kordofan and Blue Nile states (together known as the Two Areas), and has resulted in 1.1 million internally displaced persons or severely affected persons needing humanitarian assistance. A separate conflict broke out in the western region of Darfur in 2003, displacing nearly 2 million people and causing thousands of deaths. Fighting in both the Two Areas and Darfur between government forces and opposition has largely subsided, however the civilian populations are affected by low-level violence including inter-tribal conflict and banditry, largely a result of weak rule of law. The UN and the African Union have jointly commanded a Darfur peacekeeping operation (UNAMID) since 2007. Peacekeeping troops have struggled to address insecurity in Darfur and have increasingly become targets for attacks by armed groups. Sudan also has faced refugee influxes from neighboring countries, primarily Ethiopia, Eritrea, Chad, Central African Republic, and South Sudan. Armed conflict, poor transport infrastructure, and denial of access by both the government and armed opposition have impeded the provision of humanitarian assistance to affected populations.

## GEOGRAPHY :: SUDAN

### LOCATION:
north-eastern Africa, bordering the Red Sea, between Egypt and Eritrea

### GEOGRAPHIC COORDINATES:
15 00 N, 30 00 E

### MAP REFERENCES:
Africa

### AREA:
total: 1,861,484 sq km

land: NA

water: NA

country comparison to the world: 17

### AREA - COMPARATIVE:
slightly less than one-fifth the size of the US

### LAND BOUNDARIES:
total: 6,819 km

border countries (7): Central African Republic 174 km, Chad 1403 km, Egypt 1276 km, Eritrea 682 km, Ethiopia 744 km, Libya 382 km, South Sudan 2158 km

note: Sudan-South Sudan boundary represents 1 January 1956 alignment; final alignment pending negotiations and demarcation; final sovereignty status of Abyei region pending negotiations between Sudan and South Sudan

### COASTLINE:
853 km

### MARITIME CLAIMS:
territorial sea: 12 nm

contiguous zone: 18 nm

continental shelf: 200-m depth or to the depth of exploitation

### CLIMATE:
hot and dry; arid desert; rainy season varies by region (April to November)

### TERRAIN:
generally flat, featureless plain; desert dominates the north

### ELEVATION:
mean elevation: 568 m

elevation extremes: 0 m lowest point: Red Sea

3042 highest point: Jabal Marrah

### NATURAL RESOURCES:
petroleum; small reserves of iron ore, copper, chromium ore, zinc, tungsten, mica, silver, gold; hydropower

### LAND USE:
agricultural land: 100% (2011 est.)

**arable land:** 15.7% (2011 est.) / **permanent crops:** 0.2% (2011 est.) / **permanent pasture:** 84.2% (2011 est.)

**forest:** 0% (2011 est.)

**other:** 0% (2011 est.)

### IRRIGATED LAND:
18,900 sq km (2012)

### POPULATION DISTRIBUTION:
with the exception of a ribbon of settlement that corresponds to the banks of the Nile, northern Sudan, which extends into the dry Sahara, is sparsely populated; more abundant vegetation and broader access to water increases population distribution in the south extending habitable range along nearly the entire border with South Sudan; sizeable areas of population are found around Khartoum, southeast between the Blue and White Nile Rivers, and througout South Darfur

### NATURAL HAZARDS:
dust storms and periodic persistent droughts

### ENVIRONMENT - CURRENT ISSUES:
water pollution; inadequate supplies of potable water; water scarcity and periodic drought; wildlife populations threatened by excessive hunting; soil erosion; desertification; deforestation; loss of biodiversity

### ENVIRONMENT - INTERNATIONAL AGREEMENTS:
**party to:** Biodiversity, Climate Change, Climate Change-Kyoto Protocol, Desertification, Endangered Species, Hazardous Wastes, Law of the Sea, Ozone Layer Protection, Wetlands

**signed, but not ratified:** none of the selected agreements

### GEOGRAPHY - NOTE:
the Nile is Sudan's primary water source; its major tributaries, the White Nile and the Blue Nile, meet at Khartoum to form the River Nile which flows northward through Egypt to the Mediterranean Sea

# PEOPLE AND SOCIETY :: SUDAN

### POPULATION:
43,120,843 (July 2018 est.)

**country comparison to the world:** 33

### NATIONALITY:
**noun:** Sudanese (singular and plural)

**adjective:** Sudanese

### ETHNIC GROUPS:
unspecified Sudanese Arab (approximately 70%), Fur, Beja, Nuba, Fallata

### LANGUAGES:
Arabic (official), English (official), Nubian, Ta Bedawie, Fur

### RELIGIONS:
Sunni Muslim, small Christian minority

### AGE STRUCTURE:
**0-14 years:** 43.07% (male 9,434,634 /female 9,136,951)

**15-24 years:** 20.22% (male 4,459,335 /female 4,259,341)

**25-54 years:** 29.8% (male 6,236,954 /female 6,612,593)

**55-64 years:** 3.93% (male 876,614 /female 819,048)

**65 years and over:** 2.98% (male 688,391 /female 596,982) (2018 est.)

### DEPENDENCY RATIOS:
**total dependency ratio:** 81.6 (2015 est.)

**youth dependency ratio:** 75.4 (2015 est.)

**elderly dependency ratio:** 6.3 (2015 est.)

**potential support ratio:** 15.9 (2015 est.)

### MEDIAN AGE:
**total:** 17.9 years

**male:** 17.7 years

**female:** 18.1 years (2018 est.)

**country comparison to the world:** 214

### POPULATION GROWTH RATE:
2.93% (2018 est.)

**country comparison to the world:** 9

### BIRTH RATE:
34.2 births/1,000 population (2018 est.)

**country comparison to the world:** 23

### DEATH RATE:
6.7 deaths/1,000 population (2018 est.)

**country comparison to the world:** 139

### NET MIGRATION RATE:
-4.1 migrant(s)/1,000 population (2017 est.)

**country comparison to the world:** 183

### POPULATION DISTRIBUTION:
with the exception of a ribbon of settlement that corresponds to the banks of the Nile, northern Sudan, which extends into the dry Sahara, is sparsely populated; more abundant vegetation and broader access to water increases population distribution in the south extending habitable range along nearly the entire border with South Sudan; sizeable areas of population are found around Khartoum, southeast between the Blue and White Nile Rivers, and througout South Darfur

### URBANIZATION:
**urban population:** 34.6% of total population (2018)

**rate of urbanization:** 3.17% annual rate of change (2015-20 est.)

### MAJOR URBAN AREAS - POPULATION:
5.534 million KHARTOUM (capital), 834,000 Nyala (2018)

### SEX RATIO:
**at birth:** 1.04 male(s)/female (2017 est.)

**0-14 years:** 1.03 male(s)/female (2017 est.)

**15-24 years:** 1.06 male(s)/female (2017 est.)

**25-54 years:** 0.94 male(s)/female (2017 est.)

**55-64 years:** 1.1 male(s)/female (2017 est.)

**65 years and over:** 1.19 male(s)/female (2017 est.)

**total population:** 1.02 male(s)/female (2017 est.)

### MATERNAL MORTALITY RATE:
311 deaths/100,000 live births (2015 est.)

**country comparison to the world:** 41

### INFANT MORTALITY RATE:
**total:** 44.2 deaths/1,000 live births (2018 est.)

**male:** 49.2 deaths/1,000 live births (2018 est.)

**female:** 38.8 deaths/1,000 live births (2018 est.)

**country comparison to the world:** 40

### LIFE EXPECTANCY AT BIRTH:
**total population:** 65.8 years (2018 est.)

**male:** 63.7 years (2018 est.)

**female:** 68.1 years (2018 est.)

**country comparison to the world:** 177

### TOTAL FERTILITY RATE:
4.85 children born/woman (2018 est.)

**country comparison to the world:** 17

**CONTRACEPTIVE PREVALENCE RATE:**

12.2% (2014)

**HEALTH EXPENDITURES:**

8.4% of GDP (2014)

country comparison to the world: 50

**PHYSICIANS DENSITY:**

3.06 physicians/1,000 population (2014)

**HOSPITAL BED DENSITY:**

0.8 beds/1,000 population (2013)

**DRINKING WATER SOURCE:**

improved:

urban: 66% of population (2012 est.)

rural: 50.2% of population (2012 est.)

total: 55.5% of population (2012 est.)

unimproved:

urban: 34% of population (2012 est.)

rural: 49.8% of population (2012 est.)

total: 44.5% of population (2012 est.)

**SANITATION FACILITY ACCESS:**

improved:

urban: 43.9% of population (2012 est.)

rural: 13.4% of population (2012 est.)

total: 23.6% of population (2012 est.)

unimproved:

urban: 56.1% of population (2012 est.)

rural: 86.6% of population (2012 est.)

total: 76.4% of population (2012 est.)

**HIV/AIDS - ADULT PREVALENCE RATE:**

0.2% (2017 est.)

country comparison to the world: 104

**HIV/AIDS - PEOPLE LIVING WITH HIV/AIDS:**

51,000 (2017 est.)

country comparison to the world: 60

**HIV/AIDS - DEATHS:**

2,600 (2017 est.)

country comparison to the world: 44

**MAJOR INFECTIOUS DISEASES:**

degree of risk: very high (2016)

food or waterborne diseases: bacterial and protozoal diarrhea, hepatitis A and E, and typhoid fever (2016)

vectorborne diseases: malaria, dengue fever, and Rift Valley fever (2016)

water contact diseases: schistosomiasis (2016)

animal contact diseases: rabies (2016)

respiratory diseases: meningococcal meningitis (2016)

**OBESITY - ADULT PREVALENCE RATE:**

6.6% (2014)

country comparison to the world: 166

**CHILDREN UNDER THE AGE OF 5 YEARS UNDERWEIGHT:**

33% (2014)

country comparison to the world: 4

**EDUCATION EXPENDITURES:**

2.2% of GDP (2009)

country comparison to the world: 170

**LITERACY:**

definition: age 15 and over can read and write (2015 est.)

total population: 75.9% (2015 est.)

male: 83.3% (2015 est.)

female: 68.6% (2015 est.)

**SCHOOL LIFE EXPECTANCY (PRIMARY TO TERTIARY EDUCATION):**

total: 7 years (2013)

male: 7 years (2013)

female: 7 years (2013)

**UNEMPLOYMENT, YOUTH AGES 15-24:**

total: 20% (2009 est.)

male: 16% (2009 est.)

female: 32% (2009 est.)

country comparison to the world: 66

## GOVERNMENT :: SUDAN

**COUNTRY NAME:**

conventional long form: Republic of the Sudan

conventional short form: Sudan

local long form: Jumhuriyat as-Sudan

local short form: As-Sudan

former: Anglo-Egyptian Sudan, Democratic Republic of the Sudan

etymology: the name "Sudan" derives from the Arabic "bilad-as-sudan" meaning "Land of the Black [peoples]"

**GOVERNMENT TYPE:**

presidential republic

**CAPITAL:**

name: Khartoum

geographic coordinates: 15 36 N, 32 32 E

time difference: UTC+3 (8 hours ahead of Washington, DC, during Standard Time)

**ADMINISTRATIVE DIVISIONS:**

18 states (wilayat, singular - wilayah); Blue Nile, Central Darfur, East Darfur, Gedaref, Gezira, Kassala, Khartoum, North Darfur, North Kordofan, Northern, Red Sea, River Nile, Sennar, South Darfur, South Kordofan, West Darfur, West Kordofan, White Nile

**INDEPENDENCE:**

1 January 1956 (from Egypt and the UK)

**NATIONAL HOLIDAY:**

Independence Day, 1 January (1956)

**CONSTITUTION:**

history: previous 1998; latest adopted 6 July 2005, effective 9 July 2005 (interim constitution) (2017)

amendments: proposed by the National Legislature or by the president of the republic; passage requires submission of the proposal to the Legislature at least two months prior to consideration, approval by at least three-quarters majority vote in both houses of the Legislature, and assent by the president; amended 2015 (2017)

**LEGAL SYSTEM:**

mixed legal system of Islamic law and English common law

**INTERNATIONAL LAW ORGANIZATION PARTICIPATION:**

accepts compulsory ICJ jurisdiction with reservations; withdrew acceptance of ICCt jurisdiction in 2008

**CITIZENSHIP:**

citizenship by birth: no

citizenship by descent only: the father must be a citizen of Sudan

dual citizenship recognized: no

residency requirement for naturalization: 10 years

**SUFFRAGE:**

17 years of age; universal

**EXECUTIVE BRANCH:**

chief of state: President Umar Hassan Ahmad al-BASHIR (since 16 October 1993); First Vice President BAKRI Hassan Salih (since 3 December 2013); Second Vice President Osman Yousif KIBIR (since 9 September 2018); Prime Minister Mutaz MUSA Abdullah Salim (since 10 September

2018); note - the president is both chief of state and head of government

**head of government:** President Umar Hassan Ahmad al-BASHIR (since 16 October 1993); First Vice President BAKRI Hassan Salih (since 3 December 2013); Second Vice President Osman Yousif KIBIR (since 9 September 2018); Prime Minister Mutaz MUSA Abdullah Salim (since 9 September 2018)

**cabinet:** Council of Ministers appointed by the president; note - the NCP dominates al-BASHIR's cabinet

**elections/appointments:** president directly elected by absolute majority popular vote in 2 rounds if needed; last held on 13-16 April 2015 (next to be held in 2020); prime minister appointed by the president; note - the position of prime minister was reinstated in December 2016 as a result of the 2015-16 national dialogue process, and President al-BASHIR appointed BAKRI Hassan Salih to the position on 2 March 2017

**election results:** Umar Hassan Ahmad al-BASHIR reelected president; percent of vote - Umar Hassan Ahmad al-BASHIR (NCP) 94.1%, other (15 candidates) 5.9%

## LEGISLATIVE BRANCH:

**description:** bicameral National Legislature consists of:
Council of States or Majlis al-Wilayat (54 seats; members indirectly elected by the state legislatures; members serve 6-year terms)
National Assembly or Majlis Watani (426 seats; 213 members directly elected in state-level, single-seat constituencies by simple majority vote, 128 for women only directly elected by national-level, closed party-list proportional representation vote, and 85 directly elected by national-level, party-list proportional representation vote; members serve 6-year terms)

**elections:**
National Assembly - last held on 13-15 April 2015 (next to be held in 2021)

**election results:**
percent of vote by party - NA; seats by party - NCP 323, DUP 25, Democratic Unionist Party 15, other 44, independent 19

## JUDICIAL BRANCH:

**highest courts:** National Supreme Court (consists of 70 judges organized into panels of 3 judges and includes 4 circuits that operate outside the capital); Constitutional Court (consists of 9 justices including the court president); note - the Constitutional Court resides outside the national judiciary

**judge selection and term of office:** National Supreme Court and Constitutional Court judges appointed by the president of the republic upon the recommendation of the National Judicial Service Commission, an independent body chaired by the chief justice of the republic and members including other judges and judicial and legal officials; Supreme Court judge tenure NA; Constitutional Court judges appointed for 7 years

**subordinate courts:** Court of Appeal; other national courts; public courts; district, town, and rural courts

## POLITICAL PARTIES AND LEADERS:

Democratic Unionist Party or DUP [Jalal al-DIGAIR]
Democratic Unionist Party [Muhammad Uthman al-MIRGHANI]
Federal Umma Party [Dr. Ahmed Babikir NAHAR]
Muslim Brotherhood or MB
National Congress Party or NCP [Umar Hassan al-BASHIR]
National Umma Party or NUP [Saddiq al-MAHDI]
Popular Congress Party or PCP [Hassan al-TURABI]
Reform Movement Now [Dr. Ghazi Salahuddin al-ATABANI]Sudan National Front [Ali Mahmud HASANAYN]
Sudanese Communist Party or SCP [Mohammed Moktar Al-KHATEEB]
Sudanese Congress Party or SCoP [Ibrahim Al-SHEIKH]
Umma Party for Reform and Development
Unionist Movement Party or UMP

## INTERNATIONAL ORGANIZATION PARTICIPATION:

ABEDA, ACP, AfDB, AFESD, AMF, AU, CAEU, COMESA, FAO, G-77, IAEA, IBRD, ICAO, ICC (NGOs), ICRM, IDA, IDB, IFAD, IFC, IFRCS, IGAD, ILO, IMF, IMO, Interpol, IOC, IOM, IPU, ISO, ITSO, ITU, LAS, MIGA, NAM, OIC, OPCW, PCA, UN, UNCTAD, UNESCO, UNHCR, UNIDO, UNWTO, UPU, WCO, WFTU (NGOs), WHO, WIPO, WMO, WTO (observer)

## DIPLOMATIC REPRESENTATION IN THE US:

**chief of mission:** Ambassador (vacant); Charge d'Affaires Mohamed ATTA al-Moula Abbas (since July 2018)

**chancery:** 2210 Massachusetts Avenue NW, Washington, DC 20008

**telephone:** [1] (202) 338-8565

**FAX:** [1] (202) 667-2406

## DIPLOMATIC REPRESENTATION FROM THE US:

**chief of mission:** Ambassador (vacant); Charge d'Affaires Steven KOUTSIS (since July 2016)

**embassy:** Sharia Ali Abdul Latif Street, Khartoum

**mailing address:** P.O. Box 699, Kilo 10, Soba, Khartoum; APO AE 09829

**telephone:** [249] 18702-2000

**FAX:** [249] 18702-2547

## FLAG DESCRIPTION:

three equal horizontal bands of red (top), white, and black with a green isosceles triangle based on the hoist side; colors and design based on the Arab Revolt flag of World War I, but the meanings of the colors are expressed as follows: red signifies the struggle for freedom, white is the color of peace, light, and love, black represents the people of Sudan (in Arabic 'Sudan' means black), green is the color of Islam, agriculture, and prosperity

## NATIONAL SYMBOL(S):

secretary bird; national colors: red, white, black, green

## NATIONAL ANTHEM:

**name:** "Nahnu Djundulla Djundulwatan" (We Are the Army of God and of Our Land)

**lyrics/music:** Sayed Ahmad Muhammad SALIH/Ahmad MURJAN

**note:** adopted 1956; originally served as the anthem of the Sudanese military

# ECONOMY :: SUDAN

## ECONOMY - OVERVIEW:

Sudan has experienced protracted social conflict, civil war, and, in July 2011, the loss of three-quarters of its oil production due to the secession of South Sudan. The oil sector had driven much of Sudan's GDP growth since 1999. For nearly a decade, the economy boomed on the back of rising oil production, high oil prices, and significant inflows of foreign direct investment. Since the economic shock of South Sudan's secession, Sudan has struggled to stabilize its economy and make up for the loss of foreign exchange earnings. The interruption of oil production in South Sudan in 2012 for over a year and the consequent loss of oil transit fees further exacerbated the fragile state of Sudan's economy. Ongoing conflicts in Southern Kordofan, Darfur, and the Blue Nile states, lack of basic infrastructure in large areas, and reliance by much of the population on subsistence agriculture, keep close to half of the population at or below the poverty line.

Sudan was subject to comprehensive US sanctions, which were lifted in October 2017. Sudan is attempting to develop non-oil sources of revenues, such as gold mining and agriculture, while carrying out an austerity program to reduce expenditures. The world's largest exporter of gum Arabic, Sudan produces 75-80% of the world's total output. Agriculture continues to employ 80% of the work force.

Sudan introduced a new currency, still called the Sudanese pound, following South Sudan's secession, but the value of the currency has fallen since its introduction. Khartoum formally devalued the currency in June 2012, when it passed austerity measures that included gradually repealing fuel subsidies. Sudan also faces high inflation, which reached 47% on an annual basis in November 2012 but fell to about 35% per year in 2017.

**GDP (PURCHASING POWER PARITY):**

$177.4 billion (2017 est.)

$174.9 billion (2016 est.)

$169.8 billion (2015 est.)

note: data are in 2017 dollars

country comparison to the world: 71

**GDP (OFFICIAL EXCHANGE RATE):**

$45.82 billion (2017 est.) (2017 est.)

**GDP - REAL GROWTH RATE:**

1.4% (2017 est.)

3% (2016 est.)

1.3% (2015 est.)

country comparison to the world: 177

**GDP - PER CAPITA (PPP):**

$4,300 (2017 est.)

$4,400 (2016 est.)

$4,400 (2015 est.)

note: data are in 2017 dollars

country comparison to the world: 174

**GROSS NATIONAL SAVING:**

12.1% of GDP (2017 est.)

13.1% of GDP (2016 est.)

12.2% of GDP (2015 est.)

country comparison to the world: 149

**GDP - COMPOSITION, BY END USE:**

household consumption: 77.3% (2017 est.)

government consumption: 5.8% (2017 est.)

investment in fixed capital: 18.4% (2017 est.)

investment in inventories: 0.6% (2017 est.)

exports of goods and services: 9.7% (2017 est.)

imports of goods and services: -11.8% (2017 est.)

**GDP - COMPOSITION, BY SECTOR OF ORIGIN:**

agriculture: 39.6% (2017 est.)

industry: 2.6% (2017 est.)

services: 57.8% (2017 est.)

**AGRICULTURE - PRODUCTS:**

cotton, groundnuts (peanuts), sorghum, millet, wheat, gum Arabic, sugarcane, cassava (manioc, tapioca), mangoes, papaya, bananas, sweet potatoes, sesame seeds; animal feed, sheep and other livestock

**INDUSTRIES:**

oil, cotton ginning, textiles, cement, edible oils, sugar, soap distilling, shoes, petroleum refining, pharmaceuticals, armaments, automobile/light truck assembly, milling

**INDUSTRIAL PRODUCTION GROWTH RATE:**

4.5% (2017 est.)

country comparison to the world: 66

**LABOR FORCE:**

11.92 million (2007 est.)

country comparison to the world: 49

**LABOR FORCE - BY OCCUPATION:**

agriculture: 80%

industry: 7%

services: 13% (1998 est.)

**UNEMPLOYMENT RATE:**

19.6% (2017 est.)

20.6% (2016 est.)

country comparison to the world: 184

**POPULATION BELOW POVERTY LINE:**

46.5% (2009 est.)

**HOUSEHOLD INCOME OR CONSUMPTION BY PERCENTAGE SHARE:**

lowest 10%: 26.7% (2009 est.)

highest 10%: 26.7% (2009 est.)

**BUDGET:**

revenues: 8.48 billion (2017 est.)

expenditures: 13.36 billion (2017 est.)

**TAXES AND OTHER REVENUES:**

18.5% (of GDP) (2017 est.)

country comparison to the world: 159

**BUDGET SURPLUS (+) OR DEFICIT (-):**

-10.6% (of GDP) (2017 est.)

country comparison to the world: 213

**PUBLIC DEBT:**

121.6% of GDP (2017 est.)

99.5% of GDP (2016 est.)

country comparison to the world: 10

**FISCAL YEAR:**

calendar year

**INFLATION RATE (CONSUMER PRICES):**

32.4% (2017 est.)

17.8% (2016 est.)

country comparison to the world: 223

**COMMERCIAL BANK PRIME LENDING RATE:**

13% (31 December 2017 est.)

12.5% (31 December 2016 est.)

country comparison to the world: 63

**STOCK OF NARROW MONEY:**

$18.82 billion (31 December 2017 est.)

$11.7 billion (31 December 2016 est.)

country comparison to the world: 69

**STOCK OF BROAD MONEY:**

$18.82 billion (31 December 2017 est.)

$11.7 billion (31 December 2016 est.)

country comparison to the world: 70

**STOCK OF DOMESTIC CREDIT:**

$28.7 billion (31 December 2017 est.)

$20.22 billion (31 December 2016 est.)

country comparison to the world: 81

**MARKET VALUE OF PUBLICLY TRADED SHARES:**

NA

**CURRENT ACCOUNT BALANCE:**

-$4.811 billion (2017 est.)

-$4.213 billion (2016 est.)

country comparison to the world: 182

**EXPORTS:**

$4.1 billion (2017 est.)

$3.094 billion (2016 est.)

country comparison to the world: 118
**EXPORTS - PARTNERS:**
UAE 55.5%, Egypt 14.7%, Saudi Arabia 8.8% (2017)

**EXPORTS - COMMODITIES:**
gold; oil and petroleum products; cotton, sesame, livestock, peanuts, gum Arabic, sugar

**IMPORTS:**
$8.22 billion (2017 est.)

$7.48 billion (2016 est.)

country comparison to the world: 110
**IMPORTS - COMMODITIES:**
foodstuffs, manufactured goods, refinery and transport equipment, medicines, chemicals, textiles, wheat

**IMPORTS - PARTNERS:**
UAE 12.7%, Egypt 10.6%, India 10.5%, Turkey 10.2%, Japan 7.6%, Saudi Arabia 6%, Germany 4.6% (2017)

**RESERVES OF FOREIGN EXCHANGE AND GOLD:**
$198 million (31 December 2017 est.)

$168.3 million (31 December 2016 est.)

country comparison to the world: 177
**DEBT - EXTERNAL:**
$56.05 billion (31 December 2017 est.)

$51.26 billion (31 December 2016 est.)

country comparison to the world: 62
**STOCK OF DIRECT FOREIGN INVESTMENT - AT HOME:**
$25.47 billion (31 December 2016 est.)

country comparison to the world: 75
**EXCHANGE RATES:**
Sudanese pounds (SDG) per US dollar -

6.72 (2017 est.)

6.14 (2016 est.)

6.14 (2015 est.)

6.03 (2014 est.)

5.74 (2013 est.)

## ENERGY :: SUDAN

**ELECTRICITY ACCESS:**
population without electricity: 24.7 million (2013)

electrification - total population: 35% (2013)

electrification - urban areas: 63% (2013)

electrification - rural areas: 21% (2013)

**ELECTRICITY - PRODUCTION:**
13.99 billion kWh (2016 est.)

country comparison to the world: 89
**ELECTRICITY - CONSUMPTION:**
12.12 billion kWh (2016 est.)

country comparison to the world: 88
**ELECTRICITY - EXPORTS:**
0 kWh (2016 est.)

country comparison to the world: 203
**ELECTRICITY - IMPORTS:**
0 kWh (2016 est.)

country comparison to the world: 205
**ELECTRICITY - INSTALLED GENERATING CAPACITY:**
3.437 million kW (2016 est.)

country comparison to the world: 96
**ELECTRICITY - FROM FOSSIL FUELS:**
44% of total installed capacity (2016 est.)

country comparison to the world: 162
**ELECTRICITY - FROM NUCLEAR FUELS:**
0% of total installed capacity (2017 est.)

country comparison to the world: 188
**ELECTRICITY - FROM HYDROELECTRIC PLANTS:**
51% of total installed capacity (2017 est.)

country comparison to the world: 39
**ELECTRICITY - FROM OTHER RENEWABLE SOURCES:**
6% of total installed capacity (2017 est.)

country comparison to the world: 104
**CRUDE OIL - PRODUCTION:**
102,300 bbl/day (2017 est.)

country comparison to the world: 42
**CRUDE OIL - EXPORTS:**
19,540 bbl/day (2015 est.)

country comparison to the world: 50
**CRUDE OIL - IMPORTS:**
9,440 bbl/day (2015 est.)

country comparison to the world: 73
**CRUDE OIL - PROVED RESERVES:**
5 billion bbl (1 January 2018 est.)

country comparison to the world: 22
**REFINED PETROLEUM PRODUCTS - PRODUCTION:**
94,830 bbl/day (2015 est.)

country comparison to the world: 68
**REFINED PETROLEUM PRODUCTS - CONSUMPTION:**
112,000 bbl/day (2016 est.)

country comparison to the world: 75
**REFINED PETROLEUM PRODUCTS - EXPORTS:**
8,541 bbl/day (2015 est.)

country comparison to the world: 85
**REFINED PETROLEUM PRODUCTS - IMPORTS:**
24,340 bbl/day (2015 est.)

country comparison to the world: 108
**NATURAL GAS - PRODUCTION:**
0 cu m (2017 est.)

country comparison to the world: 201
**NATURAL GAS - CONSUMPTION:**
0 cu m (2017 est.)

country comparison to the world: 202
**NATURAL GAS - EXPORTS:**
0 cu m (2017 est.)

country comparison to the world: 190
**NATURAL GAS - IMPORTS:**
0 cu m (2017 est.)

country comparison to the world: 193
**NATURAL GAS - PROVED RESERVES:**
84.95 billion cu m (1 January 2018 est.)

country comparison to the world: 55
**CARBON DIOXIDE EMISSIONS FROM CONSUMPTION OF ENERGY:**
16.03 million Mt (2017 est.)

country comparison to the world: 92

## COMMUNICATIONS :: SUDAN

**TELEPHONES - FIXED LINES:**
total subscriptions: 143,280 (2017 est.)

subscriptions per 100 inhabitants: less than 1 (2017 est.)

country comparison to the world: 130
**TELEPHONES - MOBILE CELLULAR:**
total subscriptions: 28,644,139 (2017 est.)

subscriptions per 100 inhabitants: 77 (2017 est.)

country comparison to the world: 45
**TELEPHONE SYSTEM:**
general assessment: well-equipped system by regional standards and being upgraded; cellular communications started in 1996 and have expanded substantially with wide coverage of most major cities (2016)

domestic: consists of microwave radio relay, cable, fiber optic, radiotelephone communications, tropospheric scatter, and a domestic satellite system with 14 earth stations; teledensity exceeeds 75 telephones per 100 persons (2016)

*international*: country code - 249; linked to the EASSy and FLAG fiber-optic submarine cable systems; satellite earth stations - 1 Intelsat (Atlantic Ocean), 1 Arabsat (2016)

### BROADCAST MEDIA:

the Sudanese Government directly controls TV and radio, requiring that both media reflect government policies; TV has a permanent military censor; a private radio station is in operation (2007)

### INTERNET COUNTRY CODE:

.sd

### INTERNET USERS:

*total*: 10,284,260 (July 2016 est.)

*percent of population*: 28% (July 2016 est.)

*country comparison to the world*: 47

### BROADBAND - FIXED SUBSCRIPTIONS:

*total*: 31,082 (2017 est.)

*subscriptions per 100 inhabitants*: less than 1 (2017 est.)

*country comparison to the world*: 140

## TRANSPORTATION :: SUDAN

### NATIONAL AIR TRANSPORT SYSTEM:

*number of registered air carriers*: 6 (2015)

*inventory of registered aircraft operated by air carriers*: 25 (2015)

*annual passenger traffic on registered air carriers*: 496,178 (2015)

*annual freight traffic on registered air carriers*: 13,161,592 mt-km (2015)

### CIVIL AIRCRAFT REGISTRATION COUNTRY CODE PREFIX:

ST (2016)

### AIRPORTS:

74 (2013)

*country comparison to the world*: 71

### AIRPORTS - WITH PAVED RUNWAYS:

*total*: 16 (2013)

*over 3,047 m*: 2 (2013)

*2,438 to 3,047 m*: 10 (2013)

*1,524 to 2,437 m*: 2 (2013)

*under 914 m*: 2 (2013)

### AIRPORTS - WITH UNPAVED RUNWAYS:

*total*: 58 (2013)

*2,438 to 3,047 m*: 1 (2013)

*1,524 to 2,437 m*: 17 (2013)

*914 to 1,523 m*: 28 (2013)

*under 914 m*: 12 (2013)

### HELIPORTS:

6 (2013)

### PIPELINES:

156 km gas, 4070 km oil, 1613 km refined products (2013)

### RAILWAYS:

*total*: 7,251 km (2014)

*narrow gauge*: 5,851 km 1.067-m gauge (2014)

1400 0.600-m gauge for cotton plantations

*country comparison to the world*: 31

### ROADWAYS:

*total*: 11,900 km (2000)

*paved*: 4,320 km (2000)

*unpaved*: 7,580 km (2000)

*country comparison to the world*: 131

### WATERWAYS:

4,068 km (1,723 km open year-round on White and Blue Nile Rivers) (2011)

*country comparison to the world*: 24

### MERCHANT MARINE:

*total*: 17 (2017)

*by type*: general cargo 1, other 16 (2017)

*country comparison to the world*: 143

### PORTS AND TERMINALS:

*major seaport(s)*: Port Sudan

## MILITARY AND SECURITY :: SUDAN

### MILITARY EXPENDITURES:

2.83% of GDP (2016)

2.36% of GDP (2015)

*country comparison to the world*: 32

### MILITARY BRANCHES:

Sudanese Armed Forces (SAF): Land Forces, Navy (includes Marines), Sudanese Air Force (Sikakh al-Jawwiya as-Sudaniya), Rapid Support Forces, Popular Defense Forces (2016)

### MILITARY SERVICE AGE AND OBLIGATION:

18-33 years of age for male and female compulsory or voluntary military service; 1-2 year service obligation; a requirement that completion of national service was mandatory before entering public or private sector employment has been cancelled (2012)

## TRANSNATIONAL ISSUES :: SUDAN

### DISPUTES - INTERNATIONAL:

the effects of Sudan's ethnic and rebel militia fighting since the mid-20th century have penetrated all of the neighboring statesChad wishes to be a helpful mediator in resolving the Darfur conflict, and in 2010 established a joint border monitoring force with Sudan, which has helped to reduce cross-border banditry and violenceas of April 2017, more than 610,000 Sudanese refugees are being hosted in the Central African Republic, Chad, Egypt, Ethiopia, Kenya, and South SudanSudan, in turn, is hosting about 507,000 refugees, including more than 375,000 from South SudanSudan accuses South Sudan of supporting Sudanese rebel groupsSudan claims but Egypt de facto administers security and economic development of the Halaib region north of the 22nd parallel boundaryperiodic violent skirmishes with Sudanese residents over water and grazing rights persist among related pastoral populations along the border with the Central African RepublicSouth Sudan-Sudan boundary represents 1 January 1956 alignment, final alignment pending negotiations and demarcationfinal sovereignty status of Abyei Area pending negotiations between South Sudan and Sudan

### REFUGEES AND INTERNALLY DISPLACED PERSONS:

*refugees (country of origin)*: 103,176 (Eritrea), 8,502 (Chad), 6,997 (Syria) (2016), 764,400 (South Sudan) (refugees and asylum seekers) (2018)

*IDPs*: 2.072 million (civil war 1983-2005; ongoing conflict in Darfur region; government and rebel fighting along South Sudan border; inter-tribal clashes) (2017)

### TRAFFICKING IN PERSONS:

*current situation*: Sudan is a source, transit, and destination country for men, women, and children who are subjected to forced labor and sex trafficking; Sudanese women and girls, particularly those from rural areas or who are internally displaced, or refugees are vulnerable to domestic servitude in country, as well as domestic servitude and sex trafficking abroad; migrants from East and West Africa, South Sudan, Syria, and Nigeria smuggled into or through Sudan are vulnerable to exploitation; Ethiopian, Eritrean, and Filipina women are subjected to domestic servitude in Sudanese homes, and East African and possibly Thai women are forced into prostitution in Sudan; Sudanese children continue to be recruited and used as combatants by government forces and armed groups

**tier rating:** Tier 2 Watch List - Sudan does not fully comply with the minimum standards for the elimination of trafficking; however, it is making significant efforts to do so; the government increased its efforts to publically address and prevent trafficking, established a national anti-trafficking council, and began drafting a national action plan against trafficking; the government acknowledges cross-border trafficking but still denies the existence of forced labor, sex trafficking, and the recruitment of child soldiers domestically; law enforcement and judicial officials struggled to apply the national anti-trafficking law, often relying on other statutes with lesser penalties; authorities did not use systematic procedure to identify victims or refer them to care and relied on international organizations and domestic groups to provide protective services; some foreign victims were penalized for unlawful acts committed as a direct result of being trafficked, such as immigration or prostitution violations (2015)

# SOUTH AMERICA :: SURINAME

## INTRODUCTION :: SURINAME

### BACKGROUND:
First explored by the Spaniards in the 16th century and then settled by the English in the mid-17th century, Suriname became a Dutch colony in 1667. With the abolition of African slavery in 1863, workers were brought in from India and Java. The Netherlands granted the colony independence in 1975. Five years later the civilian government was replaced by a military regime that soon declared Suriname a socialist republic. It continued to exert control through a succession of nominally civilian administrations until 1987, when international pressure finally forced a democratic election. In 1990, the military overthrew the civilian leadership, but a democratically elected government - a four-party coalition - returned to power in 1991. The coalition expanded to eight parties in 2005 and ruled until August 2010, when voters returned former military leader Desire BOUTERSE and his opposition coalition to power. President BOUTERSE was reelected unopposed in 2015.

## GEOGRAPHY :: SURINAME

### LOCATION:
Northern South America, bordering the North Atlantic Ocean, between French Guiana and Guyana

### GEOGRAPHIC COORDINATES:
4 00 N, 56 00 W

### MAP REFERENCES:
South America

### AREA:
total: 163,820 sq km

land: 156,000 sq km

water: 7,820 sq km

country comparison to the world: 93

### AREA - COMPARATIVE:
slightly larger than Georgia

### LAND BOUNDARIES:
total: 1,907 km

border countries (3): Brazil 515 km, French Guiana 556 km, Guyana 836 km

### COASTLINE:
386 km

### MARITIME CLAIMS:
territorial sea: 12 nm

exclusive economic zone: 200 nm

### CLIMATE:
tropical; moderated by trade winds

### TERRAIN:
mostly rolling hills; narrow coastal plain with swamps

### ELEVATION:
mean elevation: 246 m

elevation extremes: -2 m lowest point: unnamed location in the coastal plain

1230 highest point: Juliana Top

### NATURAL RESOURCES:
timber, hydropower, fish, kaolin, shrimp, bauxite, gold, and small amounts of nickel, copper, platinum, iron ore

### LAND USE:
agricultural land: 0.5% (2011 est.)

arable land: 0.4% (2011 est.) / permanent crops: 0% (2011 est.) / permanent pasture: 0.1% (2011 est.)

forest: 94.6% (2011 est.)

other: 4.9% (2011 est.)

### IRRIGATED LAND:
570 sq km (2012)

### POPULATION DISTRIBUTION:
population concentrated along the nothern coastal strip; the remainder of the country is sparsely populated

### NATURAL HAZARDS:
flooding

### ENVIRONMENT - CURRENT ISSUES:
deforestation as timber is cut for export; pollution of inland waterways by small-scale mining activities

### ENVIRONMENT - INTERNATIONAL AGREEMENTS:
party to: Biodiversity, Climate Change, Climate Change-Kyoto Protocol, Desertification, Endangered Species, Hazardous Wastes, Law of the Sea, Marine Dumping, Ozone Layer Protection, Ship Pollution, Tropical Timber 94, Wetlands, Whaling

signed, but not ratified: none of the selected agreements

### GEOGRAPHY - NOTE:
smallest independent country on South American continent; mostly tropical rain forest; great diversity of flora and fauna that, for the most part,

is increasingly threatened by new development; relatively small population, mostly along the coast

# PEOPLE AND SOCIETY :: SURINAME

**POPULATION:**

597,927 (July 2018 est.)

country comparison to the world: 172

**NATIONALITY:**

noun: Surinamer(s)

adjective: Surinamese

**ETHNIC GROUPS:**

Hindustani (also known locally as "East Indians"; their ancestors emigrated from northern India in the latter part of the 19th century) 27.4%, "Maroon" (their African ancestors were brought to the country in the 17th and 18th centuries as slaves and escaped to the interior) 21.7%, Creole (mixed white and black) 15.7%, Javanese 13.7%, mixed 13.4%, other 7.6%, unspecified 0.6% (2012 est.)

**LANGUAGES:**

Dutch (official), English (widely spoken), Sranang Tongo (Surinamese, sometimes called Taki-Taki, is the native language of Creoles and much of the younger population and is lingua franca among others), Caribbean Hindustani (a dialect of Hindi), Javanese

**RELIGIONS:**

Protestant 23.6% (includes Evangelical 11.2%, Moravian 11.2%, Reformed .7%, Lutheran .5%), Hindu 22.3%, Roman Catholic 21.6%, Muslim 13.8%, other Christian 3.2%, Winti 1.8%, Jehovah's Witness 1.2%, other 1.7%, none 7.5%, unspecified 3.2% (2012 est.)

**DEMOGRAPHIC PROFILE:**

Suriname is a pluralistic society consisting primarily of Creoles (persons of mixed African and European heritage), the descendants of escaped African slaves known as Maroons, and the descendants of Indian and Javanese (Indonesian) contract workers. The country overall is in full, post-industrial demographic transition, with a low fertility rate, a moderate mortality rate, and a rising life expectancy. However, the Maroon population of the rural interior lags behind because of lower educational attainment and contraceptive use, higher malnutrition, and significantly less access to electricity, potable water, sanitation, infrastructure, and health care.

Some 350,000 people of Surinamese descent live in the Netherlands, Suriname's former colonial ruler. In the 19th century, better-educated, largely Dutch-speaking Surinamese began emigrating to the Netherlands. World War II interrupted the outflow, but it resumed after the war when Dutch labor demands grew - emigrants included all segments of the Creole population. Suriname still is strongly influenced by the Netherlands because most Surinamese have relatives living there and it is the largest supplier of development aid. Other emigration destinations include French Guiana and the United States. Suriname's immigration rules are flexible, and the country is easy to enter illegally because rainforests obscure its borders. Since the mid-1980s, Brazilians have settled in Suriname's capital, Paramaribo, or eastern Suriname, where they mine gold. This immigration is likely to slowly re-orient Suriname toward its Latin American roots.

**AGE STRUCTURE:**

0-14 years: 24.11% (male 73,466/female 70,704)

15-24 years: 17.36% (male 52,876/female 50,913)

25-54 years: 44.42% (male 135,282/female 130,327)

55-64 years: 7.94% (male 23,377/female 24,085)

65 years and over: 6.17% (male 16,019/female 20,878) (2018 est.)

**DEPENDENCY RATIOS:**

total dependency ratio: 50.7 (2015 est.)

youth dependency ratio: 40.6 (2015 est.)

elderly dependency ratio: 10.1 (2015 est.)

potential support ratio: 9.9 (2015 est.)

**MEDIAN AGE:**

total: 30.2 years

male: 29.8 years

female: 30.6 years (2018 est.)

country comparison to the world: 118

**POPULATION GROWTH RATE:**

1% (2018 est.)

country comparison to the world: 108

**BIRTH RATE:**

15.6 births/1,000 population (2018 est.)

country comparison to the world: 117

**DEATH RATE:**

6.1 deaths/1,000 population (2018 est.)

country comparison to the world: 161

**NET MIGRATION RATE:**

0.6 migrant(s)/1,000 population (2017 est.)

country comparison to the world: 62

**POPULATION DISTRIBUTION:**

population concentrated along the nothern coastal strip; the remainder of the country is sparsely populated

**URBANIZATION:**

urban population: 66.1% of total population (2018)

rate of urbanization: 0.9% annual rate of change (2015-20 est.)

**MAJOR URBAN AREAS - POPULATION:**

239,000 PARAMARIBO (capital) (2018)

**SEX RATIO:**

at birth: 1.04 male(s)/female (2017 est.)

0-14 years: 1.04 male(s)/female (2017 est.)

15-24 years: 1.04 male(s)/female (2017 est.)

25-54 years: 1.04 male(s)/female (2017 est.)

55-64 years: 0.96 male(s)/female (2017 est.)

65 years and over: 0.76 male(s)/female (2017 est.)

total population: 1.01 male(s)/female (2017 est.)

**MATERNAL MORTALITY RATE:**

155 deaths/100,000 live births (2015 est.)

country comparison to the world: 59

**INFANT MORTALITY RATE:**

total: 23.7 deaths/1,000 live births (2018 est.)

male: 27.6 deaths/1,000 live births (2018 est.)

female: 19.5 deaths/1,000 live births (2018 est.)

country comparison to the world: 69

**LIFE EXPECTANCY AT BIRTH:**

total population: 72.8 years (2018 est.)

male: 70.3 years (2018 est.)

female: 75.3 years (2018 est.)

country comparison to the world: 146

**TOTAL FERTILITY RATE:**

1.9 children born/woman (2018 est.)

country comparison to the world: 133

**CONTRACEPTIVE PREVALENCE RATE:**

47.6% (2010)

**HEALTH EXPENDITURES:**

5.7% of GDP (2014)

country comparison to the world: 117

**HOSPITAL BED DENSITY:**

3.1 beds/1,000 population (2010)

**DRINKING WATER SOURCE:**

improved:

urban: 98.1% of population (2015 est.)

rural: 88.4% of population (2015 est.)

total: 94.8% of population (2015 est.)

unimproved:

urban: 1.9% of population (2015 est.)

rural: 11.6% of population (2015 est.)

total: 5.2% of population (2015 est.)

**SANITATION FACILITY ACCESS:**

improved:

urban: 88.4% of population (2015 est.)

rural: 61.4% of population (2015 est.)

total: 79.2% of population (2015 est.)

unimproved:

urban: 11.6% of population (2015 est.)

rural: 38.6% of population (2015 est.)

total: 20.8% of population (2015 est.)

**HIV/AIDS - ADULT PREVALENCE RATE:**

1.3% (2017 est.)

country comparison to the world: 38

**HIV/AIDS - PEOPLE LIVING WITH HIV/AIDS:**

4,800 (2017 est.)

country comparison to the world: 117

**HIV/AIDS - DEATHS:**

<200 (2017 est.)

**MAJOR INFECTIOUS DISEASES:**

degree of risk: very high (2016)

food or waterborne diseases: bacterial and protozoal diarrhea, hepatitis A, and typhoid fever (2016)

vectorborne diseases: dengue fever and malaria (2016)

note: active local transmission of Zika virus by Aedes species mosquitoes has been identified in this country (as of August 2016); it poses an important risk (a large number of cases possible) among US citizens if bitten by an infective mosquito; other less common ways to get Zika are through sex, via blood transfusion, or during pregnancy, in which the pregnant woman passes Zika virus to her fetus

**OBESITY - ADULT PREVALENCE RATE:**

26.4% (2016)

country comparison to the world: 42

**CHILDREN UNDER THE AGE OF 5 YEARS UNDERWEIGHT:**

5.8% (2010)

country comparison to the world: 78

**EDUCATION EXPENDITURES:**

NA

**LITERACY:**

definition: age 15 and over can read and write (2015 est.)

total population: 95.6% (2015 est.)

male: 96.1% (2015 est.)

female: 95% (2015 est.)

**UNEMPLOYMENT, YOUTH AGES 15-24:**

total: 13.4% (2015 est.)

male: 9% (2015 est.)

female: 21.9% (2015 est.)

country comparison to the world: 100

## GOVERNMENT :: SURINAME

**COUNTRY NAME:**

conventional long form: Republic of Suriname

conventional short form: Suriname

local long form: Republiek Suriname

local short form: Suriname

former: Netherlands Guiana, Dutch Guiana

etymology: name may derive from the indigenous "Surinen" people who inhabited the area at the time of European contact

**GOVERNMENT TYPE:**

presidential republic

**CAPITAL:**

name: Paramaribo

geographic coordinates: 5 50 N, 55 10 W

time difference: UTC-3 (2 hours ahead of Washington, DC, during Standard Time)

**ADMINISTRATIVE DIVISIONS:**

10 districts (distrikten, singular - distrikt); Brokopondo, Commewijne, Coronie, Marowijne, Nickerie, Para, Paramaribo, Saramacca, Sipaliwini, Wanica

**INDEPENDENCE:**

25 November 1975 (from the Netherlands)

**NATIONAL HOLIDAY:**

Independence Day, 25 November (1975)

**CONSTITUTION:**

history: previous 1975; latest ratified 30 September 1987, effective 30 October 1987 (2018)

amendments: proposed by the National Assembly; passage requires at least two-thirds majority vote of the total membership; amended 1992 (2018)

**LEGAL SYSTEM:**

civil law system influenced by Dutch civil law; note - the Commissie Nieuw Surinaamse Burgerlijk Wetboek completed drafting a new civil code in February 2009

**INTERNATIONAL LAW ORGANIZATION PARTICIPATION:**

accepts compulsory ICJ jurisdiction with reservations; accepts ICCt jurisdiction

**CITIZENSHIP:**

citizenship by birth: no

citizenship by descent only: at least one parent must be a citizen of Suriname

dual citizenship recognized: no

residency requirement for naturalization: 5 years

**SUFFRAGE:**

18 years of age; universal

**EXECUTIVE BRANCH:**

chief of state: President Desire Delano BOUTERSE (since 12 August 2010); Vice President Ashwin ADHIN (since 12 August 2015); note - the president is both chief of state and head of government

head of government: President Desire Delano BOUTERSE (since 12 August 2010); Vice President Ashwin ADHIN (since 12 August 2015)

cabinet: Cabinet of Ministers appointed by the president

**elections/appointments:** president and vice president indirectly elected by the National Assembly; president and vice president serve a 5-year term (no term limits); election last held on 25 May 2015 (next to be held in May 2020)

**election results:** Desire Delano BOUTERSE reelected president unopposed; National Assembly vote - NA

### LEGISLATIVE BRANCH:

**description:** unicameral National Assembly or Nationale Assemblee (51 seats; members directly elected in multi-seat constituencies by party-list proportional representation vote to serve 5-year terms)

**elections:** last held on 25 May 2015 (next to be held in May 2020)

**election results:** percent of vote by party - NDP 45.5%, V7 37.2%, A-Com 10.5%, DOE 4.3%, PALU 0.7%, other 1.8%; seats by party - NDP 26, V7 18, A-Com 5, DOE 1, PALU 1;

**note:** seats by party as of April 2017 - seats by party - NDP 26, VHP 9, ABOP 5, PL 3, NPS 2, BEP 2, DOE 1, PALU 1, independent 2

### JUDICIAL BRANCH:

**highest courts:** High Court of Justice of Suriname (consists of the court president, vice president, and 4 judges); note - appeals beyond the High Court are referred to the Caribbean Court of Justice; human rights violations can be appealed to the Inter-American Commission on Human Rights with judgments issued by the Inter-American Court on Human Rights

**judge selection and term of office:** court judges appointed by the national president in consultation with the National Assembly, the State Advisory Council, and the Order of Private Attorneys; judges appointed for life

**subordinate courts:** cantonal courts

### POLITICAL PARTIES AND LEADERS:

Alternative Combination or A-Com (coalition includes ABOP, KTPI, Party for Democracy and Development)
Brotherhood and Unity in Politics or BEP [Celsius WATERBERG]
Democratic Alternative '91 or DA91 [Angelique DEL CASTILLO]
General Liberation and Development Party or ABOP [Ronnie BRUNSWIJK]
National Democratic Party or NDP [Desire Delano BOUTERSE]
National Party of Suriname or NPS [Gregory RUSLAND]
Party for Democracy and Development in Unity or DOE [Carl BREEVELD]
Party for National Unity and Solidarity or KTPI [Willy SOEMITA]
People's Alliance (Pertjaja Luhur) or PL [Paul SOMOHARDJO]
Progressive Workers' and Farmers' Union or PALU [Jim HOK]
Surinamese Labor Party or SPA [Guno CASTELEN]
Progressive Reform Party or VHP [Chandrikapersad SANTOKHI]
Victory 7 or V7 [Chandrikapresad SANTOKHI] (formerly the New Front for Democracy and Development or NF; an electoral coalition of NPS, VHP, DA91, PL, SPA formed only for the May 2015 election)

### INTERNATIONAL ORGANIZATION PARTICIPATION:

ACP, AOSIS, Caricom, CD, CDB, CELAC, FAO, G-77, IADB, IBRD, ICAO, ICCt, ICRM, IDA, IDB, IFAD, IFC, IFRCS, IHO, ILO, IMF, IMO, Interpol, IOC, IOM, IPU, ISO (correspondent), ITU, ITUC (NGOs), LAES, MIGA, NAM, OAS, OIC, OPANAL, OPCW, PCA, Petrocaribe, UN, UNASUR, UNCTAD, UNESCO, UNIDO, UPU, WHO, WIPO, WMO, WTO

### DIPLOMATIC REPRESENTATION IN THE US:

**chief of mission:** Ambassador Niermala Sakoentala BADRISING (since 21 July 2017)

**chancery:** Suite 460, 4301 Connecticut Avenue NW, Washington, DC 20008

**telephone:** [1] (202) 244-7488

**FAX:** [1] (202) 244-5878

**consulate(s) general:** Miami

### DIPLOMATIC REPRESENTATION FROM THE US:

**chief of mission:** Ambassador Edwin "Ned" Richard NOLAN, Jr.(since 11 January 2016)

**embassy:** 165 Kristalstraat, Paramaribo

**mailing address:** US Department of State, PO Box 1821, Paramaribo

**telephone:** [597] 472-900

**FAX:** [597] 410-972

### FLAG DESCRIPTION:

five horizontal bands of green (top, double width), white, red (quadruple width), white, and green (double width); a large, yellow, five-pointed star is centered in the red band; red stands for progress and love, green symbolizes hope and fertility, white signifies peace, justice, and freedom; the star represents the unity of all ethnic groups; from its yellow light the nation draws strength to bear sacrifices patiently while working toward a golden future

### NATIONAL SYMBOL(S):

royal palm, faya lobi (flower); national colors: green, white, red, yellow

### NATIONAL ANTHEM:

**name:** "God zij met ons Suriname!" (God Be With Our Suriname)

**lyrics/music:** Cornelis Atses HOEKSTRA and Henry DE ZIEL/Johannes Corstianus DE PUY

**note:** adopted 1959; originally adapted from a Sunday school song written in 1893 and contains lyrics in both Dutch and Sranang Tongo

# ECONOMY :: SURINAME

### ECONOMY - OVERVIEW:

Suriname's economy is dominated by the mining industry, with exports of oil and gold accounting for approximately 85% of exports and 27% of government revenues. This makes the economy highly vulnerable to mineral price volatility. The worldwide drop in international commodity prices and the cessation of alumina mining in Suriname significantly reduced government revenue and national income during the past few years. In November 2015, a major US aluminum company discontinued its mining activities in Suriname after 99 years of operation. Public sector revenues fell, together with exports, international reserves, employment, and private sector investment.

Economic growth declined annually from just under 5% in 2012 to -10.4% in 2016. In January 2011, the government devalued the currency by 20% and raised taxes to reduce the budget deficit. Suriname began instituting macro adjustments between September 2015 and 2016; these included another 20% currency devaluation in November 2015 and foreign currency interventions by the Central Bank until March 2016, after which time the Bank allowed the Surinamese dollar (SRD) to float. By December 2016, the SRD had lost 46% of its value against the dollar. Depreciation of the Surinamese dollar and increases in tariffs on electricity caused domestic prices in Suriname to rise 22.0% year-over-year by December 2017.

Suriname's economic prospects for the medium-term will depend on its commitment to responsible monetary and fiscal policies and on the introduction of structural reforms to liberalize markets and promote competition. The government's over-reliance on revenue from the extractive sector colors Suriname's economic outlook. Following two years of recession, the Fitch Credit Bureau reported a positive growth of 1.2% in 2017 and the World Bank predicted 2.2% growth in 2018. Inflation declined to 9%, down from 55% in 2016, and increased gold production helped lift exports. Yet continued budget imbalances and a heavy debt and interest burden resulted in a debt-to-GDP ratio of 83% in September 2017. Purchasing power has fallen rapidly due to the devalued local currency. The government has announced its intention to pass legislation to introduce a new value-added tax in 2018. Without this and other measures to strengthen the country's fiscal position, the government may face liquidity pressures.

**GDP (PURCHASING POWER PARITY):**

$8.688 billion (2017 est.)

$8.526 billion (2016 est.)

$8.988 billion (2015 est.)

note: data are in 2017 dollars

country comparison to the world: 162

**GDP (OFFICIAL EXCHANGE RATE):**

$3.419 billion (2017 est.) (2017 est.)

**GDP - REAL GROWTH RATE:**

1.9% (2017 est.)

-5.1% (2016 est.)

-2.6% (2015 est.)

country comparison to the world: 159

**GDP - PER CAPITA (PPP):**

$14,900 (2017 est.)

$14,800 (2016 est.)

$15,900 (2015 est.)

note: data are in 2017 dollars

country comparison to the world: 114

**GROSS NATIONAL SAVING:**

46.6% of GDP (2017 est.)

55.6% of GDP (2016 est.)

53.6% of GDP (2015 est.)

country comparison to the world: 4

**GDP - COMPOSITION, BY END USE:**

household consumption: 27.6% (2017 est.)

government consumption: 11.7% (2017 est.)

investment in fixed capital: 52.5% (2017 est.)

investment in inventories: 26.5% (2017 est.)

exports of goods and services: 68.9% (2017 est.)

imports of goods and services: -60.6% (2017 est.)

**GDP - COMPOSITION, BY SECTOR OF ORIGIN:**

agriculture: 11.6% (2017 est.)

industry: 31.1% (2017 est.)

services: 57.4% (2017 est.)

**AGRICULTURE - PRODUCTS:**

rice, bananas, seabob shrimp, yellow-fin tuna, vegetables

**INDUSTRIES:**

gold mining, oil, lumber, food processing, fishing

**INDUSTRIAL PRODUCTION GROWTH RATE:**

1% (2017 est.)

country comparison to the world: 158

**LABOR FORCE:**

144,000 (2014 est.)

country comparison to the world: 177

**LABOR FORCE - BY OCCUPATION:**

agriculture: 11.2%

industry: 19.5%

services: 69.3% (2010)

**UNEMPLOYMENT RATE:**

8.9% (2017 est.)

9.7% (2016 est.)

country comparison to the world: 129

**POPULATION BELOW POVERTY LINE:**

70% (2002 est.)

**HOUSEHOLD INCOME OR CONSUMPTION BY PERCENTAGE SHARE:**

lowest 10%: NA

highest 10%: NA

**BUDGET:**

revenues: 560.7 million (2017 est.)

expenditures: 827.8 million (2017 est.)

**TAXES AND OTHER REVENUES:**

16.4% (of GDP) (2017 est.)

country comparison to the world: 182

**BUDGET SURPLUS (+) OR DEFICIT (-):**

-7.8% (of GDP) (2017 est.)

country comparison to the world: 197

**PUBLIC DEBT:**

69.3% of GDP (2017 est.)

75.8% of GDP (2016 est.)

country comparison to the world: 52

**FISCAL YEAR:**

calendar year

**INFLATION RATE (CONSUMER PRICES):**

22% (2017 est.)

55.5% (2016 est.)

country comparison to the world: 216

**CENTRAL BANK DISCOUNT RATE:**

10% (2013)

9% (2012)

country comparison to the world: 24

**COMMERCIAL BANK PRIME LENDING RATE:**

14.43% (31 December 2017 est.)

13.49% (31 December 2016 est.)

country comparison to the world: 46

**STOCK OF NARROW MONEY:**

$1.158 billion (31 December 2017 est.)

$921.8 million (31 December 2016 est.)

country comparison to the world: 154

**STOCK OF BROAD MONEY:**

$1.158 billion (31 December 2017 est.)

$921.8 million (31 December 2016 est.)

country comparison to the world: 159

**STOCK OF DOMESTIC CREDIT:**

$1.608 billion (31 December 2017 est.)

$1.404 billion (31 December 2016 est.)

country comparison to the world: 159

**MARKET VALUE OF PUBLICLY TRADED SHARES:**

NA

**CURRENT ACCOUNT BALANCE:**

-$2 million (2017 est.)

-$169 million (2016 est.)

country comparison to the world: 69

**EXPORTS:**

$2.028 billion (2017 est.)

$1.449 billion (2016 est.)

country comparison to the world: 140

**EXPORTS - PARTNERS:**

Switzerland 38%, Hong Kong 21.9%, Belgium 10.1%, UAE 7.2%, Guyana

6.1% (2017)

**EXPORTS - COMMODITIES:**

alumina, gold, crude oil, lumber, shrimp and fish, rice, bananas

**IMPORTS:**

$1.293 billion (2017 est.)

$1.203 billion (2016 est.)

country comparison to the world: 176

**IMPORTS - COMMODITIES:**

capital equipment, petroleum, foodstuffs, cotton, consumer goods

**IMPORTS - PARTNERS:**

US 30.6%, Netherlands 14.8%, Trinidad and Tobago 11.4%, China 7.6% (2017)

**RESERVES OF FOREIGN EXCHANGE AND GOLD:**

$424.4 million (31 December 2017 est.)

$381.1 million (31 December 2016 est.)

country comparison to the world: 158

**DEBT - EXTERNAL:**

$1.7 billion (31 December 2017 est.)

$1.436 billion (31 December 2016 est.)

country comparison to the world: 156

**STOCK OF DIRECT FOREIGN INVESTMENT - AT HOME:**

(31 December 2009 est.)

**EXCHANGE RATES:**

Surinamese dollars (SRD) per US dollar -

7.53 (2017 est.)

6.229 (2016 est.)

6.229 (2015 est.)

3.4167 (2014 est.)

3.3 (2013 est.)

## ENERGY :: SURINAME

**ELECTRICITY ACCESS:**

electrification - total population: 100% (2016)

**ELECTRICITY - PRODUCTION:**

1.967 billion kWh (2016 est.)

country comparison to the world: 138

**ELECTRICITY - CONSUMPTION:**

1.75 billion kWh (2016 est.)

country comparison to the world: 144

**ELECTRICITY - EXPORTS:**

0 kWh (2016 est.)

country comparison to the world: 204

**ELECTRICITY - IMPORTS:**

0 kWh (2016 est.)

country comparison to the world: 206

**ELECTRICITY - INSTALLED GENERATING CAPACITY:**

504,000 kW (2016 est.)

country comparison to the world: 149

**ELECTRICITY - FROM FOSSIL FUELS:**

61% of total installed capacity (2016 est.)

country comparison to the world: 129

**ELECTRICITY - FROM NUCLEAR FUELS:**

0% of total installed capacity (2017 est.)

country comparison to the world: 189

**ELECTRICITY - FROM HYDROELECTRIC PLANTS:**

38% of total installed capacity (2017 est.)

country comparison to the world: 56

**ELECTRICITY - FROM OTHER RENEWABLE SOURCES:**

2% of total installed capacity (2017 est.)

country comparison to the world: 145

**CRUDE OIL - PRODUCTION:**

17,000 bbl/day (2017 est.)

country comparison to the world: 68

**CRUDE OIL - EXPORTS:**

0 bbl/day (2015 est.)

country comparison to the world: 200

**CRUDE OIL - IMPORTS:**

820 bbl/day (2015 est.)

country comparison to the world: 80

**CRUDE OIL - PROVED RESERVES:**

84.2 million bbl (1 January 2018 est.)

country comparison to the world: 70

**REFINED PETROLEUM PRODUCTS - PRODUCTION:**

7,571 bbl/day (2015 est.)

country comparison to the world: 101

**REFINED PETROLEUM PRODUCTS - CONSUMPTION:**

13,000 bbl/day (2016 est.)

country comparison to the world: 157

**REFINED PETROLEUM PRODUCTS - EXPORTS:**

14,000 bbl/day (2015 est.)

country comparison to the world: 74

**REFINED PETROLEUM PRODUCTS - IMPORTS:**

10,700 bbl/day (2015 est.)

country comparison to the world: 145

**NATURAL GAS - PRODUCTION:**

0 cu m (2017 est.)

country comparison to the world: 202

**NATURAL GAS - CONSUMPTION:**

0 cu m (2017 est.)

country comparison to the world: 203

**NATURAL GAS - EXPORTS:**

0 cu m (2017 est.)

country comparison to the world: 191

**NATURAL GAS - IMPORTS:**

0 cu m (2017 est.)

country comparison to the world: 194

**NATURAL GAS - PROVED RESERVES:**

0 cu m (1 January 2011 est.)

country comparison to the world: 198

**CARBON DIOXIDE EMISSIONS FROM CONSUMPTION OF ENERGY:**

2.075 million Mt (2017 est.)

country comparison to the world: 159

## COMMUNICATIONS :: SURINAME

**TELEPHONES - FIXED LINES:**

total subscriptions: 89,030 (2017 est.)

subscriptions per 100 inhabitants: 15 (2017 est.)

country comparison to the world: 143

**TELEPHONES - MOBILE CELLULAR:**

total subscriptions: 795,871 (2017 est.)

subscriptions per 100 inhabitants: 134 (2017 est.)

country comparison to the world: 162

**TELEPHONE SYSTEM:**

general assessment: international facilities are good (2017)

domestic: combined fixed-line and mobile-cellular teledensity exceeds 150 telephones per 100 persons; microwave radio relay network is in place (2017)

international: country code - 597; satellite earth stations - 2 Intelsat (Atlantic Ocean) (2017)

**BROADCAST MEDIA:**

2 state-owned TV stations; 1 state-owned radio station; multiple private radio and TV stations (2007)

**INTERNET COUNTRY CODE:**

.sr

**INTERNET USERS:**

total: 265,964 (July 2016 est.)

percent of population: 45.4% (July 2016 est.)

country comparison to the world: 163

**BROADBAND - FIXED SUBSCRIPTIONS:**

total: 71,217 (2017 est.)

subscriptions per 100 inhabitants: 12 (2017 est.)

country comparison to the world: 125

## TRANSPORTATION :: SURINAME

**NATIONAL AIR TRANSPORT SYSTEM:**

number of registered air carriers: 2 (2015)

inventory of registered aircraft operated by air carriers: 5 (2015)

annual passenger traffic on registered air carriers: 259,682 (2015)

annual freight traffic on registered air carriers: 29,324,319 mt-km (2015)

**CIVIL AIRCRAFT REGISTRATION COUNTRY CODE PREFIX:**

PZ (2016)

**AIRPORTS:**

55 (2013)

country comparison to the world: 86

**AIRPORTS - WITH PAVED RUNWAYS:**

total: 6 (2013)

over 3,047 m: 1 (2013)

under 914 m: 5 (2013)

**AIRPORTS - WITH UNPAVED RUNWAYS:**

total: 49 (2013)

914 to 1,523 m: 4 (2013)

under 914 m: 45 (2013)

**PIPELINES:**

50 km oil (2013)

**ROADWAYS:**

total: 4,304 km (2003)

paved: 1,130 km (2003)

unpaved: 3,174 km (2003)

country comparison to the world: 154

**WATERWAYS:**

1,200 km (most navigable by ships with drafts up to 7 m) (2011)

country comparison to the world: 59

**MERCHANT MARINE:**

total: 10 (2017)

by type: general cargo 5, oil tanker 3, other 2 (2017)

country comparison to the world: 149

**PORTS AND TERMINALS:**

major seaport(s): Paramaribo, Wageningen

## MILITARY AND SECURITY :: SURINAME

**MILITARY BRANCHES:**

Suriname Army (National Leger, NL): Army, Coast Guard, Air Force (2017)

**MILITARY SERVICE AGE AND OBLIGATION:**

18 is the legal minimum age for voluntary military service; no conscription; personnel drawn almost exclusively from the Creole community (2012)

## TRANSNATIONAL ISSUES :: SURINAME

**DISPUTES - INTERNATIONAL:**

area claimed by French Guiana between Riviere Litani and Riviere Marouini (both headwaters of the Lawa)Suriname claims a triangle of land between the New and Kutari/Koetari rivers in a historic dispute over the headwaters of the CourantyneGuyana seeks UN Convention on the Law of the Sea arbitration to resolve the longstanding dispute with Suriname over the axis of the territorial sea boundary in potentially oil-rich waters

**TRAFFICKING IN PERSONS:**

current situation: Suriname is a source, transit, and destination country for women and children subjected to sex trafficking and men, women, and children subjected to forced labor; women and girls from Suriname, Guyana, Brazil, and the Dominican Republic are subjected to sex trafficking in the country, sometimes in interior mining camps; migrant workers in agriculture and on fishing boats and children working in informal urban sectors and gold mines are vulnerable to forced labor; traffickers from Suriname exploit victims in the Netherlands

tier rating: Tier 2 Watch List – Suriname does not fully comply with the minimum standards for the elimination of trafficking; however, it is making significant efforts to do so; in 2014, Suriname was granted a waiver from an otherwise required downgrade to Tier 3 because its government has a written plan that, if implemented, would constitute making significant efforts to bring itself into compliance with the minimum standards for the elimination of trafficking; authorities increased the number of trafficking investigations, prosecutions, and convictions as compared to 2013, but resources were insufficient to conduct investigations in the country's interior; more trafficking victims were identified in 2014 than in 2013, but protective services for adults and children were inadequate, with a proposed government shelter for women and child trafficking victims remaining unopened (2015)

**ILLICIT DRUGS:**

growing transshipment point for South American drugs destined for Europe via the Netherlands and Brazil; transshipment point for arms-for-drugs dealing

# EUROPE :: SVALBARD

## INTRODUCTION :: SVALBARD

### BACKGROUND:

The archipelago may have been first discovered by Norse explorers in the 12th century; the islands served as an international whaling base during the 17th and 18th centuries. Norway's sovereignty was internationally recognized by treaty in 1920, and five years later it officially took over the territory. In the 20th century coal mining started and today a Norwegian and a Russian company are still functioning. Travel between the settlements is accomplished with snowmobiles, aircraft, and boats.

## GEOGRAPHY :: SVALBARD

### LOCATION:
Northern Europe, islands between the Arctic Ocean, Barents Sea, Greenland Sea, and Norwegian Sea, north of Norway

### GEOGRAPHIC COORDINATES:
78 00 N, 20 00 E

### MAP REFERENCES:
Arctic Region

### AREA:
total: 62,045 sq km

land: 62,045 sq km

water: 0 sq km

note: includes Spitsbergen and Bjornoya (Bear Island)

country comparison to the world: 126

### AREA - COMPARATIVE:
slightly smaller than West Virginia

### LAND BOUNDARIES:
0 km

### COASTLINE:
3,587 km

### MARITIME CLAIMS:
territorial sea: 12 nm

contiguous zone: 24 nm

continental shelf: extends to depth of exploitation

exclusive fishing zone: 200 nm

### CLIMATE:
arctic, tempered by warm North Atlantic Current; cool summers, cold winters; North Atlantic Current flows along west and north coasts of Spitsbergen, keeping water open and navigable most of the year

### TERRAIN:
rugged mountains; much of the upland areas are ice covered; west coast clear of ice about half the year; fjords along west and north coasts

### ELEVATION:
0 m lowest point: Arctic Ocean

1717 highest point: Newtontoppen

### NATURAL RESOURCES:
coal, iron ore, copper, zinc, phosphate, wildlife, fish

### LAND USE:
agricultural land: 0% (2011 est.)

arable land: 0% (2011 est.) / permanent crops: 0% (2011 est.) / permanent pasture: 0% (2011 est.)

forest: 0% (2011 est.)

other: 100% (2011 est.)

### POPULATION DISTRIBUTION:
the small population is primarily concentrated on the island of Spitsbergen in a handful of settlements on the south side of the Isfjorden, with Longyearbyen being the largest

### NATURAL HAZARDS:
ice floes often block the entrance to Bellsund (a transit point for coal export) on the west coast and occasionally make parts of the northeastern coast inaccessible to maritime traffic

### ENVIRONMENT - CURRENT ISSUES:
ice floes are a maritime hazard; past exploitation of mammal species (whale, seal, walrus, and polar bear) severely depleted the populations, but a gradual recovery seems to be occurring

### GEOGRAPHY - NOTE:
northernmost part of the Kingdom of Norway; consists of nine main islands; glaciers and snowfields cover 60% of the total area; Spitsbergen Island is the site of the Svalbard Global Seed Vault, a seed repository established by the Global Crop Diversity Trust and the Norwegian Government

## PEOPLE AND SOCIETY :: SVALBARD

### POPULATION:
2,583 (July 2017 est.)

country comparison to the world: 230

### ETHNIC GROUPS:
Norwegian 59.8%, Russian and Ukrainian 20.4%, other 19.4% (primarily Swedish, Thai, and Philippine) (2016 est.)

**LANGUAGES:**

Norwegian, Russian

**POPULATION GROWTH RATE:**

-0.03% (2014 est.)

country comparison to the world: 198

**POPULATION DISTRIBUTION:**

the small population is primarily concentrated on the island of Spitsbergen in a handful of settlements on the south side of the Isfjorden, with Longyearbyen being the largest

**SEX RATIO:**

NA

**INFANT MORTALITY RATE:**

total: NA

male: NA

female: NA

**LIFE EXPECTANCY AT BIRTH:**

total population: NA (2017 est.)

male: NA (2017 est.)

female: NA (2017 est.)

**TOTAL FERTILITY RATE:**

NA

# GOVERNMENT :: SVALBARD

**COUNTRY NAME:**

conventional long form: none

conventional short form: Svalbard (sometimes referred to as Spitsbergen, the largest island in the archipelago)

etymology: 12th century Norse accounts speak of the discovery of a "Svalbard" - literally "cold shores" - but they may have referred to Jan Mayen Island or eastern Greenland; the archipelago was traditionally known as Spitsbergen, but Norway renamed it Svalbard in the 1920s when it assumed sovereignty of the islands

**DEPENDENCY STATUS:**

territory of Norway; administered by the Polar Department of the Ministry of Justice, through a governor (sysselmann) residing in Longyearbyen, Spitsbergen; by treaty (9 February 1920), sovereignty was awarded to Norway

**GOVERNMENT TYPE:**

non-self-governing territory of Norway

**CAPITAL:**

name: Longyearbyen

geographic coordinates: 78 13 N, 15 38 E

time difference: UTC+1 (6 hours ahead of Washington, DC, during Standard Time)

daylight saving time: +1hr, begins last Sunday in March; ends last Sunday in October

**INDEPENDENCE:**

none (territory of Norway)

**LEGAL SYSTEM:**

the laws of Norway where applicable apply; only the laws of Norway made explicitly applicable to Svalbard have effect there; the Svalbard Act and the Svalbard Environmental Protection Act, and certain regulations, apply only to Svalbard; the Spitsbergen Treaty and the Svalbard Treaty grant certain rights to citizens and corporations of signatory nations; as of June 2017, 45 nations had ratified the Svalbard Treaty

**CITIZENSHIP:**

see Norway

**EXECUTIVE BRANCH:**

chief of state: King HARALD V of Norway (since 17 January 1991); Heir Apparent Crown Prince Haakon MAGNUS (son of the king, born 20 July 1973)

head of government: Governor Kjerstin ASKHOLT (since 1 October 2015); Assistant Governor Berit SAGFOSSEN (since 1 April 2016)

elections/appointments: none; the monarchy is hereditary; governor and assistant governor responsible to the Polar Department of the Ministry of Justice

**LEGISLATIVE BRANCH:**

description: unicameral Longyearbyen Community Council (15 seats; members directly elected by majority vote to serve 4-year-terms); note - the Council acts very much like a Norwegian municipality, responsible for infrastructure and utilities, including power, land-use and community planning, education, and child welfare; however, healthcare services are provided by the state

elections: last held on 6 October 2015 (next to be held in October 2019)

election results: seats by party - Conservatives 5, Labor Party 5, Liberals 3, Green Party 2; composition - men 10, women 5, percent of women 33.3%

**JUDICIAL BRANCH:**

none; note - Svalbard is subordinate to Norway's Nord-Troms District Court and Halogaland Court of Appeal, both located in Tromso

**POLITICAL PARTIES AND LEADERS:**

Svalbard Conservative Party [Kjetil FIGENSCHOU]

Svalbard Green Party [Helga Bardsdatter KRISTIANSEN, Espen Klungseth ROTEVATN]

Svalbard Labor Party [Arild OLSEN]

Svalbard Liberal Party [Erik BERGER]

**INTERNATIONAL ORGANIZATION PARTICIPATION:**

none

**FLAG DESCRIPTION:**

the flag of Norway is used

**NATIONAL ANTHEM:**

note: as a territory of Norway, "Ja, vi elsker dette landet" is official (see Norway)

# ECONOMY :: SVALBARD

**ECONOMY - OVERVIEW:**

Coal mining, tourism, and international research are Svalbard's major industries. Coal mining has historically been the dominant economic activity, and the Spitzbergen Treaty of 9 February 1920 gives the 45 countries that so far have ratified the treaty equal rights to exploit mineral deposits, subject to Norwegian regulation. Although US, UK, Dutch, and Swedish coal companies have mined in the past, the only companies still engaging in this are Norwegian and Russian. Low coal prices have forced the Norwegian coal company, Store Norske Spitsbergen Kulkompani, to close one of its two mines and to considerably reduce the activity of the other. Since the 1990s, the tourism and hospitality industry has grown rapidly, and Svalbard now receives 60,000 visitors annually.

The settlements on Svalbard were established as company towns, and at their height in the 1950s, the Norwegian state-owned coal company supported nearly 1,000 jobs. Today, only about 300 people work in the mining industry.

Goods such as alcohol, tobacco, and vehicles, normally highly taxed on mainland Norway, are considerably cheaper in Svalbard in an effort by the Norwegian Government to entice more people to live on the Arctic archipelago. By law, Norway collects only enough taxes to pay for the needs of the local government; none of tax proceeds go to the central government.

**GDP - REAL GROWTH RATE:**

NA

**LABOR FORCE:**

1,590 (2013)

country comparison to the world: 228

**BUDGET:**

revenues: NA

expenditures: NA

**TAXES AND OTHER REVENUES:**

NA

**BUDGET SURPLUS (+) OR DEFICIT (-):**

NA

**EXPORTS:**

NA

**IMPORTS:**

$NA

**EXCHANGE RATES:**

Norwegian kroner (NOK) per US dollar -

8.308 (2017 est.)

8.0646 (2016 est.)

8.0646 (2015)

8.0646 (2014 est.)

6.3021 (2013 est.)

## ENERGY :: SVALBARD

**CRUDE OIL - PRODUCTION:**

194,300 bbl/day (2014 est.)

country comparison to the world: 36

**CRUDE OIL - EXPORTS:**

16,070 bbl/day (2012 est.)

country comparison to the world: 53

**CRUDE OIL - IMPORTS:**

0 bbl/day (2012 est.)

country comparison to the world: 200

**REFINED PETROLEUM PRODUCTS - CONSUMPTION:**

80,250 bbl/day (2013 est.)

country comparison to the world: 87

**REFINED PETROLEUM PRODUCTS - EXPORTS:**

4,488 bbl/day (2012 est.)

country comparison to the world: 93

**REFINED PETROLEUM PRODUCTS - IMPORTS:**

18,600 bbl/day (2012 est.)

country comparison to the world: 127

**NATURAL GAS - PRODUCTION:**

0 cu m (2013 est.)

country comparison to the world: 203

**NATURAL GAS - CONSUMPTION:**

0 cu m (2013 est.)

country comparison to the world: 204

**NATURAL GAS - EXPORTS:**

0 cu m (2013 est.)

country comparison to the world: 192

**NATURAL GAS - IMPORTS:**

0 cu m (2013 est.)

country comparison to the world: 195

## COMMUNICATIONS :: SVALBARD

**TELEPHONE SYSTEM:**

general assessment: modern, well-developed (2017)

domestic: the Svalbard Satellite Station - connected to the mainland via the Svalbard Undersea Cable System - is the only Arctic ground station that can see low-altitude, polar-orbiting satellites; it provides ground services to more satellites than any other facility in the world (2017)

international: country code - 47-790; the Svalbard Undersea Cable System is a twin communications cable that connects Svalbard to mainland Norway; the system is the sole telecommunications link to the archipelago (2017)

**BROADCAST MEDIA:**

the Norwegian Broadcasting Corporation (NRK) began direct TV transmission to Svalbard via satellite in 1984; Longyearbyen households have access to 3 NRK radio and 2 TV stations (2008)

**INTERNET COUNTRY CODE:**

.sj

## TRANSPORTATION :: SVALBARD

**AIRPORTS:**

4 (2013)

country comparison to the world: 190

**AIRPORTS - WITH PAVED RUNWAYS:**

total: 1 (2013)

2,438 to 3,047 m: 1 (2013)

**AIRPORTS - WITH UNPAVED RUNWAYS:**

total: 3 (2013)

under 914 m: 3 (2013)

**HELIPORTS:**

1 (2013)

**PORTS AND TERMINALS:**

major seaport(s): Barentsburg, Longyearbyen, Ny-Alesund, Pyramiden

## MILITARY AND SECURITY :: SVALBARD

**MILITARY BRANCHES:**

no regular military forces

**MILITARY - NOTE:**

Svalbard is a territory of Norway, demilitarized by treaty on 9 February 1920; Norwegian military activity is limited to fisheries surveillance by the Norwegian Coast Guard

## TRANSNATIONAL ISSUES :: SVALBARD

**DISPUTES - INTERNATIONAL:**

despite recent discussions, Russia and Norway dispute their maritime limits in the Barents Sea and Russia's fishing rights beyond Svalbard's territorial limits within the Svalbard Treaty zone

# EUROPE :: SWEDEN

## INTRODUCTION :: SWEDEN

### BACKGROUND:

A military power during the 17th century, Sweden has not participated in any war for two centuries. An armed neutrality was preserved in both world wars. Sweden's long-successful economic formula of a capitalist system intermixed with substantial welfare elements was challenged in the 1990s by high unemployment and in 2000-02 and 2009 by the global economic downturns, but fiscal discipline over the past several years has allowed the country to weather economic vagaries. Sweden joined the EU in 1995, but the public rejected the introduction of the euro in a 2003 referendum.

## GEOGRAPHY :: SWEDEN

### LOCATION:
Northern Europe, bordering the Baltic Sea, Gulf of Bothnia, Kattegat, and Skagerrak, between Finland and Norway

### GEOGRAPHIC COORDINATES:
62 00 N, 15 00 E

### MAP REFERENCES:
Europe

### AREA:
total: 450,295 sq km

land: 410,335 sq km

water: 39,960 sq km

country comparison to the world: 57

### AREA - COMPARATIVE:
almost three times the size of Georgia; slightly larger than California

### LAND BOUNDARIES:
total: 2,211 km

border countries (2): Finland 545 km, Norway 1666 km

### COASTLINE:
3,218 km

### MARITIME CLAIMS:
territorial sea: 12 nm (adjustments made to return a portion of straits to high seas)

exclusive economic zone: agreed boundaries or midlines

continental shelf: 200-m depth or to the depth of exploitation

### CLIMATE:
temperate in south with cold, cloudy winters and cool, partly cloudy summers; subarctic in north

### TERRAIN:
mostly flat or gently rolling lowlands; mountains in west

### ELEVATION:
mean elevation: 320 m

elevation extremes: -2.4 m lowest point: reclaimed bay of Lake Hammarsjon, near Kristianstad

2111 highest point: Kebnekaise

### NATURAL RESOURCES:
iron ore, copper, lead, zinc, gold, silver, tungsten, uranium, arsenic, feldspar, timber, hydropower

**LAND USE:**

agricultural land: 7.5% (2011 est.)

arable land: 6.4% (2011 est.) / permanent crops: 0% (2011 est.) / permanent pasture: 1.1% (2011 est.)

forest: 68.7% (2011 est.)

other: 23.8% (2011 est.)

**IRRIGATED LAND:**

1,640 sq km (2012)

**POPULATION DISTRIBUTION:**

most Swedes live in the south where the climate is milder and there is better connectivity to mainland Europe; population clusters are found all along the Baltic coast in the east; the interior areas of the north remain sparsely populated

**NATURAL HAZARDS:**

ice floes in the surrounding waters, especially in the Gulf of Bothnia, can interfere with maritime traffic

**ENVIRONMENT - CURRENT ISSUES:**

marine pollution (Baltic Sea and North Sea); acid rain damage to soils and lakes; air pollution; inappropriate timber harvesting practices

**ENVIRONMENT - INTERNATIONAL AGREEMENTS:**

party to: Air Pollution, Air Pollution-Nitrogen Oxides, Air Pollution-Persistent Organic Pollutants, Air Pollution-Sulfur 85, Air Pollution-Sulfur 94, Air Pollution-Volatile Organic Compounds, Antarctic-Environmental Protocol, Antarctic-Marine Living Resources, Antarctic Treaty, Biodiversity, Climate Change, Climate Change-Kyoto Protocol, Desertification, Endangered Species, Environmental Modification, Hazardous Wastes, Law of the Sea, Marine Dumping, Ozone Layer Protection, Ship Pollution, Tropical Timber 83, Tropical Timber 94, Wetlands, Whaling

signed, but not ratified: none of the selected agreements

**GEOGRAPHY - NOTE:**

strategic location along Danish Straits linking Baltic and North Seas; Sweden has almost 100,000 lakes, the largest of which, Vanern, is the third largest in Europe

# PEOPLE AND SOCIETY :: SWEDEN

**POPULATION:**

10,040,995 (July 2018 est.)

country comparison to the world: 91

**NATIONALITY:**

noun: Swede(s)

adjective: Swedish

**ETHNIC GROUPS:**

Swedish 81.5%, Syrian 1.7%, Finnish 1.5%, Iraqi 1.4%, other 13.9%

(2017 est.)

note: data represent the population by country of birth; the indigenous Sami people are estimated to number between 20,000 and 40,000

**LANGUAGES:**

Swedish (official)

note: Finnish, Sami, Romani, Yiddish, and Meankieli are official minority languages

**RELIGIONS:**

Church of Sweden (Lutheran) 61.3%, other (includes Roman Catholic, Orthodox, Baptist, Muslim, Jewish, and Buddhist) 8.2%, none or unspecified 30.5% (2016 est.)

note: estimates reflect registered members of faith communities eligible for state funding (not all religions are state-funded and not all people who identify with a particular religion are registered members); an estimated 60.2% of Sweden's population were members of the Church of Sweden in 2017

**AGE STRUCTURE:**

0-14 years: 17.54% (male 904,957 /female 855,946)

15-24 years: 11.06% (male 573,595 /female 537,358)

25-54 years: 39.37% (male 2,005,422 /female 1,947,245)

55-64 years: 11.67% (male 588,314 /female 583,002)

65 years and over: 20.37% (male 946,170 /female 1,098,986) (2018 est.)

**DEPENDENCY RATIOS:**

total dependency ratio: 58.5 (2015 est.)

youth dependency ratio: 27.4 (2015 est.)

elderly dependency ratio: 31.1 (2015 est.)

potential support ratio: 3.2 (2015 est.)

**MEDIAN AGE:**

total: 41.1 years

male: 40.1 years

female: 42.2 years (2018 est.)

country comparison to the world: 45

**POPULATION GROWTH RATE:**

0.8% (2018 est.)

country comparison to the world: 129

**BIRTH RATE:**

12.1 births/1,000 population (2018 est.)

country comparison to the world: 164

**DEATH RATE:**

9.4 deaths/1,000 population (2018 est.)

country comparison to the world: 52

**NET MIGRATION RATE:**

5.3 migrant(s)/1,000 population (2017 est.)

country comparison to the world: 23

**POPULATION DISTRIBUTION:**

most Swedes live in the south where the climate is milder and there is better connectivity to mainland Europe; population clusters are found all along the Baltic coast in the east; the interior areas of the north remain sparsely populated

**URBANIZATION:**

urban population: 87.4% of total population (2018)

rate of urbanization: 1.05% annual rate of change (2015-20 est.)

**MAJOR URBAN AREAS - POPULATION:**

1.583 million STOCKHOLM (capital) (2018)

**SEX RATIO:**

at birth: 1.06 male(s)/female (2017 est.)

0-14 years: 1.06 male(s)/female (2017 est.)

15-24 years: 1.06 male(s)/female (2017 est.)

25-54 years: 1.03 male(s)/female (2017 est.)

55-64 years: 1.01 male(s)/female (2017 est.)

65 years and over: 0.85 male(s)/female (2017 est.)

total population: 1 male(s)/female (2017 est.)

**MOTHER'S MEAN AGE AT FIRST BIRTH:**

29.1 years (2015 est.)

**MATERNAL MORTALITY RATE:**

4 deaths/100,000 live births (2015 est.)

country comparison to the world: 180

**INFANT MORTALITY RATE:**

total: 2.6 deaths/1,000 live births (2018 est.)

male: 2.9 deaths/1,000 live births (2018 est.)

female: 2.3 deaths/1,000 live births (2018 est.)

country comparison to the world: 216

## LIFE EXPECTANCY AT BIRTH:

total population: 82.2 years (2018 est.)

male: 80.3 years (2018 est.)

female: 84.3 years (2018 est.)

country comparison to the world: 17

## TOTAL FERTILITY RATE:

1.87 children born/woman (2018 est.)

country comparison to the world: 141

## HEALTH EXPENDITURES:

11.9% of GDP (2014)

country comparison to the world: 6

## PHYSICIANS DENSITY:

4.19 physicians/1,000 population (2014)

## HOSPITAL BED DENSITY:

2.4 beds/1,000 population (2015)

## DRINKING WATER SOURCE:

improved:

urban: 100% of population (2015 est.)

rural: 100% of population (2015 est.)

total: 100% of population (2015 est.)

unimproved:

urban: 0% of population (2015 est.)

rural: 0% of population (2015 est.)

total: 0% of population (2015 est.)

## SANITATION FACILITY ACCESS:

improved:

urban: 99.3% of population (2015 est.)

rural: 99.6% of population (2015 est.)

total: 99.3% of population (2015 est.)

unimproved:

urban: 0.7% of population (2015 est.)

rural: 0.4% of population (2015 est.)

total: 0.7% of population (2015 est.)

## HIV/AIDS - ADULT PREVALENCE RATE:

0.2% (2016 est.)

country comparison to the world: 105

## HIV/AIDS - PEOPLE LIVING WITH HIV/AIDS:

11,000 (2016 est.)

country comparison to the world: 98

## HIV/AIDS - DEATHS:

<100 (2016 est.)

## OBESITY - ADULT PREVALENCE RATE:

20.6% (2016)

country comparison to the world: 97

## EDUCATION EXPENDITURES:

7.7% of GDP (2014)

country comparison to the world: 11

## SCHOOL LIFE EXPECTANCY (PRIMARY TO TERTIARY EDUCATION):

total: 18 years (2014)

male: 17 years (2014)

female: 20 years (2014)

## UNEMPLOYMENT, YOUTH AGES 15-24:

total: 17.9% (2017 est.)

male: 18.8% (2017 est.)

female: 17% (2017 est.)

country comparison to the world: 72

# GOVERNMENT :: SWEDEN

## COUNTRY NAME:

conventional long form: Kingdom of Sweden

conventional short form: Sweden

local long form: Konungariket Sverige

local short form: Sverige

etymology: name ultimately derives from the North Germanic Svear tribe, which inhabited central Sweden and is first mentioned in the first centuries A.D.

## GOVERNMENT TYPE:

parliamentary constitutional monarchy

## CAPITAL:

name: Stockholm

geographic coordinates: 59 20 N, 18 03 E

time difference: UTC+1 (6 hours ahead of Washington, DC, during Standard Time)

daylight saving time: +1hr, begins last Sunday in March; ends last Sunday in October

## ADMINISTRATIVE DIVISIONS:

21 counties (lan, singular and plural); Blekinge, Dalarna, Gavleborg, Gotland, Halland, Jamtland, Jonkoping, Kalmar, Kronoberg, Norrbotten, Orebro, Ostergotland, Skane, Sodermanland, Stockholm, Uppsala, Varmland, Vasterbotten, Vasternorrland, Vastmanland, Vastra Gotaland

## INDEPENDENCE:

6 June 1523 (Gustav VASA elected king of Sweden, marking the abolishment of the Kalmar Union between Denmark, Norway, and Sweden)

## NATIONAL HOLIDAY:

National Day, 6 June (1983); note - from 1916 to 1982 this date was celebrated as Swedish Flag Day

## CONSTITUTION:

history: several previous; latest adopted 1 January 1975 (2016)

amendments: proposed by Parliament; passage requires simple majority vote in two consecutive parliamentary terms with an intervening general election; passage also requires approval by simple majority vote in a referendum if Parliament approves a motion for a referendum by one-third of its members; amended several times, last in 2014 (changes to the "Instrument of Government") (2016)

## LEGAL SYSTEM:

civil law system influenced by Roman-Germanic law and customary law

## INTERNATIONAL LAW ORGANIZATION PARTICIPATION:

accepts compulsory ICJ jurisdiction with reservations; accepts ICCt jurisdiction

## CITIZENSHIP:

citizenship by birth: no

citizenship by descent only: the father must be a citizen of Sweden; in the case of a child born out of wedlock, the mother must be a citizen of Sweden and the father unknown

dual citizenship recognized: no, unless the other citizenship was acquired involuntarily

residency requirement for naturalization: 5 years

## SUFFRAGE:

18 years of age; universal

## EXECUTIVE BRANCH:

chief of state: King CARL XVI GUSTAF (since 19 September 1973); Heir Apparent Princess VICTORIA Ingrid Alice Desiree (daughter of the monarch, born 14 July 1977)

head of government: Acting Prime Minister Stefan LOFVEN (since 3 October 2014); Deputy Prime Minister

Isabella LOVIN (since 25 May 2016); note - Prime Minister Stefan LOFVEN was ousted in a no-confidence vote on 25 September 2018 and is heading a caretaker government until a new government is formed

**cabinet:** Cabinet appointed by the prime minister

**elections/appointments:** the monarchy is hereditary; following legislative elections, the leader of the majority party or majority coalition usually becomes the prime minister

## LEGISLATIVE BRANCH:

**description:** unicameral Parliament or Riksdag (349 seats; 310 members directly elected in multi-seat constituencies by closed, party-list proportional representation vote and 39 members in "at-large" seats directly elected by proportional representation vote; members serve 4-year terms)

**elections:** last held on 9 September 2018 (next to be held in 2022)

**election results:** percent of vote by party - SAP 28.31%, M 19.8%, SD 17.5%, C 8.6%, V 8%, KD 6.3%, L 5.5%, MP 4.4%, other 1.6%; seats by party - SAP 100, M 70, SD 62, C 31, V 28, KD 22, L 20, MP 16; composition - men 188, women 161, percent of women 46.1%

## JUDICIAL BRANCH:

**highest courts:** Supreme Court of Sweden (consists of 16 justices including the court chairman); Supreme Administrative Court (consists of 18 justices including the court president)

**judge selection and term of office:** Supreme Court and Supreme Administrative Court justices nominated by the Board of Judges, a 9-member nominating body consisting of high-level judges, prosecutors, and members of Parliament; justices appointed by the Government; following a probationary period, justices' appointments are permanent

**subordinate courts:** first instance, appellate, general, and administrative courts; specialized courts that handle cases such as land and environment, immigration, labor, markets, and patents

## POLITICAL PARTIES AND LEADERS:

Center Party (Centerpartiet) or C [Annie LOOF]
Christian Democrats (Kristdemokraterna) or KD [Ebba Busch THOR]
Green Party (Miljopartiet de Grona) or MP [Isabella LOVIN and Gustav FRIDOLIN]
Left Party (Vansterpartiet) or V [Jonas SJOSTEDT]
Liberal Party (Liberalerna) or L [Jan BJORKLUND]
Moderate Party (Moderaterna) or M [Ulf KRISTERSSON]
Swedish Social Democratic Party (Socialdemokraterna) or SAP [Stefan LOFVEN]
Sweden Democrats (Sverigedemokraterna) or SD [Jimmie AKESSON]

## INTERNATIONAL ORGANIZATION PARTICIPATION:

ADB (nonregional member), AfDB (nonregional member), Arctic Council, Australia Group, BIS, CBSS, CD, CE, CERN, EAPC, EBRD, ECB, EIB, EITI (implementing country), EMU, ESA, EU, FAO, FATF, G-9, G-10, IADB, IAEA, IBRD, ICAO, ICC (national committees), ICCt, ICRM, IDA, IEA, IFAD, IFC, IFRCS, IGAD (partners), IHO, ILO, IMF, IMO, IMSO, Interpol, IOC, IOM, IPU, ISO, ITSO, ITU, ITUC (NGOs), MIGA, MINUSMA, MONUSCO, NC, NEA, NIB, NSG, OAS (observer), OECD, OPCW, OSCE, Paris Club, PCA, PFP, Schengen Convention, UN, UNCTAD, UNESCO, UNHCR, UNIDO, UNMISS, UNMOGIP, UNRWA, UN Security Council (temporary), UNTSO, UPU, WCO, WFTU (NGOs), WHO, WIPO, WMO, WTO, ZC

## DIPLOMATIC REPRESENTATION IN THE US:

**chief of mission:** Ambassador Karin Ulrika OLOFSDOTTER (since 17 September 2017)

**chancery:** The House of Sweden, 2900 K Street NW, Washington, DC 20007

**telephone:** [1] (202) 467-2600

**FAX:** [1] (202) 467-2699

**consulate(s) general:** New York

## DIPLOMATIC REPRESENTATION FROM THE US:

**chief of mission:** Ambassador (vacant); Charge d'Affaires David E. LINDWALL (since 20 January 2017)

**embassy:** Dag Hammarskjolds Vag 31, SE-11589 Stockholm

**mailing address:** American Embassy Stockholm, US Department of State, 5750 Stockholm Place, Washington, DC 20521-5750

**telephone:** [46] (08) 783 53 00

**FAX:** [46] (08) 661 19 64

## FLAG DESCRIPTION:

blue with a golden yellow cross extending to the edges of the flag; the vertical part of the cross is shifted to the hoist side in the style of the Dannebrog (Danish flag); the colors reflect those of the Swedish coat of arms - three gold crowns on a blue field

## NATIONAL SYMBOL(S):

three crowns, lion; national colors: blue, yellow

## NATIONAL ANTHEM:

**name:** "Du Gamla, Du Fria" (Thou Ancient, Thou Free)

**lyrics/music:** Richard DYBECK/traditional

**note:** in use since 1844; also known as "Sang till Norden" (Song of the North), is based on a Swedish folk tune; it has never been officially adopted by the government; "Kungssangen" (The King's Song) serves as the royal anthem and is played in the presence of the royal family and during certain state ceremonies

# ECONOMY :: SWEDEN

## ECONOMY - OVERVIEW:

Sweden's small, open, and competitive economy has been thriving and Sweden has achieved an enviable standard of living with its combination of free-market capitalism and extensive welfare benefits. Sweden remains outside the euro zone largely out of concern that joining the European Economic and Monetary Union would diminish the country's sovereignty over its welfare system.

Timber, hydropower, and iron ore constitute the resource base of a manufacturing economy that relies heavily on foreign trade. Exports, including engines and other machines, motor vehicles, and telecommunications equipment, account for more than 44% of GDP. Sweden enjoys a current account surplus of about 5% of GDP, which is one of the highest margins in Europe.

GDP grew an estimated 3.3% in 2016 and 2017 driven largely by investment in the construction sector. Swedish economists expect economic growth to ease slightly in the coming years as this investment subsides. Global economic growth boosted exports of Swedish manufactures further, helping drive domestic economic growth in 2017.

The Central Bank is keeping an eye on deflationary pressures and bank observers expect it to maintain an expansionary monetary policy in 2018. Swedish prices and wages have grown only slightly over the past few years, helping to support the country's competitiveness.

In the short and medium term, Sweden's economic challenges include providing affordable housing and successfully integrating migrants into the labor market.

**GDP (PURCHASING POWER PARITY):**

$518 billion (2017 est.)

$507.3 billion (2016 est.)

$494 billion (2015 est.)

note: data are in 2017 dollars

country comparison to the world: 40

**GDP (OFFICIAL EXCHANGE RATE):**

$535.6 billion (2017 est.) (2017 est.)

**GDP - REAL GROWTH RATE:**

2.1% (2017 est.)

2.7% (2016 est.)

4.5% (2015 est.)

country comparison to the world: 148

**GDP - PER CAPITA (PPP):**

$51,200 (2017 est.)

$50,800 (2016 est.)

$50,100 (2015 est.)

note: data are in 2017 dollars

country comparison to the world: 26

**GROSS NATIONAL SAVING:**

28.9% of GDP (2017 est.)

28.8% of GDP (2016 est.)

28.8% of GDP (2015 est.)

country comparison to the world: 34

**GDP - COMPOSITION, BY END USE:**

household consumption: 44.1% (2017 est.)

government consumption: 26% (2017 est.)

investment in fixed capital: 24.9% (2017 est.)

investment in inventories: 0.8% (2017 est.)

exports of goods and services: 45.3% (2017 est.)

imports of goods and services: -41.1% (2017 est.)

**GDP - COMPOSITION, BY SECTOR OF ORIGIN:**

agriculture: 1.6% (2017 est.)

industry: 33% (2017 est.)

services: 65.4% (2017 est.)

**AGRICULTURE - PRODUCTS:**

barley, wheat, sugar beets; meat, milk

**INDUSTRIES:**

iron and steel, precision equipment (bearings, radio and telephone parts, armaments), wood pulp and paper products, processed foods, motor vehicles

**INDUSTRIAL PRODUCTION GROWTH RATE:**

4.1% (2017 est.)

country comparison to the world: 74

**LABOR FORCE:**

5.361 million (2017 est.)

country comparison to the world: 77

**LABOR FORCE - BY OCCUPATION:**

agriculture: 2%

industry: 12%

services: 86% (2014 est.)

**UNEMPLOYMENT RATE:**

6.7% (2017 est.)

7% (2016 est.)

country comparison to the world: 101

**POPULATION BELOW POVERTY LINE:**

15% (2014 est.)

**HOUSEHOLD INCOME OR CONSUMPTION BY PERCENTAGE SHARE:**

lowest 10%: 24% (2012)

highest 10%: 24% (2012)

**DISTRIBUTION OF FAMILY INCOME - GINI INDEX:**

24.9 (2013)

25 (1992)

country comparison to the world: 153

**BUDGET:**

revenues: 271.2 billion (2017 est.)

expenditures: 264.4 billion (2017 est.)

**TAXES AND OTHER REVENUES:**

50.6% (of GDP) (2017 est.)

country comparison to the world: 16

**BUDGET SURPLUS (+) OR DEFICIT (-):**

1.3% (of GDP) (2017 est.)

country comparison to the world: 27

**PUBLIC DEBT:**

40.8% of GDP (2017 est.)

42.3% of GDP (2016 est.)

note: data cover general government debt and include debt instruments issued (or owned) by government entities other than the treasury; the data include treasury debt held by foreign entities; the data include debt issued by subnational entities, as well as intragovernmental debt; intragovernmental debt consists of treasury borrowings from surpluses in the social funds, such as for retirement, medical care, and unemployment; debt instruments for the social funds are not sold at public auctions

country comparison to the world: 124

**FISCAL YEAR:**

calendar year

**INFLATION RATE (CONSUMER PRICES):**

1.9% (2017 est.)

1.1% (2016 est.)

country comparison to the world: 100

**CENTRAL BANK DISCOUNT RATE:**

-0.5% (31 December 2017)

-0.5% (31 December 2016)

note: the Discount rate was abolished in 2002, and replaced by a "Reference rate" with no bearing on monetary policy; the rate quoted here is the Reference rate

country comparison to the world: 163

**COMMERCIAL BANK PRIME LENDING RATE:**

1.93% (31 December 2017 est.)

2% (31 December 2016 est.)

country comparison to the world: 185

**STOCK OF NARROW MONEY:**

$329.2 billion (31 December 2017 est.)

$273.9 billion (31 December 2016 est.)

country comparison to the world: 14

**STOCK OF BROAD MONEY:**

$329.2 billion (31 December 2017 est.)

$273.9 billion (31 December 2016 est.)

country comparison to the world: 14

**STOCK OF DOMESTIC CREDIT:**

$929.1 billion (31 December 2017 est.)

$749.6 billion (31 December 2016 est.)

country comparison to the world: 17

**MARKET VALUE OF PUBLICLY TRADED SHARES:**

$560.5 billion (31 December 2012 est.)

$470.1 billion (31 December 2011 est.)

$581.2 billion (31 December 2010 est.)

country comparison to the world: 21

**CURRENT ACCOUNT BALANCE:**

$17.79 billion (2017 est.)

$21.84 billion (2016 est.)

country comparison to the world: 17

**EXPORTS:**

$165.6 billion (2017 est.)

$151.4 billion (2016 est.)

country comparison to the world: 31

**EXPORTS - PARTNERS:**

Germany 11%, Norway 10.2%, Finland 6.9%, US 6.9%, Denmark 6.9%, UK 6.2%, Netherlands 5.5%, China 4.5%, Belgium 4.4%, France 4.2% (2017)

**EXPORTS - COMMODITIES:**

machinery (26%), motor vehicles, paper products, pulp and wood, iron and steel products, chemicals (2016 est.)

**IMPORTS:**

$153.2 billion (2017 est.)

$140.2 billion (2016 est.)

country comparison to the world: 30

**IMPORTS - COMMODITIES:**

machinery, petroleum and petroleum products, chemicals, motor vehicles, iron and steel; foodstuffs, clothing

**IMPORTS - PARTNERS:**

Germany 18.7%, Netherlands 8.9%, Norway 7.7%, Denmark 7.2%, China 5.5%, UK 5.1%, Finland 4.7%, Belgium 4.7% (2017)

**RESERVES OF FOREIGN EXCHANGE AND GOLD:**

$62.22 billion (31 December 2017 est.)

$59.39 billion (31 December 2016 est.)

country comparison to the world: 36

**DEBT - EXTERNAL:**

$939.9 billion (31 March 2016 est.)

$929.4 billion (31 March 2015 est.)

country comparison to the world: 16

**STOCK OF DIRECT FOREIGN INVESTMENT - AT HOME:**

$458.2 billion (31 December 2017 est.)

$390.5 billion (31 December 2016 est.)

country comparison to the world: 19

**STOCK OF DIRECT FOREIGN INVESTMENT - ABROAD:**

$523.5 billion (31 December 2017 est.)

$479.3 billion (31 December 2016 est.)

country comparison to the world: 16

**EXCHANGE RATES:**

Swedish kronor (SEK) per US dollar -

8.442 (2017 est.)

8.5605 (2016 est.)

8.5605 (2015 est.)

8.4335 (2014 est.)

6.8612 (2013 est.)

# ENERGY :: SWEDEN

**ELECTRICITY ACCESS:**

electrification - total population: 100% (2016)

**ELECTRICITY - PRODUCTION:**

152.9 billion kWh (2016 est.)

country comparison to the world: 27

**ELECTRICITY - CONSUMPTION:**

133.5 billion kWh (2016 est.)

country comparison to the world: 27

**ELECTRICITY - EXPORTS:**

26.02 billion kWh (2016 est.)

country comparison to the world: 6

**ELECTRICITY - IMPORTS:**

14.29 billion kWh (2016 est.)

country comparison to the world: 16

**ELECTRICITY - INSTALLED GENERATING CAPACITY:**

40.29 million kW (2016 est.)

country comparison to the world: 26

**ELECTRICITY - FROM FOSSIL FUELS:**

5% of total installed capacity (2016 est.)

country comparison to the world: 204

**ELECTRICITY - FROM NUCLEAR FUELS:**

22% of total installed capacity (2017 est.)

country comparison to the world: 6

**ELECTRICITY - FROM HYDROELECTRIC PLANTS:**

42% of total installed capacity (2017 est.)

country comparison to the world: 50

**ELECTRICITY - FROM OTHER RENEWABLE SOURCES:**

32% of total installed capacity (2017 est.)

country comparison to the world: 16

**CRUDE OIL - PRODUCTION:**

0 bbl/day (2017 est.)

country comparison to the world: 203

**CRUDE OIL - EXPORTS:**

14,570 bbl/day (2017 est.)

country comparison to the world: 55

**CRUDE OIL - IMPORTS:**

400,200 bbl/day (2017 est.)

country comparison to the world: 23

**CRUDE OIL - PROVED RESERVES:**

0 bbl (1 January 2018 est.)

country comparison to the world: 200

**REFINED PETROLEUM PRODUCTS - PRODUCTION:**

413,200 bbl/day (2017 est.)

country comparison to the world: 36

**REFINED PETROLEUM PRODUCTS - CONSUMPTION:**

323,100 bbl/day (2017 est.)

country comparison to the world: 42

**REFINED PETROLEUM PRODUCTS - EXPORTS:**

371,100 bbl/day (2017 est.)

country comparison to the world: 23

**REFINED PETROLEUM PRODUCTS - IMPORTS:**

229,600 bbl/day (2017 est.)

country comparison to the world: 29

**NATURAL GAS - PRODUCTION:**

0 cu m (2017 est.)

country comparison to the world: 204

**NATURAL GAS - CONSUMPTION:**

764.5 million cu m (2017 est.)

country comparison to the world: 97

**NATURAL GAS - EXPORTS:**

0 cu m (2017 est.)

country comparison to the world: 193

**NATURAL GAS - IMPORTS:**

764.5 million cu m (2017 est.)

country comparison to the world: 64

**NATURAL GAS - PROVED RESERVES:**

0 cu m (1 January 2014 est.)

country comparison to the world: 199

**CARBON DIOXIDE EMISSIONS FROM CONSUMPTION OF ENERGY:**

52.31 million Mt (2017 est.)

country comparison to the world: 58

# COMMUNICATIONS :: SWEDEN

**TELEPHONES - FIXED LINES:**

total subscriptions: 2,794,418 (2017 est.)

subscriptions per 100 inhabitants: 28 (2017 est.)

country comparison to the world: 50

**TELEPHONES - MOBILE CELLULAR:**

total subscriptions: 12,435,709 (2017 est.)

subscriptions per 100 inhabitants: 125 (2017 est.)

country comparison to the world: 74

**TELEPHONE SYSTEM:**

  general assessment: highly developed telecommunications infrastructure; ranked among leading countries for fixed-line, mobile-cellular, Internet, and broadband penetration (2016)

  domestic: coaxial and multiconductor cables carry most of the voice traffic; parallel microwave radio relay systems carry some additional telephone channels (2016)

  international: country code - 46; submarine cables provide links to other Nordic countries and Europe; satellite earth stations - 1 Intelsat (Atlantic Ocean), 1 Eutelsat, and 1 Inmarsat (Atlantic and Indian Ocean regions); note - Sweden shares the Inmarsat earth station with the other Nordic countries (Denmark, Finland, Iceland, and Norway) (2016)

**BROADCAST MEDIA:**

publicly owned TV broadcaster operates 2 terrestrial networks plus regional stations; multiple privately owned TV broadcasters operating nationally, regionally, and locally; about 50 local TV stations; widespread access to pan-Nordic and international broadcasters through multi-channel cable and satellite TV; publicly owned radio broadcaster operates 3 national stations and a network of 25 regional channels; roughly 100 privately owned local radio stations with some consolidating into near national networks; an estimated 900 community and neighborhood radio stations broadcast intermittently (2008)

**INTERNET COUNTRY CODE:**

  .se

**INTERNET USERS:**

  total: 9,041,427 (July 2016 est.)

  percent of population: 91.5% (July 2016 est.)

  country comparison to the world: 50

**BROADBAND - FIXED SUBSCRIPTIONS:**

  total: 3,735,884 (2017 est.)

  subscriptions per 100 inhabitants: 38 (2017 est.)

  country comparison to the world: 33

## TRANSPORTATION :: SWEDEN

**NATIONAL AIR TRANSPORT SYSTEM:**

  number of registered air carriers: 8 (2015)

  inventory of registered aircraft operated by air carriers: 219 (2015)

  annual passenger traffic on registered air carriers: 11,623,930 (2015)

  annual freight traffic on registered air carriers: 0 mt-km (2015)

**CIVIL AIRCRAFT REGISTRATION COUNTRY CODE PREFIX:**

  SE (2016)

**AIRPORTS:**

  231 (2013)

  country comparison to the world: 25

**AIRPORTS - WITH PAVED RUNWAYS:**

  total: 149 (2013)

  over 3,047 m: 3 (2013)

  2,438 to 3,047 m: 12 (2013)

  1,524 to 2,437 m: 75 (2013)

  914 to 1,523 m: 22 (2013)

  under 914 m: 37 (2013)

**AIRPORTS - WITH UNPAVED RUNWAYS:**

  total: 82 (2013)

  914 to 1,523 m: 5 (2013)

  under 914 m: 77 (2013)

**HELIPORTS:**

  2 (2013)

**PIPELINES:**

  1626 km gas (2013)

**RAILWAYS:**

  total: 14,127 km (2016)

  standard gauge: 14,062 km 1.435-m gauge (12,322 km electrified) (2016)

  narrow gauge: 65 km 0.891-m gauge (65 km electrified) (2016)

  country comparison to the world: 20

**ROADWAYS:**

  total: 573,134 km (includes 2,050 km of expressways) (2016)

  paved: 140,100 km (2016)

  unpaved: 433,034 km (2016)

  note: includes 98,500 km of state roads, 433,034 km of private roads, and 41,600 km of municipal roads

  country comparison to the world: 13

**WATERWAYS:**

  2,052 km (2010)

  country comparison to the world: 40

**MERCHANT MARINE:**

  total: 368 (2017)

  by type: general cargo 71, oil tanker 23, other 274 (2017)

  country comparison to the world: 47

**PORTS AND TERMINALS:**

  major seaport(s): Brofjorden, Goteborg, Helsingborg, Karlshamn, Lulea, Malmo, Stockholm, Trelleborg, Visby

  LNG terminal(s) (import): Brunnsviksholme, Lysekil

## MILITARY AND SECURITY :: SWEDEN

**MILITARY EXPENDITURES:**

  1.1% of GDP (2017)

  1.04% of GDP (2016)

  1.09% of GDP (2015)

  country comparison to the world: 108

**MILITARY BRANCHES:**

Swedish Armed Forces (Forsvarsmakten): Army (Armen), Royal Swedish Navy (Marinen), Swedish Air Force (Svenska Flygvapnet) (2018)

**MILITARY SERVICE AGE AND OBLIGATION:**

18-47 years of age for male and female voluntary military service; Swedish citizenship required; service obligation: 7.5 months (Army), 7-15 months (Navy), 8-12 months (Air Force); after completing initial service, soldiers have a reserve commitment until age 47; compulsory military service, abolished in 2010, was reinstated in 2018 (2018)

## TRANSNATIONAL ISSUES :: SWEDEN

**DISPUTES - INTERNATIONAL:**

none

**REFUGEES AND INTERNALLY DISPLACED PERSONS:**

  refugees (country of origin): 96,914 (Syria), 25,968 (Eritrea), 21,693 (Iraq), 22,548 (Somalia), 16,558 (Afghanistan) (2016)

  stateless persons: 35,101 (2017); note - the majority of stateless people are from the Middle East and Somalia

# EUROPE :: SWITZERLAND

## INTRODUCTION :: SWITZERLAND

### BACKGROUND:

The Swiss Confederation was founded in 1291 as a defensive alliance among three cantons. In succeeding years, other localities joined the original three. The Swiss Confederation secured its independence from the Holy Roman Empire in 1499. A constitution of 1848, subsequently modified in 1874, replaced the confederation with a centralized federal government. Switzerland's sovereignty and neutrality have long been honored by the major European powers, and the country was not involved in either of the two world wars. The political and economic integration of Europe over the past half century, as well as Switzerland's role in many UN and international organizations, has strengthened Switzerland's ties with its neighbors. However, the country did not officially become a UN member until 2002. Switzerland remains active in many UN and international organizations but retains a strong commitment to neutrality.

## GEOGRAPHY :: SWITZERLAND

### LOCATION:
Central Europe, east of France, north of Italy

### GEOGRAPHIC COORDINATES:
47 00 N, 8 00 E

### MAP REFERENCES:
Europe

### AREA:
total: 41,277 sq km

land: 39,997 sq km

water: 1,280 sq km

country comparison to the world: 136

### AREA - COMPARATIVE:
slightly less than twice the size of New Jersey

### LAND BOUNDARIES:
total: 1,770 km

border countries (5): Austria 158 km, France 525 km, Italy 698 km, Liechtenstein 41 km, Germany 348 km

### COASTLINE:
0 km (landlocked)

### MARITIME CLAIMS:
none (landlocked)

### CLIMATE:
temperate, but varies with altitude; cold, cloudy, rainy/snowy winters; cool to warm, cloudy, humid summers with occasional showers

### TERRAIN:
mostly mountains (Alps in south, Jura in northwest) with a central plateau of rolling hills, plains, and large lakes

### ELEVATION:
mean elevation: 1,350 m

elevation extremes: 195 m lowest point: Lake Maggiore

4634 highest point: Dufourspitze

### NATURAL RESOURCES:
hydropower potential, timber, salt

### LAND USE:
agricultural land: 38.7% (2011 est.)

arable land: 10.2% (2011 est.) / permanent crops: 0.6% (2011 est.) / permanent pasture: 27.9% (2011 est.)

forest: 31.5% (2011 est.)

other: 29.8% (2011 est.)

### IRRIGATED LAND:
630 sq km (2012)

### POPULATION DISTRIBUTION:
population distribution corresponds to elevation with the northern and western areas far more heavily populated; the higher Alps of the south limit settlement

### NATURAL HAZARDS:
avalanches, landslides; flash floods

### ENVIRONMENT - CURRENT ISSUES:
air pollution from vehicle emissions; water pollution from agricultural fertilizers; chemical contaminants and erosion damage the soil and limit productivity; loss of biodiversity

### ENVIRONMENT - INTERNATIONAL AGREEMENTS:
party to: Air Pollution, Air Pollution-Nitrogen Oxides, Air Pollution-Persistent Organic Pollutants, Air Pollution-Sulfur 85, Air Pollution-Sulfur 94, Air Pollution-Volatile Organic Compounds, Antarctic Treaty, Biodiversity, Climate Change, Climate Change-Kyoto Protocol, Desertification, Endangered Species, Environmental Modification, Hazardous Wastes, Marine Dumping, Marine Life Conservation, Ozone Layer Protection, Ship Pollution, Tropical Timber 83, Tropical Timber 94, Wetlands, Whaling

signed, but not ratified: Law of the Sea

### GEOGRAPHY - NOTE:
landlocked; crossroads of northern and southern Europe; along with southeastern France, northern Italy, and southwestern Austria, has the highest elevations in the Alps

# PEOPLE AND SOCIETY :: SWITZERLAND

**POPULATION:**
8,292,809 (July 2018 est.)

country comparison to the world: 99

**NATIONALITY:**

noun: Swiss (singular and plural)

adjective: Swiss

**ETHNIC GROUPS:**
Swiss 70.3%, German 4.2%, Italian 3.2%, Portuguese 2.6%, French 2%, Kosovar 1%, other 18.7% (2017 est.)

note: data represent permanent resident population by country of birth

**LANGUAGES:**
German (or Swiss German) (official) 62.8%, French (official) 22.9%, Italian (official) 8.2%, English 5.1%, Portuguese 3.7%, Albanian 3.1%, Serbo-Croatian 2.4%, Spanish 2.3%, Romansch (official) 0.5%, other 7.5% (2016 est.)

note: German, French, Italian, and Romansch are all national and official languages; shares sum to more than 100% because some respondents gave more than one answer

**RELIGIONS:**
Roman Catholic 36.5%, Protestant 24.5%, other Christian 5.9%, Muslim 5.2%, other 1.4%, Jewish 0.3%, none 24.9%, unspecified 1.3% (2015 est.)

**AGE STRUCTURE:**

0-14 years: 15.23% (male 650,151 /female 612,479)

15-24 years: 10.69% (male 453,003 /female 433,101)

25-54 years: 42.88% (male 1,781,425 /female 1,774,124)

55-64 years: 12.88% (male 535,457 /female 532,454)

65 years and over: 18.34% (male 672,024 /female 848,591) (2018 est.)

**DEPENDENCY RATIOS:**

total dependency ratio: 48.8 (2015 est.)

youth dependency ratio: 22 (2015 est.)

elderly dependency ratio: 26.8 (2015 est.)

potential support ratio: 3.7 (2015 est.)

**MEDIAN AGE:**

total: 42.5 years

male: 41.5 years

female: 43.5 years (2018 est.)

country comparison to the world: 30

**POPULATION GROWTH RATE:**
0.68% (2018 est.)

country comparison to the world: 144

**BIRTH RATE:**
10.5 births/1,000 population (2018 est.)

country comparison to the world: 187

**DEATH RATE:**
8.4 deaths/1,000 population (2018 est.)

country comparison to the world: 81

**NET MIGRATION RATE:**
4.7 migrant(s)/1,000 population (2017 est.)

country comparison to the world: 26

**POPULATION DISTRIBUTION:**
population distribution corresponds to elevation with the northern and western areas far more heavily populated; the higher Alps of the south limit settlement

**URBANIZATION:**

urban population: 73.8% of total population (2018)

rate of urbanization: 0.88% annual rate of change (2015-20 est.)

**MAJOR URBAN AREAS - POPULATION:**
1.371 million Zurich, 422,000 BERN (capital) (2018)

**SEX RATIO:**

at birth: 1.06 male(s)/female (2017 est.)

0-14 years: 1.06 male(s)/female (2017 est.)

15-24 years: 1.04 male(s)/female (2017 est.)

25-54 years: 1.01 male(s)/female (2017 est.)

55-64 years: 1 male(s)/female (2017 est.)

65 years and over: 0.78 male(s)/female (2017 est.)

total population: 0.97 male(s)/female (2017 est.)

**MOTHER'S MEAN AGE AT FIRST BIRTH:**
30.7 years (2014 est.)

**MATERNAL MORTALITY RATE:**
5 deaths/100,000 live births (2015 est.)

country comparison to the world: 174

**INFANT MORTALITY RATE:**

total: 3.6 deaths/1,000 live births (2018 est.)

male: 3.9 deaths/1,000 live births (2018 est.)

female: 3.2 deaths/1,000 live births (2018 est.)

country comparison to the world: 198

**LIFE EXPECTANCY AT BIRTH:**

total population: 82.7 years (2018 est.)

male: 80.4 years (2018 est.)

female: 85.2 years (2018 est.)

country comparison to the world: 12

**TOTAL FERTILITY RATE:**
1.56 children born/woman (2018 est.)

country comparison to the world: 189

**CONTRACEPTIVE PREVALENCE RATE:**
72.9% (2012)

**HEALTH EXPENDITURES:**
11.7% of GDP (2014)

country comparison to the world: 7

**PHYSICIANS DENSITY:**
4.25 physicians/1,000 population (2016)

**HOSPITAL BED DENSITY:**
4.7 beds/1,000 population (2013)

**DRINKING WATER SOURCE:**

improved:

urban: 100% of population

rural: 100% of population

total: 100% of population

unimproved:

urban: 0% of population

rural: 0% of population

total: 0% of population (2015 est.)

**SANITATION FACILITY ACCESS:**

improved:

urban: 99.9% of population (2015 est.)

rural: 99.8% of population (2015 est.)

total: 99.9% of population (2015 est.)

unimproved:

urban: 0.1% of population (2015 est.)

rural: 0.2% of population (2015 est.)

total: 0.1% of population (2015 est.)

**HIV/AIDS - ADULT PREVALENCE RATE:**

NA

**HIV/AIDS - PEOPLE LIVING WITH HIV/AIDS:**

NA

**HIV/AIDS - DEATHS:**

NA

**OBESITY - ADULT PREVALENCE RATE:**

19.5% (2016)

country comparison to the world: 112

**EDUCATION EXPENDITURES:**

5.1% of GDP (2014)

country comparison to the world: 72

**SCHOOL LIFE EXPECTANCY (PRIMARY TO TERTIARY EDUCATION):**

total: 16 years (2014)

male: 16 years (2014)

female: 16 years (2014)

**UNEMPLOYMENT, YOUTH AGES 15-24:**

total: 8.1% (2017 est.)

male: 8.1% (2017 est.)

female: 8% (2017 est.)

country comparison to the world: 138

# GOVERNMENT :: SWITZERLAND

**COUNTRY NAME:**

conventional long form: Swiss Confederation

conventional short form: Switzerland

local long form: Schweizerische Eidgenossenschaft (German)

local short form: Schweiz (German)

abbreviation: CH

etymology: name derives from the canton of Schwyz, one of the founding cantons of the Old Swiss Confederacy that formed in the 14th century

Confederation Suisse (French)
Confederazione Svizzera (Italian)
Confederaziun Svizra (Romansh)
Suisse (French) Svizzera (Italian)
Svizra (Romansh)

**GOVERNMENT TYPE:**

federal republic (formally a confederation)

**CAPITAL:**

name: Bern

geographic coordinates: 46 55 N, 7 28 E

time difference: UTC+1 (6 hours ahead of Washington, DC, during Standard Time)

daylight saving time: +1hr, begins last Sunday in March; ends last Sunday in October

**ADMINISTRATIVE DIVISIONS:**

26 cantons (cantons, singular - canton in French; cantoni, singular - cantone in Italian; Kantone, singular - Kanton in German); Aargau, Appenzell Ausserrhoden, Appenzell Innerrhoden, Basel-Landschaft, Basel-Stadt, Berne/Bern, Fribourg/Freiburg, Geneve (Geneva), Glarus, Graubuenden/Grigioni/Grischun, Jura, Luzern, Neuchatel, Nidwalden, Obwalden, Sankt Gallen, Schaffhausen, Schwyz, Solothurn, Thurgau, Ticino, Uri, Valais/Wallis, Vaud, Zug, Zuerich

note: 6 of the cantons - Appenzell Ausserrhoden, Appenzell Innerrhoden, Basel-Landschaft, Basel-Stadt, Nidwalden, Obwalden - are referred to as half cantons because they elect only one member (instead of two) to the Council of States and, in popular referendums where a majority of popular votes and a majority of cantonal votes are required, these 6 cantons only have a half vote

**INDEPENDENCE:**

1 August 1291 (founding of the Swiss Confederation)

**NATIONAL HOLIDAY:**

Founding of the Swiss Confederation in 1291; note - since 1 August 1891 celebrated as Swiss National Day

**CONSTITUTION:**

history: previous 1848, 1874; latest adopted by referendum 18 April 1999, effective 1 January 2000 (2016)

amendments: proposed by the two houses of the Federal Assembly or by petition of at least one million voters (called the "federal popular initiative"); passage of proposals requires majority vote in a referendum; following drafting of an amendment by the Assembly, its passage requires approval by majority vote in a referendum and approval by the majority of cantons; amended many times, last in 2016 (2016)

**LEGAL SYSTEM:**

civil law system; judicial review of legislative acts, except for federal decrees of a general obligatory character

**INTERNATIONAL LAW ORGANIZATION PARTICIPATION:**

accepts compulsory ICJ jurisdiction with reservations; accepts ICCt jurisdiction

**CITIZENSHIP:**

citizenship by birth: no

citizenship by descent only: at least one parent must be a citizen of Switzerland

dual citizenship recognized: yes

residency requirement for naturalization: 12 years including at least 3 of the last 5 years prior to application

**SUFFRAGE:**

18 years of age; universal

**EXECUTIVE BRANCH:**

chief of state: President of the Swiss Confederation Alain BERSET (since 1 January 2018); Vice President Ueli MAURER (since 1 January 2018); note - the Federal Council, which is comprised of 7 federal councillors, constitutes the federal government of Switzerland; council members rotate the 1-year term of federal president (chief of state and head of government)

head of government: President of the Swiss Confederation Alain BERSET (since 1 January 2018); Vice President Ueli MAURER (since 1 January 2018)

cabinet: Federal Council or Bundesrat (in German), Conseil Federal (in French), Consiglio Federale (in Italian) indirectly elected, usually from among its members by the Federal Assembly for a 4-year term

elections/appointments: president and vice president elected by the Federal Assembly from among members of the Federal Council for a 1-year, non-consecutive term; election last held on 5 December 2018 (next to be held in December 2019)

election results: Ueli MAURER elected president; Federal Assembly vote - 201 of 209; Simonetta SOMMARUGA elected vice president; Federal Assembly vote - 196 of 216; MAURER and SOMMARUGA take office on 1 January 2019

**LEGISLATIVE BRANCH:**

description: bicameral Federal Assembly or Bundesversammlung (in German), Assemblee Federale (in French), Assemblea Federale (in Italian) consists of: Council of States or Staenderat (in German), Conseil des Etats (in French), Consiglio degli Stati (in Italian) (46 seats; members in multi-seat constituencies representing cantons and single-seat constituencies

representing half cantons directly elected by simple majority vote except Jura and Neuchatel cantons which use proportional representation vote; member term governed by conatonal law)
National Council or Nationalrat (in German), Conseil National (in French), Consiglio Nazionale (in Italian) (200 seats; 195 members in cantons directly elected by proportional representation vote and 6 in half cantons directly elected by simple majority vote; members serve 4-year terms)

**elections:**
Council of States - last held in most cantons on 18 October 2015 (each canton determines when the next election will be held)
National Council - last held on 18 October 2015 (next to be held in October 2019)

**election results:**
Council of States - percent of vote by party - NA; seats by party - CVP 13, FDP 13, SDP 12, SVP 5, other 3; composition - men 39, women 7, percent of women 15.2%
National Council - percent of vote by party - SVP 29.4%, SPS 18.8%, FDP 16.4%, CVP 11.6%, Green Party 7.1%, GLP 4.6%, BDP 4.1%, other 8%; seats by party - SVP 68, SPS 43, FDP 33, CVP 30, Green Party 12, GLP 7, BDP 7; composition - men 136, women 64, percent of women 32%; note - total Assembly percent of women 28.9%

## JUDICIAL BRANCH:

**highest courts:** Federal Supreme Court (consists of 38 justices and 19 deputy justices organized into 7 divisions)

**judge selection and term of office:** judges elected by the Federal Assembly for 6-year terms; note - judges are affiliated with political parties and are elected according to linguistic and regional criteria in approximate proportion to the level of party representation in the Federal Assembly

**subordinate courts:** Federal Criminal Court (began in 2004); Federal Administrative Court (began in 2007); note - each of Switzerland's 26 cantons has its own courts

## POLITICAL PARTIES AND LEADERS:

Christian Democratic People's Party (Christlichdemokratische Volkspartei der Schweiz) or CVP, Parti Democrate-Chretien Suisse or PDC, Partito Popolare Democratico Svizzero or PPD, Partida Cristiandemocratica dalla Svizra or PCD) [Gerhard PFISTER]
Conservative Democratic Party (Buergerlich-Demokratische Partei Schweiz or BDP, Parti Bourgeois Democratique Suisse or PBD, Partito Borghese Democratico Svizzero or PBD, Partido burgais democratica Svizera or PBD) [Martin LANDOLT]
Free Democratic Party or FDP.The Liberals (FDP.Die Liberalen, PLR.Les Liberaux-Radicaux, PLR.I Liberali, Ils Liberals) [Petra GOESSI]
Green Liberal Party (Grunliberale or GLP, Parti vert liberale or PVL, Partito Verde-Liberale or PVL, Partida Verde Liberale or PVL) [Jurge GROSSEN]
Green Party (Gruene Partei der Schweiz or Gruene, Parti Ecologiste Suisse or Les Verts, Partito Ecologista Svizzero or I Verdi, Partida Ecologica Svizra or La Verda) [Regula RYTZ]
Social Democratic Party (Sozialdemokratische Partei der Schweiz or SPS, Parti Socialiste Suisse or PSS, Partito Socialista Svizzero or PSS, Partida Socialdemocratica de la Svizra or PSS) [Christian LEVRAT]
Swiss People's Party (Schweizerische Volkspartei or SVP, Union Democratique du Centre or UDC, Unione Democratica di Centro or UDC, Uniun Democratica dal Center or UDC) [Albert ROESTI]
other minor parties

## INTERNATIONAL ORGANIZATION PARTICIPATION:

ADB (nonregional member), AfDB (nonregional member), Australia Group, BIS, CD, CE, CERN, EAPC, EBRD, EFTA, EITI (implementing country), ESA, FAO, FATF, G-10, IADB, IAEA, IBRD, ICAO, ICC (national committees), ICCt, ICRM, IDA, IEA, IFAD, IFC, IFRCS, IGAD (partners), ILO, IMF, IMO, IMSO, Interpol, IOC, IOM, IPU, ISO, ITSO, ITU, ITUC (NGOs), LAIA (observer), MIGA, MINUSMA, MONUSCO, NEA, NSG, OAS (observer), OECD, OIF, OPCW, OSCE, Pacific Alliance (observer), Paris Club, PCA, PFP, Schengen Convention, UN, UNCTAD, UNESCO, UNHCR, UNIDO, UNITAR, UNMISS, UNMOGIP, UNRWA, UNTSO, UNWTO, UPU, WCO, WHO, WIPO, WMO, WTO, ZC

## DIPLOMATIC REPRESENTATION IN THE US:

**chief of mission:** Ambassador Martin Werner DAHINDEN (since 18 November 2014)

**chancery:** 2900 Cathedral Avenue NW, Washington, DC 20008

**telephone:** [1] (202) 745-7900

**FAX:** [1] (202) 387-2564

**consulate(s) general:** Atlanta, Chicago, Los Angeles, New York, San Francisco

## DIPLOMATIC REPRESENTATION FROM THE US:

**chief of mission:** Ambassador Edward "Ed" MCMULLEN (since 21 November 2017) note - also accredited to Liechtenstein

**embassy:** Sulgeneckstrasse 19, CH-3007 Bern

**mailing address:** use embassy street address

**telephone:** [41] (031) 357-70-11

**FAX:** [41] (031) 357-73-20

## FLAG DESCRIPTION:

red square with a bold, equilateral white cross in the center that does not extend to the edges of the flag; various medieval legends purport to describe the origin of the flag; a white cross used as identification for troops of the Swiss Confederation is first attested at the Battle of Laupen (1339)

## NATIONAL SYMBOL(S):

Swiss cross (white cross on red field, arms equal length); national colors: red, white

## NATIONAL ANTHEM:

Leonhard WIDMER [German], Charles CHATELANAT [French], Camillo VALSANGIACOMO [Italian], and Flurin CAMATHIAS [Romansch]/Alberik ZWYSSIG

the Swiss anthem has four names: "Schweizerpsalm" [German] "Cantique Suisse" [French] "Salmo svizzero," [Italian] "Psalm svizzer" [Romansch] (Swiss Psalm)

**note:** unofficially adopted 1961, officially 1981; the anthem has been popular in a number of Swiss cantons since its composition (in German) in 1841; translated into the other three official languages of the country (French, Italian, and Romansch), it is official in each of those languages

# ECONOMY :: SWITZERLAND

## ECONOMY - OVERVIEW:

Switzerland, a country that espouses neutrality, is a prosperous and modern market economy with low unemployment, a highly skilled labor force, and a per capita GDP among the highest in the world. Switzerland's economy benefits from a highly developed service sector, led by financial services, and a manufacturing industry that specializes in high-technology, knowledge-based production. Its economic and political stability, transparent legal system, exceptional infrastructure, efficient capital markets, and low corporate tax rates also make Switzerland one of the world's most competitive economies.

The Swiss have brought their economic practices largely into conformity with the EU's to gain access to the Union's Single Market and enhance the country's international competitiveness. Some trade protectionism remains, however, particularly for its small agricultural sector. The fate of the Swiss economy is tightly linked to that of its neighbors in the euro zone, which purchases half of Swiss exports. The global financial crisis of 2008 and resulting economic downturn in 2009 stalled demand for Swiss exports and put Switzerland into a recession. During this period, the Swiss National Bank (SNB) implemented a zero-interest rate policy to boost the economy, as well as to prevent appreciation of the franc, and Switzerland's economy began to recover in 2010.

The sovereign debt crises unfolding in neighboring euro-zone countries, however, coupled with economic instability in Russia and other Eastern European economies drove up demand for the Swiss franc by investors seeking a safehaven currency. In January 2015, the SNB abandoned the Swiss franc's peg to the euro, roiling global currency markets and making active SNB intervention a necessary hallmark of present-day Swiss monetary policy. The independent SNB has upheld its zero interest rate policy and conducted major market interventions to prevent further appreciation of the Swiss franc, but parliamentarians have urged it to do more to weaken the currency. The franc's strength has made Swiss exports less competitive and weakened the country's growth outlook; GDP growth fell below 2% per year from 2011 through 2017.

In recent years, Switzerland has responded to increasing pressure from neighboring countries and trading partners to reform its banking secrecy laws, by agreeing to conform to OECD regulations on administrative assistance in tax matters, including tax evasion. The Swiss Government has also renegotiated its double taxation agreements with numerous countries, including the US, to incorporate OECD standards.

**GDP (PURCHASING POWER PARITY):**

$523.1 billion (2017 est.)

$514.5 billion (2016 est.)

$506.5 billion (2015 est.)

note: data are in 2017 dollars

country comparison to the world: 39

**GDP (OFFICIAL EXCHANGE RATE):**

$679 billion (2017 est.) (2017 est.)

**GDP - REAL GROWTH RATE:**

1.7% (2017 est.)

1.6% (2016 est.)

1.3% (2015 est.)

country comparison to the world: 165

**GDP - PER CAPITA (PPP):**

$62,100 (2017 est.)

$61,800 (2016 est.)

$61,500 (2015 est.)

note: data are in 2017 dollars

country comparison to the world: 16

**GROSS NATIONAL SAVING:**

33.8% of GDP (2017 est.)

32.3% of GDP (2016 est.)

33.9% of GDP (2015 est.)

country comparison to the world: 21

**GDP - COMPOSITION, BY END USE:**

household consumption: 53.7% (2017 est.)

government consumption: 12% (2017 est.)

investment in fixed capital: 24.5% (2017 est.)

investment in inventories: -1.4% (2017 est.)

exports of goods and services: 65.1% (2017 est.)

imports of goods and services: -54% (2017 est.)

**GDP - COMPOSITION, BY SECTOR OF ORIGIN:**

agriculture: 0.7% (2017 est.)

industry: 25.6% (2017 est.)

services: 73.7% (2017 est.)

**AGRICULTURE - PRODUCTS:**

grains, fruits, vegetables; meat, eggs, dairy products

**INDUSTRIES:**

machinery, chemicals, watches, textiles, precision instruments, tourism, banking, insurance, pharmaceuticals

**INDUSTRIAL PRODUCTION GROWTH RATE:**

3.4% (2017 est.)

country comparison to the world: 92

**LABOR FORCE:**

5.159 million (2017 est.)

country comparison to the world: 81

**LABOR FORCE - BY OCCUPATION:**

agriculture: 3.3%

industry: 19.8%

services: 76.9% (2015)

**UNEMPLOYMENT RATE:**

3.2% (2017 est.)

3.3% (2016 est.)

country comparison to the world: 40

**POPULATION BELOW POVERTY LINE:**

6.6% (2014 est.)

**HOUSEHOLD INCOME OR CONSUMPTION BY PERCENTAGE SHARE:**

lowest 10%: 19% (2007)

highest 10%: 19% (2007)

**DISTRIBUTION OF FAMILY INCOME - GINI INDEX:**

29.5 (2014 est.)

33.1 (1992)

country comparison to the world: 135

**BUDGET:**

revenues: 242.1 billion (2017 est.)

expenditures: 234.4 billion (2017 est.)

note: includes federal, cantonal, and municipal budgets

**TAXES AND OTHER REVENUES:**

35.7% (of GDP) (2017 est.)

country comparison to the world: 60

**BUDGET SURPLUS (+) OR DEFICIT (-):**

1.1% (of GDP) (2017 est.)

country comparison to the world: 33

**PUBLIC DEBT:**

41.8% of GDP (2017 est.)

41.8% of GDP (2016 est.)

note: general government gross debt; gross debt consists of all liabilities that require payment or payments of interest and/or principal by the debtor to the creditor at a date or dates in the future; includes debt liabilities in the form of Special Drawing Rights (SDRs), currency and deposits, debt securities, loans, insurance, pensions and standardized guarantee schemes, and other accounts payable; all liabilities in the GFSM (Government Financial Systems Manual) 2001 system are debt, except for equity and investment fund shares and financial derivatives and employee stock options

country comparison to the world: 119

### FISCAL YEAR:
calendar year

### INFLATION RATE (CONSUMER PRICES):
0.5% (2017 est.)

-0.4% (2016 est.)

country comparison to the world: 30

### CENTRAL BANK DISCOUNT RATE:
0.5% (31 December 2016)

0.75% (31 December 2009)

country comparison to the world: 136

### COMMERCIAL BANK PRIME LENDING RATE:
2.6% (31 December 2017 est.)

2.65% (31 December 2016 est.)

country comparison to the world: 179

### STOCK OF NARROW MONEY:
$621.8 billion (31 December 2017 est.)

$555.7 billion (31 December 2016 est.)

country comparison to the world: 10

### STOCK OF BROAD MONEY:
$621.8 billion (31 December 2017 est.)

$555.7 billion (31 December 2016 est.)

country comparison to the world: 10

### STOCK OF DOMESTIC CREDIT:
$1.253 trillion (31 December 2017 est.)

$1.166 trillion (31 December 2016 est.)

country comparison to the world: 15

### MARKET VALUE OF PUBLICLY TRADED SHARES:
$1.519 trillion (31 December 2015 est.)

$1.495 trillion (31 December 2014 est.)

$1.541 trillion (31 December 2013 est.)

country comparison to the world: 9

### CURRENT ACCOUNT BALANCE:
$66.55 billion (2017 est.)

$63.16 billion (2016 est.)

country comparison to the world: 7

### EXPORTS:
$313.5 billion (2017 est.)

$318.1 billion (2016 est.)

note: trade data exclude trade with Switzerland

country comparison to the world: 17

### EXPORTS - PARTNERS:
Germany 15.2%, US 12.3%, China 8.2%, India 6.7%, France 5.7%, UK 5.7%, Hong Kong 5.4%, Italy 5.3% (2017)

### EXPORTS - COMMODITIES:
machinery, chemicals, metals, watches, agricultural products

### IMPORTS:
$264.5 billion (2017 est.)

$266.3 billion (2016 est.)

country comparison to the world: 19

### IMPORTS - COMMODITIES:
machinery, chemicals, vehicles, metals; agricultural products, textiles

### IMPORTS - PARTNERS:
Germany 20.9%, US 7.9%, Italy 7.6%, UK 7.3%, France 6.8%, China 5% (2017)

### RESERVES OF FOREIGN EXCHANGE AND GOLD:
$811.2 billion (31 December 2017 est.)

$679.3 billion (31 December 2016 est.)

country comparison to the world: 3

### DEBT - EXTERNAL:
$1.664 trillion (31 March 2016 est.)

$1.663 trillion (31 March 2015 est.)

country comparison to the world: 12

### STOCK OF DIRECT FOREIGN INVESTMENT - AT HOME:
$1.489 trillion (31 December 2017 est.)

$1.217 trillion (31 December 2016 est.)

country comparison to the world: 8

### STOCK OF DIRECT FOREIGN INVESTMENT - ABROAD:
$1.701 trillion (31 December 2017 est.)

$1.528 trillion (31 December 2016 est.)

country comparison to the world: 6

### EXCHANGE RATES:
Swiss francs (CHF) per US dollar -

0.9875 (2017 est.)

0.9852 (2016 est.)

0.9852 (2015 est.)

0.9627 (2014 est.)

0.9152 (2013 est.)

## ENERGY :: SWITZERLAND

### ELECTRICITY ACCESS:
electrification - total population: 100% (2016)

### ELECTRICITY - PRODUCTION:
59.01 billion kWh (2016 est.)

country comparison to the world: 50

### ELECTRICITY - CONSUMPTION:
58.46 billion kWh (2016 est.)

country comparison to the world: 43

### ELECTRICITY - EXPORTS:
30.17 billion kWh (2016 est.)

country comparison to the world: 5

### ELECTRICITY - IMPORTS:
34.1 billion kWh (2016 est.)

country comparison to the world: 4

### ELECTRICITY - INSTALLED GENERATING CAPACITY:
20.84 million kW (2016 est.)

country comparison to the world: 42

### ELECTRICITY - FROM FOSSIL FUELS:
3% of total installed capacity (2016 est.)

country comparison to the world: 209

### ELECTRICITY - FROM NUCLEAR FUELS:
18% of total installed capacity (2017 est.)

country comparison to the world: 11

### ELECTRICITY - FROM HYDROELECTRIC PLANTS:
67% of total installed capacity (2017 est.)

country comparison to the world: 21

### ELECTRICITY - FROM OTHER RENEWABLE SOURCES:
13% of total installed capacity (2017 est.)

country comparison to the world: 71

### CRUDE OIL - PRODUCTION:
0 bbl/day (2017 est.)

country comparison to the world: 204

### CRUDE OIL - EXPORTS:
0 bbl/day (2017 est.)

country comparison to the world: 201

### CRUDE OIL - IMPORTS:
57,400 bbl/day (2017 est.)

country comparison to the world: 54

### CRUDE OIL - PROVED RESERVES:
0 bbl (1 January 2018 est.)

country comparison to the world: 201

**REFINED PETROLEUM PRODUCTS - PRODUCTION:**

61,550 bbl/day (2017 est.)

country comparison to the world: 79

**REFINED PETROLEUM PRODUCTS - CONSUMPTION:**

223,900 bbl/day (2017 est.)

country comparison to the world: 54

**REFINED PETROLEUM PRODUCTS - EXPORTS:**

7,345 bbl/day (2017 est.)

country comparison to the world: 88

**REFINED PETROLEUM PRODUCTS - IMPORTS:**

165,100 bbl/day (2017 est.)

country comparison to the world: 39

**NATURAL GAS - PRODUCTION:**

0 cu m (2017 est.)

country comparison to the world: 205

**NATURAL GAS - CONSUMPTION:**

3.709 billion cu m (2017 est.)

country comparison to the world: 68

**NATURAL GAS - EXPORTS:**

0 cu m (2017 est.)

country comparison to the world: 194

**NATURAL GAS - IMPORTS:**

3.681 billion cu m (2017 est.)

country comparison to the world: 42

**NATURAL GAS - PROVED RESERVES:**

NA cu m (1 January 2011 est.)

**CARBON DIOXIDE EMISSIONS FROM CONSUMPTION OF ENERGY:**

38.95 million Mt (2017 est.)

country comparison to the world: 66

## COMMUNICATIONS :: SWITZERLAND

**TELEPHONES - FIXED LINES:**

total subscriptions: 3,672,500 (2017 est.)

subscriptions per 100 inhabitants: 45 (2017 est.)

country comparison to the world: 38

**TELEPHONES - MOBILE CELLULAR:**

total subscriptions: 11.292 million (2017 est.)

subscriptions per 100 inhabitants: 137 (2017 est.)

country comparison to the world: 79

**TELEPHONE SYSTEM:**

general assessment: highly developed telecommunications infrastructure with excellent domestic and international services (2016)

domestic: ranked among leading countries for fixed-line teledensity and infrastructure; mobile-cellular subscribership roughly 140 per 100 persons; extensive cable and microwave radio relay networks (2016)

international: country code - 41; satellite earth stations - 2 Intelsat (Atlantic Ocean and Indian Ocean) (2016)

**BROADCAST MEDIA:**

the publicly owned radio and TV broadcaster, Swiss Broadcasting Corporation (SRG/SSR), operates 7 national TV networks, 3 broadcasting in German, 2 in Italian, and 2 in French; private commercial TV stations broadcast regionally and locally; TV broadcasts from stations in Germany, Italy, and France are widely available via multi-channel cable and satellite TV services; SRG/SSR operates 17 radio stations that, along with private broadcasters, provide national to local coverage (2015)

**INTERNET COUNTRY CODE:**

.ch

**INTERNET USERS:**

total: 7,312,744 (July 2016 est.)

percent of population: 89.4% (July 2016 est.)

country comparison to the world: 59

**BROADBAND - FIXED SUBSCRIPTIONS:**

total: 3.85 million (2017 est.)

subscriptions per 100 inhabitants: 47 (2017 est.)

country comparison to the world: 31

## TRANSPORTATION :: SWITZERLAND

**NATIONAL AIR TRANSPORT SYSTEM:**

number of registered air carriers: 12 (2015)

inventory of registered aircraft operated by air carriers: 163 (2015)

annual passenger traffic on registered air carriers: 26,843,991 (2015)

annual freight traffic on registered air carriers: 1,322,379,468 mt-km (2015)

**CIVIL AIRCRAFT REGISTRATION COUNTRY CODE PREFIX:**

HB (2016)

**AIRPORTS:**

63 (2013)

country comparison to the world: 78

**AIRPORTS - WITH PAVED RUNWAYS:**

total: 40 (2013)

over 3,047 m: 3 (2013)

2,438 to 3,047 m: 2 (2013)

1,524 to 2,437 m: 12 (2013)

914 to 1,523 m: 6 (2013)

under 914 m: 17 (2013)

**AIRPORTS - WITH UNPAVED RUNWAYS:**

total: 23 (2013)

under 914 m: 23 (2013)

**HELIPORTS:**

2 (2013)

**PIPELINES:**

1800 km gas, 94 km oil, 7 km refined products (2013)

**RAILWAYS:**

total: 5,652 km (2014)

standard gauge: 4,424.8 km 1.435-m gauge (3,634.1 km electrified) (2014)

narrow gauge: 2 km 1.200-m gauge (2 km electrified) (2014)

1188.3 1.000-m gauge (1,167.3 km electrified) 36.4 0.800-m gauge (36.4 km electrified)

country comparison to the world: 34

**ROADWAYS:**

total: 71,464 km (2011)

paved: 71,464 km (includes 1,415 of expressways) (2011)

country comparison to the world: 65

**WATERWAYS:**

1,292 km (there are 1,227 km of waterways on lakes and rivers for public transport and 65 km on the Rhine River between Basel-Rheinfelden and Schaffhausen-Bodensee for commercial goods transport) (2010)

country comparison to the world: 57

**MERCHANT MARINE:**

total: 51 (2017)

by type: bulk carrier 30, general cargo 12, oil tanker 1, other 8 (2017)

country comparison to the world: 116

**PORTS AND TERMINALS:**

river port(s): Basel (Rhine)

## MILITARY AND SECURITY :: SWITZERLAND

**MILITARY EXPENDITURES:**

0.71% of GDP (2016)

0.67% of GDP (2015)

0.66% of GDP (2014)

country comparison to the world: 133

**MILITARY BRANCHES:**

Swiss Armed Forces: Land Forces, Swiss Air Force (Schweizer Luftwaffe) (2013)

**MILITARY SERVICE AGE AND OBLIGATION:**

19-26 years of age for male compulsory military service; 18 years of age for voluntary male and female military service; every Swiss male has to serve at least 260 days in the armed forces; conscripts receive 18 weeks of mandatory training, followed by seven 3-week intermittent recalls for training during the next 10 years (2012)

## TRANSNATIONAL ISSUES :: SWITZERLAND

**DISPUTES - INTERNATIONAL:**

none

**REFUGEES AND INTERNALLY DISPLACED PERSONS:**

refugees (country of origin): 26,264 (Eritrea), 11,159 (Syria), 5,675 (Afghanistan), 5,458 (Sri Lanka) (2016)

stateless persons: 62 (2017)

**ILLICIT DRUGS:**

a major international financial center vulnerable to the layering and integration stages of money laundering; despite significant legislation and reporting requirements, secrecy rules persist and nonresidents are permitted to conduct business through offshore entities and various intermediaries; transit country for and consumer of South American cocaine, Southwest Asian heroin, and Western European synthetics; domestic cannabis cultivation and limited ecstasy production

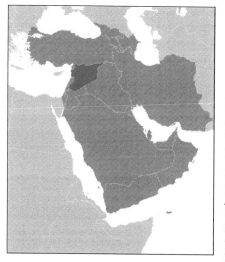

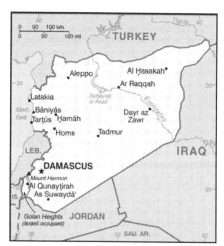

# MIDDLE EAST :: SYRIA

## INTRODUCTION :: SYRIA

**BACKGROUND:**

Following World War I, France acquired a mandate over the northern portion of the former Ottoman Empire province of Syria. The French administered the area as Syria until granting it independence in 1946. The new country lacked political stability and experienced a series of military coups. Syria united with Egypt in February 1958 to form the United Arab Republic. In September 1961, the two entities separated, and the Syrian Arab Republic was reestablished. In the 1967 Arab-Israeli War, Syria lost the Golan Heights region to Israel. During the 1990s, Syria and Israel held occasional, albeit unsuccessful, peace talks over its return. In November 1970, Hafiz al-ASAD, a member of the socialist Ba'ath Party and the minority Alawi sect, seized power in a bloodless coup and brought political stability to the country. Following the death of President Hafiz al-ASAD, his son, Bashar al-ASAD, was approved as president by popular referendum in July 2000. Syrian troops - stationed in Lebanon since 1976 in an ostensible peacekeeping role - were withdrawn in April 2005. During the July-August 2006 conflict between Israel and Hizballah, Syria placed its military forces on alert but did not intervene directly on behalf of its ally Hizballah. In May 2007, Bashar al-ASAD's second term as president was approved by popular referendum.

Influenced by major uprisings that began elsewhere in the region, and compounded by additional social and economic factors, antigovernment protests broke out first in the southern province of Dar'a in March 2011 with protesters calling for the repeal of the restrictive Emergency Law allowing arrests without charge, the legalization of political parties, and the removal of corrupt local officials. Demonstrations and violent unrest spread across Syria with the size and intensity of protests fluctuating. The government responded to unrest with a mix of concessions - including the repeal of the Emergency Law, new laws permitting new political parties, and liberalizing local and national elections - and with military force and detentions. The government's efforts to quell unrest and armed opposition activity led to extended clashes between government forces, their allies, and oppositionists.

International pressure on the ASAD regime intensified after late 2011, as the Arab League, the EU, Turkey, and the US expanded economic sanctions against the regime and those entities that support it. In December 2012, the Syrian National Coalition, was recognized by more than 130 countries as the sole legitimate representative of the Syrian people. In September 2015, Russia launched a military intervention on behalf of the ASAD regime, and government-aligned forces recaptured Aleppo city in December 2016, shifting the conflict in the regime's favor. Political negotiations between the government and opposition delegations at UN-sponsored Geneva conferences since 2014 have failed to produce a resolution of the conflict. Russia, Iran, and Turkey since early 2017 have held negotiations in Astana to establish de-escalation zones to reduce violence in Syria. Unrest continues in Syria, and according to an April 2016 UN estimate, the death toll among Syrian Government forces, opposition forces, and civilians was over 400,000, though other estimates have placed the number well over 500,000. As of December 2017, approximately 13.1 million people were in need of humanitarian assistance in Syria, with 6.3 million people displaced internally, and an additional 5.4 million registered Syrian refugees, making the Syrian situation among the largest humanitarian crises worldwide

## GEOGRAPHY :: SYRIA

**LOCATION:**

Middle East, bordering the Mediterranean Sea, between Lebanon and Turkey

**GEOGRAPHIC COORDINATES:**

35 00 N, 38 00 E

**MAP REFERENCES:**

Middle East

**AREA:**

total: 185,180 sq km

land: 183,630 sq km

water: 1,550 sq km

note: includes 1,295 sq km of Israeli-occupied territory

country comparison to the world: 90

**AREA - COMPARATIVE:**

slightly more than 1.5 times the size of Pennsylvania

**LAND BOUNDARIES:**

total: 2,363 km

**border countries (5):** Iraq 599 km, Israel 83 km, Jordan 379 km, Lebanon 403 km, Turkey 899 km

## COASTLINE:
193 km

## MARITIME CLAIMS:
**territorial sea:** 12 nm

**contiguous zone:** 24 nm

## CLIMATE:
mostly desert; hot, dry, sunny summers (June to August) and mild, rainy winters (December to February) along coast; cold weather with snow or sleet periodically in Damascus

## TERRAIN:
primarily semiarid and desert plateau; narrow coastal plain; mountains in west

## ELEVATION:
**mean elevation:** 514 m

**elevation extremes:** -208 m lowest point: unnamed location near Lake Tiberias

2814 highest point: Mount Hermon (Jabal a-Shayk)

## NATURAL RESOURCES:
petroleum, phosphates, chrome and manganese ores, asphalt, iron ore, rock salt, marble, gypsum, hydropower

## LAND USE:
**agricultural land:** 75.8% (2011 est.)

arable land: 25.4% (2011 est.) / permanent crops: 5.8% (2011 est.) / permanent pasture: 44.6% (2011 est.)

**forest:** 2.7% (2011 est.)

**other:** 21.5% (2011 est.)

## IRRIGATED LAND:
14,280 sq km (2012)

## POPULATION DISTRIBUTION:
significant population density along the Mediterranean coast; larger concentrations found in the major cities of Damascus, Aleppo (the country's largest city), and Hims (Homs); more than half of the population lives in the coastal plain, the province of Halab, and the Euphrates River valley

**note:** the ongoing civil war has altered the population distribution

## NATURAL HAZARDS:
dust storms, sandstorms

**volcanism:** Syria's two historically active volcanoes, Es Safa and an unnamed volcano near the Turkish border have not erupted in centuries

## ENVIRONMENT - CURRENT ISSUES:
deforestation; overgrazing; soil erosion; desertification; depletion of water resources; water pollution from raw sewage and petroleum refining wastes; inadequate potable water

## ENVIRONMENT - INTERNATIONAL AGREEMENTS:
**party to:** Biodiversity, Climate Change, Climate Change-Kyoto Protocol, Desertification, Endangered Species, Hazardous Wastes, Ozone Layer Protection, Ship Pollution, Wetlands

**signed, but not ratified:** Environmental Modification

## GEOGRAPHY - NOTE:
the capital of Damascus - located at an oasis fed by the Barada River - is thought to be one of the world's oldest continuously inhabited cities; there are 42 Israeli settlements and civilian land use sites in the Israeli-occupied Golan Heights (2017)

# PEOPLE AND SOCIETY :: SYRIA

## POPULATION:
19,454,263 (July 2017 est.) (July 2018 est.)

**note:** approximately 22,000 Israeli settlers live in the Golan Heights (2016)

**country comparison to the world:** 62

## NATIONALITY:
**noun:** Syrian(s)

**adjective:** Syrian

## ETHNIC GROUPS:
Arab ~50%, Alawite ~15%, Kurd ~10%, Levantine ~10%, other ~15% (includes Durze, Ismaili, Imami, Nusairi, Assyrian, Turkoman, Armenian)

## LANGUAGES:
Arabic (official), Kurdish, Armenian, Aramaic, Circassian, French, English

## RELIGIONS:
Muslim 87% (official; includes Sunni 74% and Alawi, Ismaili, and Shia 13%), Christian 10% (includes Orthodox, Uniate, and Nestorian), Druze 3%, Jewish (few remaining in Damascus and Aleppo)

**note:** the Christian population may be considerably smaller as a result of Christians fleeing the country during the ongoing civil war

## AGE STRUCTURE:
**0-14 years:** 31.39% (male 3,132,619 /female 2,974,394)

**15-24 years:** 19.52% (male 1,933,185 /female 1,863,991)

**25-54 years:** 39.26% (male 3,807,664 /female 3,829,150)

**55-64 years:** 5.52% (male 531,455 /female 542,738)

**65 years and over:** 4.31% (male 379,360 /female 459,707) (2018 est.)

## DEPENDENCY RATIOS:
**total dependency ratio:** 72.8 (2015 est.)

**youth dependency ratio:** 65.8 (2015 est.)

**elderly dependency ratio:** 7 (2015 est.)

**potential support ratio:** 14.3 (2015 est.)

## MEDIAN AGE:
**total:** 24.5 years

**male:** 24 years

**female:** 25 years (2018 est.)

**country comparison to the world:** 163

## POPULATION GROWTH RATE:
7.37% NA (2018 est.)

**country comparison to the world:** 1

## BIRTH RATE:
20.7 births/1,000 population (2018 est.)

**country comparison to the world:** 76

## DEATH RATE:
4 deaths/1,000 population (2018 est.)

**country comparison to the world:** 210

## NET MIGRATION RATE:
NA

## POPULATION DISTRIBUTION:
significant population density along the Mediterranean coast; larger concentrations found in the major cities of Damascus, Aleppo (the country's largest city), and Hims (Homs); more than half of the population lives in the coastal plain, the province of Halab, and the Euphrates River valley

**note:** the ongoing civil war has altered the population distribution

## URBANIZATION:
**urban population:** 54.2% of total population (2018)

**rate of urbanization:** 1.43% annual rate of change (2015-20 est.)

**MAJOR URBAN AREAS - POPULATION:**

2.32 million DAMASCUS (capital), 1.754 million Aleppo, 1.295 million Hims (Homs), 894,000 Hamah (2018)

**SEX RATIO:**

at birth: 1.06 male(s)/female (2017 est.)

0-14 years: 1.05 male(s)/female (2017 est.)

15-24 years: 1.03 male(s)/female (2017 est.)

25-54 years: 0.99 male(s)/female (2017 est.)

55-64 years: 0.98 male(s)/female (2017 est.)

65 years and over: 0.82 male(s)/female (2017 est.)

total population: 1.01 male(s)/female (2017 est.)

**MATERNAL MORTALITY RATE:**

68 deaths/100,000 live births (2015 est.)

country comparison to the world: 85

**INFANT MORTALITY RATE:**

total: 14.4 deaths/1,000 live births (2018 est.)

male: 16.6 deaths/1,000 live births (2018 est.)

female: 12.2 deaths/1,000 live births (2018 est.)

country comparison to the world: 100

**LIFE EXPECTANCY AT BIRTH:**

total population: 75.2 years (2018 est.)

male: 72.8 years (2018 est.)

female: 77.8 years (2018 est.)

country comparison to the world: 112

**TOTAL FERTILITY RATE:**

2.44 children born/woman (2018 est.)

country comparison to the world: 80

**CONTRACEPTIVE PREVALENCE RATE:**

53.9% (2009)

**HEALTH EXPENDITURES:**

3.3% of GDP (2014)

country comparison to the world: 180

**PHYSICIANS DENSITY:**

1.55 physicians/1,000 population (2014)

**HOSPITAL BED DENSITY:**

1.5 beds/1,000 population (2014)

**DRINKING WATER SOURCE:**

improved:

urban: 92.3% of population

rural: 87.2% of population

total: 90.1% of population

unimproved:

urban: 7.7% of population

rural: 12.8% of population

total: 9.9% of population (2015 est.)

**SANITATION FACILITY ACCESS:**

improved:

urban: 96.2% of population (2015 est.)

rural: 95.1% of population (2015 est.)

total: 95.7% of population (2015 est.)

unimproved:

urban: 3.8% of population (2015 est.)

rural: 4.9% of population (2015 est.)

total: 4.3% of population (2015 est.)

**HIV/AIDS - ADULT PREVALENCE RATE:**

NA

**HIV/AIDS - PEOPLE LIVING WITH HIV/AIDS:**

NA

**HIV/AIDS - DEATHS:**

NA

**OBESITY - ADULT PREVALENCE RATE:**

27.8% (2016)

country comparison to the world: 35

**CHILDREN UNDER THE AGE OF 5 YEARS UNDERWEIGHT:**

10.1% (2009)

country comparison to the world: 63

**EDUCATION EXPENDITURES:**

5.1% of GDP (2009)

country comparison to the world: 73

**LITERACY:**

definition: age 15 and over can read and write (2015 est.)

total population: 86.4% (2015 est.)

male: 91.7% (2015 est.)

female: 81% (2015 est.)

**SCHOOL LIFE EXPECTANCY (PRIMARY TO TERTIARY EDUCATION):**

total: 9 years (2013)

male: 9 years (2013)

female: 9 years (2013)

**UNEMPLOYMENT, YOUTH AGES 15-24:**

total: 35.8% (2011 est.)

male: 26.6% (2011 est.)

female: 71.1% (2011 est.)

country comparison to the world: 20

# GOVERNMENT :: SYRIA

**COUNTRY NAME:**

conventional long form: Syrian Arab Republic

conventional short form: Syria

local long form: Al Jumhuriyah al Arabiyah as Suriyah

local short form: Suriyah

former: United Arab Republic (with Egypt)

etymology: name ultimately derived from the ancient Assyrians who dominated northern Mesopotamia, but whose reach also extended westward to the Levant; over time, the name came to be associated more with the western area

**GOVERNMENT TYPE:**

presidential republic; highly authoritarian regime

**CAPITAL:**

name: Damascus

geographic coordinates: 33 30 N, 36 18 E

time difference: UTC+2 (7 hours ahead of Washington, DC, during Standard Time)

daylight saving time: +1hr, begins midnight on the last Friday in March; ends at midnight on the last Friday in October

**ADMINISTRATIVE DIVISIONS:**

14 provinces (muhafazat, singular - muhafazah); Al Hasakah, Al Ladhiqiyah (Latakia), Al Qunaytirah, Ar Raqqah, As Suwayda', Dar'a, Dayr az Zawr, Dimashq (Damascus), Halab (Aleppo), Hamah, Hims (Homs), Idlib, Rif Dimashq (Damascus Countryside), Tartus

**INDEPENDENCE:**

17 April 1946 (from League of Nations mandate under French administration)

**NATIONAL HOLIDAY:**

Independence Day (Evacuation Day), 17 April (1946); note - celebrates the leaving of the last French troops and the proclamation of full independence

**CONSTITUTION:**

history: several previous; latest issued 15 February 2012, passed by referendum and effective 27 February 2012 (2016)

  amendments: proposed by the president of the republic or by one-third of the People's Assembly members; following review by a special Assembly committee, passage requires at least three-quarters majority vote by the Assembly and approval by the president (2016)

## LEGAL SYSTEM:

mixed legal system of civil and Islamic law (for family courts)

## INTERNATIONAL LAW ORGANIZATION PARTICIPATION:

has not submitted an ICJ jurisdiction declaration; non-party state to the ICCt

## CITIZENSHIP:

  citizenship by birth: no

  citizenship by descent only: the father must be a citizen of Syria; if the father is unknown or stateless, the mother must be a citizen of Syria

  dual citizenship recognized: yes

  residency requirement for naturalization: 10 years

## SUFFRAGE:

18 years of age; universal

## EXECUTIVE BRANCH:

  chief of state: President Bashar al-ASAD (since 17 July 2000); Vice President Najah al-ATTAR (since 23 March 2006)

  head of government: Prime Minister Imad Muhammad Dib KHAMIS (since 22 June 2016); Deputy Prime Minister Walid al-MUALEM (since 23 June 2012)

  cabinet: Council of Ministers appointed by the president

  elections/appointments: president directly elected by simple majority popular vote for a 7-year term (eligible for a second term); election last held on 3 June 2014 (next to be held in June 2021); the president appoints the vice presidents, prime minister, and deputy prime ministers

  election results: Bashar al-ASAD elected president; percent of vote - Bashar al-ASAD (Ba'th Party) 88.7%, Hassan al-NOURI (independent) 4.3%, Maher HAJJER (independent) 3.2%, other/invalid 3.8%

## LEGISLATIVE BRANCH:

  description: unicameral People's Assembly or Majlis al-Shaab (250 seats; members directly elected in multi-seat constituencies by simple majority preferential vote to serve 4-year terms)

  elections: last held on 13 April 2016 (next to be held in 2020)

  election results: percent of vote by party - NPF 80%, other 20%; seats by party - NPF 200, other 50; composition - men 217, women 33, percent of women 13.2%

## JUDICIAL BRANCH:

  highest courts: Court of Cassation (organized into civil, criminal, religious, and military divisions, each with 3 judges); Supreme Constitutional Court (consists of 7 members)

  judge selection and term of office: Court of Cassation judges appointed by the Supreme Judicial Council or SJC, a judicial management body headed by the minister of justice with 7 members including the national president; judge tenure NA; Supreme Constitutional Court judges nominated by the president and appointed by the SJC; judges appointed for 4-year renewable terms

  subordinate courts: courts of first instance; magistrates' courts; religious and military courts; Economic Security Court; Counterterrorism Court (established June 2012)

## POLITICAL PARTIES AND LEADERS:

  legal parties/alliances: Arab Socialist Ba'ath Party [Bashar al-ASAD, regional secretary]; Arab Socialist Renaissance (Ba'th) Party [President Bashar al-ASAD]; Arab Socialist Union of Syria or ASU [Safwan al-QUDSI]; National Progressive Front or NPF [Bashar al-ASAD, Suleiman QADDAH] (alliance includes Arab Socialist Renaissance (Ba'th) Party, Socialist Unionist Democratic Party; Socialist Unionist Democratic Party [Fadlallah Nasr al-DIN]; Syrian Communist Party (two branches) [Wissal Farha BAKDASH, Yusuf Rashid FAYSAL]; Syrian Social Nationalist Party or SSNP [Ali HAIDAR]; Unionist Socialist Party [Fayez ISMAIL];

  Kurdish parties (considered illegal): Kurdish Azadi Party; Kurdish Democratic Accord Party (al Wifaq) [Fowzi SHINKALI]; Kurdish Democratic Left Party [Saleh KIDDO]; Kurdish Democratic Party (al Parti-Ibrahim wing) [Nasr al-Din IBRAHIM]; Kurdish Democratic Party (al Parti-Mustafa wing); Kurdish Democratic Party in Syria or KDP-S [Saud AL-MALA]; Kurdish Democratic Patriotic/National Party; Kurdish Democratic Peace Party [Talal MOHAMMED]; Kurdish Democratic Progressive Party or KDPP-Darwish; Kurdish Democratic Progressive Party or KDPP-Muhammad; Kurdish Democratic Union Party or PYD [Shahoz HASAN and Aysha HISSO]; Kurdish Democratic Unity Party [Kamiron Haj ABDU]; Kurdish Democratic Yekiti Party [Mahi al-Din Sheikh ALI]; Kurdish Equality Party [Namet DAOUD]; Kurdish Future Party [Rezan HASSAN]; Kurdish Green Party [ Laqman AHMI]; Kurdish Left Party [Shallal KIDDO]; Kurdish National Democratic Rally in Syria; Kurdish Reform Movement in Syria [Amjad OTHMAN]; Kurdish Reform Movement Party [Feisal AL-YUSSEF]; Kurdish Yekiti (Union) Party; Kurdistan Communist Party [Nejm al-Sin MALA'AMIR]; Kurdistan Democratic Party in Syria [Abdul Karim SAKKO]; Kurdistan Liberal Union [Farhad TILO]; Socialist Unionist Democratic Party [Fadlallah Nasr al-DIN]; Syrian Kurdish Democratic Party; Tiyar al-Mustaqbal [Narin MATINI];

  other: Syrian Democratic Party [Mustafa QALAAJI]

## INTERNATIONAL ORGANIZATION PARTICIPATION:

ABEDA, AFESD, AMF, CAEU, FAO, G-24, G-77, IAEA, IBRD, ICAO, ICC (national committees), ICRM, IDA, IDB, IFAD, IFC, IFRCS, IHO, ILO, IMF, IMO, Interpol, IOC, IPU, ISO, ITSO, ITU, LAS, MIGA, NAM, OAPEC, OIC, OPCW, UN, UNCTAD, UNESCO, UNIDO, UNRWA, UNWTO, UPU, WCO, WFTU (NGOs), WHO, WIPO, WMO, WTO (observer)

## DIPLOMATIC REPRESENTATION IN THE US:

  chief of mission: Ambassador (vacant)

  chancery: 2215 Wyoming Avenue NW, Washington, DC 20008

  telephone: [1] (202) 232-6313

FAX: [1] (202) 234-9548

note: Embassy ceased operations and closed on 18 March 2014

**DIPLOMATIC REPRESENTATION FROM THE US:**

chief of mission: ambassador (vacant); note - on 6 February 2012, the US closed its embassy in Damascus; Czechia serves as protecting power for US interests in Syria

embassy: Abou Roumaneh, 2 Al Mansour Street, Damascus

mailing address: P. O. Box 29, Damascus

telephone: [963] (11) 3391-4444

FAX: [963] (11) 3391-3999

**FLAG DESCRIPTION:**

three equal horizontal bands of red (top), white, and black; two small, green, five-pointed stars in a horizontal line centered in the white band; the band colors derive from the Arab Liberation flag and represent oppression (black), overcome through bloody struggle (red), to be replaced by a bright future (white); identical to the former flag of the United Arab Republic (1958-1961) where the two stars represented the constituent states of Syria and Egypt; the current design dates to 1980

note: similar to the flag of Yemen, which has a plain white band, Iraq, which has an Arabic inscription centered in the white band, and that of Egypt, which has a gold Eagle of Saladin centered in the white band

**NATIONAL SYMBOL(S):**

hawk; national colors: red, white, black, green

**NATIONAL ANTHEM:**

name: "Humat ad-Diyar" (Guardians of the Homeland)

lyrics/music: Khalil Mardam BEY/Mohammad Salim FLAYFEL and Ahmad Salim FLAYFEL

note: adopted 1936, restored 1961; between 1958 and 1961, while Syria was a member of the United Arab Republic with Egypt, the country had a different anthem

## ECONOMY :: SYRIA

**ECONOMY - OVERVIEW:**

Syria's economy has deeply deteriorated amid the ongoing conflict that began in 2011, declining by more than 70% from 2010 to 2017. The government has struggled to fully address the effects of international sanctions, widespread infrastructure damage, diminished domestic consumption and production, reduced subsidies, and high inflation, which have caused dwindling foreign exchange reserves, rising budget and trade deficits, a decreasing value of the Syrian pound, and falling household purchasing power. In 2017, some economic indicators began to stabilize, including the exchange rate and inflation, but economic activity remains depressed and GDP almost certainly fell.

During 2017, the ongoing conflict and continued unrest and economic decline worsened the humanitarian crisis, necessitating high levels of international assistance, as more than 13 million people remain in need inside Syria, and the number of registered Syrian refugees increased from 4.8 million in 2016 to more than 5.4 million.

Prior to the turmoil, Damascus had begun liberalizing economic policies, including cutting lending interest rates, opening private banks, consolidating multiple exchange rates, raising prices on some subsidized items, and establishing the Damascus Stock Exchange, but the economy remains highly regulated. Long-run economic constraints include foreign trade barriers, declining oil production, high unemployment, rising budget deficits, increasing pressure on water supplies caused by heavy use in agriculture, industrial contaction, water pollution, and widespread infrastructure damage.

**GDP (PURCHASING POWER PARITY):**

$50.28 billion (2015 est.)

$55.8 billion (2014 est.)

$61.9 billion (2013 est.)

note: data are in 2015 US dollars the war-driven deterioration of the economy resulted in a disappearance of quality national level statistics in the 2012-13 period

country comparison to the world: 110

**GDP (OFFICIAL EXCHANGE RATE):**

$24.6 billion (2014 est.) (2014 est.)

**GDP - REAL GROWTH RATE:**

-36.5% (2014 est.)

-30.9% (2013 est.)

note: data are in 2015 dollars

country comparison to the world: 224

**GDP - PER CAPITA (PPP):**

$2,900 (2015 est.)

$3,300 (2014 est.)

$2,800 (2013 est.)

note: data are in 2015 US dollars

country comparison to the world: 194

**GROSS NATIONAL SAVING:**

17% of GDP (2017 est.)

15.3% of GDP (2016 est.)

16.1% of GDP (2015 est.)

country comparison to the world: 121

**GDP - COMPOSITION, BY END USE:**

household consumption: 73.1% (2017 est.)

government consumption: 26% (2017 est.)

investment in fixed capital: 18.6% (2017 est.)

investment in inventories: 12.3% (2017 est.)

exports of goods and services: 16.1% (2017 est.)

imports of goods and services: -46.1% (2017 est.)

**GDP - COMPOSITION, BY SECTOR OF ORIGIN:**

agriculture: 20% (2017 est.)

industry: 19.5% (2017 est.)

services: 60.8% (2017 est.)

**AGRICULTURE - PRODUCTS:**

wheat, barley, cotton, lentils, chickpeas, olives, sugar beets; beef, mutton, eggs, poultry, milk

**INDUSTRIES:**

petroleum, textiles, food processing, beverages, tobacco, phosphate rock mining, cement, oil seeds crushing, automobile assembly

**INDUSTRIAL PRODUCTION GROWTH RATE:**

4.3% (2017 est.)

country comparison to the world: 70

**LABOR FORCE:**

3.767 million (2017 est.)

country comparison to the world: 95

**LABOR FORCE - BY OCCUPATION:**

agriculture: 17%

industry: 16%

services: 67% (2008 est.)

**UNEMPLOYMENT RATE:**

50% (2017 est.)

50% (2016 est.)

country comparison to the world: 217

**POPULATION BELOW POVERTY LINE:**

82.5% (2014 est.)

**HOUSEHOLD INCOME OR CONSUMPTION BY PERCENTAGE SHARE:**

lowest 10%: NA

highest 10%: NA

**BUDGET:**

revenues: 1.162 billion (2017 est.)

expenditures: 3.211 billion (2017 est.)

note: government projections for FY2016

**TAXES AND OTHER REVENUES:**

4.2% (of GDP) (2017 est.)

country comparison to the world: 219

**BUDGET SURPLUS (+) OR DEFICIT (-):**

-8.7% (of GDP) (2017 est.)

country comparison to the world: 203

**PUBLIC DEBT:**

94.8% of GDP (2017 est.)

91.3% of GDP (2016 est.)

country comparison to the world: 23

**FISCAL YEAR:**

calendar year

**INFLATION RATE (CONSUMER PRICES):**

28.1% (2017 est.)

47.3% (2016 est.)

country comparison to the world: 220

**CENTRAL BANK DISCOUNT RATE:**

0.75% (31 December 2017)

5% (31 December 2016)

country comparison to the world: 135

**COMMERCIAL BANK PRIME LENDING RATE:**

14% (31 December 2017 est.)

22% (31 December 2016 est.)

country comparison to the world: 49

**STOCK OF NARROW MONEY:**

$7.272 billion (31 December 2017 est.)

$4.333 billion (31 December 2016 est.)

country comparison to the world: 88

**STOCK OF BROAD MONEY:**

$7.272 billion (31 December 2017 est.)

$4.333 billion (31 December 2016 est.)

country comparison to the world: 90

**STOCK OF DOMESTIC CREDIT:**

$9.161 billion (31 December 2017 est.)

$5.786 billion (31 December 2016 est.)

country comparison to the world: 109

**MARKET VALUE OF PUBLICLY TRADED SHARES:**

NA

**CURRENT ACCOUNT BALANCE:**

-$2.123 billion (2017 est.)

-$2.077 billion (2016 est.)

country comparison to the world: 167

**EXPORTS:**

$1.85 billion (2017 est.)

$1.705 billion (2016 est.)

country comparison to the world: 144

**EXPORTS - PARTNERS:**

Lebanon 31.5%, Iraq 10.3%, Jordan 8.8%, China 7.8%, Turkey 7.5%, Spain 7.3% (2017)

**EXPORTS - COMMODITIES:**

crude oil, minerals, petroleum products, fruits and vegetables, cotton fiber, textiles, clothing, meat and live animals, wheat

**IMPORTS:**

$6.279 billion (2017 est.)

$5.496 billion (2016 est.)

country comparison to the world: 120

**IMPORTS - COMMODITIES:**

machinery and transport equipment, electric power machinery, food and livestock, metal and metal products, chemicals and chemical products, plastics, yarn, paper

**IMPORTS - PARTNERS:**

Russia 32.4%, Turkey 16.7%, China 9.5% (2017)

**RESERVES OF FOREIGN EXCHANGE AND GOLD:**

$407.3 million (31 December 2017 est.)

$504.6 million (31 December 2016 est.)

country comparison to the world: 159

**DEBT - EXTERNAL:**

$4.989 billion (31 December 2017 est.)

$5.085 billion (31 December 2016 est.)

country comparison to the world: 133

**EXCHANGE RATES:**

Syrian pounds (SYP) per US dollar -

514.6 (2017 est.)

459.2 (2016 est.)

459.2 (2015 est.)

236.41 (2014 est.)

153.695 (2013 est.)

# ENERGY :: SYRIA

**ELECTRICITY ACCESS:**

population without electricity: 1.6 million (2013)

electrification - total population: 96% (2013)

electrification - urban areas: 100% (2013)

electrification - rural areas: 81% (2013)

**ELECTRICITY - PRODUCTION:**

17.07 billion kWh (2016 est.)

country comparison to the world: 84

**ELECTRICITY - CONSUMPTION:**

14.16 billion kWh (2016 est.)

country comparison to the world: 82

**ELECTRICITY - EXPORTS:**

262 million kWh (2015 est.)

country comparison to the world: 72

**ELECTRICITY - IMPORTS:**

0 kWh (2016 est.)

country comparison to the world: 207

**ELECTRICITY - INSTALLED GENERATING CAPACITY:**

9.058 million kW (2016 est.)

country comparison to the world: 64

**ELECTRICITY - FROM FOSSIL FUELS:**

83% of total installed capacity (2016 est.)

country comparison to the world: 77

**ELECTRICITY - FROM NUCLEAR FUELS:**

0% of total installed capacity (2017 est.)

country comparison to the world: 190

**ELECTRICITY - FROM HYDROELECTRIC PLANTS:**

17% of total installed capacity (2017 est.)

country comparison to the world: 98

**ELECTRICITY - FROM OTHER RENEWABLE SOURCES:**

0% of total installed capacity (2017 est.)

country comparison to the world: 207

**CRUDE OIL - PRODUCTION:**

14,000 bbl/day (2017 est.)

country comparison to the world: 75

**CRUDE OIL - EXPORTS:**

0 bbl/day (2015 est.)

country comparison to the world: 202

**CRUDE OIL - IMPORTS:**

87,660 bbl/day (2015 est.)

country comparison to the world: 45

**CRUDE OIL - PROVED RESERVES:**

2.5 billion bbl (1 January 2018 est.)

country comparison to the world: 30

**REFINED PETROLEUM PRODUCTS - PRODUCTION:**

111,600 bbl/day (2015 est.)

country comparison to the world: 66

**REFINED PETROLEUM PRODUCTS - CONSUMPTION:**

134,000 bbl/day (2016 est.)

country comparison to the world: 71

**REFINED PETROLEUM PRODUCTS - EXPORTS:**

12,520 bbl/day (2015 est.)

country comparison to the world: 79

**REFINED PETROLEUM PRODUCTS - IMPORTS:**

38,080 bbl/day (2015 est.)

country comparison to the world: 92

**NATURAL GAS - PRODUCTION:**

3.738 billion cu m (2017 est.)

country comparison to the world: 53

**NATURAL GAS - CONSUMPTION:**

3.738 billion cu m (2017 est.)

country comparison to the world: 67

**NATURAL GAS - EXPORTS:**

0 cu m (2017 est.)

country comparison to the world: 195

**NATURAL GAS - IMPORTS:**

0 cu m (2017 est.)

country comparison to the world: 196

**NATURAL GAS - PROVED RESERVES:**

240.7 billion cu m (1 January 2018 est.)

country comparison to the world: 40

**CARBON DIOXIDE EMISSIONS FROM CONSUMPTION OF ENERGY:**

27.51 million Mt (2017 est.)

country comparison to the world: 75

## COMMUNICATIONS :: SYRIA

**TELEPHONES - FIXED LINES:**

total subscriptions: 2,726,193 (2017 est.)

subscriptions per 100 inhabitants: 15 (2017 est.)

country comparison to the world: 51

**TELEPHONES - MOBILE CELLULAR:**

total subscriptions: 15.65 million (2017 est.)

subscriptions per 100 inhabitants: 87 (2017 est.)

country comparison to the world: 65

**TELEPHONE SYSTEM:**

general assessment: the armed insurgency that began in 2011 has led to major disruptions to the network and has caused telephone and Internet outages throughout the country (2016)

domestic: the number of fixed-line connections increased markedly prior to the civil war in 2011; mobile-cellular service stands at about 70 per 100 persons (2016)

international: country code - 963; submarine cable connection to Egypt, Lebanon, and Cyprus; satellite earth stations - 1 Intelsat (Indian Ocean) and 1 Intersputnik (Atlantic Ocean region); coaxial cable and microwave radio relay to Iraq, Jordan, Lebanon, and Turkey; participant in Medarabtel (2016)

**BROADCAST MEDIA:**

state-run TV and radio broadcast networks; state operates 2 TV networks and a satellite channel; roughly two-thirds of Syrian homes have a satellite dish providing access to foreign TV broadcasts; 3 state-run radio channels; first private radio station launched in 2005; private radio broadcasters prohibited from transmitting news or political content (2007)

**INTERNET COUNTRY CODE:**

.sy

**INTERNET USERS:**

total: 5,476,850 (July 2016 est.)

percent of population: 31.9% (July 2016 est.)

country comparison to the world: 71

**BROADBAND - FIXED SUBSCRIPTIONS:**

total: 1,154,909 (2017 est.)

subscriptions per 100 inhabitants: 6 (2017 est.)

country comparison to the world: 68

## TRANSPORTATION :: SYRIA

**NATIONAL AIR TRANSPORT SYSTEM:**

number of registered air carriers: 2 (2015)

inventory of registered aircraft operated by air carriers: 11 (2015)

annual passenger traffic on registered air carriers: 475,932 (2015)

annual freight traffic on registered air carriers: 1,517,388 mt-km (2015)

**CIVIL AIRCRAFT REGISTRATION COUNTRY CODE PREFIX:**

YK (2016)

**AIRPORTS:**

90 (2013)

country comparison to the world: 62

**AIRPORTS - WITH PAVED RUNWAYS:**

total: 29 (2013)

over 3,047 m: 5 (2013)

2,438 to 3,047 m: 16 (2013)

914 to 1,523 m: 3 (2013)

under 914 m: 5 (2013)

**AIRPORTS - WITH UNPAVED RUNWAYS:**

total: 61 (2013)

1,524 to 2,437 m: 1 (2013)

914 to 1,523 m: 12 (2013)

under 914 m: 48 (2013)

**HELIPORTS:**

6 (2013)

**PIPELINES:**

3170 km gas, 2029 km oil (2013)

**RAILWAYS:**

total: 2,052 km (2014)

standard gauge: 1,801 km 1.435-m gauge (2014)

narrow gauge: 251 km 1.050-m gauge (2014)

country comparison to the world: 75

**ROADWAYS:**

total: 69,873 km (2010)

paved: 63,060 km (2010)

unpaved: 6,813 km (2010)

country comparison to the world: 68

**WATERWAYS:**

900 km (navigable but not economically significant) (2011)

country comparison to the world: 68

**MERCHANT MARINE:**

total: 21 (2017)

by type: bulk carrier 1, general cargo 7, other 13 (2017)

country comparison to the world: 137

**PORTS AND TERMINALS:**

**major seaport(s):** Baniyas, Latakia, Tartus

# MILITARY AND SECURITY :: SYRIA

## MILITARY BRANCHES:

Syrian Armed Forces: Land Forces, Naval Forces, Air Forces (includes Air Defense Forces), Intelligence Services (Air Force Intelligence, Military Intelligence),

, Ministry of Interior: Political Security Directorate, General Intelligence Directorate, National Police Force

(2017)

## MILITARY SERVICE AGE AND OBLIGATION:

18 years of age for compulsory and voluntary military service; conscript service obligation is 18 months; women are not conscripted but may volunteer to serve (2017)

# TERRORISM :: SYRIA

## TERRORIST GROUPS - HOME BASED:

### al-Nusrah Front:
**aim(s):** overthrow Syrian President Bashar al-ASAD's regime, absorb like-minded Syrian rebel groups, and ultimately, establish a regional Islamic caliphate
**area(s) of operation:** headquartered in the northwestern Idlib Governorate, with a minor presence in Halab Governorate; operational primarily in northern, western, and southern Syria; installs Sharia in areas under its control; targets primarily Syrian regime and pro-regime forces, some minorities, other Syrian insurgent groups, and occasionally Western interests (April 2018)

### Hay'at Tahrir al-Sham (HTS):
**aim(s):** an alias of the al-Nusrah Front; overthrow Syrian President Bashar al-ASAD's regime, absorb like-minded Syrian rebel groups, and, ultimately, establish a regional Islamic caliphate
**area(s) of operation:** Northwest Syria (December 2018)

### Islamic State of Iraq and ash-Sham (ISIS):
**aim(s):** replace the world order with a global Islamic state based in Iraq and Syria; expand its branches and networks in other countries; rule according to ISIS's strict interpretation of Islamic law
**area(s) of operation:** ISIS has lost most of the territory it once controlled and now its overt territorial control is limited to pockets of land along the Syria-Iraq border and in southern Syria (April 2018)

## TERRORIST GROUPS - FOREIGN BASED:

### Abdallah Azzam Brigades (AAB):
**aim(s):** disrupt and attack Shia Muslim and Western interests in Syria
**area(s) of operation:** remains operational; conducts attacks against primarily Shia Muslim organizations and individuals, including Hizballah members, and Westerners and their interests (April 2018)

### al-Qa'ida (AQ):
**aim(s):** overthrow President Bashar al-ASAD's regime; establish a regional Islamic caliphate and conduct attacks outside of Syria
**area(s) of operation:** operational primarily in Idlib Governorate and southern Syria, where it has established networks and operates paramilitary training camps (April 2018)

### Ansar al-Islam (AAI):
**aim(s):** remove Syrian President Bashar al-ASAD from power and establish a government operating according to sharia
**area(s) of operation:** operationally active in Syria since 2011; launches attacks on Syrian Government security forces and pro-Syrian Government militias; some AAI factions combat ISIS, while others are aligned with ISIS (April 2018)

### Hizballah:
**aim(s):** preserve Syrian President Bashar al-ASAD's regime
**area(s) of operation:** operational activity throughout the country since 2012; centered on providing paramilitary support to President Bashar al-ASAD's regime against armed insurgents (April 2018)

### Kata'ib Hizballah (KH):
**aim(s):** preserve Syrian President Bashar al-ASAD's regime
**area(s) of operation:** deploys combatants to Syria to fight alongside Syrian Government and Lebanese Hizballah forces (April 2018)

### Kurdistan Workers' Party (PKK):
**aim(s):** advance Kurdish autonomy, political, and cultural rights in Syria, Turkey, Iraq, and Iran
**area(s) of operation:** operational in the north and east; majority of members inside Syria are Syrian Kurds, along with Kurds from Iran, Iraq, and Turkey (April 2018)

### Mujahidin Shura Council in the Environs of Jerusalem (MSC):
**aim(s):** destroy the state of Israel; enhance its networks in Syria
**area(s) of operation:** maintains limited networks for operational planning against Israel (April 2018)

### Palestine Liberation Front (PLF):
**aim(s):** enhances its networks and, ultimately, destroy the state of Israel and establish a secular, Marxist Palestinian state with Jerusalem as its capital
**area(s) of operation:** maintains a recruitment and training presence in many refugee camps (April 2018)

### PFLP-General Command (PFLP-GC):
**aim(s):** preserve Syrian President Bashar al-ASAD's regime
**area(s) of operation:** maintains a political base in Damascus; fights with President al-ASAD's forces and Hizballah in areas where anti-regime paramilitary groups are active (April 2018)

### Popular Front for the Liberation of Palestine (PFLP):
**aim(s):** enhance its recruitment networks in Syria
**area(s) of operation:** maintains a recruitment and limited training presence in several refugee camps (April 2018)

# TRANSNATIONAL ISSUES :: SYRIA

## DISPUTES - INTERNATIONAL:

Golan Heights is Israeli-occupied with the almost 1,000-strong UN Disengagement Observer Force patrolling a buffer zone since 1964lacking a treaty or other documentation describing the boundary, portions of the Lebanon-Syria boundary are unclear with several sections in disputesince 2000, Lebanon has claimed Shab'a Farms in the Golan Heights2004 Agreement and pending demarcation would settle border dispute with Jordan

## REFUGEES AND INTERNALLY DISPLACED PERSONS:

**refugees (country of origin):** 438,000 (Palestinian Refugees), 16,879 (Iraq) (2017)

**IDPs:** 6.784 million (ongoing civil war since 2011) (2017)

**stateless persons:** 160,000 (2017); note - Syria's stateless population consists of Kurds and Palestinians; stateless persons are prevented from voting, owning land, holding certain jobs, receiving food subsidies or public healthcare, enrolling in public schools, or being legally married to Syrian citizens; in 1962, some 120,000 Syrian Kurds were stripped of their Syrian citizenship, rendering them and their descendants stateless; in 2011, the Syrian Government granted citizenship to thousands of Syrian Kurds as a means of appeasement; however, resolving the question of statelessness is not a priority given Syria's ongoing civil war

**note:** the ongoing civil war has resulted in just over 5.6 million registered Syrian refugees - dispersed in Egypt, Iraq, Jordan, Lebanon, and Turkey - as of December 2018

## TRAFFICKING IN PERSONS:

**current situation:** as conditions continue to deteriorate due to Syria's civil war, human trafficking has increased; Syrians remaining in the country and those that are refugees abroad are vulnerable to trafficking; Syria is a source and destination country for men, women and children subjected to forced labor and sex trafficking; Syrian children continue to be forcibly recruited by government forces, pro-regime militias, armed opposition groups, and terrorist organizations to serve as soldiers, human shields, and executioners; ISIL forces Syrian women and girls and Yazidi women and girls taken from Iraq to marry its fighters, where they experience domestic servitude and sexual violence; Syrian refugee women and girls are forced into exploitive marriages or prostitution in neighboring countries, while displaced children are forced into street begging domestically and abroad

**tier rating:** Tier 3 - the government does not fully comply with the minimum standards for the elimination of trafficking and is not making significant efforts to do so; in 2014, Syria's violent conditions enabled human trafficking to flourish; the government made no effort to investigate, prosecute, or convict trafficking offenders or complicit government officials, including those who forcibly recruited child soldiers; authorities did not identify victims and failed to ensure victims, including child soldiers, were protected from arrest, detention, and severe abuse as a result of being trafficked (2015)

## ILLICIT DRUGS:

a transit point for opiates, hashish, and cocaine bound for regional and Western markets; weak anti-money-laundering controls and bank privatization may leave it vulnerable to money laundering

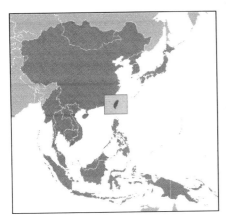

# EAST ASIA / SOUTHEAST ASIA :: TAIWAN

## INTRODUCTION :: TAIWAN

### BACKGROUND:

First inhabited by Austronesian people, Taiwan became home to Han immigrants beginning in the late Ming Dynasty (17th century). In 1895, military defeat forced China's Qing Dynasty to cede Taiwan to Japan, which then governed Taiwan for 50 years. Taiwan came under Chinese Nationalist (Kuomintang, KMT) control after World War II. With the communist victory in the Chinese civil war in 1949, the Nationalist-controlled Republic of China government and 2 million Nationalists fled to Taiwan and continued to claim to be the legitimate government for mainland China and Taiwan based on a 1947 Constitution drawn up for all of China. Until 1987, however, the Nationalist government ruled Taiwan under a civil war martial law declaration dating to 1948. Beginning in the 1970s, Nationalist authorities gradually began to incorporate the native population into the governing structure beyond the local level. The democratization process expanded rapidly in the 1980s, leading to the then illegal founding of Taiwan's first opposition party (the Democratic Progressive Party or DPP) in 1986 and the lifting of martial law the following year. Taiwan held legislative elections in 1992, the first in over forty years, and its first direct presidential election in 1996. In the 2000 presidential elections, Taiwan underwent its first peaceful transfer of power with the KMT loss to the DPP and afterwards experienced two additional democratic transfers of power in 2008 and 2016. Throughout this period, the island prospered, became one of East Asia's economic "Tigers," and after 2000 became a major investor in mainland China as cross-Strait ties matured. The dominant political issues continue to be economic reform and growth as well as management of sensitive relations between Taiwan and China.

## GEOGRAPHY :: TAIWAN

### LOCATION:

Eastern Asia, islands bordering the East China Sea, Philippine Sea, South China Sea, and Taiwan Strait, north of the Philippines, off the southeastern coast of China

### GEOGRAPHIC COORDINATES:

23 30 N, 121 00 E

### MAP REFERENCES:

Southeast Asia

### AREA:

**total:** 35,980 sq km

**land:** 32,260 sq km

**water:** 3,720 sq km

**note:** includes the Pescadores, Matsu, and Quemoy islands

**country comparison to the world:** 139

### AREA - COMPARATIVE:

slightly smaller than Maryland and Delaware combined

### LAND BOUNDARIES:

0 km

### COASTLINE:

1,566.3 km

### MARITIME CLAIMS:

**territorial sea:** 12 nm

**exclusive economic zone:** 200 nm

### CLIMATE:

tropical; marine; rainy season during southwest monsoon (June to August); persistent and extensive cloudiness all year

### TERRAIN:

eastern two-thirds mostly rugged mountains; flat to gently rolling plains in west

### ELEVATION:

**mean elevation:** 1,150 m

**elevation extremes:** 0 m lowest point: South China Sea

3952 highest point: Yu Shan

### NATURAL RESOURCES:

small deposits of coal, natural gas, limestone, marble, asbestos, arable land

### LAND USE:

**agricultural land:** 22.7% (2011 est.)

**arable land:** 16.9% (2011 est.) / **permanent crops:** 5.8% (2011 est.)

**other:** 77.3% (2011 est.)

### IRRIGATED LAND:

3,820 sq km (2012)

### POPULATION DISTRIBUTION:

distribution exhibits a peripheral coastal settlement pattern, with the largest populations on the north and west coasts

### NATURAL HAZARDS:

earthquakes; typhoons

**volcanism:** Kueishantao Island (401 m), east of Taiwan, is its only historically active volcano, although it has not erupted in centuries

### ENVIRONMENT - CURRENT ISSUES:

air pollution; water pollution from industrial emissions, raw sewage; contamination of drinking water supplies; trade in endangered species; low-level radioactive waste disposal

### ENVIRONMENT - INTERNATIONAL AGREEMENTS:

party to: none of the selected agreements because of Taiwan's international status

### GEOGRAPHY - NOTE:

strategic location adjacent to both the Taiwan Strait and the Luzon Strait

## PEOPLE AND SOCIETY :: TAIWAN

### POPULATION:

23,545,963 (July 2018 est.)

country comparison to the world: 55

### NATIONALITY:

noun: Taiwan (singular and plural)

adjective: Taiwan (or Taiwanese)

note: example - he or she is from Taiwan; they are from Taiwan

### ETHNIC GROUPS:

more than 95% Han Chinese (including Hoklo, who compose approximately 70% of Taiwan's population, Hakka, and other groups originating in mainland China), 2.3% indigenous Malayo-Polynesian peoples

note 1: there are 16 officially recognized indigenous groups: Amis, Atayal, Bunun, Hla'alua, Kanakaravu, Kavalan, Paiwan, Puyuma, Rukai, Saisiyat, Sakizaya, Seediq, Thao, Truku, Tsou, and Yami; Amis, Paiwan, and Atayal are the largest and account for roughly 70% of the indigenous population

note 2: although not definitive, the majority of current genetic, archeological, and linguistic data support the theory that Taiwan is the ultimate source for the spread of humans across the Pacific to Polynesia; the expansion (ca. 3000 B.C. to A.D. 1200) took place via the Philippines and eastern Indonesia and reached Fiji and Tonga by about 900 B.C.; from there voyagers spread across all of the rest of the Pacific islands over the next two millennia

### LANGUAGES:

Mandarin Chinese (official), Taiwanese (Min Nan), Hakka dialects

### RELIGIONS:

Buddhist 35.3%, Taoist 33.2%, Christian 3.9%, Taoist or Confucian folk religionist approximately 10%, none or unspecified 18.2% (2005 est.)

### AGE STRUCTURE:

0-14 years: 12.68% (male 1,535,365/female 1,449,336)

15-24 years: 12.52% (male 1,509,023/female 1,438,278)

25-54 years: 46.08% (male 5,412,487/female 5,437,015)

55-64 years: 14.36% (male 1,652,683/female 1,729,571)

65 years and over: 14.36% (male 1,541,716/female 1,840,489) (2018 est.)

### DEPENDENCY RATIOS:

total dependency ratio: 35.2 (2015 est.)

youth dependency ratio: 18.6 (2015 est.)

elderly dependency ratio: 16.6 (2015 est.)

potential support ratio: 6 (2015 est.)

### MEDIAN AGE:

total: 41.3 years

male: 40.5 years

female: 42 years (2018 est.)

country comparison to the world: 41

### POPULATION GROWTH RATE:

0.15% (2018 est.)

country comparison to the world: 184

### BIRTH RATE:

8.2 births/1,000 population (2018 est.)

country comparison to the world: 221

### DEATH RATE:

7.6 deaths/1,000 population (2018 est.)

country comparison to the world: 107

### NET MIGRATION RATE:

0.9 migrant(s)/1,000 population (2017 est.)

country comparison to the world: 58

### POPULATION DISTRIBUTION:

distribution exhibits a peripheral coastal settlement pattern, with the largest populations on the north and west coasts

### URBANIZATION:

urban population: 78.2% of total population (2018)

rate of urbanization: 0.8% annual rate of change (2015-20 est.)

### MAJOR URBAN AREAS - POPULATION:

4.325 million New Taipei City, 2.706 million TAIPEI (capital), 2.19 million Taiyuan, 1.532 million Kaohsiung, 1.283 million Taichung, 836,000 Tainan (2018)

### SEX RATIO:

at birth: 1.06 male(s)/female (2017 est.)

0-14 years: 1.06 male(s)/female (2017 est.)

15-24 years: 1.05 male(s)/female (2017 est.)

25-54 years: 1 male(s)/female (2017 est.)

55-64 years: 0.96 male(s)/female (2017 est.)

65 years and over: 0.86 male(s)/female (2017 est.)

total population: 0.99 male(s)/female (2017 est.)

### INFANT MORTALITY RATE:

total: 4.3 deaths/1,000 live births (2018 est.)

male: 4.7 deaths/1,000 live births (2018 est.)

female: 3.9 deaths/1,000 live births (2018 est.)

country comparison to the world: 186

### LIFE EXPECTANCY AT BIRTH:

total population: 80.4 years (2018 est.)

male: 77.2 years (2018 est.)

female: 83.7 years (2018 est.)

country comparison to the world: 43

### TOTAL FERTILITY RATE:

1.13 children born/woman (2018 est.)

country comparison to the world: 222

### HIV/AIDS - ADULT PREVALENCE RATE:

NA

### HIV/AIDS - PEOPLE LIVING WITH HIV/AIDS:

NA

### HIV/AIDS - DEATHS:

NA

### LITERACY:

definition: age 15 and over can read and write (2014 est.)

total population: 98.5% (2014 est.)

male: 99.7% (2014 est.)

female: 97.3% (2014 est.)

# GOVERNMENT :: TAIWAN

**COUNTRY NAME:**

*conventional long form:* none

*conventional short form:* Taiwan

*local long form:* none

*local short form:* Taiwan

*former:* Formosa

*etymology:* "Tayowan" was the name of the coastal sandbank where the Dutch erected their colonial headquarters on the island in the 17th century; the former name "Formosa" means "beautiful" in Portuguese

**GOVERNMENT TYPE:**

semi-presidential republic

**CAPITAL:**

*name:* Taipei

*geographic coordinates:* 25 02 N, 121 31 E

*time difference:* UTC+8 (13 hours ahead of Washington, DC, during Standard Time)

**ADMINISTRATIVE DIVISIONS:**

includes main island of Taiwan plus smaller islands nearby and off coast of China's Fujian Province; Taiwan is divided into 13 counties (xian, singular and plural), 3 cities (shi, singular and plural), and 6 special municipalities directly under the jurisdiction of the Executive Yuan

*counties:* Changhua, Chiayi, Hsinchu, Hualien, Kinmen, Lienchiang, Miaoli, Nantou, Penghu, Pingtung, Taitung, Yilan, Yunlin;

*cities:* Chiayi, Hsinchu, Keelung;

*special municipalities:* Kaohsiung (city), New Taipei (city), Taichung (city), Tainan (city), Taipei (city), Taoyuan (city)

*note:* Taiwan uses a variety of romanization systems; while a modified Wade-Giles system still dominates, the city of Taipei has adopted a Pinyin romanization for street and place names within its boundaries; other local authorities use different romanization systems

**NATIONAL HOLIDAY:**

Republic Day (National Day), 10 October (1911); note - celebrates the anniversary of the Chinese Revolution, also known as Double Ten (10-10) Day

**CONSTITUTION:**

*history:* previous 1912, 1931; latest adopted 25 December 1946, promulgated 1 January 1947, effective 25 December 1947 (2017)

*amendments:* proposed by at least one-fourth agreement of the Legislative Yuan membership; passage requires approval by at least three-fourths majority vote of at least three-fourths of the Legislative Yuan membership and approval in a referendum by more than half of eligible voters; revised several times, last in 2005 (2017)

**LEGAL SYSTEM:**

civil law system

**INTERNATIONAL LAW ORGANIZATION PARTICIPATION:**

has not submitted an ICJ jurisdiction declaration; non-party state to the ICCt

**CITIZENSHIP:**

*citizenship by birth:* no

*citizenship by descent only:* at least one parent must be a citizen of Taiwan

*dual citizenship recognized:* yes, except that citizens of Taiwan are not recognized as dual citizens of the People's Republic of China

*residency requirement for naturalization:* 5 years

**SUFFRAGE:**

20 years of age; universal; note - in mid-2016, the Legislative Yuan drafted a constitutional amendment to reduce the voting age to 18, but it has not passed as of December 2017

**EXECUTIVE BRANCH:**

*chief of state:* President TSAI Ing-wen (since 20 May 2016); Vice President CHEN Chien-jen (since 20 May 2016)

*head of government:* Premier LAI Ching-te (President of the Executive Yuan) (since 8 September 2017); Vice Premier SHIH Jun-ji, Vice President of the Executive Yuan (since 8 September 2017)

*cabinet:* Executive Yuan - ministers appointed by president on recommendation of premier

*elections/appointments:* president and vice president directly elected on the same ballot by simple majority popular vote for a 4-year term (eligible for a second term); election last held on 16 January 2016 (next to be held in early 2020); premier appointed by the president; vice premiers appointed by the president on the recommendation of the premier

*election results:* TSAI Ing-wen elected president; percent of vote - TSAI Ing-wen (DPP) 56.1%, Eric CHU Li-lun (KMT) 31.0%, James SOONG Chu-yu (PFP) 12.8%; note - TSAI is the first woman elected president of Taiwan

**LEGISLATIVE BRANCH:**

*description:* unicameral Legislative Yuan (113 seats; 73 members directly elected in single-seat constituencies by simple majority vote, 34 directly elected in a single island-wide constituency by proportional representation vote, and 6 directly elected in multi-seat aboriginal constituencies by proportional representation vote; members serve 4-year terms)

*elections:* last held on 16 January 2016 (next to be held in early 2020)

*election results:* percent of vote by party - NA; seats by party - DPP 68, KMT 35, NPP 5, PFP 3, NPSU 1, independent 1; compostion - men 70, women 43, percent of women 38.1%; note - this is the first non-KMT-led legislature in Taiwan's history

**JUDICIAL BRANCH:**

*highest courts:* Supreme Court (consists of the court president, vice president, and approximately 100 judges organized into 8 civil and 12 criminal divisions, each with a division chief justice and 4 associate justices); Constitutional Court (consists of the court president, vice president, and 13 justices)

*judge selection and term of office:* Supreme Court justices appointed by the president; Constitutional Court justices appointed by the president with approval of the Legislative Yuan; Supreme Court justices appointed for life; Constitutional Court justices appointed for 8-year terms with half the membership renewed every 4 years

*subordinate courts:* high courts; district courts; hierarchy of administrative courts

**POLITICAL PARTIES AND LEADERS:**

Democratic Progressive Party or DPP [LIN Yu-chang, acting chair]
Kuomintang or KMT (Nationalist Party) [WU Den-yih]
New Power Party or NPP [HUANG Kuo-chang]
Non-Partisan Solidarity Union or NPSU [LIN Pin-kuan]
People First Party or PFP [James SOONG Chu-yu]

**INTERNATIONAL ORGANIZATION PARTICIPATION:**

ADB (Taipei, China), APEC (Chinese Taipei), BCIE, IOC, ITUC (NGOs), SICA (observer), WTO (Taipei, China);

note - separate customs territory of Taiwan, Penghu, Kinmen, and Matsu

**DIPLOMATIC REPRESENTATION IN THE US:**

telephone: [1] 202 895-1800

office: 4201 Wisconsin Avenue NW, Washington, DC 20016

representative: Stanley KAO (since 5 June 2016)

Taipei Economic and Cultural Offices (branch offices): Atlanta, Boston, Chicago, Denver (CO), Houston, Honolulu, Los Angeles, Miami, New York, San Francisco, Seattle

none; commercial and cultural relations with its citizens in the US are maintained through an unofficial instrumentality, the Taipei Economic and Cultural Representative Office in the United States (TECRO), a private nonprofit corporation that performs citizen and consular services similar to those at diplomatic posts

**DIPLOMATIC REPRESENTATION FROM THE US:**

chief of mission: Director William Brent CHRISTIENSEN (since 11 August 2018)

telephone: [886] 7-335-5006

FAX: [886] 7-338-0551

office: #7 Lane 134, Hsin Yi Road, Section 3, Taipei 10659, Taiwan

other offices: Kaohsiung (Branch Office)

none; commercial and cultural relations with the people of Taiwan are maintained through an unofficial instrumentality, the American Institute in Taiwan (AIT), a private nonprofit corporation that performs citizen and consular services similar to those at diplomatic posts

**FLAG DESCRIPTION:**

red field with a dark blue rectangle in the upper hoist-side corner bearing a white sun with 12 triangular rays; the blue and white design of the canton (symbolizing the sun of progress) dates to 1895; it was later adopted as the flag of the Kuomintang Party; blue signifies liberty, justice, and democracy, red stands for fraternity, sacrifice, and nationalism, and white represents equality, frankness, and the people's livelihood; the 12 rays of the sun are those of the months and the twelve traditional Chinese hours (each ray equals two hours)

note: similar to the flag of Samoa

**NATIONAL SYMBOL(S):**

white, 12-rayed sun on blue field; national colors: blue, white, red

**NATIONAL ANTHEM:**

name: "Zhonghua Minguo guoge" (National Anthem of the Republic of China)

lyrics/music: HU Han-min, TAI Chi-t'ao, and LIAO Chung-k'ai/CHENG Mao-Yun

note: adopted 1930; also the song of the Kuomintang Party; it is informally known as "San Min Chu I" or "San Min Zhu Yi" (Three Principles of the People); because of political pressure from China, "Guo Qi Ge" (National Banner Song) is used at international events rather than the official anthem of Taiwan; the "National Banner Song" has gained popularity in Taiwan and is commonly used during flag raisings

# ECONOMY :: TAIWAN

**ECONOMY - OVERVIEW:**

Taiwan has a dynamic capitalist economy that is driven largely by industrial manufacturing, and especially exports of electronics, machinery, and petrochemicals. This heavy dependence on exports exposes the economy to fluctuations in global demand. Taiwan's diplomatic isolation, low birth rate, rapidly aging population, and increasing competition from China and other Asia Pacific markets are other major long-term challenges.

Following the landmark Economic Cooperation Framework Agreement (ECFA) signed with China in June 2010, Taiwan in July 2013 signed a free trade deal with New Zealand - Taipei's first-ever with a country with which it does not maintain diplomatic relations - and, in November of that year, inked a trade pact with Singapore. However, follow-on components of the ECFA, including a signed agreement on trade in services and negotiations on trade in goods and dispute resolution, have stalled. In early 2014, the government bowed to public demand and proposed a new law governing the oversight of cross-Strait agreements, before any additional deals with China are implemented; the legislature has yet to vote on such legislation, leaving the future of ECFA uncertain. President TSAI since taking office in May 2016 has promoted greater economic integration with South and Southeast Asia through the New Southbound Policy initiative and has also expressed interest in Taiwan joining the Trans-Pacific Partnership as well as bilateral trade deals with partners such as the US. These overtures have likely played a role in increasing Taiwan's total exports, which rose 11% during the first half of 2017, buoyed by strong demand for semiconductors.

Taiwan's total fertility rate of just over one child per woman is among the lowest in the world, raising the prospect of future labor shortages, falling domestic demand, and declining tax revenues. Taiwan's population is aging quickly, with the number of people over 65 expected to account for nearly 20% of the island's total population by 2025.

The island runs a trade surplus with many economies, including China and the US, and its foreign reserves are the world's fifth largest, behind those of China, Japan, Saudi Arabia, and Switzerland. In 2006, China overtook the US to become Taiwan's second-largest source of imports after Japan. China is also the island's number one destination for foreign direct investment. Taiwan since 2009 has gradually loosened rules governing Chinese investment and has also secured greater market access for its investors on the mainland. In August 2012, the Taiwan Central Bank signed a memorandum of understanding (MOU) on cross-Strait currency settlement with its Chinese counterpart. The MOU allows for the direct settlement of Chinese renminbi (RMB) and the New Taiwan dollar across the Strait, which has helped Taiwan develop into a local RMB hub.

Closer economic links with the mainland bring opportunities for Taiwan's economy but also pose challenges as political differences remain unresolved and China's economic growth is slowing. President TSAI's administration has made little progress on the domestic economic issues that loomed large when she was elected, including concerns about stagnant wages, high housing prices, youth unemployment, job security, and financial security in retirement. TSAI has made more progress on boosting trade with South and

Southeast Asia, which may help insulate Taiwan's economy from a fall in mainland demand should China's growth slow in 2018.

**GDP (PURCHASING POWER PARITY):**

$1.189 trillion (2017 est.)

$1.156 trillion (2016 est.)

$1.14 trillion (2015 est.)

note: data are in 2017 dollars

country comparison to the world: 22

**GDP (OFFICIAL EXCHANGE RATE):**

$572.6 billion (2017 est.) (2017 est.)

**GDP - REAL GROWTH RATE:**

2.9% (2017 est.)

1.4% (2016 est.)

0.8% (2015 est.)

country comparison to the world: 119

**GDP - PER CAPITA (PPP):**

$50,500 (2017 est.)

$49,100 (2016 est.)

$48,500 (2015 est.)

note: data are in 2017 dollars

country comparison to the world: 28

**GROSS NATIONAL SAVING:**

34.9% of GDP (2017 est.)

35.5% of GDP (2016 est.)

36.3% of GDP (2015 est.)

country comparison to the world: 17

**GDP - COMPOSITION, BY END USE:**

household consumption: 53% (2017 est.)

government consumption: 14.1% (2017 est.)

investment in fixed capital: 20.5% (2017 est.)

investment in inventories: -0.2% (2017 est.)

exports of goods and services: 65.2% (2017 est.)

imports of goods and services: -52.6% (2017 est.)

**GDP - COMPOSITION, BY SECTOR OF ORIGIN:**

agriculture: 1.8% (2017 est.)

industry: 36% (2017 est.)

services: 62.1% (2017 est.)

**AGRICULTURE - PRODUCTS:**

rice, vegetables, fruit, tea, flowers; pigs, poultry; fish

**INDUSTRIES:**

electronics, communications and information technology products, petroleum refining, chemicals, textiles, iron and steel, machinery, cement, food processing, vehicles, consumer products, pharmaceuticals

**INDUSTRIAL PRODUCTION GROWTH RATE:**

3.9% (2017 est.)

country comparison to the world: 79

**LABOR FORCE:**

11.78 million (2017 est.)

country comparison to the world: 51

**LABOR FORCE - BY OCCUPATION:**

agriculture: 4.9%

industry: 35.9%

services: 59.2% (2016 est.)

**UNEMPLOYMENT RATE:**

3.8% (2017 est.)

3.9% (2016 est.)

country comparison to the world: 47

**POPULATION BELOW POVERTY LINE:**

1.5% (2012 est.)

**HOUSEHOLD INCOME OR CONSUMPTION BY PERCENTAGE SHARE:**

lowest 10%: 6.4% (2010)

highest 10%: 40.3% (2010)

**DISTRIBUTION OF FAMILY INCOME - GINI INDEX:**

33.6 (2014)

32.6 (2000)

country comparison to the world: 112

**BUDGET:**

revenues: 91.62 billion (2017 est.)

expenditures: 92.03 billion (2017 est.)

**TAXES AND OTHER REVENUES:**

16% (of GDP) (2017 est.)

country comparison to the world: 184

**BUDGET SURPLUS (+) OR DEFICIT (-):**

-0.1% (of GDP) (2017 est.)

country comparison to the world: 50

**PUBLIC DEBT:**

35.7% of GDP (2017 est.)

36.2% of GDP (2016 est.)

note: data for central government

country comparison to the world: 149

**FISCAL YEAR:**

calendar year

**INFLATION RATE (CONSUMER PRICES):**

1.1% (2017 est.)

1% (2016 est.)

country comparison to the world: 61

**CENTRAL BANK DISCOUNT RATE:**

1.38% (31 December 2016)

1.63% (31 December 2015)

country comparison to the world: 129

**COMMERCIAL BANK PRIME LENDING RATE:**

2.63% (31 December 2017 est.)

2.63% (31 December 2016 est.)

country comparison to the world: 178

**STOCK OF NARROW MONEY:**

$560.9 billion (31 December 2017 est.)

$501.2 billion (31 December 2016 est.)

country comparison to the world: 11

**STOCK OF BROAD MONEY:**

$560.9 billion (31 December 2017 est.)

$501.2 billion (31 December 2016 est.)

country comparison to the world: 11

**STOCK OF DOMESTIC CREDIT:**

$880.8 billion (31 December 2017 est.)

$778.3 billion (31 December 2016 est.)

country comparison to the world: 18

**MARKET VALUE OF PUBLICLY TRADED SHARES:**

$851.2 billion (31 December 2016)

$742.5 billion (31 December 2015)

$848.3 billion (31 December 2014)

country comparison to the world: 13

**CURRENT ACCOUNT BALANCE:**

$82.88 billion (2017 est.)

$72.78 billion (2016 est.)

country comparison to the world: 5

**EXPORTS:**

$349.8 billion (2017 est.)

$310.4 billion (2016 est.)

country comparison to the world: 15

**EXPORTS - COMMODITIES:**

semiconductors, petrochemicals, automobile/auto parts, ships, wireless communication equipment, flat display displays, steel, electronics, plastics, computers

**IMPORTS:**

$269 billion (2017 est.)

$239.3 billion (2016 est.)

country comparison to the world: 18

**IMPORTS - COMMODITIES:**

oil/petroleum, semiconductors, natural gas, coal, steel, computers, wireless communication equipment, automobiles, fine chemicals, textiles

**RESERVES OF FOREIGN EXCHANGE AND GOLD:**

$456.7 billion (31 December 2017 est.)

$439 billion (31 December 2016 est.)

country comparison to the world: 5

**DEBT - EXTERNAL:**

$181.9 billion (31 December 2017 est.)

$172.2 billion (31 December 2016 est.)

country comparison to the world: 38

**STOCK OF DIRECT FOREIGN INVESTMENT - AT HOME:**

$78.3 billion (31 December 2017 est.)

$80.68 billion (31 December 2016 est.)

country comparison to the world: 51

**STOCK OF DIRECT FOREIGN INVESTMENT - ABROAD:**

$332.4 billion (31 December 2017 est.)

$354 billion (31 December 2016 est.)

country comparison to the world: 22

**EXCHANGE RATES:**

New Taiwan dollars (TWD) per US dollar -

30.68 (2017 est.)

32.325 (2016 est.)

32.325 (2015 est.)

31.911 (2014 est.)

30.363 (2013 est.)

## ENERGY :: TAIWAN

**ELECTRICITY - PRODUCTION:**

246.1 billion kWh (2016 est.)

country comparison to the world: 18

**ELECTRICITY - CONSUMPTION:**

237.4 billion kWh (2016 est.)

country comparison to the world: 16

**ELECTRICITY - EXPORTS:**

0 kWh (2016 est.)

country comparison to the world: 205

**ELECTRICITY - IMPORTS:**

0 kWh (2016 est.)

country comparison to the world: 208

**ELECTRICITY - INSTALLED GENERATING CAPACITY:**

49.52 million kW (2016 est.)

country comparison to the world: 22

**ELECTRICITY - FROM FOSSIL FUELS:**

79% of total installed capacity (2016 est.)

country comparison to the world: 88

**ELECTRICITY - FROM NUCLEAR FUELS:**

11% of total installed capacity (2017 est.)

country comparison to the world: 14

**ELECTRICITY - FROM HYDROELECTRIC PLANTS:**

4% of total installed capacity (2017 est.)

country comparison to the world: 133

**ELECTRICITY - FROM OTHER RENEWABLE SOURCES:**

6% of total installed capacity (2017 est.)

country comparison to the world: 105

**CRUDE OIL - PRODUCTION:**

196 bbl/day (2017 est.)

country comparison to the world: 96

**CRUDE OIL - EXPORTS:**

0 bbl/day (2015 est.)

country comparison to the world: 203

**CRUDE OIL - IMPORTS:**

846,400 bbl/day (2015 est.)

country comparison to the world: 13

**CRUDE OIL - PROVED RESERVES:**

2.38 million bbl (1 January 2018 est.)

country comparison to the world: 95

**REFINED PETROLEUM PRODUCTS - PRODUCTION:**

924,000 bbl/day (2015 est.)

country comparison to the world: 21

**REFINED PETROLEUM PRODUCTS - CONSUMPTION:**

962,400 bbl/day (2016 est.)

country comparison to the world: 22

**REFINED PETROLEUM PRODUCTS - EXPORTS:**

349,600 bbl/day (2015 est.)

country comparison to the world: 26

**REFINED PETROLEUM PRODUCTS - IMPORTS:**

418,300 bbl/day (2015 est.)

country comparison to the world: 20

**NATURAL GAS - PRODUCTION:**

237.9 million cu m (2017 est.)

country comparison to the world: 77

**NATURAL GAS - CONSUMPTION:**

22.45 billion cu m (2017 est.)

country comparison to the world: 34

**NATURAL GAS - EXPORTS:**

0 cu m (2017 est.)

country comparison to the world: 196

**NATURAL GAS - IMPORTS:**

22.14 billion cu m (2017 est.)

country comparison to the world: 15

**NATURAL GAS - PROVED RESERVES:**

6.229 billion cu m (1 January 2018 est.)

country comparison to the world: 86

**CARBON DIOXIDE EMISSIONS FROM CONSUMPTION OF ENERGY:**

348.8 million Mt (2017 est.)

country comparison to the world: 21

## COMMUNICATIONS :: TAIWAN

**TELEPHONES - FIXED LINES:**

total subscriptions: 13,565,064 (2017 est.)

subscriptions per 100 inhabitants: 58 (2017 est.)

country comparison to the world: 16

**TELEPHONES - MOBILE CELLULAR:**

total subscriptions: 28,777,408 (2017 est.)

subscriptions per 100 inhabitants: 122 (2017 est.)

country comparison to the world: 44

**TELEPHONE SYSTEM:**

general assessment: provides telecommunications service for every business and private need (2016)

domestic: thoroughly modern; completely digitalized (2016)

international: country code - 886; roughly 15 submarine fiber cables provide links throughout Asia, Australia, the Middle East, Europe, and the US; satellite earth stations - 2 (2016)

**BROADCAST MEDIA:**

5 nationwide television networks operating roughly 75 TV stations; about 60% of households utilize multi-channel cable TV; national and regional radio networks with about 171 radio stations (2016)

**INTERNET COUNTRY CODE:**

.tw

**INTERNET USERS:**

total: 20.601 million (July 2016 est.)

percent of population: 88% (July 2016 est.)

country comparison to the world: 32

**BROADBAND - FIXED SUBSCRIPTIONS:**

total: 5,713,568 (2017 est.)

subscriptions per 100 inhabitants: 24 (2017 est.)

country comparison to the world: 26

# TRANSPORTATION :: TAIWAN

**NATIONAL AIR TRANSPORT SYSTEM:**

number of registered air carriers: 8 (2015)

inventory of registered aircraft operated by air carriers: 221 (2015)

**CIVIL AIRCRAFT REGISTRATION COUNTRY CODE PREFIX:**

B (2016)

**AIRPORTS:**

37 (2013)

country comparison to the world: 108

**AIRPORTS - WITH PAVED RUNWAYS:**

total: 35 (2013)

over 3,047 m: 8 (2013)

2,438 to 3,047 m: 7 (2013)

1,524 to 2,437 m: 10 (2013)

914 to 1,523 m: 8 (2013)

under 914 m: 2 (2013)

**AIRPORTS - WITH UNPAVED RUNWAYS:**

total: 2 (2013)

1,524 to 2,437 m: 1 (2013)

under 914 m: 1 (2013)

**HELIPORTS:**

31 (2013)

**PIPELINES:**

25 km condensate, 802 km gas, 241 km oil (2013)

**RAILWAYS:**

total: 1,613 km (2018)

standard gauge: 345 km 1.435-m gauge (345 km electrified) (2018)

narrow gauge: 1,118.1 km 1.067-m gauge (793.9 km electrified) (2018)

150 0.762-m gauge

note: the 0.762-gauge track belongs to three entities: the Forestry Bureau, Taiwan Cement, and TaiPower

country comparison to the world: 81

**ROADWAYS:**

total: 43,365 km (2016)

paved: 42,969 km (includes 1,348 km of highways and 737 km of expressways) (2016)

unpaved: 396 km (2016)

country comparison to the world: 85

**MERCHANT MARINE:**

total: 350 (2017)

by type: bulk carrier 26, container ship 38, general cargo 59, oil tanker 24, other 203 (2017)

country comparison to the world: 49

**PORTS AND TERMINALS:**

major seaport(s): Keelung (Chi-lung), Kaohsiung, Hualian, Taichung

container port(s) (TEUs): Kaohsiung (10,464,860), Taichung (1,535,011), Taipei (1,477,330) (2016)

LNG terminal(s) (import): Yung An (Kaohsiung), Taichung

# MILITARY AND SECURITY :: TAIWAN

**MILITARY BRANCHES:**

Army, Navy (includes Marine Corps), Air Force, Military Police Command, Armed Forces Reserve Command, Coast Guard Administration (2016)

**MILITARY SERVICE AGE AND OBLIGATION:**

starting with those born in 1994, males 18-36 years of age may volunteer for military service or must complete 4 months of compulsory military training (or substitute civil service in some cases); men born before December 1993 are required to complete compulsory service for 1 year (military or civil); men are subject to training recalls up to four times for periods not to exceed 20 days for 8 years after discharge; women may enlist, but are restricted to noncombat roles in most cases; Taiwan is planning to implement an all-volunteer military in 2018 (2017)

# TRANSNATIONAL ISSUES :: TAIWAN

**DISPUTES - INTERNATIONAL:**

involved in complex dispute with Brunei, China, Malaysia, the Philippines, and Vietnam over the Spratly Islands, and with China and the Philippines over Scarborough Reefthe 2002 "Declaration on the Conduct of Parties in the South China Sea" has eased tensions but falls short of a legally binding "code of conduct" desired by several of the disputantsParacel Islands are occupied by China, but claimed by Taiwan and Vietnamin 2003, China and Taiwan became more vocal in rejecting both Japan's claims to the uninhabited islands of the Senkaku-shoto (Diaoyu Tai) and Japan's unilaterally declared exclusive economic zone in the East China Sea where all parties engage in hydrocarbon prospecting

**ILLICIT DRUGS:**

regional transit point for heroin, methamphetamine, and precursor chemicals; transshipment point for drugs to Japan; major problem with domestic consumption of methamphetamine and heroin; rising problems with use of ketamine and club drugs

# CENTRAL ASIA :: TAJIKISTAN

## INTRODUCTION :: TAJIKISTAN

### BACKGROUND:

The Tajik people came under Russian rule in the 1860s and 1870s, but Russia's hold on Central Asia weakened following the Revolution of 1917. Bands of indigenous guerrillas (called "basmachi") fiercely contested Bolshevik control of the area, which was not fully reestablished until 1925. Tajikistan was first created as an autonomous republic within Uzbekistan in 1924, but the USSR designated Tajikistan a separate republic in 1929 and transferred to it much of present-day Sughd province. Ethnic Uzbeks form a substantial minority in Tajikistan, and ethnic Tajiks an even larger minority in Uzbekistan. Tajikistan became independent in 1991 following the breakup of the Soviet Union, and experienced a civil war between political, regional, and religious factions from 1992 to 1997.

Tajikistan has endured several domestic security incidents since 2010, including armed conflict between government forces and local strongmen in the Rasht Valley and between government forces and criminal groups in Gorno-Badakhshan Autonomous Oblast. In September 2015, government security forces rebuffed attacks led by a former high-ranking official in the Ministry of Defense. President Emomali RAHMON, who came to power during the civil war, used the attacks to ban the main opposition political party in Tajikistan. In May 2016, RAHMON further strengthened his position by having himself designated "Leader of the Nation" with limitless terms and lifelong immunity through constitutional amendments ratified in a referendum. The referendum also lowered the minimum age required to run for president from 35 to 30, which would make RAHMON's son Rustam EMOMALI, the current mayor of the capital Dushanbe, eligible to run for president in 2020. The country remains the poorest in the former Soviet sphere. Tajikistan became a member of the WTO in March 2013. However, its economy continues to face major challenges, including dependence on remittances from Tajiks working in Russia, pervasive corruption, and the opiate trade emanating from neighboring Afghanistan.

## GEOGRAPHY :: TAJIKISTAN

### LOCATION:

Central Asia, west of China, south of Kyrgyzstan

### GEOGRAPHIC COORDINATES:

39 00 N, 71 00 E

### MAP REFERENCES:

Asia

### AREA:

total: 144,100 sq km

land: 141,510 sq km

water: 2,590 sq km

country comparison to the world: 97

### AREA - COMPARATIVE:

slightly smaller than Wisconsin

### LAND BOUNDARIES:

total: 4,130 km

border countries (4): Afghanistan 1357 km, China 477 km, Kyrgyzstan 984 km, Uzbekistan 1312 km

### COASTLINE:

0 km (landlocked)

### MARITIME CLAIMS:

none (landlocked)

### CLIMATE:

mid-latitude continental, hot summers, mild winters; semiarid to polar in Pamir Mountains

### TERRAIN:

mountainous region dominated by the Trans-Alay Range in the north and the Pamirs in the southeast; western Fergana Valley in north, Kofarnihon and Vakhsh Valleys in southwest

### ELEVATION:

mean elevation: 3,186 m

elevation extremes: 300 m lowest point: Syr Darya (Sirdaryo)

7495 highest point: Qullai Ismoili Somoni

### NATURAL RESOURCES:

hydropower, some petroleum, uranium, mercury, brown coal, lead, zinc, antimony, tungsten, silver, gold

### LAND USE:

agricultural land: 34.7% (2011 est.)

arable land: 6.1% (2011 est.) / permanent crops: 0.9% (2011 est.) / permanent pasture: 27.7% (2011 est.)

forest: 2.9% (2011 est.)

other: 62.4% (2011 est.)

### IRRIGATED LAND:

7,420 sq km (2012)

### POPULATION DISTRIBUTION:

the country's population is concentrated at lower elevations, with perhaps as much as 90% of the people living in valleys; overall density increases from east to west

### NATURAL HAZARDS:

earthquakes; floods

### ENVIRONMENT - CURRENT ISSUES:

areas of high air pollution from motor vehicles and industry; water pollution from agricultural runoff and disposal of untreated industrial waste and sewage; poor management of water resources; soil erosion; increasing levels of soil salinity

**ENVIRONMENT - INTERNATIONAL AGREEMENTS:**

party to: Biodiversity, Climate Change, Climate Change-Kyoto Protocol, Desertification, Environmental Modification, Hazardous Wastes, Ozone Layer Protection, Wetlands

signed, but not ratified: none of the selected agreements

**GEOGRAPHY - NOTE:**

landlocked; highest point, Qullai Ismoili Somoni (formerly Communism Peak), was the tallest mountain in the former USSR

## PEOPLE AND SOCIETY :: TAJIKISTAN

**POPULATION:**

8,604,882 (July 2018 est.)

country comparison to the world: 97

**NATIONALITY:**

noun: Tajikistani(s)

adjective: Tajikistani

**ETHNIC GROUPS:**

Tajik 84.3% (includes Pamiri and Yagnobi), Uzbek 12.2%, other 3.5% (includes Kyrgyz, Russian, Turkmen, Tatar, Arab) (2010 est.)

**LANGUAGES:**

Tajik (official) 84.4%, Uzbek 11.9%, Kyrgyz .8%, Russian .5%, other 2.4% (2010 est.)

note: Russian widely used in government and business

**RELIGIONS:**

Muslim 96.7% (Sunni ~90%, Shia ~7%), Christian 1.6%, unaffiliated 1.5%, other .2% (2010 est.)

**AGE STRUCTURE:**

0-14 years: 32.05% (male 1,404,403 /female 1,353,704)

15-24 years: 18.35% (male 801,172 /female 777,524)

25-54 years: 40.34% (male 1,721,081 /female 1,749,819)

55-64 years: 5.85% (male 231,820 /female 271,946)

65 years and over: 3.41% (male 121,405 /female 172,008) (2018 est.)

**DEPENDENCY RATIOS:**

total dependency ratio: 62.5 (2015 est.)

youth dependency ratio: 57.1 (2015 est.)

elderly dependency ratio: 5.4 (2015 est.)

potential support ratio: 18.5 (2015 est.)

**MEDIAN AGE:**

total: 24.8 years

male: 24.2 years

female: 25.4 years (2018 est.)

country comparison to the world: 160

**POPULATION GROWTH RATE:**

1.58% (2018 est.)

country comparison to the world: 65

**BIRTH RATE:**

22.8 births/1,000 population (2018 est.)

country comparison to the world: 64

**DEATH RATE:**

5.9 deaths/1,000 population (2018 est.)

country comparison to the world: 169

**NET MIGRATION RATE:**

-1.1 migrant(s)/1,000 population (2017 est.)

country comparison to the world: 141

**POPULATION DISTRIBUTION:**

the country's population is concentrated at lower elevations, with perhaps as much as 90% of the people living in valleys; overall density increases from east to west

**URBANIZATION:**

urban population: 27.1% of total population (2018)

rate of urbanization: 2.62% annual rate of change (2015-20 est.)

**MAJOR URBAN AREAS - POPULATION:**

873,000 DUSHANBE (capital) (2018)

**SEX RATIO:**

at birth: 1.04 male(s)/female (2017 est.)

0-14 years: 1.04 male(s)/female (2017 est.)

15-24 years: 1.03 male(s)/female (2017 est.)

25-54 years: 0.98 male(s)/female (2017 est.)

55-64 years: 0.85 male(s)/female (2017 est.)

65 years and over: 0.72 male(s)/female (2017 est.)

total population: 0.99 male(s)/female (2017 est.)

**MOTHER'S MEAN AGE AT FIRST BIRTH:**

22 years (2017 est.)

note: median age at first birth among women 25-29

**MATERNAL MORTALITY RATE:**

32 deaths/100,000 live births (2015 est.)

country comparison to the world: 111

**INFANT MORTALITY RATE:**

total: 30.8 deaths/1,000 live births (2018 est.)

male: 34.8 deaths/1,000 live births (2018 est.)

female: 26.5 deaths/1,000 live births (2018 est.)

country comparison to the world: 59

**LIFE EXPECTANCY AT BIRTH:**

total population: 68.4 years (2018 est.)

male: 65.2 years (2018 est.)

female: 71.7 years (2018 est.)

country comparison to the world: 168

**TOTAL FERTILITY RATE:**

2.59 children born/woman (2018 est.)

country comparison to the world: 73

**CONTRACEPTIVE PREVALENCE RATE:**

27.9% (2012)

**HEALTH EXPENDITURES:**

6.9% of GDP (2014)

country comparison to the world: 86

**PHYSICIANS DENSITY:**

1.71 physicians/1,000 population (2014)

**HOSPITAL BED DENSITY:**

4.8 beds/1,000 population (2013)

**DRINKING WATER SOURCE:**

improved:

urban: 93.1% of population

rural: 66.7% of population

total: 73.8% of population

unimproved:

urban: 6.9% of population

rural: 33.3% of population

total: 26.2% of population (2015 est.)

**SANITATION FACILITY ACCESS:**

**improved:**

urban: 93.8% of population (2015 est.)

rural: 95.5% of population (2015 est.)

total: 95% of population (2015 est.)

**unimproved:**

urban: 6.2% of population (2015 est.)

rural: 4.5% of population (2015 est.)

total: 5% of population (2015 est.)

## HIV/AIDS - ADULT PREVALENCE RATE:
0.3% (2017 est.)

country comparison to the world: 88

## HIV/AIDS - PEOPLE LIVING WITH HIV/AIDS:
15,000 (2017 est.)

country comparison to the world: 88

## HIV/AIDS - DEATHS:
<1000 (2017 est.)

## MAJOR INFECTIOUS DISEASES:
degree of risk: high (2016)

food or waterborne diseases: bacterial diarrhea, hepatitis A, and typhoid fever (2016)

vectorborne diseases: malaria (2016)

## OBESITY - ADULT PREVALENCE RATE:
14.2% (2016)

country comparison to the world: 128

## CHILDREN UNDER THE AGE OF 5 YEARS UNDERWEIGHT:
13.3% (2012)

country comparison to the world: 50

## EDUCATION EXPENDITURES:
5.2% of GDP (2015)

country comparison to the world: 65

## LITERACY:
definition: age 15 and over can read and write (2015 est.)

total population: 99.8% (2015 est.)

male: 99.8% (2015 est.)

female: 99.7% (2015 est.)

## SCHOOL LIFE EXPECTANCY (PRIMARY TO TERTIARY EDUCATION):
total: 11 years (2013)

male: 12 years (2013)

female: 11 years (2013)

## UNEMPLOYMENT, YOUTH AGES 15-24:
total: 16.7% (2009 est.)

male: 19.2% (2009 est.)

female: 13.7% (2009 est.)

country comparison to the world: 81

# GOVERNMENT :: TAJIKISTAN

## COUNTRY NAME:
conventional long form: Republic of Tajikistan

conventional short form: Tajikistan

local long form: Jumhurii Tojikiston

local short form: Tojikiston

former: Tajik Soviet Socialist Republic

etymology: the Persian suffix "-stan" means "place of" or "country," so the word Tajikistan literally means "Land of the Tajik [people]"

## GOVERNMENT TYPE:
presidential republic

## CAPITAL:
name: Dushanbe

geographic coordinates: 38 33 N, 68 46 E

time difference: UTC+5 (10 hours ahead of Washington, DC, during Standard Time)

## ADMINISTRATIVE DIVISIONS:
2 provinces (viloyatho, singular - viloyat), 1 autonomous province* (viloyati mukhtor), 1 capital region** (viloyati poytakht), and 1 area referred to as Districts Under Republic Administration***; Dushanbe**, Khatlon (Qurghonteppa), Kuhistoni Badakhshon [Gorno-Badakhshan]* (Khorugh), Nohiyahoi Tobei Jumhuri***, Sughd (Khujand)

note: the administrative center name follows in parentheses

## INDEPENDENCE:
9 September 1991 (from the Soviet Union)

## NATIONAL HOLIDAY:
Independence Day (or National Day), 9 September (1991)

## CONSTITUTION:
history: several previous; latest adopted 6 November 1994 (2017)

amendments: proposed by the president of the republic or by at least one-third of the total membership of both houses of the Supreme Assembly; adoption of any amendment requires a referendum, which includes approval by the president or approval by at least two-thirds of the Assembly of Representatives membership; passage in a referendum requires participation of an absolute majority of eligible voters and an absolute majority of votes; note – constitutional articles including Tajikistan's form of government, its territory, and its democratic nature cannot be amended; amended several times, last in 2016 (2017)

## LEGAL SYSTEM:
civil law system

## INTERNATIONAL LAW ORGANIZATION PARTICIPATION:
has not submitted an ICJ jurisdiction declaration; accepts ICCt jurisdiction

## CITIZENSHIP:
citizenship by birth: no

citizenship by descent only: at least one parent must be a citizen of Tajikistan

dual citizenship recognized: no

residency requirement for naturalization: 5 years or 3 years of continuous residence prior to application

## SUFFRAGE:
18 years of age; universal

## EXECUTIVE BRANCH:
chief of state: President Emomali RAHMON (since 6 November 1994; head of state and Supreme Assembly chairman since 19 November 1992)

head of government: Prime Minister Qohir RASULZODA (since 23 November 2013)

cabinet: Council of Ministers appointed by the president, approved by the Supreme Assembly

elections/appointments: president directly elected by simple majority popular vote for a 7-year term for a maximum of two terms; however, as the "Leader of the Nation" President RAHMON can run an unlimited number of times; election last held on 6 November 2013 (next to be held in November 2020); prime minister appointed by the president

election results: Emomali RAHMON reelected president; percent of vote - Emomali RAHMON (PDPT) 83.9%, Ismoil TALBAKOV (CPT) 5%, other 11.1%

## LEGISLATIVE BRANCH:
description: bicameral Supreme Assembly or Majlisi Oli consists of: National Assembly or Majlisi Milli (34 seats; 25 members indirectly elected by local representative assemblies or

majlisi, 8 appointed by the president, and 1 reserved for each living former president; members serve 5-year terms) Assembly of Representatives or Majlisi Namoyandagon (63 seats; 41 members directly elected in single-seat constituencies by 2-round absolute majority vote and 22 directly elected in a single nationwide constituency by proportional representation vote; members serve 5-year terms)

elections:
National Assembly - last held on 1 March 2015 (next to be held in 2020) Assembly of Representatives - last held on 1 March 2015 (next to be held in 2020)

election results:
National Assembly - percent of vote by party - NA; seats by party - NA; composition - men 32, women 2, percent of women 5.9%
Assembly of Representatives - percent of vote by party - PDPT 65.4%, APT 11.7%, PERT 7.5%, SPT 5.5%, CPT 2.2%, DPT 1.7%, other 6%; seats by party - PDPT 51, APT 5, PERT 3, CPT 2, SPT 1, DPT 1; composition - men 51, women 12, percent of women19%; note - total Supreme Assembly percent of women 14.4%

## JUDICIAL BRANCH:

highest courts: Supreme Court (consists of the chairman, deputy chairmen, and 34 judges organized into civil, criminal, and military chambers); Constitutional Court (consists of the court chairman, vice president, and 5 judges); High Economic Court (consists of 16 judicial positions)

judge selection and term of office: Supreme Court, Constitutional Court, and High Economic Court judges nominated by the president of the republic and approved by the National Assembly; judges of all 3 courts appointed for 10-year renewable terms with no limit on terms, but last appointment must occur before the age of 65

subordinate courts: regional and district courts; Dushanbe City Court; viloyat (province level) courts; Court of Gorno-Badakhshan Autonomous Region

## POLITICAL PARTIES AND LEADERS:

Agrarian Party of Tajikistan or APT [Rustam LATIFZODA]
Communist Party of Tajikistan or CPT [Miroj ABDULLOYEV]
Democratic Party of Tajikistan or DPT [Saidjafar USMONZODA]
Party of Economic Reform of Tajikistan or PERT [Olimjon BOBOEV]
People's Democratic Party of Tajikistan or PDPT [Emomali RAHMON]
Social Democratic Party of Tajikistan or SDPT [Rahmatullo ZOIROV]
Socialist Party of Tajikistan or SPT [Abduhalim GHAFFOROV]

## INTERNATIONAL ORGANIZATION PARTICIPATION:

ADB, CICA, CIS, CSTO, EAEC, EAPC, EBRD, ECO, EITI (candidate country), FAO, G-77, GCTU, IAEA, IBRD, ICAO, ICC (NGOs), ICCt, ICRM, IDA, IDB, IFAD, IFC, IFRCS, ILO, IMF, Interpol, IOC, IOM, IPU, ISO (correspondent), ITSO, ITU, MIGA, NAM (observer), OIC, OPCW, OSCE, PFP, SCO, UN, UNCTAD, UNESCO, UNIDO, UNWTO, UPU, WCO, WFTU (NGOs), WHO, WIPO, WMO, WTO

## DIPLOMATIC REPRESENTATION IN THE US:

chief of mission: Ambassador Farhod SALIM (since 21 May 2014)

chancery: 1005 New Hampshire Avenue NW, Washington, DC 20037

telephone: [1] (202) 223-6090

FAX: [1] (202) 223-6091

## DIPLOMATIC REPRESENTATION FROM THE US:

chief of mission: Ambassador (vacant); Charge d'Affaires Kevin COVERT (since 31 August 2017)

embassy: 109-A Ismoili Somoni Avenue, Dushanbe 734019

mailing address: 7090 Dushanbe Place, Dulles, VA 20189

telephone: [992] (37) 229-20-00

FAX: [992] (37) 229-20-50

## FLAG DESCRIPTION:

three horizontal stripes of red (top), a wider stripe of white, and green; a gold crown surmounted by seven gold, five-pointed stars is located in the center of the white stripe; red represents the sun, victory, and the unity of the nation, white stands for purity, cotton, and mountain snows, while green is the color of Islam and the bounty of nature; the crown symbolizes the Tajik people; the seven stars signify the Tajik magic number "seven" - a symbol of perfection and the embodiment of happiness

## NATIONAL SYMBOL(S):

crown surmounted by an arc of seven, five-pointed stars; snow leopard;
national colors: red, white, green

## NATIONAL ANTHEM:

name: "Surudi milli" (National Anthem)

lyrics/music: Gulnazar KELDI/Sulaimon YUDAKOV

note: adopted 1991; after the fall of the Soviet Union, Tajikistan kept the music of the anthem from its time as a Soviet republic but adopted new lyrics

# ECONOMY :: TAJIKISTAN

## ECONOMY - OVERVIEW:

Tajikistan is a poor, mountainous country with an economy dominated by minerals extraction, metals processing, agriculture, and reliance on remittances from citizens working abroad. Mineral resources include silver, gold, uranium, antimony, tungsten, and coal. Industry consists mainly of small obsolete factories in food processing and light industry, substantial hydropower facilities, and a large aluminum plant - currently operating well below its capacity. The 1992-97 civil war severely damaged an already weak economic infrastructure and caused a sharp decline in industrial and agricultural production. Today, Tajikistan is the poorest among the former Soviet republics. Because less than 7% of the land area is arable and cotton is the predominant crop, Tajikistan imports approximately 70% of its food.

Since the end of the civil war, the country has pursued half-hearted reforms and privatizations in the economic sphere, but its poor business climate remains a hindrance to attracting foreign investment. Some experts estimate the value of narcotics transiting Tajikistan is equivalent to 30%-50% of GDP.

Because of a lack of employment opportunities in Tajikistan, more than one million Tajik citizens work abroad - roughly 90% in Russia - supporting families back home through remittances that in 2017 were equivalent to nearly 35% of GDP. Tajikistan's large remittances from migrant workers in Russia exposes it to monetary shocks. Tajikistan often delays devaluation of its currency for fear of inflationary pressures on food and other consumables. Recent slowdowns in the Russian and Chinese economies, low commodity prices, and currency fluctuations have hampered economic growth. The dollar value of remittances from Russia to Tajikistan dropped by almost 65% in 2015, and the government spent almost $500 million in 2016 to bail out the country's still troubled banking sector.

Tajikistan's growing public debt – currently about 50% of GDP – could result in financial difficulties. Remittances from Russia increased in 2017, however, bolstering the economy somewhat. China owns about 50% of Tajikistan's outstanding debt. Tajikistan has borrowed heavily to finance investment in the country's vast hydropower potential. In 2016, Tajikistan contracted with the Italian firm Salini Impregilo to build the Roghun dam over a 13-year period for $3.9 billion. A 2017 Eurobond has largely funded Roghun's first phase, after which sales from Roghun's output are expected to fund the rest of its construction. The government has not ruled out issuing another Eurobond to generate auxiliary funding for its second phase.

**GDP (PURCHASING POWER PARITY):**

$28.43 billion (2017 est.)

$26.55 billion (2016 est.)

$24.83 billion (2015 est.)

note: data are in 2017 dollars

country comparison to the world: 135

**GDP (OFFICIAL EXCHANGE RATE):**

$7.144 billion (2017 est.) (2017 est.)

**GDP - REAL GROWTH RATE:**

7.1% (2017 est.)

6.9% (2016 est.)

6% (2015 est.)

country comparison to the world: 19

**GDP - PER CAPITA (PPP):**

$3,200 (2017 est.)

$3,000 (2016 est.)

$2,900 (2015 est.)

note: data are in 2017 dollars

country comparison to the world: 192

**GROSS NATIONAL SAVING:**

24.4% of GDP (2017 est.)

15.4% of GDP (2016 est.)

11.8% of GDP (2015 est.)

country comparison to the world: 66

**GDP - COMPOSITION, BY END USE:**

household consumption: 98.4% (2017 est.)

government consumption: 13.3% (2017 est.)

investment in fixed capital: 11.7% (2017 est.)

investment in inventories: 2.5% (2017 est.)

exports of goods and services: 10.7% (2017 est.)

imports of goods and services: -36.6% (2017 est.)

**GDP - COMPOSITION, BY SECTOR OF ORIGIN:**

agriculture: 28.6% (2017 est.)

industry: 25.5% (2017 est.)

services: 45.9% (2017 est.)

**AGRICULTURE - PRODUCTS:**

cotton, grain, fruits, grapes, vegetables; cattle, sheep, goats

**INDUSTRIES:**

aluminum, cement, coal, gold, silver, antimony, textile, vegetable oil

**INDUSTRIAL PRODUCTION GROWTH RATE:**

1% (2017 est.)

country comparison to the world: 159

**LABOR FORCE:**

2.295 million (2016 est.)

country comparison to the world: 118

**LABOR FORCE - BY OCCUPATION:**

agriculture: 43%

industry: 10.6%

services: 46.4% (2016 est.)

**UNEMPLOYMENT RATE:**

2.4% (2016 est.)

2.5% (2015 est.)

note: official rate; actual unemployment is much higher

country comparison to the world: 25

**POPULATION BELOW POVERTY LINE:**

31.5% (2016 est.)

**HOUSEHOLD INCOME OR CONSUMPTION BY PERCENTAGE SHARE:**

lowest 10%: NA (2009 est.)

highest 10%: NA (2009 est.)

**DISTRIBUTION OF FAMILY INCOME - GINI INDEX:**

32.6 (2006)

34.7 (1998)

country comparison to the world: 116

**BUDGET:**

revenues: 2.269 billion (2017 est.)

expenditures: 2.374 billion (2017 est.)

**TAXES AND OTHER REVENUES:**

31.8% (of GDP) (2017 est.)

country comparison to the world: 71

**BUDGET SURPLUS (+) OR DEFICIT (-):**

-1.5% (of GDP) (2017 est.)

country comparison to the world: 90

**PUBLIC DEBT:**

50.4% of GDP (2017 est.)

42% of GDP (2016 est.)

country comparison to the world: 101

**FISCAL YEAR:**

calendar year

**INFLATION RATE (CONSUMER PRICES):**

7.3% (2017 est.)

5.9% (2016 est.)

country comparison to the world: 193

**CENTRAL BANK DISCOUNT RATE:**

16% (20 March 2017)

6.5% (31 December 2012)

country comparison to the world: 12

**COMMERCIAL BANK PRIME LENDING RATE:**

30% (31 December 2017 est.)

24.24% (31 December 2016 est.)

country comparison to the world: 5

**STOCK OF NARROW MONEY:**

$1.389 billion (31 December 2017 est.)

$1.108 billion (31 December 2016 est.)

country comparison to the world: 145

**STOCK OF BROAD MONEY:**

$1.389 billion (31 December 2017 est.)

$1.108 billion (31 December 2016 est.)

country comparison to the world: 153

**STOCK OF DOMESTIC CREDIT:**

$1.06 billion (31 December 2017 est.)

$1.711 billion (31 December 2016 est.)

country comparison to the world: 168

**MARKET VALUE OF PUBLICLY TRADED SHARES:**

NA

**CURRENT ACCOUNT BALANCE:**

-$35 million (2017 est.)

-$362 million (2016 est.)

country comparison to the world: 78

**EXPORTS:**

$873.1 million (2017 est.)

$691.1 million (2016 est.)

country comparison to the world: 166

**EXPORTS - PARTNERS:**

Turkey 27.5%, China 17.7%, Russia 13.4%, Switzerland 12.5%, Algeria 8.2%, Iran 7.1% (2017)

**EXPORTS - COMMODITIES:**
aluminum, electricity, cotton, fruits, vegetable oil, textiles

**IMPORTS:**
$2.39 billion (2017 est.)
$2.554 billion (2016 est.)

country comparison to the world: 160

**IMPORTS - COMMODITIES:**
petroleum products, aluminum oxide, machinery and equipment, foodstuffs

**IMPORTS - PARTNERS:**
Russia 38%, Kazakhstan 19%, China 8.7%, Iran 4.4% (2017)

**RESERVES OF FOREIGN EXCHANGE AND GOLD:**
$1.292 billion (31 December 2017 est.)
$652.8 million (31 December 2016 est.)

country comparison to the world: 127

**DEBT - EXTERNAL:**
$5.75 billion (31 December 2017 est.)
$5.495 billion (31 December 2016 est.)

country comparison to the world: 130

**STOCK OF DIRECT FOREIGN INVESTMENT - AT HOME:**
$2.272 billion (31 December 2013 est.)

country comparison to the world: 118

**STOCK OF DIRECT FOREIGN INVESTMENT - ABROAD:**
$16.3 billion (31 December 2009)

country comparison to the world: 60

**EXCHANGE RATES:**
Tajikistani somoni (TJS) per US dollar -

8.764 (2017 est.)
7.8358 (2016 est.)
7.8358 (2015 est.)
6.1631 (2014 est.)
4.9348 (2013 est.)

## ENERGY :: TAJIKISTAN

**ELECTRICITY ACCESS:**
electrification - total population: 100% (2016)

**ELECTRICITY - PRODUCTION:**
17.03 billion kWh (2016 est.)

country comparison to the world: 85

**ELECTRICITY - CONSUMPTION:**
12.96 billion kWh (2016 est.)

country comparison to the world: 85

**ELECTRICITY - EXPORTS:**
1.4 billion kWh NA (2015 est.)

country comparison to the world: 52

**ELECTRICITY - IMPORTS:**
103 million kWh (2016 est.)

country comparison to the world: 98

**ELECTRICITY - INSTALLED GENERATING CAPACITY:**
5.508 million kW (2016 est.)

country comparison to the world: 78

**ELECTRICITY - FROM FOSSIL FUELS:**
6% of total installed capacity (2016 est.)

country comparison to the world: 201

**ELECTRICITY - FROM NUCLEAR FUELS:**
0% of total installed capacity (2017 est.)

country comparison to the world: 191

**ELECTRICITY - FROM HYDROELECTRIC PLANTS:**
94% of total installed capacity (2017 est.)

country comparison to the world: 6

**ELECTRICITY - FROM OTHER RENEWABLE SOURCES:**
0% of total installed capacity (2017 est.)

country comparison to the world: 208

**CRUDE OIL - PRODUCTION:**
180 bbl/day (2017 est.)

country comparison to the world: 97

**CRUDE OIL - EXPORTS:**
0 bbl/day (2015 est.)

country comparison to the world: 204

**CRUDE OIL - IMPORTS:**
0 bbl/day (2015 est.)

country comparison to the world: 201

**CRUDE OIL - PROVED RESERVES:**
12 million bbl (1 January 2018 est.)

country comparison to the world: 89

**REFINED PETROLEUM PRODUCTS - PRODUCTION:**
172 bbl/day (2015 est.)

country comparison to the world: 108

**REFINED PETROLEUM PRODUCTS - CONSUMPTION:**
24,000 bbl/day (2016 est.)

country comparison to the world: 130

**REFINED PETROLEUM PRODUCTS - EXPORTS:**
0 bbl/day (2015 est.)

country comparison to the world: 206

**REFINED PETROLEUM PRODUCTS - IMPORTS:**
22,460 bbl/day (2015 est.)

country comparison to the world: 114

**NATURAL GAS - PRODUCTION:**
19.82 million cu m (2017 est.)

country comparison to the world: 89

**NATURAL GAS - CONSUMPTION:**
19.82 million cu m (2017 est.)

country comparison to the world: 114

**NATURAL GAS - EXPORTS:**
0 cu m (2017 est.)

country comparison to the world: 197

**NATURAL GAS - IMPORTS:**
0 cu m (2017 est.)

country comparison to the world: 197

**NATURAL GAS - PROVED RESERVES:**
5.663 billion cu m (1 January 2018 est.)

country comparison to the world: 91

**CARBON DIOXIDE EMISSIONS FROM CONSUMPTION OF ENERGY:**
6.329 million Mt (2017 est.)

country comparison to the world: 126

## COMMUNICATIONS :: TAJIKISTAN

**TELEPHONES - FIXED LINES:**
total subscriptions: 468,000 (July 2016 est.)
subscriptions per 100 inhabitants: 6 (July 2016 est.)

country comparison to the world: 99

**TELEPHONES - MOBILE CELLULAR:**
total subscriptions: 9.4 million (July 2016 est.)
subscriptions per 100 inhabitants: 111 (July 2016 est.)

country comparison to the world: 87

**TELEPHONE SYSTEM:**
general assessment: foreign investment in the telephone system has resulted in major improvements; conversion of the existing fixed network from analogue to digital was completed in 2012 (2016)

domestic: fixed line availability has not changed significantly since 1998, while mobile cellular subscribership, aided by competition among multiple operators, has expanded rapidly; coverage now extends to all major cities and towns (2016) international: country code - 992; linked by cable and microwave radio relay to other CIS republics and by leased connections to the Moscow international gateway switch; Dushanbe linked by Intelsat to international gateway switch in Ankara (Turkey); satellite earth stations - 3 (2 Intelsat and 1 Orbita); established a single gateway for Internet traffic in December 2015, which is expected to limit the connectivity of nonstate-owned telecom, Internet, and mobile companies (2016)

**BROADCAST MEDIA:**

state-run TV broadcasters transmit nationally on 9 TV and 10 radio stations, and regionally on 4 stations; 31 independent TV and 20 radio stations broadcast locally and regionally; many households are able to receive Russian and other foreign stations via cable and satellite (2016)

**INTERNET COUNTRY CODE:**

.tj

**INTERNET USERS:**

total: 1,705,345 (July 2016 est.)

percent of population: 20.5% (July 2016 est.)

country comparison to the world: 119

**BROADBAND - FIXED SUBSCRIPTIONS:**

total: 6,000 (2017 est.)

subscriptions per 100 inhabitants: less than 1 (2017 est.)

country comparison to the world: 174

## TRANSPORTATION :: TAJIKISTAN

**NATIONAL AIR TRANSPORT SYSTEM:**

number of registered air carriers: 2 (2015)

inventory of registered aircraft operated by air carriers: 10 (2015)

annual passenger traffic on registered air carriers: 802,470 (2015)

annual freight traffic on registered air carriers: 105,376 mt-km (2015)

**CIVIL AIRCRAFT REGISTRATION COUNTRY CODE PREFIX:**

EY (2016)

**AIRPORTS:**

24 (2013)

country comparison to the world: 132

**AIRPORTS - WITH PAVED RUNWAYS:**

total: 17 (2013)

over 3,047 m: 2 (2013)

2,438 to 3,047 m: 4 (2013)

1,524 to 2,437 m: 5 (2013)

914 to 1,523 m: 3 (2013)

under 914 m: 3 (2013)

**AIRPORTS - WITH UNPAVED RUNWAYS:**

total: 7 (2013)

1,524 to 2,437 m: 1 (2013)

914 to 1,523 m: 1 (2013)

under 914 m: 5 (2013)

**PIPELINES:**

549 km gas, 38 km oil (2013)

**RAILWAYS:**

total: 680 km (2014)

broad gauge: 680 km 1.520-m gauge (2014)

country comparison to the world: 102

**ROADWAYS:**

total: 27,767 km (2000)

country comparison to the world: 98

**WATERWAYS:**

200 km (along Vakhsh River) (2011)

country comparison to the world: 98

## MILITARY AND SECURITY :: TAJIKISTAN

**MILITARY EXPENDITURES:**

1.19% of GDP (2017)

1.25% of GDP (2016)

1.22% of GDP (2015)

1.13% of GDP (2014)

1% of GDP (2012)

country comparison to the world: 99

**MILITARY BRANCHES:**

Ground Forces, Air and Air Defense Forces, Mobile Forces (2013)

**MILITARY SERVICE AGE AND OBLIGATION:**

18-27 years of age for compulsory or voluntary military service; 2-year conscript service obligation; males required to undergo compulsory military training between ages 16 and 55; males can enroll in military schools from at least age 15 (2012)

## TRANSNATIONAL ISSUES :: TAJIKISTAN

**DISPUTES - INTERNATIONAL:**

in 2006, China and Tajikistan pledged to commence demarcation of the revised boundary agreed to in the delimitation of 2002talks continue with Uzbekistan to delimit border and remove minefieldsdisputes in Isfara Valley delay delimitation with Kyrgyzstan

**REFUGEES AND INTERNALLY DISPLACED PERSONS:**

stateless persons: 10,500 (2017)

**ILLICIT DRUGS:**

Tajikistan sits on one of the world's highest volume illicit drug trafficking routes, between Afghan opiate production to the south and the illicit drug markets of Russia and Eastern Europe to the north; limited illicit cultivation of opium poppy for domestic consumption; significant consumer of opiates

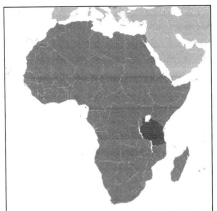

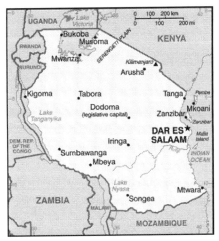

# AFRICA :: TANZANIA

## INTRODUCTION :: TANZANIA

### BACKGROUND:

Shortly after achieving independence from Britain in the early 1960s, Tanganyika and Zanzibar merged to form the United Republic of Tanzania in 1964. In 1995, the country held its first democratic elections since the 1970s. Zanzibar maintains semi-autonomy and participates in national elections; popular political opposition on the isles led to four contentious elections since 1995, in which the ruling party claimed victory despite international observers' claims of voting irregularities.

## GEOGRAPHY :: TANZANIA

### LOCATION:
Eastern Africa, bordering the Indian Ocean, between Kenya and Mozambique

### GEOGRAPHIC COORDINATES:
6 00 S, 35 00 E

### MAP REFERENCES:
Africa

### AREA:
**total:** 947,300 sq km

**land:** 885,800 sq km

**water:** 61,500 sq km

**note:** includes the islands of Mafia, Pemba, and Zanzibar

**country comparison to the world:** 32

### AREA - COMPARATIVE:
more than six times the size of Georgia; slightly larger than twice the size of California

### LAND BOUNDARIES:
**total:** 4,161 km

**border countries (8):** Burundi 589 km, Democratic Republic of the Congo 479 km, Kenya 775 km, Malawi 512 km, Mozambique 840 km, Rwanda 222 km, Uganda 391 km, Zambia 353 km

### COASTLINE:
1,424 km

### MARITIME CLAIMS:
**territorial sea:** 12 nm

**exclusive economic zone:** 200 nm

### CLIMATE:
varies from tropical along coast to temperate in highlands

### TERRAIN:
plains along coast; central plateau; highlands in north, south

### ELEVATION:
**mean elevation:** 1,018 m

**elevation extremes:** 0 m lowest point: Indian Ocean

5895 highest point: Kilimanjaro (highest point in Africa)

### NATURAL RESOURCES:
hydropower, tin, phosphates, iron ore, coal, diamonds, gemstones, gold, natural gas, nickel

### LAND USE:
**agricultural land:** 43.7% (2011 est.)

**arable land:** 14.3% (2011 est.) / **permanent crops:** 2.3% (2011 est.) / **permanent pasture:** 27.1% (2011 est.)

**forest:** 37.3% (2011 est.)

**other:** 19% (2011 est.)

### IRRIGATED LAND:
1,840 sq km (2012)

### POPULATION DISTRIBUTION:
the largest and most populous East African country; population distribution is extremely uneven, but greater population clusters occur in the northern half of country and along the east coast

### NATURAL HAZARDS:
flooding on the central plateau during the rainy season; drought

**volcanism:** limited volcanic activity; Ol Doinyo Lengai (2,962 m) has emitted lava in recent years; other historically active volcanoes include Kieyo and Meru

### ENVIRONMENT - CURRENT ISSUES:
water polution; improper management of liquid waste; indoor air pollution caused by the burning of fuel wood or charcoal for cooking and heating is a large environmental health issue; soil degradation; deforestation; desertification; destruction of coral reefs threatens marine habitats; wildlife threatened by illegal hunting and trade, especially for ivory; loss of biodiversity; solid waste disposal

### ENVIRONMENT - INTERNATIONAL AGREEMENTS:
**party to:** Biodiversity, Climate Change, Climate Change-Kyoto Protocol, Desertification, Endangered Species, Hazardous Wastes, Law of the Sea, Ozone Layer Protection, Wetlands

**signed, but not ratified:** none of the selected agreements

### GEOGRAPHY - NOTE:
Kilimanjaro is the highest point in Africa and one of only two mountains on the continent that has glaciers (the other is Mount Kenya); bordered by three of the largest lakes on the continent: Lake Victoria (the world's

second-largest freshwater lake) in the north, Lake Tanganyika (the world's second deepest) in the west, and Lake Nyasa (Lake Malawi) in the southwest

# PEOPLE AND SOCIETY :: TANZANIA

**POPULATION:**

55,451,343 (July 2018 est.)

note: estimates for this country explicitly take into account the effects of excess mortality due to AIDS; this can result in lower life expectancy, higher infant mortality, higher death rates, lower population growth rates, and changes in the distribution of population by age and sex than would otherwise be expected

country comparison to the world: 25

**NATIONALITY:**

noun: Tanzanian(s)

adjective: Tanzanian

**ETHNIC GROUPS:**

mainland - African 99% (of which 95% are Bantu consisting of more than 130 tribes), other 1% (consisting of Asian, European, and Arab); Zanzibar - Arab, African, mixed Arab and African

**LANGUAGES:**

Kiswahili or Swahili (official), Kiunguja (name for Swahili in Zanzibar), English (official, primary language of commerce, administration, and higher education), Arabic (widely spoken in Zanzibar), many local languages

note: Kiswahili (Swahili) is the mother tongue of the Bantu people living in Zanzibar and nearby coastal Tanzania; although Kiswahili is Bantu in structure and origin, its vocabulary draws on a variety of sources including Arabic and English; it has become the lingua franca of central and eastern Africa; the first language of most people is one of the local languages

**RELIGIONS:**

Christian 61.4%, Muslim 35.2%, folk religion 1.8%, other 0.2%, unaffiliated 1.4% (2010 est.)

note: Zanzibar is almost entirely Muslim

**DEMOGRAPHIC PROFILE:**

Tanzania has the largest population in East Africa and the lowest population density; almost a third of the population is urban. Tanzania's youthful population – about two-thirds of the population is under 25 – is growing rapidly because of the high total fertility rate of 4.8 children per woman. Progress in reducing the birth rate has stalled, sustaining the country's nearly 3% annual growth. The maternal mortality rate has improved since 2000, yet it remains very high because of early and frequent pregnancies, inadequate maternal health services, and a lack of skilled birth attendants – problems that are worse among poor and rural women. Tanzania has made strides in reducing under-5 and infant mortality rates, but a recent drop in immunization threatens to undermine gains in child health. Malaria is a leading killer of children under 5, while HIV is the main source of adult mortality

For Tanzania, most migration is internal, rural to urban movement, while some temporary labor migration from towns to plantations takes place seasonally for harvests. Tanzania was Africa's largest refugee-hosting country for decades, hosting hundreds of thousands of refugees from the Great Lakes region, primarily Burundi, over the last fifty years. However, the assisted repatriation and naturalization of tens of thousands of Burundian refugees between 2002 and 2014 dramatically reduced the refugee population. Tanzania is increasingly a transit country for illegal migrants from the Horn of Africa and the Great Lakes region who are heading to southern Africa for security reasons and/or economic opportunities. Some of these migrants choose to settle in Tanzania.

**AGE STRUCTURE:**

0-14 years: 43.4% (male 12,159,482 /female 11,908,654)

15-24 years: 20.03% (male 5,561,922 /female 5,543,788)

25-54 years: 30.02% (male 8,361,460 /female 8,284,229)

55-64 years: 3.51% (male 872,601 /female 1,074,480)

65 years and over: 3.04% (male 706,633 /female 978,094) (2018 est.)

**DEPENDENCY RATIOS:**

total dependency ratio: 93.4 (2015 est.)

youth dependency ratio: 87.4 (2015 est.)

elderly dependency ratio: 6 (2015 est.)

potential support ratio: 16.6 (2015 est.)

**MEDIAN AGE:**

total: 17.9 years

male: 17.6 years

female: 18.2 years (2018 est.)

country comparison to the world: 215

**POPULATION GROWTH RATE:**

2.74% (2018 est.)

country comparison to the world: 14

**BIRTH RATE:**

35.3 births/1,000 population (2018 est.)

country comparison to the world: 19

**DEATH RATE:**

7.5 deaths/1,000 population (2018 est.)

country comparison to the world: 112

**NET MIGRATION RATE:**

-0.5 migrant(s)/1,000 population (2017 est.)

country comparison to the world: 127

**POPULATION DISTRIBUTION:**

the largest and most populous East African country; population distribution is extremely uneven, but greater population clusters occur in the northern half of country and along the east coast

**URBANIZATION:**

urban population: 33.8% of total population (2018)

rate of urbanization: 5.22% annual rate of change (2015-20 est.)

**MAJOR URBAN AREAS - POPULATION:**

6.048 million DAR ES SALAAM (administrative capital), 1.003 million Mwanza, 262,000 Dodoma (legislative capital) (2018)

**SEX RATIO:**

at birth: 1.03 male(s)/female (2017 est.)

0-14 years: 1.02 male(s)/female (2017 est.)

15-24 years: 1 male(s)/female (2017 est.)

25-54 years: 1.01 male(s)/female (2017 est.)

55-64 years: 0.78 male(s)/female (2017 est.)

65 years and over: 0.75 male(s)/female (2017 est.)

total population: 0.99 male(s)/female (2017 est.)

**MOTHER'S MEAN AGE AT FIRST BIRTH:**

19.8 years (2015/16 est.)

note: median age at first birth among women 25-29

## MATERNAL MORTALITY RATE:
398 deaths/100,000 live births (2015 est.)

country comparison to the world: 27

## INFANT MORTALITY RATE:
total: 38.7 deaths/1,000 live births (2018 est.)

male: 40.8 deaths/1,000 live births (2018 est.)

female: 36.6 deaths/1,000 live births (2018 est.)

country comparison to the world: 45

## LIFE EXPECTANCY AT BIRTH:
total population: 63.1 years (2018 est.)

male: 61.6 years (2018 est.)

female: 64.6 years (2018 est.)

country comparison to the world: 196

## TOTAL FERTILITY RATE:
4.71 children born/woman (2018 est.)

country comparison to the world: 20

## CONTRACEPTIVE PREVALENCE RATE:
38.4% (2015/16)

## HEALTH EXPENDITURES:
5.6% of GDP (2014)

country comparison to the world: 122

## PHYSICIANS DENSITY:
0.02 physicians/1,000 population (2014)

## HOSPITAL BED DENSITY:
0.7 beds/1,000 population (2010)

## DRINKING WATER SOURCE:
improved:

urban: 77.2% of population

rural: 45.5% of population

total: 55.6% of population

unimproved:

urban: 22.8% of population

rural: 54.5% of population

total: 44.4% of population (2015 est.)

## SANITATION FACILITY ACCESS:
improved:

urban: 31.3% of population (2015 est.)

rural: 8.3% of population (2015 est.)

total: 15.6% of population (2015 est.)

unimproved:

urban: 68.7% of population (2015 est.)

rural: 91.7% of population (2015 est.)

total: 84.4% of population (2015 est.)

## HIV/AIDS - ADULT PREVALENCE RATE:
4.5% (2017 est.)

country comparison to the world: 13

## HIV/AIDS - PEOPLE LIVING WITH HIV/AIDS:
1.5 million (2017 est.)

country comparison to the world: 6

## HIV/AIDS - DEATHS:
32,000 (2017 est.)

country comparison to the world: 6

## MAJOR INFECTIOUS DISEASES:
degree of risk: very high (2016)

food or waterborne diseases: bacterial diarrhea, hepatitis A, and typhoid fever (2016)

vectorborne diseases: malaria, dengue fever, and Rift Valley fever (2016)

water contact diseases: schistosomiasis and leptospirosis (2016)

animal contact diseases: rabies (2016)

## OBESITY - ADULT PREVALENCE RATE:
8.4% (2016)

country comparison to the world: 151

## CHILDREN UNDER THE AGE OF 5 YEARS UNDERWEIGHT:
13.7% (2015)

country comparison to the world: 48

## EDUCATION EXPENDITURES:
3.5% of GDP (2014)

country comparison to the world: 132

## LITERACY:
definition: age 15 and over can read and write Kiswahili (Swahili), English, or Arabic (2015 est.)

total population: 77.9% (2015 est.)

male: 83.2% (2015 est.)

female: 73.1% (2015 est.)

## SCHOOL LIFE EXPECTANCY (PRIMARY TO TERTIARY EDUCATION):
total: 8 years (2013)

male: 8 years (2013)

female: 8 years (2013)

## UNEMPLOYMENT, YOUTH AGES 15-24:
total: 3.9% (2014 est.)

male: 3.1% (2014 est.)

female: 4.6% (2014 est.)

country comparison to the world: 159

# GOVERNMENT :: TANZANIA

## COUNTRY NAME:
conventional long form: United Republic of Tanzania

conventional short form: Tanzania

local long form: Jamhuri ya Muungano wa Tanzania

local short form: Tanzania

former: German East Africa, Trust Territory of Tanganyika, United Republic of Tanganyika and Zanzibar

etymology: the country's name is a combination of the first letters of Tanganyika and Zanzibar, the two states that merged to form Tanzania in 1964

## GOVERNMENT TYPE:
presidential republic

## CAPITAL:
name: Dodoma (legislative capital), Dar es Salaam (administrative capital); note - Dodoma was designated the national capital in 1996 and serves as the meeting place for the National Assembly; Dar es Salaam remains the de facto capital, the country's largest city and commercial center, and the site of the executive branch offices and diplomatic representation; the government contends that it will complete the transfer of the executive branch to Dodoma by 2020

geographic coordinates: 6 48 S, 39 17 E

time difference: UTC+3 (8 hours ahead of Washington, DC, during Standard Time)

## ADMINISTRATIVE DIVISIONS:
31 regions; Arusha, Dar es Salaam, Dodoma, Geita, Iringa, Kagera, Kaskazini Pemba (Pemba North), Kaskazini Unguja (Zanzibar North), Katavi, Kigoma, Kilimanjaro, Kusini Pemba (Pemba South), Kusini Unguja (Zanzibar Central/South), Lindi, Manyara, Mara, Mbeya, Mjini Magharibi (Zanzibar Urban/West), Morogoro, Mtwara, Mwanza, Njombe, Pwani (Coast), Rukwa, Ruvuma, Shinyanga, Simiyu, Singida, Songwe, Tabora, Tanga

## INDEPENDENCE:
26 April 1964 (Tanganyika united with Zanzibar to form the United Republic

of Tanganyika and Zanzibar); 29 October 1964 (renamed United Republic of Tanzania); notable earlier dates: 9 December 1961 (Tanganyika became independent from UK-administered UN trusteeship); 10 December 1963 (Zanzibar became independent from UK)

## NATIONAL HOLIDAY:

Union Day (Tanganyika and Zanzibar), 26 April (1964)

## CONSTITUTION:

history: several previous; latest adopted 25 April 1977; note - progress enacting a new constitution drafted in 2014 by the Constituent Assembly has been stalled (2017)

amendments: proposed by the National Assembly; passage of amendments to constitutional articles including those on sovereignty of the United Republic, the authorities and powers of the government, the president, the Assembly, and the High Court requires two-thirds majority vote of the mainland Assembly membership and of the Zanzibar House of Representatives membership; House of Representatives approval of other amendments is not required (2017)

## LEGAL SYSTEM:

English common law; judicial review of legislative acts limited to matters of interpretation

## INTERNATIONAL LAW ORGANIZATION PARTICIPATION:

has not submitted an ICJ jurisdiction declaration; accepts ICCt jurisdiction

## CITIZENSHIP:

citizenship by birth: no

citizenship by descent only: at least one parent must be a citizen of Tanzania; if a child is born abroad, the father must be a citizen of Tanzania

dual citizenship recognized: no

residency requirement for naturalization: 5 years

## SUFFRAGE:

18 years of age; universal

## EXECUTIVE BRANCH:

chief of state: President John MAGUFULI, Dr. (since 5 November 2015); Vice President Samia SULUHU (since 5 November 2015); note - the president is both chief of state and head of government

head of government: President John MAGUFULI, Dr. (since 5 November 2015); Vice President Samia SULUHU (since 5 November 2015); note - Prime Minister Kassim Majaliwa MAJALIWA (since 20 November 2015) has authority over the day-to-day functions of the government, is the leader of government business in the National Assembly, and is head of the Cabinet

cabinet: Cabinet appointed by the president from among members of the National Assembly

elections/appointments: president and vice president directly elected on the same ballot by simple majority popular vote for a 5-year term (eligible for a second term); election last held on 25 October 2015 (next to be held in October 2020); prime minister appointed by the president

election results: John MAGUFULI elected president; percent of vote - John MAGUFULI (CCM) 58.5%, Edward LOWASSA (CHADEMA) 40%, other 1.5%

note: Zanzibar elects a president as head of government for internal matters; election held on 25 October 2015 was annulled by the Zanzibar Electoral Commission and rerun on 20 March 2016; President Ali Mohamed SHEIN reelected; percent of vote - Ali Mohamed SHEIN (CCM) 91.4%, Hamad Rashid MOHAMED (ADC) 3%, other 5.6%; the main opposition party in Zanzibar CUF boycotted the 20 March 2016 election rerun

## LEGISLATIVE BRANCH:

description: unicameral National Assembly or Parliament (Bunge) (393 seats; 264 members directly elected in single-seat constituencies by simple majority vote, 113 women indirectly elected by proportional representation vote, 5 indirectly elected by simple majority vote by the Zanzibar House of Representatives, 10 appointed by the president, and 1 seat reserved for the attorney general; members serve a 5-year term); note - in addition to enacting laws that apply to the entire United Republic of Tanzania, the National Assembly enacts laws that apply only to the mainland; Zanzibar has its own House of Representatives or Baraza La Wawakilishi (82 seats; 50 members directly elected in single-seat constituencies by simple majority vote, 20 women directly elected by proportional representation vote, 10 appointed by the Zanzibar president, 1 seat for the House speaker, and 1 ex-officio seat for the attorney general; elected members serve a 5-year term)

Tanzania National Assembly and Zanzibar House of Representatives - elections last held on 25 October 2015 (next National Assembly election to be held in October 2020; next Zanzibar election either October 2020 or March 2021; note the Zanzibar Electoral Commission annulled the 2015 election; repoll held on 20 March 2016 National Assembly - percent of vote by party - CCM 55%, Chadema 31.8%, CUF 8.6%, other 4.6%; seats by party - CCM 253, Chadema 70, CUF 42, other 2 Zanzibar House of Representatives - percent of vote by party - NA; seats by party - NA

## JUDICIAL BRANCH:

highest courts: Court of Appeal of the United Republic of Tanzania (consists of the chief justice and 14 justices); High Court of the United Republic for Mainland Tanzania (consists of the principal judge and 30 judges organized into commercial, land, and labor courts); High Court of Zanzibar (consists of the chief justice and 10 justices)

judge selection and term of office: Court of Appeal and High Court justices appointed by the national president after consultation with the Judicial Service Commission for Tanzania, a judicial body of high level judges and 2 members appointed by the national president; Court of Appeal and High Court judges appointed until mandatory retirement at age 60 but terms can be extended; High Court of Zanzibar judges appointed by the national president after consultation with the Judicial Commission of Zanzibar; judges may serve until mandatory retirement at age 65

subordinate courts: Resident Magistrates Courts; Kadhi courts (for Islamic family matters); district and primary courts

## POLITICAL PARTIES AND LEADERS:

Alliance for Change and Transparency or ACT [Zitto KABWE]
Alliance for Democratic Change or ADC [Miraji ABDALLAH]Civic United Front (Chama Cha Wananchi) or CUF [Seif Shariff HAMAD, Secretary General]
National Convention for Construction and Reform-Mageuzi or NCCR-M [James Francis MBATCA]
National League for Democracy Party of Democracy and Development (Chama Cha Demokrasia na Maendeleo) or Chadema [Freeman MBOWE]

Revolutionary Party (Chama Cha Mapinduzi) or CCM [John MAGUFULI]
Tanzania Labor Party or TLP [Augustine MREMA]
United Democratic Party or UDP [John Momose CHEYO]

**note:** in March 2014, four opposition parties (CUF, CHADEMA, NCCR-Mageuzi, and NLD) united to form Coalition for the People's Constitution (Umoja wa Katiba ya Wananchi) or UKAWA; during local elections held in October, 2014, UKAWA entered one candidate representing the three parties united in the coalition

### INTERNATIONAL ORGANIZATION PARTICIPATION:

ACP, AfDB, AU, C, CD, EAC, EADB, EITI, FAO, G-77, IAEA, IBRD, ICAO, ICC (NGOs), ICCt, ICRM, IDA, IFAD, IFC, IFRCS, ILO, IMF, IMO, IMSO, Interpol, IOC, IOM, IPU, ISO, ITSO, ITU, ITUC (NGOs), MIGA, MONUSCO, NAM, OPCW, SADC, UN, UNAMID, UNCTAD, UNESCO, UNHCR, UNIDO, UNIFIL, UNISFA, UNMISS, UNWTO, UPU, WCO, WFTU (NGOs), WHO, WIPO, WMO, WTO

### DIPLOMATIC REPRESENTATION IN THE US:

**chief of mission:** Ambassador Wilson Mutagaywa MASILINGI (since 17 September 2015)

**chancery:** 1232 22nd Street NW, Washington, DC 20037

**telephone:** [1] (202) 939-6125

**FAX:** [1] (202) 797-7408

### DIPLOMATIC REPRESENTATION FROM THE US:

**chief of mission:** Ambassador (vacant); Charge d'Affaires Inmi PATTERSON (since 5 July 2017)

**embassy:** 686 Old Bagamoyo Road, Msasani, Dar es Salaam

**mailing address:** P.O. Box 9123, Dar es Salaam

**telephone:** [255] (22) 229-4000

**FAX:** [255] (22) 229-4970 or 4971

### FLAG DESCRIPTION:

divided diagonally by a yellow-edged black band from the lower hoist-side corner; the upper triangle (hoist side) is green and the lower triangle is blue; the banner combines colors found on the flags of Tanganyika and Zanzibar; green represents the natural vegetation of the country, gold its rich mineral deposits, black the native Swahili people, and blue the country's many lakes and rivers, as well as the Indian Ocean

### NATIONAL SYMBOL(S):

Uhuru (Freedom) torch, giraffe; national colors: green, yellow, blue, black

### NATIONAL ANTHEM:

**name:** "Mungu ibariki Afrika" (God Bless Africa)

**lyrics/music:** collective/Enoch Mankayi SONTONGA

**note:** adopted 1961; the anthem, which is also a popular song in Africa, shares the same melody with that of Zambia but has different lyrics; the melody is also incorporated into South Africa's anthem

# ECONOMY :: TANZANIA

### ECONOMY - OVERVIEW:

Tanzania has achieved high growth rates based on its vast natural resource wealth and tourism with GDP growth in 2009-17 averaging 6%-7% per year. Dar es Salaam used fiscal stimulus measures and easier monetary policies to lessen the impact of the global recession and in general, benefited from low oil prices. Tanzania has largely completed its transition to a market economy, though the government retains a presence in sectors such as telecommunications, banking, energy, and mining.

The economy depends on agriculture, which accounts for slightly less than one-quarter of GDP and employs about 65% of the work force, although gold production in recent years has increased to about 35% of exports. All land in Tanzania is owned by the government, which can lease land for up to 99 years. Proposed reforms to allow for land ownership, particularly foreign land ownership, remain unpopular.

The financial sector in Tanzania has expanded in recent years and foreign-owned banks account for about 48% of the banking industry's total assets. Competition among foreign commercial banks has resulted in significant improvements in the efficiency and quality of financial services, though interest rates are still relatively high, reflecting high fraud risk. Banking reforms have helped increase private-sector growth and investment.

The World Bank, the IMF, and bilateral donors have provided funds to rehabilitate Tanzania's aging infrastructure, including rail and port, which provide important trade links for inland countries. In 2013, Tanzania completed the world's largest Millennium Challenge Compact (MCC) grant, worth $698 million, but in late 2015, the MCC Board of Directors deferred a decision to renew Tanzania's eligibility because of irregularities in voting in Zanzibar and concerns over the government's use of a controversial cybercrime bill.

The new government elected in 2015 has developed an ambitious development agenda focused on creating a better business environment through improved infrastructure, access to financing, and education progress, but implementing budgets remains challenging for the government. Recent policy moves by President MAGUFULI are aimed at protecting domestic industry and have caused concern among foreign investors.

### GDP (PURCHASING POWER PARITY):

$162.5 billion (2017 est.)

$153.3 billion (2016 est.)

$143.3 billion (2015 est.)

note: data are in 2017 dollars

country comparison to the world: 75

### GDP (OFFICIAL EXCHANGE RATE):

$51.76 billion (2017 est.) (2017 est.)

### GDP - REAL GROWTH RATE:

6% (2017 est.)

7% (2016 est.)

7% (2015 est.)

country comparison to the world: 34

### GDP - PER CAPITA (PPP):

$3,200 (2017 est.)

$3,100 (2016 est.)

$3,000 (2015 est.)

note: data are in 2017 dollars

country comparison to the world: 193

### GROSS NATIONAL SAVING:

25% of GDP (2017 est.)

23.1% of GDP (2016 est.)

24.9% of GDP (2015 est.)

country comparison to the world: 60

### GDP - COMPOSITION, BY END USE:

**household consumption:** 62.4% (2017 est.)

government consumption: 12.5% (2017 est.)

investment in fixed capital: 36.1% (2017 est.)

investment in inventories: -8.7% (2017 est.)

exports of goods and services: 18.1% (2017 est.)

imports of goods and services: -20.5% (2017 est.)

### GDP - COMPOSITION, BY SECTOR OF ORIGIN:

agriculture: 23.4% (2017 est.)

industry: 28.6% (2017 est.)

services: 47.6% (2017 est.)

### AGRICULTURE - PRODUCTS:

coffee, sisal, tea, cotton, pyrethrum (insecticide made from chrysanthemums), cashew nuts, tobacco, cloves, corn, wheat, cassava (manioc, tapioca), bananas, fruits, vegetables; cattle, sheep, goats

### INDUSTRIES:

agricultural processing (sugar, beer, cigarettes, sisal twine); mining (diamonds, gold, and iron), salt, soda ash; cement, oil refining, shoes, apparel, wood products, fertilizer

### INDUSTRIAL PRODUCTION GROWTH RATE:

12% (2017 est.)

country comparison to the world: 8

### LABOR FORCE:

24.89 million (2017 est.)

country comparison to the world: 26

### LABOR FORCE - BY OCCUPATION:

agriculture: 66.9%

industry: 6.4%

services: 26.6% (2014 est.)

### UNEMPLOYMENT RATE:

10.3% (2014 est.)

country comparison to the world: 144

### POPULATION BELOW POVERTY LINE:

22.8% (2015 est.)

### HOUSEHOLD INCOME OR CONSUMPTION BY PERCENTAGE SHARE:

lowest 10%: 29.6% (2007)

highest 10%: 29.6% (2007)

### DISTRIBUTION OF FAMILY INCOME - GINI INDEX:

37.6 (2007)

34.6 (2000)

country comparison to the world: 82

### BUDGET:

revenues: 7.873 billion (2017 est.)

expenditures: 8.818 billion (2017 est.)

### TAXES AND OTHER REVENUES:

15.2% (of GDP) (2017 est.)

country comparison to the world: 192

### BUDGET SURPLUS (+) OR DEFICIT (-):

-1.8% (of GDP) (2017 est.)

country comparison to the world: 100

### PUBLIC DEBT:

37% of GDP (2017 est.)

38% of GDP (2016 est.)

country comparison to the world: 141

### FISCAL YEAR:

1 July - 30 June

### INFLATION RATE (CONSUMER PRICES):

5.3% (2017 est.)

5.2% (2016 est.)

country comparison to the world: 175

### CENTRAL BANK DISCOUNT RATE:

8.25% (31 December 2010)

3.7% (31 December 2009)

country comparison to the world: 38

### COMMERCIAL BANK PRIME LENDING RATE:

17.62% (31 December 2017 est.)

15.96% (31 December 2016 est.)

country comparison to the world: 24

### STOCK OF NARROW MONEY:

$5.002 billion (31 December 2017 est.)

$4.641 billion (31 December 2016 est.)

country comparison to the world: 105

### STOCK OF BROAD MONEY:

$5.002 billion (31 December 2017 est.)

$4.641 billion (31 December 2016 est.)

country comparison to the world: 108

### STOCK OF DOMESTIC CREDIT:

$9.045 billion (31 December 2017 est.)

$9.616 billion (31 December 2016 est.)

country comparison to the world: 110

### MARKET VALUE OF PUBLICLY TRADED SHARES:

$1.803 billion (31 December 2012 est.)

$1.539 billion (31 December 2011 est.)

$1.264 billion (31 December 2010 est.)

country comparison to the world: 101

### CURRENT ACCOUNT BALANCE:

-$1.464 billion (2017 est.)

-$2.137 billion (2016 est.)

country comparison to the world: 155

### EXPORTS:

$4.971 billion (2017 est.)

$5.697 billion (2016 est.)

country comparison to the world: 109

### EXPORTS - PARTNERS:

India 21.8%, South Africa 17.9%, Kenya 8.8%, Switzerland 6.7%, Belgium 5.9%, Democratic Republic of the Congo 5.8%, China 4.8% (2017)

### EXPORTS - COMMODITIES:

gold, coffee, cashew nuts, manufactures, cotton

### IMPORTS:

$7.869 billion (2017 est.)

$8.464 billion (2016 est.)

country comparison to the world: 112

### IMPORTS - COMMODITIES:

consumer goods, machinery and transportation equipment, industrial raw materials, crude oil

### IMPORTS - PARTNERS:

India 16.5%, China 15.8%, UAE 9.2%, Saudi Arabia 7.9%, South Africa 5.1%, Japan 4.9%, Switzerland 4.4% (2017)

### RESERVES OF FOREIGN EXCHANGE AND GOLD:

$5.301 billion (31 December 2017 est.)

$4.067 billion (31 December 2016 est.)

note: excludes gold

country comparison to the world: 94

### DEBT - EXTERNAL:

$17.66 billion (31 December 2017 est.)

$15.21 billion (31 December 2016 est.)

country comparison to the world: 97

### STOCK OF DIRECT FOREIGN INVESTMENT - AT HOME:

NA

### STOCK OF DIRECT FOREIGN INVESTMENT - ABROAD:

NA

### EXCHANGE RATES:

Tanzanian shillings (TZS) per US dollar -

2,243.8 (2017 est.)

2,177.1 (2016 est.)

2,177.1 (2015 est.)

1,989.7 (2014 est.)

1,654 (2013 est.)

## ENERGY :: TANZANIA

### ELECTRICITY ACCESS:

population without electricity: 37.4 million (2013)

electrification - total population: 24% (2013)

electrification - urban areas: 71% (2013)

electrification - rural areas: 4% (2013)

**ELECTRICITY - PRODUCTION:**
6.699 billion kWh (2016 est.)

country comparison to the world: 114

**ELECTRICITY - CONSUMPTION:**
5.682 billion kWh (2016 est.)

country comparison to the world: 118

**ELECTRICITY - EXPORTS:**
0 kWh (2016 est.)

country comparison to the world: 206

**ELECTRICITY - IMPORTS:**
102 million kWh (2016 est.)

country comparison to the world: 99

**ELECTRICITY - INSTALLED GENERATING CAPACITY:**
1.457 million kW (2016 est.)

country comparison to the world: 124

**ELECTRICITY - FROM FOSSIL FUELS:**
55% of total installed capacity (2016 est.)

country comparison to the world: 141

**ELECTRICITY - FROM NUCLEAR FUELS:**
0% of total installed capacity (2017 est.)

country comparison to the world: 192

**ELECTRICITY - FROM HYDROELECTRIC PLANTS:**
40% of total installed capacity (2017 est.)

country comparison to the world: 53

**ELECTRICITY - FROM OTHER RENEWABLE SOURCES:**
6% of total installed capacity (2017 est.)

country comparison to the world: 106

**CRUDE OIL - PRODUCTION:**
0 bbl/day (2017 est.)

country comparison to the world: 205

**CRUDE OIL - EXPORTS:**
0 bbl/day (2015 est.)

country comparison to the world: 205

**CRUDE OIL - IMPORTS:**
0 bbl/day (2015 est.)

country comparison to the world: 202

**CRUDE OIL - PROVED RESERVES:**
0 bbl (1 January 2018 est.)

country comparison to the world: 202

**REFINED PETROLEUM PRODUCTS - PRODUCTION:**
0 bbl/day (2015 est.)

country comparison to the world: 206

**REFINED PETROLEUM PRODUCTS - CONSUMPTION:**
72,000 bbl/day (2016 est.)

country comparison to the world: 92

**REFINED PETROLEUM PRODUCTS - EXPORTS:**
0 bbl/day (2015 est.)

country comparison to the world: 207

**REFINED PETROLEUM PRODUCTS - IMPORTS:**
67,830 bbl/day (2015 est.)

country comparison to the world: 69

**NATURAL GAS - PRODUCTION:**
3.115 billion cu m (2017 est.)

country comparison to the world: 56

**NATURAL GAS - CONSUMPTION:**
3.115 billion cu m (2017 est.)

country comparison to the world: 74

**NATURAL GAS - EXPORTS:**
0 cu m (2017 est.)

country comparison to the world: 198

**NATURAL GAS - IMPORTS:**
0 cu m (2017 est.)

country comparison to the world: 198

**NATURAL GAS - PROVED RESERVES:**
6.513 billion cu m (1 January 2018 est.)

country comparison to the world: 85

**CARBON DIOXIDE EMISSIONS FROM CONSUMPTION OF ENERGY:**
14.57 million Mt (2017 est.)

country comparison to the world: 93

## COMMUNICATIONS :: TANZANIA

**TELEPHONES - FIXED LINES:**
total subscriptions: 127,094 (2017 est.)

subscriptions per 100 inhabitants: less than 1 (2017 est.)

country comparison to the world: 137

**TELEPHONES - MOBILE CELLULAR:**
total subscriptions: 39,953,860 (2017 est.)

subscriptions per 100 inhabitants: 74 (2017 est.)

country comparison to the world: 36

**TELEPHONE SYSTEM:**
general assessment: telecommunications services are marginal; system operating below capacity and being modernized for better service (2016)

domestic: fixed-line telephone network inadequate with less than 1 connection per 100 persons; mobile-cellular service, aided by multiple providers, is increasing rapidly and exceeds 75 telephones per 100 persons; trunk service provided by open-wire, microwave radio relay, tropospheric scatter, and fiber-optic cable; some links being made digital (2016)

international: country code - 255; landing point for the EASSy fiber-optic submarine cable system linking East Africa with Europe and North America; satellite earth stations - 2 Intelsat (1 Indian Ocean, 1 Atlantic Ocean) (2016)

**BROADCAST MEDIA:**
a state-owned TV station and multiple privately owned TV stations; state-owned national radio station supplemented by more than 40 privately owned radio stations; transmissions of several international broadcasters are available (2007)

**INTERNET COUNTRY CODE:**
.tz

**INTERNET USERS:**
total: 6,822,754 (July 2016 est.)

percent of population: 13% (July 2016 est.)

country comparison to the world: 61

**BROADBAND - FIXED SUBSCRIPTIONS:**
total: 1,848,167 (2017 est.)

subscriptions per 100 inhabitants: 3 (2017 est.)

country comparison to the world: 52

## TRANSPORTATION :: TANZANIA

**NATIONAL AIR TRANSPORT SYSTEM:**
number of registered air carriers: 5 (2015)

inventory of registered aircraft operated by air carriers: 17 (2015)

annual passenger traffic on registered air carriers: 1,239,707 (2015)

annual freight traffic on registered air carriers: 2,337,440 mt-km (2015)

**CIVIL AIRCRAFT REGISTRATION COUNTRY CODE PREFIX:**

5H (2016)

### AIRPORTS:
166 (2013)

country comparison to the world: 34

### AIRPORTS - WITH PAVED RUNWAYS:
total: 10 (2013)

over 3,047 m: 2 (2013)

2,438 to 3,047 m: 2 (2013)

1,524 to 2,437 m: 4 (2013)

914 to 1,523 m: 2 (2013)

### AIRPORTS - WITH UNPAVED RUNWAYS:
total: 156 (2013)

over 3,047 m: 1 (2013)

1,524 to 2,437 m: 24 (2013)

914 to 1,523 m: 98 (2013)

under 914 m: 33 (2013)

### PIPELINES:
311 km gas, 891 km oil, 8 km refined products (2013)

### RAILWAYS:
total: 4,567 km (2014)

narrow gauge: 1,860 km 1.067-m gauge (2014)

2707 1.000-m gauge

country comparison to the world: 43

### ROADWAYS:
total: 86,472 km (2010)

paved: 7,092 km (2010)

unpaved: 79,380 km (2010)

country comparison to the world: 56

### WATERWAYS:
(Lake Tanganyika, Lake Victoria, and Lake Nyasa (Lake Malawi) are the principal avenues of commerce with neighboring countries; the rivers are not navigable) (2011)

### MERCHANT MARINE:
total: 279 (2017)

by type: bulk carrier 10, container ship 9, general cargo 147, oil tanker 29, other 84 (2017)

country comparison to the world: 55

### PORTS AND TERMINALS:
major seaport(s): Dar es Salaam, Zanzibar

## MILITARY AND SECURITY :: TANZANIA

### MILITARY EXPENDITURES:
1.14% of GDP (2016)

1.13% of GDP (2015)

1.05% of GDP (2014)

1% of GDP (2013)

0.93% of GDP (2012)

country comparison to the world: 105

### MILITARY BRANCHES:
Tanzania People's Defense Force (Jeshi la Wananchi la Tanzania, JWTZ): Army, Naval Wing (includes Coast Guard), Air Defense Command (includes Air Wing), National Service (2007)

### MILITARY SERVICE AGE AND OBLIGATION:
18 years of age for voluntary military service; no conscription (2012)

### MARITIME THREATS:
the International Maritime Bureau reports that shipping in territorial and offshore waters in the Indian Ocean remain at risk for piracy and armed robbery against ships, especially as Somali-based pirates extend their activities south; numerous commercial vessels have been attacked and hijacked both at anchor and while underway; crews have been robbed and stores or cargoes stolen

## TERRORISM :: TANZANIA

### TERRORIST GROUPS - FOREIGN BASED:
al-Shabaab:

aim(s): attract Tanzanian recruits to support terrorist operations in Kenya and Somalia

area(s) of operation: maintains minimal clandestine footprint in key cities (April 2018)

## TRANSNATIONAL ISSUES :: TANZANIA

### DISPUTES - INTERNATIONAL:
dispute with Tanzania over the boundary in Lake Nyasa (Lake Malawi) and the meandering Songwe River; Malawi contends that the entire lake up to the Tanzanian shoreline is its territory, while Tanzania claims the border is in the center of the lake; the conflict was reignited in 2012 when Malawi awarded a license to a British company for oil exploration in the lake

### REFUGEES AND INTERNALLY DISPLACED PERSONS:
refugees (country of origin): 222,826 (Burundi), 84,255 (Democratic Republic of the Congo) (2018)

### TRAFFICKING IN PERSONS:
current situation: Tanzania is a source, transit, and destination country for men, women, and children subjected to forced labor and sex trafficking; the exploitation of young girls in domestic servitude continues to be Tanzania's largest human trafficking problem; Tanzanian boys are subject to forced labor mainly on farms but also in mines and quarries, in the informal commercial sector, in factories, in the sex trade, and possibly on small fishing boats; Tanzanian children and adults are subjected to domestic servitude, other forms of forced labor, and sex trafficking in other African countries, the Middle East, Europe, and the US; internal trafficking is more prevalent than transnational trafficking and is usually facilitated by friends, family members, or intermediaries with false offers of education or legitimate jobs; trafficking victims from Burundi, Kenya, South Asia, and Yemen are forced to work in Tanzania's agricultural, mining, and domestic service sectors or may be sex trafficked

tier rating: Tier 2 Watch List – Tanzania does not fully comply with the minimum standards for the elimination of trafficking; however, it is making significant efforts to do so; in 2014, Tanzania was granted a waiver from an otherwise required downgrade to Tier 3 because its government has a written plan that, if implemented, would constitute making significant efforts to bring itself into compliance with the minimum standards for the elimination of trafficking; the government adopted a three-year national action plan and implementing regulations for the 2008 anti-trafficking law; authorities somewhat increased their number of trafficking investigations and prosecutions and convicted one offender, but the penalty was a fine in lieu of prison, which was inadequate given the severity of the crime; the government did not operate any shelters for victims and relied on NGOs to provide protective services (2015)

### ILLICIT DRUGS:
targeted by traffickers moving hashish, Afghan heroin, and South American cocaine transported down the East African coastline, through airports, or overland through Central Africa; Zanzibar likely used by traffickers for drug smuggling; traffickers in the past

have recruited Tanzanian couriers to
move drugs through Iran into East Asia

# EAST ASIA / SOUTHEAST ASIA :: THAILAND

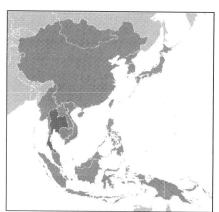

## INTRODUCTION :: THAILAND

**BACKGROUND:**

A unified Thai kingdom was established in the mid-14th century. Known as Siam until 1939, Thailand is the only Southeast Asian country never to have been colonized by a European power. A bloodless revolution in 1932 led to the establishment of a constitutional monarchy. After the Japanese invaded Thailand in 1941, the government split into a pro-Japan faction and a pro-Ally faction backed by the King. Following the war, Thailand became a US treaty ally in 1954 after sending troops to Korea and later fighting alongside the US in Vietnam. Thailand since 2005 has experienced several rounds of political turmoil including a military coup in 2006 that ousted then Prime Minister THAKSIN Shinawatra, followed by large-scale street protests by competing political factions in 2008, 2009, and 2010. THAKSIN's youngest sister, YINGLAK Chinnawat, in 2011 led the Puea Thai Party to an electoral win and assumed control of the government.

In early May 2014, after months of large-scale anti-government protests in Bangkok beginning in November 2013, YINGLAK was removed from office by the Constitutional Court and in late May 2014 the Royal Thai Army, led by Royal Thai Army Gen. PRAYUT Chan-ocha, staged a coup against the caretaker government. PRAYUT was appointed prime minister in August 2014. The interim military government created several interim institutions to promote reform and draft a new constitution, which was passed in a national referendum in August 2016. In late 2017, PRAYUT announced elections would be held by November 2018; he has subsequently suggested they might occur in February 2019. King PHUMIPHON Adunyadet passed away in October 2016 after 70 years on the throne; his only son, WACHIRALONGKON Bodinthrathepphayawarangkun, ascended the throne in December 2016. He signed the new constitution in April 2017. Thailand has also experienced violence associated with the ethno-nationalist insurgency in its southern Malay-Muslim majority provinces. Since January 2004, thousands have been killed and wounded in the insurgency.

## GEOGRAPHY :: THAILAND

**LOCATION:**

Southeastern Asia, bordering the Andaman Sea and the Gulf of Thailand, southeast of Burma

**GEOGRAPHIC COORDINATES:**

15 00 N, 100 00 E

**MAP REFERENCES:**

Southeast Asia

**AREA:**

total: 513,120 sq km

land: 510,890 sq km

water: 2,230 sq km

country comparison to the world: 52

**AREA - COMPARATIVE:**

about three times the size of Florida; slightly more than twice the size of Wyoming

**LAND BOUNDARIES:**

total: 5,673 km

border countries (4): Burma 2416 km, Cambodia 817 km, Laos 1845 km, Malaysia 595 km

**COASTLINE:**

3,219 km

**MARITIME CLAIMS:**

territorial sea: 12 nm

exclusive economic zone: 200 nm

continental shelf: 200-m depth or to the depth of exploitation

**CLIMATE:**

tropical; rainy, warm, cloudy southwest monsoon (mid-May to September); dry, cool northeast monsoon (November to mid-March); southern isthmus always hot and humid

**TERRAIN:**

central plain; Khorat Plateau in the east; mountains elsewhere

**ELEVATION:**

mean elevation: 287 m

elevation extremes: 0 m lowest point: Gulf of Thailand

2565 highest point: Doi Inthanon

**NATURAL RESOURCES:**

tin, rubber, natural gas, tungsten, tantalum, timber, lead, fish, gypsum, lignite, fluorite, arable land

**LAND USE:**

agricultural land: 41.2% (2011 est.)

arable land: 30.8% (2011 est.) / permanent crops: 8.8% (2011 est.) / permanent pasture: 1.6% (2011 est.)

forest: 37.2% (2011 est.)

other: 21.6% (2011 est.)

**IRRIGATED LAND:**

64,150 sq km (2012)

**POPULATION DISTRIBUTION:**

highest population density is found in and around Bangkok; significant population clusters found througout large parts of the country, particularly north and northeast of Bangkok and in the extreme southern region of the country

**NATURAL HAZARDS:**

land subsidence in Bangkok area resulting from the depletion of the water table; droughts

**ENVIRONMENT - CURRENT ISSUES:**

air pollution from vehicle emissions; water pollution from organic and factory wastes; water scarcity; deforestation; soil erosion; wildlife populations threatened by illegal hunting; hazardous waste disposal

**ENVIRONMENT - INTERNATIONAL AGREEMENTS:**

party to: Biodiversity, Climate Change, Climate Change-Kyoto Protocol, Desertification, Endangered Species, Hazardous Wastes, Marine Life Conservation, Ozone Layer Protection, Tropical Timber 83, Tropical Timber 94, Wetlands

signed, but not ratified: Law of the Sea

**GEOGRAPHY - NOTE:**

controls only land route from Asia to Malaysia and Singapore; ideas for the construction of a canal across the Kra Isthmus that would create a bypass to the Strait of Malacca and shorten shipping times around Asia continue to be discussed

# PEOPLE AND SOCIETY :: THAILAND

**POPULATION:**
68,615,858 (July 2018 est.)

country comparison to the world: 20

**NATIONALITY:**

noun: Thai (singular and plural)

adjective: Thai

**ETHNIC GROUPS:**

Thai 97.5%, Burmese 1.3%, other 1.1%, unspecified <.1% (2015 est.)

note: data represent population by nationality

**LANGUAGES:**

Thai (official) only 90.7%, Thai and other languages 6.4%, only other languages (includes Malay, Burmese) (2010 est.)

note: data represent population by language(s) spoken at home; English is a secondary language of the elite

**RELIGIONS:**

Buddhist 94.6%, Muslim 4.3%, Christian 1%, other (2015 est.)

**AGE STRUCTURE:**

0-14 years: 16.73% (male 5,880,026 /female 5,598,611)

15-24 years: 13.83% (male 4,840,303 /female 4,649,589)

25-54 years: 46.12% (male 15,670,881 /female 15,972,254)

55-64 years: 12.35% (male 3,970,979 /female 4,503,647)

65 years and over: 10.97% (male 3,289,576 /female 4,239,992) (2018 est.)

**DEPENDENCY RATIOS:**

total dependency ratio: 40 (2015 est.)

youth dependency ratio: 25.2 (2015 est.)

elderly dependency ratio: 14.8 (2015 est.)

potential support ratio: 6.8 (2015 est.)

**MEDIAN AGE:**

total: 38.1 years

male: 37 years

female: 39.2 years (2018 est.)

country comparison to the world: 63

**POPULATION GROWTH RATE:**

0.29% (2018 est.)

country comparison to the world: 173

**BIRTH RATE:**

11 births/1,000 population (2018 est.)

country comparison to the world: 177

**DEATH RATE:**

8.1 deaths/1,000 population (2018 est.)

country comparison to the world: 87

**NET MIGRATION RATE:**

0 migrant(s)/1,000 population (2017 est.)

country comparison to the world: 98

**POPULATION DISTRIBUTION:**

highest population density is found in and around Bangkok; significant population clusters found througout large parts of the country, particularly north and northeast of Bangkok and in the extreme southern region of the country

**URBANIZATION:**

urban population: 49.9% of total population (2018)

rate of urbanization: 1.73% annual rate of change (2015-20 est.)

**MAJOR URBAN AREAS - POPULATION:**

10.156 million BANGKOK (capital), 1.272 million Samut Prakan, 1.135 million Chiang Mai, 940,000 Songkla, 937,000 Nothaburi, 889,000 Pathum Thani (2018)

**SEX RATIO:**

at birth: 1.05 male(s)/female (2017 est.)

0-14 years: 1.05 male(s)/female (2017 est.)

15-24 years: 1.04 male(s)/female (2017 est.)

25-54 years: 0.98 male(s)/female (2017 est.)

55-64 years: 0.89 male(s)/female (2017 est.)

65 years and over: 0.78 male(s)/female (2017 est.)

total population: 0.97 male(s)/female (2017 est.)

**MOTHER'S MEAN AGE AT FIRST BIRTH:**

23.3 years (2009 est.)

**MATERNAL MORTALITY RATE:**

20 deaths/100,000 live births (2015 est.)

country comparison to the world: 129

**INFANT MORTALITY RATE:**

total: 9 deaths/1,000 live births (2018 est.)

male: 9.9 deaths/1,000 live births (2018 est.)

female: 8 deaths/1,000 live births (2018 est.)

country comparison to the world: 145

**LIFE EXPECTANCY AT BIRTH:**

total population: 75.1 years (2018 est.)

male: 71.9 years (2018 est.)

female: 78.5 years (2018 est.)

country comparison to the world: 115

**TOTAL FERTILITY RATE:**

1.52 children born/woman (2018 est.)

country comparison to the world: 194

**CONTRACEPTIVE PREVALENCE RATE:**

78.4% (2015/16)

**HEALTH EXPENDITURES:**

6.5% of GDP (2014)

country comparison to the world: 94

**PHYSICIANS DENSITY:**

0.47 physicians/1,000 population (2015)

**HOSPITAL BED DENSITY:**

2.1 beds/1,000 population (2010)

**DRINKING WATER SOURCE:**

improved:

urban: 97.6% of population

rural: 98% of population

total: 97.8% of population

unimproved:

urban: 2.4% of population

rural: 2% of population

total: 2.2% of population (2015 est.)

**SANITATION FACILITY ACCESS:**

improved:

urban: 89.9% of population (2015 est.)

rural: 96.1% of population (2015 est.)

total: 93% of population (2015 est.)

unimproved:

urban: 10.1% of population (2015 est.)

rural: 3.9% of population (2015 est.)

total: 7% of population (2015 est.)

**HIV/AIDS - ADULT PREVALENCE RATE:**

1.1% (2017 est.)

country comparison to the world: 42

**HIV/AIDS - PEOPLE LIVING WITH HIV/AIDS:**

440,000 (2017 est.)

country comparison to the world: 17

**HIV/AIDS - DEATHS:**

15,000 (2017 est.)

country comparison to the world: 17

**MAJOR INFECTIOUS DISEASES:**

degree of risk: very high (2016)

food or waterborne diseases: bacterial diarrhea (2016)

vectorborne diseases: dengue fever, Japanese encephalitis, and malaria (2016)

**OBESITY - ADULT PREVALENCE RATE:**

10% (2016)

country comparison to the world: 140

**CHILDREN UNDER THE AGE OF 5 YEARS UNDERWEIGHT:**

6.7% (2016)

country comparison to the world: 73

**EDUCATION EXPENDITURES:**

4.1% of GDP (2013)

country comparison to the world: 109

**LITERACY:**

definition: age 15 and over can read and write (2015 est.)

total population: 92.9% (2015 est.)

male: 94.7% (2015 est.)

female: 91.2% (2015 est.)

**SCHOOL LIFE EXPECTANCY (PRIMARY TO TERTIARY EDUCATION):**

total: 16 years (2015)

male: 16 years (2015)

female: 16 years (2015)

**UNEMPLOYMENT, YOUTH AGES 15-24:**

total: 3.7% (2016 est.)

male: 3% (2016 est.)

female: 4.7% (2016 est.)

country comparison to the world: 160

# GOVERNMENT :: THAILAND

**COUNTRY NAME:**

conventional long form: Kingdom of Thailand

conventional short form: Thailand

local long form: Ratcha Anachak Thai

local short form: Prathet Thai

former: Siam

etymology: Land of the Tai [People]"; the meaning of "tai" is uncertain, but may originally have meant "human beings," "people," or "free people

**GOVERNMENT TYPE:**

constitutional monarchy; note - interim military-affiliated government since May 2014

**CAPITAL:**

name: Bangkok

geographic coordinates: 13 45 N, 100 31 E

time difference: UTC+7 (12 hours ahead of Washington, DC, during Standard Time)

**ADMINISTRATIVE DIVISIONS:**

76 provinces (changwat, singular and plural) and 1 municipality* (maha nakhon); Amnat Charoen, Ang Thong, Bueng Kan, Buri Ram, Chachoengsao, Chai Nat, Chaiyaphum, Chanthaburi, Chiang Mai, Chiang Rai, Chon Buri, Chumphon, Kalasin, Kamphaeng Phet, Kanchanaburi, Khon Kaen, Krabi, Krung Thep* (Bangkok), Lampang, Lamphun, Loei, Lop Buri, Mae Hong Son, Maha Sarakham, Mukdahan, Nakhon Nayok, Nakhon Pathom, Nakhon Phanom, Nakhon Ratchasima, Nakhon Sawan, Nakhon Si Thammarat, Nan, Narathiwat, Nong Bua Lamphu, Nong Khai, Nonthaburi, Pathum Thani, Pattani, Phangnga, Phatthalung, Phayao, Phetchabun, Phetchaburi, Phichit, Phitsanulok, Phra Nakhon Si Ayutthaya, Phrae, Phuket, Prachin Buri, Prachuap Khiri Khan, Ranong, Ratchaburi, Rayong, Roi Et, Sa Kaeo, Sakon Nakhon, Samut Prakan, Samut Sakhon, Samut Songkhram, Saraburi, Satun, Sing Buri, Si Sa Ket, Songkhla, Sukhothai, Suphan Buri, Surat Thani, Surin, Tak, Trang, Trat, Ubon Ratchathani, Udon Thani, Uthai Thani, Uttaradit, Yala, Yasothon

**INDEPENDENCE:**

1238 (traditional founding date; never colonized)

**NATIONAL HOLIDAY:**

Birthday of King WACHIRALONGKON, 28 July (1952)

**CONSTITUTION:**

history: many previous; latest completed 29 March 2016, approved by referendum 7 August 2016, signed into law by the king 6 April 2017 (2017)

amendments: proposed as a joint resolution by the Council of Ministers and the National Council for Peace and Order (the junta that has ruled Thailand since the 2014 coup) and submitted as a draft to the National Legislative Assembly; passage requires majority vote of the existing Assembly members and presentation to the monarch for assent and countersignature by the prime minister (2017)

## LEGAL SYSTEM:
civil law system with common law influences

## INTERNATIONAL LAW ORGANIZATION PARTICIPATION:
has not submitted an ICJ jurisdiction declaration; non-party state to the ICCt

## CITIZENSHIP:
**citizenship by birth:** no

**citizenship by descent only:** at least one parent must be a citizen of Thailand

**dual citizenship recognized:** no

**residency requirement for naturalization:** 5 years

## SUFFRAGE:
18 years of age; universal and compulsory

## EXECUTIVE BRANCH:
**chief of state:** King WACHIRALONGKON Bodinthrathepphayawarangkun, also spelled Vajiralongkorn Bodindradebayavarangkun, (since 1 December 2016); note - King PHUMIPHON Adunyadet, also spelled BHUMIBOL Adulyadej (since 9 June 1946) died 13 October 2016

**head of government:** Interim Prime Minister Gen. PRAYUT Chan-ocha (since 25 August 2014); Deputy Prime Ministers PRAWIT Wongsuwan, Gen. (since 31 August 2014), WISSANU Kruea-ngam (since 31 August 2014), SOMKHIT Chatusiphithak (since 20 August 2015), PRACHIN Chantong, Air Chief Mar. (since 20 August 2015), CHATCHAI Sarikan, Gen. (since 23 November 2017)

**cabinet:** Council of Ministers nominated by the prime minister, appointed by the king; a Privy Council advises the king

**elections/appointments:** the monarchy is hereditary; the House of Representatives approves a person for Prime Minister who must then be appointed by the King (as stated in the transitory provision of the 2017 constitution); the office of prime minister can be held for up to a total of 8 years

**note:** Gen. Prayut Chan-ocha was appointed interim prime minister in August 2014, three months after he staged the coup that removed the previously elected government of Prime Minister YINGLAK Chinnawat

## LEGISLATIVE BRANCH:
**description:** in transition; following the May 2014 military coup, a junta-appointed National Legislative Assembly or Sapha Nitibanyat Haeng Chat of no more than 220 members replaced the bicameral National Assembly; expanded to 250 members in September 2016; the 2017 constitution calls for a 250-member military-appointed Senate with 5-year terms and a 500-member elected House of Representatives with 4-year terms

**elections:** Senate - last held on 30 March 2014 but invalidated by the coup (in future, members will be appointed); House of Representatives - last held on 2 February 2014 but later declared invalid by the Constitutional Court (next to be held 24 February 2019)

**election results:** Senate - percent of vote by party - NA; seats by party - NA; House of Representatives - percent of vote by party - NA; seats by party - NA

## JUDICIAL BRANCH:
**highest courts:** Supreme Court of Justice (consists of court president, 6 vice-presidents, and 60-70 judges, and organized into 10 divisions); Constitutional Court (consists of court president and 8 judges); Supreme Administrative Court (number of judges determined by Judicial Commission of the Administrative Courts)

**judge selection and term of office:** Supreme Court judges selected by the Judicial Commission of the Courts of Justice and approved by the monarch; judge term determined by the monarch; Constitutional Court justices - 3 judges drawn from the Supreme Court, 2 judges drawn from the Administrative Court, and 4 judge candidates selected by the Selective Committee for Judges of the Constitutional Court and confirmed by the Senate; judges appointed by the monarch to serve single 9-year terms; Supreme Administrative Court judges selected by the Judicial Commission of the Administrative Courts and appointed by the monarch; judges appointed for life

**subordinate courts:** courts of first instance and appeals courts within both the judicial and administrative systems; military courts

## POLITICAL PARTIES AND LEADERS:
Chat Thai Phatthana Party (Thai Nation Development Party) or CTP
Phumchai Thai Party (Thai Pride Party) or PJT [ANUTHIN Charnweerakul]
Puea Thai Party (For Thais Party) or PTP [WIROT Paoin]
Prachathipat Party (Democrat Party) or DP [ABHISIT Wechachiwa, also spelled ABHISIT Vejjajiva]

**note:** as of 5 April 2018, 98 new parties applied to be registered with the Election Commission in accordance with the provisions of the new organic law on political parties

## INTERNATIONAL ORGANIZATION PARTICIPATION:
ADB, APEC, ARF, ASEAN, BIMSTEC, BIS, CD, CICA, CP, EAS, FAO, G-77, IAEA, IBRD, ICAO, ICC (national committees), ICRM, IDA, IFAD, IFC, IFRCS, IHO, ILO, IMF, IMO, IMSO, Interpol, IOC, IOM, IPU, ISO, ITSO, ITU, ITUC (NGOs), MIGA, NAM, OAS (observer), OIC (observer), OIF (observer), OPCW, OSCE (partner), PCA, PIF (partner), UN, UNAMID, UNCTAD, UNESCO, UNHCR, UNIDO, UNMOGIP, UNOCI, UNWTO, UPU, WCO, WFTU (NGOs), WHO, WIPO, WMO, WTO

## DIPLOMATIC REPRESENTATION IN THE US:
**chief of mission:** Ambassador Virachai PLASAI (since 22 June 2018)

**chancery:** 1024 Wisconsin Avenue NW, Suite 401, Washington, DC 20007

**telephone:** [1] (202) 944-3600

**FAX:** [1] (202) 944-3611

**consulate(s) general:** Chicago, Los Angeles, New York

## DIPLOMATIC REPRESENTATION FROM THE US:
**chief of mission:** Ambassador (vacant); Charge d'Affaires Peter HAMMOND (since October 2018)

**embassy:** 95 Wireless Road, Bangkok 10330

**mailing address:** APO AP 96546

**telephone:** [66] 2 205-4000

FAX: [66] 2-205-4306

consulate(s) general: Chiang Mai

## FLAG DESCRIPTION:

five horizontal bands of red (top), white, blue (double width), white, and red; the red color symbolizes the nation and the blood of life, white represents religion and the purity of Buddhism, and blue stands for the monarchy

note: similar to the flag of Costa Rica but with the blue and red colors reversed

## NATIONAL SYMBOL(S):

garuda (mythical half-man, half-bird figure), elephant; national colors: red, white, blue

## NATIONAL ANTHEM:

name: "Phleng Chat Thai" (National Anthem of Thailand)

lyrics/music: Luang SARANUPRAPAN/Phra JENDURIYANG

note: music adopted 1932, lyrics adopted 1939; by law, people are required to stand for the national anthem at 0800 and 1800 every day; the anthem is played in schools, offices, theaters, and on television and radio during this time; "Phleng Sanlasoen Phra Barami" (A Salute to the Monarch) serves as the royal anthem and is played in the presence of the royal family and during certain state ceremonies

# ECONOMY :: THAILAND

## ECONOMY - OVERVIEW:

With a relatively well-developed infrastructure, a free-enterprise economy, and generally pro-investment policies, Thailand is highly dependent on international trade, with exports accounting for about two-thirds of GDP. Thailand's exports include electronics, agricultural commodities, automobiles and parts, and processed foods. The industry and service sectors produce about 90% of GDP. The agricultural sector, comprised mostly of small-scale farms, contributes only 10% of GDP but employs about one-third of the labor force. Thailand has attracted an estimated 3.0-4.5 million migrant workers, mostly from neighboring countries.

Over the last few decades, Thailand has reduced poverty substantially. In 2013, the Thai Government implemented a nationwide 300 baht (roughly $10) per day minimum wage policy and deployed new tax reforms designed to lower rates on middle-income earners.

Thailand's economy is recovering from slow growth during the years since the 2014 coup. Thailand's economic fundamentals are sound, with low inflation, low unemployment, and reasonable public and external debt levels. Tourism and government spending - mostly on infrastructure and short-term stimulus measures – have helped to boost the economy, and The Bank of Thailand has been supportive, with several interest rate reductions.

Over the longer-term, household debt levels, political uncertainty, and an aging population pose risks to growth.

## GDP (PURCHASING POWER PARITY):

$1.236 trillion (2017 est.)

$1.19 trillion (2016 est.)

$1.152 trillion (2015 est.)

note: data are in 2017 dollars

country comparison to the world: 20

## GDP (OFFICIAL EXCHANGE RATE):

$455.4 billion (2017 est.) (2017 est.)

## GDP - REAL GROWTH RATE:

3.9% (2017 est.)

3.3% (2016 est.)

3% (2015 est.)

country comparison to the world: 84

## GDP - PER CAPITA (PPP):

$17,900 (2017 est.)

$17,200 (2016 est.)

$16,700 (2015 est.)

note: data are in 2017 dollars

country comparison to the world: 98

## GROSS NATIONAL SAVING:

34.1% of GDP (2017 est.)

32.8% of GDP (2016 est.)

30.3% of GDP (2015 est.)

country comparison to the world: 19

## GDP - COMPOSITION, BY END USE:

household consumption: 48.8% (2017 est.)

government consumption: 16.4% (2017 est.)

investment in fixed capital: 23.2% (2017 est.)

investment in inventories: -0.4% (2017 est.)

exports of goods and services: 68.2% (2017 est.)

imports of goods and services: -54.6% (2017 est.)

## GDP - COMPOSITION, BY SECTOR OF ORIGIN:

agriculture: 8.2% (2017 est.)

industry: 36.2% (2017 est.)

services: 55.6% (2017 est.)

## AGRICULTURE - PRODUCTS:

rice, cassava (manioc, tapioca), rubber, corn, sugarcane, coconuts, palm oil, pineapple, livestock, fish products

## INDUSTRIES:

tourism, textiles and garments, agricultural processing, beverages, tobacco, cement, light manufacturing such as jewelry and electric appliances, computers and parts, integrated circuits, furniture, plastics, automobiles and automotive parts, agricultural machinery, air conditioning and refrigeration, ceramics, aluminum, chemical, environmental management, glass, granite and marble, leather, machinery and metal work, petrochemical, petroleum refining, pharmaceuticals, printing, pulp and paper, rubber, sugar, rice, fishing, cassava, world's second-largest tungsten producer and third-largest tin producer

## INDUSTRIAL PRODUCTION GROWTH RATE:

1.6% (2017 est.)

country comparison to the world: 141

## LABOR FORCE:

38.37 million (2017 est.)

country comparison to the world: 16

## LABOR FORCE - BY OCCUPATION:

agriculture: 31.8%

industry: 16.7%

services: 51.5% (2015 est.)

## UNEMPLOYMENT RATE:

0.7% (2017 est.)

0.8% (2016 est.)

country comparison to the world: 5

## POPULATION BELOW POVERTY LINE:

7.2% (2015 est.)

## HOUSEHOLD INCOME OR CONSUMPTION BY PERCENTAGE SHARE:

lowest 10%: 31.5% (2009 est.)

highest 10%: 31.5% (2009 est.)

## DISTRIBUTION OF FAMILY INCOME - GINI INDEX:

44.5 (2015)

48.4 (2011)

country comparison to the world: 44

**BUDGET:**

revenues: 69.23 billion (2017 est.)

expenditures: 85.12 billion (2017 est.)

**TAXES AND OTHER REVENUES:**

15.2% (of GDP) (2017 est.)

country comparison to the world: 193

**BUDGET SURPLUS (+) OR DEFICIT (-):**

-3.5% (of GDP) (2017 est.)

country comparison to the world: 148

**PUBLIC DEBT:**

41.9% of GDP (2017 est.)

41.8% of GDP (2016 est.)

note: data cover general government debt and include debt instruments issued (or owned) by government entities other than the treasury; the data include treasury debt held by foreign entities; the data include debt issued by subnational entities, as well as intragovernmental debt; intragovernmental debt consists of treasury borrowings from surpluses in the social funds, such as for retirement, medical care, and unemployment; debt instruments for the social funds are sold at public auctions

country comparison to the world: 118

**FISCAL YEAR:**

1 October - 30 September

**INFLATION RATE (CONSUMER PRICES):**

0.7% (2017 est.)

0.2% (2016 est.)

country comparison to the world: 38

**CENTRAL BANK DISCOUNT RATE:**

1.5% (31 December 2016)

1.5% (31 December 2015)

country comparison to the world: 128

**COMMERCIAL BANK PRIME LENDING RATE:**

4.42% (31 December 2017 est.)

4.47% (31 December 2016 est.)

country comparison to the world: 157

**STOCK OF NARROW MONEY:**

$62.39 billion (31 December 2017 est.)

$52.03 billion (31 December 2016 est.)

country comparison to the world: 49

**STOCK OF BROAD MONEY:**

$62.39 billion (31 December 2017 est.)

$52.03 billion (31 December 2016 est.)

country comparison to the world: 49

**STOCK OF DOMESTIC CREDIT:**

$584.9 billion (31 December 2017 est.)

$508.4 billion (31 December 2016 est.)

country comparison to the world: 24

**MARKET VALUE OF PUBLICLY TRADED SHARES:**

$348.8 billion (31 December 2015 est.)

$430.4 billion (31 December 2014 est.)

$354.4 billion (31 December 2013 est.)

country comparison to the world: 30

**CURRENT ACCOUNT BALANCE:**

$51.08 billion (2017 est.)

$48.24 billion (2016 est.)

country comparison to the world: 10

**EXPORTS:**

$235.1 billion (2017 est.)

$214.3 billion (2016 est.)

country comparison to the world: 21

**EXPORTS - PARTNERS:**

China 12.4%, US 11.2%, Japan 9.5%, Hong Kong 5.2%, Vietnam 4.9%, Australia 4.5%, Malaysia 4.4% (2017)

**EXPORTS - COMMODITIES:**

automobiles and parts, computer and parts, jewelry and precious stones, polymers of ethylene in primary forms, refine fuels, electronic integrated circuits, chemical products, rice, fish products, rubber products, sugar, cassava, poultry, machinery and parts, iron and steel and their products

**IMPORTS:**

$203.2 billion (2017 est.)

$177.7 billion (2016 est.)

country comparison to the world: 25

**IMPORTS - COMMODITIES:**

machinery and parts, crude oil, electrical machinery and parts, chemicals, iron & steel and product, electronic integrated circuit, automobile's parts, jewelry including silver bars and gold, computers and parts, electrical household appliances, soybean, soybean meal, wheat, cotton, dairy products

**IMPORTS - PARTNERS:**

China 20%, Japan 14.5%, US 6.8%, Malaysia 5.4% (2017)

**RESERVES OF FOREIGN EXCHANGE AND GOLD:**

$202.6 billion (31 December 2017 est.)

$171.9 billion (31 December 2016 est.)

country comparison to the world: 12

**DEBT - EXTERNAL:**

$132 billion (31 December 2017 est.)

$130.6 billion (31 December 2016 est.)

country comparison to the world: 44

**STOCK OF DIRECT FOREIGN INVESTMENT - AT HOME:**

$227.8 billion (31 December 2017 est.)

$193.5 billion (31 December 2016 est.)

country comparison to the world: 30

**STOCK OF DIRECT FOREIGN INVESTMENT - ABROAD:**

$117.4 billion (31 December 2017 est.)

$96.27 billion (31 December 2016 est.)

country comparison to the world: 33

**EXCHANGE RATES:**

baht per US dollar -

34.34 (2017 est.)

35.296 (2016 est.)

35.296 (2015 est.)

34.248 (2014 est.)

32.48 (2013 est.)

## ENERGY :: THAILAND

**ELECTRICITY ACCESS:**

population without electricity: 700,000 (2013)

electrification - total population: 99% (2013)

electrification - urban areas: 99.7% (2013)

electrification - rural areas: 98.3% (2013)

**ELECTRICITY - PRODUCTION:**

181.5 billion kWh (2016 est.)

country comparison to the world: 23

**ELECTRICITY - CONSUMPTION:**

187.7 billion kWh (2016 est.)

country comparison to the world: 22

**ELECTRICITY - EXPORTS:**

2.267 billion kWh (2015 est.)

country comparison to the world: 44

**ELECTRICITY - IMPORTS:**

19.83 billion kWh (2016 est.)

country comparison to the world: 11

**ELECTRICITY - INSTALLED GENERATING CAPACITY:**

44.89 million kW (2016 est.)

country comparison to the world: 24

**ELECTRICITY - FROM FOSSIL FUELS:**

76% of total installed capacity (2016 est.)

country comparison to the world: 94
**ELECTRICITY - FROM NUCLEAR FUELS:**

0% of total installed capacity (2017 est.)

country comparison to the world: 193
**ELECTRICITY - FROM HYDROELECTRIC PLANTS:**

8% of total installed capacity (2017 est.)

country comparison to the world: 124
**ELECTRICITY - FROM OTHER RENEWABLE SOURCES:**

16% of total installed capacity (2017 est.)

country comparison to the world: 55
**CRUDE OIL - PRODUCTION:**

239,700 bbl/day (2017 est.)

country comparison to the world: 34
**CRUDE OIL - EXPORTS:**

790 bbl/day (2015 est.)

country comparison to the world: 76
**CRUDE OIL - IMPORTS:**

875,400 bbl/day (2015 est.)

country comparison to the world: 12
**CRUDE OIL - PROVED RESERVES:**

349.4 million bbl (1 January 2018 est.)

country comparison to the world: 50
**REFINED PETROLEUM PRODUCTS - PRODUCTION:**

1.328 million bbl/day (2015 est.)

country comparison to the world: 14
**REFINED PETROLEUM PRODUCTS - CONSUMPTION:**

1.326 million bbl/day (2016 est.)

country comparison to the world: 16
**REFINED PETROLEUM PRODUCTS - EXPORTS:**

278,300 bbl/day (2015 est.)

country comparison to the world: 29
**REFINED PETROLEUM PRODUCTS - IMPORTS:**

134,200 bbl/day (2015 est.)

country comparison to the world: 44
**NATURAL GAS - PRODUCTION:**

38.59 billion cu m (2017 est.)

country comparison to the world: 22
**NATURAL GAS - CONSUMPTION:**

52.64 billion cu m (2017 est.)

country comparison to the world: 16
**NATURAL GAS - EXPORTS:**

0 cu m (2017 est.)

country comparison to the world: 199
**NATURAL GAS - IMPORTS:**

14.41 billion cu m (2017 est.)

country comparison to the world: 21
**NATURAL GAS - PROVED RESERVES:**

193.4 billion cu m (1 January 2018 est.)

country comparison to the world: 43
**CARBON DIOXIDE EMISSIONS FROM CONSUMPTION OF ENERGY:**

355 million Mt (2017 est.)

country comparison to the world: 19

## COMMUNICATIONS :: THAILAND

**TELEPHONES - FIXED LINES:**

total subscriptions: 2.91 million (2017 est.)

subscriptions per 100 inhabitants: 4 (2017 est.)

country comparison to the world: 49
**TELEPHONES - MOBILE CELLULAR:**

total subscriptions: 121.53 million (2017 est.)

subscriptions per 100 inhabitants: 178 (2017 est.)

country comparison to the world: 11
**TELEPHONE SYSTEM:**

general assessment: high quality system, especially in urban areas like Bangkok (2016)

domestic: fixed-line system provided by both a government-owned and commercial provider; wireless service expanding rapidly (2016)

international: country code - 66; connected to major submarine cable systems providing links throughout Asia, Australia, Middle East, Europe, and US; satellite earth stations - 2 Intelsat (1 Indian Ocean, 1 Pacific Ocean) (2016)

**BROADCAST MEDIA:**

26 digital TV stations in Bangkok broadcast nationally, 6 terrestrial TV stations in Bangkok broadcast nationally via relay stations - 2 of the stations are owned by the military, the other 4 are government-owned or controlled, leased to private enterprise, and all are required to broadcast government-produced news programs twice a day; multi-channel satellite and cable TV subscription services are available; radio frequencies have been allotted for more than 500 government and commercial radio stations; many small community radio stations operate with low-power transmitters (2017)

**INTERNET COUNTRY CODE:**

.th

**INTERNET USERS:**

total: 32,398,778 (July 2016 est.)

percent of population: 47.5% (July 2016 est.)

country comparison to the world: 21
**BROADBAND - FIXED SUBSCRIPTIONS:**

total: 8.208 million (2017 est.)

subscriptions per 100 inhabitants: 12 (2017 est.)

country comparison to the world: 18

## TRANSPORTATION :: THAILAND

**NATIONAL AIR TRANSPORT SYSTEM:**

number of registered air carriers: 19 (2015)

inventory of registered aircraft operated by air carriers: 276 (2015)

annual passenger traffic on registered air carriers: 54,259,629 (2015)

annual freight traffic on registered air carriers: 2,134,149,001 mt-km (2015)

**CIVIL AIRCRAFT REGISTRATION COUNTRY CODE PREFIX:**

HS (2016)

**AIRPORTS:**

101 (2013)

country comparison to the world: 56
**AIRPORTS - WITH PAVED RUNWAYS:**

total: 63 (2013)

over 3,047 m: 8 (2013)

2,438 to 3,047 m: 12 (2013)

1,524 to 2,437 m: 23 (2013)

914 to 1,523 m: 14 (2013)

under 914 m: 6 (2013)

**AIRPORTS - WITH UNPAVED RUNWAYS:**

total: 38 (2013)

2,438 to 3,047 m: 1 (2013)

1,524 to 2,437 m: 1 (2013)

914 to 1,523 m: 10 (2013)

under 914 m: 26 (2013)

**HELIPORTS:**

7 (2013)

**PIPELINES:**

2 km condensate, 5900 km gas, 85 km liquid petroleum gas, 1 km oil, 1097

km refined products (2013)

**RAILWAYS:**

total: 4,127 km (2017)

standard gauge: 84 km 1.435-m gauge (84 km electrified) (2017)

narrow gauge: 4,043 km 1.000-m gauge (2017)

country comparison to the world: 46

**ROADWAYS:**

total: 180,053 km (includes 450 km of expressways) (2006)

country comparison to the world: 30

**WATERWAYS:**

4,000 km (3,701 km navigable by boats with drafts up to 0.9 m) (2011)

country comparison to the world: 26

**MERCHANT MARINE:**

total: 781 (2017)

by type: bulk carrier 25, container ship 23, general cargo 94, oil tanker 240, other 399 (2017)

country comparison to the world: 27

**PORTS AND TERMINALS:**

major seaport(s): Bangkok, Laem Chabang, Map Ta Phut, Prachuap Port, Si Racha

container port(s) (TEUs): Bangkok (1,498,009), Laem Chabang (7,227,431) (2016)

LNG terminal(s) (import): Map Ta Phut

# MILITARY AND SECURITY :: THAILAND

## MILITARY EXPENDITURES:

1.5% of GDP (2017)

1.45% of GDP (2016)

1.44% of GDP (2015)

country comparison to the world: 77

## MILITARY BRANCHES:

Royal Thai Armed Forces (Kongthap Thai, RTARF): Royal Thai Army (Kongthap Bok Thai, RTA), Royal Thai Navy (Kongthap Ruea Thai, RTN, includes Royal Thai Marine Corps), Royal Thai Air Force (Kongthap Agard Thai, RTAF) (2017)

## MILITARY SERVICE AGE AND OBLIGATION:

21 years of age for compulsory military service; 18 years of age for voluntary military service; males register at 18 years of age; 2-year conscript service obligation (2012)

# TRANSNATIONAL ISSUES :: THAILAND

## DISPUTES - INTERNATIONAL:

separatist violence in Thailand's predominantly Malay-Muslim southern provinces prompt border closures and controls with Malaysia to stem insurgent activitiesSoutheast Asian states have enhanced border surveillance to check the spread of avian flutalks continue on completion of demarcation with Laos but disputes remain over several islands in the Mekong Riverdespite continuing border committee talks, Thailand must deal with Karen and other ethnic rebels, refugees, and illegal cross-border activitiesCambodia and Thailand dispute sections of boundaryin 2011, Thailand and Cambodia resorted to arms in the dispute over the location of the boundary on the precipice surmounted by Preah Vihear temple ruins, awarded to Cambodia by ICJ decision in 1962 and part of a planned UN World Heritage siteThailand is studying the feasibility of jointly constructing the Hatgyi Dam on the Salween river near the border with Burmain 2004, international environmentalist pressure prompted China to halt construction of 13 dams on the Salween River that flows through China, Burma, and Thailandapproximately 105,000 mostly Karen refugees fleeing civil strife, political upheaval, and economic stagnation in Burma live in remote camps in Thailand near the border

## REFUGEES AND INTERNALLY DISPLACED PERSONS:

refugees (country of origin): 102,633 (Burma) (2016)

IDPs: 41,000 (resurgence in ethno-nationalist violence in south of country since 2004) (2017)

stateless persons: 486,440 (2017) (estimate represents stateless persons registered with the Thai Government; actual number may be as high as 3.5 million); note - about half of Thailand's northern hill tribe people do not have citizenship and make up the bulk of Thailand's stateless population; most lack documentation showing they or one of their parents were born in Thailand; children born to Burmese refugees are not eligible for Burmese or Thai citizenship and are stateless; most Chao Lay, maritime nomadic peoples, who travel from island to island in the Andaman Sea west of Thailand are also stateless; stateless Rohingya refugees from Burma are considered illegal migrants by Thai authorities and are detained in inhumane conditions or expelled; stateless persons are denied access to voting, property, education, employment, healthcare, and driving

note: Thai nationality was granted to more than 23,000 stateless persons between 2012 and 2016; in 2016, the Government of Thailand approved changes to its citizenship laws that could make 80,000 stateless persons eligible for citizenship, as part of its effort to achieve zero statelessness by 2024 (2018)

## TRAFFICKING IN PERSONS:

current situation: Thailand is a source, transit, and destination country for men, women, and children subjected to forced labor and sex trafficking; victims from Burma, Cambodia, Laos, China, Vietnam, Uzbekistan, and India, migrate to Thailand in search of jobs but are forced, coerced, or defrauded into labor in commercial fishing, fishing-related industries, factories, domestic work, street begging, or the sex trade; some Thai, Burmese, Cambodian, and Indonesian men forced to work on fishing boats are kept at sea for years; sex trafficking of adults and children from Thailand, Laos, Vietnam, and Burma remains a significant problem; Thailand is a transit country for victims from China, Vietnam, Bangladesh, and Burma subjected to sex trafficking and forced labor in Malaysia, Indonesia, Singapore, Russia, South Korea, the US, and countries in Western Europe; Thai victims are also trafficked in North America, Europe, Africa, Asia, and the Middle East

tier rating: Tier 2 Watch List - Thailand does not fully comply with the minimum standards for the elimination of trafficking, and is not making significant efforts to do so; in 2014, authorities investigated, prosecuted, and convicted fewer traffickers and identified fewer victims; some cases of official complicity were investigated and prosecuted, but trafficking-related corruption continues to hinder progress in combatting trafficking; authorities' efforts to screen for victims among vulnerable populations remained inadequate due to a poor understanding of trafficking indicators, a failure to recognize non-physical forms of coercion, and a shortage of language interpreters; the government passed new labor laws increasing the minimum age in the fishing industry to 18 years old, guaranteeing the minimum wage, and requiring work contracts, but weak law enforcement and poor coordination among regulatory agencies enabled exploitive labor practices to continue; the government increased efforts to raise public awareness to the dangers of human trafficking and to deny entry to foreign sex tourists (2015)

**ILLICIT DRUGS:**

a minor producer of opium, heroin, and marijuana; transit point for illicit heroin en route to the international drug market from Burma and Laos; eradication efforts have reduced the area of cannabis cultivation and shifted some production to neighboring countries; opium poppy cultivation has been reduced by eradication efforts; also a drug money-laundering center; minor role in methamphetamine production for regional consumption; major consumer of methamphetamine since the 1990s despite a series of government crackdowns

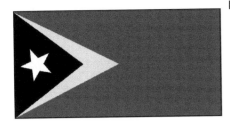

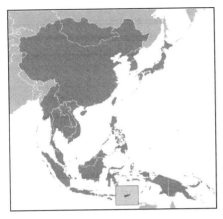

# EAST ASIA / SOUTHEAST ASIA :: TIMOR-LESTE

## INTRODUCTION :: TIMOR-LESTE

### BACKGROUND:

The Portuguese began to trade with the island of Timor in the early 16th century and colonized it in mid-century. Skirmishing with the Dutch in the region eventually resulted in an 1859 treaty in which Portugal ceded the western portion of the island. Imperial Japan occupied Portuguese Timor from 1942 to 1945, but Portugal resumed colonial authority after the Japanese defeat in World War II. East Timor declared itself independent from Portugal on 28 November 1975 and was invaded and occupied by Indonesian forces nine days later. It was incorporated into Indonesia in July 1976 as the province of Timor Timur (East Timor). An unsuccessful campaign of pacification followed over the next two decades, during which an estimated 100,000 to 250,000 people died. In an August 1999 UN-supervised popular referendum, an overwhelming majority of the people of Timor-Leste voted for independence from Indonesia. However, in the next three weeks, anti-independence Timorese militias - organized and supported by the Indonesian military - commenced a large-scale, scorched-earth campaign of retribution. The militias killed approximately 1,400 Timorese and forced 300,000 people into western Timor as refugees. Most of the country's infrastructure, including homes, irrigation systems, water supply systems, and schools, and nearly all of the country's electrical grid were destroyed. On 20 September 1999, Australian-led peacekeeping troops deployed to the country and brought the violence to an end. On 20 May 2002, Timor-Leste was internationally recognized as an independent state.

In 2006, internal tensions threatened the new nation's security when a military strike led to violence and a breakdown of law and order. At Dili's request, an Australian-led International Stabilization Force (ISF) deployed to Timor-Leste, and the UN Security Council established the UN Integrated Mission in Timor-Leste (UNMIT), which included an authorized police presence of over 1,600 personnel. The ISF and UNMIT restored stability, allowing for presidential and parliamentary elections in 2007 in a largely peaceful atmosphere. In February 2008, a rebel group staged an unsuccessful attack against the president and prime minister. The ringleader was killed in the attack, and most of the rebels surrendered in April 2008. Since the attack, the government has enjoyed one of its longest periods of post-independence stability, including successful 2012 elections for both the parliament and president and a successful transition of power in February 2015. In late 2012, the UN Security Council ended its peacekeeping mission in Timor-Leste and both the ISF and UNMIT departed the country.

## GEOGRAPHY :: TIMOR-LESTE

### LOCATION:

Southeastern Asia, northwest of Australia in the Lesser Sunda Islands at the eastern end of the Indonesian archipelago; note - Timor-Leste includes the eastern half of the island of Timor, the Oecussi (Ambeno) region on the northwest portion of the island of Timor, and the islands of Pulau Atauro and Pulau Jaco

### GEOGRAPHIC COORDINATES:

8 50 S, 125 55 E

### MAP REFERENCES:

Southeast Asia

### AREA:

total: 14,874 sq km

land: 14,874 sq km

water: 0 sq km

country comparison to the world: 160

### AREA - COMPARATIVE:

slightly larger than Connecticut

### LAND BOUNDARIES:

total: 253 km

border countries (1): Indonesia 253 km

### COASTLINE:

706 km

### MARITIME CLAIMS:

territorial sea: 12 nm

contiguous zone: 24 nm

exclusive fishing zone: 200 nm

### CLIMATE:

tropical; hot, humid; distinct rainy and dry seasons

### TERRAIN:

mountainous

### ELEVATION:

0 m lowest point: Timor Sea, Savu Sea, and Banda Sea

2963 highest point: Foho Tatamailau

**NATURAL RESOURCES:**

gold, petroleum, natural gas, manganese, marble

**LAND USE:**

agricultural land: 25.1% (2011 est.)

arable land: 10.1% (2011 est.) / permanent crops: 4.9% (2011 est.) / permanent pasture: 10.1% (2011 est.)

forest: 49.1% (2011 est.)

other: 25.8% (2011 est.)

**IRRIGATED LAND:**

350 sq km (2012)

**POPULATION DISTRIBUTION:**

most of the population concentrated in the western third of the country, particularly around Dili

**NATURAL HAZARDS:**

floods and landslides are common; earthquakes; tsunamis; tropical cyclones

**ENVIRONMENT - CURRENT ISSUES:**

air pollution and deterioration of air quality; greenhouse gas emissions; water quality, scarcity, and access; land and soil degradation; forest depletion; widespread use of slash and burn agriculture has led to deforestation and soil erosion; loss of biodiversity

**ENVIRONMENT - INTERNATIONAL AGREEMENTS:**

party to: Biodiversity, Climate Change, Climate Change-Kyoto Protocol, Desertification

signed, but not ratified: none of the selected agreements

**GEOGRAPHY - NOTE:**

Timor comes from the Malay word for "east"; the island of Timor is part of the Malay Archipelago and is the largest and easternmost of the Lesser Sunda Islands; the district of Oecussi is an exclave separated from Timor-Leste proper by Indonesia

## PEOPLE AND SOCIETY :: TIMOR-LESTE

**POPULATION:**

1,321,929 (July 2018 est.)

country comparison to the world: 156

**NATIONALITY:**

noun: Timorese

adjective: Timorese

**ETHNIC GROUPS:**

Austronesian (Malayo-Polynesian) (includes Tetun, Mambai, Tokodede, Galoli, Kemak, Baikeno), Melanesian-Papuan (includes Bunak, Fataluku, Bakasai), small Chinese minority

**LANGUAGES:**

Tetun Prasa 30.6%, Mambai 16.6%, Makasai 10.5%, Tetun Terik 6.1%, Baikenu 5.9%, Kemak 5.8%, Bunak 5.5%, Tokodede 4%, Fataluku 3.5%, Waima'a 1.8%, Galoli 1.4%, Naueti 1.4%, Idate 1.2%, Midiki 1.2%, other 4.5%

note: data represent population by mother tongue; Tetun and Portuguese are official languages; Indonesian and English are working languages; there are about 32 indigenous languages

**RELIGIONS:**

Roman Catholic 97.6%, Protestant/Evangelical 2%, Muslim 0.2%, other 0.2% (2015 est.)

**AGE STRUCTURE:**

0-14 years: 40.44% (male 274,881/female 259,736)

15-24 years: 20.46% (male 137,363/female 133,128)

25-54 years: 30.13% (male 191,290/female 206,973)

55-64 years: 5.02% (male 33,047/female 33,325)

65 years and over: 3.95% (male 25,086/female 27,100) (2018 est.)

**DEPENDENCY RATIOS:**

total dependency ratio: 90.3 (2015 est.)

youth dependency ratio: 83.7 (2015 est.)

elderly dependency ratio: 6.6 (2015 est.)

potential support ratio: 15.2 (2015 est.)

**MEDIAN AGE:**

total: 19.1 years

male: 18.5 years

female: 19.7 years (2018 est.)

country comparison to the world: 202

**POPULATION GROWTH RATE:**

2.32% (2018 est.)

country comparison to the world: 32

**BIRTH RATE:**

32.9 births/1,000 population (2018 est.)

country comparison to the world: 28

**DEATH RATE:**

5.8 deaths/1,000 population (2018 est.)

country comparison to the world: 174

**NET MIGRATION RATE:**

-3.9 migrant(s)/1,000 population (2017 est.)

country comparison to the world: 182

**POPULATION DISTRIBUTION:**

most of the population concentrated in the western third of the country, particularly around Dili

**URBANIZATION:**

urban population: 30.6% of total population (2018)

rate of urbanization: 3.35% annual rate of change (2015-20 est.)

**MAJOR URBAN AREAS - POPULATION:**

281,000 DILI (capital) (2018)

**SEX RATIO:**

at birth: 1.06 male(s)/female (2017 est.)

0-14 years: 1.06 male(s)/female (2017 est.)

15-24 years: 1.03 male(s)/female (2017 est.)

25-54 years: 0.93 male(s)/female (2017 est.)

55-64 years: 1.04 male(s)/female (2017 est.)

65 years and over: 0.91 male(s)/female (2017 est.)

total population: 1.01 male(s)/female (2017 est.)

**MOTHER'S MEAN AGE AT FIRST BIRTH:**

22.1 years (2009/10 est.)

note: median age at first birth among women 25-29

**MATERNAL MORTALITY RATE:**

215 deaths/100,000 live births (2015 est.)

country comparison to the world: 50

**INFANT MORTALITY RATE:**

total: 33.9 deaths/1,000 live births (2018 est.)

male: 36.7 deaths/1,000 live births (2018 est.)

female: 31 deaths/1,000 live births (2018 est.)

country comparison to the world: 53

**LIFE EXPECTANCY AT BIRTH:**

total population: 68.7 years (2018 est.)

male: 67.1 years (2018 est.)

female: 70.4 years (2018 est.)

country comparison to the world: 165

**TOTAL FERTILITY RATE:**

4.67 children born/woman (2018 est.)

country comparison to the world: 23

**CONTRACEPTIVE PREVALENCE RATE:**

26.1% (2016)

**HEALTH EXPENDITURES:**

1.5% of GDP (2014)

country comparison to the world: 192

**PHYSICIANS DENSITY:**

0.08 physicians/1,000 population (2011)

**HOSPITAL BED DENSITY:**

5.9 beds/1,000 population (2010)

**DRINKING WATER SOURCE:**

improved:

urban: 95.2% of population

rural: 60.5% of population

total: 71.9% of population

unimproved:

urban: 4.8% of population

rural: 39.5% of population

total: 28.1% of population (2015 est.)

**SANITATION FACILITY ACCESS:**

improved:

urban: 69% of population (2015 est.)

rural: 26.8% of population (2015 est.)

total: 40.6% of population (2015 est.)

unimproved:

urban: 31% of population (2015 est.)

rural: 73.2% of population (2015 est.)

total: 59.4% of population (2015 est.)

**HIV/AIDS - ADULT PREVALENCE RATE:**

NA

**HIV/AIDS - PEOPLE LIVING WITH HIV/AIDS:**

NA

**HIV/AIDS - DEATHS:**

NA

**MAJOR INFECTIOUS DISEASES:**

degree of risk: very high (2016)

food or waterborne diseases: bacterial diarrhea, hepatitis A, and typhoid fever (2016)

vectorborne diseases: dengue fever and malaria (2016)

**OBESITY - ADULT PREVALENCE RATE:**

3.8% (2016)

country comparison to the world: 190

**CHILDREN UNDER THE AGE OF 5 YEARS UNDERWEIGHT:**

37.7% (2013)

country comparison to the world: 2

**EDUCATION EXPENDITURES:**

7.5% of GDP (2014)

country comparison to the world: 13

**LITERACY:**

definition: age 15 and over can read and write (2015 est.)

total population: 67.5% (2015 est.)

male: 71.5% (2015 est.)

female: 63.4% (2015 est.)

**SCHOOL LIFE EXPECTANCY (PRIMARY TO TERTIARY EDUCATION):**

total: 13 years (2010)

male: 14 years (2010)

female: 13 years (2010)

**UNEMPLOYMENT, YOUTH AGES 15-24:**

total: 21.8% (2013 est.)

male: 25.1% (2013 est.)

female: 16.7% (2013 est.)

country comparison to the world: 55

## GOVERNMENT :: TIMOR-LESTE

**COUNTRY NAME:**

conventional long form: Democratic Republic of Timor-Leste

conventional short form: Timor-Leste

local long form: Republika Demokratika Timor Lorosa'e [Tetum]; Republica Democratica de Timor-Leste [Portuguese]

local short form: Timor Lorosa'e [Tetum]; Timor-Leste [Portuguese]

former: East Timor, Portuguese Timor

etymology: timor" derives from the Indonesian and Malay word "timur" meaning "east"; "leste" is the Portuguese word for "east", so "Timor-Leste" literally means "Eastern-East"; the local [Tetum] name "Timor Lorosa'e" translates as "East Rising Sun

note: pronounced TEE-mor LESS-tay

**GOVERNMENT TYPE:**

semi-presidential republic

**CAPITAL:**

name: Dili

geographic coordinates: 8 35 S, 125 36 E

time difference: UTC+9 (14 hours ahead of Washington, DC, during Standard Time)

**ADMINISTRATIVE DIVISIONS:**

12 municipalities (municipios, singular municipio) and 1 special adminstrative region* (regiao administrativa especial); Aileu, Ainaro, Baucau, Bobonaro (Maliana), Covalima (Suai), Dili, Ermera (Gleno), Lautem (Lospalos), Liquica, Manatuto, Manufahi (Same), Oe-Cusse Ambeno* (Pante Macassar), Viqueque

note: administrative divisions have the same names as their administrative centers (exceptions have the administrative center name following in parentheses)

**INDEPENDENCE:**

20 May 2002 (from Indonesia); note - 28 November 1975 was the date independence was proclaimed from Portugal; 20 May 2002 was the date of international recognition of Timor-Leste's independence from Indonesia

**NATIONAL HOLIDAY:**

Restoration of Independence Day, 20 May (2002)Proclamation of Independence Day, 28 November (1975)

**CONSTITUTION:**

history: drafted 2001, approved 22 March 2002, entered into force 20 May 2002 (2018)

amendments: proposed by Parliament and parliamentary groups; consideration of amendments requires at least four-fifths majority approval by Parliament; passage requires two-thirds majority vote by Parliament and promulgation by the president of the republic; passage of amendments to the republican form of government and the flag requires approval in a referendum (2018)

**LEGAL SYSTEM:**

civil law system based on the Portuguese model; note - penal and civil law codes to replace the Indonesian codes were passed by Parliament and promulgated in 2009 and 2011, respectively

**INTERNATIONAL LAW ORGANIZATION PARTICIPATION:**

accepts compulsory ICJ jurisdiction with reservations; accepts ICCt jurisdiction

**CITIZENSHIP:**

citizenship by birth: no

citizenship by descent only: at least one parent must be a citizen of Timor-Leste

dual citizenship recognized: no

residency requirement for naturalization: 10 years

**SUFFRAGE:**

17 years of age; universal

**EXECUTIVE BRANCH:**

chief of state: President Francisco GUTERRES (since 20 May 2017); note - the president plays a largely symbolic role but is the commander in chief of the military and is able to veto legislation, dissolve parliament, and call national elections

head of government: Prime Minister Taur Matan RUAK (since 22 June 2018); note - President GUTERRES dissolved parliament because of an impasse over passing the country's budget on 26 January 2018, with then Prime Minister Mari ALKATIRI assuming the role of caretaker prime minister until a new prime minister was appointed

cabinet: Council of Ministers proposed by the prime minister and appointed by the president

elections/appointments: president directly elected by absolute majority popular vote in 2 rounds if needed for a 5-year term (eligible for a second term); election last held on 20 March 2017 (next to be held in 2022); following parliamentary elections, the president appoints the leader of the majority party or majority coalition as the prime minister

election results: Francisco GUTERRES elected president; percent of vote - Francisco GUTERRES (FRETILIN) 57.1%, Antonio DA CONCEICAO (PD) 32.5%, Jose Luis GUTERRES (Frenti-Mudanca) 2.6%, Jose NEVES (independent) 2.3%, Luis Alves TILMAN (independent) 2.2%, other 3.4%

**LEGISLATIVE BRANCH:**

description: unicameral National Parliament (65 seats; members directly elected in a single nationwide constituency by proportional representation vote to serve 5-year terms)

elections: last held on 12 May 2018 (next to be held in July 2023)

election results: percent of vote by party - AMP - 49.6%, FRETILIN 34.2%, PD 8.1%, DDF 5.5%, other 2.6%; seats by party - AMP 34, FRETILIN 23, PD 5, DDF 3; composition - men 44, women 21, percent of women 32%

**JUDICIAL BRANCH:**

highest courts: Supreme Court of Justice (consists of the court president and NA judges)

judge selection and term of office: Supreme Court president appointed by the president of the republic from among the other court judges to serve a 4-year term; other Supreme Court judges appointed - 1 by the Parliament and the others by the Supreme Council for the Judiciary, a body presided by the Supreme Court president and includes mostly presidential and parliamentary appointees; other Supreme Court judges appointed for life

subordinate courts: Court of Appeal; High Administrative, Tax, and Audit Court; district courts; magistrates' courts; military courts

note: the UN Justice System Programme, launched in 2003 in 4 phases through 2018, is helping strengthen the country's justice system; the Programme is aligned with the country's long-range Justice Sector Strategic Plan, which includes legal reform

**POLITICAL PARTIES AND LEADERS:**

Alliance for Change and Progress or AMP [Xanana GUSMAO] (alliance includes CNRT, KHUNTO, PLP)
Democratic Development Forum or DDF
Democratic Party or PD
Frenti-Mudanca [Jose Luis GUTERRES]
Kmanek Haburas Unidade Nasional Timor Oan or KHUNTO
National Congress for Timorese Reconstruction or CNRT [Kay Rala Xanana GUSMAO]
People's Liberation Party or PLP [Taur Matan RUAK]
Revolutionary Front of Independent Timor-Leste or FRETILIN [Mari ALKATIRI]

**INTERNATIONAL ORGANIZATION PARTICIPATION:**

ACP, ADB, AOSIS, ARF, ASEAN (observer), CPLP, EITI (compliant country), FAO, G-77, IBRD, ICAO, ICCt, ICRM, IDA, IFAD, IFC, IFRCS, ILO, IMF, IMO, Interpol, IOC, IOM, IPU, ITU, MIGA, NAM, OPCW, PIF (observer), UN, UNCTAD, UNESCO, UNIDO, Union Latina, UNWTO, UPU, WCO, WHO, WMO

**DIPLOMATIC REPRESENTATION IN THE US:**

chief of mission: Ambassador Domingos Sarmento ALVES (since 21 May 2014)

chancery: 4201 Connecticut Avenue NW, Suite 504, Washington, DC 20008

telephone: [1] (202) 966-3202

FAX: [1] (202) 966-3205

**DIPLOMATIC REPRESENTATION FROM THE US:**

chief of mission: Ambassador Kathleen FITZPATRICK (since 19 January 2018)

embassy: Avenida de Portugal, Praia dos Coqueiros, Dili

mailing address: US Department of State, 8250 Dili Place, Washington, DC 20521-8250

telephone: (670) 332-4684

FAX: (670) 331-3206

**FLAG DESCRIPTION:**

red with a black isosceles triangle (based on the hoist side) superimposed on a slightly longer yellow arrowhead that extends to the center of the flag; a white star - pointing to the upper hoist-side corner of the flag - is in the center of the black triangle; yellow denotes the colonialism in Timor-Leste's past, black represents the obscurantism that needs to be overcome, red stands for the national liberation struggle; the white star symbolizes peace and serves as a guiding light

**NATIONAL SYMBOL(S):**

Mount Ramelau; national colors: red, yellow, black, white

**NATIONAL ANTHEM:**

name: "Patria" (Fatherland)

lyrics/music: Fransisco Borja DA COSTA/Afonso DE ARAUJO

note: adopted 2002; the song was first used as an anthem when Timor-Leste declared its independence from Portugal in 1975; the lyricist, Francisco Borja DA COSTA, was killed in the Indonesian invasion just days after independence was declared

# ECONOMY :: TIMOR-LESTE

**ECONOMY - OVERVIEW:**

Since independence in 1999, Timor-Leste has faced great challenges in rebuilding its infrastructure, strengthening the civil administration, and generating jobs for young people entering the work force. The development of offshore oil and gas resources has greatly supplemented government revenues. This technology-intensive industry, however, has done little to create jobs in part because there are no production facilities in Timor-Leste. Gas is currently piped to Australia for processing, but Timor-Leste has expressed interest in developing a domestic processing capability.

In June 2005, the National Parliament unanimously approved the creation of the Timor-Leste Petroleum Fund to serve as a repository for all petroleum revenues and to preserve the value of Timor-Leste's petroleum wealth for future generations. The Fund held assets of $16 billion, as of mid-2016. Oil accounts for over 90% of government revenues, and the drop in the price of oil in 2014-16 has led to concerns about the long-term sustainability of government spending. Timor-Leste compensated for the decline in price by exporting more oil. The Ministry of Finance maintains that the Petroleum Fund is sufficient to sustain government operations for the foreseeable future.

Annual government budget expenditures increased markedly between 2009 and 2012 but dropped significantly through 2016. Historically, the government failed to spend as much as its budget allowed. The government has focused significant resources on basic infrastructure, including electricity and roads, but limited experience in procurement and infrastructure building has hampered these projects. The underlying economic policy challenge the country faces remains how best to use oil-and-gas wealth to lift the non-oil economy onto a higher growth path and to reduce poverty.

## GDP (PURCHASING POWER PARITY):

$7.426 billion (2017 est.)

$7.784 billion (2016 est.)

$7.391 billion (2015 est.)

note: data are in 2017 dollars

country comparison to the world: 166

## GDP (OFFICIAL EXCHANGE RATE):

$2.775 billion (2017 est.) (2017 est.)

note: non-oil GDP

## GDP - REAL GROWTH RATE:

-4.6% (2017 est.)

5.3% (2016 est.)

4% (2015 est.)

country comparison to the world: 216

## GDP - PER CAPITA (PPP):

$6,000 (2017 est.)

$6,400 (2016 est.)

$6,200 (2015 est.)

note: data are in 2017 dollars

country comparison to the world: 164

## GDP - COMPOSITION, BY END USE:

household consumption: 33% (2017 est.)

government consumption: 30% (2017 est.)

investment in fixed capital: 10.6% (2017 est.)

investment in inventories: 0% (2017 est.)

exports of goods and services: 78.4% (2017 est.)

imports of goods and services: -52% (2017 est.)

## GDP - COMPOSITION, BY SECTOR OF ORIGIN:

agriculture: 9.1% (2017 est.)

industry: 56.7% (2017 est.)

services: 34.4% (2017 est.)

## AGRICULTURE - PRODUCTS:

coffee, rice, corn, cassava (manioc, tapioca), sweet potatoes, soybeans, cabbage, mangoes, bananas, vanilla

## INDUSTRIES:

printing, soap manufacturing, handicrafts, woven cloth

## INDUSTRIAL PRODUCTION GROWTH RATE:

2% (2017 est.)

country comparison to the world: 133

## LABOR FORCE:

286,700 (2016 est.)

country comparison to the world: 164

## LABOR FORCE - BY OCCUPATION:

agriculture: 41%

industry: 13%

services: 45.1% (2013)

## UNEMPLOYMENT RATE:

4.4% (2014 est.)

3.9% (2010 est.)

country comparison to the world: 60

## POPULATION BELOW POVERTY LINE:

41.8% (2014 est.)

## HOUSEHOLD INCOME OR CONSUMPTION BY PERCENTAGE SHARE:

lowest 10%: 27% (2007)

highest 10%: 27% (2007)

## DISTRIBUTION OF FAMILY INCOME - GINI INDEX:

31.9 (2007 est.)

38 (2002 est.)

country comparison to the world: 123

## BUDGET:

revenues: 300 million (2017 est.)

expenditures: 2.4 billion (2017 est.)

## TAXES AND OTHER REVENUES:

10.8% (of GDP) (2017 est.)

country comparison to the world: 213

## BUDGET SURPLUS (+) OR DEFICIT (-):

-75.7% (of GDP) (2017 est.)

country comparison to the world: 222

## PUBLIC DEBT:

3.8% of GDP (2017 est.)

3.1% of GDP (2016 est.)

country comparison to the world: 206

## FISCAL YEAR:

calendar year

## INFLATION RATE (CONSUMER PRICES):

0.6% (2017 est.)

-1.3% (2016 est.)

country comparison to the world: 34

## COMMERCIAL BANK PRIME LENDING RATE:

13.29% (31 December 2017 est.)

14.05% (31 December 2016 est.)

country comparison to the world: 57

## STOCK OF NARROW MONEY:

$563.3 million (31 December 2017 est.)

$464.1 million (31 December 2016 est.)

country comparison to the world: 167

## STOCK OF BROAD MONEY:

$563.3 million (31 December 2017 est.)

$464.1 million (31 December 2016 est.)

country comparison to the world: 171

## STOCK OF DOMESTIC CREDIT:

-$213 million (31 December 2017 est.)

-$212 million (31 December 2016 est.)

country comparison to the world: 191

**MARKET VALUE OF PUBLICLY TRADED SHARES:**

NA

**CURRENT ACCOUNT BALANCE:**

-$284 million (2017 est.)

-$544 million (2016 est.)

country comparison to the world: 103

**EXPORTS:**

$16.7 million (2017 est.)

$18 million (2015 est.)

country comparison to the world: 214

**EXPORTS - COMMODITIES:**

oil, coffee, sandalwood, marble

note: potential for vanilla exports

**IMPORTS:**

$681.2 million (2017 est.)

$558.6 million (2016 est.)

country comparison to the world: 192

**IMPORTS - COMMODITIES:**

food, gasoline, kerosene, machinery

**RESERVES OF FOREIGN EXCHANGE AND GOLD:**

$544.4 million (31 December 2017 est.)

$437.8 million (31 December 2015 est.)

note: excludes assets of approximately $9.7 billion in the Petroleum Fund (31 December 2010)

country comparison to the world: 150

**DEBT - EXTERNAL:**

$311.5 million (31 December 2014 est.)

$687 million (31 December 2013 est.)

country comparison to the world: 184

**STOCK OF DIRECT FOREIGN INVESTMENT - AT HOME:**

(31 December 2009 est.)

**EXCHANGE RATES:**

the US dollar is used

## ENERGY :: TIMOR-LESTE

**ELECTRICITY ACCESS:**

population without electricity: 744,032 (2012)

electrification - total population: 42% (2012)

electrification - urban areas: 78% (2012)

electrification - rural areas: 27% (2012)

**ELECTRICITY - PRODUCTION:**

0 kWh NA (2016 est.)

country comparison to the world: 219

**ELECTRICITY - CONSUMPTION:**

0 kWh (2016 est.)

country comparison to the world: 218

**ELECTRICITY - EXPORTS:**

0 kWh (2017 est.)

country comparison to the world: 207

**ELECTRICITY - IMPORTS:**

0 kWh (2016 est.)

country comparison to the world: 209

**ELECTRICITY - INSTALLED GENERATING CAPACITY:**

600 kW NA (2016 est.)

country comparison to the world: 215

**ELECTRICITY - FROM FOSSIL FUELS:**

0% of total installed capacity (2016 est.)

country comparison to the world: 215

**ELECTRICITY - FROM NUCLEAR FUELS:**

0% of total installed capacity (2017 est.)

country comparison to the world: 194

**ELECTRICITY - FROM HYDROELECTRIC PLANTS:**

0% of total installed capacity (2017 est.)

country comparison to the world: 204

**ELECTRICITY - FROM OTHER RENEWABLE SOURCES:**

100% of total installed capacity (2017 est.)

country comparison to the world: 1

**CRUDE OIL - PRODUCTION:**

40,320 bbl/day (2017 est.)

country comparison to the world: 58

**CRUDE OIL - EXPORTS:**

62,060 bbl/day (2015 est.)

country comparison to the world: 39

**CRUDE OIL - IMPORTS:**

0 bbl/day (2015 est.)

country comparison to the world: 203

**CRUDE OIL - PROVED RESERVES:**

0 bbl (1 January 2018 est.)

country comparison to the world: 203

**REFINED PETROLEUM PRODUCTS - PRODUCTION:**

0 bbl/day (2015 est.)

country comparison to the world: 207

**REFINED PETROLEUM PRODUCTS - CONSUMPTION:**

3,500 bbl/day (2016 est.)

country comparison to the world: 186

**REFINED PETROLEUM PRODUCTS - EXPORTS:**

0 bbl/day (2015 est.)

country comparison to the world: 208

**REFINED PETROLEUM PRODUCTS - IMPORTS:**

3,481 bbl/day (2015 est.)

country comparison to the world: 182

**NATURAL GAS - PRODUCTION:**

5.776 billion cu m (2017 est.)

country comparison to the world: 48

**NATURAL GAS - CONSUMPTION:**

0 cu m (2017 est.)

country comparison to the world: 205

**NATURAL GAS - EXPORTS:**

5.776 billion cu m (2017 est.)

country comparison to the world: 27

**NATURAL GAS - IMPORTS:**

0 cu m (2017 est.)

country comparison to the world: 199

**NATURAL GAS - PROVED RESERVES:**

200 billion cu m (1 January 2006 est.)

country comparison to the world: 42

**CARBON DIOXIDE EMISSIONS FROM CONSUMPTION OF ENERGY:**

533,400 Mt (2017 est.)

country comparison to the world: 184

## COMMUNICATIONS :: TIMOR-LESTE

**TELEPHONES - FIXED LINES:**

total subscriptions: 2,364 (2017 est.)

subscriptions per 100 inhabitants: less than 1 (2017 est.)

country comparison to the world: 210

**TELEPHONES - MOBILE CELLULAR:**

total subscriptions: 1,546,624 (2017 est.)

subscriptions per 100 inhabitants: 120 (2017 est.)

country comparison to the world: 153

**TELEPHONE SYSTEM:**

general assessment: rudimentary service in urban and some rural areas, which is expanding with the entrance of new competitors (2016)

domestic: system suffered significant damage during the violence associated with independence; limited fixed-line services; mobile-cellular services have been expanding and are now available in urban and most rural areas (2016)

**international:** country code - 670; international service is available (2016)

### BROADCAST MEDIA:

7 TV stations (2 nationwide satellite coverage; 3 terrestrial coverage, mostly in Dili; 2 cable) and 21 radio stations (3 nationwide coverage) (2017)

### INTERNET COUNTRY CODE:

.tl

### INTERNET USERS:

total: 318,373 (July 2016 est.)

percent of population: 25.2% (July 2016 est.)

country comparison to the world: 158

### BROADBAND - FIXED SUBSCRIPTIONS:

total: 3,346 (2017 est.)

subscriptions per 100 inhabitants: less than 1 (2017 est.)

country comparison to the world: 182

## TRANSPORTATION :: TIMOR-LESTE

### CIVIL AIRCRAFT REGISTRATION COUNTRY CODE PREFIX:

4W (2016)

### AIRPORTS:

6 (2013)

country comparison to the world: 176

### AIRPORTS - WITH PAVED RUNWAYS:

total: 2 (2013)

2,438 to 3,047 m: 1 (2013)

1,524 to 2,437 m: 1 (2013)

### AIRPORTS - WITH UNPAVED RUNWAYS:

total: 4 (2013)

914 to 1,523 m: 2 (2013)

under 914 m: 2 (2013)

### HELIPORTS:

8 (2013)

### ROADWAYS:

total: 6,040 km (2005)

paved: 2,600 km (2005)

unpaved: 3,440 km (2005)

country comparison to the world: 149

### PORTS AND TERMINALS:

major seaport(s): Dili

## MILITARY AND SECURITY :: TIMOR-LESTE

### MILITARY EXPENDITURES:

2.56% of GDP (2015)

2.12% of GDP (2014)

2.42% of GDP (2013)

country comparison to the world: 37

### MILITARY BRANCHES:

Timor-Leste Defense Force (Falintil-Forcas de Defesa de Timor-L'este, Falintil (F-FDTL)): Army, Navy (Armada) (2013)

### MILITARY SERVICE AGE AND OBLIGATION:

18 years of age for voluntary military service; 18-month service obligation; no conscription but, as of May 2013, introduction of conscription was under discussion (2013)

## TRANSNATIONAL ISSUES :: TIMOR-LESTE

### DISPUTES - INTERNATIONAL:

three stretches of land borders with Indonesia have yet to be delimited, two of which are in the Oecussi exclave area, and no maritime or Exclusive Economic Zone (EEZ) boundaries have been established between the countriesmaritime boundaries with Indonesia remain unresolvedin 2018, Australia and Timor-Leste signed a permanent maritime border treaty, scrapping a 2007 development zone and revenue sharing arrangement between the countries

### TRAFFICKING IN PERSONS:

current situation: Timor-Leste is a source and destination country for men, women, and children subjected to forced labor and sex trafficking; Timorese women and girls from rural areas are lured to the capital with promises of legitimate jobs or education prospects and are then forced into prostitution or domestic servitude, and other women and girls may be sent to Indonesia for domestic servitude; Timorese family members force children into bonded domestic or agricultural labor to repay debts; foreign migrant women are vulnerable to sex trafficking in Timor-Leste, while men and boys from Burma, Cambodia, and Thailand are forced to work on fishing boats in Timorese waters under inhumane conditions

tier rating: Tier 2 Watch List – Timor-Leste does not fully comply with the minimum standards for the elimination of trafficking; however, it is making significant efforts to do so; in 2014, legislation was drafted but not finalized or implemented that outlines procedures for screening potential trafficking victims; law enforcement made modest progress, including one conviction for sex trafficking, but efforts are hindered by prosecutors' and judges' lack of expertise in applying anti-trafficking laws effectively; the government rescued two child victims with support from an NGO but did not provide protective services (2015)

### ILLICIT DRUGS:

NA

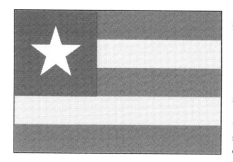

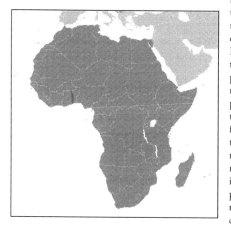

# AFRICA :: TOGO

## INTRODUCTION :: TOGO

### BACKGROUND:

French Togoland became Togo in 1960. Gen. Gnassingbe EYADEMA, installed as military ruler in 1967, ruled Togo with a heavy hand for almost four decades. Despite the facade of multi-party elections instituted in the early 1990s, the government was largely dominated by President EYADEMA, whose Rally of the Togolese People (RPT) party has been in power almost continually since 1967 and its successor, the Union for the Republic, maintains a majority of seats in today's legislature. Upon EYADEMA's death in February 2005, the military installed the president's son, Faure GNASSINGBE, and then engineered his formal election two months later. Democratic gains since then allowed Togo to hold its first relatively free and fair legislative elections in October 2007. Since 2007, President GNASSINGBE has started the country along a gradual path to political reconciliation and democratic reform, and Togo has held multiple presidential and legislative elections that were deemed generally free and fair by international observers. Despite those positive moves, political reconciliation has moved slowly and many Togolese complain that important political measures such as presidential term limits and electoral reforms remain undone, leaving the country's politics in a lethargic state. Internationally, Togo is still known as a country where the same family has been in power for five decades.

## GEOGRAPHY :: TOGO

### LOCATION:
Western Africa, bordering the Bight of Benin, between Benin and Ghana

### GEOGRAPHIC COORDINATES:
8 00 N, 1 10 E

### MAP REFERENCES:
Africa

### AREA:
total: 56,785 sq km
land: 54,385 sq km
water: 2,400 sq km
country comparison to the world: 127

### AREA - COMPARATIVE:
slightly smaller than West Virginia

### LAND BOUNDARIES:
total: 1,880 km
border countries (3): Benin 651 km, Burkina Faso 131 km, Ghana 1098 km

### COASTLINE:
56 km

### MARITIME CLAIMS:
territorial sea: 30 nm
exclusive economic zone: 200 nm

### CLIMATE:
tropical; hot, humid in south; semiarid in north

### TERRAIN:
gently rolling savanna in north; central hills; southern plateau; low coastal plain with extensive lagoons and marshes

### ELEVATION:
mean elevation: 236 m
elevation extremes: 0 m lowest point: Atlantic Ocean
986 highest point: Mont Agou

### NATURAL RESOURCES:
phosphates, limestone, marble, arable land

### LAND USE:
agricultural land: 67.4% (2011 est.)
arable land: 45.2% (2011 est.) / permanent crops: 3.8% (2011 est.) / permanent pasture: 18.4% (2011 est.)
forest: 4.9% (2011 est.)
other: 27.7% (2011 est.)

### IRRIGATED LAND:
70 sq km (2012)

### POPULATION DISTRIBUTION:
one of the more densely populated African nations with most of the population residing in rural communities, density is highest in the south on or near the Atlantic coast

### NATURAL HAZARDS:
hot, dry harmattan wind can reduce visibility in north during winter; periodic droughts

### ENVIRONMENT - CURRENT ISSUES:
deforestation attributable to slash-and-burn agriculture and the use of wood for fuel; very little rain forest still present and what remains is highly degraded; desertification; water pollution presents health hazards and hinders the fishing industry; air pollution increasing in urban areas

### ENVIRONMENT - INTERNATIONAL AGREEMENTS:
party to: Biodiversity, Climate Change, Climate Change-Kyoto Protocol, Desertification, Endangered Species, Hazardous Wastes, Law of the Sea, Ozone Layer Protection, Ship Pollution, Tropical Timber 83, Tropical Timber 94, Wetlands, Whaling

**signed, but not ratified:** none of the selected agreements

### GEOGRAPHY - NOTE:

the country's length allows it to stretch through six distinct geographic regions; climate varies from tropical to savanna

# PEOPLE AND SOCIETY :: TOGO

### POPULATION:

8,176,449 (July 2018 est.)

**note:** estimates for this country explicitly take into account the effects of excess mortality due to AIDS; this can result in lower life expectancy, higher infant mortality, higher death rates, lower population growth rates, and changes in the distribution of population by age and sex than would otherwise be expected

**country comparison to the world:** 100

### NATIONALITY:

**noun:** Togolese (singular and plural)

**adjective:** Togolese

### ETHNIC GROUPS:

African (37 tribes; largest and most important are Ewe, Mina, and Kabre) 99%, European and Syrian-Lebanese less than 1%

### LANGUAGES:

French (official, the language of commerce), Ewe and Mina (the two major African languages in the south), Kabye (sometimes spelled Kabiye) and Dagomba (the two major African languages in the north)

### RELIGIONS:

Christian 29%, Muslim 20%, indigenous beliefs 51%

### DEMOGRAPHIC PROFILE:

Togo's population is estimated to have grown to four times its size between 1960 and 2010. With nearly 60% of its populace under the age of 25 and a high annual growth rate attributed largely to high fertility, Togo's population is likely to continue to expand for the foreseeable future. Reducing fertility, boosting job creation, and improving education will be essential to reducing the country's high poverty rate. In 2008, Togo eliminated primary school enrollment fees, leading to higher enrollment but increased pressure on limited classroom space, teachers, and materials. Togo has a good chance of achieving universal primary education, but educational quality, the underrepresentation of girls, and the low rate of enrollment in secondary and tertiary schools remain concerns.

Togo is both a country of emigration and asylum. In the early 1990s, southern Togo suffered from the economic decline of the phosphate sector and ethnic and political repression at the hands of dictator Gnassingbe EYADEMA and his northern, Kabye-dominated administration. The turmoil led 300,000 to 350,000 predominantly southern Togolese to flee to Benin and Ghana, with most not returning home until relative stability was restored in 1997. In 2005, another outflow of 40,000 Togolese to Benin and Ghana occurred when violence broke out between the opposition and security forces over the disputed election of EYADEMA's son Faure GNASSINGBE to the presidency. About half of the refugees reluctantly returned home in 2006, many still fearing for their safety. Despite ethnic tensions and periods of political unrest, Togo in September 2017 was home to more than 9,600 refugees from Ghana.

### AGE STRUCTURE:

**0-14 years:** 40.13% (male 1,646,438 /female 1,634,609)

**15-24 years:** 19.1% (male 779,774 /female 782,192)

**25-54 years:** 32.96% (male 1,339,150 /female 1,356,020)

**55-64 years:** 4.34% (male 167,575 /female 187,432)

**65 years and over:** 3.46% (male 122,175 /female 161,084) (2018 est.)

### DEPENDENCY RATIOS:

**total dependency ratio:** 81.2 (2015 est.)

**youth dependency ratio:** 76.2 (2015 est.)

**elderly dependency ratio:** 5.1 (2015 est.)

**potential support ratio:** 19.8 (2015 est.)

### MEDIAN AGE:

**total:** 19.9 years

**male:** 19.6 years

**female:** 20.1 years (2018 est.)

**country comparison to the world:** 196

### POPULATION GROWTH RATE:

2.61% (2018 est.)

**country comparison to the world:** 18

### BIRTH RATE:

32.8 births/1,000 population (2018 est.)

**country comparison to the world:** 30

### DEATH RATE:

6.8 deaths/1,000 population (2018 est.)

**country comparison to the world:** 135

### NET MIGRATION RATE:

0 migrant(s)/1,000 population (2017 est.)

**country comparison to the world:** 99

### POPULATION DISTRIBUTION:

one of the more densely populated African nations with most of the population residing in rural communities, density is highest in the south on or near the Atlantic coast

### URBANIZATION:

**urban population:** 41.7% of total population (2018)

**rate of urbanization:** 3.76% annual rate of change (2015-20 est.)

### MAJOR URBAN AREAS - POPULATION:

1.746 million LOME (capital) (2018)

### SEX RATIO:

**at birth:** 1.02 male(s)/female (2017 est.)

**0-14 years:** 1.01 male(s)/female (2017 est.)

**15-24 years:** 1 male(s)/female (2017 est.)

**25-54 years:** 0.99 male(s)/female (2017 est.)

**55-64 years:** 0.89 male(s)/female (2017 est.)

**65 years and over:** 0.76 male(s)/female (2017 est.)

**total population:** 0.98 male(s)/female (2017 est.)

### MOTHER'S MEAN AGE AT FIRST BIRTH:

21 years (2013/14 est.)

**note:** median age at first birth among women 25-29

### MATERNAL MORTALITY RATE:

368 deaths/100,000 live births (2015 est.)

**country comparison to the world:** 32

### INFANT MORTALITY RATE:

**total:** 40.8 deaths/1,000 live births (2018 est.)

**male:** 47.1 deaths/1,000 live births (2018 est.)

female: 34.4 deaths/1,000 live births (2018 est.)

country comparison to the world: 43

**LIFE EXPECTANCY AT BIRTH:**

total population: 65.8 years (2018 est.)

male: 63.1 years (2018 est.)

female: 68.6 years (2018 est.)

country comparison to the world: 178

**TOTAL FERTILITY RATE:**

4.32 children born/woman (2018 est.)

country comparison to the world: 26

**CONTRACEPTIVE PREVALENCE RATE:**

19.9% (2013/14)

**HEALTH EXPENDITURES:**

5.2% of GDP (2014)

country comparison to the world: 135

**PHYSICIANS DENSITY:**

0.06 physicians/1,000 population (2008)

**HOSPITAL BED DENSITY:**

0.7 beds/1,000 population (2011)

**DRINKING WATER SOURCE:**

improved:

urban: 91.4% of population (2015 est.)

rural: 44.2% of population (2015 est.)

total: 63.1% of population (2015 est.)

unimproved:

urban: 8.6% of population (2015 est.)

rural: 55.8% of population (2015 est.)

total: 36.9% of population (2015 est.)

**SANITATION FACILITY ACCESS:**

improved:

urban: 24.7% of population (2015 est.)

rural: 2.9% of population (2015 est.)

total: 11.6% of population (2015 est.)

unimproved:

urban: 75.3% of population (2015 est.)

rural: 97.1% of population (2015 est.)

total: 88.4% of population (2015 est.)

**HIV/AIDS - ADULT PREVALENCE RATE:**

2.1% (2017 est.)

country comparison to the world: 23

**HIV/AIDS - PEOPLE LIVING WITH HIV/AIDS:**

110,000 (2017 est.)

country comparison to the world: 43

**HIV/AIDS - DEATHS:**

4,700 (2017 est.)

country comparison to the world: 31

**MAJOR INFECTIOUS DISEASES:**

degree of risk: very high (2016)

food or waterborne diseases: bacterial and protozoal diarrhea, hepatitis A, and typhoid fever (2016)

vectorborne diseases: malaria, dengue fever, and yellow fever (2016)

water contact diseases: schistosomiasis (2016)

animal contact diseases: rabies (2016)

respiratory diseases: meningococcal meningitis (2016)

**OBESITY - ADULT PREVALENCE RATE:**

8.4% (2016)

country comparison to the world: 152

**CHILDREN UNDER THE AGE OF 5 YEARS UNDERWEIGHT:**

16.2% (2014)

country comparison to the world: 38

**EDUCATION EXPENDITURES:**

5.1% of GDP (2016)

country comparison to the world: 74

**LITERACY:**

definition: age 15 and over can read and write (2015 est.)

total population: 63.7% (2015 est.)

male: 77.3% (2015 est.)

female: 51.2% (2015 est.)

**SCHOOL LIFE EXPECTANCY (PRIMARY TO TERTIARY EDUCATION):**

total: 12 years (2011)

male: NA (2011)

female: NA (2011)

**UNEMPLOYMENT, YOUTH AGES 15-24:**

total: 2.8% (2011 est.)

male: 3.4% (2011 est.)

female: 2.2% (2011 est.)

country comparison to the world: 165

# GOVERNMENT :: TOGO

**COUNTRY NAME:**

conventional long form: Togolese Republic

conventional short form: Togo

local long form: Republique Togolaise

local short form: none

former: French Togoland

etymology: derived from the Ewe words "to" (river) and "godo" (on the other side) to give the sense of "on the other side of the river"; originally, this designation applied to the town of Togodo (now Togoville) on the northern shore of Lake Togo, but the name was eventually extended to the entire nation

**GOVERNMENT TYPE:**

presidential republic

**CAPITAL:**

name: Lome

geographic coordinates: 6 07 N, 1 13 E

time difference: UTC 0 (5 hours ahead of Washington, DC, during Standard Time)

**ADMINISTRATIVE DIVISIONS:**

5 regions (regions, singular - region); Centrale, Kara, Maritime, Plateaux, Savanes

**INDEPENDENCE:**

27 April 1960 (from French-administered UN trusteeship)

**NATIONAL HOLIDAY:**

Independence Day, 27 April (1960)

**CONSTITUTION:**

history: several previous; latest adopted 27 September 1992, effective 14 October 1992 (2017)

amendments: proposed by the president of the republic or supported by at least one-fifth of the National Assembly membership; passage requires four-fifths majority vote by the Assembly; a referendum is required if approved by only two-thirds majority of the Assembly or if requested by the president; constitutional articles on the republican and secular form of government cannot be amended; amended 2002, 2007; note - a September 2017 Assembly vote on a package of amendments including presidential term limits failed the four-fifths majority vote required for passage but met the two-thirds majority vote required for holding a referendeum (2017)

**LEGAL SYSTEM:**

customary law system

**INTERNATIONAL LAW ORGANIZATION PARTICIPATION:**

accepts compulsory ICJ jurisdiction with reservations; non-party state to the ICCt

## CITIZENSHIP:

**citizenship by birth:** no

**citizenship by descent only:** at least one parent must be a citizen of Togo

**dual citizenship recognized:** yes

**residency requirement for naturalization:** 5 years

## SUFFRAGE:

18 years of age; universal

## EXECUTIVE BRANCH:

**chief of state:** President Faure GNASSINGBE (since 4 May 2005)

**head of government:** Prime Minister Komi KLASSOU (since 5 June 2015)

**cabinet:** Council of Ministers appointed by the president on the advice of the prime minister

**elections/appointments:** president directly elected by simple majority popular vote for a 5-year term (no term limits); election last held on 25 April 2015 (next to be held in 2020); prime minister appointed by the president

**election results:** Faure GNASSINGBE reelected president; percent of vote - Faure GNASSINGBE (UNIR) 58.8%, Jean-Pierre FABRE (ANC) 35.2%, Tchaboure GOGUE (ADDI) 4%, other 2%

## LEGISLATIVE BRANCH:

**description:** unicameral National Assembly or Assemblee Nationale (91 seats; members directly elected in multi-seat constituencies by closed, party-list proportional representation vote to serve 5-year terms)

**elections:** last held on 25 July 2013 (next originally scheduled in July 2018, rescheduled for 20 December 2018)

**election results:** percent of vote by coalition/party - UNIR 46.7%, CST 28.9%, Rainbow Alliance 10.8%, UFC 7.7%, independent 0.8%, other 5.1%; seats by coalition/party - UNIR 62, CST 19, Rainbow Alliance 6, UFC 3, independent 1

## JUDICIAL BRANCH:

**highest courts:** Supreme Court or Cour Supreme (organized into criminal and administrative chambers, each with a chamber president and advisors); Constitutional Court (consists of 9 judges including the court president)

**judge selection and term of office:** Supreme Court president appointed by decree of the president of the republic upon the proposal of the Supreme Council of the Magistracy, a 9-member judicial, advisory, and disciplinary body; other judge appointments and judge tenure NA; Constitutional Court judges appointed by the National Assembly; judge tenure NA

**subordinate courts:** Court of Assizes (sessions court); Appeal Court; tribunals of first instance (divided into civil, commercial, and correctional chambers; Court of State Security; military tribunal

## POLITICAL PARTIES AND LEADERS:

Action Committee for Renewal or CAR [Yaovi AGBOYIBO]
Alliance of Democrats for Integral Development or ADDI [Tchaboure GOGUE]
Combat for Political Change in 2015 or CAP 2015 (coalition of 7 parties) [Jean-Pierre FABRE]
Democratic Convention of African Peoples or CDPA [Brigitte ADJAMAGBO-JOHNSON]
Democratic Forces for the Republic or FDR [Dodji APEVON]
National Alliance for Change or ANC [Jean-Pierre FABRE]
New Togolese Commitment [Gerry TAAMA]
Pan-African National Party or PNP [Tikpi ATCHADAM]
Pan-African Patriotic Convergence or CPP [Edem KODJO]
Rainbow Alliance [Brigitte ADJAMAGBO-JOHNSON] (a coalition of 6 parties)
Save Togo Collective (Collectif Sauvons le Togo) or CST [Ata MESAN, Ajavaon ZEUS](alliance established in 2012 includes ADDI, ANC, Organization to Build a United Togo, the Socialist Pact for Renewal, the Movement of Centrist Republicans, Worker's Party)
Socialist Pact for Renewal or PSR [Abi TCHESSA]
The Togolese Party [Nathaniel OLYMPIO]
Union of Forces for Change or UFC [Gilchrist OLYMPIO]
Union for the Republic or UNIR [Faure GNASSINGBE]

## INTERNATIONAL ORGANIZATION PARTICIPATION:

ACP, AfDB, AU, ECOWAS, EITI (compliant country), Entente, FAO, FZ, G-77, IAEA, IBRD, ICAO, ICRM, IDA, IDB, IFAD, IFC, IFRCS, ILO, IMF, IMO, Interpol, IOC, IOM, IPU, ISO (correspondent), ITSO, ITU, ITUC (NGOs), MIGA, MINURSO, MINUSMA, NAM, OIC, OIF, OPCW, PCA, UN, UNAMID, UNCTAD, UNESCO, UNHCR, UNIDO, UNMIL, UNOCI, UNWTO, UPU, WADB (regional), WAEMU, WCO, WFTU (NGOs), WHO, WIPO, WMO, WTO

## DIPLOMATIC REPRESENTATION IN THE US:

**chief of mission:** Ambassador Frederic Edem HEGBE (since 24 April 2017)

**chancery:** 2208 Massachusetts Avenue NW, Washington, DC 20008

**telephone:** [1] (202) 234-4212

**FAX:** [1] (202) 232-3190

## DIPLOMATIC REPRESENTATION FROM THE US:

**chief of mission:** Ambassador David R. GILMOUR (20 December 2015)

**embassy:** 4332 Blvd. Gnassingbe Eyadema, Cite OUA, Lome

**mailing address:** B.P. 852, Lome; 2300 Lome Place, Washington, DC 20521-2300

**telephone:** [228] 2261-5470

**FAX:** [228] 2261-5501

## FLAG DESCRIPTION:

five equal horizontal bands of green (top and bottom) alternating with yellow; a white five-pointed star on a red square is in the upper hoist-side corner; the five horizontal stripes stand for the five different regions of the country; the red square is meant to express the loyalty and patriotism of the people, green symbolizes hope, fertility, and agriculture, while yellow represents mineral wealth and faith that hard work and strength will bring prosperity; the star symbolizes life, purity, peace, dignity, and Togo's independence

**note:** uses the popular Pan-African colors of Ethiopia

## NATIONAL SYMBOL(S):

lion; national colors: green, yellow, red, white

## NATIONAL ANTHEM:

**name:** "Salut a toi, pays de nos aieux" (Hail to Thee, Land of Our Forefathers)

**lyrics/music:** Alex CASIMIR-DOSSEH

**note:** adopted 1960, restored 1992; this anthem was replaced by another during one-party rule between 1979 and 1992

## ECONOMY :: TOGO

## ECONOMY - OVERVIEW:

Togo has enjoyed a period of steady economic growth fueled by political stability and a concerted effort by the government to modernize the country's commercial infrastructure, but discontent with President Faure GNASSINGBE has led to a rapid rise in protests, creating downside risks. The country completed an ambitious large-scale infrastructure improvement program, including new principal roads, a new airport terminal, and a new seaport. The economy depends heavily on both commercial and subsistence agriculture, providing employment for around 60% of the labor force. Some basic foodstuffs must still be imported. Cocoa, coffee, and cotton and other agricultural products generate about 20% of export earnings with cotton being the most important cash crop. Togo is among the world's largest producers of phosphate and seeks to develop its carbonate phosphate reserves, which provide more than 20% of export earnings.

Supported by the World Bank and the IMF, the government's decade-long effort to implement economic reform measures, encourage foreign investment, and bring revenues in line with expenditures has moved slowly. Togo completed its IMF Extended Credit Facility in 2011 and reached a Heavily Indebted Poor Country debt relief completion point in 2010 at which 95% of the country's debt was forgiven. Togo continues to work with the IMF on structural reforms, and in January 2017, the IMF signed an Extended Credit Facility arrangement consisting of a three-year $238 million loan package. Progress depends on follow through on privatization, increased transparency in government financial operations, progress toward legislative elections, and continued support from foreign donors.

Togo's 2017 economic growth probably remained steady at 5.0%, largely driven by infusions of foreign aid, infrastructure investment in its port and mineral industry, and improvements in the business climate. Foreign direct investment inflows have slowed in recent years.

## GDP (PURCHASING POWER PARITY):

$12.97 billion (2017 est.)

$12.42 billion (2016 est.)

$11.82 billion (2015 est.)

note: data are in 2017 dollars

country comparison to the world: 155

## GDP (OFFICIAL EXCHANGE RATE):

$4.767 billion (2017 est.) (2017 est.)

## GDP - REAL GROWTH RATE:

4.4% (2017 est.)

5.1% (2016 est.)

5.7% (2015 est.)

country comparison to the world: 66

## GDP - PER CAPITA (PPP):

$1,700 (2017 est.)

$1,600 (2016 est.)

$1,600 (2015 est.)

note: data are in 2017 dollars

country comparison to the world: 215

## GROSS NATIONAL SAVING:

16.1% of GDP (2017 est.)

21.8% of GDP (2016 est.)

21.2% of GDP (2015 est.)

country comparison to the world: 129

## GDP - COMPOSITION, BY END USE:

household consumption: 84.5% (2017 est.)

government consumption: 11.4% (2017 est.)

investment in fixed capital: 23.4% (2017 est.)

investment in inventories: -1.4% (2017 est.)

exports of goods and services: 43.1% (2017 est.)

imports of goods and services: -61% (2017 est.)

## GDP - COMPOSITION, BY SECTOR OF ORIGIN:

agriculture: 28.8% (2017 est.)

industry: 21.8% (2017 est.)

services: 49.8% (2017 est.)

## AGRICULTURE - PRODUCTS:

coffee, cocoa, cotton, yams, cassava (manioc, tapioca), corn, beans, rice, millet, sorghum; livestock; fish

## INDUSTRIES:

phosphate mining, agricultural processing, cement, handicrafts, textiles, beverages

## INDUSTRIAL PRODUCTION GROWTH RATE:

5% (2017 est.)

country comparison to the world: 58

## LABOR FORCE:

2.595 million (2007 est.)

country comparison to the world: 114

## LABOR FORCE - BY OCCUPATION:

agriculture: 65%

industry: 5%

services: 30% (1998 est.)

## UNEMPLOYMENT RATE:

6.9% (2016 est.)

country comparison to the world: 105

## POPULATION BELOW POVERTY LINE:

55.1% (2015 est.)

## HOUSEHOLD INCOME OR CONSUMPTION BY PERCENTAGE SHARE:

lowest 10%: 27.1% (2006)

highest 10%: 27.1% (2006)

## DISTRIBUTION OF FAMILY INCOME - GINI INDEX:

46 (2011)

country comparison to the world: 35

## BUDGET:

revenues: 1.023 billion (2017 est.)

expenditures: 1.203 billion (2017 est.)

## TAXES AND OTHER REVENUES:

21.5% (of GDP) (2017 est.)

country comparison to the world: 137

## BUDGET SURPLUS (+) OR DEFICIT (-):

-3.8% (of GDP) (2017 est.)

country comparison to the world: 154

## PUBLIC DEBT:

75.7% of GDP (2017 est.)

81.6% of GDP (2016 est.)

country comparison to the world: 40

## FISCAL YEAR:

calendar year

## INFLATION RATE (CONSUMER PRICES):

-0.7% (2017 est.)

0.9% (2016 est.)

country comparison to the world: 4

## CENTRAL BANK DISCOUNT RATE:

2.5% (31 December 2010)

4.25% (31 December 2009)

country comparison to the world: 116

## COMMERCIAL BANK PRIME LENDING RATE:

5.3% (31 December 2016 est.)

8.29% (31 December 2015 est.)

country comparison to the world: 142

## STOCK OF NARROW MONEY:

$1.335 billion (31 December 2017 est.)

$1.119 billion (31 December 2016 est.)

country comparison to the world: 146

**STOCK OF BROAD MONEY:**

$1.335 billion (31 December 2017 est.)

$1.119 billion (31 December 2016 est.)

country comparison to the world: 154

**STOCK OF DOMESTIC CREDIT:**

$1.95 billion (31 December 2017 est.)

$1.624 billion (31 December 2016 est.)

country comparison to the world: 152

**MARKET VALUE OF PUBLICLY TRADED SHARES:**

NA

**CURRENT ACCOUNT BALANCE:**

-$383 million (2017 est.)

-$416 million (2016 est.)

country comparison to the world: 111

**EXPORTS:**

$1.046 billion (2017 est.)

$967.4 million (2016 est.)

country comparison to the world: 159

**EXPORTS - PARTNERS:**

Benin 16.7%, Burkina Faso 15.2%, Niger 8.9%, India 7.3%, Mali 6.7%, Ghana 5.5%, Cote dIvoire 5.4%, Nigeria 4.1% (2017)

**EXPORTS - COMMODITIES:**

reexports, cotton, phosphates, coffee, cocoa

**IMPORTS:**

$1.999 billion (2017 est.)

$2 billion (2016 est.)

country comparison to the world: 166

**IMPORTS - COMMODITIES:**

machinery and equipment, foodstuffs, petroleum products

**IMPORTS - PARTNERS:**

China 27.5%, France 9.1%, Netherlands 4.4%, Japan 4.3% (2017)

**RESERVES OF FOREIGN EXCHANGE AND GOLD:**

$77.8 million (31 December 2017 est.)

$42.6 million (31 December 2016 est.)

country comparison to the world: 182

**DEBT - EXTERNAL:**

$1.442 billion (31 December 2017 est.)

$1.22 billion (31 December 2016 est.)

country comparison to the world: 161

**STOCK OF DIRECT FOREIGN INVESTMENT - AT HOME:**

(31 December 2009 est.)

**EXCHANGE RATES:**

Communaute Financiere Africaine francs (XOF) per US dollar -

617.4 (2017 est.)

593.01 (2016 est.)

593.01 (2015 est.)

591.45 (2014 est.)

494.42 (2013 est.)

## ENERGY :: TOGO

**ELECTRICITY ACCESS:**

population without electricity: 5 million (2013)

electrification - total population: 27% (2013)

electrification - urban areas: 35% (2013)

electrification - rural areas: 21% (2013)

**ELECTRICITY - PRODUCTION:**

232.6 million kWh (2016 est.)

country comparison to the world: 189

**ELECTRICITY - CONSUMPTION:**

1.261 billion kWh (2016 est.)

country comparison to the world: 151

**ELECTRICITY - EXPORTS:**

0 kWh (2016 est.)

country comparison to the world: 208

**ELECTRICITY - IMPORTS:**

1.14 billion kWh (2016 est.)

country comparison to the world: 67

**ELECTRICITY - INSTALLED GENERATING CAPACITY:**

230,000 kW (2016 est.)

country comparison to the world: 164

**ELECTRICITY - FROM FOSSIL FUELS:**

70% of total installed capacity (2016 est.)

country comparison to the world: 110

**ELECTRICITY - FROM NUCLEAR FUELS:**

0% of total installed capacity (2017 est.)

country comparison to the world: 195

**ELECTRICITY - FROM HYDROELECTRIC PLANTS:**

29% of total installed capacity (2017 est.)

country comparison to the world: 71

**ELECTRICITY - FROM OTHER RENEWABLE SOURCES:**

1% of total installed capacity (2017 est.)

country comparison to the world: 169

**CRUDE OIL - PRODUCTION:**

0 bbl/day (2017 est.)

country comparison to the world: 206

**CRUDE OIL - EXPORTS:**

0 bbl/day (2015 est.)

country comparison to the world: 206

**CRUDE OIL - IMPORTS:**

0 bbl/day (2015 est.)

country comparison to the world: 204

**CRUDE OIL - PROVED RESERVES:**

0 bbl (1 January 2018 est.)

country comparison to the world: 204

**REFINED PETROLEUM PRODUCTS - PRODUCTION:**

0 bbl/day (2015 est.)

country comparison to the world: 208

**REFINED PETROLEUM PRODUCTS - CONSUMPTION:**

15,000 bbl/day (2016 est.)

country comparison to the world: 152

**REFINED PETROLEUM PRODUCTS - EXPORTS:**

0 bbl/day (2015 est.)

country comparison to the world: 209

**REFINED PETROLEUM PRODUCTS - IMPORTS:**

13,100 bbl/day (2015 est.)

country comparison to the world: 142

**NATURAL GAS - PRODUCTION:**

0 cu m (2017 est.)

country comparison to the world: 206

**NATURAL GAS - CONSUMPTION:**

0 cu m (2017 est.)

country comparison to the world: 206

**NATURAL GAS - EXPORTS:**

0 cu m (2017 est.)

country comparison to the world: 200

**NATURAL GAS - IMPORTS:**

0 cu m (2017 est.)

country comparison to the world: 200

**NATURAL GAS - PROVED RESERVES:**

0 cu m (1 January 2014 est.)

country comparison to the world: 200

**CARBON DIOXIDE EMISSIONS FROM CONSUMPTION OF ENERGY:**

2.651 million Mt (2017 est.)

country comparison to the world: 151

## COMMUNICATIONS :: TOGO

**TELEPHONES - FIXED LINES:**

total subscriptions: 36,111 (2017 est.)

subscriptions per 100 inhabitants: less than 1 (2017 est.)

country comparison to the world: 165

**TELEPHONES - MOBILE CELLULAR:**

total subscriptions: 6,219,981 (2017 est.)

subscriptions per 100 inhabitants: 78 (2017 est.)

country comparison to the world: 113

**TELEPHONE SYSTEM:**

general assessment: fair system based on a network of microwave radio relay routes supplemented by open-wire lines and a mobile-cellular system (2016)

domestic: microwave radio relay and open-wire lines for conventional system; combined fixed-line and mobile-cellular teledensity roughly 70 telephones per 100 persons with mobile-cellular use predominating (2016)

international: country code - 228; satellite earth stations - 1 Intelsat (Atlantic Ocean), 1 Symphonie (2016)

**BROADCAST MEDIA:**

1 state-owned TV station with multiple transmission sites; 5 private TV stations broadcast locally; cable TV service is available; state-owned radio network with 2 stations (in Lome and Kara); several dozen private radio stations and a few community radio stations; transmissions of multiple international broadcasters available (2018)

**INTERNET COUNTRY CODE:**

.tg

**INTERNET USERS:**

total: 877,310 (July 2016 est.)

percent of population: 11.3% (July 2016 est.)

country comparison to the world: 135

**BROADBAND - FIXED SUBSCRIPTIONS:**

total: 45,756 (2017 est.)

subscriptions per 100 inhabitants: 1 (2017 est.)

country comparison to the world: 131

# TRANSPORTATION :: TOGO

**NATIONAL AIR TRANSPORT SYSTEM:**

number of registered air carriers: 1 (2015)

inventory of registered aircraft operated by air carriers: 8 (2015)

annual passenger traffic on registered air carriers: 769,904 (2015)

annual freight traffic on registered air carriers: 0 mt-km (2015)

**CIVIL AIRCRAFT REGISTRATION COUNTRY CODE PREFIX:**

5V (2016)

**AIRPORTS:**

8 (2013)

country comparison to the world: 163

**AIRPORTS - WITH PAVED RUNWAYS:**

total: 2 (2013)

2,438 to 3,047 m: 2 (2013)

**AIRPORTS - WITH UNPAVED RUNWAYS:**

total: 6 (2013)

914 to 1,523 m: 4 (2013)

under 914 m: 2 (2013)

**PIPELINES:**

62 km gas

**RAILWAYS:**

total: 568 km (2014)

narrow gauge: 568 km 1.000-m gauge (2014)

country comparison to the world: 111

**ROADWAYS:**

total: 11,652 km (2007)

paved: 2,447 km (2007)

unpaved: 9,205 km (2007)

country comparison to the world: 132

**WATERWAYS:**

50 km (seasonally navigable by small craft on the Mono River depending on rainfall) (2011)

country comparison to the world: 102

**MERCHANT MARINE:**

total: 308 (2017)

by type: bulk carrier 11, container ship 3, general cargo 199, oil tanker 44, other 51 (2017)

country comparison to the world: 51

**PORTS AND TERMINALS:**

major seaport(s): Kpeme, Lome

# MILITARY AND SECURITY :: TOGO

**MILITARY EXPENDITURES:**

1.86% of GDP (2016)

1.71% of GDP (2015)

1.85% of GDP (2014)

country comparison to the world: 56

**MILITARY BRANCHES:**

Togolese Armed Forces (Forces Armees Togolaise, FAT): Togolese Army (l'Armee de Terre), Togolese Navy (Forces Naval Togolaises), Togolese Air Force (Armee de l'Air), National Gendarmerie (2018)

**MILITARY SERVICE AGE AND OBLIGATION:**

18 years of age for military service; 2-year service obligation; currently the military is only an all-volunteer force (2017)

# TRANSNATIONAL ISSUES :: TOGO

**DISPUTES - INTERNATIONAL:**

in 2001, Benin claimed Togo moved boundary monuments - joint commission continues to resurvey the boundarytalks continue between Benin and Togo on funding the Adjrala hydroelectric dam on the Mona River

**REFUGEES AND INTERNALLY DISPLACED PERSONS:**

refugees (country of origin): 9,727 (Ghana) (2018)

**ILLICIT DRUGS:**

transit hub for Nigerian heroin and cocaine traffickers; money laundering not a significant problem

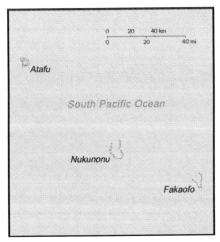

# AUSTRALIA - OCEANIA :: TOKELAU

## INTRODUCTION :: TOKELAU

### BACKGROUND:
Originally settled by Polynesian emigrants from surrounding island groups, the Tokelau Islands were made a British protectorate in 1889. They were transferred to New Zealand administration in 1925. Referenda held in 2006 and 2007 to change the status of the islands from that of a New Zealand territory to one of free association with New Zealand did not meet the needed threshold for approval.

## GEOGRAPHY :: TOKELAU

### LOCATION:
Oceania, group of three atolls in the South Pacific Ocean, about one-half of the way from Hawaii to New Zealand

### GEOGRAPHIC COORDINATES:
9 00 S, 172 00 W

### MAP REFERENCES:
Oceania

### AREA:
total: 12 sq km

land: 12 sq km

water: 0 sq km

country comparison to the world: 242

### AREA - COMPARATIVE:
about 17 times the size of the National Mall in Washington, DC

### LAND BOUNDARIES:
0 km

### COASTLINE:
101 km

### MARITIME CLAIMS:
territorial sea: 12 nm

exclusive economic zone: 200 nm

### CLIMATE:
tropical; moderated by trade winds (April to November)

### TERRAIN:
low-lying coral atolls enclosing large lagoons

### ELEVATION:
0 m lowest point: Pacific Ocean

5 highest point: unnamed location

### NATURAL RESOURCES:
NEGL

### LAND USE:
agricultural land: 60% (2011 est.)

arable land: 0% (2011 est.) / permanent crops: 60% (2011 est.) / permanent pasture: 0% (2011 est.)

forest: 0% (2011 est.)

other: 40% (2011 est.)

### IRRIGATED LAND:
0 sq km (2012)

### POPULATION DISTRIBUTION:
the country's small population is fairly evenly distributed amongst the three atolls

### NATURAL HAZARDS:
lies in Pacific cyclone belt

### ENVIRONMENT - CURRENT ISSUES:
overexploitation of certain fish and other marine species, coastal sand, and forest resources; pollution of freshwater lenses and coastal waters from improper disposal of chemicals

### GEOGRAPHY - NOTE:
consists of three atolls (Atafu, Fakaofo, Nukunonu), each with a lagoon surrounded by a number of reef-bound islets of varying length and rising to over 3 m above sea level

## PEOPLE AND SOCIETY :: TOKELAU

### POPULATION:
1,285 (2016 est.)

country comparison to the world: 235

### NATIONALITY:
noun: Tokelauan(s)

adjective: Tokelauan

### ETHNIC GROUPS:
Tokelauan 64.5%, part Tokelauan/Samoan 9.7%, part Tokelauan/Tuvaluan 2.8%, Tuvaluan 7.5%, Samoan 5.8%, other Pacific islander 3.4%, other 5.6%, unspecified 0.8% (2016 est.)

### LANGUAGES:
Tokelauan 88.1% (a Polynesian language), English 48.6%, Samoan 26.7%, Tuvaluan 11.2%, Kiribati 1.5%, other 2.8%, none 2.8%, unspecified 0.8% (2016 ests.)

note: shares sum to more than 100% because some respondents gave more than one answer on the census

### RELIGIONS:
Congregational Christian Church 50.4%, Roman Catholic 38.7%, Presbyterian 5.9%, other Christian 4.2%, unspecified 0.8% (2016 est.)

### POPULATION GROWTH RATE:
-0.01% (2014 est.)

country comparison to the world: 196

### POPULATION DISTRIBUTION:
the country's small population is fairly evenly distributed amongst the three atolls

**URBANIZATION:**

urban population: 0% of total population (2018)

rate of urbanization: 0% annual rate of change (2015-20 est.)

**SEX RATIO:**

NA

**INFANT MORTALITY RATE:**

total: NA

male: NA

female: NA

**LIFE EXPECTANCY AT BIRTH:**

total population: NA (2017 est.)

male: NA (2017 est.)

female: NA (2017 est.)

**TOTAL FERTILITY RATE:**

NA

**PHYSICIANS DENSITY:**

2.72 physicians/1,000 population (2010)

**DRINKING WATER SOURCE:**

improved:

rural: 100% of population

total: 100% of population

unimproved:

rural: 0% of population

total: 0% of population (2015 est.)

**SANITATION FACILITY ACCESS:**

improved:

rural: 90.5% of population (2015 est.)

total: 90.5% of population (2015 est.)

unimproved:

rural: 9.5% of population (2015 est.)

total: 9.5% of population (2015 est.)

**HIV/AIDS - ADULT PREVALENCE RATE:**

NA

**HIV/AIDS - PEOPLE LIVING WITH HIV/AIDS:**

NA

**HIV/AIDS - DEATHS:**

NA

**EDUCATION EXPENDITURES:**

NA

## GOVERNMENT :: TOKELAU

**COUNTRY NAME:**

conventional long form: none

conventional short form: Tokelau

former: Union Islands, Tokelau Islands

etymology: tokelau" is a Polynesian word meaning "north wind

**DEPENDENCY STATUS:**

self-administering territory of New Zealand; note - Tokelau and New Zealand have agreed to a draft constitution as Tokelau moves toward free association with New Zealand; a UN-sponsored referendum on self governance in October 2007 did not produce the two-thirds majority vote necessary for changing the political status

**GOVERNMENT TYPE:**

parliamentary democratic dependency (General Fono); a territory of New Zealand

**CAPITAL:**

UTC+13 (18 hours ahead of Washington, DC during Standard Time)

**ADMINISTRATIVE DIVISIONS:**

none (territory of New Zealand)

**INDEPENDENCE:**

none (territory of New Zealand)

**NATIONAL HOLIDAY:**

Waitangi Day (Treaty of Waitangi established British sovereignty over New Zealand), 6 February (1840)

**CONSTITUTION:**

history: many previous; latest effective 1 January 1949 (Tokelau Islands Act 1948) (2018)

amendments: proposed as a resolution by the General Fono; passage requires support by each village and approval by the General Fono; amended many times, last in 2007 (2018)

**LEGAL SYSTEM:**

common law system of New Zealand

**CITIZENSHIP:**

see New Zealand

**SUFFRAGE:**

21 years of age; universal

**EXECUTIVE BRANCH:**

chief of state: Queen ELIZABETH II (since 6 February 1952); represented by Governor General of New Zealand Governor General Dame Patricia Lee REDDY (since 28 September 2016); New Zealand is represented by Administrator Jonathan KINGS (since 30 August 2017)

head of government: Afega GAULOFA (since 10 March 2016); note - position rotates annually among the three Faipule (village leaders)

cabinet: Council for the Ongoing Government of Tokelau (or Tokelau Council) functions as a cabinet; consists of 3 Faipule (village leaders) and 3 Pulenuku (village mayors)

elections/appointments: the monarchy is hereditary; governor general appointed by the monarch; administrator appointed by the Minister of Foreign Affairs and Trade in New Zealand; head of government chosen from the Council of Faipule to serve a 1-year term

note: the meeting place of the Tokelau Council rotates annually among the three atolls; this tradition has given rise to the somewhat misleading description that the capital rotates yearly between the three atolls; in actuality, it is the seat of the government councillors that rotates since Tokelau has no capital

**LEGISLATIVE BRANCH:**

description: unicameral General Fono (20 seats apportioned by island - Atafu 7, Fakaofo 7, Nukunonu 6; members directly elected by simple majority vote to serve 3-year terms); note - the Tokelau Amendment Act of 1996 confers limited legislative power to the General Fono

elections: last held on 23, 27, and 31 January 2017 depending on island (next to be held in 2020)

election results: percent of vote by party - NA; seats by party - independent 20; composition - men 17, women 3, percent of women 15%

**JUDICIAL BRANCH:**

highest courts: Court of Appeal in New Zealand (consists of the court president and 8 judges sitting in 3- or 5-judge panels depending on the case)

judge selection and term of office: judges nominated by the Judicial Selection Committee and approved by three-quarters majority of the Parliament; judges appointed for life

subordinate courts: High Court, in New Zealand; Council of Elders or Taupulega

**POLITICAL PARTIES AND LEADERS:**

none

**INTERNATIONAL ORGANIZATION PARTICIPATION:**

PIF (associate member), SPC, UNESCO (associate), UPU

**DIPLOMATIC REPRESENTATION IN THE US:**

none (territory of New Zealand)

**DIPLOMATIC REPRESENTATION FROM THE US:**

none (territory of New Zealand)

**FLAG DESCRIPTION:**

a yellow stylized Tokelauan canoe on a dark blue field sails toward the manu - the Southern Cross constellation of four, white, five-pointed stars at the hoist side; the Southern Cross represents the role of Christianity in Tokelauan culture and, in conjunction with the canoe, symbolizes the country navigating into the future; the color yellow indicates happiness and peace, and the blue field represents the ocean on which the community relies

**NATIONAL SYMBOL(S):**

tuluma (fishing tackle box); national colors: blue, yellow, white

**NATIONAL ANTHEM:**

name: "Te Atua" (For the Almighty)

lyrics/music: unknown/Falani KALOLO

note: adopted 2008; in preparation for eventual self governance, Tokelau held a national contest to choose an anthem; as a territory of New Zealand, "God Defend New Zealand" and "God Save the Queen" are official (see New Zealand)

## ECONOMY :: TOKELAU

**ECONOMY - OVERVIEW:**

Tokelau's small size (three villages), isolation, and lack of resources greatly restrain economic development and confine agriculture to the subsistence level. The principal sources of revenue are from sales of copra, postage stamps, souvenir coins, and handicrafts. Money is also remitted to families from relatives in New Zealand.

The people rely heavily on aid from New Zealand - about $15 million annually in FY12/13 and FY13/14 - to maintain public services. New Zealand's support amounts to 80% of Tokelau's recurrent government budget. An international trust fund, currently worth nearly $32 million, was established in 2004 by New Zealand to provide Tokelau an independent source of revenue.

**GDP (PURCHASING POWER PARITY):**

$1.5 million (1993 est.)

country comparison to the world: 229

**GDP (OFFICIAL EXCHANGE RATE):**

NA

**GDP - REAL GROWTH RATE:**

NA

**GDP - PER CAPITA (PPP):**

$1,000 (1993 est.)

country comparison to the world: 225

**GDP - COMPOSITION, BY SECTOR OF ORIGIN:**

agriculture: NA

industry: NA

services: NA

**AGRICULTURE - PRODUCTS:**

coconuts, copra, breadfruit, papayas, bananas; pigs, poultry, goats; fish

**INDUSTRIES:**

small-scale enterprises for copra production, woodworking, plaited craft goods; stamps, coins; fishing

**LABOR FORCE:**

440 (2001)

country comparison to the world: 231

**UNEMPLOYMENT RATE:**

NA

**POPULATION BELOW POVERTY LINE:**

NA

**BUDGET:**

revenues: 430,800 (1987 est.)

expenditures: 2.8 million (1987 est.)

**FISCAL YEAR:**

1 April - 31 March

**INFLATION RATE (CONSUMER PRICES):**

NA

**EXPORTS:**

$0 (2002 est.)

country comparison to the world: 224

**EXPORTS - COMMODITIES:**

stamps, copra, handicrafts

**IMPORTS:**

$969,200 (2002 est.)

country comparison to the world: 223

**IMPORTS - COMMODITIES:**

foodstuffs, building materials, fuel

**EXCHANGE RATES:**

New Zealand dollars (NZD) per US dollar -

1.416 (2017 est.)

1.4279 (2016 est.)

1.4279 (2015)

1.4279 (2014 est.)

1.2039 (2013 est.)

## ENERGY :: TOKELAU

**CRUDE OIL - PROVED RESERVES:**

0 bbl (1 January 2010 est.)

country comparison to the world: 205

## COMMUNICATIONS :: TOKELAU

**TELEPHONES - FIXED LINES:**

total subscriptions: 300 (July 2016 est.)

subscriptions per 100 inhabitants: 21 (July 2016 est.)

country comparison to the world: 218

**TELEPHONE SYSTEM:**

general assessment: modern satellite-based communications system (2015)

domestic: radiotelephone service between islands (2015)

international: country code - 690; radiotelephone service to Samoa; government-regulated telephone service (TeleTok); satellite earth stations - 3 (2015)

**BROADCAST MEDIA:**

Sky TV access for around 30% of the population; each atoll operates a radio service that provides shipping news and weather reports (2011)

**INTERNET COUNTRY CODE:**

.tk

**INTERNET USERS:**

total: 805 (July 2016 est.)

percent of population: 60.2% (July 2016 est.)

country comparison to the world: 224

## TRANSPORTATION :: TOKELAU

**PORTS AND TERMINALS:**

none; offshore anchorage only

## MILITARY AND SECURITY :: TOKELAU

**MILITARY - NOTE:**
defense is the responsibility of New Zealand

## TRANSNATIONAL ISSUES :: TOKELAU

**DISPUTES - INTERNATIONAL:**
Tokelau included American Samoa's Swains Island (Olosega) in its 2006 draft independence constitution

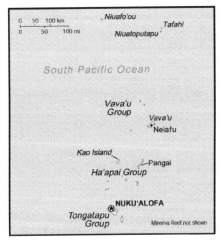

# AUSTRALIA - OCEANIA :: TONGA

## INTRODUCTION :: TONGA

### BACKGROUND:
Tonga - unique among Pacific nations - never completely lost its indigenous governance. The archipelagos of "The Friendly Islands" were united into a Polynesian kingdom in 1845. Tonga became a constitutional monarchy in 1875 and a British protectorate in 1900; it withdrew from the protectorate and joined the Commonwealth of Nations in 1970. Tonga remains the only monarchy in the Pacific; in 2010 it began implementing steps to conduct more representative elections. Tropical Cyclone Gita, the strongest-ever recorded storm to impact Tonga, hit the islands in February 2018 causing extensive damage.

## GEOGRAPHY :: TONGA

### LOCATION:
Oceania, archipelago in the South Pacific Ocean, about two-thirds of the way from Hawaii to New Zealand

### GEOGRAPHIC COORDINATES:
20 00 S, 175 00 W

### MAP REFERENCES:
Oceania

### AREA:
total: 747 sq km

land: 717 sq km

water: 30 sq km

country comparison to the world: 190

### AREA - COMPARATIVE:
four times the size of Washington, DC

### LAND BOUNDARIES:
0 km

### COASTLINE:
419 km

### MARITIME CLAIMS:
territorial sea: 12 nm

exclusive economic zone: 200 nm

continental shelf: 200-m depth or to the depth of exploitation

### CLIMATE:
tropical; modified by trade winds; warm season (December to May), cool season (May to December)

### TERRAIN:
mostly flat islands with limestone bedrock formed from uplifted coral formation; others have limestone overlying volcanic rock

### ELEVATION:
0 m lowest point: Pacific Ocean

1046 highest point: Kao Volcano on Kao Island

### NATURAL RESOURCES:
arable land, fish

### LAND USE:
agricultural land: 43.1% (2011 est.)

arable land: 22.2% (2011 est.) / permanent crops: 15.3% (2011 est.) / permanent pasture: 5.6% (2011 est.)

forest: 12.5% (2011 est.)

other: 44.4% (2011 est.)

### IRRIGATED LAND:
0 sq km (2012)

### POPULATION DISTRIBUTION:
over two-thirds of the population lives on the island of Tongatapu; only 45 of the nation's 171 islands are occupied

### NATURAL HAZARDS:
cyclones (October to April); earthquakes and volcanic activity on Fonuafo'ou

volcanism: moderate volcanic activity; Fonualei (180 m) has shown frequent activity in recent years, while Niuafo'ou (260 m), which last erupted in 1985, has forced evacuations; other historically active volcanoes include Late and Tofua

### ENVIRONMENT - CURRENT ISSUES:
deforestation from land being cleared for agriculture and settlement; soil exhaustion; water pollution due to salinization, sewage, and toxic chemicals from farming activities; coral reefs and marine populations threatened

### ENVIRONMENT - INTERNATIONAL AGREEMENTS:
party to: Biodiversity, Climate Change, Climate Change-Kyoto Protocol, Desertification, Hazardous Wastes, Law of the Sea, Marine Dumping, Marine Life Conservation, Ozone Layer Protection, Ship Pollution

signed, but not ratified: none of the selected agreements

### GEOGRAPHY - NOTE:
the western islands (making up the Tongan Volcanic Arch) are all of volcanic origin; the eastern islands are nonvolcanic and are composed of coral limestone and sand

## PEOPLE AND SOCIETY :: TONGA

### POPULATION:
106,398 (July 2018 est.)

country comparison to the world: 193

### NATIONALITY:
noun: Tongan(s)

adjective: Tongan

**ETHNIC GROUPS:**

Tongan 97%, part-Tongan 0.8%, other 2.2%, unspecified (2016 est.)

**LANGUAGES:**

Tongan and English 76.8%, Tongan, English, and other language 10.6%, Tongan only (official) 8.7%, English only (official) 0.7%, other 1.7%, none 2.2% (2016 est.)

note: data represent persons aged 5 and older who can read and write a simple sentence in Tongan, English, or another language

**RELIGIONS:**

Protestant 64.1% (includes Free Wesleyan Church 35%, Free Church of Tonga 11.9%, Church of Tonga 6.8%, Assembly of God 2.3%, Seventh Day Adventist 2.2%, Tokaikolo Christian Church 1.6%, other 4.3%), Mormon 18.6%, Roman Catholic 14.2%, other 2.4%, none 0.5%, unspecified 0.1% (2016 est.)

**AGE STRUCTURE:**

0-14 years: 33.26% (male 17,979 /female 17,404)

15-24 years: 19.69% (male 10,725 /female 10,223)

25-54 years: 34.69% (male 18,436 /female 18,469)

55-64 years: 5.81% (male 3,098 /female 3,089)

65 years and over: 6.56% (male 3,140 /female 3,835) (2018 est.)

**DEPENDENCY RATIOS:**

total dependency ratio: 74.2 (2015 est.)

youth dependency ratio: 63.9 (2015 est.)

elderly dependency ratio: 10.2 (2015 est.)

potential support ratio: 9.8 (2015 est.)

**MEDIAN AGE:**

total: 23.3 years

male: 22.9 years

female: 23.8 years (2018 est.)

country comparison to the world: 174

**POPULATION GROWTH RATE:**

-0.1% (2018 est.)

country comparison to the world: 204

**BIRTH RATE:**

21.8 births/1,000 population (2018 est.)

country comparison to the world: 69

**DEATH RATE:**

4.9 deaths/1,000 population (2018 est.)

country comparison to the world: 199

**NET MIGRATION RATE:**

-17.8 migrant(s)/1,000 population (2017 est.)

country comparison to the world: 218

**POPULATION DISTRIBUTION:**

over two-thirds of the population lives on the island of Tongatapu; only 45 of the nation's 171 islands are occupied

**URBANIZATION:**

urban population: 23.1% of total population (2018)

rate of urbanization: 0.71% annual rate of change (2015-20 est.)

**MAJOR URBAN AREAS - POPULATION:**

23,000 NUKU'ALOFA (2018)

**SEX RATIO:**

at birth: 1.03 male(s)/female (2017 est.)

0-14 years: 1.03 male(s)/female (2017 est.)

15-24 years: 1.05 male(s)/female (2017 est.)

25-54 years: 1 male(s)/female (2017 est.)

55-64 years: 0.98 male(s)/female (2017 est.)

65 years and over: 0.84 male(s)/female (2017 est.)

total population: 1.01 male(s)/female (2017 est.)

**MOTHER'S MEAN AGE AT FIRST BIRTH:**

24.9 years (2012 est.)

note: median age at first birth among women 25-49

**MATERNAL MORTALITY RATE:**

124 deaths/100,000 live births (2015 est.)

country comparison to the world: 68

**INFANT MORTALITY RATE:**

total: 10.9 deaths/1,000 live births (2018 est.)

male: 11.3 deaths/1,000 live births (2018 est.)

female: 10.5 deaths/1,000 live births (2018 est.)

country comparison to the world: 127

**LIFE EXPECTANCY AT BIRTH:**

total population: 76.6 years (2018 est.)

male: 75 years (2018 est.)

female: 78.3 years (2018 est.)

country comparison to the world: 85

**TOTAL FERTILITY RATE:**

3.03 children born/woman (2018 est.)

country comparison to the world: 51

**CONTRACEPTIVE PREVALENCE RATE:**

34.1% (2012)

**HEALTH EXPENDITURES:**

5.2% of GDP (2014)

country comparison to the world: 136

**PHYSICIANS DENSITY:**

0.56 physicians/1,000 population (2010)

**HOSPITAL BED DENSITY:**

2.6 beds/1,000 population (2010)

**DRINKING WATER SOURCE:**

improved:

urban: 99.7% of population

rural: 99.6% of population

total: 99.6% of population

unimproved:

urban: 0.3% of population

rural: 0.4% of population

total: 0.4% of population (2015 est.)

**SANITATION FACILITY ACCESS:**

improved:

urban: 97.6% of population (2015 est.)

rural: 89% of population (2015 est.)

total: 91% of population (2015 est.)

unimproved:

urban: 2.4% of population (2015 est.)

rural: 11% of population (2015 est.)

total: 9% of population (2015 est.)

**HIV/AIDS - ADULT PREVALENCE RATE:**

NA

**HIV/AIDS - PEOPLE LIVING WITH HIV/AIDS:**

NA

**HIV/AIDS - DEATHS:**

NA

**MAJOR INFECTIOUS DISEASES:**

note: active local transmission of Zika virus by Aedes species mosquitoes has been identified in this country (as of August 2016); it poses an important risk (a large number of cases possible) among US citizens if bitten by an infective mosquito; other less common ways to get Zika are through sex, via blood transfusion, or during pregnancy, in which the pregnant woman passes Zika virus to her fetus

**OBESITY - ADULT PREVALENCE RATE:**

48.2% (2016)

country comparison to the world: 7

**CHILDREN UNDER THE AGE OF 5 YEARS UNDERWEIGHT:**

1.9% (2012)

country comparison to the world: 112

**LITERACY:**

definition: can read and write Tongan and/or English (2015 est.)

total population: 99.4% (2015 est.)

male: 99.3% (2015 est.)

female: 99.4% (2015 est.)

# GOVERNMENT :: TONGA

**COUNTRY NAME:**

conventional long form: Kingdom of Tonga

conventional short form: Tonga

local long form: Pule'anga Fakatu'i 'o Tonga

local short form: Tonga

former: Friendly Islands

etymology: "tonga" means "south" in the Tongan language and refers to the country's geographic position in relation to central Polynesia

**GOVERNMENT TYPE:**

constitutional monarchy

**CAPITAL:**

name: Nuku'alofa

geographic coordinates: 21 08 S, 175 12 W

time difference: UTC+13 (18 hours ahead of Washington, DC, during Standard Time)

daylight saving time: +1hr, begins first Sunday in November; ends second Sunday in January

**ADMINISTRATIVE DIVISIONS:**

5 island divisions; 'Eua, Ha'apai, Ongo Niua, Tongatapu, Vava'u

**INDEPENDENCE:**

4 June 1970 (from UK protectorate)

**NATIONAL HOLIDAY:**

Official Birthday of King TUPOU VI, 4 July (1959); note - actual birthday of the monarch is 12 July 1959; 4 July (2015) is the day the king was crownedConstitution Day (National Day), 4 November (1875)

**CONSTITUTION:**

history: adopted 4 November 1875 (2018)

amendments: proposed by the Legislative Assembly; passage requires approval by the Assembly in each of three readings, the unanimous approval of the Privy Council (a high-level advisory body to the monarch), the Cabinet, and assent to by the monarch; revised 1988; amended many times, last in 2016 (2018)

**LEGAL SYSTEM:**

English common law

**INTERNATIONAL LAW ORGANIZATION PARTICIPATION:**

has not submitted an ICJ jurisdiction declaration; non-party state to the ICCt

**CITIZENSHIP:**

citizenship by birth: no

citizenship by descent only: the father must be a citizen of Tonga; if a child is born out of wedlock, the mother must be a citizen of Tonga

dual citizenship recognized: yes

residency requirement for naturalization: 5 years

**SUFFRAGE:**

21 years of age; universal

**EXECUTIVE BRANCH:**

chief of state: King TUPOU VI (since 18 March 2012); Heir Apparent Crown Prince Siaosi Manumataogo 'Alaivahamama'o 'Ahoeitu Konstantin Tuku'aho, son of the king (born 17 September 1985); note - on 18 March 2012, King George TUPOU V died and his brother, Crown Prince TUPOUTO'A Lavaka, assumed the throne as TUPOU VI

head of government: Interim Prime Minister 'Akilisi POHIVA (since 30 December 2014); note - King TUPOU VI dissolved the parliament on 26 August 2017

cabinet: Cabinet nominated by the prime minister and appointed by the monarch

elections/appointments: the monarchy is hereditary; prime minister and deputy prime minister indirectly elected by the Legislative Assembly and appointed by the monarch; election last held on 18 December 2017 (next to be held in November 2021); note - King TUPOU VI's dissolution of parliament in August 2017 triggered an early election

election results: 'Akilisi POHIVA (Democratic Party of the Friendly Islands) reelected prime minister by parliament receiving 14 of 26 votes

note: a Privy Council advises the monarch

**LEGISLATIVE BRANCH:**

description: unicameral Legislative Assembly or Fale Alea (up to 30 seats - currently 28; 17 people's representatives directly elected in single-seat constituencies by simple majority vote, 9 indirectly elected by hereditary leaders, and 2 non-elected; members serve 3-year terms)

elections: last held on 16 November 2017 (next to be held in 2020)

election results: percent of vote - NA; seats by party - Democratic Party 14, nobles' representatives 9, other 2, independent 3; composition - men 27, women 1, percent of women 3.6%

**JUDICIAL BRANCH:**

highest courts: Court of Appeal (consists of the court president and a number of judges determined by the monarch); note - appeals beyond the Court of Appeal are brought before the King in Privy Council, the monarch's advisory organ that has both judicial and legislative powers

judge selection and term of office: judge appointments and tenures made by the King in Privy Council, judge appointments subject to consent of the Legislative Assembly

subordinate courts: Supreme Court; Magistrate's Courts; Land Courts

**POLITICAL PARTIES AND LEADERS:**

Democratic Party of the Friendly Islands [Samuela 'Akilisi POHIVA]
People's Democratic Party or PDP [Tesina FUKO]
Sustainable Nation-Building Party [Sione FONUA]
Tonga Democratic Labor Party
Tonga Human Rights and Democracy Movement or THRDM

**INTERNATIONAL ORGANIZATION PARTICIPATION:**

ACP, ADB, AOSIS, C, FAO, G-77, IBRD, ICAO, ICRM, IDA, IFAD, IFC, IFRCS, IHO, IMF, IMO, IMSO, Interpol, IOC, IPU, ITU, ITUC (NGOs), OPCW, PIF, Sparteca, SPC, UN, UNCTAD, UNESCO, UNIDO, UPU, WCO, WHO, WIPO, WMO, WTO

**DIPLOMATIC REPRESENTATION IN THE US:**

chief of mission: Ambassador Mahe'uli'uli Sandhurst TUPOUNIUA (since 17 September 2013)

chancery: 250 E. 51st Street, New York, NY, 10022

telephone: [1] (917) 369-1025

FAX: [1] (917) 369-1024

consulate(s) general: San Francisco

**DIPLOMATIC REPRESENTATION FROM THE US:**

the US does not have an embassy in Tonga; the US Ambassador to Fiji is accredited to Tonga

**FLAG DESCRIPTION:**

red with a bold red cross on a white rectangle in the upper hoist-side corner; the cross reflects the deep-rooted Christianity in Tonga, red represents the blood of Christ and his sacrifice, and white signifies purity

**NATIONAL SYMBOL(S):**

red cross on white field, arms equal length; national colors: red, white

**NATIONAL ANTHEM:**

name: "Ko e fasi 'o e tu"i 'o e 'Otu Tonga" (Song of the King of the Tonga Islands)

lyrics/music: Uelingatoni Ngu TUPOUMALOHI/Karl Gustavus SCHMITT

note: in use since 1875; more commonly known as "Fasi Fakafonua" (National Song)

## ECONOMY :: TONGA

**ECONOMY - OVERVIEW:**

Tonga has a small, open island economy and is the last constitutional monarchy among the Pacific Island countries. It has a narrow export base in agricultural goods. Squash, vanilla beans, and yams are the main crops. Agricultural exports, including fish, make up two-thirds of total exports. Tourism is the second-largest source of hard currency earnings following remittances. Tonga had 53,800 visitors in 2015. The country must import a high proportion of its food, mainly from New Zealand.

The country remains dependent on external aid and remittances from overseas Tongans to offset its trade deficit. The government is emphasizing the development of the private sector, encouraging investment, and is committing increased funds for health care and education. Tonga's English-speaking and educated workforce offers a viable labor market, and the tropical climate provides fertile soil. Renewable energy and deep-sea mining also offer opportunities for investment.

Tonga has a reasonably sound basic infrastructure and well developed social services. But the government faces high unemployment among the young, moderate inflation, pressures for democratic reform, and rising civil service expenditures.

**GDP (PURCHASING POWER PARITY):**

$591 million (2017 est.)

$576.6 million (2016 est.)

$553.6 million (2015 est.)

note: data are in 2017 dollars

country comparison to the world: 211

**GDP (OFFICIAL EXCHANGE RATE):**

$455 million (2017 est.) (2017 est.)

**GDP - REAL GROWTH RATE:**

2.5% (2017 est.)

4.2% (2016 est.)

3.5% (2015 est.)

country comparison to the world: 134

**GDP - PER CAPITA (PPP):**

$5,900 (2017 est.)

$5,700 (2016 est.)

$5,400 (2015 est.)

note: data are in 2017 dollars

country comparison to the world: 167

**GDP - COMPOSITION, BY END USE:**

household consumption: 99.4% (2017 est.)

government consumption: 21.9% (2017 est.)

investment in fixed capital: 24.1% (2017 est.)

investment in inventories: 0% (2017 est.)

exports of goods and services: 22.8% (2017 est.)

imports of goods and services: -68.5% (2017 est.)

**GDP - COMPOSITION, BY SECTOR OF ORIGIN:**

agriculture: 19.9% (2017 est.)

industry: 20.3% (2017 est.)

services: 59.8% (2017 est.)

**AGRICULTURE - PRODUCTS:**

squash, coconuts, copra, bananas, vanilla beans, cocoa, coffee, sweet potatoes, cassava, taro, and kava

**INDUSTRIES:**

tourism, construction, fishing

**INDUSTRIAL PRODUCTION GROWTH RATE:**

5% (2017 est.)

country comparison to the world: 59

**LABOR FORCE:**

33,800 (2011 est.)

country comparison to the world: 201

**LABOR FORCE - BY OCCUPATION:**

agriculture: 2,006% (2006 est.)

industry: 27.5% (2006 est.)

services: 2,006% (2006 est.)

**UNEMPLOYMENT RATE:**

1.1% (2011 est.)

1.1% (2006)

country comparison to the world: 12

**POPULATION BELOW POVERTY LINE:**

22.5% (2010 est.)

**HOUSEHOLD INCOME OR CONSUMPTION BY PERCENTAGE SHARE:**

lowest 10%: NA

highest 10%: NA

**BUDGET:**

revenues: 181.2 million (2017 est.)

expenditures: 181.2 million (2017 est.)

**TAXES AND OTHER REVENUES:**

39.8% (of GDP) (2017 est.)

country comparison to the world: 42

**BUDGET SURPLUS (+) OR DEFICIT (-):**

0% (of GDP) (2017 est.)

country comparison to the world: 47

**PUBLIC DEBT:**

48% of GDP (FY2017 est.)

51.8% of GDP (FY2016 est.)

country comparison to the world: 109

**FISCAL YEAR:**

1 July - 30 June

**INFLATION RATE (CONSUMER PRICES):**

7.4% (2017 est.)

2.6% (2016 est.)

country comparison to the world: 195

**COMMERCIAL BANK PRIME LENDING RATE:**

8% (31 December 2017 est.)

7.9% (31 December 2016 est.)

country comparison to the world: 110

**STOCK OF NARROW MONEY:**

$130.8 million (31 December 2017 est.)

$112.7 million (31 December 2016 est.)

country comparison to the world: 187

**STOCK OF BROAD MONEY:**

$130.8 million (31 December 2017 est.)

$112.7 million (31 December 2016 est.)

country comparison to the world: 192

**STOCK OF DOMESTIC CREDIT:**

$139.2 million (31 December 2017 est.)

$135.2 million (31 December 2016 est.)

country comparison to the world: 187

**MARKET VALUE OF PUBLICLY TRADED SHARES:**

NA

**CURRENT ACCOUNT BALANCE:**

-$53 million (2017 est.)

-$30 million (2016 est.)

country comparison to the world: 80

**EXPORTS:**

$18.4 million (2017 est.)

$19.4 million (2016 est.)

country comparison to the world: 213

**EXPORTS - PARTNERS:**

Hong Kong 25.1%, NZ 22.6%, US 14.3%, Japan 12.8%, Australia 10.5% (2017)

**EXPORTS - COMMODITIES:**

squash, fish, vanilla beans, root crops, kava

**IMPORTS:**

$250.2 million (2017 est.)

$269.8 million (2016 est.)

country comparison to the world: 207

**IMPORTS - COMMODITIES:**

foodstuffs, machinery and transport equipment, fuels, chemicals

**IMPORTS - PARTNERS:**

NZ 33.3%, Fiji 11.7%, US 9.8%, Singapore 9%, Australia 8.9%, China 7.9%, Japan 5.9% (2017)

**RESERVES OF FOREIGN EXCHANGE AND GOLD:**

$198.5 million (31 December 2017 est.)

$176.5 million (31 December 2016 est.)

country comparison to the world: 176

**DEBT - EXTERNAL:**

$189.9 million (31 December 2017 est.)

$198.2 million (31 December 2016 est.)

country comparison to the world: 190

**STOCK OF DIRECT FOREIGN INVESTMENT - AT HOME:**

$127.2 million (31 December 2017 est.)

$117.2 million (31 December 2016 est.)

country comparison to the world: 137

**EXCHANGE RATES:**

pa'anga (TOP) per US dollar -

2.228 (2017 est.)

2.216 (2016 est.)

2.216 (2015 est.)

2.106 (2014 est.)

1.847 (2013 est.)

## ENERGY :: TONGA

**ELECTRICITY ACCESS:**

population without electricity: 5,325 (2012)

electrification - total population: 96% (2012)

electrification - urban areas: 100% (2012)

electrification - rural areas: 83% (2012)

**ELECTRICITY - PRODUCTION:**

52 million kWh (2016 est.)

country comparison to the world: 205

**ELECTRICITY - CONSUMPTION:**

48.36 million kWh (2016 est.)

country comparison to the world: 205

**ELECTRICITY - EXPORTS:**

0 kWh (2016)

country comparison to the world: 209

**ELECTRICITY - IMPORTS:**

0 kWh (2016 est.)

country comparison to the world: 210

**ELECTRICITY - INSTALLED GENERATING CAPACITY:**

20,300 kW (2016 est.)

country comparison to the world: 204

**ELECTRICITY - FROM FOSSIL FUELS:**

74% of total installed capacity (2016 est.)

country comparison to the world: 98

**ELECTRICITY - FROM NUCLEAR FUELS:**

0% of total installed capacity (2017 est.)

country comparison to the world: 196

**ELECTRICITY - FROM HYDROELECTRIC PLANTS:**

0% of total installed capacity (2017 est.)

country comparison to the world: 205

**ELECTRICITY - FROM OTHER RENEWABLE SOURCES:**

26% of total installed capacity (2017 est.)

country comparison to the world: 28

**CRUDE OIL - PRODUCTION:**

71,800 bbl/day (2017 est.)

country comparison to the world: 48

**CRUDE OIL - EXPORTS:**

0 bbl/day (2015 est.)

country comparison to the world: 207

**CRUDE OIL - IMPORTS:**

0 bbl/day (2015 est.)

country comparison to the world: 205

**CRUDE OIL - PROVED RESERVES:**

0 bbl (1 January 2018 est.)

country comparison to the world: 206

**REFINED PETROLEUM PRODUCTS - PRODUCTION:**

0 bbl/day (2017 est.)

country comparison to the world: 209

**REFINED PETROLEUM PRODUCTS - CONSUMPTION:**

900 bbl/day (2016 est.)

country comparison to the world: 207

**REFINED PETROLEUM PRODUCTS - EXPORTS:**

0 bbl/day (2015 est.)

country comparison to the world: 210

**REFINED PETROLEUM PRODUCTS - IMPORTS:**

910 bbl/day (2015 est.)

country comparison to the world: 203

**NATURAL GAS - PRODUCTION:**

0 cu m (2017 est.)

country comparison to the world: 207

**NATURAL GAS - CONSUMPTION:**

0 cu m (2017 est.)

country comparison to the world: 207

**NATURAL GAS - EXPORTS:**

0 cu m (2017 est.)

country comparison to the world: 201

**NATURAL GAS - IMPORTS:**

0 cu m (2017 est.)

country comparison to the world: 201

**NATURAL GAS - PROVED RESERVES:**

0 cu m (1 January 2014 est.)

country comparison to the world: 201

**CARBON DIOXIDE EMISSIONS FROM CONSUMPTION OF ENERGY:**

139,700 Mt (2017 est.)

country comparison to the world: 205

## COMMUNICATIONS :: TONGA

**TELEPHONES - FIXED LINES:**

total subscriptions: 11,000 (July 2016 est.)

subscriptions per 100 inhabitants: 10 (July 2016 est.)

country comparison to the world: 192

**TELEPHONES - MOBILE CELLULAR:**

total subscriptions: 80,000 (July 2016 est.)

subscriptions per 100 inhabitants: 75 (July 2016 est.)

country comparison to the world: 194

**TELEPHONE SYSTEM:**

general assessment: competition between Tonga Telecommunications Corporation (TCC) and Digicel Tonga Limited is accelerating expansion of telecommunications; both parties provide high speed Internet, mobile telephone networks, and international telecom services; Digicel also holds a telecommunication license after its acquisition of TonFon (a subsidiary of former Shoreline Communications Tonga); submarine cable infrastructure, managed by Tonga Cable Limited, has also been brought to the country by Asian Development Bank and World Bank aid (2016)

domestic: combined fixed-line and mobile-cellular teledensity about 85 telephones per 100 persons; fully automatic switched network (2016)

international: country code - 676; satellite earth station - 1 Intelsat (Pacific Ocean) (2016)

**BROADCAST MEDIA:**

1 state-owned TV station and 3 privately owned TV stations; satellite and cable TV services are available; 1 state-owned and 3 privately owned radio stations; Radio Australia broadcasts available via satellite (2015)

**INTERNET COUNTRY CODE:**

.to

**INTERNET USERS:**

total: 42,552 (July 2016 est.)

percent of population: 40% (July 2016 est.)

country comparison to the world: 198

**BROADBAND - FIXED SUBSCRIPTIONS:**

total: 3,000 (2017 est.)

subscriptions per 100 inhabitants: 3 (2017 est.)

country comparison to the world: 183

## TRANSPORTATION :: TONGA

**NATIONAL AIR TRANSPORT SYSTEM:**

number of registered air carriers: 1 (2015)

inventory of registered aircraft operated by air carriers: 1 (2015)

annual passenger traffic on registered air carriers: 75,416 (2015)

annual freight traffic on registered air carriers: 0 mt-km (2015)

**CIVIL AIRCRAFT REGISTRATION COUNTRY CODE PREFIX:**

A3 (2016)

**AIRPORTS:**

6 (2013)

country comparison to the world: 177

**AIRPORTS - WITH PAVED RUNWAYS:**

total: 1 (2013)

2,438 to 3,047 m: 1 (2013)

**AIRPORTS - WITH UNPAVED RUNWAYS:**

total: 5 (2013)

1,524 to 2,437 m: 1 (2013)

914 to 1,523 m: 3 (2013)

under 914 m: 1 (2013)

**ROADWAYS:**

total: 680 km (2011)

paved: 184 km (2011)

unpaved: 496 km (2011)

country comparison to the world: 191

**MERCHANT MARINE:**

total: 34 (2017)

by type: bulk carrier 1, container ship 1, general cargo 14, oil tanker 1, other 17 (2017)

country comparison to the world: 124

**PORTS AND TERMINALS:**

major seaport(s): Nuku'alofa, Neiafu, Pangai

## MILITARY AND SECURITY :: TONGA

**MILITARY BRANCHES:**

Tonga Defense Services (TDS): Land Force (Royal Guard), Maritime Force (includes Royal Marines, Air Wing) (2013)

**MILITARY SERVICE AGE AND OBLIGATION:**

16 years of age for voluntary enlistment (with parental consent); no conscription; the king retains the right to call up "all those capable of bearing arms" in wartime (2012)

## TRANSNATIONAL ISSUES :: TONGA

**DISPUTES - INTERNATIONAL:**

none

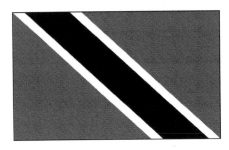

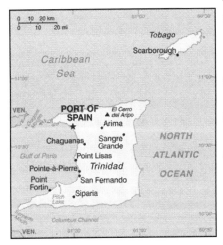

# CENTRAL AMERICA :: TRINIDAD AND TOBAGO

## INTRODUCTION :: TRINIDAD AND TOBAGO

### BACKGROUND:

First colonized by the Spanish, the islands came under British control in the early 19th century. The islands' sugar industry was hurt by the emancipation of the slaves in 1834. Manpower was replaced with the importation of contract laborers from India between 1845 and 1917, which boosted sugar production as well as the cocoa industry. The discovery of oil on Trinidad in 1910 added another important export. Independence was attained in 1962. The country is one of the most prosperous in the Caribbean thanks largely to petroleum and natural gas production and processing. Tourism, mostly in Tobago, is targeted for expansion and is growing. The government is struggling to reverse a surge in violent crime.

## GEOGRAPHY :: TRINIDAD AND TOBAGO

### LOCATION:
Caribbean, islands between the Caribbean Sea and the North Atlantic Ocean, northeast of Venezuela

### GEOGRAPHIC COORDINATES:
11 00 N, 61 00 W

### MAP REFERENCES:
Central America and the Caribbean

### AREA:
total: 5,128 sq km

land: 5,128 sq km

water: 0 sq km

country comparison to the world: 174

### AREA - COMPARATIVE:
slightly smaller than Delaware

### LAND BOUNDARIES:
0 km

### COASTLINE:
362 km

### MARITIME CLAIMS:
territorial sea: 12 nm

exclusive economic zone: 200 nm

contiguous zone: 24 nm

continental shelf: 200 nm or to the outer edge of the continental margin

measured from claimed archipelagic baselines

### CLIMATE:
tropical; rainy season (June to December)

### TERRAIN:
mostly plains with some hills and low mountains

### ELEVATION:
mean elevation: 83 m

elevation extremes: 0 m lowest point: Caribbean Sea

940 highest point: El Cerro del Aripo

### NATURAL RESOURCES:
petroleum, natural gas, asphalt

### LAND USE:
agricultural land: 10.6% (2011 est.)

arable land: 4.9% (2011 est.) / permanent crops: 4.3% (2011 est.) / permanent pasture: 1.4% (2011 est.)

forest: 44% (2011 est.)

other: 45.4% (2011 est.)

### IRRIGATED LAND:
70 sq km (2012)

### POPULATION DISTRIBUTION:
population on Trinidad is concentrated in the western half of the island, on Tobago in the southern half

### NATURAL HAZARDS:
outside usual path of hurricanes and other tropical storms

### ENVIRONMENT - CURRENT ISSUES:
water pollution from agricultural chemicals, industrial wastes, and raw sewage; widespread pollution of waterways and coastal areas; illegal dumping; deforestation; soil erosion; fisheries and wildlife depletion

### ENVIRONMENT - INTERNATIONAL AGREEMENTS:
party to: Biodiversity, Climate Change, Climate Change-Kyoto Protocol, Desertification, Endangered Species, Hazardous Wastes, Law of the Sea, Marine Dumping, Marine Life Conservation, Ozone Layer Protection, Ship Pollution, Tropical Timber 83, Tropical Timber 94, Wetlands

signed, but not ratified: none of the selected agreements

### GEOGRAPHY - NOTE:
Pitch Lake, on Trinidad's southwestern coast, is the world's largest natural reservoir of asphalt

## PEOPLE AND SOCIETY :: TRINIDAD AND TOBAGO

### POPULATION:
1,215,527 (July 2018 est.)

country comparison to the world: 159
**NATIONALITY:**
noun: Trinidadian(s), Tobagonian(s)
adjective: Trinidadian, Tobagonian
note: Trinbagonian is used on occasion to describe a citizen of the country without specifying the island of origin

**ETHNIC GROUPS:**
East Indian 35.4%, African 34.2%, mixed - other 15.3%, mixed - African/East Indian 7.7%, other 1.3%, unspecified 6.2% (2011 est.)

**LANGUAGES:**
English (official), Trinidadian Creole English, Tobagonian Creole English, Caribbean Hindustani (a dialect of Hindi), Trinidadian Creole French, Spanish, Chinese

**RELIGIONS:**
Protestant 32.1% (Pentecostal/Evangelical/Full Gospel 12%, Baptist 6.9%, Anglican 5.7%, Seventh-Day Adventist 4.1%, Presbyterian/Congregational 2.5%, other Protestant 0.9%), Roman Catholic 21.6%, Hindu 18.2%, Muslim 5%, Jehovah's Witness 1.5%, other 8.4%, none 2.2%, unspecified 11.1% (2011 est.)

**AGE STRUCTURE:**
0-14 years: 19.24% (male 119,093 /female 114,830)
15-24 years: 11.55% (male 73,171 /female 67,164)
25-54 years: 44.99% (male 285,376 /female 261,517)
55-64 years: 13.12% (male 79,596 /female 79,890)
65 years and over: 11.1% (male 58,866 /female 76,024) (2018 est.)

**DEPENDENCY RATIOS:**
total dependency ratio: 43.2 (2015 est.)
youth dependency ratio: 29.8 (2015 est.)
elderly dependency ratio: 13.5 (2015 est.)
potential support ratio: 7.4 (2015 est.)

**MEDIAN AGE:**
total: 36.6 years
male: 36.1 years
female: 37.1 years (2018 est.)
country comparison to the world: 74

**POPULATION GROWTH RATE:**
-0.23% (2018 est.)

country comparison to the world: 210
**BIRTH RATE:**
12.3 births/1,000 population (2018 est.)
country comparison to the world: 159

**DEATH RATE:**
8.9 deaths/1,000 population (2018 est.)
country comparison to the world: 66

**NET MIGRATION RATE:**
-5.9 migrant(s)/1,000 population (2017 est.)
country comparison to the world: 196

**POPULATION DISTRIBUTION:**
population on Trinidad is concentrated in the western half of the island, on Tobago in the southern half

**URBANIZATION:**
urban population: 53.2% of total population (2018)
rate of urbanization: 0.22% annual rate of change (2015-20 est.)

**MAJOR URBAN AREAS - POPULATION:**
544,000 PORT-OF-SPAIN (capital) (2018)

**SEX RATIO:**
at birth: 1.03 male(s)/female (2017 est.)
0-14 years: 1.04 male(s)/female (2017 est.)
15-24 years: 1.09 male(s)/female (2017 est.)
25-54 years: 1.09 male(s)/female (2017 est.)
55-64 years: 0.99 male(s)/female (2017 est.)
65 years and over: 0.77 male(s)/female (2017 est.)
total population: 1.03 male(s)/female (2017 est.)

**MATERNAL MORTALITY RATE:**
63 deaths/100,000 live births (2015 est.)
country comparison to the world: 88

**INFANT MORTALITY RATE:**
total: 21.6 deaths/1,000 live births (2018 est.)
male: 22.8 deaths/1,000 live births (2018 est.)
female: 20.3 deaths/1,000 live births (2018 est.)
country comparison to the world: 74

**LIFE EXPECTANCY AT BIRTH:**
total population: 73.4 years (2018 est.)
male: 70.5 years (2018 est.)
female: 76.4 years (2018 est.)
country comparison to the world: 138

**TOTAL FERTILITY RATE:**
1.7 children born/woman (2018 est.)
country comparison to the world: 172

**CONTRACEPTIVE PREVALENCE RATE:**
40.3% (2011)

**HEALTH EXPENDITURES:**
5.9% of GDP (2014)
country comparison to the world: 108

**PHYSICIANS DENSITY:**
1.82 physicians/1,000 population (2011)

**HOSPITAL BED DENSITY:**
3 beds/1,000 population (2014)

**DRINKING WATER SOURCE:**
improved:
urban: 95.1% of population (2015 est.)
rural: 95.1% of population (2015 est.)
total: 95.1% of population (2015 est.)
unimproved:
urban: 4.9% of population (2015 est.)
rural: 4.9% of population (2015 est.)
total: 4.9% of population (2015 est.)

**SANITATION FACILITY ACCESS:**
improved:
urban: 91.5% of population (2015 est.)
rural: 91.5% of population (2015 est.)
total: 91.5% of population (2015 est.)
unimproved:
urban: 8.5% of population (2015 est.)
rural: 8.5% of population (2015 est.)
total: 8.5% of population (2015 est.)

**HIV/AIDS - ADULT PREVALENCE RATE:**
1.1% (2017 est.)
country comparison to the world: 43

**HIV/AIDS - PEOPLE LIVING WITH HIV/AIDS:**
11,000 (2017 est.)
country comparison to the world: 99

**HIV/AIDS - DEATHS:**
<500 (2017 est.)

**MAJOR INFECTIOUS DISEASES:**
note: active local transmission of Zika virus by Aedes species mosquitoes has

been identified in this country (as of August 2016); it poses an important risk (a large number of cases possible) among US citizens if bitten by an infective mosquito; other less common ways to get Zika are through sex, via blood transfusion, or during pregnancy, in which the pregnant woman passes Zika virus to her fetus

## OBESITY - ADULT PREVALENCE RATE:

18.6% (2016)

country comparison to the world: 116

## CHILDREN UNDER THE AGE OF 5 YEARS UNDERWEIGHT:

5.5% (2011)

country comparison to the world: 80

## LITERACY:

definition: age 15 and over can read and write (2015 est.)

total population: 99% (2015 est.)

male: 99.2% (2015 est.)

female: 98.7% (2015 est.)

## UNEMPLOYMENT, YOUTH AGES 15-24:

total: 7.1% (2016 est.)

male: 7.2% (2016 est.)

female: 6.9% (2016 est.)

country comparison to the world: 145

# GOVERNMENT :: TRINIDAD AND TOBAGO

## COUNTRY NAME:

conventional long form: Republic of Trinidad and Tobago

conventional short form: Trinidad and Tobago

etymology: explorer Christopher COLUMBUS named the larger island "La Isla de la Trinidad" (The Island of the Trinity) on 31 July 1498 on his third voyage; the tobacco grown and smoked by the natives of the smaller island or its elongated cigar shape may account for the "tobago" name, which is spelled "tobaco" in Spanish

## GOVERNMENT TYPE:

parliamentary republic

## CAPITAL:

name: Port of Spain

geographic coordinates: 10 39 N, 61 31 W

time difference: UTC-4 (1 hour ahead of Washington, DC, during Standard Time)

## ADMINISTRATIVE DIVISIONS:

9 regions, 3 boroughs, 2 cities, 1 ward

regions: Couva/Tabaquite/Talparo, Diego Martin, Mayaro/Rio Claro, Penal/Debe, Princes Town, Sangre Grande, San Juan/Laventille, Siparia, Tunapuna/Piarco;

borough: Arima, Chaguanas, Point Fortin;

cities: Port of Spain, San Fernando;

ward: Tobago

## INDEPENDENCE:

31 August 1962 (from the UK)

## NATIONAL HOLIDAY:

Independence Day, 31 August (1962)

## CONSTITUTION:

history: previous 1962; latest 1976 (2018)

amendments: proposed by Parliament; passage of amendments affecting constitutional provisions such as human rights and freedoms or citizenship requires at least two-thirds majority vote by the membership of both houses and assent to by the president; passage of amendments such as the powers and authorities of the executive, legislative, and judicial branches of government, and the procedure for amending the constitution requires at least three-quarters majority vote by the House membership, two-thirds majority vote by the Senate membership, and assent to by the president; amended many times, last in 2007 (2018)

## LEGAL SYSTEM:

English common law; judicial review of legislative acts in the Supreme Court

## INTERNATIONAL LAW ORGANIZATION PARTICIPATION:

has not submitted an ICJ jurisdiction declaration; accepts ICCt jurisdiction

## CITIZENSHIP:

citizenship by birth: yes

citizenship by descent only: yes

dual citizenship recognized: yes

residency requirement for naturalization: 8 years

## SUFFRAGE:

18 years of age; universal

## EXECUTIVE BRANCH:

chief of state: President Paula-Mae WEEKES (since 19 March 2018)

head of government: Prime Minister Keith ROWLEY (since 9 September 2015)

cabinet: Cabinet appointed from among members of Parliament

elections/appointments: president indirectly elected by an electoral college of selected Senate and House of Representatives members for a 5-year term (eligible for a second term); election last held on 19 January 2018 (next to be held by February 2023); the president usually appoints the leader of the majority party in the House of Representatives as prime minister

election results: Paula-Mae WEEKES (independent) elected president; ran unopposed and was elected without a vote; she is Trinidad and Tabago's first female head of state

## LEGISLATIVE BRANCH:

description: bicameral Parliament consists of:
Senate (31 seats; 16 members appointed by the ruling party, 9 by the president, and 6 by the opposition party; members serve 5-year terms;) House of Representatives 42 seats; 41 members directly elected in single-seat constituencies by simple majority vote and the house speaker - usually designated from outside Parliament; members serve 5-year terms)

elections:
House of Representatives - last held on 7 September 2015 (next to be held in 2020)

election results:
House of Representatives - percent of vote - PNM 51.7%, People's Partnership coalition 46.6% (UNC 39.6%, COP 6%, other coalition 1%), other 1.7%; seats by party - PNM 23, UNC 17, COP 1

note: Tobago has a unicameral House of Assembly (16 seats; 12 assemblymen directly elected by simple majority vote and 4 appointed councillors - 3 on the advice of the chief secretary and 1 on the advice of the minority leader; members serve 4-year terms)

## JUDICIAL BRANCH:

highest courts: Supreme Court of the Judicature (consists of a chief justice for both the Court of Appeal with 12 judges and the High Court with 24 judges); note - Trinidad and Tobago can file appeals beyond its Supreme Court to the Caribbean Court of Justice, with final appeal to the Judicial Committee of the Privy Council (in London)

**judge selection and term of office:** Supreme Court chief justice appointed by the president after consultation with the prime minister and the parliamentary leader of the opposition; other judges appointed by the Judicial Legal Services Commission, headed by the chief justice and 5 members with judicial experience; all judges appointed for life with mandatory retirement normally at age 65

**subordinate courts:** Courts of Summary Criminal Jurisdiction; Petty Civil Courts; Family Court

## POLITICAL PARTIES AND LEADERS:

Congress of the People or COP
People's National Movement or PNM [Keith ROWLEY]
People's Partnership [Kamla PERSAD-BISSESSAR] (coalition includes UNC, COP, TOP, NJAC)
National Joint Action Committee or NJAC [Kwasi MUTEMA]
Tobago Organization of the People or TOP [Ashworth JACK]
United National Congress or UNC [Kamla PERSAD-BISSESSAR]

## INTERNATIONAL ORGANIZATION PARTICIPATION:

ACP, AOSIS, C, Caricom, CDB, CELAC, EITI (compliant country), FAO, G-24, G-77, IADB, IAEA, IBRD, ICAO, ICC (NGOs), ICCt, ICRM, IDA, IFAD, IFC, IFRCS, IHO, ILO, IMF, IMO, Interpol, IOC, IOM, IPU, ISO, ITSO, ITU, ITUC (NGOs), LAES, MIGA, NAM, OAS, OPANAL, OPCW, Pacific Alliance (observer), Paris Club (associate), UN, UNCTAD, UNESCO, UNIDO, UPU, WCO, WFTU (NGOs), WHO, WIPO, WMO, WTO

## DIPLOMATIC REPRESENTATION IN THE US:

**chief of mission:** Ambassador Anthony Wayne Jerome PHILLIPS-SPENCER, Brig. Gen. (Ret.) (since 27 June 2016)

**chancery:** 1708 Massachusetts Avenue NW, Washington, DC 20036

**telephone:** [1] (202) 467-6490

**FAX:** [1] (202) 785-3130

**consulate(s) general:** Miami, New York

## DIPLOMATIC REPRESENTATION FROM THE US:

**chief of mission:** Ambassador (vacant); Charge d'Affaires John W. MCINTYRE (since 20 January 2017)

**embassy:** 15 Queen's Park West, Port of Spain

**mailing address:** P. O. Box 752, Port of Spain

**telephone:** [1] (868) 622-6371 through 6376

**FAX:** [1] (868) 822-5905

## FLAG DESCRIPTION:

red with a white-edged black diagonal band from the upper hoist side to the lower fly side; the colors represent the elements of earth, water, and fire; black stands for the wealth of the land and the dedication of the people; white symbolizes the sea surrounding the islands, the purity of the country's aspirations, and equality; red symbolizes the warmth and energy of the sun, the vitality of the land, and the courage and friendliness of its people

## NATIONAL SYMBOL(S):

scarlet ibis (bird of Trinidad), cocrico (bird of Tobago), Chaconia flower; national colors: red, white, black

## NATIONAL ANTHEM:

**name:** Forged From the Love of Liberty

**lyrics/music:** Patrick Stanislaus CASTAGNE

**note:** adopted 1962; song originally created to serve as an anthem for the West Indies Federation; adopted by Trinidad and Tobago following the Federation's dissolution in 1962

# ECONOMY :: TRINIDAD AND TOBAGO

## ECONOMY - OVERVIEW:

Trinidad and Tobago relies on its energy sector for much of its economic activity, and has one of the highest per capita incomes in Latin America. Economic growth between 2000 and 2007 averaged slightly over 8% per year, significantly above the regional average of about 3.7% for that same period; however, GDP has slowed down since then, contracting during 2009-12, making small gains in 2013 and contracting again in 2014-17. Trinidad and Tobago is buffered by considerable foreign reserves and a sovereign wealth fund that equals about one-and-a-half times the national budget, but the country is still in a recession and the government faces the dual challenge of gas shortages and a low price environment. Large-scale energy projects in the last quarter of 2017 are helping to mitigate the gas shortages.

Energy production and downstream industrial use dominate the economy. Oil and gas typically account for about 40% of GDP and 80% of exports but less than 5% of employment. Trinidad and Tobago is home to one of the largest natural gas liquefaction facilities in the Western Hemisphere. The country produces about nine times more natural gas than crude oil on an energy equivalent basis with gas contributing about two-thirds of energy sector government revenue. The US is the country's largest trading partner, accounting for 28% of its total imports and 48% of its exports.

Economic diversification is a longstanding government talking point, and Trinidad and Tobago has much potential due to its stable, democratic government and its educated, English speaking workforce. The country is also a regional financial center with a well-regulated and stable financial system. Other sectors the Government of Trinidad and Tobago has targeted for increased investment and projected growth include tourism, agriculture, information and communications technology, and shipping. Unfortunately, a host of other factors, including low labor productivity, inefficient government bureaucracy, and corruption, have hampered economic development.

## GDP (PURCHASING POWER PARITY):

$42.85 billion (2017 est.)

$43.99 billion (2016 est.)

$46.83 billion (2015 est.)

note: data are in 2017 dollars

country comparison to the world: 114

## GDP (OFFICIAL EXCHANGE RATE):

$22.78 billion (2017 est.) (2017 est.)

## GDP - REAL GROWTH RATE:

-2.6% (2017 est.)

-6.1% (2016 est.)

1.7% (2015 est.)

country comparison to the world: 210

## GDP - PER CAPITA (PPP):

$31,300 (2017 est.)

$32,200 (2016 est.)

$34,400 (2015 est.)

note: data are in 2017 dollars

country comparison to the world: 65

## GROSS NATIONAL SAVING:

26.4% of GDP (2017 est.)

16.8% of GDP (2016 est.)

29% of GDP (2015 est.)

country comparison to the world: 50

**GDP - COMPOSITION, BY END USE:**

household consumption: 78.9% (2017 est.)

government consumption: 16.4% (2017 est.)

investment in fixed capital: 8.2% (2017 est.)

investment in inventories: 0.6% (2017 est.)

exports of goods and services: 45.4% (2017 est.)

imports of goods and services: -48.7% (2017 est.)

**GDP - COMPOSITION, BY SECTOR OF ORIGIN:**

agriculture: 0.4% (2017 est.)

industry: 47.8% (2017 est.)

services: 51.7% (2017 est.)

**AGRICULTURE - PRODUCTS:**

cocoa, dasheen, pumpkin, cassava, tomatoes, cucumbers, eggplant, hot pepper, pommecythere, coconut water, poultry

**INDUSTRIES:**

petroleum and petroleum products, liquefied natural gas, methanol, ammonia, urea, steel products, beverages, food processing, cement, cotton textiles

**INDUSTRIAL PRODUCTION GROWTH RATE:**

-4.3% (2017 est.)

country comparison to the world: 195

**LABOR FORCE:**

629,400 (2017 est.)

country comparison to the world: 154

**LABOR FORCE - BY OCCUPATION:**

agriculture: 3.1%

industry: 11.5%

services: 85.4% (2016 est.)

**UNEMPLOYMENT RATE:**

4.9% (2017 est.)

4% (2016 est.)

country comparison to the world: 72

**POPULATION BELOW POVERTY LINE:**

20% (2014 est.)

**HOUSEHOLD INCOME OR CONSUMPTION BY PERCENTAGE SHARE:**

lowest 10%: NA

highest 10%: NA

**BUDGET:**

revenues: 5.581 billion (2017 est.)

expenditures: 7.446 billion (2017 est.)

**TAXES AND OTHER REVENUES:**

24.5% (of GDP) (2017 est.)

country comparison to the world: 121

**BUDGET SURPLUS (+) OR DEFICIT (-):**

-8.2% (of GDP) (2017 est.)

country comparison to the world: 200

**PUBLIC DEBT:**

41.8% of GDP (2017 est.)

37% of GDP (2016 est.)

country comparison to the world: 120

**FISCAL YEAR:**

1 October - 30 September

**INFLATION RATE (CONSUMER PRICES):**

1.9% (2017 est.)

3.1% (2016 est.)

country comparison to the world: 101

**CENTRAL BANK DISCOUNT RATE:**

6.75% (4 March 2016 est.)

6.75% (31 December 2015 est.)

country comparison to the world: 54

**COMMERCIAL BANK PRIME LENDING RATE:**

9% (31 December 2017 est.)

9% (31 December 2016 est.)

country comparison to the world: 94

**STOCK OF NARROW MONEY:**

$7.247 billion (31 December 2017 est.)

$6.72 billion (31 December 2016 est.)

country comparison to the world: 89

**STOCK OF BROAD MONEY:**

$7.247 billion (31 December 2017 est.)

$6.72 billion (31 December 2016 est.)

country comparison to the world: 91

**STOCK OF DOMESTIC CREDIT:**

$10.55 billion (31 December 2017 est.)

$9.718 billion (31 December 2016 est.)

country comparison to the world: 106

**MARKET VALUE OF PUBLICLY TRADED SHARES:**

$177.4 million (31 December 2015 est.)

$171.6 million (31 December 2014 est.)

$170 million (31 December 2013 est.)

country comparison to the world: 118

**CURRENT ACCOUNT BALANCE:**

$2.325 billion (2017 est.)

-$653 million (2016 est.)

country comparison to the world: 37

**EXPORTS:**

$9.927 billion (2017 est.)

$8.714 billion (2016 est.)

country comparison to the world: 94

**EXPORTS - PARTNERS:**

US 34.8%, Argentina 9% (2017)

**EXPORTS - COMMODITIES:**

petroleum and petroleum products, liquefied natural gas, methanol, ammonia, urea, steel products, beverages, cereal and cereal products, cocoa, fish, preserved fruits, cosmetics, household cleaners, plastic packaging

**IMPORTS:**

$6.105 billion (2017 est.)

$6.858 billion (2016 est.)

country comparison to the world: 121

**IMPORTS - COMMODITIES:**

mineral fuels, lubricants, machinery, transportation equipment, manufactured goods, food, chemicals, live animals

**IMPORTS - PARTNERS:**

US 23.8%, Russia 15.3%, Colombia 11.1%, Gabon 10.5%, China 7.3% (2017)

**RESERVES OF FOREIGN EXCHANGE AND GOLD:**

$8.892 billion (31 December 2017 est.)

$9.995 billion (31 December 2016 est.)

country comparison to the world: 77

**DEBT - EXTERNAL:**

$8.238 billion (31 December 2017 est.)

$8.746 billion (31 December 2016 est.)

country comparison to the world: 120

**STOCK OF DIRECT FOREIGN INVESTMENT - AT HOME:**

$382.9 million (31 December 2014 est.)

$311.7 million (31 December 2013 est.)

country comparison to the world: 131

**STOCK OF DIRECT FOREIGN INVESTMENT - ABROAD:**

$1.266 billion (2014 est.)

$2.061 billion (2013 est.)

country comparison to the world: 87

**EXCHANGE RATES:**

Trinidad and Tobago dollars (TTD) per US dollar -

6.78 (2017 est.)
6.669 (2016 est.)
6.669 (2015 est.)
6.4041 (2014 est.)
6.4041 (2013 est.)

## ENERGY :: TRINIDAD AND TOBAGO

**ELECTRICITY ACCESS:**
population without electricity: 12,452 (2012)
electrification - total population: 99.8% (2012)
electrification - urban areas: 100% (2012)
electrification - rural areas: 99% (2012)

**ELECTRICITY - PRODUCTION:**
10.07 billion kWh (2016 est.)
country comparison to the world: 103

**ELECTRICITY - CONSUMPTION:**
9.867 billion kWh (2016 est.)
country comparison to the world: 97

**ELECTRICITY - EXPORTS:**
0 kWh (2016 est.)
country comparison to the world: 210

**ELECTRICITY - IMPORTS:**
0 kWh (2016 est.)
country comparison to the world: 211

**ELECTRICITY - INSTALLED GENERATING CAPACITY:**
2.608 million kW (2016 est.)
country comparison to the world: 104

**ELECTRICITY - FROM FOSSIL FUELS:**
100% of total installed capacity (2016 est.)
country comparison to the world: 19

**ELECTRICITY - FROM NUCLEAR FUELS:**
0% of total installed capacity (2017 est.)
country comparison to the world: 197

**ELECTRICITY - FROM HYDROELECTRIC PLANTS:**
0% of total installed capacity (2017 est.)
country comparison to the world: 206

**ELECTRICITY - FROM OTHER RENEWABLE SOURCES:**
0% of total installed capacity (2017 est.)
country comparison to the world: 209

**CRUDE OIL - PRODUCTION:**
36,620 bbl/day (2017 est.)
country comparison to the world: 59

**CRUDE OIL - EXPORTS:**
31,030 bbl/day (2015 est.)
country comparison to the world: 45

**CRUDE OIL - IMPORTS:**
80,860 bbl/day (2015 est.)
country comparison to the world: 47

**CRUDE OIL - PROVED RESERVES:**
243 million bbl (1 January 2018 est.)
country comparison to the world: 53

**REFINED PETROLEUM PRODUCTS - PRODUCTION:**
134,700 bbl/day (2015 est.)
country comparison to the world: 63

**REFINED PETROLEUM PRODUCTS - CONSUMPTION:**
51,000 bbl/day (2016 est.)
country comparison to the world: 105

**REFINED PETROLEUM PRODUCTS - EXPORTS:**
106,100 bbl/day (2015 est.)
country comparison to the world: 40

**REFINED PETROLEUM PRODUCTS - IMPORTS:**
0 bbl/day (2015 est.)
country comparison to the world: 213

**NATURAL GAS - PRODUCTION:**
36.73 billion cu m (2017 est.)
country comparison to the world: 23

**NATURAL GAS - CONSUMPTION:**
21.24 billion cu m (2017 est.)
country comparison to the world: 37

**NATURAL GAS - EXPORTS:**
15.49 billion cu m (2017 est.)
country comparison to the world: 14

**NATURAL GAS - IMPORTS:**
0 cu m (2017 est.)
country comparison to the world: 202

**NATURAL GAS - PROVED RESERVES:**
447.4 billion cu m (1 January 2018 est.)
country comparison to the world: 33

**CARBON DIOXIDE EMISSIONS FROM CONSUMPTION OF ENERGY:**
48.92 million Mt (2017 est.)
country comparison to the world: 61

## COMMUNICATIONS :: TRINIDAD AND TOBAGO

**TELEPHONES - FIXED LINES:**
total subscriptions: 257,445 (2017 est.)
subscriptions per 100 inhabitants: 21 (2017 est.)
country comparison to the world: 121

**TELEPHONES - MOBILE CELLULAR:**
total subscriptions: 2,030,637 (2017 est.)
subscriptions per 100 inhabitants: 167 (2017 est.)
country comparison to the world: 149

**TELEPHONE SYSTEM:**
general assessment: excellent international service; good local service (2016)
domestic: combined fixed-line and mobile-cellular teledensity over 190 telephones per 100 persons (2016)
international: country code - 1-868; submarine cable systems provide connectivity to US and parts of the Caribbean and South America; satellite earth station - 1 Intelsat (Atlantic Ocean); tropospheric scatter to Barbados and Guyana (2016)

**BROADCAST MEDIA:**
6 free-to-air TV networks, 2 of which are state-owned; 24 subscription providers (cable and satellite); over 36 radio frequencies (2016)

**INTERNET COUNTRY CODE:**
.tt

**INTERNET USERS:**
total: 846,000 (July 2016 est.)
percent of population: 69.2% (July 2016 est.)
country comparison to the world: 137

**BROADBAND - FIXED SUBSCRIPTIONS:**
total: 326,776 (2017 est.)
subscriptions per 100 inhabitants: 27 (2017 est.)
country comparison to the world: 92

## TRANSPORTATION :: TRINIDAD AND TOBAGO

**NATIONAL AIR TRANSPORT SYSTEM:**
number of registered air carriers: 1 (2015)
inventory of registered aircraft operated by air carriers: 17 (2015)
annual passenger traffic on registered air carriers: 2,617,842 (2015)

annual freight traffic on registered air carriers: 43,198,176 mt-km (2015)

**CIVIL AIRCRAFT REGISTRATION COUNTRY CODE PREFIX:**

9Y (2016)

**AIRPORTS:**

4 (2013)

country comparison to the world: 191

**AIRPORTS - WITH PAVED RUNWAYS:**

total: 2 (2013)

over 3,047 m: 1 (2013)

2,438 to 3,047 m: 1 (2013)

**AIRPORTS - WITH UNPAVED RUNWAYS:**

total: 2 (2013)

914 to 1,523 m: 1 (2013)

under 914 m: 1 (2013)

**PIPELINES:**

257 km condensate, 11 km condensate/gas, 1567 km gas, 587 km oil (2013)

**ROADWAYS:**

total: 9,592 km (2015)

paved: 5,524 km (2015)

unpaved: 4,068 km (2015)

country comparison to the world: 137

**MERCHANT MARINE:**

total: 105 (2017)

by type: general cargo 1, other 104 (2017)

country comparison to the world: 83

**PORTS AND TERMINALS:**

major seaport(s): Point Fortin, Point Lisas, Port of Spain, Scarborough

oil terminal(s): Galeota Point terminal

LNG terminal(s) (export): Port Fortin

# MILITARY AND SECURITY :: TRINIDAD AND TOBAGO

**MILITARY EXPENDITURES:**

1.12% of GDP (2016)

0.88% of GDP (2015)

0.72% of GDP (2014)

country comparison to the world: 106

**MILITARY BRANCHES:**

Trinidad and Tobago Defense Force (TTDF): Trinidad and Tobago Army, Coast Guard, Air Guard, Defense Force Reserves (2010)

**MILITARY SERVICE AGE AND OBLIGATION:**

18-25 years of age for voluntary military service (16 years of age with parental consent); no conscription; Trinidad and Tobago citizenship and completion of secondary school required (2012)

# TRANSNATIONAL ISSUES :: TRINIDAD AND TOBAGO

**DISPUTES - INTERNATIONAL:**

Barbados and Trinidad and Tobago abide by the April 2006 Permanent Court of Arbitration decision delimiting a maritime boundary and limiting catches of flying fish in Trinidad and Tobago's EEZin 2005, Barbados and Trinidad and Tobago agreed to compulsory international arbitration under UN Convention on the Law of the Sea challenging whether the northern limit of Trinidad and Tobago's and Venezuela's maritime boundary extends into Barbadian watersGuyana has expressed its intention to include itself in the arbitration, as the Trinidad and Tobago-Venezuela maritime boundary may also extend into its waters

**REFUGEES AND INTERNALLY DISPLACED PERSONS:**

refugees (country of origin): 5,760 (Venezuela) (economic and political crisis; includes Venezuelans who have claimed asylum or have received alternative legal stay) (2018)

**TRAFFICKING IN PERSONS:**

current situation: Trinidad and Tobago is a destination, transit, and possible source country for adults and children subjected to sex trafficking and forced labor; women and girls from Venezuela, the Dominican Republic, Guyana, and Colombia have been subjected to sex trafficking in Trinidad and Tobago's brothels and clubs; some economic migrants from the Caribbean region and Asia are vulnerable to forced labor in domestic service and the retail sector; the steady flow of vessels transiting Trinidad and Tobago's territorial waters may also increase opportunities for forced labor for fishing; international crime organizations are increasingly involved in trafficking, and boys are coerced to sell drugs and guns; corruption among police and immigration officials impedes anti-trafficking efforts

tier rating: Tier 2 Watch List – Trinidad and Tobago does not fully comply with the minimum standards for the elimination of trafficking; however, it is making significant efforts to do so; anti-trafficking law enforcement efforts decreased from the initiation of 12 prosecutions in 2013 to 1 in 2014; the government has yet to convict anyone under its 2011 anti-trafficking law, and all prosecutions from previous years remain pending; the government sustained efforts to identify victims and to refer them for care at NGO facilities, which it provided with funding; the government failed to draft a national action plan as mandated under the 2011 anti-trafficking law and did not launch a sufficiently robust awareness campaign to educate the public and officials (2015)

**ILLICIT DRUGS:**

transshipment point for South American drugs destined for the US and Europe; producer of cannabis

# AFRICA :: TUNISIA

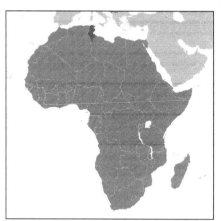

## INTRODUCTION :: TUNISIA

**BACKGROUND:**

Rivalry between French and Italian interests in Tunisia culminated in a French invasion in 1881 and the creation of a protectorate. Agitation for independence in the decades following World War I was finally successful in convincing the French to recognize Tunisia as an independent state in 1956. The country's first president, Habib BOURGUIBA, established a strict one-party state. He dominated the country for 31 years, repressing Islamic fundamentalism and establishing rights for women unmatched by any other Arab nation. In November 1987, BOURGUIBA was removed from office and replaced by Zine el Abidine BEN ALI in a bloodless coup. Street protests that began in Tunis in December 2010 over high unemployment, corruption, widespread poverty, and high food prices escalated in January 2011, culminating in rioting that led to hundreds of deaths. On 14 January 2011, the same day BEN ALI dismissed the government, he fled the country, and by late January 2011, a "national unity government" was formed. Elections for the new Constituent Assembly were held in late October 2011, and in December, it elected human rights activist Moncef MARZOUKI as interim president. The Assembly began drafting a new constitution in February 2012 and, after several iterations and a months-long political crisis that stalled the transition, ratified the document in January 2014. Parliamentary and presidential elections for a permanent government were held at the end of 2014. Beji CAID ESSEBSI was elected as the first president under the country's new constitution. CAID ESSEBSI's term, as well as that of Tunisia's 217-member Parliament, expires in 2019.

## GEOGRAPHY :: TUNISIA

**LOCATION:**

Northern Africa, bordering the Mediterranean Sea, between Algeria and Libya

**GEOGRAPHIC COORDINATES:**

34 00 N, 9 00 E

**MAP REFERENCES:**

Africa

**AREA:**

total: 163,610 sq km

land: 155,360 sq km

water: 8,250 sq km

country comparison to the world: 94

**AREA - COMPARATIVE:**

slightly larger than Georgia

**LAND BOUNDARIES:**

total: 1,495 km

border countries (2): Algeria 1034 km, Libya 461 km

**COASTLINE:**

1,148 km

**MARITIME CLAIMS:**

territorial sea: 12 nm

exclusive economic zone: 12 nm

contiguous zone: 24 nm

**CLIMATE:**

temperate in north with mild, rainy winters and hot, dry summers; desert in south

**TERRAIN:**

mountains in north; hot, dry central plain; semiarid south merges into the Sahara

**ELEVATION:**

mean elevation: 246 m

elevation extremes: -17 m lowest point: Shatt al Gharsah

1544 highest point: Jebel ech Chambi

**NATURAL RESOURCES:**

petroleum, phosphates, iron ore, lead, zinc, salt

**LAND USE:**

agricultural land: 64.8% (2011 est.)

arable land: 18.3% (2011 est.) / permanent crops: 15.4% (2011 est.) / permanent pasture: 31.1% (2011 est.)

forest: 6.6% (2011 est.)

other: 28.6% (2011 est.)

**IRRIGATED LAND:**

4,590 sq km (2012)

**POPULATION DISTRIBUTION:**

the overwhelming majority of the population is located in the northern half of the country; the south remains largely underpopulated

**NATURAL HAZARDS:**

flooding; earthquakes; droughts

**ENVIRONMENT - CURRENT ISSUES:**

toxic and hazardous waste disposal is ineffective and poses health risks; water pollution from raw sewage; limited natural freshwater resources; deforestation; overgrazing; soil erosion; desertification

**ENVIRONMENT - INTERNATIONAL AGREEMENTS:**

party to: Biodiversity, Climate Change, Climate Change-Kyoto Protocol, Desertification, Endangered Species, Environmental Modification, Hazardous Wastes, Law of the Sea, Marine Dumping, Ozone Layer Protection, Ship Pollution, Wetlands

signed, but not ratified: Marine Life Conservation

**GEOGRAPHY - NOTE:**

strategic location in central Mediterranean; Malta and Tunisia are discussing the commercial exploitation of the continental shelf between their countries, particularly for oil exploration

# PEOPLE AND SOCIETY :: TUNISIA

**POPULATION:**

11,516,189 (July 2018 est.)

country comparison to the world: 78

**NATIONALITY:**

noun: Tunisian(s)

adjective: Tunisian

**ETHNIC GROUPS:**

Arab 98%, European 1%, Jewish and other 1%

**LANGUAGES:**

Arabic (official, one of the languages of commerce), French (commerce), Berber (Tamazight)

note: despite having no official status, French plays a major role in the country and is spoken by about two-thirds of the population

**RELIGIONS:**

Muslim (official; Sunni) 99.1%, other (includes Christian, Jewish, Shia Muslim, and Baha'i) 1%

**DEMOGRAPHIC PROFILE:**

The Tunisian Government took steps in the 1960s to decrease population growth and gender inequality in order to improve socioeconomic development. Through its introduction of a national family planning program (the first in Africa) and by raising the legal age of marriage, Tunisia rapidly reduced its total fertility rate from about 7 children per woman in 1960 to 2 today. Unlike many of its North African and Middle Eastern neighbors, Tunisia will soon be shifting from being a youth-bulge country to having a transitional age structure, characterized by lower fertility and mortality rates, a slower population growth rate, a rising median age, and a longer average life expectancy.

Currently, the sizable young working-age population is straining Tunisia's labor market and education and health care systems. Persistent high unemployment among Tunisia's growing workforce, particularly its increasing number of university graduates and women, was a key factor in the uprisings that led to the overthrow of the BEN ALI regime in 2011. In the near term, Tunisia's large number of jobless young, working-age adults; deficiencies in primary and secondary education; and the ongoing lack of job creation and skills mismatches could contribute to future unrest. In the longer term, a sustained low fertility rate will shrink future youth cohorts and alleviate demographic pressure on Tunisia's labor market, but employment and education hurdles will still need to be addressed.

Tunisia has a history of labor emigration. In the 1960s, workers migrated to European countries to escape poor economic conditions and to fill Europe's need for low-skilled labor in construction and manufacturing. The Tunisian Government signed bilateral labor agreements with France, Germany, Belgium, Hungary, and the Netherlands, with the expectation that Tunisian workers would eventually return home. At the same time, growing numbers of Tunisians headed to Libya, often illegally, to work in the expanding oil industry. In the mid-1970s, with European countries beginning to restrict immigration and Tunisian-Libyan tensions brewing, Tunisian economic migrants turned toward the Gulf countries. After mass expulsions from Libya in 1983, Tunisian migrants increasingly sought family reunification in Europe or moved illegally to southern Europe, while Tunisia itself developed into a transit point for sub-Saharan migrants heading to Europe.

Following the ousting of BEN ALI in 2011, the illegal migration of unemployed Tunisian youths to Italy and onward to France soared into the tens of thousands. Thousands more Tunisian and foreign workers escaping civil war in Libya flooded into Tunisia and joined the exodus. A readmission agreement signed by Italy and Tunisia in April 2011 helped stem the outflow, leaving Tunisia and international organizations to repatriate, resettle, or accommodate some 1 million Libyans and third-country nationals.

**AGE STRUCTURE:**

0-14 years: 25.25% (male 1,502,655 /female 1,405,310)

15-24 years: 13.53% (male 787,178 /female 770,929)

25-54 years: 43.25% (male 2,426,011 /female 2,554,253)

55-64 years: 9.75% (male 560,233 /female 562,436)

65 years and over: 8.22% (male 448,784 /female 498,400) (2018 est.)

**DEPENDENCY RATIOS:**

total dependency ratio: 45.6 (2015 est.)

youth dependency ratio: 34.5 (2015 est.)

elderly dependency ratio: 11.1 (2015 est.)

potential support ratio: 9 (2015 est.)

**MEDIAN AGE:**

total: 32 years

male: 31.3 years

female: 32.5 years (2018 est.)

country comparison to the world: 106

**POPULATION GROWTH RATE:**

0.95% (2018 est.)

country comparison to the world: 116

**BIRTH RATE:**

17.4 births/1,000 population (2018 est.)

country comparison to the world: 103

**DEATH RATE:**

6.4 deaths/1,000 population (2018 est.)

country comparison to the world: 148

**NET MIGRATION RATE:**

-1.7 migrant(s)/1,000 population (2017 est.)

country comparison to the world: 153

**POPULATION DISTRIBUTION:**

the overwhelming majority of the population is located in the northern half of the country; the south remains largely underpopulated

**URBANIZATION:**

urban population: 68.9% of total population (2018)

rate of urbanization: 1.53% annual rate of change (2015-20 est.)

**MAJOR URBAN AREAS - POPULATION:**

2.291 million TUNIS (capital) (2018)

**SEX RATIO:**

at birth: 1.06 male(s)/female (2017 est.)

0-14 years: 1.06 male(s)/female (2017 est.)

15-24 years: 1.01 male(s)/female (2017 est.)

25-54 years: 0.94 male(s)/female (2017 est.)

55-64 years: 1.03 male(s)/female (2017 est.)

65 years and over: 0.97 male(s)/female (2017 est.)

total population: 0.99 male(s)/female (2017 est.)

**MATERNAL MORTALITY RATE:**

62 deaths/100,000 live births (2015 est.)

country comparison to the world: 89

**INFANT MORTALITY RATE:**

total: 11.7 deaths/1,000 live births (2018 est.)

male: 12.8 deaths/1,000 live births (2018 est.)

female: 10.5 deaths/1,000 live births (2018 est.)

country comparison to the world: 123

**LIFE EXPECTANCY AT BIRTH:**

total population: 75.9 years (2018 est.)

male: 74.3 years (2018 est.)

female: 77.6 years (2018 est.)

country comparison to the world: 99

**TOTAL FERTILITY RATE:**

2.17 children born/woman (2018 est.)

country comparison to the world: 96

**CONTRACEPTIVE PREVALENCE RATE:**

62.5% (2011/12)

**HEALTH EXPENDITURES:**

7% of GDP (2014)

country comparison to the world: 83

**PHYSICIANS DENSITY:**

1.29 physicians/1,000 population (2015)

**HOSPITAL BED DENSITY:**

2.2 beds/1,000 population (2014)

**DRINKING WATER SOURCE:**

improved:

urban: 100% of population (2015 est.)

rural: 93.2% of population (2015 est.)

total: 97.7% of population (2015 est.)

unimproved:

urban: 0% of population (2015 est.)

rural: 6.8% of population (2015 est.)

total: 2.3% of population (2015 est.)

**SANITATION FACILITY ACCESS:**

improved:

urban: 97.4% of population (2015 est.)

rural: 79.8% of population (2015 est.)

total: 91.6% of population (2015 est.)

unimproved:

urban: 2.6% of population (2015 est.)

rural: 20.2% of population (2015 est.)

total: 8.4% of population (2015 est.)

**HIV/AIDS - ADULT PREVALENCE RATE:**

<.1% (2017 est.)

**HIV/AIDS - PEOPLE LIVING WITH HIV/AIDS:**

3,000 (2017 est.)

country comparison to the world: 122

**HIV/AIDS - DEATHS:**

<200 (2017 est.)

**OBESITY - ADULT PREVALENCE RATE:**

26.9% (2016)

country comparison to the world: 40

**CHILDREN UNDER THE AGE OF 5 YEARS UNDERWEIGHT:**

2.3% (2012)

country comparison to the world: 109

**EDUCATION EXPENDITURES:**

6.6% of GDP (2015)

country comparison to the world: 25

**LITERACY:**

definition: age 15 and over can read and write (2015 est.)

total population: 81.8% (2015 est.)

male: 89.6% (2015 est.)

female: 74.2% (2015 est.)

**SCHOOL LIFE EXPECTANCY (PRIMARY TO TERTIARY EDUCATION):**

total: 15 years (2015)

male: NA (2015)

female: NA (2015)

**UNEMPLOYMENT, YOUTH AGES 15-24:**

total: 34.7% (2013 est.)

male: 33.4% (2013 est.)

female: 37.7% (2013 est.)

country comparison to the world: 23

## GOVERNMENT :: TUNISIA

**COUNTRY NAME:**

conventional long form: Republic of Tunisia

conventional short form: Tunisia

local long form: Al Jumhuriyah at Tunisiyah

local short form: Tunis

etymology: the country name derives from the capital city of Tunis

**GOVERNMENT TYPE:**

parliamentary republic

**CAPITAL:**

name: Tunis

geographic coordinates: 36 48 N, 10 11 E

time difference: UTC+1 (6 hours ahead of Washington, DC, during Standard Time)

**ADMINISTRATIVE DIVISIONS:**

24 governorates (wilayat, singular - wilayah); Beja (Bajah), Ben Arous (Bin 'Arus), Bizerte (Banzart), Gabes (Qabis), Gafsa (Qafsah), Jendouba (Jundubah), Kairouan (Al Qayrawan), Kasserine (Al Qasrayn), Kebili (Qibili), Kef (Al Kaf), L'Ariana (Aryanah), Mahdia (Al Mahdiyah), Manouba (Manubah), Medenine (Madanin), Monastir (Al Munastir), Nabeul (Nabul), Sfax (Safaqis), Sidi Bouzid (Sidi Bu Zayd), Siliana (Silyanah), Sousse (Susah), Tataouine (Tatawin), Tozeur (Tawzar), Tunis, Zaghouan (Zaghwan)

**INDEPENDENCE:**

20 March 1956 (from France)

**NATIONAL HOLIDAY:**

Independence Day, 20 March (1956)Revolution and Youth Day, 14

January (2011)

## CONSTITUTION:

**history:** several previous; latest approved by Constituent Assembly 26 January 2014, signed by the president, prime minister, and Constituent Assembly speaker 27 January 2014 (2017)

**amendments:** proposed by the president of the republic or by one-third of members of the Assembly of the Representatives of the People; following review by the Constitutional Court, approval to proceed requires an absolute majority vote by the Assembly and final passage requires a two-thirds majority vote by the Assembly; the president can opt to submit an amendment to a referendum, which requires an absolute majority of votes cast for passage (2017)

## LEGAL SYSTEM:

mixed legal system of civil law, based on the French civil code and Islamic law; some judicial review of legislative acts in the Supreme Court in joint session

## INTERNATIONAL LAW ORGANIZATION PARTICIPATION:

has not submitted an ICJ jurisdiction declaration; accepts ICCt jurisdiction

## CITIZENSHIP:

**citizenship by birth:** no

**citizenship by descent only:** at least one parent must be a citizen of Tunisia

**dual citizenship recognized:** yes

**residency requirement for naturalization:** 5 years

## SUFFRAGE:

18 years of age; universal except for active government security forces (including the police and the military), people with mental disabilities, people who have served more than three months in prison (criminal cases only), and people given a suspended sentence of more than six months

## EXECUTIVE BRANCH:

**chief of state:** President Beji CAID ESSEBSI (since 31 December 2014)

**head of government:** Prime Minister Youssef CHAHED (since 27 August 2016)

**cabinet:** selected by the prime minister and approved by the Assembly of the Representatives of the People

**elections/appointments:** president directly elected by absolute majority popular vote in 2 rounds if needed for a 5-year term (eligible for a second term); election last held on 23 November with a runoff on 21 December 2014 (next to be held in 2019); following legislative elections, the prime minister is selected by the majority party or majority coalition and appointed by the president

**election results:** Beji CAID ESSEBSI elected president in second round; percent of vote - Beji CAID ESSEBSI (Call for Tunisia) 55.7%, Moncef MARZOUKI (CPR) 44.3%

## LEGISLATIVE BRANCH:

**description:** unicameral Assembly of the Representatives of the People or Majlis Nuwwab ash-Sha'b (Assemblee des representants du peuple) (217 seats; 199 members directly elected in Tunisian multi-seat constituencies and 18 members in multi-seat constituencies abroad by party-list proportional representation vote; members serve 5-year terms)

**elections:** initial election held on 26 October 2014 (next to be held in 2019)

**election results:** percent of vote by party - Call for Tunisia 37.6%, Ennahdha 27.8%, UPL 4.1%, Popular Front 3.6%, Afek Tounes 3%, CPR 2.1%, other 21.8%; seats by party - Call to Tunisia 86, Nahda 69, UPL 16, Popular Front 15, Afek Tounes 8, CPR 4, other 17, independent 2; composition - men 149, women 68, percent of women 31.3%

## JUDICIAL BRANCH:

**highest courts:** Court of Cassation or Cour de Cassation (organized into 1 civil and 3 criminal chambers); Constitutional Court (consists of 12 members)

**judge selection and term of office:** Supreme Court judges nominated by the SJC; judge tenure based on terms of appointment; Constitutional Court members appointed 3 each by the president of the republic, the Chamber of the People's Deputies, and the SJC; members serve 9-year terms with one-third of the membership renewed every 3 years

**subordinate courts:** Courts of Appeal; administrative courts; Court of Audit; Housing Court; courts of first instance; lower district courts; military courts

**note:** the new Tunisian constitution of January 2014 called for the creation of a constitutional court by the end of 2015; the court will consist of 12 members - 4 each appointed by the president, the Supreme Judicial Council or SJC (an independent 4-part body consisting mainly of elected judges and the remainder legal specialists), and the Chamber of the People's Deputies (parliament); members will serve 9-year terms with one-third of the membership renewed every 3 years; in late 2015, the International Commission of Jurists called on Tunisia's parliament to revise the draft on the Constitutional Court to ensure compliance with international standards; as of spring 2018 the court had not been appointed

## POLITICAL PARTIES AND LEADERS:

Afek Tounes [Yassine BRAHIM]
Al Badil Al-Tounisi (The Tunisian Alternative) [Mehdi JOMAA]
Call for Tunisia (Nidaa Tounes) [Hafedh CAID ESSEBSI]
Congress for the Republic or CPR [Imed DAIMI]
Current of Love [Hachemi HAMDI] (formerly the Popular Petition party)
Democratic Alliance Party [Mohamed HAMDI]
Democratic Current [Mohamed ABBOU]
Democratic Patriots' Unified Party [Zied LAKHDHAR]
Free Patriotic Union or UPL (Union patriotique libre) [Slim RIAHI]
Green Tunisia Party [Abdelkader ZITOUNI]
Machrou Tounes (Tunisia Project) [Mohsen MARZOUK]
Movement of Socialist Democrats or MDS [Ahmed KHASKHOUSSI]
Nahda Movement (The Renaissance) [Rachid GHANNOUCHI]
National Destourian Initiative or El Moubadra [Kamel MORJANE]
Party of the Democratic Arab Vanguard [Ahmed JEDDICK, Kheireddine SOUABNI]
People's Movement [Zouheir MAGHZAOUI]
Popular Front (coalition includes Democratic Patriots' Unified Party, Workers' Party, Green Tunisia, Tunisian Ba'ath Movement, and Party of the Democratic Arab Vanguard)
Republican Party [Maya JRIBI]
Tunisian Ba'ath Movement [OMAR Othman BELHADJ]
Tunisia First (Tunis Awlan) [Ridha BELHAJ]
Workers' Party [Hamma HAMMAMI]

## INTERNATIONAL ORGANIZATION PARTICIPATION:

ABEDA, AfDB, AFESD, AMF, AMU, AU, BSEC (observer), CAEU, CD, EBRD, FAO, G-11, G-77, IAEA, IBRD, ICAO, ICC (national committees), ICCt, ICRM, IDA, IDB, IFAD, IFC, IFRCS, IHO, ILO, IMF, IMO, IMSO, Interpol, IOC, IOM, IPU, ISO, ITSO, ITU, ITUC (NGOs), LAS, MIGA, MONUSCO, NAM, OAS (observer), OIC, OIF, OPCW, OSCE (partner), UN, UNCTAD, UNESCO, UNHCR, UNIDO, UNOCI, UNWTO, UPU, WCO, WFTU (NGOs), WHO, WIPO, WMO, WTO

### DIPLOMATIC REPRESENTATION IN THE US:

chief of mission: Ambassador Faycal GOUIA (since 18 May 2015)

chancery: 1515 Massachusetts Avenue NW, Washington, DC 20005

telephone: [1] (202) 862-1850

FAX: [1] (202) 862-1858

### DIPLOMATIC REPRESENTATION FROM THE US:

chief of mission: Ambassador Daniel H. RUBINSTEIN (since 26 October 2015)

embassy: Zone Nord-Est des Berges du Lac Nord de Tunis 1053

mailing address: Zone Nord-Est des Berges du Lac Nord de Tunis 1053

telephone: [216] 71 107-000

FAX: [216] 71 107-090

### FLAG DESCRIPTION:

red with a white disk in the center bearing a red crescent nearly encircling a red five-pointed star; resembles the Ottoman flag (red banner with white crescent and star) and recalls Tunisia's history as part of the Ottoman Empire; red represents the blood shed by martyrs in the struggle against oppression, white stands for peace; the crescent and star are traditional symbols of Islam

note: the flag is based on that of Turkey, itself a successor state to the Ottoman Empire

### NATIONAL SYMBOL(S):

encircled red star and crescent; national colors: red, white

### NATIONAL ANTHEM:

name: "Humat Al Hima" (Defenders of the Homeland)

lyrics/music: Mustafa Sadik AL-RAFII and Aboul-Qacem ECHEBBI/Mohamad Abdel WAHAB

note: adopted 1957, replaced 1958, restored 1987; Mohamad Abdel WAHAB also composed the music for the anthem of the United Arab Emirates

# ECONOMY :: TUNISIA

### ECONOMY - OVERVIEW:

Tunisia's economy – structurally designed to favor vested interests – faced an array of challenges exposed by the 2008 global financial crisis that helped precipitate the 2011 Arab Spring revolution. After the revolution and a series of terrorist attacks, including on the country's tourism sector, barriers to economic inclusion continued to add to slow economic growth and high unemployment.

Following an ill-fated experiment with socialist economic policies in the 1960s, Tunisia focused on bolstering exports, foreign investment, and tourism, all of which have become central to the country's economy. Key exports now include textiles and apparel, food products, petroleum products, chemicals, and phosphates, with about 80% of exports bound for Tunisia's main economic partner, the EU. Tunisia's strategy, coupled with investments in education and infrastructure, fueled decades of 4-5% annual GDP growth and improved living standards. Former President Zine el Abidine BEN ALI (1987-2011) continued these policies, but as his reign wore on cronyism and corruption stymied economic performance, unemployment rose, and the informal economy grew. Tunisia's economy became less and less inclusive. These grievances contributed to the January 2011 overthrow of BEN ALI, further depressing Tunisia's economy as tourism and investment declined sharply.

Tunisia's government remains under pressure to boost economic growth quickly to mitigate chronic socio-economic challenges, especially high levels of youth unemployment, which has persisted since the 2011 revolution. Successive terrorist attacks against the tourism sector and worker strikes in the phosphate sector, which combined account for nearly 15% of GDP, slowed growth from 2015 to 2017. Tunis is seeking increased foreign investment and working with the IMF through an Extended Fund Facility agreement to fix fiscal deficiencies.

### GDP (PURCHASING POWER PARITY):

$137.7 billion (2017 est.)

$135 billion (2016 est.)

$133.5 billion (2015 est.)

note: data are in 2017 dollars

country comparison to the world: 78

### GDP (OFFICIAL EXCHANGE RATE):

$39.96 billion (2017 est.) (2017 est.)

### GDP - REAL GROWTH RATE:

2% (2017 est.)

1.1% (2016 est.)

1.2% (2015 est.)

country comparison to the world: 155

### GDP - PER CAPITA (PPP):

$11,900 (2017 est.)

$11,800 (2016 est.)

$11,800 (2015 est.)

note: data are in 2017 dollars

country comparison to the world: 131

### GROSS NATIONAL SAVING:

12% of GDP (2017 est.)

13.4% of GDP (2016 est.)

12.5% of GDP (2015 est.)

country comparison to the world: 152

### GDP - COMPOSITION, BY END USE:

household consumption: 71.7% (2017 est.)

government consumption: 20.8% (2017 est.)

investment in fixed capital: 19.4% (2017 est.)

investment in inventories: 0% (2017 est.)

exports of goods and services: 43.2% (2017 est.)

imports of goods and services: -55.2% (2017 est.)

### GDP - COMPOSITION, BY SECTOR OF ORIGIN:

agriculture: 10.1% (2017 est.)

industry: 26.2% (2017 est.)

services: 63.8% (2017 est.)

### AGRICULTURE - PRODUCTS:

olives, olive oil, grain, tomatoes, citrus fruit, sugar beets, dates, almonds; beef, dairy products

### INDUSTRIES:

petroleum, mining (particularly phosphate, iron ore), tourism, textiles, footwear, agribusiness, beverages

### INDUSTRIAL PRODUCTION GROWTH RATE:

0.5% (2017 est.)

country comparison to the world: 166
**LABOR FORCE:**

4.054 million (2017 est.)

country comparison to the world: 92
**LABOR FORCE - BY OCCUPATION:**

agriculture: 14.8%

industry: 33.2%

services: 51.7% (2014 est.)
**UNEMPLOYMENT RATE:**

15.5% (2017 est.)

15.5% (2016 est.)

country comparison to the world: 174
**POPULATION BELOW POVERTY LINE:**

15.5% (2010 est.)
**HOUSEHOLD INCOME OR CONSUMPTION BY PERCENTAGE SHARE:**

lowest 10%: 27% (2010 est.)

highest 10%: 27% (2010 est.)
**DISTRIBUTION OF FAMILY INCOME - GINI INDEX:**

40 (2005 est.)

41.7 (1995 est.)

country comparison to the world: 68
**BUDGET:**

revenues: 9.876 billion (2017 est.)

expenditures: 12.21 billion (2017 est.)
**TAXES AND OTHER REVENUES:**

24.7% (of GDP) (2017 est.)

country comparison to the world: 120
**BUDGET SURPLUS (+) OR DEFICIT (-):**

-5.8% (of GDP) (2017 est.)

country comparison to the world: 180
**PUBLIC DEBT:**

70.3% of GDP (2017 est.)

62.3% of GDP (2016 est.)

country comparison to the world: 51
**FISCAL YEAR:**

calendar year
**INFLATION RATE (CONSUMER PRICES):**

5.3% (2017 est.)

3.7% (2016 est.)

country comparison to the world: 176
**CENTRAL BANK DISCOUNT RATE:**

5.75% (31 December 2010)

country comparison to the world: 73
**COMMERCIAL BANK PRIME LENDING RATE:**

7.31% (31 December 2016 est.)

6.76% (31 December 2013 est.)

country comparison to the world: 114
**STOCK OF NARROW MONEY:**

$12.92 billion (31 December 2017 est.)

$11.83 billion (31 December 2016 est.)

country comparison to the world: 77
**STOCK OF BROAD MONEY:**

$12.92 billion (31 December 2017 est.)

$11.83 billion (31 December 2016 est.)

country comparison to the world: 78
**STOCK OF DOMESTIC CREDIT:**

$36.19 billion (31 December 2017 est.)

$34.18 billion (31 December 2016 est.)

country comparison to the world: 73
**MARKET VALUE OF PUBLICLY TRADED SHARES:**

$8.887 billion (31 December 2012 est.)

$9.662 billion (31 December 2011 est.)

$10.68 billion (31 December 2010 est.)

country comparison to the world: 75
**CURRENT ACCOUNT BALANCE:**

-$4.191 billion (2017 est.)

-$3.694 billion (2016 est.)

country comparison to the world: 179
**EXPORTS:**

$13.82 billion (2017 est.)

$13.57 billion (2016 est.)

country comparison to the world: 80
**EXPORTS - PARTNERS:**

France 32.1%, Italy 17.3%, Germany 12.4% (2017)
**EXPORTS - COMMODITIES:**

clothing, semi-finished goods and textiles, agricultural products, mechanical goods, phosphates and chemicals, hydrocarbons, electrical equipment
**IMPORTS:**

$19.09 billion (2017 est.)

$18.37 billion (2016 est.)

country comparison to the world: 80
**IMPORTS - COMMODITIES:**

textiles, machinery and equipment, hydrocarbons, chemicals, foodstuffs
**IMPORTS - PARTNERS:**

Italy 15.8%, France 15.1%, China 9.2%, Germany 8.1%, Turkey 4.8%, Algeria 4.7%, Spain 4.5% (2017)
**RESERVES OF FOREIGN EXCHANGE AND GOLD:**

$5.594 billion (31 December 2017 est.)

$5.941 billion (31 December 2016 est.)

country comparison to the world: 93
**DEBT - EXTERNAL:**

$30.19 billion (31 December 2017 est.)

$28.95 billion (31 December 2016 est.)

country comparison to the world: 79
**STOCK OF DIRECT FOREIGN INVESTMENT - AT HOME:**

$37.95 billion (31 December 2017 est.)

$37.15 billion (31 December 2016 est.)

country comparison to the world: 64
**STOCK OF DIRECT FOREIGN INVESTMENT - ABROAD:**

$285 million (31 December 2017 est.)

$285 million (31 December 2016 est.)

country comparison to the world: 104
**EXCHANGE RATES:**

Tunisian dinars (TND) per US dollar -

2.48 (2017 est.)

2.148 (2016 est.)

2.148 (2015 est.)

1.9617 (2014 est.)

1.6976 (2013 est.)

## ENERGY :: TUNISIA

**ELECTRICITY ACCESS:**

electrification - total population: 100% (2016)
**ELECTRICITY - PRODUCTION:**

18.44 billion kWh (2016 est.)

country comparison to the world: 78
**ELECTRICITY - CONSUMPTION:**

15.27 billion kWh (2016 est.)

country comparison to the world: 79
**ELECTRICITY - EXPORTS:**

500 million kWh (2015 est.)

country comparison to the world: 68
**ELECTRICITY - IMPORTS:**

134 million kWh (2016 est.)

country comparison to the world: 96
**ELECTRICITY - INSTALLED GENERATING CAPACITY:**

5.768 million kW (2016 est.)

country comparison to the world: 77
**ELECTRICITY - FROM FOSSIL FUELS:**

94% of total installed capacity (2016 est.)

country comparison to the world: 49
**ELECTRICITY - FROM NUCLEAR FUELS:**

0% of total installed capacity (2017 est.)

country comparison to the world: 198

**ELECTRICITY - FROM HYDROELECTRIC PLANTS:**

1% of total installed capacity (2017 est.)

country comparison to the world: 151

**ELECTRICITY - FROM OTHER RENEWABLE SOURCES:**

5% of total installed capacity (2017 est.)

country comparison to the world: 109

**CRUDE OIL - PRODUCTION:**

49,170 bbl/day (2017 est.)

country comparison to the world: 53

**CRUDE OIL - EXPORTS:**

39,980 bbl/day (2015 est.)

country comparison to the world: 42

**CRUDE OIL - IMPORTS:**

17,580 bbl/day (2015 est.)

country comparison to the world: 66

**CRUDE OIL - PROVED RESERVES:**

425 million bbl (1 January 2018 est.)

country comparison to the world: 48

**REFINED PETROLEUM PRODUCTS - PRODUCTION:**

27,770 bbl/day (2015 est.)

country comparison to the world: 85

**REFINED PETROLEUM PRODUCTS - CONSUMPTION:**

102,000 bbl/day (2016 est.)

country comparison to the world: 79

**REFINED PETROLEUM PRODUCTS - EXPORTS:**

13,660 bbl/day (2015 est.)

country comparison to the world: 75

**REFINED PETROLEUM PRODUCTS - IMPORTS:**

85,340 bbl/day (2015 est.)

country comparison to the world: 58

**NATURAL GAS - PRODUCTION:**

1.274 billion cu m (2017 est.)

country comparison to the world: 64

**NATURAL GAS - CONSUMPTION:**

5.125 billion cu m (2017 est.)

country comparison to the world: 59

**NATURAL GAS - EXPORTS:**

0 cu m (2017 est.)

country comparison to the world: 202

**NATURAL GAS - IMPORTS:**

3.851 billion cu m (2017 est.)

country comparison to the world: 41

**NATURAL GAS - PROVED RESERVES:**

65.13 billion cu m (1 January 2018 est.)

country comparison to the world: 58

**CARBON DIOXIDE EMISSIONS FROM CONSUMPTION OF ENERGY:**

23.42 million Mt (2017 est.)

country comparison to the world: 82

## COMMUNICATIONS :: TUNISIA

**TELEPHONES - FIXED LINES:**

total subscriptions: 1,113,168 (2017 est.)

subscriptions per 100 inhabitants: 10 (2017 est.)

country comparison to the world: 76

**TELEPHONES - MOBILE CELLULAR:**

total subscriptions: 14,334,080 (2017 est.)

subscriptions per 100 inhabitants: 126 (2017 est.)

country comparison to the world: 67

**TELEPHONE SYSTEM:**

general assessment: above the African average and continuing to be upgraded; key centers are Sfax, Sousse, Bizerte, and Tunis; telephone network is completely digitized; Internet access available throughout the country (2016)

domestic: in an effort to jumpstart expansion of the fixed-line network, the government awarded a concession to build and operate a VSAT network with international connectivity; rural areas are served by wireless local loops; competition between several mobile-cellular service providers has resulted in lower activation and usage charges and a strong surge in subscribership; overall fixed-line and mobile-cellular teledensity has reached about 135 telephones per 100 persons (2016)

international: country code - 216; a landing point for the SEA-ME-WE-4 submarine cable system that provides links to Europe, Middle East, and Asia; satellite earth stations - 1 Intelsat (Atlantic Ocean) and 1 Arabsat; coaxial cable and microwave radio relay to Algeria and Libya; participant in Medarabtel; 2 international gateway digital switches (2016)

**BROADCAST MEDIA:**

broadcast media is mainly government-controlled; the state-run Tunisian Radio and Television Establishment (ERTT) operates 2 national TV networks, several national radio networks, and a number of regional radio stations; 1 TV and 3 radio stations are privately owned and report domestic news stories directly from the official Tunisian news agency; the state retains control of broadcast facilities and transmitters through L'Office National de la Telediffusion; Tunisians also have access to Egyptian, pan-Arab, and European satellite TV channels (2007)

**INTERNET COUNTRY CODE:**

.tn

**INTERNET USERS:**

total: 5,665,242 (July 2016 est.)

percent of population: 50.9% (July 2016 est.)

country comparison to the world: 70

**BROADBAND - FIXED SUBSCRIPTIONS:**

total: 801,785 (2017 est.)

subscriptions per 100 inhabitants: 7 (2017 est.)

country comparison to the world: 71

## TRANSPORTATION :: TUNISIA

**NATIONAL AIR TRANSPORT SYSTEM:**

number of registered air carriers: 3 (2015)

inventory of registered aircraft operated by air carriers: 41 (2015)

annual passenger traffic on registered air carriers: 3,496,190 (2015)

annual freight traffic on registered air carriers: 10,354,241 mt-km (2015)

**CIVIL AIRCRAFT REGISTRATION COUNTRY CODE PREFIX:**

TS (2016)

**AIRPORTS:**

29 (2013)

country comparison to the world: 120

**AIRPORTS - WITH PAVED RUNWAYS:**

total: 15 (2013)

over 3,047 m: 4 (2013)

2,438 to 3,047 m: 6 (2013)

1,524 to 2,437 m: 2 (2013)

914 to 1,523 m: 3 (2013)

**AIRPORTS - WITH UNPAVED RUNWAYS:**

total: 14 (2013)

1,524 to 2,437 m: 1 (2013)

914 to 1,523 m: 5 (2013)

under 914 m: 8 (2013)

**PIPELINES:**

68 km condensate, 3111 km gas, 1381 km oil, 453 km refined products (2013)

**RAILWAYS:**

total: 2,173 km (1,991 in use) (2014)

standard gauge: 471 km 1.435-m gauge (2014)

narrow gauge: 1,694 km 1.000-m gauge (65 km electrified) (2014)

dual gauge: 8 km 1.435-1.000-m gauge (2014)

country comparison to the world: 71

**ROADWAYS:**

total: 19,418 km (2010)

paved: 14,756 km (includes 357 km of expressways) (2010)

unpaved: 4,662 km (2010)

country comparison to the world: 113

**MERCHANT MARINE:**

total: 62 (2017)

by type: general cargo 13, oil tanker 1, other 48 (2017)

country comparison to the world: 106

**PORTS AND TERMINALS:**

major seaport(s): Bizerte, Gabes, Rades, Sfax, Skhira

## MILITARY AND SECURITY :: TUNISIA

**MILITARY EXPENDITURES:**

2.32% of GDP (2016)

2.27% of GDP (2015)

1.91% of GDP (2014)

country comparison to the world: 42

**MILITARY BRANCHES:**

Tunisian Armed Forces (Forces Armees Tunisiens, FAT): Tunisian Army (includes Tunisian Air Defense Force), Tunisian Navy, Republic of Tunisia Air Force (Al-Quwwat al-Jawwiya al-Jamahiriyah At'Tunisia) (2012)

**MILITARY SERVICE AGE AND OBLIGATION:**

20-23 years of age for compulsory service, 1-year service obligation; 18-23 years of age for voluntary service; Tunisian nationality required (2012)

## TERRORISM :: TUNISIA

**TERRORIST GROUPS - HOME BASED:**

al-Qa'ida in the Islamic Maghreb (AQIM):
aim(s): overthrow various African regimes and replace them with one ruled by sharia; establish a regional Islamic caliphate across all of North and West Africa
area(s) of operation: leadership headquartered in Algeria; operates in Tunisia and Libya
note: al-Qa'ida's affiliate in North Africa; Tunisia-based branch known as the Uqbah bin Nafi Battalion; Mali-based cadre merged with allies to form JNIM in March 2017, which pledged allegiance to AQIM and al-Qa'ida (April 2018)

Ansar al-Sharia in Tunisia (AAS-T):
aim(s): expand its influence in Tunisia and, ultimately, replace the Tunisian Government with sharia
area(s) of operation: headquartered in Tunisia; members instigate riots and violent demonstrations and engage in attacks, targeting Tunisian military and security personnel, Tunisian politicians, religious sites, and Western interests (April 2018)

Islamic State of Iraq and ash-Sham (ISIS) network in Tunisia (to include pro-ISIS cells and designated Jund al-Khilafah (JAK-T)):
aim(s): replace the Tunisian Government with an Islamic state and implement ISIS's strict interpretation of sharia
area(s) of operation: Tunisian ISIS fighters stage attacks just across the border in Libya against government facilities and personnel and foreign tourists in Tunisia (April 2018)

## TRANSNATIONAL ISSUES :: TUNISIA

**DISPUTES - INTERNATIONAL:**

none

**TRAFFICKING IN PERSONS:**

current situation: Tunisia is a source, destination, and possible transit country for men, women, and children subjected to forced labor and sex trafficking; Tunisia's increased number of street children, rural children working to support their families, and migrants who have fled unrest in neighboring countries are vulnerable to human trafficking; organized gangs force street children to serve as thieves, beggars, and drug transporters; Tunisian women have been forced into prostitution domestically and elsewhere in the region under false promises of legitimate work; East and West African women may be subjected to forced labor as domestic workers

tier rating: Tier 2 Watch List – Tunisia does not fully comply with the minimum standards for the elimination of trafficking; however, it is making significant efforts to do so; in 2014, Tunisia was granted a waiver from an otherwise required downgrade to Tier 3 because its government has a written plan that, if implemented would constitute making significant efforts to bring itself into compliance with the minimum standards for the elimination of trafficking; in early 2015, the government drafted a national anti-trafficking action plan outlining proposals to raise awareness and enact draft anti-trafficking legislation; authorities did not provide data on the prosecution and conviction of offenders but reportedly identified 24 victims, as opposed to none in 2013, and operated facilities specifically dedicated to trafficking victims, regardless of nationality and gender; the government did not fully implement its national victim referral mechanism; some unidentified victims were not protected from punishment for unlawful acts directly resulting from being trafficked (2015)

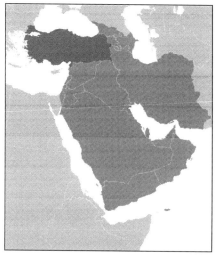

# MIDDLE EAST :: TURKEY

## INTRODUCTION :: TURKEY

**BACKGROUND:**

Modern Turkey was founded in 1923 from the remnants of the defeated Ottoman Empire by national hero Mustafa KEMAL, who was later honored with the title Ataturk or "Father of the Turks." Under his leadership, the country adopted radical social, legal, and political reforms. After a period of one-party rule, an experiment with multi-party politics led to the 1950 election victory of the opposition Democrat Party and the peaceful transfer of power. Since then, Turkish political parties have multiplied, but democracy has been fractured by periods of instability and military coups (1960, 1971, 1980), which in each case eventually resulted in a return of formal political power to civilians. In 1997, the military again helped engineer the ouster - popularly dubbed a "post-modern coup" - of the then Islamic-oriented government. A coup attempt was made in July 2016 by a faction of the Turkish Armed Forces.

Turkey intervened militarily on Cyprus in 1974 to prevent a Greek takeover of the island and has since acted as patron state to the "Turkish Republic of Northern Cyprus," which only Turkey recognizes. A separatist insurgency begun in 1984 by the Kurdistan Workers' Party (PKK), a US-designated terrorist organization, has long dominated the attention of Turkish security forces and claimed more than 40,000 lives. In 2013, the Turkish Government and the PKK conducted negotiations aimed at ending the violence, however intense fighting resumed in 2015. Turkey joined the UN in 1945 and in 1952 it became a member of NATO. In 1963, Turkey became an associate member of the European Community; it began accession talks with the EU in 2005. Over the past decade, economic reforms, coupled with some political reforms, have contributed to a growing economy, although economic growth slowed in recent years.

From 2015 and continuing through 2016, Turkey witnessed an uptick in terrorist violence, including major attacks in Ankara, Istanbul, and throughout the predominantly Kurdish southeastern region of Turkey. On 15 July 2016, elements of the Turkish Armed forces attempted a coup that ultimately failed following widespread popular resistance. More than 240 people were killed and over 2,000 injured when Turkish citizens took to the streets en masse to confront the coup forces. In response, Turkish Government authorities arrested, suspended, or dismissed more than 100,000 security personnel, journalists, judges, academics, and civil servants due to their alleged connection with the attempted coup. The government accused followers of an Islamic transnational religious and social movement for allegedly instigating the failed coup and designates the followers as terrorists. Following the failed coup, the Turkish Government instituted a State of Emergency in July 2016 that has been extended to July 2017. The Turkish Government conducted a referendum on 16 April 2017 that will, when implemented, change Turkey from a parliamentary to a presidential system.

## GEOGRAPHY :: TURKEY

**LOCATION:**

Southeastern Europe and Southwestern Asia (that portion of Turkey west of the Bosporus is geographically part of Europe), bordering the Black Sea, between Bulgaria and Georgia, and bordering the Aegean Sea and the Mediterranean Sea, between Greece and Syria

**GEOGRAPHIC COORDINATES:**

39 00 N, 35 00 E

**MAP REFERENCES:**

Middle East

**AREA:**

total: 783,562 sq km

land: 769,632 sq km

water: 13,930 sq km

country comparison to the world: 38

**AREA - COMPARATIVE:**

slightly larger than Texas

**LAND BOUNDARIES:**

total: 2,816 km

border countries (8): Armenia 311 km, Azerbaijan 17 km, Bulgaria 223 km, Georgia 273 km, Greece 192 km, Iran 534 km, Iraq 367 km, Syria 899 km

**COASTLINE:**

7,200 km

**MARITIME CLAIMS:**

territorial sea: 6 nm in the Aegean Sea

exclusive economic zone: in Black Sea only: to the maritime boundary agreed upon with the former USSR

12 nm in Black Sea and in Mediterranean Sea

**CLIMATE:**

temperate; hot, dry summers with mild, wet winters; harsher in interior

**TERRAIN:**

high central plateau (Anatolia); narrow coastal plain; several mountain ranges

**ELEVATION:**

mean elevation: 1,132 m

elevation extremes: 0 m lowest point: Mediterranean Sea

5137 highest point: Mount Ararat

**NATURAL RESOURCES:**

coal, iron ore, copper, chromium, antimony, mercury, gold, barite, borate, celestite (strontium), emery, feldspar, limestone, magnesite, marble, perlite, pumice, pyrites (sulfur), clay, arable land, hydropower

**LAND USE:**

agricultural land: 49.7% (2011 est.)

arable land: 26.7% (2011 est.) / permanent crops: 4% (2011 est.) / permanent pasture: 19% (2011 est.)

forest: 14.9% (2011 est.)

other: 35.4% (2011 est.)

**IRRIGATED LAND:**

52,150 sq km (2012)

**POPULATION DISTRIBUTION:**

the most densely populated area is found around the Bosporus in the northwest where 20% of the population lives in Istanbul; with the exception of Ankara, urban centers remain small and scattered throughout the interior of Anatolia; an overall pattern of peripheral development exists, particularly along the Aegean Sea coast in the west, and the Tigris and Euphrates River systems in the southeast

**NATURAL HAZARDS:**

severe earthquakes, especially in northern Turkey, along an arc extending from the Sea of Marmara to Lake Van; landslides; flooding

volcanism: limited volcanic activity; its three historically active volcanoes; Ararat, Nemrut Dagi, and Tendurek Dagi have not erupted since the 19th century or earlier

**ENVIRONMENT - CURRENT ISSUES:**

water pollution from dumping of chemicals and detergents; air pollution, particularly in urban areas; deforestation; land degradation; concern for oil spills from increasing Bosporus ship traffic; conservation of biodiversity

**ENVIRONMENT - INTERNATIONAL AGREEMENTS:**

party to: Air Pollution, Antarctic Treaty, Biodiversity, Climate Change, Desertification, Endangered Species, Hazardous Wastes, Ozone Layer Protection, Ship Pollution, Wetlands

signed, but not ratified: Environmental Modification

**GEOGRAPHY - NOTE:**

strategic location controlling the Turkish Straits (Bosporus, Sea of Marmara, Dardanelles) that link the Black and Aegean Seas; the 3% of Turkish territory north of the Straits lies in Europe and goes by the names of European Turkey, Eastern Thrace, or Turkish Thrace; the 97% of the country in Asia is referred to as Anatolia; Mount Ararat, the legendary landing place of Noah's ark, is in the far eastern portion of the country

## PEOPLE AND SOCIETY :: TURKEY

**POPULATION:**

81,257,239 (July 2018 est.)

country comparison to the world: 18

**NATIONALITY:**

noun: Turk(s)

adjective: Turkish

**ETHNIC GROUPS:**

Turkish 70-75%, Kurdish 19%, other minorities 7-12% (2016 est.)

**LANGUAGES:**

Turkish (official), Kurdish, other minority languages

**RELIGIONS:**

Muslim 99.8% (mostly Sunni), other 0.2% (mostly Christians and Jews)

**AGE STRUCTURE:**

0-14 years: 24.26% (male 10,085,558 /female 9,627,967)

15-24 years: 15.88% (male 6,589,039 /female 6,311,113)

25-54 years: 43.26% (male 17,798,864 /female 17,349,228)

55-64 years: 8.82% (male 3,557,329 /female 3,606,120)

65 years and over: 7.79% (male 2,825,738 /female 3,506,283) (2018 est.)

**DEPENDENCY RATIOS:**

total dependency ratio: 50.1 (2015 est.)

youth dependency ratio: 38.4 (2015 est.)

elderly dependency ratio: 11.7 (2015 est.)

potential support ratio: 8.5 (2015 est.)

**MEDIAN AGE:**

total: 31.4 years

male: 30.9 years

female: 31.9 years (2018 est.)

country comparison to the world: 110

**POPULATION GROWTH RATE:**

0.49% (2018 est.)

country comparison to the world: 155

**BIRTH RATE:**

15.4 births/1,000 population (2018 est.)

country comparison to the world: 119

**DEATH RATE:**

6 deaths/1,000 population (2018 est.)

country comparison to the world: 165

**NET MIGRATION RATE:**

-4.5 migrant(s)/1,000 population (2017 est.)

country comparison to the world: 185

**POPULATION DISTRIBUTION:**

the most densely populated area is found around the Bosporus in the northwest where 20% of the population lives in Istanbul; with the exception of Ankara, urban centers remain small and scattered throughout the interior of Anatolia; an overall pattern of peripheral development exists, particularly along the Aegean Sea coast in the west, and the Tigris and Euphrates River systems in the southeast

**URBANIZATION:**

urban population: 75.1% of total population (2018)

rate of urbanization: 2.04% annual rate of change (2015-20 est.)

**MAJOR URBAN AREAS - POPULATION:**

14.751 million Istanbul, 4.919 million ANKARA (capital), 2.937 million Izmir, 1.916 million Bursa, 1.73 million Adana, 1.632 million Gaziantep (2018)

**SEX RATIO:**

at birth: 1.05 male(s)/female (2017 est.)

0-14 years: 1.05 male(s)/female (2017 est.)

15-24 years: 1.04 male(s)/female (2017 est.)

25-54 years: 1.03 male(s)/female (2017 est.)

**55-64 years:** 0.99 male(s)/female (2017 est.)

**65 years and over:** 0.8 male(s)/female (2017 est.)

**total population:** 1.01 male(s)/female (2017 est.)

## MOTHER'S MEAN AGE AT FIRST BIRTH:
22.3 years (2010 est.)

## MATERNAL MORTALITY RATE:
16 deaths/100,000 live births (2015 est.)

country comparison to the world: 134

## INFANT MORTALITY RATE:
**total:** 16.9 deaths/1,000 live births (2018 est.)

**male:** 18.1 deaths/1,000 live births (2018 est.)

**female:** 15.7 deaths/1,000 live births (2018 est.)

country comparison to the world: 92

## LIFE EXPECTANCY AT BIRTH:
**total population:** 75.3 years (2018 est.)

**male:** 72.9 years (2018 est.)

**female:** 77.7 years (2018 est.)

country comparison to the world: 109

## TOTAL FERTILITY RATE:
2 children born/woman (2018 est.)

country comparison to the world: 118

## CONTRACEPTIVE PREVALENCE RATE:
73.5% (2013)

## HEALTH EXPENDITURES:
5.4% of GDP (2014)

country comparison to the world: 131

## PHYSICIANS DENSITY:
1.75 physicians/1,000 population (2014)

## HOSPITAL BED DENSITY:
2.7 beds/1,000 population (2013)

## DRINKING WATER SOURCE:
**improved:**

urban: 100% of population

rural: 100% of population

total: 100% of population

**unimproved:**

urban: 0% of population

rural: 0% of population

total: 0% of population (2015 est.)

## SANITATION FACILITY ACCESS:
**improved:**

urban: 98.3% of population (2015 est.)

rural: 85.5% of population (2015 est.)

total: 94.9% of population (2015 est.)

**unimproved:**

urban: 1.7% of population (2015 est.)

rural: 14.5% of population (2015 est.)

total: 5.1% of population (2015 est.)

## HIV/AIDS - ADULT PREVALENCE RATE:
NA

## HIV/AIDS - PEOPLE LIVING WITH HIV/AIDS:
NA

## HIV/AIDS - DEATHS:
NA

## OBESITY - ADULT PREVALENCE RATE:
32.1% (2016)

country comparison to the world: 17

## CHILDREN UNDER THE AGE OF 5 YEARS UNDERWEIGHT:
1.9% (2013)

country comparison to the world: 113

## EDUCATION EXPENDITURES:
4.4% of GDP (2014)

country comparison to the world: 99

## LITERACY:
**definition:** age 15 and over can read and write (2015 est.)

**total population:** 95.6% (2015 est.)

**male:** 98.6% (2015 est.)

**female:** 92.6% (2015 est.)

## SCHOOL LIFE EXPECTANCY (PRIMARY TO TERTIARY EDUCATION):
**total:** 16 years (2013)

**male:** 17 years (2013)

**female:** 16 years (2013)

## UNEMPLOYMENT, YOUTH AGES 15-24:
**total:** 20.5% (2017 est.)

**male:** 17.7% (2017 est.)

**female:** 25.6% (2017 est.)

country comparison to the world: 63

# GOVERNMENT :: TURKEY

## COUNTRY NAME:
**conventional long form:** Republic of Turkey

**conventional short form:** Turkey

**local long form:** Turkiye Cumhuriyeti

**local short form:** Turkiye

**etymology:** the name means "Land of the Turks"

## GOVERNMENT TYPE:
parliamentary republic

## CAPITAL:
**name:** Ankara

**geographic coordinates:** 39 56 N, 32 52 E

**time difference:** UTC+2 (7 hours ahead of Washington, DC, during Standard Time)

## ADMINISTRATIVE DIVISIONS:
81 provinces (iller, singular - ili); Adana, Adiyaman, Afyonkarahisar, Agri, Aksaray, Amasya, Ankara, Antalya, Ardahan, Artvin, Aydin, Balikesir, Bartin, Batman, Bayburt, Bilecik, Bingol, Bitlis, Bolu, Burdur, Bursa, Canakkale, Cankiri, Corum, Denizli, Diyarbakir, Duzce, Edirne, Elazig, Erzincan, Erzurum, Eskisehir, Gaziantep, Giresun, Gumushane, Hakkari, Hatay, Igdir, Isparta, Istanbul, Izmir (Smyrna), Kahramanmaras, Karabuk, Karaman, Kars, Kastamonu, Kayseri, Kilis, Kirikkale, Kirklareli, Kirsehir, Kocaeli, Konya, Kutahya, Malatya, Manisa, Mardin, Mersin, Mugla, Mus, Nevsehir, Nigde, Ordu, Osmaniye, Rize, Sakarya, Samsun, Sanliurfa, Siirt, Sinop, Sirnak, Sivas, Tekirdag, Tokat, Trabzon (Trebizond), Tunceli, Usak, Van, Yalova, Yozgat, Zonguldak

## INDEPENDENCE:
29 October 1923 (republic proclaimed succeeding the Ottoman Empire)

## NATIONAL HOLIDAY:
Republic Day, 29 October (1923)

## CONSTITUTION:
**history:** several previous; latest ratified 9 November 1982 (2018)

**amendments:** proposed by written consent of at least one-third of Grand National Assembly (GNA) members; adoption of draft amendments requires two debates in plenary GNA session and three-fifths majority vote of all GNA members; the president of the republic can request GNA reconsideration of the amendment and, if readopted by two-thirds majority GNA vote, the president may submit the amendment to a referendum; passage by referendum requires absolute majority vote;

amended several times, last in 2017 (2018)

**LEGAL SYSTEM:**

civil law system based on various European legal systems, notably the Swiss civil code

**INTERNATIONAL LAW ORGANIZATION PARTICIPATION:**

has not submitted an ICJ jurisdiction declaration; non-party state to the ICCt

**CITIZENSHIP:**

citizenship by birth: no

citizenship by descent only: at least one parent must be a citizen of Turkey

dual citizenship recognized: yes, but requires prior permission from the government

residency requirement for naturalization: 5 years

**SUFFRAGE:**

18 years of age; universal

**EXECUTIVE BRANCH:**

chief of state: President Recep Tayyip ERDOGAN (since 10 August 2014); Vice President Fuat OKTAY (since 9 July 2018)

head of government: President Recep Tayyip ERDOGAN (since 10 August 2014); note - a 2017 constitutional referendum eliminated the post of prime minister after the 2018 general election

cabinet: Council of Ministers nominated by the prime minister, appointed by the president (until the next parliamentary or presidential election following the April 2017 referendum)

elections/appointments: president directly elected by absolute majority popular vote in 2 rounds if needed for a 5-year term (eligible for a second term); prime minister appointed by the president from among members of parliament; note - a 2007 constitutional amendment changed the presidential electoral process to direct popular vote; prime minister appointed by the president from among members of the Grand National Assembly of Turkey; election last held on 24 June 2018 (next to be held in June 2022)

election results: Recep Tayyip ERDOGAN reelected president in the first round; Recep Tayyip ERDOGAN (AKP) 52.6%, Muharrem INCE (CHP) 30.6%, Salahattin DIMIRTAS (HDP) 8.4%, Meral AKSENER (IYI) 7.3%, other 1.1%

**LEGISLATIVE BRANCH:**

description: unicameral Grand National Assembly of Turkey or Turkiye Buyuk Millet Meclisi (600 seats - increased from 560 seats beginning with June 2018 election; members directly elected in multi-seat constituencies by proportional representation vote to serve 5-year terms - increased from 4 to 5 years beginning with June 2018 election)

elections: last held on 24 June 2018 (next to be held on June 2023)

election results: percent of vote by party - People's Alliance (AKP and MHP) 53.7%, National Alliance (CHP, SP, IVI) 33.9%, HDP 11.7%, other 0.7%; seats by party - People's Alliance 344, National Alliance 189, HDP 67; composition - men 496, women 104, percent of women 17.3%; note - only parties surpassing a 10% threshold can win parliamentary seats

**JUDICIAL BRANCH:**

highest courts: Constitutional Court or Anayasa Mahkemesi (consists of 17 members - a constitutional referendum held in 2017 approved an amendment to reduce to 15 from 17 the number of Constitutional Court judges); Court of Cassation (consists of about 390 judges and is organized into civil and penal chambers); Council of State (organized into 15 divisions - 14 judicial and 1 consultative - each with a division head and at least 5 members)

judge selection and term of office: Constitutional Court members - 3 appointed by the Grand National Assembly and 12 by the president of the republic; court president and 2 deputy presidents appointed from among its members for 4-year terms; judges appointed for 12-year, nonrenewable terms with mandatory retirement at age 65; Court of Cassation judges appointed by the Board of Judges and Prosecutors, a 13-member body of judicial officials; Court of Cassation judges appointed until retirement at age 65; Council of State members appointed by the Board and by the president of the republic; members appointed for renewable, 4-year terms

subordinate courts: regional appeals courts; basic (first instance) courts, peace courts; military courts; state security courts; specialized courts, including administrative and audit; note - a constitutional amendment in 2017 abolished military courts unless established to investigate military personnel actions during war conditions

**POLITICAL PARTIES AND LEADERS:**

Democrat Party or DP [Gultekin UYSAL]
Democratic Left Party or DSP [Onder AKSAKAL]
Felicity Party or SP [Temel KARAMOLLAOGLU]
Good Party or IYI [Meral AKSENER]
Grand Unity Party or BBP [Mustafa DESTICI]
Justice and Development Party or AKP [Recep Tayyip ERDOGAN]
Nationalist Movement Party or MHP [Devlet BAHCELI]
Patriotic Party or VP [Dogu PERINCEK]
People's Democratic Party or HDP [Selahattin DEMIRTAS and Serpil KEMALBAY]; note - DEMIRTAS was detained by Turkish authorities in November 2016 over his alleged links to the PKK
Republican People's Party or CHP [Kemal KILICDAROGLU]
True Path Party or DYP [Cetin OZACIRGOZ]

**INTERNATIONAL ORGANIZATION PARTICIPATION:**

ADB (nonregional member), Australia Group, BIS, BSEC, CBSS (observer), CD, CE, CERN (observer), CICA, CPLP (associate observer), D-8, EAPC, EBRD, ECO, EU (candidate country), FAO, FATF, G-20, IAEA, IBRD, ICAO, ICC (national committees), ICRM, IDA, IDB, IEA, IFAD, IFC, IFRCS, IHO, ILO, IMF, IMO, IMSO, Interpol, IOC, IOM, IPU, ISO, ITSO, ITU, ITUC (NGOs), MIGA, NATO, NEA, NSG, OAS (observer), OECD, OIC, OPCW, OSCE, Pacific Alliance (observer), Paris Club (associate), PCA, PIF (partner), SCO (dialogue member), SELEC, UN, UNCTAD, UNESCO, UNHCR, UNIDO, UNIFIL, UNRWA, UNWTO, UPU, WCO, WFTU (NGOs), WHO, WIPO, WMO, WTO, ZC

**DIPLOMATIC REPRESENTATION IN THE US:**

chief of mission: Ambassador Serdar KILIC (since 21 May 2014)

chancery: 2525 Massachusetts Avenue NW, Washington, DC 20008

telephone: [1] (202) 612-6700

FAX: [1] (202) 612-6744

consulate(s) general: Boston, Chicago, Houston, Los Angeles, Miami, New York

## DIPLOMATIC REPRESENTATION FROM THE US:

**chief of mission:** Ambassador (vacant); Charge d'Affairs Philip KOSNETT (since 16 October 2017)

**embassy:** 110 Ataturk Boulevard, Kavaklidere, 06100 Ankara

**mailing address:** PSC 93, Box 5000, APO AE 09823

**telephone:** [90] (312) 455-5555

**FAX:** [90] (312) 467-0019

**consulate(s) general:** Istanbul

**consulate(s):** Adana

## FLAG DESCRIPTION:

red with a vertical white crescent moon (the closed portion is toward the hoist side) and white five-pointed star centered just outside the crescent opening; the flag colors and designs closely resemble those on the banner of the Ottoman Empire, which preceded modern-day Turkey; the crescent moon and star serve as insignia for Turkic peoples; according to one interpretation, the flag represents the reflection of the moon and a star in a pool of blood of Turkish warriors

## NATIONAL SYMBOL(S):

star and crescent; national colors: red, white

## NATIONAL ANTHEM:

**name:** "Istiklal Marsi" (Independence March)

**lyrics/music:** Mehmet Akif ERSOY/Zeki UNGOR

**note:** lyrics adopted 1921, music adopted 1932; the anthem's original music was adopted in 1924; a new composition was agreed upon in 1932

# ECONOMY :: TURKEY

## ECONOMY - OVERVIEW:

Turkey's largely free-market economy is driven by its industry and, increasingly, service sectors, although its traditional agriculture sector still accounts for about 25% of employment. The automotive, petrochemical, and electronics industries have risen in importance and surpassed the traditional textiles and clothing sectors within Turkey's export mix. However, the recent period of political stability and economic dynamism has given way to domestic uncertainty and security concerns, which are generating financial market volatility and weighing on Turkey's economic outlook.

Current government policies emphasize populist spending measures and credit breaks, while implementation of structural economic reforms has slowed. The government is playing a more active role in some strategic sectors and has used economic institutions and regulators to target political opponents, undermining private sector confidence in the judicial system. Between July 2016 and March 2017, three credit ratings agencies downgraded Turkey's sovereign credit ratings, citing concerns about the rule of law and the pace of economic reforms.

Turkey remains highly dependent on imported oil and gas but is pursuing energy relationships with a broader set of international partners and taking steps to increase use of domestic energy sources including renewables, nuclear, and coal. The joint Turkish-Azerbaijani Trans-Anatolian Natural Gas Pipeline is moving forward to increase transport of Caspian gas to Turkey and Europe, and when completed will help diversify Turkey's sources of imported gas.

After Turkey experienced a severe financial crisis in 2001, Ankara adopted financial and fiscal reforms as part of an IMF program. The reforms strengthened the country's economic fundamentals and ushered in an era of strong growth, averaging more than 6% annually until 2008. An aggressive privatization program also reduced state involvement in basic industry, banking, transport, power generation, and communication. Global economic conditions and tighter fiscal policy caused GDP to contract in 2009, but Turkey's well-regulated financial markets and banking system helped the country weather the global financial crisis, and GDP growth rebounded to around 9% in 2010 and 2011, as exports and investment recovered following the crisis.

The growth of Turkish GDP since 2016 has revealed the persistent underlying imbalances in the Turkish economy. In particular, Turkey's large current account deficit means it must rely on external investment inflows to finance growth, leaving the economy vulnerable to destabilizing shifts in investor confidence. Other troublesome trends include rising unemployment and inflation, which increased in 2017, given the Turkish lira's continuing depreciation against the dollar. Although government debt remains low at about 30% of GDP, bank and corporate borrowing has almost tripled as a percent of GDP during the past decade, outpacing its emerging-market peers and prompting investor concerns about its long-term sustainability.

## GDP (PURCHASING POWER PARITY):

$2.186 trillion (2017 est.)

$2.034 trillion (2016 est.)

$1.972 trillion (2015 est.)

**note:** data are in 2017 dollars

**country comparison to the world:** 13

## GDP (OFFICIAL EXCHANGE RATE):

$851.5 billion (2017 est.) (2017 est.)

## GDP - REAL GROWTH RATE:

7.4% (2017 est.)

3.2% (2016 est.)

6.1% (2015 est.)

**country comparison to the world:** 16

## GDP - PER CAPITA (PPP):

$27,000 (2017 est.)

$25,500 (2016 est.)

$25,000 (2015 est.)

**note:** data are in 2017 dollars

**country comparison to the world:** 77

## GROSS NATIONAL SAVING:

25.5% of GDP (2017 est.)

24.5% of GDP (2016 est.)

24.8% of GDP (2015 est.)

**country comparison to the world:** 57

## GDP - COMPOSITION, BY END USE:

**household consumption:** 59.1% (2017 est.)

**government consumption:** 14.5% (2017 est.)

**investment in fixed capital:** 29.8% (2017 est.)

**investment in inventories:** 1.1% (2017 est.)

**exports of goods and services:** 24.9% (2017 est.)

**imports of goods and services:** -29.4% (2017 est.)

## GDP - COMPOSITION, BY SECTOR OF ORIGIN:

**agriculture:** 6.8% (2017 est.)

**industry:** 32.3% (2017 est.)

**services:** 60.7% (2017 est.)

## AGRICULTURE - PRODUCTS:

tobacco, cotton, grain, olives, sugar beets, hazelnuts, pulses, citrus; livestock

**INDUSTRIES:**

textiles, food processing, automobiles, electronics, mining (coal, chromate, copper, boron), steel, petroleum, construction, lumber, paper

**INDUSTRIAL PRODUCTION GROWTH RATE:**

9.1% (2017 est.)

country comparison to the world: 18

**LABOR FORCE:**

31.3 million (2017 est.)

note: this number is for the domestic labor force only; number does not include about 1.2 million Turks working abroad, nor refugees

country comparison to the world: 19

**LABOR FORCE - BY OCCUPATION:**

agriculture: 18.4%

industry: 26.6%

services: 54.9% (2016)

**UNEMPLOYMENT RATE:**

10.9% (2017 est.)

10.9% (2016 est.)

country comparison to the world: 147

**POPULATION BELOW POVERTY LINE:**

21.9% (2015 est.)

**HOUSEHOLD INCOME OR CONSUMPTION BY PERCENTAGE SHARE:**

lowest 10%: 30.3% (2008)

highest 10%: 30.3% (2008)

**DISTRIBUTION OF FAMILY INCOME - GINI INDEX:**

40.2 (2010)

43.6 (2003)

country comparison to the world: 65

**BUDGET:**

revenues: 172.8 billion (2017 est.)

expenditures: 185.8 billion (2017 est.)

**TAXES AND OTHER REVENUES:**

20.3% (of GDP) (2017 est.)

country comparison to the world: 151

**BUDGET SURPLUS (+) OR DEFICIT (-):**

-1.5% (of GDP) (2017 est.)

country comparison to the world: 91

**PUBLIC DEBT:**

28.3% of GDP (2017 est.)

28.3% of GDP (2016 est.)

country comparison to the world: 169

**FISCAL YEAR:**

calendar year

**INFLATION RATE (CONSUMER PRICES):**

11.1% (2017 est.)

7.8% (2016 est.)

country comparison to the world: 204

**CENTRAL BANK DISCOUNT RATE:**

5.25% (31 December 2011)

15% (22 December 2009)

country comparison to the world: 79

**COMMERCIAL BANK PRIME LENDING RATE:**

15.77% (31 December 2017 est.)

14.74% (31 December 2016 est.)

country comparison to the world: 33

**STOCK OF NARROW MONEY:**

$119.4 billion (31 December 2017 est.)

$108.7 billion (31 December 2016 est.)

country comparison to the world: 33

**STOCK OF BROAD MONEY:**

$119.4 billion (31 December 2017 est.)

$108.7 billion (31 December 2016 est.)

country comparison to the world: 33

**STOCK OF DOMESTIC CREDIT:**

$610.4 billion (31 December 2017 est.)

$549.9 billion (31 December 2016 est.)

country comparison to the world: 23

**MARKET VALUE OF PUBLICLY TRADED SHARES:**

$188.9 billion (31 December 2015 est.)

$219.8 billion (31 December 2014 est.)

$195.7 billion (31 December 2013 est.)

country comparison to the world: 36

**CURRENT ACCOUNT BALANCE:**

-$47.44 billion (2017 est.)

-$33.14 billion (2016 est.)

country comparison to the world: 202

**EXPORTS:**

$166.2 billion (2017 est.)

$150.2 billion (2016 est.)

country comparison to the world: 30

**EXPORTS - PARTNERS:**

Germany 9.6%, UK 6.1%, UAE 5.9%, Iraq 5.8%, US 5.5%, Italy 5.4%, France 4.2%, Spain 4% (2017)

**EXPORTS - COMMODITIES:**

apparel, foodstuffs, textiles, metal manufactures, transport equipment

**IMPORTS:**

$225.1 billion (2017 est.)

$191.1 billion (2016 est.)

country comparison to the world: 22

**IMPORTS - COMMODITIES:**

machinery, chemicals, semi-finished goods, fuels, transport equipment

**IMPORTS - PARTNERS:**

China 10%, Germany 9.1%, Russia 8.4%, US 5.1%, Italy 4.8% (2017)

**RESERVES OF FOREIGN EXCHANGE AND GOLD:**

$107.7 billion (31 December 2017 est.)

$106.1 billion (31 December 2016 est.)

country comparison to the world: 24

**DEBT - EXTERNAL:**

$452.4 billion (31 December 2017 est.)

$404.9 billion (31 December 2016 est.)

country comparison to the world: 26

**STOCK OF DIRECT FOREIGN INVESTMENT - AT HOME:**

$180.3 billion (31 December 2017 est.)

$133.2 billion (31 December 2016 est.)

country comparison to the world: 35

**STOCK OF DIRECT FOREIGN INVESTMENT - ABROAD:**

$47.44 billion (31 December 2017 est.)

$38.31 billion (31 December 2016 est.)

country comparison to the world: 45

**EXCHANGE RATES:**

Turkish liras (TRY) per US dollar -

3.628 (2017 est.)

3.0201 (2016 est.)

3.0201 (2015 est.)

2.72 (2014 est.)

2.1885 (2013 est.)

## ENERGY :: TURKEY

**ELECTRICITY ACCESS:**

electrification - total population: 100% (2016)

**ELECTRICITY - PRODUCTION:**

261.9 billion kWh (2016 est.)

country comparison to the world: 16

**ELECTRICITY - CONSUMPTION:**

231.1 billion kWh (2016 est.)

country comparison to the world: 18

**ELECTRICITY - EXPORTS:**

1.442 billion kWh (2016 est.)

country comparison to the world: 49

**ELECTRICITY - IMPORTS:**

6.33 billion kWh (2016 est.)

country comparison to the world: 31

**ELECTRICITY - INSTALLED GENERATING CAPACITY:**

78.5 million kW (2016 est.)

country comparison to the world: 15

**ELECTRICITY - FROM FOSSIL FUELS:**

53% of total installed capacity (2016 est.)

country comparison to the world: 144

**ELECTRICITY - FROM NUCLEAR FUELS:**

0% of total installed capacity (2017 est.)

country comparison to the world: 199

**ELECTRICITY - FROM HYDROELECTRIC PLANTS:**

33% of total installed capacity (2017 est.)

country comparison to the world: 64

**ELECTRICITY - FROM OTHER RENEWABLE SOURCES:**

14% of total installed capacity (2017 est.)

country comparison to the world: 64

**CRUDE OIL - PRODUCTION:**

245,000 bbl/day (2017 est.)

country comparison to the world: 32

**CRUDE OIL - EXPORTS:**

0 bbl/day (2017 est.)

country comparison to the world: 208

**CRUDE OIL - IMPORTS:**

521,500 bbl/day (2017 est.)

country comparison to the world: 17

**CRUDE OIL - PROVED RESERVES:**

341.6 million bbl (1 January 2018 est.)

country comparison to the world: 51

**REFINED PETROLEUM PRODUCTS - PRODUCTION:**

657,900 bbl/day (2017 est.)

country comparison to the world: 27

**REFINED PETROLEUM PRODUCTS - CONSUMPTION:**

989,900 bbl/day (2017 est.)

country comparison to the world: 21

**REFINED PETROLEUM PRODUCTS - EXPORTS:**

141,600 bbl/day (2017 est.)

country comparison to the world: 37

**REFINED PETROLEUM PRODUCTS - IMPORTS:**

560,000 bbl/day (2017 est.)

country comparison to the world: 16

**NATURAL GAS - PRODUCTION:**

368.1 million cu m (2017 est.)

country comparison to the world: 75

**NATURAL GAS - CONSUMPTION:**

53.6 billion cu m (2017 est.)

country comparison to the world: 15

**NATURAL GAS - EXPORTS:**

622.9 million cu m (2017 est.)

country comparison to the world: 42

**NATURAL GAS - IMPORTS:**

55.13 billion cu m (2017 est.)

country comparison to the world: 6

**NATURAL GAS - PROVED RESERVES:**

5.097 billion cu m (1 January 2018 est.)

country comparison to the world: 92

**CARBON DIOXIDE EMISSIONS FROM CONSUMPTION OF ENERGY:**

379.5 million Mt (2017 est.)

country comparison to the world: 17

## COMMUNICATIONS :: TURKEY

**TELEPHONES - FIXED LINES:**

total subscriptions: 11,308,444 (2017 est.)

subscriptions per 100 inhabitants: 14 (2017 est.)

country comparison to the world: 17

**TELEPHONES - MOBILE CELLULAR:**

total subscriptions: 77,800,170 (2017 est.)

subscriptions per 100 inhabitants: 96 (2017 est.)

country comparison to the world: 21

**TELEPHONE SYSTEM:**

general assessment: comprehensive telecommunications network undergoing rapid modernization and expansion, especially in mobile-cellular services (2016)

domestic: additional digital exchanges are permitting a rapid increase in subscribers; the construction of a network of technologically advanced intercity trunk lines, using both fiber-optic cable and digital microwave radio relay, is facilitating communication between urban centers; remote areas are reached by a domestic satellite system; combined fixed-line and mobile-cellular teledensity is roughly 105 telephones per 100 persons (2016)

international: country code - 90; international service is provided by the SEA-ME-WE-3 submarine cable and by submarine fiber-optic cables in the Mediterranean and Black Seas that link Turkey with Italy, Greece, Israel, Bulgaria, Romania, and Russia; satellite earth stations - 12 Intelsat; mobile satellite terminals - 328 in the Inmarsat and Eutelsat systems (2016)

**BROADCAST MEDIA:**

Turkish Radio and Television Corporation (TRT) operates multiple TV and radio networks and stations; multiple privately owned national television stations and up to 300 private regional and local television stations; multi-channel cable TV subscriptions available; more than 1,000 private radio broadcast stations (2009)

**INTERNET COUNTRY CODE:**

.tr

**INTERNET USERS:**

total: 46,838,412 (July 2016 est.)

percent of population: 58.3% (July 2016 est.)

country comparison to the world: 15

**BROADBAND - FIXED SUBSCRIPTIONS:**

total: 11,924,905 (2017 est.)

subscriptions per 100 inhabitants: 15 (2017 est.)

country comparison to the world: 15

## TRANSPORTATION :: TURKEY

**NATIONAL AIR TRANSPORT SYSTEM:**

number of registered air carriers: 15 (2015)

inventory of registered aircraft operated by air carriers: 531 (2015)

annual passenger traffic on registered air carriers: 96,604,665 (2015)

annual freight traffic on registered air carriers: 2,882,162,000 mt-km (2015)

**CIVIL AIRCRAFT REGISTRATION COUNTRY CODE PREFIX:**

TC (2016)

**AIRPORTS:**

98 (2013)

country comparison to the world: 58

**AIRPORTS - WITH PAVED RUNWAYS:**

total: 91 (2013)

over 3,047 m: 16 (2013)

2,438 to 3,047 m: 38 (2013)

1,524 to 2,437 m: 17 (2013)

914 to 1,523 m: 16 (2013)

under 914 m: 4 (2013)

**AIRPORTS - WITH UNPAVED RUNWAYS:**

total: 7 (2013)

1,524 to 2,437 m: 1 (2013)

914 to 1,523 m: 4 (2013)

under 914 m: 2 (2013)

**HELIPORTS:**

20 (2013)

**PIPELINES:**

12603 km gas, 3038 km oil (2016)

**RAILWAYS:**

total: 12,008 km (2014)

standard gauge: 12,008 km 1.435-m gauge (3,216 km electrified) (2014)

country comparison to the world: 21

**ROADWAYS:**

total: 385,754 km (2012)

paved: 352,268 km (includes 2,127 km of expressways) (2012)

unpaved: 33,486 km (2012)

country comparison to the world: 19

**WATERWAYS:**

1,200 km (2010)

country comparison to the world: 60

**MERCHANT MARINE:**

total: 1,285 (2017)

by type: bulk carrier 78, container ship 50, general cargo 432, oil tanker 121, other 604 (2017)

country comparison to the world: 22

**PORTS AND TERMINALS:**

major seaport(s): Aliaga, Ambarli, Diliskelesi, Eregli, Izmir, Kocaeli (Izmit), Mersin (Icel), Limani, Yarimca

container port(s) (TEUs): Ambarli (2,803,133), Mersin (Icel) (1,453,000) (2016)

LNG terminal(s) (import): Izmir Aliaga, Marmara Ereglisi

# MILITARY AND SECURITY :: TURKEY

**MILITARY EXPENDITURES:**

1.73% of GDP (2016)

1.85% of GDP (2015)

1.9% of GDP (2014)

country comparison to the world: 64

**MILITARY BRANCHES:**

Turkish Armed Forces (TSK): Turkish Land Forces (Turk Kara Kuvvetleri), Turkish Naval Forces (Turk Deniz Kuvvetleri; includes naval air and naval infantry), Turkish Air Forces (Turk Hava Kuvvetleri) (2013)

**MILITARY SERVICE AGE AND OBLIGATION:**

21-41 years of age for male compulsory military service (in case of mobilization, up to 65 years of age); 18 years of age for voluntary service; 12-month conscript obligation for non-university graduates, 6-12 months for university graduates (graduates of higher education may perform 6 months of military service as short-term privates, or 12 months as reserve officers); conscripts are called to register at age 20, for service at 21; women serve in the Turkish Armed Forces only as officers; reserve obligation to age 41; Turkish citizens with a residence or work permit who have worked abroad for at least 3 years (1095 days) can be exempt from military service in exchange for 6,000 EUR or its equivalent in foreign currencies; a law passed in December 2014 introduced a one-time payment scheme which exempted Turkish citizens 27 and older from conscription in exchange for a payment of $8,150 (2013)

**MILITARY - NOTE:**

the ruling Justice and Development Party (AKP) has actively pursued the goal of asserting civilian control over the military since first taking power in 2002; the Turkish Armed Forces (TSK) role in internal security has been significantly reduced; the TSK leadership continues to be an influential institution within Turkey, but plays a much smaller role in politics; the Turkish military remains focused on the threats emanating from the Syrian civil war, Russia's actions in Ukraine, and the PKK insurgency; primary domestic threats are listed as fundamentalism (with the definition in some dispute with the civilian government), separatism (Kurdish discontent), and the extreme left wing; Ankara strongly opposed establishment of an autonomous Kurdish region in Iraq; an overhaul of the Turkish Land Forces Command (TLFC) taking place under the "Force 2014" program is to produce 20-30% smaller, more highly trained forces characterized by greater mobility and firepower and capable of joint and combined operations; the TLFC has taken on increasing international peacekeeping responsibilities including in Afghanistan; the Turkish Navy is a regional naval power that wants to develop the capability to project power beyond Turkey's coastal waters; the Navy is heavily involved in NATO, multinational, and UN operations; its roles include control of territorial waters and security for sea lines of communications; the Turkish Air Force adopted an "Aerospace and Missile Defense Concept" in 2002 and has initiated project work on an integrated missile defense system; Air Force priorities include attaining a modern deployable, survivable, and sustainable force structure, and establishing a sustainable command and control system; Turkey is a NATO ally and hosts NATO's Land Forces Command in Izmir, as well as the AN/TPY-2 radar as part of NATO Missile Defense (2014)

# TERRORISM :: TURKEY

**TERRORIST GROUPS - HOME BASED:**

Islamic State of Iraq and ash-Sham (ISIS) networks in Turkey:
aim(s): replace the Turkish Government with an Islamic state and implement ISIS's strict interpretation of sharia
area(s) of operation: moves fighters and supplies across the Turkey-Syria border; has periodically conducted attacks against civilian and government security targets (April 2018)

Revolutionary People's Liberation Party/Front (DHKP/C):
aim(s): install a Marxist-Leninist government in Turkey
area(s) of operation: membership centered in Turkey, leadership primarily spread throughout Europe; in recent years has revived its attacks against Turkish Government elements, primarily in Istanbul; outlawed in Turkey (April 2018)

**TERRORIST GROUPS - FOREIGN BASED:**

al-Nusrah Front:
aim(s): overthrow Syrian President Bashar al-ASAD's regime, absorb like-minded Syrian rebel groups, and ultimately, establish a regional Islamic caliphate
area(s) of operation: some facilitation networks (April 2018)

al-Qa'ida (AQ):
aim(s): radicalize the Turkish populace and eventually overthrow the Turkish Government as part of a long-term plan to establish a pan-Islamic caliphate under a strict Salafi Muslim

interpretation of sharia
**area(s) of operation**: maintains facilitation networks (April 2018)

**Kurdistan Workers' Party (PKK)**:
**aim(s)**: advance Kurdish autonomy, political, and cultural rights in Turkey, Iran, Iraq, and Syria
**area(s) of operation**: operational predominantly in the southeast; the group's primary targets include government, military, and security personnel and facilities; majority of members inside Turkey are Turkish Kurds, along with Kurds from Iran, Iraq, and Syria; the group is outlawed in Turkey (April 2018)

# TRANSNATIONAL ISSUES :: TURKEY

## DISPUTES - INTERNATIONAL:

complex maritime, air, and territorial disputes with Greece in the Aegean Seastatus of north Cyprus question remainsTurkey has expressed concern over the status of Kurds in Iraqin 2009, Swiss mediators facilitated an accord reestablishing diplomatic ties between Armenia and Turkey, but neither side has ratified the agreement and the rapprochement effort has falteredTurkish authorities have complained that blasting from quarries in Armenia might be damaging the medieval ruins of Ani, on the other side of the Arpacay valley

## REFUGEES AND INTERNALLY DISPLACED PERSONS:

**refugees (country of origin)**: 3,611,834 (Syria), 170,000 (Afghanistan), 142,000 (Iraq), 39,000 (Iran), 5,700 (Somalia) (2018)

**IDPs**: 1.113 million (displaced from 1984-2005 because of fighting between the Kurdish PKK and Turkish military; most IDPs are Kurds from eastern and southeastern provinces; no information available on persons displaced by development projects) (2017)

**stateless persons**: 117 (2017)

## ILLICIT DRUGS:

key transit route for Southwest Asian heroin to Western Europe and, to a lesser extent, the US - via air, land, and sea routes; major Turkish and other international trafficking organizations operate out of Istanbul; laboratories to convert imported morphine base into heroin exist in remote regions of Turkey and near Istanbul; government maintains strict controls over areas of legal opium poppy cultivation and over output of poppy straw concentrate; lax enforcement of money-laundering controls

# CENTRAL ASIA :: TURKMENISTAN

## INTRODUCTION :: TURKMENISTAN

### BACKGROUND:

Present-day Turkmenistan covers territory that has been at the crossroads of civilizations for centuries. The area was ruled in antiquity by various Persian empires, and was conquered by Alexander the Great, Muslim armies, the Mongols, Turkic warriors, and eventually the Russians. In medieval times, Merv (located in present-day Mary province) was one of the great cities of the Islamic world and an important stop on the Silk Road. Annexed by Russia in the late 1800s, Turkmenistan later figured prominently in the anti-Bolshevik movement in Central Asia. In 1924, Turkmenistan became a Soviet republic; it achieved independence upon the dissolution of the USSR in 1991. Extensive hydrocarbon/natural gas reserves, which have yet to be fully exploited, have begun to transform the country. The Government of Turkmenistan is moving to expand its extraction and delivery projects and has attempted to diversify its gas export routes beyond Russia's pipeline network. In 2010, new gas export pipelines that carry Turkmen gas to China and to northern Iran began operating, effectively ending the Russian monopoly on Turkmen gas exports. In 2016 and 2017, Turkmen sales of natural gas were halted to Russia and Iran, respectively, making China the sole major buyer of Turkmen gas. President for Life Saparmurat NYYAZOW died in December 2006, and Turkmenistan held its first multi-candidate presidential election in February 2007. Gurbanguly BERDIMUHAMEDOW, a deputy cabinet chairman under NYYAZOW, emerged as the country's new president. He was reelected in 2012 and again in 2017 with over 97% of the vote in both instances, in elections widely regarded as undemocratic.

## GEOGRAPHY :: TURKMENISTAN

### LOCATION:

Central Asia, bordering the Caspian Sea, between Iran and Kazakhstan

### GEOGRAPHIC COORDINATES:

40 00 N, 60 00 E

### MAP REFERENCES:

Asia

### AREA:

total: 488,100 sq km

land: 469,930 sq km

water: 18,170 sq km

country comparison to the world: 54

### AREA - COMPARATIVE:

slightly more than three times the size of Georgia; slightly larger than California

### LAND BOUNDARIES:

total: 4,158 km

border countries (4): Afghanistan 804 km, Iran 1148 km, Kazakhstan 413 km, Uzbekistan 1793 km

### COASTLINE:

0 km (landlocked); note - Turkmenistan borders the Caspian Sea (1,768 km)

### MARITIME CLAIMS:

none (landlocked)

### CLIMATE:

subtropical desert

### TERRAIN:

flat-to-rolling sandy desert with dunes rising to mountains in the south; low mountains along border with Iran; borders Caspian Sea in west

### ELEVATION:

mean elevation: 230 m

elevation extremes: -81 m lowest point: Vpadina Akchanaya (Sarygamysh Koli is a lake in northern Turkmenistan with a water level that fluctuates above and below the elevation of Vpadina Akchanaya, the lake has dropped as low as -110 m)

3139 highest point: Gora Ayribaba

### NATURAL RESOURCES:

petroleum, natural gas, sulfur, salt

### LAND USE:

agricultural land: 72% (2011 est.)

arable land: 4.1% (2011 est.) / permanent crops: 0.1% (2011 est.) / permanent pasture: 67.8% (2011 est.)

forest: 8.8% (2011 est.)

other: 19.2% (2011 est.)

### IRRIGATED LAND:

19,950 sq km (2012)

### POPULATION DISTRIBUTION:

the most densely populated areas are the southern, eastern, and northeastern oases; approximately 50% of the population lives in and around the capital of Ashgabat

### NATURAL HAZARDS:

earthquakes; mudslides; droughts; dust storms; floods

**ENVIRONMENT - CURRENT ISSUES:**

contamination of soil and groundwater with agricultural chemicals, pesticides; salination, water logging of soil due to poor irrigation methods; Caspian Sea pollution; diversion of a large share of the flow of the Amu Darya into irrigation contributes to that river's inability to replenish the Aral Sea; soil erosion; desertification

**ENVIRONMENT - INTERNATIONAL AGREEMENTS:**

party to: Biodiversity, Climate Change, Climate Change-Kyoto Protocol, Desertification, Hazardous Wastes, Ozone Layer Protection

signed, but not ratified: none of the selected agreements

**GEOGRAPHY - NOTE:**

landlocked; the western and central low-lying desolate portions of the country make up the great Garagum (Kara-Kum) desert, which occupies over 80% of the country; eastern part is plateau

# PEOPLE AND SOCIETY :: TURKMENISTAN

**POPULATION:**

5,411,012 (July 2018 est.)

country comparison to the world: 119

**NATIONALITY:**

noun: Turkmen(s)

adjective: Turkmen

**ETHNIC GROUPS:**

Turkmen 85%, Uzbek 5%, Russian 4%, other 6% (2003)

**LANGUAGES:**

Turkmen (official) 72%, Russian 12%, Uzbek 9%, other 7%

**RELIGIONS:**

Muslim 89%, Eastern Orthodox 9%, unknown 2%

**AGE STRUCTURE:**

0-14 years: 25.66% (male 704,067 /female 684,581)

15-24 years: 17.71% (male 482,094 /female 476,080)

25-54 years: 43.52% (male 1,169,965 /female 1,185,159)

55-64 years: 8.17% (male 208,328 /female 233,902)

65 years and over: 4.93% (male 116,218 /female 150,618) (2018 est.)

**DEPENDENCY RATIOS:**

total dependency ratio: 52.7 (2015 est.)

youth dependency ratio: 46.5 (2015 est.)

elderly dependency ratio: 6.2 (2015 est.)

potential support ratio: 16.1 (2015 est.)

**MEDIAN AGE:**

total: 28.3 years

male: 27.8 years

female: 28.8 years (2018 est.)

country comparison to the world: 139

**POPULATION GROWTH RATE:**

1.1% (2018 est.)

country comparison to the world: 100

**BIRTH RATE:**

18.9 births/1,000 population (2018 est.)

country comparison to the world: 85

**DEATH RATE:**

6.1 deaths/1,000 population (2018 est.)

country comparison to the world: 162

**NET MIGRATION RATE:**

-1.8 migrant(s)/1,000 population (2017 est.)

country comparison to the world: 156

**POPULATION DISTRIBUTION:**

the most densely populated areas are the southern, eastern, and northeastern oases; approximately 50% of the population lives in and around the capital of Ashgabat

**URBANIZATION:**

urban population: 51.6% of total population (2018)

rate of urbanization: 2.46% annual rate of change (2015-20 est.)

**MAJOR URBAN AREAS - POPULATION:**

810,000 ASHGABAT (capital) (2018)

**SEX RATIO:**

at birth: 1.04 male(s)/female (2017 est.)

0-14 years: 1.03 male(s)/female (2017 est.)

15-24 years: 1.01 male(s)/female (2017 est.)

25-54 years: 0.98 male(s)/female (2017 est.)

55-64 years: 0.89 male(s)/female (2017 est.)

65 years and over: 0.77 male(s)/female (2017 est.)

total population: 0.98 male(s)/female (2017 est.)

**MATERNAL MORTALITY RATE:**

42 deaths/100,000 live births (2015 est.)

country comparison to the world: 104

**INFANT MORTALITY RATE:**

total: 33.1 deaths/1,000 live births (2018 est.)

male: 39.8 deaths/1,000 live births (2018 est.)

female: 26 deaths/1,000 live births (2018 est.)

country comparison to the world: 55

**LIFE EXPECTANCY AT BIRTH:**

total population: 70.7 years (2018 est.)

male: 67.6 years (2018 est.)

female: 73.9 years (2018 est.)

country comparison to the world: 159

**TOTAL FERTILITY RATE:**

2.06 children born/woman (2018 est.)

country comparison to the world: 107

**CONTRACEPTIVE PREVALENCE RATE:**

50.2% (2015/16)

**HEALTH EXPENDITURES:**

2.1% of GDP (2014)

country comparison to the world: 190

**PHYSICIANS DENSITY:**

2.29 physicians/1,000 population (2014)

**HOSPITAL BED DENSITY:**

7.4 beds/1,000 population (2013)

**DRINKING WATER SOURCE:**

improved:

urban: 89.1% of population (2012 est.)

rural: 53.7% of population (2012 est.)

total: 71.1% of population (2012 est.)

unimproved:

urban: 10.9% of population (2012 est.)

rural: 46.3% of population (2012 est.)

total: 28.9% of population (2012 est.)

**SANITATION FACILITY ACCESS:**

improved:

urban: 100% of population (2012 est.)

rural: 98.2% of population (2012 est.)

total: 99.1% of population (2012 est.)

**unimproved:**

urban: 0% of population (2012 est.)

rural: 1.8% of population (2012 est.)

total: 0.9% of population (2012 est.)

### HIV/AIDS - ADULT PREVALENCE RATE:

NA

### HIV/AIDS - PEOPLE LIVING WITH HIV/AIDS:

NA

### HIV/AIDS - DEATHS:

NA

### OBESITY - ADULT PREVALENCE RATE:

18.6% (2016)

country comparison to the world: 117

### CHILDREN UNDER THE AGE OF 5 YEARS UNDERWEIGHT:

3.2% (2015)

country comparison to the world: 96

### EDUCATION EXPENDITURES:

3% of GDP (2012)

country comparison to the world: 145

### LITERACY:

definition: age 15 and over can read and write (2015 est.)

total population: 99.7% (2015 est.)

male: 99.8% (2015 est.)

female: 99.6% (2015 est.)

### SCHOOL LIFE EXPECTANCY (PRIMARY TO TERTIARY EDUCATION):

total: 11 years (2014)

male: 11 years (2014)

female: 11 years (2014)

# GOVERNMENT :: TURKMENISTAN

### COUNTRY NAME:

conventional long form: none

conventional short form: Turkmenistan

local long form: none

local short form: Turkmenistan

former: Turkmen Soviet Socialist Republic

etymology: the suffix "-stan" means "place of" or "country," so Turkmenistan literally means the "Land of the Turkmen [people]"

### GOVERNMENT TYPE:

presidential republic; authoritarian

### CAPITAL:

name: Ashgabat (Ashkhabad)

geographic coordinates: 37 57 N, 58 23 E

time difference: UTC+5 (10 hours ahead of Washington, DC, during Standard Time)

### ADMINISTRATIVE DIVISIONS:

5 provinces (welayatlar, singular - welayat) and 1 independent city*: Ahal Welayaty (Anew), Ashgabat*, Balkan Welayaty (Balkanabat), Dasoguz Welayaty, Lebap Welayaty (Turkmenabat), Mary Welayaty

note: administrative divisions have the same names as their administrative centers (exceptions have the administrative center name following in parentheses)

### INDEPENDENCE:

27 October 1991 (from the Soviet Union)

### NATIONAL HOLIDAY:

Independence Day, 27 October (1991)

### CONSTITUTION:

history: adopted 18 May 1992 (2017)

amendments: proposed by the National Assembly; passage requires two-thirds majority vote of the total Assembly membership or absolute majority approval in a referendum; amended several times, last in 2016; note - in mid-2014, the president established a Constitutional Commission to initiate a process for developing constitutional reforms (2017)

### LEGAL SYSTEM:

civil law system with Islamic law influences

### INTERNATIONAL LAW ORGANIZATION PARTICIPATION:

has not submitted an ICJ jurisdiction declaration; non-party state to the ICCt

### CITIZENSHIP:

citizenship by birth: no

citizenship by descent only: at least one parent must be a citizen of Turkmenistan

dual citizenship recognized: yes

residency requirement for naturalization: 7 years

### SUFFRAGE:

18 years of age; universal

### EXECUTIVE BRANCH:

chief of state: President Gurbanguly BERDIMUHAMEDOW (since 14 February 2007); note - the president is both chief of state and head of government

head of government: President Gurbanguly BERDIMUHAMEDOW (since 14 February 2007)

cabinet: Cabinet of Ministers appointed by the president

elections/appointments: president directly elected by absolute majority popular vote in 2 rounds if needed for a 7-year term (no term limits); election last held on 12 February 2017 (next to be held in February 2024)

election results: Gurbanguly BERDIMUHAMEDOW reelected president in the first round; percent of vote - Gurbanguly BERDIMUHAMEDOW (DPT) 97.7%, other 2.3%

### LEGISLATIVE BRANCH:

description: unicameral National Assembly or Mejlis (125 seats; members directly elected from single-seat constituencies by absolute majority vote; members serve 5-year terms)

elections: last held on 25 March 2018, although interim elections are held on an ad hoc basis to fill vacant sets

election results: percent of vote by party - NA; seats by party - DPT 55, APT 11, PIE 11, independent 48 (individuals nominated by citizen groups); composition - men 94, women 31, percent of women 24.8%

### JUDICIAL BRANCH:

highest courts: Supreme Court of Turkmenistan (consists of the court president and 21 associate judges and organized into civil, criminal, and military chambers)

judge selection and term of office: judges appointed by the president for 5-year terms

subordinate courts: High Commercial Court; appellate courts; provincial, district, and city courts; military courts

### POLITICAL PARTIES AND LEADERS:

Agrarian Party of Turkmenistan or APT [Bashim ANNAGURBANOW]

Democratic Party of Turkmenistan or

DPT [Ata SERDAROW]
Organization of Trade Unions of Turkmenistan
Magtymguly Youth Organization
Party of Industrialists and Entrepreneurs or PIE [Saparmyrat OVGANOW]
Women's Union of Turkmenistan

**note:** all of these parties support President BERDIMUHAMEDOW; a law authorizing the registration of political parties went into effect in January 2012; unofficial, small opposition movements exist abroad

## INTERNATIONAL ORGANIZATION PARTICIPATION:

ADB, CIS (associate member, has not ratified the 1993 CIS charter although it participates in meetings and held the chairmanship of the CIS in 2012), EAPC, EBRD, ECO, FAO, G-77, IBRD, ICAO, ICRM, IDA, IDB, IFC, IFRCS, ILO, IMF, IMO, Interpol, IOC, IOM (observer), ISO (correspondent), ITU, MIGA, NAM, OIC, OPCW, OSCE, PFP, UN, UNCTAD, UNESCO, UNHCR, UNIDO, UNWTO, UPU, WCO, WFTU (NGOs), WHO, WIPO, WMO

## DIPLOMATIC REPRESENTATION IN THE US:

**chief of mission:** Ambassador Meret Bairamovich ORAZOW (since 14 February 2001)

**chancery:** 2207 Massachusetts Avenue NW, Washington, DC 20008

**telephone:** [1] (202) 588-1500

**FAX:** [1] (202) 588-0697

## DIPLOMATIC REPRESENTATION FROM THE US:

**chief of mission:** Ambassador Allan MUSTARD (since 20 January 2015)

**embassy:** No. 9 1984 Street (formerly Pushkin Street), Ashgabat, Turkmenistan 744000

**mailing address:** 7070 Ashgabat Place, Washington, DC 20521-7070

**telephone:** [993] (12) 94-00-45

**FAX:** [993] (12) 94-26-14

## FLAG DESCRIPTION:

green field with a vertical red stripe near the hoist side, containing five tribal guls (designs used in producing carpets) stacked above two crossed olive branches; five white stars and a white crescent moon appear in the upper corner of the field just to the fly side of the red stripe; the green color and crescent moon represent Islam; the five stars symbolize the regions or welayats of Turkmenistan; the guls reflect the national identity of Turkmenistan where carpet-making has long been a part of traditional nomadic life

**note:** the flag of Turkmenistan is the most intricate of all national flags

## NATIONAL SYMBOL(S):

Akhal-Teke horse; national colors: green, white

## NATIONAL ANTHEM:

**name:** "Garassyz, Bitarap Turkmenistanyn" (Independent, Neutral, Turkmenistan State Anthem)

**lyrics/music:** collective/Veli MUKHATOV

**note:** adopted 1997, lyrics revised in 2008, to eliminate references to deceased President Saparmurat NYYAZOW

# ECONOMY :: TURKMENISTAN

## ECONOMY - OVERVIEW:

Turkmenistan is largely a desert country with intensive agriculture in irrigated oases and significant natural gas and oil resources. The two largest crops are cotton, most of which is produced for export, and wheat, which is domestically consumed. Although agriculture accounts for almost 8% of GDP, it continues to employ nearly half of the country's workforce. Hydrocarbon exports, the bulk of which is natural gas going to China, make up 25% of Turkmenistan's GDP. Ashgabat has explored two initiatives to bring gas to new markets: a trans-Caspian pipeline that would carry gas to Europe and the Turkmenistan-Afghanistan-Pakistan-India gas pipeline. Both face major financing, political, and security hurdles and are unlikely to be completed soon.

Turkmenistan's autocratic governments under presidents NIYAZOW (1991-2006) and BERDIMUHAMEDOW (since 2007) have made little progress improving the business climate, privatizing state-owned industries, combatting corruption, and limiting economic development outside the energy sector. High energy prices in the mid-2000s allowed the government to undertake extensive development and social spending, including providing heavy utility subsidies.

Low energy prices since mid-2014 are hampering Turkmenistan's economic growth and reducing government revenues. The government has cut subsidies in several areas, and wage arrears have increased. In January 2014, the Central Bank of Turkmenistan devalued the manat by 19%, and downward pressure on the currency continues. There is a widening spread between the official exchange rate (3.5 TMM per US dollar) and the black market exchange rate (approximately 14 TMM per US dollar). Currency depreciation and conversion restrictions, corruption, isolationist policies, and declining spending on public services have resulted in a stagnate economy that is nearing crisis. Turkmenistan claims substantial foreign currency reserves, but non-transparent data limit international institutions' ability to verify this information.

## GDP (PURCHASING POWER PARITY):

$103.7 billion (2017 est.)

$97.41 billion (2016 est.)

$91.72 billion (2015 est.)

**note:** data are in 2017 dollars

**country comparison to the world:** 84

## GDP (OFFICIAL EXCHANGE RATE):

$37.93 billion (2017 est.) (2017 est.)

## GDP - REAL GROWTH RATE:

6.5% (2017 est.)

6.2% (2016 est.)

6.5% (2015 est.)

**country comparison to the world:** 30

## GDP - PER CAPITA (PPP):

$18,200 (2017 est.)

$17,300 (2016 est.)

$16,500 (2015 est.)

**note:** data are in 2017 dollars

**country comparison to the world:** 96

## GROSS NATIONAL SAVING:

23.9% of GDP (2017 est.)

24.3% of GDP (2016 est.)

18.9% of GDP (2015 est.)

**country comparison to the world:** 70

## GDP - COMPOSITION, BY END USE:

**household consumption:** 50% (2017 est.)

**government consumption:** 10% (2017 est.)

**investment in fixed capital:** 28.2% (2017 est.)

**investment in inventories:** 0% (2017 est.)

exports of goods and services: 26.2% (2017 est.)

imports of goods and services: -14.3% (2017 est.)

## GDP - COMPOSITION, BY SECTOR OF ORIGIN:

agriculture: 7.5% (2017 est.)

industry: 44.9% (2017 est.)

services: 47.7% (2017 est.)

## AGRICULTURE - PRODUCTS:

cotton, grain, melons; livestock

## INDUSTRIES:

natural gas, oil, petroleum products, textiles, food processing

## INDUSTRIAL PRODUCTION GROWTH RATE:

1% (2017 est.)

country comparison to the world: 160

## LABOR FORCE:

2.305 million (2013 est.)

country comparison to the world: 116

## LABOR FORCE - BY OCCUPATION:

agriculture: 48.2%

industry: 14%

services: 37.8% (2004 est.)

## UNEMPLOYMENT RATE:

11% (2014 est.)

10.6% (2013)

country comparison to the world: 149

## POPULATION BELOW POVERTY LINE:

0.2% (2012 est.)

## HOUSEHOLD INCOME OR CONSUMPTION BY PERCENTAGE SHARE:

lowest 10%: 31.7% (1998)

highest 10%: 31.7% (1998)

## DISTRIBUTION OF FAMILY INCOME - GINI INDEX:

40.8 (1998)

country comparison to the world: 62

## BUDGET:

revenues: 5.657 billion (2017 est.)

expenditures: 6.714 billion (2017 est.)

## TAXES AND OTHER REVENUES:

14.9% (of GDP) (2017 est.)

country comparison to the world: 197

## BUDGET SURPLUS (+) OR DEFICIT (-):

-2.8% (of GDP) (2017 est.)

country comparison to the world: 126

## PUBLIC DEBT:

28.8% of GDP (2017 est.)

24.1% of GDP (2016 est.)

country comparison to the world: 167

## FISCAL YEAR:

calendar year

## INFLATION RATE (CONSUMER PRICES):

8% (2017 est.)

3.6% (2016 est.)

country comparison to the world: 198

## CENTRAL BANK DISCOUNT RATE:

5% (31 December 2014)

5% (31 December 2013)

country comparison to the world: 83

## COMMERCIAL BANK PRIME LENDING RATE:

19% (31 December 2017 est.)

16% (31 December 2016 est.)

country comparison to the world: 17

## STOCK OF NARROW MONEY:

$1.326 billion (31 December 2015 est.)

$1.255 billion (31 December 2014 est.)

country comparison to the world: 148

## STOCK OF BROAD MONEY:

$12.23 billion (31 December 2015 est.)

$5.632 billion (31 December 2014 est.)

country comparison to the world: 82

## STOCK OF DOMESTIC CREDIT:

$28.4 billion (31 December 2015 est.)

$13.09 billion (31 December 2014 est.)

country comparison to the world: 82

## MARKET VALUE OF PUBLICLY TRADED SHARES:

NA

## CURRENT ACCOUNT BALANCE:

-$4.359 billion (2017 est.)

-$7.207 billion (2016 est.)

country comparison to the world: 181

## EXPORTS:

$7.458 billion (2017 est.)

$6.987 billion (2016 est.)

country comparison to the world: 101

## EXPORTS - PARTNERS:

China 83.7%, Turkey 5.1% (2017)

## EXPORTS - COMMODITIES:

gas, crude oil, petrochemicals, textiles, cotton fiber

## IMPORTS:

$4.571 billion (2017 est.)

$5.215 billion (2016 est.)

country comparison to the world: 135

## IMPORTS - COMMODITIES:

machinery and equipment, chemicals, foodstuffs

## IMPORTS - PARTNERS:

Turkey 24.2%, Algeria 14.4%, Germany 9.8%, China 8.9%, Russia 8%, US 6.6% (2017)

## RESERVES OF FOREIGN EXCHANGE AND GOLD:

$24.91 billion (31 December 2017 est.)

$25.05 billion (31 December 2016 est.)

country comparison to the world: 56

## DEBT - EXTERNAL:

$539.4 million (31 December 2017 est.)

$425.3 million (31 December 2016 est.)

country comparison to the world: 177

## STOCK OF DIRECT FOREIGN INVESTMENT - AT HOME:

$3.061 billion (2013 est.)

$3.117 billion (2012 est.)

country comparison to the world: 115

## EXCHANGE RATES:

Turkmen manat (TMM) per US dollar -

4.125 (2017 est.)

3.5 (2016 est.)

3.5 (2015 est.)

3.5 (2014 est.)

2.85 (2013 est.)

# ENERGY :: TURKMENISTAN

## ELECTRICITY ACCESS:

electrification - total population: 100% (2016)

## ELECTRICITY - PRODUCTION:

21.18 billion kWh (2016 est.)

country comparison to the world: 74

## ELECTRICITY - CONSUMPTION:

15.09 billion kWh (2016 est.)

country comparison to the world: 80

## ELECTRICITY - EXPORTS:

3.201 billion kWh (2015 est.)

country comparison to the world: 41

## ELECTRICITY - IMPORTS:

0 kWh (2016 est.)

country comparison to the world: 212

## ELECTRICITY - INSTALLED GENERATING CAPACITY:

4.001 million kW (2016 est.)

country comparison to the world: 88
### ELECTRICITY - FROM FOSSIL FUELS:
100% of total installed capacity (2016 est.)

country comparison to the world: 20
### ELECTRICITY - FROM NUCLEAR FUELS:
0% of total installed capacity (2017 est.)

country comparison to the world: 200
### ELECTRICITY - FROM HYDROELECTRIC PLANTS:
0% of total installed capacity (2017 est.)

country comparison to the world: 207
### ELECTRICITY - FROM OTHER RENEWABLE SOURCES:
0% of total installed capacity (2017 est.)

country comparison to the world: 210
### CRUDE OIL - PRODUCTION:
0 bbl/day (2017 est.)

country comparison to the world: 207
### CRUDE OIL - EXPORTS:
67,790 bbl/day (2015 est.)

country comparison to the world: 38
### CRUDE OIL - IMPORTS:
0 bbl/day (2015 est.)

country comparison to the world: 206
### CRUDE OIL - PROVED RESERVES:
600 million bbl (1 January 2018 est.)

country comparison to the world: 43
### REFINED PETROLEUM PRODUCTS - PRODUCTION:
191,100 bbl/day (2015 est.)

country comparison to the world: 52
### REFINED PETROLEUM PRODUCTS - CONSUMPTION:
160,000 bbl/day (2016 est.)

country comparison to the world: 63
### REFINED PETROLEUM PRODUCTS - EXPORTS:
53,780 bbl/day (2015 est.)

country comparison to the world: 53
### REFINED PETROLEUM PRODUCTS - IMPORTS:
0 bbl/day (2015 est.)

country comparison to the world: 214
### NATURAL GAS - PRODUCTION:
77.45 billion cu m (2017 est.)

country comparison to the world: 11
### NATURAL GAS - CONSUMPTION:
39.31 billion cu m (2017 est.)

country comparison to the world: 27

### NATURAL GAS - EXPORTS:
38.14 billion cu m (2017 est.)

country comparison to the world: 10
### NATURAL GAS - IMPORTS:
0 cu m (2017 est.)

country comparison to the world: 203
### NATURAL GAS - PROVED RESERVES:
7.504 trillion cu m (1 January 2018 est.)

country comparison to the world: 5
### CARBON DIOXIDE EMISSIONS FROM CONSUMPTION OF ENERGY:
100.5 million Mt (2017 est.)

country comparison to the world: 44

## COMMUNICATIONS :: TURKMENISTAN

### TELEPHONES - FIXED LINES:
total subscriptions: 665,000 (July 2016 est.)

subscriptions per 100 inhabitants: 13 (July 2016 est.)

country comparison to the world: 90
### TELEPHONES - MOBILE CELLULAR:
total subscriptions: 8.575 million (July 2016 est.)

subscriptions per 100 inhabitants: 160 (July 2016 est.)

country comparison to the world: 95
### TELEPHONE SYSTEM:
general assessment: telecommunications network is gradually improving (2018)

domestic: Turkmentelekom, in cooperation with foreign partners, has installed high-speed fiber-optic lines and has upgraded most of the country's telephone exchanges and switching centers with new digital technology; combined fixed-line and mobile teledensity is about 170 per 100 persons; Russia's Mobile TeleSystems (MTS), the only foreign mobile-cellular service provider in Turkmenistan, suspended operations in September 2017 due to the state-owned telecom company cutting MTS' access to international and long-distance communication services and Internet; Turkmenistan's first telecommunication satellite was launched in 2015 and is expected to greatly improve connectivity in the country (2018)

international: country code - 993; linked by fiber-optic cable and microwave radio relay to other CIS republics and to other countries by leased connections to the Moscow international gateway switch; an exchange in Ashgabat switches international traffic through Turkey via Intelsat; satellite earth stations - 1 Orbita and 1 Intelsat (2018)

### BROADCAST MEDIA:
broadcast media is government controlled and censored; 7 state-owned TV and 4 state-owned radio networks; satellite dishes and programming provide an alternative to the state-run media; officials sometimes limit access to satellite TV by removing satellite dishes (2007)

### INTERNET COUNTRY CODE:
.tm

### INTERNET USERS:
total: 951,925 (July 2016 est.)

percent of population: 18% (July 2016 est.)

country comparison to the world: 133
### BROADBAND - FIXED SUBSCRIPTIONS:
total: 4,000 (2017 est.)

subscriptions per 100 inhabitants: less than 1 (2017 est.)

country comparison to the world: 177

## TRANSPORTATION :: TURKMENISTAN

### NATIONAL AIR TRANSPORT SYSTEM:
number of registered air carriers: 1 (2015)

inventory of registered aircraft operated by air carriers: 23 (2015)

annual passenger traffic on registered air carriers: 2,138,389 (2015)

annual freight traffic on registered air carriers: 0 mt-km (2015)

### CIVIL AIRCRAFT REGISTRATION COUNTRY CODE PREFIX:
EZ (2016)

### AIRPORTS:
26 (2013)

country comparison to the world: 127
### AIRPORTS - WITH PAVED RUNWAYS:
total: 21 (2013)

over 3,047 m: 1 (2013)

2,438 to 3,047 m: 9 (2013)

1,524 to 2,437 m: 9 (2013)

**914 to 1,523 m:** 2 (2013)

## AIRPORTS - WITH UNPAVED RUNWAYS:

**total:** 5 (2013)

**1,524 to 2,437 m:** 1 (2013)

**under 914 m:** 4 (2013)

## HELIPORTS:

1 (2013)

## PIPELINES:

7500 km gas, 1501 km oil (2013)

## RAILWAYS:

**total:** 5,113 km (2017)

**broad gauge:** 5,113 km 1.520-m gauge (2017)

**country comparison to the world:** 38

## ROADWAYS:

**total:** 58,592 km (2002)

**paved:** 47,577 km (2002)

**unpaved:** 11,015 km (2002)

**country comparison to the world:** 72

## WATERWAYS:

1,300 km (Amu Darya River and Kara Kum Canal are important inland waterways) (2011)

**country comparison to the world:** 55

## MERCHANT MARINE:

**total:** 73 (2017)

**by type:** general cargo 8, oil tanker 8, other 57 (2017)

**country comparison to the world:** 102

## PORTS AND TERMINALS:

**major seaport(s):** Caspian Sea - Turkmenbasy

# MILITARY AND SECURITY :: TURKMENISTAN

## MILITARY BRANCHES:

Turkmen Armed Forces: Ground Forces, Navy, Air and Air Defense Forces (2013)

## MILITARY SERVICE AGE AND OBLIGATION:

18-27 years of age for compulsory male military service; 2-year conscript service obligation; 20 years of age for voluntary service; males may enroll in military schools from age 15 (2015)

# TRANSNATIONAL ISSUES :: TURKMENISTAN

## DISPUTES - INTERNATIONAL:

cotton monoculture in Uzbekistan and Turkmenistan creates water-sharing difficulties for Amu Darya river statesfield demarcation of the boundaries with Kazakhstan commenced in 2005 and with Uzbekistan in 2017, but Caspian seabed delimitation remains stalled with Azerbaijan, Iran, Russia, and Kazakhstan due to indecision over how to allocate the sea's waters and seabedbilateral talks continue with Azerbaijan on dividing the seabed and contested oilfields in the middle of the Caspian

## REFUGEES AND INTERNALLY DISPLACED PERSONS:

**stateless persons:** 3,851 (2017)

## TRAFFICKING IN PERSONS:

**current situation:** Turkmenistan is a source country for men, women, and children subjected to forced labor and sex trafficking; Turkmen who migrate abroad are forced to work in the textile, agriculture, construction, and domestic service industries, while women and girls may also be sex trafficked; in 2014, men surpassed women as victims; Turkey and Russia are primary trafficking destinations, followed by the Middle East, South and Central Asia, and other parts of Europe; Turkmen also experience forced labor domestically in the informal construction industry; participation in the cotton harvest is still mandatory for some public sector employees

**tier rating:** Tier 2 Watch List – Turkmenistan does not fully comply with the minimum standards for the elimination of trafficking; however, it is making significant efforts to do so; in 2014, Turkmenistan was granted a waiver from an otherwise required downgrade to Tier 3 because its government has a written plan that, if implemented, would constitute making significant efforts to bring itself into compliance with the minimum standards for the elimination of trafficking; the government made some progress in its law enforcement efforts in 2014, convicting more offenders than in 2013; authorities did not make adequate efforts to identify and protect victims and did not fund international organizations or NGOs that offered protective services; some victims were punished for crimes as a result of being trafficked (2015)

## ILLICIT DRUGS:

transit country for Afghan narcotics bound for Russian and Western European markets; transit point for heroin precursor chemicals bound for Afghanistan

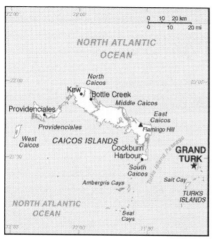

# CENTRAL AMERICA :: TURKS AND CAICOS ISLANDS

## INTRODUCTION :: TURKS AND CAICOS ISLANDS

### BACKGROUND:
The islands were part of the UK's Jamaican colony until 1962, when they assumed the status of a separate Crown colony upon Jamaica's independence. The governor of The Bahamas oversaw affairs from 1965 to 1973. With Bahamian independence, the islands received a separate governor in 1973. Although independence was agreed upon for 1982, the policy was reversed and the islands remain a British overseas territory. Grand Turk island suffered extensive damage from Hurricane Maria on 22 September 2017 resulting in loss of power and communications as well as damage to housing and businesses.

## GEOGRAPHY :: TURKS AND CAICOS ISLANDS

### LOCATION:
two island groups in the North Atlantic Ocean, southeast of The Bahamas, north of Haiti

### GEOGRAPHIC COORDINATES:
21 45 N, 71 35 W

### MAP REFERENCES:
Central America and the Caribbean

### AREA:
total: 948 sq km

land: 948 sq km

water: 0 sq km

country comparison to the world: 186

### AREA - COMPARATIVE:
2.5 times the size of Washington, DC

### LAND BOUNDARIES:
0 km

### COASTLINE:
389 km

### MARITIME CLAIMS:
territorial sea: 12 nm

exclusive fishing zone: 200 nm

### CLIMATE:
tropical; marine; moderated by trade winds; sunny and relatively dry

### TERRAIN:
low, flat limestone; extensive marshes and mangrove swamps

### ELEVATION:
0 m lowest point: Caribbean Sea

48 highest point: Blue Hill on Providenciales and Flamingo Hill on East Caicos

### NATURAL RESOURCES:
spiny lobster, conch

### LAND USE:
agricultural land: 1.1% (2011 est.)

arable land: 1.1% (2011 est.) / permanent crops: 0% (2011 est.) / permanent pasture: 0% (2011 est.)

forest: 36.2% (2011 est.)

other: 62.7% (2011 est.)

### IRRIGATED LAND:
0 sq km (2012)

### POPULATION DISTRIBUTION:
eight of the thirty islands are inhabited; the island of Providenciales is the most populated, but the most densely populated is Grand Turk

### NATURAL HAZARDS:
frequent hurricanes

### ENVIRONMENT - CURRENT ISSUES:
limited natural freshwater resources, private cisterns collect rainwater

### GEOGRAPHY - NOTE:
include eight large islands and numerous smaller cays, islets, and reefs; only two of the Caicos Islands and six of the Turks group are inhabited

## PEOPLE AND SOCIETY :: TURKS AND CAICOS ISLANDS

### POPULATION:
53,701 (July 2018 est.)

country comparison to the world: 207

### NATIONALITY:
noun: none

adjective: none

### ETHNIC GROUPS:
black 87.6%, white 7.9%, mixed 2.5%, East Indian 1.3%, other 0.7% (2006 est.)

### LANGUAGES:
English (official)

### RELIGIONS:
Protestant 72.8% (Baptist 35.8%, Church of God 11.7%, Anglican 10%, Methodist 9.3%, Seventh-Day Adventist 6%), Roman Catholic 11.4%, Jehovah's Witnesses 1.8%, other 14% (2006 est.)

### AGE STRUCTURE:
0-14 years: 21.62% (male 5,916 /female 5,694)

15-24 years: 13.7% (male 3,657 /female 3,698)

**25-54 years:** 52.97% (male 14,316 /female 14,128)

**55-64 years:** 6.96% (male 1,988 /female 1,748)

**65 years and over:** 4.76% (male 1,181 /female 1,375) (2018 est.)

### MEDIAN AGE:
**total:** 33.8 years

**male:** 34.1 years

**female:** 33.5 years (2018 est.)

**country comparison to the world:** 91

### POPULATION GROWTH RATE:
2.09% (2018 est.)

**country comparison to the world:** 44

### BIRTH RATE:
14.9 births/1,000 population (2018 est.)

**country comparison to the world:** 127

### DEATH RATE:
3.3 deaths/1,000 population (2018 est.)

**country comparison to the world:** 221

### NET MIGRATION RATE:
9.5 migrant(s)/1,000 population (2017 est.)

**country comparison to the world:** 10

### POPULATION DISTRIBUTION:
eight of the thirty islands are inhabited; the island of Providenciales is the most populated, but the most densely populated is Grand Turk

### URBANIZATION:
**urban population:** 93.1% of total population (2018)

**rate of urbanization:** 1.77% annual rate of change (2015-20 est.)

### MAJOR URBAN AREAS - POPULATION:
5,000 GRAND TURK (capital) (2018)

### SEX RATIO:
**at birth:** 1.05 male(s)/female (2017 est.)

**0-14 years:** 1.04 male(s)/female (2017 est.)

**15-24 years:** 0.97 male(s)/female (2017 est.)

**25-54 years:** 1.02 male(s)/female (2017 est.)

**55-64 years:** 1.18 male(s)/female (2017 est.)

**65 years and over:** 0.8 male(s)/female (2017 est.)

**total population:** 1.02 male(s)/female (2017 est.)

### INFANT MORTALITY RATE:
**total:** 9.8 deaths/1,000 live births (2018 est.)

**male:** 12.2 deaths/1,000 live births (2018 est.)

**female:** 7.3 deaths/1,000 live births (2018 est.)

**country comparison to the world:** 135

### LIFE EXPECTANCY AT BIRTH:
**total population:** 80.1 years (2018 est.)

**male:** 77.3 years (2018 est.)

**female:** 83 years (2018 est.)

**country comparison to the world:** 44

### TOTAL FERTILITY RATE:
1.7 children born/woman (2018 est.)

**country comparison to the world:** 173

### HIV/AIDS - ADULT PREVALENCE RATE:
NA

### HIV/AIDS - PEOPLE LIVING WITH HIV/AIDS:
NA

### HIV/AIDS - DEATHS:
NA

### MAJOR INFECTIOUS DISEASES:
**note:** active local transmission of Zika virus by Aedes species mosquitoes has been identified in this country (as of August 2016); it poses an important risk (a large number of cases possible) among US citizens if bitten by an infective mosquito; other less common ways to get Zika are through sex, via blood transfusion, or during pregnancy, in which the pregnant woman passes Zika virus to her fetus

### EDUCATION EXPENDITURES:
3.3% of GDP (2015)

**country comparison to the world:** 137

### PEOPLE - NOTE:
destination and transit point for illegal Haitian immigrants bound for the Bahamas and the US

## GOVERNMENT :: TURKS AND CAICOS ISLANDS

### COUNTRY NAME:
**conventional long form:** none

**conventional short form:** Turks and Caicos Islands

**abbreviation:** TCI

**etymology:** the Turks Islands are named after the Turk's cap cactus (native to the islands and appearing on the flag and coat of arms), while the Caicos Islands derive from the native term "caya hico" meaning "string of islands"

### DEPENDENCY STATUS:
overseas territory of the UK

### GOVERNMENT TYPE:
parliamentary democracy (House of Assembly); self-governing overseas territory of the UK

### CAPITAL:
**name:** Grand Turk (Cockburn Town)

**geographic coordinates:** 21 28 N, 71 08 W

**time difference:** UTC-5 (same time as Washington, DC, during Standard Time)

### ADMINISTRATIVE DIVISIONS:
none (overseas territory of the UK)

### INDEPENDENCE:
none (overseas territory of the UK)

### NATIONAL HOLIDAY:
Birthday of Queen ELIZABETH II, usually celebrated the Monday after the second Saturday in June

### CONSTITUTION:
several previous; latest signed 7 August 2012, effective 15 October 2012 (The Turks and Caicos Constitution Order 2011) (2018)

### LEGAL SYSTEM:
mixed legal system of English common law and civil law

### CITIZENSHIP:
see United Kingdom

### SUFFRAGE:
18 years of age; universal

### EXECUTIVE BRANCH:
**chief of state:** Queen ELIZABETH II (since 6 February 1952); represented by Governor John FREEMAN (since 17 October 2016)

**head of government:** Premier Sharlene CARTWRIGHT-ROBINSON (since 20 December 2016); first female Premier of Turks and Caicos

**cabinet:** Cabinet appointed by the governor from among members of the House of Assembly

**elections/appointments:** the monarch is hereditary; governor appointed by the monarch; following legislative elections, the leader of the majority party is appointed premier by the governor

### LEGISLATIVE BRANCH:

description: unicameral House of Assembly (19 seats; 15 members in multi-seat constituencies and a single all-islands constituency directly elected by simple majority vote, 1 member nominated by the premier and appointed by the governor, 1 nominated by the opposition party leader and appointed by the governor, and 2 from the Turks and Caicos Islands Civic Society directly appointed by the governor; members serve 4-year terms)

elections: last held on 15 December 2016 (next to be held in 2020)

election results: percent of vote - NA; seats by party - PDM 10, PNP 5

### JUDICIAL BRANCH:

highest courts: Supreme Court (consists of the chief justice and such number of other judges as determined by the governor); Court of Appeal (consists of the court president and 2 justices); note - appeals beyond the Supreme Court are referred to the Judicial Committee of the Privy Council (in London)

judge selection and term of office: Supreme Court and Appeals Court judges appointed by the governor in accordance with the Judicial Service Commission, a 3-member body of high level judicial officials; Supreme Court judges appointed until mandatory retirement at age 65, but terms can be extended to age 70; Appeals Court judge tenure determined by individual terms of appointment

subordinate courts: magistrates' courts

### POLITICAL PARTIES AND LEADERS:

People's Democratic Movement or PDM [Sharlene CARTWRIGHT-ROBINSON]
Progressive National Party or PNP [Washington MISICK]

### INTERNATIONAL ORGANIZATION PARTICIPATION:

Caricom (associate), CDB, Interpol (subbureau), UPU

### DIPLOMATIC REPRESENTATION IN THE US:

none (overseas territory of the UK)

### DIPLOMATIC REPRESENTATION FROM THE US:

none (overseas territory of the UK)

### FLAG DESCRIPTION:

blue with the flag of the UK in the upper hoist-side quadrant and the colonial shield centered on the outer half of the flag; the shield is yellow and displays a conch shell, a spiny lobster, and Turk's cap cactus - three common elements of the islands' biota

### NATIONAL SYMBOL(S):

conch shell, Turk's cap cactus

### NATIONAL ANTHEM:

name: This Land of Ours

lyrics/music: Conrad HOWELL

note: serves as a local anthem; as a territory of the UK, "God Save the Queen" is the official anthem (see United Kingdom)

# ECONOMY :: TURKS AND CAICOS ISLANDS

### ECONOMY - OVERVIEW:

The Turks and Caicos economy is based on tourism, offshore financial services, and fishing. Most capital goods and food for domestic consumption are imported. The US is the leading source of tourists, accounting for more than three-quarters of the more than 1 million visitors that arrive annually. Three-quarters of the visitors come by ship. Major sources of government revenue also include fees from offshore financial activities and customs receipts.

### GDP (PURCHASING POWER PARITY):

$632 million (2007 est.)

$568.3 million (2006 est.)

country comparison to the world: 210

### GDP (OFFICIAL EXCHANGE RATE):

NA

### GDP - REAL GROWTH RATE:

11.2% (2007 est.)

country comparison to the world: 4

### GDP - PER CAPITA (PPP):

$29,100 (2007 est.)

country comparison to the world: 72

### GDP - COMPOSITION, BY END USE:

household consumption: 49% (2017 est.)

government consumption: 21.5% (2017 est.)

investment in fixed capital: 16.5% (2017 est.)

investment in inventories: -0.1% (2017 est.)

exports of goods and services: 69.5% (2017 est.)

imports of goods and services: -56.4% (2017 est.)

### GDP - COMPOSITION, BY SECTOR OF ORIGIN:

agriculture: 0.5% (2017 est.)

industry: 8.9% (2017 est.)

services: 90.6% (2017 est.)

### AGRICULTURE - PRODUCTS:

corn, beans, cassava (manioc, tapioca), citrus fruits; fish

### INDUSTRIES:

tourism, offshore financial services

### INDUSTRIAL PRODUCTION GROWTH RATE:

3% (2017 est.)

country comparison to the world: 106

### LABOR FORCE:

4,848 (1990 est.)

country comparison to the world: 220

### LABOR FORCE - BY OCCUPATION:

note: about 33% in government and 20% in agriculture and fishing; significant numbers in tourism, financial, and other services

### UNEMPLOYMENT RATE:

10% (1997 est.)

country comparison to the world: 139

### POPULATION BELOW POVERTY LINE:

NA

### HOUSEHOLD INCOME OR CONSUMPTION BY PERCENTAGE SHARE:

lowest 10%: NA

highest 10%: NA

### BUDGET:

revenues: 247.3 million (2017 est.)

expenditures: 224.3 million (2017 est.)

### FISCAL YEAR:

calendar year

### INFLATION RATE (CONSUMER PRICES):

4% (2017 est.)

0.7% (2016 est.)

country comparison to the world: 158

### EXPORTS:

$24.77 million (2008 est.)

country comparison to the world: 208

### EXPORTS - COMMODITIES:

lobster, dried and fresh conch, conch shells

### IMPORTS:

$591.3 million (2008 est.)

country comparison to the world: 196

**IMPORTS - COMMODITIES:**

food and beverages, tobacco, clothing, manufactures, construction materials

**DEBT - EXTERNAL:**

NA

**EXCHANGE RATES:**

the US dollar is used

# ENERGY :: TURKS AND CAICOS ISLANDS

**ELECTRICITY ACCESS:**

population without electricity: 5,143 (2012)

electrification - total population: 91% (2012)

electrification - urban areas: 92% (2012)

electrification - rural areas: 80% (2012)

**ELECTRICITY - PRODUCTION:**

235 million kWh (2016 est.)

country comparison to the world: 188

**ELECTRICITY - CONSUMPTION:**

218.6 million kWh (2016 est.)

country comparison to the world: 191

**ELECTRICITY - EXPORTS:**

0 kWh (2016 est.)

country comparison to the world: 211

**ELECTRICITY - IMPORTS:**

0 kWh (2016 est.)

country comparison to the world: 213

**ELECTRICITY - INSTALLED GENERATING CAPACITY:**

82,000 kW (2016 est.)

country comparison to the world: 183

**ELECTRICITY - FROM FOSSIL FUELS:**

100% of total installed capacity (2016 est.)

country comparison to the world: 21

**ELECTRICITY - FROM NUCLEAR FUELS:**

0% of total installed capacity (2017 est.)

country comparison to the world: 201

**ELECTRICITY - FROM HYDROELECTRIC PLANTS:**

0% of total installed capacity (2017 est.)

country comparison to the world: 208

**ELECTRICITY - FROM OTHER RENEWABLE SOURCES:**

0% of total installed capacity (2017 est.)

country comparison to the world: 211

**CRUDE OIL - PRODUCTION:**

0 bbl/day (2017 est.)

country comparison to the world: 208

**CRUDE OIL - EXPORTS:**

0 bbl/day (2015 est.)

country comparison to the world: 209

**CRUDE OIL - IMPORTS:**

0 bbl/day (2015 est.)

country comparison to the world: 207

**CRUDE OIL - PROVED RESERVES:**

0 bbl (1 January 2018 est.)

country comparison to the world: 207

**REFINED PETROLEUM PRODUCTS - PRODUCTION:**

0 bbl/day (2015 est.)

country comparison to the world: 210

**REFINED PETROLEUM PRODUCTS - CONSUMPTION:**

1,420 bbl/day (2016 est.)

country comparison to the world: 201

**REFINED PETROLEUM PRODUCTS - EXPORTS:**

0 bbl/day (2015 est.)

country comparison to the world: 211

**REFINED PETROLEUM PRODUCTS - IMPORTS:**

1,369 bbl/day (2015 est.)

country comparison to the world: 197

**NATURAL GAS - PRODUCTION:**

0 cu m (2017 est.)

country comparison to the world: 208

**NATURAL GAS - CONSUMPTION:**

0 cu m (2017 est.)

country comparison to the world: 208

**NATURAL GAS - EXPORTS:**

0 cu m (2017 est.)

country comparison to the world: 203

**NATURAL GAS - IMPORTS:**

0 cu m (2017 est.)

country comparison to the world: 204

**NATURAL GAS - PROVED RESERVES:**

0 cu m (1 January 2014 est.)

country comparison to the world: 202

**CARBON DIOXIDE EMISSIONS FROM CONSUMPTION OF ENERGY:**

221,800 Mt (2017 est.)

country comparison to the world: 198

# COMMUNICATIONS :: TURKS AND CAICOS ISLANDS

**TELEPHONE SYSTEM:**

general assessment: fully digital system with international direct dialing (2015)

domestic: full range of services available; GSM wireless service available (2015)

international: country code - 1-649; the Americas Region Caribbean Ring System (ARCOS-1) fiber-optic telecommunications submarine cable provides connectivity to South and Central America, parts of the Caribbean, and the US; satellite earth station - 1 Intelsat (Atlantic Ocean) (2015)

**BROADCAST MEDIA:**

no local terrestrial TV stations, broadcasts from the Bahamas can be received and multi-channel cable and satellite TV services are available; government-run radio network operates alongside private broadcasters with a total of about 15 stations (2007)

**INTERNET COUNTRY CODE:**

.tc

# TRANSPORTATION :: TURKS AND CAICOS ISLANDS

**NATIONAL AIR TRANSPORT SYSTEM:**

number of registered air carriers: 1 (2015)

inventory of registered aircraft operated by air carriers: 16 (2015)

**CIVIL AIRCRAFT REGISTRATION COUNTRY CODE PREFIX:**

VQ-T (2016)

**AIRPORTS:**

8 (2013)

country comparison to the world: 164

**AIRPORTS - WITH PAVED RUNWAYS:**

total: 6 (2013)

2,438 to 3,047 m: 1 (2013)

1,524 to 2,437 m: 3 (2013)

914 to 1,523 m: 1 (2013)

under 914 m: 1 (2013)

**AIRPORTS - WITH UNPAVED RUNWAYS:**

total: 2 (2013)

under 914 m: 2 (2013)

**ROADWAYS:**

total: 121 km (2003)

paved: 24 km (2003)

unpaved: 97 km (2003)

country comparison to the world: 214

**MERCHANT MARINE:**

total: 4 (2017)

by type: general cargo 1, other 3 (2017)

country comparison to the world: 166

**PORTS AND TERMINALS:**

major seaport(s): Cockburn Harbour, Grand Turk, Providenciales

## MILITARY AND SECURITY :: TURKS AND CAICOS ISLANDS

**MILITARY - NOTE:**

defense is the responsibility of the UK

## TRANSNATIONAL ISSUES :: TURKS AND CAICOS ISLANDS

**DISPUTES - INTERNATIONAL:**

have received Haitians fleeing economic and civil disorder

**ILLICIT DRUGS:**

transshipment point for South American narcotics destined for the US and Europe

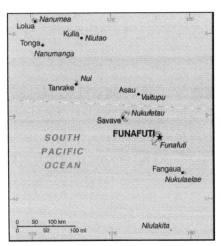

# AUSTRALIA - OCEANIA :: TUVALU

## INTRODUCTION :: TUVALU

### BACKGROUND:
In 1974, ethnic differences within the British colony of the Gilbert and Ellice Islands caused the Polynesians of the Ellice Islands to vote for separation from the Micronesians of the Gilbert Islands. The following year, the Ellice Islands became the separate British colony of Tuvalu. Independence was granted in 1978. In 2000, Tuvalu negotiated a contract leasing its Internet domain name ".tv" for $50 million in royalties over a 12-year period. The agreement was subsequently renegotiated but details were not disclosed.

## GEOGRAPHY :: TUVALU

### LOCATION:
Oceania, island group consisting of nine coral atolls in the South Pacific Ocean, about half way from Hawaii to Australia

### GEOGRAPHIC COORDINATES:
8 00 S, 178 00 E

### MAP REFERENCES:
Oceania

### AREA:
total: 26 sq km

land: 26 sq km

water: 0 sq km

country comparison to the world: 238

### AREA - COMPARATIVE:
0.1 times the size of Washington, DC

### LAND BOUNDARIES:
0 km

### COASTLINE:
24 km

### MARITIME CLAIMS:
territorial sea: 12 nm

exclusive economic zone: 200 nm

contiguous zone: 24 nm

### CLIMATE:
tropical; moderated by easterly trade winds (March to November); westerly gales and heavy rain (November to March)

### TERRAIN:
low-lying and narrow coral atolls

### ELEVATION:
mean elevation: 2 m

elevation extremes: 0 m lowest point: Pacific Ocean

5 highest point: unnamed location

### NATURAL RESOURCES:
fish, coconut (copra)

### LAND USE:
agricultural land: 60% (2011 est.)

arable land: 0% (2011 est.) / permanent crops: 60% (2011 est.) / permanent pasture: 0% (2011 est.)

forest: 33.3% (2011 est.)

other: 6.7% (2011 est.)

### IRRIGATED LAND:
0 sq km (2012)

### POPULATION DISTRIBUTION:
over half of the population resides on the atoll of Funafuti

### NATURAL HAZARDS:
severe tropical storms are usually rare, but in 1997 there were three cyclones; low levels of islands make them sensitive to changes in sea level

### ENVIRONMENT - CURRENT ISSUES:
water needs met by catchment systems; the use of sand as a building material has led to beachhead erosion; deforestation; damage to coral reefs from increasing ocean temperatures and acidification; rising sea levels threaten water table; in 2000, the government appealed to Australia and New Zealand to take in Tuvaluans if rising sea levels should make evacuation necessary

### ENVIRONMENT - INTERNATIONAL AGREEMENTS:
party to: Biodiversity, Climate Change, Climate Change-Kyoto Protocol, Desertification, Law of the Sea, Ozone Layer Protection, Ship Pollution, Whaling

signed, but not ratified: none of the selected agreements

### GEOGRAPHY - NOTE:
one of the smallest and most remote countries on Earth; six of the nine coral atolls - Nanumea, Nui, Vaitupu, Nukufetau, Funafuti, and Nukulaelae - have lagoons open to the ocean; Nanumaya and Niutao have landlocked lagoons; Niulakita does not have a lagoon

## PEOPLE AND SOCIETY :: TUVALU

### POPULATION:
11,147 (July 2018 est.)

country comparison to the world: 222

### NATIONALITY:
noun: Tuvaluan(s)

adjective: Tuvaluan

### ETHNIC GROUPS:
Tuvaluan 86.8%, Tuvaluan/I-Kiribati 5.6%, Tuvaluan/other 6.7%, other 0.9% (2012 est.)

### LANGUAGES:

Tuvaluan (official), English (official), Samoan, Kiribati (on the island of Nui)

**RELIGIONS:**

Protestant 92.4% (Congregational Christian Church of Tuvalu 85.7%, Brethren 3%, Seventh Day Adventist 2.8%, Assemblies of God .9%), Baha'i 2%, Jehovah's Witness 1.3%, Mormon 1%, other 3.1%, none 0.2% (2012 est.)

**AGE STRUCTURE:**

 0-14 years: 29.32% (male 1,675 /female 1,593)

 15-24 years: 18.63% (male 1,078 /female 999)

 25-54 years: 36.91% (male 2,080 /female 2,034)

 55-64 years: 8.86% (male 404 /female 584)

 65 years and over: 6.28% (male 274 /female 426) (2018 est.)

**MEDIAN AGE:**

 total: 26 years

 male: 25 years

 female: 27.2 years (2018 est.)

 country comparison to the world: 152

**POPULATION GROWTH RATE:**

0.86% (2018 est.)

 country comparison to the world: 124

**BIRTH RATE:**

23.7 births/1,000 population (2018 est.)

 country comparison to the world: 55

**DEATH RATE:**

8.4 deaths/1,000 population (2018 est.)

 country comparison to the world: 82

**NET MIGRATION RATE:**

-6.7 migrant(s)/1,000 population (2017 est.)

 country comparison to the world: 202

**POPULATION DISTRIBUTION:**

over half of the population resides on the atoll of Funafuti

**URBANIZATION:**

 urban population: 62.4% of total population (2018)

 rate of urbanization: 2.27% annual rate of change (2015-20 est.)

**MAJOR URBAN AREAS - POPULATION:**

7,000 FUNAFUTI (capital) (2018)

**SEX RATIO:**

 at birth: 1.05 male(s)/female (2017 est.)

 0-14 years: 1.05 male(s)/female (2017 est.)

 15-24 years: 1.1 male(s)/female (2017 est.)

 25-54 years: 0.99 male(s)/female (2017 est.)

 55-64 years: 0.69 male(s)/female (2017 est.)

 65 years and over: 0.69 male(s)/female (2017 est.)

 total population: 0.98 male(s)/female (2017 est.)

**INFANT MORTALITY RATE:**

 total: 28.2 deaths/1,000 live births (2018 est.)

 male: 30.6 deaths/1,000 live births (2018 est.)

 female: 25.7 deaths/1,000 live births (2018 est.)

 country comparison to the world: 66

**LIFE EXPECTANCY AT BIRTH:**

 total population: 67.2 years (2018 est.)

 male: 65 years (2018 est.)

 female: 69.5 years (2018 est.)

 country comparison to the world: 173

**TOTAL FERTILITY RATE:**

2.93 children born/woman (2018 est.)

 country comparison to the world: 56

**HEALTH EXPENDITURES:**

16.5% of GDP (2014)

 country comparison to the world: 3

**PHYSICIANS DENSITY:**

1.22 physicians/1,000 population (2009)

**DRINKING WATER SOURCE:**

 improved:

 urban: 98.3% of population

 rural: 97% of population

 total: 97.7% of population

 unimproved:

 urban: 1.7% of population

 rural: 3% of population

 total: 2.3% of population (2015 est.)

**SANITATION FACILITY ACCESS:**

 improved:

 urban: 86.3% of population (2012 est.)

 rural: 80.2% of population (2012 est.)

 total: 83.3% of population (2012 est.)

 unimproved:

 urban: 13.7% of population (2012 est.)

 rural: 19.8% of population (2012 est.)

 total: 16.7% of population (2012 est.)

**HIV/AIDS - ADULT PREVALENCE RATE:**

NA

**HIV/AIDS - PEOPLE LIVING WITH HIV/AIDS:**

NA

**HIV/AIDS - DEATHS:**

NA

**OBESITY - ADULT PREVALENCE RATE:**

51.6% (2016)

 country comparison to the world: 5

**EDUCATION EXPENDITURES:**

NA

## GOVERNMENT :: TUVALU

**COUNTRY NAME:**

 conventional long form: none

 conventional short form: Tuvalu

 local long form: none

 local short form: Tuvalu

 former: Ellice Islands

 etymology: "tuvalu" means "group of eight" or "eight standing together" referring to the country's eight traditionally inhabited islands

**GOVERNMENT TYPE:**

parliamentary democracy (House of Assembly) under a constitutional monarchy; a Commonwealth realm

**CAPITAL:**

 name: Funafuti; note - the capital is an atoll of some 29 islets; administrative offices are in Vaiaku Village on Fongafale Islet

 geographic coordinates: 8 31 S, 179 13 E

 time difference: UTC+12 (17 hours ahead of Washington, DC, during Standard Time)

**ADMINISTRATIVE DIVISIONS:**

7 island councils and 1 town council*; Funafuti*, Nanumaga, Nanumea, Niutao, Nui, Nukufetau, Nukulaelae, Vaitupu

**INDEPENDENCE:**

1 October 1978 (from the UK)

**NATIONAL HOLIDAY:**

Independence Day, 1 October (1978)

## CONSTITUTION:

**history:** previous 1978 (at independence); latest effective 1 October 1986 (2017)

**amendments:** proposed by the House of Assembly; passage requires at least two-thirds majority vote by the Assembly membership in the final reading; amended 2007, 2010, 2013 (2017)

## LEGAL SYSTEM:

mixed legal system of English common law and local customary law

## INTERNATIONAL LAW ORGANIZATION PARTICIPATION:

has not submitted an ICJ jurisdiction declaration; non-party state to the ICCt

## CITIZENSHIP:

**citizenship by birth:** yes

**citizenship by descent only:** yes; for a child born abroad, at least one parent must be a citizen of Tuvalu

**dual citizenship recognized:** yes

**residency requirement for naturalization:** na

## SUFFRAGE:

18 years of age; universal

## EXECUTIVE BRANCH:

**chief of state:** Queen ELIZABETH II (since 6 February 1952); represented by Governor General Iakoba TAEIA Italeli (since 16 April 2010)

**head of government:** Prime Minister Enele SOPOAGA (since 5 August 2013)

**cabinet:** Cabinet appointed by the governor general on recommendation of the prime minister

**elections/appointments:** the monarchy is hereditary; governor general appointed by the monarch on recommendation of the prime minister; prime minister and deputy prime minister elected by and from members of House of Assembly following parliamentary elections

**election results:** Enele SOPOAGA elected prime minister by House of Assembly; House of Assembly vote count on 4 August 2013 - 8 to 5; note - Willie TELAVI removed as prime minister by the governor general on 1 August 2013

## LEGISLATIVE BRANCH:

**description:** unicameral House of Assembly or Fale I Fono (15 seats; members directly elected in single- and multi-seat constituencies by simple majority vote to serve 4-year terms)

**elections:** last held on 31 March 2015 (next to be held in 2019)

**election results:** percent of vote - NA; seats - independent 15 (12 members reelected); composition - men 14, women 1, percent of women 6.7%

## JUDICIAL BRANCH:

**highest courts:** Court of Appeal (consists of the chief justice and not less than 3 appeals judges); High Court (consists of the chief justice); appeals beyond the Court of Appeal are heard by the Judicial Committee of the Privy Council (in London)

**judge selection and term of office:** Appeal Court judges appointed by the governor general on the advice of the Cabinet; judges' tenure based on terms of appointment; High Court chief justice appointed by the governor general on the advice of the Cabinet; chief justice appointed for life; other judges appointed by the governor-general on the advice of the Cabinet after consultation with chief justice; tenure of judges set by terms of appointment

**subordinate courts:** magistrates' courts; island courts; land courts

## POLITICAL PARTIES AND LEADERS:

there are no political parties but members of parliament usually align themselves in informal groupings

## INTERNATIONAL ORGANIZATION PARTICIPATION:

ACP, ADB, AOSIS, C, FAO, IBRD, IDA, IFAD, IFRCS (observer), ILO, IMF, IMO, IOC, ITU, OPCW, PIF, Sparteca, SPC, UN, UNCTAD, UNESCO, UNIDO, UPU, WHO, WIPO, WMO

## DIPLOMATIC REPRESENTATION IN THE US:

none; the Tuvalu Permanent Mission to the UN serves as the Embassy; it is headed by Samuelu LALONIU (since 21 July 2017); address: 685 Third Avenue, Suite 1104, New York, NY 10017; telephone: [1](212)490-0534; FAX: [1](212)808-4975

## DIPLOMATIC REPRESENTATION FROM THE US:

the US does not have an embassy in Tuvalu; the US Ambassador to Fiji is accredited to Tuvalu

## FLAG DESCRIPTION:

light blue with the flag of the UK in the upper hoist-side quadrant; the outer half of the flag represents a map of the country with nine yellow, five-pointed stars on a blue field symbolizing the nine atolls in the ocean

## NATIONAL SYMBOL(S):

maneapa (native meeting house); national colors: light blue, yellow

## NATIONAL ANTHEM:

**name:** "Tuvalu mo te Atua" (Tuvalu for the Almighty)

**lyrics/music:** Afaese MANOA

**note:** adopted 1978; the anthem's name is also the nation's motto

# ECONOMY :: TUVALU

## ECONOMY - OVERVIEW:

Tuvalu consists of a densely populated, scattered group of nine coral atolls with poor soil. Only eight of the atolls are inhabited. It is one of the smallest countries in the world, with its highest point at 4.6 meters above sea level. The country is isolated, almost entirely dependent on imports, particularly of food and fuel, and vulnerable to climate change and rising sea levels, which pose significant challenges to development.

The public sector dominates economic activity. Tuvalu has few natural resources, except for its fisheries. Earnings from fish exports and fishing licenses for Tuvalu's territorial waters are a significant source of government revenue. In 2013, revenue from fishing licenses doubled and totaled more than 45% of GDP.

Official aid from foreign development partners has also increased. Tuvalu has substantial assets abroad. The Tuvalu Trust Fund, an international trust fund established in 1987 by development partners, has grown to $104 million (A$141 million) in 2014 and is an important cushion for meeting shortfalls in the government's budget. While remittances are another substantial source of income, the value of remittances has declined since the 2008-09 global financial crisis, but has stabilized at nearly $4 million per year. The financial impact of climate change and the cost of climate related adaptation projects is one of many concerns for the nation.

## GDP (PURCHASING POWER PARITY):

$42 million (2017 est.)

$40.68 million (2016 est.)

$39.48 million (2015 est.)

note: data are in 2017 dollars

country comparison to the world: 226

**GDP (OFFICIAL EXCHANGE RATE):**

$40 million (2017 est.) (2017 est.)

**GDP - REAL GROWTH RATE:**

3.2% (2017 est.)

3% (2016 est.)

9.1% (2015 est.)

country comparison to the world: 107

**GDP - PER CAPITA (PPP):**

$3,800 (2017 est.)

$3,700 (2016 est.)

$3,600 (2015 est.)

note: data are in 2017 dollars

country comparison to the world: 180

**GDP - COMPOSITION, BY END USE:**

government consumption: 87% (2016 est.)

investment in fixed capital: 24.3% (2016 est.)

exports of goods and services: 43.7% (2016 est.)

imports of goods and services: -66.1% (2016 est.)

**GDP - COMPOSITION, BY SECTOR OF ORIGIN:**

agriculture: 24.5% (2012 est.)

industry: 5.6% (2012 est.)

services: 70% (2012 est.)

**AGRICULTURE - PRODUCTS:**

coconuts; fish

**INDUSTRIES:**

fishing

**INDUSTRIAL PRODUCTION GROWTH RATE:**

-26.1% (2012 est.)

country comparison to the world: 202

**LABOR FORCE:**

3,615 (2004 est.)

country comparison to the world: 225

**LABOR FORCE - BY OCCUPATION:**

note: most people make a living through exploitation of the sea, reefs, and atolls - and through overseas remittances (mostly from workers in the phosphate industry and sailors)

**UNEMPLOYMENT RATE:**

NA

**POPULATION BELOW POVERTY LINE:**

26.3% (2010 est.)

**HOUSEHOLD INCOME OR CONSUMPTION BY PERCENTAGE SHARE:**

lowest 10%: NA

highest 10%: NA

**BUDGET:**

revenues: 42.68 million (2013 est.)

expenditures: 32.46 million (2012 est.)

note: revenue data include Official Development Assistance from Australia

**TAXES AND OTHER REVENUES:**

106.7% (of GDP) (2013 est.)

note: revenue data include Official Development Assistance from Australia

country comparison to the world: 1

**BUDGET SURPLUS (+) OR DEFICIT (-):**

25.6% (of GDP) (2013 est.)

country comparison to the world: 1

**PUBLIC DEBT:**

37% of GDP (2017 est.)

47.2% of GDP (2016 est.)

country comparison to the world: 142

**FISCAL YEAR:**

calendar year

**INFLATION RATE (CONSUMER PRICES):**

4.1% (2017 est.)

3.5% (2016 est.)

country comparison to the world: 162

**COMMERCIAL BANK PRIME LENDING RATE:**

10.6% (31 December 2013 est.)

10.6% (31 December 2012 est.)

country comparison to the world: 79

**MARKET VALUE OF PUBLICLY TRADED SHARES:**

$0 (2014)

country comparison to the world: 124

**CURRENT ACCOUNT BALANCE:**

$2 million (2017 est.)

$8 million (2016 est.)

country comparison to the world: 65

**EXPORTS:**

$600,000 (2010 est.)

$1 million (2004 est.)

country comparison to the world: 220

**EXPORTS - PARTNERS:**

US 18.2%, Bosnia and Herzegovina 17%, Fiji 14.8%, Nigeria 14.2%, Germany 8.2%, South Africa 5.9%, Colombia 5.1% (2017)

**EXPORTS - COMMODITIES:**

copra, fish

**IMPORTS:**

$20.69 billion (2018 est.)

$19.09 billion (2017 est.)

country comparison to the world: 75

**IMPORTS - COMMODITIES:**

food, animals, mineral fuels, machinery, manufactured goods

**IMPORTS - PARTNERS:**

Singapore 33.4%, South Korea 11.5%, Australia 10.8%, NZ 8%, Fiji 7.5%, Chile 6.1%, South Africa 5%, Japan 5% (2017)

**DEBT - EXTERNAL:**

NA

**EXCHANGE RATES:**

Tuvaluan dollars or Australian dollars (AUD) per US dollar -

1.311 (2017 est.)

1.3442 (2016 est.)

## ENERGY :: TUVALU

**ELECTRICITY ACCESS:**

population without electricity: 6,137 (2012)

electrification - total population: 45% (2012)

electrification - urban areas: 57% (2012)

electrification - rural areas: 32% (2012)

**ELECTRICITY - PRODUCTION:**

11.8 million kWh (2011 est.)

country comparison to the world: 214

**ELECTRICITY - EXPORTS:**

0 kWh (2014 est.)

country comparison to the world: 212

**ELECTRICITY - IMPORTS:**

0 kWh (2014 est.)

country comparison to the world: 214

**ELECTRICITY - INSTALLED GENERATING CAPACITY:**

5,100 kW (2011 est.)

country comparison to the world: 212

**ELECTRICITY - FROM FOSSIL FUELS:**

96% of total installed capacity (2015 est.)

country comparison to the world: 43
**ELECTRICITY - FROM NUCLEAR FUELS:**
0% of total installed capacity (2014)
country comparison to the world: 202
**ELECTRICITY - FROM HYDROELECTRIC PLANTS:**
0% of total installed capacity (2014)
country comparison to the world: 209
**CRUDE OIL - PRODUCTION:**
0 bbl/day (2014 est.)
country comparison to the world: 209
**CRUDE OIL - EXPORTS:**
0 bbl/day (2014 est.)
country comparison to the world: 210
**CRUDE OIL - IMPORTS:**
0 bbl/day (2014 est.)
country comparison to the world: 208
**CRUDE OIL - PROVED RESERVES:**
0 bbl (2014 est.)
country comparison to the world: 208
**REFINED PETROLEUM PRODUCTS - PRODUCTION:**
0 bbl/day (2014 est.)
country comparison to the world: 211
**REFINED PETROLEUM PRODUCTS - EXPORTS:**
0 bbl/day
country comparison to the world: 212
**NATURAL GAS - PRODUCTION:**
0 cu m (2014 est.)
country comparison to the world: 209
**NATURAL GAS - CONSUMPTION:**
0 cu m (2014)
country comparison to the world: 209
**NATURAL GAS - EXPORTS:**
0 cu m (2014 est.)
country comparison to the world: 204
**NATURAL GAS - IMPORTS:**
0 cu m (2014 est.)
country comparison to the world: 205

## COMMUNICATIONS :: TUVALU

**TELEPHONES - FIXED LINES:**
total subscriptions: 2,000 (July 2016 est.)
subscriptions per 100 inhabitants: 18 (July 2016 est.)
country comparison to the world: 213
**TELEPHONES - MOBILE CELLULAR:**
total subscriptions: 7,600 (July 2016 est.)
subscriptions per 100 inhabitants: 69 (July 2016 est.)
country comparison to the world: 213
**TELEPHONE SYSTEM:**
general assessment: serves particular needs for internal communications (2015)
domestic: radiotelephone communications between islands (2015)
international: country code - 688; international calls can be made by satellite (2015)
**BROADCAST MEDIA:**
no TV stations; many households use satellite dishes to watch foreign TV stations; 1 government-owned radio station, Radio Tuvalu, includes relays of programming from international broadcasters (2009)
**INTERNET COUNTRY CODE:**
.tv
**INTERNET USERS:**
total: 5,042 (July 2016 est.)
percent of population: 46% (July 2016 est.)
country comparison to the world: 215
**BROADBAND - FIXED SUBSCRIPTIONS:**
total: 1,000 (2017 est.)
subscriptions per 100 inhabitants: 9 (2017 est.)
country comparison to the world: 193

## TRANSPORTATION :: TUVALU

**CIVIL AIRCRAFT REGISTRATION COUNTRY CODE PREFIX:**
T2 (2016)
**AIRPORTS:**
1 (2013)
country comparison to the world: 237
**AIRPORTS - WITH UNPAVED RUNWAYS:**
total: 1 (2013)
1,524 to 2,437 m: 1 (2013)
**ROADWAYS:**
total: 8 km (2011)
paved: 8 km (2011)
country comparison to the world: 223
**MERCHANT MARINE:**
total: 245 (2017)
by type: bulk carrier 18, container ship 2, general cargo 36, oil tanker 27, other 162 (2017)
country comparison to the world: 62
**PORTS AND TERMINALS:**
major seaport(s): Funafuti

## MILITARY AND SECURITY :: TUVALU

**MILITARY BRANCHES:**
no regular military forces; Tuvalu Police Force (2012)

## TRANSNATIONAL ISSUES :: TUVALU

**DISPUTES - INTERNATIONAL:**
none

# AFRICA :: UGANDA

## INTRODUCTION :: UGANDA

### BACKGROUND:

The colonial boundaries created by Britain to delimit Uganda grouped together a wide range of ethnic groups with different political systems and cultures. These differences complicated the establishment of a working political community after independence was achieved in 1962. The dictatorial regime of Idi AMIN (1971-79) was responsible for the deaths of some 300,000 opponents; guerrilla war and human rights abuses under Milton OBOTE (1980-85) claimed at least another 100,000 lives. The rule of Yoweri MUSEVENI since 1986 has brought relative stability and economic growth to Uganda. In December 2017, parliament approved the removal of presidential age limits, thereby making it possible for MUSEVENI to continue standing for office.

## GEOGRAPHY :: UGANDA

### LOCATION:
East-Central Africa, west of Kenya, east of the Democratic Republic of the Congo

### GEOGRAPHIC COORDINATES:
1 00 N, 32 00 E

### MAP REFERENCES:
Africa

### AREA:
total: 241,038 sq km
land: 197,100 sq km
water: 43,938 sq km
country comparison to the world: 82

### AREA - COMPARATIVE:
slightly more than two times the size of Pennsylvania; slightly smaller than Oregon

### LAND BOUNDARIES:
total: 2,729 km
border countries (5): Democratic Republic of the Congo 877 km, Kenya 814 km, Rwanda 172 km, South Sudan 475 km, Tanzania 391 km

### COASTLINE:
0 km (landlocked)

### MARITIME CLAIMS:
none (landlocked)

### CLIMATE:
tropical; generally rainy with two dry seasons (December to February, June to August); semiarid in northeast

### TERRAIN:
mostly plateau with rim of mountains

### ELEVATION:
614 m lowest point: Albert Nile 5110 highest point: Margherita Peak on Mount Stanley

### NATURAL RESOURCES:
copper, cobalt, hydropower, limestone, salt, arable land, gold

### LAND USE:
agricultural land: 71.2% (2011 est.)
arable land: 34.3% (2011 est.) / permanent crops: 11.3% (2011 est.) / permanent pasture: 25.6% (2011 est.)
forest: 14.5% (2011 est.)
other: 14.3% (2011 est.)

### IRRIGATED LAND:
140 sq km (2012)

### POPULATION DISTRIBUTION:
population density is relatively high in comparison to other African nations; most of the population is concentrated in the central and southern parts of the country, particularly along the shores of Lake Victoria and Lake Albert; the northeast is least populated

### NATURAL HAZARDS:
droughts; floods; earthquakes; landslides; hailstorms

### ENVIRONMENT - CURRENT ISSUES:
draining of wetlands for agricultural use; deforestation; overgrazing; soil erosion; water pollution from industrial discharge and water hyacinth infestation in Lake Victoria; widespread poaching

### ENVIRONMENT - INTERNATIONAL AGREEMENTS:
party to: Biodiversity, Climate Change, Climate Change-Kyoto Protocol, Desertification, Endangered Species, Hazardous Wastes, Law of the Sea, Marine Life Conservation, Ozone Layer Protection, Wetlands
signed, but not ratified: Environmental Modification

### GEOGRAPHY - NOTE:
landlocked; fertile, well-watered country with many lakes and rivers

## PEOPLE AND SOCIETY :: UGANDA

### POPULATION:
40,853,749 (July 2018 est.)
note: estimates for this country explicitly take into account the effects of excess mortality due to AIDS; this can result in lower life expectancy, higher infant mortality, higher death

rates, lower population growth rates, and changes in the distribution of population by age and sex than would otherwise be expected

country comparison to the world: 35

**NATIONALITY:**

noun: Ugandan(s)

adjective: Ugandan

**ETHNIC GROUPS:**

Baganda 16.5%, Banyankole 9.6%, Basoga 8.8%, Bakiga 7.1%, Iteso 7%, Langi 6.3%, Bagisu 4.9%, Acholi 4.4%, Lugbara 3.3%, other 32.1% (2014 est.)

**LANGUAGES:**

English (official national language, taught in grade schools, used in courts of law and by most newspapers and some radio broadcasts), Ganda or Luganda (most widely used of the Niger-Congo languages, preferred for native language publications in the capital and may be taught in school), other Niger-Congo languages, Nilo-Saharan languages, Swahili, Arabic

**RELIGIONS:**

Protestant 45.1% (Anglican 32.0%, Pentecostal/Born Again/Evangelical 11.1%, Seventh Day Adventist 1.7%, Baptist .3%), Roman Catholic 39.3%, Muslim 13.7%, other 1.6%, none 0.2% (2014 est.)

**DEMOGRAPHIC PROFILE:**

Uganda has one of the youngest and most rapidly growing populations in the world; its total fertility rate is among the world's highest at 5.8 children per woman. Except in urban areas, actual fertility exceeds women's desired fertility by one or two children, which is indicative of the widespread unmet need for contraception, lack of government support for family planning, and a cultural preference for large families. High numbers of births, short birth intervals, and the early age of childbearing contribute to Uganda's high maternal mortality rate. Gender inequities also make fertility reduction difficult; women on average are less-educated, participate less in paid employment, and often have little say in decisions over childbearing and their own reproductive health. However, even if the birth rate were significantly reduced, Uganda's large pool of women entering reproductive age ensures rapid population growth for decades to come.

Unchecked, population increase will further strain the availability of arable land and natural resources and overwhelm the country's limited means for providing food, employment, education, health care, housing, and basic services. The country's north and northeast lag even further behind developmentally than the rest of the country as a result of long-term conflict (the Ugandan Bush War 1981-1986 and more than 20 years of fighting between the Lord's Resistance Army (LRA) and Ugandan Government forces), ongoing inter-communal violence, and periodic natural disasters.

Uganda has been both a source of refugees and migrants and a host country for refugees. In 1972, then President Idi AMIN, in his drive to return Uganda to Ugandans, expelled the South Asian population that composed a large share of the country's business people and bankers. Since the 1970s, thousands of Ugandans have emigrated, mainly to southern Africa or the West, for security reasons, to escape poverty, to search for jobs, and for access to natural resources. The emigration of Ugandan doctors and nurses due to low wages is a particular concern given the country's shortage of skilled health care workers. Africans escaping conflicts in neighboring states have found refuge in Uganda since the 1950s; the country currently struggles to host tens of thousands from the Democratic Republic of the Congo, South Sudan, and other nearby countries.

**AGE STRUCTURE:**

0-14 years: 47.84% (male 9,753,880 /female 9,789,455)

15-24 years: 21.04% (male 4,250,222 /female 4,347,313)

25-54 years: 26.52% (male 5,422,096 /female 5,412,112)

55-64 years: 2.64% (male 522,637 /female 554,287)

65 years and over: 1.96% (male 351,481 /female 450,266) (2018 est.)

**DEPENDENCY RATIOS:**

total dependency ratio: 101.6 (2015 est.)

youth dependency ratio: 97.2 (2015 est.)

elderly dependency ratio: 4.4 (2015 est.)

potential support ratio: 22.8 (2015 est.)

**MEDIAN AGE:**

total: 15.9 years

male: 15.8 years

female: 16 years (2018 est.)

country comparison to the world: 225

**POPULATION GROWTH RATE:**

3.18% (2018 est.)

country comparison to the world: 6

**BIRTH RATE:**

42.4 births/1,000 population (2018 est.)

country comparison to the world: 5

**DEATH RATE:**

9.9 deaths/1,000 population (2018 est.)

country comparison to the world: 40

**NET MIGRATION RATE:**

-0.7 migrant(s)/1,000 population (2017 est.)

country comparison to the world: 130

**POPULATION DISTRIBUTION:**

population density is relatively high in comparison to other African nations; most of the population is concentrated in the central and southern parts of the country, particularly along the shores of Lake Victoria and Lake Albert; the northeast is least populated

**URBANIZATION:**

urban population: 23.8% of total population (2018)

rate of urbanization: 5.7% annual rate of change (2015-20 est.)

**MAJOR URBAN AREAS - POPULATION:**

2.986 million KAMPALA (capital) (2018)

**SEX RATIO:**

at birth: 1.02 male(s)/female (2017 est.)

0-14 years: 1 male(s)/female (2017 est.)

15-24 years: 0.98 male(s)/female (2017 est.)

25-54 years: 1 male(s)/female (2017 est.)

55-64 years: 0.93 male(s)/female (2017 est.)

65 years and over: 0.79 male(s)/female (2017 est.)

total population: 0.99 male(s)/female (2017 est.)

**MOTHER'S MEAN AGE AT FIRST BIRTH:**

18.9 years (2011 est.)

note: median age at first birth among women 25-29

**MATERNAL MORTALITY RATE:**

343 deaths/100,000 live births (2015 est.)

country comparison to the world: 36

**INFANT MORTALITY RATE:**

total: 54.6 deaths/1,000 live births (2018 est.)

male: 63.3 deaths/1,000 live births (2018 est.)

female: 45.7 deaths/1,000 live births (2018 est.)

country comparison to the world: 22

**LIFE EXPECTANCY AT BIRTH:**

total population: 56.3 years (2018 est.)

male: 54.8 years (2018 est.)

female: 57.8 years (2018 est.)

country comparison to the world: 217

**TOTAL FERTILITY RATE:**

5.62 children born/woman (2018 est.)

country comparison to the world: 7

**CONTRACEPTIVE PREVALENCE RATE:**

38.4% (2017)

**HEALTH EXPENDITURES:**

7.2% of GDP (2014)

country comparison to the world: 78

**PHYSICIANS DENSITY:**

0.09 physicians/1,000 population (2015)

**HOSPITAL BED DENSITY:**

0.5 beds/1,000 population (2010)

**DRINKING WATER SOURCE:**

improved:

urban: 95.5% of population

rural: 75.8% of population

total: 79% of population

unimproved:

urban: 4.5% of population

rural: 24.2% of population

total: 21% of population (2015 est.)

**SANITATION FACILITY ACCESS:**

improved:

urban: 28.5% of population (2015 est.)

rural: 17.3% of population (2015 est.)

total: 19.1% of population (2015 est.)

unimproved:

urban: 71.5% of population (2015 est.)

rural: 82.7% of population (2015 est.)

total: 80.9% of population (2015 est.)

**HIV/AIDS - ADULT PREVALENCE RATE:**

5.9% (2017 est.)

country comparison to the world: 11

**HIV/AIDS - PEOPLE LIVING WITH HIV/AIDS:**

1.3 million (2017 est.)

country comparison to the world: 7

**HIV/AIDS - DEATHS:**

26,000 (2017 est.)

country comparison to the world: 8

**MAJOR INFECTIOUS DISEASES:**

degree of risk: very high (2016)

food or waterborne diseases: bacterial diarrhea, hepatitis A and E, and typhoid fever (2016)

vectorborne diseases: malaria, dengue fever, and trypanosomiasis-Gambiense (African sleeping sickness) (2016)

water contact diseases: schistosomiasis (2016)

animal contact diseases: rabies (2016)

**OBESITY - ADULT PREVALENCE RATE:**

5.3% (2016)

country comparison to the world: 181

**CHILDREN UNDER THE AGE OF 5 YEARS UNDERWEIGHT:**

10.5% (2016)

country comparison to the world: 61

**EDUCATION EXPENDITURES:**

2.3% of GDP (2014)

country comparison to the world: 169

**LITERACY:**

definition: age 15 and over can read and write (2015 est.)

total population: 78.4% (2015 est.)

male: 85.3% (2015 est.)

female: 71.5% (2015 est.)

**SCHOOL LIFE EXPECTANCY (PRIMARY TO TERTIARY EDUCATION):**

total: 10 years (2011)

male: 10 years (2011)

female: 10 years (2011)

**UNEMPLOYMENT, YOUTH AGES 15-24:**

total: 2.6% (2013 est.)

male: 2% (2013 est.)

female: 3.2% (2013 est.)

country comparison to the world: 166

# GOVERNMENT :: UGANDA

**COUNTRY NAME:**

conventional long form: Republic of Uganda

conventional short form: Uganda

etymology: from the name "Buganda," adopted by the British as the designation for their East African colony in 1894; Buganda had been a powerful East African state during the 18th and 19th centuries

**GOVERNMENT TYPE:**

presidential republic

**CAPITAL:**

name: Kampala

geographic coordinates: 0 19 N, 32 33 E

time difference: UTC+3 (8 hours ahead of Washington, DC, during Standard Time)

**ADMINISTRATIVE DIVISIONS:**

121 districts and 1 capital city*; Abim, Adjumani, Agago, Alebtong, Amolatar, Amudat, Amuria, Amuru, Apac, Arua, Budaka, Bududa, Bugiri, Buhweju, Buikwe, Bukedea, Bukomansimbi, Bukwa, Bulambuli, Buliisa, Bundibugyo, Bunyangabu, Bushenyi, Busia, Butaleja, Butambala, Butebo, Buvuma, Buyende, Dokolo, Gomba, Gulu, Hoima, Ibanda, Iganga, Isingiro, Jinja, Kaabong, Kabale, Kabarole, Kaberamaido, Kagadi, Kakumiro, Kalangala, Kaliro, Kalungu, Kampala*, Kamuli, Kamwenge, Kanungu, Kapchorwa, Kasese, Katakwi, Kayunga, Kibaale, Kiboga, Kibuku, Kiruhura, Kiryandongo, Kisoro, Kitgum, Koboko, Kole, Kotido, Kumi, Kween, Kyankwanzi, Kyegegwa, Kyenjojo, Kyotera, Lamwo, Lira, Luuka, Luwero, Lwengo, Lyantonde, Manafwa, Maracha, Masaka, Masindi, Mayuge, Mbale, Mbarara, Mitooma, Mityana, Moroto, Moyo, Mpigi, Mubende, Mukono, Nakapiripirit, Nakaseke, Nakasongola, Namayingo, Namisindwa, Namutumba, Napak, Nebbi, Ngora, Ntoroko, Ntungamo, Nwoya, Omoro, Otuke, Oyam, Pader, Pakwach, Pallisa, Rakai, Rubanda, Rubirizi, Rukiga, Rukungiri, Sembabule, Serere, Sheema, Sironko, Soroti, Tororo, Wakiso, Yumbe, Zombo

**INDEPENDENCE:**

9 October 1962 (from the UK)

**NATIONAL HOLIDAY:**

Independence Day, 9 October (1962)

## CONSTITUTION:

**history:** several previous; latest adopted 27 September 1995, promulgated 8 October 1995 (2018)

**amendments:** proposed by the National Assembly; passage requires at least two-thirds majority vote of the Assembly membership in the second and third readings; proposals affecting "entrenched clauses" including the sovereignty of the people, supremacy of the constitution, human rights and freedoms, the democratic and multiparty form of government, presidential term of office, independence of the judiciary, and the institutions of traditional or cultural leaders also requires passage by referendum, ratification by at least two-thirds majority vote of district council members in at least two-thirds of Uganda's districts, and assent by the president of the republic; amended many times, last in 2017 (2018)

## LEGAL SYSTEM:

mixed legal system of English common law and customary law

## INTERNATIONAL LAW ORGANIZATION PARTICIPATION:

accepts compulsory ICJ jurisdiction; accepts ICCt jurisdiction

## CITIZENSHIP:

**citizenship by birth:** no

**citizenship by descent only:** at least one parent or grandparent must be a native-born citizen of Uganda

**dual citizenship recognized:** yes

**residency requirement for naturalization:** an aggregate of 20 years and continuously for the last 2 years prior to applying for citizenship

## SUFFRAGE:

18 years of age; universal

## EXECUTIVE BRANCH:

**head of government:** President Yoweri Kaguta MUSEVENI (since seizing power on 26 January 1986); Vice President Edward SSEKANDI (since 24 May 2011); Prime Minister Ruhakana RUGUNDA (since 19 September 2014); First Deputy Prime Minister Moses ALI (since 6 June 2016); Second Deputy Prime Minister Kirunda KIVEJINJA (since 6 June 2016)

**cabinet:** Cabinet appointed by the president from among elected members of the National Assembly or persons who qualify to be elected as members of the National Assembly

**elections/appointments:** president directly elected by absolute majority popular vote in 2 rounds if needed for a 5-year term (no term limits); election last held on 18 February 2016 (next to be held in 2021)

**election results:** Yoweri Kaguta MUSEVENI reelected president in the first round; percent of vote - Yoweri Kaguta MUSEVENI (NRM) 60.6%, Kizza BESIGYE (FDC) 35.6%, other 3.8%

**head of state:** President Yoweri Kaguta MUSEVENI (since seizing power on 26 January 1986); Vice President Edward SSEKANDI (since 24 May 2011); note - the president is both head of state and head of government

## LEGISLATIVE BRANCH:

**description:** unicameral National Assembly or Parliament (445 seats; 290 members directly elected in single-seat constituencies by simple majority vote, 112 for women directly elected in single-seat districts by simple majority vote, and 25 "representatives" reserved for special interest groups - army 10, disabled 5, youth 5, labor 5; up to 18 ex officio members appointed by the president; members serve 5-year terms)

**elections:** last held on 18 February 2016 (next to be held in 2021)

**election results:** percent of vote by party - NA; seats by party - NRM 292, FDC 37, DP 5, UPDF 10, UPC 6, independent 66 (excludes 19 ex-officio members)

## JUDICIAL BRANCH:

**highest courts:** Supreme Court of Uganda (consists of the chief justice and at least 6 justices)

**judge selection and term of office:** justices appointed by the president of the republic in consultation with the Judicial Service Commission (an 8-member independent advisory body) and approved by the National Assembly; justices serve until mandatory retirement at age 70

**subordinate courts:** Court of Appeal (also sits as the Constitutional Court); High Court (includes 12 High Court Circuits and 8 High Court Divisions); Industrial Court; Chief Magistrate Grade One and Grade Two Courts throughout the country; qadhis courts; local council courts; family and children courts

## POLITICAL PARTIES AND LEADERS:

Conservative Party or CP [Ken LUKYAMUZI]
Democratic Party or DP [Norbert MAO]
Forum for Democratic Change or FDC [Patrick Oboi AMURIAT]
Justice Forum or JEEMA [Asuman BASALIRWA]
National Resistance Movement or NRM [Yoweri MUSEVENI]
Uganda People's Congress or UPC [James AKENA]

## INTERNATIONAL ORGANIZATION PARTICIPATION:

ACP, AfDB, AU, C, COMESA, EAC, EADB, FAO, G-77, IAEA, IBRD, ICAO, ICC (national committees), ICCt, IDA, IDB, IFAD, IFC, IFRCS, IGAD, ILO, IMF, IMO, Interpol, IOC, IOM, IPU, ISO (correspondent), ITSO, ITU, ITUC (NGOs), MIGA, NAM, OIC, OPCW, PCA, UN, UNCTAD, UNESCO, UNHCR, UNIDO, UNOCI, UNWTO, UPU, WCO, WFTU (NGOs), WHO, WIPO, WMO, WTO

## DIPLOMATIC REPRESENTATION IN THE US:

**chief of mission:** Ambassador Mull Sebujja KATENDE (since 8 September 2017)

**chancery:** 5911 16th Street NW, Washington, DC 20011

**telephone:** [1] (202) 726-7100 through 7102, 0416

**FAX:** [1] (202) 726-1727

## DIPLOMATIC REPRESENTATION FROM THE US:

**chief of mission:** Ambassador Deborah R. MALAC (since 27 February 2016)

**embassy:** 1577 Ggaba Road, Kampala

**mailing address:** P.O. Box 7007, Kampala

**telephone:** [256] 414-306001

**FAX:** [256] 414-306-009

## FLAG DESCRIPTION:

six equal horizontal bands of black (top), yellow, red, black, yellow, and red; a white disk is superimposed at the center and depicts a grey crowned crane (the national symbol) facing the hoist side; black symbolizes the African people, yellow sunshine and vitality, red African brotherhood; the crane was the military badge of Ugandan soldiers under the UK

## NATIONAL SYMBOL(S):

grey crowned crane; national colors: black, yellow, red

**NATIONAL ANTHEM:**

*name:* Oh Uganda, Land of Beauty!

*lyrics/music:* George Wilberforce KAKOMOA

*note:* adopted 1962

## ECONOMY :: UGANDA

**ECONOMY - OVERVIEW:**

Uganda has substantial natural resources, including fertile soils, regular rainfall, substantial reserves of recoverable oil, and small deposits of copper, gold, and other minerals. Agriculture is one of the most important sectors of the economy, employing 72% of the work force. The country's export market suffered a major slump following the outbreak of conflict in South Sudan, but has recovered lately, largely due to record coffee harvests, which account for 16% of exports, and increasing gold exports, which account for 10% of exports. Uganda has a small industrial sector that is dependent on imported inputs such as refined oil and heavy equipment. Overall, productivity is hampered by a number of supply-side constraints, including insufficient infrastructure, lack of modern technology in agriculture, and corruption.

Uganda's economic growth has slowed since 2016 as government spending and public debt has grown. Uganda's budget is dominated by energy and road infrastructure spending, while Uganda relies on donor support for long-term drivers of growth, including agriculture, health, and education. The largest infrastructure projects are externally financed through concessional loans, but at inflated costs. As a result, debt servicing for these loans is expected to rise.

Oil revenues and taxes are expected to become a larger source of government funding as oil production starts in the next three to 10 years. Over the next three to five years, foreign investors are planning to invest $9 billion in production facilities projects, $4 billion in an export pipeline, as well as in a $2-3 billion refinery to produce petroleum products for the domestic and East African Community markets. Furthermore, the government is looking to build several hundred million dollars' worth of highway projects to the oil region.

Uganda faces many economic challenges. Instability in South Sudan has led to a sharp increase in Sudanese refugees and is disrupting Uganda's main export market. Additional economic risks include: poor economic management, endemic corruption, and the government's failure to invest adequately in the health, education, and economic opportunities for a burgeoning young population. Uganda has one of the lowest electrification rates in Africa - only 22% of Ugandans have access to electricity, dropping to 10% in rural areas.

**GDP (PURCHASING POWER PARITY):**

$89.19 billion (2017 est.)

$85.07 billion (2016 est.)

$83.14 billion (2015 est.)

*note:* data are in 2017 dollars

*country comparison to the world:* 89

**GDP (OFFICIAL EXCHANGE RATE):**

$26.62 billion (2017 est.) (2017 est.)

**GDP - REAL GROWTH RATE:**

4.8% (2017 est.)

2.3% (2016 est.)

5.7% (2015 est.)

*country comparison to the world:* 59

**GDP - PER CAPITA (PPP):**

$2,400 (2017 est.)

$2,300 (2016 est.)

$2,300 (2015 est.)

*note:* data are in 2017 dollars

*country comparison to the world:* 200

**GROSS NATIONAL SAVING:**

20.6% of GDP (2017 est.)

21.5% of GDP (2016 est.)

17.7% of GDP (2015 est.)

*country comparison to the world:* 93

**GDP - COMPOSITION, BY END USE:**

*household consumption:* 74.3% (2017 est.)

*government consumption:* 8% (2017 est.)

*investment in fixed capital:* 23.9% (2017 est.)

*investment in inventories:* 0.3% (2017 est.)

*exports of goods and services:* 18.8% (2017 est.)

*imports of goods and services:* -25.1% (2017 est.)

**GDP - COMPOSITION, BY SECTOR OF ORIGIN:**

*agriculture:* 28.2% (2017 est.)

*industry:* 21.1% (2017 est.)

*services:* 50.7% (2017 est.)

**AGRICULTURE - PRODUCTS:**

coffee, tea, cotton, tobacco, cassava (manioc, tapioca), potatoes, corn, millet, pulses, cut flowers; beef, goat meat, milk, poultry, and fish

**INDUSTRIES:**

sugar processing, brewing, tobacco, cotton textiles; cement, steel production

**INDUSTRIAL PRODUCTION GROWTH RATE:**

4.4% (2017 est.)

*country comparison to the world:* 69

**LABOR FORCE:**

15.84 million (2015 est.)

*country comparison to the world:* 38

**LABOR FORCE - BY OCCUPATION:**

*agriculture:* 71%

*industry:* 7%

*services:* 22% (2013 est.)

**UNEMPLOYMENT RATE:**

9.4% (2014 est.)

*country comparison to the world:* 137

**POPULATION BELOW POVERTY LINE:**

21.4% (2017 est.)

**HOUSEHOLD INCOME OR CONSUMPTION BY PERCENTAGE SHARE:**

*lowest 10%:* 36.1% (2009 est.)

*highest 10%:* 36.1% (2009 est.)

**DISTRIBUTION OF FAMILY INCOME - GINI INDEX:**

39.5 (2013)

45.7 (2002)

*country comparison to the world:* 71

**BUDGET:**

*revenues:* 3.848 billion (2017 est.)

*expenditures:* 4.928 billion (2017 est.)

**TAXES AND OTHER REVENUES:**

14.5% (of GDP) (2017 est.)

*country comparison to the world:* 199

**BUDGET SURPLUS (+) OR DEFICIT (-):**

-4.1% (of GDP) (2017 est.)

*country comparison to the world:* 158

**PUBLIC DEBT:**

40% of GDP (2017 est.)

37.4% of GDP (2016 est.)

country comparison to the world: 127
### FISCAL YEAR:
1 July - 30 June
### INFLATION RATE (CONSUMER PRICES):
5.6% (2017 est.)

5.5% (2016 est.)

country comparison to the world: 181
### CENTRAL BANK DISCOUNT RATE:
9% (February 2018)

9.5% (December 2017)

country comparison to the world: 34
### COMMERCIAL BANK PRIME LENDING RATE:
21.28% (31 December 2017 est.)

23.89% (31 December 2016 est.)

country comparison to the world: 11
### STOCK OF NARROW MONEY:
$2.519 billion (31 December 2017 est.)

$2.167 billion (31 December 2016 est.)

country comparison to the world: 127
### STOCK OF BROAD MONEY:
$2.519 billion (31 December 2017 est.)

$2.167 billion (31 December 2016 est.)

country comparison to the world: 134
### STOCK OF DOMESTIC CREDIT:
$4.297 billion (31 December 2017 est.)

$3.989 billion (31 December 2016 est.)

country comparison to the world: 132
### MARKET VALUE OF PUBLICLY TRADED SHARES:
$7.294 billion (31 December 2012 est.)

$7.727 billion (31 December 2011 est.)

$1.788 billion (31 December 2011 est.)

country comparison to the world: 77
### CURRENT ACCOUNT BALANCE:
-$1.212 billion (2017 est.)

-$707 million (2016 est.)

country comparison to the world: 148
### EXPORTS:
$3.339 billion (2017 est.)

$2.921 billion (2016 est.)

country comparison to the world: 125
### EXPORTS - PARTNERS:
Kenya 17.7%, UAE 16.7%, Democratic Republic of the Congo 6.6%, Rwanda 6.1%, Italy 4.8% (2017)
### EXPORTS - COMMODITIES:
coffee, fish and fish products, tea, cotton, flowers, horticultural products; gold
### IMPORTS:
$5.036 billion (2017 est.)

$4.424 billion (2016 est.)

country comparison to the world: 127
### IMPORTS - COMMODITIES:
capital equipment, vehicles, petroleum, medical supplies; cereals
### IMPORTS - PARTNERS:
China 17.4%, India 13.4%, UAE 12.2%, Kenya 7.9%, Japan 6.4%, Saudi Arabia 6.3%, Indonesia 4.4%, South Africa 4.1% (2017)
### RESERVES OF FOREIGN EXCHANGE AND GOLD:
$3.654 billion (31 December 2017 est.)

$3.034 billion (31 December 2016 est.)

note: excludes gold

country comparison to the world: 101
### DEBT - EXTERNAL:
$10.8 billion (22 March 2018 est.)

$11.54 billion (31 December 2017 est.)

$6.241 billion (31 December 2016 est.)

country comparison to the world: 112
### STOCK OF DIRECT FOREIGN INVESTMENT - AT HOME:
$541 million (2017)

NA

country comparison to the world: 128
### STOCK OF DIRECT FOREIGN INVESTMENT - ABROAD:
NA
### EXCHANGE RATES:
Ugandan shillings (UGX) per US dollar -

3,695 (2017 est.)

3,420.1 (2016 est.)

3,420.1 (2015 est.)

3,234.1 (2014 est.)

2,599.8 (2013 est.)

## ENERGY :: UGANDA

### ELECTRICITY ACCESS:
population without electricity: 32.1 million (2013)

electrification - total population: 22% (2013)

electrification - urban areas: 55% (2013)

electrification - rural areas: 10% (2013)
### ELECTRICITY - PRODUCTION:
3.463 billion kWh (2016 est.)

country comparison to the world: 130
### ELECTRICITY - CONSUMPTION:
3.106 billion kWh (2016 est.)

country comparison to the world: 135
### ELECTRICITY - EXPORTS:
121 million kWh (2015 est.)

country comparison to the world: 81
### ELECTRICITY - IMPORTS:
50 million kWh (2016 est.)

country comparison to the world: 107
### ELECTRICITY - INSTALLED GENERATING CAPACITY:
1.02 million kW (2016 est.)

country comparison to the world: 127
### ELECTRICITY - FROM FOSSIL FUELS:
19% of total installed capacity (2016 est.)

country comparison to the world: 195
### ELECTRICITY - FROM NUCLEAR FUELS:
0% of total installed capacity (2017 est.)

country comparison to the world: 203
### ELECTRICITY - FROM HYDROELECTRIC PLANTS:
68% of total installed capacity (2017 est.)

country comparison to the world: 19
### ELECTRICITY - FROM OTHER RENEWABLE SOURCES:
12% of total installed capacity (2017 est.)

country comparison to the world: 75
### CRUDE OIL - PRODUCTION:
0 bbl/day (2017 est.)

country comparison to the world: 210
### CRUDE OIL - EXPORTS:
0 bbl/day (2015 est.)

country comparison to the world: 211
### CRUDE OIL - IMPORTS:
0 bbl/day (2015 est.)

country comparison to the world: 209
### CRUDE OIL - PROVED RESERVES:
2.5 billion bbl (1 January 2018 est.)

country comparison to the world: 31
### REFINED PETROLEUM PRODUCTS - PRODUCTION:
0 bbl/day (2015 est.)

country comparison to the world: 212
### REFINED PETROLEUM PRODUCTS - CONSUMPTION:
32,000 bbl/day (2016 est.)

country comparison to the world: 119
### REFINED PETROLEUM PRODUCTS - EXPORTS:

0 bbl/day (2015 est.)

country comparison to the world: 213

**REFINED PETROLEUM PRODUCTS - IMPORTS:**

31,490 bbl/day (2015 est.)

country comparison to the world: 99

**NATURAL GAS - PRODUCTION:**

0 cu m (2017 est.)

country comparison to the world: 210

**NATURAL GAS - CONSUMPTION:**

0 cu m (2017 est.)

country comparison to the world: 210

**NATURAL GAS - EXPORTS:**

0 cu m (2017 est.)

country comparison to the world: 205

**NATURAL GAS - IMPORTS:**

0 cu m (2017 est.)

country comparison to the world: 206

**NATURAL GAS - PROVED RESERVES:**

14.16 billion cu m (1 January 2018 est.)

country comparison to the world: 76

**CARBON DIOXIDE EMISSIONS FROM CONSUMPTION OF ENERGY:**

4.703 million Mt (2017 est.)

country comparison to the world: 135

# COMMUNICATIONS :: UGANDA

**TELEPHONES - FIXED LINES:**

total subscriptions: 262,286 (2017 est.)

subscriptions per 100 inhabitants: 1 (2017 est.)

country comparison to the world: 120

**TELEPHONES - MOBILE CELLULAR:**

total subscriptions: 24,948,878 (2017 est.)

subscriptions per 100 inhabitants: 63 (2017 est.)

country comparison to the world: 49

**TELEPHONE SYSTEM:**

general assessment: in recent years, telecommunications infrastructure has developed through private partnerships; private companies have laid over 1,800 km of fiber optics in Uganda since 2015; as of 2018, fixed fiber backbone infrastructure is available in over half of Uganda's districts; mobile phone companies now provide 4G networks across all major cities and national parks, while offering 3G coverage in second-tier cities and most rural areas with road access; between 2016 and 2018, commercial Internet services dropped in price from $300/Mbps to $80/Mbps. (2018) (2018)

domestic: intercity traffic by wire, microwave radio relay, and radiotelephone communication stations, fixed-line and mobile- cellular systems for short-range traffic; mobile-cellular teledensity about 65 per 100 persons (September 2017) (2018)

international: country code - 256; satellite earth stations - 1 Intelsat (Atlantic Ocean) and 1 Inmarsat; analog and digital links to Kenya and Tanzania (2018)

**BROADCAST MEDIA:**

public broadcaster, Uganda Broadcasting Corporation (UBC), operates radio and TV networks; 31 Free-To-Air (FTA) TV stations, 2 digital terrestrial TV stations, 3 cable TV stations, and 5 digital satellite TV stations; 258 operational FM stations (2017)

**INTERNET COUNTRY CODE:**

.ug

**INTERNET USERS:**

total: 18,148,923 (September 2017)

percent of population: 45.9% (September 2017)

country comparison to the world: 36

**BROADBAND - FIXED SUBSCRIPTIONS:**

total: 145,765 (2017 est.)

subscriptions per 100 inhabitants: less than 1 (2017 est.)

country comparison to the world: 113

# TRANSPORTATION :: UGANDA

**NATIONAL AIR TRANSPORT SYSTEM:**

number of registered air carriers: 1 (2015)

inventory of registered aircraft operated by air carriers: 1 (2015)

annual passenger traffic on registered air carriers: 41,812 (2015)

annual freight traffic on registered air carriers: 23,472 mt-km (2015)

**CIVIL AIRCRAFT REGISTRATION COUNTRY CODE PREFIX:**

5X (2016)

**AIRPORTS:**

47 (2013)

country comparison to the world: 94

**AIRPORTS - WITH PAVED RUNWAYS:**

total: 5 (2013)

over 3,047 m: 3 (2013)

1,524 to 2,437 m: 1 (2013)

914 to 1,523 m: 1 (2013)

**AIRPORTS - WITH UNPAVED RUNWAYS:**

total: 42 (2013)

over 3,047 m: 1 (2013)

1,524 to 2,437 m: 8 (2013)

914 to 1,523 m: 26 (2013)

under 914 m: 7 (2013)

**RAILWAYS:**

total: 1,244 km (2014)

narrow gauge: 1,244 km 1.000-m gauge (2014)

country comparison to the world: 85

**ROADWAYS:**

total: 20,544 km (excludes local roads) (2017)

paved: 4,257 km (2017)

unpaved: 16,287 km (2017)

country comparison to the world: 108

**WATERWAYS:**

(there are no long navigable stretches of river in Uganda; parts of the Albert Nile that flow out of Lake Albert in the northwestern part of the country are navigable; several lakes including Lake Victoria and Lake Kyoga have substantial traffic; Lake Albert is navigable along a 200-km stretch from its northern tip to its southern shores) (2011)

**MERCHANT MARINE:**

total: 1 (2017)

by type: bulk carrier 1 (2017)

country comparison to the world: 175

**PORTS AND TERMINALS:**

lake port(s): Entebbe, Jinja, Port Bell (Lake Victoria)

# MILITARY AND SECURITY :: UGANDA

**MILITARY EXPENDITURES:**

1.57% of GDP (2016)

1.6% of GDP (2015)

1.71% of GDP (2014)

1.74% of GDP (2013)

1.79% of GDP (2012)

country comparison to the world: 72

## MILITARY BRANCHES:

Uganda People's Defense Force (UPDF): Land Forces (includes Marine Unit), Uganda Air Force (2013)

## MILITARY SERVICE AGE AND OBLIGATION:

18-26 years of age for voluntary military duty; 18-30 years of age for professionals; no conscription; 9-year service obligation; the government has stated that while recruitment under 18 years of age could occur with proper consent, "no person under the apparent age of 18 years shall be enrolled in the armed forces"; Ugandan citizenship and secondary education required (2012)

# TERRORISM :: UGANDA

## TERRORIST GROUPS - FOREIGN BASED:

al-Shabaab:
aim(s): punish Ugandan Government for participating in African Union military operations against al-Shabaab; compel Uganda to withdraw forces from Somalia
area(s) of operation: aspires to renew attacks in Kampala; no permanent presence (April 2018)

# TRANSNATIONAL ISSUES :: UGANDA

## DISPUTES - INTERNATIONAL:

Uganda is subject to armed fighting among hostile ethnic groups, rebels, armed gangs, militias, and various government forces that extend across its bordersUgandan refugees as well as members of the Lord's Resistance Army (LRA) seek shelter in southern Sudan and the Democratic Republic of the Congo's Garamba National ParkLRA forces have also attacked Kenyan villages across the border

## REFUGEES AND INTERNALLY DISPLACED PERSONS:

refugees (country of origin): 785,114 (South Sudan) (refugees and asylum seekers), 299,850 (Democratic Republic of the Congo) (refugees and asylum seekers), 33,657 (Burundi) (refugee and asylum seekers), 22,064 (Somalia) (refugees and asylum seekers), 14,313 (Rwanda) (refugees and asylum seekers), 8,854 (Eritrea) (2018)

IDPs: 24,000 (displaced in northern Uganda because of fighting between government forces and the Lord's Resistance Army; as of 2011, most of the 1.8 million people displaced to IDP camps at the height of the conflict had returned home or resettled, but many had not found durable solutions; intercommunal violence and cattle raids) (2017)

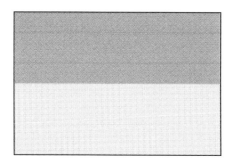

# EUROPE :: UKRAINE

## INTRODUCTION :: UKRAINE

**BACKGROUND:**

Ukraine was the center of the first eastern Slavic state, Kyivan Rus, which during the 10th and 11th centuries was the largest and most powerful state in Europe. Weakened by internecine quarrels and Mongol invasions, Kyivan Rus was incorporated into the Grand Duchy of Lithuania and eventually into the Polish-Lithuanian Commonwealth. The cultural and religious legacy of Kyivan Rus laid the foundation for Ukrainian nationalism through subsequent centuries. A new Ukrainian state, the Cossack Hetmanate, was established during the mid-17th century after an uprising against the Poles. Despite continuous Muscovite pressure, the Hetmanate managed to remain autonomous for well over 100 years. During the latter part of the 18th century, most Ukrainian ethnographic territory was absorbed by the Russian Empire. Following the collapse of czarist Russia in 1917, Ukraine achieved a short-lived period of independence (1917-20), but was reconquered and endured a brutal Soviet rule that engineered two forced famines (1921-22 and 1932-33) in which over 8 million died. In World War II, German and Soviet armies were responsible for 7 to 8 million more deaths. Although Ukraine achieved independence in 1991 with the dissolution of the USSR, democracy and prosperity remained elusive as the legacy of state control and endemic corruption stalled efforts at economic reform, privatization, and civil liberties.

A peaceful mass protest referred to as the "Orange Revolution" in the closing months of 2004 forced the authorities to overturn a rigged presidential election and to allow a new internationally monitored vote that swept into power a reformist slate under Viktor YUSHCHENKO. Subsequent internal squabbles in the YUSHCHENKO camp allowed his rival Viktor YANUKOVYCH to stage a comeback in parliamentary (Rada) elections, become prime minister in August 2006, and be elected president in February 2010. In October 2012, Ukraine held Rada elections, widely criticized by Western observers as flawed due to use of government resources to favor ruling party candidates, interference with media access, and harassment of opposition candidates. President YANUKOVYCH's backtracking on a trade and cooperation agreement with the EU in November 2013 - in favor of closer economic ties with Russia - and subsequent use of force against students, civil society activists, and other civilians in favor of the agreement led to a three-month protest occupation of Kyiv's central square. The government's use of violence to break up the protest camp in February 2014 led to all out pitched battles, scores of deaths, international condemnation, and the president's abrupt departure for Russia. New elections in the spring allowed pro-West president Petro POROSHENKO to assume office on 7 June 2014.

Shortly after YANUKOVYCH's departure in late February 2014, Russian President PUTIN ordered the invasion of Ukraine's Crimean Peninsula claiming the action was to protect ethnic Russians living there. Two weeks later, a "referendum" was held regarding the integration of Crimea into the Russian Federation. The "referendum" was condemned as illegitimate by the Ukrainian Government, the EU, the US, and the UN General Assembly (UNGA). In response to Russia's purported annexation of Crimea, 100 members of the UN passed UNGA resolution 68/262, rejecting the "referendum" as baseless and invalid and confirming the sovereignty, political independence, unity, and territorial integrity of Ukraine. Russia also continues to supply proxies in two of Ukraine's eastern provinces with manpower, funding, and materiel resulting in an armed conflict with the Ukrainian Government. Representatives from Ukraine, Russia, and the unrecognized Russia proxy republics signed the Minsk Protocol and Memorandum in September 2014 to end the conflict. However, this agreement failed to stop the fighting. In a renewed attempt to alleviate ongoing clashes, leaders of Ukraine, Russia, France, and Germany negotiated a follow-on package of measures in February 2015 to implement the Minsk Agreements. Representatives from Ukraine, Russia, and the Organization for Security and Cooperation in Europe also meet regularly to facilitate implementation of the peace deal. More than 34,000 civilians have been killed or wounded in the fighting resulting from Russian aggression in eastern Ukraine.

## GEOGRAPHY :: UKRAINE

**LOCATION:**

Eastern Europe, bordering the Black Sea, between Poland, Romania, and Moldova in the west and Russia in the east

**GEOGRAPHIC COORDINATES:**

49 00 N, 32 00 E

**MAP REFERENCES:**

AsiaEurope

**AREA:**

**total:** 603,550 sq km

**land:** 579,330 sq km

**water:** 24,220 sq km

**note:** approximately 43,133 sq km, or about 7.1% of Ukraine's area, is Russian occupied; the seized area includes all of Crimea and about one-third of both Luhans'k and Donets'k oblasts

**country comparison to the world:** 47

### AREA - COMPARATIVE:
almost four times the size of Georgia; slightly smaller than Texas

### LAND BOUNDARIES:
**total:** 5,618 km

**border countries (7):** Belarus 1111 km, Hungary 128 km, Moldova 1202 km, Poland 535 km, Romania 601 km, Russia 1944 km, Slovakia 97 km

### COASTLINE:
2,782 km

### MARITIME CLAIMS:
**territorial sea:** 12 nm

**exclusive economic zone:** 200 nm

**continental shelf:** 200 m or to the depth of exploitation

### CLIMATE:
temperate continental; Mediterranean only on the southern Crimean coast; precipitation disproportionately distributed, highest in west and north, lesser in east and southeast; winters vary from cool along the Black Sea to cold farther inland; warm summers across the greater part of the country, hot in the south

### TERRAIN:
mostly fertile plains (steppes) and plateaus, with mountains found only in the west (the Carpathians) or in the extreme south of the Crimean Peninsula

### ELEVATION:
**mean elevation:** 175 m

**elevation extremes:** 0 m lowest point: Black Sea

2061 highest point: Hora Hoverla

### NATURAL RESOURCES:
iron ore, coal, manganese, natural gas, oil, salt, sulfur, graphite, titanium, magnesium, kaolin, nickel, mercury, timber, arable land

### LAND USE:
**agricultural land:** 71.2% (2011 est.)

arable land: 56.1% (2011 est.) / permanent crops: 1.5% (2011 est.) / permanent pasture: 13.6% (2011 est.)

**forest:** 16.8% (2011 est.)

**other:** 12% (2011 est.)

### IRRIGATED LAND:
21,670 sq km (2012)

### POPULATION DISTRIBUTION:
densest settlement in the eastern (Donbas) and western regions; noteable concentrations in and around major urban areas of Kyiv, Kharkiv, Donets'k, Dnipropetrovs'k, and Odesa

### NATURAL HAZARDS:
occasional floods; occasional droughts

### ENVIRONMENT - CURRENT ISSUES:
air and water pollution; land degradation; solid waste management; biodiversity loss; deforestation; radiation contamination in the northeast from 1986 accident at Chornobyl' Nuclear Power Plant

### ENVIRONMENT - INTERNATIONAL AGREEMENTS:
**party to:** Air Pollution, Air Pollution-Nitrogen Oxides, Air Pollution-Sulfur 85, Antarctic-Environmental Protocol, Antarctic-Marine Living Resources, Antarctic Treaty, Biodiversity, Climate Change, Climate Change-Kyoto Protocol, Desertification, Endangered Species, Environmental Modification, Hazardous Wastes, Law of the Sea, Marine Dumping, Ozone Layer Protection, Ship Pollution, Wetlands

**signed, but not ratified:** Air Pollution-Persistent Organic Pollutants, Air Pollution-Sulfur 94, Air Pollution-Volatile Organic Compounds

### GEOGRAPHY - NOTE:
strategic position at the crossroads between Europe and Asia; second-largest country in Europe after Russia

## PEOPLE AND SOCIETY :: UKRAINE

### POPULATION:
43,952,299 (July 2018 est.)

**country comparison to the world:** 32

### NATIONALITY:
**noun:** Ukrainian(s)

**adjective:** Ukrainian

### ETHNIC GROUPS:
Ukrainian 77.8%, Russian 17.3%, Belarusian 0.6%, Moldovan 0.5%, Crimean Tatar 0.5%, Bulgarian 0.4%, Hungarian 0.3%, Romanian 0.3%, Polish 0.3%, Jewish 0.2%, other 1.8% (2001 est.)

### LANGUAGES:
Ukrainian (official) 67.5%, Russian (regional language) 29.6%, other (includes small Crimean Tatar-, Moldovan/Romanian-, and Hungarian-speaking minorities) 2.9% (2001 est.)

**note:** in February 2018, the Constitutional Court ruled that 2012 language legislation entitling a language spoken by at least 10% of an oblast's population to be given the status of "regional language" - allowing for its use in courts, schools, and other government institutions - was unconstitutional, thus making the law invalid; Ukrainian remains the country's only official nationwide language

### RELIGIONS:
Orthodox (includes Ukrainian Autocephalous Orthodox (UAOC), Ukrainian Orthodox - Kyiv Patriarchate (UOC-KP), Ukrainian Orthodox - Moscow Patriarchate (UOC-MP)), Ukrainian Greek Catholic, Roman Catholic, Protestant, Muslim, Jewish (2013 est.)

**note:** Ukraine's population is overwhelmingly Christian; the vast majority - up to two-thirds - identify themselves as Orthodox, but many do not specify a particular branch; the UOC-KP and the UOC-MP each represent less than a quarter of the country's population, the Ukrainian Greek Catholic Church accounts for 8-10%, and the UAOC accounts for 1-2%; Muslim and Jewish adherents each compose less than 1% of the total population

### AGE STRUCTURE:
**0-14 years:** 15.95% (male 3,609,386 /female 3,400,349)

**15-24 years:** 9.57% (male 2,156,338 /female 2,047,821)

**25-54 years:** 44.03% (male 9,522,108 /female 9,831,924)

**55-64 years:** 13.96% (male 2,638,173 /female 3,499,718)

**65 years and over:** 16.49% (male 2,433,718 /female 4,812,764) (2018 est.)

### DEPENDENCY RATIOS:
**total dependency ratio:** 44.8 (2015 est.)

**youth dependency ratio:** 21.8 (2015 est.)

**elderly dependency ratio:** 23 (2015 est.)

potential support ratio: 4.3 (2015 est.)

note: data include Crimea

**MEDIAN AGE:**

total: 40.8 years

male: 37.7 years

female: 43.9 years (2018 est.)

country comparison to the world: 47

**POPULATION GROWTH RATE:**

0.04% (2018 est.)

country comparison to the world: 187

**BIRTH RATE:**

10.1 births/1,000 population (2018 est.)

country comparison to the world: 190

**DEATH RATE:**

14.3 deaths/1,000 population (2018 est.)

country comparison to the world: 6

**NET MIGRATION RATE:**

0 migrant(s)/1,000 population (2017 est.)

country comparison to the world: 100

**POPULATION DISTRIBUTION:**

densest settlement in the eastern (Donbas) and western regions; noteable concentrations in and around major urban areas of Kyiv, Kharkiv, Donets'k, Dnipropetrovs'k, and Odesa

**URBANIZATION:**

urban population: 69.4% of total population (2018)

rate of urbanization: -0.33% annual rate of change (2015-20 est.)

**MAJOR URBAN AREAS - POPULATION:**

2.957 million KYIV (capital), 1.436 million Kharkiv, 1.01 million Odesa, 969,000 Dnipropetrovsk, 919,000 Donetsk (2018)

**SEX RATIO:**

at birth: 1.06 male(s)/female (2017 est.)

0-14 years: 1.06 male(s)/female (2017 est.)

15-24 years: 1.05 male(s)/female (2017 est.)

25-54 years: 0.96 male(s)/female (2017 est.)

55-64 years: 0.75 male(s)/female (2017 est.)

65 years and over: 0.5 male(s)/female (2017 est.)

total population: 0.86 male(s)/female (2017 est.)

**MOTHER'S MEAN AGE AT FIRST BIRTH:**

24.9 years (2014 est.)

**MATERNAL MORTALITY RATE:**

24 deaths/100,000 live births (2015 est.)

country comparison to the world: 125

**INFANT MORTALITY RATE:**

total: 7.7 deaths/1,000 live births (2018 est.)

male: 8.6 deaths/1,000 live births (2018 est.)

female: 6.7 deaths/1,000 live births (2018 est.)

country comparison to the world: 157

**LIFE EXPECTANCY AT BIRTH:**

total population: 72.4 years (2018 est.)

male: 67.7 years (2018 est.)

female: 77.4 years (2018 est.)

country comparison to the world: 148

**TOTAL FERTILITY RATE:**

1.55 children born/woman (2018 est.)

country comparison to the world: 190

**CONTRACEPTIVE PREVALENCE RATE:**

65.4% (2012)

**HEALTH EXPENDITURES:**

7.1% of GDP (2014)

country comparison to the world: 80

**PHYSICIANS DENSITY:**

3 physicians/1,000 population (2014)

**HOSPITAL BED DENSITY:**

8.8 beds/1,000 population (2013)

**DRINKING WATER SOURCE:**

improved:

urban: 95.5% of population

rural: 97.8% of population

total: 96.2% of population

unimproved:

urban: 4.5% of population

rural: 2.2% of population

total: 3.8% of population (2015 est.)

**SANITATION FACILITY ACCESS:**

improved:

urban: 97.4% of population (2015 est.)

rural: 92.6% of population (2015 est.)

total: 95.9% of population (2015 est.)

unimproved:

urban: 2.6% of population (2015 est.)

rural: 7.4% of population (2015 est.)

total: 4.1% of population (2015 est.)

**HIV/AIDS - ADULT PREVALENCE RATE:**

0.9% (2017 est.)

country comparison to the world: 49

**HIV/AIDS - PEOPLE LIVING WITH HIV/AIDS:**

240,000 (2017 est.)

country comparison to the world: 24

**HIV/AIDS - DEATHS:**

9,000 (2017 est.)

country comparison to the world: 21

**OBESITY - ADULT PREVALENCE RATE:**

24.1% (2016)

country comparison to the world: 61

**EDUCATION EXPENDITURES:**

5.9% of GDP (2014)

country comparison to the world: 41

**LITERACY:**

definition: age 15 and over can read and write (2015 est.)

total population: 99.8% (2015 est.)

male: 99.8% (2015 est.)

female: 99.7% (2015 est.)

**SCHOOL LIFE EXPECTANCY (PRIMARY TO TERTIARY EDUCATION):**

total: 15 years (2014)

male: 15 years (2014)

female: 16 years (2014)

**UNEMPLOYMENT, YOUTH AGES 15-24:**

total: 23% (2016 est.)

male: 24% (2016 est.)

female: 21.5% (2016 est.)

country comparison to the world: 53

## GOVERNMENT :: UKRAINE

**COUNTRY NAME:**

conventional long form: none

conventional short form: Ukraine

local long form: none

local short form: Ukrayina

former: Ukrainian National Republic, Ukrainian State, Ukrainian Soviet Socialist Republic

etymology: name derives from the Old East Slavic word "ukraina" meaning "borderland or march (militarized border region)" and began to be used extensively in the 19th century; originally Ukrainians referred to themselves as Rusyny (Rusyns, Ruthenians, or Ruthenes), an endonym derived from the medieval Rus state (Kyivan Rus)

## GOVERNMENT TYPE:
semi-presidential republic

## CAPITAL:
name: Kyiv (Kiev)

geographic coordinates: 50 26 N,

time difference: UTC+2 (7 hours ahead of Washington, DC, during Standard Time)

daylight saving time: +1hr, begins last Sunday in March; ends last Sunday in October

note: pronounced KAY-yiv
30 31 E

## ADMINISTRATIVE DIVISIONS:
24 provinces (oblasti, singular - oblast'), 1 autonomous republic* (avtonomna respublika), and 2 municipalities** (mista, singular - misto) with oblast status; Cherkasy, Chernihiv, Chernivtsi, Crimea or Avtonomna Respublika Krym* (Simferopol'), Dnipropetrovs'k (Dnipro), Donets'k, Ivano-Frankivs'k, Kharkiv, Kherson, Khmel'nyts'kyy, Kirovohrad (Kropyvnyts'kyy), Kyiv**, Kyiv, Luhans'k, L'viv, Mykolayiv, Odesa, Poltava, Rivne, Sevastopol'**, Sumy, Ternopil', Vinnytsya, Volyn' (Luts'k), Zakarpattya (Uzhhorod), Zaporizhzhya, Zhytomyr

note: administrative divisions have the same names as their administrative centers (exceptions have the administrative center name following in parentheses); plans include the eventual renaming of Dnipropetrovsk and Kirovohrad oblasts, but because these names are mentioned in the Constitution of Ukraine, the change will require a constitutional amendment

note: the US Government does not recognize Russia's annexation of Ukraine's Autonomous Republic of Crimea and the municipality of Sevastopol, nor their redesignation as the "Republic of Crimea" and the "Federal City of Sevastopol"

## INDEPENDENCE:
24 August 1991 (from the Soviet Union); notable earlier dates: ca. 982 (VOLODYMYR I consolidates Kyivan Rus); 1199 (Principality (later Kingdom) of Ruthenia formed; 1648 (establishment of the Cossack Hetmanate)

## NATIONAL HOLIDAY:
Independence Day, 24 August (1991); note - 22 January 1918, the day Ukraine first declared its independence from Soviet Russia, and the date the short-lived Western and Greater (Eastern) Ukrainian republics united (1919), is now celebrated as Unity Day

## CONSTITUTION:
history: several previous; latest adopted and ratified 28 June 1996 (2018)

amendments: proposed by the president of Ukraine or by at least one-third of the Supreme Council members; adoption requires simple majority vote by the Council and at least two-thirds majority vote in its next regular session; adoption of proposals relating to general constitutional principles, elections, and amendment procedures requires two-thirds majority vote by the Council and approval in a referendum; constitutional articles on personal rights and freedoms, national independence, and territorial integrity cannot be amended; amended 2004, 2010, 2015, latest in 2016 (2018)

## LEGAL SYSTEM:
civil law system; judicial review of legislative acts

## INTERNATIONAL LAW ORGANIZATION PARTICIPATION:
has not submitted an ICJ jurisdiction declaration; non-party state to the ICCt

## CITIZENSHIP:
citizenship by birth: no

citizenship by descent only: at least one parent must be a citizen of Ukraine

dual citizenship recognized: no

residency requirement for naturalization: 5 years

## SUFFRAGE:
18 years of age; universal

## EXECUTIVE BRANCH:
chief of state: President Petro POROSHENKO (since 7 June 2014)

head of government: Prime Minister Volodymyr HROYSMAN (since 14 April 2016); First Deputy Prime Minister Stepan KUBIV (since 14 April 2016)

cabinet: Cabinet of Ministers nominated by the prime minister, approved by the Verkhovna Rada

elections/appointments: president directly elected by absolute majority popular vote in 2 rounds if needed for a 5-year term (eligible for a second term); election last held on 25 May 2014 (next to be held on 31 March 2019); prime minister nominated by the president, confirmed by the Verkhovna Rada

election results: Petro POROSHENKO elected president in the first round; percent of vote - Petro POROSHENKO (independent) 54.5%, Yuliya TYMOSHENKO (Fatherland) 12.9%, Oleh LYASHKO (Radical Party) 8.4%, other 24.2%; Volodymyr HROYSMAN (BPP) elected prime minister; Verkhovna Rada vote - 257-50

note: there is also a National Security and Defense Council or NSDC originally created in 1992 as the National Security Council; the NSDC staff is tasked with developing national security policy on domestic and international matters and advising the president; a presidential administration helps draft presidential edicts and provides policy support to the president

## LEGISLATIVE BRANCH:
description: unicameral Supreme Council or Verkhovna Rada (450 seats; 225 members directly elected in single-seat constituencies by simple majority vote and 225 directly elected in a single nationwide constituency by closed, party-list proportional representation vote; members serve 5-year terms)

elections: last held on 26 October 2014 (next to be held by 27 October 2019)

election results: percent of vote by party/coalition - NF 22.1%, BPP 21.8%, Samopomich 11%, OB 9.4%, Radical 7.4%, Batkivshchyna 5.7%, Svoboda 4.7%, CPU 3.9%, other 14%; seats by party/coalition - BPP 132, NF 82, Samopomich 33, OB 29, Radical 22, Batkivshchyna 19, Svoboda 6, other 4, independent 96, vacant 27; composition - men 374, women 49, percent of women 12%; note - voting not held in Crimea and parts of two Russian-occupied eastern oblasts leaving 27 seats vacant

note: seats by party/coalition as of December 2018 - BPP 135, NF 81, OB 38, Samopomich 25, Vidrodzhennya 24, Radical 21, Batkivshchyna 20, VN 19, independent 60, vacant 27;

composition - men 371, women 52, percent of women 12.3%

## JUDICIAL BRANCH:

**highest courts:** Supreme Court of Ukraine or SCU (consists of 113 judges, with the possibility of up to 200, organized into civil, criminal, commercial, and administrative chambers, and a grand chamber); Constitutional Court (consists of 18 justices)

**judge selection and term of office:** Supreme Court judges recommended by the High Qualification Commission of Judges of Ukraine (a 16-member state body responsible for judicial candidate testing and assessment, and judicial administration), proposed by the Supreme Council of Justice or SCJ (a 21-member independent body of judicial officials and other appointees), and appointed by the president; judges serve until mandatory retirement at age 65; Constitutional Court justices appointed - 6 each by the president, by the SCU, and by the Verkhovna Rada; justices appointed for 9-year nonrenewable terms

**subordinate courts:** Courts of Appeal; district courts; note - specialized courts were abolished as part of Ukraine's judicial reform program

**note:** in 2014, President POROSHENKO initiated a national judicial reform program with the formation of the Judicial Reform Council; it produced a multi-year strategy for judicial reform that the president approved that same year

## POLITICAL PARTIES AND LEADERS:

Batkivshchyna (Fatherland) [Yuliya TYMOSHENKO]
Bloc of Petro Poroshenko – Solidarnist or BPP [Vitaliy KLYCHKO] (formed from the merger of Solidarnist and UDAR)
Hromadyanska Positsiya (Civic Position) [Anatoliy HRYTSENKO]
Narodnyy Front (People's Front) or NF [Arseniy YATSENIUK]
Opposition Bloc or OB [Vadym NOVINSKYY]
Radical Party [Oleh LYASHKO]
Samopomich (Self Reliance) [Andriy SADOVYY]
Svoboda (Freedom) [Oleh TYAHNYBOK]
Ukrainian Association of Patriots or UKROP [Taras BATENKO]
Vidrodzhennya (Revival) [Vitaliy KHOMUTYNNIK]
Volya Narodu (People's Will) or VN [Yaroslav MOSKALENKO] (parliamentary group)
Za Zhyttya (For Life) [Vadym RABYNOVICH]

## INTERNATIONAL ORGANIZATION PARTICIPATION:

Australia Group, BSEC, CBSS (observer), CD, CE, CEI, CICA (observer), CIS (participating member, has not signed the 1993 CIS charter), EAEC (observer), EAPC, EBRD, FAO, GCTU, GUAM, IAEA, IBRD, ICAO, ICC (national committees), ICRM, IDA, IFC, IFRCS, IHO, ILO, IMF, IMO, IMSO, Interpol, IOC, IOM, IPU, ISO, ITU, ITUC (NGOs), LAIA (observer), MIGA, MONUSCO, NAM (observer), NSG, OAS (observer), OIF (observer), OPCW, OSCE, PCA, PFP, SELEC (observer), UN, UNCTAD, UNESCO, UNFICYP, UNIDO, UNISFA, UNMIL, UNMISS, UNOCI, UNWTO, UPU, WCO, WFTU (NGOs), WHO, WIPO, WMO, WTO, ZC

## DIPLOMATIC REPRESENTATION IN THE US:

**chief of mission:** Ambassador Valeriy CHALYY (since 3 August 2015)

**chancery:** 3350 M Street NW, Washington, DC 20007

**telephone:** [1] (202) 349-2920

**FAX:** [1] (202) 333-0817

**consulate(s) general:** Chicago, New York, San Francisco, Seattle

## DIPLOMATIC REPRESENTATION FROM THE US:

**chief of mission:** Ambassador Marie YOVANOVITCH (since 29 August 2016)

**embassy:** 4 Igor Sikorsky Street, 04112 Kyiv

**mailing address:** 5850 Kyiv Place, Washington, DC 20521-5850

**telephone:** [380] (44) 521-5000

**FAX:** [380] (44) 521-5155

## FLAG DESCRIPTION:

two equal horizontal bands of azure (top) and golden yellow represent grain fields under a blue sky

## NATIONAL SYMBOL(S):

tryzub (trident); national colors: blue, yellow

## NATIONAL ANTHEM:

**name:** "Shche ne vmerla Ukraina" (Ukraine Has Not Yet Perished)

**lyrics/music:** Paul CHUBYNSKYI/Mikhail VERBYTSKYI

**note:** music adopted 1991, lyrics adopted 2003; song first performed in 1864 at the Ukraine Theatre in Lviv; the lyrics, originally written in 1862, were revised in 2003

# ECONOMY :: UKRAINE

## ECONOMY - OVERVIEW:

After Russia, the Ukrainian Republic was the most important economic component of the former Soviet Union, producing about four times the output of the next-ranking republic. Its fertile black soil accounted for more than one-fourth of Soviet agricultural output, and its farms provided substantial quantities of meat, milk, grain, and vegetables to other republics. Likewise, its diversified heavy industry supplied unique equipment such as large diameter pipes and vertical drilling apparatus, and raw materials to industrial and mining sites in other regions of the former USSR.

Shortly after independence in August 1991, the Ukrainian Government liberalized most prices and erected a legal framework for privatization, but widespread resistance to reform within the government and the legislature soon stalled reform efforts and led to some backtracking. Output by 1999 had fallen to less than 40% of the 1991 level. Outside institutions - particularly the IMF encouraged Ukraine to quicken the pace and scope of reforms to foster economic growth. Ukrainian Government officials eliminated most tax and customs privileges in a March 2005 budget law, bringing more economic activity out of Ukraine's large shadow economy. From 2000 until mid-2008, Ukraine's economy was buoyant despite political turmoil between the prime minister and president. The economy contracted nearly 15% in 2009, among the worst economic performances in the world. In April 2010, Ukraine negotiated a price discount on Russian gas imports in exchange for extending Russia's lease on its naval base in Crimea.

Ukraine's oligarch-dominated economy grew slowly from 2010 to 2013, but remained behind peers in the region and among Europe's poorest. After former President YANUKOVYCH fled the country during the Revolution of Dignity, Ukraine's economy fell into crisis because of Russia's annexation of Crimea, military conflict in the eastern part of the country, and a trade war with Russia, resulting in a 17% decline in GDP, inflation at nearly 60%, and dwindling foreign currency reserves. The international community began efforts to stabilize the Ukrainian economy, including a March 2014 IMF assistance package of $17.5 billion, of which Ukraine has received four disbursements, most recently in April 2017, bringing the total disbursed as of that date to approximately $8.4 billion. Ukraine has made significant progress on reforms designed to make the country prosperous, democratic, and transparent, including creation of a national anti-corruption agency, overhaul of the banking sector, establishment of a transparent VAT refund system, and increased transparency in government procurement. But more improvements are needed, including fighting corruption, developing capital markets, improving the business environment to attract foreign investment, privatizing state-owned enterprises, and land reform. The fifth tranche of the IMF program, valued at $1.9 billion, was delayed in mid-2017 due to lack of progress on outstanding reforms, including adjustment of gas tariffs to import parity levels and adoption of legislation establishing an independent anti-corruption court.

Russia's occupation of Crimea in March 2014 and ongoing aggression in eastern Ukraine have hurt economic growth. With the loss of a major portion of Ukraine's heavy industry in Donbas and ongoing violence, the economy contracted by 6.6% in 2014 and by 9.8% in 2015, but it returned to low growth in in 2016 and 2017, reaching 2.3% and 2.0%, respectively, as key reforms took hold. Ukraine also redirected trade activity towards the EU following the implementation of a bilateral Deep and Comprehensive Free Trade Agreement, displacing Russia as its largest trading partner. A prohibition on commercial trade with separatist-controlled territories in early 2017 has not impacted Ukraine's key industrial sectors as much as expected, largely because of favorable external conditions. Ukraine returned to international debt markets in September 2017, issuing a $3 billion sovereign bond.

## GDP (PURCHASING POWER PARITY):

$369.6 billion (2017 est.)

$360.5 billion (2016 est.)

$351.9 billion (2015 est.)

note: data are in 2017 dollars

country comparison to the world: 50

## GDP (OFFICIAL EXCHANGE RATE):

$112.1 billion (2017 est.) (2017 est.)

## GDP - REAL GROWTH RATE:

2.5% (2017 est.)

2.4% (2016 est.)

-9.8% (2015 est.)

country comparison to the world: 135

## GDP - PER CAPITA (PPP):

$8,800 (2017 est.)

$8,500 (2016 est.)

$8,300 (2015 est.)

note: data are in 2017 dollars

country comparison to the world: 146

## GROSS NATIONAL SAVING:

18.9% of GDP (2017 est.)

20.2% of GDP (2016 est.)

17.7% of GDP (2015 est.)

country comparison to the world: 105

## GDP - COMPOSITION, BY END USE:

**household consumption:** 66.5% (2017 est.)

**government consumption:** 20.4% (2017 est.)

**investment in fixed capital:** 16% (2017 est.)

**investment in inventories:** 4.7% (2017 est.)

**exports of goods and services:** 47.9% (2017 est.)

**imports of goods and services:** -55.6% (2017 est.)

## GDP - COMPOSITION, BY SECTOR OF ORIGIN:

**agriculture:** 12.2% (2017 est.)

**industry:** 28.6% (2017 est.)

**services:** 60% (2017 est.)

## AGRICULTURE - PRODUCTS:

grain, sugar beets, sunflower seeds, vegetables; beef, milk

## INDUSTRIES:

coal, electric power, ferrous and nonferrous metals, machinery and transport equipment, chemicals, food processing

## INDUSTRIAL PRODUCTION GROWTH RATE:

3.1% (2017 est.)

country comparison to the world: 100

## LABOR FORCE:

17.99 million (2017 est.)

country comparison to the world: 34

## LABOR FORCE - BY OCCUPATION:

**agriculture:** 5.8%

**industry:** 26.5%

**services:** 67.8% (2014)

## UNEMPLOYMENT RATE:

9.2% (2017 est.)

9.3% (2016 est.)

note: officially registered workers; large number of unregistered or underemployed workers

country comparison to the world: 133

## POPULATION BELOW POVERTY LINE:

3.8% (2016 est.)

## HOUSEHOLD INCOME OR CONSUMPTION BY PERCENTAGE SHARE:

**lowest 10%:** 21.6% (2015 est.)

**highest 10%:** 21.6% (2015 est.)

## DISTRIBUTION OF FAMILY INCOME - GINI INDEX:

25.5 (2015)

28.2 (2009)

country comparison to the world: 151

## BUDGET:

**revenues:** 29.82 billion (2017 est.)

**expenditures:** 31.55 billion (2017 est.)

note: this is the planned, consolidated budget

## TAXES AND OTHER REVENUES:

26.6% (of GDP) (2017 est.)

country comparison to the world: 108

## BUDGET SURPLUS (+) OR DEFICIT (-):

-1.5% (of GDP) (2017 est.)

country comparison to the world: 92

## PUBLIC DEBT:

71% of GDP (2017 est.)

81.2% of GDP (2016 est.)

note: the total public debt of $64.5 billion consists of: domestic public debt ($23.8 billion); external public debt ($26.1 billion); and sovereign guarantees ($14.6 billion)

country comparison to the world: 48

## FISCAL YEAR:

calendar year

## INFLATION RATE (CONSUMER PRICES):

14.4% (2017 est.)

13.9% (2016 est.)

note: Excluding the temporarily occupied territories of the Autonomous Republic of Crimea, the city of Sevastopol and part of the anti-terrorist operation zone

country comparison to the world: 210

**CENTRAL BANK DISCOUNT RATE:**

22% (23 December 2015)

7.5% (31 January 2012)

country comparison to the world: 3

**COMMERCIAL BANK PRIME LENDING RATE:**

16.38% (31 December 2017 est.)

19.24% (31 December 2016 est.)

country comparison to the world: 30

**STOCK OF NARROW MONEY:**

$21.92 billion (31 December 2017 est.)

$19.49 billion (31 December 2016 est.)

country comparison to the world: 67

**STOCK OF BROAD MONEY:**

$21.92 billion (31 December 2017 est.)

$19.49 billion (31 December 2016 est.)

country comparison to the world: 68

**STOCK OF DOMESTIC CREDIT:**

$63.63 billion (31 December 2017 est.)

$61.65 billion (31 December 2016 est.)

country comparison to the world: 61

**MARKET VALUE OF PUBLICLY TRADED SHARES:**

$20.71 billion (31 December 2012 est.)

$25.56 billion (31 December 2011 est.)

$39.46 billion (31 December 2010 est.)

country comparison to the world: 62

**CURRENT ACCOUNT BALANCE:**

-$2.088 billion (2017 est.)

-$1.394 billion (2016 est.)

country comparison to the world: 166

**EXPORTS:**

$39.69 billion (2017 est.)

$33.56 billion (2016 est.)

country comparison to the world: 55

**EXPORTS - PARTNERS:**

Russia 9.2%, Poland 6.5%, Turkey 5.6%, India 5.5%, Italy 5.2%, China 4.6%, Germany 4.3% (2017)

**EXPORTS - COMMODITIES:**

ferrous and nonferrous metals, fuel and petroleum products, chemicals, machinery and transport equipment, foodstuffs

**IMPORTS:**

$49.06 billion (2017 est.)

$40.5 billion (2016 est.)

country comparison to the world: 53

**IMPORTS - COMMODITIES:**

energy, machinery and equipment, chemicals

**IMPORTS - PARTNERS:**

Russia 14.5%, China 11.3%, Germany 11.2%, Poland 7%, Belarus 6.7%, US 5.1% (2017)

**RESERVES OF FOREIGN EXCHANGE AND GOLD:**

$18.81 billion (31 December 2017 est.)

$15.54 billion (31 December 2016 est.)

country comparison to the world: 61

**DEBT - EXTERNAL:**

$130 billion (31 December 2017 est.)

$121.1 billion (31 December 2016 est.)

country comparison to the world: 45

**STOCK OF DIRECT FOREIGN INVESTMENT - AT HOME:**

$67.22 billion (31 December 2017 est.)

$64.95 billion (31 December 2016 est.)

country comparison to the world: 54

**STOCK OF DIRECT FOREIGN INVESTMENT - ABROAD:**

$7.59 billion (31 December 2017 est.)

$7.983 billion (31 December 2016 est.)

country comparison to the world: 68

**EXCHANGE RATES:**

hryvnia (UAH) per US dollar -

26.71 (2017 est.)

25.5513 (2016 est.)

25.5513 (2015 est.)

21.8447 (2014 est.)

11.8867 (2013 est.)

## ENERGY :: UKRAINE

**ELECTRICITY ACCESS:**

electrification - total population: 100% (2016)

**ELECTRICITY - PRODUCTION:**

153.6 billion kWh (2016 est.)

country comparison to the world: 26

**ELECTRICITY - CONSUMPTION:**

133.2 billion kWh (2016 est.)

country comparison to the world: 28

**ELECTRICITY - EXPORTS:**

3.591 billion kWh (2015 est.)

country comparison to the world: 39

**ELECTRICITY - IMPORTS:**

77 million kWh (2016 est.)

country comparison to the world: 103

**ELECTRICITY - INSTALLED GENERATING CAPACITY:**

57.28 million kW (2016 est.)

country comparison to the world: 20

**ELECTRICITY - FROM FOSSIL FUELS:**

65% of total installed capacity (2016 est.)

country comparison to the world: 120

**ELECTRICITY - FROM NUCLEAR FUELS:**

23% of total installed capacity (2017 est.)

country comparison to the world: 4

**ELECTRICITY - FROM HYDROELECTRIC PLANTS:**

8% of total installed capacity (2017 est.)

country comparison to the world: 125

**ELECTRICITY - FROM OTHER RENEWABLE SOURCES:**

3% of total installed capacity (2017 est.)

country comparison to the world: 129

**CRUDE OIL - PRODUCTION:**

29,650 bbl/day (2017 est.)

country comparison to the world: 62

**CRUDE OIL - EXPORTS:**

413 bbl/day (2015 est.)

country comparison to the world: 79

**CRUDE OIL - IMPORTS:**

4,720 bbl/day (2015 est.)

country comparison to the world: 76

**CRUDE OIL - PROVED RESERVES:**

395 million bbl (1 January 2018 est.)

country comparison to the world: 49

**REFINED PETROLEUM PRODUCTS - PRODUCTION:**

63,670 bbl/day (2017 est.)

country comparison to the world: 77

**REFINED PETROLEUM PRODUCTS - CONSUMPTION:**

233,000 bbl/day (2016 est.)

country comparison to the world: 53

**REFINED PETROLEUM PRODUCTS - EXPORTS:**

1,828 bbl/day (2015 est.)

country comparison to the world: 105

**REFINED PETROLEUM PRODUCTS - IMPORTS:**

167,000 bbl/day (2015 est.)

country comparison to the world: 37

**NATURAL GAS - PRODUCTION:**

19.73 billion cu m (2017 est.)

country comparison to the world: 31

**NATURAL GAS - CONSUMPTION:**

30.92 billion cu m (2017 est.)

country comparison to the world: 30

**NATURAL GAS - EXPORTS:**

0 cu m (2017 est.)

country comparison to the world: 206

**NATURAL GAS - IMPORTS:**

12.97 billion cu m (2017 est.)

country comparison to the world: 25

**NATURAL GAS - PROVED RESERVES:**

1.104 trillion cu m (1 January 2018 est.)

country comparison to the world: 24

**CARBON DIOXIDE EMISSIONS FROM CONSUMPTION OF ENERGY:**

238.9 million Mt (2017 est.)

country comparison to the world: 28

## COMMUNICATIONS :: UKRAINE

**TELEPHONES - FIXED LINES:**

total subscriptions: 7,186,579 (2017 est.)

subscriptions per 100 inhabitants: 16 (2017 est.)

country comparison to the world: 22

**TELEPHONES - MOBILE CELLULAR:**

total subscriptions: 55,714,733 (2017 est.)

subscriptions per 100 inhabitants: 127 (2017 est.)

country comparison to the world: 27

**TELEPHONE SYSTEM:**

general assessment: Ukraine's telecommunication development plan emphasizes improving domestic trunk lines, international connections, and the mobile-cellular system (2016)

domestic: the country's former sole telephone provider, Ukrtelekom, was successfully privatized 2011 and independent foreign-invested private companies now provide substantial telecommunications services; the mobile-cellular telephone system's expansion has slowed, largely due to saturation of the market that is now about 130 mobile phones per 100 persons (2016)

international: country code - 380; 2 new domestic trunk lines are a part of the fiber-optic Trans-Asia-Europe (TAE) system and 3 Ukrainian links have been installed in the fiber-optic Trans-European Lines (TEL) project that connects 18 countries; additional international service is provided by the Italy-Turkey-Ukraine-Russia (ITUR) fiber-optic submarine cable and by an unknown number of earth stations in the Intelsat, Inmarsat, and Intersputnik satellite systems (2016)

**BROADCAST MEDIA:**

state-controlled nationwide TV broadcast channel (UT1) and a number of privately owned TV networks provide basic TV coverage; multi-channel cable and satellite TV services are available; Russian television broadcasts have a small audience nationwide, but larger audiences in the eastern and southern regions; the radio broadcast market, a mix of independent and state-owned networks, is comprised of some 300 stations (2007)

**INTERNET COUNTRY CODE:**

.ua

**INTERNET USERS:**

total: 23,202,067 (July 2016 est.)

percent of population: 52.5% (July 2016 est.)

country comparison to the world: 30

**BROADBAND - FIXED SUBSCRIPTIONS:**

total: 5,239,743 (2017 est.)

subscriptions per 100 inhabitants: 12 (2017 est.)

country comparison to the world: 27

## TRANSPORTATION :: UKRAINE

**NATIONAL AIR TRANSPORT SYSTEM:**

number of registered air carriers: 17 (2015)

inventory of registered aircraft operated by air carriers: 92 (2015)

annual passenger traffic on registered air carriers: 4,613,224 (2015)

annual freight traffic on registered air carriers: 37,721,565 mt-km (2015)

**CIVIL AIRCRAFT REGISTRATION COUNTRY CODE PREFIX:**

UR (2016)

**AIRPORTS:**

187 (2013)

country comparison to the world: 31

**AIRPORTS - WITH PAVED RUNWAYS:**

total: 108 (2013)

over 3,047 m: 13 (2013)

2,438 to 3,047 m: 42 (2013)

1,524 to 2,437 m: 22 (2013)

914 to 1,523 m: 3 (2013)

under 914 m: 28 (2013)

**AIRPORTS - WITH UNPAVED RUNWAYS:**

total: 79 (2013)

1,524 to 2,437 m: 5 (2013)

914 to 1,523 m: 5 (2013)

under 914 m: 69 (2013)

**HELIPORTS:**

9 (2013)

**PIPELINES:**

36720 km gas, 4514 km oil, 4363 km refined products (2013)

**RAILWAYS:**

total: 21,733 km (2014)

standard gauge: 49 km 1.435-m gauge (49 km electrified) (2014)

broad gauge: 21,684 km 1.524-m gauge (9,250 km electrified) (2014)

country comparison to the world: 12

**ROADWAYS:**

total: 169,694 km (2012)

paved: 166,095 km (includes 17 km of expressways) (2012)

unpaved: 3,599 km (2012)

country comparison to the world: 31

**WATERWAYS:**

1,672 km (most on Dnieper River) (2012)

country comparison to the world: 46

**MERCHANT MARINE:**

total: 419 (2017)

by type: general cargo 91, oil tanker 15, other 313 (2017)

country comparison to the world: 45

**PORTS AND TERMINALS:**

major seaport(s): Feodosiya (Theodosia), Illichivsk, Mariupol', Mykolayiv, Odesa, Yuzhnyy

## MILITARY AND SECURITY :: UKRAINE

**MILITARY EXPENDITURES:**

3.5% of GDP (2017)

3.67% of GDP (2016)

3.97% of GDP (2015)

3.02% of GDP (2014)

2.39% of GDP (2013)

country comparison to the world: 21

**MILITARY BRANCHES:**

Ground Forces, High Mobility Assault Troops, Naval Forces, Air Forces (2017)

## MILITARY SERVICE AGE AND OBLIGATION:

20-27 years of age for compulsory military service; conscript service obligation is 18 months (2015)

# TRANSNATIONAL ISSUES :: UKRAINE

## DISPUTES - INTERNATIONAL:

1997 boundary delimitation treaty with Belarus remains unratified due to unresolved financial claims, stalling demarcation and reducing border securitydelimitation of land boundary with Russia is complete and demarcation began in 2012the dispute over the boundary between Russia and Ukraine through the Kerch Strait and Sea of Azov is suspended due to the occupation of Crimea by RussiaUkraine and Moldova signed an agreement officially delimiting their border in 1999, but the border has not been demarcated due to Moldova's difficulties with the break-away region of TransnistriaMoldova and Ukraine operate joint customs posts to monitor transit of people and commodities through Moldova's Transnistria Region, which remains under the auspices of an Organization for Security and Cooperation in Europe-mandated peacekeeping mission comprised of Moldovan, Transnistrian, Russian, and Ukrainian troopsthe ICJ ruled largely in favor of Romania in its dispute submitted in 2004 over Ukrainian-administered Zmiyinyy/Serpilor (Snake) Island and Black Sea maritime boundary delimitationRomania opposes Ukraine's reopening of a navigation canal from the Danube border through Ukraine to the Black Sea

## REFUGEES AND INTERNALLY DISPLACED PERSONS:

**IDPs:** 1.5 million (Russian-sponsored separatist violence in Crimea and eastern Ukraine) (2018)

**stateless persons:** 35,294 (2017); note - citizens of the former USSR who were permanently resident in Ukraine were granted citizenship upon Ukraine's independence in 1991, but some missed this window of opportunity; people arriving after 1991, Crimean Tatars, ethnic Koreans, people with expired Soviet passports, and people with no documents have difficulty acquiring Ukrainian citizenship; following the fall of the Soviet Union in 1989, thousands of Crimean Tatars and their descendants deported from Ukraine under the STALIN regime returned to their homeland, some being stateless and others holding the citizenship of Uzbekistan or other former Soviet republics; a 1998 bilateral agreement between Ukraine and Uzbekistan simplified the process of renouncing Uzbek citizenship and obtaining Ukrainian citizenship

## TRAFFICKING IN PERSONS:

**current situation:** Ukraine is a source, transit, and destination country for men, women, and children subjected to forced labor and sex trafficking; Ukrainian victims are sex trafficked within Ukraine as well as in Russia, Poland, Iraq, Spain, Turkey, Cyprus, Greece, Seychelles, Portugal, the Czech Republic, Israel, Italy, South Korea, Moldova, China, the United Arab Emirates, Montenegro, UK, Kazakhstan, Tunisia, and other countries; small numbers of foreigners from Moldova, Russia, Vietnam, Uzbekistan, Pakistan, Cameroon, and Azerbaijan were victims of labor trafficking in Ukraine; Ukrainian recruiters most often target Ukrainians from rural areas with limited job prospects using fraud, coercion, and debt bondage

**tier rating:** Tier 2 Watch List – Ukraine does not fully comply with the minimum standards for the elimination of trafficking; however, it is making significant efforts to do so; the government's focus on its security situation constrained its anti-trafficking capabilities; law enforcement efforts to pursue trafficking cases weakened in 2014, continuing a multi-year decline, and no investigations, prosecutions, or convictions of government officials were made, despite reports of official complicity in the sex and labor trafficking of children living in state-run institutions; fewer victims were identified and referred to NGOs, which continued to provide and to fund the majority of victims' services (2015)

## ILLICIT DRUGS:

limited cultivation of cannabis and opium poppy, mostly for CIS consumption; some synthetic drug production for export to the West; limited government eradication program; used as transshipment point for opiates and other illicit drugs from Africa, Latin America, and Turkey to Europe and Russia; Ukraine has improved anti-money-laundering controls, resulting in its removal from the Financial Action Task Force's (FATF's) Noncooperative Countries and Territories List in February 2004; Ukraine's anti-money-laundering regime continues to be monitored by FATF

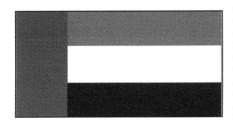

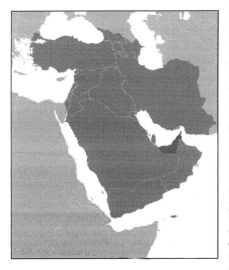

# MIDDLE EAST :: UNITED ARAB EMIRATES

## INTRODUCTION :: UNITED ARAB EMIRATES

### BACKGROUND:

The Trucial States of the Persian Gulf coast granted the UK control of their defense and foreign affairs in 19th century treaties. In 1971, six of these states - Abu Dhabi, 'Ajman, Al Fujayrah, Ash Shariqah, Dubayy, and Umm al Qaywayn - merged to form the United Arab Emirates (UAE). They were joined in 1972 by Ra's al Khaymah. The UAE's per capita GDP is on par with those of leading West European nations. For more than three decades, oil and global finance drove the UAE's economy. However, in 2008-09, the confluence of falling oil prices, collapsing real estate prices, and the international banking crisis hit the UAE especially hard. The UAE essentially avoided the "Arab Spring" unrest seen elsewhere in the Middle East in 2010-11 and in an effort to stem potential unrest, the government announced a multi-year, $1.6-billion infrastructure investment plan for the poorer northern emirates and aggressively pursued advocates of political reform. The UAE in recent years has played a growing role in regional affairs. In addition to donating billions of dollars in economic aid to help stabilize Egypt, the UAE was one of the first countries to join the Defeat-ISIS coalition, and is a key partner in a Saudi-led military campaign in Yemen.

## GEOGRAPHY :: UNITED ARAB EMIRATES

### LOCATION:
Middle East, bordering the Gulf of Oman and the Persian Gulf, between Oman and Saudi Arabia

### GEOGRAPHIC COORDINATES:
24 00 N, 54 00 E

### MAP REFERENCES:
Middle East

### AREA:
total: 83,600 sq km

land: 83,600 sq km

water: 0 sq km

country comparison to the world: 116

### AREA - COMPARATIVE:
slightly larger than South Carolina; slightly smaller than Maine

### LAND BOUNDARIES:
total: 1,066 km

border countries (2): Oman 609 km, Saudi Arabia 457 km

### COASTLINE:
1,318 km

### MARITIME CLAIMS:
territorial sea: 12 nm

exclusive economic zone: 200 nm

contiguous zone: 24 nm

continental shelf: 200 nm or to the edge of the continental margin

### CLIMATE:
desert; cooler in eastern mountains

### TERRAIN:
flat, barren coastal plain merging into rolling sand dunes of vast desert; mountains in east

### ELEVATION:
mean elevation: 149 m

elevation extremes: 0 m lowest point: Persian Gulf

1527 highest point: Jabal Yibir

### NATURAL RESOURCES:
petroleum, natural gas

### LAND USE:
agricultural land: 4.6% (2011 est.)

arable land: 0.5% (2011 est.) / permanent crops: 0.5% (2011 est.) / permanent pasture: 3.6% (2011 est.)

forest: 3.8% (2011 est.)

other: 91.6% (2011 est.)

### IRRIGATED LAND:
923 sq km (2012)

### POPULATION DISTRIBUTION:
population is heavily concentrated to the northeast on the Musandam Peninsula; the three largest emirates - Abu Dhabi, Dubai, and Sharjah - are home to nearly 85% of the population

### NATURAL HAZARDS:
frequent sand and dust storms

### ENVIRONMENT - CURRENT ISSUES:
air pollution; rapid population growth and high energy demand contribute to water scarcity; lack of natural freshwater resources compensated by desalination plants; land degradation and desertification; waste generation, beach pollution from oil spills

### ENVIRONMENT - INTERNATIONAL AGREEMENTS:
party to: Biodiversity, Climate Change, Climate Change-Kyoto Protocol, Desertification, Endangered Species, Hazardous Wastes, Marine Dumping, Ozone Layer Protection

signed, but not ratified: Law of the Sea

### GEOGRAPHY - NOTE:

strategic location along southern approaches to Strait of Hormuz, a vital transit point for world crude oil

# PEOPLE AND SOCIETY :: UNITED ARAB EMIRATES

**POPULATION:**

9,701,315 (July 2017 est.) (July 2018 est.)

note: the UN estimated the country's total population was 9,400,145 as of mid-year 2017; immigrants make up more than 88% of the total population, according to UN data (2017)

country comparison to the world: 93

**NATIONALITY:**

noun: Emirati(s)

adjective: Emirati

**ETHNIC GROUPS:**

Emirati 11.6%, South Asian 59.4% (includes Indian 38.2%, Bangladeshi 9.5%, Pakistani 9.4%, other 2.3%), Egyptian 10.2%, Philippine 6.1%, other 12.8% (2015 est.)

**LANGUAGES:**

Arabic (official), Persian, English, Hindi, Urdu

**RELIGIONS:**

Muslim (official) 76%, Christian 9%, other (primarily Hindu and Buddhist, less than 5% of the population consists of Parsi, Baha'i, Druze, Sikh, Ahmadi, Ismaili, Dawoodi Bohra Muslim, and Jewish) 15% (2005 est.)

note: represents the total population; about 85% of the population consists of noncitizens

**AGE STRUCTURE:**

0-14 years: 14.39% (male 724,904 /female 671,524)

15-24 years: 7.64% (male 408,376 /female 332,986)

25-54 years: 70.45% (male 5,297,201 /female 1,537,300)

55-64 years: 6.05% (male 499,579 /female 87,037)

65 years and over: 1.47% (male 106,739 /female 35,669) (2018 est.)

**DEPENDENCY RATIOS:**

total dependency ratio: 17.4 (2015 est.)

youth dependency ratio: 16.2 (2015 est.)

elderly dependency ratio: 1.2 (2015 est.)

potential support ratio: 83.4 (2015 est.)

**MEDIAN AGE:**

total: 37.2 years

male: 39 years

female: 31.1 years (2018 est.)

country comparison to the world: 69

**POPULATION GROWTH RATE:**

1.44% (2018 est.)

country comparison to the world: 78

**BIRTH RATE:**

9.8 births/1,000 population (2018 est.)

country comparison to the world: 196

**DEATH RATE:**

1.7 deaths/1,000 population (2018 est.)

country comparison to the world: 225

**NET MIGRATION RATE:**

10.5 migrant(s)/1,000 population (2017 est.)

country comparison to the world: 9

**POPULATION DISTRIBUTION:**

population is heavily concentrated to the northeast on the Musandam Peninsula; the three largest emirates - Abu Dhabi, Dubai, and Sharjah - are home to nearly 85% of the population

**URBANIZATION:**

urban population: 86.5% of total population (2018)

rate of urbanization: 1.71% annual rate of change (2015-20 est.)

**MAJOR URBAN AREAS - POPULATION:**

2.785 million Dubai, 1.571 million Sharjah, 1.42 million ABU DHABI (capital) (2018)

**SEX RATIO:**

at birth: 1.05 male(s)/female (2017 est.)

0-14 years: 1.05 male(s)/female (2017 est.)

15-24 years: 1.47 male(s)/female (2017 est.)

25-54 years: 3.2 male(s)/female (2017 est.)

55-64 years: 2.93 male(s)/female (2017 est.)

65 years and over: 1.69 male(s)/female (2017 est.)

total population: 2.18 male(s)/female (2017 est.)

**MATERNAL MORTALITY RATE:**

6 deaths/100,000 live births (2015 est.)

country comparison to the world: 169

**INFANT MORTALITY RATE:**

total: 5.5 deaths/1,000 live births (2018 est.)

male: 6 deaths/1,000 live births (2018 est.)

female: 4.9 deaths/1,000 live births (2018 est.)

country comparison to the world: 171

**LIFE EXPECTANCY AT BIRTH:**

total population: 78.7 years (2018 est.)

male: 77.3 years (2018 est.)

female: 80.1 years (2018 est.)

country comparison to the world: 59

**TOTAL FERTILITY RATE:**

1.73 children born/woman (2018 est.)

country comparison to the world: 166

**HEALTH EXPENDITURES:**

3.6% of GDP (2014)

country comparison to the world: 172

**PHYSICIANS DENSITY:**

1.56 physicians/1,000 population (2014)

**HOSPITAL BED DENSITY:**

1.2 beds/1,000 population (2013)

**DRINKING WATER SOURCE:**

improved:

urban: 99.6% of population (2015 est.)

rural: 100% of population (2015 est.)

total: 99.6% of population (2015 est.)

unimproved:

urban: 0.4% of population (2015 est.)

rural: 0% of population (2015 est.)

total: 0.4% of population (2015 est.)

**SANITATION FACILITY ACCESS:**

improved:

urban: 98% of population (2015 est.)

rural: 95.2% of population (2015 est.)

total: 97.6% of population (2015 est.)

unimproved:

urban: 2% of population (2015 est.)

rural: 4.8% of population (2015 est.)

total: 2.4% of population (2015 est.)

**HIV/AIDS - ADULT PREVALENCE RATE:**

NA

**HIV/AIDS - PEOPLE LIVING WITH HIV/AIDS:**
NA

**HIV/AIDS - DEATHS:**
NA

**OBESITY - ADULT PREVALENCE RATE:**
31.7% (2016)

country comparison to the world: 20

**EDUCATION EXPENDITURES:**
NA

**LITERACY:**

definition: age 15 and over can read and write (2015 est.)

total population: 93.8% (2015 est.)

male: 93.1% (2015 est.)

female: 95.8% (2015 est.)

**UNEMPLOYMENT, YOUTH AGES 15-24:**

total: 12.1% (2008 est.)

male: 7.9% (2008 est.)

female: 21.8% (2008 est.)

country comparison to the world: 108

# GOVERNMENT :: UNITED ARAB EMIRATES

**COUNTRY NAME:**

conventional long form: United Arab Emirates

conventional short form: none

local long form: Al Imarat al Arabiyah al Muttahidah

local short form: none

former: Trucial Oman, Trucial States

abbreviation: UAE

etymology: self-descriptive country name; the name "Arabia" can be traced back many centuries B.C., the ancient Egyptians referred to the region as "Ar Rabi"; "emirates" derives from "amir" the Arabic word for "commander," "lord," or "prince"

**GOVERNMENT TYPE:**
federation of monarchies

**CAPITAL:**

name: Abu Dhabi

geographic coordinates: 24 28 N, 54 22 E

time difference: UTC+4 (9 hours ahead of Washington, DC, during Standard Time)

**ADMINISTRATIVE DIVISIONS:**

7 emirates (imarat, singular - imarah); Abu Zaby (Abu Dhabi), 'Ajman, Al Fujayrah, Ash Shariqah (Sharjah), Dubayy (Dubai), Ra's al Khaymah, Umm al Qaywayn

**INDEPENDENCE:**

2 December 1971 (from the UK)

**NATIONAL HOLIDAY:**

Independence Day (National Day), 2 December (1971)

**CONSTITUTION:**

history: previous 1971 (provisional); latest drafted in 1979, became permanent May 1996 (2016)

amendments: proposed by the Supreme Council and submitted to the Federal National Council; passage requires at least a two-thirds majority vote of Federal National Council members present, and approval by the Supreme Council president; amended 2009 (2016)

**LEGAL SYSTEM:**

mixed legal system of Islamic law and civil law

**INTERNATIONAL LAW ORGANIZATION PARTICIPATION:**

has not submitted an ICJ jurisdiction declaration; non-party state to the ICCt

**CITIZENSHIP:**

citizenship by birth: no

citizenship by descent only: the father must be a citizen of the United Arab Emirates; if the father is unknown, the mother must be a citizen

dual citizenship recognized: no

residency requirement for naturalization: 30 years

**SUFFRAGE:**

limited; note - rulers of the seven emirates each select a proportion of voters for the Federal National Council (FNC) that together account for about 12 percent of Emirati citizens

**EXECUTIVE BRANCH:**

chief of state: President KHALIFA bin Zayid Al-Nuhayyan (since 3 November 2004), ruler of Abu Zaby (Abu Dhabi) (since 4 November 2004); Vice President and Prime Minister MUHAMMAD BIN RASHID Al-Maktum (since 5 January 2006)

head of government: Prime Minister Vice President MUHAMMAD BIN RASHID Al-Maktum (since 5 January 2006); Deputy Prime Ministers SAIF bin Zayid Al-Nuhayyan, MANSUR bin Zayid Al-Nuhayyan (both since 11 May 2009)

cabinet: Council of Ministers announced by the prime minister and approved by the president

elections/appointments: president and vice president indirectly elected by the Federal Supreme Council - composed of the rulers of the 7 emirates - for a 5-year term (no term limits); election last held 3 November 2009 (next election NA); prime minister and deputy prime minister appointed by the president

election results: KHALIFA bin Zayid Al-Nuhayyan reelected president; FSC vote NA

note: there is also a Federal Supreme Council (FSC) composed of the 7 emirate rulers; the FSC is the highest constitutional authority in the UAE; establishes general policies and sanctions federal legislation; meets 4 times a year; Abu Zaby (Abu Dhabi) and Dubayy (Dubai) rulers have effective veto power

**LEGISLATIVE BRANCH:**

description: unicameral Federal National Council (FNC) or Majlis al-Ittihad al-Watani (40 seats; 20 members indirectly elected by an electoral college whose members are selected by each emirate ruler proportional to its FNC membership, and 20 members appointed by the rulers of the 7 constituent states; members serve 4-year terms)

elections: last held on 3 October 2015 (next to be held in 2019); note - the electoral college was expanded from 129,274 electors in the December 2011 election to 224,279 in the October 2015 election; 347 candidates including 78 women ran for 20 contested seats in the 40-member FNC

election results: 19 men and 1 woman were elected; seats by emirate - Abu Dhabi 4, Dubai 4, Sharjah 3, Ras al-Khaimah 3, Ajman 2, Fujairah 2, Umm al-Quwain 2; note - only 1 woman (from Ras Al Khaimah) won an FNC seat

**JUDICIAL BRANCH:**

highest courts: Federal Supreme Court (consists of the court president and 4 judges; jurisdiction limited to federal cases)

judge selection and term of office: judges appointed by the federal president following approval by the Federal Supreme Council, the highest executive and legislative authority consisting of the 7 emirate rulers; judges serve until retirement age or the expiry of their appointment terms

**subordinate courts:** Federal Court of Cassation (determines the constitutionality of laws promulgated at the federal and emirate level; federal level courts of first instance and appeals courts; the emirates of Abu Dhabi, Dubai, and Ra's al Khaymah have parallel court systems; the other 4 emirates have incorporated their courts into the federal system; note - the Abu Dhabi Global Market Courts and the Dubai International Financial Center Courts, the country's two largest financial free zones, both adjudicate civil and commercial disputes.

## POLITICAL PARTIES AND LEADERS:

none; political parties are banned

## INTERNATIONAL ORGANIZATION PARTICIPATION:

ABEDA, AfDB (nonregional member), AFESD, AMF, BIS, CAEU, CICA, FAO, G-77, GCC, IAEA, IBRD, ICAO, ICC (national committees), ICRM, IDA, IDB, IFAD, IFC, IFRCS, IHO, ILO, IMF, IMO, IMSO, Interpol, IOC, IPU, ISO, ITSO, ITU, LAS, MIGA, NAM, OAPEC, OIC, OIF (observer), OPCW, OPEC, PCA, UN, UNCTAD, UNESCO, UNIDO, UNRWA, UNWTO, UPU, WCO, WHO, WIPO, WMO, WTO

## DIPLOMATIC REPRESENTATION IN THE US:

**chief of mission:** Ambassador Yusif bin Mani bin Said al-UTAYBA (since 28 July 2008)

**chancery:** 3522 International Court NW, Suite 400, Washington, DC 20008

**telephone:** [1] (202) 243-2400

**FAX:** [1] (202) 243-2432

**consulate(s) general:** Boston, Los Angeles, New York

## DIPLOMATIC REPRESENTATION FROM THE US:

**chief of mission:** Ambassador (vanant); Charge d'Affaires Steven C. BONDY (since 22 March 2018)

**embassy:** Embassies District, Plot 38 Sector W59-02, Street No. 4, Abu Dhabi

**mailing address:** P. O. Box 4009, Abu Dhabi

**telephone:** [971] (2) 414-2200

**FAX:** [971] (2) 414-2603

**consulate(s) general:** Dubai

## FLAG DESCRIPTION:

three equal horizontal bands of green (top), white, and black with a wider vertical red band on the hoist side; the flag incorporates all four Pan-Arab colors, which in this case represent fertility (green), neutrality (white), petroleum resources (black), and unity (red); red was the traditional color incorporated into all flags of the emirates before their unification

## NATIONAL SYMBOL(S):

golden falcon; national colors: green, white, black, red

## NATIONAL ANTHEM:

**name:** "Nashid al-watani al-imarati" (National Anthem of the UAE)

**lyrics/music:** AREF Al Sheikh Abdullah Al Hassan/Mohamad Abdel WAHAB

**note:** music adopted 1971, lyrics adopted 1996; Mohamad Abdel WAHAB also composed the music for the anthem of Tunisia

# ECONOMY :: UNITED ARAB EMIRATES

## ECONOMY - OVERVIEW:

The UAE has an open economy with a high per capita income and a sizable annual trade surplus. Successful efforts at economic diversification have reduced the portion of GDP from the oil and gas sector to 30%.

Since the discovery of oil in the UAE nearly 60 years ago, the country has undergone a profound transformation from an impoverished region of small desert principalities to a modern state with a high standard of living. The government has increased spending on job creation and infrastructure expansion and is opening up utilities to greater private sector involvement. The country's free trade zones - offering 100% foreign ownership and zero taxes - are helping to attract foreign investors.

The global financial crisis of 2008-09, tight international credit, and deflated asset prices constricted the economy in 2009. UAE authorities tried to blunt the crisis by increasing spending and boosting liquidity in the banking sector. The crisis hit Dubai hardest, as it was heavily exposed to depressed real estate prices. Dubai lacked sufficient cash to meet its debt obligations, prompting global concern about its solvency and ultimately a $20 billion bailout from the UAE Central Bank and Abu Dhabi Government that was refinanced in March 2014.

The UAE's dependence on oil is a significant long-term challenge, although the UAE is one of the most diversified countries in the Gulf Cooperation Council. Low oil prices have prompted the UAE to cut expenditures, including on some social programs, but the UAE has sufficient assets in its sovereign investment funds to cover its deficits. The government reduced fuel subsidies in August 2015, and introduced excise taxes (50% on sweetened carbonated beverages and 100% on energy drinks and tobacco) in October 2017. A five-percent value-added tax was introduced in January 2018. The UAE's strategic plan for the next few years focuses on economic diversification, promoting the UAE as a global trade and tourism hub, developing industry, and creating more job opportunities for nationals through improved education and increased private sector employment.

## GDP (PURCHASING POWER PARITY):

$696 billion (2017 est.)

$690.5 billion (2016 est.)

$670.5 billion (2015 est.)

**note:** data are in 2017 dollars

**country comparison to the world:** 32

## GDP (OFFICIAL EXCHANGE RATE):

$382.6 billion (2017 est.) (2017 est.)

## GDP - REAL GROWTH RATE:

0.8% (2017 est.)

3% (2016 est.)

5.1% (2015 est.)

**country comparison to the world:** 188

## GDP - PER CAPITA (PPP):

$68,600 (2017 est.)

$70,100 (2016 est.)

$70,000 (2015 est.)

**note:** data are in 2017 dollars

**country comparison to the world:** 13

## GROSS NATIONAL SAVING:

28.5% of GDP (2017 est.)

30.9% of GDP (2016 est.)

30.7% of GDP (2015 est.)

**country comparison to the world:** 39

## GDP - COMPOSITION, BY END USE:

household consumption: 34.9% (2017 est.)

government consumption: 12.3% (2017 est.)

investment in fixed capital: 23% (2017 est.)

investment in inventories: 1.8% (2017 est.)

exports of goods and services: 100.4% (2017 est.)

imports of goods and services: -72.4% (2017 est.)

**GDP - COMPOSITION, BY SECTOR OF ORIGIN:**

agriculture: 0.9% (2017 est.)

industry: 49.8% (2017 est.)

services: 49.2% (2017 est.)

**AGRICULTURE - PRODUCTS:**

dates, vegetables, watermelons; poultry, eggs, dairy products; fish

**INDUSTRIES:**

petroleum and petrochemicals; fishing, aluminum, cement, fertilizer, commercial ship repair, construction materials, handicrafts, textiles

**INDUSTRIAL PRODUCTION GROWTH RATE:**

1.8% (2017 est.)

country comparison to the world: 138

**LABOR FORCE:**

5.344 million (2017 est.)

note: expatriates account for about 85% of the workforce

country comparison to the world: 78

**LABOR FORCE - BY OCCUPATION:**

agriculture: 7%

industry: 15%

services: 78% (2000 est.)

**UNEMPLOYMENT RATE:**

1.6% (2016 est.)

3.6% (2014 est.)

country comparison to the world: 14

**POPULATION BELOW POVERTY LINE:**

19.5% (2003 est.)

**HOUSEHOLD INCOME OR CONSUMPTION BY PERCENTAGE SHARE:**

lowest 10%: NA

highest 10%: NA

**BUDGET:**

revenues: 110.2 billion (2017 est.)

expenditures: 111.1 billion (2017 est.)

note: the UAE federal budget does not account for emirate-level spending in Abu Dhabi and Dubai

**TAXES AND OTHER REVENUES:**

28.8% (of GDP) (2017 est.)

country comparison to the world: 90

**BUDGET SURPLUS (+) OR DEFICIT (-):**

-0.2% (of GDP) (2017 est.)

country comparison to the world: 51

**PUBLIC DEBT:**

19.7% of GDP (2017 est.)

20.2% of GDP (2016 est.)

country comparison to the world: 190

**FISCAL YEAR:**

calendar year

**INFLATION RATE (CONSUMER PRICES):**

2% (2017 est.)

1.6% (2016 est.)

country comparison to the world: 108

**CENTRAL BANK DISCOUNT RATE:**

NA

**COMMERCIAL BANK PRIME LENDING RATE:**

6% (31 December 2017 est.)

5.7% (31 December 2016 est.)

country comparison to the world: 126

**STOCK OF NARROW MONEY:**

$134 billion (31 December 2017 est.)

$129.1 billion (31 December 2016 est.)

country comparison to the world: 32

**STOCK OF BROAD MONEY:**

$134 billion (31 December 2017 est.)

$129.1 billion (31 December 2016 est.)

country comparison to the world: 32

**STOCK OF DOMESTIC CREDIT:**

$395.5 billion (31 December 2017 est.)

$396 billion (31 December 2016 est.)

country comparison to the world: 31

**MARKET VALUE OF PUBLICLY TRADED SHARES:**

$195.9 billion (31 December 2015 est.)

$201.6 billion (31 December 2014 est.)

$180.3 billion (31 December 2013 est.)

country comparison to the world: 33

**CURRENT ACCOUNT BALANCE:**

$26.47 billion (2017 est.)

$13.23 billion (2016 est.)

country comparison to the world: 13

**EXPORTS:**

$308.5 billion (2017 est.)

$298.6 billion (2016 est.)

country comparison to the world: 18

**EXPORTS - PARTNERS:**

India 10.1%, Iran 9.9%, Japan 9.3%, China 5.4%, Oman 5%, Switzerland 4.4%, South Korea 4.1% (2017)

**EXPORTS - COMMODITIES:**

crude oil 45%, natural gas, reexports, dried fish, dates (2012 est.)

**IMPORTS:**

$229.2 billion (2017 est.)

$226.5 billion (2016 est.)

country comparison to the world: 21

**IMPORTS - COMMODITIES:**

machinery and transport equipment, chemicals, food

**IMPORTS - PARTNERS:**

China 8.5%, US 6.8%, India 6.6% (2017)

**RESERVES OF FOREIGN EXCHANGE AND GOLD:**

$95.37 billion (31 December 2017 est.)

$85.39 billion (31 December 2016 est.)

country comparison to the world: 27

**DEBT - EXTERNAL:**

$237.6 billion (31 December 2017 est.)

$218.7 billion (31 December 2016 est.)

country comparison to the world: 32

**STOCK OF DIRECT FOREIGN INVESTMENT - AT HOME:**

$129.9 billion (31 December 2017 est.)

$134.8 billion (31 December 2016 est.)

country comparison to the world: 41

**STOCK OF DIRECT FOREIGN INVESTMENT - ABROAD:**

$124.4 billion (31 December 2017 est.)

$114.6 billion (31 December 2016 est.)

country comparison to the world: 32

**EXCHANGE RATES:**

Emirati dirhams (AED) per US dollar -

3.673 (2017 est.)

3.673 (2016 est.)

3.673 (2015 est.)

3.673 (2014 est.)

3.673 (2013 est.)

## ENERGY :: UNITED ARAB EMIRATES

**ELECTRICITY ACCESS:**

population without electricity: 177,824 (2012)

electrification - total population: 98% (2012)

electrification - urban areas: 99% (2012)

electrification - rural areas: 93% (2012)

### ELECTRICITY - PRODUCTION:
121.8 billion kWh (2016 est.)

country comparison to the world: 31

### ELECTRICITY - CONSUMPTION:
113.2 billion kWh (2016 est.)

country comparison to the world: 31

### ELECTRICITY - EXPORTS:
0 kWh (2016 est.)

country comparison to the world: 213

### ELECTRICITY - IMPORTS:
1.141 billion kWh (2016 est.)

country comparison to the world: 66

### ELECTRICITY - INSTALLED GENERATING CAPACITY:
28.91 million kW (2016 est.)

country comparison to the world: 33

### ELECTRICITY - FROM FOSSIL FUELS:
99% of total installed capacity (2016 est.)

country comparison to the world: 26

### ELECTRICITY - FROM NUCLEAR FUELS:
0% of total installed capacity (2017 est.)

country comparison to the world: 204

### ELECTRICITY - FROM HYDROELECTRIC PLANTS:
0% of total installed capacity (2017 est.)

country comparison to the world: 210

### ELECTRICITY - FROM OTHER RENEWABLE SOURCES:
1% of total installed capacity (2017 est.)

country comparison to the world: 170

### CRUDE OIL - PRODUCTION:
3.174 million bbl/day (2017 est.)

country comparison to the world: 8

### CRUDE OIL - EXPORTS:
2.552 million bbl/day (2015 est.)

country comparison to the world: 5

### CRUDE OIL - IMPORTS:
0 bbl/day (2015 est.)

country comparison to the world: 210

### CRUDE OIL - PROVED RESERVES:
97.8 billion bbl (1 January 2018 est.)

country comparison to the world: 7

### REFINED PETROLEUM PRODUCTS - PRODUCTION:
943,500 bbl/day (2017 est.)

country comparison to the world: 19

### REFINED PETROLEUM PRODUCTS - CONSUMPTION:
896,000 bbl/day (2016 est.)

country comparison to the world: 24

### REFINED PETROLEUM PRODUCTS - EXPORTS:
817,700 bbl/day (2015 est.)

country comparison to the world: 10

### REFINED PETROLEUM PRODUCTS - IMPORTS:
392,000 bbl/day (2015 est.)

country comparison to the world: 23

### NATURAL GAS - PRODUCTION:
62.01 billion cu m (2017 est.)

country comparison to the world: 14

### NATURAL GAS - CONSUMPTION:
74.48 billion cu m (2017 est.)

country comparison to the world: 12

### NATURAL GAS - EXPORTS:
7.504 billion cu m (2017 est.)

country comparison to the world: 25

### NATURAL GAS - IMPORTS:
20.22 billion cu m (2017 est.)

country comparison to the world: 16

### NATURAL GAS - PROVED RESERVES:
6.091 trillion cu m (1 January 2018 est.)

country comparison to the world: 6

### CARBON DIOXIDE EMISSIONS FROM CONSUMPTION OF ENERGY:
289.4 million Mt (2017 est.)

country comparison to the world: 24

## COMMUNICATIONS :: UNITED ARAB EMIRATES

### TELEPHONES - FIXED LINES:
total subscriptions: 2,320,837 (2017 est.)

subscriptions per 100 inhabitants: 38 (2017 est.)

country comparison to the world: 56

### TELEPHONES - MOBILE CELLULAR:
total subscriptions: 19,826,224 (2017 est.)

subscriptions per 100 inhabitants: 326 (2017 est.)

country comparison to the world: 58

### TELEPHONE SYSTEM:
general assessment: modern fiber-optic integrated services; digital network with rapidly growing use of mobile-cellular telephones; key centers are Abu Dhabi and Dubai (2016)

domestic: microwave radio relay, fiber-optic and coaxial cable (2016)

international: country code - 971; linked to the international submarine cable FLAG (Fiber-Optic Link Around the Globe); landing point for both the SEA-ME-WE-3 and SEA-ME-WE-4 submarine cable networks; satellite earth stations - 3 Intelsat (1 Atlantic Ocean and 2 Indian) (2016)

### BROADCAST MEDIA:
except for the many organizations now operating in media free zones in Abu Dhabi and Dubai, most TV and radio stations remain government-owned; widespread use of satellite dishes provides access to pan-Arab and other international broadcasts; restrictions since June 2017 on some satellite channels and websites originating from or otherwise linked to Qatar (2018)

### INTERNET COUNTRY CODE:
.ae

### INTERNET USERS:
total: 5,370,299 (July 2016 est.)

percent of population: 90.6% (July 2016 est.)

country comparison to the world: 73

### BROADBAND - FIXED SUBSCRIPTIONS:
total: 1,297,585 (2017 est.)

subscriptions per 100 inhabitants: 21 (2017 est.)

country comparison to the world: 66

## TRANSPORTATION :: UNITED ARAB EMIRATES

### NATIONAL AIR TRANSPORT SYSTEM:
number of registered air carriers: 12 (2015)

inventory of registered aircraft operated by air carriers: 498 (2015)

annual passenger traffic on registered air carriers: 84,738,479 (2015)

annual freight traffic on registered air carriers: 16.647 billion mt-km (2015)

### CIVIL AIRCRAFT REGISTRATION COUNTRY CODE PREFIX:

A6 (2016)

## AIRPORTS:
43 (2013)

country comparison to the world: 100

## AIRPORTS - WITH PAVED RUNWAYS:
total: 25 (2013)

over 3,047 m: 12 (2013)

2,438 to 3,047 m: 3 (2013)

1,524 to 2,437 m: 5 (2013)

914 to 1,523 m: 3 (2013)

under 914 m: 2 (2013)

## AIRPORTS - WITH UNPAVED RUNWAYS:
total: 18 (2013)

over 3,047 m: 1 (2013)

2,438 to 3,047 m: 1 (2013)

1,524 to 2,437 m: 4 (2013)

914 to 1,523 m: 6 (2013)

under 914 m: 6 (2013)

## HELIPORTS:
5 (2013)

## PIPELINES:
533 km condensate, 3277 km gas, 300 km liquid petroleum gas, 3287 km oil, 24 km oil/gas/water, 218 km refined products, 99 km water (2013)

## ROADWAYS:
total: 4,080 km (2008)

paved: 4,080 km (includes 253 km of expressways) (2008)

country comparison to the world: 157

## MERCHANT MARINE:
total: 618 (2017)

by type: general cargo 97, oil tanker 26, other 495 (2017)

country comparison to the world: 34

## PORTS AND TERMINALS:
major seaport(s): Al Fujayrah, Mina' Jabal 'Ali (Dubai), Khor Fakkan (Khawr Fakkan) (Sharjah), Mubarraz Island (Abu Dhabi), Mina' Rashid (Dubai), Mina' Saqr (Ra's al Khaymah)

container port(s) (TEUs): Mubarraz Island (Abu Dhabi) (1,550,000), Dubai Port (14,772,000), Khor Fakkan (Khawr Fakkan) (Sharjah) (4,330,200) (2016)

LNG terminal(s) (export): Das Island

# MILITARY AND SECURITY :: UNITED ARAB EMIRATES

## MILITARY EXPENDITURES:
4.86% of GDP (2017)

4.99% of GDP (2016)

5.66% of GDP (2014)

country comparison to the world: 8

## MILITARY BRANCHES:
United Arab Emirates Armed Forces: Critical Infrastructure Coastal Patrol Agency (CICPA), Land Forces, Navy, Air Force and Air Defense, Presidential Guard, Joint Aviation Command (2018)

## MILITARY SERVICE AGE AND OBLIGATION:
18-30 years of age for compulsory military service for men, optional service for women; 17 years of age for male volunteers with parental approval; 2-year general obligation, 12 months for secondary school graduates; women may train for 9 months regardless of education (2016)

# TRANSNATIONAL ISSUES :: UNITED ARAB EMIRATES

## DISPUTES - INTERNATIONAL:
boundary agreement was signed and ratified with Oman in 2003 for entire border, including Oman's Musandam Peninsula and Al Madhah enclaves, but contents of the agreement and detailed maps showing the alignment have not been publishedIran and UAE dispute Tunb Islands and Abu Musa Island, which Iran occupies

## ILLICIT DRUGS:
the UAE is a drug transshipment point for traffickers given its proximity to Southwest Asian drug-producing countries; the UAE's position as a major financial center makes it vulnerable to money laundering; anti-money-laundering controls improving, but informal banking remains unregulated

# EUROPE :: UNITED KINGDOM

## INTRODUCTION :: UNITED KINGDOM

### BACKGROUND:

The United Kingdom has historically played a leading role in developing parliamentary democracy and in advancing literature and science. At its zenith in the 19th century, the British Empire stretched over one-fourth of the earth's surface. The first half of the 20th century saw the UK's strength seriously depleted in two world wars and the Irish Republic's withdrawal from the union. The second half witnessed the dismantling of the Empire and the UK rebuilding itself into a modern and prosperous European nation. As one of five permanent members of the UN Security Council and a founding member of NATO and the Commonwealth, the UK pursues a global approach to foreign policy. The Scottish Parliament, the National Assembly for Wales, and the Northern Ireland Assembly were established in 1998.

The UK has been an active member of the EU since its accession in 1973, although it chose to remain outside the Economic and Monetary Union. However, motivated in part by frustration at a remote bureaucracy in Brussels and massive migration into the country, UK citizens on 23 June 2016 narrowly voted to leave the EU. The UK and the EU are currently negotiating the terms of the UK's withdrawal and will discuss a framework for their future relationship ahead of the UK's scheduled departure from the bloc on 29 March 2019.

## GEOGRAPHY :: UNITED KINGDOM

### LOCATION:

Western Europe, islands - including the northern one-sixth of the island of Ireland - between the North Atlantic Ocean and the North Sea; northwest of France

### GEOGRAPHIC COORDINATES:

54 00 N, 2 00 W

### MAP REFERENCES:

Europe

### AREA:

total: 243,610 sq km

land: 241,930 sq km

water: 1,680 sq km

note: includes Rockall and Shetland Islands

country comparison to the world: 81

### AREA - COMPARATIVE:

twice the size of Pennsylvania; slightly smaller than Oregon

### LAND BOUNDARIES:

total: 443 km

border countries (1): Ireland 443 km

### COASTLINE:

12,429 km

### MARITIME CLAIMS:

territorial sea: 12 nm

continental shelf: as defined in continental shelf orders or in accordance with agreed upon boundaries

exclusive fishing zone: 200 nm

### CLIMATE:

temperate; moderated by prevailing southwest winds over the North Atlantic Current; more than one-half of the days are overcast

### TERRAIN:

mostly rugged hills and low mountains; level to rolling plains in east and southeast

### ELEVATION:

mean elevation: 162 m

elevation extremes: -4 m lowest point: The Fens

1343 highest point: Ben Nevis

### NATURAL RESOURCES:

coal, petroleum, natural gas, iron ore, lead, zinc, gold, tin, limestone, salt, clay, chalk, gypsum, potash, silica sand, slate, arable land

### LAND USE:

agricultural land: 71% (2011 est.)

arable land: 25.1% (2011 est.) / permanent crops: 0.2% (2011 est.) / permanent pasture: 45.7% (2011 est.)

forest: 11.9% (2011 est.)

other: 17.1% (2011 est.)

**IRRIGATED LAND:**

950 sq km (2012)

**POPULATION DISTRIBUTION:**

the core of the population lies in and around London, with significant clusters found in central Britain around Manchester and Liverpool, in the Scotish lowlands between Endinburgh and Glasgow, southern Wales in and around Cardiff, and far eastern Northern Ireland centered on Belfast

**NATURAL HAZARDS:**

winter windstorms; floods

**ENVIRONMENT - CURRENT ISSUES:**

air pollution improved but remains a concern, particularly in the London region; soil pollution from pesticides and heavy metals; decline in marine and coastal habitats brought on by pressures from housing, tourism, and industry

**ENVIRONMENT - INTERNATIONAL AGREEMENTS:**

party to: Air Pollution, Air Pollution-Nitrogen Oxides, Air Pollution-Persistent Organic Pollutants, Air Pollution-Sulfur 94, Air Pollution-Volatile Organic Compounds, Antarctic-Environmental Protocol, Antarctic-Marine Living Resources, Antarctic Seals, Antarctic Treaty, Biodiversity, Climate Change, Climate Change-Kyoto Protocol, Desertification, Endangered Species, Environmental Modification, Hazardous Wastes, Law of the Sea, Marine Dumping, Marine Life Conservation, Ozone Layer Protection, Ship Pollution, Tropical Timber 83, Tropical Timber 94, Wetlands, Whaling

signed, but not ratified: none of the selected agreements

**GEOGRAPHY - NOTE:**

lies near vital North Atlantic sea lanes; only 35 km from France and linked by tunnel under the English Channel (the Channel Tunnel or Chunnel); because of heavily indented coastline, no location is more than 125 km from tidal waters

# PEOPLE AND SOCIETY :: UNITED KINGDOM

**POPULATION:**

65,105,246 United Kingdom (July 2018 est.)

constituent countries:
England 55,268,100
Scotland 5,404,700
Wales 3,113,200
Northern Ireland 1,862,10

country comparison to the world: 22

**NATIONALITY:**

noun: Briton(s), British (collective plural)

adjective: British

**ETHNIC GROUPS:**

white 87.2%, black/African/Caribbean/black British 3%, Asian/Asian British: Indian 2.3%, Asian/Asian British: Pakistani 1.9%, mixed 2%, other 3.7% (2011 est.)

**LANGUAGES:**

English, Scottish Gaelic (about 60,000 in Scotland), Welsh (about 20% of the population of Wales), Irish (about 10% of the population of Northern Ireland), Cornish (some 2,000 to 3,000 people in Cornwall) (2012 est.)

note: the following are recognized regional languages: Scots (about 30% of the population of Scotland)

**RELIGIONS:**

Christian (includes Anglican, Roman Catholic, Presbyterian, Methodist) 59.5%, Muslim 4.4%, Hindu 1.3%, other 2%, unspecified 7.2%, none 25.7% (2011 est.)

**AGE STRUCTURE:**

0-14 years: 17.59% (male 5,871,268 /female 5,582,107)

15-24 years: 11.71% (male 3,895,850 /female 3,726,311)

25-54 years: 40.29% (male 13,387,119 /female 12,843,549)

55-64 years: 12.22% (male 3,936,466 /female 4,022,245)

65 years and over: 18.19% (male 5,321,392 /female 6,518,939) (2018 est.)

**DEPENDENCY RATIOS:**

total dependency ratio: 55.5 (2015 est.)

youth dependency ratio: 27.4 (2015 est.)

elderly dependency ratio: 28.2 (2015 est.)

potential support ratio: 3.5 (2015 est.)

**MEDIAN AGE:**

total: 40.5 years

male: 39.3 years

female: 41.7 years (2018 est.)

country comparison to the world: 48

**POPULATION GROWTH RATE:**

0.51% (2018 est.)

country comparison to the world: 154

**BIRTH RATE:**

12 births/1,000 population (2018 est.)

country comparison to the world: 167

**DEATH RATE:**

9.4 deaths/1,000 population (2018 est.)

country comparison to the world: 53

**NET MIGRATION RATE:**

2.5 migrant(s)/1,000 population (2017 est.)

country comparison to the world: 38

**POPULATION DISTRIBUTION:**

the core of the population lies in and around London, with significant clusters found in central Britain around Manchester and Liverpool, in the Scotish lowlands between Endinburgh and Glasgow, southern Wales in and around Cardiff, and far eastern Northern Ireland centered on Belfast

**URBANIZATION:**

urban population: 83.4% of total population (2018)

rate of urbanization: 0.89% annual rate of change (2015-20 est.)

**MAJOR URBAN AREAS - POPULATION:**

9.046 million LONDON (capital), 2.69 million Manchester, 2.57 million Birmingham, 1.864 million West Yorkshire, 1.661 million Glasgow, 912,000 Southampton/Portsmouth (2018)

**SEX RATIO:**

at birth: 1.05 male(s)/female (2017 est.)

0-14 years: 1.05 male(s)/female (2017 est.)

15-24 years: 1.04 male(s)/female (2017 est.)

25-54 years: 1.04 male(s)/female (2017 est.)

55-64 years: 0.98 male(s)/female (2017 est.)

65 years and over: 0.81 male(s)/female (2017 est.)

total population: 0.99 male(s)/female (2017 est.)

**MOTHER'S MEAN AGE AT FIRST BIRTH:**

28.5 years (2014 est.)

note: data represent England and Wales only

**MATERNAL MORTALITY RATE:**

9 deaths/100,000 live births (2015 est.)

country comparison to the world: 155

**INFANT MORTALITY RATE:**

total: 4.2 deaths/1,000 live births (2018 est.)

male: 4.6 deaths/1,000 live births (2018 est.)

female: 3.8 deaths/1,000 live births (2018 est.)

country comparison to the world: 190

**LIFE EXPECTANCY AT BIRTH:**

total population: 80.9 years (2018 est.)

male: 78.7 years (2018 est.)

female: 83.2 years (2018 est.)

country comparison to the world: 39

**TOTAL FERTILITY RATE:**

1.88 children born/woman (2018 est.)

country comparison to the world: 137

**CONTRACEPTIVE PREVALENCE RATE:**

84% (2008)

note: percent of women aged 16-49

**HEALTH EXPENDITURES:**

9.1% of GDP (2014)

country comparison to the world: 38

**PHYSICIANS DENSITY:**

2.83 physicians/1,000 population (2016)

**HOSPITAL BED DENSITY:**

2.8 beds/1,000 population (2013)

**DRINKING WATER SOURCE:**

improved:

urban: 100% of population

rural: 100% of population

total: 100% of population

unimproved:

urban: 0% of population

rural: 0% of population

total: 0% of population (2015 est.)

**SANITATION FACILITY ACCESS:**

improved:

urban: 99.1% of population (2015 est.)

rural: 99.6% of population (2015 est.)

total: 99.2% of population (2015 est.)

unimproved:

urban: 0.9% of population (2015 est.)

rural: 0.4% of population (2015 est.)

total: 0.8% of population (2015 est.)

**HIV/AIDS - ADULT PREVALENCE RATE:**

NA

**HIV/AIDS - PEOPLE LIVING WITH HIV/AIDS:**

NA

**HIV/AIDS - DEATHS:**

NA

**OBESITY - ADULT PREVALENCE RATE:**

27.8% (2016)

country comparison to the world: 36

**EDUCATION EXPENDITURES:**

5.6% of GDP (2015)

country comparison to the world: 48

**SCHOOL LIFE EXPECTANCY (PRIMARY TO TERTIARY EDUCATION):**

total: 18 years (2014)

male: 17 years (2014)

female: 18 years (2014)

**UNEMPLOYMENT, YOUTH AGES 15-24:**

total: 13% (2016 est.)

male: 14.8% (2016 est.)

female: 11.1% (2016 est.)

country comparison to the world: 102

# GOVERNMENT :: UNITED KINGDOM

**COUNTRY NAME:**

conventional long form: United Kingdom of Great Britain and Northern Ireland; note - the island of Great Britain includes England, Scotland, and Wales

conventional short form: United Kingdom

abbreviation: UK

etymology: self-descriptive country name; the designation "Great Britain," in the sense of "Larger Britain," dates back to medieval times and was used to distinguish the island from "Little Britain," or Brittany in modern France; the name Ireland derives from the Gaelic "Eriu," the matron goddess of Ireland (goddess of the land)

**GOVERNMENT TYPE:**

parliamentary constitutional monarchy; a Commonwealth realm

**CAPITAL:**

name: London

geographic coordinates: 51 30 N, 0 05 W

time difference: UTC 0 (5 hours ahead of Washington, DC, during Standard Time)

daylight saving time: +1hr, begins last Sunday in March; ends last Sunday in October

note: applies to the United Kingdom proper, not to its Crown dependencies or overseas territories

**ADMINISTRATIVE DIVISIONS:**

England: 27 two-tier counties, 32 London boroughs and 1 City of London or Greater London, 36 metropolitan districts, 56 unitary authorities (including 4 single-tier counties*);

two-tier counties: Buckinghamshire, Cambridgeshire, Cumbria, Derbyshire, Devon, Dorset, East Sussex, Essex, Gloucestershire, Hampshire, Hertfordshire, Kent, Lancashire, Leicestershire, Lincolnshire, Norfolk, North Yorkshire, Northamptonshire, Nottinghamshire, Oxfordshire, Somerset, Staffordshire, Suffolk, Surrey, Warwickshire, West Sussex, Worcestershire;

London boroughs and City of London or Greater London: Barking and Dagenham, Barnet, Bexley, Brent, Bromley, Camden, Croydon, Ealing, Enfield, Greenwich, Hackney, Hammersmith and Fulham, Haringey, Harrow, Havering, Hillingdon, Hounslow, Islington, Kensington and Chelsea, Kingston upon Thames, Lambeth, Lewisham, City of London, Merton, Newham, Redbridge, Richmond upon Thames, Southwark, Sutton, Tower Hamlets, Waltham Forest, Wandsworth, Westminster;

metropolitan districts: Barnsley, Birmingham, Bolton, Bradford, Bury, Calderdale, Coventry, Doncaster, Dudley, Gateshead, Kirklees, Knowlsey, Leeds, Liverpool, Manchester, Newcastle upon Tyne, North Tyneside, Oldham, Rochdale, Rotherham, Salford, Sandwell, Sefton, Sheffield, Solihull, South Tyneside, St. Helens, Stockport, Sunderland, Tameside, Trafford, Wakefield, Walsall, Wigan, Wirral, Wolverhampton;

unitary authorities: Bath and North East Somerset, Blackburn with Darwen, Bedford, Blackpool, Bournemouth, Bracknell Forest,

Brighton and Hove, City of Bristol, Central Bedfordshire, Cheshire East, Cheshire West and Chester, Cornwall, Darlington, Derby, Durham County*, East Riding of Yorkshire, Halton, Hartlepool, Herefordshire*, Isle of Wight*, Isles of Scilly, City of Kingston upon Hull, Leicester, Luton, Medway, Middlesbrough, Milton Keynes, North East Lincolnshire, North Lincolnshire, North Somerset, Northumberland*, Nottingham, Peterborough, Plymouth, Poole, Portsmouth, Reading, Redcar and Cleveland, Rutland, Shropshire, Slough, South Gloucestershire, Southampton, Southend-on-Sea, Stockton-on-Tees, Stoke-on-Trent, Swindon, Telford and Wrekin, Thurrock, Torbay, Warrington, West Berkshire, Wiltshire, Windsor and Maidenhead, Wokingham, York;

**Northern Ireland:** 5 borough councils, 4 district councils, 2 city councils;

**borough councils:** Antrim and Newtownabbey; Ards and North Down; Armagh City, Banbridge, and Craigavon; Causeway Coast and Glens; Mid and East Antrim;

**district councils:** Derry City and Strabane; Fermanagh and Omagh; Mid Ulster; Newry, Murne, and Down;

**city councils:** Belfast; Lisburn and Castlereagh;

**Scotland:** 32 council areas;

**council areas:** Aberdeen City, Aberdeenshire, Angus, Argyll and Bute, Clackmannanshire, Dumfries and Galloway, Dundee City, East Ayrshire, East Dunbartonshire, East Lothian, East Renfrewshire, City of Edinburgh, Eilean Siar (Western Isles), Falkirk, Fife, Glasgow City, Highland, Inverclyde, Midlothian, Moray, North Ayrshire, North Lanarkshire, Orkney Islands, Perth and Kinross, Renfrewshire, Shetland Islands, South Ayrshire, South Lanarkshire, Stirling, The Scottish Borders, West Dunbartonshire, West Lothian

**Wales:** 22 unitary authorities;

**unitary authorities:** Blaenau Gwent, Bridgend, Caerphilly, Cardiff, Carmarthenshire, Ceredigion, Conwy, Denbighshire, Flintshire, Gwynedd, Isle of Anglesey, Merthyr Tydfil, Monmouthshire, Neath Port Talbot, Newport, Pembrokeshire, Powys, Rhondda Cynon Taff, Swansea, The Vale of Glamorgan, Torfaen, Wrexham

## DEPENDENT AREAS:

Anguilla, Bermuda, British Indian Ocean Territory, British Virgin Islands, Cayman Islands, Falkland Islands, Gibraltar, Montserrat, Pitcairn Islands, Saint Helena, Ascension, and Tristan da Cunha, South Georgia and the South Sandwich Islands, Turks and Caicos Islands

## INDEPENDENCE:

no official date of independence: 927 (minor English kingdoms united);3 March 1284 (enactment of the Statute of Rhuddlan uniting England and Wales);1536 (Act of Union formally incorporates England and Wales);1 May 1707 (Acts of Union formally unite England, Scotland, and Wales as Great Britain);1 January 1801 (Acts of Union formally unite Great Britain and Ireland as the United Kingdom of Great Britain and Ireland);6 December 1921 (Anglo-Irish Treaty formalizes partition of Ireland; six counties remain part of the United Kingdom and Northern Ireland);12 April 1927 (Royal and Parliamentary Titles Act establishes current name of the United Kingdom of Great Britain and Northern Ireland)

## NATIONAL HOLIDAY:

the UK does not celebrate one particular national holiday

## CONSTITUTION:

**history:** unwritten; partly statutes, partly common law and practice (2016)

**amendments:** proposed as a bill for an Act of Parliament by the government, by the House of Commons, or by the House of Lords; passage requires agreement by both houses and by the monarch (Royal Assent); note - additions include the Human Rights Act of 1998, the Constitutional Reform and Governance Act 2010, the Parliamentary Voting System and Constituencies Act 2011, the Fixed-term Parliaments Act 2011, and the House of Lords (Expulsion and Suspension) Act 2015 (2016)

## LEGAL SYSTEM:

common law system; has nonbinding judicial review of Acts of Parliament under the Human Rights Act of 1998

## INTERNATIONAL LAW ORGANIZATION PARTICIPATION:

accepts compulsory ICJ jurisdiction with reservations; accepts ICCt jurisdiction

## CITIZENSHIP:

**citizenship by birth:** no

**citizenship by descent only:** at least one parent must be a citizen of the United Kingdom

**dual citizenship recognized:** yes

**residency requirement for naturalization:** 5 years

## SUFFRAGE:

18 years of age; universal

## EXECUTIVE BRANCH:

**chief of state:** Queen ELIZABETH II (since 6 February 1952); Heir Apparent Prince CHARLES (son of the queen, born 14 November 1948)

**head of government:** Prime Minister Theresa MAY (Conservative) (since 13 July 2016)

**cabinet:** Cabinet appointed by the prime minister

**elections/appointments:** the monarchy is hereditary; following legislative elections, the leader of the majority party or majority coalition usually becomes the prime minister; election last held on 8 June 2017 (next to be held by 5 May 2022)

**note:** in addition to serving as the UK head of state, the British sovereign is the constitutional monarch for 15 additional Commonwealth countries (these 16 states are each referred to as a Commonwealth realm)

## LEGISLATIVE BRANCH:

**description:** bicameral Parliament consists of:
House of Lords (membership not fixed; as of May 2018, 780 lords were eligible to participate in the work of the House of Lords - 664 life peers, 90 hereditary peers, and 26 clergy; members are appointed by the monarch on the advice of the prime minister and non-party political members recommended by the House of Lords Appointments Commission); note - House of Lords total does not include ineligible members or members on leave of absence
House of Commons (650 seats; members directly elected in single-seat constituencies by simple majority popular vote to serve 5-year terms unless the House is dissolved earlier)

**elections:**
House of Lords - no elections; note - in 1999, as provided by the House of Lords Act, elections were held in the House of Lords to determine the 92 hereditary peers who would remain; elections held only as vacancies in the hereditary peerage arise)

House of Commons - last held on 8 June 2017 (next to be held by 5 May 2022)

election results:
House of Lords - composition - men 583, women 208, percent of women 26.3%
House of Commons - percent of vote by party - Conservative 42.3%, Labor 40.0%, SNP 43.0%, Lib Dems 7.4%, DUP 0.9%, Sinn Fein 0.7%, Plaid Cymru 0.5%, other 0.6%; seats by party - Conservative 317, Labor 262, SNP 35, Lib Dems 12, DUP 10, Sinn Fein 7, Plaid Cymru 4, other 3; composition - men 442, women 208, percent of women 32%; total Parliament percent of women 28.9%

## JUDICIAL BRANCH:

highest courts: Supreme Court (consists of 12 justices including the court president and deputy president); note - the Supreme Court was established by the Constitutional Reform Act 2005 and implemented in October 2009, replacing the Appellate Committee of the House of Lords as the highest court in the United Kingdom

judge selection and term of office: judge candidates selected by an independent committee of several judicial commissions, followed by their recommendations to the prime minister, and appointed by the monarch; justices appointed for life

subordinate courts: England and Wales - Court of Appeal (civil and criminal divisions); High Court; Crown Court; County Courts; Magistrates' Courts; Scotland - Court of Sessions; Sheriff Courts; High Court of Justiciary; tribunals; Northern Ireland - Court of Appeal in Northern Ireland; High Court; county courts; magistrates' courts; specialized tribunals

## POLITICAL PARTIES AND LEADERS:

Alliance Party (Northern Ireland) [Naomi LONG]
Conservative and Unionist Party [Theresa MAY]
Democratic Unionist Party or DUP (Northern Ireland) [Arlene FOSTER]
Green Party of England and Wales or Greens [Caroline LUCAS and Jonathan BARTLEY]
Labor (Labour) Party [Jeremy CORBYN]
Liberal Democrats (Lib Dems) [Sir Vince CABLE]
Party of Wales (Plaid Cymru) [Adam PRICE]
Scottish National Party or SNP [Nicola STURGEON]
Sinn Fein (Northern Ireland) [Gerry ADAMS]
Social Democratic and Labor Party or SDLP (Northern Ireland) [Colum EASTWOOD]
Ulster Unionist Party or UUP (Northern Ireland) [Robin SWANN]
UK Independence Party or UKIP [Gerard BATTEN]

## INTERNATIONAL ORGANIZATION PARTICIPATION:

ADB (nonregional member), AfDB (nonregional member), Arctic Council (observer), Australia Group, BIS, C, CBSS (observer), CD, CDB, CE, CERN, EAPC, EBRD, ECB, EIB, EITI (implementing country), ESA, EU, FAO, FATF, G-5, G-7, G-8, G-10, G-20, IADB, IAEA, IBRD, ICAO, ICC (national committees), ICCt, ICRM, IDA, IEA, IFAD, IFC, IFRCS, IGAD (partners), IHO, ILO, IMF, IMO, IMSO, Interpol, IOC, IOM, IPU, ISO, ITSO, ITU, ITUC (NGOs), MIGA, MINUSMA, MONUSCO, NATO, NEA, NSG, OAS (observer), OECD, OPCW, OSCE, Pacific Alliance (observer), Paris Club, PCA, PIF (partner), SELEC (observer), SICA (observer), UN, UNCTAD, UNESCO, UNFICYP, UNHCR, UNMISS, UNRWA, UN Security Council (permanent), UPU, WCO, WHO, WIPO, WMO, WTO, ZC

## DIPLOMATIC REPRESENTATION IN THE US:

chief of mission: Ambassador Sir Nigel Kim DARROCH (since 28 January 2016)

chancery: 3100 Massachusetts Avenue NW, Washington, DC 20008

telephone: [1] (202) 588-6500

FAX: [1] (202) 588-7870

consulate(s) general: Atlanta, Boston, Chicago, Denver, Houston, Los Angeles, Miami, New York, San Francisco

consulate(s): Orlando (FL), San Juan (Puerto Rico)

## DIPLOMATIC REPRESENTATION FROM THE US:

chief of mission: Ambassador Robert Wood (Woody) JOHNSON IV (since 29 August 2017)

embassy:

33 Nine Elms Lane, London, SW11 7US United Kingdom

mailing address: PSC 801, Box 40, FPO AE 09498-4040

telephone: [44] 20-7499-9000

FAX: [44] 20-7891-3151

consulate(s) general: Belfast, Edinburgh

## FLAG DESCRIPTION:

blue field with the red cross of Saint George (patron saint of England) edged in white superimposed on the diagonal red cross of Saint Patrick (patron saint of Ireland), which is superimposed on the diagonal white cross of Saint Andrew (patron saint of Scotland); properly known as the Union Flag, but commonly called the Union Jack; the design and colors (especially the Blue Ensign) have been the basis for a number of other flags including other Commonwealth countries and their constituent states or provinces, and British overseas territories

## NATIONAL SYMBOL(S):

lion (Britain in general); lion, Tudor rose, oak (England); lion, unicorn, thistle (Scotland); dragon, daffodil, leek (Wales); shamrock, flax (Northern Ireland); national colors: red, white, blue (Britain in general); red, white (England); blue, white (Scotland); red, white, green (Wales)

## NATIONAL ANTHEM:

name: God Save the Queen

lyrics/music: unknown

note: in use since 1745; by tradition, the song serves as both the national and royal anthem of the UK; it is known as either "God Save the Queen" or "God Save the King," depending on the gender of the reigning monarch; it also serves as the royal anthem of many Commonwealth nations

# ECONOMY :: UNITED KINGDOM

## ECONOMY - OVERVIEW:

The UK, a leading trading power and financial center, is the third largest economy in Europe after Germany and France. Agriculture is intensive, highly mechanized, and efficient by European standards, producing about 60% of food needs with less than 2% of the labor force. The UK has large coal, natural gas, and oil resources, but its oil and natural gas reserves are declining; the UK has been a net importer of energy since 2005. Services, particularly banking, insurance, and business services, are key drivers of British GDP growth. Manufacturing, meanwhile, has declined in importance but still accounts for about 10% of economic output.

In 2008, the global financial crisis hit the economy particularly hard, due to the importance of its financial sector. Falling home prices, high consumer debt, and the global economic slowdown compounded the UK's economic problems, pushing the economy into recession in the latter half of 2008 and prompting the then BROWN (Labour) government to implement a number of measures to stimulate the economy and stabilize the financial markets. Facing burgeoning public deficits and debt levels, in 2010 the then CAMERON-led coalition government (between Conservatives and Liberal Democrats) initiated an austerity program, which has continued under the Conservative government. However, the deficit still remains one of the highest in the G7, standing at 3.6% of GDP as of 2017, and the UK has pledged to lower its corporation tax from 20% to 17% by 2020. The UK had a debt burden of 90.4% GDP at the end of 2017.

The UK economy has begun to slow since the referendum vote to leave the EU in June 2016. A sustained depreciation of the British pound has increased consumer and producer prices, weighing on consumer spending without spurring a meaningful increase in exports. The UK has an extensive trade relationship with other EU members through its single market membership, and economic observers have warned the exit will jeopardize its position as the central location for European financial services. Prime Minister MAY is seeking a new "deep and special" trade relationship with the EU following the UK's exit. However, economists doubt that the UK will be able to preserve the benefits of EU membership without the obligations. The UK is expected to officially leave the EU by the end of March 2019.

**GDP (PURCHASING POWER PARITY):**

$2.925 trillion (2017 est.)

$2.877 trillion (2016 est.)

$2.827 trillion (2015 est.)

note: data are in 2017 dollars

country comparison to the world: 9

**GDP (OFFICIAL EXCHANGE RATE):**

$2.628 trillion (2017 est.) (2017 est.)

**GDP - REAL GROWTH RATE:**

1.7% (2017 est.)

1.8% (2016 est.)

2.3% (2015 est.)

country comparison to the world: 166

**GDP - PER CAPITA (PPP):**

$44,300 (2017 est.)

$43,800 (2016 est.)

$43,400 (2015 est.)

note: data are in 2017 dollars

country comparison to the world: 39

**GROSS NATIONAL SAVING:**

13.6% of GDP (2017 est.)

12% of GDP (2016 est.)

12.3% of GDP (2015 est.)

country comparison to the world: 142

**GDP - COMPOSITION, BY END USE:**

household consumption: 65.8% (2017 est.)

government consumption: 18.3% (2017 est.)

investment in fixed capital: 17.2% (2017 est.)

investment in inventories: 0.2% (2017 est.)

exports of goods and services: 30.2% (2017 est.)

imports of goods and services: -31.5% (2017 est.)

**GDP - COMPOSITION, BY SECTOR OF ORIGIN:**

agriculture: 0.7% (2017 est.)

industry: 20.2% (2017 est.)

services: 79.2% (2017 est.)

**AGRICULTURE - PRODUCTS:**

cereals, oilseed, potatoes, vegetables; cattle, sheep, poultry; fish; milk, eggs

**INDUSTRIES:**

machine tools, electric power equipment, automation equipment, railroad equipment, shipbuilding, aircraft, motor vehicles and parts, electronics and communications equipment, metals, chemicals, coal, petroleum, paper and paper products, food processing, textiles, clothing, other consumer goods

**INDUSTRIAL PRODUCTION GROWTH RATE:**

3.4% (2017 est.)

country comparison to the world: 93

**LABOR FORCE:**

33.5 million (2017 est.)

country comparison to the world: 17

**LABOR FORCE - BY OCCUPATION:**

agriculture: 1.3%

industry: 15.2%

services: 83.5% (2014 est.)

**UNEMPLOYMENT RATE:**

4.4% (2017 est.)

4.9% (2016 est.)

country comparison to the world: 61

**POPULATION BELOW POVERTY LINE:**

15% (2013 est.)

**HOUSEHOLD INCOME OR CONSUMPTION BY PERCENTAGE SHARE:**

lowest 10%: 31.1% (2012)

highest 10%: 31.1% (2012)

**DISTRIBUTION OF FAMILY INCOME - GINI INDEX:**

32.4 (2012)

33.4 (2010)

country comparison to the world: 117

**BUDGET:**

revenues: 1.028 trillion (2017 est.)

expenditures: 1.079 trillion (2017 est.)

**TAXES AND OTHER REVENUES:**

39.1% (of GDP) (2017 est.)

country comparison to the world: 49

**BUDGET SURPLUS (+) OR DEFICIT (-):**

-1.9% (of GDP) (2017 est.)

country comparison to the world: 102

**PUBLIC DEBT:**

87.5% of GDP (2017 est.)

87.9% of GDP (2016 est.)

note: data cover general government debt and include debt instruments issued (or owned) by government entities other than the treasury; the data include treasury debt held by foreign entities; the data include debt issued by subnational entities, as well as intragovernmental debt; intragovernmental debt consists of treasury borrowings from surpluses in the social funds, such as for retirement, medical care, and unemployment; debt instruments for the social funds are not sold at public auctions

country comparison to the world: 29

**FISCAL YEAR:**

6 April - 5 April

**INFLATION RATE (CONSUMER PRICES):**

2.7% (2017 est.)

0.7% (2016 est.)

country comparison to the world: 126
**CENTRAL BANK DISCOUNT RATE:**
0.25% (31 December 2016)
0.5% (31 December 2015)
country comparison to the world: 141
**COMMERCIAL BANK PRIME LENDING RATE:**
4.38% (31 December 2017 est.)
4.44% (31 December 2016 est.)
country comparison to the world: 159
**STOCK OF NARROW MONEY:**
$110.9 billion (31 December 2017 est.)
$96.15 billion (31 December 2016 est.)
country comparison to the world: 34
**STOCK OF BROAD MONEY:**
$110.9 billion (31 December 2017 est.)
$96.15 billion (31 December 2016 est.)
country comparison to the world: 34
**STOCK OF DOMESTIC CREDIT:**
$3.22 trillion (31 December 2017 est.)
$2.785 trillion (31 December 2016 est.)
country comparison to the world: 7
**MARKET VALUE OF PUBLICLY TRADED SHARES:**
$3.019 trillion (31 December 2012 est.)
$2.903 trillion (31 December 2011 est.)
$3.107 trillion (31 December 2010 est.)
country comparison to the world: 5
**CURRENT ACCOUNT BALANCE:**
-$99.21 billion (2017 est.)
-$139.3 billion (2016 est.)
country comparison to the world: 205
**EXPORTS:**
$441.2 billion (2017 est.)
$407.3 billion (2016 est.)
country comparison to the world: 10
**EXPORTS - PARTNERS:**
US 13.2%, Germany 10.5%, France 7.4%, Netherlands 6.2%, Ireland 5.6%, China 4.8%, Switzerland 4.5% (2017)
**EXPORTS - COMMODITIES:**
manufactured goods, fuels, chemicals; food, beverages, tobacco
**IMPORTS:**
$615.9 billion (2017 est.)
$591 billion (2016 est.)
country comparison to the world: 5
**IMPORTS - COMMODITIES:**
manufactured goods, machinery, fuels; foodstuffs
**IMPORTS - PARTNERS:**
Germany 13.7%, US 9.5%, China 9.3%, Netherlands 8%, France 5.4%, Belgium 5% (2017)
**RESERVES OF FOREIGN EXCHANGE AND GOLD:**
$150.8 billion (31 December 2017 est.)
$129.6 billion (31 December 2015 est.)
country comparison to the world: 17
**DEBT - EXTERNAL:**
$8.126 trillion (31 March 2016 est.)
$8.642 trillion (31 March 2015 est.)
country comparison to the world: 2
**STOCK OF DIRECT FOREIGN INVESTMENT - AT HOME:**
$2.078 trillion (31 December 2017 est.)
$1.858 trillion (31 December 2016 est.)
country comparison to the world: 4
**STOCK OF DIRECT FOREIGN INVESTMENT - ABROAD:**
$2.11 trillion (31 December 2017 est.)
$1.611 trillion (31 December 2016 est.)
country comparison to the world: 4
**EXCHANGE RATES:**
British pounds (GBP) per US dollar -
0.7836 (2017 est.)
0.738 (2016 est.)
0.738 (2015 est.)
0.607 (2014 est.)
0.6391 (2013 est.)

## ENERGY :: UNITED KINGDOM

**ELECTRICITY ACCESS:**
electrification - total population: 100% (2016)
**ELECTRICITY - PRODUCTION:**
318.2 billion kWh (2016 est.)
country comparison to the world: 12
**ELECTRICITY - CONSUMPTION:**
309.2 billion kWh (2016 est.)
country comparison to the world: 11
**ELECTRICITY - EXPORTS:**
2.153 billion kWh (2016 est.)
country comparison to the world: 45
**ELECTRICITY - IMPORTS:**
19.7 billion kWh (2016 est.)
country comparison to the world: 12
**ELECTRICITY - INSTALLED GENERATING CAPACITY:**
97.06 million kW (2016 est.)
country comparison to the world: 13
**ELECTRICITY - FROM FOSSIL FUELS:**
50% of total installed capacity (2016 est.)
country comparison to the world: 152
**ELECTRICITY - FROM NUCLEAR FUELS:**
9% of total installed capacity (2017 est.)
country comparison to the world: 17
**ELECTRICITY - FROM HYDROELECTRIC PLANTS:**
2% of total installed capacity (2017 est.)
country comparison to the world: 143
**ELECTRICITY - FROM OTHER RENEWABLE SOURCES:**
39% of total installed capacity (2017 est.)
country comparison to the world: 7
**CRUDE OIL - PRODUCTION:**
910,500 bbl/day (2017 est.)
country comparison to the world: 20
**CRUDE OIL - EXPORTS:**
710,600 bbl/day (2017 est.)
country comparison to the world: 20
**CRUDE OIL - IMPORTS:**
907,100 bbl/day (2017 est.)
country comparison to the world: 11
**CRUDE OIL - PROVED RESERVES:**
2.069 billion bbl (1 January 2018 est.)
country comparison to the world: 33
**REFINED PETROLEUM PRODUCTS - PRODUCTION:**
1.29 million bbl/day (2017 est.)
country comparison to the world: 16
**REFINED PETROLEUM PRODUCTS - CONSUMPTION:**
1.584 million bbl/day (2017 est.)
country comparison to the world: 15
**REFINED PETROLEUM PRODUCTS - EXPORTS:**
613,800 bbl/day (2017 est.)
country comparison to the world: 14
**REFINED PETROLEUM PRODUCTS - IMPORTS:**
907,500 bbl/day (2017 est.)
country comparison to the world: 7
**NATURAL GAS - PRODUCTION:**
42.11 billion cu m (2017 est.)
country comparison to the world: 19

**NATURAL GAS - CONSUMPTION:**

79.17 billion cu m (2017 est.)

country comparison to the world: 10

**NATURAL GAS - EXPORTS:**

11.27 billion cu m (2017 est.)

country comparison to the world: 19

**NATURAL GAS - IMPORTS:**

47 billion cu m (2017 est.)

country comparison to the world: 11

**NATURAL GAS - PROVED RESERVES:**

176 billion cu m (1 January 2018 est.)

country comparison to the world: 46

**CARBON DIOXIDE EMISSIONS FROM CONSUMPTION OF ENERGY:**

424 million Mt (2017 est.)

country comparison to the world: 16

## COMMUNICATIONS :: UNITED KINGDOM

**TELEPHONES - FIXED LINES:**

total subscriptions: 33,140,662 (2017 est.)

subscriptions per 100 inhabitants: 50 (2017 est.)

country comparison to the world: 7

**TELEPHONES - MOBILE CELLULAR:**

total subscriptions: 79,173,658 (2017 est.)

subscriptions per 100 inhabitants: 121 (2017 est.)

country comparison to the world: 20

**TELEPHONE SYSTEM:**

general assessment: technologically advanced domestic and international system (2016)

domestic: equal mix of buried cables, microwave radio relay, and fiber-optic systems (2016)

international: country code - 44; numerous submarine cables provide links throughout Europe, Asia, Australia, the Middle East, and US; satellite earth stations - 10 Intelsat (7 Atlantic Ocean and 3 Indian Ocean), 1 Inmarsat (Atlantic Ocean region), and 1 Eutelsat; at least 8 large international switching centers (2016)

**BROADCAST MEDIA:**

public service broadcaster, British Broadcasting Corporation (BBC), is the largest broadcasting corporation in the world; BBC operates multiple TV networks with regional and local TV service; a mixed system of public and commercial TV broadcasters along with satellite and cable systems provide access to hundreds of TV stations throughout the world; BBC operates multiple national, regional, and local radio networks with multiple transmission sites; a large number of commercial radio stations, as well as satellite radio services are available (2018)

**INTERNET COUNTRY CODE:**

.uk

**INTERNET USERS:**

total: 61,064,454 (July 2016 est.)

percent of population: 94.8% (July 2016 est.)

country comparison to the world: 10

**BROADBAND - FIXED SUBSCRIPTIONS:**

total: 26,015,818 (2017 est.)

subscriptions per 100 inhabitants: 40 (2017 est.)

country comparison to the world: 8

**COMMUNICATIONS - NOTE:**

the British Library claims to be the largest library in the world with well over 150 million items and in most known languages; it receives copies of all books produced in the UK or Ireland, as well as a significant proportion of overseas titles distributed in the UK; in addition to books (print and digital), holdings include: journals, manuscripts, newspapers, magazines, sound and music recordings, videos, maps, prints, patents, and drawings (2018)

## TRANSPORTATION :: UNITED KINGDOM

**NATIONAL AIR TRANSPORT SYSTEM:**

number of registered air carriers: 28 (2015)

inventory of registered aircraft operated by air carriers: 1,242 (2015)

annual passenger traffic on registered air carriers: 131,449,680 (2015)

annual freight traffic on registered air carriers: 5,466,504,676 mt-km (2015)

**CIVIL AIRCRAFT REGISTRATION COUNTRY CODE PREFIX:**

G (2016)

**AIRPORTS:**

460 (2013)

country comparison to the world: 18

**AIRPORTS - WITH PAVED RUNWAYS:**

total: 271 (2013)

over 3,047 m: 7 (2013)

2,438 to 3,047 m: 29 (2013)

1,524 to 2,437 m: 89 (2013)

914 to 1,523 m: 80 (2013)

under 914 m: 66 (2013)

**AIRPORTS - WITH UNPAVED RUNWAYS:**

total: 189 (2013)

1,524 to 2,437 m: 3 (2013)

914 to 1,523 m: 26 (2013)

under 914 m: 160 (2013)

**HELIPORTS:**

9 (2013)

**PIPELINES:**

502 km condensate, 9 km condensate/gas, 28603 km gas, 59 km liquid petroleum gas, 5256 km oil, 175 km oil/gas/water, 4919 km refined products, 255 km water (2013)

**RAILWAYS:**

total: 16,837 km (2015)

standard gauge: 16,534 km 1.435-m gauge (5,357 km electrified) (2015)

broad gauge: 303 km 1.600-m gauge (in Northern Ireland) (2015)

country comparison to the world: 16

**ROADWAYS:**

total: 394,428 km (2009)

paved: 394,428 km (includes 3,519 km of expressways) (2009)

country comparison to the world: 18

**WATERWAYS:**

3,200 km (620 km used for commerce) (2009)

country comparison to the world: 31

**MERCHANT MARINE:**

total: 1,551 (2017)

by type: bulk carrier 117, container ship 112, general cargo 175, oil tanker 173, other 974 (2017)

country comparison to the world: 17

**PORTS AND TERMINALS:**

major seaport(s): Dover, Felixstowe, Immingham, Liverpool, London, Southampton, Teesport (England); Forth Ports (Scotland); Milford Haven (Wales)

oil terminal(s): Fawley Marine terminal, Liverpool Bay terminal (England); Braefoot Bay terminal, Finnart oil terminal, Hound Point terminal (Scotland) container port(s) (TEUs): Felixstowe (4,000,000), London (2,537,000), Southampton (1,957,000) (2016)

LNG terminal(s) (import): Isle of Grain, Milford Haven, Teesside

## MILITARY AND SECURITY :: UNITED KINGDOM

### MILITARY EXPENDITURES:

2.2% of GDP (2016)

2.05% of GDP (2015)

2.22% of GDP (2014)

country comparison to the world: 46

### MILITARY BRANCHES:

Army, Royal Navy (includes Royal Marines), Royal Air Force (2013)

### MILITARY SERVICE AGE AND OBLIGATION:

16-33 years of age (officers 17-28) for voluntary military service (with parental consent under 18); no conscription; women serve in military services including ground combat roles; must be citizen of the UK, Commonwealth, or Republic of Ireland; reservists serve a minimum of 3 years, to age 45 or 55; 17 years 6 months of age for voluntary military service by Nepalese citizens in the Brigade of Gurkhas; 16-34 years of age for voluntary military service by Papua New Guinean citizens (2016)

## TERRORISM :: UNITED KINGDOM

### TERRORIST GROUPS - HOME BASED:

Continuity Irish Republican Army (CIRA):
aim(s): disrupt the Northern Ireland peace process; remove British rule in Northern Ireland and, ultimately, unify Ireland
area(s) of operation: based and operationally active primarily in Belfast and along the Northern Ireland-Ireland border, where operatives continue to carry out bombings, assassinations, kidnappings, hijackings, extortion, and robberies (April 2018)

New Irish Republican Army (NIRA):
aim(s): use violence to remove British rule in Northern Ireland, disrupt the Northern Ireland peace process, and unify Ireland
area(s) of operation: based and operationally active in Northern Ireland, where operatives continue to conduct occasional shootings and small-scale bombings; maintains a presence in Great Britain
note: formerly known as the Real Irish Republican Army (RIRA) (April 2018)

## TRANSNATIONAL ISSUES :: UNITED KINGDOM

### DISPUTES - INTERNATIONAL:

in 2002, Gibraltar residents voted overwhelmingly by referendum to reject any "shared sovereignty" arrangement between the UK and Spain; the Government of Gibraltar insisted on equal participation in talks between the two countriesSpain disapproved of UK plans to grant Gibraltar greater autonomyMauritius and Seychelles claim the Chagos Archipelago (British Indian Ocean Territory)in 2001, the former inhabitants of the archipelago, evicted 1967 - 1973, were granted UK citizenship and the right of return, followed by Orders in Council in 2004 that banned rehabitation, a High Court ruling reversed the ban, a Court of Appeal refusal to hear the case, and a Law Lords' decision in 2008 denied the right of returnin addition, the UK created the world's largest marine protection area around the Chagos islands prohibiting the extraction of any natural resources thereinUK rejects sovereignty talks requested by Argentina, which still claims the Falkland Islands (Islas Malvinas) and South Georgia and the South Sandwich Islandsterritorial claim in Antarctica (British Antarctic Territory) overlaps Argentine claim and partially overlaps Chilean claimIceland, the UK, and Ireland dispute Denmark's claim that the Faroe Islands' continental shelf extends beyond 200 nm

### REFUGEES AND INTERNALLY DISPLACED PERSONS:

refugees (country of origin): 14,363 (Iran), 13,720 (Eritrea), 9,752 (Afghanistan), 8,790 (Zimbabwe), 8,269 (Syria), 7,326 (Sudan), 6,814 (Pakistan), 5,954 (Somalia), 5,809 (Sri Lanka) (2016)

stateless persons: 97 (2017)

### ILLICIT DRUGS:

producer of limited amounts of synthetic drugs and synthetic precursor chemicals; major consumer of Southwest Asian heroin, Latin American cocaine, and synthetic drugs; money-laundering center

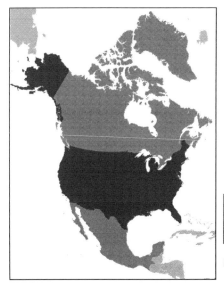

# NORTH AMERICA :: UNITED STATES

## INTRODUCTION :: UNITED STATES

### BACKGROUND:

Britain's American colonies broke with the mother country in 1776 and were recognized as the new nation of the United States of America following the Treaty of Paris in 1783. During the 19th and 20th centuries, 37 new states were added to the original 13 as the nation expanded across the North American continent and acquired a number of overseas possessions. The two most traumatic experiences in the nation's history were the Civil War (1861-65), in which a northern Union of states defeated a secessionist Confederacy of 11 southern slave states, and the Great Depression of the 1930s, an economic downturn during which about a quarter of the labor force lost its jobs. Buoyed by victories in World Wars I and II and the end of the Cold War in 1991, the US remains the world's most powerful nation state. Since the end of World War II, the economy has achieved relatively steady growth, low unemployment and inflation, and rapid advances in technology.

UNITED STATES SUMMARY

## GEOGRAPHY :: UNITED STATES

### LOCATION:
North America, bordering both the North Atlantic Ocean and the North Pacific Ocean, between Canada and Mexico

### GEOGRAPHIC COORDINATES:
38 00 N, 97 00 W

### MAP REFERENCES:
North America

### AREA:
total: 9,833,517 sq km (2010)

land: 9,147,593 sq km (2010)

water: 685,924 sq km (2010)

note: includes only the 50 states and District of Columbia, no overseas territories

country comparison to the world: 4

### AREA - COMPARATIVE:
about half the size of Russia; about three-tenths the size of Africa; about half the size of South America (or slightly larger than Brazil); slightly larger than China; more than twice the size of the European Union

### LAND BOUNDARIES:
total: 12,048 km

border countries (2): Canada 8893 km (including 2477 km with Alaska), Mexico 3155 km

note: US Naval Base at Guantanamo Bay, Cuba is leased by the US and is part of Cuba; the base boundary is 28.5 km

### COASTLINE:
19,924 km

### MARITIME CLAIMS:
territorial sea: 12 nm

exclusive economic zone: 200 nm

contiguous zone: 24 nm

continental shelf: not specified

### CLIMATE:
mostly temperate, but tropical in Hawaii and Florida, arctic in Alaska, semiarid in the great plains west of the Mississippi River, and arid in the Great Basin of the southwest; low winter temperatures in the northwest are ameliorated occasionally in January and February by warm chinook winds from the eastern slopes of the Rocky Mountains

### TERRAIN:
vast central plain, mountains in west, hills and low mountains in east; rugged mountains and broad river valleys in Alaska; rugged, volcanic topography in Hawaii

### ELEVATION:
mean elevation: 760 m

elevation extremes: -86 m lowest point: Death Valley (lowest point in North America)

6190 highest point: Denali (Mount McKinley) (highest point in North America)

note: the peak of Mauna Kea (4,205 m above sea level) on the island of Hawaii rises about 10,200 m above the Pacific Ocean floor; by this measurement, it is the world's tallest mountain - higher than Mount Everest (8,850 m), which is recognized as the tallest mountain above sea level

### NATURAL RESOURCES:
coal, copper, lead, molybdenum, phosphates, rare earth elements, uranium, bauxite, gold, iron, mercury, nickel, potash, silver, tungsten, zinc, petroleum, natural gas, timber, arable land, note, the US has the world's largest coal reserves with 491 billion short tons accounting for 27% of the world's total

### LAND USE:
agricultural land: 44.5% (2011 est.)

arable land: 16.8% (2011 est.) / permanent crops: 0.3% (2011 est.) / permanent pasture: 27.4% (2011 est.)

**forest:** 33.3% (2011 est.)

**other:** 22.2% (2011 est.)

### IRRIGATED LAND:
264,000 sq km (2012)

### POPULATION DISTRIBUTION:
large urban clusters are spread throughout the eastern half of the US (particularly the Great Lakes area, northeast, east, and southeast) and the western tier states; mountainous areas, principally the Rocky Mountains and Appalachian chain, deserts in the southwest, the dense boreal forests in the extreme north, and the central prarie states are less densely populated; Alaska's population is concentrated along its southern coast - with particular emphasis on the city of Anchorage - and Hawaii's is centered on the island of Oahu

### NATURAL HAZARDS:
tsunamis; volcanoes; earthquake activity around Pacific Basin; hurricanes along the Atlantic and Gulf of Mexico coasts; tornadoes in the Midwest and Southeast; mud slides in California; forest fires in the west; flooding; permafrost in northern Alaska, a major impediment to development

**volcanism:** volcanic activity in the Hawaiian Islands, Western Alaska, the Pacific Northwest, and in the Northern Mariana Islands; both Mauna Loa (4,170 m) in Hawaii and Mount Rainier (4,392 m) in Washington have been deemed Decade Volcanoes by the International Association of Volcanology and Chemistry of the Earth's Interior, worthy of study due to their explosive history and close proximity to human populations; Pavlof (2,519 m) is the most active volcano in Alaska's Aleutian Arc and poses a significant threat to air travel since the area constitutes a major flight path between North America and East Asia; St. Helens (2,549 m), famous for the devastating 1980 eruption, remains active today; numerous other historically active volcanoes exist, mostly concentrated in the Aleutian arc and Hawaii; they include: in Alaska: Aniakchak, Augustine, Chiginagak, Fourpeaked, Iliamna, Katmai, Kupreanof, Martin, Novarupta, Redoubt, Spurr, Wrangell, Trident, Ugashik-Peulik, Ukinrek Maars, Veniaminof; in Hawaii: Haleakala, Kilauea, Loihi; in the Northern Mariana Islands: Anatahan; and in the Pacific Northwest: Mount Baker, Mount Hood; see note 2 under "Geography - note"

### ENVIRONMENT - CURRENT ISSUES:
air pollution; large emitter of carbon dioxide from the burning of fossil fuels; water pollution from runoff of pesticides and fertilizers; limited natural freshwater resources in much of the western part of the country require careful management; deforestation; mining; desertification; species conservation; invasive species

### ENVIRONMENT - INTERNATIONAL AGREEMENTS:
**party to:** Air Pollution, Air Pollution-Nitrogen Oxides, Antarctic-Environmental Protocol, Antarctic-Marine Living Resources, Antarctic Seals, Antarctic Treaty, Climate Change, Desertification, Endangered Species, Environmental Modification, Marine Dumping, Marine Life Conservation, Ozone Layer Protection, Ship Pollution, Tropical Timber 83, Tropical Timber 94, Wetlands, Whaling

**signed, but not ratified:** Air Pollution-Persistent Organic Pollutants, Air Pollution-Volatile Organic Compounds, Biodiversity, Climate Change-Kyoto Protocol, Hazardous Wastes

### GEOGRAPHY - NOTE:
**note 1:** world's third-largest country by size (after Russia and Canada) and by population (after China and India); Denali (Mt. McKinley) is the highest point in North America and Death Valley the lowest point on the continent

**note 2:** the western coast of the United States and southern coast of Alaska lie along the Ring of Fire, a belt of active volcanoes and earthquake epicenters bordering the Pacific Ocean; up to 90% of the world's earthquakes and some 75% of the world's volcanoes occur within the Ring of Fire

**note 3:** the Aleutian Islands are a chain of volcanic islands that divide the Bering Sea (north) from the main Pacific Ocean (south); they extend about 1,800 km westward from the Alaskan Peninsula; the archipelago consists of 14 larger islands, 55 smaller islands, and hundreds of islets; there are 41 active volcanoes on the islands, which together form a large northern section of the Ring of Fire

## PEOPLE AND SOCIETY :: UNITED STATES

### POPULATION:
329,256,465 (July 2018 est.)

**country comparison to the world:** 3

### NATIONALITY:
**noun:** American(s)

**adjective:** American

### ETHNIC GROUPS:
white 72.4%, black 12.6%, Asian 4.8%, Amerindian and Alaska native 0.9%, native Hawaiian and other Pacific islander 0.2%, other 6.2%, two or more races 2.9% (2010 est.)

**note:** a separate listing for Hispanic is not included because the US Census Bureau considers Hispanic to mean persons of Spanish/Hispanic/Latino origin including those of Mexican, Cuban, Puerto Rican, Dominican Republic, Spanish, and Central or South American origin living in the US who may be of any race or ethnic group (white, black, Asian, etc.); an estimated 16.3% of the total US population is Hispanic as of 2010

### LANGUAGES:
English only 78.2%, Spanish 13.4%, Chinese 1.1%, other 7.3% (2017 est.)

**note:** data represent the language spoken at home; the US has no official national language, but English has acquired official status in 32 of the 50 states; Hawaiian is an official language in the state of Hawaii, and 20 indigenous languages are official in Alaska

### RELIGIONS:
Protestant 46.5%, Roman Catholic 20.8%, Jewish 1.9%, Mormon 1.6%, other Christian 0.9%, Muslim 0.9%, Jehovah's Witness 0.8%, Buddhist 0.7%, Hindu 0.7%, other 1.8%, unaffiliated 22.8%, don't know/refused 0.6% (2014 est.)

### AGE STRUCTURE:
**0-14 years:** 18.62% (male 31,329,121 /female 29,984,705)

**15-24 years:** 13.12% (male 22,119,340 /female 21,082,599)

**25-54 years:** 39.29% (male 64,858,646 /female 64,496,889)

**55-64 years:** 12.94% (male 20,578,432 /female 22,040,267)

**65 years and over:** 16.03% (male 23,489,515 /female 29,276,951) (2018 est.)

**DEPENDENCY RATIOS:**

  total dependency ratio: 51.2 (2015 est.)

  youth dependency ratio: 29 (2015 est.)

  elderly dependency ratio: 22.1 (2015 est.)

  potential support ratio: 4.5 (2015 est.)

**MEDIAN AGE:**

  total: 38.2 years

  male: 37 years

  female: 39.5 years (2018 est.)

  country comparison to the world: 61

**POPULATION GROWTH RATE:**

0.8% (2018 est.)

  country comparison to the world: 130

**BIRTH RATE:**

12.4 births/1,000 population (2018 est.)

  country comparison to the world: 157

**DEATH RATE:**

8.2 deaths/1,000 population (2018 est.)

  country comparison to the world: 86

**NET MIGRATION RATE:**

3.9 migrant(s)/1,000 population (2017 est.)

  country comparison to the world: 30

**POPULATION DISTRIBUTION:**

large urban clusters are spread throughout the eastern half of the US (particularly the Great Lakes area, northeast, east, and southeast) and the western tier states; mountainous areas, principally the Rocky Mountains and Appalachian chain, deserts in the southwest, the dense boreal forests in the extreme north, and the central prarie states are less densely populated; Alaska's population is concentrated along its southern coast - with particular emphasis on the city of Anchorage - and Hawaii's is centered on the island of Oahu

**URBANIZATION:**

  urban population: 82.3% of total population (2018)

  rate of urbanization: 0.95% annual rate of change (2015-20 est.)

**MAJOR URBAN AREAS - POPULATION:**

18.819 million New York-Newark, 12.458 million Los Angeles-Long Beach-Santa Ana, 8.864 million Chicago, 6.115 million Houston, 5.817 million Miami, 5.207 million WASHINGTON, D.C. (capital) (2018)

**SEX RATIO:**

  at birth: NA (2017 est.)

  0-14 years: 1.04 male(s)/female (2017 est.)

  15-24 years: 1.05 male(s)/female (2017 est.)

  25-54 years: 1 male(s)/female (2017 est.)

  55-64 years: 0.93 male(s)/female (2017 est.)

  65 years and over: 0.79 male(s)/female (2017 est.)

  total population: 0.97 male(s)/female (2017 est.)

**MOTHER'S MEAN AGE AT FIRST BIRTH:**

26.4 years (2015 est.)

**MATERNAL MORTALITY RATE:**

14 deaths/100,000 live births (2015 est.)

  country comparison to the world: 139

**INFANT MORTALITY RATE:**

  total: 5.7 deaths/1,000 live births (2018 est.)

  male: 6.2 deaths/1,000 live births (2018 est.)

  female: 5.2 deaths/1,000 live births (2018 est.)

  country comparison to the world: 170

**LIFE EXPECTANCY AT BIRTH:**

  total population: 80.1 years (2018 est.)

  male: 77.8 years (2018 est.)

  female: 82.3 years (2018 est.)

  country comparison to the world: 45

**TOTAL FERTILITY RATE:**

1.87 children born/woman (2017 est.)

  country comparison to the world: 142

**CONTRACEPTIVE PREVALENCE RATE:**

72.7% (2013/15)

  note: percent of women aged 15-44

**HEALTH EXPENDITURES:**

17.1% of GDP (2014)

  country comparison to the world: 2

**PHYSICIANS DENSITY:**

2.57 physicians/1,000 population (2014)

**HOSPITAL BED DENSITY:**

2.9 beds/1,000 population (2013)

**DRINKING WATER SOURCE:**

  improved:

  urban: 99.4% of population

  rural: 98.2% of population

  total: 99.2% of population

  unimproved:

  urban: 0.6% of population

  rural: 1.8% of population

  total: 0.8% of population (2015 est.)

**SANITATION FACILITY ACCESS:**

  improved:

  urban: 100% of population (2015 est.)

  rural: 100% of population (2015 est.)

  total: 100% of population (2015 est.)

  unimproved:

  urban: 0% of population (2015 est.)

  rural: 0% of population (2015 est.)

  total: 0% of population (2015 est.)

**HIV/AIDS - ADULT PREVALENCE RATE:**

NA

**HIV/AIDS - PEOPLE LIVING WITH HIV/AIDS:**

NA

**HIV/AIDS - DEATHS:**

NA

**OBESITY - ADULT PREVALENCE RATE:**

36.2% (2016)

  country comparison to the world: 12

**CHILDREN UNDER THE AGE OF 5 YEARS UNDERWEIGHT:**

0.5% (2012)

  country comparison to the world: 126

**EDUCATION EXPENDITURES:**

5% of GDP (2014)

  country comparison to the world: 78

**SCHOOL LIFE EXPECTANCY (PRIMARY TO TERTIARY EDUCATION):**

  total: 17 years (2014)

  male: 16 years (2014)

  female: 17 years (2014)

**UNEMPLOYMENT, YOUTH AGES 15-24:**

  total: 9.2% (2017 est.)

  male: 10.3% (2017 est.)

  female: 8.1% (2017 est.)

  country comparison to the world: 131

## GOVERNMENT :: UNITED STATES

**COUNTRY NAME:**

**conventional long form:** United States of America

**conventional short form:** United States

**abbreviation:** US or USA

**etymology:** the name America is derived from that of Amerigo VESPUCCI (1454-1512) - Italian explorer, navigator, and cartographer - using the Latin form of his name, Americus, feminized to America

## GOVERNMENT TYPE:
constitutional federal republic

## CAPITAL:
**name:** Washington, DC

**geographic coordinates:** 38 53 N, 77 02 W

**time difference:** UTC-5 (during Standard Time)

**daylight saving time:** +1hr, begins second Sunday in March; ends first Sunday in November

**note:** the 50 United States cover six time zones

## ADMINISTRATIVE DIVISIONS:
50 states and 1 district*; Alabama, Alaska, Arizona, Arkansas, California, Colorado, Connecticut, Delaware, District of Columbia*, Florida, Georgia, Hawaii, Idaho, Illinois, Indiana, Iowa, Kansas, Kentucky, Louisiana, Maine, Maryland, Massachusetts, Michigan, Minnesota, Mississippi, Missouri, Montana, Nebraska, Nevada, New Hampshire, New Jersey, New Mexico, New York, North Carolina, North Dakota, Ohio, Oklahoma, Oregon, Pennsylvania, Rhode Island, South Carolina, South Dakota, Tennessee, Texas, Utah, Vermont, Virginia, Washington, West Virginia, Wisconsin, Wyoming

## DEPENDENT AREAS:
American Samoa, Baker Island, Guam, Howland Island, Jarvis Island, Johnston Atoll, Kingman Reef, Midway Islands, Navassa Island, Northern Mariana Islands, Palmyra Atoll, Puerto Rico, Virgin Islands, Wake Island

**note:** from 18 July 1947 until 1 October 1994, the US administered the Trust Territory of the Pacific Islands; it entered into a political relationship with all four political entities: the Northern Mariana Islands is a commonwealth in political union with the US (effective 3 November 1986); the Republic of the Marshall Islands signed a Compact of Free Association with the US (effective 21 October 1986); the Federated States of Micronesia signed a Compact of Free Association with the US (effective 3 November 1986); Palau concluded a Compact of Free Association with the US (effective 1 October 1994)

## INDEPENDENCE:
4 July 1776 (declared independence from Great Britain); 3 September 1783 (recognized by Great Britain)

## NATIONAL HOLIDAY:
Independence Day, 4 July (1776)

## CONSTITUTION:
**history:** previous 1781 (Articles of Confederation and Perpetual Union); latest drafted July - September 1787, submitted to the Congress of the Confederation 20 September 1787, submitted for states' ratification 28 September 1787, ratification completed by nine of the 13 states 21 June 1788, effective 4 March 1789 (2018)

**amendments:** proposed as a "joint resolution" by Congress, which requires a two-thirds majority vote in both the House of Representatives and the Senate or by a constitutional convention called for by at least two-thirds of the state legislatures; passage requires ratification by three-fourths of the state legislatures or passage in state-held constitutional conventions as specified by Congress; the US president has no role in the constitutional amendment process; amended many times, last in 1992 (2018)

## LEGAL SYSTEM:
common law system based on English common law at the federal level; state legal systems based on common law except Louisiana, which is based on Napoleonic civil code; judicial review of legislative acts

## INTERNATIONAL LAW ORGANIZATION PARTICIPATION:
withdrew acceptance of compulsory ICJ jurisdiction in 2005; withdrew acceptance of ICCt jurisdiction in 2002

## CITIZENSHIP:
**citizenship by birth:** yes

**citizenship by descent only:** yes

**dual citizenship recognized:** no, but the US government acknowledges such situtations exist; US citizens are not encouraged to seek dual citizenship since it limits protection by the US

**residency requirement for naturalization:** 5 years

## SUFFRAGE:
18 years of age; universal

## EXECUTIVE BRANCH:
**chief of state:** President Donald J. TRUMP (since 20 January 2017); Vice President Michael R. PENCE (since 20 January 2017); note - the president is both chief of state and head of government

**head of government:** President Donald J. TRUMP (since 20 January 2017); Vice President Michael R. PENCE (since 20 January 2017)

**cabinet:** Cabinet appointed by the president, approved by the Senate

**elections/appointments:** president and vice president indirectly elected on the same ballot by the Electoral College of 'electors' chosen from each state; president and vice president serve a 4-year term (eligible for a second term); election last held on 8 November 2016 (next to be held on 3 November 2020)

**election results:** Donald J. TRUMP elected president; electoral vote - Donald J. TRUMP (Republican Party) 304, Hillary D. CLINTON (Democratic Party) 227, other 7; percent of direct popular vote - Hillary D. CLINTON 48.2%, Donald J. TRUMP 46.1%, other 5.7%

## LEGISLATIVE BRANCH:
**description:** bicameral Congress consists of:
Senate (100 seats; 2 members directly elected in each of the 50 state constituencies by simple majority vote except in Georgia and Louisiana which require an absolute majority vote with a second round if needed; members serve 6-year terms with one-third of membership renewed every 2 years)
House of Representatives (435 seats; members directly elected in single-seat constituencies by simple majority vote except in Georgia which requires an absolute majority vote with a second round if needed; members serve 2-year terms)

**elections:**
Senate - last held on 6 November 2018 (next to be held on 3 November 2020)
House of Representatives - last held on 6 November 2018 (next to be held on 3 November 2020)

**election results:**
Senate - percent of vote by party - NA; seats by party - Republican Party 53, Democratic Party 45, independent 2; House of Representatives - percent of vote by party - NA; seats by party - Democratic Party 234, Republican

Party 200; note - 1 seat has yet to be decided

note: in addition to the regular members of the House of Representatives there are 6 non-voting delegates elected from the District of Columbia and the US territories of American Samoa, Guam, Puerto Rico, the Northern Mariana Islands, and the Virgin Islands; these are single seat constituencies directly elected by simple majority vote to serve a 2-year term (except for the resident commissioner of Puerto Rico who serves a 4-year term); the delegate can vote when serving on a committee and when the House meets as the Committee of the Whole House, but not when legislation is submitted for a "full floor" House vote; election of delegates last held on 8 November 2016 (next to be held on 6 November 2018)

## JUDICIAL BRANCH:

**highest courts:** US Supreme Court (consists of 9 justices - the chief justice and 8 associate justices)

**judge selection and term of office:** president nominates and, with the advice and consent of the Senate, appoints Supreme Court justices; justices appointed for life

**subordinate courts:** Courts of Appeal (includes the US Court of Appeal for the Federal District and 12 regional appeals courts); 94 federal district courts in 50 states and territories

note: the US court system consists of the federal court system and the state court systems; although each court system is responsible for hearing certain types of cases, neither is completely independent of the other, and the systems often interact

## POLITICAL PARTIES AND LEADERS:

Democratic Party [Tom PEREZ]
Green Party [collective leadership]
Libertarian Party [Nicholas SARWARK]
Republican Party [Ronna Romney MCDANIEL]

## INTERNATIONAL ORGANIZATION PARTICIPATION:

ADB (nonregional member), AfDB (nonregional member), ANZUS, APEC, Arctic Council, ARF, ASEAN (dialogue partner), Australia Group, BIS, BSEC (observer), CBSS (observer), CD, CE (observer), CERN (observer), CICA (observer), CP, EAPC, EAS, EBRD, EITI (implementing country), FAO, FATF, G-5, G-7, G-8, G-10, G-20, IADB, IAEA, IBRD, ICAO, ICC (national committees), ICRM, IDA, IEA, IFAD, IFC, IFRCS, IGAD (partners), IHO, ILO, IMF, IMO, IMSO, Interpol, IOC, IOM, ISO, ITSO, ITU, ITUC (NGOs), MIGA, MINUSMA, MINUSTAH, MONUSCO, NAFTA, NATO, NEA, NSG, OAS, OECD, OPCW, OSCE, Pacific Alliance (observer), Paris Club, PCA, PIF (partner), SAARC (observer), SELEC (observer), SICA (observer), SPC, UN, UNCTAD, UNESCO, UNHCR, UNITAR, UNMIL, UNMISS, UNRWA, UN Security Council (permanent), UNTSO, UPU, WCO, WHO, WIPO, WMO, WTO, ZC

## FLAG DESCRIPTION:

13 equal horizontal stripes of red (top and bottom) alternating with white; there is a blue rectangle in the upper hoist-side corner bearing 50 small, white, five-pointed stars arranged in nine offset horizontal rows of six stars (top and bottom) alternating with rows of five stars; the 50 stars represent the 50 states, the 13 stripes represent the 13 original colonies; blue stands for loyalty, devotion, truth, justice, and friendship, red symbolizes courage, zeal, and fervency, while white denotes purity and rectitude of conduct; commonly referred to by its nickname of Old Glory

note: the design and colors have been the basis for a number of other flags, including Chile, Liberia, Malaysia, and Puerto Rico

## NATIONAL SYMBOL(S):

bald eagle; national colors: red, white, blue

## NATIONAL ANTHEM:

**name:** The Star-Spangled Banner

**lyrics/music:** Francis Scott KEY/John Stafford SMITH

note: adopted 1931; during the War of 1812, after witnessing the successful American defense of Fort McHenry in Baltimore following British naval bombardment, Francis Scott KEY wrote the lyrics to what would become the national anthem; the lyrics were set to the tune of "The Anacreontic Song"; only the first verse is sung

# ECONOMY :: UNITED STATES

## ECONOMY - OVERVIEW:

The US has the most technologically powerful economy in the world, with a per capita GDP of $59,500. US firms are at or near the forefront in technological advances, especially in computers, pharmaceuticals, and medical, aerospace, and military equipment; however, their advantage has narrowed since the end of World War II. Based on a comparison of GDP measured at purchasing power parity conversion rates, the US economy in 2014, having stood as the largest in the world for more than a century, slipped into second place behind China, which has more than tripled the US growth rate for each year of the past four decades.

In the US, private individuals and business firms make most of the decisions, and the federal and state governments buy needed goods and services predominantly in the private marketplace. US business firms enjoy greater flexibility than their counterparts in Western Europe and Japan in decisions to expand capital plant, to lay off surplus workers, and to develop new products. At the same time, businesses face higher barriers to enter their rivals' home markets than foreign firms face entering US markets.

Long-term problems for the US include stagnation of wages for lower-income families, inadequate investment in deteriorating infrastructure, rapidly rising medical and pension costs of an aging population, energy shortages, and sizable current account and budget deficits.

The onrush of technology has been a driving factor in the gradual development of a "two-tier" labor market in which those at the bottom lack the education and the professional/technical skills of those at the top and, more and more, fail to get comparable pay raises, health insurance coverage, and other benefits. But the globalization of trade, and especially the rise of low-wage producers such as China, has put additional downward pressure on wages and upward pressure on the return to capital. Since 1975, practically all the gains in household income have gone to the top 20% of households. Since 1996, dividends and capital gains have grown faster than wages or any other category of after-tax income.

Imported oil accounts for more than 50% of US consumption and oil has a major impact on the overall health of the economy. Crude oil prices doubled between 2001 and 2006, the year home prices peaked; higher gasoline prices ate into consumers' budgets and many individuals fell behind in their mortgage payments. Oil prices climbed another 50% between 2006 and 2008, and bank foreclosures more than doubled in the same period. Besides dampening the housing market, soaring oil prices caused a drop in the value of the dollar and a deterioration in the US merchandise trade deficit, which peaked at $840 billion in 2008. Because the US economy is energy-intensive, falling oil prices since 2013 have alleviated many of the problems the earlier increases had created.

The sub-prime mortgage crisis, falling home prices, investment bank failures, tight credit, and the global economic downturn pushed the US into a recession by mid-2008. GDP contracted until the third quarter of 2009, the deepest and longest downturn since the Great Depression. To help stabilize financial markets, the US Congress established a $700 billion Troubled Asset Relief Program in October 2008. The government used some of these funds to purchase equity in US banks and industrial corporations, much of which had been returned to the government by early 2011. In January 2009, Congress passed and former President Barack OBAMA signed a bill providing an additional $787 billion fiscal stimulus to be used over 10 years - two-thirds on additional spending and one-third on tax cuts - to create jobs and to help the economy recover. In 2010 and 2011, the federal budget deficit reached nearly 9% of GDP. In 2012, the Federal Government reduced the growth of spending and the deficit shrank to 7.6% of GDP. US revenues from taxes and other sources are lower, as a percentage of GDP, than those of most other countries.

Wars in Iraq and Afghanistan required major shifts in national resources from civilian to military purposes and contributed to the growth of the budget deficit and public debt. Through FY 2018, the direct costs of the wars will have totaled more than $1.9 trillion, according to US Government figures.

In March 2010, former President OBAMA signed into law the Patient Protection and Affordable Care Act (ACA), a health insurance reform that was designed to extend coverage to an additional 32 million Americans by 2016, through private health insurance for the general population and Medicaid for the impoverished. Total spending on healthcare - public plus private - rose from 9.0% of GDP in 1980 to 17.9% in 2010.

In July 2010, the former president signed the DODD-FRANK Wall Street Reform and Consumer Protection Act, a law designed to promote financial stability by protecting consumers from financial abuses, ending taxpayer bailouts of financial firms, dealing with troubled banks that are "too big to fail," and improving accountability and transparency in the financial system - in particular, by requiring certain financial derivatives to be traded in markets that are subject to government regulation and oversight.

The Federal Reserve Board (Fed) announced plans in December 2012 to purchase $85 billion per month of mortgage-backed and Treasury securities in an effort to hold down long-term interest rates, and to keep short-term rates near zero until unemployment dropped below 6.5% or inflation rose above 2.5%. The Fed ended its purchases during the summer of 2014, after the unemployment rate dropped to 6.2%, inflation stood at 1.7%, and public debt fell below 74% of GDP. In December 2015, the Fed raised its target for the benchmark federal funds rate by 0.25%, the first increase since the recession began. With continued low growth, the Fed opted to raise rates several times since then, and in December 2017, the target rate stood at 1.5%.

In December 2017, Congress passed and President Donald TRUMP signed the Tax Cuts and Jobs Act, which, among its various provisions, reduces the corporate tax rate from 35% to 21%; lowers the individual tax rate for those with the highest incomes from 39.6% to 37%, and by lesser percentages for those at lower income levels; changes many deductions and credits used to calculate taxable income; and eliminates in 2019 the penalty imposed on taxpayers who do not obtain the minimum amount of health insurance required under the ACA. The new taxes took effect on 1 January 2018; the tax cut for corporations are permanent, but those for individuals are scheduled to expire after 2025. The Joint Committee on Taxation (JCT) under the Congressional Budget Office estimates that the new law will reduce tax revenues and increase the federal deficit by about $1.45 trillion over the 2018-2027 period. This amount would decline if economic growth were to exceed the JCT's estimate.

**GDP (PURCHASING POWER PARITY):**

$19.49 trillion (2017 est.)

$19.06 trillion (2016 est.)

$18.77 trillion (2015 est.)

note: data are in 2017 dollars

country comparison to the world: 2

**GDP (OFFICIAL EXCHANGE RATE):**

$19.49 trillion (2017 est.) (2017 est.)

**GDP - REAL GROWTH RATE:**

2.2% (2017 est.)

1.6% (2016 est.)

2.9% (2015 est.)

country comparison to the world: 145

**GDP - PER CAPITA (PPP):**

$59,800 (2017 est.)

$58,900 (2016 est.)

$58,400 (2015 est.)

note: data are in 2017 dollars

country comparison to the world: 19

**GROSS NATIONAL SAVING:**

18.9% of GDP (2017 est.)

18.6% of GDP (2016 est.)

20.1% of GDP (2015 est.)

country comparison to the world: 106

**GDP - COMPOSITION, BY END USE:**

household consumption: 68.4% (2017 est.)

government consumption: 17.3% (2017 est.)

investment in fixed capital: 17.2% (2017 est.)

investment in inventories: 0.1% (2017 est.)

exports of goods and services: 12.1% (2017 est.)

imports of goods and services: -15% (2017 est.)

**GDP - COMPOSITION, BY SECTOR OF ORIGIN:**

agriculture: 0.9% (2017 est.)

industry: 19.1% (2017 est.)

services: 80% (2017 est.)

**AGRICULTURE - PRODUCTS:**

wheat, corn, other grains, fruits, vegetables, cotton; beef, pork, poultry, dairy products; fish; forest products

**INDUSTRIES:**

highly diversified, world leading, high-technology innovator, second-largest industrial output in the world; petroleum, steel, motor vehicles, aerospace, telecommunications, chemicals, electronics, food processing, consumer goods, lumber, mining

**INDUSTRIAL PRODUCTION GROWTH RATE:**

2.3% (2017 est.)

country comparison to the world: 122

**LABOR FORCE:**

160.4 million (2017 est.)

note: includes unemployed

country comparison to the world: 3

**LABOR FORCE - BY OCCUPATION:**

agriculture: 0.7% (2009)

industry: 20.3% (2009)

services: 37.3% (2009)

industry and services: 24.2% (2009)

manufacturing: 17.6% (2009)

farming, forestry, and fishing: 0.7% (2009)

manufacturing, extraction, transportation, and crafts: 20.3% (2009)

managerial, professional, and technical: 37.3% (2009)

sales and office: 24.2% (2009)

other services: 17.6% (2009)

note: figures exclude the unemployed

**UNEMPLOYMENT RATE:**

4.4% (2017 est.)

4.9% (2016 est.)

country comparison to the world: 62

**POPULATION BELOW POVERTY LINE:**

15.1% (2010 est.)

**HOUSEHOLD INCOME OR CONSUMPTION BY PERCENTAGE SHARE:**

lowest 10%: 30% (2007 est.)

highest 10%: 30% (2007 est.)

**DISTRIBUTION OF FAMILY INCOME - GINI INDEX:**

45 (2007)

40.8 (1997)

country comparison to the world: 41

**BUDGET:**

revenues: 3.315 trillion (2017 est.)

expenditures: 3.981 trillion (2017 est.)

note: revenues exclude social contributions of approximately $1.0 trillion; expenditures exclude social benefits of approximately $2.3 trillion

**TAXES AND OTHER REVENUES:**

17% (of GDP) (2017 est.)

note: excludes contributions for social security and other programs; if social contributions were added, taxes and other revenues would amount to approximately 22% of GDP

country comparison to the world: 172

**BUDGET SURPLUS (+) OR DEFICIT (-):**

-3.4% (of GDP) (2017 est.)

country comparison to the world: 145

**PUBLIC DEBT:**

78.8% of GDP (2017 est.)

81.2% of GDP (2016 est.)

note: data cover only what the United States Treasury denotes as "Debt Held by the Public," which includes all debt instruments issued by the Treasury that are owned by non-US Government entities; the data include Treasury debt held by foreign entities; the data exclude debt issued by individual US states, as well as intragovernmental debt; intragovernmental debt consists of Treasury borrowings from surpluses in the trusts for Federal Social Security, Federal Employees, Hospital and Supplemental Medical Insurance (Medicare), Disability and Unemployment, and several other smaller trusts; if data for intragovernment debt were added, "gross debt" would increase by about one-third of GDP

country comparison to the world: 36

**FISCAL YEAR:**

1 October - 30 September

**INFLATION RATE (CONSUMER PRICES):**

2.1% (2017 est.)

1.3% (2016 est.)

country comparison to the world: 110

**CENTRAL BANK DISCOUNT RATE:**

0.5% (31 December 2010)

0.5% (31 December 2009)

country comparison to the world: 137

**COMMERCIAL BANK PRIME LENDING RATE:**

4.1% (31 December 2017 est.)

3.51% (31 December 2016 est.)

country comparison to the world: 165

**STOCK OF NARROW MONEY:**

$3.512 trillion (31 December 2017 est.)

$3.251 trillion (31 December 2016 est.)

country comparison to the world: 3

**STOCK OF BROAD MONEY:**

$3.512 trillion (31 December 2017 est.)

$3.251 trillion (31 December 2016 est.)

country comparison to the world: 3

**STOCK OF DOMESTIC CREDIT:**

$21.59 trillion (31 December 2017 est.)

$20.24 trillion (31 December 2016 est.)

country comparison to the world: 2

**MARKET VALUE OF PUBLICLY TRADED SHARES:**

$25.07 trillion (31 December 2015 est.)

$26.33 trillion (31 December 2014 est.)

$24.03 trillion (31 December 2013 est.)

country comparison to the world: 1

**CURRENT ACCOUNT BALANCE:**

-$449.1 billion (2017 est.)

-$432.9 billion (2016 est.)

country comparison to the world: 206

**EXPORTS:**

$1.553 trillion (2017 est.)

$1.456 trillion (2016 est.)

country comparison to the world: 2

**EXPORTS - PARTNERS:**

Canada 18.3%, Mexico 15.7%, China 8.4%, Japan 4.4% (2017)

**EXPORTS - COMMODITIES:**

agricultural products (soybeans, fruit, corn) 9.2%, industrial supplies (organic chemicals) 26.8%, capital goods (transistors, aircraft, motor vehicle parts, computers, telecommunications equipment) 49.0%, consumer goods (automobiles, medicines) 15.0% (2008 est.)

**IMPORTS:**

$2.361 trillion (2017 est.)

$2.208 trillion (2016 est.)

country comparison to the world: 1

**IMPORTS - COMMODITIES:**

agricultural products 4.9%, industrial supplies 32.9% (crude oil 8.2%), capital goods 30.4% (computers, telecommunications equipment, motor vehicle parts, office machines, electric power machinery), consumer goods 31.8% (automobiles, clothing, medicines, furniture, toys) (2008 est.)

**IMPORTS - PARTNERS:**

China 21.6%, Mexico 13.4%, Canada 12.8%, Japan 5.8%, Germany 5% (2017)

**RESERVES OF FOREIGN EXCHANGE AND GOLD:**

$123.3 billion (31 December 2017 est.)

$117.6 billion (31 December 2015 est.)

country comparison to the world: 20

**DEBT - EXTERNAL:**

$17.91 trillion (31 March 2016 est.)

$17.85 trillion (31 March 2015 est.)

note: approximately 4/5ths of US external debt is denominated in US dollars; foreign lenders have been willing to hold US dollar denominated debt instruments because they view the dollar as the world's reserve currency

country comparison to the world: 1

**STOCK OF DIRECT FOREIGN INVESTMENT - AT HOME:**

$4.08 trillion (31 December 2017 est.)

$3.614 trillion (31 December 2016 est.)

country comparison to the world: 2

**STOCK OF DIRECT FOREIGN INVESTMENT - ABROAD:**

$5.711 trillion (31 December 2017 est.)

$5.352 trillion (31 December 2016 est.)

country comparison to the world: 2

**EXCHANGE RATES:**

British pounds per US dollar: 0.7836 (2017 est.), 0.738 (2016 est.), 0.738 (2015 est.), 0.607 (2014 est), 0.6391 (2013 est.)

Canadian dollars per US dollar: 1, 1.308 (2017 est.), 1.3256 (2016 est.), 1.3256 (2015 est.), 1.2788 (2014 est.), 1.0298 (2013 est.)

Chinese yuan per US dollar: 1, 6.7588 (2017 est.), 6.6445 (2016 est.), 6.2275 (2015 est.), 6.1434 (2014 est.), 6.1958 (2013 est.)

euros per US dollar: 0.885 (2017 est.), 0.903 (2016 est.), 0.9214 (2015 est.), 0.885 (2014 est.), 0.7634 (2013 est.)

Japanese yen per US dollar: 111.10 (2017 est.), 108.76 (2016 est.), 108.76 (2015 est.), 121.02 (2014 est.), 97.44 (2013 est.)

# ENERGY :: UNITED STATES

**ELECTRICITY ACCESS:**

electrification - total population: 100% (2016)

**ELECTRICITY - PRODUCTION:**

4.095 trillion kWh (2016 est.)

country comparison to the world: 2

**ELECTRICITY - CONSUMPTION:**

3.902 trillion kWh (2016 est.)

country comparison to the world: 2

**ELECTRICITY - EXPORTS:**

9.695 billion kWh (2016 est.)

country comparison to the world: 22

**ELECTRICITY - IMPORTS:**

72.72 billion kWh (2016 est.)

country comparison to the world: 1

**ELECTRICITY - INSTALLED GENERATING CAPACITY:**

1.087 billion kW (2016 est.)

country comparison to the world: 2

**ELECTRICITY - FROM FOSSIL FUELS:**

70% of total installed capacity (2016 est.)

country comparison to the world: 111

**ELECTRICITY - FROM NUCLEAR FUELS:**

9% of total installed capacity (2017 est.)

country comparison to the world: 18

**ELECTRICITY - FROM HYDROELECTRIC PLANTS:**

7% of total installed capacity (2017 est.)

country comparison to the world: 128

**ELECTRICITY - FROM OTHER RENEWABLE SOURCES:**

14% of total installed capacity (2017 est.)

country comparison to the world: 65

**CRUDE OIL - PRODUCTION:**

9.352 million bbl/day (2017 est.)

country comparison to the world: 3

**CRUDE OIL - EXPORTS:**

1.158 million bbl/day (2017 est.)

country comparison to the world: 12

**CRUDE OIL - IMPORTS:**

7.969 million bbl/day (2017 est.)

country comparison to the world: 1

**CRUDE OIL - PROVED RESERVES:**

NA bbl (1 January 2018 est.)

**REFINED PETROLEUM PRODUCTS - PRODUCTION:**

20.3 million bbl/day (2017 est.)

country comparison to the world: 1

**REFINED PETROLEUM PRODUCTS - CONSUMPTION:**

19.96 million bbl/day (2017 est.)

country comparison to the world: 1

**REFINED PETROLEUM PRODUCTS - EXPORTS:**

5.218 million bbl/day (2017 est.)

country comparison to the world: 1

**REFINED PETROLEUM PRODUCTS - IMPORTS:**

2.175 million bbl/day (2017 est.)

country comparison to the world: 2

**NATURAL GAS - PRODUCTION:**

772.8 billion cu m (2017 est.)

country comparison to the world: 1

**NATURAL GAS - CONSUMPTION:**

767.6 billion cu m (2017 est.)

country comparison to the world: 1

**NATURAL GAS - EXPORTS:**

89.7 billion cu m (2017 est.)

country comparison to the world: 4

**NATURAL GAS - IMPORTS:**

86.15 billion cu m (2017 est.)

country comparison to the world: 4

**NATURAL GAS - PROVED RESERVES:**

0 cu m (1 January 2017 est.)

country comparison to the world: 203

**CARBON DIOXIDE EMISSIONS FROM CONSUMPTION OF ENERGY:**

5.242 billion Mt (2017 est.)

country comparison to the world: 2

# COMMUNICATIONS :: UNITED STATES

**TELEPHONES - FIXED LINES:**

total subscriptions: 119.902 million (2017 est.)

subscriptions per 100 inhabitants: 37 (2017 est.)

country comparison to the world: 2

**TELEPHONES - MOBILE CELLULAR:**

total subscriptions: 395.881 million (2017 est.)

subscriptions per 100 inhabitants: 121 (2017 est.)

country comparison to the world: 4

**TELEPHONE SYSTEM:**

**general assessment:** a large, technologically advanced, multipurpose communications system (2016)

**domestic:** a large system of fiber-optic cable, microwave radio relay, coaxial cable, and domestic satellites carries every form of telephone traffic; a rapidly growing cellular system carries mobile telephone traffic throughout the country (2016)

**international:** country code - 1; multiple ocean cable systems provide international connectivity; satellite earth stations - 61 Intelsat (45 Atlantic Ocean and 16 Pacific Ocean), 5 Intersputnik (Atlantic Ocean region), and 4 Inmarsat (Pacific and Atlantic Ocean regions) (2016)

## BROADCAST MEDIA:

4 major terrestrial TV networks with affiliate stations throughout the country, plus cable and satellite networks, independent stations, and a limited public broadcasting sector that is largely supported by private grants; overall, thousands of TV stations broadcasting; multiple national radio networks with many affiliate stations; while most stations are commercial, National Public Radio (NPR) has a network of some 900 member stations; satellite radio available; in total, over 15,000 radio stations operating (2018)

## INTERNET COUNTRY CODE:

.us

## INTERNET USERS:

**total:** 246,809,221 (July 2016 est.)

**percent of population:** 76.2% (July 2016 est.)

**country comparison to the world:** 3

## BROADBAND - FIXED SUBSCRIPTIONS:

**total:** 109.838 million (2017 est.)

**subscriptions per 100 inhabitants:** 34 (2017 est.)

**country comparison to the world:** 2

## COMMUNICATIONS - NOTE:

**note 1:** The Library of Congress, Washington DC, USA, claims to be the largest library in the world with more than 167 million items (as of 2018); its collections are universal, not limited by subject, format, or national boundary, and include materials from all parts of the world and in over 450 languages; collections include: books, newspapers, magazines, sheet music, sound and video recordings, photographic images, artwork, architectural drawings, and copyright data

**note 2:** Cape Canaveral, Florida, USA, hosts one of four dedicated ground antennas that assist in the operation of the Global Positioning System (GPS) navigation system (the others are on Ascension (Saint Helena, Ascension, and Tistan da Cunha), Diego Garcia (British Indian Ocean Territory), and at Kwajalein (Marshall Islands)

# TRANSPORTATION :: UNITED STATES

## NATIONAL AIR TRANSPORT SYSTEM:

**number of registered air carriers:** 92 (2015)

**inventory of registered aircraft operated by air carriers:** 6,817 (2015)

**annual passenger traffic on registered air carriers:** 798.23 million (2015)

**annual freight traffic on registered air carriers:** 37.219 billion mt-km (2015)

## CIVIL AIRCRAFT REGISTRATION COUNTRY CODE PREFIX:

N (2016)

## AIRPORTS:

13,513 (2013)

**country comparison to the world:** 1

## AIRPORTS - WITH PAVED RUNWAYS:

**total:** 5,054 (2013)

**over 3,047 m:** 189 (2013)

**2,438 to 3,047 m:** 235 (2013)

**1,524 to 2,437 m:** 1,478 (2013)

**914 to 1,523 m:** 2,249 (2013)

**under 914 m:** 903 (2013)

## AIRPORTS - WITH UNPAVED RUNWAYS:

**total:** 8,459 (2013)

**over 3,047 m:** 1 (2013)

**2,438 to 3,047 m:** 6 (2013)

**1,524 to 2,437 m:** 140 (2013)

**914 to 1,523 m:** 1,552 (2013)

**under 914 m:** 6,760 (2013)

## HELIPORTS:

5,287 (2013)

## PIPELINES:

1984321 km natural gas, 240711 km petroleum products (2013)

## RAILWAYS:

**total:** 293,564 km (2014)

**standard gauge:** 293,564.2 km 1.435-m gauge (2014)

**country comparison to the world:** 1

## ROADWAYS:

**total:** 6,586,610 km (2012)

**paved:** 4,304,715 km (includes 76,334 km of expressways) (2012)

**unpaved:** 2,281,895 km (2012)

**country comparison to the world:** 1

## WATERWAYS:

41,009 km (19,312 km used for commerce; Saint Lawrence Seaway of 3,769 km, including the Saint Lawrence River of 3,058 km, is shared with Canada) (2012)

**country comparison to the world:** 5

## MERCHANT MARINE:

**total:** 3,611 (2017)

**by type:** bulk carrier 5, container ship 61, general cargo 114, oil tanker 66, other 3365 (2017)

**country comparison to the world:** 5

## PORTS AND TERMINALS:

**oil terminal(s):** LOOP terminal, Haymark terminal

**container port(s) (TEUs):** Charleston (1,996,282), Hampton Roads (2,655,705), Houston (2,174,000), Long Beach (6,775,171), Los Angeles (8,856,783), New York/New Jersey (6,251,953), Oakland (2,370,000), Savannah (3,737,521), Seattle (3,615,752) (2016)

**LNG terminal(s) (export):** Kenai (AK)

**LNG terminal(s) (import):** Cove Point (MD), Elba Island (GA), Everett (MA), Freeport (TX), Golden Pass (TX), Hackberry (LA), Lake Charles (LA), Neptune (offshore), Northeast Gateway (offshore), Pascagoula (MS), Sabine Pass (TX)

**cargo ports:** Baton Rouge, Corpus Christi, Hampton Roads, Houston, Long Beach, Los Angeles, New Orleans, New York, Plaquemines (LA), Tampa, Texas City

**cruise departure ports (passengers):** Miami (2,032,000), Port Everglades (1,277,000), Port Canaveral (1,189,000), Seattle (430,000), Long Beach (415,000) (2009)

# MILITARY AND SECURITY :: UNITED STATES

## MILITARY EXPENDITURES:

3.29% of GDP (2016)

3.3% of GDP (2015)

3.51% of GDP (2014)

country comparison to the world: 25

## MILITARY BRANCHES:

United States Armed Forces: US Army, US Navy (includes Marine Corps), US Air Force, US Coast Guard; note - Coast Guard administered in peacetime by the Department of Homeland Security, but in wartime reports to the Department of the Navy (2017)

## MILITARY SERVICE AGE AND OBLIGATION:

18 years of age (17 years of age with parental consent) for male and female voluntary service; no conscription; maximum enlistment age 42 (Army), 27 (Air Force), 34 (Navy), 28 (Marines); 8-year service obligation, including 2-5 years active duty (Army), 2 years active (Navy), 4 years active (Air Force, Marines); all military occupations and positions open to women (2016)

# TRANSNATIONAL ISSUES :: UNITED STATES

## DISPUTES - INTERNATIONAL:

the US has intensified domestic security measures and is collaborating closely with its neighbors, Canada and Mexico, to monitor and control legal and illegal personnel, transport, and commodities across the international bordersabundant rainfall in recent years along much of the Mexico-US border region has ameliorated periodically strained water-sharing arrangements1990 Maritime Boundary Agreement in the Bering Sea still awaits Russian Duma ratificationCanada and the United States dispute how to divide the Beaufort Sea and the status of the Northwest Passage but continue to work cooperatively to survey the Arctic continental shelfThe Bahamas and US have not been able to agree on a maritime boundaryUS Naval Base at Guantanamo Bay is leased from Cuba and only mutual agreement or US abandonment of the area can terminate the leaseHaiti claims US-administered Navassa IslandUS has made no territorial claim in Antarctica (but has reserved the right to do so) and does not recognize the claims of any other statesMarshall Islands claims Wake IslandTokelau included American Samoa's Swains Island among the islands listed in its 2006 draft constitution

## REFUGEES AND INTERNALLY DISPLACED PERSONS:

refugees (country of origin): the US admitted 53,716 refugees during FY2017 including: 9,377 (Democratic Republic of the Congo), 6,886 (Iraq), 6,557 (Syria), 6,130 (Somalia), 5,078 (Burma), 3,550 (Bhutan), 2,577 (Iran)

note: more than 46,000 Venezuelans have claimed asylum since 2014 because of the economic and political crisis (2017)

## ILLICIT DRUGS:

world's largest consumer of cocaine (shipped from Colombia through Mexico and the Caribbean), Colombian heroin, and Mexican heroin and marijuana; major consumer of ecstasy and Mexican methamphetamine; minor consumer of high-quality Southeast Asian heroin; illicit producer of cannabis, marijuana, depressants, stimulants, hallucinogens, and methamphetamine; money-laundering center

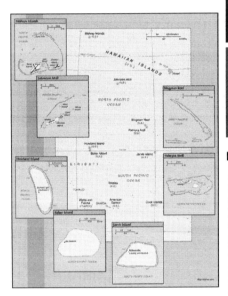

# AUSTRALIA - OCEANIA :: UNITED STATES PACIFIC ISLAND WILDLIFE REFUGES

## INTRODUCTION :: UNITED STATES PACIFIC ISLAND WILDLIFE REFUGES

**BACKGROUND:**

All of the following US Pacific island territories except Midway Atoll constitute the Pacific Remote Islands National Wildlife Refuge (NWR) Complex and as such are managed by the Fish and Wildlife Service of the US Department of the Interior. Midway Atoll NWR has been included in a Refuge Complex with the Hawaiian Islands NWR and also designated as part of Papahanaumokuakea Marine National Monument. These remote refuges are the most widespread collection of marine- and terrestrial-life protected areas on the planet under a single country's jurisdiction. They sustain many endemic species including corals, fish, shellfish, marine mammals, seabirds, water birds, land birds, insects, and vegetation not found elsewhere.

**Baker Island:** The US took possession of the island in 1857. Its guano deposits were mined by US and British companies during the second half of the 19th century. In 1935, a short-lived attempt at colonization began on this island but was disrupted by World War II and thereafter abandoned. The island was established as a NWR in 1974.;

**Howland Island:** Discovered by the US early in the 19th century, the uninhabited atoll was officially claimed by the US in 1857. Both US and British companies mined for guano deposits until about 1890. In 1935, a short-lived attempt at colonization began on this island, similar to the effort on nearby Baker Island, but was disrupted by World War II and thereafter abandoned. The famed American aviatrix Amelia EARHART disappeared while seeking out Howland Island as a refueling stop during her 1937 round-the-world flight; Earhart Light, a day beacon near the middle of the west coast, was named in her memory. The island was established as a NWR in 1974.;

**Jarvis Island:** First discovered by the British in 1821, the uninhabited island was annexed by the US in 1858 but abandoned in 1879 after tons of guano had been removed. The UK annexed the island in 1889 but never carried out plans for further exploitation. The US occupied and reclaimed the island in 1935. It was abandoned in 1942 during World War II. The island was established as a NWR in 1974.;

**Johnston Atoll:** Both the US and the Kingdom of Hawaii annexed Johnston Atoll in 1858, but it was the US that mined the guano deposits until the late 1880s. Johnston and Sand Islands were designated wildlife refuges in 1926. The US Navy took over the atoll in 1934. Subsequently, the US Air Force assumed control in 1948. The site was used for high-altitude nuclear tests in the 1950s and 1960s. Until late in 2000 the atoll was maintained as a storage and disposal site for chemical weapons. Munitions destruction, cleanup, and closure of the facility were completed by May 2005. The Fish and Wildlife Service and the US Air Force are currently discussing future management options; in the interim, Johnston Atoll and the three-mile Naval Defensive Sea around it remain under the jurisdiction and administrative control of the US Air Force.;

**Kingman Reef:** The US annexed the reef in 1922. Its sheltered lagoon served as a way station for flying boats on Hawaii-to-American Samoa flights during the late 1930s. There are no terrestrial plants on the reef, which is frequently awash, but it does support abundant and diverse marine fauna and flora. In 2001, the waters surrounding the reef out to 12 nm were designated a NWR.;

**Midway Islands:** The US took formal possession of the islands in 1867. The laying of the transpacific cable, which passed through the islands, brought the first residents in 1903. Between 1935 and 1947, Midway was used as a refueling stop for transpacific flights. The US naval victory over a Japanese fleet off Midway in 1942 was one of the turning points of World War II. The islands continued to serve as a naval station until closed in 1993. Today the islands are a NWR and are the site of the world's largest Laysan albatross colony.;

**Palmyra Atoll:** The Kingdom of Hawaii claimed the atoll in 1862, and the US included it among the Hawaiian Islands when it annexed the archipelago in 1898. The Hawaii Statehood Act of 1959 did not include Palmyra Atoll, which is now partly privately owned by the Nature Conservancy with the rest owned by the Federal government and managed by the US Fish and Wildlife Service. These organizations are managing the atoll as a wildlife refuge. The lagoons and surrounding waters within the 12-nm US territorial seas were transferred to the US Fish and Wildlife Service and designated a NWR in January 2001.

# GEOGRAPHY :: UNITED STATES PACIFIC ISLAND WILDLIFE REFUGES

## LOCATION:
Oceania

**Baker Island:** atoll in the North Pacific Ocean 3,390 km southwest of Honolulu, about halfway between Hawaii and Australia;

**Howland Island:** island in the North Pacific Ocean 3,360 km southwest of Honolulu, about halfway between Hawaii and Australia;

**Jarvis Island:** island in the South Pacific Ocean 2,415 km south of Honolulu, about halfway between Hawaii and Cook Islands;

**Johnston Atoll:** atoll in the North Pacific Ocean 1,330 km southwest of Honolulu, about one-third of the way from Hawaii to the Marshall Islands;

**Kingman Reef:** reef in the North Pacific Ocean 1,720 km south of Honolulu, about halfway between Hawaii and American Samoa;

**Midway Islands:** atoll in the North Pacific Ocean 2,335 km northwest of Honolulu near the end of the Hawaiian Archipelago, about one-third of the way from Honolulu to Tokyo;

**Palmyra Atoll:** atoll in the North Pacific Ocean 1,780 km south of Honolulu, about halfway between Hawaii and American Samoa

## GEOGRAPHIC COORDINATES:
**Baker Island:** 0 13 N, 176 28 W;

**Howland Island:** 0 48 N, 176 38 W;

**Jarvis Island:** 0 23 S, 160 01 W;

**Johnston Atoll:** 16 45 N, 169 31 W;

**Kingman Reef:** 6 23 N, 162 25 W;

**Midway Islands:** 28 12 N, 177 22 W;

**Palmyra Atoll:** 5 53 N, 162 05 W

## MAP REFERENCES:
Oceania

## AREA:
**land:** 6,959.41 sq km (emergent land - 22.41 sq km; submerged - 6,937 sq km)

**Baker Island:** total - 129.1 sq km; emergent land - 2.1 sq km; submerged - 127 sq km

**Howland Island:** total - 138.6 sq km; emergent land - 2.6 sq km; submerged - 136 sq km

**Jarvis Island:** total - 152 sq km; emergent land - 5 sq km; submerged - 147 sq km

**Johnston Atoll:** total - 276.6 sq km; emergent land - 2.6 sq km; submerged - 274 sq km

**Kingman Reef:** total - 1,958.01 sq km; emergent land - 0.01 sq km; submerged - 1,958 sq km

**Midway Islands:** total - 2,355.2 sq km; emergent land - 6.2 sq km; submerged - 2,349 sq km

**Palmyra Atoll:** total - 1,949.9 sq km; emergent land - 3.9 sq km; submerged - 1,946 sq km

## AREA - COMPARATIVE:
**Baker Island:** about 2.5 times the size of the National Mall in Washington, DC;

**Howland Island:** about three times the size of the National Mall in Washington, DC;

**Jarvis Island:** about eight times the size of the National Mall in Washington, DC;

**Johnston Atoll:** about 4.5 times the size of the National Mall in Washington, DC;

**Kingman Reef:** a little more than 1.5 times the size of the National Mall in Washington, DC;

**Midway Islands:** about nine times the size of the National Mall in Washington, DC;

**Palmyra Atoll:** about 20 times the size of the National Mall in Washington, DC

## LAND BOUNDARIES:
0 km

## COASTLINE:
**Baker Island:** 4.8 km
**Howland Island:** 6.4 km
**Jarvis Island:** 8 km
**Johnston Atoll:** 34 km
**Kingman Reef:** 3 km
**Midway Islands:** 15 km
**Palmyra Atoll:** 14.5 km

## MARITIME CLAIMS:
**territorial sea:** 12 nm

**exclusive economic zone:** 200 nm

## CLIMATE:
**Baker, Howland, and Jarvis Islands:** equatorial; scant rainfall, constant wind, burning sun;

**Johnston Atoll and Kingman Reef:** tropical, but generally dry; consistent northeast trade winds with little seasonal temperature variation;

**Midway Islands:** subtropical with cool, moist winters (December to February) and warm, dry summers (May to October); moderated by prevailing easterly winds; most of the 107 cm of annual rainfall occurs during the winter;

**Palmyra Atoll:** equatorial, hot; located within the low pressure area of the Intertropical Convergence Zone (ITCZ) where the northeast and southeast trade winds meet, it is extremely wet with between 400-500 cm of rainfall each year

## TERRAIN:
low and nearly flat sandy coral islands with narrow fringing reefs that have developed at the top of submerged volcanic mountains, which in most cases rise steeply from the ocean floor

## ELEVATION:

0 m lowest point: Pacific Ocean

8 highest point: Baker Island, unnamed location - 3 Howland Island, unnamed location - 7 Jarvis Island, unnamed location - 10 Johnston Atoll, Sand Island - 2 Kingman Reef, unnamed location - less than 13 Midway Islands, unnamed location - 3 Palmyra Atoll, unnamed location -

### NATURAL RESOURCES:
terrestrial and aquatic wildlife

### LAND USE:
agricultural land: 0% (2011 est.)

arable land: 0% (2011 est.) / permanent crops: 0% (2011 est.) / permanent pasture: 0% (2011 est.)

forest: 0% (2011 est.)

other: 100% (2011 est.)

### NATURAL HAZARDS:
Baker, Howland, and Jarvis Islands: the narrow fringing reef surrounding the island poses a maritime hazard;

Kingman Reef: wet or awash most of the time, maximum elevation of less than 2 m makes Kingman Reef a maritime hazard;

Midway Islands, Johnston, and Palmyra Atolls: NA

### ENVIRONMENT - CURRENT ISSUES:
Baker Island: no natural freshwater resources; feral cats, introduced in 1937 during a short-lived colonization effort, ravaged the avian population and were eradicated in 1965

Howland Island: no natural freshwater resources; the island habitat has suffered from invasive exotic species; black rats, introduced in 1854, were eradicated by feral cats within a year of their introduction in 1937; the cats preyed on the bird population and were eliminated by 1985

Jarvis Island : no natural freshwater resources; feral cats, introduced in the 1930s during a short-lived colonization venture, were not completely removed until 1990

Johnston Atoll: no natural freshwater resources; the seven decades under US military administration (1934-2004) left the atoll environmentally degraded and required large-scale remediation efforts; a swarm of Anoplolepis (crazy) ants invaded the island in 2010 damaging native wildlife; eradication has been largely, but not completely, successful

Midway Islands: many exotic species introduced, 75% of the roughly 200 plant species on the island are non-native; plastic pollution harms wildlife, via entanglement, ingestion, and toxic contamination

Kingman Reef: none

Palmyra Atoll: black rats, believed to have been introduced to the atoll during the US military occupation of the 1940s, severely degraded the ecosystem outcompeting native species (seabirds, crabs); following a successful rat removal project in 2011, native flora and fauna have begun to recover

### GEOGRAPHY - NOTE:
Baker, Howland, and Jarvis Islands: scattered vegetation consisting of grasses, prostrate vines, and low growing shrubs; primarily a nesting, roosting, and foraging habitat for seabirds, shorebirds, and marine wildlife; closed to the public;

Johnston Atoll: Johnston Island and Sand Island are natural islands, which have been expanded by coral dredging; North Island (Akau) and East Island (Hikina) are manmade islands formed from coral dredging; the egg-shaped reef is 34 km in circumference; closed to the public;

Kingman Reef: barren coral atoll with deep interior lagoon; closed to the public;

Midway Islands: a coral atoll managed as a National Wildlife Refuge and open to the public for wildlife-related recreation in the form of wildlife observation and photography;

Palmyra Atoll: the high rainfall and resulting lush vegetation make the environment of this atoll unique among the US Pacific Island territories; supports a large undisturbed stand of Pisonia beach forest

# PEOPLE AND SOCIETY :: UNITED STATES PACIFIC ISLAND WILDLIFE REFUGES

### POPULATION:
no indigenous inhabitants

note: public entry is only by special-use permit from US Fish and Wildlife Service and generally restricted to scientists and educators; visited annually by US Fish and Wildlife Service

Jarvis Island: Millersville settlement on western side of island occasionally used as a weather station from 1935 until World War II, when it was abandoned; reoccupied in 1957 during the International Geophysical Year by scientists who left in 1958; currently unoccupied

Johnston Atoll: in previous years, an average of 1,100 US military and civilian contractor personnel were present; as of May 2005, all US Government personnel had left the island

Midway Islands: approximately 40 people make up the staff of US Fish and Wildlife Service and their services contractor living at the atoll

Palmyra Atoll: four to 20 Nature Conservancy, US Fish and Wildlife staff, and researchers

# GOVERNMENT :: UNITED STATES PACIFIC ISLAND WILDLIFE REFUGES

### COUNTRY NAME:
conventional long form: none

conventional short form: Baker Island

etymology: self-descriptive name specifying the territories' affiliation and location

Howland Island Jarvis Island Johnston Atoll Kingman Reef Midway Islands Palmyra Atoll

### DEPENDENCY STATUS:
unincorporated unorganized territories of the US; administered from Washington, DC, by the Fish and Wildlife Service of the US Department of the Interior as part of the National Wildlife Refuge System

note: incorporated unorganized territory of the US; partly privately owned and partly federally owned; administered from Washington, DC, by the Fish and Wildlife Service of the US Department of the Interior; the Office of Insular Affairs of the US Department of the Interior continues to administer nine excluded areas comprising certain tidal and submerged lands within the 12 nm territorial sea or within the lagoon

**LEGAL SYSTEM:**

the laws of the US, where applicable, apply

**DIPLOMATIC REPRESENTATION FROM THE US:**

none (territories of the US)

**FLAG DESCRIPTION:**

the flag of the US is used

# ECONOMY :: UNITED STATES PACIFIC ISLAND WILDLIFE REFUGES

**ECONOMY - OVERVIEW:**

no economic activity

# TRANSPORTATION :: UNITED STATES PACIFIC ISLAND WILDLIFE REFUGES

**AIRPORTS:**

Baker Island: one abandoned World War II runway of 1,665 m covered with vegetation and unusable (2013)

Howland Island: airstrip constructed in 1937 for scheduled refueling stop on the round-the-world flight of Amelia EARHART and Fred NOONAN; the aviators left Lae, New Guinea, for Howland Island but were never seen again; the airstrip is no longer serviceable (2013)

Johnston Atoll: one closed and not maintained (2013)

Kingman Reef: lagoon was used as a halfway station between Hawaii and American Samoa by Pan American Airways for flying boats in 1937 and 1938 (2013)

Midway Islands: 3 - one operational (2,377 m paved); no fuel for sale except emergencies (2013)

Palmyra Atoll: 1 - 1,846 m unpaved runway; privately owned (2013)

**AIRPORTS - WITH PAVED RUNWAYS:**

2,438 to 3,047 m: 1 - Johnston Atoll; (2016)

note - abandoned but usable

**AIRPORTS - WITH UNPAVED RUNWAYS:**

1 - Palmyra Atoll (2016)

**PORTS AND TERMINALS:**

major seaport(s): Baker, Howland, and Jarvis Islands, and Kingman Reef

Baker, Howland, and Jarvis Islands, and Kingman Reef: none; offshore anchorage only

Johnston Atoll: Johnston Island

Midway Islands: Sand Island

Palmyra Atoll: West Lagoon

# MILITARY AND SECURITY :: UNITED STATES PACIFIC ISLAND WILDLIFE REFUGES

**MILITARY - NOTE:**

defense is the responsibility of the US

# TRANSNATIONAL ISSUES :: UNITED STATES PACIFIC ISLAND WILDLIFE REFUGES

**DISPUTES - INTERNATIONAL:**

none

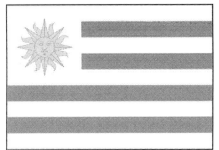

## INTRODUCTION :: URUGUAY

### BACKGROUND:
Montevideo, founded by the Spanish in 1726 as a military stronghold, soon took advantage of its natural harbor to become an important commercial center. Claimed by Argentina but annexed by Brazil in 1821, Uruguay declared its independence four years later and secured its freedom in 1828 after a three-year struggle. The administrations of President Jose BATLLE in the early 20th century launched widespread political, social, and economic reforms that established a statist tradition. A violent Marxist urban guerrilla movement named the Tupamaros, launched in the late 1960s, led Uruguay's president to cede control of the government to the military in 1973. By yearend, the rebels had been crushed, but the military continued to expand its hold over the government. Civilian rule was restored in 1985. In 2004, the left-of-center Frente Amplio Coalition won national elections that effectively ended 170 years of political control previously held by the Colorado and National (Blanco) parties. Uruguay's political and labor conditions are among the freest on the continent.

## GEOGRAPHY :: URUGUAY

### LOCATION:
Southern South America, bordering the South Atlantic Ocean, between Argentina and Brazil

### GEOGRAPHIC COORDINATES:
33 00 S, 56 00 W

### MAP REFERENCES:
South America

### AREA:
total: 176,215 sq km
land: 175,015 sq km
water: 1,200 sq km
country comparison to the world: 92

### AREA - COMPARATIVE:
about the size of Virginia and West Virginia combined; slightly smaller than the state of Washington

### LAND BOUNDARIES:
total: 1,591 km
border countries (2): Argentina 541 km, Brazil 1050 km

### COASTLINE:
660 km

### MARITIME CLAIMS:
territorial sea: 12 nm
exclusive economic zone: 200 nm
contiguous zone: 24 nm
continental shelf: 200 nm or the edge of continental margin

### CLIMATE:
warm temperate; freezing temperatures almost unknown

### TERRAIN:
mostly rolling plains and low hills; fertile coastal lowland

### ELEVATION:
mean elevation: 109 m
elevation extremes: 0 m lowest point: Atlantic Ocean
514 highest point: Cerro Catedral

### NATURAL RESOURCES:
arable land, hydropower, minor minerals, fish

### LAND USE:
agricultural land: 87.2% (2011 est.)
arable land: 10.1% (2011 est.) / permanent crops: 0.2% (2011 est.) / permanent pasture: 76.9% (2011 est.)
forest: 10.2% (2011 est.)
other: 2.6% (2011 est.)

### IRRIGATED LAND:
2,380 sq km (2012)

### POPULATION DISTRIBUTION:
most of the country's population resides in the southern half of the country; approximately 80% of the populace is urban, living in towns or cities; nearly half of the population lives in and around the capital of Montevideo

### NATURAL HAZARDS:
seasonally high winds (the pampero is a chilly and occasional violent wind that blows north from the Argentine pampas), droughts, floods; because of the absence of mountains, which act as weather barriers, all locations are particularly vulnerable to rapid changes from weather fronts

### ENVIRONMENT - CURRENT ISSUES:
water pollution from meat packing/tannery industry; heavy metal pollution; inadequate solid/hazardous waste disposal; deforestation

**ENVIRONMENT - INTERNATIONAL AGREEMENTS:**

party to: Antarctic-Environmental Protocol, Antarctic-Marine Living Resources, Antarctic Treaty, Biodiversity, Climate Change, Climate Change-Kyoto Protocol, Desertification, Endangered Species, Environmental Modification, Hazardous Wastes, Law of the Sea, Ozone Layer Protection, Ship Pollution, Wetlands

signed, but not ratified: Marine Dumping, Marine Life Conservation

**GEOGRAPHY - NOTE:**

second-smallest South American country (after Suriname); most of the low-lying landscape (three-quarters of the country) is grassland, ideal for cattle and sheep raising

## PEOPLE AND SOCIETY :: URUGUAY

**POPULATION:**

3,369,299 (July 2018 est.)

country comparison to the world: 133

**NATIONALITY:**

noun: Uruguayan(s)

adjective: Uruguayan

**ETHNIC GROUPS:**

white 87.7%, black 4.6%, indigenous 2.4%, other 0.3%, none or unspecified 5% (2011 est.)

note: data represent primary ethnic identity

**LANGUAGES:**

Spanish (official)

**RELIGIONS:**

Roman Catholic 47.1%, non-Catholic Christians 11.1%, nondenominational 23.2%, Jewish 0.3%, atheist or agnostic 17.2%, other 1.1% (2006 est.)

**DEMOGRAPHIC PROFILE:**

Uruguay rates high for most development indicators and is known for its secularism, liberal social laws, and well-developed social security, health, and educational systems. It is one of the few countries in Latin America and the Caribbean where the entire population has access to clean water. Uruguay's provision of free primary through university education has contributed to the country's high levels of literacy and educational attainment. However, the emigration of human capital has diminished the state's return on its investment in education. Remittances from the roughly 18% of Uruguayans abroad amount to less than 1 percent of national GDP. The emigration of young adults and a low birth rate are causing Uruguay's population to age rapidly.

In the 1960s, Uruguayans for the first time emigrated en masse - primarily to Argentina and Brazil - because of economic decline and the onset of more than a decade of military dictatorship. Economic crises in the early 1980s and 2002 also triggered waves of emigration, but since 2002 more than 70% of Uruguayan emigrants have selected the US and Spain as destinations because of better job prospects. Uruguay had a tiny population upon its independence in 1828 and welcomed thousands of predominantly Italian and Spanish immigrants, but the country has not experienced large influxes of new arrivals since the aftermath of World War II. More recent immigrants include Peruvians and Arabs.

**AGE STRUCTURE:**

0-14 years: 19.91% (male 341,402 /female 329,474)

15-24 years: 15.56% (male 265,486 /female 258,611)

25-54 years: 39.48% (male 658,871 /female 671,172)

55-64 years: 10.68% (male 169,385 /female 190,392)

65 years and over: 14.38% (male 194,269 /female 290,237) (2018 est.)

**DEPENDENCY RATIOS:**

total dependency ratio: 55.9 (2015 est.)

youth dependency ratio: 33.4 (2015 est.)

elderly dependency ratio: 22.5 (2015 est.)

potential support ratio: 4.4 (2015 est.)

**MEDIAN AGE:**

total: 35.1 years

male: 33.3 years

female: 36.9 years (2018 est.)

country comparison to the world: 82

**POPULATION GROWTH RATE:**

0.27% (2018 est.)

country comparison to the world: 175

**BIRTH RATE:**

13 births/1,000 population (2018 est.)

country comparison to the world: 150

**DEATH RATE:**

9.4 deaths/1,000 population (2018 est.)

country comparison to the world: 54

**NET MIGRATION RATE:**

-0.9 migrant(s)/1,000 population (2017 est.)

country comparison to the world: 137

**POPULATION DISTRIBUTION:**

most of the country's population resides in the southern half of the country; approximately 80% of the populace is urban, living in towns or cities; nearly half of the population lives in and around the capital of Montevideo

**URBANIZATION:**

urban population: 95.3% of total population (2018)

rate of urbanization: 0.46% annual rate of change (2015-20 est.)

**MAJOR URBAN AREAS - POPULATION:**

1.737 million MONTEVIDEO (capital) (2018)

**SEX RATIO:**

at birth: 1.04 male(s)/female (2017 est.)

0-14 years: 1.04 male(s)/female (2017 est.)

15-24 years: 1.03 male(s)/female (2017 est.)

25-54 years: 0.98 male(s)/female (2017 est.)

55-64 years: 0.89 male(s)/female (2017 est.)

65 years and over: 0.66 male(s)/female (2017 est.)

total population: 0.94 male(s)/female (2017 est.)

**MATERNAL MORTALITY RATE:**

15 deaths/100,000 live births (2015 est.)

country comparison to the world: 137

**INFANT MORTALITY RATE:**

total: 8.1 deaths/1,000 live births (2018 est.)

male: 9 deaths/1,000 live births (2018 est.)

female: 7.2 deaths/1,000 live births (2018 est.)

country comparison to the world: 151

**LIFE EXPECTANCY AT BIRTH:**

total population: 77.6 years (2018 est.)

male: 74.4 years (2018 est.)

female: 80.8 years (2018 est.)

country comparison to the world: 69

**TOTAL FERTILITY RATE:**

1.79 children born/woman (2018 est.)

country comparison to the world: 149

**CONTRACEPTIVE PREVALENCE RATE:**

79.6% (2015)

note: percent of women aged 15-44

**HEALTH EXPENDITURES:**

8.6% of GDP (2014)

country comparison to the world: 47

**PHYSICIANS DENSITY:**

3.94 physicians/1,000 population (2008)

**HOSPITAL BED DENSITY:**

2.8 beds/1,000 population (2014)

**DRINKING WATER SOURCE:**

improved:

urban: 100% of population (2015 est.)

rural: 93.9% of population (2015 est.)

total: 99.7% of population (2015 est.)

unimproved:

urban: 0% of population (2015 est.)

rural: 6.1% of population (2015 est.)

total: 0.3% of population (2015 est.)

**SANITATION FACILITY ACCESS:**

improved:

urban: 96.6% of population (2015 est.)

rural: 92.6% of population (2015 est.)

total: 96.4% of population (2015 est.)

unimproved:

urban: 3.4% of population (2015 est.)

rural: 7.4% of population (2015 est.)

total: 3.6% of population (2015 est.)

**HIV/AIDS - ADULT PREVALENCE RATE:**

0.6% (2017 est.)

country comparison to the world: 62

**HIV/AIDS - PEOPLE LIVING WITH HIV/AIDS:**

13,000 (2017 est.)

country comparison to the world: 94

**HIV/AIDS - DEATHS:**

<500 (2017 est.)

**OBESITY - ADULT PREVALENCE RATE:**

27.9% (2016)

country comparison to the world: 34

**CHILDREN UNDER THE AGE OF 5 YEARS UNDERWEIGHT:**

4% (2011)

country comparison to the world: 88

**EDUCATION EXPENDITURES:**

4.4% of GDP (2011)

country comparison to the world: 100

**LITERACY:**

definition: age 15 and over can read and write (2015 est.)

total population: 98.5% (2015 est.)

male: 98.1% (2015 est.)

female: 98.9% (2015 est.)

**SCHOOL LIFE EXPECTANCY (PRIMARY TO TERTIARY EDUCATION):**

total: 16 years (2010)

male: 14 years (2010)

female: 17 years (2010)

**UNEMPLOYMENT, YOUTH AGES 15-24:**

total: 23.8% (2016 est.)

male: 20.2% (2016 est.)

female: 28.7% (2016 est.)

country comparison to the world: 52

# GOVERNMENT :: URUGUAY

**COUNTRY NAME:**

conventional long form: Oriental Republic of Uruguay

conventional short form: Uruguay

local long form: Republica Oriental del Uruguay

local short form: Uruguay

former: Banda Oriental, Cisplatine Province

etymology: name derives from the Spanish pronunciation of the Guarani Indian designation of the Uruguay River, which makes up the western border of the country and whose name later came to be applied to the entire country

**GOVERNMENT TYPE:**

presidential republic

**CAPITAL:**

name: Montevideo

geographic coordinates: 34 51 S, 56 10 W

time difference: UTC-3 (2 hours ahead of Washington, DC, during Standard Time)

**ADMINISTRATIVE DIVISIONS:**

19 departments (departamentos, singular - departamento); Artigas, Canelones, Cerro Largo, Colonia, Durazno, Flores, Florida, Lavalleja, Maldonado, Montevideo, Paysandu, Rio Negro, Rivera, Rocha, Salto, San Jose, Soriano, Tacuarembo, Treinta y Tres

**INDEPENDENCE:**

25 August 1825 (from Brazil)

**NATIONAL HOLIDAY:**

Independence Day, 25 August (1825)

**CONSTITUTION:**

history: several previous; latest approved by plebiscite 27 November 1966, effective 15 February 1967 (2018)

amendments: initiated by public petition of at least 10% of qualified voters, proposed by agreement of at least two-fifths of the General Assembly membership, or by existing "constitutional laws" sanctioned by at least two-thirds of the membership in both houses of the Assembly; proposals can also be submitted by senators, representatives, or by the executive power and require the formation of and approval in a national constituent convention; final passage by either method requires approval by absolute majority of votes cast in a referendum; amended many times, last in 2004 (2018)

**LEGAL SYSTEM:**

civil law system based on the Spanish civil code

**INTERNATIONAL LAW ORGANIZATION PARTICIPATION:**

accepts compulsory ICJ jurisdiction; accepts ICCt jurisdiction

**CITIZENSHIP:**

citizenship by birth: yes

citizenship by descent only: yes

dual citizenship recognized: yes

residency requirement for naturalization: 3-5 years

**SUFFRAGE:**

18 years of age; universal and compulsory

**EXECUTIVE BRANCH:**

chief of state: President Tabare VAZQUEZ (since 1 March 2015); Vice President Lucia TOPOLANSKY (since 13 September 2017); note - Vice President Raul Fernando SENDIC Rodriguez (since 1 March 2015) stepped down on 9 September amid accusations of misuse of public funds; the president is both chief of state and head of government

**head of government:** President Tabare VAZQUEZ (since 1 March 2015); Vice President Lucia TOPOLANSKY (since 13 September 2017)

**cabinet:** Council of Ministers appointed by the president with approval of the General Assembly

**elections/appointments:** president and vice president directly elected on the same ballot by absolute majority vote in 2 rounds if needed for a 5-year term (eligible for nonconsecutive terms); election last held on 26 October 2014 with a runoff election on 30 November 2014 (next to be held on 27 October 2019, and a runoff if needed on 24 November 2019)

**election results:** Tabare VAZQUEZ elected president in second round; percent of vote - Tabare VAZQUEZ (Socialist Party) 56.5%, Luis Alberto LACALLE Pou (Blanco) 43.4%

## LEGISLATIVE BRANCH:

**description:** bicameral General Assembly or Asamblea General consists of:
Chamber of Senators or Camara de Senadores (31 seats; members directly elected in a single nationwide constituency by proportional representation vote; the vice-president serves as the presiding ex-officio member; elected members serve 5-year terms)
Chamber of Representatives or Camara de Representantes (99 seats; members directly elected in multi-seat constituencies by proportional representation vote to serve 5-year terms)

**elections:**
Chamber of Senators - last held on 26 October 2014 (next to be held in October 2019); Chamber of Representatives - last held on 26 October 2014 (next to be held in October 2019)

**election results:**
Chamber of Senators - percent of vote by coalition/party - Frente Amplio 49.5%, National Party 31.9%, Colorado Party 13.3%, Independent Party 3.2%, other 2.1%; seats by coalition/party - Frente Amplio 15, National Party 10, Colorado Party 4, Independent Party 1
Chamber of Representatives - percent of vote by coalition/party - Frente Amplio 49.5%, National Party 31.9%, Colorado Party 13.3%, Independent Party 3.2%, AP 1.2%, other 0.9%; seats by coalition/party - Frente Amplio 50, National Party 32, Colorado Party 13, Independent Party 3, AP 1

## JUDICIAL BRANCH:

**highest courts:** Supreme Court of Justice (consists of 5 judges)

**judge selection and term of office:** judges nominated by the president and appointed in joint conference of the General Assembly; judges appointed for 10-year terms, with reelection after a lapse of 5 years following the previous term

**subordinate courts:** Courts of Appeal; District Courts (Juzgados Letrados); Peace Courts (Juzgados de Paz); Rural Courts (Juzgados Rurales)

## POLITICAL PARTIES AND LEADERS:

Broad Front or FA (Frente Amplio) - (a broad governing coalition that includes Uruguay Assembly [Danilo ASTORI], Progressive Alliance [Rodolfo NIN NOVOA], New Space [Rafael MICHELINI], Socialist Party [Monica XAVIER], Vertiente Artiguista [Enrique RUBIO], Christian Democratic Party [Juan Andres ROBALLO], For the People's Victory [Luis PUIG], Popular Participation Movement (MPP) [Jose MUJICA], Broad Front Commitment [Raul SENDIC], Big House [Constanza MOREIRA], Communist Party [Marcos CARAMBULA], The Federal League [Dario PEREZ]
Colorado Party (including Vamos Uruguay (or Let's Go Uruguay) [Pedro BORDABERRY], Open Space [Tabare VIERA], and Open Batllism [Ope PASQUET])
Independent Party [Pablo MIERES]
National Party or Blanco (including All Forward [Luis LACALLE POU] and National Alliance [Jorge LARRANAGA])
Popular Assembly [Gonzalo ABELLA]

## INTERNATIONAL ORGANIZATION PARTICIPATION:

CAN (associate), CD, CELAC, FAO, G-77, IADB, IAEA, IBRD, ICAO, ICC (national committees), ICCt, ICRM, IDA, IFAD, IFC, IFRCS, IHO, ILO, IMF, IMO, Interpol, IOC, IOM, IPU, ISO, ITSO, ITU, LAES, LAIA, Mercosur, MIGA, MINUSTAH, MONUSCO, NAM (observer), OAS, OIF (observer), OPANAL, OPCW, Pacific Alliance (observer), PCA, SICA (observer), UN, UNASUR, UNCTAD, UNESCO, UNIDO, Union Latina, UNMOGIP, UNOCI, UNWTO, UPU, WCO, WFTU (NGOs), WHO, WIPO, WMO, WTO

## DIPLOMATIC REPRESENTATION IN THE US:

**chief of mission:** Ambassador Carlos Alberto GIANELLI Derois (since 3 August 2015)

**chancery:** 1913 I Street NW, Washington, DC 20006

**telephone:** [1] (202) 331-1313

**FAX:** [1] (202) 331-8142

**consulate(s) general:** Chicago, Los Angeles, Miami, New York

## DIPLOMATIC REPRESENTATION FROM THE US:

**chief of mission:** Ambassador Kelly Ann KEIDERLING-FRANZ (since 23 June 2016)

**embassy:** Lauro Muller 1776, Montevideo 11200

**mailing address:** APO AA 34035

**telephone:** [598] (2) 1770-2000

**FAX:** [598] (2) 1770-2128

## FLAG DESCRIPTION:

nine equal horizontal stripes of white (top and bottom) alternating with blue; a white square in the upper hoist-side corner with a yellow sun bearing a human face (delineated in black) known as the Sun of May with 16 rays that alternate between triangular and wavy; the stripes represent the nine original departments of Uruguay; the sun symbol evokes the legend of the sun breaking through the clouds on 25 May 1810 as independence was first declared from Spain (Uruguay subsequently won its independence from Brazil); the sun features are said to represent those of Inti, the Inca god of the sun

**note:** the banner was inspired by the national colors of Argentina and by the design of the US flag

## NATIONAL SYMBOL(S):

Sun of May (a sun-with-face symbol); national colors: blue, white, yellow

## NATIONAL ANTHEM:

**name:** "Himno Nacional" (National Anthem of Uruguay)

**lyrics/music:** Francisco Esteban ACUNA de Figueroa/Francisco Jose DEBALI

**note:** adopted 1848; the anthem is also known as "Orientales, la Patria o la tumba!" ("Uruguayans, the Fatherland or Death!"); it is the world's longest national anthem in terms of music (105 bars; almost five minutes); generally only the first verse and chorus are sung

# ECONOMY :: URUGUAY

## ECONOMY - OVERVIEW:

Uruguay has a free market economy characterized by an export-oriented agricultural sector, a well-educated workforce, and high levels of social spending. Uruguay has sought to expand trade within the Common Market of the South (Mercosur) and with non-Mercosur members, and President VAZQUEZ has maintained his predecessor's mix of pro-market policies and a strong social safety net.

Following financial difficulties in the late 1990s and early 2000s, Uruguay's economic growth averaged 8% annually during the 2004-08 period. The 2008-09 global financial crisis put a brake on Uruguay's vigorous growth, which decelerated to 2.6% in 2009. Nevertheless, the country avoided a recession and kept growth rates positive, mainly through higher public expenditure and investment; GDP growth reached 8.9% in 2010 but slowed markedly in the 2012-16 period as a result of a renewed slowdown in the global economy and in Uruguay's main trade partners and Mercosur counterparts, Argentina and Brazil. Reforms in those countries should give Uruguay an economic boost. Growth picked up in 2017.

## GDP (PURCHASING POWER PARITY):

$78.16 billion (2017 est.)

$76.14 billion (2016 est.)

$74.87 billion (2015 est.)

note: data are in 2017 dollars

country comparison to the world: 96

## GDP (OFFICIAL EXCHANGE RATE):

$59.18 billion (2017 est.) (2017 est.)

## GDP - REAL GROWTH RATE:

2.7% (2017 est.)

1.7% (2016 est.)

0.4% (2015 est.)

country comparison to the world: 127

## GDP - PER CAPITA (PPP):

$22,400 (2017 est.)

$21,900 (2016 est.)

$21,600 (2015 est.)

note: data are in 2017 dollars

country comparison to the world: 85

## GROSS NATIONAL SAVING:

17.2% of GDP (2017 est.)

18.6% of GDP (2016 est.)

18.7% of GDP (2015 est.)

country comparison to the world: 119

## GDP - COMPOSITION, BY END USE:

household consumption: 66.8% (2017 est.)

government consumption: 14.3% (2017 est.)

investment in fixed capital: 16.7% (2017 est.)

investment in inventories: -1% (2017 est.)

exports of goods and services: 21.6% (2017 est.)

imports of goods and services: -18.4% (2017 est.)

## GDP - COMPOSITION, BY SECTOR OF ORIGIN:

agriculture: 6.2% (2017 est.)

industry: 24.1% (2017 est.)

services: 69.7% (2017 est.)

## AGRICULTURE - PRODUCTS:

Cellulose, beef, soybeans, rice, wheat; dairy products; fish; lumber, tobacco, wine

## INDUSTRIES:

food processing, electrical machinery, transportation equipment, petroleum products, textiles, chemicals, beverages

## INDUSTRIAL PRODUCTION GROWTH RATE:

-3.6% (2017 est.)

country comparison to the world: 190

## LABOR FORCE:

1.748 million (2017 est.)

country comparison to the world: 127

## LABOR FORCE - BY OCCUPATION:

agriculture: 13%

industry: 14%

services: 73% (2010 est.)

## UNEMPLOYMENT RATE:

7.6% (2017 est.)

7.9% (2016 est.)

country comparison to the world: 112

## POPULATION BELOW POVERTY LINE:

9.7% (2015 est.)

## HOUSEHOLD INCOME OR CONSUMPTION BY PERCENTAGE SHARE:

lowest 10%: 30.8% (2014 est.)

highest 10%: 30.8% (2014 est.)

## DISTRIBUTION OF FAMILY INCOME - GINI INDEX:

41.6 (2014)

41.9 (2013)

country comparison to the world: 55

## BUDGET:

revenues: 17.66 billion (2017 est.)

expenditures: 19.72 billion (2017 est.)

## TAXES AND OTHER REVENUES:

29.8% (of GDP) (2017 est.)

country comparison to the world: 79

## BUDGET SURPLUS (+) OR DEFICIT (-):

-3.5% (of GDP) (2017 est.)

country comparison to the world: 149

## PUBLIC DEBT:

65.7% of GDP (2017 est.)

61.6% of GDP (2016 est.)

note: data cover general government debt and include debt instruments issued (or owned) by government entities other than the treasury; the data include treasury debt held by foreign entities; the data include debt issued by subnational entities, as well as intragovernmental debt; intragovernmental debt consists of treasury borrowings from surpluses in the social funds, such as for retirement, medical care, and unemployment; debt instruments for the social funds are not sold at public auctions.

country comparison to the world: 57

## FISCAL YEAR:

calendar year

## INFLATION RATE (CONSUMER PRICES):

6.2% (2017 est.)

9.6% (2016 est.)

country comparison to the world: 189

## CENTRAL BANK DISCOUNT RATE:

9% (31 December 2012)

8.75% (31 December 2011)

note: Uruguay's central bank uses the benchmark interest rate, rather than the discount rate, to conduct monetary policy; the rates shown here are the benchmark rates

country comparison to the world: 35

## COMMERCIAL BANK PRIME LENDING RATE:

13.83% (31 December 2017 est.)

16.17% (31 December 2016 est.)

country comparison to the world: 51

**STOCK OF NARROW MONEY:**

$5.068 billion (31 December 2017 est.)

$4.516 billion (31 December 2016 est.)

country comparison to the world: 104

**STOCK OF BROAD MONEY:**

$5.068 billion (31 December 2017 est.)

$4.516 billion (31 December 2016 est.)

country comparison to the world: 107

**STOCK OF DOMESTIC CREDIT:**

$20.84 billion (31 December 2017 est.)

$19.03 billion (31 December 2016 est.)

country comparison to the world: 91

**MARKET VALUE OF PUBLICLY TRADED SHARES:**

$175.4 million (31 December 2012 est.)

$174.6 million (31 December 2011 est.)

$156.9 million (31 December 2010 est.)

country comparison to the world: 119

**CURRENT ACCOUNT BALANCE:**

$879 million (2017 est.)

$410 million (2016 est.)

country comparison to the world: 51

**EXPORTS:**

$11.41 billion (2017 est.)

$8.387 billion (2016 est.)

country comparison to the world: 88

**EXPORTS - PARTNERS:**

China 19%, Brazil 16.1%, US 5.7%, Argentina 5.4% (2017)

**EXPORTS - COMMODITIES:**

beef, soybeans, cellulose, rice, wheat, wood, dairy products, wool

**IMPORTS:**

$8.607 billion (2017 est.)

$8.463 billion (2016 est.)

country comparison to the world: 107

**IMPORTS - COMMODITIES:**

refined oil, crude oil, passenger and other transportation vehicles, vehicle parts, cellular phones

**IMPORTS - PARTNERS:**

China 20%, Brazil 19.5%, Argentina 12.6%, US 10.9% (2017)

**RESERVES OF FOREIGN EXCHANGE AND GOLD:**

$15.96 billion (31 December 2017 est.)

$13.47 billion (31 December 2016 est.)

country comparison to the world: 66

**DEBT - EXTERNAL:**

$28.37 billion (31 December 2017 est.)

$27.9 billion (31 December 2016 est.)

country comparison to the world: 84

**STOCK OF DIRECT FOREIGN INVESTMENT - AT HOME:**

$44.84 billion (31 December 2017 est.)

$22.81 billion (31 December 2016 est.)

country comparison to the world: 60

**STOCK OF DIRECT FOREIGN INVESTMENT - ABROAD:**

$19.97 billion (31 December 2017 est.)

$136.1 million (31 December 2016 est.)

country comparison to the world: 54

**EXCHANGE RATES:**

Uruguayan pesos (UYU) per US dollar -

28.77 (2017 est.)

30.16 (2016 est.)

30.16 (2015 est.)

27.52 (2014 est.)

23.25 (2013 est.)

## ENERGY :: URUGUAY

**ELECTRICITY ACCESS:**

population without electricity: 20,106 (2012)

electrification - total population: 99.4% (2012)

electrification - urban areas: 99.7% (2012)

electrification - rural areas: 93.8% (2012)

**ELECTRICITY - PRODUCTION:**

13.13 billion kWh (2016 est.)

country comparison to the world: 92

**ELECTRICITY - CONSUMPTION:**

10.77 billion kWh (2016 est.)

country comparison to the world: 93

**ELECTRICITY - EXPORTS:**

1.321 billion kWh (2015 est.)

country comparison to the world: 53

**ELECTRICITY - IMPORTS:**

24 million kWh (2016 est.)

country comparison to the world: 111

**ELECTRICITY - INSTALLED GENERATING CAPACITY:**

4.808 million kW (2016 est.)

country comparison to the world: 81

**ELECTRICITY - FROM FOSSIL FUELS:**

29% of total installed capacity (2016 est.)

country comparison to the world: 185

**ELECTRICITY - FROM NUCLEAR FUELS:**

0% of total installed capacity (2017 est.)

country comparison to the world: 205

**ELECTRICITY - FROM HYDROELECTRIC PLANTS:**

29% of total installed capacity (2017 est.)

country comparison to the world: 72

**ELECTRICITY - FROM OTHER RENEWABLE SOURCES:**

42% of total installed capacity (2017 est.)

country comparison to the world: 5

**CRUDE OIL - PRODUCTION:**

0 bbl/day (2017 est.)

country comparison to the world: 211

**CRUDE OIL - EXPORTS:**

0 bbl/day (2015 est.)

country comparison to the world: 212

**CRUDE OIL - IMPORTS:**

40,200 bbl/day (2015 est.)

country comparison to the world: 57

**CRUDE OIL - PROVED RESERVES:**

0 bbl (1 January 2018 est.)

country comparison to the world: 209

**REFINED PETROLEUM PRODUCTS - PRODUCTION:**

42,220 bbl/day (2015 est.)

country comparison to the world: 81

**REFINED PETROLEUM PRODUCTS - CONSUMPTION:**

53,000 bbl/day (2016 est.)

country comparison to the world: 101

**REFINED PETROLEUM PRODUCTS - EXPORTS:**

0 bbl/day (2015 est.)

country comparison to the world: 214

**REFINED PETROLEUM PRODUCTS - IMPORTS:**

9,591 bbl/day (2015 est.)

country comparison to the world: 150

**NATURAL GAS - PRODUCTION:**

0 cu m (2017 est.)

country comparison to the world: 211

**NATURAL GAS - CONSUMPTION:**

70.79 million cu m (2017 est.)

country comparison to the world: 110

**NATURAL GAS - EXPORTS:**

0 cu m (2017 est.)

country comparison to the world: 207

**NATURAL GAS - IMPORTS:**

70.79 million cu m (2017 est.)

country comparison to the world: 75

**NATURAL GAS - PROVED RESERVES:**

0 cu m (1 January 2014 est.)

country comparison to the world: 204

**CARBON DIOXIDE EMISSIONS FROM CONSUMPTION OF ENERGY:**

7.554 million Mt (2017 est.)

country comparison to the world: 122

## COMMUNICATIONS :: URUGUAY

**TELEPHONES - FIXED LINES:**

total subscriptions: 1,136,977 (2017 est.)

subscriptions per 100 inhabitants: 34 (2017 est.)

country comparison to the world: 74

**TELEPHONES - MOBILE CELLULAR:**

total subscriptions: 5,097,569 (2017 est.)

subscriptions per 100 inhabitants: 152 (2017 est.)

country comparison to the world: 119

**TELEPHONE SYSTEM:**

general assessment: fully digitalized (2016)

domestic: most modern facilities concentrated in Montevideo; nationwide microwave radio relay network; overall fixed-line and mobile-cellular teledensity over 185 telephones per 100 persons (2016)

international: country code - 598; the UNISOR submarine cable system provides direct connectivity to Brazil and Argentina; satellite earth stations - 2 Intelsat (Atlantic Ocean) (2016)

**BROADCAST MEDIA:**

mixture of privately owned and state-run broadcast media; more than 100 commercial radio stations and about 20 TV channels; cable TV is available; many community radio and TV stations; adopted the hybrid Japanese/Brazilian HDTV standard (ISDB-T) in December 2010 (2010)

**INTERNET COUNTRY CODE:**

.uy

**INTERNET USERS:**

total: 2,225,075 (July 2016 est.)

percent of population: 66.4% (July 2016 est.)

country comparison to the world: 108

**BROADBAND - FIXED SUBSCRIPTIONS:**

total: 949,974 (2017 est.)

subscriptions per 100 inhabitants: 28 (2017 est.)

country comparison to the world: 70

## TRANSPORTATION :: URUGUAY

**NATIONAL AIR TRANSPORT SYSTEM:**

number of registered air carriers: 2 (2015)

inventory of registered aircraft operated by air carriers: 3 (2015)

**CIVIL AIRCRAFT REGISTRATION COUNTRY CODE PREFIX:**

CX (2016)

**AIRPORTS:**

133 (2013)

country comparison to the world: 43

**AIRPORTS - WITH PAVED RUNWAYS:**

total: 11 (2013)

over 3,047 m: 1 (2013)

1,524 to 2,437 m: 4 (2013)

914 to 1,523 m: 4 (2013)

under 914 m: 2 (2013)

**AIRPORTS - WITH UNPAVED RUNWAYS:**

total: 122 (2013)

1,524 to 2,437 m: 3 (2013)

914 to 1,523 m: 40 (2013)

under 914 m: 79 (2013)

**PIPELINES:**

257 km gas, 160 km oil (2013)

**RAILWAYS:**

total: 1,673 km (operational; government claims overall length is 2,961 km) (2016)

standard gauge: 1,673 km 1.435-m gauge (2016)

country comparison to the world: 80

**ROADWAYS:**

total: 77,732 km (2010)

paved: 7,743 km (2010)

unpaved: 69,989 km (2010)

country comparison to the world: 63

**WATERWAYS:**

1,600 km (2011)

country comparison to the world: 50

**MERCHANT MARINE:**

total: 56 (2017)

by type: container ship 1, general cargo 6, oil tanker 4, other 45 (2017)

country comparison to the world: 109

**PORTS AND TERMINALS:**

major seaport(s): Montevideo

## MILITARY AND SECURITY :: URUGUAY

**MILITARY EXPENDITURES:**

1.85% of GDP (2016)

1.82% of GDP (2015)

1.81% of GDP (2014)

country comparison to the world: 59

**MILITARY BRANCHES:**

Uruguayan Armed Forces: Uruguayan National Army (Ejercito Nacional Uruguayo, ENU), Uruguayan National Navy (Armada Nacional del Uruguay, includes naval air arm, Naval Rifle Corps (Cuerpo de Fusileros Navales, Fusna), Maritime Prefecture in wartime), Uruguayan Air Force (Fuerza Aerea Uruguaya, FAU) (2012)

**MILITARY SERVICE AGE AND OBLIGATION:**

18-30 years of age (18-22 years of age for navy) for male or female voluntary military service; up to 40 years of age for specialists; enlistment is voluntary in peacetime, but the government has the authority to conscript in emergencies; minimum 6-year education (2013)

## TRANSNATIONAL ISSUES :: URUGUAY

**DISPUTES - INTERNATIONAL:**

in 2010, the ICJ ruled in favor of Uruguay's operation of two paper mills on the Uruguay River, which forms the border with Argentina; the two countries formed a joint pollution monitoring regimeuncontested boundary dispute between Brazil and Uruguay over Braziliera/Brasiliera Island in the Quarai/Cuareim River leaves the tripoint with Argentina in questionsmuggling of firearms and narcotics continues to be an issue along the Uruguay-Brazil border

**REFUGEES AND INTERNALLY DISPLACED PERSONS:**

refugees (country of origin): 9,186 (Venezuela) (economic and political crisis; includes Venezuelans who have claimed asylum or have received alternative legal stay) (2018)

**ILLICIT DRUGS:** small-scale transit country for drugs mainly bound for Europe, often through sea-borne containers; law enforcement corruption; money laundering because of strict banking secrecy laws; weak border control along Brazilian frontier; increasing consumption of cocaine base and synthetic drugs

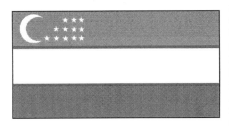

# CENTRAL ASIA :: UZBEKISTAN

## INTRODUCTION :: UZBEKISTAN

### BACKGROUND:

Russia conquered the territory of present-day Uzbekistan in the late 19th century. Stiff resistance to the Red Army after the Bolshevik Revolution was eventually suppressed and a socialist republic established in 1924. During the Soviet era, intensive production of "white gold" (cotton) and grain led to overuse of agrochemicals and the depletion of water supplies, which have left the land degraded and the Aral Sea and certain rivers half dry. Independent since 1991 upon the dissolution of the USSR, the country has reduced its dependence on the cotton monoculture by diversifying agricultural production while developing its mineral and petroleum export capacity and increasing its manufacturing base. Uzbekistan's first president, Islom KARIMOV, led Uzbekistan for 25 years until his death in September 2016. The political transition to his successor, then-Prime Minister Shavkat MIRZIYOYEV was peaceful, but sidelined the constitutional process where the chairman of the Senate would have served as the acting president. MIRZIYOYEV, who won the presidential election in December 2016, has improved relations with Uzbekistan's neighbors and introduced wide-ranging economic and judicial reforms.

## GEOGRAPHY :: UZBEKISTAN

### LOCATION:
Central Asia, north of Turkmenistan, south of Kazakhstan

### GEOGRAPHIC COORDINATES:
41 00 N, 64 00 E

### MAP REFERENCES:
Asia

### AREA:
total: 447,400 sq km

land: 425,400 sq km

water: 22,000 sq km

country comparison to the world: 58

### AREA - COMPARATIVE:
about four times the size of Virginia; slightly larger than California

### LAND BOUNDARIES:
total: 6,893 km

border countries (5): Afghanistan 144 km, Kazakhstan 2330 km, Kyrgyzstan 1314 km, Tajikistan 1312 km, Turkmenistan 1793 km

### COASTLINE:
0 km (doubly landlocked); note - Uzbekistan includes the southern portion of the Aral Sea with a 420 km shoreline

### MARITIME CLAIMS:
none (doubly landlocked)

### CLIMATE:
mostly mid-latitude desert, long, hot summers, mild winters; semiarid grassland in east

### TERRAIN:
mostly flat-to-rolling sandy desert with dunes; broad, flat intensely irrigated river valleys along course of Amu Darya, Syr Darya (Sirdaryo), and Zarafshon; Fergana Valley in east surrounded by mountainous Tajikistan and Kyrgyzstan; shrinking Aral Sea in west

### ELEVATION:
-12 m lowest point: Sariqamish Kuli

4301 highest point: Adelunga Toghi

### NATURAL RESOURCES:
natural gas, petroleum, coal, gold, uranium, silver, copper, lead and zinc, tungsten, molybdenum

### LAND USE:
agricultural land: 62.6% (2011 est.)

arable land: 10.1% (2011 est.) / permanent crops: 0.8% (2011 est.) / permanent pasture: 51.7% (2011 est.)

forest: 7.7% (2011 est.)

other: 29.7% (2011 est.)

### IRRIGATED LAND:
42,150 sq km (2012)

### POPULATION DISTRIBUTION:
most of the population is concentrated in the fertile Fergana Valley in the easternmost arm of the country; the south has significant clusters of people, while the central and western deserts are sparsely populated

### NATURAL HAZARDS:
earthquakes; floods; landslides or mudslides; avalanches; droughts

### ENVIRONMENT - CURRENT ISSUES:
shrinkage of the Aral Sea has resulted in growing concentrations of chemical pesticides and natural salts; these substances are then blown from the increasingly exposed lake bed and contribute to desertification and respiratory health problems; water pollution from industrial wastes and the heavy use of fertilizers and pesticides is the cause of many human health disorders; increasing soil salination; soil contamination from buried nuclear processing and agricultural chemicals, including DDT

### ENVIRONMENT - INTERNATIONAL AGREEMENTS:
party to: Biodiversity, Climate Change, Climate Change-Kyoto Protocol, Desertification, Endangered

Species, Environmental Modification, Hazardous Wastes, Ozone Layer Protection, Wetlands

signed, but not ratified: none of the selected agreements

### GEOGRAPHY - NOTE:
along with Liechtenstein, one of the only two doubly landlocked countries in the world

## PEOPLE AND SOCIETY :: UZBEKISTAN

### POPULATION:
30,023,709 (July 2018 est.)

country comparison to the world: 46

### NATIONALITY:
noun: Uzbekistani

adjective: Uzbekistani

### ETHNIC GROUPS:
Uzbek 80%, Russian 5.5%, Tajik 5%, Kazakh 3%, Karakalpak 2.5%, Tatar 1.5%, other 2.5% (1996 est.)

### LANGUAGES:
Uzbek (official) 74.3%, Russian 14.2%, Tajik 4.4%, other 7.1%

note: in the Karakalpakstan Republic, both the Karakalpak language and Uzbek have official status

### RELIGIONS:
Muslim 88% (mostly Sunni), Eastern Orthodox 9%, other 3%

### AGE STRUCTURE:
0-14 years: 23.61% (male 3,631,957 /female 3,457,274)

15-24 years: 17.85% (male 2,735,083 /female 2,623,511)

25-54 years: 44.95% (male 6,714,567 /female 6,781,485)

55-64 years: 8.15% (male 1,156,462 /female 1,289,703)

65 years and over: 5.44% (male 698,610 /female 935,057) (2018 est.)

### DEPENDENCY RATIOS:
total dependency ratio: 47.7 (2015 est.)

youth dependency ratio: 41.4 (2015 est.)

elderly dependency ratio: 6.2 (2015 est.)

potential support ratio: 16 (2015 est.)

### MEDIAN AGE:
total: 29.1 years

male: 28.5 years

female: 29.7 years (2018 est.)

country comparison to the world: 128

### POPULATION GROWTH RATE:
0.91% (2018 est.)

country comparison to the world: 119

### BIRTH RATE:
16.6 births/1,000 population (2018 est.)

country comparison to the world: 108

### DEATH RATE:
5.4 deaths/1,000 population (2018 est.)

country comparison to the world: 183

### NET MIGRATION RATE:
-2.2 migrant(s)/1,000 population (2017 est.)

country comparison to the world: 167

### POPULATION DISTRIBUTION:
most of the population is concentrated in the fertile Fergana Valley in the easternmost arm of the country; the south has significant clusters of people, while the central and western deserts are sparsely populated

### URBANIZATION:
urban population: 50.5% of total population (2018)

rate of urbanization: 1.28% annual rate of change (2015-20 est.)

### MAJOR URBAN AREAS - POPULATION:
2.464 million TASHKENT (capital) (2018)

### SEX RATIO:
at birth: 1.05 male(s)/female (2017 est.)

0-14 years: 1.05 male(s)/female (2017 est.)

15-24 years: 1.03 male(s)/female (2017 est.)

25-54 years: 0.99 male(s)/female (2017 est.)

55-64 years: 0.9 male(s)/female (2017 est.)

65 years and over: 0.74 male(s)/female (2017 est.)

total population: 0.99 male(s)/female (2017 est.)

### MOTHER'S MEAN AGE AT FIRST BIRTH:
23.4 years (2014 est.)

### MATERNAL MORTALITY RATE:
36 deaths/100,000 live births (2015 est.)

country comparison to the world: 109

### INFANT MORTALITY RATE:
total: 17.4 deaths/1,000 live births (2018 est.)

male: 20.7 deaths/1,000 live births (2018 est.)

female: 14 deaths/1,000 live births (2018 est.)

country comparison to the world: 90

### LIFE EXPECTANCY AT BIRTH:
total population: 74.3 years (2018 est.)

male: 71.2 years (2018 est.)

female: 77.5 years (2018 est.)

country comparison to the world: 126

### TOTAL FERTILITY RATE:
1.75 children born/woman (2018 est.)

country comparison to the world: 161

### HEALTH EXPENDITURES:
5.8% of GDP (2014)

country comparison to the world: 112

### PHYSICIANS DENSITY:
2.45 physicians/1,000 population (2014)

### HOSPITAL BED DENSITY:
4 beds/1,000 population (2013)

### DRINKING WATER SOURCE:
improved:

urban: 98.5% of population

rural: 80.9% of population

total: 87.3% of population

unimproved:

urban: 1.5% of population

rural: 19.1% of population

total: 12.7% of population (2012 est.)

### SANITATION FACILITY ACCESS:
improved:

urban: 100% of population (2015 est.)

rural: 100% of population (2015 est.)

total: 100% of population (2015 est.)

unimproved:

urban: 0% of population (2015 est.)

rural: 0% of population (2015 est.)

total: 0% of population (2015 est.)

### HIV/AIDS - ADULT PREVALENCE RATE:
0.3% (2017 est.)

country comparison to the world: 89

### HIV/AIDS - PEOPLE LIVING WITH HIV/AIDS:
52,000 (2017 est.)

country comparison to the world: 59

### HIV/AIDS - DEATHS:
1,900 (2017 est.)

**country comparison to the world:** 54

### OBESITY - ADULT PREVALENCE RATE:
16.6% (2016)

**country comparison to the world:** 123

### EDUCATION EXPENDITURES:
NA

### LITERACY:
**definition:** age 15 and over can read and write (2015 est.)

**total population:** 100% (2015 est.)

**male:** 100% (2015 est.)

**female:** 100% (2015 est.)

### SCHOOL LIFE EXPECTANCY (PRIMARY TO TERTIARY EDUCATION):
**total:** 12 years (2016)

**male:** 13 years (2016)

**female:** 12 years (2016)

## GOVERNMENT :: UZBEKISTAN

### COUNTRY NAME:
**conventional long form:** Republic of Uzbekistan

**conventional short form:** Uzbekistan

**local long form:** O'zbekiston Respublikasi

**local short form:** O'zbekiston

**former:** Uzbek Soviet Socialist Republic

**etymology:** a combination of the Turkic words "uz" (self) and "bek" (master) with the Persian suffix "-stan" (country) to give the meaning "Land of the Free"

### GOVERNMENT TYPE:
presidential republic; highly authoritarian

### CAPITAL:
**name:** Tashkent (Toshkent)

**geographic coordinates:** 41 19 N, 69 15 E

**time difference:** UTC+5 (10 hours ahead of Washington, DC, during Standard Time)

### ADMINISTRATIVE DIVISIONS:
12 provinces (viloyatlar, singular - viloyat), 1 autonomous republic* (avtonom respublikasi), and 1 city** (shahar); Andijon Viloyati, Buxoro Viloyati [Bukhara Province], Farg'ona Viloyati [Fergana Province], Jizzax Viloyati, Namangan Viloyati, Navoiy Viloyati, Qashqadaryo Viloyati (Qarshi), Qoraqalpog'iston Respublikasi [Karakalpakstan Republic]* (Nukus), Samarqand Viloyati [Samarkand Province], Sirdaryo Viloyati (Guliston), Surxondaryo Viloyati (Termiz), Toshkent Shahri [Tashkent City]**, Toshkent Viloyati [Tashkent Province], Xorazm Viloyati (Urganch)

**note:** administrative divisions have the same names as their administrative centers (exceptions have the administrative center name following in parentheses)

### INDEPENDENCE:
1 September 1991 (from the Soviet Union)

### NATIONAL HOLIDAY:
Independence Day, 1 September (1991)

### CONSTITUTION:
**history:** several previous; latest adopted 8 December 1992 (2017)

**amendments:** proposed by the Supreme Assembly or by referendum; passage requires two-thirds majority vote of both houses of the Assembly or passage in a referendum; amended several times, last in 2014 (2017)

### LEGAL SYSTEM:
civil law system

### INTERNATIONAL LAW ORGANIZATION PARTICIPATION:
has not submitted an ICJ jurisdiction declaration; non-party state to the ICCt

### CITIZENSHIP:
**citizenship by birth:** no

**citizenship by descent only:** at least one parent must be a citizen of Uzbekistan

**dual citizenship recognized:** no

**residency requirement for naturalization:** 5 years

### SUFFRAGE:
18 years of age; universal

### EXECUTIVE BRANCH:
**chief of state:** President Shavkat MIRZIYOYEV (interim president from 8 September 2016; formally elected president on 4 December 2016 to succeed longtime President Islom KARIMOV, who died on 2 September 2016)

**head of government:** Prime Minister Abdulla ARIPOV (since 14 December 2016); First Deputy Prime Minister Achilbay RAMATOV (since 15 December 2016)

**cabinet:** Cabinet of Ministers appointed by the president with most requiring approval of the Senate chamber of the Supreme Assembly (Oliy Majlis)

**elections/appointments:** president directly elected by absolute majority popular vote in 2 rounds if needed for a 5-year term (eligible for a second term; previously a 5-year term, extended by a 2002 constitutional amendment to 7 years, and reverted to 5 years in 2011); election last held on 4 December 2016 (next to be held in 2021); prime minister nominated by majority party in legislature since 2011, but appointed along with the ministers and deputy ministers by the president

**election results:** Shavkat MIRZIYOYEV elected president in first round; percent of vote - Shavkat MIRZIYOYEV (LDPU) 88.6%, Khatamjon KETMONOV (NDP) 3.7%, Narimon UMAROV (Adolat) 3.5%, Sarvar OTAMURADOV (Milliy Tiklanish/National Revival) 2.4%, other 1.8%

### LEGISLATIVE BRANCH:
**description:** bicameral Supreme Assembly or Oliy Majlis consists of: Senate (100 seats; 84 members indirectly elected by regional governing councils and 16 appointed by the president; members serve 5-year terms) Legislative Chamber or Qonunchilik Palatasi (150 seats; 135 members directly elected in single-seat constituencies by absolute majority vote with a second round, if needed, and 15 indirectly elected by the Ecological Movement of Uzbekistan; members serve 5-year terms)

**elections:**
Senate - last held 13-14 January 2015 (next to be held in 2020)
Legislative Chamber - last held on 21 December 2014 and 4 January 2015 (next to be held in December 2019)

**election results:**
Senate - percent of vote by party - NA; seats by party - NA; composition - men 83, women 17, percent of women 17%
Legislative Chamber - percent of vote by party - NA; seats by party - LDPU 52, National Revival Democratic Party 36, NDP 27, Adolat 20, Ecological

Movement 15; composition - men 126, women 24, percent of women 16%; note - total Supreme Assembly percent of women 16.4%

note: all parties in the Supreme Assembly support President Shavkat MIRZIYOYEV

## JUDICIAL BRANCH:

highest courts: Supreme Court (consists of 67 judges organized into administrative, civil, criminal, economic, and military sections); Constitutional Court (consists of 7 judges)

judge selection and term of office: judges of the highest courts nominated by the president and confirmed by the Oliy Majlis; judges appointed for initial 5-year term, subsequent 10-year term, and lifetime term subject to reappointment

subordinate courts: regional, district, city, and town courts; economic courts

## POLITICAL PARTIES AND LEADERS:

Ecological Movement of Uzbekistan (O'zbekiston Ekologik Harakati) [Boriy ALIKHANOV]
Justice (Adolat) Social Democratic Party of Uzbekistan [Narimon UMAROV]
Liberal Democratic Party of Uzbekistan (O'zbekiston Liberal-Demokratik Partiyasi) or LDPU [Shavkat MIRZIYOYEV]
National Revival Democratic Party of Uzbekistan (O'zbekiston Milliy Tiklanish Demokratik Partiyasi) [Sarvar OTAMURATOV]
People's Democratic Party of Uzbekistan (Xalq Demokratik Partiyas) or NDP [Hotamjon KETMONOV] (formerly Communist Party)

## INTERNATIONAL ORGANIZATION PARTICIPATION:

ADB, CICA, CIS, EAPC, EBRD, ECO, FAO, IAEA, IBRD, ICAO, ICC (national committees), ICCt, ICRM, IDA, IDB, IFAD, IFC, IFRCS, ILO, IMF, Interpol, IOC, ISO, ITSO, ITU, MIGA, NAM, OIC, OPCW, OSCE, PFP, SCO, UN, UN Security Council (temporary), UNCTAD, UNESCO, UNIDO, UNWTO, UPU, WCO, WFTU (NGOs), WHO, WIPO, WMO, WTO (observer)

## DIPLOMATIC REPRESENTATION IN THE US:

chief of mission: Ambassador Javlon VAKHABOV (since 29 November 2017)

chancery: 1746 Massachusetts Avenue NW, Washington, DC 20036

telephone: [1] (202) 887-5300

FAX: [1] (202) 293-6804

consulate(s) general: New York

## DIPLOMATIC REPRESENTATION FROM THE US:

chief of mission: Ambassador Pamela L. SPRATLEN (since 27 January 2015)

embassy: 3 Moyqo'rq'on, 5th Block, Yunusobod District, Tashkent 100093

mailing address: use embassy street address

telephone: [998] (71) 120-5450

FAX: [998] (71) 120-6335

## FLAG DESCRIPTION:

three equal horizontal bands of blue (top), white, and green separated by red fimbriations with a white crescent moon (closed side to the hoist) and 12 white stars shifted to the hoist on the top band; blue is the color of the Turkic peoples and of the sky, white signifies peace and the striving for purity in thoughts and deeds, while green represents nature and is the color of Islam; the red stripes are the vital force of all living organisms that links good and pure ideas with the eternal sky and with deeds on earth; the crescent represents Islam and the 12 stars the months and constellations of the Uzbek calendar

## NATIONAL SYMBOL(S):

khumo (mythical bird); national colors: blue, white, red, green

## NATIONAL ANTHEM:

name: "O'zbekiston Respublikasining Davlat Madhiyasi" (National Anthem of the Republic of Uzbekistan)

lyrics/music: Abdulla ARIPOV/Mutal BURHANOV

note: adopted 1992; after the fall of the Soviet Union, Uzbekistan kept the music of the anthem from its time as a Soviet Republic but adopted new lyrics

# ECONOMY :: UZBEKISTAN

## ECONOMY - OVERVIEW:

Uzbekistan is a doubly landlocked country in which 51% of the population lives in urban settlements; the agriculture-rich Fergana Valley, in which Uzbekistan's eastern borders are situated, has been counted among the most densely populated parts of Central Asia. Since its independence in September 1991, the government has largely maintained its Soviet-style command economy with subsidies and tight controls on production, prices, and access to foreign currency. Despite ongoing efforts to diversify crops, Uzbek agriculture remains largely centered on cotton; Uzbekistan is the world's fifth-largest cotton exporter and seventh-largest producer. Uzbekistan's growth has been driven primarily by state-led investments, and export of natural gas, gold, and cotton provides a significant share of foreign exchange earnings.

Recently, lower global commodity prices and economic slowdowns in neighboring Russia and China have hurt Uzbekistan's trade and investment and worsened its foreign currency shortage. Aware of the need to improve the investment climate, the government is taking incremental steps to reform the business sector and address impediments to foreign investment in the country. Since the death of first President Islam KARIMOV and election of President Shavkat MIRZIYOYEV, emphasis on such initiatives and government efforts to improve the private sector have increased. In the past, Uzbek authorities accused US and other foreign companies operating in Uzbekistan of violating Uzbek laws and have frozen and seized their assets.

As a part of its economic reform efforts, the Uzbek Government is looking to expand opportunities for small and medium enterprises and prioritizes increasing foreign direct investment. In September 2017, the government devalued the official currency rate by almost 50% and announced the loosening of currency restrictions to eliminate the currency black market, increase access to hard currency, and boost investment.

## GDP (PURCHASING POWER PARITY):

$223 billion (2017 est.)

$211.8 billion (2016 est.)

$196.5 billion (2015 est.)

note: data are in 2017 dollars

country comparison to the world: 63

## GDP (OFFICIAL EXCHANGE RATE):

$48.83 billion (2017 est.) (2017 est.)

## GDP - REAL GROWTH RATE:

5.3% (2017 est.)

7.8% (2016 est.)
7.9% (2015 est.)

country comparison to the world: 44

## GDP - PER CAPITA (PPP):
$6,900 (2017 est.)
$6,700 (2016 est.)
$6,300 (2015 est.)

note: data are in 2017 dollars

country comparison to the world: 158

## GROSS NATIONAL SAVING:
32.7% of GDP (2017 est.)
25.4% of GDP (2016 est.)
27.6% of GDP (2015 est.)

country comparison to the world: 24

## GDP - COMPOSITION, BY END USE:
household consumption: 59.5% (2017 est.)

government consumption: 16.3% (2017 est.)

investment in fixed capital: 25.3% (2017 est.)

investment in inventories: 3% (2017 est.)

exports of goods and services: 19% (2017 est.)

imports of goods and services: -20% (2017 est.)

## GDP - COMPOSITION, BY SECTOR OF ORIGIN:
agriculture: 17.9% (2017 est.)

industry: 33.7% (2017 est.)

services: 48.5% (2017 est.)

## AGRICULTURE - PRODUCTS:
cotton, vegetables, fruits, grain; livestock

## INDUSTRIES:
textiles, food processing, machine building, metallurgy, mining, hydrocarbon extraction, chemicals

## INDUSTRIAL PRODUCTION GROWTH RATE:
4.5% (2017 est.)

country comparison to the world: 67

## LABOR FORCE:
18.12 million (2017 est.)

country comparison to the world: 32

## LABOR FORCE - BY OCCUPATION:
agriculture: 25.9%

industry: 13.2%

services: 60.9% (2012 est.)

## UNEMPLOYMENT RATE:
5% (2017 est.)

5.1% (2016 est.)

note: official data; another 20% are underemployed

country comparison to the world: 75

## POPULATION BELOW POVERTY LINE:
14% (2016 est.)

## HOUSEHOLD INCOME OR CONSUMPTION BY PERCENTAGE SHARE:
lowest 10%: 29.6% (2003)

highest 10%: 29.6% (2003)

## DISTRIBUTION OF FAMILY INCOME - GINI INDEX:
36.8 (2003)

44.7 (1998)

country comparison to the world: 85

## BUDGET:
revenues: 15.22 billion (2017 est.)

expenditures: 15.08 billion (2017 est.)

## TAXES AND OTHER REVENUES:
31.2% (of GDP) (2017 est.)

country comparison to the world: 74

## BUDGET SURPLUS (+) OR DEFICIT (-):
0.3% (of GDP) (2017 est.)

country comparison to the world: 42

## PUBLIC DEBT:
24.3% of GDP (2017 est.)

10.5% of GDP (2016 est.)

country comparison to the world: 178

## FISCAL YEAR:
calendar year

## INFLATION RATE (CONSUMER PRICES):
12.5% (2017 est.)

8% (2016 est.)

note: official data; based on independent analysis of consumer prices, inflation reached 22% in 2012

country comparison to the world: 208

## CENTRAL BANK DISCOUNT RATE:
9% (2016)

9% (2015)

country comparison to the world: 36

## COMMERCIAL BANK PRIME LENDING RATE:
16% (31 December 2016 est.)

11.2% (31 December 2012 est.)

country comparison to the world: 31

## STOCK OF NARROW MONEY:
$4.173 billion (31 December 2017 est.)

$7.729 billion (31 December 2016 est.)

country comparison to the world: 110

## STOCK OF BROAD MONEY:
$4.173 billion (31 December 2017 est.)

$7.729 billion (31 December 2016 est.)

country comparison to the world: 115

## STOCK OF DOMESTIC CREDIT:
$5.558 billion (31 December 2017 est.)

$11.63 billion (31 December 2016 est.)

country comparison to the world: 128

## MARKET VALUE OF PUBLICLY TRADED SHARES:
$NA (31 December 2012)

$715.3 million (31 December 2006)

country comparison to the world: 108

## CURRENT ACCOUNT BALANCE:
$1.713 billion (2017 est.)

$384 million (2016 est.)

country comparison to the world: 43

## EXPORTS:
$11.48 billion (2017 est.)

$11.2 billion (2016 est.)

country comparison to the world: 86

## EXPORTS - PARTNERS:
Switzerland 38.7%, China 15.5%, Russia 10.7%, Turkey 8.6%, Kazakhstan 7.7%, Afghanistan 4.7% (2017)

## EXPORTS - COMMODITIES:
energy products, cotton, gold, mineral fertilizers, ferrous and nonferrous metals, textiles, foodstuffs, machinery, automobiles

## IMPORTS:
$11.42 billion (2017 est.)

$10.92 billion (2016 est.)

country comparison to the world: 95

## IMPORTS - COMMODITIES:
machinery and equipment, foodstuffs, chemicals, ferrous and nonferrous metals

## IMPORTS - PARTNERS:
China 23.7%, Russia 22.5%, Kazakhstan 10.7%, South Korea 9.8%, Turkey 5.8%, Germany 5.6% (2017)

## RESERVES OF FOREIGN EXCHANGE AND GOLD:
$16 billion (31 December 2017 est.)

$14 billion (31 December 2016 est.)

country comparison to the world: 65

## DEBT - EXTERNAL:
$16.9 billion (31 December 2017 est.)

$16.76 billion (31 December 2016 est.)

country comparison to the world: 101

**STOCK OF DIRECT FOREIGN INVESTMENT - AT HOME:**

NA

**STOCK OF DIRECT FOREIGN INVESTMENT - ABROAD:**

NA

**EXCHANGE RATES:**

Uzbekistani soum (UZS) per US dollar -

3,906.1 (2017 est.)

2,966.6 (2016 est.)

2,966.6 (2015 est.)

2,569.6 (2014 est.)

2,311.4 (2013 est.)

## ENERGY :: UZBEKISTAN

**ELECTRICITY ACCESS:**

electrification - total population: 100% (2016)

**ELECTRICITY - PRODUCTION:**

55.55 billion kWh (2016 est.)

country comparison to the world: 52

**ELECTRICITY - CONSUMPTION:**

49.07 billion kWh (2016 est.)

country comparison to the world: 50

**ELECTRICITY - EXPORTS:**

13 billion kWh (2014 est.)

country comparison to the world: 15

**ELECTRICITY - IMPORTS:**

10.84 billion kWh (2016 est.)

country comparison to the world: 23

**ELECTRICITY - INSTALLED GENERATING CAPACITY:**

12.96 million kW (2016 est.)

country comparison to the world: 54

**ELECTRICITY - FROM FOSSIL FUELS:**

86% of total installed capacity (2016 est.)

country comparison to the world: 69

**ELECTRICITY - FROM NUCLEAR FUELS:**

0% of total installed capacity (2017 est.)

country comparison to the world: 206

**ELECTRICITY - FROM HYDROELECTRIC PLANTS:**

14% of total installed capacity (2017 est.)

country comparison to the world: 109

**ELECTRICITY - FROM OTHER RENEWABLE SOURCES:**

0% of total installed capacity (2017 est.)

country comparison to the world: 212

**CRUDE OIL - PRODUCTION:**

46,070 bbl/day (2017 est.)

country comparison to the world: 54

**CRUDE OIL - EXPORTS:**

27,000 bbl/day (2015 est.)

country comparison to the world: 46

**CRUDE OIL - IMPORTS:**

420 bbl/day (2015 est.)

country comparison to the world: 81

**CRUDE OIL - PROVED RESERVES:**

594 million bbl (1 January 2018 est.)

country comparison to the world: 44

**REFINED PETROLEUM PRODUCTS - PRODUCTION:**

61,740 bbl/day (2015 est.)

country comparison to the world: 78

**REFINED PETROLEUM PRODUCTS - CONSUMPTION:**

60,000 bbl/day (2016 est.)

country comparison to the world: 95

**REFINED PETROLEUM PRODUCTS - EXPORTS:**

3,977 bbl/day (2015 est.)

country comparison to the world: 95

**REFINED PETROLEUM PRODUCTS - IMPORTS:**

0 bbl/day (2015 est.)

country comparison to the world: 215

**NATURAL GAS - PRODUCTION:**

52.1 billion cu m (2017 est.)

country comparison to the world: 15

**NATURAL GAS - CONSUMPTION:**

43.07 billion cu m (2017 est.)

country comparison to the world: 22

**NATURAL GAS - EXPORTS:**

9.401 billion cu m (2017 est.)

country comparison to the world: 22

**NATURAL GAS - IMPORTS:**

0 cu m (2017 est.)

country comparison to the world: 207

**NATURAL GAS - PROVED RESERVES:**

1.841 trillion cu m (1 January 2018 est.)

country comparison to the world: 18

**CARBON DIOXIDE EMISSIONS FROM CONSUMPTION OF ENERGY:**

95.58 million Mt (2017 est.)

country comparison to the world: 46

## COMMUNICATIONS :: UZBEKISTAN

**TELEPHONES - FIXED LINES:**

total subscriptions: 3,444,330 (2017 est.)

subscriptions per 100 inhabitants: 12 (2017 est.)

country comparison to the world: 41

**TELEPHONES - MOBILE CELLULAR:**

total subscriptions: 24,265,460 (2017 est.)

subscriptions per 100 inhabitants: 82 (2017 est.)

country comparison to the world: 51

**TELEPHONE SYSTEM:**

general assessment: digital exchanges in large cities and in rural areas (2018)

domestic: the state-owned telecommunications company, Uzbektelecom, owner of the fixed-line telecommunications system, has used loans from the Japanese government and the China Development Bank to upgrade fixed-line services including conversion to digital exchanges; mobile-cellular services are provided by 3 private and 2 state-owned operators with a total subscriber base of 22.8 million as of January 2018 (2018)

international: country code - 998; linked by fiber-optic cable or microwave radio relay with CIS member states and to other countries by leased connection via the Moscow international gateway switch; the country also has a link to the Trans-Asia-Europe (TAE) fiber-optic cable; Uzbekistan has supported the national fiber- optic backbone project of Afghanistan since 2008 (2018)

**BROADCAST MEDIA:**

government controls media; 18 state-owned broadcasters - 14 TV and 4 radio - provide service to virtually the entire country; about 20 privately owned TV stations, overseen by local officials, broadcast to local markets; privately owned TV stations are required to lease transmitters from the government-owned Republic TV and Radio Industry Corporation; in 2013, the government closed TV and radio broadcasters affiliated with the National Association of Electronic Mass Media (NAEMM) of Uzbekistan, a government-sponsored NGO for private broadcast media; in 2015, the

NAEMM relaunched its TV channel under a different name (2017)

**INTERNET COUNTRY CODE:**

.uz

**INTERNET USERS:**

total: 13,791,083 (July 2016 est.)

percent of population: 46.8% (July 2016 est.)

country comparison to the world: 43

**BROADBAND - FIXED SUBSCRIPTIONS:**

total: 3,320,210 (2017 est.)

subscriptions per 100 inhabitants: 11 (2017 est.)

country comparison to the world: 36

## TRANSPORTATION :: UZBEKISTAN

**NATIONAL AIR TRANSPORT SYSTEM:**

number of registered air carriers: 2 (2015)

inventory of registered aircraft operated by air carriers: 29 (2015)

annual passenger traffic on registered air carriers: 2,486,673 (2015)

annual freight traffic on registered air carriers: 114,334,520 mt-km (2015)

**CIVIL AIRCRAFT REGISTRATION COUNTRY CODE PREFIX:**

UK (2016)

**AIRPORTS:**

53 (2013)

country comparison to the world: 89

**AIRPORTS - WITH PAVED RUNWAYS:**

total: 33 (2013)

over 3,047 m: 6 (2013)

2,438 to 3,047 m: 13 (2013)

1,524 to 2,437 m: 6 (2013)

914 to 1,523 m: 4 (2013)

under 914 m: 4 (2013)

**AIRPORTS - WITH UNPAVED RUNWAYS:**

total: 20 (2013)

2,438 to 3,047 m: 2 (2013)

under 914 m: 18 (2013)

**PIPELINES:**

13700 km gas, 944 km oil (2016)

**RAILWAYS:**

total: 4,642 km (2018)

broad gauge: 4,642 km 1.520-m gauge (1,684 km electrified) (2018)

country comparison to the world: 42

**ROADWAYS:**

total: 86,496 km (2000)

paved: 75,511 km (2000)

unpaved: 10,985 km (2000)

country comparison to the world: 55

**WATERWAYS:**

1,100 km (2012)

country comparison to the world: 62

**PORTS AND TERMINALS:**

river port(s): Termiz (Amu Darya)

## MILITARY AND SECURITY :: UZBEKISTAN

**MILITARY BRANCHES:**

Armed Forces: Army, Air and Air Defense Forces, National Guard (2017)

**MILITARY SERVICE AGE AND OBLIGATION:**

18 years of age for compulsory military service; 1-month or 1-year conscript service obligation for males; moving toward a professional military, but conscription in some form will continue; the military cannot accommodate everyone who wishes to enlist, and competition for entrance into the military is similar to the competition for admission to universities; note - widely considered to have one of the strongest militaries in Central Asia, although it is untested (2016)

## TRANSNATIONAL ISSUES :: UZBEKISTAN

**DISPUTES - INTERNATIONAL:**

prolonged drought and cotton monoculture in Uzbekistan and Turkmenistan created water-sharing difficulties for Amu Darya river statesfield demarcation of the boundaries with Kazakhstan commenced in 2004border delimitation of 130 km of border with Kyrgyzstan is hampered by serious disputes around enclaves and other areas

**REFUGEES AND INTERNALLY DISPLACED PERSONS:**

stateless persons: 85,555 (2017)

**TRAFFICKING IN PERSONS:**

current situation: Uzbekistan is a source country for men, women, and children subjected to forced labor and women and children subjected to sex trafficking; government-compelled forced labor of adults remained endemic during the 2014 cotton harvest; despite a decree banning the use of persons under 18, children were mobilized to harvest cotton by local officials in some districts; in some regions, local officials forced teachers, students, private business employees, and others to work in construction, agriculture, and cleaning parks; Uzbekistani women and children are victims of sex trafficking domestically and in the Middle East, Eurasia, and Asia; Uzbekistani men and, to a lesser extent, women are subjected to forced labor in Kazakhstan, Russia, and Ukraine in the construction, oil, agriculture, retail, and food sectors

tier rating: Tier 2 Watch List – Uzbekistan does not fully comply with the minimum standards for the elimination of trafficking; however, it is making significant efforts to do so; law enforcement efforts in 2014 were mixed; the government made efforts to combat sex and transnational labor trafficking, but government-compelled forced labor of adults in the cotton harvest went unaddressed, and the decree prohibiting forced child labor was not applied universally; official complicity in human trafficking in the cotton harvest remained prevalent; authorities made efforts to identify and protect sex and transnational labor victims, although a systematic process is still lacking; minimal efforts were made to assist victims of forced labor in the cotton harvest, as the government does not openly acknowledge the existence of this forced labor; the ILO did not have permission or funding to monitor the 2014 harvest, but the government authorized the UN's International Labour Organization to conduct a survey on recruitment practices and working conditions in agriculture, particularly the cotton sector, and to monitor the 2015-17 cotton harvests for child and forced labor in project areas (2015)

**ILLICIT DRUGS:**

transit country for Afghan narcotics bound for Russian and, to a lesser extent, Western European markets; limited illicit cultivation of cannabis and small amounts of opium poppy for domestic consumption; poppy cultivation almost wiped out by government crop eradication program;

transit point for heroin precursor chemicals bound for Afghanistan

# AUSTRALIA - OCEANIA :: VANUATU

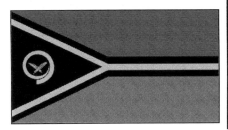

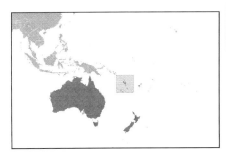

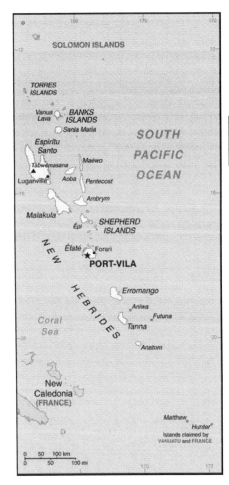

## INTRODUCTION :: VANUATU

### BACKGROUND:
Multiple waves of colonizers, each speaking a distinct language, migrated to the New Hebrides in the millennia preceding European exploration in the 18th century. This settlement pattern accounts for the complex linguistic diversity found on the archipelago to this day. The British and French, who settled the New Hebrides in the 19th century, agreed in 1906 to an Anglo-French Condominium, which administered the islands until independence in 1980, when the new name of Vanuatu was adopted.

## GEOGRAPHY :: VANUATU

### LOCATION:
Oceania, group of islands in the South Pacific Ocean, about three-quarters of the way from Hawaii to Australia

### GEOGRAPHIC COORDINATES:
16 00 S, 167 00 E

### MAP REFERENCES:
Oceania

### AREA:
total: 12,189 sq km
land: 12,189 sq km
water: 0 sq km
note: includes more than 80 islands, about 65 of which are inhabited
country comparison to the world: 163

### AREA - COMPARATIVE:
slightly larger than Connecticut

### LAND BOUNDARIES:
0 km

### COASTLINE:
2,528 km

### MARITIME CLAIMS:
territorial sea: 12 nm
exclusive economic zone: 200 nm
contiguous zone: 24 nm
continental shelf: 200 nm or to the edge of the continental margin
measured from claimed archipelagic baselines

### CLIMATE:
tropical; moderated by southeast trade winds from May to October; moderate rainfall from November to April; may be affected by cyclones from December to April

### TERRAIN:
mostly mountainous islands of volcanic origin; narrow coastal plains

### ELEVATION:
0 m lowest point: Pacific Ocean
1877 highest point: Tabwemasana

### NATURAL RESOURCES:
manganese, hardwood forests, fish

### LAND USE:
agricultural land: 15.3% (2011 est.)
arable land: 1.6% (2011 est.) / permanent crops: 10.3% (2011 est.) / permanent pasture: 3.4% (2011 est.)
forest: 36.1% (2011 est.)
other: 48.6% (2011 est.)

### IRRIGATED LAND:
0 sq km (2012)

### POPULATION DISTRIBUTION:
three-quarters of the population lives in rural areas; the urban populace lives primarily in two cities, Port-Vila and Lugenville; three largest islands - Espiritu Santo, Malakula, and Efate - accomodate over half of the populace

### NATURAL HAZARDS:
tropical cyclones (January to April); volcanic eruption on Aoba (Ambae) island began on 27 November 2005, volcanism also causes minor earthquakes; tsunamis

volcanism: significant volcanic activity with multiple eruptions in recent years; Yasur (361 m), one of the world's most active volcanoes, has experienced continuous activity in recent centuries; other historically active volcanoes include Aoba, Ambrym, Epi, Gaua, Kuwae, Lopevi, Suretamatai, and Traitor's Head

### ENVIRONMENT - CURRENT ISSUES:
population growth; water pollution, most of the population does not have access to a reliable supply of potable

water; inadequate sanitation; deforestation

**ENVIRONMENT - INTERNATIONAL AGREEMENTS:**

party to: Antarctic-Marine Living Resources, Biodiversity, Climate Change, Climate Change-Kyoto Protocol, Desertification, Endangered Species, Law of the Sea, Marine Dumping, Ozone Layer Protection, Ship Pollution, Tropical Timber 94

signed, but not ratified: none of the selected agreements

**GEOGRAPHY - NOTE:**

a Y-shaped chain of four main islands and 80 smaller islands; several of the islands have active volcanoes and there are several underwater volcanoes as well

## PEOPLE AND SOCIETY :: VANUATU

**POPULATION:**

288,037 (July 2018 est.)

country comparison to the world: 182

**NATIONALITY:**

noun: Ni-Vanuatu (singular and plural)

adjective: Ni-Vanuatu

**ETHNIC GROUPS:**

Melanesian 99.2%, non-Melanesian 0.8% (2016 est.)

**LANGUAGES:**

local languages (more than 100) 63.2%, Bislama (official; creole) 33.7%, English (official) 2%, French (official) 0.6%, other 0.5% (2009 est.)

**RELIGIONS:**

Protestant 70% (includes Presbyterian 27.9%, Anglican 15.1%, Seventh Day Adventist 12.5%, Assemblies of God 4.7%, Church of Christ 4.5%, Neil Thomas Ministry 3.1%, and Apostolic 2.2%), Roman Catholic 12.4%, customary beliefs 3.7% (including Jon Frum cargo cult), other 12.6%, none 1.1%, unspecified 0.2% (2009 est.)

**AGE STRUCTURE:**

0-14 years: 34.89% (male 51,313 /female 49,190)

15-24 years: 20.03% (male 28,631 /female 29,053)

25-54 years: 35.39% (male 49,803 /female 52,140)

55-64 years: 5.57% (male 7,973 /female 8,072)

65 years and over: 4.12% (male 5,968 /female 5,894) (2018 est.)

**DEPENDENCY RATIOS:**

total dependency ratio: 68.7 (2015 est.)

youth dependency ratio: 61.6 (2015 est.)

elderly dependency ratio: 7.1 (2015 est.)

potential support ratio: 14.1 (2015 est.)

**MEDIAN AGE:**

total: 22.3 years

male: 21.9 years

female: 22.7 years (2018 est.)

country comparison to the world: 180

**POPULATION GROWTH RATE:**

1.81% (2018 est.)

country comparison to the world: 55

**BIRTH RATE:**

23.5 births/1,000 population (2018 est.)

country comparison to the world: 57

**DEATH RATE:**

4 deaths/1,000 population (2018 est.)

country comparison to the world: 211

**NET MIGRATION RATE:**

-1.4 migrant(s)/1,000 population (2017 est.)

country comparison to the world: 147

**POPULATION DISTRIBUTION:**

three-quarters of the population lives in rural areas; the urban populace lives primarily in two cities, Port-Vila and Lugenville; three largest islands - Espiritu Santo, Malakula, and Efate - accomodate over half of the populace

**URBANIZATION:**

urban population: 25.3% of total population (2018)

rate of urbanization: 2.55% annual rate of change (2015-20 est.)

**MAJOR URBAN AREAS - POPULATION:**

53,000 PORT-VILA (capital) (2018)

**SEX RATIO:**

at birth: 1.05 male(s)/female (2017 est.)

0-14 years: 1.04 male(s)/female (2017 est.)

15-24 years: 0.99 male(s)/female (2017 est.)

25-54 years: 0.96 male(s)/female (2017 est.)

55-64 years: 1 male(s)/female (2017 est.)

65 years and over: 1.04 male(s)/female (2017 est.)

total population: 1 male(s)/female (2017 est.)

**MATERNAL MORTALITY RATE:**

78 deaths/100,000 live births (2015 est.)

country comparison to the world: 81

**INFANT MORTALITY RATE:**

total: 13.9 deaths/1,000 live births (2018 est.)

male: 14.8 deaths/1,000 live births (2018 est.)

female: 12.9 deaths/1,000 live births (2018 est.)

country comparison to the world: 102

**LIFE EXPECTANCY AT BIRTH:**

total population: 74 years (2018 est.)

male: 72.4 years (2018 est.)

female: 75.7 years (2018 est.)

country comparison to the world: 130

**TOTAL FERTILITY RATE:**

2.97 children born/woman (2018 est.)

country comparison to the world: 55

**CONTRACEPTIVE PREVALENCE RATE:**

49% (2013)

**HEALTH EXPENDITURES:**

5% of GDP (2014)

country comparison to the world: 142

**PHYSICIANS DENSITY:**

0.19 physicians/1,000 population (2012)

**HOSPITAL BED DENSITY:**

1.7 beds/1,000 population (2008)

**DRINKING WATER SOURCE:**

improved:

urban: 98.9% of population (2015 est.)

rural: 92.9% of population (2015 est.)

total: 94.5% of population (2015 est.)

unimproved:

urban: 1.1% of population (2015 est.)

rural: 7.1% of population (2015 est.)

total: 5.5% of population (2015 est.)

**SANITATION FACILITY ACCESS:**

improved:

urban: 65.1% of population (2015 est.)

rural: 55.4% of population (2015 est.)

total: 57.9% of population (2015 est.)

**unimproved:**

urban: 34.9% of population (2015 est.)

rural: 44.6% of population (2015 est.)

total: 42.1% of population (2015 est.)

## HIV/AIDS - ADULT PREVALENCE RATE:

NA

## HIV/AIDS - PEOPLE LIVING WITH HIV/AIDS:

NA

## HIV/AIDS - DEATHS:

NA

## OBESITY - ADULT PREVALENCE RATE:

25.2% (2016)

country comparison to the world: 52

## CHILDREN UNDER THE AGE OF 5 YEARS UNDERWEIGHT:

10.7% (2013)

country comparison to the world: 60

## EDUCATION EXPENDITURES:

5.5% of GDP (2015)

country comparison to the world: 52

## LITERACY:

definition: age 15 and over can read and write (2015 est.)

total population: 85.2% (2015 est.)

male: 86.6% (2015 est.)

female: 83.8% (2015 est.)

## UNEMPLOYMENT, YOUTH AGES 15-24:

total: 10.6% (2009 est.)

male: 10.2% (2009 est.)

female: 11.2% (2009 est.)

country comparison to the world: 121

# GOVERNMENT :: VANUATU

## COUNTRY NAME:

conventional long form: Republic of Vanuatu

conventional short form: Vanuatu

local long form: Ripablik blong Vanuatu

local short form: Vanuatu

former: New Hebrides

etymology: derived from the words "vanua" (home or land) and "tu" (stand) that occur in several of the Austonesian languages spoken on the islands and which provide a meaning of "the land remains" but which also convey a sense of "independence" or "our land"

## GOVERNMENT TYPE:

parliamentary republic

## CAPITAL:

name: Port-Vila (on Efate)

geographic coordinates: 17 44 S, 168 19 E

time difference: UTC+11 (16 hours ahead of Washington, DC, during Standard Time)

## ADMINISTRATIVE DIVISIONS:

6 provinces; Malampa, Penama, Sanma, Shefa, Tafea, Torba

## INDEPENDENCE:

30 July 1980 (from France and the UK)

## NATIONAL HOLIDAY:

Independence Day, 30 July (1980)

## CONSTITUTION:

history: draft completed August 1979, finalized by constitution conference 19 September 1979, ratified by French and British Governments 23 October 1979, effective 30 July 1980 at independence

amendments: proposed by the prime minister or by the Parliament membership; passage requires at least two-thirds majority vote by Parliament in special session with at least three-fourths of the membership; passage of amendments affecting the national and official languages, or the electoral and parliamentary system also requires approval in a referendum; amended several times, last in 2013

## LEGAL SYSTEM:

mixed legal system of English common law, French law, and customary law

## INTERNATIONAL LAW ORGANIZATION PARTICIPATION:

has not submitted an ICJ jurisdiction declaration; accepts ICCt jurisdiction

## CITIZENSHIP:

citizenship by birth: no

citizenship by descent only: both parents must be citizens of Vanuatu; in the case of only one parent, it must be the father who is a citizen

dual citizenship recognized: no

residency requirement for naturalization: 10 years

## SUFFRAGE:

18 years of age; universal

## EXECUTIVE BRANCH:

chief of state: President Tallis Obed MOSES (since 6 July 2017)

head of government: Prime Minister Charlot SALWAI (since 11 February 2016)

cabinet: Council of Ministers appointed by the prime minister, responsible to parliament

elections/appointments: president indirectly elected by an electoral college consisting of Parliament and presidents of the 6 provinces; Vanuatu president serves a 5-year term; election last held on 17 June 2017 (next to be held in 2022); following legislative elections, the leader of the majority party or majority coalition usually elected prime minister by parliament from among its members; election for prime minister last held on 11 February 2016 (next to be held following general elections in 2020)

election results: Baldwin LONSDALE (independent) died suddenly on 17 June 2017; Parliament elected Tallis Obed MOSES on 6 July 2017 with a 39 to 17 vote in the fourth round; Charlot SALWAI elected prime minister on 11 February 2016 with 46 votes

## LEGISLATIVE BRANCH:

description: unicameral Parliament (52 seats; members directly elected in multi-seat constituencies by simple majority vote to serve 4-year terms)

elections: last held on 22 January 2016 (next to be held in 2020)

election results: percent of vote by party - NA; seats by party - VP 8, PPP 6, UMP 5, GJP 4, NUP 4, IG 3, GC 3, NAG 3, RMC 3, MPP 2, NIPDP 2, PSP 1, VLDP 1, VNP 1, VPDP 1, VRP 1, and independent 4; note - political party associations are fluid

note: the National Council of Chiefs advises on matters of culture and language

## JUDICIAL BRANCH:

highest courts: Court of Appeal (consists of 2 or more judges of the Supreme Court designated by the chief justice); Supreme Court (consists of the chief justice and 6 puisne judges - 3 local and 3 expatriate)

judge selection and term of office: Supreme Court chief justice appointed by the president after consultation with the prime minister and the leader of the opposition; other judges are appointed by the president on the advice of the Judicial Service Commission, a 4-member advisory body; judges appointed until age of retirement

**subordinate courts:** Magistrates Courts; Island Courts

## POLITICAL PARTIES AND LEADERS:

Greens Confederation or GC [Moana CARCASSES Kalosil]
Iauko Group or IG [Tony NARI]
Land and Justice Party (Graon mo Jastis Pati) or GJP [Ralph REGENVANU]
Melanesian Progressive Party or MPP [Barak SOPE]
Nagriamel movement or NAG [Frankie STEVENS]
Natatok Indigenous People's Democratic Party or (NATATOK) or NIPDP [Alfred Roland CARLOT]
National United Party or NUP [Ham LINI]
People's Progressive Party or PPP [Sato KILMAN]
People's Service Party or PSP [Don KEN]
Reunification of Movement for Change or RMC [Charlot SALWAI]
Union of Moderate Parties or UMP [Serge VOHOR]
Vanua'aku Pati (Our Land Party) or VP [Edward NATAPEI]
Vanuatu Democratic Party [Maxime Carlot KORMAN]
Vanuatu Liberal Democratic Party or VLDP [Tapangararua WILLIE]
Vanuatu National Party or VNP [Issac HAMARILIU]
Vanuatu National Development Party or VNDP [Robert Bohn SIKOL]
Vanuatu Republican Party or VRP [Marcellino PIPITE]

## INTERNATIONAL ORGANIZATION PARTICIPATION:

ACP, ADB, AOSIS, C, FAO, G-77, IBRD, ICAO, ICRM, IDA, IFC, IFRCS, ILO, IMF, IMO, IMSO, IOC, IOM, ITU, ITUC (NGOs), MIGA, NAM, OAS (observer), OIF, OPCW, PIF, Sparteca, SPC, UN, UNCTAD, UNESCO, UNIDO, UNWTO, UPU, WCO, WFTU (NGOs), WHO, WIPO, WMO, WTO

## DIPLOMATIC REPRESENTATION IN THE US:

none; the Vanuatu Permanent Mission to the UN serves as the Embassy; it is headed by Odo TEVI (since 2014); address: 800 Second Avenue, Suite 400B, New York, NY 10017; telephone: [1](212)661-4303; FAX: [1](212)422-2437

## DIPLOMATIC REPRESENTATION FROM THE US:

the US does not have an embassy in Vanuatu; the US Ambassador to Papua New Guinea is accredited to Vanuatu

## FLAG DESCRIPTION:

two equal horizontal bands of red (top) and green with a black isosceles triangle (based on the hoist side) all separated by a black-edged yellow stripe in the shape of a horizontal Y (the two points of the Y face the hoist side and enclose the triangle); centered in the triangle is a boar's tusk encircling two crossed namele fern fronds, all in yellow; red represents the blood of boars and men, as well as unity, green the richness of the islands, and black the ni-Vanuatu people; the yellow Y-shape - which reflects the pattern of the islands in the Pacific Ocean - symbolizes the light of the Gospel spreading through the islands; the boar's tusk is a symbol of prosperity frequently worn as a pendant on the islands; the fern fronds represent peace

**note:** one of several flags where a prominent component of the design reflects the shape of the country; other such flags are those of Bosnia and Herzegovina, Brazil, and Eritrea

## NATIONAL SYMBOL(S):

boar's tusk with crossed fern fronds; national colors: red, black, green, yellow

## NATIONAL ANTHEM:

**name:** "Yumi, Yumi, Yumi" (We, We, We)

**lyrics/music:** Francois Vincent AYSSAV

**note:** adopted 1980; the anthem is written in Bislama, a Creole language that mixes Pidgin English and French

# ECONOMY :: VANUATU

## ECONOMY - OVERVIEW:

This South Pacific island economy is based primarily on small-scale agriculture, which provides a living for about two thirds of the population. Fishing, offshore financial services, and tourism, with more than 330,000 visitors in 2017, are other mainstays of the economy. Tourism has struggled after Efate, the most populous and most popular island for tourists, was damaged by Tropical Cyclone Pam in 2015. Ongoing infrastructure difficulties at Port Vila's Bauerfield Airport have caused air travel disruptions, further hampering tourism numbers. Australia and New Zealand are the main source of tourists and foreign aid. A small light industry sector caters to the local market. Tax revenues come mainly from import duties. Mineral deposits are negligible; the country has no known petroleum deposits.

Economic development is hindered by dependence on relatively few commodity exports, vulnerability to natural disasters, and long distances from main markets and between constituent islands. In response to foreign concerns, the government has promised to tighten regulation of its offshore financial center.

Since 2002, the government has stepped up efforts to boost tourism through improved air connections, resort development, and cruise ship facilities. Agriculture, especially livestock farming, is a second target for growth.

## GDP (PURCHASING POWER PARITY):

$772 million (2017 est.)

$740.9 million (2016 est.)

$716.1 million (2015 est.)

note: data are in 2017 dollars

country comparison to the world: 207

## GDP (OFFICIAL EXCHANGE RATE):

$870 million (2017 est.) (2017 est.)

## GDP - REAL GROWTH RATE:

4.2% (2017 est.)

3.5% (2016 est.)

0.2% (2015 est.)

country comparison to the world: 73

## GDP - PER CAPITA (PPP):

$2,700 (2017 est.)

$2,700 (2016 est.)

$2,700 (2015 est.)

note: data are in 2017 dollars

country comparison to the world: 196

## GDP - COMPOSITION, BY END USE:

**household consumption:** 59.9% (2017 est.)

**government consumption:** 17.4% (2017 est.)

**investment in fixed capital:** 28.7% (2017 est.)

**investment in inventories:** 0% (2017 est.)

**exports of goods and services:** 42.5% (2017 est.)

imports of goods and services: -48.5% (2017 est.)

### GDP - COMPOSITION, BY SECTOR OF ORIGIN:
agriculture: 27.3% (2017 est.)

industry: 11.8% (2017 est.)

services: 60.8% (2017 est.)

### AGRICULTURE - PRODUCTS:
copra, coconuts, cocoa, coffee, taro, yams, fruits, vegetables; beef; fish

### INDUSTRIES:
food and fish freezing, wood processing, meat canning

### INDUSTRIAL PRODUCTION GROWTH RATE:
4.5% (2017 est.)

country comparison to the world: 68

### LABOR FORCE:
115,900 (2007 est.)

country comparison to the world: 182

### LABOR FORCE - BY OCCUPATION:
agriculture: 65%

industry: 5%

services: 30% (2000 est.)

### UNEMPLOYMENT RATE:
1.7% (1999 est.)

country comparison to the world: 16

### POPULATION BELOW POVERTY LINE:
NA

### HOUSEHOLD INCOME OR CONSUMPTION BY PERCENTAGE SHARE:
lowest 10%: NA

highest 10%: NA

### BUDGET:
revenues: 236.7 million (2017 est.)

expenditures: 244.1 million (2017 est.)

### TAXES AND OTHER REVENUES:
27.2% (of GDP) (2017 est.)

country comparison to the world: 102

### BUDGET SURPLUS (+) OR DEFICIT (-):
-0.9% (of GDP) (2017 est.)

country comparison to the world: 73

### PUBLIC DEBT:
48.4% of GDP (2017 est.)

46.1% of GDP (2016 est.)

country comparison to the world: 107

### FISCAL YEAR:
calendar year

### INFLATION RATE (CONSUMER PRICES):
3.1% (2017 est.)

0.8% (2016 est.)

country comparison to the world: 134

### CENTRAL BANK DISCOUNT RATE:
20% (31 December 2010)

6% (31 December 2009)

country comparison to the world: 6

### COMMERCIAL BANK PRIME LENDING RATE:
3.2% (31 December 2017 est.)

2.95% (31 December 2016 est.)

country comparison to the world: 173

### STOCK OF NARROW MONEY:
$424.7 million (31 December 2017 est.)

$379.9 million (31 December 2016 est.)

country comparison to the world: 173

### STOCK OF BROAD MONEY:
$424.7 million (31 December 2017 est.)

$379.9 million (31 December 2016 est.)

country comparison to the world: 177

### STOCK OF DOMESTIC CREDIT:
$494 million (31 December 2017 est.)

$463.4 million (31 December 2016 est.)

country comparison to the world: 178

### MARKET VALUE OF PUBLICLY TRADED SHARES:
NA

### CURRENT ACCOUNT BALANCE:
-$13 million (2017 est.)

-$37 million (2016 est.)

country comparison to the world: 70

### EXPORTS:
$44.7 million (2017 est.)

$53.5 million (2016 est.)

country comparison to the world: 204

### EXPORTS - PARTNERS:
Philippines 23.9%, Australia 16.5%, US 10.4%, Japan 8.8%, Venezuela 8%, France 4.8%, Fiji 4.5%, Hong Kong 4.4% (2017)

### EXPORTS - COMMODITIES:
copra, beef (veal), cocoa, timber, kava, coffee, coconut oil, shell, cowhides, coconut meal, fish

### IMPORTS:
$273.7 million (2017 est.)

$308.5 million (2016 est.)

country comparison to the world: 206

### IMPORTS - COMMODITIES:
machinery and equipment, foodstuffs, fuels

### IMPORTS - PARTNERS:
Russia 35.2%, Australia 19.8%, NZ 9.8%, China 6.3%, Fiji 5.5% (2017)

### RESERVES OF FOREIGN EXCHANGE AND GOLD:
$395.1 million (31 December 2017 est.)

$267.4 million (31 December 2016 est.)

country comparison to the world: 160

### DEBT - EXTERNAL:
$200.5 million (31 December 2017 est.)

$182.5 million (31 December 2016 est.)

country comparison to the world: 188

### STOCK OF DIRECT FOREIGN INVESTMENT - AT HOME:
$590.9 million (31 December 2017 est.)

$535.9 million (31 December 2016 est.)

country comparison to the world: 127

### STOCK OF DIRECT FOREIGN INVESTMENT - ABROAD:
$22.3 million (31 December 2017 est.)

$22.4 million (31 December 2016 est.)

country comparison to the world: 116

### EXCHANGE RATES:
vatu (VUV) per US dollar -

109.7 (2017 est.)

112.28 (2016 est.)

108.48 (2015 est.)

108.99 (2014 est.)

97.07 (2013 est.)

## ENERGY :: VANUATU

### ELECTRICITY ACCESS:
population without electricity: 202,614 (2012)

electrification - total population: 27% (2012)

electrification - urban areas: 55% (2012)

electrification - rural areas: 18% (2012)

### ELECTRICITY - PRODUCTION:
63 million kWh (2016 est.)

country comparison to the world: 204

**ELECTRICITY - CONSUMPTION:**

58.59 million kWh (2016 est.)

country comparison to the world: 204

**ELECTRICITY - EXPORTS:**

0 kWh (2016 est.)

country comparison to the world: 214

**ELECTRICITY - IMPORTS:**

0 kWh (2016 est.)

country comparison to the world: 215

**ELECTRICITY - INSTALLED GENERATING CAPACITY:**

37,000 kW (2016 est.)

country comparison to the world: 199

**ELECTRICITY - FROM FOSSIL FUELS:**

71% of total installed capacity (2016 est.)

country comparison to the world: 107

**ELECTRICITY - FROM NUCLEAR FUELS:**

0% of total installed capacity (2017 est.)

country comparison to the world: 207

**ELECTRICITY - FROM HYDROELECTRIC PLANTS:**

0% of total installed capacity (2017 est.)

country comparison to the world: 211

**ELECTRICITY - FROM OTHER RENEWABLE SOURCES:**

29% of total installed capacity (2017 est.)

country comparison to the world: 21

**CRUDE OIL - PRODUCTION:**

0 bbl/day (2017 est.)

country comparison to the world: 212

**CRUDE OIL - EXPORTS:**

0 bbl/day (2015 est.)

country comparison to the world: 213

**CRUDE OIL - IMPORTS:**

0 bbl/day (2015 est.)

country comparison to the world: 211

**CRUDE OIL - PROVED RESERVES:**

0 bbl (1 January 2018 est.)

country comparison to the world: 210

**REFINED PETROLEUM PRODUCTS - PRODUCTION:**

0 bbl/day (2015 est.)

country comparison to the world: 213

**REFINED PETROLEUM PRODUCTS - CONSUMPTION:**

1,100 bbl/day (2016 est.)

country comparison to the world: 205

**REFINED PETROLEUM PRODUCTS - EXPORTS:**

0 bbl/day (2015 est.)

country comparison to the world: 215

**REFINED PETROLEUM PRODUCTS - IMPORTS:**

1,073 bbl/day (2015 est.)

country comparison to the world: 201

**NATURAL GAS - PRODUCTION:**

0 cu m (2017 est.)

country comparison to the world: 212

**NATURAL GAS - CONSUMPTION:**

0 cu m (2017 est.)

country comparison to the world: 211

**NATURAL GAS - EXPORTS:**

0 cu m (2017 est.)

country comparison to the world: 208

**NATURAL GAS - IMPORTS:**

0 cu m (2017 est.)

country comparison to the world: 208

**NATURAL GAS - PROVED RESERVES:**

0 cu m (1 January 2014 est.)

country comparison to the world: 205

**CARBON DIOXIDE EMISSIONS FROM CONSUMPTION OF ENERGY:**

164,800 Mt (2017 est.)

country comparison to the world: 203

## COMMUNICATIONS :: VANUATU

**TELEPHONES - FIXED LINES:**

total subscriptions: 3,499 (2017 est.)

subscriptions per 100 inhabitants: 1 (2017 est.)

country comparison to the world: 207

**TELEPHONES - MOBILE CELLULAR:**

total subscriptions: 228,016 (2017 est.)

subscriptions per 100 inhabitants: 81 (2017 est.)

country comparison to the world: 180

**TELEPHONE SYSTEM:**

general assessment: telecom services have progressed significantly in recent years; mobile phones are now the primary means of communication and more than 90% of the population is covered by a mobile network (2016)

domestic: 2016 saw the launch of LTE services by Digicel and the introduction of rural satellite broadband services by Kacific; mobile phone use in some rural areas is constrained by electricity shortages (2016)

international: country code - 678; satellite earth station - 1 Intelsat (Pacific Ocean) (2016)

**BROADCAST MEDIA:**

1 state-owned TV station; multi-channel pay TV is available; state-owned Radio Vanuatu operates 2 radio stations; 2 privately owned radio broadcasters; programming from multiple international broadcasters is available (2008)

**INTERNET COUNTRY CODE:**

.vu

**INTERNET USERS:**

total: 66,613 (July 2016 est.)

percent of population: 24% (July 2016 est.)

country comparison to the world: 183

**BROADBAND - FIXED SUBSCRIPTIONS:**

total: 5,841 (2017 est.)

subscriptions per 100 inhabitants: 2 (2017 est.)

country comparison to the world: 175

## TRANSPORTATION :: VANUATU

**NATIONAL AIR TRANSPORT SYSTEM:**

number of registered air carriers: 1 (2015)

inventory of registered aircraft operated by air carriers: 6 (2015)

annual passenger traffic on registered air carriers: 287,526 (2015)

annual freight traffic on registered air carriers: 1,510,732 mt-km (2015)

**CIVIL AIRCRAFT REGISTRATION COUNTRY CODE PREFIX:**

YJ (2016)

**AIRPORTS:**

31 (2013)

country comparison to the world: 114

**AIRPORTS - WITH PAVED RUNWAYS:**

total: 3 (2013)

2,438 to 3,047 m: 1 (2013)

1,524 to 2,437 m: 1 (2013)

914 to 1,523 m: 1 (2013)

**AIRPORTS - WITH UNPAVED RUNWAYS:**

total: 28 (2013)

914 to 1,523 m: 7 (2013)

under 914 m: 21 (2013)

**ROADWAYS:**

*total:* 1,070 km (2000)

*paved:* 256 km (2000)

*unpaved:* 814 km (2000)

*country comparison to the world:* 185

**MERCHANT MARINE:**

*total:* 421 (2017)

*by type:* bulk carrier 22, container ship 1, general cargo 27, other 371 (2017)

*country comparison to the world:* 44

**PORTS AND TERMINALS:**

*major seaport(s):* Forari Bay, Luganville (Santo, Espiritu Santo), Port-Vila

## MILITARY AND SECURITY :: VANUATU

**MILITARY BRANCHES:**

no regular military forces; Vanuatu Police Force (VPF), Vanuatu Mobile Force (VMF; includes Police Maritime Wing (PMW)) (2013)

## TRANSNATIONAL ISSUES :: VANUATU

**DISPUTES - INTERNATIONAL:**

Matthew and Hunter Islands east of New Caledonia claimed by Vanuatu and France

## INTRODUCTION :: VENEZUELA

### BACKGROUND:

Venezuela was one of three countries that emerged from the collapse of Gran Colombia in 1830 (the others being Ecuador and New Granada, which became Colombia). For most of the first half of the 20th century, Venezuela was ruled by generally benevolent military strongmen who promoted the oil industry and allowed for some social reforms. Democratically elected governments have held sway since 1959. Under Hugo CHAVEZ, president from 1999 to 2013, and his hand-picked successor, President Nicolas MADURO, the executive branch has exercised increasingly authoritarian control over other branches of government. In 2016, President MADURO issued a decree to hold an election to form a "Constituent Assembly." A 30 July 2017 poll approved the formation of a 545-member Constituent Assembly and elected its delegates, empowering them to change the constitution and dismiss government institutions and officials. The US Government does not recognize the Assembly, which has generally used its powers to rule by decree rather than to reform the constitution. Simultaneously, democratic institutions continue to deteriorate, freedoms of expression and the press are curtailed, and political polarization has grown. The ruling party's economic policies have expanded the state's role in the economy through expropriations of major enterprises, strict currency exchange and price controls that discourage private sector investment and production, and overdependence on the petroleum industry for revenues, among others. Current concerns include human rights abuses, rampant violent crime, high inflation, and widespread shortages of basic consumer goods, medicine, and medical supplies.

## GEOGRAPHY :: VENEZUELA

### LOCATION:
Northern South America, bordering the Caribbean Sea and the North Atlantic Ocean, between Colombia and Guyana

### GEOGRAPHIC COORDINATES:
8 00 N, 66 00 W

### MAP REFERENCES:
South America

### AREA:
total: 912,050 sq km

land: 882,050 sq km

water: 30,000 sq km

country comparison to the world: 34

### AREA - COMPARATIVE:
almost six times the size of Georgia; slightly more than twice the size of California

### LAND BOUNDARIES:
total: 5,267 km

border countries (3): Brazil 2137 km, Colombia 2341 km, Guyana 789 km

### COASTLINE:
2,800 km

### MARITIME CLAIMS:
territorial sea: 12 nm

exclusive economic zone: 200 nm

contiguous zone: 15 nm

continental shelf: 200-m depth or to the depth of exploitation

### CLIMATE:
tropical; hot, humid; more moderate in highlands

### TERRAIN:
Andes Mountains and Maracaibo Lowlands in northwest; central plains (llanos); Guiana Highlands in southeast

### ELEVATION:
mean elevation: 450 m

elevation extremes: 0 m lowest point: Caribbean Sea

4978 highest point: Pico Bolivar

### NATURAL RESOURCES:
petroleum, natural gas, iron ore, gold, bauxite, other minerals, hydropower, diamonds

### LAND USE:
agricultural land: 24.5% (2011 est.)

arable land: 3.1% (2011 est.) / permanent crops: 0.8% (2011 est.) / permanent pasture: 20.6% (2011 est.)

forest: 52.1% (2011 est.)

other: 23.4% (2011 est.)

### IRRIGATED LAND:
10,550 sq km (2012)

**POPULATION DISTRIBUTION:**

most of the population is concentrated in the northern and western highlands along an eastern spur at the northern end of the Andes, an area that includes the capital of Caracas

**NATURAL HAZARDS:**

subject to floods, rockslides, mudslides; periodic droughts

**ENVIRONMENT - CURRENT ISSUES:**

sewage pollution of Lago de Valencia; oil and urban pollution of Lago de Maracaibo; deforestation; soil degradation; urban and industrial pollution, especially along the Caribbean coast; threat to the rainforest ecosystem from irresponsible mining operations

**ENVIRONMENT - INTERNATIONAL AGREEMENTS:**

party to: Antarctic Treaty, Biodiversity, Climate Change, Climate Change-Kyoto Protocol, Desertification, Endangered Species, Hazardous Wastes, Marine Life Conservation, Ozone Layer Protection, Ship Pollution, Tropical Timber 83, Tropical Timber 94, Wetlands

signed, but not ratified: none of the selected agreements

**GEOGRAPHY - NOTE:**

note 1: the country lies on major sea and air routes linking North and South America

note 2: Venezuela has some of the most unique geology in the world; tepuis are massive table-top mountains of the western Guiana Highlands that tend to be isolated and thus support unique endemic plant and animal species; their sheer cliffsides account for some of the most spectacular waterfalls in the world including Angel Falls, the world's highest (979 m) that drops off Auyan Tepui

## PEOPLE AND SOCIETY :: VENEZUELA

**POPULATION:**

31,689,176 (July 2018 est.)

country comparison to the world: 43

**NATIONALITY:**

noun: Venezuelan(s)

adjective: Venezuelan

**ETHNIC GROUPS:**

unspecified Spanish, Italian, Portuguese, Arab, German, African, indigenous people

**LANGUAGES:**

Spanish (official), numerous indigenous dialects

**RELIGIONS:**

nominally Roman Catholic 96%, Protestant 2%, other 2%

**DEMOGRAPHIC PROFILE:**

Social investment in Venezuela during the CHAVEZ administration reduced poverty from nearly 50% in 1999 to about 27% in 2011, increased school enrollment, substantially decreased infant and child mortality, and improved access to potable water and sanitation through social investment. "Missions" dedicated to education, nutrition, healthcare, and sanitation were funded through petroleum revenues. The sustainability of this progress remains questionable, however, as the continuation of these social programs depends on the prosperity of Venezuela's oil industry. In the long-term, education and health care spending may increase economic growth and reduce income inequality, but rising costs and the staffing of new health care jobs with foreigners are slowing development.

While CHAVEZ was in power, more than one million predominantly middle- and upper-class Venezuelans are estimated to have emigrated. The brain drain is attributed to a repressive political system, lack of economic opportunities, steep inflation, a high crime rate, and corruption. Thousands of oil engineers emigrated to Canada, Colombia, and the United States following CHAVEZ's firing of over 20,000 employees of the state-owned petroleum company during a 2002-03 oil strike. Additionally, thousands of Venezuelans of European descent have taken up residence in their ancestral homelands. Nevertheless, Venezuela has attracted hundreds of thousands of immigrants from South America and southern Europe because of its lenient migration policy and the availability of education and health care. Venezuela also has been a fairly accommodating host to Colombian refugees, numbering about 170,000 as of year-end 2016. However, since 2014, falling oil prices have driven a major economic crisis that has pushed Venezuelans from all walks of life to migrate or to seek asylum abroad to escape severe shortages of food, water, and medicine; soaring inflation; unemployment; and violence. As of October 2018, an estimate 3 million Venezuelans were refugees or migrants worldwide, with 2.4 million in Latin America and the Caribbean (notably Colombia, Brazil, Mexico, Panama, Chile, Guyana, the Dominican Republic, Aruba, and Curacao). Asylum applications increased significantly in the US and Brazil in 2016 and 2017. Several receiving countries are making efforts to increase immigration restrictions and to deport illegal Venezuelan migrants - Ecuador and Peru in August 2018 began requiring valid passports for entry, which are diffult to obtain for Venezuelans. Nevertheless, Venezuelans continue to migrate to avoid economic collapse at home.

**AGE STRUCTURE:**

0-14 years: 27.04% (male 4,392,305 /female 4,176,518)

15-24 years: 16.82% (male 2,709,250 /female 2,621,681)

25-54 years: 40.65% (male 6,393,114 /female 6,487,570)

55-64 years: 8.11% (male 1,233,524 /female 1,336,963)

65 years and over: 7.38% (male 1,056,864 /female 1,281,387) (2018 est.)

**DEPENDENCY RATIOS:**

total dependency ratio: 52.6 (2015 est.)

youth dependency ratio: 43 (2015 est.)

elderly dependency ratio: 9.5 (2015 est.)

potential support ratio: 10.5 (2015 est.)

**MEDIAN AGE:**

total: 28.7 years

male: 28 years

female: 29.4 years (2018 est.)

country comparison to the world: 132

**POPULATION GROWTH RATE:**

1.21% (2018 est.)

country comparison to the world: 90

**BIRTH RATE:**

18.5 births/1,000 population (2018 est.)

country comparison to the world: 90

**DEATH RATE:**

5.3 deaths/1,000 population (2018 est.)

country comparison to the world: 187

**NET MIGRATION RATE:**

-1.2 migrant(s)/1,000 population (2017 est.)

country comparison to the world: 143

**POPULATION DISTRIBUTION:**

most of the population is concentrated in the northern and western highlands along an eastern spur at the northern end of the Andes, an area that includes the capital of Caracas

**URBANIZATION:**

urban population: 88.2% of total population (2018)

rate of urbanization: 1.28% annual rate of change (2015-20 est.)

**MAJOR URBAN AREAS - POPULATION:**

2.935 million CARACAS (capital), 2.179 million Maracaibo, 1.734 million Valencia, 1.178 million Maracay, 1.189 million Barquisimeto (2018)

**SEX RATIO:**

at birth: 1.05 male(s)/female (2017 est.)

0-14 years: 1.05 male(s)/female (2017 est.)

15-24 years: 1.03 male(s)/female (2017 est.)

25-54 years: 0.98 male(s)/female (2017 est.)

55-64 years: 0.92 male(s)/female (2017 est.)

65 years and over: 0.79 male(s)/female (2017 est.)

total population: 0.99 male(s)/female (2017 est.)

**MATERNAL MORTALITY RATE:**

95 deaths/100,000 live births (2015 est.)

country comparison to the world: 73

**INFANT MORTALITY RATE:**

total: 11.9 deaths/1,000 live births (2018 est.)

male: 12.5 deaths/1,000 live births (2018 est.)

female: 11.2 deaths/1,000 live births (2018 est.)

country comparison to the world: 117

**LIFE EXPECTANCY AT BIRTH:**

total population: 76.2 years (2018 est.)

male: 73.2 years (2018 est.)

female: 79.3 years (2018 est.)

country comparison to the world: 93

**TOTAL FERTILITY RATE:**

2.3 children born/woman (2018 est.)

country comparison to the world: 87

**CONTRACEPTIVE PREVALENCE RATE:**

75% (2010)

**HEALTH EXPENDITURES:**

5.3% of GDP (2014)

country comparison to the world: 132

**HOSPITAL BED DENSITY:**

0.8 beds/1,000 population (2014)

**DRINKING WATER SOURCE:**

improved:

urban: 95% of population

rural: 77.9% of population

total: 93.1% of population

unimproved:

urban: 5% of population

rural: 22.1% of population

total: 6.9% of population (2015 est.)

**SANITATION FACILITY ACCESS:**

improved:

urban: 97.5% of population (2015 est.)

rural: 69.9% of population (2015 est.)

total: 94.4% of population (2015 est.)

unimproved:

urban: 2.5% of population (2015 est.)

rural: 30.1% of population (2015 est.)

total: 5.6% of population (2015 est.)

**HIV/AIDS - ADULT PREVALENCE RATE:**

0.6% (2016 est.)

country comparison to the world: 63

**HIV/AIDS - PEOPLE LIVING WITH HIV/AIDS:**

120,000 (2016 est.)

country comparison to the world: 40

**HIV/AIDS - DEATHS:**

2,500 (2016 est.)

country comparison to the world: 47

**MAJOR INFECTIOUS DISEASES:**

degree of risk: high (2016)

food or waterborne diseases: bacterial diarrhea and hepatitis A (2016)

vectorborne diseases: dengue fever and malaria (2016)

note: active local transmission of Zika virus by Aedes species mosquitoes has been identified in this country (as of August 2016); it poses an important risk (a large number of cases possible) among US citizens if bitten by an infective mosquito; other less common ways to get Zika are through sex, via blood transfusion, or during pregnancy, in which the pregnant woman passes Zika virus to her fetus

**OBESITY - ADULT PREVALENCE RATE:**

25.6% (2016)

country comparison to the world: 50

**CHILDREN UNDER THE AGE OF 5 YEARS UNDERWEIGHT:**

2.9% (2009)

country comparison to the world: 102

**EDUCATION EXPENDITURES:**

6.9% of GDP (2009)

country comparison to the world: 22

**LITERACY:**

definition: age 15 and over can read and write (2016 est.)

total population: 97.1% (2016 est.)

male: 97% (2016 est.)

female: 97.2% (2016 est.)

**SCHOOL LIFE EXPECTANCY (PRIMARY TO TERTIARY EDUCATION):**

total: 14 years (2009)

male: NA (2009)

female: NA (2009)

**UNEMPLOYMENT, YOUTH AGES 15-24:**

total: 14.6% (2015 est.)

male: NA (2015 est.)

female: NA (2015 est.)

country comparison to the world: 92

## GOVERNMENT :: VENEZUELA

**COUNTRY NAME:**

conventional long form: Bolivarian Republic of Venezuela

conventional short form: Venezuela

local long form: Republica Bolivariana de Venezuela

local short form: Venezuela

etymology: native stilt-houses built on Lake Maracaibo reminded early explorers Alonso de OJEDA and Amerigo VESPUCCI in 1499 of buildings in Venice and so they named the region "Venezuola," which in Italian means "Little Venice"

**GOVERNMENT TYPE:**

federal presidential republic

**CAPITAL:**

name: Caracas

**geographic coordinates:** 10 29 N, 66 52 W

**time difference:** UTC-4 (1 hour ahead of Washington, DC, during Standard Time)

## ADMINISTRATIVE DIVISIONS:

23 states (estados, singular - estado), 1 capital district* (distrito capital), and 1 federal dependency** (dependencia federal); Amazonas, Anzoategui, Apure, Aragua, Barinas, Bolivar, Carabobo, Cojedes, Delta Amacuro, Dependencias Federales (Federal Dependencies)**, Distrito Capital (Capital District)*, Falcon, Guarico, Lara, Merida, Miranda, Monagas, Nueva Esparta, Portuguesa, Sucre, Tachira, Trujillo, Vargas, Yaracuy, Zulia

**note:** the federal dependency consists of 11 federally controlled island groups with a total of 72 individual islands

## INDEPENDENCE:

5 July 1811 (from Spain)

## NATIONAL HOLIDAY:

Independence Day, 5 July (1811)

## CONSTITUTION:

**history:** many previous; latest adopted 15 December 1999, effective 30 December 1999 (2018)

**amendments:** proposed through agreement by at least 39% of the National Assembly membership, by the president of the republic in session with the cabinet of ministers, or by petition of at least 15% of registered voters; passage requires simple majority vote by the Assembly and simple majority approval in a referendum; amended 2009; note - in 2016, President MADURO issued a decree to hold an election to form a constituent assembly to change the constution; the election in July 2017 approved the formation of a 545-member constituent assembly and elected its delegates, empowering them to change the constitution and dismiss government institutions and officials (2018)

## LEGAL SYSTEM:

civil law system based on the Spanish civil code

## INTERNATIONAL LAW ORGANIZATION PARTICIPATION:

has not submitted an ICJ jurisdiction declaration; accepts ICCt jurisdiction

## CITIZENSHIP:

**citizenship by birth:** yes

**citizenship by descent only:** yes

**dual citizenship recognized:** no

**residency requirement for naturalization:** 5 years

## SUFFRAGE:

18 years of age; universal

## EXECUTIVE BRANCH:

**chief of state:** President Nicolas MADURO Moros (since 19 April 2013); Executive Vice President Delcy RODRIGUEZ Gomez(since 14 June 2018); note - the president is both chief of state and head of government

**head of government:** President Nicolas MADURO Moros (since 19 April 2013); Executive Vice President Delcy RODRIGUEZ Gomez (since 14 June 2018)

**cabinet:** Council of Ministers appointed by the president

**elections/appointments:** president directly elected by simple majority popular vote for a 6-year term (no term limits); election last held on 20 May 2018 (next election scheduled for 2024)

**election results:** Nicolas MADURO Moros reelected president; percent of vote - Nicolas MADURO Moros (PSUV) 68%, Henri FALCON (AP) 21%, Javier BERTUCCI 11%; note - the election was marked by serious shortcomings and electoral fraud; voter turnout was approximately 46% due largely to an opposition boycott of the election

## LEGISLATIVE BRANCH:

**description:** unicameral National Assembly or Asamblea Nacional (167 seats; 113 members directly elected in single- and multi-seat constituencies by simple majority vote, 51 directly elected in multi-seat constituencies by proportional representation vote, and 3 seats reserved for indigenous peoples of Venezuela; members serve 5-year terms)

**elections:** last held on 6 December 2015 (next expected to be held in 2018)

**election results:** percent of vote by party - MUD (opposition coalition) 56.2%, PSUV (pro-government) 40.9%, other 2.9%; seats by party - MUD 109, PSUV 55, indigenous peoples 3

## JUDICIAL BRANCH:

**highest courts:** Supreme Tribunal of Justice (consists of 32 judges organized into 6 divisions - constitutional, political administrative, electoral, civil appeals, criminal appeals, and social (mainly agrarian and labor issues)

**judge selection and term of office:** judges proposed by the Committee of Judicial Postulation (an independent body of organizations dealing with legal issues and of the organs of citizen power) and appointed by the National Assembly; judges serve nonrenewable 12-year terms; note - in July 2017, the National Assembly named 33 judges to the court to replace a series of judges, it argued, had been illegally appointed in late 2015 by the outgoing, socialist-party-led Assembly; the Government of President MADURO and the socialist-party-appointed judges refused to recognize these appointments, however, and many of the new judges have since been imprisoned or forced into exile

**subordinate courts:** Superior or Appeals Courts (Tribunales Superiores); District Tribunals (Tribunales de Distrito); Courts of First Instance (Tribunales de Primera Instancia); Parish Courts (Tribunales de Parroquia); Justices of the Peace (Justicia de Paz) Network

## POLITICAL PARTIES AND LEADERS:

A New Time or UNT [Manuel ROSALES]
Brave People's Alliance or ABP [Richard BLANCO]
Christian Democrats or COPEI [Roberto ENRIQUEZ]
Coalition of opposition parties -- The Democratic Unity Table or MUD [Jose Luis CARTAYA]
Communist Party of Venezuela or PCV [Oscar FIGUERA]
Democratic Action or AD [Henry RAMOS ALLUP]
Fatherland for All or PPT [Rafael UZCATEGUI]
For Social Democracy or PODEMOS [Didalco Antonio BOLIVAR GRATEROL]
Justice First or PJ [Julio BORGES]
Movement Toward Socialism or MAS [Segundo MELENDEZ]
Popular Will or VP [Leopoldo LOPEZ]
Progressive Wave or AP [Henri FALCON]
The Radical Cause or La Causa R [Americo DE GRAZIA]
United Socialist Party of Venezuela or PSUV [Nicolas MADURO]
Venezuelan Progressive Movement or MPV [Simon CALZADILLA]
Venezuela Project or PV [Henrique Fernando SALAS FEO]

## INTERNATIONAL ORGANIZATION PARTICIPATION:

Caricom (observer), CD, CDB, CELAC, FAO, G-15, G-24, G-77, IADB, IAEA, IBRD, ICAO, ICC (national committees), ICCt (signatory), ICRM, IDA, IFAD, IFC, IFRCS, IHO, ILO, IMF, IMO, IMSO, Interpol, IOC, IOM, IPU, ITSO, ITU, ITUC (NGOs), LAES, LAIA, LAS (observer), MIGA, NAM, OAS, OPANAL, OPCW, OPEC, PCA, Petrocaribe, UN, UNASUR, UNCTAD, UNESCO, UNHCR, UNIDO, Union Latina, UNWTO, UPU, WCO, WFTU (NGOs), WHO, WIPO, WMO, WTO

## DIPLOMATIC REPRESENTATION IN THE US:

**chief of mission:** Ambassador (vacant); Charge d'Affaires Carlos Julio RON Martinez (since February 2017)

**chancery:** 1099 30th Street NW, Washington, DC 20007

**telephone:** [1] (202) 342-2214

**FAX:** [1] (202) 342-6820

**consulate(s) general:** Boston, Chicago, Houston, New Orleans, New York, San Francisco, San Juan (Puerto Rico)

## DIPLOMATIC REPRESENTATION FROM THE US:

**chief of mission:** Ambassador (vacant); Charge d'Affaires James "Jimmy" STORY (since July 2018); note - due to strained relations between the US and Venezuelan Governments, neither country has shared ambassadors since 2010; on 22 May 2018, Venezuelan President Nicolas MADURO declared Charge d'Affaires Todd D. ROBINSON and his deputy persona non grata and ordered them expelled

**embassy:** Calle F con Calle Suapure, Urbanizacion Colinas de Valle Arriba, Caracas 1080

**mailing address:** P. O. Box 62291, Caracas 1060-A; APO AA 34037

**telephone:** [58] (212) 975-6411, 907-8400 (after hours)

**FAX:** [58] (212) 907-8106

## FLAG DESCRIPTION:

three equal horizontal bands of yellow (top), blue, and red with the coat of arms on the hoist side of the yellow band and an arc of eight white five-pointed stars centered in the blue band; the flag retains the three equal horizontal bands and three main colors of the banner of Gran Colombia, the South American republic that broke up in 1830; yellow is interpreted as standing for the riches of the land, blue for the courage of its people, and red for the blood shed in attaining independence; the seven stars on the original flag represented the seven provinces in Venezuela that united in the war of independence; in 2006, then President Hugo CHAVEZ ordered an eighth star added to the star arc - a decision that sparked much controversy - to conform with the flag proclaimed by Simon Bolivar in 1827 and to represent the historic province of Guayana

## NATIONAL SYMBOL(S):

troupial (bird); national colors: yellow, blue, red

## NATIONAL ANTHEM:

**name:** "Gloria al bravo pueblo" (Glory to the Brave People)

**lyrics/music:** Vicente SALIAS/Juan Jose LANDAETA

**note:** adopted 1881; lyrics written in 1810, the music some years later; both SALIAS and LANDAETA were executed in 1814 during Venezuela's struggle for independence

# ECONOMY :: VENEZUELA

## ECONOMY - OVERVIEW:

Venezuela remains highly dependent on oil revenues, which account for almost all export earnings and nearly half of the government's revenue, despite a continued decline in oil production in 2017. In the absence of official statistics, foreign experts estimate that GDP contracted 12% in 2017, inflation exceeded 2000%, people faced widespread shortages of consumer goods and medicine, and the central bank's international reserves dwindled. In late 2017, Venezuela also entered selective default on some of its sovereign and state oil company, Petroleos de Venezuela, S.A., (PDVSA) bonds. Domestic production and industry continues to severely underperform and the Venezuelan Government continues to rely on imports to meet its basic food and consumer goods needs.

Falling oil prices since 2014 have aggravated Venezuela's economic crisis. Insufficient access to dollars, price controls, and rigid labor regulations have led some US and multinational firms to reduce or shut down their Venezuelan operations. Market uncertainty and PDVSA's poor cash flow have slowed investment in the petroleum sector, resulting in a decline in oil production.

Under President Nicolas MADURO, the Venezuelan Government's response to the economic crisis has been to increase state control over the economy and blame the private sector for shortages. MADURO has given authority for the production and distribution of basic goods to the military and to local socialist party member committees. The Venezuelan Government has maintained strict currency controls since 2003. The government has been unable to sustain its mechanisms for distributing dollars to the private sector, in part because it needed to withhold some foreign exchange reserves to make its foreign bond payments. As a result of price and currency controls, local industries have struggled to purchase production inputs necessary to maintain their operations or sell goods at a profit on the local market. Expansionary monetary policies and currency controls have created opportunities for arbitrage and corruption and fueled a rapid increase in black market activity.

## GDP (PURCHASING POWER PARITY):

$381.6 billion (2017 est.)

$443.7 billion (2016 est.)

$531.1 billion (2015 est.)

**note:** data are in 2017 dollars

**country comparison to the world:** 47

## GDP (OFFICIAL EXCHANGE RATE):

$210.1 billion (2017 est.) (2017 est.)

## GDP - REAL GROWTH RATE:

-14% (2017 est.)

-16.5% (2016 est.)

-6.2% (2015 est.)

**country comparison to the world:** 222

## GDP - PER CAPITA (PPP):

$12,500 (2017 est.)

$14,400 (2016 est.)

$17,300 (2015 est.)

**note:** data are in 2017 dollars

**country comparison to the world:** 126

## GROSS NATIONAL SAVING:

12.1% of GDP (2017 est.)

8.6% of GDP (2016 est.)

31.8% of GDP (2015 est.)

**country comparison to the world:** 150

## GDP - COMPOSITION, BY END USE:

household consumption: 68.5% (2017 est.)

government consumption: 19.6% (2017 est.)

investment in fixed capital: 13.9% (2017 est.)

investment in inventories: 1.7% (2017 est.)

exports of goods and services: 7% (2017 est.)

imports of goods and services: -10.7% (2017 est.)

**GDP - COMPOSITION, BY SECTOR OF ORIGIN:**

agriculture: 4.7% (2017 est.)

industry: 40.4% (2017 est.)

services: 54.9% (2017 est.)

**AGRICULTURE - PRODUCTS:**

corn, sorghum, sugarcane, rice, bananas, vegetables, coffee; beef, pork, milk, eggs; fish

**INDUSTRIES:**

agricultural products, livestock, raw materials, machinery and equipment, transport equipment, construction materials, medical equipment, pharmaceuticals, chemicals, iron and steel products, crude oil and petroleum products

**INDUSTRIAL PRODUCTION GROWTH RATE:**

-2% (2017 est.)

country comparison to the world: 183

**LABOR FORCE:**

14.21 million (2017 est.)

country comparison to the world: 40

**LABOR FORCE - BY OCCUPATION:**

agriculture: 7.3%

industry: 21.8%

services: 70.9% (4th quarter, 2011 est.)

**UNEMPLOYMENT RATE:**

27.1% (2017 est.)

20.6% (2016 est.)

country comparison to the world: 199

**POPULATION BELOW POVERTY LINE:**

19.7% (2015 est.)

**HOUSEHOLD INCOME OR CONSUMPTION BY PERCENTAGE SHARE:**

lowest 10%: 32.7% (2006)

highest 10%: 32.7% (2006)

**DISTRIBUTION OF FAMILY INCOME - GINI INDEX:**

39 (2011)

49.5 (1998)

country comparison to the world: 74

**BUDGET:**

revenues: 92.8 billion (2017 est.)

expenditures: 189.7 billion (2017 est.)

**TAXES AND OTHER REVENUES:**

44.2% (of GDP) (2017 est.)

country comparison to the world: 25

**BUDGET SURPLUS (+) OR DEFICIT (-):**

-46.1% (of GDP) (2017 est.)

country comparison to the world: 220

**PUBLIC DEBT:**

38.9% of GDP (2017 est.)

31.3% of GDP (2016 est.)

note: data cover central government debt, as well as the debt of state-owned oil company PDVSA; the data include treasury debt held by foreign entities; the data include some debt issued by subnational entities, as well as intragovernmental debt; intragovernmental debt consists of treasury borrowings from surpluses in the social funds, such as for retirement, medical care, and unemployment; some debt instruments for the social funds are sold at public auctions

country comparison to the world: 135

**FISCAL YEAR:**

calendar year

**INFLATION RATE (CONSUMER PRICES):**

1,087.5% (2017 est.)

254.4% (2016 est.)

country comparison to the world: 226

**CENTRAL BANK DISCOUNT RATE:**

29.5% (2015)

country comparison to the world: 1

**COMMERCIAL BANK PRIME LENDING RATE:**

21.1% (31 December 2017 est.)

20.78% (31 December 2016 est.)

country comparison to the world: 12

**STOCK OF NARROW MONEY:**

$149.8 billion (31 December 2017 est.)

$163.3 billion (31 December 2016 est.)

country comparison to the world: 29

**STOCK OF BROAD MONEY:**

$149.8 billion (31 December 2017 est.)

$163.3 billion (31 December 2016 est.)

country comparison to the world: 29

**STOCK OF DOMESTIC CREDIT:**

$66.97 billion (31 December 2017 est.)

$148.5 billion (31 December 2016 est.)

country comparison to the world: 60

**MARKET VALUE OF PUBLICLY TRADED SHARES:**

$25.3 billion (31 December 2012 est.)

$5.143 billion (31 December 2011 est.)

$3.991 billion (31 December 2011 est.)

country comparison to the world: 60

**CURRENT ACCOUNT BALANCE:**

$4.277 billion (2017 est.)

-$3.87 billion (2016 est.)

country comparison to the world: 32

**EXPORTS:**

$32.06 billion (2017 est.)

$27.2 billion (2016 est.)

country comparison to the world: 64

**EXPORTS - PARTNERS:**

US 34.8%, India 17.2%, China 16%, Netherlands Antilles 8.2%, Singapore 6.3%, Cuba 4.2% (2017)

**EXPORTS - COMMODITIES:**

petroleum and petroleum products, bauxite and aluminum, minerals, chemicals, agricultural products

**IMPORTS:**

$11 billion (2017 est.)

$16.34 billion (2016 est.)

country comparison to the world: 100

**IMPORTS - COMMODITIES:**

agricultural products, livestock, raw materials, machinery and equipment, transport equipment, construction materials, medical equipment, petroleum products, pharmaceuticals, chemicals, iron and steel products

**IMPORTS - PARTNERS:**

US 24.8%, China 14.2%, Mexico 9.5% (2017)

**RESERVES OF FOREIGN EXCHANGE AND GOLD:**

$9.661 billion (31 December 2017 est.)

$11 billion (31 December 2016 est.)

country comparison to the world: 75

**DEBT - EXTERNAL:**

$100.3 billion (31 December 2017 est.)

$109.8 billion (31 December 2016 est.)

country comparison to the world: 47

**STOCK OF DIRECT FOREIGN INVESTMENT - AT HOME:**

$32.74 billion (31 December 2017 est.)

$33.78 billion (31 December 2016 est.)

country comparison to the world: 70
**STOCK OF DIRECT FOREIGN INVESTMENT - ABROAD:**
$35.15 billion (31 December 2017 est.)
$31.12 billion (31 December 2016 est.)
country comparison to the world: 47
**EXCHANGE RATES:**
bolivars (VEB) per US dollar -
3,345 (2017 est.)
673.76 (2016 est.)
48.07 (2015 est.)
13.72 (2014 est.)
6.284 (2013 est.)

## ENERGY :: VENEZUELA

**ELECTRICITY ACCESS:**
population without electricity: 100,000 (2013)
electrification - total population: 99.7% (2013)
electrification - urban areas: 99.8% (2013)
electrification - rural areas: 98.6% (2013)

**ELECTRICITY - PRODUCTION:**
109.3 billion kWh (2016 est.)
country comparison to the world: 34

**ELECTRICITY - CONSUMPTION:**
71.96 billion kWh (2016 est.)
country comparison to the world: 39

**ELECTRICITY - EXPORTS:**
0 kWh (2015 est.)
country comparison to the world: 215

**ELECTRICITY - IMPORTS:**
0 kWh (2016 est.)
country comparison to the world: 216

**ELECTRICITY - INSTALLED GENERATING CAPACITY:**
31 million kW (2016 est.)
country comparison to the world: 32

**ELECTRICITY - FROM FOSSIL FUELS:**
51% of total installed capacity (2016 est.)
country comparison to the world: 150

**ELECTRICITY - FROM NUCLEAR FUELS:**
0% of total installed capacity (2017 est.)
country comparison to the world: 208

**ELECTRICITY - FROM HYDROELECTRIC PLANTS:**
49% of total installed capacity (2017 est.)
country comparison to the world: 43

**ELECTRICITY - FROM OTHER RENEWABLE SOURCES:**
0% of total installed capacity (2017 est.)
country comparison to the world: 213

**CRUDE OIL - PRODUCTION:**
2.007 million bbl/day (2017 est.)
country comparison to the world: 11

**CRUDE OIL - EXPORTS:**
1.656 million bbl/day (2015 est.)
country comparison to the world: 8

**CRUDE OIL - IMPORTS:**
0 bbl/day (2015 est.)
country comparison to the world: 212

**CRUDE OIL - PROVED RESERVES:**
302.3 billion bbl (1 January 2018 est.)
country comparison to the world: 1

**REFINED PETROLEUM PRODUCTS - PRODUCTION:**
926,300 bbl/day (2015 est.)
country comparison to the world: 20

**REFINED PETROLEUM PRODUCTS - CONSUMPTION:**
659,000 bbl/day (2016 est.)
country comparison to the world: 29

**REFINED PETROLEUM PRODUCTS - EXPORTS:**
325,800 bbl/day (2015 est.)
country comparison to the world: 27

**REFINED PETROLEUM PRODUCTS - IMPORTS:**
20,640 bbl/day (2015 est.)
country comparison to the world: 117

**NATURAL GAS - PRODUCTION:**
27.07 billion cu m (2017 est.)
country comparison to the world: 28

**NATURAL GAS - CONSUMPTION:**
24.21 billion cu m (2017 est.)
country comparison to the world: 33

**NATURAL GAS - EXPORTS:**
0 cu m (2017 est.)
country comparison to the world: 209

**NATURAL GAS - IMPORTS:**
0 cu m (2017 est.)
country comparison to the world: 209

**NATURAL GAS - PROVED RESERVES:**
5.739 trillion cu m (1 January 2018 est.)
country comparison to the world: 7

**CARBON DIOXIDE EMISSIONS FROM CONSUMPTION OF ENERGY:**
129.9 million Mt (2017 est.)
country comparison to the world: 36

## COMMUNICATIONS :: VENEZUELA

**TELEPHONES - FIXED LINES:**
total subscriptions: 5,928,714 (2017 est.)
subscriptions per 100 inhabitants: 19 (2017 est.)
country comparison to the world: 27

**TELEPHONES - MOBILE CELLULAR:**
total subscriptions: 24,493,687 (2017 est.)
subscriptions per 100 inhabitants: 78 (2017 est.)
country comparison to the world: 50

**TELEPHONE SYSTEM:**
general assessment: modern and expanding (2016)
domestic: two domestic satellite systems with three earth stations; recent substantial improvement in telephone service in rural areas; installation of a national interurban fiber-optic network capable of digital multimedia services; three major providers operate the mobile market; combined fixed-line and mobile-cellular telephone subscribership about 115 per 100 persons (2016)
international: country code - 58; submarine cable systems provide connectivity to Cuba and the Caribbean, Central and South America, and US; satellite earth stations - 1 Intelsat (Atlantic Ocean) and 1 PanAmSat; participating with Colombia, Ecuador, Peru, and Bolivia in the construction of an international fiber-optic network (2016)

**BROADCAST MEDIA:**
government supervises a mixture of state-run and private broadcast media; 13 public service networks, 61 privately owned TV networks, a privately owned news channel with limited national coverage, and a government-backed Pan-American channel; state-run radio network includes roughly 65 news stations and another 30 stations targeted at specific audiences; state-sponsored community broadcasters include 235 radio stations and 44 TV stations; the number of private broadcast radio stations has been declining, but many still remain in operation (2014)

**INTERNET COUNTRY CODE:**

.ve

**INTERNET USERS:**

total: 18,547,381 (July 2016 est.)

percent of population: 60% (July 2016 est.)

country comparison to the world: 35

**BROADBAND - FIXED SUBSCRIPTIONS:**

total: 2,610,118 (2017 est.)

subscriptions per 100 inhabitants: 8 (2017 est.)

country comparison to the world: 44

## TRANSPORTATION :: VENEZUELA

**NATIONAL AIR TRANSPORT SYSTEM:**

number of registered air carriers: 17 (2015)

inventory of registered aircraft operated by air carriers: 122 (2015)

annual passenger traffic on registered air carriers: 6,456,853 (2015)

annual freight traffic on registered air carriers: 6,204,085 mt-km (2015)

**CIVIL AIRCRAFT REGISTRATION COUNTRY CODE PREFIX:**

YV (2016)

**AIRPORTS:**

444 (2013)

country comparison to the world: 19

**AIRPORTS - WITH PAVED RUNWAYS:**

total: 127 (2013)

over 3,047 m: 6 (2013)

2,438 to 3,047 m: 9 (2013)

1,524 to 2,437 m: 33 (2013)

914 to 1,523 m: 62 (2013)

under 914 m: 17 (2013)

**AIRPORTS - WITH UNPAVED RUNWAYS:**

total: 317 (2013)

2,438 to 3,047 m: 3 (2013)

1,524 to 2,437 m: 57 (2013)

914 to 1,523 m: 127 (2013)

under 914 m: 130 (2013)

**HELIPORTS:**

3 (2013)

**PIPELINES:**

981 km extra heavy crude, 5941 km gas, 7588 km oil, 1778 km refined products (2013)

**RAILWAYS:**

total: 447 km (2014)

standard gauge: 447 km 1.435-m gauge (41.4 km electrified) (2014)

country comparison to the world: 115

**ROADWAYS:**

total: 96,189 km (2014)

country comparison to the world: 50

**WATERWAYS:**

7,100 km (Orinoco River (400 km) and Lake de Maracaibo navigable by oceangoing vessels) (2011)

country comparison to the world: 20

**MERCHANT MARINE:**

total: 267 (2017)

by type: bulk carrier 4, container ship 1, general cargo 31, oil tanker 24, other 207 (2017)

country comparison to the world: 58

**PORTS AND TERMINALS:**

major seaport(s): La Guaira, Maracaibo, Puerto Cabello, Punta Cardon

oil terminal(s): Jose terminal

## MILITARY AND SECURITY :: VENEZUELA

**MILITARY EXPENDITURES:**

1% of GDP (2015)

1.16% of GDP (2014)

1.43% of GDP (2013)

country comparison to the world: 112

**MILITARY BRANCHES:**

Bolivarian National Armed Forces (Fuerza Armada Nacional Bolivariana, FANB): Bolivarian Army (Ejercito Bolivariano, EB), Bolivarian Navy (Armada Bolivariana, AB; includes Naval Infantry, Coast Guard, Naval Aviation), Bolivarian Military Aviation (Aviacion Militar Bolivariana, AMB; includes Air National Guard), Bolivarian National Guard (Guardia Nacional Bolivaria, GNB), Bolivarian Militia (Milicia Bolivariana, NMB) (2016)

**MILITARY SERVICE AGE AND OBLIGATION:**

all citizens of military service age (18-60 years old) are obligated to register for military service, though mandatory recruitment is forbidden; the minimum service obligation is 12 months (2016)

**MARITIME THREATS:**

the International Maritime Bureau continues to report the territorial and offshore waters in the Caribbean Sea as at risk for piracy and armed robbery against ships; numerous vessels, including commercial shipping and pleasure craft, have been attacked and hijacked both at anchor and while underway; crews have been robbed and stores or cargoes stolen; in 2016, there were five attacks reported and this increased to 12 attacks in 2017 making Venezuela the fourth most dangerous area in the World

## TERRORISM :: VENEZUELA

**TERRORIST GROUPS - FOREIGN BASED:**

National Liberation Army (Ejercito de Liberacion Nacional, ELN):

aim(s): enhance its narcotics trafficking networks in Venezuela

area(s) of operation: maintains a narcotics trafficking presence, facilitating the transshipment of narcotics through the country (April 2018)

## TRANSNATIONAL ISSUES :: VENEZUELA

**DISPUTES - INTERNATIONAL:**

claims all of the area west of the Essequibo River in Guyana, preventing any discussion of a maritime boundaryGuyana has expressed its intention to join Barbados in asserting claims before the UN Convention on the Law of the Sea that Trinidad and Tobago's maritime boundary with Venezuela extends into their watersdispute with Colombia over maritime boundary and Venezuelan administered Los Monjes Islands near the Gulf of VenezuelaColombian organized illegal narcotics and paramilitary activities penetrate Venezuela's shared border regionUS, France, and the Netherlands recognize Venezuela's granting full effect to Aves Island, thereby claiming a Venezuelan Economic Exclusion Zone/continental shelf extending over a large portion of the eastern Caribbean SeaDominica, Saint Kitts and Nevis, Saint Lucia, and Saint Vincent and the Grenadines protest Venezuela's full effect claim

**REFUGEES AND INTERNALLY DISPLACED PERSONS:**

refugees (country of origin): 171,920 (Colombia) (2016)

**TRAFFICKING IN PERSONS:**

**current situation:** Venezuela is a source and destination country for men, women, and children subjected to sex trafficking and forced labor; Venezuelan women and girls, sometimes lured from poor interior regions to urban and tourist areas, are trafficked for sexual exploitation within the country, as well as in the Caribbean; Venezuelan children are exploited, frequently by their families, in domestic servitude; people from South America, the Caribbean, Asia, and Africa are sex and labor trafficking victims in Venezuela; thousands of Cuban citizens, particularly doctors, who work in Venezuela on government social programs in exchange for the provision of resources to the Cuban Government experience conditions of forced labor

**tier rating:** Tier 3 – Venezuela does not fully comply with the minimum standards for the elimination of trafficking and is not making significant efforts to do so; in 2014, the government appeared to increase efforts to hold traffickers criminally accountable, but a lack of government data made anti-trafficking law enforcement efforts difficult to assess; publically available information indicated many cases pursued under anti-trafficking law involved illegal adoption rather than sex and labor trafficking; authorities identified a small number of trafficking victims, and victim referrals to limited government services were made on an ad hoc basis; because no specialized facilities are available for trafficking victims, women and child victims accessed centers for victims of domestic violence or at-risk youth, and services for men were virtually non-existent; NGOs provided some services to sex and labor trafficking victims; Venezuela has no permanent anti-trafficking interagency body, no national anti-trafficking plan, and still has not passed anti-trafficking legislation drafted in 2010 (2015)

**ILLICIT DRUGS:**

small-scale illicit producer of opium and coca for the processing of opiates and coca derivatives; however, large quantities of cocaine, heroin, and marijuana transit the country from Colombia bound for US and Europe; significant narcotics-related money-laundering activity, especially along the border with Colombia and on Margarita Island; active eradication program primarily targeting opium; increasing signs of drug-related activities by Colombian insurgents on border

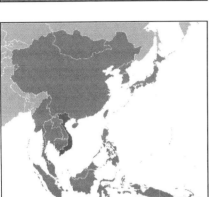

# EAST ASIA / SOUTHEAST ASIA :: VIETNAM

## INTRODUCTION :: VIETNAM

### BACKGROUND:

The conquest of Vietnam by France began in 1858 and was completed by 1884. It became part of French Indochina in 1887. Vietnam declared independence after World War II, but France continued to rule until its 1954 defeat by communist forces under Ho Chi MINH. Under the Geneva Accords of 1954, Vietnam was divided into the communist North and anti-communist South. US economic and military aid to South Vietnam grew through the 1960s in an attempt to bolster the government, but US armed forces were withdrawn following a cease-fire agreement in 1973. Two years later, North Vietnamese forces overran the South reuniting the country under communist rule. Despite the return of peace, for over a decade the country experienced little economic growth because of conservative leadership policies, the persecution and mass exodus of individuals - many of them successful South Vietnamese merchants - and growing international isolation. However, since the enactment of Vietnam's "doi moi" (renovation) policy in 1986, Vietnamese authorities have committed to increased economic liberalization and enacted structural reforms needed to modernize the economy and to produce more competitive, export-driven industries. The communist leaders maintain tight control on political expression but have demonstrated some modest steps toward better protection of human rights. The country continues to experience small-scale protests, the vast majority connected to either land-use issues, calls for increased political space, or the lack of equitable mechanisms for resolving disputes. The small-scale protests in the urban areas are often organized by human rights activists, but many occur in rural areas and involve various ethnic minorities such as the Montagnards of the Central Highlands, Hmong in the Northwest Highlands, and the Khmer Krom in the southern delta region.

## GEOGRAPHY :: VIETNAM

### LOCATION:
Southeastern Asia, bordering the Gulf of Thailand, Gulf of Tonkin, and South China Sea, as well as China, Laos, and Cambodia

### GEOGRAPHIC COORDINATES:
16 10 N, 107 50 E

### MAP REFERENCES:
Southeast Asia

### AREA:
total: 331,210 sq km

land: 310,070 sq km

water: 21,140 sq km

country comparison to the world: 67

### AREA - COMPARATIVE:
about three times the size of Tennessee; slightly larger than New Mexico

### LAND BOUNDARIES:
total: 4,616 km

border countries (3): Cambodia 1158 km, China 1297 km, Laos 2161 km

### COASTLINE:
3,444 km (excludes islands)

### MARITIME CLAIMS:
territorial sea: 12 nm

exclusive economic zone: 200 nm

contiguous zone: 24 nm

continental shelf: 200 nm or to the edge of the continental margin

### CLIMATE:
tropical in south; monsoonal in north with hot, rainy season (May to September) and warm, dry season (October to March)

### TERRAIN:
low, flat delta in south and north; central highlands; hilly, mountainous in far north and northwest

### ELEVATION:
mean elevation: 398 m

elevation extremes: 0 m lowest point: South China Sea

3144 highest point: Fan Si Pan

**NATURAL RESOURCES:**

antimony, phosphates, coal, manganese, rare earth elements, bauxite, chromate, offshore oil and gas deposits, timber, hydropower, arable land

**LAND USE:**

agricultural land: 34.8% (2011 est.)

arable land: 20.6% (2011 est.) / permanent crops: 12.1% (2011 est.) / permanent pasture: 2.1% (2011 est.)

forest: 45% (2011 est.)

other: 20.2% (2011 est.)

**IRRIGATED LAND:**

46,000 sq km (2012)

**POPULATION DISTRIBUTION:**

though it has one of the highest population densities in the world, the population is not evenly dispersed; clustering is heaviest along the South China Sea and Gulf of Tonkin, with the Mekong Delta (in the south) and the Red River Valley (in the north) having the largest concentrations of people

**NATURAL HAZARDS:**

occasional typhoons (May to January) with extensive flooding, especially in the Mekong River delta

**ENVIRONMENT - CURRENT ISSUES:**

logging and slash-and-burn agricultural practices contribute to deforestation and soil degradation; water pollution and overfishing threaten marine life populations; groundwater contamination limits potable water supply; air pollution; growing urban industrialization and population migration are rapidly degrading environment in Hanoi and Ho Chi Minh City

**ENVIRONMENT - INTERNATIONAL AGREEMENTS:**

party to: Biodiversity, Climate Change, Climate Change-Kyoto Protocol, Desertification, Endangered Species, Environmental Modification, Hazardous Wastes, Law of the Sea, Ozone Layer Protection, Ship Pollution, Wetlands

signed, but not ratified: none of the selected agreements

**GEOGRAPHY - NOTE:**

extending 1,650 km north to south, the country is only 50 km across at its narrowest point

# PEOPLE AND SOCIETY :: VIETNAM

**POPULATION:**

97,040,334 (July 2018 est.)

country comparison to the world: 15

**NATIONALITY:**

noun: Vietnamese (singular and plural)

adjective: Vietnamese

**ETHNIC GROUPS:**

Kinh (Viet) 85.7%, Tay 1.9%, Thai 1.8%, Muong 1.5%, Khmer 1.5%, Mong 1.2%, Nung 1.1%, Hoa 1%, other 4.3% (2009 est.)

note: 54 ethnic groups are recognized by the Vietnamese Government

**LANGUAGES:**

Vietnamese (official), English (increasingly favored as a second language), some French, Chinese, and Khmer, mountain area languages (Mon-Khmer and Malayo-Polynesian)

**RELIGIONS:**

Buddhist 7.9%, Catholic 6.6%, Hoa Hao 1.7%, Cao Dai 0.9%, Protestant 0.9%, Muslim 0.1%, none 81.8% (2009 est.)

**AGE STRUCTURE:**

0-14 years: 23.27% (male 11,876,141 /female 10,704,895)

15-24 years: 15.81% (male 7,967,981 /female 7,371,016)

25-54 years: 45.67% (male 22,378,768 /female 21,939,925)

55-64 years: 8.9% (male 4,014,622 /female 4,620,177)

65 years and over: 6.35% (male 2,404,304 /female 3,762,505) (2018 est.)

**DEPENDENCY RATIOS:**

total dependency ratio: 42.5 (2015 est.)

youth dependency ratio: 32.9 (2015 est.)

elderly dependency ratio: 9.6 (2015 est.)

potential support ratio: 10.4 (2015 est.)

**MEDIAN AGE:**

total: 30.9 years

male: 29.9 years

female: 32.1 years (2018 est.)

country comparison to the world: 113

**POPULATION GROWTH RATE:**

0.9% (2018 est.)

country comparison to the world: 120

**BIRTH RATE:**

15.2 births/1,000 population (2018 est.)

country comparison to the world: 123

**DEATH RATE:**

5.9 deaths/1,000 population (2018 est.)

country comparison to the world: 170

**NET MIGRATION RATE:**

-0.3 migrant(s)/1,000 population (2017 est.)

country comparison to the world: 117

**POPULATION DISTRIBUTION:**

though it has one of the highest population densities in the world, the population is not evenly dispersed; clustering is heaviest along the South China Sea and Gulf of Tonkin, with the Mekong Delta (in the south) and the Red River Valley (in the north) having the largest concentrations of people

**URBANIZATION:**

urban population: 35.9% of total population (2018)

rate of urbanization: 2.98% annual rate of change (2015-20 est.)

**MAJOR URBAN AREAS - POPULATION:**

8.145 million Ho Chi Minh City, 1.444 million Da Nang, 1.219 million Hai Phong, 1.175 million Can Tho, 1.075 million Haiphong, 1.064 million HANOI (capital) (2018)

**SEX RATIO:**

at birth: 1.1 male(s)/female (2017 est.)

0-14 years: 1.11 male(s)/female (2017 est.)

15-24 years: 1.08 male(s)/female (2017 est.)

25-54 years: 1.01 male(s)/female (2017 est.)

55-64 years: 0.85 male(s)/female (2017 est.)

65 years and over: 0.63 male(s)/female (2017 est.)

total population: 1 male(s)/female (2017 est.)

**MATERNAL MORTALITY RATE:**

54 deaths/100,000 live births (2015 est.)

country comparison to the world: 92

**INFANT MORTALITY RATE:**

total: 16.7 deaths/1,000 live births (2018 est.)

male: 17.1 deaths/1,000 live births (2018 est.)

female: 16.3 deaths/1,000 live births (2018 est.)

country comparison to the world: 94

### LIFE EXPECTANCY AT BIRTH:

total population: 73.9 years (2018 est.)

male: 71.4 years (2018 est.)

female: 76.7 years (2018 est.)

country comparison to the world: 132

### TOTAL FERTILITY RATE:

1.79 children born/woman (2018 est.)

country comparison to the world: 150

### CONTRACEPTIVE PREVALENCE RATE:

75.7% (2015)

### HEALTH EXPENDITURES:

7.1% of GDP (2014)

country comparison to the world: 81

### PHYSICIANS DENSITY:

0.82 physicians/1,000 population (2016)

### HOSPITAL BED DENSITY:

2.6 beds/1,000 population (2014)

### DRINKING WATER SOURCE:

improved:

urban: 99.1% of population

rural: 96.9% of population

total: 97.6% of population

unimproved:

urban: 0.9% of population

rural: 3.1% of population

total: 2.4% of population (2015 est.)

### SANITATION FACILITY ACCESS:

improved:

urban: 94.4% of population (2015 est.)

rural: 69.7% of population (2015 est.)

total: 78% of population (2015 est.)

unimproved:

urban: 5.6% of population (2015 est.)

rural: 30.3% of population (2015 est.)

total: 22% of population (2015 est.)

### HIV/AIDS - ADULT PREVALENCE RATE:

0.3% (2017 est.)

country comparison to the world: 90

### HIV/AIDS - PEOPLE LIVING WITH HIV/AIDS:

250,000 (2017 est.)

country comparison to the world: 23

### HIV/AIDS - DEATHS:

8,600 (2017 est.)

country comparison to the world: 22

### MAJOR INFECTIOUS DISEASES:

degree of risk: very high (2016)

food or waterborne diseases: bacterial diarrhea, hepatitis A, and typhoid fever (2016)

vectorborne diseases: dengue fever, malaria, and Japanese encephalitis (2016)

### OBESITY - ADULT PREVALENCE RATE:

2.1% (2016)

country comparison to the world: 192

### CHILDREN UNDER THE AGE OF 5 YEARS UNDERWEIGHT:

14.1% (2015)

country comparison to the world: 46

### EDUCATION EXPENDITURES:

5.7% of GDP (2013)

country comparison to the world: 46

### LITERACY:

definition: age 15 and over can read and write (2015 est.)

total population: 94.5% (2015 est.)

male: 96.3% (2015 est.)

female: 92.8% (2015 est.)

### UNEMPLOYMENT, YOUTH AGES 15-24:

total: 7.2% (2016 est.)

male: 7.1% (2016 est.)

female: 7.2% (2016 est.)

country comparison to the world: 143

## GOVERNMENT :: VIETNAM

### COUNTRY NAME:

conventional long form: Socialist Republic of Vietnam

conventional short form: Vietnam

local long form: Cong Hoa Xa Hoi Chu Nghia Viet Nam

local short form: Viet Nam

abbreviation: SRV

etymology: "Viet nam" translates as "Viet south," where "Viet" is an ethnic self identification dating to a second century B.C. kingdom and "nam" refers to its location in relation to other Viet kingdoms

### GOVERNMENT TYPE:

communist state

### CAPITAL:

name: Hanoi (Ha Noi)

geographic coordinates: 21 02 N, 105 51 E

time difference: UTC+7 (12 hours ahead of Washington, DC, during Standard Time)

### ADMINISTRATIVE DIVISIONS:

58 provinces (tinh, singular and plural) and 5 municipalities (thanh pho, singular and plural)

provinces: An Giang, Bac Giang, Bac Kan, Bac Lieu, Bac Ninh, Ba Ria-Vung Tau, Ben Tre, Binh Dinh, Binh Duong, Binh Phuoc, Binh Thuan, Ca Mau, Cao Bang, Dak Lak, Dak Nong, Dien Bien, Dong Nai, Dong Thap, Gia Lai, Ha Giang, Ha Nam, Ha Tinh, Hai Duong, Hau Giang, Hoa Binh, Hung Yen, Khanh Hoa, Kien Giang, Kon Tum, Lai Chau, Lam Dong, Lang Son, Lao Cai, Long An, Nam Dinh, Nghe An, Ninh Binh, Ninh Thuan, Phu Tho, Phu Yen, Quang Binh, Quang Nam, Quang Ngai, Quang Ninh, Quang Tri, Soc Trang, Son La, Tay Ninh, Thai Binh, Thai Nguyen, Thanh Hoa, Thua Thien-Hue, Tien Giang, Tra Vinh, Tuyen Quang, Vinh Long, Vinh Phuc, Yen Bai;

municipalities: Can Tho, Da Nang, Ha Noi (Hanoi), Hai Phong, Ho Chi Minh City (Saigon)

### INDEPENDENCE:

2 September 1945 (from France)

### NATIONAL HOLIDAY:

Independence Day (National Day), 2 September (1945)

### CONSTITUTION:

history: several previous; latest adopted 15 April 1992, effective 1 January 1995 (2018)

amendments: proposed by the president, by the National Assembly's Standing Committee, or supported by at least two-thirds of the National Assembly membership; a decision to draft an amendment requires approval by at least a two-thirds majority of the Assembly membership, followed by the formation of a constitutional drafting committee to write a draft and collect citizens' opinions; passage requires at least two-thirds majority of the Assembly membership; the Assembly can opt to conduct a referendum; amended 2001, 2013 (2018)

**LEGAL SYSTEM:**

civil law system; note - the civil code of 2005 reflects a European-style civil law

**INTERNATIONAL LAW ORGANIZATION PARTICIPATION:**

has not submitted an ICJ jurisdiction declaration; non-party state to the ICCt

**CITIZENSHIP:**

citizenship by birth: no

citizenship by descent only: at least one parent must be a citizen of Vietnam

dual citizenship recognized: no

residency requirement for naturalization: 5 years

**SUFFRAGE:**

18 years of age; universal

**EXECUTIVE BRANCH:**

chief of state: President Nguyen Phu TRONG (since 23 October 2018); note - President Tran Dai QUANG (since 2 April 2016) died on 21 September 2018

head of government: Prime Minister Nguyen Xuan PHUC (since 7 April 2016); Deputy Prime Ministers Truong Hoa BINH (since 9 April 2016), Vuong Dinh HUE (since 9 April 2016), Vu Duc DAM (since 13 November 2013), Trinh Dinh DUNG (since 9 April 2016), Pham Binh MINH (since 13 November 2013)

cabinet: Cabinet proposed by prime minister, appointed by the president, and confirmed by the National Assembly

elections/appointments: president indirectly elected by National Assembly from among its members for a single 5-year term; election last held on 2 April 2016 (next to be held in spring 2021); prime minister appointed by the president from among members of the National Assembly, confirmed by National Assembly; deputy prime ministers appointed by the prime minister, confirmed by National Assembly

election results: Nguyen Phu TRONG (CPV) elected president; percent of National Assembly vote - 99.8%; Nguyen Xuan PHUC elected prime minister; percent of National Assembly vote - 91%

**LEGISLATIVE BRANCH:**

description: unicameral National Assembly or Quoc Hoi (500 seats - current number following 2016 election - 496; members directly elected by absolute majority vote with a second round if needed; members serve 5-year terms)

elections: last held on 22 May 2016 (next to be held in May 2021)

election results: percent of vote by party - CPV 95.8%, non-party members 4.2%; seats by party - CPV 473, non-party CPV-approved 19, self-nominated 2; note - 496 candidates elected, 2 CPV candidates-elect were disqualified; composition - men 374, women 122, percent of women 24.6%

**JUDICIAL BRANCH:**

highest courts: Supreme People's Court (consists of the chief justice and 13 judges)

judge selection and term of office: chief justice elected by the National Assembly on the recommendation of the president for a 5-year, renewable term; other judges appointed by the president for 5-year terms

subordinate courts: Court of Appeals; administrative, civil, criminal, economic, and labor courts; Central Military Court; People's Special Courts; note - the National Assembly can establish special tribunals

**POLITICAL PARTIES AND LEADERS:**

Communist Party of Vietnam or CPV [Nguyen Phu TRONG]

note: other parties proscribed

**INTERNATIONAL ORGANIZATION PARTICIPATION:**

ADB, APEC, ARF, ASEAN, CICA, CP, EAS, FAO, G-77, IAEA, IBRD, ICAO, ICC (NGOs), ICRM, IDA, IFAD, IFC, IFRCS, ILO, IMF, IMO, IMSO, Interpol, IOC, IOM, IPU, ISO, ITSO, ITU, MIGA, NAM, OIF, OPCW, PCA, UN, UNCTAD, UNESCO, UNIDO, UNWTO, UPU, WCO, WFTU (NGOs), WHO, WIPO, WMO, WTO

**DIPLOMATIC REPRESENTATION IN THE US:**

chief of mission: Ambassador Ha Kim NGOC (since 17 September 2018)

chancery: 1233 20th Street NW, Suite 400, Washington, DC 20036

telephone: [1] (202) 861-0737

FAX: [1] (202) 861-0917

consulate(s) general: Houston, San Francisco

consulate(s): New York

**DIPLOMATIC REPRESENTATION FROM THE US:**

chief of mission: Ambassador Daniel KRITENBRINK (since 6 November 2017)

embassy: 7 Lang Ha Street, Hanoi

mailing address: 7 Lang Ha Street, Ba Dinh District, Hanoi; 4550 Hanoi Place, Washington, DC 20521-4550

telephone: [84] (24) 3850-5000

FAX: [84] (24) 3850-5010

consulate(s) general: Ho Chi Minh City

**FLAG DESCRIPTION:**

red field with a large yellow five-pointed star in the center; red symbolizes revolution and blood, the five-pointed star represents the five elements of the populace - peasants, workers, intellectuals, traders, and soldiers - that unite to build socialism

**NATIONAL SYMBOL(S):**

yellow, five-pointed star on red field; lotus blossom; national colors: red, yellow

**NATIONAL ANTHEM:**

name: "Tien quan ca" (The Song of the Marching Troops)

lyrics/music: Nguyen Van CAO

note: adopted as the national anthem of the Democratic Republic of Vietnam in 1945; it became the national anthem of the unified Socialist Republic of Vietnam in 1976; although it consists of two verses, only the first is used as the official anthem

## ECONOMY :: VIETNAM

**ECONOMY - OVERVIEW:**

Vietnam is a densely populated developing country that has been transitioning since 1986 from the rigidities of a centrally planned, highly agrarian economy to a more industrial and market based economy, and it has raised incomes substantially. Vietnam exceeded its 2017 GDP growth target of 6.7% with growth of 6.8%, primarily due to unexpected increases in domestic demand, and strong manufacturing exports.

Vietnam has a young population, stable political system, commitment to sustainable growth, relatively low inflation, stable currency, strong FDI inflows, and strong manufacturing sector. In addition, the country is committed to continuing its global economic integration. Vietnam joined the WTO in January 2007 and concluded several free trade agreements in 2015-16, including the EU-Vietnam Free Trade Agreement (which the EU has not yet ratified), the Korean Free Trade Agreement, and the Eurasian Economic Union Free Trade Agreement. In 2017, Vietnam successfully chaired the Asia-Pacific Economic Cooperation (APEC) Conference with its key priorities including inclusive growth, innovation, strengthening small and medium enterprises, food security, and climate change. Seeking to diversify its opportunities, Vietnam also signed the Comprehensive and Progressive Agreement for the Transpacific Partnership in 2018 and continued to pursue the Regional Comprehensive Economic Partnership.

To continue its trajectory of strong economic growth, the government acknowledges the need to spark a 'second wave' of reforms, including reforming state-owned-enterprises, reducing red tape, increasing business sector transparency, reducing the level of non-performing loans in the banking sector, and increasing financial sector transparency. Vietnam's public debt to GDP ratio is nearing the government mandated ceiling of 65%.

In 2016, Vietnam cancelled its civilian nuclear energy development program, citing public concerns about safety and the high cost of the program; it faces growing pressure on energy infrastructure. Overall, the country's infrastructure fails to meet the needs of an expanding middle class. Vietnam has demonstrated a commitment to sustainable growth over the last several years, but despite the recent speed-up in economic growth the government remains cautious about the risk of external shocks.

## GDP (PURCHASING POWER PARITY):

$648.7 billion (2017 est.)

$607.4 billion (2016 est.)

$571.9 billion (2015 est.)

note: data are in 2017 dollars

country comparison to the world: 35

## GDP (OFFICIAL EXCHANGE RATE):

$220.4 billion (2017 est.) (2017 est.)

## GDP - REAL GROWTH RATE:

6.8% (2017 est.)

6.2% (2016 est.)

6.7% (2015 est.)

country comparison to the world: 25

## GDP - PER CAPITA (PPP):

$6,900 (2017 est.)

$6,600 (2016 est.)

$6,200 (2015 est.)

note: data are in 2017 dollars

country comparison to the world: 159

## GROSS NATIONAL SAVING:

29% of GDP (2017 est.)

29.5% of GDP (2016 est.)

27.5% of GDP (2015 est.)

country comparison to the world: 33

## GDP - COMPOSITION, BY END USE:

household consumption: 66.9% (2017 est.)

government consumption: 6.5% (2017 est.)

investment in fixed capital: 24.2% (2017 est.)

investment in inventories: 2.8% (2017 est.)

exports of goods and services: 100% (2017 est.)

imports of goods and services: -101% (2017 est.)

## GDP - COMPOSITION, BY SECTOR OF ORIGIN:

agriculture: 15.3% (2017 est.)

industry: 33.3% (2017 est.)

services: 51.3% (2017 est.)

## AGRICULTURE - PRODUCTS:

rice, coffee, rubber, tea, pepper, soybeans, cashews, sugar cane, peanuts, bananas; pork; poultry; seafood

## INDUSTRIES:

food processing, garments, shoes, machine-building; mining, coal, steel; cement, chemical fertilizer, glass, tires, oil, mobile phones

## INDUSTRIAL PRODUCTION GROWTH RATE:

8% (2017 est.)

country comparison to the world: 24

## LABOR FORCE:

54.8 million (2017 est.)

country comparison to the world: 11

## LABOR FORCE - BY OCCUPATION:

agriculture: 40.3%

industry: 25.7%

services: 34% (2017)

## UNEMPLOYMENT RATE:

2.2% (2017 est.)

2.3% (2016 est.)

country comparison to the world: 22

## POPULATION BELOW POVERTY LINE:

8% (2017 est.)

## HOUSEHOLD INCOME OR CONSUMPTION BY PERCENTAGE SHARE:

lowest 10%: 26.8% (2014)

highest 10%: 26.8% (2014)

## DISTRIBUTION OF FAMILY INCOME - GINI INDEX:

34.8 (2014)

37.6 (2008)

country comparison to the world: 101

## BUDGET:

revenues: 54.59 billion (2017 est.)

expenditures: 69.37 billion (2017 est.)

## TAXES AND OTHER REVENUES:

24.8% (of GDP) (2017 est.)

country comparison to the world: 119

## BUDGET SURPLUS (+) OR DEFICIT (-):

-6.7% (of GDP) (2017 est.)

country comparison to the world: 191

## PUBLIC DEBT:

58.5% of GDP (2017 est.)

59.9% of GDP (2016 est.)

note: official data; data cover general government debt and include debt instruments issued (or owned) by government entities other than the treasury; the data include treasury debt held by foreign entities; the data include debt issued by subnational entities, as well as intragovernmental debt; intragovernmental debt consists of treasury borrowings from surpluses in the social funds, such as for retirement, medical care, and unemployment; debt instruments for the social funds are not sold at public auctions

country comparison to the world: 76

## FISCAL YEAR:

calendar year

## INFLATION RATE (CONSUMER PRICES):

3.5% (2017 est.)

2.7% (2016 est.)

country comparison to the world: 142

## CENTRAL BANK DISCOUNT RATE:

4.25% (7 October 2017)

15% (31 December 2011)

country comparison to the world: 98

**COMMERCIAL BANK PRIME LENDING RATE:**

7.07% (31 December 2017 est.)

6.96% (31 December 2016 est.)

country comparison to the world: 117

**STOCK OF NARROW MONEY:**

$85.96 billion (31 December 2017 est.)

$73.48 billion (31 December 2016 est.)

country comparison to the world: 43

**STOCK OF BROAD MONEY:**

$85.96 billion (31 December 2017 est.)

$73.48 billion (31 December 2016 est.)

country comparison to the world: 43

**STOCK OF DOMESTIC CREDIT:**

$313 billion (31 December 2017 est.)

$277.3 billion (31 December 2016 est.)

country comparison to the world: 35

**MARKET VALUE OF PUBLICLY TRADED SHARES:**

$156.7 billion (29 December 2017 est.)

$87.95 billion (31 December 2016 est.)

$52.39 billion (31 December 2015 est.)

country comparison to the world: 37

**CURRENT ACCOUNT BALANCE:**

$5.401 billion (2017 est.)

$5.924 billion (2016 est.)

country comparison to the world: 28

**EXPORTS:**

$214.1 billion (2017 est.)

$176.6 billion (2016 est.)

country comparison to the world: 27

**EXPORTS - PARTNERS:**

US 20.1%, China 14.5%, Japan 8%, South Korea 6.8% (2017)

**EXPORTS - COMMODITIES:**

clothes, shoes, electronics, seafood, crude oil, rice, coffee, wooden products, machinery

**IMPORTS:**

$202.6 billion (2017 est.)

$162.6 billion (2016 est.)

country comparison to the world: 26

**IMPORTS - COMMODITIES:**

machinery and equipment, petroleum products, steel products, raw materials for the clothing and shoe industries, electronics, plastics, automobiles

**IMPORTS - PARTNERS:**

China 25.8%, South Korea 20.5%, Japan 7.8%, Thailand 4.9% (2017)

**RESERVES OF FOREIGN EXCHANGE AND GOLD:**

$49.5 billion (31 December 2017 est.)

$36.91 billion (31 December 2016 est.)

country comparison to the world: 40

**DEBT - EXTERNAL:**

$96.58 billion (31 December 2017 est.)

$84.34 billion (31 December 2016 est.)

country comparison to the world: 48

**STOCK OF DIRECT FOREIGN INVESTMENT - AT HOME:**

$129.5 billion (31 December 2017 est.)

$293.2 billion (31 December 2016 est.)

country comparison to the world: 42

**STOCK OF DIRECT FOREIGN INVESTMENT - ABROAD:**

$19.75 billion (31 December 2015 est.)

$18.97 billion (31 December 2014 est.)

country comparison to the world: 55

**EXCHANGE RATES:**

dong (VND) per US dollar -

22,425 (2017 est.)

22,159 (2016 est.)

22,355 (2015 est.)

21,909 (2014 est.)

21,189 (2013 est.)

## ENERGY :: VIETNAM

**ELECTRICITY ACCESS:**

population without electricity: 2.6 million (2013)

electrification - total population: 99% (2013)

electrification - urban areas: 100% (2013)

electrification - rural areas: 98% (2013)

**ELECTRICITY - PRODUCTION:**

158.2 billion kWh (2016 est.)

country comparison to the world: 24

**ELECTRICITY - CONSUMPTION:**

143.2 billion kWh (2016 est.)

country comparison to the world: 25

**ELECTRICITY - EXPORTS:**

713 million kWh (2017 est.)

country comparison to the world: 63

**ELECTRICITY - IMPORTS:**

2.733 billion kWh (2016 est.)

country comparison to the world: 51

**ELECTRICITY - INSTALLED GENERATING CAPACITY:**

40.77 million kW (2016 est.)

country comparison to the world: 25

**ELECTRICITY - FROM FOSSIL FUELS:**

56% of total installed capacity (2016 est.)

country comparison to the world: 140

**ELECTRICITY - FROM NUCLEAR FUELS:**

0% of total installed capacity (2017 est.)

country comparison to the world: 209

**ELECTRICITY - FROM HYDROELECTRIC PLANTS:**

43% of total installed capacity (2017 est.)

country comparison to the world: 47

**ELECTRICITY - FROM OTHER RENEWABLE SOURCES:**

1% of total installed capacity (2017 est.)

country comparison to the world: 171

**CRUDE OIL - PRODUCTION:**

271,400 bbl/day (2017 est.)

country comparison to the world: 30

**CRUDE OIL - EXPORTS:**

324,600 bbl/day (2015 est.)

country comparison to the world: 25

**CRUDE OIL - IMPORTS:**

0 bbl/day (2015 est.)

country comparison to the world: 213

**CRUDE OIL - PROVED RESERVES:**

4.4 billion bbl (1 January 2018 est.)

country comparison to the world: 25

**REFINED PETROLEUM PRODUCTS - PRODUCTION:**

153,800 bbl/day (2015 est.)

country comparison to the world: 58

**REFINED PETROLEUM PRODUCTS - CONSUMPTION:**

438,000 bbl/day (2016 est.)

country comparison to the world: 35

**REFINED PETROLEUM PRODUCTS - EXPORTS:**

25,620 bbl/day (2015 est.)

country comparison to the world: 67

**REFINED PETROLEUM PRODUCTS - IMPORTS:**

282,800 bbl/day (2015 est.)

country comparison to the world: 25

**NATURAL GAS - PRODUCTION:**

8.098 billion cu m (2017 est.)

country comparison to the world: 44

**NATURAL GAS - CONSUMPTION:**

8.098 billion cu m (2017 est.)

country comparison to the world: 52

**NATURAL GAS - EXPORTS:**

0 cu m (2017 est.)

country comparison to the world: 210

**NATURAL GAS - IMPORTS:**

0 cu m (2017 est.)

country comparison to the world: 210

**NATURAL GAS - PROVED RESERVES:**

699.4 billion cu m (1 January 2018 est.)

country comparison to the world: 27

**CARBON DIOXIDE EMISSIONS FROM CONSUMPTION OF ENERGY:**

235.3 million Mt (2017 est.)

country comparison to the world: 29

## COMMUNICATIONS :: VIETNAM

**TELEPHONES - FIXED LINES:**

total subscriptions: 4,526,077 (2017 est.)

subscriptions per 100 inhabitants: 5 (2017 est.)

country comparison to the world: 30

**TELEPHONES - MOBILE CELLULAR:**

total subscriptions: 120,016,181 (2017 est.)

subscriptions per 100 inhabitants: 125 (2017 est.)

country comparison to the world: 12

**TELEPHONE SYSTEM:**

general assessment: Vietnam is putting considerable effort into modernization and expansion of its telecommunication system (2016)

domestic: all provincial exchanges are digitalized and connected to Hanoi, Da Nang, and Ho Chi Minh City by fiber-optic cable or microwave radio relay networks; main lines have been increased, and the use of mobile telephones is growing rapidly (2016)

international: country code - 84; a landing point for the SEA-ME-WE-3, the C2C, and Thailand-Vietnam-Hong Kong submarine cable systems; the Asia-America Gateway submarine cable system, completed in 2009, provided new access links to Asia and the US; satellite earth stations - 2 Intersputnik (Indian Ocean region) (2016)

**BROADCAST MEDIA:**

government controls all broadcast media exercising oversight through the Ministry of Information and Communication (MIC); government-controlled national TV provider, Vietnam Television (VTV), operates a network of several channels with regional broadcasting centers; programming is relayed nationwide via a network of provincial and municipal TV stations; law limits access to satellite TV but many households are able to access foreign programming via home satellite equipment; government-controlled Voice of Vietnam, the national radio broadcaster, broadcasts on several channels and is repeated on AM, FM, and shortwave stations throughout Vietnam (2018)

**INTERNET COUNTRY CODE:**

.vn

**INTERNET USERS:**

total: 49.741 million (July 2016 est.)

percent of population: 52.7% (July 2016 est.)

country comparison to the world: 13

**BROADBAND - FIXED SUBSCRIPTIONS:**

total: 11,269,936 (2017 est.)

subscriptions per 100 inhabitants: 12 (2017 est.)

country comparison to the world: 16

## TRANSPORTATION :: VIETNAM

**NATIONAL AIR TRANSPORT SYSTEM:**

number of registered air carriers: 4 (2015)

inventory of registered aircraft operated by air carriers: 140 (2015)

annual passenger traffic on registered air carriers: 29,944,771 (2015)

annual freight traffic on registered air carriers: 384,470,240 mt-km (2015)

**CIVIL AIRCRAFT REGISTRATION COUNTRY CODE PREFIX:**

VN (2016)

**AIRPORTS:**

45 (2013)

country comparison to the world: 96

**AIRPORTS - WITH PAVED RUNWAYS:**

total: 38 (2013)

over 3,047 m: 10 (2013)

2,438 to 3,047 m: 6 (2013)

1,524 to 2,437 m: 13 (2013)

914 to 1,523 m: 9 (2013)

**AIRPORTS - WITH UNPAVED RUNWAYS:**

total: 7 (2013)

1,524 to 2,437 m: 1 (2013)

914 to 1,523 m: 3 (2013)

under 914 m: 3 (2013)

**HELIPORTS:**

1 (2013)

**PIPELINES:**

72 km condensate, 398 km condensate/gas, 955 km gas, 128 km oil, 33 km oil/gas/water, 206 km refined products, 13 km water (2013)

**RAILWAYS:**

total: 2,600 km (2014)

standard gauge: 178 km 1.435-m gauge; 253 km mixed gauge (2014)

narrow gauge: 2,169 km 1.000-m gauge (2014)

country comparison to the world: 66

**ROADWAYS:**

total: 195,468 km (2013)

paved: 148,338 km (2013)

unpaved: 47,130 km (2013)

country comparison to the world: 28

**WATERWAYS:**

47,130 km (30,831 km weight under 50 tons) (2011)

country comparison to the world: 4

**MERCHANT MARINE:**

total: 1,818 (2017)

by type: bulk carrier 81, container ship 34, general cargo 1259, oil tanker 109, other 335 (2017)

country comparison to the world: 13

**PORTS AND TERMINALS:**

major seaport(s): Cam Pha Port, Da Nang, Haiphong, Phu My, Quy Nhon

container port(s) (TEUs): Saigon (5,986,747) (2016)

river port(s): Ho Chi Minh (Mekong)

## MILITARY AND SECURITY :: VIETNAM

**MILITARY EXPENDITURES:**

2.44% of GDP (2016)

2.36% of GDP (2015)

2.29% of GDP (2014)

country comparison to the world: 40

**MILITARY BRANCHES:**

People's Armed Forces: People's Army of Vietnam (PAVN, includes Vietnam People's Navy (with Naval Infantry), Vietnam People's Air and Air Defense

Force, Border Defense Command, Coast Guard) (2013)

## MILITARY SERVICE AGE AND OBLIGATION:

18-25 years of age for male compulsory and voluntary military service; females may volunteer for active duty military service; conscription typically takes place twice annually and service obligation is 18 months (Army, Air Defense), 2 years (Navy and Air Force); 18-45 years of age (male) or 18-40 years of age (female) for Militia Force or Self Defense Force service; males may enroll in military schools at age 17 (2013)

## MARITIME THREATS:

the International Maritime Bureau reports the territorial and offshore waters in the South China Sea as high risk for piracy and armed robbery against ships; numerous commercial vessels have been attacked and hijacked both at anchor and while underway; hijacked vessels are often disguised and cargo diverted to ports in East Asia; crews have been murdered or cast adrift; the number of reported incidents declined from nine in 2016 to two in 2017, primarily near the port of Vung Tau

# TRANSNATIONAL ISSUES :: VIETNAM

## DISPUTES - INTERNATIONAL:

southeast Asian states have enhanced border surveillance to check the spread of avian fluCambodia and Laos protest Vietnamese squatters and armed encroachments along borderCambodia accuses Vietnam of a wide variety of illicit cross-border activitiesprogress on a joint development area with Cambodia is hampered by an unresolved dispute over sovereignty of offshore islandsan estimated 300,000 Vietnamese refugees reside in Chinaestablishment of a maritime boundary with Cambodia is hampered by unresolved dispute over the sovereignty of offshore islandsthe decade-long demarcation of the China-Vietnam land boundary was completed in 2009China occupies the Paracel Islands also claimed by Vietnam and TaiwanBrunei claims a maritime boundary extending beyond as far as a median with Vietnam, thus asserting an implicit claim to Lousia Reefthe 2002 "Declaration on the Conduct of Parties in the South China Sea" has eased tensions but falls short of a legally binding "code of conduct" desired by several of the disputantsVietnam continues to expand construction of facilities in the Spratly Islandsin March 2005, the national oil companies of China, the Philippines, and Vietnam signed a joint accord to conduct marine seismic activities in the Spratly IslandsEconomic Exclusion Zone negotiations with Indonesia are ongoing, and the two countries in Fall 2011 agreed to work together to reduce illegal fishing along their maritime boundary

## REFUGEES AND INTERNALLY DISPLACED PERSONS:

**stateless persons:** 29,522 (2017); note - Vietnam's stateless ethnic Chinese Cambodian population dates to the 1970s when thousands of Cambodians fled to Vietnam to escape the Khmer Rouge and were no longer recognized as Cambodian citizens; Vietnamese women who gave up their citizenship to marry foreign men have found themselves stateless after divorcing and returning home to Vietnam; the government addressed this problem in 2009, and Vietnamese women are beginning to reclaim their citizenship

## ILLICIT DRUGS:

minor producer of opium poppy; probable minor transit point for Southeast Asian heroin; government continues to face domestic opium/heroin/methamphetamine addiction problems despite longstanding crackdowns; enforces the death penalty for drug trafficking

# CENTRAL AMERICA :: VIRGIN ISLANDS

## INTRODUCTION :: VIRGIN ISLANDS

### BACKGROUND:

The Danes secured control over the southern Virgin Islands of Saint Thomas, Saint John, and Saint Croix during the 17th and early 18th centuries. Sugarcane, produced by African slave labor, drove the islands' economy during the 18th and early 19th centuries. In 1917, the US purchased the Danish holdings, which had been in economic decline since the abolition of slavery in 1848. On 6 September 2017, Hurricane Irma passed over the northern Virgin Islands of Saint Thomas and Saint John and inflicted severe damage to structures, roads, the airport on Saint Thomas, communications, and electricity. Less than two weeks later, Hurricane Maria passed over the island of Saint Croix in the southern Virgin Islands, inflicting considerable damage with heavy winds and flooding rains.

## GEOGRAPHY :: VIRGIN ISLANDS

### LOCATION:
Caribbean, islands between the Caribbean Sea and the North Atlantic Ocean, east of Puerto Rico

### GEOGRAPHIC COORDINATES:
18 20 N, 64 50 W

### MAP REFERENCES:
Central America and the Caribbean

### AREA:
**total:** 1,910 sq km

**land:** 346 sq km

**water:** 1,564 sq km

**country comparison to the world:** 182

### AREA - COMPARATIVE:
twice the size of Washington, DC

### LAND BOUNDARIES:
0 km

### COASTLINE:
188 km

### MARITIME CLAIMS:
**territorial sea:** 12 nm

**exclusive economic zone:** 200 nm

### CLIMATE:
subtropical, tempered by easterly trade winds, relatively low humidity, little seasonal temperature variation; rainy season September to November

### TERRAIN:
mostly hilly to rugged and mountainous with little flat land

### ELEVATION:
0 m lowest point: Caribbean Sea

474 highest point: Crown Mountain

### NATURAL RESOURCES:
pleasant climate, beaches foster tourism

### LAND USE:
**agricultural land:** 11.5% (2011 est.)

**arable land:** 2.9% (2011 est.) / **permanent crops:** 2.9% (2011 est.) / **permanent pasture:** 5.7% (2011 est.)

**forest:** 57.4% (2011 est.)

**other:** 31.1% (2011 est.)

### IRRIGATED LAND:
1 sq km (2012)

### POPULATION DISTRIBUTION:
while overall population density throughout the islands is relatively low, concentrations appear around Charlotte Amalie on St. Thomas and Christiansted on St. Croix

### NATURAL HAZARDS:
several hurricanes in recent years; frequent and severe droughts and floods; occasional earthquakes

### ENVIRONMENT - CURRENT ISSUES:
lack of natural freshwater resources; protection of coral reefs; solid waste management; coastal development; increased boating and overfishing

### GEOGRAPHY - NOTE:
important location along the Anegada Passage - a key shipping lane for the Panama Canal; Saint Thomas has one of the best natural deepwater harbors in the Caribbean

## PEOPLE AND SOCIETY :: VIRGIN ISLANDS

### POPULATION:
106,977 (July 2018 est.)

**country comparison to the world:** 192

### NATIONALITY:
**noun:** Virgin Islander(s) (US citizens)

**adjective:** Virgin Islander

### ETHNIC GROUPS:
black 76%, white 15.6%, Asian 1.4%, other 4.9%, mixed 2.1% (2010 est.)

**note:** 17.4% self-identify as latino

### LANGUAGES:
English 71.6%, Spanish or Spanish Creole 17.2%, French or French Creole 8.6%, other 2.5% (2010 est.)

### RELIGIONS:
Protestant 59% (Baptist 42%, Episcopalian 17%), Roman Catholic 34%, other 7%

**AGE STRUCTURE:**

0-14 years: 20.26% (male 11,102/female 10,570)

15-24 years: 10.87% (male 5,665/female 5,965)

25-54 years: 36.87% (male 18,454/female 20,987)

55-64 years: 13.92% (male 7,039/female 7,851)

65 years and over: 18.08% (male 8,802/female 10,542) (2018 est.)

**DEPENDENCY RATIOS:**

total dependency ratio: 60.8 (2015 est.)

youth dependency ratio: 32.8 (2015 est.)

elderly dependency ratio: 28 (2015 est.)

potential support ratio: 3.6 (2015 est.)

**MEDIAN AGE:**

total: 41.3 years

male: 40.1 years

female: 42.2 years (2018 est.)

country comparison to the world: 42

**POPULATION GROWTH RATE:**

-0.3% (2018 est.)

country comparison to the world: 217

**BIRTH RATE:**

12.5 births/1,000 population (2018 est.)

country comparison to the world: 155

**DEATH RATE:**

8.1 deaths/1,000 population (2018 est.)

country comparison to the world: 88

**NET MIGRATION RATE:**

-7.5 migrant(s)/1,000 population (2017 est.)

country comparison to the world: 204

**POPULATION DISTRIBUTION:**

while overall population density throughout the islands is relatively low, concentrations appear around Charlotte Amalie on St. Thomas and Christiansted on St. Croix

**URBANIZATION:**

urban population: 95.7% of total population (2018)

rate of urbanization: 0.1% annual rate of change (2015-20 est.)

**MAJOR URBAN AREAS - POPULATION:**

52,000 CHARLOTTE AMALIE (capital) (2018)

**SEX RATIO:**

at birth: 1.06 male(s)/female (2017 est.)

0-14 years: 1.02 male(s)/female (2017 est.)

15-24 years: 0.82 male(s)/female (2017 est.)

25-54 years: 0.82 male(s)/female (2017 est.)

55-64 years: 0.93 male(s)/female (2017 est.)

65 years and over: 0.83 male(s)/female (2017 est.)

total population: 0.87 male(s)/female (2017 est.)

**INFANT MORTALITY RATE:**

total: 7.7 deaths/1,000 live births (2018 est.)

male: 8.8 deaths/1,000 live births (2018 est.)

female: 6.7 deaths/1,000 live births (2018 est.)

country comparison to the world: 158

**LIFE EXPECTANCY AT BIRTH:**

total population: 79.5 years (2018 est.)

male: 76.3 years (2018 est.)

female: 83 years (2018 est.)

country comparison to the world: 49

**TOTAL FERTILITY RATE:**

2.06 children born/woman (2018 est.)

country comparison to the world: 108

**DRINKING WATER SOURCE:**

improved:

urban: 100% of population (2015 est.)

rural: 100% of population (2015 est.)

total: 100% of population (2015 est.)

unimproved:

urban: 0% of population (2015 est.)

rural: 0% of population (2015 est.)

total: 0% of population (2015 est.)

**SANITATION FACILITY ACCESS:**

improved:

urban: 96.4% of population (2015 est.)

rural: 96.4% of population (2015 est.)

total: 96.4% of population (2015 est.)

unimproved:

urban: 3.6% of population (2015 est.)

rural: 3.6% of population (2015 est.)

total: 3.6% of population (2015 est.)

**HIV/AIDS - ADULT PREVALENCE RATE:**

NA

**HIV/AIDS - PEOPLE LIVING WITH HIV/AIDS:**

NA

**HIV/AIDS - DEATHS:**

NA

**MAJOR INFECTIOUS DISEASES:**

note: active local transmission of Zika virus by Aedes species mosquitoes has been identified in this country (as of August 2016); it poses an important risk (a large number of cases possible) among US citizens if bitten by an infective mosquito; other less common ways to get Zika are through sex, via blood transfusion, or during pregnancy, in which the pregnant woman passes Zika virus to her fetus

# GOVERNMENT :: VIRGIN ISLANDS

**COUNTRY NAME:**

conventional long form: none

conventional short form: Virgin Islands

former: Danish West Indies

abbreviation: VI

etymology: the myriad islets, cays, and rocks surrounding the major islands reminded Christopher COLUMBUS in 1493 of Saint Ursula and her 11,000 virgin followers (Santa Ursula y las Once Mil Virgenes), which over time shortened to the Virgins (las Virgenes)

**DEPENDENCY STATUS:**

unincorporated organized territory of the US with policy relations between the Virgin Islands and the US under the jurisdiction of the Office of Insular Affairs, US Department of the Interior

**GOVERNMENT TYPE:**

presidential democracy; a self-governing territory of the US

**CAPITAL:**

name: Charlotte Amalie

geographic coordinates: 18 21 N, 64 56 W

time difference: UTC-4 (1 hour ahead of Washington, DC, during Standard Time)

**ADMINISTRATIVE DIVISIONS:**

none (territory of the US); there are no first-order administrative divisions as defined by the US Government, but there are 3 islands at the second order; Saint Croix, Saint John, Saint Thomas

### INDEPENDENCE:
none (territory of the US)

### NATIONAL HOLIDAY:
Transfer Day (from Denmark to the US), 31 March (1917)

### CONSTITUTION:
history: 22 July 1954 - the Revised Organic Act of the Virgin Islands functions as a constitution for this territory of the US (2018)

amendments: revised 1962, 2000 (2018)

### LEGAL SYSTEM:
US common law

### CITIZENSHIP:
see United States

### SUFFRAGE:
18 years of age; universal; note - island residents are US citizens but do not vote in US presidential elections

### EXECUTIVE BRANCH:
chief of state: President Donald J. TRUMP (since 20 January 2017); Vice President Michael R. PENCE (since 20 January 2017)

head of government: Governor Kenneth MAPP (since 5 January 2015), Lieutenant Governor Osbert POTTER (since 5 January 2015)

cabinet: Territorial Cabinet appointed by the governor and confirmed by the Senate

elections/appointments: president and vice president indirectly elected on the same ballot by an Electoral College of 'electors' chosen from each state; president and vice president serve a 4-year term (eligible for a second term); under the US Constitution, residents of the Virgin Islands do not vote in elections for US president and vice president; however, they may vote in the Democratic and Republican presidential primary elections; governor and lieutenant governor directly elected on the same ballot by absolute majority vote in 2 rounds if needed for a 4-year term (eligible for a second term); election last held on 6 November 2018 (next to be held in November 2022)

election results:

Albert BRYAN (Democratic Party) 37.9%, incumbent Kenneth MAPP (independent) 33.7%, Adlah Donastorg, Jr. (independent) 16.4%; a runoff will be held 20 November 2018

### LEGISLATIVE BRANCH:
description: unicameral Senate (15 seats; members directly elected in single- and multi-seat constituencies by simple majority popular vote to serve 2-year terms)

elections: last held on 6 November 2018 (next to be held in November 2020)

election results: percent of vote by party - NA; seats by party - Democratic Party 13, independent 2

note: the Virgin Islands directly elects 1 member by simple majority vote to serve a 2-year term as a delegate to the US House of Representatives; the delegate can vote when serving on a committee and when the House meets as the Committee of the Whole House, but not when legislation is submitted for a "full floor" House vote; election of delegate last held on 6 November 2018 (next to be held in November 2020)

### JUDICIAL BRANCH:
highest courts: Supreme Court of the Virgin Islands (consists of the chief justice and 2 associate justices); note - court established by US Congress in 2004 and assumed appellate jurisdiction in 2007

judge selection and term of office: justices appointed by the governor and confirmed by the Virgin Islands Senate; justices initially serve renewable 10-year terms; chief justice elected to position by peers for a 3-year term

subordinate courts: Superior Court (Territorial Court renamed in 2004); US Court of Appeals for the Third Circuit (has appellate jurisdiction over the District Court of the Virgin Islands; it is a territorial court and is not associated with a US federal judicial district); District Court of the Virgin Islands

### POLITICAL PARTIES AND LEADERS:
Democratic Party [Donna M. CHRISTENSEN]
Independent Citizens' Movement or ICM [Dale BLYDEN]
Republican Party [John CANEGATA]

### INTERNATIONAL ORGANIZATION PARTICIPATION:
AOSIS (observer), Interpol (subbureau), IOC, UPU, WFTU (NGOs)

### DIPLOMATIC REPRESENTATION IN THE US:
none (territory of the US)

### DIPLOMATIC REPRESENTATION FROM THE US:
none (territory of the US)

### FLAG DESCRIPTION:
white field with a modified US coat of arms in the center between the large blue initials V and I; the coat of arms shows a yellow eagle holding an olive branch in its right talon and three arrows in the left with a superimposed shield of seven red and six white vertical stripes below a blue panel; white is a symbol of purity, the letters stand for the Virgin Islands

### NATIONAL ANTHEM:
name: Virgin Islands March

lyrics/music: multiple/Alton Augustus ADAMS, Sr.

note: adopted 1963; serves as a local anthem; as a territory of the US, "The Star-Spangled Banner" is official (see United States)

## ECONOMY :: VIRGIN ISLANDS

### ECONOMY - OVERVIEW:
Tourism, trade, other services, and rum production are the primary economic activities of the US Virgin Islands (USVI), accounting for most of its GDP and employment. The USVI receives between 2.5 and 3 million tourists a year, mostly from visiting cruise ships. The islands are vulnerable to damage from storms, as evidenced by the destruction from two major hurricanes in 2017. Recovery and rebuilding have continued, but full recovery from these back-to-back hurricanes is years away. The USVI government estimates it will need $7.5 billion, almost twice the territory's GDP, to rebuild the territory.

The agriculture sector is small and most food is imported. In 2016, government spending (both federal and territorial together) accounted for about 27% of GDP while exports of goods and services, including spending by tourists, accounted for nearly 47%. Federal programs and grants, including rum tax cover-over totaling $482.3 million in 2016, contributed 32.2% of the territory's total revenues. The economy picked up 0.9% in 2016 and had appeared to be progressing before the 2017 hurricanes severely damaged the territory's infrastructure and the economy.

## GDP (PURCHASING POWER PARITY):

$3.872 billion (2016 est.)

$3.759 billion (2015 est.)

$3.622 billion (2014 est.)

note: data are in 2013 dollars

country comparison to the world: 181

## GDP (OFFICIAL EXCHANGE RATE):

$5.182 billion (2016 est.) (2016 est.)

## GDP - REAL GROWTH RATE:

0.9% (2016 est.)

0.3% (2015 est.)

-1% (2014 est.)

country comparison to the world: 185

## GDP - PER CAPITA (PPP):

$37,000 (2016 est.)

$35,800 (2015 est.)

$34,500 (2014 est.)

country comparison to the world: 54

## GDP - COMPOSITION, BY END USE:

household consumption: 68.2% (2016 est.)

government consumption: 26.8% (2016 est.)

investment in fixed capital: 7.5% (2016 est.)

investment in inventories: 15% NA (2016 est.)

exports of goods and services: 46.7% (2016 est.)

imports of goods and services: -64.3% (2016 est.)

## GDP - COMPOSITION, BY SECTOR OF ORIGIN:

agriculture: 2% (2012 est.)

industry: 20% (2012 est.)

services: 78% (2012 est.)

## AGRICULTURE - PRODUCTS:

fruit, vegetables, sorghum; Senepol cattle

## INDUSTRIES:

tourism, watch assembly, rum distilling, construction, pharmaceuticals, electronics

## INDUSTRIAL PRODUCTION GROWTH RATE:

NA

## LABOR FORCE:

48,550 (2016 est.)

country comparison to the world: 193

## LABOR FORCE - BY OCCUPATION:

agriculture: 1%

industry: 19%

services: 80% (2003 est.)

## UNEMPLOYMENT RATE:

10.4% (2017 est.)

11% (2016 est.)

country comparison to the world: 145

## POPULATION BELOW POVERTY LINE:

28.9% (2002 est.)

## HOUSEHOLD INCOME OR CONSUMPTION BY PERCENTAGE SHARE:

lowest 10%: NA

highest 10%: NA

## BUDGET:

revenues: 1.496 billion (2016 est.)

expenditures: 1.518 billion (2016 est.)

## TAXES AND OTHER REVENUES:

28.9% (of GDP) (2016 est.)

country comparison to the world: 89

## BUDGET SURPLUS (+) OR DEFICIT (-):

-0.4% (of GDP) (2016 est.)

country comparison to the world: 59

## PUBLIC DEBT:

53.3% of GDP (2016 est.)

45.9% of GDP (2014 est.)

country comparison to the world: 91

## FISCAL YEAR:

1 October - 30 September

## INFLATION RATE (CONSUMER PRICES):

1% (2016 est.)

2.6% (2015 est.)

country comparison to the world: 54

## EXPORTS:

$1.81 billion (2016 est.)

$1.537 billion (2015 est.)

country comparison to the world: 147

## EXPORTS - COMMODITIES:

rum

## IMPORTS:

$2.489 billion (2016 est.)

$1.549 billion (2015 est.)

country comparison to the world: 159

## IMPORTS - COMMODITIES:

foodstuffs, consumer goods, building materials

## DEBT - EXTERNAL:

NA

## STOCK OF DIRECT FOREIGN INVESTMENT - AT HOME:

(31 December 2009 est.)

## EXCHANGE RATES:

the US dollar is used

# ENERGY :: VIRGIN ISLANDS

## ELECTRICITY ACCESS:

population without electricity: 10,295 (2012)

electrification - total population: 91% (2012)

electrification - urban areas: 91% (2012)

electrification - rural areas: 80% (2012)

## ELECTRICITY - PRODUCTION:

704 million kWh (2016 est.)

country comparison to the world: 157

## ELECTRICITY - CONSUMPTION:

654.7 million kWh (2016 est.)

country comparison to the world: 162

## ELECTRICITY - EXPORTS:

0 kWh (2016 est.)

country comparison to the world: 216

## ELECTRICITY - IMPORTS:

0 kWh (2016 est.)

country comparison to the world: 217

## ELECTRICITY - INSTALLED GENERATING CAPACITY:

325,000 kW (2016 est.)

country comparison to the world: 157

## ELECTRICITY - FROM FOSSIL FUELS:

98% of total installed capacity (2016 est.)

country comparison to the world: 30

## ELECTRICITY - FROM NUCLEAR FUELS:

0% of total installed capacity (2017 est.)

country comparison to the world: 210

## ELECTRICITY - FROM HYDROELECTRIC PLANTS:

0% of total installed capacity (2017 est.)

country comparison to the world: 212

## ELECTRICITY - FROM OTHER RENEWABLE SOURCES:

2% of total installed capacity (2017 est.)

country comparison to the world: 146

## CRUDE OIL - PRODUCTION:

0 bbl/day (2017 est.)

country comparison to the world: 213

**CRUDE OIL - EXPORTS:**

0 bbl/day (2015 est.)

country comparison to the world: 214

**CRUDE OIL - IMPORTS:**

0 bbl/day (2015 est.)

country comparison to the world: 214

**CRUDE OIL - PROVED RESERVES:**

0 bbl (1 January 2018 est.)

country comparison to the world: 211

**REFINED PETROLEUM PRODUCTS - PRODUCTION:**

0 bbl/day (2015 est.)

country comparison to the world: 214

**REFINED PETROLEUM PRODUCTS - CONSUMPTION:**

1,240 bbl/day (2016 est.)

country comparison to the world: 204

**REFINED PETROLEUM PRODUCTS - EXPORTS:**

3,285 bbl/day (2015 est.)

country comparison to the world: 97

**REFINED PETROLEUM PRODUCTS - IMPORTS:**

23,480 bbl/day (2015 est.)

country comparison to the world: 112

**NATURAL GAS - PRODUCTION:**

0 cu m (2017 est.)

country comparison to the world: 213

**NATURAL GAS - CONSUMPTION:**

0 cu m (2017 est.)

country comparison to the world: 212

**NATURAL GAS - EXPORTS:**

0 cu m (2017 est.)

country comparison to the world: 211

**NATURAL GAS - IMPORTS:**

0 cu m (2017 est.)

country comparison to the world: 211

**NATURAL GAS - PROVED RESERVES:**

0 cu m (1 January 2014 est.)

country comparison to the world: 206

**CARBON DIOXIDE EMISSIONS FROM CONSUMPTION OF ENERGY:**

2.764 million Mt (2017 est.)

country comparison to the world: 150

## COMMUNICATIONS :: VIRGIN ISLANDS

**TELEPHONES - FIXED LINES:**

total subscriptions: 76,000 (July 2016 est.)

subscriptions per 100 inhabitants: 73 (July 2016 est.)

country comparison to the world: 146

**TELEPHONE SYSTEM:**

general assessment: modern system with total digital switching, uses fiber-optic cable and microwave radio relay (2016)

domestic: full range of services available (2016)

international: country code - 1-340; submarine cable connections to US, the Caribbean, Central and South America; satellite earth stations - NA (2016)

**BROADCAST MEDIA:**

about a dozen TV broadcast stations including 1 public TV station; multi-channel cable and satellite TV services are available; 24 radio stations (2009)

**INTERNET COUNTRY CODE:**

.vi

**INTERNET USERS:**

total: 57,000 (July 2016 est.)

percent of population: 54.8% (July 2016 est.)

country comparison to the world: 190

## TRANSPORTATION :: VIRGIN ISLANDS

**AIRPORTS:**

2 (2013)

country comparison to the world: 208

**AIRPORTS - WITH PAVED RUNWAYS:**

total: 2 (2013)

over 3,047 m: 1 (2013)

1,524 to 2,437 m: 1 (2013)

**ROADWAYS:**

total: 1,260 km (2008)

country comparison to the world: 180

**PORTS AND TERMINALS:**

major seaport(s): Charlotte Amalie, Christiansted, Cruz Bay, Frederiksted, Limetree Bay

## MILITARY AND SECURITY :: VIRGIN ISLANDS

**MILITARY - NOTE:**

defense is the responsibility of the US

## TRANSNATIONAL ISSUES :: VIRGIN ISLANDS

**DISPUTES - INTERNATIONAL:**

none

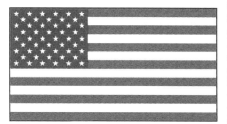

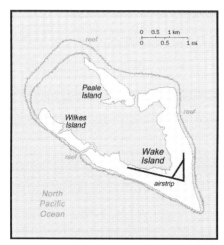

# AUSTRALIA - OCEANIA :: WAKE ISLAND

## INTRODUCTION :: WAKE ISLAND

### BACKGROUND:

The US annexed Wake Island in 1899 for a cable station. An important air and naval base was constructed in 1940-41. In December 1941, the island was captured by the Japanese and held until the end of World War II. In subsequent years, Wake became a stopover and refueling site for military and commercial aircraft transiting the Pacific. Since 1974, the island's airstrip has been used by the US military, as well as for emergency landings. Operations on the island were temporarily suspended and all personnel evacuated in 2006 with the approach of super typhoon IOKE (category 5), but resultant damage was comparatively minor. A US Air Force repair team restored full capability to the airfield and facilities, and the island remains a vital strategic link in the Pacific region.

## GEOGRAPHY :: WAKE ISLAND

### LOCATION:
Oceania, atoll in the North Pacific Ocean, about two-thirds of the way from Hawaii to the Northern Mariana Islands

### GEOGRAPHIC COORDINATES:
19 17 N, 166 39 E

### MAP REFERENCES:
Oceania

### AREA:
total: 6.5 sq km

land: 6.5 sq km

water: 0 sq km

country comparison to the world: 246

### AREA - COMPARATIVE:
about 11 times the size of the National Mall in Washington, DC

### LAND BOUNDARIES:
0 km

### COASTLINE:
19.3 km

### MARITIME CLAIMS:
territorial sea: 12 nm

exclusive economic zone: 200 nm

### CLIMATE:
tropical

### TERRAIN:
atoll of three low coral islands, Peale, Wake, and Wilkes, built up on an underwater volcano; central lagoon is former crater, islands are part of the rim

### ELEVATION:
0 m lowest point: Pacific Ocean

8 highest point: unnamed location

### NATURAL RESOURCES:
none

### LAND USE:
agricultural land: 0% (2011 est.)

arable land: 0% (2011 est.) / permanent crops: 0% (2011 est.) / permanent pasture: 0% (2011 est.)

forest: 0% (2011 est.)

other: 100% (2011 est.)

### IRRIGATED LAND:
0 sq km (2012)

### NATURAL HAZARDS:
subject to occasional typhoons

### ENVIRONMENT - CURRENT ISSUES:
potable water obtained through a catchment rainwater system and a desalinization plant for brackish ground water; hazardous wastes moved to an accumulation site for storage and eventual transport off site via barge

### GEOGRAPHY - NOTE:
strategic location in the North Pacific Ocean; emergency landing location for transpacific flights

## PEOPLE AND SOCIETY :: WAKE ISLAND

### POPULATION:
no indigenous inhabitants (2018 est.)

note: approximately 100 military personnel and civilian contractors maintain and operate the airfield and communications facilities

## GOVERNMENT :: WAKE ISLAND

### COUNTRY NAME:
conventional long form: none

conventional short form: Wake Island

etymology: although first discovered by British Captain William WAKE in 1792, the island is named after British Captain Samuel WAKE who rediscovered the island in 1796

### DEPENDENCY STATUS:
unincorporated unorganized territory of the US; administered from Washington, DC, by the Department of the Interior; activities in the atoll are currently conducted by the 11th US Air Force and managed from Pacific Air Force Support Center

### LEGAL SYSTEM:

US common law

**CITIZENSHIP:**
see United States

**FLAG DESCRIPTION:**
the flag of the US is used

## ECONOMY :: WAKE ISLAND

**ECONOMY - OVERVIEW:**
Economic activity is limited to providing services to military personnel and contractors located on the island. All food and manufactured goods must be imported.

## COMMUNICATIONS :: WAKE ISLAND

**TELEPHONE SYSTEM:**
general assessment: satellite communications; 2 Defense Switched Network circuits off the Overseas Telephone System (OTS); located in the Hawaii area code - 808

**BROADCAST MEDIA:**
American Armed Forces Radio and Television Service (AFRTS) provides satellite radio/TV broadcasts (2018)

## TRANSPORTATION :: WAKE ISLAND

**AIRPORTS:**
1 (2018)

country comparison to the world: 238

**AIRPORTS - WITH PAVED RUNWAYS:**
total: 1 (2018)

2,438 to 3,047 m: 1 (2018)

**PORTS AND TERMINALS:**
none; two offshore anchorages for large ships

**TRANSPORTATION - NOTE:**
there are no commercial or civilian flights to and from Wake Island, except in direct support of island missions; emergency landing is available

## MILITARY AND SECURITY :: WAKE ISLAND

**MILITARY - NOTE:**
defense is the responsibility of the US; the US Air Force is responsible for overall administration and operation of the island facilities; the launch support facility is administered by the US Missile Defense Agency (MDA)

## TRANSNATIONAL ISSUES :: WAKE ISLAND

**DISPUTES - INTERNATIONAL:**
claimed by Marshall Islands

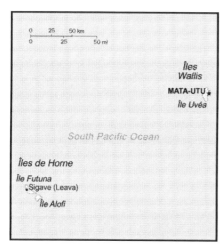

# AUSTRALIA - OCEANIA :: WALLIS AND FUTUNA

## INTRODUCTION :: WALLIS AND FUTUNA

### BACKGROUND:

The Futuna island group was discovered by the Dutch in 1616 and Wallis by the British in 1767, but it was the French who declared a protectorate over the islands in 1842, and took official control of them between 1886 and 1888. Notably, Wallis and Futuna was the only French colony to side with the Vichy regime during World War II, a phase that ended in May of 1942 with the arrival of 2,000 American troops. In 1959, the inhabitants of the islands voted to become a French overseas territory and officially assumed that status in 1961. In 2003, Wallis and Futuna's designation changed to that of an overseas collectivity.

## GEOGRAPHY :: WALLIS AND FUTUNA

### LOCATION:
Oceania, islands in the South Pacific Ocean, about two-thirds of the way from Hawaii to New Zealand

### GEOGRAPHIC COORDINATES:
13 18 S, 176 12 W

### MAP REFERENCES:
Oceania

### AREA:
total: 142 sq km

land: 142 sq km

water: 0 sq km

note: includes Ile Uvea (Wallis Island), Ile Futuna (Futuna Island), Ile Alofi, and 20 islets

country comparison to the world: 221

### AREA - COMPARATIVE:
1.5 times the size of Washington, DC

### LAND BOUNDARIES:
0 km

### COASTLINE:
129 km

### MARITIME CLAIMS:
territorial sea: 12 nm

exclusive economic zone: 200 nm

### CLIMATE:
tropical; hot, rainy season (November to April); cool, dry season (May to October); rains 250-300 cm per year (80% humidity); average temperature 26.6 degrees Celsius

### TERRAIN:
volcanic origin; low hills

### ELEVATION:
0 m lowest point: Pacific Ocean

522 highest point: Mont Singavi (on Futuna)

### NATURAL RESOURCES:
NEGL

### LAND USE:
agricultural land: 42.8% (2011 est.)

arable land: 7.1% (2011 est.) / permanent crops: 35.7% (2011 est.) / permanent pasture: 0% (2011 est.)

forest: 41.9% (2011 est.)

other: 15.3% (2011 est.)

### IRRIGATED LAND:
0 sq km (2012)

### NATURAL HAZARDS:
cyclones; tsunamis

### ENVIRONMENT - CURRENT ISSUES:
deforestation (only small portions of the original forests remain) largely as a result of the continued use of wood as the main fuel source; as a consequence of cutting down the forests, the mountainous terrain of Futuna is particularly prone to erosion; there are no permanent settlements on Alofi because of the lack of natural freshwater resources; lack of soil fertility on the islands of Uvea and Futuna negatively impacts agricultural producitivity

### GEOGRAPHY - NOTE:
both island groups have fringing reefs; Wallis contains several prominent crater lakes

## PEOPLE AND SOCIETY :: WALLIS AND FUTUNA

### POPULATION:
15,763 (July 2018 est.)

country comparison to the world: 221

### NATIONALITY:
noun: Wallisian(s), Futunan(s), or Wallis and Futuna Islanders

adjective: Wallisian, Futunan, or Wallis and Futuna Islander

### ETHNIC GROUPS:
Polynesian

### LANGUAGES:
Wallisian (indigenous Polynesian language) 58.9%, Futunian 30.1%, French (official) 10.8%, other 0.2% (2003 census)

### RELIGIONS:
Roman Catholic 99%, other 1%

### AGE STRUCTURE:
0-14 years: 21.28% (male 1,749 /female 1,606)

**15-24 years:** 15.87% (male 1,336 /female 1,165)

**25-54 years:** 42.65% (male 3,391 /female 3,332)

**55-64 years:** 9.76% (male 752 /female 787)

**65 years and over:** 10.44% (male 782 /female 863) (2018 est.)

### MEDIAN AGE:

total: 32.8 years

male: 31.9 years

female: 34 years (2018 est.)

country comparison to the world: 98

### POPULATION GROWTH RATE:

0.3% (2018 est.)

country comparison to the world: 171

### BIRTH RATE:

13 births/1,000 population (2018 est.)

country comparison to the world: 151

### DEATH RATE:

5.5 deaths/1,000 population (2018 est.)

country comparison to the world: 178

### NET MIGRATION RATE:

-4.7 migrant(s)/1,000 population (2017 est.)

note: there has been steady emigration from Wallis and Futuna to New Caledonia

country comparison to the world: 188

### URBANIZATION:

urban population: 0% of total population (2018)

rate of urbanization: 0% annual rate of change (2015-20 est.)

### MAJOR URBAN AREAS - POPULATION:

1,000 MATA-UTU (capital) (2018)

### SEX RATIO:

at birth: 1.05 male(s)/female (2017 est.)

0-14 years: 1.09 male(s)/female (2017 est.)

15-24 years: 1.11 male(s)/female (2017 est.)

25-54 years: 1.01 male(s)/female (2017 est.)

55-64 years: 0.97 male(s)/female (2017 est.)

65 years and over: 0.92 male(s)/female (2017 est.)

total population: 1.03 male(s)/female (2017 est.)

### INFANT MORTALITY RATE:

total: 4.3 deaths/1,000 live births (2018 est.)

male: 4.5 deaths/1,000 live births (2018 est.)

female: 4 deaths/1,000 live births (2018 est.)

country comparison to the world: 187

### LIFE EXPECTANCY AT BIRTH:

total population: 80 years (2018 est.)

male: 77 years (2018 est.)

female: 83.1 years (2018 est.)

country comparison to the world: 46

### TOTAL FERTILITY RATE:

1.72 children born/woman (2018 est.)

country comparison to the world: 169

### PHYSICIANS DENSITY:

1.1 physicians/1,000 population (2008)

### SANITATION FACILITY ACCESS:

improved:

rural: 96% of population (2008 est.)

total: 96% of population (2008 est.)

unimproved:

rural: 4% of population (2008 est.)

total: 4% of population (2008 est.)

### HIV/AIDS - ADULT PREVALENCE RATE:

NA

### HIV/AIDS - PEOPLE LIVING WITH HIV/AIDS:

NA

### HIV/AIDS - DEATHS:

NA

## GOVERNMENT :: WALLIS AND FUTUNA

### COUNTRY NAME:

conventional long form: Territory of the Wallis and Futuna Islands

conventional short form: Wallis and Futuna

local long form: Territoire des Iles Wallis et Futuna

local short form: Wallis et Futuna

former: Hoorn Islands is the former name of the Futuna Islands

etymology: Wallis Island is named after British Captain Samuel WALLIS who discovered it in 1767; Futuna is derived from the native word "futu," which is the name of the fish-poison tree found on the island

### DEPENDENCY STATUS:

overseas collectivity of France

### GOVERNMENT TYPE:

parliamentary democracy (Territorial Assembly); overseas collectivity of France

### CAPITAL:

name: Mata-Utu (on Ile Uvea)

geographic coordinates: 13 57 S, 171 56 W

time difference: UTC+12 (17 hours ahead of Washington, DC, during Standard Time)

### ADMINISTRATIVE DIVISIONS:

3 administrative precincts (circonscriptions, singular - circonscription) Alo, Sigave, Uvea

### INDEPENDENCE:

none (overseas collectivity of France)

### NATIONAL HOLIDAY:

Bastille Day, 14 July (1789)

### CONSTITUTION:

history: 4 October 1958 (French Constitution)

amendments: French constitution amendment procedures apply

### LEGAL SYSTEM:

French civil law

### CITIZENSHIP:

see France

### SUFFRAGE:

18 years of age; universal

### EXECUTIVE BRANCH:

chief of state: President Emmanuel MACRON (since 14 May 2017); represented by High Administrator Jean-Francis TREFFEL (since 6 February 2017)

head of government: President of the Territorial Assembly David VERGE (since 4 April 2017)

cabinet: Council of the Territory appointed by the high administrator on the advice of the Territorial Assembly

elections/appointments: French president elected by absolute majority popular vote in 2 rounds if needed for a 5-year term (eligible for a second term); high administrator appointed by the French president on the advice of the French Ministry of the Interior; the presidents of the Territorial Government and the Territorial Assembly elected by assembly members note: there are 3 traditional kings with limited powers

## LEGISLATIVE BRANCH:

description: unicameral Territorial Assembly or Assemblee Territoriale (20 seats - Wallis 13, Futuna 7; members directly elected in multi-seat constituencies by party-list proportional representation vote to serve 5-year terms) Wallis and Futuna indirectly elects 1 senator to the French Senate by an electoral college by absolute majority vote in 2 rounds if needed for a 6-year term, and 1 deputy directly elected to the French National Assembly by absolute majority vote for a 5-year term

elections: Territorial Assembly - last held on 26 March 2017 (next to be held in March 2022)

election results: Territorial Assembly - percent of vote by party - NA; seats by party - 2 members are elected from the list Fia gaue fakatahi kihe kaha'u e lelei and 1 each from 18 other lists; composition - men 14, women 6, percent of women 30%

French Senate - last held on 28 September 2014 (next to be held by September 2020) French National Assembly - last held on 11 June 2017 (next to be held in June 2022) French Senate - 1 seat: LR 1 French National Assembly - 1 seat: independent 1

## JUDICIAL BRANCH:

highest courts: Court of Assizes or Cour d'Assizes (consists of 1 judge; court hears primarily serious criminal cases); note - appeals beyond the Court of Assizes are heard before the Court of Appeal or Cour d'Appel, located in Noumea, New Caledonia

judge selection and term of office: NA

subordinate courts: courts of first instance; labor court; note - justice generally administered under French law by the high administrator, but the 3 traditional kings administer customary law, and there is a magistrate in Mata-Utu

## POLITICAL PARTIES AND LEADERS:

Left Radical Party or PRG [Sylvia PINEL] (formerly Radical Socialist Party or PRS and the Left Radical Movement or MRG) Lua Kae Tahi (Giscardians) Rally for Wallis and Futuna-The Republicans (Rassemblement pour Wallis and Futuna) or RPWF-LR [Clovis LOGOLOGOFOLAU] Socialist Party or PS Taumu'a Lelei [Soane Muni UHILA] Union Pour la Democratie Francaise or UDF

## INTERNATIONAL ORGANIZATION PARTICIPATION:

PIF (observer), SPC, UPU

## DIPLOMATIC REPRESENTATION IN THE US:

none (overseas collectivity of France)

## DIPLOMATIC REPRESENTATION FROM THE US:

none (overseas collectivity of France)

## FLAG DESCRIPTION:

unofficial, local flag has a red field with four white isosceles triangles in the middle, representing the three native kings of the islands and the French administrator; the apexes of the triangles are oriented inward and at right angles to each other; the flag of France, outlined in white on two sides, is in the upper hoist quadrant

note: the design is derived from an original red banner with a white cross pattee that was introduced in the 19th century by French missionaries; the flag of France is used for official occasions

## NATIONAL SYMBOL(S):

red saltire (Saint Andrew's Cross) on a white square on a red field; national colors: red, white

## NATIONAL ANTHEM:

note: as a territory of France, "La Marseillaise" is official (see France)

# ECONOMY :: WALLIS AND FUTUNA

## ECONOMY - OVERVIEW:

The economy is limited to traditional subsistence agriculture, with about 80% of labor force earnings coming from agriculture (coconuts and vegetables), livestock (mostly pigs), and fishing. However, roughly 70% of the labor force is employed in the public sector, although only about a third of the population is in salaried employment.

Revenues come from French Government subsidies, licensing of fishing rights to Japan and South Korea, import taxes, and remittances from expatriate workers in New Caledonia. France directly finances the public sector and health-care and education services. It also provides funding for key development projects in a range of areas, including infrastructure, economic development, environmental management, and health-care facilities.

A key concern for Wallis and Futuna is an aging population with consequent economic development issues. Very few people aged 18-30 live on the islands due to the limited formal employment opportunities. Improving job creation is a current priority for the territorial government.

## GDP (PURCHASING POWER PARITY):

$60 million (2004 est.)

country comparison to the world: 225

## GDP (OFFICIAL EXCHANGE RATE):

$195 million (2005) (2005)

## GDP - REAL GROWTH RATE:

NA

## GDP - PER CAPITA (PPP):

$3,800 (2004 est.)

country comparison to the world: 181

## GDP - COMPOSITION, BY END USE:

household consumption: 26% (2005)

government consumption: 54% (2005)

## GDP - COMPOSITION, BY SECTOR OF ORIGIN:

agriculture: NA

industry: NA

services: NA

## AGRICULTURE - PRODUCTS:

coconuts, breadfruit, yams, taro, bananas; pigs, goats; fish

## INDUSTRIES:

copra, handicrafts, fishing, lumber

## INDUSTRIAL PRODUCTION GROWTH RATE:

NA

## LABOR FORCE:

4,482 (2013)

country comparison to the world: 223

## LABOR FORCE - BY OCCUPATION:

agriculture: 74%

industry: 3%

services: 23% (2015 est.)

## UNEMPLOYMENT RATE:

8.8% (2013 est.)

12.2% (2008 est.)

country comparison to the world: 126

## POPULATION BELOW POVERTY LINE:

NA

**HOUSEHOLD INCOME OR CONSUMPTION BY PERCENTAGE SHARE:**

lowest 10%: NA

highest 10%: NA

**BUDGET:**

revenues: 32.54 million NA (2015 est.)

expenditures: 34.18 million NA (2015 est.)

**TAXES AND OTHER REVENUES:**

16.7% (of GDP) NA (2015 est.)

country comparison to the world: 175

**BUDGET SURPLUS (+) OR DEFICIT (-):**

-0.8% (of GDP) NA (2015 est.)

country comparison to the world: 70

**PUBLIC DEBT:**

5.6% of GDP (2004 est.)

note: offical data; data cover general government debt and include debt instruments issued (or owned) by government entities other than the treasury; the data include treasury debt held by foreign entities; the data include debt issued by subnational entities, as well as intragovernmental debt; intragovernmental debt consists of treasury borrowings from surpluses in the social funds, such as for retirement, medical care, and unemployment; debt instruments for the social funds are not sold at public auctions

country comparison to the world: 204

**FISCAL YEAR:**

calendar year

**INFLATION RATE (CONSUMER PRICES):**

0.9% (2015)

2.8% (2005)

country comparison to the world: 48

**EXPORTS:**

$47,450 (2004 est.)

country comparison to the world: 222

**EXPORTS - COMMODITIES:**

copra, chemicals, construction materials

**IMPORTS:**

$61.17 million (2004 est.)

country comparison to the world: 219

**IMPORTS - COMMODITIES:**

chemicals, machinery, consumer goods

**DEBT - EXTERNAL:**

$3.67 million (2004)

country comparison to the world: 201

**STOCK OF DIRECT FOREIGN INVESTMENT - AT HOME:**

(31 December 2009 est.)

**EXCHANGE RATES:**

Comptoirs Francais du Pacifique francs (XPF) per US dollar -

110.2 (2015 est.)

89.8 (2014 est.)

89.85 (2013 est.)

90.56 (2012 est.)

## COMMUNICATIONS :: WALLIS AND FUTUNA

**TELEPHONES - FIXED LINES:**

total subscriptions: 3,132 (July 2016 est.)

subscriptions per 100 inhabitants: 20 (July 2016 est.)

country comparison to the world: 208

**TELEPHONE SYSTEM:**

international: country code - 681

**BROADCAST MEDIA:**

the publicly owned French Overseas Network (RFO), which broadcasts to France's overseas departments, collectivites, and territories, is carried on the RFO Wallis and Fortuna TV and radio stations (2008)

**INTERNET COUNTRY CODE:**

.wf

**INTERNET USERS:**

total: 3,450 (July 2016 est.)

percent of population: 22.1% (July 2016 est.)

country comparison to the world: 218

## TRANSPORTATION :: WALLIS AND FUTUNA

**AIRPORTS:**

2 (2013)

country comparison to the world: 209

**AIRPORTS - WITH PAVED RUNWAYS:**

total: 2 (2013)

1,524 to 2,437 m: 1 (2013)

914 to 1,523 m: 1 (2013)

**PORTS AND TERMINALS:**

major seaport(s): Leava, Mata-Utu

## MILITARY AND SECURITY :: WALLIS AND FUTUNA

**MILITARY - NOTE:**

defense is the responsibility of France

## TRANSNATIONAL ISSUES :: WALLIS AND FUTUNA

**DISPUTES - INTERNATIONAL:**

none

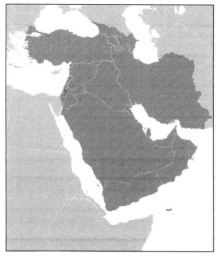

# MIDDLE EAST :: WEST BANK

## INTRODUCTION :: WEST BANK

### BACKGROUND:

From the early 16th century through 1917, the area now known as the West Bank fell under Ottoman rule. Following World War I, the Allied powers (France, UK, Russia) allocated the area to the British Mandate of Palestine. After World War II, the UN passed a resolution to establish two states within the Mandate, and designated a territory including what is now known as the West Bank as part of the proposed Arab state. During the 1948 Arab-Israeli War, the West Bank was captured by Transjordan (later renamed Jordan), which annexed the West Bank in 1950. In June 1967, Israel captured the West Bank and East Jerusalem during the 1967 Six-Day War. Israel transferred security and civilian responsibility for a number of Palestinian-populated areas of the West Bank and Gaza Strip to the Palestinian Authority (PA) under a series of agreements signed between 1993 and 1999, the so-called "Oslo Accords." Roughly 60% of the West Bank (excluding East Jerusalem) remains under Israeli military control. Follow-on negotiations to determine the permanent status of the West Bank and Gaza Strip stalled after the outbreak of an intifada in mid-2000. Since HAMAS's violent seizure of military and governmental institutions in the Gaza Strip in 2007, the PA has administered those areas of the West Bank under its control while Hamas maintains de facto control of Gaza. Fatah and HAMAS have made several attempts at reconciliation, but the factions have been unable to implement any agreements reached.

## GEOGRAPHY :: WEST BANK

### LOCATION:

Middle East, west of Jordan, east of Israel

### GEOGRAPHIC COORDINATES:

32 00 N, 35 15 E

### MAP REFERENCES:

Middle East

### AREA:

total: 5,860 sq km

land: 5,640 sq km

water: 220 sq km

note: includes West Bank, Latrun Salient, and the northwest quarter of the Dead Sea, but excludes Mt. Scopus; East Jerusalem and Jerusalem No Man's Land are also included only as a means of depicting the entire area occupied by Israel in 1967

country comparison to the world: 172

### AREA - COMPARATIVE:

slightly smaller than Delaware

### LAND BOUNDARIES:

total: 478 km

border countries (2): Israel 330 km, Jordan 148 km

### COASTLINE:

0 km (landlocked)

### MARITIME CLAIMS:

none (landlocked)

### CLIMATE:

temperate; temperature and precipitation vary with altitude, warm to hot summers, cool to mild winters

### TERRAIN:

mostly rugged, dissected upland in west, flat plains descending to Jordan River Valley to the east

### ELEVATION:

-431 m lowest point: Dead Sea

1020 highest point: Khallat al Batrakh

### NATURAL RESOURCES:

arable land

### LAND USE:

agricultural land: 43.3% (2011 est.)

arable land: 7.4% (2011 est.) / permanent crops: 11% (2011 est.) / permanent pasture: 24.9% (2011 est.)

forest: 1.5% (2011 est.)

other: 55.2% (2011 est.)

note: includes Gaza Strip

### IRRIGATED LAND:

240 sq km; note - includes Gaza Strip (2012)

### POPULATION DISTRIBUTION:

Palestinian settlements are primarily located in the central to western half of the territory; Jewish settlements are found in pockets throughout, particularly in the northeast, north-central, and around Jerusalem

### NATURAL HAZARDS:

droughts

### ENVIRONMENT - CURRENT ISSUES:
adequacy of freshwater supply; sewage treatment

### GEOGRAPHY - NOTE:
landlocked; highlands are main recharge area for Israel's coastal aquifers; there are about 380 Israeli civilian sites, including about 213 settlements and 132 small outpost communities in the West Bank and 35 sites in East Jerusalem (2017)

## PEOPLE AND SOCIETY :: WEST BANK

### POPULATION:
2,798,494 (July 2017 est.) (July 2018 est.)

note: approximately 391,000 Israeli settlers live in the West Bank (2016); approximately 201,200 Israeli settlers live in East Jerusalem (2014)

country comparison to the world: 140

### NATIONALITY:
noun: NA

adjective: NA

### ETHNIC GROUPS:
Palestinian Arab, Jewish, other

### LANGUAGES:
Arabic, Hebrew (spoken by Israeli settlers and many Palestinians), English (widely understood)

### RELIGIONS:
Muslim 80-85% (predominantly Sunni), Jewish 12-14%, Christian 1-2.5% (mainly Greek Orthodox), other, unaffiliated, unspecified <1% (2012 est.)

### AGE STRUCTURE:
0-14 years: 36.09% (male 518,376 /female 491,676)

15-24 years: 21.17% (male 302,474 /female 289,852)

25-54 years: 34.48% (male 489,559 /female 475,402)

55-64 years: 4.74% (male 68,317 /female 64,233)

65 years and over: 3.52% (male 44,662 /female 53,943) (2018 est.)

### DEPENDENCY RATIOS:
total dependency ratio: 75.8 (2015 est.)

youth dependency ratio: 70.5 (2015 est.)

elderly dependency ratio: 5.2 (2015 est.)

potential support ratio: 19.1 (2015 est.)

note: data represent Gaza Strip and the West Bank

### MEDIAN AGE:
total: 21.4 years

male: 21.2 years

female: 21.6 years (2018 est.)

country comparison to the world: 183

### POPULATION GROWTH RATE:
1.81% (2018 est.)

country comparison to the world: 56

### BIRTH RATE:
26 births/1,000 population (2018 est.)

country comparison to the world: 47

### DEATH RATE:
3.5 deaths/1,000 population (2018 est.)

country comparison to the world: 217

### NET MIGRATION RATE:
-4.5 migrant(s)/1,000 population (2017 est.)

country comparison to the world: 186

### POPULATION DISTRIBUTION:
Palestinian settlements are primarily located in the central to western half of the territory; Jewish settlements are found in pockets throughout, particularly in the northeast, north-central, and around Jerusalem

### URBANIZATION:
urban population: 76.2% of total population (2018)

rate of urbanization: 3% annual rate of change (2015-20 est.)

note: data represent Gaza Strip and the West Bank

### SEX RATIO:
at birth: 1.06 male(s)/female (2017 est.)

0-14 years: 1.05 male(s)/female (2017 est.)

15-24 years: 1.04 male(s)/female (2017 est.)

25-54 years: 1.03 male(s)/female (2017 est.)

55-64 years: 1.06 male(s)/female (2017 est.)

65 years and over: 0.73 male(s)/female (2017 est.)

total population: 1.04 male(s)/female (2017 est.)

### MATERNAL MORTALITY RATE:
45 deaths/100,000 live births (2015 est.)

note: data represent Gaza Strip and the West Bank

country comparison to the world: 100

### INFANT MORTALITY RATE:
total: 13.6 deaths/1,000 live births (2018 est.)

male: 15.3 deaths/1,000 live births (2018 est.)

female: 11.9 deaths/1,000 live births (2018 est.)

country comparison to the world: 104

### LIFE EXPECTANCY AT BIRTH:
total population: 75.4 years (2018 est.)

male: 73.4 years (2018 est.)

female: 77.6 years (2018 est.)

country comparison to the world: 108

### TOTAL FERTILITY RATE:
3.2 children born/woman (2018 est.)

country comparison to the world: 48

### CONTRACEPTIVE PREVALENCE RATE:
57.2% (includes Gaza Strip and the West Bank) (2014)

### PHYSICIANS DENSITY:
1.3 physicians/1,000 population (2014)

### HOSPITAL BED DENSITY:
1.26 beds/1,000 population (2015)

### DRINKING WATER SOURCE:
improved:

urban: 50.7% of population

rural: 81.5% of population

total: 58.4% of population

unimproved:

urban: 49.3% of population

rural: 18.5% of population

total: 41.6% of population (2015 est.)

note: includes Gaza Strip and the West Bank

### SANITATION FACILITY ACCESS:
improved:

urban: 93% of population (2015 est.)

rural: 90.2% of population (2015 est.)

total: 92.3% of population (2015 est.)

unimproved:

urban: 7% of population (2015 est.)

rural: 9.8% of population (2015 est.)

total: 7.7% of population (2015 est.)

note: note includes Gaza Strip and the West Bank

**HIV/AIDS - ADULT PREVALENCE RATE:**

NA

**HIV/AIDS - PEOPLE LIVING WITH HIV/AIDS:**

NA

**HIV/AIDS - DEATHS:**

NA

**CHILDREN UNDER THE AGE OF 5 YEARS UNDERWEIGHT:**

1.4% (2014)

note: estimate is for Gaza Strip and the West Bank

country comparison to the world: 118

**EDUCATION EXPENDITURES:**

5.7% of GDP (2015)

note: includes Gaza Strip and the West Bank

country comparison to the world: 47

**LITERACY:**

definition: age 15 and over can read and write (2016 est.)

total population: 96.9% (2016 est.)

male: 98.6% (2016 est.)

female: 95.2% (2016 est.)

note: estimates are for Gaza and the West Bank

**SCHOOL LIFE EXPECTANCY (PRIMARY TO TERTIARY EDUCATION):**

total: 13 years (2015)

male: 12 years (2015)

female: 14 years (2015)

note: data represent Gaza Strip and the West Bank

**UNEMPLOYMENT, YOUTH AGES 15-24:**

total: 40.7% (2015 est.)

male: 36.4% (2015 est.)

female: 60.8% (2015 est.)

note: includes Gaza Strip

country comparison to the world: 12

## GOVERNMENT :: WEST BANK

**COUNTRY NAME:**

conventional long form: none

conventional short form: West Bank

etymology: name refers to the location of the region - occupied and administered by Jordan after 1948 - that fell on the far side (west bank) of the Jordan River in relation to Jordan proper; the designation was retained following the 1967 Six-Day War and the subsequent changes in government

## ECONOMY :: WEST BANK

**ECONOMY - OVERVIEW:**

In 2017, the economic outlook in the West Bank - the larger of the two areas comprising the Palestinian Territories – remained fragile, as security concerns and political friction slowed economic growth. Unemployment in the West Bank remained high at 19.0% in the third quarter of 2017, only slightly better than 19.6% at the same point the previous year, while the labor force participation rate remained flat, year-on-year.

Longstanding Israeli restrictions on imports, exports, and movement of goods and people continue to disrupt labor and trade flows and the territory's industrial capacity, and constrain private sector development. The PA's budget benefited from an effort to improve tax collection, coupled with lower spending in 2017, but the PA for the foreseeable future will continue to rely heavily on donor aid for its budgetary needs and infrastructure development.

**GDP (PURCHASING POWER PARITY):**

$21.22 billion (2014 est.)

$20.15 billion (2013 est.)

$19.95 billion (2012 est.)

note: data are in 2014 US dollars; includes Gaza Strip

country comparison to the world: 147

**GDP (OFFICIAL EXCHANGE RATE):**

$9.828 billion (2014 est.) (2014 est.)

note: excludes Gaza Strip

**GDP - REAL GROWTH RATE:**

5.3% (2014 est.)

1% (2013 est.)

6% (2012 est.)

note: excludes Gaza Strip

country comparison to the world: 45

**GDP - PER CAPITA (PPP):**

$4,300 (2014 est.)

$4,400 (2013 est.)

$4,600 (2012 est.)

note: includes Gaza Strip

country comparison to the world: 175

**GROSS NATIONAL SAVING:**

7.8% of GDP (2014 est.)

9.5% of GDP (2013 est.)

5% of GDP (2012 est.)

note: includes Gaza Strip

country comparison to the world: 170

**GDP - COMPOSITION, BY END USE:**

household consumption: 91.3% (2017 est.)

government consumption: 26.7% (2017 est.)

investment in fixed capital: 23% (2017 est.)

investment in inventories: 0% (2017 est.)

exports of goods and services: 20% (2017 est.)

imports of goods and services: -61% (2017 est.)

note: excludes Gaza Strip

**GDP - COMPOSITION, BY SECTOR OF ORIGIN:**

agriculture: 2.9% (2017 est.)

industry: 19.5% (2017 est.)

services: 77.6% (2017 est.)

note: excludes Gaza Strip

**AGRICULTURE - PRODUCTS:**

olives, citrus fruit, vegetables; beef, dairy products

**INDUSTRIES:**

small-scale manufacturing, quarrying, textiles, soap, olive-wood carvings, and mother-of-pearl souvenirs

**INDUSTRIAL PRODUCTION GROWTH RATE:**

2.2% (2017 est.)

note: includes Gaza Strip

country comparison to the world: 127

**LABOR FORCE:**

1.24 million (2017 est.)

note: excludes Gaza Strip

country comparison to the world: 139

**LABOR FORCE - BY OCCUPATION:**

agriculture: 11.5%

industry: 34.4%

services: 54.1% (2013 est.)

note: excludes Gaza Strip

**UNEMPLOYMENT RATE:**

27.9% (2017 est.)

27% (2016 est.)

note: excludes Gaza Strip

country comparison to the world: 202

**POPULATION BELOW POVERTY LINE:**

18% (2011 est.)

**HOUSEHOLD INCOME OR CONSUMPTION BY PERCENTAGE SHARE:**

lowest 10%: 28.2% (2009 est.)

highest 10%: 28.2% (2009 est.)

note: includes Gaza Strip

**DISTRIBUTION OF FAMILY INCOME - GINI INDEX:**

34.5 (2009 est.)

38.7 (2007 est.)

note: includes Gaza Strip

country comparison to the world: 103

**BUDGET:**

revenues: 1.314 billion (2017 est.)

expenditures: 1.278 billion (2017 est.)

note: includes Palestinian Authority expenditures in the Gaza Strip

**TAXES AND OTHER REVENUES:**

13.4% (of GDP) (2017 est.)

country comparison to the world: 207

**BUDGET SURPLUS (+) OR DEFICIT (-):**

0.4% (of GDP) (2017 est.)

country comparison to the world: 39

**PUBLIC DEBT:**

24.4% of GDP (2014 est.)

23.8% of GDP (2013 est.)

country comparison to the world: 177

**FISCAL YEAR:**

calendar year

**INFLATION RATE (CONSUMER PRICES):**

0.2% (2017 est.)

-0.2% (2016 est.)

note: excludes Gaza Strip

country comparison to the world: 18

**COMMERCIAL BANK PRIME LENDING RATE:**

5.8% (31 December 2017 est.)

6.15% (31 December 2016 est.)

country comparison to the world: 128

**STOCK OF NARROW MONEY:**

$416.5 million (31 December 2017 est.)

$317.8 million (31 December 2016 est.)

country comparison to the world: 176

**STOCK OF BROAD MONEY:**

$416.5 million (31 December 2017 est.)

$317.8 million (31 December 2016 est.)

country comparison to the world: 180

**STOCK OF DOMESTIC CREDIT:**

$2.211 billion (31 December 2017 est.)

$1.712 billion (31 December 2016 est.)

country comparison to the world: 147

**MARKET VALUE OF PUBLICLY TRADED SHARES:**

$3.339 billion (31 December 2015 est.)

$3.187 billion (31 December 2014 est.)

$3.247 billion (31 December 2013 est.)

country comparison to the world: 91

**CURRENT ACCOUNT BALANCE:**

-$1.444 billion (2017 est.)

-$1.348 billion (2016 est.)

country comparison to the world: 153

**EXPORTS:**

$2.126 billion (2017 est.)

$1.827 billion (2016 est.)

note: excludes Gaza Strip

country comparison to the world: 139

**EXPORTS - COMMODITIES:**

stone, olives, fruit, vegetables, limestone

**IMPORTS:**

$6.565 billion (2017 est.)

$6.207 billion (2016 est.)

note: data include the Gaza Strip

country comparison to the world: 118

**IMPORTS - COMMODITIES:**

food, consumer goods, construction materials, petroleum, chemicals

**RESERVES OF FOREIGN EXCHANGE AND GOLD:**

$0 (31 December 2017 est.)

$583 million (31 December 2015 est.)

country comparison to the world: 195

**DEBT - EXTERNAL:**

$1.662 billion (31 March 2016 est.)

$1.467 billion (31 March 2015 est.)

note: data include the Gaza Strip

country comparison to the world: 158

**EXCHANGE RATES:**

new Israeli shekels (ILS) per US dollar -

3.606 (2017 est.)

3.841 (2016 est.)

3.841 (2015 est.)

3.8869 (2014 est.)

3.5779 (2013 est.)

## ENERGY :: WEST BANK

**ELECTRICITY ACCESS:**

population without electricity: 80,930 (2012)

electrification - total population: 98% (2012)

electrification - urban areas: 99% (2012)

electrification - rural areas: 93% (2012)

note: data for West Bank and Gaza Strip combined

**ELECTRICITY - PRODUCTION:**

1.093 billion kWh (2016 est.)

country comparison to the world: 148

**ELECTRICITY - CONSUMPTION:**

6.489 billion kWh (2016 est.)

country comparison to the world: 110

**ELECTRICITY - EXPORTS:**

0 kWh (2016)

country comparison to the world: 217

**ELECTRICITY - IMPORTS:**

5.473 billion kWh (2016 est.)

country comparison to the world: 36

**ELECTRICITY - INSTALLED GENERATING CAPACITY:**

170,000 kW (2016 est.)

note: includes Gaza Strip

country comparison to the world: 170

**ELECTRICITY - FROM FOSSIL FUELS:**

78% of total installed capacity (2016 est.)

country comparison to the world: 91

**ELECTRICITY - FROM NUCLEAR FUELS:**

0% of total installed capacity (2017 est.)

country comparison to the world: 211

**ELECTRICITY - FROM HYDROELECTRIC PLANTS:**

0% of total installed capacity (2017 est.)

country comparison to the world: 213

**ELECTRICITY - FROM OTHER RENEWABLE SOURCES:**

22% of total installed capacity (2017 est.)

country comparison to the world: 34

**CRUDE OIL - PRODUCTION:**

0 bbl/day (2017 est.)

country comparison to the world: 214
**CRUDE OIL - EXPORTS:**
0 bbl/day (2015 est.)
country comparison to the world: 215
**CRUDE OIL - IMPORTS:**
0 bbl/day (2015 est.)
country comparison to the world: 215
**CRUDE OIL - PROVED RESERVES:**
0 bbl (1 January 2018)
country comparison to the world: 212
**REFINED PETROLEUM PRODUCTS - PRODUCTION:**
0 bbl/day (2015 est.)
country comparison to the world: 215
**REFINED PETROLEUM PRODUCTS - CONSUMPTION:**
24,000 bbl/day (2016 est.)
country comparison to the world: 131
**REFINED PETROLEUM PRODUCTS - EXPORTS:**
19 bbl/day (2015 est.)
country comparison to the world: 123
**REFINED PETROLEUM PRODUCTS - IMPORTS:**
22,740 bbl/day (2015 est.)
country comparison to the world: 113
**NATURAL GAS - PRODUCTION:**
0 cu m (2017 est.)
country comparison to the world: 214
**NATURAL GAS - CONSUMPTION:**
0 cu m (2017 est.)
country comparison to the world: 213
**NATURAL GAS - EXPORTS:**
0 cu m (2017 est.)
country comparison to the world: 212
**NATURAL GAS - IMPORTS:**
0 cu m (2017 est.)
country comparison to the world: 212
**NATURAL GAS - PROVED RESERVES:**
0 cu m (1 January 2014 est.)
country comparison to the world: 207
**CARBON DIOXIDE EMISSIONS FROM CONSUMPTION OF ENERGY:**
3.113 million Mt (2017 est.)
country comparison to the world: 146

## COMMUNICATIONS :: WEST BANK

**TELEPHONES - FIXED LINES:**
total subscriptions: 472,293 (includes Gaza Strip) (2017 est.)
subscriptions per 100 inhabitants: 17 (includes Gaza Strip) (2017 est.)
country comparison to the world: 98
**TELEPHONES - MOBILE CELLULAR:**
total subscriptions: 4,135,363 (includes Gaza Strip) (2017 est.)
subscriptions per 100 inhabitants: 150 (includes Gaza Strip) (2017 est.)
country comparison to the world: 126
**TELEPHONE SYSTEM:**
general assessment: continuing political and economic instability has impeded liberalization of the telecommunications industry (2018)
domestic: Israeli company BEZEK and the Palestinian company PALTEL are responsible for fixed-line services; two Palestinian cellular providers, JAWWAL and WATANIYA MOBILE, launched 3G mobile networks in the West Bank in January 2018 after Israel lifted its ban (2018)
international: country code - 970; 1 international switch in Ramallah (2018)
**BROADCAST MEDIA:**
the Palestinian Authority operates 1 TV and 1 radio station; about 20 private TV and 40 radio stations; both Jordanian TV and satellite TV are accessible (2013)
**INTERNET COUNTRY CODE:**
.ps note - same as Gaza Strip
**INTERNET USERS:**
total: 2.673 million (includes Gaza Strip) (July 2016 est.)
percent of population: 57.4% (July 2016 est.)
country comparison to the world: 102
**BROADBAND - FIXED SUBSCRIPTIONS:**
total: 371,299 (2017 est.)
subscriptions per 100 inhabitants: 14 (2017 est.)
note: includes Gaza Strip
country comparison to the world: 89

## TRANSPORTATION :: WEST BANK

**AIRPORTS:**
2 (2013)
country comparison to the world: 210
**AIRPORTS - WITH PAVED RUNWAYS:**
total: 2 (2013)
1,524 to 2,437 m: 1 (2013)
under 914 m: 1 (2013)
**HELIPORTS:**
1 (2013)
**ROADWAYS:**
total: 4,686 km (2010)
paved: 4,686 km (2010)
note: includes Gaza Strip
country comparison to the world: 153

## MILITARY AND SECURITY :: WEST BANK

**MILITARY BRANCHES:**
in accordance with the Interim Agreement, the PA is not permitted a conventional military but can maintain security forces; PA security forces have operated almost exclusively in the West Bank since Hamas seized power in the Gaza Strip in 2007

## TERRORISM :: WEST BANK

**TERRORIST GROUPS - HOME BASED:**

Kahane Chai (Kach):
aim(s): restore the biblical state of Israel; expel Arabs from Israel's biblical lands
area(s) of operation: present in West Bank Jewish settlements, especially the Qiryat Arba' settlement in Hebron, where operatives have conducted bombings and shootings against Muslim and Christian Palestinians; operationally inactive in recent years (April 2018)

**TERRORIST GROUPS - FOREIGN BASED:**

HAMAS:
aim(s): grow its political and operational presence in the West Bank
area(s) of operation: mostly political activity; small cells scattered throughout the West Bank for militant and illicit finance purposes (April 2018)

Palestine Islamic Jihad (PIJ):
aim(s): enhance its staging capabilities in the West Bank to launch attacks against Israel
area(s) of operation: mostly political activity; strives to maintain an operational presence (April 2018)

Palestine Liberation Front (PLF):
aim(s): enhance its networks in the

West Bank and, ultimately, destroy the state of Israel; establish a secular, Marxist Palestinian state with Jerusalem as its capital
**area(s) of operation:** maintains a recruitment and training presence in some of the West Bank's refugee camps (April 2018)

**Popular Front for the Liberation of Palestine (PFLP):**
**aim(s):** bolster its recruitment networks in the West Bank
**area(s) of operation:** mostly political activity, maintains a recruitment presence targeting youths (April 2018)

# TRANSNATIONAL ISSUES :: WEST BANK

## DISPUTES - INTERNATIONAL:

the current status of the West Bank is subject to the Israeli-Palestinian Interim Agreement - permanent status to be determined through further negotiationIsrael continues construction of a "seam line" separation barrier along parts of the Green Line and within the West BankIsrael withdrew from Gaza and four settlements in the northern West Bank in August 2005since 1948, about 350 peacekeepers from the UN Truce Supervision Organization (UNTSO), headquartered in Jerusalem, monitor ceasefires, supervise armistice agreements, prevent isolated incidents from escalating, and assist other UN personnel in the region

## REFUGEES AND INTERNALLY DISPLACED PERSONS:

**refugees (country of origin):** 809,738 (Palestinian refugees) (2017)

**IDPs:** 131,000 (includes persons displaced within the Gaza strip due to the intensification of the Israeli-Palestinian conflict since June 2014 and other Palestinian IDPs in the Gaza Strip and West Bank who fled as long ago as 1967, although confirmed cumulative data do not go back beyond 2006) (2017)

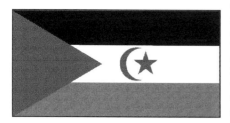

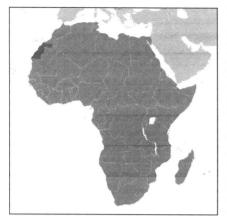

# AFRICA :: WESTERN SAHARA

## INTRODUCTION :: WESTERN SAHARA

### BACKGROUND:

Western Sahara is a non-self governing territory on the northwest coast of Africa bordered by Morocco, Mauritania, and Algeria. After Spain withdrew from its former colony of Spanish Sahara in 1976, Morocco annexed the northern two-thirds of Western Sahara and claimed the rest of the territory in 1979, following Mauritania's withdrawal. A guerrilla war with the Polisario Front contesting Morocco's sovereignty ended in a 1991 cease-fire and the establishment of a UN peacekeeping operation. As part of this effort, the UN sought to offer a choice to the peoples of Western Sahara between independence (favored by the Polisario Front) or integration into Morocco. A proposed referendum never took place due to lack of agreement on voter eligibility. The approximately 1,600 km- (almost 1,000 mi-) long defensive sand berm, built by the Moroccans from 1980 to 1987 and running the length of the territory, continues to separate the opposing forces with Morocco controlling the roughly three-quarters of the territory west of the berm. There are periodic ethnic tensions between the native Sahrawi population and Moroccan immigrants. Morocco maintains a heavy security presence in the territory.

## GEOGRAPHY :: WESTERN SAHARA

### LOCATION:
Northern Africa, bordering the North Atlantic Ocean, between Mauritania and Morocco

### GEOGRAPHIC COORDINATES:
24 30 N, 13 00 W

### MAP REFERENCES:
Africa

### AREA:
total: 266,000 sq km
land: 266,000 sq km
water: 0 sq km
country comparison to the world: 79

### AREA - COMPARATIVE:
about the size of Colorado

### LAND BOUNDARIES:
total: 2,049 km
border countries (3): Algeria 41 km, Mauritania 1564 km, Morocco 444 km

### COASTLINE:
1,110 km

### MARITIME CLAIMS:
contingent upon resolution of sovereignty issue

### CLIMATE:
hot, dry desert; rain is rare; cold offshore air currents produce fog and heavy dew

### TERRAIN:
mostly low, flat desert with large areas of rocky or sandy surfaces rising to small mountains in south and northeast

### ELEVATION:
mean elevation: 256 m
elevation extremes: -55 m lowest point: Sebjet Tah
805 highest point: unnamed elevation

### NATURAL RESOURCES:
phosphates, iron ore

### LAND USE:
agricultural land: 18.8% (2011 est.)
arable land: 0% (2011 est.) / permanent crops: 0% (2011 est.) / permanent pasture: 18.8% (2011 est.)
forest: 2.7% (2011 est.)
other: 78.5% (2011 est.)

### IRRIGATED LAND:
0 sq km (2012)

### POPULATION DISTRIBUTION:
most of the population lives in the two-thirds of the area west of the berm (Moroccan-occupied) that divides the territory; about 40% of that populace resides in Laayoune

### NATURAL HAZARDS:
hot, dry, dust/sand-laden sirocco wind can occur during winter and spring; widespread harmattan haze exists 60% of time, often severely restricting visibility

### ENVIRONMENT - CURRENT ISSUES:
desertification; overgrazing; sparse water and lack of arable land

### GEOGRAPHY - NOTE:
the waters off the coast are particularly rich fishing areas

## PEOPLE AND SOCIETY :: WESTERN SAHARA

### POPULATION:
619,551 (July 2018 est.)
note: estimate is based on projections by age, sex, fertility, mortality, and migration; fertility and mortality are based on data from neighboring countries
country comparison to the world: 168

**NATIONALITY:**

noun: Sahrawi(s), Sahraoui(s)

adjective: Sahrawi, Sahrawian, Sahraouian

**ETHNIC GROUPS:**

Arab, Berber

**LANGUAGES:**

Standard Arabic, Hassaniya Arabic, Moroccan Arabic, Berber, Spanish, French

**RELIGIONS:**

Muslim

**DEMOGRAPHIC PROFILE:**

Western Sahara is a non-self governing territory; approximately 75% is under Moroccan control. It was inhabited almost entirely by Sahrawi pastoral nomads until the mid-20th century. Their traditional vast migratory ranges, based on following unpredictable rainfall, did not coincide with colonial and later international borders. Since the 1930s, most Sahrawis have been compelled to adopt a sedentary lifestyle and to live in urban settings as a result of fighting, the presence of minefields, job opportunities in the phosphate industry, prolonged drought, the closure of Western Sahara's border with Mauritania from 1979-2002, and the construction of the defensive berm separating Moroccan- and Polisario-controlled (Sahrawi liberalization movement) areas. Morocco supported rapid urbanization to facilitate surveillance and security.

Today more than 80% of Western Sahara's population lives in urban areas; more than 40% live in the administrative center Laayoune. Moroccan immigration has altered the composition and dramatically increased the size of Western Sahara's population. Morocco maintains a large military presence in Western Sahara and has encouraged its citizens to settle there, offering bonuses, pay raises, and food subsidies to civil servants and a tax exemption, in order to integrate Western Sahara into the Moroccan Kingdom and, Sahrawis contend, to marginalize the native population.

Western Saharan Sahrawis have been migrating to Europe, principally to former colonial ruler Spain, since the 1950s. Many who moved to refugee camps in Tindouf, Algeria, also have migrated to Spain and Italy, usually alternating between living in cities abroad with periods back at the camps. The Polisario claims that the population of the Tindouf camps is about 155,000, but this figure may include thousands of Arabs and Tuaregs from neighboring countries. Because international organizations have been unable to conduct an independent census in Tindouf, the UNHCR bases its aid on a figure of 90,000 refugees. Western Saharan coastal towns emerged as key migration transit points (for reaching Spain's Canary Islands) in the mid-1990s, when Spain's and Italy's tightening of visa restrictions and EU pressure on Morocco and other North African countries to control illegal migration pushed sub-Saharan African migrants to shift their routes to the south.

**AGE STRUCTURE:**

0-14 years: 36.93% (male 115,703 /female 113,121)

15-24 years: 19.49% (male 60,793 /female 59,948)

25-54 years: 34.52% (male 105,420 /female 108,462)

55-64 years: 5.11% (male 14,773 /female 16,880)

65 years and over: 3.95% (male 10,787 /female 13,664) (2018 est.)

**DEPENDENCY RATIOS:**

total dependency ratio: 45 (2015 est.)

youth dependency ratio: 41.4 (2015 est.)

elderly dependency ratio: 3.7 (2015 est.)

potential support ratio: 27.1 (2015 est.)

**MEDIAN AGE:**

total: 21.5 years

male: 21 years

female: 21.9 years (2018 est.)

country comparison to the world: 181

**POPULATION GROWTH RATE:**

2.64% (2018 est.)

country comparison to the world: 17

**BIRTH RATE:**

28.9 births/1,000 population (2018 est.)

country comparison to the world: 41

**DEATH RATE:**

7.9 deaths/1,000 population (2018 est.)

country comparison to the world: 95

**POPULATION DISTRIBUTION:**

most of the population lives in the two-thirds of the area west of the berm (Moroccan-occupied) that divides the territory; about 40% of that populace resides in Laayoune

**URBANIZATION:**

urban population: 86.7% of total population (2018)

rate of urbanization: 2.61% annual rate of change (2015-20 est.)

**MAJOR URBAN AREAS - POPULATION:**

232,000 Laayoune (2018)

**SEX RATIO:**

at birth: 1.03 male(s)/female (2017 est.)

0-14 years: 1.02 male(s)/female (2017 est.)

15-24 years: 1.01 male(s)/female (2017 est.)

25-54 years: 0.97 male(s)/female (2017 est.)

55-64 years: 0.87 male(s)/female (2017 est.)

65 years and over: 0.78 male(s)/female (2017 est.)

total population: 0.99 male(s)/female (2017 est.)

**INFANT MORTALITY RATE:**

total: 50.5 deaths/1,000 live births (2018 est.)

male: 55.3 deaths/1,000 live births (2018 est.)

female: 45.6 deaths/1,000 live births (2018 est.)

country comparison to the world: 27

**LIFE EXPECTANCY AT BIRTH:**

total population: 63.8 years (2018 est.)

male: 61.4 years (2018 est.)

female: 66.2 years (2018 est.)

country comparison to the world: 195

**TOTAL FERTILITY RATE:**

3.79 children born/woman (2018 est.)

country comparison to the world: 40

**HIV/AIDS - ADULT PREVALENCE RATE:**

NA

**HIV/AIDS - PEOPLE LIVING WITH HIV/AIDS:**

NA

**HIV/AIDS - DEATHS:**

NA

# GOVERNMENT :: WESTERN SAHARA

**COUNTRY NAME:**

conventional long form: none

conventional short form: Western Sahara

former: Rio de Oro, Saguia el Hamra, Spanish Sahara

etymology: self-descriptive name specifying the territory's western location on the African continent's vast desert

**GOVERNMENT TYPE:**

legal status of territory and issue of sovereignty unresolved - territory contested by Morocco and Polisario Front (Popular Front for the Liberation of the Saguia el Hamra and Rio de Oro), which in February 1976 formally proclaimed a government-in-exile of the Sahrawi Arab Democratic Republic (SADR), near Tindouf, Algeria, was led by President Mohamed ABDELAZIZ until his death in May 2016; current President Brahim GHALI elected in July 2016; territory partitioned between Morocco and Mauritania in April 1976 when Spain withdrew, with Morocco acquiring northern two-thirds; Mauritania, under pressure from Polisario guerrillas, abandoned all claims to its portion in August 1979; Morocco moved to occupy that sector shortly thereafter and has since asserted administrative control; the Polisario's government-in-exile was seated as an Organization of African Unity (OAU) member in 1984 - Morocco between 1980 and 1987 built a fortified sand berm delineating the roughly 75% of Western Sahara west of the barrier that currently is controlled by Morocco; guerrilla activities continued sporadically until a UN-monitored cease-fire was implemented on 6 September 1991 (Security Council Resolution 690) by the United Nations Mission for the Referendum in Western Sahara (MINURSO)

**CAPITAL:**

time difference: UTC 0 (5 hours ahead of Washington, DC, during Standard Time)

daylight saving time: +1hr, begins last Sunday in March; ends last Sunday in October

**ADMINISTRATIVE DIVISIONS:**

none officially; the territory west of the Moroccan berm falls under de facto Moroccan control; Morocco claims the territory of Western Sahara, the political status of which is considered undetermined by the US Government; portions of the regions Guelmim-Es Smara and Laayoune-Boujdour-Sakia El Hamra, as claimed by Morocco, lie within Western Sahara; Morocco also claims Oued Eddahab-Lagouira, another region that falls entirely within Western Sahara

**SUFFRAGE:**

none; (residents of Moroccan-controlled Western Sahara participate in Moroccan elections)

**EXECUTIVE BRANCH:**

none

**INTERNATIONAL ORGANIZATION PARTICIPATION:**

AU, CAN (observer), WFTU (NGOs)

**DIPLOMATIC REPRESENTATION IN THE US:**

none

**DIPLOMATIC REPRESENTATION FROM THE US:**

none

# ECONOMY :: WESTERN SAHARA

**ECONOMY - OVERVIEW:**

Western Sahara has a small market-based economy whose main industries are fishing, phosphate mining, tourism, and pastoral nomadism. The territory's arid desert climate makes sedentary agriculture difficult, and much of its food is imported. The Moroccan Government administers Western Sahara's economy and is a key source of employment, infrastructure development, and social spending in the territory.

Western Sahara's unresolved legal status makes the exploitation of its natural resources a contentious issue between Morocco and the Polisario. Morocco and the EU in December 2013 finalized a four-year agreement allowing European vessels to fish off the coast of Morocco, including disputed waters off the coast of Western Sahara. As of April 2018, Moroccan and EU authorities were negotiating an amendment to renew the agreement.

Oil has never been found in Western Sahara in commercially significant quantities, but Morocco and the Polisario have quarreled over rights to authorize and benefit from oil exploration in the territory. Western Sahara's main long-term economic challenge is the development of a more diverse set of industries capable of providing greater employment and income to the territory. However, following King MOHAMMED VI's November 2015 visit to Western Sahara, the Government of Morocco announced a series of investments aimed at spurring economic activity in the region, while the General Confederation of Moroccan Enterprises announced a $609 million investment initiative in the region in March 2015.

**GDP (PURCHASING POWER PARITY):**

$906.5 million (2007 est.)

country comparison to the world: 205

**GDP (OFFICIAL EXCHANGE RATE):**

NA

**GDP - REAL GROWTH RATE:**

NA

**GDP - PER CAPITA (PPP):**

$2,500 (2007 est.)

country comparison to the world: 198

**GDP - COMPOSITION, BY SECTOR OF ORIGIN:**

agriculture: NA (2007 est.)

industry: NA (2007 est.)

services: 40% (2007 est.)

**AGRICULTURE - PRODUCTS:**

fruits and vegetables (grown in the few oases); camels, sheep, goats (kept by nomads); fish

**INDUSTRIES:**

phosphate mining, handicrafts

**INDUSTRIAL PRODUCTION GROWTH RATE:**

NA

**LABOR FORCE:**

144,000 (2010 est.)

country comparison to the world: 178

**LABOR FORCE - BY OCCUPATION:**

agriculture: 50%

industry: 50%

industry and services: 50% (2005 est.)

**UNEMPLOYMENT RATE:**

NA

**POPULATION BELOW POVERTY LINE:**

NA

**HOUSEHOLD INCOME OR CONSUMPTION BY PERCENTAGE SHARE:**

lowest 10%: NA

highest 10%: NA

**BUDGET:**

revenues: NA

expenditures: NA

**TAXES AND OTHER REVENUES:**

NA

**BUDGET SURPLUS (+) OR DEFICIT (-):**

NA

**FISCAL YEAR:**

calendar year

**INFLATION RATE (CONSUMER PRICES):**

NA

**EXPORTS:**

NA

**EXPORTS - COMMODITIES:**

phosphates 62% (2012 est.)

**IMPORTS:**

NA

**IMPORTS - COMMODITIES:**

fuel for fishing fleet, foodstuffs

**DEBT - EXTERNAL:**

NA

**EXCHANGE RATES:**

Moroccan dirhams (MAD) per US dollar -

9.639 (2017 est.)

9.7351 (2016 est.)

9.7351 (2015)

9.7351 (2014 est.)

8.3798 (2013 est.)

## ENERGY :: WESTERN SAHARA

**ELECTRICITY - PRODUCTION:**

0 kWh NA (2016 est.)

country comparison to the world: 220

**ELECTRICITY - CONSUMPTION:**

0 kWh (2016 est.)

country comparison to the world: 219

**ELECTRICITY - EXPORTS:**

0 kWh (2016 est.)

country comparison to the world: 218

**ELECTRICITY - IMPORTS:**

0 kWh (2016 est.)

country comparison to the world: 218

**ELECTRICITY - INSTALLED GENERATING CAPACITY:**

58,000 kW (2016 est.)

country comparison to the world: 188

**ELECTRICITY - FROM FOSSIL FUELS:**

100% of total installed capacity (2016 est.)

country comparison to the world: 22

**ELECTRICITY - FROM NUCLEAR FUELS:**

0% of total installed capacity (2017 est.)

country comparison to the world: 212

**ELECTRICITY - FROM HYDROELECTRIC PLANTS:**

0% of total installed capacity (2017 est.)

country comparison to the world: 214

**ELECTRICITY - FROM OTHER RENEWABLE SOURCES:**

0% of total installed capacity (2017 est.)

country comparison to the world: 214

**CRUDE OIL - PRODUCTION:**

0 bbl/day (2017 est.)

country comparison to the world: 215

**CRUDE OIL - EXPORTS:**

0 bbl/day (2015 est.)

country comparison to the world: 216

**CRUDE OIL - IMPORTS:**

0 bbl/day (2015 est.)

country comparison to the world: 216

**CRUDE OIL - PROVED RESERVES:**

0 bbl (1 January 2018 est.)

country comparison to the world: 213

**REFINED PETROLEUM PRODUCTS - PRODUCTION:**

0 bbl/day (2015 est.)

country comparison to the world: 216

**REFINED PETROLEUM PRODUCTS - CONSUMPTION:**

1,700 bbl/day (2016 est.)

country comparison to the world: 197

**REFINED PETROLEUM PRODUCTS - EXPORTS:**

0 bbl/day (2015 est.)

country comparison to the world: 216

**REFINED PETROLEUM PRODUCTS - IMPORTS:**

1,702 bbl/day (2015 est.)

country comparison to the world: 193

**NATURAL GAS - PRODUCTION:**

0 cu m (2017 est.)

country comparison to the world: 215

**NATURAL GAS - CONSUMPTION:**

0 cu m (2017 est.)

country comparison to the world: 214

**NATURAL GAS - EXPORTS:**

0 cu m (2017 est.)

country comparison to the world: 213

**NATURAL GAS - IMPORTS:**

0 cu m (2017 est.)

country comparison to the world: 213

**NATURAL GAS - PROVED RESERVES:**

0 cu m (1 January 2014 est.)

country comparison to the world: 208

**CARBON DIOXIDE EMISSIONS FROM CONSUMPTION OF ENERGY:**

268,400 Mt (2017 est.)

country comparison to the world: 194

## COMMUNICATIONS :: WESTERN SAHARA

**TELEPHONE SYSTEM:**

general assessment: sparse and limited system (2015)

international: country code - 212; tied into Morocco's system by microwave radio relay, tropospheric scatter, and satellite; satellite earth stations - 2 Intelsat (Atlantic Ocean) linked to Rabat, Morocco (2015)

**BROADCAST MEDIA:**

Morocco's state-owned broadcaster, Radio-Television Marocaine (RTM), operates a radio service from Laayoune and relays TV service; a Polisario-backed radio station also broadcasts (2008)

**INTERNET COUNTRY CODE:**

.eh

## TRANSPORTATION :: WESTERN SAHARA

**AIRPORTS:**

6 (2013)

country comparison to the world: 178

**AIRPORTS - WITH PAVED RUNWAYS:**

total: 3 (2013)

**2,438 to 3,047 m:** 3 (2013)

**AIRPORTS - WITH UNPAVED RUNWAYS:**

total: 3 (2013)

**1,524 to 2,437 m:** 1 (2013)

**914 to 1,523 m:** 1 (2013)

under 914 m: 1 (2013)

**PORTS AND TERMINALS:**

major seaport(s): Ad Dakhla, Laayoune (El Aaiun)

# TRANSNATIONAL ISSUES :: WESTERN SAHARA

**DISPUTES - INTERNATIONAL:** no country has recognized Morocco's claim to the Western Sahara several states have extended diplomatic relations to the "Sahrawi Arab Democratic Republic" represented by the Polisario Front in exile in Algeria more than 100,000 Sahrawi refugees continue to be sheltered in camps in Tindouf, Algeria, which has hosted Sahrawi refugees since the 1980s

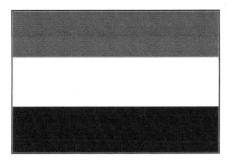

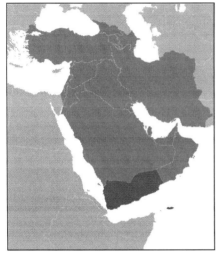

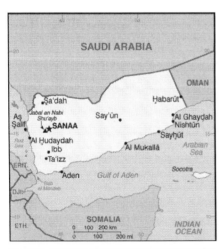

# MIDDLE EAST :: YEMEN

## INTRODUCTION :: YEMEN

### BACKGROUND:

North Yemen became independent from the Ottoman Empire in 1918. The British, who had set up a protectorate area around the southern port of Aden in the 19th century, withdrew in 1967 from what became South Yemen. Three years later, the southern government adopted a Marxist orientation. The massive exodus of hundreds of thousands of Yemenis from the south to the north contributed to two decades of hostility between the states. The two countries were formally unified as the Republic of Yemen in 1990. A southern secessionist movement and brief civil war in 1994 was quickly subdued. In 2000, Saudi Arabia and Yemen agreed to delineate their border. Fighting in the northwest between the government and the Huthis, a Zaydi Shia Muslim minority, continued intermittently from 2004 to 2010. The southern secessionist movement was revitalized in 2007.

Public rallies in Sana'a against then President SALIH - inspired by similar demonstrations in Tunisia and Egypt - slowly built momentum starting in late January 2011 fueled by complaints over high unemployment, poor economic conditions, and corruption. By the following month, some protests had resulted in violence, and the demonstrations had spread to other major cities. By March the opposition had hardened its demands and was unifying behind calls for SALIH's immediate ouster. In April 2011, the Gulf Cooperation Council (GCC), in an attempt to mediate the crisis in Yemen, proposed the GGC Initiative, an agreement in which the president would step down in exchange for immunity from prosecution. SALIH's refusal to sign an agreement led to further violence. The UN Security Council passed Resolution 2014 in October 2011 calling for an end to the violence and completing a power transfer deal. In November 2011, SALIH signed the GCC Initiative to step down and to transfer some of his powers to Vice President Abd Rabuh Mansur HADI. Following HADI's uncontested election victory in February 2012, SALIH formally transferred his powers. In accordance with the GCC initiative, Yemen launched a National Dialogue Conference (NDC) in March 2013 to discuss key constitutional, political, and social issues. HADI concluded the NDC in January 2014 and planned to begin implementing subsequent steps in the transition process, including constitutional drafting, a constitutional referendum, and national elections.

The Huthis, perceiving their grievances were not addressed in the NDC, joined forces with SALIH and expanded their influence in northwestern Yemen, culminating in a major offensive against military units and rival tribes and enabling their forces to overrun the capital, Sanaa, in September 2014. In January 2015, the Huthis surrounded the presidential palace, HADI's residence, and key government facilities, prompting HADI and the cabinet to submit their resignations. HADI fled to Aden in February 2015 and rescinded his resignation. He subsequently escaped to Oman and then moved to Saudi Arabia and asked the GCC to intervene militarily in Yemen to protect the legitimate government from the Huthis. In March, Saudi Arabia assembled a coalition of Arab militaries and began airstrikes against the Huthis and Huthi-affiliated forces. Ground fighting between Huthi-aligned forces and resistance groups backed by the Saudi-led coalition continued through 2016. In 2016, the UN brokered a months-long cessation of hostilities that reduced airstrikes and fighting, and initiated peace talks in Kuwait. However, the talks ended without agreement. The Huthis and SALIH's political party announced a Supreme Political Council in August 2016 and a National Salvation Government, including a prime minister and several dozen cabinet members, in November 2016, to govern in Sanaa and further challenge the legitimacy of HADI's government. Further attempts at peace have failed while neither side has made decisive battlefield gains, perpetuating the conflict and deepening the divisions between northern and southern Yemen. Amid rising tensions between the Huthis and SALIH, sporadic clashes erupted in mid-2017, and Huthi forces killed SALIH in early December 2017.

## GEOGRAPHY :: YEMEN

### LOCATION:

Middle East, bordering the Arabian Sea, Gulf of Aden, and Red Sea, between Oman and Saudi Arabia

### GEOGRAPHIC COORDINATES:

15 00 N, 48 00 E

**MAP REFERENCES:**
Middle East

**AREA:**
total: 527,968 sq km
land: 527,968 sq km
water: 0 sq km
note: includes Perim, Socotra, the former Yemen Arab Republic (YAR or North Yemen), and the former People's Democratic Republic of Yemen (PDRY or South Yemen)
country comparison to the world: 51

**AREA - COMPARATIVE:**
almost four times the size of Alabama; slightly larger than twice the size of Wyoming

**LAND BOUNDARIES:**
total: 1,601 km
border countries (2): Oman 294 km, Saudi Arabia 1307 km

**COASTLINE:**
1,906 km

**MARITIME CLAIMS:**
territorial sea: 12 nm
exclusive economic zone: 200 nm
contiguous zone: 24 nm
continental shelf: 200 nm or to the edge of the continental margin

**CLIMATE:**
mostly desert; hot and humid along west coast; temperate in western mountains affected by seasonal monsoon; extraordinarily hot, dry, harsh desert in east

**TERRAIN:**
narrow coastal plain backed by flat-topped hills and rugged mountains; dissected upland desert plains in center slope into the desert interior of the Arabian Peninsula

**ELEVATION:**
mean elevation: 999 m
elevation extremes: 0 m lowest point: Arabian Sea
3666 highest point: Jabal an Nabi Shu'ayb

**NATURAL RESOURCES:**
petroleum, fish, rock salt, marble; small deposits of coal, gold, lead, nickel, and copper; fertile soil in west

**LAND USE:**
agricultural land: 44.5% (2011 est.)
arable land: 2.2% (2011 est.) / permanent crops: 0.6% (2011 est.) / permanent pasture: 41.7% (2011 est.)
forest: 1% (2011 est.)
other: 54.5% (2011 est.)

**IRRIGATED LAND:**
6,800 sq km (2012)

**POPULATION DISTRIBUTION:**
the vast majority of the population is found in the Asir Mountains (part of the larger Sarawat Mountain system), located in the far western region of the country

**NATURAL HAZARDS:**
sandstorms and dust storms in summer
volcanism: limited volcanic activity; Jebel at Tair (Jabal al-Tair, Jebel Teir, Jabal al-Tayr, Jazirat at-Tair) (244 m), which forms an island in the Red Sea, erupted in 2007 after awakening from dormancy; other historically active volcanoes include Harra of Arhab, Harras of Dhamar, Harra es-Sawad, and Jebel Zubair, although many of these have not erupted in over a century

**ENVIRONMENT - CURRENT ISSUES:**
limited natural freshwater resources; inadequate supplies of potable water; overgrazing; soil erosion; desertification

**ENVIRONMENT - INTERNATIONAL AGREEMENTS:**
party to: Biodiversity, Climate Change, Climate Change-Kyoto Protocol, Desertification, Endangered Species, Environmental Modification, Hazardous Wastes, Law of the Sea, Ozone Layer Protection
signed, but not ratified: none of the selected agreements

**GEOGRAPHY - NOTE:**
strategic location on Bab el Mandeb, the strait linking the Red Sea and the Gulf of Aden, one of world's most active shipping lanes

## PEOPLE AND SOCIETY :: YEMEN

**POPULATION:**
28,667,230 (July 2018 est.)
country comparison to the world: 48

**NATIONALITY:**
noun: Yemeni(s)
adjective: Yemeni

**ETHNIC GROUPS:**
European predominantly Arab; but also Afro-Arab, South Asians, Europeans

**LANGUAGES:**
Arabic (official)
note: a distinct Socotri language is widely used on Socotra Island and Archipelago; Mahri is still fairly widely spoken in eastern Yemen

**RELIGIONS:**
Muslim 99.1% (official; virtually all are citizens, an estimated 65% are Sunni and 35% are Shia), other 0.9% (includes Jewish, Baha'i, Hindu, and Christian; many are refugees or temporary foreign residents) (2010 est.)

**AGE STRUCTURE:**
0-14 years: 39.16% (male 5,711,709 /female 5,513,526)
15-24 years: 21.26% (male 3,089,817 /female 3,005,693)
25-54 years: 32.78% (male 4,805,059 /female 4,591,811)
55-64 years: 4% (male 523,769 /female 623,100)
65 years and over: 2.8% (male 366,891 /female 435,855) (2018 est.)

**DEPENDENCY RATIOS:**
total dependency ratio: 76.8 (2015 est.)
youth dependency ratio: 71.7 (2015 est.)
elderly dependency ratio: 5.1 (2015 est.)
potential support ratio: 19.8 (2015 est.)

**MEDIAN AGE:**
total: 19.8 years
male: 19.6 years
female: 19.9 years (2018 est.)
country comparison to the world: 198

**POPULATION GROWTH RATE:**
2.17% (2018 est.)
country comparison to the world: 39

**BIRTH RATE:**
27.6 births/1,000 population (2018 est.)
country comparison to the world: 44

**DEATH RATE:**
5.9 deaths/1,000 population (2018 est.)
country comparison to the world: 171

**NET MIGRATION RATE:**
0.4 migrant(s)/1,000 population (2017 est.)
country comparison to the world: 65

**POPULATION DISTRIBUTION:**

the vast majority of the population is found in the Asir Mountains (part of the larger Sarawat Mountain system), located in the far western region of the country

**URBANIZATION:**

urban population: 36.6% of total population (2018)

rate of urbanization: 4.06% annual rate of change (2015-20 est.)

**MAJOR URBAN AREAS - POPULATION:**

2.779 million SANAA (capital), 922,000 Aden (2018)

**SEX RATIO:**

at birth: 1.04 male(s)/female (2017 est.)

0-14 years: 1.04 male(s)/female (2017 est.)

15-24 years: 1.03 male(s)/female (2017 est.)

25-54 years: 1.05 male(s)/female (2017 est.)

55-64 years: 0.85 male(s)/female (2017 est.)

65 years and over: 0.87 male(s)/female (2017 est.)

total population: 1.02 male(s)/female (2017 est.)

**MOTHER'S MEAN AGE AT FIRST BIRTH:**

21.4 years (2013 est.)

median age at first birth among women 25-29

**MATERNAL MORTALITY RATE:**

385 deaths/100,000 live births (2015 est.)

country comparison to the world: 30

**INFANT MORTALITY RATE:**

total: 44.6 deaths/1,000 live births (2018 est.)

male: 48.6 deaths/1,000 live births (2018 est.)

female: 40.4 deaths/1,000 live births (2018 est.)

country comparison to the world: 37

**LIFE EXPECTANCY AT BIRTH:**

total population: 66.2 years (2018 est.)

male: 64 years (2018 est.)

female: 68.5 years (2018 est.)

country comparison to the world: 176

**TOTAL FERTILITY RATE:**

3.48 children born/woman (2018 est.)

country comparison to the world: 43

**CONTRACEPTIVE PREVALENCE RATE:**

33.5% (2013)

**HEALTH EXPENDITURES:**

5.6% of GDP (2014)

country comparison to the world: 123

**PHYSICIANS DENSITY:**

0.31 physicians/1,000 population (2014)

**HOSPITAL BED DENSITY:**

0.7 beds/1,000 population (2014)

**DRINKING WATER SOURCE:**

improved:

urban: 72% of population (2012 est.)

rural: 46.5% of population (2012 est.)

total: 54.9% of population (2012 est.)

unimproved:

urban: 28% of population (2012 est.)

rural: 53.5% of population (2012 est.)

total: 45.1% of population (2012 est.)

**SANITATION FACILITY ACCESS:**

improved:

urban: 92.5% of population (2012 est.)

rural: 34.1% of population (2012 est.)

total: 53.3% of population (2012 est.)

unimproved:

urban: 7.5% of population (2012 est.)

rural: 65.9% of population (2012 est.)

total: 46.7% of population (2012 est.)

**HIV/AIDS - ADULT PREVALENCE RATE:**

<.1% (2016 est.)

**HIV/AIDS - PEOPLE LIVING WITH HIV/AIDS:**

9,900 (2016 est.)

country comparison to the world: 100

**HIV/AIDS - DEATHS:**

<500 (2016 est.)

**MAJOR INFECTIOUS DISEASES:**

degree of risk: high (2016)

food or waterborne diseases: bacterial diarrhea, hepatitis A, and typhoid fever (2016)

vectorborne diseases: dengue fever and malaria (2016)

water contact diseases: schistosomiasis (2016)

**OBESITY - ADULT PREVALENCE RATE:**

17.1% (2016)

country comparison to the world: 120

**CHILDREN UNDER THE AGE OF 5 YEARS UNDERWEIGHT:**

16.3% (2013)

country comparison to the world: 37

**EDUCATION EXPENDITURES:**

4.6% of GDP (2008)

country comparison to the world: 91

**LITERACY:**

definition: age 15 and over can read and write (2015 est.)

total population: 70.1% (2015 est.)

male: 85.1% (2015 est.)

female: 55% (2015 est.)

**SCHOOL LIFE EXPECTANCY (PRIMARY TO TERTIARY EDUCATION):**

total: 9 years (2011)

male: 10 years (2011)

female: 8 years (2011)

**UNEMPLOYMENT, YOUTH AGES 15-24:**

total: 24.5% (2014 est.)

male: 23.5% (2014 est.)

female: 34.6% (2014 est.)

country comparison to the world: 48

## GOVERNMENT :: YEMEN

**COUNTRY NAME:**

conventional long form: Republic of Yemen

conventional short form: Yemen

local long form: Al Jumhuriyah al Yamaniyah

local short form: Al Yaman

former: Yemen Arab Republic [Yemen (Sanaa) or North Yemen] and People's Democratic Republic of Yemen [Yemen (Aden) or South Yemen]

etymology: name derivation remains unclear but may come from the Arab term "yumn" (happiness) and be related to the region's classical name "Arabia Felix" (Fertile or Happy Arabia); the Romans referred to the rest of the peninsula as "Arabia Deserta" (Deserted Arabia)

**GOVERNMENT TYPE:**

in transition

**CAPITAL:**

name: Sanaa

geographic coordinates: 15 21 N, 44 12 E

**time difference:** UTC+3 (8 hours ahead of Washington, DC, during Standard Time)

**ADMINISTRATIVE DIVISIONS:**

22 governorates (muhafazat, singular - muhafazah); Abyan, 'Adan (Aden), Ad Dali', Al Bayda', Al Hudaydah, Al Jawf, Al Mahrah, Al Mahwit, Amanat al 'Asimah (Sanaa City), 'Amran, Arkhabil Suqutra (Socotra Archipelago), Dhamar, Hadramawt, Hajjah, Ibb, Lahij, Ma'rib, Raymah, Sa'dah, San'a' (Sanaa), Shabwah, Ta'izz

**INDEPENDENCE:**

22 May 1990 (Republic of Yemen was established with the merger of the Yemen Arab Republic [Yemen (Sanaa) or North Yemen] and the Marxist-dominated People's Democratic Republic of Yemen [Yemen (Aden) or South Yemen]); notable earlier dates: North Yemen became independent on 1 November 1918 (from the Ottoman Empire) and became a republic with the overthrow of the theocratic Imamate on 27 September 1962; South Yemen became independent on 30 November 1967 (from the UK)

**NATIONAL HOLIDAY:**

Unification Day, 22 May (1990)

**CONSTITUTION:**

adopted by referendum 16 May 1991 (following unification); amended several times, last in 2009; note - after the National Dialogue ended in January 2015, a presidentially appointed Constitutional Drafting Committee worked to prepare a new draft constitution that was expected to be put to a national referendum before being adopted; however, the president's resignation in January 2015 and subsequent conflict have interrupted the process (2016)

**LEGAL SYSTEM:**

mixed legal system of Islamic law, Napoleonic law, English common law, and customary law

**INTERNATIONAL LAW ORGANIZATION PARTICIPATION:**

has not submitted an ICJ jurisdiction declaration; non-party state to the ICCt

**CITIZENSHIP:**

citizenship by birth: no

citizenship by descent only: the father must be a citizen of Yemen; if the father is unknown, the mother must be a citizen

dual citizenship recognized: no

residency requirement for naturalization: 10 years

**SUFFRAGE:**

18 years of age; universal

**EXECUTIVE BRANCH:**

chief of state: President Abd Rabuh Mansur HADI (since 21 February 2012); Vice President ALI MUHSIN al-Ahmar, Lt. Gen. (since 3 April 2016)

head of government: Prime Minister Ahmad Obaid bin DAGHIR (since 3 April 2016)

cabinet: appointed by the president

elections/appointments: president directly elected by absolute majority popular vote in 2 rounds if needed for a 7-year term (eligible for a second term); election last held on 21 February 2012 (next election NA); note - a special election was held on 21 February 2012 to remove Ali Abdallah SALIH under the terms of a Gulf Cooperation Council-mediated deal during the political crisis of 2011; vice president appointed by the president; prime minister appointed by the president

election results: Abd Rabuh Mansur HADI (GPC) elected as a consensus president with about 50% popular participation; no other candidates

**LEGISLATIVE BRANCH:**

description: bicameral Parliament or Majlis consists of:
Shura Council or Majlis Alshoora (111 seats; members appointed by the president; member tenure NA)
House of Representatives or Majlis al Nuwaab (301 seats; members directly elected in single-seat constituencies by simple majority vote to serve 6-year terms)

elections:
House of Representatives - last held on 27 April 2003 (next scheduled for April 2009 but postponed indefinitely)

election results:
percent of vote by party - GPC 58.0%, Islah 22.6%, YSP 3.8%, Unionist Party 1.9%, other 13.7%; seats by party - GPC 238, Islah 46, YSP 8, Nasserist Unionist Party 3, National Arab Socialist Ba'ath Party 2, independent 4

**JUDICIAL BRANCH:**

highest courts: Supreme Court (consists of the president of the Court, 2 deputies, and nearly 50 judges; court organized into constitutional, civil, commercial, family, administrative, criminal, military, and appeals scrutiny divisions)

judge selection and term of office: judges appointed by the Supreme Judicial Council, chaired by the president of the republic and consisting of 10 high-ranking judicial officers; judges appointed for life with mandatory retirement at age 65

subordinate courts: appeal courts; district or first instance courts; commercial courts

**POLITICAL PARTIES AND LEADERS:**

General People's Congress or GPC – Aden [Abd Rabuh Mansur HADI]
General People's Congress or GPC - Sana'a [Sadiq Ameen Abu RAS]
National Arab Socialist Ba'ath Party [Qassem Salam SAID]
Nasserist Unionist People's Organization [Abdulmalik al-MEKHLAFI]
Yemeni Reform Grouping or Islah [Muhammed Abdallah al-YADUMI]
Yemeni Socialist Party or YSP [Dr. Abd al-Rahman Umar al-SAQQAF]

**INTERNATIONAL ORGANIZATION PARTICIPATION:**

AFESD, AMF, CAEU, CD, EITI (temporarily suspended), FAO, G-77, IAEA, IBRD, ICAO, ICRM, IDA, IDB, IFAD, IFC, IFRCS, ILO, IMF, IMO, IMSO, Interpol, IOC, IOM, IPU, ISO, ITSO, ITU, ITUC (NGOs), LAS, MIGA, MINURSO, MINUSMA, MONUSCO, NAM, OAS (observer), OIC, OPCW, UN, UNAMID, UNCTAD, UNESCO, UNHCR, UNIDO, UNISFA, UNMIL, UNMIS, UNOCI, UNWTO, UPU, WCO, WFTU (NGOs), WHO, WIPO, WMO, WTO

**DIPLOMATIC REPRESENTATION IN THE US:**

chief of mission: Ambassador Ahmad Awadh BIN MUBARAK (since 3 August 2015)

chancery: 2319 Wyoming Avenue NW, Washington, DC 20008

telephone: [1] (202) 965-4760

FAX: [1] (202) 337-2017

**DIPLOMATIC REPRESENTATION FROM THE US:**

chief of mission: Ambassador Matthew H. TUELLER (since 10 June 2014)

embassy: Sa'awan Street, Sanaa; note - Embassy closed in March 2015; relocated to Jeddah, Saudia Arabia

mailing address: P. O. Box 22347, Sanaa

**telephone:** Suspended Operations [966] 11-488-3800 (Embassy Riyadh)

**FAX:** Suspended Operations [966] 11-488-7360 (Embassy Riyadh)

## FLAG DESCRIPTION:

three equal horizontal bands of red (top), white, and black; the band colors derive from the Arab Liberation flag and represent oppression (black), overcome through bloody struggle (red), to be replaced by a bright future (white)

note: similar to the flag of Syria, which has two green stars in the white band, and of Iraq, which has an Arabic inscription centered in the white band; also similar to the flag of Egypt, which has a heraldic eagle centered in the white band

## NATIONAL SYMBOL(S):

golden eagle; national colors: red, white, black

## NATIONAL ANTHEM:

name: "al-qumhuriyatu l-muttahida" (United Republic)

lyrics/music: Abdullah Abdulwahab NOA'MAN/Ayyoab Tarish ABSI

note: adopted 1990; the music first served as the anthem for South Yemen before unification with North Yemen in 1990

# ECONOMY :: YEMEN

## ECONOMY - OVERVIEW:

Yemen is a low-income country that faces difficult long-term challenges to stabilizing and growing its economy, and the current conflict has only exacerbated those issues. The ongoing war has halted Yemen's exports, pressured the currency's exchange rate, accelerated inflation, severely limited food and fuel imports, and caused widespread damage to infrastructure. The conflict has also created a severe humanitarian crisis - the world's largest cholera outbreak currently at nearly 1 million cases, more than 7 million people at risk of famine, and more than 80% of the population in need of humanitarian assistance.

Prior to the start of the conflict in 2014, Yemen was highly dependent on declining oil and gas resources for revenue. Oil and gas earnings accounted for roughly 25% of GDP and 65% of government revenue. The Yemeni Government regularly faced annual budget shortfalls and tried to diversify the Yemeni economy through a reform program designed to bolster non-oil sectors of the economy and foreign investment. In July 2014, the government continued reform efforts by eliminating some fuel subsidies and in August 2014, the IMF approved a three-year, $570 million Extended Credit Facility for Yemen.

However, the conflict that began in 2014 stalled these reform efforts and ongoing fighting continues to accelerate the country's economic decline. In September 2016, President HADI announced the move of the main branch of Central Bank of Yemen from Sanaa to Aden where his government could exert greater control over the central bank's dwindling resources. Regardless of which group controls the main branch, the central bank system is struggling to function. Yemen's Central Bank's foreign reserves, which stood at roughly $5.2 billion prior to the conflict, have declined to negligible amounts. The Central Bank can no longer fully support imports of critical goods or the country's exchange rate. The country also is facing a growing liquidity crisis and rising inflation. The private sector is hemorrhaging, with almost all businesses making substantial layoffs. Access to food and other critical commodities such as medical equipment is limited across the country due to security issues on the ground. The Social Welfare Fund, a cash transfer program for Yemen's neediest, is no longer operational and has not made any disbursements since late 2014.

Yemen will require significant international assistance during and after the protracted conflict to stabilize its economy. Long-term challenges include a high population growth rate, high unemployment, declining water resources, and severe food scarcity.

## GDP (PURCHASING POWER PARITY):

$73.63 billion (2017 est.)

$78.28 billion (2016 est.)

$90.63 billion (2015 est.)

note: data are in 2017 dollars

country comparison to the world: 97

## GDP (OFFICIAL EXCHANGE RATE):

$31.27 billion (2017 est.) (2017 est.)

## GDP - REAL GROWTH RATE:

-5.9% (2017 est.)

-13.6% (2016 est.)

-16.7% (2015 est.)

country comparison to the world: 219

## GDP - PER CAPITA (PPP):

$2,500 (2017 est.)

$2,700 (2016 est.)

$3,200 (2015 est.)

note: data are in 2017 dollars

country comparison to the world: 199

## GROSS NATIONAL SAVING:

-1.9% of GDP (2017 est.)

-3.7% of GDP (2016 est.)

-4.5% of GDP (2015 est.)

country comparison to the world: 182

## GDP - COMPOSITION, BY END USE:

household consumption: 116.6% (2017 est.)

government consumption: 17.6% (2017 est.)

investment in fixed capital: 2.2% (2017 est.)

investment in inventories: 0% (2017 est.)

exports of goods and services: 7.5% (2017 est.)

imports of goods and services: -43.9% (2017 est.)

## GDP - COMPOSITION, BY SECTOR OF ORIGIN:

agriculture: 20.3% (2017 est.)

industry: 11.8% (2017 est.)

services: 67.9% (2017 est.)

## AGRICULTURE - PRODUCTS:

grain, fruits, vegetables, pulses, qat, coffee, cotton; dairy products, livestock (sheep, goats, cattle, camels), poultry; fish

## INDUSTRIES:

crude oil production and petroleum refining; small-scale production of cotton textiles, leather goods; food processing; handicrafts; aluminum products; cement; commercial ship repair; natural gas production

## INDUSTRIAL PRODUCTION GROWTH RATE:

8.9% (2017 est.)

country comparison to the world: 21

## LABOR FORCE:

7.425 million (2017 est.)

country comparison to the world: 65

## LABOR FORCE - BY OCCUPATION:

note: most people are employed in agriculture and herding; services, construction, industry, and commerce account for less than one-fourth of the labor force

**UNEMPLOYMENT RATE:**

27% (2014 est.)

35% (2003 est.)

country comparison to the world: 198

**POPULATION BELOW POVERTY LINE:**

54% (2014 est.)

**HOUSEHOLD INCOME OR CONSUMPTION BY PERCENTAGE SHARE:**

lowest 10%: 30.3% (2008 est.)

highest 10%: 30.3% (2008 est.)

**DISTRIBUTION OF FAMILY INCOME - GINI INDEX:**

37.9 (2009 est.)

37.3 (1999 est.)

country comparison to the world: 81

**BUDGET:**

revenues: 2.821 billion (2017 est.)

expenditures: 4.458 billion (2017 est.)

**TAXES AND OTHER REVENUES:**

9% (of GDP) (2017 est.)

country comparison to the world: 216

**BUDGET SURPLUS (+) OR DEFICIT (-):**

-5.2% (of GDP) (2017 est.)

country comparison to the world: 171

**PUBLIC DEBT:**

74.5% of GDP (2017 est.)

68.1% of GDP (2016 est.)

country comparison to the world: 41

**FISCAL YEAR:**

calendar year

**INFLATION RATE (CONSUMER PRICES):**

24.7% (2017 est.)

-12.6% (2016 est.)

country comparison to the world: 218

**CENTRAL BANK DISCOUNT RATE:**

NA

**COMMERCIAL BANK PRIME LENDING RATE:**

30% (31 December 2017 est.)

27% (31 December 2016 est.)

country comparison to the world: 6

**STOCK OF NARROW MONEY:**

$4.736 billion (31 December 2017 est.)

$6.718 billion (31 December 2016 est.)

country comparison to the world: 108

**STOCK OF BROAD MONEY:**

$4.736 billion (31 December 2017 est.)

$6.718 billion (31 December 2016 est.)

country comparison to the world: 112

**STOCK OF DOMESTIC CREDIT:**

$2.326 billion (31 December 2017 est.)

$4.515 billion (31 December 2016 est.)

country comparison to the world: 146

**MARKET VALUE OF PUBLICLY TRADED SHARES:**

NA

**CURRENT ACCOUNT BALANCE:**

-$1.236 billion (2017 est.)

-$1.868 billion (2016 est.)

country comparison to the world: 149

**EXPORTS:**

$384.5 million (2017 est.)

$940 million (2016 est.)

country comparison to the world: 184

**EXPORTS - PARTNERS:**

Egypt 29.4%, Thailand 16.7%, Belarus 13.5%, Oman 10.5%, UAE 6.5%, Saudi Arabia 5% (2017)

**EXPORTS - COMMODITIES:**

crude oil, coffee, dried and salted fish, liquefied natural gas

**IMPORTS:**

$4.079 billion (2017 est.)

$3.117 billion (2016 est.)

country comparison to the world: 140

**IMPORTS - COMMODITIES:**

food and live animals, machinery and equipment, chemicals

**IMPORTS - PARTNERS:**

UAE 12.2%, China 12.1%, Turkey 8.7%, Brazil 7.3%, Saudi Arabia 6.5%, Argentina 5.5%, India 4.7% (2017)

**RESERVES OF FOREIGN EXCHANGE AND GOLD:**

$245.4 million (31 December 2017 est.)

$592.6 million (31 December 2016 est.)

country comparison to the world: 170

**DEBT - EXTERNAL:**

$7.068 billion (31 December 2017 est.)

$7.181 billion (31 December 2016 est.)

country comparison to the world: 124

**STOCK OF DIRECT FOREIGN INVESTMENT - AT HOME:**

NA

**EXCHANGE RATES:**

Yemeni rials (YER) per US dollar -

275 (2017 est.)

214.9 (2016 est.)

214.9 (2015 est.)

228 (2014 est.)

214.89 (2013 est.)

## ENERGY :: YEMEN

**ELECTRICITY ACCESS:**

population without electricity: 13.3 million (2013)

electrification - total population: 48% (2013)

electrification - urban areas: 79% (2013)

electrification - rural areas: 33% (2013)

**ELECTRICITY - PRODUCTION:**

4.784 billion kWh (2016 est.)

country comparison to the world: 122

**ELECTRICITY - CONSUMPTION:**

3.681 billion kWh (2016 est.)

country comparison to the world: 130

**ELECTRICITY - EXPORTS:**

0 kWh (2016 est.)

country comparison to the world: 219

**ELECTRICITY - IMPORTS:**

0 kWh (2016 est.)

country comparison to the world: 219

**ELECTRICITY - INSTALLED GENERATING CAPACITY:**

1.819 million kW (2016 est.)

country comparison to the world: 116

**ELECTRICITY - FROM FOSSIL FUELS:**

79% of total installed capacity (2016 est.)

country comparison to the world: 89

**ELECTRICITY - FROM NUCLEAR FUELS:**

0% of total installed capacity (2017 est.)

country comparison to the world: 213

**ELECTRICITY - FROM HYDROELECTRIC PLANTS:**

0% of total installed capacity (2017 est.)

country comparison to the world: 215

**ELECTRICITY - FROM OTHER RENEWABLE SOURCES:**

21% of total installed capacity (2017 est.)

country comparison to the world: 37

**CRUDE OIL - PRODUCTION:**

12,260 bbl/day (2017 est.)

country comparison to the world: 76

**CRUDE OIL - EXPORTS:**

8,990 bbl/day (2015 est.)

country comparison to the world: 60

**CRUDE OIL - IMPORTS:**

0 bbl/day (2015 est.)

country comparison to the world: 217

**CRUDE OIL - PROVED RESERVES:**

3 billion bbl (1 January 2018 est.)

country comparison to the world: 29

**REFINED PETROLEUM PRODUCTS - PRODUCTION:**

20,180 bbl/day (2015 est.)

country comparison to the world: 89

**REFINED PETROLEUM PRODUCTS - CONSUMPTION:**

104,000 bbl/day (2016 est.)

country comparison to the world: 78

**REFINED PETROLEUM PRODUCTS - EXPORTS:**

12,670 bbl/day (2015 est.)

country comparison to the world: 78

**REFINED PETROLEUM PRODUCTS - IMPORTS:**

75,940 bbl/day (2015 est.)

country comparison to the world: 65

**NATURAL GAS - PRODUCTION:**

481.4 million cu m (2017 est.)

country comparison to the world: 72

**NATURAL GAS - CONSUMPTION:**

481.4 million cu m (2017 est.)

country comparison to the world: 99

**NATURAL GAS - EXPORTS:**

0 cu m (2017 est.)

country comparison to the world: 214

**NATURAL GAS - IMPORTS:**

0 cu m (2017 est.)

country comparison to the world: 214

**NATURAL GAS - PROVED RESERVES:**

478.5 billion cu m (1 January 2018 est.)

country comparison to the world: 31

**CARBON DIOXIDE EMISSIONS FROM CONSUMPTION OF ENERGY:**

13.68 million Mt (2017 est.)

country comparison to the world: 95

# COMMUNICATIONS :: YEMEN

**TELEPHONES - FIXED LINES:**

total subscriptions: 1,165,828 (July 2016 est.)

subscriptions per 100 inhabitants: 4 (July 2016 est.)

country comparison to the world: 72

**TELEPHONES - MOBILE CELLULAR:**

total subscriptions: 16,433,055 (July 2016 est.)

subscriptions per 100 inhabitants: 59 (July 2016 est.)

country comparison to the world: 63

**TELEPHONE SYSTEM:**

general assessment: cell phone penetration growing rapidly (2016)

domestic: the national network consists of microwave radio relay, cable, tropospheric scatter, GSM and CDMA mobile-cellular telephone systems; fixed-line teledensity remains low by regional standards but mobile cellular use expanding apace (2016)

international: country code - 967; landing point for the international submarine cable Fiber-Optic Link Around the Globe (FLAG); satellite earth stations - 3 Intelsat (2 Indian Ocean and 1 Atlantic Ocean), 1 Intersputnik (Atlantic Ocean region), and 2 Arabsat; microwave radio relay to Saudi Arabia and Djibouti (2016)

**BROADCAST MEDIA:**

state-run TV with 2 stations; state-run radio with 2 national radio stations and 5 local stations; stations from Oman and Saudi Arabia can be accessed (2007)

**INTERNET COUNTRY CODE:**

.ye

**INTERNET USERS:**

total: 6,732,928 (July 2016 est.)

percent of population: 24.6% (July 2016 est.)

country comparison to the world: 63

**BROADBAND - FIXED SUBSCRIPTIONS:**

total: 430,400 (2017 est.)

subscriptions per 100 inhabitants: 2 (2017 est.)

country comparison to the world: 85

# TRANSPORTATION :: YEMEN

**NATIONAL AIR TRANSPORT SYSTEM:**

number of registered air carriers: 2 (2015)

inventory of registered aircraft operated by air carriers: 10 (2015)

annual passenger traffic on registered air carriers: 1,387,999 (2015)

annual freight traffic on registered air carriers: 0 mt-km (2015)

**CIVIL AIRCRAFT REGISTRATION COUNTRY CODE PREFIX:**

7O (2016)

**AIRPORTS:**

57 (2013)

country comparison to the world: 84

**AIRPORTS - WITH PAVED RUNWAYS:**

total: 17 (2013)

over 3,047 m: 4 (2013)

2,438 to 3,047 m: 9 (2013)

1,524 to 2,437 m: 3 (2013)

914 to 1,523 m: 1 (2013)

**AIRPORTS - WITH UNPAVED RUNWAYS:**

total: 40 (2013)

over 3,047 m: 3 (2013)

2,438 to 3,047 m: 5 (2013)

1,524 to 2,437 m: 7 (2013)

914 to 1,523 m: 16 (2013)

under 914 m: 9 (2013)

**PIPELINES:**

641 km gas, 22 km liquid petroleum gas, 1370 km oil (2013)

**ROADWAYS:**

total: 71,300 km (2005)

paved: 6,200 km (2005)

unpaved: 65,100 km (2005)

country comparison to the world: 66

**MERCHANT MARINE:**

total: 31 (2017)

by type: general cargo 3, oil tanker 4, other 24 (2017)

country comparison to the world: 128

**PORTS AND TERMINALS:**

major seaport(s): Aden, Al Hudaydah, Al Mukalla

# MILITARY AND SECURITY :: YEMEN

**MILITARY EXPENDITURES:**

3.97% of GDP (2014)

4.08% of GDP (2013)

4.57% of GDP (2012)

note - no reliable information exists following the start of renewed conflict in 2015

country comparison to the world: 16

**MILITARY BRANCHES:**

Land Forces (includes seven Military Regional Commands, supported by Strategic Reserve Units), Naval and Coastal Defense Forces (includes Navy Infantry or Marine units and Coast Guard), Air and Air Defense Force (although it still exists in name, in practice many of the officers and soldiers in this branch have been distributed to other military branches and jobs), Border Guards, Strategic Reserve Forces (supports the Land Forces at the discretion of the Armed Forces Commander-in-Chief and also includes a Missile Group, Presidential Protection Brigades, and Special Operations Forces), Minister of Defense Intelligence Authority (consists of the Department of Military Intelligence [active], Department of Reconnaissance [active], Department of Military Security [inactive], and the Electronic Warfare Department [inactive]) (March 2018)

**MILITARY SERVICE AGE AND OBLIGATION:**

18 is the legal minimum age for voluntary military service; no conscription; 2-year service obligation (2018)

**MARITIME THREATS:**

the International Maritime Bureau reports offshore waters in the Gulf of Aden are high risk for piracy; numerous vessels, including commercial shipping and pleasure craft, have been attacked and hijacked both at anchor and while underway; crew, passengers, and cargo have been held for ransom; the presence of several naval task forces in the Gulf of Aden and additional anti-piracy measures on the part of ship operators reduced the incidence of piracy in that body of water; one attack was reported in 2016 while three ships reported being fired upon in 2017

## TERRORISM :: YEMEN

**TERRORIST GROUPS - HOME BASED:**

al-Qa'ida in the Arabian Peninsula (AQAP):
aim(s): overthrow the Yemen Government and Huthi forces and, ultimately, establish an Islamic caliphate; eradicate US and Western influence and presence from Yemen and the rest of the Arabian Peninsula
area(s) of operation: a core al-Qa'ida affiliate; most active in southern, eastern, and central Yemen (April 2018)

Islamic State of Iraq and ash-Sham-Yemen (ISIS-Yemen):
aim(s): replace the Yemen Government and Huthi forces with an Islamic state and implement ISIS's strict interpretation of sharia
area(s) of operation: operational primarily in south and central Yemen, where operatives conduct attacks against Huthi forces, Shia Muslims, and government facilities and personnel (April 2018)

## TRANSNATIONAL ISSUES :: YEMEN

**DISPUTES - INTERNATIONAL:**

Saudi Arabia has reinforced its concrete-filled security barrier along sections of the fully demarcated border with Yemen to stem illegal cross-border activities

**REFUGEES AND INTERNALLY DISPLACED PERSONS:**

refugees (country of origin): 256,363 (Somalia), 13,107 (Ethiopia) (2018)

IDPs: 2,331,264 (conflict in Sa'ada Governorate; clashes between al-Qa'ida in the Arabian Peninsula and government forces) (2018)

**TRAFFICKING IN PERSONS:**

current situation: Yemen is a source and, to a lesser extent, transit and destination country for men, women, and children subjected to forced labor and women and children subjected to sex trafficking; trafficking activities grew in Yemen in 2014, as the country's security situation deteriorated and poverty worsened; armed groups increased their recruitment of Yemeni children as combatants or checkpoint guards, and the Yemeni military and security forces continue to use child soldiers; some other Yemeni children, mostly boys, migrate to Yemeni cities or Saudi Arabia and, less frequently Oman, where they end up as beggars, drug smugglers, prostitutes, or forced laborers in domestic service or small shops; Yemeni children increasingly are also subjected to sex trafficking in country and in Saudi Arabia; tens of thousands of Yemeni migrant workers deported from Saudi Arabia and thousands of Syrian refugees are vulnerable to trafficking; additionally, Yemen is a destination and transit country for women and children from the Horn of Africa who are looking for work or receive fraudulent job offers in the Gulf states but are subjected to sexual exploitation or forced labor upon arrival; reports indicate that adults and children are still sold or inherited as slaves in Yemen

tier rating: Tier 3 – Yemen does not fully comply with the minimum standards for the elimination of trafficking and is not making significant efforts to do so; weak government institutions, corruption, economic problems, security threats, and poor law enforcement capabilities impeded the government's ability to combat human trafficking; not all forms of trafficking are criminalized, and officials continue to conflate trafficking and smuggling; the status of an anti-trafficking law drafted with assistance from an international organization remains unknown following the dissolution of the government in January 2015; the government did not report efforts to investigate, prosecute, or convict anyone of trafficking or slavery offenses, including complicit officials, despite reports of officials willfully ignoring trafficking crimes and using child soldiers in the government's armed forces; the government acknowledged the use of child soldiers and signed a UN action plan to end the practice in 2014 but made no efforts to release child soldiers from the military and provide them with rehabilitative services; authorities failed to identify victims and refer them to protective services; the status of a draft national anti-trafficking strategy remains unknown (2015)

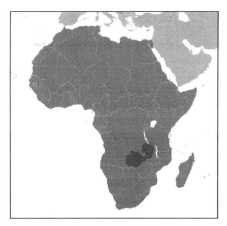

# AFRICA :: ZAMBIA

## INTRODUCTION :: ZAMBIA

### BACKGROUND:

The territory of Northern Rhodesia was administered by the former British South Africa Company from 1891 until it was taken over by the UK in 1923. During the 1920s and 1930s, advances in mining spurred development and immigration. The name was changed to Zambia upon independence in 1964. In the 1980s and 1990s, declining copper prices, economic mismanagement, and a prolonged drought hurt the economy. Elections in 1991 brought an end to one-party rule and propelled the Movement for Multiparty Democracy (MMD) to government. The subsequent vote in 1996, however, saw increasing harassment of opposition parties and abuse of state media and other resources. The election in 2001 was marked by administrative problems, with three parties filing a legal petition challenging the election of ruling party candidate Levy MWANAWASA. MWANAWASA was reelected in 2006 in an election that was deemed free and fair. Upon his death in August 2008, he was succeeded by his vice president, Rupiah BANDA, who won a special presidential byelection later that year. The MMD and BANDA lost to the Patriotic Front (PF) and Michael SATA in the 2011 general elections. SATA, however, presided over a period of haphazard economic management and attempted to silence opposition to PF policies. SATA died in October 2014 and was succeeded by his vice president, Guy SCOTT, who served as interim president until January 2015, when Edgar LUNGU won the presidential byelection and completed SATA's term. LUNGU then won a full term in August 2016 presidential elections.

## GEOGRAPHY :: ZAMBIA

### LOCATION:
Southern Africa, east of Angola, south of the Democratic Republic of the Congo

### GEOGRAPHIC COORDINATES:
15 00 S, 30 00 E

### MAP REFERENCES:
Africa

### AREA:
total: 752,618 sq km

land: 743,398 sq km

water: 9,220 sq km

country comparison to the world: 40

### AREA - COMPARATIVE:
almost five times the size of Georgia; slightly larger than Texas

### LAND BOUNDARIES:
total: 6,043.15 km

border countries (8): Angola 1065 km, Botswana 0.15 km, Democratic Republic of the Congo 2332 km, Malawi 847 km, Mozambique 439 km, Namibia 244 km, Tanzania 353 km, Zimbabwe 763 km

### COASTLINE:
0 km (landlocked)

### MARITIME CLAIMS:
none (landlocked)

### CLIMATE:
tropical; modified by altitude; rainy season (October to April)

### TERRAIN:
mostly high plateau with some hills and mountains

### ELEVATION:
mean elevation: 1,138 m

elevation extremes: 329 m lowest point: Zambezi river

2301 highest point: unnamed elevation in Mafinga Hills

### NATURAL RESOURCES:
copper, cobalt, zinc, lead, coal, emeralds, gold, silver, uranium, hydropower

### LAND USE:
agricultural land: 31.7% (2011 est.)

arable land: 4.8% (2011 est.) / permanent crops: 0% (2011 est.) / permanent pasture: 26.9% (2011 est.)

forest: 66.3% (2011 est.)

other: 2% (2011 est.)

### IRRIGATED LAND:
1,560 sq km (2012)

### POPULATION DISTRIBUTION:
one of the highest levels of urbanization in Africa; high density in the central area, particularly around the cities of Lusaka, Ndola, Kitwe, and Mufulira

### NATURAL HAZARDS:
periodic drought; tropical storms (November to April)

### ENVIRONMENT - CURRENT ISSUES:
air pollution and resulting acid rain in the mineral extraction and refining region; chemical runoff into watersheds; loss of biodiversity; poaching seriously threatens rhinoceros, elephant, antelope, and large cat populations; deforestation; soil erosion; desertification; lack of

adequate water treatment presents human health risks

### ENVIRONMENT - INTERNATIONAL AGREEMENTS:

**party to:** Biodiversity, Climate Change, Climate Change-Kyoto Protocol, Desertification, Endangered Species, Hazardous Wastes, Law of the Sea, Ozone Layer Protection, Wetlands

**signed, but not ratified:** none of the selected agreements

### GEOGRAPHY - NOTE:

landlocked; the Zambezi forms a natural riverine boundary with Zimbabwe; Lake Kariba on the Zambia-Zimbabwe border forms the world's largest reservoir by volume (180 cu km; 43 cu mi)

## PEOPLE AND SOCIETY :: ZAMBIA

### POPULATION:

16,445,079 (July 2018 est.)

**note:** estimates for this country explicitly take into account the effects of excess mortality due to AIDS; this can result in lower life expectancy, higher infant mortality, higher death rates, lower population growth rates, and changes in the distribution of population by age and sex than would otherwise be expected

**country comparison to the world:** 70

### NATIONALITY:

**noun:** Zambian(s)

**adjective:** Zambian

### ETHNIC GROUPS:

Bemba 21%, Tonga 13.6%, Chewa 7.4%, Lozi 5.7%, Nsenga 5.3%, Tumbuka 4.4%, Ngoni 4%, Lala 3.1%, Kaonde 2.9%, Namwanga 2.8%, Lunda (north Western) 2.6%, Mambwe 2.5%, Luvale 2.2%, Lamba 2.1%, Ushi 1.9%, Lenje 1.6%, Bisa 1.6%, Mbunda 1.2%, other 13.8%, unspecified 0.4% (2010 est.)

### LANGUAGES:

Bemba 33.4%, Nyanja 14.7%, Tonga 11.4%, Lozi 5.5%, Chewa 4.5%, Nsenga 2.9%, Tumbuka 2.5%, Lunda (North Western) 1.9%, Kaonde 1.8%, Lala 1.8%, Lamba 1.8%, English (official) 1.7%, Luvale 1.5%, Mambwe 1.3%, Namwanga 1.2%, Lenje 1.1%, Bisa 1%, other 9.7%, unspecified 0.2% (2010 est.)

**note:** Zambia is said to have over 70 languages, although many of these may be considered dialects; all of Zambia's major languages are members of the Bantu family

### RELIGIONS:

Protestant 75.3%, Roman Catholic 20.2%, other 2.7% (includes Muslim Buddhist, Hindu, and Baha'i), none 1.8% (2010 est.)

### DEMOGRAPHIC PROFILE:

Zambia's poor, youthful population consists primarily of Bantu-speaking people representing nearly 70 different ethnicities. Zambia's high fertility rate continues to drive rapid population growth, averaging almost 3 percent annually between 2000 and 2010. The country's total fertility rate has fallen by less than 1.5 children per woman during the last 30 years and still averages among the world's highest, almost 6 children per woman, largely because of the country's lack of access to family planning services, education for girls, and employment for women. Zambia also exhibits wide fertility disparities based on rural or urban location, education, and income. Poor, uneducated women from rural areas are more likely to marry young, to give birth early, and to have more children, viewing children as a sign of prestige and recognizing that not all of their children will live to adulthood. HIV/AIDS is prevalent in Zambia and contributes to its low life expectancy.

Zambian emigration is low compared to many other African countries and is comprised predominantly of the well-educated. The small amount of brain drain, however, has a major impact in Zambia because of its limited human capital and lack of educational infrastructure for developing skilled professionals in key fields. For example, Zambia has few schools for training doctors, nurses, and other health care workers. Its spending on education is low compared to other sub-Saharan countries.

### AGE STRUCTURE:

**0-14 years:** 45.95% (male 3,796,548 /female 3,759,624)

**15-24 years:** 20% (male 1,643,364 /female 1,645,713)

**25-54 years:** 28.79% (male 2,384,765 /female 2,349,877)

**55-64 years:** 2.95% (male 225,586 /female 260,252)

**65 years and over:** 2.31% (male 166,224 /female 213,126) (2018 est.)

### DEPENDENCY RATIOS:

**total dependency ratio:** 91.9 (2015 est.)

**youth dependency ratio:** 87.1 (2015 est.)

**elderly dependency ratio:** 4.8 (2015 est.)

**potential support ratio:** 20.8 (2015 est.)

### MEDIAN AGE:

**total:** 16.8 years

**male:** 16.7 years

**female:** 16.9 years (2018 est.)

**country comparison to the world:** 222

### POPULATION GROWTH RATE:

2.91% (2018 est.)

**country comparison to the world:** 10

### BIRTH RATE:

41.1 births/1,000 population (2018 est.)

**country comparison to the world:** 6

### DEATH RATE:

12 deaths/1,000 population (2018 est.)

**country comparison to the world:** 18

### NET MIGRATION RATE:

0 migrant(s)/1,000 population (2017 est.)

**country comparison to the world:** 101

### POPULATION DISTRIBUTION:

one of the highest levels of urbanization in Africa; high density in the central area, particularly around the cities of Lusaka, Ndola, Kitwe, and Mufulira

### URBANIZATION:

**urban population:** 43.5% of total population (2018)

**rate of urbanization:** 4.23% annual rate of change (2015-20 est.)

### MAJOR URBAN AREAS - POPULATION:

2.524 million LUSAKA (capital) (2018)

### SEX RATIO:

**at birth:** 1.02 male(s)/female (2017 est.)

**0-14 years:** 1.01 male(s)/female (2017 est.)

**15-24 years:** 1 male(s)/female (2017 est.)

**25-54 years:** 1.02 male(s)/female (2017 est.)

**55-64 years:** 0.88 male(s)/female (2017 est.)

**65 years and over:** 0.76 male(s)/female (2017 est.)

total population: 1 male(s)/female (2017 est.)

**MOTHER'S MEAN AGE AT FIRST BIRTH:**

19.2 years (2013/14 est.)

note: median age at first birth among women 25-29

**MATERNAL MORTALITY RATE:**

224 deaths/100,000 live births (2015 est.)

country comparison to the world: 48

**INFANT MORTALITY RATE:**

total: 59.3 deaths/1,000 live births (2018 est.)

male: 64.6 deaths/1,000 live births (2018 est.)

female: 53.9 deaths/1,000 live births (2018 est.)

country comparison to the world: 15

**LIFE EXPECTANCY AT BIRTH:**

total population: 53 years (2018 est.)

male: 51.4 years (2018 est.)

female: 54.7 years (2018 est.)

country comparison to the world: 222

**TOTAL FERTILITY RATE:**

5.58 children born/woman (2018 est.)

country comparison to the world: 8

**CONTRACEPTIVE PREVALENCE RATE:**

49% (2013/14)

**HEALTH EXPENDITURES:**

5% of GDP (2014)

country comparison to the world: 143

**PHYSICIANS DENSITY:**

0.09 physicians/1,000 population (2016)

**HOSPITAL BED DENSITY:**

2 beds/1,000 population (2010)

**DRINKING WATER SOURCE:**

improved:

urban: 85.6% of population

rural: 51.3% of population

total: 65.4% of population

unimproved:

urban: 14.4% of population

rural: 48.7% of population

total: 34.6% of population (2015 est.)

**SANITATION FACILITY ACCESS:**

improved:

urban: 55.6% of population (2015 est.)

rural: 35.7% of population (2015 est.)

total: 43.9% of population (2015 est.)

unimproved:

urban: 44.4% of population (2015 est.)

rural: 64.3% of population (2015 est.)

total: 56.1% of population (2015 est.)

**HIV/AIDS - ADULT PREVALENCE RATE:**

11.5% (2017 est.)

country comparison to the world: 8

**HIV/AIDS - PEOPLE LIVING WITH HIV/AIDS:**

1.1 million (2017 est.)

country comparison to the world: 9

**HIV/AIDS - DEATHS:**

16,000 (2017 est.)

country comparison to the world: 15

**MAJOR INFECTIOUS DISEASES:**

degree of risk: very high (2016)

food or waterborne diseases: bacterial and protozoal diarrhea, hepatitis A, and typhoid fever (2016)

vectorborne diseases: malaria and dengue fever (2016)

water contact diseases: schistosomiasis (2016)

animal contact diseases: rabies (2016)

**OBESITY - ADULT PREVALENCE RATE:**

8.1% (2016)

country comparison to the world: 155

**CHILDREN UNDER THE AGE OF 5 YEARS UNDERWEIGHT:**

14.8% (2013)

country comparison to the world: 45

**EDUCATION EXPENDITURES:**

1.1% of GDP (2008)

country comparison to the world: 178

**LITERACY:**

definition: age 15 and over can read and write English (2015 est.)

total population: 63.4% (2015 est.)

male: 70.9% (2015 est.)

female: 56% (2015 est.)

**UNEMPLOYMENT, YOUTH AGES 15-24:**

total: 15.2% (2012 est.)

male: 14.6% (2012 est.)

female: 15.8% (2012 est.)

country comparison to the world: 90

# GOVERNMENT :: ZAMBIA

**COUNTRY NAME:**

conventional long form: Republic of Zambia

conventional short form: Zambia

former: Northern Rhodesia

etymology: name derived from the Zambezi River, which flows through the western part of the country and forms its southern border with neighboring Zimbabwe

**GOVERNMENT TYPE:**

presidential republic

**CAPITAL:**

name: Lusaka; note - a proposal to build a new capital city in Ngabwe was announced in May 2017

geographic coordinates: 15 25 S, 28 17 E

time difference: UTC+2 (7 hours ahead of Washington, DC, during Standard Time)

**ADMINISTRATIVE DIVISIONS:**

10 provinces; Central, Copperbelt, Eastern, Luapula, Lusaka, Muchinga, Northern, North-Western, Southern, Western

**INDEPENDENCE:**

24 October 1964 (from the UK)

**NATIONAL HOLIDAY:**

Independence Day, 24 October (1964)

**CONSTITUTION:**

history: several previous; latest adopted 24 August 1991, promulgated 30 August 1991 (2017)

amendments: proposed by the National Assembly; passage requires two-thirds majority vote by the Assembly in two separate readings at least 30 days apart; passage of amendments affecting fundamental rights and freedoms requires approval by at least one-half of votes cast in a referendum prior to consideration and voting by the Assembly; amended 1996, 2015, last in 2016 (2017)

**LEGAL SYSTEM:**

mixed legal system of English common law and customary law

**INTERNATIONAL LAW ORGANIZATION PARTICIPATION:**

has not submitted an ICJ jurisdiction declaration; accepts ICCt jurisdiction

**CITIZENSHIP:**

**citizenship by birth:** only if at least one parent is a citizen of Zambia

**citizenship by descent only:** yes, if at least one parent was a citizen of Zambia

**dual citizenship recognized:** yes

**residency requirement for naturalization:** 5 years for those with an ancestor who was a citizen of Zambia, otherwise 10 years residency is required

## SUFFRAGE:

18 years of age; universal

## EXECUTIVE BRANCH:

**chief of state:** President Edgar LUNGU (since 25 January 2015); Vice President Inonge WINA (since 26 January 2015); note - the president is both chief of state and head of government

**head of government:** President Edgar LUNGU (since 25 January 2015); Vice President Inonge WINA (since 26 January 2015)

**cabinet:** Cabinet appointed by president from among members of the National Assembly

**elections/appointments:** president directly elected by absolute majority popular vote in 2 rounds if needed for a 5-year term (eligible for a second term); last held on 11 August 2016 (next to be held in 2021)

**election results:** Edgar LUNGU reelected president in the first round; percent of vote - Edgar LUNGU (PF) 50.4%, Hakainde HICHILEMA (UPND) 47.6%, other 2.0%

## LEGISLATIVE BRANCH:

**description:** unicameral National Assembly (164 seats; 156 members directly elected in single-seat constituencies by simple majority vote in 2 rounds if needed, and 8 appointed by the president; members serve 5-year terms); note - 6 additional electoral seats were added for the 11 August 2016 election, up from 150 electoral seats in the 2011 election

**elections:** last held on 11 August 2016 (next to be held in 2021)

**election results:** percent of vote by party - PF 42%, UPND 41.7%, MMD 2.7%, FDD 2.2%, other 1.9%,independent 9.5%; seats by party - PF 80, UPND 58, MMD 3, FDD 1, independent 14

## JUDICIAL BRANCH:

**highest courts:** Supreme Court (consists of the chief justice and deputy chief justice, and at least 11 judges); Constitutional Court (consists of the court president, vice-president, and 11 judges); note - the Constitutional Court began operation in June 2016

**judge selection and term of office:** Supreme Court and Constitutional Court judges appointed by the president upon the advice of the 9-member Judicial Service Commission headed by the chief justice, and ratified by the National Assembly; judges normally serve until age 65

**subordinate courts:** Court of Appeal; High Court; Industrial Relations Court; subordinate courts 3 levels, based on upper limit of money involved); Small Claims Court; local courts (2 grades, based on upper limit of money involved)

## POLITICAL PARTIES AND LEADERS:

Alliance for Democracy and Development or ADD [Charles MILUPI]
Forum for Democracy and Development or FDD [Edith NAWAKWI]
Movement for Multiparty Democracy or MMD [Felix MUTATI]
Patriotic Front or PF [Edgar LUNGU]
United Party for National Development or UPND [Hakainde HICHILEMA]

## INTERNATIONAL ORGANIZATION PARTICIPATION:

ACP, AfDB, AU, C, COMESA, EITI (compliant country), FAO, G-77, IAEA, IBRD, ICAO, ICCt, ICRM, IDA, IFAD, IFC, IFRCS, ILO, IMF, Interpol, IOC, IOM, IPU, ISO (correspondent), ITSO, ITU, ITUC (NGOs), MIGA, MONUSCO, NAM, OPCW, PCA, SADC, UN, UNAMID, UNCTAD, UNESCO, UNHCR, UNIDO, UNISFA, UNMIL, UNMISS, UNOCI, UNWTO, UPU, WCO, WHO, WIPO, WMO, WTO

## DIPLOMATIC REPRESENTATION IN THE US:

**chief of mission:** Ambassador Ngosa SIMBYAKULA (since 29 November 2017)

**chancery:** 2200 R Street NW, Washington, DC 20008

**telephone:** [1] (202) 265-9717 through 9719

**FAX:** [1] (202) 332-0826

## DIPLOMATIC REPRESENTATION FROM THE US:

**chief of mission:** Ambassador Daniel L. FOOTE (since December 2017)

**embassy:** Eastern end of Kabulonga Road, Ibex Hill, Lusaka

**mailing address:** P. O. Box 320065, Lusaka

**telephone:** [260] 211-357-000

**FAX:** [260] 211-357-224

## FLAG DESCRIPTION:

green field with a panel of three vertical bands of red (hoist side), black, and orange below a soaring orange eagle, on the outer edge of the flag; green stands for the country's natural resources and vegetation, red symbolizes the struggle for freedom, black the people of Zambia, and orange the country's mineral wealth; the eagle represents the people's ability to rise above the nation's problems

## NATIONAL SYMBOL(S):

African fish eagle; national colors: green, red, black, orange

## NATIONAL ANTHEM:

**name:** "Lumbanyeni Zambia" (Stand and Sing of Zambia, Proud and Free)

**lyrics/music:** multiple/Enoch Mankayi SONTONGA

**note:** adopted 1964; the melody, from the popular song "God Bless Africa," is the same as that of Tanzania but with different lyrics; the melody is also incorporated into South Africa's anthem

# ECONOMY :: ZAMBIA

## ECONOMY - OVERVIEW:

Zambia had one of the world's fastest growing economies for the ten years up to 2014, with real GDP growth averaging roughly 6.7% per annum, though growth slowed during the period 2015 to 2017, due to falling copper prices, reduced power generation, and depreciation of the kwacha. Zambia's lack of economic diversification and dependency on copper as its sole major export makes it vulnerable to fluctuations in the world commodities market and prices turned downward in 2015 due to declining demand from China; Zambia was overtaken by the Democratic Republic of Congo as Africa's largest copper producer. GDP growth picked up in 2017 as mineral prices rose.

Despite recent strong economic growth and its status as a lower middle-income country, widespread and extreme rural poverty and high unemployment levels remain significant problems, made worse by a high birth rate, a relatively high HIV/AIDS burden, by market-distorting agricultural and energy policies, and growing government debt. Zambia raised $7 billion from international investors by issuing separate sovereign bonds in 2012, 2014, and 2015. Concurrently, it issued over $4 billion in domestic debt and agreed to Chinese-financed infrastructure projects, significantly increasing the country's public debt burden to more than 60% of GDP. The government has considered refinancing $3 billion worth of Eurobonds and significant Chinese loans to cut debt servicing costs.

**GDP (PURCHASING POWER PARITY):**

$68.93 billion (2017 est.)

$66.66 billion (2016 est.)

$64.25 billion (2015 est.)

note: data are in 2017 dollars

country comparison to the world: 102

**GDP (OFFICIAL EXCHANGE RATE):**

$25.71 billion (2017 est.) (2017 est.)

**GDP - REAL GROWTH RATE:**

3.4% (2017 est.)

3.8% (2016 est.)

2.9% (2015 est.)

country comparison to the world: 103

**GDP - PER CAPITA (PPP):**

$4,000 (2017 est.)

$4,000 (2016 est.)

$4,000 (2015 est.)

note: data are in 2017 dollars

country comparison to the world: 178

**GROSS NATIONAL SAVING:**

38.3% of GDP (2017 est.)

37.3% of GDP (2016 est.)

38.9% of GDP (2015 est.)

country comparison to the world: 11

**GDP - COMPOSITION, BY END USE:**

household consumption: 52.6% (2017 est.)

government consumption: 21% (2017 est.)

investment in fixed capital: 27.1% (2017 est.)

investment in inventories: 1.2% (2017 est.)

exports of goods and services: 43% (2017 est.)

imports of goods and services: -44.9% (2017 est.)

**GDP - COMPOSITION, BY SECTOR OF ORIGIN:**

agriculture: 7.5% (2017 est.)

industry: 35.3% (2017 est.)

services: 57% (2017 est.)

**AGRICULTURE - PRODUCTS:**

corn, sorghum, rice, peanuts, sunflower seeds, vegetables, flowers, tobacco, cotton, sugarcane, cassava (manioc, tapioca), coffee; cattle, goats, pigs, poultry, milk, eggs, hides

**INDUSTRIES:**

copper mining and processing, emerald mining, construction, foodstuffs, beverages, chemicals, textiles, fertilizer, horticulture

**INDUSTRIAL PRODUCTION GROWTH RATE:**

4.7% (2017 est.)

country comparison to the world: 62

**LABOR FORCE:**

6.898 million (2017 est.)

country comparison to the world: 68

**LABOR FORCE - BY OCCUPATION:**

agriculture: 54.8%

industry: 9.9%

services: 35.3% (2017 est.)

**UNEMPLOYMENT RATE:**

15% (2008 est.)

50% (2000 est.)

country comparison to the world: 173

**POPULATION BELOW POVERTY LINE:**

54.4% (2015 est.)

**HOUSEHOLD INCOME OR CONSUMPTION BY PERCENTAGE SHARE:**

lowest 10%: 47.4% (2010)

highest 10%: 47.4% (2010)

**DISTRIBUTION OF FAMILY INCOME - GINI INDEX:**

57.5 (2013)

50.8 (2004)

country comparison to the world: 7

**BUDGET:**

revenues: 4.473 billion (2017 est.)

expenditures: 6.357 billion (2017 est.)

**TAXES AND OTHER REVENUES:**

17.4% (of GDP) (2017 est.)

country comparison to the world: 169

**BUDGET SURPLUS (+) OR DEFICIT (-):**

-7.3% (of GDP) (2017 est.)

country comparison to the world: 195

**PUBLIC DEBT:**

63.1% of GDP (2017 est.)

60.7% of GDP (2016 est.)

country comparison to the world: 66

**FISCAL YEAR:**

calendar year

**INFLATION RATE (CONSUMER PRICES):**

6.6% (2017 est.)

17.9% (2016 est.)

country comparison to the world: 192

**CENTRAL BANK DISCOUNT RATE:**

9.1% (31 December 2012)

19% (31 December 2011)

country comparison to the world: 29

**COMMERCIAL BANK PRIME LENDING RATE:**

12.5% (31 December 2017 est.)

15.5% (31 December 2016 est.)

country comparison to the world: 66

**STOCK OF NARROW MONEY:**

$1.764 billion (31 December 2017 est.)

$1.582 billion (31 December 2016 est.)

country comparison to the world: 137

**STOCK OF BROAD MONEY:**

$1.764 billion (31 December 2017 est.)

$1.582 billion (31 December 2016 est.)

country comparison to the world: 146

**STOCK OF DOMESTIC CREDIT:**

$5.401 billion (31 December 2017 est.)

$4.167 billion (31 December 2016 est.)

country comparison to the world: 129

**MARKET VALUE OF PUBLICLY TRADED SHARES:**

$3.004 billion (31 December 2012 est.)

$4.009 billion (31 December 2011 est.)

$2.817 billion (31 December 2010 est.)

country comparison to the world: 93

**CURRENT ACCOUNT BALANCE:**

-$1.006 billion (2017 est.)

-$934 million (2016 est.)

country comparison to the world: 142

**EXPORTS:**

$8.216 billion (2017 est.)

$6.514 billion (2016 est.)

country comparison to the world: 98

**EXPORTS - PARTNERS:**

Switzerland 44.8%, China 16.1%, Democratic Republic of the Congo 6.2%, Singapore 6%, South Africa 5.9% (2017)

**EXPORTS - COMMODITIES:**

copper/cobalt, cobalt, electricity; tobacco, flowers, cotton

**IMPORTS:**

$7.852 billion (2017 est.)

$6.539 billion (2016 est.)

country comparison to the world: 113

**IMPORTS - COMMODITIES:**

machinery, transportation equipment, petroleum products, electricity, fertilizer, foodstuffs, clothing

**IMPORTS - PARTNERS:**

South Africa 28.2%, Democratic Republic of the Congo 20.8%, China 12.9%, Kuwait 5.4%, UAE 4.6% (2017)

**RESERVES OF FOREIGN EXCHANGE AND GOLD:**

$2.082 billion (31 December 2017 est.)

$2.353 billion (31 December 2016 est.)

country comparison to the world: 121

**DEBT - EXTERNAL:**

$11.66 billion (31 December 2017 est.)

$9.562 billion (31 December 2016 est.)

country comparison to the world: 108

**STOCK OF DIRECT FOREIGN INVESTMENT - AT HOME:**

NA

**STOCK OF DIRECT FOREIGN INVESTMENT - ABROAD:**

NA

**EXCHANGE RATES:**

Zambian kwacha (ZMK) per US dollar -

9.2 (2017 est.)

10.3 (2016 est.)

10.3 (2015 est.)

8.6 (2014 est.)

6.2 (2013 est.)

## ENERGY :: ZAMBIA

**ELECTRICITY ACCESS:**

population without electricity: 10.7 million (2013)

electrification - total population: 26% (2013)

electrification - urban areas: 45% (2013)

electrification - rural areas: 14% (2013)

**ELECTRICITY - PRODUCTION:**

11.55 billion kWh (2016 est.)

country comparison to the world: 98

**ELECTRICITY - CONSUMPTION:**

11.04 billion kWh (2016 est.)

country comparison to the world: 91

**ELECTRICITY - EXPORTS:**

1.176 billion kWh (2015 est.)

country comparison to the world: 56

**ELECTRICITY - IMPORTS:**

2.185 billion kWh (2016 est.)

country comparison to the world: 56

**ELECTRICITY - INSTALLED GENERATING CAPACITY:**

2.573 million kW (2016 est.)

country comparison to the world: 107

**ELECTRICITY - FROM FOSSIL FUELS:**

5% of total installed capacity (2016 est.)

country comparison to the world: 205

**ELECTRICITY - FROM NUCLEAR FUELS:**

0% of total installed capacity (2017 est.)

country comparison to the world: 214

**ELECTRICITY - FROM HYDROELECTRIC PLANTS:**

93% of total installed capacity (2017 est.)

country comparison to the world: 9

**ELECTRICITY - FROM OTHER RENEWABLE SOURCES:**

2% of total installed capacity (2017 est.)

country comparison to the world: 147

**CRUDE OIL - PRODUCTION:**

0 bbl/day (2017 est.)

country comparison to the world: 216

**CRUDE OIL - EXPORTS:**

0 bbl/day (2015 est.)

country comparison to the world: 217

**CRUDE OIL - IMPORTS:**

12,860 bbl/day (2015 est.)

country comparison to the world: 70

**CRUDE OIL - PROVED RESERVES:**

0 bbl (1 January 2018 est.)

country comparison to the world: 214

**REFINED PETROLEUM PRODUCTS - PRODUCTION:**

13,120 bbl/day (2015 est.)

country comparison to the world: 98

**REFINED PETROLEUM PRODUCTS - CONSUMPTION:**

23,000 bbl/day (2016 est.)

country comparison to the world: 133

**REFINED PETROLEUM PRODUCTS - EXPORTS:**

371 bbl/day (2015 est.)

country comparison to the world: 113

**REFINED PETROLEUM PRODUCTS - IMPORTS:**

10,150 bbl/day (2015 est.)

country comparison to the world: 149

**NATURAL GAS - PRODUCTION:**

0 cu m (2017 est.)

country comparison to the world: 216

**NATURAL GAS - CONSUMPTION:**

0 cu m (2017 est.)

country comparison to the world: 215

**NATURAL GAS - EXPORTS:**

0 cu m (2017 est.)

country comparison to the world: 215

**NATURAL GAS - IMPORTS:**

0 cu m (2017 est.)

country comparison to the world: 215

**NATURAL GAS - PROVED RESERVES:**

0 cu m (1 January 2014 est.)

country comparison to the world: 209

**CARBON DIOXIDE EMISSIONS FROM CONSUMPTION OF ENERGY:**

3.777 million Mt (2017 est.)

country comparison to the world: 140

## COMMUNICATIONS :: ZAMBIA

**TELEPHONES - FIXED LINES:**

total subscriptions: 101,444 (2017 est.)

subscriptions per 100 inhabitants: 1 (2017 est.)

country comparison to the world: 141

**TELEPHONES - MOBILE CELLULAR:**

total subscriptions: 13,438,539 (2017 est.)

subscriptions per 100 inhabitants: 84 (2017 est.)

country comparison to the world: 70

**TELEPHONE SYSTEM:**

general assessment: among the best in sub-Saharan Africa (2015)

domestic: high-capacity microwave radio relay connects most larger towns and cities; several cellular telephone services in operation and network coverage is improving; domestic satellite system being installed to improve telephone service in rural areas; Internet service is widely available; very small aperture terminal (VSAT) networks are operated by private firms (2015)

*international:* country code - 260; satellite earth stations - 2 Intelsat (1 Indian Ocean and 1 Atlantic Ocean), 3 owned by Zamtel (2015)

## BROADCAST MEDIA:

state-owned Zambia National Broadcasting Corporation (ZNBC) operates 3 TV stations, is the principal local-content provider, and owns about 45% of multi-channel Zambia shares; several private TV stations and multi-channel subscription TV services are available; ZNBC operates 4 radio networks; 64 private radio stations are available (most regionally) and relays of at least 2 international broadcasters — including BBC and Radio France International – are accessible in Lusaka and Kitwe (2015)

## INTERNET COUNTRY CODE:

.zm

## INTERNET USERS:

total: 3,956,252 (July 2016 est.)

percent of population: 25.5% (July 2016 est.)

country comparison to the world: 89

## BROADBAND - FIXED SUBSCRIPTIONS:

total: 35,912 (2017 est.)

subscriptions per 100 inhabitants: less than 1 (2017 est.)

country comparison to the world: 136

# TRANSPORTATION :: ZAMBIA

## NATIONAL AIR TRANSPORT SYSTEM:

number of registered air carriers: 1 (2015)

inventory of registered aircraft operated by air carriers: 1 (2015)

annual passenger traffic on registered air carriers: 11,796 (2015)

annual freight traffic on registered air carriers: 79,092,826 mt-km (2015)

## CIVIL AIRCRAFT REGISTRATION COUNTRY CODE PREFIX:

9J (2016)

## AIRPORTS:

88 (2013)

country comparison to the world: 63

## AIRPORTS - WITH PAVED RUNWAYS:

total: 8 (2013)

over 3,047 m: 1 (2013)

2,438 to 3,047 m: 3 (2013)

1,524 to 2,437 m: 3 (2013)

914 to 1,523 m: 1 (2013)

## AIRPORTS - WITH UNPAVED RUNWAYS:

total: 80 (2013)

2,438 to 3,047 m: 1 (2013)

1,524 to 2,437 m: 5 (2013)

914 to 1,523 m: 53 (2013)

under 914 m: 21 (2013)

## PIPELINES:

771 km oil (2013)

## RAILWAYS:

total: 3,126 km (2014)

narrow gauge: 3,126 km 1.067-m gauge (2014)

note: includes 1,860 km of the Tanzania-Zambia Railway Authority (TAZARA)

country comparison to the world: 59

## ROADWAYS:

total: 40,454 km (2005)

paved: 9,403 km (2005)

unpaved: 31,051 km (2005)

country comparison to the world: 87

## WATERWAYS:

2,250 km (includes Lake Tanganyika and the Zambezi and Luapula Rivers) (2010)

country comparison to the world: 38

## MERCHANT MARINE:

total: 1 (2017)

by type: other 1 (2017)

country comparison to the world: 176

## PORTS AND TERMINALS:

river port(s): Mpulungu (Zambezi)

# MILITARY AND SECURITY :: ZAMBIA

## MILITARY EXPENDITURES:

1.53% of GDP (2016)

1.75% of GDP (2015)

1.63% of GDP (2014)

country comparison to the world: 74

## MILITARY BRANCHES:

Zambian Defense Force (ZDF): Zambia Army, Zambia Air Force, Zambia National Service (support organization) (2015)

## MILITARY SERVICE AGE AND OBLIGATION:

national registration required at age 16; 18-25 years of age for male and female voluntary military service (16 years of age with parental consent); no conscription; Zambian citizenship required; grade 12 certification required; mandatory HIV testing on enlistment; mandatory retirement for officers at age 65 (Army, Air Force) (2012)

# TRANSNATIONAL ISSUES :: ZAMBIA

## DISPUTES - INTERNATIONAL:

in 2004, Zimbabwe dropped objections to plans between Botswana and Zambia to build a bridge over the Zambezi River, thereby de facto recognizing a short, but not clearly delimited, Botswana-Zambia boundary in the river

## REFUGEES AND INTERNALLY DISPLACED PERSONS:

refugees (country of origin): 42,308 (Democratic Republic of the Congo) (refugees and asylum seekers), 5,000 (Burundi) (refugees and asylum seekers) (2018)

## ILLICIT DRUGS:

transshipment point for moderate amounts of methaqualone, small amounts of heroin, and cocaine bound for southern Africa and possibly Europe; a poorly developed financial infrastructure coupled with a government commitment to combating money laundering make it an unattractive venue for money launderers; major consumer of cannabis

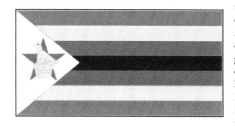

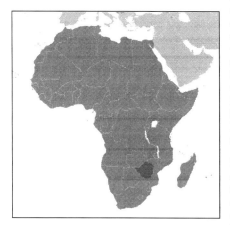

# AFRICA :: ZIMBABWE

## INTRODUCTION :: ZIMBABWE

### BACKGROUND:

The UK annexed Southern Rhodesia from the former British South Africa Company in 1923. A 1961 constitution was formulated that favored whites in power. In 1965 the government unilaterally declared its independence, but the UK did not recognize the act and demanded more complete voting rights for the black African majority in the country (then called Rhodesia). UN sanctions and a guerrilla uprising finally led to free elections in 1979 and independence (as Zimbabwe) in 1980. Robert MUGABE, the nation's first prime minister, has been the country's only ruler (as president since 1987) and has dominated the country's political system since independence. His chaotic land redistribution campaign, which began in 1997 and intensified after 2000, caused an exodus of white farmers, crippled the economy, and ushered in widespread shortages of basic commodities. Ignoring international condemnation, MUGABE rigged the 2002 presidential election to ensure his reelection.

In 2005, the capital city of Harare embarked on Operation Restore Order, ostensibly an urban rationalization program, which resulted in the destruction of the homes or businesses of 700,000 mostly poor supporters of the opposition. MUGABE in 2007 instituted price controls on all basic commodities causing panic buying and leaving store shelves empty for months. General elections held in March 2008 contained irregularities but still amounted to a censure of the ZANU-PF-led government with the opposition winning a majority of seats in parliament. Movement for Democratic Change - Tsvangirai opposition leader Morgan TSVANGIRAI won the most votes in the presidential poll, but not enough to win outright. In the lead up to a run-off election in June 2008, considerable violence against opposition party members led to the withdrawal of TSVANGIRAI from the ballot. Extensive evidence of violence and intimidation resulted in international condemnation of the process. Difficult negotiations over a power-sharing "government of national unity," in which MUGABE remained president and TSVANGIRAI became prime minister, were finally settled in February 2009, although the leaders failed to agree upon many key outstanding governmental issues. MUGABE was reelected president in 2013 in balloting that was severely flawed and internationally condemned. As a prerequisite to holding the election, Zimbabwe enacted a new constitution by referendum, although many provisions in the new constitution have yet to be codified in law. In November 2017, Vice President Emmerson MNANGAGWA took over following a military intervention that forced MUGABE to resign. MNANGAGWA was inaugurated president days later, promising to hold presidential elections in 2018.

## GEOGRAPHY :: ZIMBABWE

### LOCATION:
Southern Africa, between South Africa and Zambia

### GEOGRAPHIC COORDINATES:
20 00 S, 30 00 E

### MAP REFERENCES:
Africa

### AREA:
total: 390,757 sq km

land: 386,847 sq km

water: 3,910 sq km

country comparison to the world: 62

### AREA - COMPARATIVE:
about four times the size of Indiana; slightly larger than Montana

### LAND BOUNDARIES:
total: 3,229 km

border countries (4): Botswana 834 km, Mozambique 1402 km, South Africa 230 km, Zambia 763 km

### COASTLINE:
0 km (landlocked)

### MARITIME CLAIMS:
none (landlocked)

### CLIMATE:
tropical; moderated by altitude; rainy season (November to March)

### TERRAIN:
mostly high plateau with higher central plateau (high veld); mountains in east

### ELEVATION:
mean elevation: 961 m

elevation extremes: 162 m lowest point: junction of the Runde and Save Rivers

2592 highest point: Inyangani

### NATURAL RESOURCES:
coal, chromium ore, asbestos, gold, nickel, copper, iron ore, vanadium, lithium, tin, platinum group metals

### LAND USE:

**agricultural land:** 42.5% (2011 est.)

**arable land:** 10.9% (2011 est.) / **permanent crops:** 0.3% (2011 est.) / **permanent pasture:** 31.3% (2011 est.)

**forest:** 39.5% (2011 est.)

**other:** 18% (2011 est.)

## IRRIGATED LAND:
1,740 sq km (2012)

## POPULATION DISTRIBUTION:
Aside from major urban agglomerations in Harare and Bulawayo, population distribution is fairly even, with slightly greater overall numbers in the eastern half

## NATURAL HAZARDS:
recurring droughts; floods and severe storms are rare

## ENVIRONMENT - CURRENT ISSUES:
deforestation; soil erosion; land degradation; air and water pollution; the black rhinoceros herd - once the largest concentration of the species in the world - has been significantly reduced by poaching; poor mining practices have led to toxic waste and heavy metal pollution

## ENVIRONMENT - INTERNATIONAL AGREEMENTS:
**party to:** Biodiversity, Climate Change, Desertification, Endangered Species, Hazardous Wastes, Law of the Sea, Ozone Layer Protection

**signed, but not ratified:** none of the selected agreements

## GEOGRAPHY - NOTE:
landlocked; the Zambezi forms a natural riverine boundary with Zambia; in full flood (February-April) the massive Victoria Falls on the river forms the world's largest curtain of falling water; Lake Kariba on the Zambia-Zimbabwe border forms the world's largest reservoir by volume (180 cu km; 43 cu mi)

# PEOPLE AND SOCIETY :: ZIMBABWE

## POPULATION:
14,030,368 (July 2018 est.)

**note:** estimates for this country explicitly take into account the effects of excess mortality due to AIDS; this can result in lower life expectancy, higher infant mortality, higher death rates, lower population growth rates, and changes in the distribution of population by age and sex than would otherwise be expected

**country comparison to the world:** 73

## NATIONALITY:
**noun:** Zimbabwean(s)

**adjective:** Zimbabwean

## ETHNIC GROUPS:
African 99.4% (predominantly Shona; Ndebele is the second largest ethnic group), other 0.4%, unspecified 0.2% (2012 est.)

## LANGUAGES:
Shona (official; most widely spoken), Ndebele (official, second most widely spoken), English (official; traditionally used for official business), 13 minority languages (official; includes Chewa, Chibarwe, Kalanga, Koisan, Nambya, Ndau, Shangani, sign language, Sotho, Tonga, Tswana, Venda, and Xhosa)

## RELIGIONS:
Protestant 74.8% (includes Apostolic 37.5%, Pentecostal 21.8%, other 15.5%), Roman Catholic 7.3%, other Christian 5.3%, traditional 1.5%, Muslim 0.5%, other 0.1%, none 10.5% (2015 est.)

## DEMOGRAPHIC PROFILE:
Zimbabwe's progress in reproductive, maternal, and child health has stagnated in recent years. According to a 2010 Demographic and Health Survey, contraceptive use, the number of births attended by skilled practitioners, and child mortality have either stalled or somewhat deteriorated since the mid-2000s. Zimbabwe's total fertility rate has remained fairly stable at about 4 children per woman for the last two decades, although an uptick in the urban birth rate in recent years has caused a slight rise in the country's overall fertility rate. Zimbabwe's HIV prevalence rate dropped from approximately 29% to 15% since 1997 but remains among the world's highest and continues to suppress the country's life expectancy rate. The proliferation of HIV/AIDS information and prevention programs and personal experience with those suffering or dying from the disease have helped to change sexual behavior and reduce the epidemic.

Historically, the vast majority of Zimbabwe's migration has been internal – a rural-urban flow. In terms of international migration, over the last 40 years Zimbabwe has gradually shifted from being a destination country to one of emigration and, to a lesser degree, one of transit (for East African illegal migrants traveling to South Africa). As a British colony, Zimbabwe attracted significant numbers of permanent immigrants from the UK and other European countries, as well as temporary economic migrants from Malawi, Mozambique, and Zambia. Although Zimbabweans have migrated to South Africa since the beginning of the 20th century to work as miners, the first major exodus from the country occurred in the years before and after independence in 1980. The outward migration was politically and racially influenced; a large share of the white population of European origin chose to leave rather than live under a new black-majority government.

In the 1990s and 2000s, economic mismanagement and hyperinflation sparked a second, more diverse wave of emigration. This massive out migration – primarily to other southern African countries, the UK, and the US – has created a variety of challenges, including brain drain, illegal migration, and human smuggling and trafficking. Several factors have pushed highly skilled workers to go abroad, including unemployment, lower wages, a lack of resources, and few opportunities for career growth.

## AGE STRUCTURE:
**0-14 years:** 38.62% (male 2,681,192 /female 2,736,876)

**15-24 years:** 20.42% (male 1,403,715 /female 1,461,168)

**25-54 years:** 32.22% (male 2,286,915 /female 2,234,158)

**55-64 years:** 4.24% (male 233,021 /female 361,759)

**65 years and over:** 4.5% (male 255,704 /female 375,860) (2018 est.)

## DEPENDENCY RATIOS:
**total dependency ratio:** 79.5 (2015 est.)

**youth dependency ratio:** 74.4 (2015 est.)

**elderly dependency ratio:** 5.1 (2015 est.)

**potential support ratio:** 19.7 (2015 est.)

## MEDIAN AGE:
**total:** 20.2 years

**male:** 19.9 years

**female:** 20.4 years (2018 est.)

**country comparison to the world:** 190

## POPULATION GROWTH RATE:
1.68% (2018 est.)

country comparison to the world: 60

**BIRTH RATE:**

34 births/1,000 population (2018 est.)

country comparison to the world: 25

**DEATH RATE:**

9.9 deaths/1,000 population (2018 est.)

country comparison to the world: 41

**NET MIGRATION RATE:**

-8.5 migrant(s)/1,000 population (2017 est.)

country comparison to the world: 209

**POPULATION DISTRIBUTION:**

Aside from major urban agglomerations in Harare and Bulawayo, population distribution is fairly even, with slightly greater overall numbers in the eastern half

**URBANIZATION:**

urban population: 32.2% of total population (2018)

rate of urbanization: 2.19% annual rate of change (2015-20 est.)

**MAJOR URBAN AREAS - POPULATION:**

1.515 million HARARE (capital) (2018)

**SEX RATIO:**

at birth: 1.03 male(s)/female (2017 est.)

0-14 years: 1.02 male(s)/female (2017 est.)

15-24 years: 1.02 male(s)/female (2017 est.)

25-54 years: 1.1 male(s)/female (2017 est.)

55-64 years: 0.58 male(s)/female (2017 est.)

65 years and over: 0.64 male(s)/female (2017 est.)

total population: 1.01 male(s)/female (2017 est.)

**MOTHER'S MEAN AGE AT FIRST BIRTH:**

20 years (2015 est.)

note: median age at first birth among women 25-29

**MATERNAL MORTALITY RATE:**

443 deaths/100,000 live births (2015 est.)

country comparison to the world: 24

**INFANT MORTALITY RATE:**

total: 31.9 deaths/1,000 live births (2018 est.)

male: 35.9 deaths/1,000 live births (2018 est.)

female: 27.7 deaths/1,000 live births (2018 est.)

country comparison to the world: 57

**LIFE EXPECTANCY AT BIRTH:**

total population: 61.1 years (2018 est.)

male: 59 years (2018 est.)

female: 63.2 years (2018 est.)

country comparison to the world: 205

**TOTAL FERTILITY RATE:**

3.97 children born/woman (2018 est.)

country comparison to the world: 33

**CONTRACEPTIVE PREVALENCE RATE:**

66.8% (2015)

**HEALTH EXPENDITURES:**

6.4% of GDP (2014)

country comparison to the world: 99

**PHYSICIANS DENSITY:**

0.08 physicians/1,000 population (2014)

**HOSPITAL BED DENSITY:**

1.7 beds/1,000 population (2011)

**DRINKING WATER SOURCE:**

improved:

urban: 97% of population

rural: 67.3% of population

total: 76.9% of population

unimproved:

urban: 3% of population

rural: 32.7% of population

total: 23.1% of population (2015 est.)

**SANITATION FACILITY ACCESS:**

improved:

urban: 49.3% of population (2015 est.)

rural: 30.8% of population (2015 est.)

total: 36.8% of population (2015 est.)

unimproved:

urban: 50.7% of population (2015 est.)

rural: 69.2% of population (2015 est.)

total: 63.2% of population (2015 est.)

**HIV/AIDS - ADULT PREVALENCE RATE:**

13.3% (2017 est.)

country comparison to the world: 5

**HIV/AIDS - PEOPLE LIVING WITH HIV/AIDS:**

1.3 million (2017 est.)

country comparison to the world: 8

**HIV/AIDS - DEATHS:**

22,000 (2017 est.)

country comparison to the world: 11

**MAJOR INFECTIOUS DISEASES:**

degree of risk: high (2016)

food or waterborne diseases: bacterial and protozoal diarrhea, hepatitis A, and typhoid fever (2016)

vectorborne diseases: malaria and dengue fever (2016)

water contact diseases: schistosomiasis (2016)

animal contact diseases: rabies (2016)

**OBESITY - ADULT PREVALENCE RATE:**

15.5% (2016)

country comparison to the world: 126

**CHILDREN UNDER THE AGE OF 5 YEARS UNDERWEIGHT:**

8.4% (2015)

country comparison to the world: 69

**EDUCATION EXPENDITURES:**

8.4% of GDP (2014)

country comparison to the world: 7

**LITERACY:**

definition: age 15 and over can read and write English (2015 est.)

total population: 86.5% (2015 est.)

male: 88.5% (2015 est.)

female: 84.6% (2015 est.)

**SCHOOL LIFE EXPECTANCY (PRIMARY TO TERTIARY EDUCATION):**

total: 10 years (2013)

male: 10 years (2013)

female: 10 years (2013)

**UNEMPLOYMENT, YOUTH AGES 15-24:**

total: 16.5% (2014 est.)

male: 11.7% (2014 est.)

female: 21.1% (2014 est.)

country comparison to the world: 82

## GOVERNMENT :: ZIMBABWE

**COUNTRY NAME:**

conventional long form: Republic of Zimbabwe

conventional short form: Zimbabwe

**former:** Southern Rhodesia, Rhodesia, Zimbabwe-Rhodesia

**etymology:** takes its name from the Kingdom of Zimbabwe (13th-15th century) and its capital of Great Zimbabwe, the largest stone structure in pre-colonial southern Africa

## GOVERNMENT TYPE:
semi-presidential republic

## CAPITAL:
**name:** Harare

**geographic coordinates:** 17 49 S, 31 02 E

**time difference:** UTC+2 (7 hours ahead of Washington, DC, during Standard Time)

## ADMINISTRATIVE DIVISIONS:
8 provinces and 2 cities* with provincial status; Bulawayo*, Harare*, Manicaland, Mashonaland Central, Mashonaland East, Mashonaland West, Masvingo, Matabeleland North, Matabeleland South, Midlands

## INDEPENDENCE:
18 April 1980 (from the UK)

## NATIONAL HOLIDAY:
Independence Day, 18 April (1980)

## CONSTITUTION:
**history:** previous 1965 (at Rhodesian independence), 1979 (Lancaster House Agreement), 1980 (at Zimbabwean independence); latest final draft completed January 2013, approved by referendum 16 March 2013, approved by Parliament 9 May 2013, effective 22 May 2013 (2017)

**amendments:** proposed by the Senate or by the National Assembly; passage requires two-thirds majority vote by the membership of both houses of Parliament and assent by the president of the republic; amendments to constitutional chapters on fundamental human rights and freedoms and on agricultural lands also require approval by a majority of votes cast in a referendum; amended many times, last in 2017 (2017)

## LEGAL SYSTEM:
mixed legal system of English common law, Roman-Dutch civil law, and customary law

## INTERNATIONAL LAW ORGANIZATION PARTICIPATION:
has not submitted an ICJ jurisdiction declaration; non-party state to the ICCt

## CITIZENSHIP:
**citizenship by birth:** no

**citizenship by descent only:** the father must be a citizen of Zimbabwe; in the case of a child born out of wedlock, the mother must be a citizen

**dual citizenship recognized:** no

**residency requirement for naturalization:** 5 years

## SUFFRAGE:
18 years of age; universal

## EXECUTIVE BRANCH:
**chief of state:** President Emmerson Dambudzo MNANGAGWA (since 24 November 2017); First Vice President Constantino CHIWENGA (since 28 December 2017); note - Robert Gabriel MUGABE resigned on 21 November 2017, after ruling for 37 years

**head of government:** President Emmerson Dambudzo MNANGAGWA (since 24 November 2017); First Vice President Constantino CHIWENGA (since 28 December 2017)

**cabinet:** Cabinet appointed by president, responsible to National Assembly

**elections/appointments:** each presidential candidate nominated with a nomination paper signed by at least 10 registered voters (at least 1 candidate from each province) and directly elected by absolute majority popular vote in 2 rounds if needed for a 5-year term (no term limits); election last held on 3 July 2018 (next to be held in 2023); co-vice presidents drawn from party leadership

**election results:** Emmerson MNANGAGWA reelected president in 1st round of voting; percent of vote - Emmerson MNANGAGWA (ZANU-PF) 50.8%, Nelson CHAMISA (MDC-T) 44.3%, Thokozani KHUP (MDC-N) .9%, other 3%

## LEGISLATIVE BRANCH:
**description:** bicameral Parliament consists of:
Senate (80 seats; 60 members directly elected in multi-seat constituencies - 6 seats in each of the 10 provinces - by proportional representation vote, 16 indirectly elected by the regional governing councils, 2 reserved for the National Council Chiefs, and 2 reserved for members with disabilities; members serve 5-year terms)
National Assembly (270 seats; 210 members directly elected in single-seat constituencies by simple majority vote and 60 seats reserved for women directly elected by proportional representation vote; members serve 5-year terms)

**elections:**
Senate - last held for elected member on 30 July 2018 (next to be held in 2023)
National Assembly - last held on 31 July 2013 (next to be held in 2018)

**election results:**
Senate - percent of vote by party - NA; seats by party - ZANU-PF 34, MDC Alliance 25, Chiefs 18, people with disabilities 2, MDC-T 1
National Assembly - percent of vote by party - NA; seats by party - ZANU-PF 170, MDC Alliance 85, MDC-T 1, NPF 1, independent 1

## JUDICIAL BRANCH:
**highest courts:** Supreme Court (consists of the chief justice and 4 judges); Constitutional Court (consists of the chief and deputy chief justices and 9 judges)

**judge selection and term of office:** Supreme Court judges appointed by the president upon recommendation of the Judicial Service Commission, an independent body consisting of the chief justice, Public Service Commission chairman, attorney general, and 2-3 members appointed by the president; judges normally serve until age 65 but can elect to serve until age 70; Constitutional Court judge appointment NA; judges serve nonrenewable 15-year terms

**subordinate courts:** High Court; Labor Court; Administrative Court; regional magistrate courts; customary law courts; special courts

## POLITICAL PARTIES AND LEADERS:
Freedom Front [Cosmas MPONDA]
MDC Alliance [Nelson CHAMISA]
Movement for Democratic Change - Ncube or MDC-N [Welshman NCUBE]
Movement for Democratic Change - MDC-T [leadership contested between Nelson CHAMISA and Thokozani KHUPE]
National People's Party or NPP [Joyce MUJURU] formerly Zimbabwe People First or ZimPF)
National Patriotic Front or NPF [Ambrose MUTINHIRI]
Peoples Democratic Party or PDP [Tendai BITI]
Transform Zimbabwe or TZ [Jacob NGARIVHUME]
Zimbabwe African National Union-Patriotic Front or ZANU-PF [Emmerson Dambudzo MNANGAGWA]

Zimbabwe African Peoples Union or ZAPU [Dumiso DABENGWA]
Zimbabwe People First or ZimFirst [Maxwell SHUMBA]

**INTERNATIONAL ORGANIZATION PARTICIPATION:**

ACP, AfDB, AU, COMESA, FAO, G-15, G-77, IAEA, IBRD, ICAO, ICRM, IDA, IFAD, IFC, IFRCS, ILO, IMF, IMO, Interpol, IOC, IOM, IPU, ISO, ITSO, ITU, ITUC (NGOs), MIGA, NAM, OPCW, PCA, SADC, UN, UNAMID, UNCTAD, UNESCO, UNIDO, UNMIL, UNMISS, UNOCI, UNWTO, UPU, WCO, WFTU (NGOs), WHO, WIPO, WMO, WTO

**DIPLOMATIC REPRESENTATION IN THE US:**

chief of mission: Ambassador Ammon MUTEMBWA (since 18 November 2014)

chancery: 1608 New Hampshire Avenue NW, Washington, DC 20009

telephone: [1] (202) 332-7100

FAX: [1] (202) 483-9326

**DIPLOMATIC REPRESENTATION FROM THE US:**

chief of mission: Ambassador Brian A. NICHOLS (since 19 July 2018)

embassy: 172 Herbert Chitepo Avenue, Harare

mailing address: P.O. Box 3340, Harare

telephone: [263] (4) 250-593 through 250-594

FAX: [263] (4) 796-488

**FLAG DESCRIPTION:**

seven equal horizontal bands of green (top), yellow, red, black, red, yellow, and green with a white isosceles triangle edged in black with its base on the hoist side; a yellow Zimbabwe bird representing the long history of the country is superimposed on a red five-pointed star in the center of the triangle, which symbolizes peace; green represents agriculture, yellow mineral wealth, red the blood shed to achieve independence, and black stands for the native people

**NATIONAL SYMBOL(S):**

Zimbabwe bird symbol, African fish eagle, flame lily; national colors: green, yellow, red, black, white

**NATIONAL ANTHEM:**

name: "Kalibusiswe Ilizwe leZimbabwe" [Northern Ndebele language] "Simudzai Mureza WeZimbabwe" [Shona] (Blessed Be the Land of Zimbabwe)

lyrics/music: Solomon MUTSWAIRO/Fred Lecture CHANGUNDEGA

note: adopted 1994

# ECONOMY :: ZIMBABWE

**ECONOMY - OVERVIEW:**

Zimbabwe's economy depends heavily on its mining and agriculture sectors. Following a contraction from 1998 to 2008, the economy recorded real growth of more than 10% per year in the period 2010-13, before falling below 3% in the period 2014-17, due to poor harvests, low diamond revenues, and decreased investment. Lower mineral prices, infrastructure and regulatory deficiencies, a poor investment climate, a large public and external debt burden, and extremely high government wage expenses impede the country's economic performance.

Until early 2009, the Reserve Bank of Zimbabwe (RBZ) routinely printed money to fund the budget deficit, causing hyperinflation. Adoption of a multi-currency basket in early 2009 - which allowed currencies such as the Botswana pula, the South Africa rand, and the US dollar to be used locally - reduced inflation below 10% per year. In January 2015, as part of the government's effort to boost trade and attract foreign investment, the RBZ announced that the Chinese renmimbi, Indian rupee, Australian dollar, and Japanese yen would be accepted as legal tender in Zimbabwe, though transactions were predominantly carried out in US dollars and South African rand until 2016, when the rand's devaluation and instability led to near-exclusive use of the US dollar. The government in November 2016 began releasing bond notes, a parallel currency legal only in Zimbabwe which the government claims will have a one-to-one exchange ratio with the US dollar, to ease cash shortages. Bond notes began trading at a discount of up to 10% in the black market by the end of 2016.

Zimbabwe's government entered a second Staff Monitored Program with the IMF in 2014 and undertook other measures to reengage with international financial institutions. Zimbabwe repaid roughly $108 million in arrears to the IMF in October 2016, but financial observers note that Zimbabwe is unlikely to gain new financing because the government has not disclosed how it plans to repay more than $1.7 billion in arrears to the World Bank and African Development Bank. International financial institutions want Zimbabwe to implement significant fiscal and structural reforms before granting new loans. Foreign and domestic investment continues to be hindered by the lack of land tenure and titling, the inability to repatriate dividends to investors overseas, and the lack of clarity regarding the government's Indigenization and Economic Empowerment Act.

**GDP (PURCHASING POWER PARITY):**

$34.27 billion (2017 est.)

$33.04 billion (2016 est.)

$32.82 billion (2015 est.)

note: data are in 2017 dollars

country comparison to the world: 127

**GDP (OFFICIAL EXCHANGE RATE):**

$17.64 billion (2017 est.) (2017 est.)

**GDP - REAL GROWTH RATE:**

3.7% (2017 est.)

0.7% (2016 est.)

1.4% (2015 est.)

country comparison to the world: 93

**GDP - PER CAPITA (PPP):**

$2,300 (2017 est.)

$2,300 (2016 est.)

$2,300 (2015 est.)

note: data are in 2017 dollars

country comparison to the world: 203

**GROSS NATIONAL SAVING:**

23.3% of GDP (2017 est.)

19.1% of GDP (2016 est.)

8% of GDP (2015 est.)

country comparison to the world: 74

**GDP - COMPOSITION, BY END USE:**

household consumption: 77.6% (2017 est.)

government consumption: 24% (2017 est.)

investment in fixed capital: 12.6% (2017 est.)

investment in inventories: 0% (2017 est.)

exports of goods and services: 25.6% (2017 est.)

imports of goods and services: -39.9% (2017 est.)

**GDP - COMPOSITION, BY SECTOR OF ORIGIN:**

agriculture: 12% (2017 est.)

industry: 22.2% (2017 est.)

services: 65.8% (2017 est.)

**AGRICULTURE - PRODUCTS:**

tobacco, corn, cotton, wheat, coffee, sugarcane, peanuts; sheep, goats, pigs

**INDUSTRIES:**

mining (coal, gold, platinum, copper, nickel, tin, diamonds, clay, numerous metallic and nonmetallic ores), steel; wood products, cement, chemicals, fertilizer, clothing and footwear, foodstuffs, beverages

**INDUSTRIAL PRODUCTION GROWTH RATE:**

0.3% (2017 est.)

country comparison to the world: 167

**LABOR FORCE:**

7.907 million (2017 est.)

country comparison to the world: 64

**LABOR FORCE - BY OCCUPATION:**

agriculture: 67.5%

industry: 7.3%

services: 25.2% (2017 est.)

**UNEMPLOYMENT RATE:**

11.3% (2014 est.)

80% (2005 est.)

note: data include both unemployment and underemployment; true unemployment is unknown and, under current economic conditions, unknowable

country comparison to the world: 154

**POPULATION BELOW POVERTY LINE:**

72.3% (2012 est.)

**HOUSEHOLD INCOME OR CONSUMPTION BY PERCENTAGE SHARE:**

lowest 10%: 40.4% (1995)

highest 10%: 40.4% (1995)

**DISTRIBUTION OF FAMILY INCOME - GINI INDEX:**

43.2 (2011 est.)

50.1 (2006)

country comparison to the world: 48

**BUDGET:**

revenues: 3.8 billion (2017 est.)

expenditures: 5.5 billion (2017 est.)

**TAXES AND OTHER REVENUES:**

21.5% (of GDP) (2017 est.)

country comparison to the world: 138

**BUDGET SURPLUS (+) OR DEFICIT (-):**

-9.6% (of GDP) (2017 est.)

country comparison to the world: 208

**PUBLIC DEBT:**

82.3% of GDP (2017 est.)

69.9% of GDP (2016 est.)

country comparison to the world: 34

**FISCAL YEAR:**

calendar year

**INFLATION RATE (CONSUMER PRICES):**

0.9% (2017 est.)

-1.6% (2016 est.)

country comparison to the world: 49

**CENTRAL BANK DISCOUNT RATE:**

7.17% (31 December 2010)

975% (31 December 2007)

country comparison to the world: 46

**COMMERCIAL BANK PRIME LENDING RATE:**

18% (31 December 2017 est.)

7.1% (31 December 2016 est.)

country comparison to the world: 22

**STOCK OF NARROW MONEY:**

$4.322 billion (31 December 2017 est.)

$4.104 billion (31 December 2016 est.)

note: Zimbabwe's central bank no longer publishes data on monetary aggregates, except for bank deposits, which amounted to $2.1 billion in November 2010; the Zimbabwe dollar stopped circulating in early 2009; since then, the US dollar and South African rand have been the most frequently used currencies; there are no reliable estimates of the amount of foreign currency circulating in Zimbabwe

country comparison to the world: 109

**STOCK OF BROAD MONEY:**

$4.322 billion (31 December 2017 est.)

$4.104 billion (31 December 2016 est.)

country comparison to the world: 114

**STOCK OF DOMESTIC CREDIT:**

$8.389 billion (31 December 2017 est.)

$5.358 billion (31 December 2016 est.)

country comparison to the world: 115

**MARKET VALUE OF PUBLICLY TRADED SHARES:**

$4.073 billion (13 April 2015 est.)

$11.82 billion (31 December 2012 est.)

$10.9 billion (31 December 2011 est.)

country comparison to the world: 88

**CURRENT ACCOUNT BALANCE:**

-$716 million (2017 est.)

-$553 million (2016 est.)

country comparison to the world: 130

**EXPORTS:**

$4.353 billion (2017 est.)

$3.366 billion (2016 est.)

country comparison to the world: 115

**EXPORTS - PARTNERS:**

South Africa 50.3%, Mozambique 22.5%, UAE 9.8%, Zambia 4.9% (2017)

**EXPORTS - COMMODITIES:**

platinum, cotton, tobacco, gold, ferroalloys, textiles/clothing

**IMPORTS:**

$5.472 billion (2017 est.)

$5.236 billion (2016 est.)

country comparison to the world: 122

**IMPORTS - COMMODITIES:**

machinery and transport equipment, other manufactures, chemicals, fuels, food products

**IMPORTS - PARTNERS:**

South Africa 47.8%, Zambia 20.5% (2017)

**RESERVES OF FOREIGN EXCHANGE AND GOLD:**

$431.8 million (31 December 2017 est.)

$407.2 million (31 December 2016 est.)

country comparison to the world: 157

**DEBT - EXTERNAL:**

$9.357 billion (31 December 2017 est.)

$10.14 billion (31 December 2016 est.)

country comparison to the world: 116

**STOCK OF DIRECT FOREIGN INVESTMENT - AT HOME:**

$3.86 billion (31 December 2017 est.)

$3.518 billion (31 December 2016 est.)

country comparison to the world: 110

**STOCK OF DIRECT FOREIGN INVESTMENT - ABROAD:**

$309.6 million (31 December 2017 est.)

$271.6 million (31 December 2016 est.)

country comparison to the world: 102

**EXCHANGE RATES:**

Zimbabwean dollars (ZWD) per US dollar -

1 (2017 est.)

1 (2016 est.)

(2013)

234.25 (2010)

note: the dollar was adopted as a legal currency in 2009; since then the Zimbabwean dollar has experienced hyperinflation and is essentially worthless

## ENERGY :: ZIMBABWE

**ELECTRICITY ACCESS:**

population without electricity: 8.5 million (2013)

electrification - total population: 40% (2013)

electrification - urban areas: 80% (2013)

electrification - rural areas: 21% (2013)

**ELECTRICITY - PRODUCTION:**

6.8 billion kWh (2016 est.)

country comparison to the world: 113

**ELECTRICITY - CONSUMPTION:**

7.118 billion kWh (2016 est.)

country comparison to the world: 108

**ELECTRICITY - EXPORTS:**

1.239 billion kWh (2015 est.)

country comparison to the world: 54

**ELECTRICITY - IMPORTS:**

2.22 billion kWh (2016 est.)

country comparison to the world: 54

**ELECTRICITY - INSTALLED GENERATING CAPACITY:**

2.122 million kW (2016 est.)

country comparison to the world: 111

**ELECTRICITY - FROM FOSSIL FUELS:**

58% of total installed capacity (2016 est.)

country comparison to the world: 136

**ELECTRICITY - FROM NUCLEAR FUELS:**

0% of total installed capacity (2017 est.)

country comparison to the world: 215

**ELECTRICITY - FROM HYDROELECTRIC PLANTS:**

37% of total installed capacity (2017 est.)

country comparison to the world: 58

**ELECTRICITY - FROM OTHER RENEWABLE SOURCES:**

5% of total installed capacity (2017 est.)

country comparison to the world: 110

**CRUDE OIL - PRODUCTION:**

0 bbl/day (2017 est.)

country comparison to the world: 217

**CRUDE OIL - EXPORTS:**

0 bbl/day (2015 est.)

country comparison to the world: 218

**CRUDE OIL - IMPORTS:**

0 bbl/day (2015 est.)

country comparison to the world: 218

**CRUDE OIL - PROVED RESERVES:**

0 bbl (1 January 2018 est.)

country comparison to the world: 215

**REFINED PETROLEUM PRODUCTS - PRODUCTION:**

0 bbl/day (2015 est.)

country comparison to the world: 217

**REFINED PETROLEUM PRODUCTS - CONSUMPTION:**

27,000 bbl/day (2016 est.)

country comparison to the world: 127

**REFINED PETROLEUM PRODUCTS - EXPORTS:**

0 bbl/day (2015 est.)

country comparison to the world: 217

**REFINED PETROLEUM PRODUCTS - IMPORTS:**

26,400 bbl/day (2015 est.)

country comparison to the world: 104

**NATURAL GAS - PRODUCTION:**

0 cu m (2017 est.)

country comparison to the world: 217

**NATURAL GAS - CONSUMPTION:**

0 cu m (2017 est.)

country comparison to the world: 216

**NATURAL GAS - EXPORTS:**

0 cu m (2017 est.)

country comparison to the world: 216

**NATURAL GAS - IMPORTS:**

0 cu m (2017 est.)

country comparison to the world: 216

**NATURAL GAS - PROVED RESERVES:**

0 cu m (1 January 2014 est.)

country comparison to the world: 210

**CARBON DIOXIDE EMISSIONS FROM CONSUMPTION OF ENERGY:**

12.06 million Mt (2017 est.)

country comparison to the world: 100

## COMMUNICATIONS :: ZIMBABWE

**TELEPHONES - FIXED LINES:**

total subscriptions: 264,150 (2017 est.)

subscriptions per 100 inhabitants: 2 (2017 est.)

country comparison to the world: 119

**TELEPHONES - MOBILE CELLULAR:**

total subscriptions: 14,092,104 (2017 est.)

subscriptions per 100 inhabitants: 102 (2017 est.)

country comparison to the world: 68

**TELEPHONE SYSTEM:**

general assessment: competition has driven rapid expansion of telecommunications, particularly cellular voice and mobile broadband, in recent years; continued economic instability and infrastructure limitations, such as reliable power, hinder progress (2017)

domestic: consists of microwave radio relay links, open-wire lines, radiotelephone communication stations, fixed wireless local loop installations, fiber-optic cable, VSAT terminals, and a substantial mobile-cellular network; Internet connection is most readily available in Harare and major towns; two government owned and two private cellular providers; 3G and VoIP services are widely available with 4G/LTE service being deployed (2017)

international: country code - 263; satellite earth stations - 2 Intelsat; 5 international digital gateway exchanges; fiber-optic connections to neighboring states provide access to international networks via undersea cable (2017)

**BROADCAST MEDIA:**

government owns all local radio and TV stations; foreign shortwave broadcasts and satellite TV are available to those who can afford antennas and receivers; in rural areas, access to TV broadcasts is extremely limited; analog TV only, no digital service (2017)

**INTERNET COUNTRY CODE:**

.zw

**INTERNET USERS:**

total: 3,363,256 (July 2016 est.)

percent of population: 23.1% (July 2016 est.)

country comparison to the world: 94

**BROADBAND - FIXED SUBSCRIPTIONS:**

total: 187,310 (2017 est.)

subscriptions per 100 inhabitants: 1 (2017 est.)

country comparison to the world: 109

## TRANSPORTATION :: ZIMBABWE

**NATIONAL AIR TRANSPORT SYSTEM:**

number of registered air carriers: 2 (2015)

inventory of registered aircraft operated by air carriers: 4 (2015)

annual passenger traffic on registered air carriers: 370,164 (2015)

annual freight traffic on registered air carriers: 962,642 mt-km (2015)

**CIVIL AIRCRAFT REGISTRATION COUNTRY CODE PREFIX:**

Z (2016)

**AIRPORTS:**

196 (2013)

country comparison to the world: 29

**AIRPORTS - WITH PAVED RUNWAYS:**

total: 17 (2013)

over 3,047 m: 3 (2013)

2,438 to 3,047 m: 2 (2013)

1,524 to 2,437 m: 5 (2013)

914 to 1,523 m: 7 (2013)

**AIRPORTS - WITH UNPAVED RUNWAYS:**

total: 179 (2013)

1,524 to 2,437 m: 3 (2013)

914 to 1,523 m: 104 (2013)

under 914 m: 72 (2013)

**PIPELINES:**

270 km refined products (2013)

**RAILWAYS:**

total: 3,427 km (2014)

narrow gauge: 3,427 km 1.067-m gauge (313 km electrified) (2014)

country comparison to the world: 57

**ROADWAYS:**

total: 97,267 km (2002)

paved: 18,481 km (2002)

unpaved: 78,786 km (2002)

country comparison to the world: 49

**WATERWAYS:**

(some navigation possible on Lake Kariba) (2011)

**PORTS AND TERMINALS:**

river port(s): Binga, Kariba (Zambezi)

## MILITARY AND SECURITY :: ZIMBABWE

**MILITARY EXPENDITURES:**

2.2% of GDP (2016)

2.34% of GDP (2015)

2.32% of GDP (2014)

2.34% of GDP (2013)

2.26% of GDP (2012)

country comparison to the world: 47

**MILITARY BRANCHES:**

Zimbabwe Defense Forces (ZDF): Zimbabwe National Army (ZNA), Air Force of Zimbabwe (AFZ) (2012)

**MILITARY SERVICE AGE AND OBLIGATION:**

18-24 years of age for voluntary military service; no conscription; women are eligible to serve (2012)

## TRANSNATIONAL ISSUES :: ZIMBABWE

**DISPUTES - INTERNATIONAL:**

Namibia has supported, and in 2004 Zimbabwe dropped objections to, plans between Botswana and Zambia to build a bridge over the Zambezi River, thereby de facto recognizing a short, but not clearly delimited, Botswana-Zambia boundary in the riverSouth Africa has placed military units to assist police operations along the border of Lesotho, Zimbabwe, and Mozambique to control smuggling, poaching, and illegal migration

**REFUGEES AND INTERNALLY DISPLACED PERSONS:**

refugees (country of origin): 9,997 (Democratic Republic of Congo) (refugees and asylum seekers), Mozambique 8,312 (refugees and asylum seekers) (2018)

IDPs: undetermined (political violence, violence in association with the 2008 election, human rights violations, land reform, and economic collapse) (2015)

stateless persons: 300,000 (2016)

**TRAFFICKING IN PERSONS:**

current situation: Zimbabwe is a source, transit, and destination country for men, women, and children subjected to forced labor and sex trafficking; Zimbabwean women and girls from towns bordering South Africa, Mozambique, and Zambia are subjected to forced labor, including domestic servitude, and prostitution catering to long-distance truck drivers; Zimbabwean men, women, and children experience forced labor in agriculture and domestic servitude in rural areas; family members may recruit children and other relatives from rural areas with promises of work or education in cities and towns where they end up in domestic servitude and sex trafficking; Zimbabwean women and men are lured into exploitative labor situations in South Africa and other neighboring countries

tier rating: Tier 3 - Zimbabwe does not fully comply with the minimum standards for the elimination of trafficking and is not making significant efforts to do so; the government passed an anti-trafficking law in 2014 defining trafficking in persons as a crime of transportation and failing to capture the key element of the international definition of human trafficking – the purpose of exploitation – which prevents the law from being comprehensive or consistent with the 2000 UN TIP Protocol that Zimbabwe acceded to in 2013; the government did not report on anti-trafficking law enforcement efforts during 2014, and corruption in law enforcement and the judiciary remain a concern; authorities made minimal efforts to identify and protect trafficking victims, relying on NGOs to identify and assist victims; Zimbabwe's 2014 anti-trafficking law required the opening of 10 centers for trafficking victims, but none were established during the year; five existing shelters for vulnerable children and orphans may have accommodated child victims; in January 2015, an inter-ministerial anti-trafficking committee was established, but it is unclear if the committee ever met or initiated any activities (2015)

**ILLICIT DRUGS:**

transit point for cannabis and South Asian heroin, mandrax, and methamphetamines en route to South Africa

# APPENDIX A :: ABBREVIATIONS

### ABEDA
Arab Bank for Economic Development in Africa

### ACP GROUP
African, Caribbean, and Pacific Group of States

### ADB
Asian Development Bank

### AFDB
African Development Bank

### AFESD
Arab Fund for Economic and Social Development

### AG
Australia Group

### AIR POLLUTION
Convention on Long-Range Transboundary Air Pollution

### AIR POLLUTION-NITROGEN OXIDES
Protocol to the 1979 Convention on Long-Range Transboundary Air Pollution Concerning the Control of Emissions of Nitrogen Oxides or Their Transboundary Fluxes

### AIR POLLUTION-PERSISTENT ORGANIC POLLUTANTS
Protocol to the 1979 Convention on Long-Range Transboundary Air Pollution on Persistent Organic Pollutants

### AIR POLLUTION-SULPHUR 85
Protocol to the 1979 Convention on Long-Range Transboundary Air Pollution on the Reduction of Sulphur Emissions or Their Transboundary Fluxes by at Least 30%

### AIR POLLUTION-SULPHUR 94
Protocol to the 1979 Convention on Long-Range Transboundary Air Pollution on Further Reduction of Sulphur Emissions

### AIR POLLUTION-VOLATILE ORGANIC COMPOUNDS
Protocol to the 1979 Convention on Long-Range Transboundary Air Pollution Concerning the Control of Emissions of Volatile Organic Compounds or Their Transboundary Fluxes

### AMF
Arab Monetary Fund

### AMU
Arab Maghreb Union

### ANTARCTIC MARINE LIVING RESOURCES
Convention on the Conservation of Antarctic Marine Living Resources

### ANTARCTIC SEALS
Convention for the Conservation of Antarctic Seals

### ANTARCTIC-ENVIRONMENTAL PROTOCOL
Protocol on Environmental Protection to the Antarctic Treaty

### ANZUS
Australia-New Zealand-United States Security Treaty

### AOSIS
Alliance of Small Island States

### APEC
Asia-Pacific Economic Cooperation

### ARABSAT
Arab Satellite Communications Organization

### ARF
ASEAN Regional Forum

## ASEAN
Association of Southeast Asian Nations

## AU
African Union

## AUTODIN
Automatic Digital Network

## BA
Baltic Assembly

## BBL/DAY
barrels per day

## BCIE
Central American Bank for Economic Integration

## BDEAC
Central African States Development Bank

## BENELUX
Benelux Union

## BGN
United States Board on Geographic Names

## BIMSTEC
Bay of Bengal Initiative for Multi-sectoral Technical and Economic Cooperation

## BIODIVERSITY
Convention on Biological Diversity

## BIS
Bank for International Settlements

## BRICS
(Brazil, Russia, India, China, and South Africa)

## BSEC
Black Sea Economic Cooperation Zone

## C
Commonwealth

## C.I.F.
cost, insurance, and freight

## CACM
Central American Common Market

## CAEU
Council of Arab Economic Unity

## CAN
Andean Community

## CARICOM
Caribbean Community and Common Market

## CB
citizen's band mobile radio communications

## CBSS
Council of the Baltic Sea States

## CCC
Customs Cooperation Council

## CD
Community of Democracies

## CDB
Caribbean Development Bank

## CE
Council of Europe

## CEI
Central European Initiative

## CELAC
Community of Latin American and Caribbean States

### CEMA
Council for Mutual Economic Assistance

### CEMAC
Economic and Monetary Community of Central Africa

### CEPGL
Economic Community of the Great Lakes Countries

### CERN
European Organization for Nuclear Research

### CIA
Central Intelligence Agency

### CICA
Conference of Interaction and Confidence-Building Measures in Asia

### CIS
Commonwealth of Independent States

### CITES
see Endangered Species

### CLIMATE CHANGE
United Nations Framework Convention on Climate Change

### CLIMATE CHANGE-KYOTO PROTOCOL
Kyoto Protocol to the United Nations Framework Convention on Climate Change

### COCOM
Coordinating Committee on Export Controls

### COMESA
Common Market for Eastern and Southern Africa

### COMSAT
Communications Satellite Corporation

### CP
Colombo Plan

### CPLP
Comunidade dos Paises de Lingua Portuguesa

### CSN
South American Community of Nations became UNASUL - Union of South American Nations

### CSTO
Collective Security Treaty Organization

### CTBTO
Preparatory Commission for the Nuclear-Test-Ban Treaty Organization

### CY
calendar year

### D-8
Developing Eight

### DC
developed country

### DDT
dichloro-diphenyl-trichloro-ethane

### DESERTIFICATION
United Nations Convention to Combat Desertification in Those Countries Experiencing Serious Drought and/or Desertification, Particularly in Africa

### DIA
United States Defense Intelligence Agency

### DSN
Defense Switched Network

### DST
daylight savings time

### DWT

deadweight ton

**EAC**
East African Community

**EADB**
East African Development Bank

**EAEC**
Eurasian Economic Community

**EAPC**
Euro-Atlantic Partnership Council

**EAS**
East Asia Summit

**EBRD**
European Bank for Reconstruction and Development

**EC**
European Community or European Commission

**ECA**
Economic Commission for Africa

**ECB**
European Central Bank

**ECE**
Economic Commission for Europe

**ECLAC**
Economic Commission for Latin America and the Caribbean

**ECO**
Economic Cooperation Organization

**ECOSOC**
Economic and Social Council

**ECOWAS**
Economic Community of West African States

**ECSC**
European Coal and Steel Community

**EE**
Eastern Europe

**EEC**
European Economic Community

**EEZ**
exclusive economic zone

**EFTA**
European Free Trade Association

**EIB**
European Investment Bank

**EITI**
Extractive Industry Transparency Initiative

**EMU**
European Monetary Union

**ENDANGERED SPECIES**
Convention on the International Trade in Endangered Species of Wild Flora and Fauna (CITES)

**ENTENTE**
Council of the Entente

**ENVIRONMENTAL MODIFICATION**
Convention on the Prohibition of Military or Any Other Hostile Use of Environmental Modification Techniques

**ESA**
European Space Agency

**ESCAP**

Economic and Social Commission for Asia and the Pacific

**ESCWA**

Economic and Social Commission for Western Asia

**EST.**

estimate

**EU**

European Union

**EURATOM**

European Atomic Energy Community

**EUTELSAT**

European Telecommunications Satellite Organization

**EX-IM**

Export-Import Bank of the United States

**F.O.B.**

free on board

**FAO**

Food and Agriculture Organization

**FATF**

Financial Action Task Force

**FAX**

facsimile

**FLS**

Front Line States

**FOC**

flags of convenience

**FSU**

former Soviet Union

**FY**

fiscal year

**FZ**

Franc Zone

**G-10**

Group of 10

**G-11**

Group of 11

**G-15**

Group of 15

**G-20**

Group of 20

**G-24**

Group of 24

**G-3**

Group of 3

**G-5**

Group of 5

**G-6**

Group of 6

**G-7**

Group of 7

**G-77**

Group of 77

**G-8**

Group of 8

**G-9**

Group of 9

**GATT**

General Agreement on Tariffs and Trade; now WTO

**GCC**

Gulf Cooperation Council

**GCN**

Global Caribbean Network

**GCTU**

General Confederation of Trade Unions

**GDP**

gross domestic product

**GMT**

Greenwich Mean Time

**GNP**

gross national product

**GRT**

gross register ton

**GSM**

global system for mobile cellular communications

**GUAM**

Organization for Democracy and Economic Development; acronym for member states - Georgia, Ukraine, Azerbaijan, Moldova

**GWP**

gross world product

**HAZARDOUS WASTES**

Basel Convention on the Control of Transboundary Movements of Hazardous Wastes and Their Disposal

**HF**

high-frequency

**HIV/AIDS**

human immunodeficiency virus/acquired immune deficiency syndrome

**IADB**

Inter-American Development Bank

**IAEA**

International Atomic Energy Agency

**IANA**

Internet Assigned Numbers Authority

**IBRD**

International Bank for Reconstruction and Development (World Bank)

**ICAO**

International Civil Aviation Organization

**ICC**

International Chamber of Commerce

**ICCT**

International Criminal Court

**ICJ**

International Court of Justice (World Court)

**ICRC**

International Committee of the Red Cross

**ICRM**

International Red Cross and Red Crescent Movement

**ICSID**

International Center for Settlement of Investment Disputes

**ICTR**

International Criminal Tribunal for Rwanda

**ICTY**

International Criminal Tribunal for the former Yugoslavia

**IDA**

International Development Association

**IDB**

Islamic Development Bank

**IDP**

Internally Displaced Person

**IEA**

International Energy Agency

**IFAD**

International Fund for Agricultural Development

**IFC**

International Finance Corporation

**IFRCS**

International Federation of Red Cross and Red Crescent Societies

**IGAD**

Inter-Governmental Authority on Development

**IHO**

International Hydrographic Organization

**ILO**

International Labor Organization

**IMF**

International Monetary Fund

**IMO**

International Maritime Organization

**IMSO**

International Mobile Satellite Organization

**INMARSAT**

International Maritime Satellite Organization

**INOC**

Indian Ocean Commission

**INTELSAT**

International Telecommunications Satellite Organization

**INTERPOL**

International Criminal Police Organization

**INTERSPUTNIK**

International Organization of Space Communications

**IOC**

International Olympic Committee

**IOM**

International Organization for Migration

**IPU**

Inter-Parliamentary Union

**ISO**

International Organization for Standardization

**ISP**

Internet Service Provider

**ITC**

International Trade Center

**ITSO**

International Telecommunications Satellite Organization

**ITU**

International Telecommunication Union

**ITUC**

International Trade Union Confederation, the successor to ICFTU (International Confederation of Free Trade Unions) and the WCL (World Confederation of Labor)

## KHZ
kilohertz

## KM
kilometer

## KW
kilowatt

## KWH
kilowatt-hour

## LAES
Latin American and Caribbean Economic System

## LAIA
Latin American Integration Association

## LAS
League of Arab States

## LAW OF THE SEA
United Nations Convention on the Law of the Sea (LOS)

## LDC
less developed country

## LLDC
least developed country

## LONDON CONVENTION
see Marine Dumping

## LOS
see Law of the Sea

## M
meter

## MARECS
Maritime European Communications Satellite

## MARINE DUMPING
Convention on the Prevention of Marine Pollution by Dumping Wastes and Other Matter

## MARINE LIFE CONSERVATION
Convention on Fishing and Conservation of Living Resources of the High Seas

## MARPOL
see Ship Pollution

## MEDARABTEL
Middle East Telecommunications Project of the International Telecommunications Union

## MERCOSUR
Southern Cone Common Market

## MHZ
megahertz

## MICAH
International Civilian Support Mission in Haiti

## MIGA
Multilateral Investment Guarantee Agency

## MINURCAT
United Nations Mission in the Central African Republic and Chad

## MINURSO
United Nations Mission for the Referendum in Western Sahara

## MINUSTAH
United Nations Stabilization Mission in Haiti

## MONUSCO

United Nations Organization Stabilization Mission in the Democratic Republic of the Congo

**NA**

not available

**NAFTA**

North American Free Trade Agreement

**NAM**

Nonaligned Movement

**NATO**

North Atlantic Treaty Organization

**NC**

Nordic Council

**NEA**

Nuclear Energy Agency

**NEGL**

negligible

**NGA**

National Geospatial-Intelligence Agency

**NGO**

nongovernmental organization

**NIB**

Nordic Investment Bank

**NIC**

newly industrializing country

**NIE**

newly industrializing economy

**NIS**

new independent states

**NM**

nautical mile

**NMT**

Nordic Mobile Telephone

**NSG**

Nuclear Suppliers Group

**NUCLEAR TEST BAN**

Treaty Banning Nuclear Weapons Tests in the Atmosphere, in Outer Space, and Under Water

**NZ**

New Zealand

**OAPEC**

Organization of Arab Petroleum Exporting Countries

**OAS**

Organization of American States

**OAU**

Organization of African Unity; see African Union

**ODA**

official development assistance

**OECD**

Organization for Economic Cooperation and Development

**OECS**

Organization of Eastern Caribbean States

**OHCHR**

Office of the United Nations High Commissioner for Human Rights

**OIC**

Organization of the Islamic Conference

**OIF**

International Organization of the French-speaking World

**OOF**

other official flows

**OPANAL**

Agency for the Prohibition of Nuclear Weapons in Latin America and the Caribbean

**OPCW**

Organization for the Prohibition of Chemical Weapons

**OPEC**

Organization of Petroleum Exporting Countries

**OSCE**

Organization for Security and Cooperation in Europe

**OZONE LAYER PROTECTION**

Montreal Protocol on Substances That Deplete the Ozone Layer

**PCA**

Permanent Court of Arbitration

**PFP**

Partnership for Peace

**PIF**

Pacific Islands Forum

**PPP**

purchasing power parity

**RAMSAR**

see Wetlands

**RG**

Rio Group

**SAARC**

South Asian Association for Regional Cooperation

**SACEP**

South Asia Co-operative Environment Program

**SACU**

Southern African Customs Union

**SADC**

Southern African Development Community

**SAFE**

South African Far East Cable

**SCO**

Shanghai Cooperation Organization

**SECI**

Southeast European Cooperative Initiative

**SELEC**

Convention of the Southeast European Law Enforcement Centers (successor to SECI)

**SHF**

super-high-frequency

**SHIP POLLUTION**

Protocol of 1978 Relating to the International Convention for the Prevention of Pollution From Ships, 1973 (MARPOL)

**SICA**

Central American Integration System

**SPARTECA**

South Pacific Regional Trade and Economic Cooperation Agreement

**SPC**

Secretariat of the Pacific Communities

**SPF**

South Pacific Forum

**SQ KM**

square kilometer

**SQ MI**

square mile

**TAT**

Trans-Atlantic Telephone

**TEU**

Twenty-Foot Equivalent Unit, a unit of measure for containerized cargo capacity

**TROPICAL TIMBER 83**

International Tropical Timber Agreement, 1983

**TROPICAL TIMBER 94**

International Tropical Timber Agreement, 1994

**UAE**

United Arab Emirates

**UDEAC**

Central African Customs and Economic Union

**UHF**

ultra-high-frequency

**UK**

United Kingdom

**UN**

United Nations

**UN-AIDS**

Joint United Nations Program on HIV/AIDS

**UN-HABITAT**

United Nations Center for Human Settlements

**UNAMA**

United Nations Assistance Mission in Afghanistan

**UNAMID**

African Union/United Nations Hybrid Operation in Darfur

**UNASUR**

Union of South American Nations

**UNCLOS**

United Nations Convention on the Law of the Sea, also known as LOS

**UNCTAD**

United Nations Conference on Trade and Development

**UNDCP**

United Nations Drug Control Program

**UNDEF**

United Nations Democracy Fund

**UNDOF**

United Nations Disengagement Observer Force

**UNDP**

United Nations Development Program

**UNEP**

United Nations Environment Program

**UNESCO**

United Nations Educational, Scientific, and Cultural Organization

**UNFICYP**

United Nations Peace-keeping Force in Cyprus

**UNFPA**

United Nations Population Fund

**UNHCR**

United Nations High Commissioner for Refugees

**UNICEF**

United Nations Children's Fund

**UNICRI**

United Nations Interregional Crime and Justice Research Institute

**UNIDIR**

United Nations Institute for Disarmament Research

**UNIDO**

United Nations Industrial Development Organization

**UNIFIL**

United Nations Interim Force in Lebanon

**UNISFA**

United Nations Interim Force for Abyei

**UNITAR**

United Nations Institute for Training and Research

**UNMIK**

United Nations Interim Administration Mission in Kosovo

**UNMIL**

United Nations Mission in Liberia

**UNMIS**

United Nations Mission in the Sudan

**UNMISS**

United Nations Mission in South Sudan

**UNMIT**

United Nations Integrated Mission in Timor-Leste

**UNMOGIP**

United Nations Military Observer Group in India and Pakistan

**UNOCI**

United Nations Operation in Cote d'Ivoire

**UNODC**

United Nations Office of Drugs and Crime

**UNOPS**

United Nations Office of Project Services

**UNRISD**

United Nations Research Institute for Social Development

**UNRWA**

United Nations Relief and Works Agency for Palestine Refugees in the Near East

**UNSC**

United Nations Security Council

**UNSSC**

United Nations System Staff College

**UNTSO**

United Nations Truce Supervision Organization

**UNU**

United Nations University

**UNWTO**

World Tourism Organization

**UPU**

Universal Postal Union

**US**

United States

**USSR**

Union of Soviet Socialist Republics (Soviet Union); used for information dated before 25 December 1991

**UTC**

Coordinated Universal Time

**UV**

ultraviolet

**VHF**

very-high-frequency

**VSAT**

very small aperture terminal

**WADB**

West African Development Bank

**WAEMU**

West African Economic and Monetary Union

**WCL**

World Confederation of Labor

**WCO**

World Customs Organization

**WETLANDS**

Convention on Wetlands of International Importance Especially As Waterfowl Habitat

**WEU**

Western European Union

**WFP**

World Food Program

**WFTU**

World Federation of Trade Unions

**WHALING**

International Convention for the Regulation of Whaling

**WHO**

World Health Organization

**WIPO**

World Intellectual Property Organization

**WMO**

World Meteorological Organization

**WP**

Warsaw Pact

**WTO**

World Trade Organization

**ZC**

Zangger Committee

# APPENDIX B :: INTERNATIONAL ORGANIZATIONS AND GROUPS

## ADVANCED DEVELOPING COUNTRIES

another term for those less developed countries (LDCs) with particularly rapid industrial development; see newly industrializing economies (NIEs)

## ADVANCED ECONOMIES

a term used by the International Monetary FUND (IMF) for the top group in its hierarchy of advanced economies, countries in transition, and developing countries; it includes the following 33 advanced economies: Australia, Austria, Belgium, Canada, Cyprus, Czechia, Denmark, Estonia, Finland, France, Germany, Greece, Hong Kong, Iceland, Ireland, Israel, Italy, Japan, South Korea, Latvia, Lithuania, Luxembourg, Malta, Netherlands, NZ, Norway, Portugal, Singapore, Slovakia, Slovenia, Spain, Sweden, Switzerland, Taiwan, UK, US; note - this group would presumably also cover the following nine smaller countries of Andorra, Bermuda, Faroe Islands, Guernsey, Holy See, Jersey, Liechtenstein, Monaco, and San Marino that are included in the more comprehensive group of "developed countries"

## AFRICAN DEVELOPMENT BANK GROUP (AFDB)

**note** - regional multilateral development finance institution temporarily located in Tunis, Tunisia; the Bank Group consists of the African Development Bank, the African Development Fund, and the Nigerian Trust Fund
10 September 1964
to promote economic development and social progress
**regional members** - (54) Algeria, Angola, Benin, Botswana, Burkina Faso, Burundi, Cabo Verde, Cameroon, Central African Republic, Chad, Comoros, Democratic Republic of the Congo, Republic of the Congo, Cote d'Ivoire, Djibouti, Egypt, Equatorial Guinea, Eritrea, Ethiopia, Gabon, The Gambia, Ghana, Guinea, Guinea-Bissau, Kenya, Lesotho, Liberia, Libya, Madagascar, Malawi, Mali, Mauritania, Mauritius, Morocco, Mozambique, Namibia, Niger, Nigeria, Rwanda, Sao Tome and Principe, Senegal, Seychelles, Sierra Leone, Somalia, South Africa, South Sudan, Sudan, Swaziland, Tanzania, Togo, Tunisia, Uganda, Zambia, Zimbabwe
**nonregional members** - (27) Argentina, Austria, Belgium, Brazil, Canada, China, Denmark, Finland, France, Germany, India, Italy, Japan, South Korea, Kuwait, Luxembourg, Netherlands, Norway, Portugal, Saudi Arabia, Spain, Sweden, Switzerland, Turkey, UAE (ADF members only), UK, US

## AFRICAN UNION (AU)

**note** - replaces Organization of African Unity (OAU)
8 July 2001
to achieve greater unity among African States; to defend states' integrity and independence; to accelerate political, social, and economic integration; to encourage international cooperation; to promote democratic principles and institutions
**members** - (54) Algeria, Angola, Benin, Botswana, Burkina Faso, Burundi, Cabo Verde, Cameroon, Central African Republic (suspended), Chad, Comoros, Democratic Republic of the Congo, Republic of the Congo, Cote d'Ivoire, Djibouti, Egypt (suspended), Equatorial Guinea, Eritrea, Ethiopia, Gabon, The Gambia, Ghana, Guinea , Guinea-Bissau (suspended), Kenya, Lesotho, Liberia, Libya, Madagascar, Malawi, Mali, Mauritania, Mauritius, Mozambique, Namibia, Niger, Nigeria, Rwanda, Sahrawi Arab Democratic Republic (Western Sahara), Sao Tome and Principe, Senegal, Seychelles, Sierra Leone, Somalia, South Africa, South Sudan, Sudan, Swaziland, Tanzania, Togo, Tunisia, Uganda, Zambia, Zimbabwe

## AFRICAN UNION/UNITED NATIONS HYBRID OPERATION IN DARFUR (UNAMID)

31 July 2007
to contribute to the restoration of security conditions which will allow safe humanitarian assistance throughout Darfur, to contribute to the protection of civilian populations under imminent threat of physical attack, to monitor, observe compliance with, and verify the implementation of various ceasefire agreements
**members** - (41) Bangladesh, Bolivia, Burkina Faso, Burundi, Cambodia, Cameroon, China, Djibouti, Ecuador, Egypt, Ethiopia, The Gambia, Germany, Ghana, Indonesia, Iran, Jordan, Kenya, Kyrgyzstan, Malawi, Malaysia, Mali, Mongolia, Namibia, Nepal, Nigeria, Pakistan, Papua New Guinea, Peru, Rwanda, Senegal, Sierra Leone, South Africa, Tanzania, Thailand, Togo, Tunisia, Turkey, Yemen, Zambia, Zimbabwe

## AFRICAN, CARIBBEAN, AND PACIFIC GROUP OF STATES (ACP GROUP)

6 June 1975
to manage their preferential economic and aid relationship with the EU

**members** - (79) Angola, Antigua and Barbuda, The Bahamas, Barbados, Belize, Benin, Botswana, Burkina Faso, Burundi, Cabo Verde, Cameroon, Central African Republic, Chad, Comoros, Democratic Republic of the Congo, Republic of the Congo, Cook Islands, Cote d'Ivoire, Cuba, Djibouti, Dominica, Dominican Republic, Equatorial Guinea, Eritrea, Ethiopia, Fiji, Gabon, The Gambia, Ghana, Grenada, Guinea, Guinea-Bissau, Guyana, Haiti, Jamaica, Kenya, Kiribati, Lesotho, Liberia, Madagascar, Malawi, Mali, Marshall Islands, Mauritania, Mauritius, Federated States of Micronesia, Mozambique, Namibia, Nauru, Niger, Nigeria, Niue, Palau, Papua New Guinea, Rwanda, Saint Kitts and Nevis, Saint Lucia, Saint Vincent and the Grenadines, Samoa, Sao Tome and Principe, Senegal, Seychelles, Sierra Leone, Solomon Islands, Somalia, South Africa, Sudan, Suriname, Swaziland, Tanzania, Timor-Leste, Togo, Tonga, Trinidad and Tobago, Tuvalu, Uganda, Vanuatu, Zambia, Zimbabwe

## AGENCY FOR THE PROHIBITION OF NUCLEAR WEAPONS IN LATIN AMERICA AND THE CARIBBEAN (OPANAL)

**note** - acronym from Organismo para la Proscripcion de las Armas Nucleares en la America Latina y el Caribe (OPANAL)
14 February 1967 under the Treaty of Tlatelolco; effective - 25 April 1969 on the 11th ratification
to encourage the peaceful uses of atomic energy and prohibit nuclear weapons
**members** - (33) Antigua and Barbuda, Argentina, The Bahamas, Barbados, Belize, Bolivia, Brazil, Chile, Colombia, Costa Rica, Cuba, Dominica, Dominican Republic, Ecuador, El Salvador, Grenada, Guatemala, Guyana, Haiti, Honduras, Jamaica, Mexico, Nicaragua, Panama, Paraguay, Peru, Saint Kitts and Nevis, Saint Lucia, Saint Vincent and the Grenadines, Suriname, Trinidad and Tobago, Uruguay, Venezuela

## ALLIANCE OF SMALL ISLAND STATES (AOSIS)

November 1990
to call attention to threats of sea-level rise and coral bleaching to small islands and low-lying coastal developing states from global warming; to emphasize the importance of information and information technology in the process of achieving sustainable development
**members** - (39) Antigua and Barbuda, The Bahamas, Barbados, Belize, Cabo Verde, Comoros, Cook Islands, Cuba, Dominica, Dominican Republic, Fiji, Grenada, Guinea-Bissau, Guyana, Haiti, Jamaica, Kiribati, Maldives, Marshall Islands, Mauritius, Federated States of Micronesia, Nauru, Niue, Palau, Papua New Guinea, St. Kitts and Nevis, St. Lucia, St. Vincent and the Grenadines, Samoa, Sao Tome and Principe, Seychelles, Singapore, Solomon Islands, Suriname, Timor-Leste, Tonga, Trinidad and Tobago, Tuvalu, Vanuatu

**observers** - (5) American Samoa, Guam, Netherlands Antilles, Puerto Rico, U.S. Virgin Islands

## ANDEAN COMMUNITY (CAN)

**note** - formerly known as the Andean Group (AG) and the Andean Common Market (Ancom)
26 May 1969; present name established 1 October 1992; effective - 16 October 1969
to promote harmonious development through economic integration
**members** - (4) Bolivia, Colombia, Ecuador, Peru
**associate members** - (5) Argentina, Brazil, Chile, Paraguay, Uruguay
**observers** - (3) Mexico, Panama, Spain

## ARAB BANK FOR ECONOMIC DEVELOPMENT IN AFRICA (ABEDA)

**note** - also known as Banque Arabe de Developpement Economique en Afrique (BADEA)
18 February 1974; effective - 16 September 1974
to promote economic development
**members** - (17 plus the State of Palestine) Algeria, Bahrain, Egypt, Iraq, Jordan, Kuwait, Lebanon, Libya, Mauritania, Morocco, Oman, Qatar, Saudi Arabia, Sudan, Syria, Tunisia, UAE, State of Palestine; note - these are all the members of the Arab League excluding Comoros, Djibouti, Somalia, Yemen

## ARAB FUND FOR ECONOMIC AND SOCIAL DEVELOPMENT (AFESD)

16 May 1968
to promote economic and social development
**members** - (20 plus Palestine) Algeria, Bahrain, Djibouti, Egypt, Iraq, Jordan, Kuwait, Lebanon, Libya, Mauritania, Morocco, Oman, Palestine, Qatar, Saudi Arabia, Somalia (suspended 1993), Sudan, Syria, Tunisia, UAE, Yemen

## ARAB MAGHREB UNION (AMU)

17 February 1989
to promote cooperation and integration among the Arab states of northern Africa
**members** - (5) Algeria, Libya, Mauritania, Morocco, Tunisia

## ARAB MONETARY FUND (AMF)

27 April 1976; effective - 2 February 1977
to promote Arab cooperation, development, and integration in monetary and economic affairs
**members** - (21 plus Palestine) Algeria, Bahrain, Comoros, Djibouti, Egypt, Iraq, Jordan, Kuwait, Lebanon, Libya, Mauritania, Morocco, Oman, Palestine,

Qatar, Saudi Arabia, Somalia, Sudan, Syria, Tunisia, UAE, Yemen

## ARCTIC COUNCIL

18 September 1996
to address the common concerns and challenges faced by Arctic governments and the people of the Arctic; to protect the Arctic environment
**members** - (8) Canada, Denmark (Greenland, Faroe Islands), Finland, Iceland, Norway, Russia, Sweden, US
**permanent participants** - (6) Aleut International Association, Arctic Athabaskan Council, Gwich'in Council International, Inuit Circumpolar Conference, Russian Association of Indigenous People of the North, Saami Council
**observers** - (12) China, France, Germany, India, Italy, Japan, South Korea, Netherlands, Poland, Singapore, Spain, UK

## ASEAN REGIONAL FORUM (ARF)

25 July 1994
to foster constructive dialogue and consultation on political and security issues of common interest and concern
**members** - (27) Australia, Bangladesh, Brunei, Burma, Cambodia, Canada, China, EU, India, Indonesia, Japan, North Korea, South Korea, Laos, Malaysia, Mongolia, NZ, Pakistan, Papua New Guinea, Philippines, Russia, Singapore, Sri Lanka, Thailand, Timor-Leste, US, Vietnam

## ASIA-PACIFIC ECONOMIC COOPERATION (APEC)

7 November 1989
to promote trade and investment in the Pacific basin
**members** - (21) Australia, Brunei, Canada, Chile, China, Hong Kong, Indonesia, Japan, South Korea, Malaysia, Mexico, NZ, Papua New Guinea, Peru, Philippines, Russia, Singapore, Taiwan, Thailand, US, Vietnam
**observers** - (3) Association of Southeast Asian Nations, Pacific Economic Cooperation Council, Pacific Islands Forum Secretariat

## ASIAN DEVELOPMENT BANK (ADB)

19 December 1966
to promote regional economic cooperation
**members** - (48) Afghanistan, Armenia, Australia, Azerbaijan, Bangladesh, Bhutan, Brunei, Burma, Cambodia, China, Cook Islands, Fiji, Georgia, Hong Kong, India, Indonesia, Japan, Kazakhstan, Kiribati, South Korea, Kyrgyzstan, Laos, Malaysia, Maldives, Marshall Islands, Federated States of Micronesia, Mongolia, Nauru, Nepal, NZ, Pakistan, Palau, Papua New Guinea, Philippines, Samoa, Singapore, Solomon Islands, Sri Lanka, Taiwan, Tajikistan, Thailand, Timor-Leste, Tonga, Turkmenistan, Tuvalu, Uzbekistan, Vanuatu, Vietnam
**nonregional members** - (19) Austria, Belgium, Canada, Denmark, Finland, France, Germany, Ireland, Italy, Luxembourg, Netherlands, Norway, Portugal, Spain, Sweden, Switzerland, Turkey, UK, US

## ASSOCIATION OF SOUTHEAST ASIAN NATIONS (ASEAN)

8 August 1967
to encourage regional economic, social, and cultural cooperation among the non-Communist countries of Southeast Asia
**members** - (10) Brunei, Burma, Cambodia, Indonesia, Laos, Malaysia, Philippines, Singapore, Thailand, Vietnam
**dialogue partners** - (11) Australia, Canada, China, EU, India, Japan, South Korea, NZ, Pakistan, Russia, US
**observers** - (2) Papua New Guinea, Timor-Leste

## AUSTRALIA GROUP (AG)

June, 1985
to consult on and coordinate export controls related to chemical and biological weapons
**members** - (42) Argentina, Australia, Austria, Belgium, Bulgaria, Canada, Croatia, Cyprus, Czechia, Denmark, Estonia, European Union, Finland, France, Germany, Greece, Hungary, Iceland, Ireland, Italy, Japan, South Korea, Latvia, Lithuania, Luxembourg, Malta, Mexico, Netherlands, NZ, Norway, Poland, Portugal, Romania, Slovakia, Slovenia, Spain, Sweden, Switzerland, Turkey, Ukraine, UK, US

## AUSTRALIA-NEW ZEALAND-UNITED STATES SECURITY TREATY (ANZUS)

1 September 1951; effective - 29 April 1952
to implement a trilateral mutual security agreement, although the US suspended security obligations to NZ on 11 August 1986; Australia and the US continue to hold annual meetings
**members** - (3) Australia, NZ, US

## BALTIC ASSEMBLY (BA)

12 May 1990
to thoroughly discuss various cooperation issues between Baltic states
**members** - (3) Estonia, Latvia, Lithuania

## BANK FOR INTERNATIONAL SETTLEMENTS (BIS)

20 January 1930; effective - 17 March 1930
to promote cooperation among central banks in international financial settlements
**members** - (60) Algeria, Argentina, Australia, Austria, Belgium, Bosnia and Herzegovina, Brazil, Bulgaria, Canada, Chile, China, Colombia, Croatia, Czechia, Denmark, European Central Bank, Estonia, Finland, France, Germany, Greece, Hong Kong, Hungary, Iceland, India, Indonesia, Ireland, Israel, Italy, Japan, South Korea, Latvia, Lithuania, Luxembourg, Macedonia, Malaysia, Mexico, Netherlands, NZ, Norway, Peru, Philippines, Poland, Portugal, Romania, Russia, Saudi Arabia, Serbia, Singapore, Slovakia, Slovenia, South Africa, Spain, Sweden, Switzerland, Thailand, Turkey, UAE, UK, US; note - Montenegro has a separate central bank; its links with BIS are currently under review

## BAY OF BENGAL INITIATIVE FOR MULTI-SECTORAL TECHNICAL AND ECONOMIC COOPERATION (BIMSTEC)

June 1997
to foster socio-economic cooperation among members
**members** - (7) Bangladesh, Bhutan, Burma, India, Nepal, Sri Lanka, Thailand

## BENELUX UNION (BENELUX)

**note** - acronym from Belgium, Netherlands, and Luxembourg; was formerly known as Benelux Economic Union
3 February 1958; effective - 1 November 1960; changed names 17 June 2008
to develop closer economic and legal cooperation and integration
**members** - (3) Belgium, Luxembourg, Netherlands

## BIG SEVEN

**note** - membership is the same as the Group of 7
1975
to discuss and coordinate major economic policies
**members** - (7) Big Six (Canada, France, Germany, Italy, Japan, UK) plus the US

## BLACK SEA ECONOMIC COOPERATION ZONE (BSEC)

25 June 1992
to enhance regional stability through economic cooperation
**members** - (12) Albania, Armenia, Azerbaijan, Bulgaria, Georgia, Greece, Moldova, Romania, Russia, Serbia, Turkey, Ukraine; note - Macedonia is in the process of joining
**observers** - (17) Austria, Belarus, Black Sea Commission, EU, Croatia, Czechia, Egypt, Energy Charter Secretariat, France, Germany, International Black Sea Club, Israel, Italy, Poland, Slovakia, Tunisia, US; note - Bosnia and Herzegovina and Slovenia have applied for observer status

## BRICS

**note** - note: the name of the organization stands for the first letter of each of the five members' names
BRIC established 16 June 2009; BRICS established 24 December 2011
to seek common ground in political and economic venues; to achieve peace, security, development, and cooperation; to contribute significantly to the development of humanity and to establish a more equitable world
**members** - (5) Brazil, Russia, India, China, South Africa

## CARIBBEAN COMMUNITY AND COMMON MARKET (CARICOM)

4 July 1973; effective - 1 August 1973
to promote economic integration and development, especially among the less developed countries
**members** - (15) Antigua and Barbuda, The Bahamas, Barbados, Belize, Dominica, Grenada, Guyana, Haiti, Jamaica, Montserrat, Saint Kitts and Nevis, Saint Lucia, Saint Vincent and the Grenadines, Suriname, Trinidad and Tobago
**associate members** - (5) Anguilla, Bermuda, British Virgin Islands, Cayman Islands, Turks and Caicos Islands
**observers** - (8) Aruba, Colombia, Curacao, Dominican Republic, Mexico, Puerto Rico, Sint Maarten, Venezuela

## CARIBBEAN DEVELOPMENT BANK (CDB)

18 October 1969; effective - 26 January 1970
to promote economic development and cooperation
**regional members** - (19) Anguilla, Antigua and Barbuda, The Bahamas, Barbados, Belize, British Virgin Islands, Cayman Islands, Dominica, Grenada, Guyana, Haiti, Jamaica, Montserrat, Saint Kitts and Nevis, Saint Lucia, Saint Vincent and the Grenadines, Suriname, Trinidad and Tobago, Turks and Caicos Islands
**other regional members** - (4) Brazil, Colombia, Mexico, Venezuela (not entitled to borrow funds from the bank)
**nonregional members** - (5) Canada, China, Germany, Italy, UK

## CENTRAL AFRICAN CUSTOMS AND ECONOMIC UNION (UDEAC)

see Economic and Monetary Community of Central Africa (CEMAC)

## CENTRAL AFRICAN STATES DEVELOPMENT BANK (BDEAC)

**note** - acronym from Banque de Developpement des Etats de l'Afrique Centrale
3 December 1975
to provide loans for economic development
**members** - (11) African Development Bank (AfDB), Cameroon, Central African States Bank (BEAC), Central African Republic, Chad, Republic of the Congo, Equatorial Guinea, France, Gabon, Kuwait, Libya

## CENTRAL AMERICAN BANK FOR ECONOMIC INTEGRATION (BCIE)

**note** - acronym from Banco Centroamericano de Integracion Economico
13 December 1960 signature of Articles of Agreement; 31 May 1961 began operations
to promote economic integration and development
**members** - (7) Costa Rica, Dominican Republic, El Salvador, Guatemala, Honduras, Nicaragua, Panama
**nonregional members** - (5) Argentina, Colombia, Mexico, Spain, Taiwan

## CENTRAL AMERICAN COMMON MARKET (CACM)

13 December 1960, collapsed in 1969, reinstated in 1991
to promote establishment of a Central American Common Market
**members** - (5) Costa Rica, El Salvador, Guatemala, Honduras, Nicaragua

## CENTRAL AMERICAN INTEGRATION SYSTEM (SICA)

13 December 1991; operational 1 February 1993
to strengthen democracy; to set up a new model of regional security; to promote freedom; to achieve a regional system of welfare and economic and social justice; to attain economic unity and strengthen the area as an economic bloc; to act as a bloc in international matters
**members** - (8) Belize, Costa Rica, Dominican Republic, El Salvador, Guatemala, Honduras, Nicaragua, Panama
**associated member** - (1) Dominican Republic
**observers** - ( (18) Argentina, Australia, Brazil, Chile, China, Colombia, France, Germany, Holy See, Italy, Japan, South Korea, Mercosur, Mexico, Peru, Spain, Taiwan, US

## CENTRAL EUROPEAN INITIATIVE (CEI)

**note** - evolved from the Quadrilateral Initiative and the Hexagonal Initiative
11 November 1989 as the Quadrilateral Initiative, 27 July 1991 became the Hexagonal Initiative, July 1992 its present name was adopted
to form an economic and political cooperation group for the region between the Adriatic and the Baltic Seas
**members** - (18) Albania, Austria, Belarus, Bosnia and Herzegovina, Bulgaria, Croatia, Czechia, Hungary, Italy, Macedonia, Moldova, Montenegro, Poland, Romania, Serbia, Slovakia, Slovenia, Ukraine

## CENTRALLY PLANNED ECONOMIES

a term applied mainly to the traditionally communist states that looked to the former USSR for leadership; most have now evolved toward more democratic and market-oriented systems; also known formerly as the Second World or as the communist countries; through the 1980s, this group included Albania, Bulgaria, Cambodia, China, Cuba, Czechoslovakia, German Democratic Republic, Hungary, North Korea, Laos, Mongolia, Poland, Romania, USSR, Vietnam, Yugoslavia, but now is limited to Cuba and North Korea, and less so to China

## COLLECTIVE SECURITY TREATY ORGANIZATION (CSTO)

7 October 2002
to coordinate military and political cooperation, to develop multilateral structures and mechanisms of cooperation for ensuring national security of the member states
**members** - (7) Armenia, Belarus, Kazakhstan, Kyrgyzstan, Russia, Tajikistan, Uzbekistan

## COLOMBO PLAN (CP)

May 1950 proposal was adopted; 1 July 1951 commenced full operations
to promote economic and social development in Asia and the Pacific
**members** - (27) Afghanistan, Australia, Bangladesh, Bhutan, Brunei, Burma, Fiji, India, Indonesia, Iran, Japan, South Korea, Laos, Malaysia, Maldives, Mongolia, Nepal, NZ, Pakistan, Papua New Guinea, Philippines, Saudi Arabia, Singapore, Sri Lanka, Thailand, US, Vietnam

## COMMON MARKET FOR EASTERN AND SOUTHERN AFRICA (COMESA)

**note** - formerly known as Preferential Trade Area for Eastern and Southern Africa (PTA)

treaty signed 5 November 1993; treaty ratified 8 December 1994
recognizing, promoting and protecting fundamental human rights, commitment to the principles of liberty and rule of law, maintaining peace and stability through the promotion and strengthening of good neighborliness, commitment to peaceful settlement of disputes among member states
**members** - (19) Burundi, Comoros, Democratic Republic of the Congo, Djibouti, Egypt, Eritrea, Ethiopia, Kenya, Libya, Madagascar, Malawi, Mauritius, Rwanda, Seychelles, Sudan, Swaziland, Uganda, Zambia, Zimbabwe

## COMMONWEALTH (C)

**note** - also known as Commonwealth of Nations
31 December 1931
to foster multinational cooperation and assistance, as a voluntary association that evolved from the British Empire
**members** - (53) Antigua and Barbuda, Australia, The Bahamas, Bangladesh, Barbados, Belize, Botswana, Brunei, Cameroon, Canada, Cyprus, Dominica, Fiji (suspended), Ghana, Grenada, Guyana, India, Jamaica, Kenya, Kiribati, Lesotho, Malawi, Malaysia, Maldives, Malta, Mauritius, Mozambique, Namibia, Nauru, NZ, Nigeria, Pakistan (reinstated 2004), Papua New Guinea, Rwanda, Saint Kitts and Nevis, Saint Lucia, Saint Vincent and the Grenadines, Samoa, Seychelles, Sierra Leone, Singapore, Solomon Islands, South Africa, Sri Lanka, Swaziland, Tanzania, Tonga, Trinidad and Tobago, Tuvalu, Uganda, UK, Vanuatu, Zambia; note - on 7 December 2003 Zimbabwe withdrew its membership from the Commonwealth

## COMMONWEALTH OF INDEPENDENT STATES (CIS)

8 December 1991; effective - 21 December 1991
to coordinate intercommonwealth relations and to provide a mechanism for the orderly dissolution of the USSR
**members** - (11) Armenia, Azerbaijan, Belarus, Kazakhstan, Kyrgyzstan, Moldova, Russia, Tajikistan, Turkmenistan (unofficial), Ukraine (unofficial), Uzbekistan; note - neither Ukraine as a participating member nor Turkmenistan as an associate member have signed the 1993 CIS charter, although both participate in meetings; Georgia left the organization in August 2009

## COMMUNIST COUNTRIES

traditionally the Marxist-Leninist states with authoritarian governments and command economies based on the Soviet model; most of the original and the successor states are no longer communist; see centrally planned economies

## COMMUNITY OF DEMOCRACIES (CD)

27 June 2000
"to respect and uphold core democratic principles and practices" including free and fair elections, freedom of speech and expression, equal access to education, rule of law, and freedom of peaceful assembly
**signatories of the Warsaw Declaration** - (110) Albania, Algeria, Argentina, Armenia, Australia, Austria, Azerbaijan, Bangladesh, Belgium, Belize, Benin, Bolivia, Bosnia and Herzegovina, Botswana, Brazil, Bulgaria, Burkina Faso, Cabo Verde, Canada, Chile, Colombia, Costa Rica, Croatia, Cyprus, Czechia, Denmark, Dominica, Dominican Republic, Ecuador, Egypt, El Salvador, Estonia, Finland, Georgia, Germany, Greece, Guatemala, Guyana, Haiti, Honduras, Hungary, Iceland, India, Indonesia, Ireland, Israel, Italy, Japan, Jordan, Kenya, South Korea, Kuwait, Latvia, Lesotho, Liechtenstein, Lithuania, Luxembourg, Macedonia, Madagascar, Malawi, Mali, Malta, Mauritius, Mexico, Moldova, Monaco, Mongolia, Morocco, Mozambique, Namibia, Nepal, Netherlands, NZ, Nicaragua, Niger, Nigeria, Norway, Panama, Papua New Guinea, Paraguay, Peru, Philippines, Poland, Portugal, Qatar, Romania, Russia, Saint Lucia, Sao Tome and Principe, Senegal, Seychelles, Slovakia, Slovenia, South Africa, Spain, Sri Lanka, Suriname, Sweden, Switzerland, Tanzania, Thailand, Tunisia, Turkey, Ukraine, UK, US, Uruguay, Venezuela, Yemen, Yugoslavia

## COMMUNITY OF LATIN AMERICAN AND CARIBBEAN STATES (CELAC)

**note** - successor to the Rio Group and the Latin America and Caribbean Summit on Integration and Development
created 23 February 2010; established July 2011
to deepen the integration within Latin American and to reduce the influence of the US in the politics and economics of that part of the world
**members** - (33) Antigua and Barbuda, Argentina, The Bahamas, Barbados, Belize, Bolivia, Brazil, Chile, Colombia, Costa Rica, Cuba, Dominica, Dominican Republic, Ecuador, El Salvador, Grenada, Guatemala, Guyana, Haiti, Honduras, Jamaica, Mexico, Nicaragua, Panama, Paraguay, Peru, St. Kitts and Nevis, St. Lucia, St. Vincent and the Grenadines, Suriname, Trinidad and Tobago, Uruguay, Venezuela

## COMUINIDADE DOS PAISES DE LINGUA PORTUGUESA (CPLP)

1996
to establish a forum for friendship among Portuguese-speaking nations where Portuguese is an official language

**members** - (9) Angola, Brazil, Cabo Verde, Equatorial Guinea, Guinea-Bissau, Mozambique, Portugal, Sao Tome and Principe, Timor-Leste
**associate observers** - (6) Georgia, Japan, Mauritius, Namibia, Senegal, Turkey

## CONFERENCE OF INTERACTION AND CONFIDENCE-BUILDING MEASURES IN ASIA (CICA)

proposed 5 October 1992; established 14 September 1999
promoting a multi-national forum for enhancing cooperation towards promoting peace, security, and stability in Asia
**members** - (25 and Palestine) Afghanistan, Azerbaijan, Bahrain, Bangladesh, Cambodia, China, Egypt, India, Iraq, Iran, Israel, Jordan, Kazakhstan, Kyrgyzstan, Mongolia, Pakistan, Palestine, Qatar, South Korea, Russia, Tajikistan, Thailand, Turkey, UAE, Uzbekistan, Vietnam
**observers** - (11) Indonesia, Japan, League of Arab States, Malaysia, OSCE, Parliamentary Assembly of the Turkic Speaking Countries, Philippines, Sri Lanka, Ukraine, UN, US

## CONVENTION OF THE SOUTHEAST EUROPEAN LAW ENFORCEMENT CENTER (SELEC)

**note** - successor to Southeast European Cooperative Initiative (SECI) formed in 1996 to help the Southeast European countries rebuild and stabilize through access to resources
7 October 2011
to provide support for Member States and enhance coordination in preventing and combating crime in trans-border activity
**members** - (13) Albania, Bosnia and Herzegovina, Bulgaria, Croatia, Greece, Hungary, Macedonia, Moldova, Montenegro, Romania, Serbia, Slovenia, Turkey
**observers** - (15) Austria, Belgium, Czechia, France, Georgia, Germany, Israel, Italy, Japan, The Netherlands, Slovakia, Spain, Ukraine, UK, US

## COORDINATING COMMITTEE ON EXPORT CONTROLS (COCOM)

established in 1949 to control the export of strategic products and technical data from member countries to proscribed destinations; members were: Australia, Belgium, Canada, Denmark, France, Germany, Greece, Italy, Japan, Luxembourg, Netherlands, Norway, Portugal, Spain, Turkey, UK, US; abolished 31 March 1994; COCOM members established a new organization, the Wassenaar Arrangement, with expanded membership on 12 July 1996 that focuses on nonproliferation export controls as opposed to East-West control of advanced technology

## COUNCIL FOR MUTUAL ECONOMIC ASSISTANCE (CEMA)

**note** - also known as CMEA or Comecon
established 25 January 1949 to promote the development of socialist economies and abolished 1 January 1991; members included Afghanistan (observer), Albania (had not participated since 1961 break with USSR), Angola (observer), Bulgaria, Cuba, Czechoslovakia, Ethiopia (observer), GDR, Hungary, Laos (observer), Mongolia, Mozambique (observer), Nicaragua (observer), Poland, Romania, USSR, Vietnam, Yemen (observer), Yugoslavia (associate)

## COUNCIL OF ARAB ECONOMIC UNITY (CAEU)

3 June 1957; effective - 30 May 1964
to promote economic integration among Arab nations
**members** - (17 plus Palestine) Algeria, Bahrain, Egypt, Iraq, Jordan, Kuwait, Lebanon, Libya, Morocco, Oman, Palestine, Qatar, Saudi Arabia, Sudan, Syria, Tunisia, UAE, Yemen
**candidates** - (4) Comoros, Djibouti, Mauritania, Somalia

## COUNCIL OF EUROPE (CE)

5 May 1949; effective - 3 August 1949
to promote increased unity and quality of life in Europe
**members** - (47) Albania, Andorra, Armenia, Austria, Azerbaijan, Belgium, Bosnia and Herzegovina, Bulgaria, Croatia, Cyprus, Czechia, Denmark, Estonia, Finland, France, Georgia, Germany, Greece, Hungary, Iceland, Ireland, Italy, Latvia, Liechtenstein, Lithuania, Luxembourg, Macedonia, Malta, Moldova, Monaco, Montenegro, Netherlands, Norway, Poland, Portugal, Romania, Russia, San Marino, Serbia, Slovakia, Slovenia, Spain, Sweden, Switzerland, Turkey, Ukraine, UK
**observers** - (6) Canada, Holy See, Israel, Japan, Mexico, US

## COUNCIL OF THE BALTIC SEA STATES (CBSS)

6 March 1992
to promote cooperation among the Baltic Sea states in the areas of aid to new democratic institutions, economic development, humanitarian aid, energy and the environment, cultural programs and education, and transportation and communication
**members** - (12) Denmark, Estonia, EC, Finland, Germany, Iceland, Latvia, Lithuania, Norway, Poland, Russia, Sweden
**observers** - (13) Belarus, France, Ireland, Italy,

Netherlands, Norway, Romania, Slovakia, Spain, Turkey, Ukraine, UK, US

## COUNCIL OF THE ENTENTE (ENTENTE)

29 May 1959
to promote economic, social, and political coordination
**members** - (5) Benin, Burkina Faso, Cote d'Ivoire, Niger, Togo

## COUNTRIES IN TRANSITION

a term used by the International Monetary Fund (IMF) for the middle group in its hierarchy of formerly centrally planned economies; IMF statistics include the following 29 countries in transition: Albania, Armenia, Azerbaijan, Belarus, Bosnia and Herzegovina, Bulgaria, Croatia, Czechia, Estonia, Georgia, Hungary, Kazakhstan, Kyrgyzstan, Latvia, Lithuania, Macedonia, Moldova, Mongolia, Montenegro, Poland, Romania, Russia, Serbia, Slovakia, Slovenia, Tajikistan, Turkmenistan, Ukraine, Uzbekistan; note - this group is identical to the group traditionally referred to as the "former USSR/Eastern Europe" except for the addition of Mongolia

## CUSTOMS COOPERATION COUNCIL (CCC)

**note** - see World Customs Organization (WCO)

## DEVELOPED COUNTRIES (DCS)

the top group in the hierarchy of developed countries (DCs), former USSR/Eastern Europe (former USSR/EE), and less developed countries (LDCs); includes the market-oriented economies of the mainly democratic nations in the Organization for Economic Cooperation and Development (OECD), Bermuda, Israel, South Africa, and the European ministates; also known as the First World, high-income countries, the North, industrial countries; generally have a per capita GDP in excess of $15,000 although four OECD countries and South Africa have figures well under $15,000 and eight of the excluded OPEC countries have figures of more than $20,000; the DCs include: Andorra, Australia, Austria, Belgium, Bermuda, Canada, Denmark, Faroe Islands, Finland, France, Germany, Greece, Holy See, Iceland, Ireland, Israel, Italy, Japan, Liechtenstein, Luxembourg, Malta, Monaco, Netherlands, NZ, Norway, Portugal, San Marino, South Africa, Spain, Sweden, Switzerland, Turkey, UK, US; note - similar to the International Monetary Fund (IMF) term "advanced economies" that adds Hong Kong, South Korea, Singapore, and Taiwan but drops Malta, Mexico, South Africa, and Turkey

## DEVELOPING COUNTRIES

a term used by the International Monetary Fund (IMF) for the bottom group in its hierarchy of advanced economies, countries in transition, and developing countries; IMF statistics include the following 126 developing countries: Afghanistan, Algeria, Angola, Antigua and Barbuda, Argentina, Aruba, The Bahamas, Bahrain, Bangladesh, Barbados, Belize, Benin, Bhutan, Bolivia, Botswana, Brazil, Burkina Faso, Burma, Burundi, Cambodia, Cabo Verde, Cameroon, Central African Republic, Chad, Chile, China, Colombia, Comoros, Democratic Republic of the Congo, Republic of the Congo, Costa Rica, Cote d'Ivoire, Cyprus, Djibouti, Dominica, Dominican Republic, Ecuador, Egypt, El Salvador, Equatorial Guinea, Ethiopia, Fiji, Gabon, The Gambia, Ghana, Grenada, Guatemala, Guinea, Guinea-Bissau, Guyana, Haiti, Honduras, India, Indonesia, Iran, Iraq, Jamaica, Jordan, Kenya, Kiribati, Kuwait, Laos, Lebanon, Lesotho, Liberia, Libya, Madagascar, Malawi, Malaysia, Maldives, Mali, Malta, Marshall Islands, Mauritania, Mauritius, Mexico, Federated States of Micronesia, Morocco, Mozambique, Namibia, Nepal, Netherlands Antilles, Nicaragua, Niger, Nigeria, Oman, Pakistan, Panama, Papua New Guinea, Paraguay, Peru, Philippines, Qatar, Rwanda, Saint Kitts and Nevis, Saint Lucia, Saint Vincent and the Grenadines, Samoa, Sao Tome and Principe, Saudi Arabia, Senegal, Seychelles, Sierra Leone, Solomon Islands, Somalia, South Africa, Sri Lanka, Sudan, Suriname, Swaziland, Syria, Tanzania, Thailand, Togo, Trinidad and Tobago, Tunisia, Turkey, UAE, Uganda, Uruguay, Vanuatu, Venezuela, Vietnam, Yemen, Zambia, Zimbabwe; note - this category would presumably also cover the following 46 other countries that are traditionally included in the more comprehensive group of "less developed countries": American Samoa, Anguilla, British Virgin Islands, Brunei, Cayman Islands, Christmas Island, Cocos Islands, Cook Islands, Cuba, Eritrea, Falkland Islands, French Guiana, French Polynesia, Gaza Strip, Gibraltar, Greenland, Grenada, Guadeloupe, Guam, Guernsey, Isle of Man, Jersey, North Korea, Macau, Martinique, Mayotte, Montserrat, Nauru, New Caledonia, Niue, Norfolk Island, Northern Mariana Islands, Palau, Pitcairn Islands, Puerto Rico, Reunion, Saint Helena, Ascension, and Tristan da Cunha, Saint Pierre and Miquelon, Tokelau, Tonga, Turks and Caicos Islands, Tuvalu, Virgin Islands, Wallis and Futuna, West Bank, Western Sahara

## DEVELOPING EIGHT (D-8)

15 June 1997
to improve developing countries' positions in the world economy, diversify and create new opportunities in trade relations, enhance participation in decision-making at the international level, provide better standards of living
**member** - (8) Bangladesh, Egypt, Indonesia, Iran, Malaysia, Nigeria, Pakistan, Turkey

## EAST AFRICAN COMMUNITY (EAC)

**note** - originally established in 1967, it was disbanded in 1977
January 2001
to establish a political and economic union among the countries
**members** - (5) Burundi, Kenya, Rwanda, Tanzania, Uganda

## EAST AFRICAN DEVELOPMENT BANK (EADB)

6 June 1967; effective - 1 December 1967
to promote economic development
**members** - (4) Kenya, Rwanda, Tanzania, Uganda

## EAST ASIA SUMMIT (EAS)

14 December 2005
to promote cooperation in political and security issues; to promote development, financial stability, energy security, economic integration and growth; to eradicate poverty and narrow the development gap in East Asia, and to promote deeper cultural understanding
**members** - (18) Australia, Brunei, Burma, Cambodia, China, India, Indonesia, Japan, South Korea, Laos, Malaysia, NZ, Philippines, Russia, Singapore, Thailand, US, Vietnam

## ECONOMIC AND MONETARY COMMUNITY OF CENTRAL AFRICA (CEMAC)

**note** - was formerly the Central African Customs and Economic Union (UDEAC)
8 December 1964; effective - 1 January 1966
to promote the establishment of a Central African Common Market
**members** - (11) Angola, Burundi, Cameroon, Central African Republic, Chad, Democratic Republic of the Congo, Republic of the Congo, Equatorial Guinea, Gabon, Sao Tome and Principe, Rwanda

## ECONOMIC AND MONETARY UNION (EMU)

**note** - an integral part of the European Union; also known as the European Economic and Monetary Union
1-2 December 1969 (proposed at summit conference of heads of government; 7 February 1992 (Maastricht Treaty signed)
to promote a single market by creating a single currency, the euro; timetable - 2 May 1998: European exchange rates fixed for 1 January 1999; 1 January 1999: all banks and stock exchanges begin using euros; 1 January 2002: the euro goes into circulation; 1 July 2002 local currencies no longer accepted
**members** - (28) Austria, Belgium, Bulgaria, Croatia, Cyprus, Czechia, Denmark, Estonia, Finland, France, Germany, Greece, Hungary, Ireland, Italy, Latvia, Lithuania, Luxembourg, Malta, Netherlands, Poland, Portugal, Romania, Slovakia, Slovenia, Spain, Sweden, UK

## ECONOMIC AND SOCIAL COUNCIL (ECOSOC)

26 June 1945; effective - 24 October 1945
to coordinate the economic and social work of the UN; includes five regional commissions (Economic Commission for Africa, Economic Commission for Europe, Economic Commission for Latin America and the Caribbean, Economic and Social Commission for Asia and the Pacific, Economic and Social Commission for Western Asia) and nine functional commissions (Commission for Social Development, Commission on Human Rights, Commission on Narcotic Drugs, Commission on the Status of Women, Commission on Population and Development, Statistical Commission, Commission on Science and Technology for Development, Commission on Sustainable Development, and Commission on Crime Prevention and Criminal Justice)
**members** - (54) selected on a rotating basis from all regions

## ECONOMIC COMMUNITY OF THE GREAT LAKES COUNTRIES (CEPGL)

**note** - acronym from Communaute Economique des Pays des Grands Lacs
20 September 1976
to promote regional economic cooperation and integration
**members** - (3) Burundi, Democratic Republic of the Congo, Rwanda; note - organization collapsed because of fighting in 1998; reactivated in 2006

## ECONOMIC COMMUNITY OF WEST AFRICAN STATES (ECOWAS)

28 May 1975
to promote regional economic cooperation
**members** - (15) Benin, Burkina Faso, Cabo Verde, Cote d'Ivoire, The Gambia, Ghana, Guinea, Guinea-Bissau, Liberia, Mali, Niger, Nigeria, Senegal, Sierra Leone, Togo

## ECONOMIC COOPERATION ORGANIZATION (ECO)

27-29 January 1985
to promote regional cooperation in trade, transportation, communications, tourism, cultural affairs, and economic development
**members** - (10) Afghanistan, Azerbaijan, Iran, Kazakhstan, Kyrgyzstan, Pakistan, Tajikistan, Turkey, Turkmenistan, Uzbekistan

## EURASIAN ECONOMIC COMMUNITY (EAEC OR EURASEC)

**note** - merged with Central Asian Cooperation Organization (CACO) in 2005
May 2001
to create a common economic and energy policy
**members** - (6) Belarus, Kazakhstan, Kyrgyzstan, Russia, Tajikistan, Uzbekistan (suspended)
**observers** - (3) Armenia, Moldova, Ukraine

## EURASIAN ECONOMIC UNION (EAEU)

treaty signed 29 May 2014; came into being 1 January 2015
to form a large economic market for its members
*members* - (5) Armenia, Belarus, Kazakstan, Kyrgyzstan, Russia

## EURO-ATLANTIC PARTNERSHIP COUNCIL (EAPC)

**note** - began as the North Atlantic Cooperation Council (NACC); an extension of NATO
8 November 1991; effective - 20 December 1991
to discuss cooperation on mutual political and security issues
**members** - (50) Albania, Armenia, Austria, Azerbaijan, Belarus, Belgium, Bosnia and Herzegovina, Bulgaria, Canada, Croatia, Czechia, Denmark, Estonia, Finland, France, Georgia, Germany, Greece, Hungary, Iceland, Ireland, Italy, Kazakhstan, Kyrgyzstan, Latvia, Lithuania, Luxembourg, Macedonia, Malta, Moldova, Montenegro, Netherlands, Norway, Poland, Portugal, Romania, Russia, Serbia, Slovakia, Slovenia, Spain, Sweden, Switzerland, Tajikistan, Turkey, Turkmenistan, Ukraine, UK, US, Uzbekistan

## EUROPEAN BANK FOR RECONSTRUCTION AND DEVELOPMENT (EBRD)

8-9 January 1990 (proposals made); 15 April 1991 (bank inaugurated)
to facilitate the transition of seven centrally planned economies in Europe (Bulgaria, former Czechoslovakia, Hungary, Poland, Romania, former USSR, and former Yugoslavia) to market economies by committing 60% of its loans to privatization
**members** - (67) Albania, Armenia, Australia, Austria, Azerbaijan, Belarus, Belgium, Bosnia and Herzegovina, Bulgaria, Canada, China, Croatia, Cyprus, Czechia, Denmark, Egypt, EU, European Investment Bank (EIB), Estonia, Finland, France, Georgia, Germany, Greece, Hungary, Iceland, Ireland, Israel, Italy, Japan, Jordan, Kazakhstan, South Korea, Kosovo, Kyrgyzstan, Latvia, Liechtenstein, Lithuania, Luxembourg, Macedonia, Malta, Mexico, Moldova, Mongolia, Montenegro, Morocco, Netherlands, NZ, Norway, Poland, Portugal, Romania, Russia, Serbia, Slovakia, Slovenia, Spain, Sweden, Switzerland, Tajikistan, Tunisia, Turkey, Turkmenistan, Ukraine, UK, US, Uzbekistan

## EUROPEAN CENTRAL BANK (ECB)

1 June 1998
to administer the monetary policy of the EU Eurozone member states
**Eurozone members** - (19) Austria, Belgium, Cyprus, Estonia, Finland, France, Germany, Greece, Ireland, Italy, Latvia, Lithuania, Luxembourg, Malta, Netherlands, Portugal, Slovakia, Slovenia, Spain
**non-Eurozone members** (10) Bulgaria, Croatia, Czechia, Denmark, Hungary, Lithuania, Poland, Romania, Sweden, UK

## EUROPEAN COMMUNITY (OR EUROPEAN COMMUNITIES, EC)

established 8 April 1965 to integrate the European Atomic Energy Community (Euratom), the European Coal and Steel Community (ECSC), the European Economic Community (EEC or Common Market), and to establish a completely integrated common market and an eventual federation of Europe; merged into the European Union (EU) on 7 February 1992; member states at the time of merger were Belgium, Denmark, France, Germany, Greece, Ireland, Italy, Luxembourg, Netherlands, Portugal, Spain, UK

## EUROPEAN FREE TRADE ASSOCIATION (EFTA)

4 January 1960; effective - 3 May 1960
to promote expansion of free trade
**members** - (4) Iceland, Liechtenstein, Norway, Switzerland

## EUROPEAN INVESTMENT BANK (EIB)

25 March 1957; effective - 1 January 1958
to promote economic development of the EU and its predecessors, the EEC and the EC
**members** - (28) Austria, Belgium, Bulgaria, Croatia, Cyprus, Czechia, Denmark, Estonia, Finland, France, Germany, Greece, Hungary, Ireland, Italy, Latvia, Lithuania, Luxembourg, Malta, Netherlands, Poland, Portugal, Romania, Slovakia, Slovenia, Spain, Sweden, UK

## EUROPEAN ORGANIZATION FOR NUCLEAR RESEARCH (CERN)

**note** - acronym retained from the predecessor organization Conseil Europeenne pour la Recherche Nucleaire
1 July 1953; effective - 29 September 1954

to foster nuclear research for peaceful purposes only
**members** - (21) Austria, Belgium, Bulgaria, Czechia, Denmark, Finland, France, Germany, Greece, Hungary, Israel, Italy, Netherlands, Norway, Poland, Portugal, Slovakia, Spain, Sweden, Switzerland, UK
**associate members** - (2) Pakistan, Turkey
**observers** - (6) EC, India, Japan, Russia, United Nations Educational, Scientific, and Cultural Organization (UNESCO), US

## EUROPEAN SPACE AGENCY (ESA)

31 May 1975
to promote peaceful cooperation in space research and technology
**members** - (22) Austria, Belgium, Czechia, Denmark, Estonia, Finland, France, Germany, Greece, Hungary, Ireland, Italy, Luxembourg, Netherlands, Norway, Poland, Portugal, Romania, Spain, Sweden, Switzerland, UK
**cooperating states** - (8) Bulgaria, Canada, Cyprus, Latvia, Lithuania, Malta, Slovakia, Slovenia

## EUROPEAN UNION (EU)

**note** - see European Union entry at the end of the "country" listings

## EXTRACTIVE INDUSTRY TRANSPARENCY INITIATIVE (EITI)

October 2002 Initiative announced; June 2003 first EITC Plenary Conference
to set a global standard for transparency in the extractive industries in an effort to make natural resources benefit all
**compliant countries** - (30) Albania, Burkina Faso, Cameroon, Central African Republic (suspended), Chad, Cote d'Ivoire, Democratic Republic of the Congo, Republic of the Congo, Ghana, Guatemala, Guinea, Indonesia, Iraq, Kazakhstan, Kyrgyzstan, Liberia, Mali, Mauritania, Mongolia, Mozambique, Niger, Nigeria, Norway, Peru, Sierra Leone, Tanzania, Timor-Leste, Togo, Trinidad and Tobago, Yemen (suspended), Zambia
**candidate countries** - (20) Afghanistan, Azerbaijan, Burma, Colombia, Dominican Republic, Ethiopia, Germany, Honduras, Madagascar, Malawi, Papua New Guinea, Philippines, Sao Tome and Principe, Senegal, Seychelles, Solomon Islands, Tajikistan, Ukraine, UK, US

## FINANCIAL ACTION TASK FORCE (FATF)

by G-7 Summit in Paris in 1989
to develop and promote policies to combat money laundering and terrorist financing
**members** - (37) Argentina, Australia, Austria, Belgium, Brazil, Canada, China, Denmark, EC, Finland, France, Germany, Greece, Gulf Cooperation Council, Hong Kong, Iceland, India, Ireland, Italy, Japan, South Korea, Luxembourg, Malaysia, Mexico, Netherlands (Aruba, Curacao, Sint Maarten), NZ, Norway, Portugal, Russia, Singapore, South Africa, Spain, Sweden, Switzerland, Turkey, UK, US

## FIRST WORLD

another term for countries with advanced, industrialized economies; this term is fading from use; see developed countries (DCs)

## FOOD AND AGRICULTURE ORGANIZATION (FAO)

16 October 1945
to raise living standards and increase availability of agricultural products; a UN specialized agency
**members** - (195) includes all UN member countries except Liechtenstein (192 total); plus Cook Islands, EU, and Niue
**associate members** - (2) Faroe Islands, Tokelau

## FORMER SOVIET UNION (FSU)

former term often used to identify as a group the successor nations to the Soviet Union or USSR; this group of 15 countries consists of: Armenia, Azerbaijan, Belarus, Estonia, Georgia, Kazakhstan, Kyrgyzstan, Latvia, Lithuania, Moldova, Russia, Tajikistan, Turkmenistan, Ukraine, Uzbekistan

## FORMER USSR/EASTERN EUROPE (FORMER USSR/EE)

the middle group in the hierarchy of developed countries (DCs), former USSR/Eastern Europe (former USSR/EE), and less developed countries (LDCs); these countries are in political and economic transition and may well be grouped differently in the near future; this group of 29 countries consists of: Albania, Armenia, Azerbaijan, Belarus, Bosnia and Herzegovina, Bulgaria, Croatia, Czechia, Estonia, Georgia, Hungary, Kazakhstan, Kosovo, Kyrgyzstan, Latvia, Lithuania, Macedonia, Moldova, Montenegro, Poland, Romania, Russia, Serbia, Slovakia, Slovenia, Tajikistan, Turkmenistan, Ukraine, Uzbekistan; this group is identical to the IMF group "countries in transition" except for the IMF's inclusion of Mongolia

## FOUR DRAGONS

the four small Asian less developed countries (LDCs) that have experienced unusually rapid economic growth; also known as the Four Tigers; this group consists of Hong Kong, South Korea, Singapore, Taiwan; these countries are included in the IMF's "advanced economies" group

## FRANC ZONE (FZ)

**note** - also known as Conference des Ministres des Finances des Pays de la Zone Franc
1964
to form a monetary union among countries whose currencies were linked to the French franc
**members** - (16) Benin, Burkina Faso, Cameroon, Central African Republic, Chad, Comoros, Republic of the Congo, Cote d'Ivoire, Equatorial Guinea, France, Gabon, Guinea-Bissau, Mali, Niger, Senegal, Togo

## FRONT LINE STATES (FLS)

established to achieve black majority rule in South Africa; has since gone out of existence; members included Angola, Botswana, Mozambique, Namibia, Tanzania, Zambia, Zimbabwe

## GENERAL AGREEMENT ON TARIFFS AND TRADE (GATT)

see the World Trade Organization (WTO)

## GENERAL CONFEDERATION OF TRADE UNIONS (GCTU)

16 April 1992
to consolidate trade union actions to protect citizens' social and labor rights and interests, to help secure trade unions' rights and guarantees, and to strengthen international trade union solidarity
**members** - (10) Armenia, Azerbaijan, Belarus, Georgia, Kazakhstan, Kyrgyzstan, Moldova, Russia, Tajikistan, Ukraine

## GROUP OF 10 (G-10)

**note** - also known as the Paris Club; includes the wealthiest members of the IMF who provide most of the money to be loaned and act as the informal steering committee; name persists despite increased membership
October 1962
to coordinate credit policy
**members** - (11) Belgium, Canada, France, Germany, Italy, Japan, Netherlands, Sweden, Switzerland, UK, US
**observers** - (4) BIS, EC, IMF, OECD

## GROUP OF 11 (G-11)

2006
to narrow the income gap with the world's richest nations
**members** - (11) Croatia, Ecuador, El Salvador, Georgia, Honduras, Indonesia, Jordan, Morocco, Pakistan, Paraguay, Sri Lanka

## GROUP OF 15 (G-15)

**note** - byproduct of the Nonaligned Movement; name persists despite increased membership
September 1989
to promote economic cooperation among developing nations; to act as the main political organ for the Nonaligned Movement
**members** - (17) Algeria, Argentina, Brazil, Chile, Egypt, India, Indonesia, Iran, Jamaica, Kenya, Malaysia, Mexico, Nigeria, Senegal, Sri Lanka, Venezuela, Zimbabwe

## GROUP OF 20 (G-20)

created 1999; inaugurated 15-16 December 1999
to promote open and constructive discussion between industrial and emerging-market countries on any issues related to global economic stability; helps to support growth and development across the globe
**members** - (20) Argentina, Australia, Brazil, Canada, China, EU, France, Germany, India, Indonesia, Italy, Japan, South Korea, Mexico, Russia, Saudi Arabia, South Africa, Turkey, UK, US

## GROUP OF 24 (G-24)

1 August 1989
to promote the interests of developing countries in Africa, Asia, and Latin America within the IMF
**members** - (24) Algeria, Argentina, Brazil, Colombia, Democratic Republic of the Congo, Cote d'Ivoire, Egypt, Ethiopia, Gabon, Ghana, Guatemala, India, Iran, Lebanon, Mexico, Nigeria, Pakistan, Peru, Philippines, South Africa, Sri Lanka, Syria, Trinidad and Tobago, Venezuela
**special invitee** - (1) China

## GROUP OF 3 (G-3)

September 1990
mechanism for policy coordination
**members** - (2) Colombia, Mexico; note - Venezuela was an original member until 2006; in 2004, Panama was invited to join but has not

## GROUP OF 5 (G-5)

**note** - with the addition of Italy, Canada, and Russia, it is now known as the Group of 8 or G-8; meanwhile the Group of 5 now refers to Brazil, China, India, Mexico, and South Africa
22 September 1985
to coordinate the economic policies of five major

noncommunist economic powers
**members** - (5) France, Germany, Japan, UK, US

## GROUP OF 6 (G-6)

also known as Groupe des Six Sur le Desarmement (not to be confused with the Big Six) was established in 22 May 1984 with the aim of achieving nuclear disarmement; its members were Argentina, Greece, India, Mexico, Sweden, Tanzania

## GROUP OF 7 (G-7)

**note** - membership is the same as the Big Seven
22 September 1985
to facilitate economic cooperation among the seven major noncommunist economic powers
**members** - (8) Group of 5 (France, Germany, Japan, UK, US) plus Canada, EU, and Italy

## GROUP OF 77 (G-77)

15 June 1964; October 1967 first ministerial meeting
to promote economic cooperation among developing countries; name persists in spite of increased membership
**members** - (133 plus the Palestine Liberation Organization) Afghanistan, Algeria, Angola, Antigua and Barbuda, Argentina, The Bahamas, Bahrain, Bangladesh, Barbados, Belize, Benin, Bhutan, Bolivia, Bosnia and Herzegovina, Botswana, Brazil, Brunei, Burkina Faso, Burma, Burundi, Cambodia, Cabo Verde, Cameroon, Central African Republic, Chad, Chile, China, Colombia, Comoros, Democratic Republic of the Congo, Republic of the Congo, Costa Rica, Cote d'Ivoire, Cuba, Djibouti, Dominica, Dominican Republic, Ecuador, Egypt, El Salvador, Equatorial Guinea, Eritrea, Ethiopia, Fiji, Gabon, The Gambia, Ghana, Grenada, Guatemala, Guinea, Guinea-Bissau, Guyana, Haiti, Honduras, India, Indonesia, Iran, Iraq, Jamaica, Jordan, Kenya, Kiribati, North Korea, Kuwait, Laos, Lebanon, Lesotho, Liberia, Libya, Madagascar, Malawi, Malaysia, Maldives, Mali, Marshall Islands, Mauritania, Mauritius, Federated States of Micronesia, Mongolia, Morocco, Mozambique, Namibia, Nauru, Nepal, Nicaragua, Niger, Nigeria, Oman, Pakistan, Panama, Papua New Guinea, Paraguay, Peru, Philippines, Qatar, Rwanda, Saint Kitts and Nevis, Saint Lucia, Saint Vincent and the Grenadines, Samoa, Sao Tome and Principe, Saudi Arabia, Senegal, Seychelles, Sierra Leone, Singapore, Solomon Islands, Somalia, South Africa, South Sudan, Sri Lanka, Sudan, Suriname, Swaziland, Syria, Tajikistan, Tanzania, Thailand, Timor-Leste, Togo, Tonga, Trinidad and Tobago, Tunisia, Turkmenistan, Uganda, UAE, Uruguay, Vanuatu, Venezuela, Vietnam, Yemen, Zambia, Zimbabwe, Palestine Liberation Organization

## GROUP OF 8 (G-8)

October 1975
to facilitate economic cooperation among the developed countries (DCs) that participated in the Conference on International Economic Cooperation (CIEC), held in several sessions between December 1975 and 3 June 1977; Russia admitted in 1997 but suspended in 2014 following the annexation of Crimea in Ukraine; the EU has been represented in the G-8 since the 1980s
**members** - (9) Canada, EU, France, Germany, Italy, Japan, Russia, UK, US

## GROUP OF 9 (G-9)

NA
to discuss matters of mutual interest on an informal basis
**members** - (9) Austria, Belgium, Bulgaria, Denmark, Finland, Hungary, Romania, Serbia, Sweden; may not be active

## GULF COOPERATION COUNCIL (GCC)

**note** - also known as the Cooperation Council for the Arab States of the Gulf
25 May 1981
to promote regional cooperation in economic, social, political, and military affairs
**members** - (6) Bahrain, Kuwait, Oman, Qatar, Saudi Arabia, UAE

## HIGH INCOME COUNTRIES

another term for the industrialized countries with high per capita GDPs; see developed countries (DCs)

## INDIAN OCEAN COMMISSION (INOC)

21 December 1982
to organize and promote regional cooperation in all sectors, especially economic
**members** - (5) Comoros, France (for Reunion), Madagascar, Mauritius, Seychelles

## INDUSTRIAL COUNTRIES

another term for the developed countries; see developed countries (DCs)

## INTER-AMERICAN DEVELOPMENT BANK (IADB)

**note** - also known as Banco Interamericano de Desarrollo (BID)
8 April 1959; effective - 30 December 1959
to promote economic and social development in Latin America

**members** - (48) Argentina, Austria, The Bahamas, Barbados, Belgium, Belize, Bolivia, Brazil, Canada, Chile, China, Colombia, Costa Rica, Croatia, Denmark, Dominican Republic, Ecuador, El Salvador, Finland, France, Germany, Guatemala, Guyana, Haiti, Honduras, Israel, Italy, Jamaica, Japan, South Korea, Mexico, Netherlands, Nicaragua, Norway, Panama, Paraguay, Peru, Portugal, Slovenia, Spain, Suriname, Sweden, Switzerland, Trinidad and Tobago, UK, US, Uruguay, Venezuela

## INTER-GOVERNMENTAL AUTHORITY ON DEVELOPMENT (IGAD)

**note** - formerly known as Inter-Governmental Authority on Drought and Development (IGADD) 15-16 January 1986 as the Inter-Governmental Authority on Drought and Development; revitalized - 21 March 1996 as the Inter-Governmental Authority on Development
to promote a social, economic, and scientific community among its members
**members** - (6) Djibouti, Ethiopia, Kenya, Somalia, Sudan, Uganda
**partners** - (20) Austria, Belgium, Canada, Denmark, EC, France, Germany, Greece, International Organization for Migration, Ireland, Italy, Japan, Netherlands, Norway, Sweden, Switzerland, UK, UN Development Program, US, World Bank

## INTER-PARLIAMENTARY UNION (IPU)

1889
fosters contacts among parliamentarians, considers and expresses views of international interest and concern with the purpose of bringing about action by parliaments and parliamentarians, contributes to the defense and promotion of human rights, contributes to better knowledge of representative institutions
**members** - (165 and Palestine) Afghanistan, Albania, Algeria, Andorra, Angola, Argentina, Armenia, Australia, Austria, Azerbaijan, Bahrain, Bangladesh, Belarus, Belgium, Benin, Bhutan, Bolivia, Bosnia and Herzegovina, Botswana, Brazil, Bulgaria, Burkina Faso, Burma, Burundi, Cambodia, Cabo Verde, Cameroon, Canada, Chad, Chile, China, Colombia, Democratic Republic of the Congo, Republic of the Congo, Costa Rica, Cote d'Ivoire, Croatia, Cuba, Cyprus, Czechia, Denmark, Djibouti, Dominican Republic, Ecuador, El Salvador, Equatorial Guinea, Estonia, Ethiopia, Finland, France, Gabon, The Gambia, Georgia, Germany, Ghana, Greece, Guatemala, Guinea, Guinea-Bissau, Haiti, Honduras, Hungary, Iceland, India, Indonesia, Iran, Iraq, Ireland, Israel, Italy, Japan, Jordan, Kazakhstan, Kenya, North Korea, South Korea, Kuwait, Kyrgyzstan, Laos, Latvia, Lebanon, Lesotho, Libya, Liechtenstein, Lithuania, Luxembourg, Macedonia, Madagascar, Malawi, Malaysia, Maldives, Mali, Malta, Mauritania, Mauritius, Mexico, Federated States of Micronesia, Moldova, Monaco, Mongolia, Montenegro, Morocco, Mozambique, Namibia, Nepal, Netherlands, NZ, Nicaragua, Niger, Nigeria, Norway, Oman, Pakistan, Palau, Palestine, Panama, Papua New Guinea, Paraguay, Peru, Philippines, Poland, Portugal, Qatar, Romania, Russia, Rwanda, Samoa, San Marino, Sao Tome and Principe, Saudi Arabia, Senegal, Serbia, Seychelles, Sierra Leone, Singapore, Slovakia, Slovenia, Somalia, South Africa, South Sudan, Spain, Sri Lanka, Sudan, Suriname, Sweden, Switzerland, Syria, Tanzania, Tajikistan, Thailand, Timor-Leste, Togo, Tonga, Trinidad and Tobago, Tunisia, Turkey, Uganda, Ukraine, UAE, UK, Uruguay, Venezuela, Vietnam, Yemen, Zambia, Zimbabwe
**associate members** - (11) Andean Parliament, Central American Parliament, East African Legislative Assembly, European Parliament, Interparliamentary Assembly of Member States of the Commonwealth of Independent States, Inter-Parliamentary Committee of the West African Economic and Monetary Union, Latin American Parliament, Parliament of the Economic Community of West African States, Parliament of the Economic and Monetary Community of Central Africa, Parliamentary Assembly of the Council of Europe

## INTERNATIONAL ATOMIC ENERGY AGENCY (IAEA)

26 October 1956; effective - 29 July 1957
to promote peaceful uses of atomic energy
**members** - (171) Afghanistan, Albania, Algeria, Angola, Antiqua and Barbuda, Argentina, Armenia, Australia, Austria, Azerbaijan, The Bahamas, Bahrain, Bangladesh, Barbados, Belarus, Belgium, Belize, Benin, Bolivia, Bosnia and Herzegovina, Botswana, Brazil, Brunei, Bulgaria, Burkina Faso, Burma, Burundi, Cabo Verde, Cambodia, Cameroon, Canada, Central African Republic, Chad, Chile, China, Colombia, Comoros, Democratic Republic of the Congo, Republic of the Congo, Costa Rica, Cote d'Ivoire, Croatia, Cuba, Cyprus, Czechia, Denmark, Djibouti, Dominica, Dominican Republic, Ecuador, Egypt, El Salvador, Eritrea, Estonia, Ethiopia, Fiji, Finland, France, Gabon, Georgia, Germany, Ghana, Greece, Guatemala, Guyana, Haiti, Holy See, Honduras, Hungary, Iceland, India, Indonesia, Iran, Iraq, Ireland, Israel, Italy, Jamaica, Japan, Jordan, Kazakhstan, Kenya, South Korea, Kuwait, Kyrgyzstan, Laos, Latvia, Lebanon, Lesotho, Liberia, Libya, Liechtenstein, Lithuania, Luxembourg, Macedonia, Madagascar, Malawi, Malaysia, Mali, Malta, Marshall Islands, Mauritania, Mauritius, Mexico, Moldova, Monaco, Mongolia, Montenegro, Morocco, Mozambique, Namibia, Nepal, Netherlands, NZ, Nicaragua, Niger, Nigeria, Norway, Oman, Pakistan, Palau, Panama, Papua New Guinea, Paraguay, Peru, Philippines, Poland, Portugal, Qatar, Romania, Russia, Rwanda, San Marino, Saudi Arabia, Senegal, Serbia,

Seychelles, Sierra Leone, Singapore, Slovakia, Slovenia, South Africa, Spain, Sri Lanka, Sudan, Swaziland, Sweden, Switzerland, Syria, Tajikistan, Tanzania, Thailand, Togo, Tonga, Trinidad and Tobago, Tunisia, Turkey, Turkmenistan, Uganda, Ukraine, UAE, UK, US, Uruguay, Uzbekistan, Vanuatu, Venezuela, Vietnam, Yemen, Zambia, Zimbabwe

## INTERNATIONAL BANK FOR RECONSTRUCTION AND DEVELOPMENT (IBRD)

**note** - also known as the World Bank
22 July 1944; effective - 27 December 1945
to provide economic development loans; a UN specialized agency
**members** - (189) includes all UN member countries except Andorra, Cuba, North Korea, Liechtenstein, Monaco; plus Kosovo

## INTERNATIONAL CHAMBER OF COMMERCE (ICC)

1919
to promote free trade and private enterprise and to represent business interests at national and international levels
**members** - 128 plus Palestine
**countries with national committees** - (96 and the Palestine Liberation Organization) Albania, Algeria, Argentina, Australia, Austria, Bahrain, Bangladesh, Belgium, Bolivia, Brazil, Bulgaria, Burkina Faso, Cameroon, Canada, Caribbean, Chile, China, Colombia, Costa Rica, Croatia, Cuba, Cyprus, Czechia, Denmark, Dominican Republic, Ecuador, Egypt, El Salvador, Estonia, Finland, France, Georgia, Germany, Ghana, Greece, Guatemala, Hong Kong, Hungary, Iceland, India, Indonesia, Iran, Ireland, Israel, Italy, Japan, Jordan, Kenya, South Korea, Kuwait, Lebanon, Lithuania, Luxembourg, Macao, Macedonia, Madagascar, Malaysia, Mexico, Monaco, Morocco, Netherlands, NZ, Nigeria, Norway, Pakistan, Panama, Paraguay, Philippines, Poland, Portugal, Qatar, Romania, Russia, Saudi Arabia, Senegal, Serbia, Singapore, Slovakia, Slovenia, South Africa, Spain, Sri Lanka, Sweden, Switzerland, Syria, Taiwan, Thailand, Togo, Tunisia, Turkey, Ukraine, UAE, UK, US, Uruguay, Venezuela, Palestine Liberation Organization; note - Peru is restructuring
**countries with no national committees having direct members** - (39) Afghanistan, Andorra, Armenia, Azerbaijan, The Bahamas, Belarus, Bermuda, Bosnia and Herzegovina, Botswana, Burma, Democratic Republic of the Congo, Cote d'Ivoire, Eritrea, Ethiopia, Gibraltar, Haiti, Honduras, Iraq, Jamaica, North Korea, Latvia, Liberia, Malta, Mauritania, Mauritius, Moldova, Mongolia, Montenegro, Mozambique, Nepal, Oman, Peru, Seychelles, Sudan, Tajikistan, Tanzania, Turkey, Uganda, Vietnam

## INTERNATIONAL CIVIL AVIATION ORGANIZATION (ICAO)

7 December 1944; effective - 4 April 1947
to promote international cooperation in civil aviation; a UN specialized agency
**members** - (191) includes all UN member countries except Dominica, Liechtenstein, and Tuvalu (190 total); plus Cook Islands

## INTERNATIONAL CIVILIAN SUPPORT MISSION IN HAITI (MICAH)

established 17 December 1999 to promote respect for human rights; members included Argentina, Benin, Canada, France, India, Mali, Niger, Senegal, Togo, Tunisia, US; closed 2001

## INTERNATIONAL COMMITTEE OF THE RED CROSS (ICRC)

17 February 1863
to provide humanitarian aid in wartime
**members** - (15-25 members of the Assembly Council) all Swiss nationals

## INTERNATIONAL COURT OF JUSTICE (ICJ)

also known as the World Court; primary judicial organ of the UN
26 June 1945 with the signing of the UN Charter (inaugural sitting of the Court was on 18 April 1946); superseded Permanent Court of International Justice (attached to the League of Nations)
to settle disputes submitted by member states and to provide advice to UN organs and other international agencies
**members** - (15 judges) elected by the UN General Assembly and Security Council to represent all principal legal systems; judges elected to nine-year terms (eligible for two additional terms); elections held every three years for one-third of the judges
**jurisdiction** - based on the principle of consent in contentious issues; consent to compulsory jurisdiction is outlined in Statute 36 of the ICJ; states provide declarations of consent to compulsory jurisdiction of the ICJ either with or without reservations (date in parens after each state is when the declaration was deposited with the UN Secretary-General); Haiti, Luxembourg, Nicaragua, and Uruguay deposited declarations with the Permanent Court of International Justice prior to 1945 and these were later transferred to the ICJ)
**states accepting compulsory jurisdiction with reservations** - (61) Australia (22 March 2002),

Barbados (1 August 1980), Belgium (17 June 1958), Botswana (16 March 1970), Bulgaria (21 June 1992), Cambodia (19 September 1957), Canada (10 May 1994), Democratic Republic of the Congo (8 February 1989), Cote d'Ivoire ( 29 September 2001), Cyprus (3 September 2002), Denmark (10 December 1956), Djibouti (2 September 2005), Egypt (22 July 1957), Estonia (31 October 1991), Finland (25 June 1958), The Gambia (22 June 1966), Germany (30 April 2008), Greece (10 January 1994), Guinea (4 December 1998), Honduras (6 June 1986), Hungary (22 October 1992), India (18 September 1974), Ireland (15 December 2011), Japan (9 July 2007), Italy (25 November 2014), Kenya (19 April 1965), Lesotho (6 September 2000), Liberia (20 March 1952), Liechtenstein (29 March 1950), Lithuania (26 September 2012), Madagascar (2 July 1992), Malawi (12 December 1966), Malta (2 September 1983), Marshall Islands (23 April 2013), Mauritius (23 September 1968), Mexico (28 October 1947), Netherlands (1 August 1956), New Zealand (23 September 1977), Nicaragua (24 September 1929), Nigeria (30 April 1998), Norway (25 June 1996), Pakistan (13 September 1960), Panama (25 October 1921), Peru (7 July 2003), Philippines (18 January 1972), Poland (25 March 1996), Portugal (25 February 2005), Romania (23 June 2015), Senegal (2 December 1985), Slovakia (28 May 2004), Somalia (11 April 1963), Spain (20 October 1990), Sudan (2 January 1958), Suriname (31 August 1987), Swaziland (26 May 1969), Sweden (6 April 1957), Switzerland (28 July 1948), Timor-Leste (21 September 2012), Togo (25 October 1979), Uganda (3 October 1963), United Kingdom (5 July 2004)
**states accepting compulsory jurisdiction without reservations** - (11) Austria (19 May 1971), Cameroon (3 March 1994), Costa Rica (20 February 1973), Dominica (31 March 2006), Dominican Republic (30 September 1924), Georgia (20 June 1995), Guinea-Bissau (7 August 1989), Haiti (4 October 1921), Luxembourg (15 September 1930), Paraguay (25 September 1996), Uruguay (28 January 1921)

## INTERNATIONAL CRIMINAL COURT (ICCT)

1 July 2002
to hold all individuals and countries accountable to international laws of conduct; to specify international standards of conduct; to provide an important mechanism for implementing these standards; to ensure that perpetrators are brought to justice
**members** - 21 judges (three judges form the Presidency) and six judges each in the Pre-trial, Trial, and Appeals Divisions; judges elected by secret ballot by the Assembly of States Parties to the Rome Statute for nine-year terms (not eligible for reelection)
governed by the Statute of the International Criminal Court treaty (or Rome Statute), adopted 17 July 1998 at the UN Conference of Plenipotentiaries in Rome and entered into force 1 July 2002
**states accepting jurisdiction** - (124 with the Palestine Liberation Organization) Afghanistan, Albania, Andorra, Antigua and Barbuda, Argentina, Australia, Austria, Bangladesh, Barbados, Belgium, Belize, Benin, Bolivia, Bosnia and Herzegovina, Botswana, Brazil, Bulgaria, Burkina Faso, Burundi, Cabo Verde, Cambodia, Canada, Central African Republic, Chad, Chile, Colombia, Comoros, Cook Islands, Democratic Republic of the Congo, Republic of the Congo, Costa Rica, Cote d'Ivoire, Croatia, Cyprus, Czechia, Denmark, Djibouti, Dominica, Dominican Republic, Ecuador, El Salvador, Estonia, Fiji, Finland, France, Gabon, The Gambia, Georgia, Germany, Ghana, Greece, Grenada, Guatemala, Guinea, Guyana, Honduras, Hungary, Iceland, Ireland, Italy, Japan, Jordan, Kenya, South Korea, Latvia, Lesotho, Liberia, Liechtenstein, Lithuania, Luxembourg, Macedonia, Madagascar, Malawi, Maldives, Mali, Malta, Marshall Islands, Mauritius, Mexico, Moldova, Mongolia, Montenegro, Namibia, Nauru, Netherlands, NZ, Niger, Nigeria, Norway, Panama, Paraguay, Peru, Philippines, Poland, Portugal, Romania, Saint Kitts and Nevis, Saint Lucia, Saint Vincent and the Grenadines, Samoa, San Marino, Senegal, Serbia, Seychelles, Sierra Leone, Slovakia, Slovenia, South Africa, Spain, Suriname, Sweden, Switzerland, Tajikistan, Tanzania, Timor-Leste, Trinidad and Tobago, Tunisia, Uganda, UK, Uruguay, Vanuatu, Venezuela, Zambia, Palestine Liberation Organization

## INTERNATIONAL CRIMINAL POLICE ORGANIZATION (INTERPOL)

September 1923 set up as the International Criminal Police Commission; 13 June 1956 constitution modified and present name adopted
to promote international cooperation among police authorities in fighting crime
**members** - (190) Afghanistan, Albania, Algeria, Andorra, Angola, Antigua and Barbuda, Argentina, Armenia, Aruba, Australia, Austria, Azerbaijan, The Bahamas, Bahrain, Bangladesh, Barbados, Belarus, Belgium, Belize, Benin, Bhutan, Bolivia, Bosnia and Herzegovina, Botswana, Brazil, Brunei, Bulgaria, Burkina Faso, Burma, Burundi, Cabo Verde, Cambodia, Cameroon, Canada, Central African Republic, Chad, Chile, China, Colombia, Comoros, Democratic Republic of the Congo, Republic of the Congo, Costa Rica, Cote d'Ivoire, Croatia, Cuba, Curacao, Cyprus, Czechia, Denmark, Djibouti, Dominica, Dominican Republic, Ecuador, Egypt, El Salvador, Equatorial Guinea, Eritrea, Estonia, Ethiopia, Fiji, Finland, France, Gabon, The Gambia, Georgia, Germany, Ghana, Greece, Grenada, Guatemala, Guinea, Guinea-Bissau, Guyana, Haiti, Holy See, Honduras, Hungary, Iceland, India, Indonesia, Iran, Iraq, Ireland, Israel, Italy, Jamaica, Japan, Jordan, Kazakhstan, Kenya, South Korea, Kuwait,

Kyrgyzstan, Laos, Latvia, Lebanon, Lesotho, Liberia, Libya, Liechtenstein, Lithuania, Luxembourg, Macedonia, Madagascar, Malawi, Malaysia, Maldives, Mali, Malta, Marshall Islands, Mauritania, Mauritius, Mexico, Moldova, Monaco, Mongolia, Montenegro, Morocco, Mozambique, Namibia, Nauru, Nepal, Netherlands, NZ, Nicaragua, Niger, Nigeria, Norway, Oman, Pakistan, Panama, Papua New Guinea, Paraguay, Peru, Philippines, Poland, Portugal, Qatar, Romania, Russia, Rwanda, Saint Kitts and Nevis, Saint Lucia, Saint Vincent and the Grenadines, Samoa, San Marino, Sao Tome and Principe, Saudi Arabia, Senegal, Serbia, Seychelles, Sierra Leone, Singapore, Sint Maarten, Slovakia, Slovenia, Somalia, South Africa, South Sudan, Spain, Sri Lanka, Sudan, Suriname, Swaziland, Sweden, Switzerland, Syria, Tajikistan, Tanzania, Thailand, Timor-Leste, Togo, Tonga, Trinidad and Tobago, Tunisia, Turkey, Turkmenistan, Uganda, Ukraine, UAE, UK, US, Uruguay, Uzbekistan, Venezuela, Vietnam, Yemen, Zambia, Zimbabwe
**subbureaus** - (11) American Samoa, Anguilla, Bermuda, British Virgin Islands, Cayman Islands, Gibraltar, Hong Kong, Macau, Montserrat, Puerto Rico, Turks and Caicos Islands

## INTERNATIONAL DEVELOPMENT ASSOCIATION (IDA)

26 January 1960; effective - 24 September 1960
to provide economic loans for low-income countries; UN specialized agency and IBRD affiliate
**members** - (180) Afghanistan, Albania, Algeria, Angola, Antigua and Barbuda, Argentina, Armenia, , Austria, Azerbaijan, Bahrain, Bangladesh, Belarus, Belgium, Belize, Benin, Bhutan, Bolivia, Bosnia and Herzegovina, Botswana, Brazil, Bulgaria, Burkina Faso, Burma, Burundi, Cabo Verde, Cambodia, Cameroon, Canada, Central African Republic, Chad, Chile, China, Colombia, Comoros, Democratic Republic of the Congo, Republic of the Congo, Costa Rica, Cote d'Ivoire, Croatia, Czechia, Denmark, Djibouti, Dominica, Dominican Republic, Ecuador, Egypt, El Salvador, Equatorial Guinea, Eritrea, Estonia, Ethiopia, EU, Fiji, Finland, France, Gabon, The Gambia, Georgia, Germany, Ghana, Greece, Grenada, Guatemala, Guinea, Guinea-Bissau, Guyana, Haiti, Honduras, Hungary, Iceland, India, Indonesia, Iran, Iraq, Israel, Italy, Jamaica, Japan, Jordan, Kazakhstan, Kenya, Kiribati, South Korea, Kosovo, Kuwait, Kyrgyzstan, Laos, Latvia, Lebanon, Lesotho, Liberia, Libya, Lithuania, Luxembourg, Macedonia, Madagascar, Malawi, Malaysia, Maldives, Mali, Marshall Islands, Mauritania, Mauritius, Mexico, Federated States of Micronesia, Moldova, Mongolia, Montenegro, Morocco, Mozambique, Namibia, Nepal, Netherlands, Nicaragua, Niger, Nigeria, Norway, Oman, Pakistan, Palau, Panama, Papua New Guinea, Paraguay, Peru, Philippines, Poland, Portugal, Qatar, Romania, Russia, Rwanda, Saint Kitts and Nevis, Saint Lucia, Saint Vincent and the Grenadines, Samoa, Sao Tome and Principe, Senegal, Serbia, Seychelles, Sierra Leone, Singapore, Slovakia, Slovenia, Solomon Islands, Somalia, South Africa, South Sudan, Spain, Sri Lanka, Sudan, Suriname, Swaziland, Sweden, Switzerland, Syria, Tajikistan, Tanzania, Thailand, Timor-Leste, Togo, Tonga, Trinidad and Tobago, Tunisia, Turkey, Turkmenistan, Tuvalu, Uganda, Ukraine, UAE, UK, US, Uruguay, Uzbekistan, Vanuatu, Venezuela, Vietnam, West Bank and Gaza, Yemen, Zambia, Zimbabwe

## INTERNATIONAL ENERGY AGENCY (IEA)

15 November 1974
to promote cooperation on energy matters, especially emergency oil sharing and relations between oil consumers and oil producers; established by the OECD
**members** - (30) Australia, Austria, Belgium, Canada, Czechia, Denmark, Estonia, EC, Estonia, Finland, France, Germany, Greece, Hungary, Ireland, Italy, Japan, South Korea, Luxembourg, Netherlands, NZ, Norway, Poland, Portugal, Slovakia, Spain, Sweden, Switzerland, Turkey, UK, US

## INTERNATIONAL FEDERATION OF RED CROSS AND RED CRESCENT SOCIETIES (IFRCS)

**note** - formerly known as League of Red Cross and Red Crescent Societies (LORCS)
5 May 1919
to organize, coordinate, and direct international relief actions; to promote humanitarian activities; to represent and encourage the development of National Societies; to bring help to victims of armed conflicts, refugees, and displaced people; to reduce the vulnerability of people through development programs
**members** - (190 plus the Palestine Liberation Organization) Afghanistan, Albania, Algeria, Andorra, Angola, Antigua and Barbuda, Argentina, Armenia, Australia, Austria, Azerbaijan, The Bahamas, Bahrain, Bangladesh, Barbados, Belarus, Belgium, Belize, Benin, Bolivia, Bosnia and Herzegovina, Botswana, Brazil, Brunei, Bulgaria, Burkina Faso, Burma, Burundi, Cabo Verde, Cambodia, Cameroon, Canada, Central African Republic, Chad, Chile, China, Colombia, Comoros, Democratic Republic of the Congo, Republic of the Congo, Cook Islands, Costa Rica, Cote d'Ivoire, Croatia, Cuba, Cyprus, Czechia, Denmark, Djibouti, Dominica, Dominican Republic, Ecuador, Egypt, El Salvador, Equatorial Guinea, Eritrea, Estonia, Ethiopia, Fiji, Finland, France, Gabon, The Gambia, Georgia, Germany, Ghana, Greece, Grenada, Guatemala, Guinea, Guinea-Bissau, Guyana, Haiti, Honduras, Hungary, Iceland, India, Indonesia, Iran, Iraq, Ireland, Israel, Italy, Jamaica, Japan, Jordan, Kazakhstan, Kenya, Kiribati, North Korea, South Korea, Kuwait, Kyrgyzstan, Laos, Latvia, Lebanon, Lesotho, Liberia,

Libya, Liechtenstein, Lithuania, Luxembourg, Macedonia, Madagascar, Malawi, Malaysia, Maldives, Mali, Malta, Mauritania, Mauritius, Mexico, Federated States of Micronesia, Moldova, Monaco, Mongolia, Montenegro, Morocco, Mozambique, Namibia, Nepal, Netherlands, NZ, Nicaragua, Niger, Nigeria, Norway, Pakistan, Palau, Panama, Papua New Guinea, Paraguay, Peru, Philippines, Poland, Portugal, Qatar, Romania, Russia, Rwanda, Saint Kitts and Nevis, Saint Lucia, Saint Vincent and the Grenadines, Samoa, San Marino, Sao Tome and Principe, Saudi Arabia, Senegal, Serbia, Seychelles, Sierra Leone, Singapore, Slovakia, Slovenia, Solomon Islands, Somalia, South Africa, South Sudan, Spain, Sri Lanka, Sudan, Suriname, Swaziland, Sweden, Switzerland, Syria, Tajikistan, Tanzania, Thailand, Timor-Leste, Togo, Tonga, Trinidad and Tobago, Tunisia, Turkey, Turkmenistan, Tuvalu, Uganda, Ukraine, UAE, UK, US, Uruguay, Uzbekistan, Vanuatu, Venezuela, Vietnam, Yemen, Zambia, Zimbabwe, Palestine Liberatin Organization

## INTERNATIONAL FINANCE CORPORATION (IFC)

25 May 1955; effective - 24 July 1956
to support private enterprise in international economic development; a UN specialized agency and IBRD affiliate
**members** - (184) includes all UN member countries except Andorra, Brunei, Cuba, North Korea, Liechtenstein, Monaco, Nauru, Saint Vincent and the Grenadines, San Marino, Tuvalu; plus Kosovo

## INTERNATIONAL FUND FOR AGRICULTURAL DEVELOPMENT (IFAD)

November 1974
to promote agricultural development; a UN specialized agency
**members** - (176)
**List A** - (25 industrialized aid contributors) Austria, Belgium, Canada, Denmark, Estonia, Finland, France, Germany, Greece, Hungary, Iceland, Ireland, Italy, Japan, Luxembourg, Netherlands, NZ, Norway, Portugal, Russia, Spain, Sweden, Switzerland, UK, US
**List B** - (12 petroleum-exporting aid contributors) Algeria, Gabon, Indonesia, Iran, Iraq, Kuwait, Libya, Nigeria, Qatar, Saudi Arabia, UAE, Venezuela
**List C** - (139 aid recipients) Afghanistan, Albania, Angola, Antigua and Barbuda, Argentina, Armenia, Azerbaijan, The Bahamas, Bangladesh, Barbados, Belize, Benin, Bhutan, Bolivia, Bosnia and Herzegovina, Botswana, Brazil, Burkina Faso, Burma, Burundi, Cabo Verde, Cambodia, Cameroon, Central African Republic, Chad, Chile, China, Colombia, Comoros, Democratic Republic of the Congo, Republic of the Congo, Cook Islands, Costa Rica, Côte d'Ivoire, Croatia, Cuba, Cyprus, Djibouti, Dominica, Dominican Republic, Ecuador, Egypt, El Salvador, Equatorial Guinea, Eritrea, Ethiopia, Fiji, The Gambia, Georgia, Ghana, Grenada, Guatemala, Guinea, Guinea-Bissau, Guyana, Haiti, Honduras, India, Israel, Jamaica, Jordan, Kazakhstan, Kenya, Kiribati, North Korea, South Korea, Kyrgyzstan, Laos, Lebanon, Lesotho, Liberia, Macedonia, Madagascar, Malawi, Malaysia, Maldives, Mali, Malta, Marshall Islands, Mauritania, Mauritius, Mexico, Federated States of Micronesia, Moldova, Mongolia, Montenegro, Morocco, Mozambique, Namibia, Nauru, Nepal, Nicaragua, Niger, Niue, Oman, Pakistan, Palau, Panama, Papua New Guinea, Paraguay, Peru, Philippines, Romania, Rwanda, Saint Kitts and Nevis, Saint Lucia, Saint Vincent and the Grenadines, Samoa, Sao Tome and Principe, Senegal, Seychelles, Sierra Leone, Solomon Islands, Somalia, South Africa, South Sudan, Sri Lanka, Sudan, Suriname, Swaziland, Syria, Tajikistan, Tanzania, Thailand, Timor-Leste, Togo, Tonga, Trinidad and Tobago, Tunisia, Turkey, Tuvalu, Uganda, Uruguay, Uzbekistan, Vanuatu, Vietnam, Yemen, Zambia, Zimbabwe
**note** - Andorra and Australia are members but have not been assiged to a list

## INTERNATIONAL HYDROGRAPHIC ORGANIZATION (IHO)

**note** - name changed from International Hydrographic Bureau on 22 September 1970
June 1919; effective - June 1921
to train hydrographic surveyors and nautical cartographers to achieve standardization in nautical charts and electronic chart displays; to provide advice on nautical cartography and hydrography; to develop the sciences in the field of hydrography and techniques used for descriptive oceanography
**members** - (85) Algeria, Argentina, Australia, Bahrain, Bangladesh, Belgium, Brazil, Brunei, Burma, Cameroon, Canada, Chile, China (including Hong Kong and Macau), Colombia, Democratic Republic of the Congo, Croatia, Cuba, Cyprus, Denmark, Dominican Republic, Ecuador, Egypt, Estonia, Fiji, Finland, France, Georgia, Germany, Greece, Guatemala, Iceland, India, Indonesia, Iran, Ireland, Italy, Jamaica, Japan, North Korea, South Korea, Kuwait, Latvia, Malaysia, Mauritius, Mexico, Monaco, Montenegro, Morocco, Mozambique, Netherlands, NZ, Nigeria, Norway, Oman, Pakistan, Papua New Guinea, Peru, Philippines, Poland, Portugal, Qatar, Romania, Russia, Saudi Arabia, Serbia, Singapore, Slovenia, South Africa, Spain, Sri Lanka, Suriname, Sweden, Syria, Thailand, Tonga, Trinidad and Tobago, Tunisia, Turkey, Ukraine, UAE, UK, US, Uruguay, Venezuela, Vietnam

## INTERNATIONAL LABOR ORGANIZATION (ILO)

28 June 1919 set up as part of Treaty of Versailles; 11 April 1919 became operative; 14 December 1946 affiliated with the UN

to deal with world labor issues; a UN specialized agency
**members** - (190) includes all UN member countries except Andorra, Bhutan, North Korea, Liechtenstein, Federated States of Micronesia, Monaco, Nauru; note - includes the following dependencies: Netherlands (Aruba, Curacao, Sint Maarten), New Zealand (Cook Islands)

## INTERNATIONAL MARITIME ORGANIZATION (IMO)

**note** - name changed from Intergovernmental Maritime Consultative Organization (IMCO) on 22 May 1982
6 March 1948 set up as the Inter-Governmental Maritime Consultative Organization; effective - 17 March 1958
to deal with international maritime affairs; a UN specialized agency
**members** - (171) includes all UN member countries except Afghanistan, Andorra, Armenia, Belarus, Bhutan, Botswana, Burkina Faso, Burundi, Central African Republic, Chad, Kyrgyzstan, Laos, Lesotho, Liechtenstein, Mali, Federated States of Micronesia, Nauru, Niger, Rwanda, South Sudan, Swaziland, Tajikistan, Uzbekistan; and the Cook Islands
**associate members** - (3) Faroe Islands, Hong Kong, Macau

## INTERNATIONAL MOBILE SATELLITE ORGANIZATION (IMSO)

15 April 1999
acts as watchdog over Inmarsat (International Maritime Satellite Organization), a private company, to make sure it follows ICAO standards and recommended practices; plays an active role in the development of international telecommunications policies
**members** - (102) Algeria, Antigua and Barbuda, Argentina, Australia, The Bahamas, Bahrain, Bangladesh, Belarus, Belgium, Bosnia and Herzegovina, Brazil, Brunei, Bulgaria, Cameroon, Canada, Chile, China, Colombia, Comoros, Cook Islands, Costa Rica, Croatia, Cuba, Cyprus, Czechia, Denmark, Ecuador, Egypt, Fiji, Finland, France, Gabon, Georgia, Germany, Ghana, Greece, Hungary, Iceland, India, Indonesia, Iran, Iraq, Israel, Italy, Japan, Jordan, Kenya, North Korea, South Korea, Kuwait, Latvia, Lebanon, Liberia, Libya, Malaysia, Malta, Marshall Islands, Mauritius, Mexico, Monaco, Mongolia, Montenegro, Morocco, Mozambique, Netherlands, NZ, Nigeria, Norway, Oman, Pakistan, Palau, Panama, Peru, Philippines, Poland, Portugal, Qatar, Romania, Russia, Saudi Arabia, Senegal, Serbia, Singapore, Slovakia, South Africa, Spain, Sri Lanka, Sweden, Switzerland, Tanzania, Thailand, Tonga, Tunisia, Turkey, Ukraine, UAE, UK, US, Vanuatu, Venezuela, Vietnam, Yemen

## INTERNATIONAL MONETARY FUND (IMF)

22 July 1944; effective - 27 December 1945
to promote world monetary stability and economic development; a UN specialized agency
**members** - (188) includes all UN member countries except Andorra, Cuba, North Korea, Liechtenstein, Monaco; plus Kosovo; note - includes the following dependencies or areas of special interest: China (Hong Kong and Macau), Netherlands (Aruba, Curacao, Sint Maarten), UK (Anguilla, Montserrat)

## INTERNATIONAL OLYMPIC COMMITTEE (IOC)

23 June 1894
to promote the Olympic ideals and administer the Olympic games: 2016 Summer Olympics in Rio de Janeiro, Brazil; 2018 Winter Olympics in PyeongChang, South Korea; 2020 Summer Olympics in Tokyo, Japan; 2022 Winter Olympics in Beijing, China
**National Olympic Committees** - (205 and the Palestine Liberation Organization) Afghanistan, Albania, Algeria, American Samoa, Andorra, Angola, Antigua and Barbuda, Argentina, Armenia, Aruba, Australia, Austria, Azerbaijan, The Bahamas, Bahrain, Bangladesh, Barbados, Belarus, Belgium, Belize, Benin, Bermuda, Bhutan, Bolivia, Bosnia and Herzegovina, Botswana, Brazil, British Virgin Islands, Brunei, Bulgaria, Burkina Faso, Burma, Burundi, Cabo Verde, Cambodia, Cameroon, Canada, Cayman Islands, Central African Republic, Chad, Chile, China, Colombia, Comoros, Democratic Republic of the Congo, Republic of the Congo, Cook Islands, Costa Rica, Cote d'Ivoire, Croatia, Cuba, Cyprus, Czechia, Denmark, Djibouti, Dominica, Dominican Republic, Ecuador, Egypt, El Salvador, Equatorial Guinea, Eritrea, Estonia, Ethiopia, Fiji, Finland, France, Gabon, The Gambia, Georgia, Germany, Ghana, Greece, Grenada, Guam, Guatemala, Guinea, Guinea-Bissau, Guyana, Haiti, Honduras, Hong Kong, Hungary, Iceland, India, Indonesia, Iran, Iraq, Ireland, Israel, Italy, Jamaica, Japan, Jordan, Kazakhstan, Kenya, Kiribati, North Korea, South Korea, Kosovo, Kuwait, Kyrgyzstan, Laos, Latvia, Lebanon, Lesotho, Liberia, Libya, Liechtenstein, Lithuania, Luxembourg, Macedonia, Madagascar, Malawi, Malaysia, Maldives, Mali, Malta, Marshall Islands, Mauritania, Mauritius, Mexico, Federated States of Micronesia, Moldova, Monaco, Mongolia, Montenegro, Morocco, Mozambique, Namibia, Nauru, Nepal, Netherlands, NZ, Nicaragua, Niger, Nigeria, Norway, Oman, Pakistan, Palau, Panama, Papua New Guinea, Paraguay, Peru, Philippines, Poland, Portugal, Puerto Rico, Qatar, Romania, Russia, Rwanda, Saint Kitts and Nevis, Saint Lucia, Saint Vincent and the Grenadines, Samoa, San Marino, Sao Tome and Principe, Saudi Arabia, Senegal, Serbia, Seychelles, Sierra Leone, Singapore, Slovakia, Slovenia, Solomon Islands, Somalia, South Africa, South Sudan, Spain, Sri Lanka, Sudan, Suriname, Swaziland, Sweden, Switzerland, Syria, Taiwan, Tajikistan, Tanzania,

Thailand, Timor-Leste, Togo, Tonga, Trinidad and Tobago, Tunisia, Turkey, Turkmenistan, Tuvalu, Uganda, Ukraine, UAE, UK, US, Uruguay, Uzbekistan, Vanuatu, Venezuela, Vietnam, Virgin Islands, Yemen, Zambia, Zimbabwe, Palestine Liberation Organization

## INTERNATIONAL ORGANIZATION FOR MIGRATION (IOM)

**note** - established as Provisional Intergovernmental Committee for the Movement of Migrants from Europe; renamed Intergovernmental Committee for European Migration (ICEM) on 15 November 1952; renamed Intergovernmental Committee for Migration (ICM) in November 1980; current name adopted 14 November 1989
5 December 1951
to facilitate orderly international emigration and immigration
**members** - (161) Afghanistan, Albania, Algeria, Angola, Antigua and Barbuda, Argentina, Armenia, Australia, Austria, Azerbaijan, The Bahamas, Bangladesh, Belarus, Belgium, Belize, Benin, Bolivia, Bosnia and Herzegovina, Botswana, Brazil, Bulgaria, Burkina Faso, Burma, Burundi, Cabo Verde, Cambodia, Cameroon, Canada, Central African Republic, Chad, Chile, Colombia, Comoros, Democratic Republic of the Congo, Republic of the Congo, Costa Rica, Cote d'Ivoire, Croatia, Cyprus, Czechia, Denmark, Djibouti, Dominican Republic, Ecuador, Egypt, El Salvador, Eritrea, Estonia, Ethiopia, Fiji, Finland, France, Gabon, The Gambia, Georgia, Germany, Ghana, Greece, Guatemala, Guinea, Guinea-Bissau, Guyana, Haiti, Holy See, Honduras, Hungary, India, Iran, Ireland, Israel, Italy, Jamaica, Japan, Jordan, Kazakhstan, Kenya, Kiribati, South Korea, Kyrgyzstan, Latvia, Lesotho, Liberia, Libya, Lithuania, Luxembourg, Macedonia, Madagascar, Malawi, Maldives, Mali, Malta, Marshall Islands, Mauritania, Mauritius, Mexico, Federation of Micronesia, Moldova, Mongolia, Montenegro, Morocco, Mozambique, Namibia, Nauru, Nepal, Netherlands, NZ, Nicaragua, Niger, Nigeria, Norway, Pakistan, Panama, Papua New Guinea, Paraguay, Peru, Philippines, Poland, Portugal, Romania, Rwanda, Saint Kitts and Nevis, Saint Lucia, Saint Vincent and the Grenadines, Samoa, Sao Tome and Principe, Senegal, Serbia, Seychelles, Sierra Leone, Slovakia, Slovenia, Somalia, South Africa, South Sudan, Spain, Sri Lanka, Sudan, Suriname, Swaziland, Sweden, Switzerland, Tajikistan, Tanzania, Thailand, Timor-Leste, Togo, Trinidad and Tobago, Tunisia, Turkey, Turkmenistan, Uganda, Ukraine, UK, US, Uruguay, Vanuatu, Venezuela, Vietnam, Yemen, Zambia, Zimbabwe
**observers** - (9) Bahrain, Bhutan, China, Cuba, Indonesia, Qatar, Russia, San Marino, Saudi Arabia

## INTERNATIONAL ORGANIZATION FOR STANDARDIZATION (ISO)

February 1947
to promote the development of international standards with a view to facilitating international exchange of goods and services and to developing cooperation in the sphere of intellectual, scientific, technological and economic activity
**members** - (119 national standards organizations) Afghanistan, Algeria, Argentina, Armenia, Australia, Austria, Azerbaijan, Bahrain, Bangladesh, Barbados, Belarus, Belgium, Benin, Bosnia and Herzegovina, Botswana, Brazil, Bulgaria, Burkina Faso, Cameroon, Canada, Chile, China, Colombia, Democratic Republic of the Congo, Costa Rica, Cote d'Ivoire, Croatia, Cuba, Cyprus, Czechia, Denmark, Ecuador, Egypt, El Salvador, Estonia, Ethiopia, Fiji, Finland, France, Gabon, Germany, Ghana, Greece, Hungary, Iceland, India, Indonesia, Iran, Iraq, Ireland, Israel, Italy, Jamaica, Japan, Jordan, Kazakhstan, Kenya, North Korea, South Korea, Kuwait, Latvia, Lebanon, Libya, Lithuania, Luxembourg, Macedonia, Malaysia, Mali, Malta, Mauritius, Mexico, Mongolia, Morocco, Namibia, Nepal, Netherlands, NZ, Nigeria, Norway, Oman, Pakistan, Panama, Peru, Philippines, Poland, Portugal, Qatar, Romania, Russia, Rwanda, Saint Lucia, Saudi Arabia, Senegal, Serbia, Singapore, Slovakia, Slovenia, South Africa, Spain, Sri Lanka, Sudan, Sweden, Switzerland, Syria, Tanzania, Thailand, Trinidad and Tobago, Tunisia, Turkey, Uganda, Ukraine, UAE, UK, US, Uruguay, Uzbekistan, Vietnam, Yemen, Zimbabwe
**correspondent members** - (38 plus the Palestine Liberation Organization) Albania, Angola, The Bahamas, Bhutan, Bolivia, Brunei, Burma, Burundi, Cambodia, Republic of the Congo, Dominica, Dominican Republic, Eritrea, The Gambia, Georgia, Guatemala, Guyana, Haiti, Honduras, Hong Kong, Kyrgyzstan, Lesotho, Macau, Madagascar, Moldova, Montenegro, Mozambique, Nicaragua, Niger, Papua New Guinea, Paraguay, Seychelles, Sierra Leone, Suriname, Swaziland, Tajikistan, Turkmenistan, Zambia, Palestine Liberation Organization
**subscriber members** - (4) Antigua and Barbuda, Belize, Laos, Saint Vincent and the Grenadines

## INTERNATIONAL ORGANIZATION OF THE FRENCH-SPEAKING WORLD (OIF)

**note** - name changed from Agency of Cultural and Technical Cooperation (ACCT) in 1997; also known as Organisation Internationale de la Francophonie
20 March 1970
founded around a common language to promote and spread the cultures of its members and to reinforce cultural and technical cooperation between them
**members** - (57) Albania, Andorra, Armenia, Belgium, Benin, Bulgaria, Burkina Faso, Burundi, Cabo Verde, Cambodia, Cameroon, Canada, Canada - New Brunswick, Canada - Quebec, Central African Republic,

Chad, Comoros, Democratic Republic of Congo, Republic of Congo, Cote d'Ivoire, Cyprus, Djibouti, Dominica, Egypt, Equatorial Guinea, France, French Community of Belgium, Gabon, Ghana, Greece, Guinea, Guinea-Bissau, Haiti, Laos, Lebanon, Luxembourg, Macedonia, Madagascar, Mali, Mauritania, Mauritius, Moldova, Monaco, Morocco, Niger, Qatar, Romania, Rwanda, Saint Lucia, Sao Tome and Principe, Senegal, Seychelles, Switzerland, Togo, Tunisia, Vanuatu, Vietnam
**observers** - (23) Austria, Bosnia and Herzegovina, Costa Rica, Croatia, Czechia, Dominican Republic, Estonia, Georgia, Hungary, Kosovo, Latvia, Lithuania, Mexico, Montenegro, Mozambique, Poland, Serbia, Slovakia, Slovenia, Thailand, Ukraine, UAE, Uruguay

## INTERNATIONAL RED CROSS AND RED CRESCENT MOVEMENT (ICRM)

1928
to promote worldwide humanitarian aid through the International Committee of the Red Cross (ICRC) in wartime, and International Federation of Red Cross and Red Crescent Societies (IFRCS; formerly League of Red Cross and Red Crescent Societies or LORCS) in peacetime
**National Societies** - (190 countries and the Palestine Liberation Organization); note - same as membership for International Federation of Red Cross and Red Crescent Societies (IFRCS)

## INTERNATIONAL TELECOMMUNICATION SATELLITE ORGANIZATION (ITSO)

August 1964
to act as a watchdog over Intelsat, Ltd., a private company, to make sure it provides on a global and non-discriminatory basis public telecommunication services
**members** - (149) Afghanistan, Algeria, Angola, Argentina, Armenia, Australia, Austria, Azerbaijan, The Bahamas, Bahrain, Bangladesh, Barbados, Belgium, Benin, Bhutan, Bolivia, Bosnia and Herzegovina, Botswana, Brazil, Brunei, Burkina Faso, Cabo Verde, Cameroon, Canada, Central African Republic, Chad, Chile, China, Colombia, Comoros, Democratic Republic of the Congo, Republic of the Congo, Costa Rica, Cote d'Ivoire, Croatia, Cuba, Cyprus, Czechia, Denmark, Dominican Republic, Ecuador, Egypt, El Salvador, Equatorial Guinea, Estonia, Ethiopia, Fiji, Finland, France, Gabon, The Gambia, Georgia, Germany, Ghana, Greece, Guatemala, Guinea, Guinea-Bissau, Haiti, Holy See, Honduras, Hungary, Iceland, India, Indonesia, Iran, Iraq, Ireland, Israel, Italy, Jamaica, Japan, Jordan, Kazakhstan, Kenya, North Korea, South Korea, Kuwait, Kyrgyzstan, Lebanon, Libya, Liechtenstein, Luxembourg, Madagascar, Malawi, Malaysia, Mali, Malta, Mauritania, Mauritius, Mexico, the Federated States of Micronesia, Monaco, Mongolia, Montenegro, Morocco, Mozambique, Namibia, Nepal, Netherlands, NZ, Nicaragua, Niger, Nigeria, Norway, Oman, Pakistan, Panama, Papua New Guinea, Paraguay, Peru, Philippines, Poland, Portugal, Qatar, Romania, Russia, Rwanda, Saudi Arabia, Senegal, Serbia, Singapore, Somalia, South Africa, Spain, Sri Lanka, Sudan, Swaziland, Sweden, Switzerland, Syria, Tajikistan, Tanzania, Thailand, Togo, Trinidad and Tobago, Tunisia, Turkey, Uganda, UAE, UK, US, Uruguay, Uzbekistan, Venezuela, Vietnam, Yemen, Zambia, Zimbabwe

## INTERNATIONAL TELECOMMUNICATION UNION (ITU)

17 May 1865 set up as the International Telegraph Union; 9 December 1932 adopted present name; effective - 1 January 1934; affiliated with the UN - 15 November 1947
to deal with world telecommunications issues; a UN specialized agency
**members** - (193) includes all UN member countries except Palau (192 total); plus Holy See

## INTERNATIONAL TRADE UNION CONFEDERATION (ITUC)

**note** - its predecessors were the International Confederation of Free Trade Unions (ICFTU) and the World Confederation of Labor (WCL)
3 November 2006
to promote the trade union movement
**members** - (333 affiliated organizations in 164 countries or territories and the Palestine Liberation Organization as of 2013) Afghanistan, Albania, Algeria, Angola, Antigua and Barbuda, Armenia, Aruba, Argentina, Australia, Austria, Azerbaijan, Bahrain, Bangladesh, Barbados, Belarus, Belgium, Belize, Benin, Bermuda, Bonaire, Bosnia and Herzegovina, Botswana, Brazil, Bulgaria, Burkina Faso, Burma, Burundi, Cabo Verde, Cambodia, Cameroon, Canada, Central African Republic, Chad, Chile, Colombia, Comoros, Democratic Republic of the Congo, Republic of the Congo, Cook Islands, Costa Rica, Cote d'Ivoire, Croatia, Curacao, Cyprus, Czechia, Denmark, Djibouti, Dominica, Dominican Republic, Ecuador, Egypt, El Salvador, Eritrea, Estonia, Ethiopia, Fiji, Finland, France, French Polynesia, Gabon, The Gambia, Georgia, Germany, Ghana, Greece, Grenada, Guatemala, Guinea, Guinea-Bissau, Haiti, Holy See, Honduras, Hong Kong, Hungary, Iceland, India, Indonesia, Ireland, Israel, Italy, Japan, Jordan, Kazakhstan, Kenya, Kiribati, South Korea, Kosovo, Kuwait, Latvia, Lesotho, Liberia, Liechtenstein, Lithuania, Luxembourg, Macedonia, Madagascar, Malawi, Malaysia, Mali, Malta, Mauritania, Mauritius, Mexico, Moldova, Mongolia, Montenegro, Morocco, Mozambique, Namibia, Nepal, Netherlands, New Caledonia, NZ, Nicaragua, Niger, Nigeria,

Norway, Oman, Pakistan, Panama, Paraguay, Peru, Philippines, Poland, Portugal, Romania, Russia, Rwanda, Saint Lucia, Samoa, San Marino, Sao Tome and Principe, Senegal, Serbia, Sierra Leone, Singapore, Slovakia, Somalia, South Africa, Spain, Sri Lanka, Sudan, Suriname, Swaziland, Sweden, Switzerland, Taiwan, Tanzania, Thailand, Togo, Tonga, Trinidad and Tobago, Tunisia, Turkey, Uganda, Ukraine, UK, US, Vanuatu, Venezuela, Yemen, Zambia, Zimbabwe, and the Palestine Liberation Organization

## ISLAMIC DEVELOPMENT BANK (IDB)

15 December 1973 by declaration of intent; effective - 12 August 1974
to promote Islamic economic aid and social development
**members** - (55 plus the Palestine Liberation Organization) Afghanistan, Albania, Algeria, Azerbaijan, Bahrain, Bangladesh, Benin, Brunei, Burkina Faso, Cameroon, Chad, Comoros, Cote d'Ivoire, Djibouti, Egypt, Gabon, The Gambia, Guinea, Guinea-Bissau, Indonesia, Iran, Iraq, Jordan, Kazakhstan, Kuwait, Kyrgyzstan, Lebanon, Libya, Malaysia, Maldives, Mali, Mauritania, Morocco, Mozambique, Niger, Nigeria, Oman, Pakistan, Qatar, Saudi Arabia, Senegal, Sierra Leone, Somalia, Sudan, Suriname, Syria, Tajikistan, Togo, Tunisia, Turkey, Turkmenistan, Uganda, UAE, Uzbekistan, Yemen, Palestine Liberation Organization

## LATIN AMERICAN AND CARIBBEAN ECONOMIC SYSTEM (LAES)

**note** - also known as Sistema Economico Latinoamericana (SELA)
17 October 1975
to promote economic and social development through regional cooperation
**members** - (28) Argentina, the Bahamas, Barbados, Belize, Bolivia, Brazil, Chile, Colombia, Costa Rica, Cuba, Dominican Republic, Ecuador, El Salvador, Grenada, Guatemala, Guyana, Haiti, Honduras, Jamaica, Mexico, Nicaragua, Panama, Paraguay, Peru, Suriname, Trinidad and Tobago, Uruguay, Venezuela

## LATIN AMERICAN INTEGRATION ASSOCIATION (LAIA)

**note** - also known as Asociacion Latinoamericana de Integracion (ALADI)
12 August 1980; effective - 18 March 1981
to promote freer regional trade
**members** - (13) Argentina, Bolivia, Brazil, Chile, Colombia, Cuba, Ecuador, Mexico, Panama, Paraguay, Peru, Uruguay, Venezuela
**observers** - (25) China, Costa Rica, Dominican Republic, EC, El Salvador, Guatemala, Honduras, Inter-American Development Bank, Inter-American Institute for Cooperation on Agriculture, Italy, Japan, South Korea, Latin America Economic System, Nicaragua, Organizacion Panamericana de la Salud, Organization of American States, Panama, Portugal, Romania, Russia, Spain, Switzerland, Ukraine, United Nations Development Program, United Nations Economic Commission for Latin America and the Caribbean

## LEAGUE OF ARAB STATES (LAS)

**note** - also known as Arab League (AL)
22 March 1945
to promote economic, social, political, and military cooperation
**members** - (21 plus Palestine) Algeria, Bahrain, Comoros, Djibouti, Egypt, Iraq, Jordan, Kuwait, Lebanon, Libya, Mauritania, Morocco, Oman, Palestine, Qatar, Saudi Arabia, Somalia, Sudan, Syria (suspended), Tunisia, UAE, Yemen
**observers** - (4) Brazil, Eritrea, India, Venezuela

## LEAST DEVELOPED COUNTRIES (LLDCS)

that subgroup of the less developed countries (LDCs) initially identified by the UN General Assembly in 1971 as having no significant economic growth, per capita GDPs normally less than $1,000, and low literacy rates; also known as the undeveloped countries; the 44 LLDCs are: Afghanistan, Bangladesh, Benin, Bhutan, Burkina Faso, Burma, Burundi, Cambodia, Cameroon, Central African Republic, Chad, Comoros, Democratic Republic of the Congo, Cote d'Ivoire, Equatorial Guinea, Eritrea, Ethiopia, The Gambia, Ghana, Guinea, Guinea-Bissau, Haiti, Kenya, Lesotho, Liberia, Malawi, Mali, Moldova, Mozambique, Nepal, Niger, Rwanda, Sao Tome and Principe, Senegal, Sierra Leone, Somalia, Sudan, Tajikistan, Tanzania, Togo, Tokelau, Tuvalu, Uganda, Zambia

## LESS DEVELOPED COUNTRIES (LDCS)

the bottom group in the hierarchy of developed countries (DCs), former USSR/Eastern Europe (former USSR/EE), and less developed countries (LDCs); mainly countries and dependent areas with low levels of output, living standards, and technology; per capita GDPs are generally below $5,000 and often less than $1,500; however, the group also includes a number of countries with high per capita incomes, areas of advanced technology, and rapid rates of growth; includes the advanced developing countries, developing countries, Four Dragons (Four Tigers), least developed countries (LLDCs), low-income countries, middle-income countries, newly industrializing economies (NIEs), the South, Third World, underdeveloped countries, undeveloped countries; the 172 LDCs are: Afghanistan, Algeria, American Samoa, Angola, Anguilla, Antigua and Barbuda, Argentina, Aruba, The Bahamas, Bahrain, Bangladesh, Barbados, Belize, Benin, Bhutan, Bolivia, Botswana, Brazil, British Virgin Islands, Brunei, Burkina Faso, Burma, Burundi, Cabo Verde, Cambodia, Cameroon, Cayman Islands, Central African Republic, Chad, Chile, China, Christmas Island, Cocos Islands, Colombia, Comoros, Democratic Republic of the Congo, Republic of the Congo, Cook Islands, Costa Rica, Cote d'Ivoire, Cuba, Cyprus, Djibouti, Dominica, Dominican Republic, Ecuador, Egypt, El Salvador, Equatorial Guinea, Eritrea, Ethiopia, Falkland Islands, Fiji, French Guiana, French Polynesia, Gabon, The Gambia, Gaza Strip, Ghana, Gibraltar, Greenland, Grenada, Guadeloupe, Guam, Guatemala, Guernsey, Guinea, Guinea-Bissau, Guyana, Haiti, Honduras, Hong Kong, India, Indonesia, Iran, Iraq, Isle of Man, Jamaica, Jersey, Jordan, Kenya, Kiribati, North Korea, South Korea, Kuwait, Laos, Lebanon, Lesotho, Liberia, Libya, Macau, Madagascar, Malawi, Malaysia, Maldives, Mali, Marshall Islands, Martinique, Mauritania, Mauritius, Mayotte, Federated States of Micronesia, Mongolia, Montserrat, Morocco, Mozambique, Namibia, Nauru, Nepal, Netherlands Antilles, New Caledonia, Nicaragua, Niger, Nigeria, Niue, Norfolk Island, Northern Mariana Islands, Oman, Palau, Pakistan, Panama, Papua New Guinea, Paraguay, Peru, Philippines, Pitcairn Islands, Puerto Rico, Qatar, Reunion, Rwanda, Saint Helena, Ascension, and Tristan da Cunha, Saint Kitts and Nevis, Saint Lucia, Saint Pierre and Miquelon, Saint Vincent and the Grenadines, Samoa, Sao Tome and Principe, Saudi Arabia, Senegal, Seychelles, Sierra Leone, Singapore, Solomon Islands, Somalia, Sri Lanka, Sudan, Suriname, Swaziland, Syria, Taiwan, Tanzania, Thailand, Togo, Tokelau, Tonga, Trinidad and Tobago, Tunisia, Turks and Caicos Islands, Tuvalu, UAE, Uganda, Uruguay, Vanuatu, Venezuela, Vietnam, Virgin Islands, Wallis and Futuna, West Bank, Western Sahara, Yemen, Zambia, Zimbabwe; note - similar to the new International Monetary Fund (IMF) term "developing countries" which adds Malta, Mexico, South Africa, and Turkey but omits in its recently published statistics American Samoa, Anguilla, British Virgin Islands, Brunei, Cayman Islands, Christmas Island, Cocos Islands, Cook Islands, Cuba, Eritrea, Falkland Islands, French Guiana, French Polynesia, Gaza Strip, Gibraltar, Greenland, Grenada, Guadeloupe, Guam, Guernsey, Isle of Man, Jersey, North Korea, Macau, Martinique, Mayotte, Montserrat, Nauru, New Caledonia, Niue, Norfolk Island, Northern Mariana Islands, Palau, Pitcairn Islands, Puerto Rico, Reunion, Saint Helena, Ascension, and Tristan da Cunha, Saint Pierre and Miquelon, Tokelau, Tonga, Turks and Caicos Islands, Tuvalu, Virgin Islands, Wallis and Futuna, West Bank, Western Sahara

## LOW-INCOME COUNTRIES

another term for those less developed countries with below-average per capita GDPs; see less developed countries (LDCs)

## MIDDLE-INCOME COUNTRIES

another term for those less developed countries with above-average per capita GDPs; see less developed countries (LDCs)

## MULTILATERAL INVESTMENT GUARANTEE AGENCY (MIGA)

12 April 1988
encourages flow of foreign direct investment among member countries by offering investment insurance, consultation, and negotiation on conditions for foreign investment and technical assistance; a UN specialized agency
**members** - (181) includes all UN member countries except Andorra, Brunei, Cuba, Kiribati, North Korea, Liechtenstein, Marshall Islands, Monaco, Nauru, San Marino, Somalia, Tonga, Tuvalu; plus Kosovo

## NEAR ABROAD

Russian term for the 14 non-Russian successor states of the USSR, in which 25 million ethnic Russians live and in which Moscow has expressed a strong national security interest; the 14 countries are Armenia, Azerbaijan, Belarus, Estonia, Georgia, Kazakhstan, Kyrgyzstan, Latvia, Lithuania, Moldova, Tajikistan, Turkmenistan, Ukraine, Uzbekistan

## NEW INDEPENDENT STATES (NIS)

a term referring to all the countries of the FSU except the Baltic countries (Estonia, Latvia, Lithuania)

## NEWLY INDUSTRIALIZING COUNTRIES (NICS)

former term for the newly industrializing economies; see newly industrializing economies (NIEs)

## NEWLY INDUSTRIALIZING ECONOMIES (NIES)

that subgroup of the less developed countries (LDCs) that has experienced particularly rapid industrialization of their economies; formerly known as the newly industrializing countries (NICs); also known as advanced developing countries; usually includes the Four Dragons (Hong Kong, South Korea, Singapore, Taiwan), and Brazil

## NONALIGNED MOVEMENT (NAM)

1-6 September 1961
to establish political and military cooperation apart from the traditional East or West blocs
**members** - (114 plus Palestine) Afghanistan, Algeria, Angola, Antigua and Barbuda, Azerbaijan, The Bahamas, Bahrain, Bangladesh, Barbados, Belarus, Belize, Benin, Bhutan, Bolivia, Botswana, Brunei, Burkina Faso, Burma, Burundi, Cabo Verde, Cambodia, Cameroon, Central African Republic, Chad, Chile, Colombia, Comoros, Democratic Republic of the Congo, Republic of the Congo, Cote d'Ivoire, Cuba, Djibouti, Dominica, Dominican Republic, Ecuador, Egypt, Equatorial Guinea, Eritrea, Ethiopia, Fiji, Gabon, The Gambia, Ghana, Grenada, Guatemala, Guinea, Guinea-Bissau, Guyana, Haiti, Honduras, India, Indonesia, Iran, Iraq, Jamaica, Jordan, Kenya, North Korea, Kuwait, Laos, Lebanon, Lesotho, Liberia, Libya, Madagascar, Malawi, Malaysia, Maldives, Mali, Mauritania, Mauritius, Mongolia, Morocco, Mozambique, Namibia, Nepal, Nicaragua, Niger, Nigeria, Oman, Pakistan, Palestine, Panama, Papua New Guinea, Peru, Philippines, Qatar, Rwanda, Saint Kitts and Nevis, Saint Lucia, Saint Vincent and the Grenadines, Sao Tome and Principe, Saudi Arabia, Senegal, Seychelles, Sierra Leone, Singapore, Somalia, South Africa, Sri Lanka, Sudan, Suriname, Swaziland, Syria, Tanzania, Thailand, Timor-Leste, Togo, Trinidad and Tobago, Tunisia, Turkmenistan, Uganda, UAE, Uzbekistan, Vanuatu, Venezuela, Vietnam, Yemen, Zambia, Zimbabwe
**observers** - (17) Argentina, Armenia, Bosnia and Herzegovina, Brazil, China, Costa Rica, Croatia, El Salvador, Kazakhstan, Kyrgyzstan, Mexico, Montenegro, Paraguay, Serbia, Tajikistan, Ukraine, Uruguay

## NORDIC COUNCIL (NC)

16 March 1952; effective - 12 February 1953
to promote regional economic, cultural, and environmental cooperation
**members** - (5) Denmark (including Faroe Islands and Greenland), Finland (including Aland Islands), Iceland, Norway, Sweden
**observers** - (6) Estonia, Latvia, Lithuania, and the Sami (Lapp) local parliaments of Finland, Norway, and Sweden

## NORDIC INVESTMENT BANK (NIB)

4 December 1975; effective - 1 June 1976
to promote economic cooperation and development
**members** - (8) Denmark (including Faroe Islands and Greenland), Estonia, Finland (including Aland Islands), Iceland, Latvia, Lithuania, Norway, Sweden

## NORTH

a popular term for the rich industrialized countries generally located in the northern portion of the Northern Hemisphere; the counterpart of the South; see developed countries (DCs)

## NORTH AMERICAN FREE TRADE AGREEMENT (NAFTA)

17 December 1992
to eliminate trade barriers, promote fair competition, increase investment opportunities, provide protection of intellectual property rights, and create procedures to settle disputes
**members** - (3) Canada, Mexico, US

## NORTH ATLANTIC TREATY ORGANIZATION (NATO)

4 April 1949
to promote mutual defense and cooperation
**members** - (28) Albania, Belgium, Bulgaria, Canada, Croatia, Czechia, Denmark, Estonia, France, Germany, Greece, Hungary, Iceland, Italy, Latvia, Lithuania, Luxembourg, Netherlands, Norway, Poland, Portugal, Romania, Slovakia, Slovenia, Spain, Turkey, UK, US

## NUCLEAR ENERGY AGENCY (NEA)

**note** - also known as OECD Nuclear Energy Agency
1 February 1958
to promote the peaceful uses of nuclear energy; associated with OECD
**members** - (31) Australia, Austria, Belgium, Canada, Czechia, Denmark, Finland, France, Germany, Greece, Hungary, Iceland, Ireland, Italy, Japan, South Korea, Luxembourg, Mexico, Netherlands, Norway, Poland, Portugal, Russia, Slovakia, Slovenia, Spain, Sweden, Switzerland, Turkey, UK, US

## NUCLEAR SUPPLIERS GROUP (NSG)

**note** - also known as the London Suppliers Group or the London Group
1974; effective - 1975
to establish guidelines for exports of nuclear materials, processing equipment for uranium enrichment, and technical information to countries of proliferation concern and regions of conflict and instability
**members** - (48) Argentina, Australia, Austria, Belarus, Belgium, Brazil, Bulgaria, Canada, China, Croatia, Cyprus, Czechia, Denmark, Estonia, Finland, France, Germany, Greece, Hungary, Iceland, Ireland, Italy, Japan, Kazakhstan, South Korea, Latvia, Lithuania, Luxembourg, Malta, Mexico, Netherlands, NZ, Norway, Poland, Portugal, Romania, Russia, Serbia, Slovakia, Slovenia, South Africa, Spain, Sweden, Switzerland, Turkey, Ukraine, UK, US

**observer** - (2) Chairman of the Zangger Committee, European Commission (a policy-planning body for the EU)

## ORGANISATION FOR ECONOMIC COOPERATION AND DEVELOPMENT (OECD)

14 December 1960; effective - 30 September 1961
to promote economic cooperation and development
**members** - (34) Australia, Austria, Belgium, Canada, Chile, Czechia, Denmark, Estonia, Finland, France, Germany, Greece, Hungary, Iceland, Ireland, Israel, Italy, Japan, South Korea, Luxembourg, Mexico, Netherlands, NZ, Norway, Poland, Portugal, Slovakia, Slovenia, Spain, Sweden, Switzerland, Turkey, UK, US
**special member** - (1) EC

## ORGANIZATION FOR DEMOCRACY AND ECONOMIC DEVELOPMENT (GUAM)

**note** - acronym standing for the member countries, Georgia, Ukraine, Azerbaijan, Moldova; formerly known as GUUAM before Uzbekistan withdrew in 5 May 2005
7 June 2001
commits the countries to cooperation and assistance in social and economic development, the strengthening and broadening of trade and economic relations, and the development and effective use of transport and communications, highways, and related infrastructure crossing the boundaries of the member states
**members** - (4) Azerbaijan, Georgia, Moldova, Ukraine

## ORGANIZATION FOR SECURITY AND COOPERATION IN EUROPE (OSCE)

**note** - formerly the Conference on Security and Cooperation in Europe (CSCE) established 3 July 1975
1 January 1995
to foster the implementation of human rights, fundamental freedoms, democracy, and the rule of law; to act as an instrument of early warning, conflict prevention, and crisis management; and to serve as a framework for conventional arms control and confidence building measures
**members** - (57) Albania, Andorra, Armenia, Austria, Azerbaijan, Belarus, Belgium, Bosnia and Herzegovina, Bulgaria, Canada, Croatia, Cyprus, Czechia, Denmark, Estonia, Finland, France, Georgia, Germany, Greece, Holy See, Hungary, Iceland, Ireland, Italy, Kazakhstan, Kyrgyzstan, Latvia, Liechtenstein, Lithuania, Luxembourg, Macedonia, Malta, Moldova, Monaco, Mongolia, Montenegro, Netherlands, Norway, Poland, Portugal, Romania, Russia, San Marino, Serbia, Slovakia, Slovenia, Spain, Sweden, Switzerland, Tajikistan, Turkey, Turkmenistan, Ukraine, UK, US, Uzbekistan
**partners for cooperation** - (11) Afghanistan, Algeria, Australia, Egypt, Israel, Japan, Jordan, South Korea, Morocco, Thailand, Tunisia

## ORGANIZATION FOR THE PROHIBITION OF CHEMICAL WEAPONS (OPCW)

29 April 1997
to enforce the Convention on the Prohibition of the Development, Production, Stockpiling, and Use of Chemical Weapons and on Their Destruction; to provide a forum for consultation and cooperation among the signatories of the Convention
**members (countries that have ratified the Convention)** - (192) Afghanistan, Albania, Algeria, Andorra, Angola, Antigua and Barbuda, Argentina, Armenia, Australia, Austria, Azerbaijan, The Bahamas, Bahrain, Bangladesh, Barbados, Belarus, Belgium, Belize, Benin, Bhutan, Bolivia, Bosnia and Herzegovina, Botswana, Brazil, Brunei, Bulgaria, Burkina Faso, Burma, Burundi, Cabo Verde, Cambodia, Cameroon, Canada, Central African Republic, Chad, Chile, China, Colombia, Comoros, Democratic Republic of the Congo, Republic of the Congo, Cook Islands, Costa Rica, Cote d'Ivoire, Croatia, Cuba, Cyprus, Czechia, Denmark, Djibouti, Dominica, Dominican Republic, Ecuador, El Salvador, Equatorial Guinea, Eritrea, Estonia, Ethiopia, Fiji, Finland, France, Gabon, The Gambia, Georgia, Germany, Ghana, Greece, Grenada, Guatemala, Guinea, Guinea-Bissau, Guyana, Haiti, Holy See, Honduras, Hungary, Iceland, India, Indonesia, Iran, Iraq, Ireland, Italy, Jamaica, Japan, Jordan, Kazakhstan, Kenya, Kiribati, South Korea, Kuwait, Kyrgyzstan, Laos, Latvia, Lebanon, Lesotho, Liberia, Libya, Liechtenstein, Lithuania, Luxembourg, Macedonia, Madagascar, Malawi, Malaysia, Maldives, Mali, Malta, Marshall Islands, Mauritania, Mauritius, Mexico, Federated States of Micronesia, Moldova, Monaco, Mongolia, Montenegro, Morocco, Mozambique, Namibia, Nauru, Nepal, Netherlands, NZ, Nicaragua, Niger, Nigeria, Niue, Norway, Oman, Pakistan, Palau, Panama, Papua New Guinea, Paraguay, Peru, Philippines, Poland, Portugal, Qatar, Romania, Russia, Rwanda, Saint Kitts and Nevis, Saint Lucia, Saint Vincent and the Grenadines, Samoa, San Marino, Sao Tome and Principe, Saudi Arabia, Senegal, Serbia, Seychelles, Sierra Leone, Singapore, Slovakia, Slovenia, Solomon Islands, Somalia, South Africa, Spain, Sri Lanka, Sudan, Suriname, Swaziland, Sweden, Switzerland, Syria, Tajikistan, Tanzania, Thailand, Timor-Leste, Togo, Tonga, Trinidad and Tobago, Tunisia, Turkey, Turkmenistan, Tuvalu, Uganda, Ukraine, UAE, UK, US, Uruguay, Uzbekistan, Vanuatu, Venezuela, Vietnam, Yemen, Zambia, Zimbabwe
**signatory states** (countries that have signed, but not ratified, the Convention) - (1) Israel

## ORGANIZATION OF AFRICAN UNITY (OAU)

see African Union

## ORGANIZATION OF AMERICAN STATES (OAS)

14 April 1890 as the International Union of American Republics; 30 April 1948 adopted present charter; effective - 13 December 1951
to promote regional peace and security as well as economic and social development
**members** - (35) Antigua and Barbuda, Argentina, The Bahamas, Barbados, Belize, Bolivia, Brazil, Canada, Chile, Colombia, Costa Rica, Cuba (suspended), Dominica, Dominican Republic, Ecuador, El Salvador, Grenada, Guatemala, Guyana, Haiti, Honduras, Jamaica, Mexico, Nicaragua, Panama, Paraguay, Peru, Saint Kitts and Nevis, Saint Lucia, Saint Vincent and the Grenadines, Suriname, Trinidad and Tobago, US, Uruguay, Venezuela
**observers** - (70) Albania, Algeria, Angola, Armenia, Austria, Azerbaijan, Belgium, Benin, Bosnia and Herzegovina, Bulgaria, China, Croatia, Cyprus, Czechia, Denmark, Egypt, Equatorial Guinea, Estonia, EU, Finland, France, Georgia, Germany, Ghana, Greece, Holy See, Hungary, Iceland, India, Ireland, Israel, Italy, Japan, Kazakhstan, South Korea, Latvia, Lebanon, Liechtenstein, Lithuania, Luxembourg, Macedonia, Malta, Monaco, Montenegro, Morocco, Netherlands, Nigeria, Norway, Pakistan, Philippines, Poland, Portugal, Qatar, Romania, Russia, Saudi Arabia, Serbia, Slovakia, Slovenia, Spain, Sri Lanka, Sweden, Switzerland, Thailand, Tunisia, Turkey, Ukraine, UK, Vanuatu, Yemen

## ORGANIZATION OF ARAB PETROLEUM EXPORTING COUNTRIES (OAPEC)

9 January 1968
to promote cooperation in the petroleum industry
**members** - (11) Algeria, Bahrain, Egypt, Iraq, Kuwait, Libya, Qatar, Saudi Arabia, Syria, Tunisia (suspended), UAE

## ORGANIZATION OF EASTERN CARIBBEAN STATES (OECS)

18 June 1981; effective - 4 July 1981
to promote political, economic, and defense cooperation
**members** - (9) Anguilla, Antigua and Barbuda, British Virgin Islands, Dominica, Grenada, Montserrat, Saint Kitts and Nevis, Saint Lucia, Saint Vincent and the Grenadines

## ORGANIZATION OF ISLAMIC COOPERATION (OIC)

**note** - formerly the Organization of the Islamic Conference

22-25 September 1969
to promote Islamic solidarity in economic, social, cultural, and political affairs
**members** - (56 plus Palestine) Afghanistan, Albania, Algeria, Azerbaijan, Bahrain, Bangladesh, Benin, Brunei, Burkina Faso, Cameroon, Chad, Comoros, Cote d'Ivoire, Djibouti, Egypt, Gabon, The Gambia, Guinea, Guinea-Bissau, Guyana, Indonesia, Iran, Iraq, Jordan, Kazakhstan, Kuwait, Kyrgyzstan, Lebanon, Libya, Malaysia, Maldives, Mali, Mauritania, Morocco, Mozambique, Niger, Nigeria, Oman, Pakistan, Palestine, Qatar, Saudi Arabia, Senegal, Sierra Leone, Somalia, Sudan, Suriname, Syria, Tajikistan, Togo, Tunisia, Turkey, Turkmenistan, Uganda, UAE, Uzbekistan, Yemen
**observers** - (12) AU, Bosnia and Herzegovina, Central African Republic, ECO, LAS, Moro National Liberation Front, NAM, Parliamentary Union of the OIC Member States, Russia, Thailand, Turkish Muslim Community of Kibris, UN

## ORGANIZATION OF PETROLEUM EXPORTING COUNTRIES (OPEC)

14 September 1960
to coordinate petroleum policies
**members** - (13) Algeria, Angola, Ecuador, Indonesia, Iran, Iraq, Kuwait, Libya, Nigeria, Qatar, Saudi Arabia, UAE, Venezuela; note - Indonesia left OPEC in 2008 but returned on 1 January 2016

## PACIFIC ALLIANCE

28 April 2011
to reduce trade barriers between member countries, to install visa-free travel, to install a common stock exchange, and to set up joint embassies in some countries
**members** - (4) Chile, Columbia, Mexico, Peru
**observers** - (44) Argentina, Australia, Austria, Belgium, Canada, China, Costa Rica, Denmark, Dominica, Dominican Republic, Ecuador, El Salvador, Finland, France, Georgia, Germany, Greece, Guatemala, Haiti, Honduras, Hungary, India, Indonesia, Israel, Italy, Japan, Morocco, Netherlands, New Zealand, Panama, Paraguay, Poland, Portugal, Singapore, South Korea, Spain, Sweden, Switzerland, Thailand, Trinidad and Tobago, Turkey, UK, US, Uruguay

## PACIFIC COMMUNITY (SPC)

local name of the Secretariat of the Pacific Community

## PACIFIC ISLANDS FORUM (PIF)

**note** - formerly known as South Pacific Forum (SPF)
5 August 1971
to promote regional cooperation in political matters

**members** - (16) Australia, Cook Islands, Fiji, Kiribati, Marshall Islands, Federated States of Micronesia, Nauru, NZ, Niue, Palau, Papua New Guinea, Samoa, Solomon Islands, Tonga, Tuvalu, Vanuatu
**associate members** - (3) French Polynesia, New Caledonia, Tokelau
**partners** - (17) Canada, China, Cuba, EU, France, India, Indonesia, Italy, Japan, South Korea, Malaysia, Philippines, Spain, Thailand, Turkey, UK, US
**observers** - (12) ACP Group, American Samoa, Asia Development Bank, The Commonwealth, Commonwealth of the Northern Marianas, Guam, international Organization for Migration, Timor-Leste (special observer), UN, Wallis and Futuna, Western and Central Pacific Fisheries Commission, the World Bank

## PARIS CLUB

1956
to provide a forum for debtor countries to negotiate rescheduling of debt service payments or loans extended by governments or official agencies of participating countries; to help restore normal trade and project finance to debtor countries
**members** - (20) Australia, Austria, Belgium, Canada, Denmark, Finland, France, Germany, Ireland, Israel, Italy, Japan, Netherlands, Norway, Russia, Spain, Sweden, Switzerland, UK, US
**associate members** - (13) Abu Dhabi, Argentina, Brazil, China, South Korea, Kuwait, Mexico, Morocco, NZ, Portugal, South Africa, Trinidad and Tobago, Turkey

## PARTNERSHIP FOR PEACE (PFP)

10-11 January 1994
to expand and intensify political and military cooperation throughout Europe, increase stability, diminish threats to peace, and build relationships by promoting the spirit of practical cooperation and commitment to democratic principles that underpin NATO; program under the auspices of NATO
**members** - (22) Armenia, Austria, Azerbaijan, Belarus, Bosnia and Herzegovina, Finland, Georgia, Ireland, Kazakhstan, Kyrgyzstan, Macedonia, Malta, Moldova, Montenegro, Russia, Serbia, Sweden, Switzerland, Tajikistan, Turkmenistan, Ukraine, Uzbekistan; note - a nation that becomes a member of NATO is no longer a member of PFP

## PERMANENT COURT OF ARBITRATION (PCA)

29 July 1899
to facilitate the settlement of international disputes
**members** - (118 and the Palestine Liberation Organization) Albania, Argentina, Australia, Austria, Bahrain, Bangladesh, Belarus, Belgium, Belize, Benin, Bolivia, Brazil, Bulgaria, Burkina Faso, Cambodia, Cameroon, Canada, Chile, China, Colombia, Democratic Republic of the Congo, Costa Rica, Croatia, Cuba, Cyprus, Czechia, Denmark, Djibouti, Dominican Republic, Ecuador, Egypt, El Salvador, Eritrea, Estonia, Ethiopia, Fiji, Finland, France, Georgia, Germany, Greece, Guatemala, Guyana, Haiti, Honduras, Hungary, Iceland, India, Iran, Iraq, Ireland, Israel, Italy, Japan, Jordan, Kenya, South Korea, Kuwait, Kyrgyzstan, Laos, Latvia, Lebanon, Libya, Liechtenstein, Lithuania, Luxembourg, Macedonia, Madagascar, Malaysia, Malta, Mauritius, Mexico, Montenegro, Morocco, Netherlands, NZ, Nicaragua, Nigeria, Norway, Pakistan, Panama, Paraguay, Peru, Philippines, Poland, Portugal, Qatar, Romania, Russia, Rwanda, Sao Tome and Principe, Saudi Arabia, Senegal, Serbia, Singapore, Slovakia, Slovenia, South Africa, Spain, Sri Lanka, Sudan, Suriname, Swaziland, Sweden, Switzerland, Thailand, Togo, Turkey, Uganda, Ukraine, UAE, UK, US, Uruguay, Venezuela, Vietnam, Zambia, Zimbabwe, Palestine Liberation Organization

## PETROCARIBE

29 June 2005
to eliminate existing social inequities, to foster high standards of living, to promote effective people's participation in shaping their own destiny
**members** - (19) Antigua and Barbuda, The Bahamas, Belize, Cuba, Dominica, Dominican Republic, El Salvador, Grenada, Guatemala, Guyana, Haiti, Honduras, Jamaica, Nicaragua, St. Kitts and Nevis, St. Lucia, St. Vincent and the Grenadines, Suriname, Venezuela
fb_test

## RIO GROUP (RG)

**note** - formerly known as Grupo de los Ocho, established NA December 1986; composed of the Contadora Group and the Lima Group
established in 1988 to consult on regional Latin American issues; its members were Argentina, Belize, Bolivia, Brazil, Chile, Colombia, Costa Rica, Cuba, Dominican Republic, Ecuador, El Salvador, Guatemala, Guyana, Haiti, Honduras, Jamaica (representing CARICOM), Mexico, Nicaragua, Panama, Paraguay, Peru, Uruguay, Venezuela; in 2010 joined with the Caribbean Summit on Integration and Development (CALC) to form the Community of Latin American and Caribbean States (CELAC)

## SCHENGEN CONVENTION

signed June 1990; effective March 1995
to allow free movement within an area without internal border controls
**members** - (26) Austria, Belgium, Czechia, Denmark, Estonia, Finland, France, Germany, Greece, Hungary,

Iceland, Italy, Latvia, Liechtenstein, Lithuania, Luxembourg, Malta, Netherlands, Norway, Poland, Portugal, Slovakia, Slovenia, Spain, Sweden, Switzerland; note - UK and Ireland have not joined; Cyprus will probably join in the near future; Bulgaria and Romania are still not fully implemented
**De Facto members (microstates within or between Schengen states)** - (4) Andorra, Holy See, Monaco, San Marino

## SECOND WORLD

another term for the traditionally Marxist-Leninist states of the USSR and Eastern Europe, with authoritarian governments and command economies based on the Soviet model; the term is fading from use; see centrally planned economies

## SECRETARIAT OF THE PACIFIC COMMUNITY (SPC)

6 February 1947; effective 29 July 1948
to serve island development in 22 Pacific countries; to develop technical assistance and professional, scientific, and research support; to build planning and management capability
**members** - (26) America Samoa, Australia, Cook Islands, Fiji, France, French Polynesia, Guam, Kiribati, Marshall Islands, Federated States of Micronesia, Nauru, New Caledonia, Niue, Northern Mariana Islands, NZ, Palau, Papua New Guinea, Pitcairn Islands, Samoa, Solomon Islands, Tokelau, Tonga, Tuvalu, Vanuatu, US, Wallis and Futuna

## SHANGHAI COOPERATION ORGANIZATION (SCO)

15 June 2001
to combat terrorism, extremism, and separatism; to safeguard regional security through mutual trust, disarmament, and cooperative security; and to increase cooperation in political, trade, economic, scientific and technological, cultural, and educational fields
**members** - (6) China, Kazakhstan, Kyrgyzstan, Russia, Tajikistan, Uzbekistan
**dialogue members** - (3) Belarus, Sri Lanka Turkey
**observers** - (5) Afghanistan, India, Iran, Mongolia, Pakistan

## SOCIALIST COUNTRIES

in general, countries in which the government owns and plans the use of the major factors of production; note - the term is sometimes used incorrectly as a synonym for communist countries

## SOUTH

a popular term for the poorer, less industrialized countries generally located south of the developed countries; the counterpart of the North; see less developed countries (LDCs)

## SOUTH AMERICAN COMMUNITY OF NATIONS (CSN)

established on 9 December 2004; its aim was to coordinate common policies regarding multilateral organizations, to integrate physical infrastructure, and to consolidate the merger of CAN and Mercosur; the members were Argentina, Bolivia, Brazil, Chile, Colombia, Ecuador, Guyana, Paraguay, Peru, Surinam, Uruguay, Venezuela; in 2008 it became Union of South American Nations (UNASUR)

## SOUTH ASIA CO-OPERATIVE ENVIRONMENT PROGRAM (SACEP)

January 1983
to promote regional cooperation in South Asia in the field of environment, both natural and human, and on issues of economic and social development; to support conservation and management of natural resources of the region
**members** - (8) Afghanistan, Bangladesh, Bhutan, India, Maldives, Nepal, Pakistan, Sri Lanka

## SOUTH ASIAN ASSOCIATION FOR REGIONAL COOPERATION (SAARC)

8 December 1985
to promote economic, social, and cultural cooperation
**members** - (8) Afghanistan, Bangladesh, Bhutan, India, Maldives, Nepal, Pakistan, Sri Lanka
**observers** - (9) Australia, Burma, China, EU, Iran, Japan, South Korea, Mauritius, US

## SOUTH PACIFIC FORUM (SPF)

**note** - see Pacific Island Forum

## SOUTH PACIFIC REGIONAL TRADE AND ECONOMIC COOPERATION AGREEMENT (SPARTECA)

1981
to redress unequal trade relationships of Australia and New Zealand with small island economies in the Pacific region
**members** - (16) Australia, Cook Islands, Fiji (suspended), Kiribati, Marshall Islands, Federated States of Micronesia, Nauru, NZ, Niue, Palau, Papua New Guinea, Samoa, Solomon Islands, Tonga, Tuvalu, Vanuatu

## SOUTHERN AFRICAN CUSTOMS UNION (SACU)

11 December 1969
to promote free trade and cooperation in customs matters
**members** - (5) Botswana, Lesotho, Namibia, South Africa, Swaziland

## SOUTHERN AFRICAN DEVELOPMENT COMMUNITY (SADC)

**note** - evolved from the Southern African Development Coordination Conference (SADCC)
17 August 1992
to promote regional economic development and integration
**members** - (15) Angola, Botswana, Democratic Republic of the Congo, Lesotho, Madagascar, Malawi, Mauritius, Mozambique, Namibia, Seychelles, South Africa, Swaziland, Tanzania, Zambia, Zimbabwe

## SOUTHERN CONE COMMON MARKET (MERCOSUR) OR SOUTHERN COMMON MARKET

**note** - also known as Mercado Comun del Sur (Mercosur - Spanish); Mercado Comum Sol (Mercosol - Portuguese)
26 March 1991
to increase regional economic cooperation
**members** - (4) Argentina, Brazil, Paraguay, Uruguay
**associate members** - (7) Bolivia, Chile, Colombia, Ecuador, Buyana, Peru, Suriname

## THIRD WORLD

another term for the less developed countries; the term is obsolescent; see less developed countries (LDCs)

## UNDERDEVELOPED COUNTRIES

refers to those less developed countries with the potential for above-average economic growth; see less developed countries (LDCs)

## UNDEVELOPED COUNTRIES

refers to those extremely poor less developed countries (LDCs) with little prospect for economic growth; see least developed countries (LLDCs)

## UNION LATINA

established on 15 May 1954, became functional 1983; its aim was to project, protect, and promote the common heritage and unifying identities of the Latin and Latin-influenced world; on 26 January 2012, because of financial difficulties, it announced the suspension of activities; the 36 members were: Angola, Bolivia, Brazil, Cabo Verde, Chile, Colombia, Cote d'Ivoire, Costa Rica, Cuba, Dominican Republic, Ecuador, El Salvador, France, Guatemala, Guinea-Bissau, Haiti, Honduras, Italy, Moldova, Monaco, Mozambique, Nicaragua, Panama, Paraguay, Peru, Philippines, Portugal, Romania, San Marino, Sao Tome and Principe, Senegal, Spain, Timor-Leste, Uruguay, and Venezuela; 4 observers were: Argentina, Holy See, Mexico, Order of Malta

## UNION OF SOUTH AMERICAN NATIONS (UNASUR - SPANISH; UNASUL - PORTUGUESE)

formerly South American Community of Nations (CSN) which terminated on 16 April 2007
23 May 2008
to model a community after the European Union which will include a common currency, parliament, passport, and defense policy
**members** - (12) Argentina, Bolivia, Brazil, Chile, Colombia, Ecuador, Guyana, Paraguay, Peru, Suriname, Uruguay, Venezuela
**observers** - (2) Mexico, Panama

## UNITED NATIONS (UN)

26 June 1945; effective - 24 October 1945
to maintain international peace and security and to promote cooperation involving economic, social, cultural, and humanitarian problems
**constituent organizations** - the UN is composed of six principal organs and numerous subordinate agencies and bodies as follows:
**1) Secretariat**
**2) General Assembly:** International Computing Center (ICC), International Trade Center (ITC), Joint United Nations Program on HIV/AIDS (UN-AIDS), Office of the United Nations High Commissioner for Refugees (UNHCR), United Nations Center for Human Settlements (UN-Habitat), United Nations Children's Fund (UNICEF), United Nations Conference on Trade and Development (UNCTAD), United Nations Development Program (UNDP), United Nations Environment Program (UNEP), United Nations Institute for Disarmament Research (UNIDIR), United Nations Institute for Training and Research (UNITAR), United Nations Interregional Crime and Justice Research Institute (UNICRI), United Nations Office on Drugs and Crime (UNODC), United Nations Population Fund (UNFPA), United Nations Office of Project Services (UNOPS), United Nations Relief and Works Agency for Palestine Refugees in the Near East (UNRWA), United Nations Research Institute for Social Development (UNRISD), United Nations System Staff College (UNSSC), United Nations University (UNU), United Nations Women, World Food Program (WFP)

**3) Security Council:** International Criminal Tribunal for the Former Yugoslavia (ICTY), International Criminal Tribunal for Rwanda (ICTR), United Nations Compensation Commission, United Nations Disengagement Observer Force (UNDOF), African Union/United Nations Hybrid Operation in Darfur (UNAMID), United Nations Assistance Mission in Afghanistan (UNAMA), United Nations Interim Administration Mission in Kosovo (UNMIK), United Nations Interim Force for Abyei (UNIFSA), United Nations Interim Force in Lebanon (UNIFIL), United Nations Mission in Liberia (UNMIL), United Nations Military Observer Group in India and Pakistan (UNMOGIP), United Nations Multidimensional Integrated Stabilization Mission in Mali (MINUSMA), United Nations Operation in Cote d'Ivoire (UNOCI), United Nations Mission for the Referendum in Western Sahara (MINURSO), United Nations Mission in South Sudan (UNMISS), United Nations Organization Stabilization Mission in the Democratic Republic of the Congo (MONUSCO), United Nations Peace-Keeping Force in Cyprus (UNFICYP), United Nations Stabilization Mission in Haiti (MINUSTAH), and United Nations Truce Supervision Organization (UNTSO)

**4) Economic and Social Council (ECOSOC):** Commission for Social Development, Commission on Crime Prevention and Criminal Justice, Commission on Narcotics Drugs, Commission on Population and Development, Commission on Science and Technology for Development, Commission on Sustainable Development, Commission on the Status of Women, Economic and Social Commission for Asia and the Pacific (ESCAP), Economic and Social Commission for Western Asia (ESCWA), Economic Commission for Africa (ECA), Economic Commission for Europe (ECE), Economic Commission for Latin America and the Caribbean (ECLAC), Statistical Commission, Food and Agriculture Organization of the United Nations (FAO), International Atomic Energy Agency (IAEA), Preparatory Commission for the Nuclear-Test-Ban Treaty Organization (CTBTO), International Bank for Reconstruction and Development (IBRD), International Center for Secretariat of Investment Disputes (ICSID), International Civil Aviation Organization (ICAO), International Development Association (IDA), International Finance Corporation (IFC), International Fund for Agricultural Development (IFAD), International Labor Organization (ILO), International Maritime Organization (IMO), International Monetary Fund (IMF), International Telecommunication Union (ITU), Multilateral Investment Guarantee Agency (MIGA), Statistical Commission, United Nations Educational, Scientific, and Cultural Organization (UNESCO), United Nations Forum on Forests, United Nations Industrial Development Organization (UNIDO), Universal Postal Union (UPU), World Health Organization (WHO), World Intellectual Property Organization (WIPO), World Meteorological Organization (WMO), World Tourism Organization (UNWTO), and World Trade Organization (WTO), Statistical Commission, UN Forum on Forests

**5) Trusteeship Council** (inactive; no trusteeships at this time)

**6) International Court of Justice (ICJ)**

**UN members -** (193) Afghanistan, Albania, Algeria, Andorra, Angola, Antigua and Barbuda, Argentina, Armenia, Australia, Austria, Azerbaijan, The Bahamas, Bahrain, Bangladesh, Barbados, Belarus, Belgium, Belize, Benin, Bhutan, Bolivia, Bosnia and Herzegovina, Botswana, Brazil, Brunei, Bulgaria, Burkina Faso, Burma, Burundi, Cabo Verde, Cambodia, Cameroon, Canada, Central African Republic, Chad, Chile, China, Colombia, Comoros, Democratic Republic of the Congo, Republic of the Congo, Costa Rica, Cote d'Ivoire, Croatia, Cuba, Cyprus, Czechia, Denmark, Djibouti, Dominica, Dominican Republic, Ecuador, Egypt, El Salvador, Equatorial Guinea, Eritrea, Estonia, Eswatini, Ethiopia, Fiji, Finland, France, Gabon, The Gambia, Georgia, Germany, Ghana, Greece, Grenada, Guatemala, Guinea, Guinea-Bissau, Guyana, Haiti, Honduras, Hungary, Iceland, India, Indonesia, Iran, Iraq, Ireland, Israel, Italy, Jamaica, Japan, Jordan, Kazakhstan, Kenya, Kiribati, North Korea, South Korea, Kuwait, Kyrgyzstan, Laos, Latvia, Lebanon, Lesotho, Liberia, Libya, Liechtenstein, Lithuania, Luxembourg, Macedonia, Madagascar, Malawi, Malaysia, Maldives, Mali, Malta, Marshall Islands, Mauritania, Mauritius, Mexico, Federated States of Micronesia, Moldova, Monaco, Mongolia, Montenegro, Morocco, Mozambique, Namibia, Nauru, Nepal, Netherlands, NZ, Nicaragua, Niger, Nigeria, Norway, Oman, Pakistan, Palau, Panama, Papua New Guinea, Paraguay, Peru, Philippines, Poland, Portugal, Qatar, Romania, Russia, Rwanda, Saint Kitts and Nevis, Saint Lucia, Saint Vincent and the Grenadines, Samoa, San Marino, Sao Tome and Principe, Saudi Arabia, Senegal, Serbia, Seychelles, Sierra Leone, Singapore, Slovakia, Slovenia, Solomon Islands, Somalia, South Africa, South Sudan, Spain, Sri Lanka, Sudan, Suriname, Sweden, Switzerland, Syria, Tajikistan, Tanzania, Thailand, Timor-Leste, Togo, Tonga, Trinidad and Tobago, Tunisia, Turkey, Turkmenistan, Tuvalu, Uganda, Ukraine, UAE, UK, US, Uruguay, Uzbekistan, Vanuatu, Venezuela

**observers** - (1 plus Palestine Liberation Organization) Holy See, Palestine Liberation Organization

## UNITED NATIONS ASSISTANCE MISSION IN AFGHANISTAN (UNAMA)

January 2010
to support the government of Afghanistan, in its attempt to improve security, governance, and economic development and regional cooperation; protect civilians

and support efforts to support human rights
**note** - gives civilian support only

## UNITED NATIONS CHILDREN'S FUND (UNICEF)

**note** - acronym retained from the predecessor organization, UN International Children's Emergency Fund
11 December 1946
to help establish child health and welfare services
**executive board members** - (36) selected on a rotating basis from all regions

## UNITED NATIONS CONFERENCE ON TRADE AND DEVELOPMENT (UNCTAD)

30 December 1964
to promote international trade
**members** - (194) all UN members plus Holy See

## UNITED NATIONS DEVELOPMENT PROGRAM (UNDP)

22 November 1965
to provide technical assistance to stimulate economic and social development
**members (executive board)** - (36) selected on a rotating basis from all regions

## UNITED NATIONS DISENGAGEMENT OBSERVER FORCE (UNDOF)

31 May 1974
to observe the 1973 Arab-Israeli cease-fire; established by the UN Security Council
**members** -(7) Bhutan, Czechia, Fiji, India, Ireland, Nepal, Netherlands

## UNITED NATIONS EDUCATIONAL, SCIENTIFIC, AND CULTURAL ORGANIZATION (UNESCO)

16 November 1945; effective - 4 November 1946
to promote cooperation in education, science, and culture
**members** - (194 plus Palestine) includes all UN member countries except Liechtenstein (192 total); plus Cook Islands, Niue, Palestine
**associate members** - (9) Anguilla, Aruba, British Virgin Islands, Cayman Islands, Curacao, Faroe Islands, Macau, Sint Maarten, Tokelau

## UNITED NATIONS ENVIRONMENT PROGRAM (UNEP)

15 December 1972
to promote international cooperation on all environmental matters

**members** - (58) Governing Council selected on a rotating basis from all regions

## UNITED NATIONS GENERAL ASSEMBLY

26 June 1945; effective - 24 October 1945
to function as the primary deliberative organ of the UN
**members** - (193) all UN members are represented in the General Assembly

## UNITED NATIONS HIGH COMMISSIONER FOR REFUGEES (UNHCR)

3 December 1949; effective - 1 January 1951
to ensure the humanitarian treatment of refugees and find permanent solutions to refugee problems
**members (executive committee)** - (98) Afghanistan, Algeria, Argentina, Armenia, Australia, Austria, Azerbaijan, Bangladesh, Belarus, Belgium, Benin, Brazil, Bulgaria, Cameroon, Canada, Chad, Chile, China, Colombia, Democratic Republic of the Congo, Republic of the Congo, Costa Rica, Cote d'Ivoire, Croatia, Cyprus, Czechia, Denmark, Djibouti, Ecuador, Egypt, Estonia, Ethiopia, Finland, France, Georgia, Germany, Ghana, Greece, Guinea, Holy See, Hungary, India, Iran, Ireland, Israel, Italy, Japan, Jordan, Kenya, South Korea, Latvia, Lebanon, Lesotho, Luxembourg, Macedonia, Madagascar, Mexico, Moldova, Montenegro, Morocco, Mozambique, Namibia, Netherlands, NZ, Nicaragua, Nigeria, Norway, Pakistan, Peru, Philippines, Poland, Portugal, Romania, Russia, Rwanda, Senegal, Serbia, Slovakia, Slovenia, Somalia, South Africa, Spain, Sudan, Sweden, Switzerland, Tanzania, Thailand, Togo, Tunisia, Turkey, Turkmenistan, Uganda, Uruguay, UK, US, Venezuela, Yemen, Zambia

## UNITED NATIONS INDUSTRIAL DEVELOPMENT ORGANIZATION (UNIDO)

17 November 1966; effective - 1 January 1967
UN specialized agency that promotes industrial development especially among the members
**members** - (170) includes all UN member countries except Andorra, Antigua and Barbuda, Australia, Belgium, Brunei, Canada, Estonia, France, Iceland, Latvia, Liechtenstein, Lithuania, Federated States of Micronesia, Nauru, NZ, Palau, Portugal, San Marino, Singapore, Solomon Islands, South Sudan, UK, US

## UNITED NATIONS INSTITUTE FOR TRAINING AND RESEARCH (UNITAR)

11 December 1963 adoption of the resolution establishing the Institute; effective - 24 March 1965
to help the UN become more effective through training and research
**members (Board of Trustees)** - (14) Algeria, Chile,

China, Denmark, Germany, Guatemala, India, Japan, Nigeria, Russia, Sweden, Switzerland, UK, US; note - the UN Secretary General can appoint up to 30 members

## UNITED NATIONS INTEGRATED MISSION IN TIMOR-LESTE (UNMIT)

25 August 2006 - 31 December 2012
established on 25 August 2006; to support the Government, to support the electoral process, to ensure the restoration and maintenance of public security
**members were** - Australia, Bangladesh, Brazil, China, Fiji, Japan, India, Malaysia, Nepal, NZ, Pakistan, Philippines, Portugal, Sierra Leone, Singapore; UNMIT was dissolved on 31 December 2012

## UNITED NATIONS INTERIM ADMINISTRATION MISSION IN KOSOVO (UNMIK)

10 June 1999
to promote the establishment of substantial autonomy and self-government in Kosovo; to perform basic civilian administrative functions; to support the reconstruction of key infrastructure and humanitarian and disaster relief
**note** - gives civilian support only; works closely with NATO Kosovo Force (KFOR)

## UNITED NATIONS INTERIM FORCE IN LEBANON (UNIFIL)

19 March 1978
to confirm the withdrawal of Israeli forces, and assist in reestablishing Lebanese authority in southern Lebanon; established by the UN Security Council
**members** - (40) Armenia, Austria, Bangladesh, Belarus, Belgium, Brazil, Brunei, Cambodia, China, Croatia, Cyprus, El Salvador, Estonia, Fiji, Finland, France, Germany, Ghana, Greece, Guatemala, Hungary, India, Indonesia, Ireland, Italy, Kenya, South Korea, Macedonia, Malaysia, Mexico, Nepal, Nigeria, Qatar, Serbia, Sierra Leone, Slovenia, Spain, Sri Lanka, Tanzania, Turkey

## UNITED NATIONS INTERIM SECURITY FORCE FOR ABYEI (UNISFA)

27 June 2011
to protect civilians and humanitarian workers in Abyei
**members** - (32) Benin, Bhutan, Brazil, Burkina Faso, Burundi, Cambodia, Ecuador, El Salvador, Ethiopia, Ghana, Guatemala, Guinea, India, Indonesia, Kyrgyzstan, Malawi, Malaysia, Mongolia, Mozambique, Namibia, Nepal, Nigeria, Peru, Russia, Rwanda, Sierra Leone, Sri Lanka, Tanzania, Ukraine, Yemen, Zambia, Zimbabwe

## UNITED NATIONS MILITARY OBSERVER GROUP IN INDIA AND PAKISTAN (UNMOGIP)

24 January 1949
to observe the 1949 India-Pakistan cease-fire; established by the UN Security Council
**members** - (10) Chile, Croatia, Finland, Ghana, South Korea, Philippines, Sweden, Switzerland, Thailand, Uruguay

## UNITED NATIONS MISSION FOR THE REFERENDUM IN WESTERN SAHARA (MINURSO)

29 April 1991
to supervise the cease-fire and conduct a referendum in Western Sahara; established by the UN Security Council
**members** - (34) Argentina, Austria, Bangladesh, Bhutan, Brazil, China, Croatia, Djibouti, Egypt, El Salvador, France, Germany, Ghana, Guinea, Honduras, Hungary, India, Indonesia, Ireland, Kazakhstan, South Korea, Malawi, Malaysia, Mexico, Mongolia, Nepal, Nigeria, Pakistan, Poland, Russia, Sri Lanka, Switzerland, Togo, Yemen

## UNITED NATIONS MISSION IN LIBERIA (UNMIL)

19 September 2003
to support the cease-fire agreement and peace process, protect UN facilities and people, support humanitarian activities, and assist in national security reform
**members** - (32) Bangladesh, Benin, Bolivia, Brazil, Bulgaria, Burma, China, Ecuador, Egypt, Ethiopia, France, The Gambia, Germany, Ghana, Indonesia, Kyrgyzstan, Malaysia, Moldova, Namibia, Nepal, Niger, Nigeria, Pakistan, Poland, Russia, Serbia, Togo, Ukraine, US, Yemen, Zambia, Zimbabwe

## UNITED NATIONS MISSION IN THE CENTRAL AFRICAN REPUBLIC AND CHAD (MINURCAT)

established on 25 September 2007; to create the security and conditions which will to contribute to the protection of refugees, displaced persons, and citizens in danger, to facilitate the provision of humanitarian assistance in eastern Chad and the northeastern Central African Republic, to create favorable conditions for the reconstruction and economic and social development of these areas; members were Bangladesh, Benin, Burkina Faso, Democratic Republic of the Congo, Egypt, Ethiopia, Ghana, Ireland, Kenya, Mali, Mongolia, Namibia, Nepal, Nigeria, Norway, Pakistan, Poland, Russia, Rwanda, Senegal, Serbia, Sri Lanka, Togo, Tunisia, US; MINURCAT was dissolved in December 2010

## UNITED NATIONS MISSION IN THE REPUBLIC OF SOUTH SUDAN (UNMISS)

8 July 2011
to consolidate peace and security and to establish the conditions in South Sudan which will strengthen its ability to govern effectively and democratically and establish good relations with its neighbors
**members** - (55) Australia, Bangladesh, Benin, Bhutan, Bolivia, Brazil, Burma, Cambodia, Canada, China, Denmark, Egypt, El Salvador, Ethiopia, Fiji, Germany, Ghana, Guatemala, Guinea, India, Indonesia, Japan, Jordan, Kenya, South Korea, Kyrgyzstan, Moldova, Mongolia, Namibia, Nepal, Netherlands, NZ, Nigeria, Norway, Papua New Guinea, Paraguay, Peru, Poland, Romania, Russia, Rwanda, Senegal, Sri Lanka, Sweden, Switzerland, Tanzania, Togo, Uganda, Ukraine, UK, US, Vietnam, Yemen, Zambia, Zimbabwe

## UNITED NATIONS MISSION IN THE SUDAN (UNMIS)

established in March 2005 to support implementation of the comprehensive Peace Agreement by monitoring and verifying the implementation of the Cease Fire Agreement, by observing and monitoring movements of armed groups, and by helping disarm, demobilizing and reintegrating armed bands; members were Australia, Bangladesh, Belgium, Benin, Bolivia, Brazil, Burkina Faso, Cambodia, Canada, China, Croatia, Denmark, Ecuador, Egypt, El Salvador, Fiji, Finland, Germany, Greece, Guatemala, Guinea, India, Indonesia, Iran, Japan, Jordan, Kenya, Kyrgyzstan, Malaysia, Moldova, Mongolia, Morocco, Namibia, Nepal, Netherland, NZ, Niger, Norway, Pakistan, Paraguay, Peru, Philippines, Poland, Qatar, Romania, Russia, Rwanda, Sierra Leone, Spain, Sweden, Switzerland, Tanzania, Thailand, Turkey, Uganda, Ukraine, UK, Yemen, Zambia, Zimbabwe; UNMIS was dissolved on 9 July 2011

## UNITED NATIONS MULTIDIMENSIONAL INTEGRATED STABILIZATION MISSION IN MALI (MINUSMA)

25 April 2013
to support political processes and carry out a number of security-related tasks
**members** - (44) Armenia, Austria, Bangladesh, Belgium, Benin, Bhutan, Bosnia and Herzegovina, Cambodia, Cameroon, Chad, Cote d'Ivoire, Czechia, Denmark, Egypt, El Salvador, France, The Gambia, Germany, Ghana, Guinea, Guinea-Bissau, Indonesia, Italy, Jordan, Kenya, Latvia, Liberia, Mauritania, Nepal, Netherlands, Niger, Nigeria, Norway, Portugal, Romania, Rwanda, Senegal, Sierra Leone, Sweden, Switzerland, Togo, UK, US, Yemen

## UNITED NATIONS OPERATION IN COTE D'IVOIRE (UNOCI)

27 February 2004
to facilitate the implementation by the Ivorian parties of the peace agreement signed by them in January 2003
**members** - (47) Bangladesh, Benin, Bolivia, Brazil, Cameroon, Chad, China, Ecuador, Egypt, El Salvador, Ethiopia, France, The Gambia, Ghana, Guatemala, Guinea, India, Ireland, Jordan, Kazakhston, South Korea, Malawi, Moldova, Morocco, Namibia, Nepal, Niger, Nigeria, Pakistan, Paraguay, Peru, Philippines, Poland, Romania, Russia, Senegal, Serbia, Spain, Tanzania, Togo, Tunisia, Uganda, Ukraine, Uruguay, Yemen, Zambia, Zimbabwe

## UNITED NATIONS ORGANIZATION STABILIZATION MISSION IN THE DEMOCRATIC REPUBLIC OF THE CONGO (MONUSCO)

28 May 2010
to protect the civilians; to assist the government in the areas of stabilization and peace consolidation
**members** - (50) Algeria, Bangladesh, Belgium, Benin, Bolivia, Bosnia and Herzegovina, Brazil, Burkina Faso, Cameroon, Canada, China, Cote d'Ivoire, Czechia, Egypt, France, Ghana, Guatemala, Guinea, India, Indonesia, Ireland, Jordan, Kenya, Malawi, Malaysia, Mali, Mongolia, Morocco, Nepal, Niger, Nigeria, Pakistan, Paraguay, Peru, Poland, Romania, Russia, Senegal, Serbia, South Africa, Sri Lanka, Sweden, Switzerland, Tunisia, Ukraine, UK, US, Uruguay, Yemen, Zambia

## UNITED NATIONS PEACEKEEPING FORCE IN CYPRUS (UNFICYP)

4 March 1964
to serve as a peacekeeping force between Greek Cypriots and Turkish Cypriots in Cyprus; established by the UN Security Council
**members** - (12) Argentina, Austria, Brazil, Canada, Chile, Hungary, Norway, Paraguay, Serbia, Slovakia, Ukraine, UK

## UNITED NATIONS POPULATION FUND (UNFPA)

**note** - acronym retained from predecessor organization UN Fund for Population Activities
July 1967
to assist both developed and developing countries to deal with their population problems
**members (executive board )** - (36) selected on a rotating basis from all regions

## UNITED NATIONS RELIEF AND WORKS AGENCY FOR PALESTINE REFUGEES IN THE

## NEAR EAST (UNRWA)

8 December 1949
to provide assistance to Palestinian refugees
**members (advisory commission)** - (27) Australia, Belgium, Brazil, Canada, Denmark, Egypt, Finland, France, Germany, Ireland, Italy, Japan, Jordan, Kuwait, Lebanon, Luxembourg, Netherlands, Norway, Saudi Arabia, Spain, Sweden, Switzerland, Syria, Turkey, UAE, UK, US
**observers** - (3) EC, League of Arab States, Palestine Liberation Organization

## UNITED NATIONS RESEARCH INSTITUTE FOR SOCIAL DEVELOPMENT (UNRISD)

1963
to conduct research into the problems of economic development during different phases of economic growth
**members** - no country members, but a Board of Directors currently consisting of a chairman appointed by the UN Secretary General and 8 members confirmed by ECOSOC and a representative of the Secretary General

## UNITED NATIONS SECRETARIAT

26 June 1945; effective - 24 October 1945
to serve as the primary administrative organ of the UN; a Secretary General is appointed for a five-year term by the General Assembly on the recommendation of the Security Council
**members** - the UN Secretary General and staff

## UNITED NATIONS SECURITY COUNCIL (UNSC)

26 June 1945; effective - 24 October 1945
to maintain international peace and security
**permanent members** - (5) China, France, Russia, UK, US
**nonpermanent members** - (10) elected for two-year terms by the UN General Assembly; Angola (2015-16), Egypt (2016-17), Japan (2016-17), Malaysia (2016-17), NZ (2015-16), Senegal (2016-17), Spain (2015-16), Ukraine (2016-17), Uruguay (2016-17), Venezuela (2015-16)

## UNITED NATIONS TRUCE SUPERVISION ORGANIZATION (UNTSO)

June 1948
to supervise the 1948 Arab-Israeli cease-fire; currently supports timely deployment of reinforcements to other peacekeeping operations in the region as needed; initially established by the UN Security Council
**members** - (26) Argentina, Australia, Austria, Belgium, Bhutan, Canada, Chile, China, Denmark, Estonia, Fiji, Finland, France, India, Ireland, Nepal, Netherlands, NZ, Norway, Russia, Serbia, Slovakia, Slovenia, Sweden, Switzerland, US

## UNITED NATIONS TRUSTEESHIP COUNCIL

established on 26 June 1945, effective on 24 October 1945, to supervise the administration of the 11 UN trust territories; members were China, France, Russia, UK, US; it formally suspended operations 1 November 1994 after the Trust Territory of the Pacific Islands (Palau) became the Republic of Palau, a constitutional government in free association with the US; the Trusteeship Council was not dissolved

## UNITED NATIONS UNIVERSITY (UNU)

3 December 1973
to conduct research in development, welfare, and human survival and to train scholars
**members** - (12 members of UNU Council and the Rector are appointed by the Secretary General of the United Nations and the Director General of UNESCO)

## UNIVERSAL POSTAL UNION (UPU)

9 October 1874, affiliated with the UN 15 November 1947; effective - 1 July 1948
to promote international postal cooperation; a UN specialized agency
**members** - (192) includes all UN member countries except Andorra, Marshall Islands, Federated States of Micronesia, Palau (189 total); plus Aruba, Curacao, and Sint Maarten; the Holy See; and Overseas Territories of the UK; note - includes the following dependencies or areas of special interest: Australia (Norfolk Island), China (Hong Kong, Macau), Denmark (Faroe Islands, Greenland), France (French Guiana, French Polynesia including Clipperton Island, French Southern and Antarctic Lands, Guadeloupe, Martinique, Mayotte, New Caledonia, Reunion, Saint Barthelemy, Saint Martin, Saint Pierre and Miquelon, Scattered Islands [Bassas da India, Europe, Juan de Nova, Glorioso Islands, Tromelin], Wallis and Futuna), Netherlands (Aruba, Curacao, Sint Maarten), NZ (Cook Island, Niue, Tokelau), UK (Guernsey, Isle of Man, Jersey; Anguilla, Bermuda, British Indian Ocean Territory, British Virgin Islands, Cayman Islands, Falkland Islands, Gibraltar, Montserrat, Pitcairn Islands, Saint Helena, Ascension, and Tristan da Cunha, South Georgia and South Sandwich Islands, Turks and Caicos), US (American Samoa, Guam, Northern Mariana Islands, Puerto Rico, Virgin Islands)

## WARSAW PACT (WP)

established 14 May 1955 to promote mutual defense; members met 1 July 1991 to dissolve the alliance;

member states at the time of dissolution were: Bulgaria, Czechoslovakia, Hungary, Poland, Romania, and the USSR; earlier members included German Democratic Republic (GDR) and Albania

## WEST AFRICAN DEVELOPMENT BANK (WADB)

**note** - also known as Banque Ouest-Africaine de Developpement (BOAD); is a financial institution of WAEMU
14 November 1973
to promote regional economic development and integration
**regional members** - (8) Benin, Burkina Faso, Cote d'Ivoire, Guinea-Bissau, Mali, Niger, Senegal, Togo

## WEST AFRICAN ECONOMIC AND MONETARY UNION (WAEMU)

**note** - also known as Union Economique et Monetaire Ouest Africaine (UEMOA)
1 August 1994
to increase competitiveness of members' economic markets; to create a common market
**members** - (8) Benin, Burkina Faso, Cote d'Ivoire, Guinea-Bissau, Mali, Niger, Senegal, Togo

## WESTERN EUROPEAN UNION (WEU)

established 23 October 1954; effective - 6 May 1955; aim to provide mutual defense and to move toward political unification; 10 members: Belgium, France, Germany, Greece, Italy, Luxembourg, Netherlands, Portugal, Spain, UK; 6 associate members: Czechia, Hungary, Iceland, Norway, Poland, Turkey; 7 associate partners: Bulgaria, Estonia, Latvia, Lithuania, Romania, Slovakia, Slovenia; 5 observers: Austria, Denmark, Finland, Ireland, Sweden; note - ceased existence completely on 30 June 2011

## WORLD BANK GROUP

includes International Bank for Reconstruction and Development (IBRD), International Development Association (IDA), International Finance Corporation (IFC), and Multilateral Investment Guarantee Agency (MIGA)

## WORLD CONFEDERATION OF LABOR (WCL)

established 19 June 1920 as the International Federation of Christian Trade Unions (IFCTU), renamed 4 October 1968; aim was to promote the trade union movement; on 31 October 2006 it merged with the International Confederation of Free Trade Unions (ICFTU) to form the International Trade Union Confederation (ITUC); members were (105 national organizations) Antigua and Barbuda, Argentina, Aruba, Austria, Bangladesh, Belgium, Belize, Benin, Bolivia, Brazil, Bulgaria, Burkina Faso, Cameroon, Canada, Central African Republic, Chad, Chile, Colombia, Democratic Republic of the Congo, Republic of the Congo, Costa Rica, Cote d'Ivoire, Cuba, Cyprus, Czechia, Denmark, Dominica, Dominican Republic, Ecuador, El Salvador, France, French Guiana, Gabon, The Gambia, Ghana, Guadeloupe, Guatemala, Guinea, Guyana, Haiti, Honduras, Hong Kong, Hungary, India, Indonesia, Iran, Italy, Japan, Kazakhstan, South Korea, Liberia, Libya, Liechtenstein, Lithuania, Luxembourg, Macedonia, Madagascar, Malawi, Malaysia, Malta, Martinique, Mauritania, Mauritius, Mexico, Morocco, Namibia, Nepal, Netherlands, Nicaragua, Niger, Pakistan, Panama, Paraguay, Peru, Philippines, Poland, Portugal, Puerto Rico, Romania, Rwanda, Saint Lucia, Saint Vincent and the Grenadines, Sao Tome and Principe, Senegal, Serbia, Sierra Leone, Singapore, Slovakia, South Africa, Spain, Sri Lanka, Suriname, Switzerland, Taiwan, Thailand, Togo, Trinidad and Tobago, Ukraine, US, Uruguay, Venezuela, Vietnam, Zambia, Zimbabwe

## WORLD CUSTOMS ORGANIZATION (WCO)

**note** - began as the Customs Cooperation Council (CCC)
15 December 1950
to promote international cooperation in customs matters
**members** - (179) Afghanistan, Albania, Algeria, Andorra, Angola, Argentina, Armenia, Australia, Austria, Azerbaijan, The Bahamas, Bahrain, Bangladesh, Barbados, Belarus, Belgium, Belize, Benin, Bermuda, Bhutan, Bolivia, Bosnia and Herzegovina, Botswana, Brazil, Brunei, Bulgaria, Burkina Faso, Burma, Burundi, Cabo Verde, Cambodia, Cameroon, Canada, Central African Republic, Chad, Chile, China, Colombia, Comoros, Democratic Republic of the Congo, Republic of the Congo, Costa Rica, Cote d'Ivoire, Croatia, Cuba, Curacao, Cyprus, Czechia, Denmark, Djibouti, Dominican Republic, EU, Ecuador, Egypt, El Salvador, Eritrea, Estonia, Ethiopia, Fiji, Finland, France, Gabon, The Gambia, Georgia, Germany, Ghana, Greece, Guatemala, Guinea, Guinea-Bissau, Guyana, Haiti, Honduras, Hong Kong, Hungary, Iceland, India, Indonesia, Iran, Iraq, Ireland, Israel, Italy, Jamaica, Japan, Jordan, Kazakhstan, Kenya, South Korea, Kuwait, Kyrgyzstan, Laos, Latvia, Lebanon, Lesotho, Liberia, Libya, Lithuania, Luxembourg, Macau, Macedonia, Madagascar, Malawi, Malaysia, Maldives, Mali, Malta, Mauritania, Mauritius, Mexico, Moldova, Mongolia, Montenegro, Morocco, Mozambique, Namibia, Nepal, Netherlands, NZ, Nicaragua, Niger, Nigeria, Norway, Oman, Pakistan, Panama, Papua New Guinea, Paraguay, Peru, Philippines, Poland, Portugal, Qatar, Romania, Russia, Rwanda, Saint Lucia, Samoa, Sao Tome and Principe, Saudi Arabia, Senegal, Serbia, Seychelles,

Sierra Leone, Singapore, Slovakia, Slovenia, Somalia, South Africa, South Sudan, Spain, Sri Lanka, Sudan, Swaziland, Sweden, Switzerland, Syria, Tajikistan, Tanzania, Thailand, Timor-Leste, Togo, Tonga, Trinidad and Tobago, Tunisia, Turkey, Turkmenistan, Uganda, Ukraine, UAE, UK, US, Uruguay, Uzbekistan, Vanuatu, Venezuela, Vietnam, Yemen, Zambia, Zimbabwe

## WORLD FEDERATION OF TRADE UNIONS (WFTU)

3 October 1945
to promote the trade union movement
**members** - (125 participating nations and territories and the PalestineLiberation Union); Afghanistan, Albania, Angola, Antigua and Barbuda, Argentina, Armenia, Australia, Austria, Azerbaijan, Bahrain, Bangladesh, Barbados, Belarus, Benin, Bolivia, Botswana, Brazil, Bulgaria, Burkina Faso, Cambodia, Cameroon, Canada, Chile, Colombia, Democratic Republic of the Congo, Republic of the Congo, Costa Rica, Cote d'Ivoire, Cuba, Cyprus, Czechia, Djibouti, Dominican Republic, Ecuador, Egypt, El Salvador, Eritrea, Ethiopia, Fiji, Finland, France, French Guiana, The Gambia, Ghana, Greece, Guadeloupe, Guatemala, Guinea, Guinea-Bissau, Guyana, Haiti, Honduras, Hungary, India, Indonesia, Iran, Iraq, Jamaica, Japan, Jordan, Kazakhstan, North Korea, Kuwait, Kyrgyzstan, Laos, Lebanon, Lesotho, Liberia, Libya, Madagascar, Malawi, Malaysia, Mali, Martinique, Mauritius, Mexico, Mozambique, Nepal, New Caledonia, NZ, Niger, Nigeria, Oman, Pakistan, Palestine, Panama, Papua New Guinea, Peru, Philippines, Poland, Portugal, Puerto Rico, Reunion, Romania, Russia, Saint Lucia, Saint Pierre and Miquelon, Saint Vincent and the Grenadines, Saudi Arabia, Senegal, Sierra Leone, Slovakia, Solomon Islands, Somalia, South Africa, Sri Lanka, Sudan, Sweden, Syria, Tajikistan, Tanzania, Thailand, Togo, Trinidad and Tobago, Tunisia, Turkey, Turkmenistan, Uganda, Ukraine, Uruguay, Uzbekistan, Vanuatu, Venezuela, Vietnam, Yemen, Zimbabwe

## WORLD FOOD PROGRAM (WFP)

24 November 1961
to provide food aid in support of economic development or disaster relief; an ECOSOC organization
**members (Executive Board)** - (36) selected on a rotating basis from all regions

## WORLD HEALTH ORGANIZATION (WHO)

22 July 1946; effective - 7 April 1948
to deal with health matters worldwide; a UN specialized agency
**members** - (194) includes all UN member countries except Liechtenstein (192 total); plus Cook Islands and Niue

## WORLD INTELLECTUAL PROPERTY ORGANIZATION (WIPO)

14 July 1967; effective - 26 April 1970
to furnish protection for literary, artistic, and scientific works; a UN specialized agency
**members** - (188) includes all UN member countries except Marshall Islands, Federated States of Micronesia, Nauru, Palau, Solomon Islands, South Sudan, Timor-Leste (186 total); plus Holy See

## WORLD METEOROLOGICAL ORGANIZATION (WMO)

11 October 1947; effective - 4 April 1951
to sponsor meteorological cooperation; a UN specialized agency
**members** - (185) includes all UN member countries except Andorra, Equatorial Guinea, Grenada, Liechtenstein, Marshall Islands, Nauru, Palau, Saint Kitts and Nevis, Saint Vincent and the Grenadines, San Marino (183 total); plus Cook Islands and Niue

## WORLD TOURISM ORGANIZATION (UNWTO)

2 January 1975
to promote tourism as a means of contributing to economic development, international understanding, and peace
**members** - (157) Afghanistan, Albania, Algeria, Andorra, Angola, Argentina, Armenia, Australia, Austria, Azerbaijan, The Bahamas, Bahrain, Bangladesh, Barbados, Belarus, Benin, Bhutan, Bolivia, Bosnia and Herzegovina, Botswana, Brazil, Brunei, Bulgaria, Burkina Faso, Burma, Burundi, Cabo Verde, Cambodia, Cameroon, Central African Republic, Chad, Chile, China, Colombia, Democratic Republic of the Congo, Republic of the Congo, Costa Rica, Cote d'Ivoire, Croatia, Cuba, Cyprus, Czechia, Djibouti, Dominican Republic, Ecuador, Egypt, El Salvador, Equatorial Guinea, Eritrea, Ethiopia, Fiji, France, Gabon, The Gambia, Georgia, Germany, Ghana, Greece, Guatemala, Guinea, Guinea-Bissau, Haiti, Honduras, Hungary, India, Indonesia, Iran, Iraq, Israel, Italy, Jamaica, Japan, Jordan, Kazakhstan, Kenya, North Korea, South Korea, Kuwait, Kyrgyzstan, Laos, Lebanon, Lesotho, Liberia, Libya, Lithuania, Macedonia, Madagascar, Malawi, Malaysia, Maldives, Mali, Malta, Mauritania, Mauritius, Mexico, Moldova, Monaco, Mongolia, Montenegro, Morocco, Mozambique, Namibia, Nepal, Netherlands, Nicaragua, Niger, Nigeria, Oman, Pakistan, Panama, Papua New Guinea, Paraguay, Peru, Philippines, Poland, Portugal, Qatar, Romania, Russia, Rwanda, Samoa, San Marino, Sao Tome and Principe, Saudi Arabia, Senegal, Serbia, Seychelles, Sierra Leone, Slovakia, Slovenia,

South Africa, Spain, Sri Lanka, Sudan, Swaziland, Switzerland, Syria, Tajikistan, Tanzania, Thailand, Timor-Leste, Togo, Trinidad and Tobago, Tunisia, Turkey, Turkmenistan, Uganda, Ukraine, UAE, Uruguay, Uzbekistan, Vanuatu, Venezuela, Vietnam, Yemen, Zambia, Zimbabwe
**associate members** - (6) Aruba, Flemish Community of Belgium, Hong Kong, Macau, Madeira Islands, Puerto Rico
**observers** - (1 plus Palestine Liberation Organization) Holy See, Palestine Liberation Organization

## WORLD TRADE ORGANIZATION (WTO)

**note** - succeeded General Agreement on Tariff and Trade (GATT)
15 April 1994; effective - 1 January 1995
to provide a forum to resolve trade conflicts between members and to carry on negotiations with the goal of further lowering and/or eliminating tariffs and other trade barriers
**members** - (163) Afghanistan, Albania, Angola, Antigua and Barbuda, Argentina, Armenia, Australia, Austria, Bahrain, Bangladesh, Barbados, Belgium, Belize, Benin, Bolivia, Botswana, Brazil, Brunei, Bulgaria, Burkina Faso, Burma, Burundi, Cabo Verde, Cambodia, Cameroon, Canada, Central African Republic, Chad, Chile, China, Colombia, Democratic Republic of the Congo, Republic of the Congo, Costa Rica, Cote d'Ivoire, Croatia, Cuba, Cyprus, Czechia, Denmark, Djibouti, Dominica, Dominican Republic, Ecuador, Egypt, El Salvador, Estonia, EU, Fiji, Finland, France, Gabon, The Gambia, Georgia, Germany, Ghana, Greece, Grenada, Guatemala, Guinea, Guinea-Bissau, Guyana, Haiti, Honduras, Hong Kong, Hungary, Iceland, India, Indonesia, Ireland, Israel, Italy, Jamaica, Japan, Jordan, Kazakhstan, Kenya, South Korea, Kuwait, Kyrgyzstan, Laos, Latvia, Lesotho, Liechtenstein, Lithuania, Luxembourg, Macau, Macedonia, Madagascar, Malawi, Malaysia, Maldives, Mali, Malta, Mauritania, Mauritius, Mexico, Moldova, Mongolia, Montenegro, Morocco, Mozambique, Namibia, Nepal, Netherlands, NZ, Nicaragua, Niger, Nigeria, Norway, Oman, Pakistan, Panama, Papua New Guinea, Paraguay, Peru, Philippines, Poland, Portugal, Qatar, Romania, Russia, Rwanda, Saint Kitts and Nevis, Saint Lucia, Saint Vincent and the Grenadines, Samoa, Saudi Arabia, Senegal, Seychelles, Sierra Leone, Singapore, Slovakia, Slovenia, Solomon Islands, South Africa, Spain, Sri Lanka, Suriname, Swaziland, Sweden, Switzerland, Chinese Taipei, Tajikistan, Tanzania, Thailand, Togo, Tonga, Trinidad and Tobago, Tunisia, Turkey, Uganda, Ukraine, UAE, UK, US, Uruguay, Vanuatu, Venezuela, Vietnam, Yemen, Zambia, Zimbabwe
**observers** - (21) Algeria, Andorra, Azerbaijan, The Bahamas, Belarus, Bhutan, Bosnia and Herzegovina, Comoros, Equatorial Guinea, Ethiopia, Holy See, Iran, Iraq, Lebanon, Liberia, Libya, Sao Tome and Principe, Serbia, Sudan, Syria, Uzbekistan; note - with the exception of the Holy See, an observer must start accession negotiations within five years of becoming an observer

## ZANGGER COMMITTEE (ZC)

early 1970s
to establish guidelines for the export control provisions of the Nonproliferation of Nuclear Weapons Treaty (NPT)
**members** - (38) Argentina, Australia, Austria, Belarus, Belgium, Bulgaria, Canada, China, Croatia, Czechia, Denmark, Finland, France, Germany, Greece, Hungary, Ireland, Italy, Japan, Kazakhstan, South Korea, Luxembourg, Netherlands, Norway, Poland, Portugal, Romania, Russia, Slovakia, Slovenia, South Africa, Spain, Sweden, Switzerland, Turkey, Ukraine, UK, US
**observers** - (1) EU

# APPENDIX C :: SELECTED INTERNATIONAL ENVIRONMENTAL AGREEMENTS

## AIR POLLUTION

see Convention on Long-Range Transboundary Air Pollution

## AIR POLLUTION-HEAVY METALS

see Protocol to the 1979 Convention on Long-Range Transboundary Air Pollution on Heavy Metals

## AIR POLLUTION-NITROGEN OXIDES

see Protocol to the 1979 Convention on Long-Range Transboundary Air Pollution Concerning the Control of Emissions of Nitrogen Oxides or Their Transboundary Fluxes

## AIR POLLUTION-PERSISTENT ORGANIC POLLUTANTS

see Protocol to the 1979 Convention on Long-Range Transboundary Air Pollution on Persistent Organic Pollutants

## AIR POLLUTION-SULPHUR 85

see Protocol to the 1979 Convention on Long-Range Transboundary Air Pollution on the Reduction of Sulphur Emissions or Their Transboundary Fluxes by at least 30%

## AIR POLLUTION-SULPHUR 94

see Protocol to the 1979 Convention on Long-Range Transboundary Air Pollution on Further Reduction of Sulphur Emissions

## AIR POLLUTION-VOLATILE ORGANIC COMPOUNDS

see Protocol to the 1979 Convention on Long-Range Transboundary Air Pollution Concerning the Control of Emissions of Volatile Organic Compounds or Their Transboundary Fluxes

## ANTARCTIC - ENVIRONMENTAL PROTOCOL

see Protocol on Environmental Protection to the Antarctic Treaty

## ANTARCTIC TREATY

**opened for signature -** 1 December 1959
**entered into force -** 23 June 1961
**objective -** to ensure that Antarctica is used for peaceful purposes only (such as international cooperation in scientific research); to defer the question of territorial claims asserted by some nations and not recognized by others; to provide an international forum for management of the region; applies to land and ice shelves south of 60 degrees south latitude
**parties -** (53) Argentina, Australia, Austria, Belarus, Belgium, Brazil, Bulgaria, Canada, Chile, China, Colombia, Cuba, Czechia, Denmark, Ecuador, Estonia, Finland, France, Germany, Greece, Guatemala, Hungary, Iceland, India, Italy, Japan, Kazakhstan, North Korea, South Korea, Malaysia, Monaco, Mongolia, Netherlands, NZ, Norway, Pakistan, Papua New Guinea, Peru, Poland, Portugal, Romania, Russia, Slovakia, South Africa, Spain, Sweden, Switzerland, Turkey, Ukraine, UK, US, Uruguay, Venezuela

## BASEL CONVENTION ON THE CONTROL OF TRANSBOUNDARY MOVEMENTS OF HAZARDOUS WASTES AND THEIR DISPOSAL

**note** - abbreviated as Hazardous Wastes
**opened for signature -** 22 March 1989
**entered into force -** 5 May 1992
**objective -** to reduce transboundary movements of wastes subject to the Convention to a minimum consistent with the environmentally sound and efficient management of such wastes; to minimize the amount and toxicity of wastes generated and ensure their environmentally sound management as closely as possible to the source of generation; and to assist LDCs in environmentally sound management of the hazardous and other wastes they generate
**parties -** (186 and the Palestine Liberation Organization) Afghanistan, Albania, Algeria, Andorra, Angola, Antigua and Barbuda, Argentina, Armenia, Australia, Austria, Azerbaijan, The Bahamas, Bahrain, Bangladesh, Barbados, Belarus, Belgium, Belize, Benin, Bhutan, Bolivia, Bosnia and Herzegovina, Botswana, Brazil, Brunei, Bulgaria, Burkina Faso, Burma, Burundi, Cambodia, Cameroon, Canada, Cape Verde, Central African Republic, Chad, Chile, China, Colombia, Comoros, Democratic Republic of the Congo, Republic of the Congo, Cook Islands, Costa Rica, Cote d'Ivoire,

Croatia, Cuba, Cyprus, Czechia, Denmark, Djibouti, Dominica, Dominican Republic, Ecuador, Egypt, El Salvador, Equatorial Guinea, Eritrea, Estonia, Ethiopia, EU, Finland, France, Gabon, The Gambia, Georgia, Germany, Ghana, Greece, Guatemala, Guinea, Guinea-Bissau, Guyana, Haiti, Honduras, Hungary, Iceland, India, Indonesia, Iran, Iraq, Ireland, Israel, Italy, Jamaica, Japan, Jordan, Kazakhstan, Kenya, Kiribati, North Korea, South Korea, Kuwait, Kyrgyzstan, Latvia, Laos, Lebanon, Lesotho, Liberia, Libya, Liechtenstein, Lithuania, Luxembourg, Macedonia, Madagascar, Malawi, Malaysia, Maldives, Mali, Malta, Marshall Islands, Mauritania, Mauritius, Mexico, Federated States of Micronesia, Moldova, Monaco, Mongolia, Montenegro, Morocco, Mozambique, Namibia, Nauru, Nepal, Netherlands, NZ, Nicaragua, Niger, Nigeria, Norway, Oman, Pakistan, Palau, Panama, Papua New Guinea, Paraguay, Peru, Philippines, Poland, Portugal, Qatar, Romania, Russia, Rwanda, Saint Kitts and Nevis, Saint Lucia, Saint Vincent and the Grenadines, Samoa, Sao Tome and Principe, Saudi Arabia, Senegal, Serbia, Seychelles, Sierra Leone, Singapore, Slovakia, Slovenia, Somalia, South Africa, Spain, Sri Lanka, Sudan, Suriname, Swaziland, Sweden, Switzerland, Syria, Tajikistan, Tanzania, Thailand, Togo, Tonga, Trinidad and Tobago, Tunisia, Turkey, Turkmenistan, Uganda, Ukraine, UAE, UK, Uruguay, Uzbekistan, Venezuela, Vietnam, Yemen, Zambia, Zimbabwe, Palestine Liberation Organization
**countries that have signed, but not yet ratified** - (1) US

## BIODIVERSITY

see Convention on Biological Diversity

## CLIMATE CHANGE

see United Nations Framework Convention on Climate Change

## CLIMATE CHANGE-KYOTO PROTOCOL

see Kyoto Protocol to the United Nations Framework Convention on Climate Change

## CONVENTION FOR THE CONSERVATION OF ANTARCTIC SEALS

**note** - abbreviated as Antarctic Seals
**opened for signature** - 1 June 1972
**entered into force** - 11 March 1978
**objective** - to promote and achieve the protection, scientific study, and rational use of Antarctic seals, and to maintain a satisfactory balance within the ecological system of Antarctica
**parties** - (17) Argentina, Australia, Belgium, Brazil, Canada, Chile, France, Germany, Italy, Japan, Norway, Pakistan, Poland, Russia, South Africa, UK, US
**countries that have signed, but not yet ratified** - (1) NZ

## CONVENTION ON BIOLOGICAL DIVERSITY

**note** - abbreviated as Biodiversity
**opened for signature** - 5 June 1992
**entered into force** - 29 December 1993
**objective** - to develop national strategies for the conservation and sustainable use of biological diversity and to address the fair and equitable sharing of benefits arising out of the utilization of genetic resources
**parties** - (195 and the Palestine Liberation Organization) Afghanistan, Albania, Algeria, Andorra, Angola, Antigua and Barbuda, Argentina, Armenia, Australia, Austria, Azerbaijan, The Bahamas, Bahrain, Bangladesh, Barbados, Belarus, Belgium, Belize, Benin, Bhutan, Bolivia, Bosnia and Herzegovina, Botswana, Brazil, Brunei, Bulgaria, Burkina Faso, Burma, Burundi, Cambodia, Cameroon, Canada, Cape Verde, Central African Republic, Chad, Chile, China, Colombia, Comoros, Democratic Republic of the Congo, Republic of the Congo, Cook Islands, Costa Rica, Cote d'Ivoire, Croatia, Cuba, Cyprus, Czechia, Denmark, Djibouti, Dominica, Dominican Republic, Ecuador, Egypt, El Salvador, Equatorial Guinea, Eritrea, Estonia, Ethiopia, EU, Fiji, Finland, France, Gabon, The Gambia, Georgia, Germany, Ghana, Greece, Grenada, Guatemala, Guinea, Guinea-Bissau, Guyana, Haiti, Honduras, Hungary, Iceland, India, Indonesia, Iran, Iraq, Ireland, Israel, Italy, Jamaica, Japan, Jordan, Kazakhstan, Kenya, Kiribati, North Korea, South Korea, Kuwait, Kyrgyzstan, Laos, Latvia, Lebanon, Lesotho, Liberia, Libya, Liechtenstein, Lithuania, Luxembourg, Macedonia, Madagascar, Malawi, Malaysia, Maldives, Mali, Malta, Marshall Islands, Mauritania, Mauritius, Mexico, Federated States of Micronesia, Moldova, Monaco, Mongolia, Montenegro, Morocco, Mozambique, Namibia, Nauru, Nepal, Netherlands, NZ, Nicaragua, Niger, Nigeria, Niue, Norway, Oman, Pakistan, Palau, Panama, Papua New Guinea, Paraguay, Peru, Philippines, Poland, Portugal, Qatar, Romania, Russia, Rwanda, Saint Kitts and Nevis, Saint Lucia, Saint Vincent and the Grenadines, Samoa, San Marino, Sao Tome and Principe, Saudi Arabia, Senegal, Serbia, Seychelles, Sierra Leone, Singapore, Slovakia, Slovenia, Solomon Islands, Somalia, South Africa, South Sudan, Spain, Sri Lanka, Sudan, Suriname, Swaziland, Sweden, Switzerland, Syria, Tajikistan, Tanzania, Thailand, Timor-Leste, Togo, Tonga, Trinidad and Tobago, Tunisia, Turkey, Turkmenistan, Tuvalu, Uganda, Ukraine, UAE, UK, Uruguay, Uzbekistan, Vanuatu, Venezuela, Vietnam, Yemen, Zambia, Zimbabwe, Palestine Liberation Organization
**countries that have signed, but not yet ratified** - (1) US

## CONVENTION ON FISHING AND CONSERVATION OF LIVING RESOURCES OF THE HIGH SEAS

**note** - abbreviated as Marine Life Conservation
**opened for signature** - 29 April 1958
**entered into force** - 20 March 1966
**objective** - to solve through international cooperation the problems involved in the conservation of living resources of the high seas, considering that because of the development of modern technology some of these resources are in danger of being overexploited
**parties** - (39) Australia, Belgium, Bosnia and Herzegovina, Burkina Faso, Cambodia, Colombia, Republic of the Congo, Denmark, Dominican Republic, Fiji, Finland, France, Haiti, Jamaica, Kenya, Lesotho, Madagascar, Malawi, Malaysia, Mauritius, Mexico, Montenegro, Netherlands, Nigeria, Portugal, Senegal, Serbia, Sierra Leone, Solomon Islands, South Africa, Spain, Switzerland, Thailand, Tonga, Trinidad and Tobago, Uganda, UK, US, Venezuela
**countries that have signed, but not yet ratified** - (21) Afghanistan, Argentina, Bolivia, Canada, Costa Rica, Cuba, Ghana, Iceland, Indonesia, Iran, Ireland, Israel, Lebanon, Liberia, Nepal, NZ, Pakistan, Panama, Sri Lanka, Tunisia, Uruguay

## CONVENTION ON LONG-RANGE TRANSBOUNDARY AIR POLLUTION

**note** - abbreviated as Air Pollution
**opened for signature** - 13 November 1979
**entered into force** - 16 March 1983
**objective** - to protect the human environment against air pollution and, as far as possible, to gradually reduce and prevent air pollution, including long-range transboundary air pollution
**parties** - (51) Albania, Armenia, Austria, Azerbaijan, Belarus, Belgium, Bosnia and Herzegovina, Bulgaria, Canada, Croatia, Cyprus, Czechia, Denmark, Estonia, EU, Finland, France, Georgia, Germany, Greece, Hungary, Iceland, Ireland, Italy, Kazakhstan, Kyrgyzstan, Latvia, Liechtenstein, Lithuania, Luxembourg, Macedonia, Malta, Moldova, Monaco, Montenegro, Netherlands, Norway, Poland, Portugal, Romania, Russia, Serbia, Slovakia, Slovenia, Spain, Sweden, Switzerland, Turkey, Ukraine, UK, US
**countries that have signed, but not yet ratified** - (1) Holy See, San Marino

## CONVENTION ON THE CONSERVATION OF ANTARCTIC MARINE LIVING RESOURCES

**note** - abbreviated as Antarctic-Marine Living Resources
**opened for signature** - 5 May 1980
**entered into force** - 7 April 1982
**objective** - to safeguard the environment and protect the integrity of the ecosystem of the seas surrounding Antarctica, and to conserve Antarctic marine living resources
**members** - (25) Argentina, Australia, Belgium, Brazil, Chile, China, EU, France, Germany, India, Italy, Japan, South Korea, Namibia, NZ, Norway, Poland, Russia, South Africa, Spain, Sweden, Ukraine, UK, US, Uruguay
**acceding states** - (11) Bulgaria, Canada, Cook Islands, Finland, Greece, Mauritius, Netherlands, Pakistan, Panama, Peru, Vanuatu

## CONVENTION ON THE INTERNATIONAL TRADE IN ENDANGERED SPECIES OF WILD FLORA AND FAUNA (CITES)

**note** - abbreviated as Endangered Species
**opened for signature** - 3 March 1973
**entered into force** - 1 July 1975
**objective** - to protect certain endangered species from overexploitation by means of a system of import/export permits
**parties** - (183) Afghanistan, Albania, Algeria, Angola, Antigua and Barbuda, Argentina, Armenia, Australia, Austria, Azerbaijan, The Bahamas, Bahrain, Bangladesh, Barbados, Belarus, Belgium, Belize, Benin, Bhutan, Bolivia, Bosnia and Herzegovina, Botswana, Brazil, Brunei, Bulgaria, Burkina Faso, Burma, Burundi, Cambodia, Cameroon, Canada, Cape Verde, Central African Republic, Chad, Chile, China, Colombia, Comoros, Democratic Republic of the Congo, Republic of the Congo, Costa Rica, Cote d'Ivoire, Croatia, Cuba, Cyprus, Czechia, Denmark, Djibouti, Dominica, Dominican Republic, Ecuador, Egypt, El Salvador, Equatorial Guinea, Eritrea, Estonia, Ethiopia, EU, Fiji, Finland, France, Gabon, The Gambia, Georgia, Germany, Ghana, Greece, Grenada, Guatemala, Guinea, Guinea-Bissau, Guyana, Honduras, Hungary, Iceland, India, Indonesia, Iran, Iraq, Ireland, Israel, Italy, Jamaica, Japan, Jordan, Kazakhstan, Kenya, South Korea, Kuwait, Kyrgyzstan, Laos, Latvia, Lebanon, Lesotho, Liberia, Libya, Liechtenstein, Lithuania, Luxembourg, Macedonia, Madagascar, Malawi, Malaysia, Maldives, Mali, Malta, Mauritania, Mauritius, Mexico, Moldova, Monaco, Mongolia, Montenegro, Morocco, Mozambique, Namibia, Nepal, Netherlands, NZ, Nicaragua, Niger, Nigeria, Norway, Oman, Palau, Pakistan, Panama, Papua New Guinea, Paraguay, Peru, Philippines, Poland, Portugal, Qatar, Romania, Russia, Rwanda, Saint Kitts and Nevis, Saint Lucia, Saint Vincent and the Grenadines, Samoa, San Marino, Sao Tome and Principe, Saudi Arabia, Senegal, Serbia, Seychelles, Sierra Leone, Singapore, Slovakia, Slovenia, Solomon Islands, Somalia, South Africa, Spain, Sri Lanka, Sudan, Suriname, Swaziland, Sweden, Switzerland, Syria, Tajikistan, Tanzania, Thailand, Togo, Tonga, Trinidad and Tobago, Tunisia, Turkey, Uganda, Ukraine, UAE, UK, US, Uruguay, Uzbekistan,

Vanuatu, Venezuela, Vietnam, Yemen, Zambia, Zimbabwe

## CONVENTION ON THE PREVENTION OF MARINE POLLUTION BY DUMPING WASTES AND OTHER MATTER (LONDON CONVENTION)

**note** - abbreviated as Marine Dumping
**opened for signature** - 29 December 1972
**entered into force** - 30 August 1975
**objective** - to promote effective control of all sources of marine pollution and to take all practicable steps to prevent pollution of the sea by dumping and to encourage regional agreements supplementary to the Convention
**parties** - (87) Afghanistan, Antigua and Barbuda, Argentina, Australia, Azerbaijan, Barbados, Belarus, Belgium, Benin, Bolivia, Brazil, Bulgaria, Canada, Cape Verde, Chile, China, Democratic Republic of the Congo, Costa Rica, Cote d'Ivoire, Croatia, Cuba, Cyprus, Denmark, Dominican Republic, Egypt, Equatorial Guinea, Finland, France, Gabon, Germany, Greece, Guatemala, Haiti, Honduras, Hungary, Iceland, Iran, Ireland, Italy, Jamaica, Japan, Jordan, Kenya, Kiribati, South Korea, Libya, Luxembourg, Malta, Mexico, Monaco, Montenegro, Morocco, Nauru, Netherlands, NZ, Nigeria, Norway, Oman, Pakistan, Panama, Papua New Guinea, Peru, Philippines, Poland, Portugal, Russia, Saint Lucia, Saint Vincent and the Grenadines, Serbia, Seychelles, Sierra Leon, Slovenia, Solomon Islands, South Africa, Spain, Suriname, Sweden, Switzerland, Syria, Tanzania, Tonga, Tunisia, Ukraine, UAE, UK, US, Vanuatu
**associate members to the London Convention** - (3) Faroe Islands, Hong Kong, Macau
i>countries that have signed, but not yet ratified - (3) Chad, Kuwait, Uruguay

## CONVENTION ON THE PROHIBITION OF MILITARY OR ANY OTHER HOSTILE USE OF ENVIRONMENTAL MODIFICATION TECHNIQUES

**note** - abbreviated as Environmental Modification
**opened for signature** - 18 May 1977
**entered into force** - 5 October 1978
**objective** - to prohibit the military or other hostile use of environmental modification techniques in order to further world peace and trust among nations
**parties** - (77 and the Palestine Liberation Organization) Afghanistan, Algeria, Antigua and Barbuda, Argentina, Armenia, Australia, Austria, Bangladesh, Belarus, Belgium, Benin, Brazil, Bulgaria, Canada, Cameroon, Cape Verde, Chile, China, Costa Rica, Cuba, Cyprus, Czechia, Denmark, Dominica, Egypt, Estonia, Finland, Germany, Ghana, Greece, Guatemala, Honduras, Hungary, India, Ireland, Italy, Japan, Kazakhstan, North Korea, South Korea, Kuwait, Kyrgyzstan, Laos, Lithuania, Malawi, Mauritius, Mongolia, Netherlands, NZ, Nicaragua, Niger, Norway, Pakistan, Panama, Papua New Guinea, Poland, Romania, Russia, Saint Lucia, Saint Vincent and the Grenadines, Sao Tome and Principe, Slovakia, Slovenia, Solomon Islands, Spain, Sri Lanka, Sweden, Switzerland, Tajikistan, Tunisia, Ukraine, UK, US, Uruguay, Uzbekistan, Vietnam, Yemen, Palestine Liberation Organization
**countries that have signed, but not yet ratified** - (16) Bolivia, Democratic Republic of the Congo, Ethiopia, Holy See, Iceland, Iran, Iraq, Lebanon, Liberia, Luxembourg, Morocco, Portugal, Sierra Leone, Syria, Turkey, Uganda

## CONVENTION ON WETLANDS OF INTERNATIONAL IMPORTANCE ESPECIALLY AS WATERFOWL HABITAT (RAMSAR)

**note** - abbreviated as Wetlands
**opened for signature** - 2 February 1971
**entered into force** - 21 December 1975
**objective** - to stem the progressive encroachment on and loss of wetlands now and in the future
**parties** - (170) Albania, Algeria, Andorra, Antigua and Barbuda, Argentina, Armenia, Australia, Austria, Azerbaijan, The Bahamas, Bahrain, Bangladesh, Barbados, Belarus, Belgium, Belize, Benin, Bhutan, Bolivia, Bosnia and Herzegovina, Botswana, Brazil, Bulgaria, Burkina Faso, Burma, Burundi, Cabo Verde, Cambodia, Cameroon, Canada, Central African Republic, Chad, Chile, China, Colombia, Comoros, Democratic Republic of the Congo, Republic of the Congo, Costa Rica, Cote d'Ivoire, Croatia, Cuba, Cyprus, Czechia, Denmark, Djibouti, Dominican Republic, Ecuador, Egypt, El Salvador, Equatorial Guinea, Estonia, Eswatini, Fiji, Finland, France, Gabon, The Gambia, Georgia, Germany, Ghana, Greece, Grenada, Guatemala, Guinea, Guinea-Bissau, Honduras, Hungary, Iceland, India, Indonesia, Iran, Iraq, Ireland, Israel, Italy, Jamaica, Japan, Jordan, Kazakhstan, Kenya, Kiribati, South Korea, Kyrgyzstan, Kuwait, Laos, Latvia, Lebanon, Lesotho, Liberia, Libya, Liechtenstein, Lithuania, Luxembourg, Macedonia, Madagascar, Malawi, Malaysia, Mali, Malta, Marshall Islands, Mauritania, Mauritius, Mexico, Moldova, Monaco, Mongolia, Montenegro, Morocco, Mozambique, Namibia, Nepal, Netherlands, NZ, Nicaragua, Niger, Nigeria, Norway, Oman, Pakistan, Palau, Panama, Papua New Guinea, Paraguay, Peru, Philippines, Poland, Portugal, Romania, Russia, Rwanda, Saint Lucia, Samoa, Sao Tome and Principe, Senegal, Serbia, Seychelles, Sierra Leone, Slovakia, Slovenia, South Africa, South Sudan, Spain, Sri Lanka, Sudan, Suriname, Sweden, Switzerland, Syria, Tanzania, Tajikistan, Thailand, Togo, Trinidad and Tobago, Tunisia, Turkey, Turkmenistan, Uganda, Ukraine, UAE, UK, US, Uruguay, Uzbekistan, Venezuela, Vietnam, Yemen, Zambia, Zimbabwe

## DESERTIFICATION

see United Nations Convention to Combat Desertification in those Countries Experiencing Serious Drought and/or Desertification, Particularly in Africa

## ENDANGERED SPECIES

see Convention on the International Trade in Endangered Species of Wild Flora and Fauna (CITES)

## ENVIRONMENTAL MODIFICATION

see Convention on the Prohibition of Military or Any Other Hostile Use of Environmental Modification Techniques

## HAZARDOUS WASTES

see Basel Convention on the Control of Transboundary Movements of Hazardous Wastes and Their Disposal

## INTERNATIONAL CONVENTION FOR THE REGULATION OF WHALING

**note** - abbreviated as Whaling
**opened for signature** - 2 December 1946
**entered into force** - 10 November 1948
**objective** - to protect all species of whales from overhunting; to establish a system of international regulation for the whale fisheries to ensure proper conservation and development of whale stocks; and to safeguard for future generations the great natural resources represented by whale stocks
**parties** - (89) Antigua and Barbuda, Argentina, Australia, Austria, Belgium, Belize, Benin, Brazil, Bulgaria, Cambodia, Cameroon, Chile, China, Colombia, Republic of the Congo, Costa Rica, Cote D'Ivoire, Croatia, Cyprus, Czechia, Denmark, Dominica, Dominican Republic, Ecuador, Eritrea, Estonia, Finland, France, Gabon, The Gambia, Germany, Ghana, Grenada, Guinea, Guinea-Bissau, Hungary, Iceland, India, Ireland, Israel, Italy, Japan, Kenya, Kiribati, South Korea, Laos, Liberia, Lithuania, Luxembourg, Mali, Marshall Islands, Mauritania, Mexico, Monaco, Mongolia, Morocco, Nauru, Netherlands, NZ, Nicaragua, Norway, Oman, Palau, Panama, Peru, Poland, Portugal, Romania, Russia, Saint Kitts and Nevis, Saint Lucia, Saint Vincent and the Grenadines, San Marino, Sao Tome and Principe, Senegal, Slovakia, Slovenia, Solomon Islands, South Africa, Spain, Suriname, Sweden, Switzerland, Tanzania, Togo, Tuvalu, UK, US, Uruguay

## INTERNATIONAL TROPICAL TIMBER AGREEMENT, 2006

**note** - abbreviated as Tropical Timber, 2006; ITTA, 2006; or ITTA3
**opened for signature** - 3 April 2006
**entered into force** - 7 December 2011; note - superseded the International Tropical Timber Agreement, 1994, which itself superseded the International Tropical Timber Agreement, 1983
**objective** - to promote the expansion and diversification of international trade in tropical timber from sustainably managed and legally harvested forests and to promote the sustainable management of tropical timber producing forests
**parties** - (74) Abania, Australia, Austria, Belgium, Benin, Brazil, Bulgaria, Burma, Cambodia, Cameroon, Central African Republic, China, Colombia, Democratic Republic of the Congo, Republic of the Congo, Costa Rica, Cote d'Ivoire, Croatia, Cyprus, Czechia, Denmark, Ecuador, Estonia, EU, Fiji, Finland, France, Gabon, Germany, Ghana, Greece, Guatemala, Guyana, Honduras, Hungary, India, Indonesia, Ireland, Italy, Japan, South Korea, Latvia, Liberia, Lithuania, Luxembourg, Madagascar, Malaysia, Mali, Malta, Mexico, Mozambique, Netherlands, NZ, Norway, Panama, Papua New Guinea, Peru, Philippines, Poland, Portugal, Romania, Slovakia, Slovenia, Spain, Suriname, Sweden, Switzerland, Thailand, Togo, Trinidad and Tobago, UK, US, Venezuela, Vietnam
**countries that have signed, but not yet ratified** - (2) Nigeria, Paraguay

## KYOTO PROTOCOL TO THE UNITED NATIONS FRAMEWORK CONVENTION ON CLIMATE CHANGE

**note** - abbreviated as Climate Change-Kyoto Protocol
**opened for signature** - 16 March 1998
**entered into force** - 16 February 2005
**objective** - to further reduce greenhouse gas emissions by enhancing the national programs of developed countries aimed at this goal and by establishing percentage reduction targets for the developed countries
**parties** - (192) Afghanistan, Albania, Algeria, Angola, Antigua and Barbuda, Argentina, Armenia, Australia, Austria, Azerbaijan, The Bahamas, Bahrain, Bangladesh, Barbados, Belarus, Belgium, Belize, Benin, Bhutan, Bolivia, Bosnia and Herzegovina, Botswana, Brazil, Brunei, Bulgaria, Burkina Faso, Burma, Burundi, Cabo Verde, Cambodia, Cameroon, Central African Republic, Chad, Chile, China, Colombia, Comoros, Democratic Republic of the Congo, Republic of the Congo, Cook Islands, Costa Rica, Cote d'Ivoire, Croatia, Cuba, Cyprus, Czechia, Denmark, Djibouti, Dominica, Dominican Republic, Ecuador, Egypt, El Salvador, Equatorial Guinea, Eritrea, Estonia, Ethiopia, EU, Fiji, Finland, France, Gabon, The Gambia, Georgia, Germany, Ghana, Greece, Grenada, Guatemala, Guinea, Guinea-Bissau, Guyana, Haiti, Honduras, Hungary, Iceland, India, Indonesia, Iran, Iraq, Ireland, Israel,

Italy, Jamaica, Japan, Jordan, Kazakhstan, Kenya, Kiribati, North Korea, South Korea, Kuwait, Kyrgyzstan, Laos, Latvia, Lebanon, Lesotho, Liberia, Libya, Liechtenstein, Lithuania, Luxembourg, Macedonia, Madagascar, Malawi, Malaysia, Maldives, Mali, Malta, Marshall Islands, Mauritania, Mauritius, Mexico, Federated States of Micronesia, Moldova, Monaco, Mongolia, Montenegro, Morocco, Mozambique, Namibia, Nauru, Nepal, Netherlands, NZ, Nicaragua, Niger, Nigeria, Niue, Norway, Oman, Pakistan, Palau, Panama, Papua New Guinea, Paraguay, Peru, Philippines, Poland, Portugal, Qatar, Romania, Russia, Rwanda, Saint Kitts and Nevis, Saint Lucia, Saint Vincent and the Grenadines, Samoa, San Marino, Sao Tome and Principe, Saudi Arabia, Senegal, Serbia, Seychelles, Sierra Leone, Singapore, Slovakia, Slovenia, Solomon Islands, Somalia, South Africa, Spain, Sri Lanka, Sudan, Suriname, Swaziland, Sweden, Switzerland, Syria, Tajikistan, Tanzania, Thailand, Timor-Leste, Togo, Tonga, Trinidad and Tobago, Tunisia, Turkey, Turkmenistan, Tuvalu, Uganda, Ukraine, UAE, UK, Uruguay, Uzbekistan, Vanuatu, Venezuela, Vietnam, Yemen, Zambia, Zimbabwe
**countries that have signed, but not yet ratified** - (1) US

## LAW OF THE SEA

see United Nations Convention on the Law of the Sea (LOS)

## MARINE DUMPING

see Convention on the Prevention of Marine Pollution by Dumping Wastes and Other Matter (London Convention)

## MARINE LIFE CONSERVATION

see Convention on Fishing and Conservation of Living Resources of the High Seas

## MONTREAL PROTOCOL ON SUBSTANCES THAT DEPLETE THE OZONE LAYER

**note** - abbreviated as Ozone Layer Protection
**opened for signature** - 16 September 1987
**entered into force** - 1 January 1989
**objective** - to protect the ozone layer by controlling emissions of substances that deplete it
**parties** - (197) Afghanistan, Albania, Algeria, Andorra, Angola, Antigua and Barbuda, Argentina, Armenia, Australia, Austria, Azerbaijan, The Bahamas, Bahrain, Bangladesh, Barbados, Belarus, Belgium, Belize, Benin, Bhutan, Bolivia, Bosnia and Herzegovina, Botswana, Brazil, Brunei, Bulgaria, Burkina Faso, Burma, Burundi, Cambodia, Cameroon, Canada, Cape Verde, Central African Republic, Chad, Chile, China, Colombia, Comoros, Democratic Republic of the Congo, Republic of the Congo, Cook Islands, Costa Rica, Cote d'Ivoire, Croatia, Cuba, Cyprus, Czechia, Denmark, Djibouti, Dominica, Dominican Republic, Ecuador, Egypt, El Salvador, Equatorial Guinea, Eritrea, Estonia, Ethiopia, EU, Fiji, Finland, France, Gabon, The Gambia, Georgia, Germany, Ghana, Greece, Grenada, Guatemala, Guinea, Guinea-Bissau, Guyana, Haiti, Holy See, Honduras, Hungary, Iceland, India, Indonesia, Iran, Iraq, Ireland, Israel, Italy, Jamaica, Japan, Jordan, Kazakhstan, Kenya, Kiribati, North Korea, South Korea, Kuwait, Kyrgyzstan, Laos, Latvia, Lebanon, Lesotho, Liberia, Libya, Liechtenstein, Lithuania, Luxembourg, Macedonia, Madagascar, Malawi, Malaysia, Maldives, Mali, Malta, Marshall Islands, Mauritania, Mauritius, Mexico, Federated States of Micronesia, Moldova, Monaco, Mongolia, Montenegro, Morocco, Mozambique, Namibia, Nauru, Nepal, Netherlands, NZ, Nicaragua, Niger, Nigeria, Niue, Norway, Oman, Pakistan, Palau, Panama, Papua New Guinea, Paraguay, Peru, Philippines, Poland, Portugal, Qatar, Romania, Russia, Rwanda, Saint Kitts and Nevis, Saint Lucia, Saint Vincent and the Grenadines, Samoa, San Marino, Sao Tome and Principe, Saudi Arabia, Senegal, Serbia, Seychelles, Sierra Leone, Singapore, Slovakia, Slovenia, Solomon Islands, Somalia, South Africa, South Sudan, Spain, Sri Lanka, Sudan, Suriname, Swaziland, Sweden, Switzerland, Syria, Tajikistan, Tanzania, Thailand, Timor-Leste, Togo, Tonga, Trinidad and Tobago, Tunisia, Turkey, Turkmenistan, Tuvalu, Uganda, Ukraine, UAE, UK, US, Uruguay, Uzbekistan, Vanuatu, Venezuela, Vietnam, Yemen, Zambia, Zimbabwe

## MULTI-EFFECT PROTOCOL

see Protocol to the 1979 Convention on Long-Range Transboundary Air Pollution to Abate Acidification, Eutrophication, and Ground-Level Ozone

## NUCLEAR TEST BAN

see Treaty Banning Nuclear Weapons Tests in the Atmosphere, in Outer Space, and Under Water

## OZONE LAYER PROTECTION

see Montreal Protocol on Substances That Deplete the Ozone Layer

## PROTOCOL OF 1978 RELATING TO THE INTERNATIONAL CONVENTION FOR THE PREVENTION OF POLLUTION FROM SHIPS, 1973 (MARPOL)

**note** - abbreviated as Ship Pollution
**opened for signature** - 1 June 1978
**entered into force** - 2 October 1983

**objective** - to preserve the marine environment in an attempt to completely eliminate pollution by oil and other harmful substances and to minimize accidental spillage of such substances
**parties** - (153) Albania, Algeria, Angola, Antigua and Barbuda, Argentina, Australia, Austria, Azerbaijan, The Bahamas, Bahrain, Bangladesh, Barbados, Belarus, Belgium, Belize, Benin, Bolivia, Brazil, Brunei, Bulgaria, Burma, Cabo Verde, Cambodia, Cameroon, Canada, Chile, China, Colombia, Comoros, Republic of Congo, Cook Islands, Cote d'Ivoire, Croatia, Cuba, Cyprus, Czechia, Denmark, Djibouti, Dominica, Dominican Republic, Ecuador, Egypt, El Salvador, Equatorial Guinea, Estonia, Fiji, Finland, France, Gabon, The Gambia, Georgia, Germany, Ghana, Greece, Guatemala, Guinea, Guinea-Bissau, Guyana, Honduras, Hungary, Iceland, India, Indonesia, Iran, Iraq, Ireland, Israel, Italy, Jamaica, Japan, Jordan, Kazakhstan, Kenya, Kiribati, North Korea, South Korea, Kuwait, Latvia, Lebanon, Liberia, Libya, Lithuania, Luxembourg, Madagascar, Malawi, Malaysia, Maldives, Malta, Marshall Islands, Mauritania, Mauritius, Mexico, Moldova, Monaco, Mongolia, Montenegro, Morocco, Mozambique, Namibia, Netherlands, NZ, Nicaragua, Nigeria, Niue, Norway, Oman, Pakistan, Palau, Panama, Papua New Guinea, Peru, Philippines, Poland, Portugal, Qatar, Romania, Russia, Saint Kitts and Nevis, Saint Lucia, Saint Vincent and the Grenadines, Samoa, Sao Tome and Principe, Saudi Arabia, Senegal, Serbia, Sierra Leone, Singapore, Slovakia, Slovenia, Solomon Islands, South Africa, Spain, Sri Lanka, Sudan, Suriname, Sweden, Switzerland, Syria, Tanzania, Togo, Tonga, Trinidad and Tobago, Tunisia, Turkey, Tuvalu, Ukraine, UAE, UK, US, Uruguay, Vanuatu, Venezuela, Vietnam

## PROTOCOL ON ENVIRONMENTAL PROTECTION TO THE ANTARCTIC TREATY

**note** - abbreviated as Antarctic-Environmental Protocol
**opened for signature** - 4 October 1991
**entered into force** - 14 January 1998
**objective** - to provide for comprehensive protection of the Antarctic environment and dependent and associated ecosystems; applies to the area covered by the Antarctic Treaty
**consultative parties** - (29) Argentina, Australia, Belgium, Brazil, Bulgaria, Chile, China, Czechia, Ecuador, Finland, France, Germany, India, Italy, Japan, South Korea, Netherlands, NZ, Norway, Peru, Poland, Russia, South Africa, Spain, Sweden, Ukraine, UK, US, Uruguay
**non consultative parties** - (24) Austria, Belarus, Canada, Colombia, Cuba, Denmark, Estonia, Greece, Guatemala, Hungary, Iceland, Kazakhstan, North Korea, Malaysia, Monaco, Mongolia, Pakistan, Papua New Guinea, Portugal, Romania, Slovakia, Switzerland, Turkey, Venezuela

## PROTOCOL TO THE 1979 CONVENTION ON LONG-RANGE TRANSBOUNDARY AIR POLLUTION CONCERNING THE CONTROL OF EMISSIONS OF NITROGEN OXIDES OR THEIR TRANSBOUNDARY FLUXES

**note** - abbreviated as Air Pollution-Nitrogen Oxides
**opened for signature** - 31 October 1988
**entered into force** - 14 February 1991
**objective** - to provide for the control or reduction national of nitrogen oxide emissions and their transboundary fluxes
**parties** - (35) Albania, Austria, Belarus, Belgium, Bulgaria, Canada, Croatia, Cyprus, Czechia, Denmark, Estonia, EU, Finland, France, Germany, Greece, Hungary, Ireland, Italy, Liechtenstein, Lithuania, Luxembourg, Macedonia, Netherlands, Norway, Poland, Russia, Slovakia, Slovenia, Spain, Sweden, Switzerland, Ukraine, UK, US

## PROTOCOL TO THE 1979 CONVENTION ON LONG-RANGE TRANSBOUNDARY AIR POLLUTION CONCERNING THE CONTROL OF EMISSIONS OF VOLATILE ORGANIC COMPOUNDS OR THEIR TRANSBOUNDARY FLUXES

**note** - abbreviated as Air Pollution-Volatile Organic Compounds
**opened for signature** - 18 November 1991
**entered into force** - 29 September 1997
**objective** - to provide for the control and reduction of national emissions of volatile organic compounds in order to reduce their transboundary fluxes
**parties** - (24) Austria, Belgium, Bulgaria, Croatia, Czechia, Denmark, Estonia, Finland, France, Germany, Hungary, Italy, Liechtenstein, Lithuania, Luxembourg, Macedonia, Monaco, Netherlands, Norway, Slovakia, Spain, Sweden, Switzerland, UK
**countries that have signed, but not yet ratified** - (6) Canada, EU, Greece, Portugal, Ukraine, US

## PROTOCOL TO THE 1979 CONVENTION ON LONG-RANGE TRANSBOUNDARY AIR POLLUTION ON FURTHER REDUCTION OF SULPHUR EMISSIONS

**note** - abbreviated as Air Pollution-Sulphur 94
**opened for signature** - 14 June 1994
**entered into force** - 5 August 1998
**objective** - to provide for a further reduction in national sulfur emissions or transboundary fluxes on a regional basis within Europe
**parties** - (30) Austria, Belgium, Bulgaria, Canada, Croatia, Cyprus, Czechia, Denmark, EU, Finland, France, Germany, Greece, Hungary, Ireland, Italy,

Liechtenstein, Lithuania, Luxembourg, Macedonia, Monaco, Netherlands, Norway, Poland, Slovakia, Slovenia, Spain, Sweden, Switzerland, UK
**countries that have signed, but not yet ratified** - (2) Russia, Ukraine

## PROTOCOL TO THE 1979 CONVENTION ON LONG-RANGE TRANSBOUNDARY AIR POLLUTION ON HEAVY METALS

**note** - abbreviated as Air Pollution-Heavy Metals
**opened for signature** - 24 June 1998
**entered into force** - 29 December 2003
**objective** - to reduce emissions of the heavy metals cadmium, lead, and mercury from industrial sources, combustion processes, and waste incineration
**parties** - (34) Austria, Belgium, Bulgaria, Canada, Croatia, Cyprus, Czechia, Denmark, Estonia, EU, Finland, France, Germany, Hungary, Iceland, Latvia, Liechtenstein, Lithuania, Luxembourg, Macedonia, Moldova, Monaco, Montenegro, Netherlands, Norway, Portugal, Romania, Serbia, Slovakia, Slovenia, Spain, Sweden, Switzerland, UK, US
**countries that have signed, but not yet ratified** - (7) Armenia, Greece, Iceland, Ireland, Italy, Poland, Ukraine

## PROTOCOL TO THE 1979 CONVENTION ON LONG-RANGE TRANSBOUNDARY AIR POLLUTION ON PERSISTENT ORGANIC POLLUTANTS

**note** - abbreviated as Air Pollution-Persistent Organic Pollutants
**opened for signature** - 24 June 1998
**entered into force** - 23 October 2003
**objective** - to provide for the control, reduction, or elimination of discharges, emissions of persistent organic pollutants
**parties** - (33) Austria, Belgium, Bulgaria, Canada, Croatia, Cyprus, Czechia, Denmark, Estonia, EU, Finland, France, Germany, Hungary, Iceland, Italy, Latvia, Liechtenstein, Lithuania, Luxembourg, Macedonia, Moldova, Montenegro, Netherlands, Norway, Romania, Serbia, Slovakia, Slovenia, Spain, Sweden, Switzerland, UK
**countries that have signed, but not yet ratified** - (7) Armenia, Greece, Ireland, Poland, Portugal, Ukraine, US

## PROTOCOL TO THE 1979 CONVENTION ON LONG-RANGE TRANSBOUNDARY AIR POLLUTION ON THE REDUCTION OF SULPHUR EMISSIONS OR THEIR TRANSBOUNDARY FLUXES BY AT LEAST 30%

**note** - abbreviated as Air Pollution-Sulphur 85
**opened for signature** - 8 July 1985
**entered into force** - 2 September 1987
**objective** - to provide for national reductions in sulfur emissions or transboundary fluxes by 30% of 1980 emission or transboundary flux levels by no later than 1993
**parties** - (25) Albania, Austria, Belarus, Belgium, Bulgaria, Canada, Czechia, Denmark, Estonia, Finland, France, Germany, Hungary, Italy, Liechtenstein, Lithuania, Luxembourg, Macedonia, Netherlands, Norway, Russia, Slovakia, Sweden, Switzerland, Ukraine
**note** - Albania and Macedonia listed as non-compliant

## PROTOCOL TO THE 1979 CONVENTION ON LONG-RANGE TRANSBOUNDARY AIR POLLUTION TO ABATE ACIDIFICATION, EUTROPHICATION, AND GROUND-LEVEL OZONE

**note** - abbreviated as Multi-effect Protocol
**opened for signature** - 30 November 1999
**entered into force** - 17 May 2005
**objective** - to reduce acidification, eutrophication, and ground-level ozone by setting emissions ceilings for sulphur dioxide, nitrogen oxides, volatile organic compounds, and ammonia
**parties** - (27) Belgium, Bulgaria, Canada, Croatia, Cyprus, Czechia, Denmark, EU, Finland, France, Germany, Hungary, Latvia, Lithuania, Luxembourg, Macedonia, Netherlands, Norway, Portugal, Romania, Slovakia, Slovenia, Spain, Sweden, Switzerland, UK, US
**countries that have signed, but not yet ratified** - (8) Armenia, Austria, Greece, Ireland, Italy, Liechtenstein, Moldova, Poland

## SHIP POLLUTION

see Protocol of 1978 Relating to the International Convention for the Prevention of Pollution From Ships, 1973 (MARPOL)

## TREATY BANNING NUCLEAR WEAPON TESTS IN THE ATMOSPHERE, IN OUTER SPACE, AND UNDER WATER

**note** - abbreviated as Nuclear Test Ban
**opened for signature** - 5 August 1963
**entered into force** - 10 October 1963
**objective** - to ban nuclear weapons testing in the atmosphere, outer space, or under water
**parties** - (125) Afghanistan, Antigua and Barbuda, Argentina, Armenia, Australia, Austria, The Bahamas, Bangladesh, Belarus, Belgium, Benin, Bhutan, Bolivia, Bosnia and Herzegovina, Botswana, Brazil, Bulgaria, Burma, Cabo Verde, Canada, Central African Republic, Chad, Chile, Colombia, Democratic Republic of the

Congo, Costa Rica, Cote d'Ivoire, Croatia, Cyprus, Czechia, Denmark, Dominican Republic, Ecuador, Egypt, El Salvador, Eswatini, Equatorial Guinea, Fiji, Finland, Gabon, The Gambia, Germany, Ghana, Greece, Guatemala, Guinea-Bissau, Honduras, Hungary, Iceland, India, Indonesia, Iran, Iraq, Ireland, Israel, Italy, Jamaica, Japan, Jordan, Kenya, South Korea, Kuwait, Laos, Lebanon, Liberia, Libya, Luxembourg, Madagascar, Malawi, Malaysia, Malta, Mauritania, Mauritius, Mexico, Mongolia, Montenegro, Morocco, Nepal, Netherlands, NZ, Nicaragua, Niger, Nigeria, Norway, Pakistan, Panama, Papua New Guinea, Peru, Philippines, Poland, Romania, Russia, Rwanda, Samoa, San Marino, Senegal, Serbia, Seychelles, Sierra Leone, Singapore, Slovakia, Slovenia, South Africa, Spain, Sri Lanka, Sudan, Suriname, Sweden, Switzerland, Syria, Tanzania, Thailand, Togo, Tonga, Trinidad and Tobago, Tunisia, Turkey, Uganda, Ukraine, UK, US, Uruguay, Venezuela, Yemen, Zambia
**countries that have signed, but not yet ratified** - (10) Algeria, Burkina-Faso, Burundi, Cameroon, Ethiopia, Haiti, Mali, Paraguay, Portugal, Somalia

## TROPICAL TIMBER, 2006

see International Tropical Timber Agreement, 2006

## UNITED NATIONS CONVENTION ON THE LAW OF THE SEA (LOS)

**note** - abbreviated as Law of the Sea
**opened for signature** - 10 December 1982
**entered into force** - 16 November 1994
**objective** - to provide a comprehensive legal regime for the sea and oceans
**parties** - (167 and the Palestine Liberation Organization) Albania, Algeria, Angola, Antigua and Barbuda, Argentina, Armenia, Australia, Austria, Azerbaijan, The Bahamas, Bahrain, Bangladesh, Barbados, Belarus, Belgium, Belize, Benin, Bolivia, Bosnia and Herzegovina, Botswana, Brazil, Brunei, Bulgaria, Burkina Faso, Burma, Burundi, Cabo Verde, Cameroon, Canada, Chad, Chile, China, Comoros, Democratic Republic of the Congo, Republic of the Congo, Cook Islands, Costa Rica, Cote d'Ivoire, Croatia, Cuba, Cyprus, Czechia, Denmark, Djibouti, Dominica, Dominican Republic, Ecuador, Egypt, Equatorial Guinea, Estonia, EU, Fiji, Finland, France, Gabon, The Gambia, Georgia, Germany, Ghana, Greece, Grenada, Guatemala, Guinea, Guinea-Bissau, Guyana, Haiti, Honduras, Hungary, Iceland, India, Indonesia, Iraq, Ireland, Italy, Jamaica, Japan, Jordan, Kenya, Kiribati, South Korea, Kuwait, Laos, Latvia, Lebanon, Lesotho, Liberia, Lithuania, Luxembourg, Macedonia, Madagascar, Malawi, Malaysia, Maldives, Mali, Malta, Marshall Islands, Mauritania, Mauritius, Mexico, Federated States of Micronesia, Moldova, Monaco, Mongolia, Montenegro, Morocco, Mozambique, Namibia, Nauru, Nepal, Netherlands, NZ, Nicaragua, Niger, Nigeria, Niue, Norway, Oman, Pakistan, Palau, Panama, Papua New Guinea, Paraguay, Philippines, Poland, Portugal, Qatar, Romania, Russia, Rwanda, Saint Kitts and Nevis, Saint Lucia, Saint Vincent and the Grenadines, Samoa, Sao Tome and Principe, Saudi Arabia, Senegal, Serbia, Seychelles, Sierra Leone, Singapore, Slovakia, Slovenia, Solomon Islands, Somalia, South Africa, Spain, Sri Lanka, Sudan, Suriname, Swaziland, Sweden, Switzerland, Tanzania, Thailand, Timor-Leste, Togo, Tonga, Trinidad and Tobago, Tunisia, Tuvalu, Uganda, Ukraine, UK, Uruguay, Vanuatu, Vietnam, Yemen, Zambia, Zimbabwe, Palestine Liberation Organization
**countries that have signed, but not yet ratified** - (14) Afghanistan, Bhutan, Burundi, Cambodia, Central African Republic, Colombia, El Salvador, Ethiopia, Iran, North Korea, Libya, Liechtenstein, Rwanda, UAE

## UNITED NATIONS CONVENTION TO COMBAT DESERTIFICATION IN THOSE COUNTRIES EXPERIENCING SERIOUS DROUGHT AND/OR DESERTIFICATION, PARTICULARLY IN AFRICA

**note** - abbreviated as Desertification
**opened for signature** - 14 October 1994
**entered into force** - 26 December 1996
**objective** - to combat desertification and mitigate the effects of drought through an integrated framework that is consistent with Agenda 21, employing international cooperation and partnership arrangements, and effective action at all levels
**parties** - (196 and the Palestine Liberation Organization) Afghanistan, Albania, Algeria, Andorra, Angola, Antigua and Barbuda, Argentina, Armenia, Australia, Austria, Azerbaijan, The Bahamas, Bahrain, Bangladesh, Barbados, Belarus, Belgium, Belize, Benin, Bhutan, Bolivia, Bosnia and Herzegovina, Botswana, Brazil, Brunei, Bulgaria, Burkina Faso, Burma, Burundi, Cambodia, Cameroon, Canada, Cape Verde, Central African Republic, Chad, Chile, China, Colombia, Comoros, Democratic Republic of the Congo, Republic of the Congo, Cook Islands, Costa Rica, Cote d'Ivoire, Croatia, Cuba, Cyprus, Czechia, Denmark, Djibouti, Dominica, Dominican Republic, Ecuador, Egypt, El Salvador, Equatorial Guinea, Eritrea, Estonia, Ethiopia, EU, Fiji, Finland, France, Gabon, The Gambia, Georgia, Germany, Ghana, Greece, Grenada, Guatemala, Guinea, Guinea-Bissau, Guyana, Haiti, Honduras, Hungary, Iceland, India, Indonesia, Iran, Iraq, Ireland, Israel, Italy, Jamaica, Japan, Jordan, Kazakhstan, Kenya, Kiribati, North Korea, South Korea, Kuwait, Kyrgyzstan, Laos, Latvia, Lebanon, Lesotho, Liberia, Libya, Liechtenstein, Lithuania, Luxembourg, Macedonia, Madagascar, Malawi, Malaysia, Maldives, Mali, Malta, Marshall Islands, Mauritania, Mauritius, Mexico, Federated States of Micronesia, Moldova,

## UNITED NATIONS FRAMEWORK CONVENTION ON CLIMATE CHANGE

**note** - abbreviated as Climate Change
**opened for signature** - 9 May 1992
**entered into force** - 21 March 1994
**objective** - to achieve stabilization of greenhouse gas concentrations in the atmosphere at a low enough level to prevent dangerous anthropogenic interference with the climate system
**parties** - (196 and the Palestine Liberation Organization) Afghanistan, Albania, Algeria, Andorra, Angola, Antigua and Barbuda, Argentina, Armenia, Australia, Austria, Azerbaijan, The Bahamas, Bahrain, Bangladesh, Barbados, Belarus, Belgium, Belize, Benin, Bhutan, Bolivia, Bosnia and Herzegovina, Botswana, Brazil, Brunei, Bulgaria, Burkina Faso, Burma, Burundi, Cambodia, Cameroon, Canada, Cape Verde, Central African Republic, Chad, Chile, China, Colombia, Comoros, Democratic Republic of the Congo, Republic of the Congo, Cook Islands, Costa Rica, Cote d'Ivoire, Croatia, Cuba, Cyprus, Czechia, Denmark, Djibouti, Dominica, Dominican Republic, Ecuador, Egypt, El Salvador, Equatorial Guinea, Eritrea, Estonia, Ethiopia, EU, Fiji, Finland, France, Gabon, The Gambia, Georgia, Germany, Ghana, Greece, Grenada, Guatemala, Guinea, Guinea-Bissau, Guyana, Haiti, Honduras, Hungary, Iceland, India, Indonesia, Iran, Iraq, Ireland, Israel, Italy, Jamaica, Japan, Jordan, Kazakhstan, Kenya, Kiribati, North Korea, South Korea, Kuwait, Kyrgyzstan, Laos, Latvia, Lebanon, Lesotho, Liberia, Libya, Liechtenstein, Lithuania, Luxembourg, Macedonia, Madagascar, Malawi, Malaysia, Maldives, Mali, Malta, Marshall Islands, Mauritania, Mauritius, Mexico, Federated States of Micronesia, Moldova, Monaco, Mongolia, Montenegro, Morocco, Mozambique, Namibia, Nauru, Nepal, Netherlands, NZ, Nicaragua, Niger, Nigeria, Niue, Norway, Oman, Pakistan, Palau, Panama, Papua New Guinea, Paraguay, Peru, Philippines, Poland, Portugal, Qatar, Romania, Russia, Rwanda, Saint Kitts and Nevis, Saint Lucia, Saint Vincent and the Grenadines, Samoa, San Marino, Sao Tome and Principe, Saudi Arabia, Senegal, Serbia, Seychelles, Sierra Leone, Singapore, Slovakia, Slovenia, Solomon Islands, Somalia, South Africa, South Sudan, Spain, Sri Lanka, Sudan, Suriname, Swaziland, Sweden, Switzerland, Syria, Tajikistan, Tanzania, Thailand, Timor-Leste, Togo, Tonga, Trinidad and Tobago, Tunisia, Turkey, Turkmenistan, Tuvalu, Uganda, Ukraine, UAE, UK, US, Uruguay, Uzbekistan, Vanuatu, Venezuela, Vietnam, Yemen, Zambia, Zimbabwe, Palestine Liberation Organization

## WETLANDS

see Convention on Wetlands of International Importance Especially As Waterfowl Habitat (Ramsar)

## WHALING

see International Convention for the Regulation of Whaling

# APPENDIX D :: CROSS-REFERENCE LIST OF COUNTRY DATA CODES

**GEOPOLITICAL ENTITIES and CODES (formerly FIPS PUB 10-4)**: FIPS PUB 10-4 was withdrawn by the National Institute of Standards and Technology on 2 September 2008 based on Public Law 104-113 (codified OMB Circular A-119 and the National Technology Transfer and Advancement Act of 1995). The National Geospatial-Intelligence Agency (NGA), as the maintenance authority for FIPS PUB 10-4, has continued to maintain and provide regular updates to its content in a document known as Geopolitical Entities and Codes (GEC) (Formerly FIPS 1PUB 10-4).

**ISO 3166**: Codes for the Representation of Names of Countries (ISO 3166) is prepared by the International Organization for Standardization. ISO 3166 includes two- and three-character alphabetic codes and three-digit numeric codes that may be needed for activities involving exchange of data with international organizations that have adopted that standard. Except for the numeric codes, ISO 3166 codes have been adopted in the US as FIPS 104-1: American National Standard Codes for the Representation of Names of Countries, Dependencies, and Areas of Special Sovereignty for Information Interchange.

**STANAG 1059**: Letter Codes for Geographical Entities (8th edition, 2004) is a Standardization Agreement (STANAG) established and maintained by the North Atlantic Treaty Organization (NATO/OTAN) for the purpose of providing a common set of geo-spatial identifiers for countries, territories, and possessions. The 8th edition established trigraph codes for each country based upon the ISO 3166-1 alpha-3 character sets. These codes are used throughout NATO.

**Internet**: The Internet country code is the two-letter digraph maintained by the International Organization for Standardization (ISO) in the ISO 3166 Alpha-2 list and used by the Internet Assigned Numbers Authority (IANA) to establish country-coded top-level domains (ccTLDs).

| ENTITY | GEC | ISO 3166 | | | STANAG | INTERNET | COMMENT |
|---|---|---|---|---|---|---|---|
| Afghanistan | AF | AF | AFG | 004 | AFG | .af | |
| Akrotiri | AX | - | - | - | - | - | |
| Albania | AL | AL | ALB | 008 | ALB | .al | |
| Algeria | AG | DZ | DZA | 012 | DZA | .dz | |
| American Samoa | AQ | AS | ASM | 016 | ASM | .as | |
| Andorra | AN | AD | AND | 020 | AND | .ad | |
| Angola | AO | AO | AGO | 024 | AGO | .ao | |
| Anguilla | AV | AI | AIA | 660 | AIA | .ai | |
| Antarctica | AY | AQ | ATA | 010 | ATA | .aq | ISO defines as the territory south of 60 degrees south latitude |
| Antigua and Barbuda | AC | AG | ATG | 028 | ATG | .ag | |
| Argentina | AR | AR | ARG | 032 | ARG | .ar | |
| Armenia | AM | AM | ARM | 051 | ARM | .am | |
| Aruba | AA | AW | ABW | 533 | ABW | .aw | |
| Ashmore and Cartier Islands | AT | - | - | - | AUS | - | ISO includes with Australia |
| Australia | AS | AU | AUS | 036 | AUS | .au | ISO includes Ashmore and Cartier Islands, Coral Sea Islands |

| ENTITY | GEC | ISO 3166 | | STANAG | INTERNET | COMMENT |
|---|---|---|---|---|---|---|
| Austria | AU | AT | AUT | 040 | AUT | .at | |
| Azerbaijan | AJ | AZ | AZE | 031 | AZE | .az | |
| Bahamas, The | BF | BS | BHS | 044 | BHS | .bs | |
| Bahrain | BA | BH | BHR | 048 | BHR | .bh | |
| Baker Island | FQ | - | - | - | UMI | - | ISO includes with the US Minor Outlying Islands |
| Bangladesh | BG | BD | BGD | 050 | BGD | .bd | |
| Barbados | BB | BB | BRB | 052 | BRB | .bb | |
| Bassas da India | BS | - | - | - | - | - | administered as part of French Southern and Antarctic Lands; no ISO codes assigned |
| Belarus | BO | BY | BLR | 112 | BLR | .by | |
| Belgium | BE | BE | BEL | 056 | BEL | .be | |
| Belize | BH | BZ | BLZ | 084 | BLZ | .bz | |
| Benin | BN | BJ | BEN | 204 | BEN | .bj | |
| Bermuda | BD | BM | BMU | 060 | BMU | .bm | |
| Bhutan | BT | BT | BTN | 064 | BTN | .bt | |
| Bolivia | BL | BO | BOL | 068 | BOL | .bo | |
| Bosnia and Herzegovina | BK | BA | BIH | 070 | BIH | .ba | |
| Botswana | BC | BW | BWA | 072 | BWA | .bw | |
| Bouvet Island | BV | BV | BVT | 074 | BVT | .bv | |
| Brazil | BR | BR | BRA | 076 | BRA | .br | |
| British Indian Ocean Territory | IO | IO | IOT | 086 | IOT | .io | |
| British Virgin Islands | VI | VG | VGB | 092 | VGB | .vg | |
| Brunei | BX | BN | BRN | 096 | BRN | .bn | |
| Bulgaria | BU | BG | BGR | 100 | BGR | .bg | |
| Burkina Faso | UV | BF | BFA | 854 | BFA | .bf | |
| Burma | BM | MM | MMR | 104 | MMR | .mm | ISO uses the name Myanmar |
| Burundi | BY | BI | BDI | 108 | BDI | .bi | |
| Cabo Verde | CV | CV | CPV | 132 | CPV | .cv | |
| Cambodia | CB | KH | KHM | 116 | KHM | .kh | |
| Cameroon | CM | CM | CMR | 120 | CMR | .cm | |
| Canada | CA | CA | CAN | 124 | CAN | .ca | |
| Cayman Islands | CJ | KY | CYM | 136 | CYM | .ky | |
| Central African Republic | CT | CF | CAF | 140 | CAF | .cf | |

| ENTITY | GEC | ISO 3166 | | STANAG | INTERNET | COMMENT |
|---|---|---|---|---|---|---|
| Chad | CD | TD | TCD | 148 | TCD | .td | |
| Chile | CI | CL | CHL | 152 | CHL | .cl | |
| China | CH | CN | CHN | 156 | CHN | .cn | see also Taiwan |
| Christmas Island | KT | CX | CXR | 162 | CXR | .cx | |
| Clipperton Island | IP | - | - | - | FYP | - | ISO includes with France |
| Cocos (Keeling) Islands | CK | CC | CCK | 166 | AUS | .cc | |
| Colombia | CO | CO | COL | 170 | COL | .co | |
| Comoros | CN | KM | COM | 174 | COM | .km | |
| Congo, Democratic Republic of the | CG | CD | COD | 180 | COD | .cd | formerly Zaire |
| Congo, Republic of the | CF | CG | COG | 178 | COG | .cg | |
| Cook Islands | CW | CK | COK | 184 | COK | .ck | |
| Coral Sea Islands | CR | - | - | - | AUS | - | ISO includes with Australia |
| Costa Rica | CS | CR | CRI | 188 | CRI | .cr | |
| Cote d'Ivoire | IV | CI | CIV | 384 | CIV | .ci | |
| Croatia | HR | HR | HRV | 191 | HRV | .hr | |
| Cuba | CU | CU | CUB | 192 | CUB | .cu | |
| Curacao | UC | CW | CUW | 531 | - | .cw | |
| Cyprus | CY | CY | CYP | 196 | CYP | .cy | |
| Czechia | EZ | CZ | CZE | 203 | CZE | .cz | |
| Denmark | DA | DK | DNK | 208 | DNK | .dk | |
| Dhekelia | DX | - | - | - | - | - | |
| Djibouti | DJ | DJ | DJI | 262 | DJI | .dj | |
| Dominica | DO | DM | DMA | 212 | DMA | .dm | |
| Dominican Republic | DR | DO | DOM | 214 | DOM | .do | |
| Ecuador | EC | EC | ECU | 218 | ECU | .ec | |
| Egypt | EG | EG | EGY | 818 | EGY | .eg | |
| El Salvador | ES | SV | SLV | 222 | SLV | .sv | |
| Equatorial Guinea | EK | GQ | GNQ | 226 | GNQ | .gq | |
| Eritrea | ER | ER | ERI | 232 | ERI | .er | |
| Estonia | EN | EE | EST | 233 | EST | .ee | |
| Ethiopia | ET | ET | ETH | 231 | ETH | .et | |
| Europa Island | EU | - | - | - | - | - | administered as part of French Southern and Antarctic Lands; no ISO codes assigned |

| ENTITY | GEC | ISO 3166 | | STANAG | INTERNET | COMMENT |
|---|---|---|---|---|---|---|
| Falkland Islands (Islas Malvinas) | FK | FK | FLK | 238 | FLK | .fk | |
| Faroe Islands | FO | FO | FRO | 234 | FRO | .fo | |
| Fiji | FJ | FJ | FJI | 242 | FJI | .fj | |
| Finland | FI | FI | FIN | 246 | FIN | .fi | |
| France | FR | FR | FRA | 250 | FRA | .fr | ISO includes metropolitan France along with the dependencies of Clipperton Island, French Guiana, French Polynesia, French Southern and Antarctic Lands, Guadeloupe, Martinique, Mayotte, New Caledonia, Reunion, Saint Pierre and Miquelon, Wallis and Futuna |
| France, Metropolitan | - | FX | FXX | 249 | - | .fx | ISO limits to the European part of France |
| French Guiana | FG | GF | GUF | 254 | GUF | .gf | |
| French Polynesia | FP | PF | PYF | 258 | PYF | .pf | |
| French Southern and Antarctic Lands | FS | TF | ATF | 260 | ATF | .tf | GEC does not include the French-claimed portion of Antarctica (Terre Adelie) |
| Gabon | GB | GA | GAB | 266 | GAB | .ga | |
| Gambia, The | GA | GM | GMB | 270 | GMB | .gm | |
| Gaza Strip | GZ | PS | PSE | 275 | PSE | .ps | ISO identifies as Occupied Palestinian Territory |
| Georgia | GG | GE | GEO | 268 | GEO | .ge | |
| Germany | GM | DE | DEU | 276 | DEU | .de | |
| Ghana | GH | GH | GHA | 288 | GHA | .gh | |
| Gibraltar | GI | GI | GIB | 292 | GIB | .gi | |
| Glorioso Islands | GO | - | - | - | - | - | administered as part of French Southern and Antarctic Lands; no ISO codes assigned |
| Greece | GR | GR | GRC | 300 | GRC | .gr | For its internal communications, the European Union recommends the use of the code EL in lieu of the ISO 3166-2 code of GR |
| Greenland | GL | GL | GRL | 304 | GRL | .gl | |
| Grenada | GJ | GD | GRD | 308 | GRD | .gd | |
| Guadeloupe | GP | GP | GLP | 312 | GLP | .gp | |
| Guam | GQ | GU | GUM | 316 | GUM | .gu | |
| Guatemala | GT | GT | GTM | 320 | GTM | .gt | |
| Guernsey | GK | GG | GGY | 831 | UK | .gg | |
| Guinea | GV | GN | GIN | 324 | GIN | .gn | |
| Guinea-Bissau | PU | GW | GNB | 624 | GNB | .gw | |

| ENTITY | GEC | ISO 3166 | | STANAG | INTERNET | COMMENT |
|---|---|---|---|---|---|---|
| Guyana | GY | GY | GUY | 328 | GUY | .gy | |
| Haiti | HA | HT | HTI | 332 | HTI | .ht | |
| Heard Island and McDonald Islands | HM | HM | HMD | 334 | HMD | .hm | |
| Holy See (Vatican City) | VT | VA | VAT | 336 | VAT | .va | |
| Honduras | HO | HN | HND | 340 | HND | .hn | |
| Hong Kong | HK | HK | HKG | 344 | HKG | .hk | |
| Howland Island | HQ | - | - | - | UMI | - | ISO includes with the US Minor Outlying Islands |
| Hungary | HU | HU | HUN | 348 | HUN | .hu | |
| Iceland | IC | IS | ISL | 352 | ISL | .is | |
| India | IN | IN | IND | 356 | IND | .in | |
| Indonesia | ID | ID | IDN | 360 | IDN | .id | |
| Iran | IR | IR | IRN | 364 | IRN | .ir | |
| Iraq | IZ | IQ | IRQ | 368 | IRQ | .iq | |
| Ireland | EI | IE | IRL | 372 | IRL | .ie | |
| Isle of Man | IM | IM | IMN | 833 | UK | .im | |
| Israel | IS | IL | ISR | 376 | ISR | .il | |
| Italy | IT | IT | ITA | 380 | ITA | .it | |
| Jamaica | JM | JM | JAM | 388 | JAM | .jm | |
| Jan Mayen | JN | - | - | - | SJM | - | ISO includes with Svalbard |
| Japan | JA | JP | JPN | 392 | JPN | .jp | |
| Jarvis Island | DQ | - | - | - | UMI | - | ISO includes with the US Minor Outlying Islands |
| Jersey | JE | JE | JEY | 832 | UK | .je | |
| Johnston Atoll | JQ | - | - | - | UMI | - | ISO includes with the US Minor Outlying Islands |
| Jordan | JO | JO | JOR | 400 | JOR | .jo | |
| Juan de Nova Island | JU | - | - | - | - | - | administered as part of French Southern and Antarctic Lands; no ISO codes assigned |
| Kazakhstan | KZ | KZ | KAZ | 398 | KAZ | .kz | |
| Kenya | KE | KE | KEN | 404 | KEN | .ke | |
| Kingman Reef | KQ | - | - | - | UMI | - | ISO includes with the US Minor Outlying Islands |
| Kiribati | KR | KI | KIR | 296 | KIR | .ki | |
| Korea, North | KN | KP | PRK | 408 | PRK | .kp | |
| Korea, South | KS | KR | KOR | 410 | KOR | .kr | |

| ENTITY | GEC | ISO 3166 | | STANAG | INTERNET | COMMENT |
|---|---|---|---|---|---|---|
| Kosovo | KV | XK | XKS | - | - | - | XK and XKS are ISO 3166 user assigned codes; ISO 3166 Maintenace Authority has not assigned codes |
| Kuwait | KU | KW | KWT | 414 | KWT | .kw | |
| Kyrgyzstan | KG | KG | KGZ | 417 | KGZ | .kg | |
| Laos | LA | LA | LAO | 418 | LAO | .la | |
| Latvia | LG | LV | LVA | 428 | LVA | .lv | |
| Lebanon | LE | LB | LBN | 422 | LBN | .lb | |
| Lesotho | LT | LS | LSO | 426 | LSO | .ls | |
| Liberia | LI | LR | LBR | 430 | LBR | .lr | |
| Libya | LY | LY | LBY | 434 | LBY | .ly | |
| Liechtenstein | LS | LI | LIE | 438 | LIE | .li | |
| Lithuania | LH | LT | LTU | 440 | LTU | .lt | |
| Luxembourg | LU | LU | LUX | 442 | LUX | .lu | |
| Macau | MC | MO | MAC | 446 | MAC | .mo | |
| Macedonia | MK | MK | MKD | 807 | FYR | .mk | |
| Madagascar | MA | MG | MDG | 450 | MDG | .mg | |
| Malawi | MI | MW | MWI | 454 | MWI | .mw | |
| Malaysia | MY | MY | MYS | 458 | MYS | .my | |
| Maldives | MV | MV | MDV | 462 | MDV | .mv | |
| Mali | ML | ML | MLI | 466 | MLI | .ml | |
| Malta | MT | MT | MLT | 470 | MLT | .mt | |
| Marshall Islands | RM | MH | MHL | 584 | MHL | .mh | |
| Martinique | MB | MQ | MTQ | 474 | MTQ | .mq | |
| Mauritania | MR | MR | MRT | 478 | MRT | .mr | |
| Mauritius | MP | MU | MUS | 480 | MUS | .mu | |
| Mayotte | MF | YT | MYT | 175 | FRA | .yt | |
| Mexico | MX | MX | MEX | 484 | MEX | .mx | |
| Micronesia, Federated States of | FM | FM | FSM | 583 | FSM | .fm | |
| Midway Islands | MQ | - | - | - | UMI | - | ISO includes with the US Minor Outlying Islands |
| Moldova | MD | MD | MDA | 498 | MDA | .md | |
| Monaco | MN | MC | MCO | 492 | MCO | .mc | |
| Mongolia | MG | MN | MNG | 496 | MNG | .mn | |

| ENTITY | GEC | ISO 3166 | | STANAG | INTERNET | COMMENT |
|---|---|---|---|---|---|---|
| Montenegro | MJ | ME | MNE | 499 | MNE | .me | |
| Montserrat | MH | MS | MSR | 500 | MSR | .ms | |
| Morocco | MO | MA | MAR | 504 | MAR | .ma | |
| Mozambique | MZ | MZ | MOZ | 508 | MOZ | .mz | |
| Myanmar | - | - | - | - | - | - | see Burma |
| Namibia | WA | NA | NAM | 516 | NAM | .na | |
| Nauru | NR | NR | NRU | 520 | NRU | .nr | |
| Navassa Island | BQ | - | - | - | UMI | - | ISO includes with the US Minor Outlying Islands |
| Nepal | NP | NP | NPL | 524 | NPL | .np | |
| Netherlands | NL | NL | NLD | 528 | NLD | .nl | |
| Netherlands Antilles | NT | | | | ANT | .an | disestablished in October 2010 this entity no longer exists; ISO deleted the codes in December 2010 |
| New Caledonia | NC | NC | NCL | 540 | NCL | .nc | |
| New Zealand | NZ | NZ | NZL | 554 | NZL | .nz | |
| Nicaragua | NU | NI | NIC | 558 | NIC | .ni | |
| Niger | NG | NE | NER | 562 | NER | .ne | |
| Nigeria | NI | NG | NGA | 566 | NGA | .ng | |
| Niue | NE | NU | NIU | 570 | NIU | .nu | |
| Norfolk Island | NF | NF | NFK | 574 | NFK | .nf | |
| Northern Mariana Islands | CQ | MP | MNP | 580 | MNP | .mp | |
| Norway | NO | NO | NOR | 578 | NOR | .no | |
| Oman | MU | OM | OMN | 512 | OMN | .om | |
| Pakistan | PK | PK | PAK | 586 | PAK | .pk | |
| Palau | PS | PW | PLW | 585 | PLW | .pw | |
| Palmyra Atoll | LQ | - | - | - | UMI | - | ISO includes with the US Minor Outlying Islands |
| Panama | PM | PA | PAN | 591 | PAN | .pa | |
| Papua New Guinea | PP | PG | PNG | 598 | PNG | .pg | |
| Paracel Islands | PF | - | - | - | - | - | |
| Paraguay | PA | PY | PRY | 600 | PRY | .py | |
| Peru | PE | PE | PER | 604 | PER | .pe | |
| Philippines | RP | PH | PHL | 608 | PHL | .ph | |
| Pitcairn Islands | PC | PN | PCN | 612 | PCN | .pn | |
| Poland | PL | PL | POL | 616 | POL | .pl | |

| ENTITY | GEC | ISO 3166 | | | STANAG | INTERNET | COMMENT |
|---|---|---|---|---|---|---|---|
| Portugal | PO | PT | PRT | 620 | PRT | .pt | |
| Puerto Rico | RQ | PR | PRI | 630 | PRI | .pr | |
| Qatar | QA | QA | QAT | 634 | QAT | .qa | |
| Reunion | RE | RE | REU | 638 | REU | .re | |
| Romania | RO | RO | ROU | 642 | ROU | .ro | |
| Russia | RS | RU | RUS | 643 | RUS | .ru | |
| Rwanda | RW | RW | RWA | 646 | RWA | .rw | |
| Saint Barthelemy | TB | BL | BLM | 652 | - | .bl | ccTLD .fr and .gp may also be used |
| Saint Helena, Ascension, and Tristan da Cunha | SH | SH | SHN | 654 | SHN | .sh | includes Saint Helena Island, Ascension Island, and the Tristan da Cunha archipelago |
| Saint Kitts and Nevis | SC | KN | KNA | 659 | KNA | .kn | |
| Saint Lucia | ST | LC | LCA | 662 | LCA | .lc | |
| Saint Martin | RN | MF | MAF | 663 | - | .mf | ccTLD .fr and .gp may also be used |
| Saint Pierre and Miquelon | SB | PM | SPM | 666 | SPM | .pm | |
| Saint Vincent and the Grenadines | VC | VC | VCT | 670 | VCT | .vc | |
| Samoa | WS | WS | WSM | 882 | WSM | .ws | |
| San Marino | SM | SM | SMR | 674 | SMR | .sm | |
| Sao Tome and Principe | TP | ST | STP | 678 | STP | .st | |
| Saudi Arabia | SA | SA | SAU | 682 | SAU | .sa | |
| Senegal | SG | SN | SEN | 686 | SEN | .sn | |
| Serbia | RI | RS | SRB | 688 | - | .rs | |
| Seychelles | SE | SC | SYC | 690 | SYC | .sc | |
| Sierra Leone | SL | SL | SLE | 694 | SLE | .sl | |
| Singapore | SN | SG | SGP | 702 | SGP | .sg | |
| Sint Maarten | NN | SX | SXM | 534 | - | .sx | |
| Slovakia | LO | SK | SVK | 703 | SVK | .sk | |
| Slovenia | SI | SI | SVN | 705 | SVN | .si | |
| Solomon Islands | BP | SB | SLB | 090 | SLB | .sb | |
| Somalia | SO | SO | SOM | 706 | SOM | .so | |
| South Africa | SF | ZA | ZAF | 710 | ZAF | .za | |
| South Georgia and the Islands | SX | GS | SGS | 239 | SGS | .gs | |

| ENTITY | GEC | ISO 3166 | | STANAG | INTERNET | COMMENT |
|---|---|---|---|---|---|---|
| South Sudan | OD | SS | SSD | 728 | - | - | IANA has designated .ss as the ccTLD for South Sudan, however it has not been activated in DNS root zone |
| Spain | SP | ES | ESP | 724 | ESP | .es | |
| Spratly Islands | PG | - | - | - | - | - | |
| Sri Lanka | CE | LK | LKA | 144 | LKA | .lk | |
| Sudan | SU | SD | SDN | 729 | SDN | .sd | |
| Suriname | NS | SR | SUR | 740 | SUR | .sr | |
| Svalbard | SV | SJ | SJM | 744 | SJM | .sj | ISO includes Jan Mayen |
| Swaziland | WZ | SZ | SWZ | 748 | SWZ | .sz | |
| Sweden | SW | SE | SWE | 752 | SWE | .se | |
| Switzerland | SZ | CH | CHE | 756 | CHE | .ch | |
| Syria | SY | SY | SYR | 760 | SYR | .sy | |
| Taiwan | TW | TW | TWN | 158 | TWN | .tw | |
| Tajikistan | TI | TJ | TJK | 762 | TJK | .tj | |
| Tanzania | TZ | TZ | TZA | 834 | TZA | .tz | |
| Thailand | TH | TH | THA | 764 | THA | .th | |
| Timor-Leste | TT | TL | TLS | 626 | TLS | .tl | |
| Togo | TO | TG | TGO | 768 | TGO | .tg | |
| Tokelau | TL | TK | TKL | 772 | TKL | .tk | |
| Tonga | TN | TO | TON | 776 | TON | .to | |
| Trinidad and Tobago | TD | TT | TTO | 780 | TTO | .tt | |
| Tromelin Island | TE | - | - | - | - | - | administered as part of French Southern and Antarctic Lands; no ISO codes assigned |
| Tunisia | TS | TN | TUN | 788 | TUN | .tn | |
| Turkey | TU | TR | TUR | 792 | TUR | .tr | |
| Turkmenistan | TX | TM | TKM | 795 | TKM | .tm | |
| Turks and Caicos Islands | TK | TC | TCA | 796 | TCA | .tc | |
| Tuvalu | TV | TV | TUV | 798 | TUV | .tv | |
| Uganda | UG | UG | UGA | 800 | UGA | .ug | |
| Ukraine | UP | UA | UKR | 804 | UKR | .ua | |
| United Arab Emirates | AE | AE | ARE | 784 | ARE | .ae | |
| United Kingdom | UK | GB | GBR | 826 | GBR | .uk | for its internal communications, the European Union recommends the use of the code UK in lieu of the ISO 3166-2 code of GB |

| ENTITY | GEC | ISO 3166 | | STANAG | INTERNET | COMMENT |
|---|---|---|---|---|---|---|
| United States | US | US | USA | 840 | USA | .us | |
| United States Minor Outlying Islands | - | UM | UMI | 581 | - | .um | ISO includes Baker Island, Howland Island, Jarvis Island, Johnston Atoll, Kingman Reef, Midway Islands, Navassa Island, Palmyra Atoll, Wake Island |
| Uruguay | UY | UY | URY | 858 | URY | .uy | |
| Uzbekistan | UZ | UZ | UZB | 860 | UZB | .uz | |
| Vanuatu | NH | VU | VUT | 548 | VUT | .vu | |
| Venezuela | VE | VE | VEN | 862 | VEN | .ve | |
| Vietnam | VM | VN | VNM | 704 | VNM | .vn | |
| Virgin Islands | VQ | VI | VIR | 850 | VIR | .vi | |
| Virgin Islands (UK) | - | - | - | - | - | .vg | see British Virgin Islands |
| Virgin Islands (US) | - | - | - | - | - | .vi | see Virgin Islands |
| Wake Island | WQ | - | - | - | UMI | - | ISO includes with the US Minor Outlying Islands |
| Wallis and Futuna | WF | WF | WLF | 876 | WLF | .wf | |
| West Bank | WE | PS | PSE | 275 | PSE | .ps | ISO identifies as Occupied Palestinian Territory |
| Western Sahara | WI | EH | ESH | 732 | ESH | .eh | |
| Western Samoa | - | - | - | - | - | .ws | see Samoa |
| World | - | - | - | - | - | - | the Factbook uses the W data code from DIAM 65-18 Geopolitical Data Elements and Related Features, Data Standard No. 3, December 1994, published by the Defense Intelligence Agency |
| Yemen | YM | YE | YEM | 887 | YEM | .ye | |
| Zaire | - | - | - | - | - | - | see Democratic Republic of the Congo |
| Zambia | ZA | ZM | ZMB | 894 | ZMB | .zm | |
| Zimbabwe | ZI | ZW | ZWE | 716 | ZWE | .zw | |

# APPENDIX E :: CROSS-REFERENCE LIST OF HYDROGRAPHIC DATA CODES

**IHO 23-4th:** *Limits of Oceans and Seas*, Special Publication 23, Draft 4th Edition 1986, published by the International Hydrographic Bureau of the International Hydrographic Organization.

**IHO 23-3rd:** *Limits of Oceans and Seas*, Special Publication 23, 3rd Edition 1953, published by the International Hydrographic Organization.

**ACIC M 49-1:** *Chart of Limits of Seas and Oceans*, revised January 1958, published by the Aeronautical Chart and Information Center (ACIC), United States Air Force.

**DIAM 65-18:** *Geopolitical Data Elements and Related Features*, Data Standard No. 4, Defense Intelligence Agency Manual 65-18, December 1994, published by the Defense Intelligence Agency.

The US Government has not yet adopted a standard for hydrographic codes similar to the Federal Information Processing Standards (FIPS) 10-4 country codes. The names and limits of the following oceans and seas are not always directly comparable because of differences in the customers, needs, and requirements of the individual organizations. Even the number of principal water bodies varies from organization to organization. *Factbook* users, for example, find the Atlantic Ocean and Pacific Ocean entries useful, but none of the following standards include those oceans in their entirety. Nor is there any provision for combining codes or overcodes to aggregate water bodies. The recently delimited Southern Ocean is not included.

### Principal Oceans and Seas of the World With Hydrographic Codes by Institution

| BODY OF WATER | IHO 23-4TH | IHO 23-3RD* | ACIC M 49-1 | DIAM 65-18 |
|---|---|---|---|---|
| Arctic Ocean | 9 | 17 | A | 5A |
| Atlantic Ocean | - | - | - | - |
| Baltic Sea | 2 | 1 | B26 | 7B |
| Eastern Mediterranean | 3.1.2 | 28 B | - | 8E |
| Indian Ocean | 5 | 45 | F | 6A |
| Mediterranean Sea | 3.1 | 28 | B11 | - |
| North Atlantic Ocean | 1 | 23 | B | 1A |
| North Pacific Ocean | 7 | 57 | D | 3A |
| Pacific Ocean | - | - | - | - |
| South Atlantic Ocean | 4 | 32 | C | 2A |
| South China and Eastern Archipelagic Seas | 6 | 49, 48 | D18 plus others | 3U plus others |
| South Pacific Ocean | 8 | 61 | E | 4A |
| Western Mediterranean | 3.1.1 | 28 A | - | 8W |

*The letters after the numbers are subdivisions, not footnotes.

# APPENDIX F :: CROSS-REFERENCE LIST OF GEOGRAPHIC NAMES

This appendix cross-references a wide variety of geographic names to the appropriate Factbook 'country' entry. Additional information is included in parentheses.

| NAME | ENTRY IN THE WORLD FACTBOOK | LATITUDE (DEG MIN) | LONGITUDE (DEG MIN) |
|---|---|---|---|
| Abidjan (capital) | Cote d'Ivoire | 5 19 N | 4 02 W |
| Abkhazia (region) | Georgia | 43 00 N | 41 00 E |
| Abu Dhabi (capital) | United Arab Emirates | 24 28 N | 54 22 E |
| Abu Musa (island) | Iran | 25 52 N | 55 03 E |
| Abuja (capital) | Nigeria | 9 12 N | 7 11 E |
| Abyssinia (former name for Ethiopia) | Ethiopia | 8 00 N | 38 00 E |
| Acapulco (city) | Mexico | 16 51 N | 99 55 W |
| Accra (capital) | Ghana | 5 33 N | 0 13 W |
| Adamstown (capital) | Pitcairn Islands | 25 04 S | 130 05 W |
| Addis Ababa (capital) | Ethiopia | 9 02 N | 38 42 E |
| Adelie Land (claimed by France; also Terre Adelie) | Antarctica | 66 30 S | 139 00 E |
| Aden (city) | Yemen | 12 46 N | 45 01 E |
| Aden, Gulf of | Indian Ocean | 12 30 N | 48 00 E |
| Admiralty Island | United States (Alaska) | 57 44 N | 134 20 W |
| Admiralty Islands | Papua New Guinea | 2 10 S | 147 00 E |
| Adriatic Sea | Atlantic Ocean | 42 30 N | 16 00 E |
| Adygey (region) | Russia | 44 30 N | 40 10 E |
| Aegean Islands | Greece | 38 00 N | 25 00 E |
| Aegean Sea | Atlantic Ocean | 38 30 N | 25 00 E |
| Afars and Issas, French Territory of the (or FTAI; former name for Djibouti) | Djibouti | 11 30 N | 43 00 E |
| Afghanestan (local name for Afghanistan) | Afghanistan | 33 00 N | 65 00 E |
| Agalega Islands | Mauritius | 10 25 S | 56 40 E |
| Agana (city; former name for Hagatna) | Guam | 13 28 N | 144 45 E |
| Ajaccio (city) | France (Corsica) | 41 55 N | 8 44 E |
| Ajaria (region) | Georgia | 41 45 N | 42 10 E |
| Akmola (city; former name for Astana) | Kazakhstan | 51 10 N | 71 30 E |
| Aksai Chin (region) | China (de facto), India (claimed) | 35 00 N | 79 00 E |

| NAME | ENTRY IN THE WORLD FACTBOOK | LATITUDE (DEG MIN) | LONGITUDE (DEG MIN) |
| --- | --- | --- | --- |
| Al Arabiyah as Suudiyah (local name for Saudi Arabia) | Saudi Arabia | 25 00 N | 45 00 E |
| Al Bahrayn (local name for Bahrain) | Bahrain | 26 00 N | 50 33 E |
| Al Imarat al Arabiyah al Muttahidah (local name for the United Arab Emirates) | United Arab Emirates | 24 00 N | 54 00 E |
| Al Iraq (local name for Iraq) | Iraq | 33 00 N | 44 00 E |
| Al Jaza'ir (local name for Algeria) | Algeria | 28 00 N | 3 00 E |
| Al Kuwayt (local name for Kuwait) | Kuwait | 29 30 N | 45 45 E |
| Al Maghrib (local name for Morocco) | Morocco | 32 00 N | 5 00 W |
| Al Urdun (local name for Jordan) | Jordan | 31 00 N | 36 00 E |
| Al Yaman (local name for Yemen) | Yemen | 15 00 N | 48 00 E |
| Aland Islands | Finland | 60 15 N | 20 00 E |
| Alaska (state) | United States | 65 00 N | 153 00 W |
| Alaska, Gulf of | Pacific Ocean | 58 00 N | 145 00 W |
| Alboran Sea | Atlantic Ocean | 36 00 N | 2 30 W |
| Aldabra Islands (Groupe d'Aldabra) | Seychelles | 9 25 S | 46 22 E |
| Alderney (island) | Guernsey | 49 43 N | 2 12 W |
| Aleutian Islands | United States (Alaska) | 52 00 N | 176 00 W |
| Alexander Archipelago (island group) | United States (Alaska) | 57 00 N | 134 00 W |
| Alexander Island | Antarctica | 71 00 S | 70 00 W |
| Alexandretta (region; former name for Iskenderun) | Turkey | 36 34 N | 36 08 E |
| Alexandria (city) | Egypt | 31 12 N | 29 54 E |
| Algiers (capital) | Algeria | 36 47 N | 2 03 E |
| Alhucemas, Penon de (island group) | Spain | 35 13 N | 3 53 W |
| Alma-Ata (city; former name for Almaty) | Kazakhstan | 43 15 N | 76 57 E |
| Almaty (former capital) | Kazakhstan | 43 15 N | 76 57 E |
| Alofi (capital) | Niue | 19 01 S | 169 55 W |
| Alphonse Island | Seychelles | 7 01 S | 52 45 E |
| Alsace (region) | France | 48 30 N | 7 20 E |
| Amami Strait | Pacific Ocean | 28 40 N | 129 30 E |
| Amindivi Islands (former name for Laccadive Islands) | India | 11 30 N | 72 30 E |
| Amirante Isles (island group; also Les Amirantes) | Seychelles | 6 00 S | 53 10 E |
| Amman (capital) | Jordan | 31 57 N | 35 56 E |

| NAME | ENTRY IN THE WORLD FACTBOOK | LATITUDE (DEG MIN) | LONGITUDE (DEG MIN) |
|---|---|---|---|
| Amsterdam (capital) | Netherlands | 52 23 N | 4 54 E |
| Amsterdam Island (Ile Amsterdam) | French Southern and Antarctic Lands | 37 52 S | 77 32 E |
| Amundsen Sea | Southern Ocean | 72 30 S | 112 00 W |
| Amur River | China, Russia | 52 56 N | 141 10 E |
| Amurskiy Liman (strait) | Pacific Ocean | 53 00 N | 141 30 E |
| Anadyrskiy Zaliv (gulf) | Pacific Ocean | 64 00 N | 177 00 E |
| Anatolia (region) | Turkey | 39 00 N | 35 00 E |
| Andaman Islands | India | 12 00 N | 92 45 E |
| Andaman Sea | Indian Ocean | 10 00 N | 95 00 E |
| Andorra la Vella (capital) | Andorra | 42 30 N | 1 30 E |
| Andros (island) | Greece | 37 45 N | 24 42 E |
| Andros Island | The Bahamas | 24 26 N | 77 57 W |
| Anegada Passage | Atlantic Ocean | 18 30 N | 63 40 W |
| Angkor Wat (ruins) | Cambodia | 13 26 N | 103 50 E |
| Anglo-Egyptian Sudan (former name for Sudan) | Sudan | 15 00 N | 30 00 E |
| Anjouan (island) | Comoros | 12 15 S | 44 25 E |
| Ankara (capital) | Turkey | 39 56 N | 32 52 E |
| Annobon (island) | Equatorial Guinea | 1 25 S | 5 36 E |
| Antananarivo (capital) | Madagascar | 18 52 S | 47 30 E |
| Antigua (island) | Antigua and Barbuda | 14 34 N | 90 44 W |
| Antipodes Islands | New Zealand | 49 41 S | 178 43 E |
| Antwerp (city) | Belgium | 51 13 N | 4 25 E |
| Aomen (local Chinese short-form name for Macau) | Macau | 22 10 N | 113 33 E |
| Aozou Strip (region) | Chad | 22 00 N | 18 00 E |
| Apia (capital) | Samoa | 13 50 S | 171 44 W |
| Aqaba, Gulf of | Indian Ocean | 29 00 N | 34 30 E |
| Arab, Shatt al (river) | Iran, Iraq | 29 57 N | 48 34 E |
| Arabian Sea | Indian Ocean | 15 00 N | 65 00 E |
| Arafura Sea | Pacific Ocean | 9 00 S | 133 00 E |
| Aral Sea | Kazakhstan, Uzbekistan | 45 00 N | 60 00 E |
| Argun River | China, Russia | 53 20 N | 121 28 E |
| Aru Sea | Pacific Ocean | 6 15 S | 135 00 E |

| NAME | ENTRY IN THE WORLD FACTBOOK | LATITUDE (DEG MIN) | LONGITUDE (DEG MIN) |
|---|---|---|---|
| As-Sudan (local name for Sudan) | Sudan | 15 00 N | 30 00 E |
| Ascension Island | Saint Helena, Ascension, and Tristan da Cunha | 7 57 S | 14 22 W |
| Ashgabat, Ashkhabad (capital) | Turkmenistan | 37 57 N | 58 23 E |
| Asmara, Asmera (capital) | Eritrea | 15 20 N | 38 53 E |
| Assumption Island | Seychelles | 9 46 S | 46 34 E |
| Astana (capital; formerly Akmola) | Kazakhstan | 51 10 N | 71 30 E |
| Asuncion (capital) | Paraguay | 25 16 S | 57 40 W |
| Asuncion Island | Northern Mariana Islands | 19 40 N | 145 24 E |
| Atacama (desert) | Chile | 23 00 S | 70 10 W |
| Atacama (region) | Chile | 24 30 S | 69 15 W |
| Athens (capital) | Greece | 37 59 N | 23 44 E |
| Attu Island | United States | 52 55 N | 172 57 E |
| Auckland (city) | New Zealand | 36 52 S | 174 46 E |
| Auckland Islands | New Zealand | 51 00 S | 166 30 E |
| Australes, Iles (island group; also Iles Tubuai) | French Polynesia | 23 20 S | 151 00 W |
| Avarua (capital) | Cook Islands | 21 12 S | 159 46 W |
| Axel Heiberg Island | Canada | 79 30 N | 90 00 W |
| Azad Kashmir (region) | Pakistan | 34 30 N | 74 00 E |
| Azarbaycan, Azerbaidzhan (local name for Azerbaijan) | Azerbaijan | 40 30 N | 47 30 E |
| Azores (islands) | Portugal | 38 30 N | 28 00 W |
| Azov, Sea of | Atlantic Ocean | 49 00 N | 36 00 E |
| Bab el Mandeb (strait) | Indian Ocean | 12 40 N | 43 20 E |
| Babuyan Channel | Pacific Ocean | 18 44 N | 121 40 E |
| Babuyan Islands | Philippines | 19 10 N | 121 40 E |
| Baffin Bay | Arctic Ocean | 73 00 N | 66 00 W |
| Baffin Island | Canada | 68 00 N | 70 00 W |
| Baghdad (capital) | Iraq | 33 21 N | 44 25 E |
| Baku (capital; also Baki, Baky) | Azerbaijan | 40 23 N | 49 51 E |
| Balabac Strait | Pacific Ocean | 7 35 N | 117 00 E |
| Balearic Islands | Spain | 39 30 N | 3 00 E |
| Balearic Sea (Iberian Sea) | Atlantic Ocean (Mediterranean Sea) | 40 30 N | 2 00 E |
| Bali (island) | Indonesia | 8 20 S | 115 00 E |

| NAME | ENTRY IN THE WORLD FACTBOOK | LATITUDE (DEG MIN) | LONGITUDE (DEG MIN) |
|---|---|---|---|
| Bali Sea | Indian Ocean | 7 45 S | 115 30 E |
| Balintang Channel | Pacific Ocean | 19 49 N | 121 40 E |
| Balintang Islands | Philippines | 19 55 N | 122 10 E |
| Balkan Peninsula | Albania, Bosnia and Herzegovina, Bulgaria, Croatia, Greece, Kosovo, Macedonia, Montenegro, Romania, Serbia, Slovenia, Turkey (European part) | 42 00 N | 23 00 E |
| Balleny Islands | Antarctica | 67 00 S | 163 00 E |
| Balochistan (region) | Pakistan | 28 00 N | 63 00 E |
| Baltic Sea | Atlantic Ocean | 57 00 N | 19 00 E |
| Bamako (capital) | Mali | 12 39 N | 8 00 W |
| Banaba (Ocean Island) | Kiribati | 0 52 S | 169 35 E |
| Banat (region) | Hungary, Romania, Serbia | 45 30 N | 21 00 E |
| Banda Sea | Pacific Ocean | 5 00 S | 128 00 E |
| Bandar Seri Begawan (capital) | Brunei | 4 53 N | 114 56 E |
| Bangka (island) | Indonesia | 2 30 S | 106 00 E |
| Bangkok (capital) | Thailand | 13 45 N | 100 31 E |
| Bangui (capital) | Central African Republic | 4 22 N | 18 35 E |
| Banjul (capital) | The Gambia | 13 28 N | 16 39 W |
| Banks Island | Australia | 10 12 S | 142 16 E |
| Banks Islands (Iles Banks) | Vanuatu | 14 00 S | 167 30 E |
| Barbuda (island) | Antigua and Barbuda | 17 38 N | 61 48 W |
| Barcelona (city) | Spain | 41 25 N | 2 13 E |
| Barents Sea | Arctic Ocean | 74 00 N | 36 00 E |
| Barranquilla (city) | Colombia | 10 59 N | 74 48 W |
| Bashi Channel | Pacific Ocean | 22 00 N | 121 00 E |
| Basilan Strait | Pacific Ocean | 6 49 N | 122 05 E |
| Basque Provinces | Spain | 43 00 N | 2 30 W |
| Bass Strait | Pacific Ocean | 39 20 S | 145 30 E |
| Bassas da India | Indian Ocean | 21 30 S | 39 50 E |
| Basse-Terre (regional capital) | France (Guadeloupe) | 16 00 N | 61 43 W |
| Basseterre (capital) | Saint Kitts and Nevis | 17 18 N | 62 43 W |
| Bastia (city) | France (Corsica) | 42 42 N | 9 27 E |
| Basutoland (former name for Lesotho) | Lesotho | 29 30 S | 28 30 E |

| NAME | ENTRY IN THE WORLD FACTBOOK | LATITUDE (DEG MIN) | LONGITUDE (DEG MIN) |
|---|---|---|---|
| Batan Islands | Philippines | 20 30 N | 121 50 E |
| Bavaria (region; also Bayern) | Germany | 48 30 N | 11 30 E |
| Beagle Channel | Atlantic Ocean | 54 53 S | 68 10 W |
| Bear Island (see Bjornoya) | Svalbard | 74 26 N | 19 05 E |
| Beaufort Sea | Arctic Ocean | 73 00 N | 140 00 W |
| Bechuanaland (former name for Botswana) | Botswana | 22 00 S | 24 00 E |
| Beijing (capital) | China | 39 56 N | 116 24 E |
| Beirut (capital) | Lebanon | 33 53 N | 35 30 E |
| Bekaa Valley | Lebanon | 34 00 N | 36 05 E |
| Belau (Palau Islands) | Palau | 7 30 N | 134 30 E |
| Belep Islands (Iles Belep) | New Caledonia | 19 45 S | 163 40 E |
| Belfast (city) | United Kingdom | 54 36 N | 5 55 W |
| Belgian Congo (former name for Democratic Republic of the Congo) | Democratic Republic of the Congo | 0 00 N | 25 00 E |
| Belgie, Belgique (local name for Belgium) | Belgium | 50 50 N | 4 00 E |
| Belgrade (capital) | Serbia | 44 50 N | 20 30 E |
| Belize City | Belize | 17 30 N | 88 12 W |
| Belle Isle, Strait of | Atlantic Ocean | 51 35 N | 56 30 W |
| Bellingshausen Sea | Southern Ocean | 71 00 S | 85 00 W |
| Belmopan (capital) | Belize | 17 15 N | 88 46 W |
| Belorussia (former name for Belarus) | Belarus | 53 00 N | 28 00 E |
| Benadir (region; former name of Italian Somaliland) | Somalia | 4 00 N | 46 00 E |
| Bengal (region) | Bangladesh, India | 24 30 N | 88 15 E |
| Bengal, Bay of | Indian Ocean | 15 00 N | 90 00 E |
| Berau, Gulf of | Pacific Ocean | 2 30 S | 132 30 E |
| Bering Island | Russia | 55 00 N | 166 30 E |
| Bering Sea | Pacific Ocean | 60 00 N | 175 00 W |
| Bering Strait | Pacific Ocean | 65 30 N | 169 00 W |
| Berkner Island | Antarctica | 79 30 S | 49 30 W |
| Berlin (capital) | Germany | 52 31 N | 13 24 E |
| Berlin, East (former name for eastern sector of Berlin) | Germany | 52 30 N | 13 33 E |
| Berlin, West (former name for western sector of Berlin) | Germany | 52 30 N | 13 20 E |
| Bern (capital) | Switzerland | 46 57 N | 7 26 E |

| NAME | ENTRY IN THE WORLD FACTBOOK | LATITUDE (DEG MIN) | LONGITUDE (DEG MIN) |
|---|---|---|---|
| Bessarabia (region) | Moldova, Romania, Ukraine | 47 00 N | 28 30 E |
| Bharat (local name for India) | India | 20 00 N | 77 00 E |
| Bhopal (city) | India | 23 16 N | 77 24 E |
| Biafra (region) | Nigeria | 5 30 N | 7 30 E |
| Big Diomede Island | Russia | 65 46 N | 169 06 W |
| Bijagos, Arquipelago dos (island group) | Guinea-Bissau | 11 25 N | 16 20 W |
| Bikini Atoll | Marshall Islands | 11 35 N | 165 23 E |
| Bilbao (city) | Spain | 43 15 N | 2 58 W |
| Bioko (island) | Equatorial Guinea | 3 30 N | 8 42 E |
| Biscay, Bay of | Atlantic Ocean | 44 00 N | 4 00 W |
| Bishkek (capital) | Kyrgyzstan | 42 54 N | 74 36 E |
| Bishop Rock | United Kingdom | 49 52 N | 6 27 W |
| Bismarck Archipelago (island group) | Papua New Guinea | 5 00 S | 150 00 E |
| Bismarck Sea | Pacific Ocean | 4 00 S | 148 00 E |
| Bissau (capital) | Guinea-Bissau | 11 51 N | 15 35 W |
| Bjornoya (Bear Island) | Svalbard | 74 26 N | 19 05 E |
| Black Forest (region) | Germany | 48 00 N | 8 15 E |
| Black Rock (island) | South Georgia and the South Sandwich Islands | 53 39 S | 41 48 W |
| Black Sea | Atlantic Ocean | 43 00 N | 35 00 E |
| Bloemfontein (judicial capital) | South Africa | 29 12 S | 26 07 E |
| Bo Hai (gulf) | Pacific Ocean | 38 00 N | 120 00 E |
| Boa Vista (island) | Cabo Verde | 16 05 N | 22 50 W |
| Bogota (capital) | Colombia | 4 36 N | 74 05 W |
| Bohemia (region) | Czech Republic | 50 00 N | 14 30 E |
| Bombay (city; see Mumbai) | India | 18 58 N | 72 50 E |
| Bonaire (island) | Netherlands | 12 10 N | 68 15 W |
| Bonifacio, Strait of | Atlantic Ocean (Mediterranean Sea) | 41 01 N | 14 00 E |
| Bonin Islands | Japan | 27 00 N | 142 10 E |
| Bonn (former capital) | Germany | 50 44 N | 7 05 E |
| Bophuthatswana (region; enclave) | South Africa | 26 30 S | 25 30 E |
| Bora-Bora (island) | French Polynesia | 16 30 S | 151 45 W |
| Bordeaux (city) | France | 44 50 N | 0 34 W |
| Borneo (island) | Brunei, Indonesia, Malaysia | 0 30 N | 114 00 E |

| NAME | ENTRY IN THE WORLD FACTBOOK | LATITUDE (DEG MIN) | LONGITUDE (DEG MIN) |
| --- | --- | --- | --- |
| Bornholm (island) | Denmark | 55 10 N | 15 00 E |
| Bosna i Hercegovina (local name for Bosnia and Herzegovina) | Bosnia and Herzegovina | 44 00 N | 18 00 E |
| Bosnia (political region) | Bosnia and Herzegovina | 44 00 N | 18 00 E |
| Bosporus (strait) | Atlantic Ocean | 41 00 N | 29 00 E |
| Bothnia, Gulf of | Atlantic Ocean | 63 00 N | 20 00 E |
| Bougainville (island) | Papua New Guinea | 6 00 S | 155 00 E |
| Bougainville Strait | Pacific Ocean | 6 40 S | 156 10 E |
| Bounty Islands | New Zealand | 47 43 S | 174 00 E |
| Bourbon Island (former name of Reunion) | Reunion | 21 06 S | 55 36 E |
| Brasilia (capital) | Brazil | 15 47 S | 47 55 W |
| Bratislava (capital) | Slovakia | 48 09 N | 17 07 E |
| Brazzaville (capital) | Republic of the Congo | 4 16 S | 15 17 E |
| Bridgetown (capital) | Barbados | 13 06 N | 59 37 W |
| Brisbane (city) | Australia | 27 28 S | 153 02 E |
| Bristol Bay | Pacific Ocean | 57 00 N | 160 00 W |
| Bristol Channel | Atlantic Ocean | 51 18 N | 3 30 W |
| Britain (see Great Britain) | United Kingdom | 54 00 N | 2 00 W |
| British Bechuanaland (region; former name for northwest South Africa) | South Africa | 27 30 S | 23 30 E |
| British Central African Protectorate (former name of Nyasaland) | Malawi | 13 30 S | 34 00 E |
| British East Africa (former name for British possessions in eastern Africa) | Kenya, Tanzania, Uganda | 1 00 N | 38 00 E |
| British Guiana (former name for Guyana) | Guyana | 5 00 N | 59 00 W |
| British Honduras (former name for Belize) | Belize | 17 15 N | 88 45 W |
| British Solomon Islands (former name for Solomon Islands) | Solomon Islands | 8 00 S | 159 00 E |
| British Somaliland (former name for northern Somalia) | Somalia | 10 00 N | 49 00 E |
| Brussels (capital) | Belgium | 50 50 N | 4 20 E |
| Bubiyan (island) | Kuwait | 29 47 N | 48 10 E |
| Bucharest (capital) | Romania | 44 26 N | 26 06 E |
| Budapest (capital) | Hungary | 47 30 N | 19 05 E |
| Buenos Aires (capital) | Argentina | 34 36 S | 58 27 W |
| Bujumbura (capital) | Burundi | 3 23 S | 29 22 E |

| NAME | ENTRY IN THE WORLD FACTBOOK | LATITUDE (DEG MIN) | LONGITUDE (DEG MIN) |
|---|---|---|---|
| Bukovina (region) | Romania, Ukraine | 48 00 N | 26 00 E |
| Byelarus (local name for Belarus) | Belarus | 53 00 N | 28 00 E |
| Byelorussia (former name for Belarus) | Belarus | 53 00 N | 28 00 E |
| Cabinda (province) | Angola | 5 33 S | 12 12 E |
| Cabot Strait | Atlantic Ocean | 47 20 N | 59 30 W |
| Caicos Islands | Turks and Caicos Islands | 21 56 N | 71 58 W |
| Cairo (capital) | Egypt | 30 03 N | 31 15 E |
| Calcutta (city) | India | 22 32 N | 88 21 E |
| Calgary (city) | Canada | 51 02 N | 114 04 W |
| California, Gulf of | Pacific Ocean | 28 00 N | 112 00 W |
| Cameroun (local name for Cameroon) | Cameroon | 6 00 N | 12 00 E |
| Campbell Island | New Zealand | 52 33 S | 169 09 E |
| Campeche, Bay of | Atlantic Ocean (Gulf of Mexico) | 20 00 N | 94 00 W |
| Canal Zone (former name for US possessions in Panama) | Panama | 9 00 N | 79 45 W |
| Canarias Sea | Atlantic Ocean | 28 00 N | 16 00 W |
| Canary Islands | Spain | 28 00 N | 15 30 W |
| Canberra (capital) | Australia | 35 17 S | 149 08 E |
| Cancun (city) | Mexico | 21 10 N | 86 50 W |
| Canton (city; now Guangzhou) | China | 23 06 N | 113 16 E |
| Canton Island (Kanton Island) | Kiribati | 2 49 S | 171 40 W |
| Cape Juby (region; former name for Southern Morocco) | Morocco | 27 53 N | 12 58 W |
| Cape of Good Hope (cape; also alternate name for Cape Province of South Africa) | South Africa | 34 15 S | 18 20 E |
| Cape Province (region; former name for Northern, Western, and Eastern Cape Provinces of South Africa) | South Africa | 31 30 S | 22 30 E |
| Cape Town (legislative capital) | South Africa | 33 57 S | 18 25 E |
| Caracas (capital) | Venezuela | 10 30 N | 66 56 W |
| Cargados Carajos Shoals | Mauritius | 16 25 S | 59 38 E |
| Caribbean Sea | Atlantic Ocean | 15 00 N | 73 00 W |
| Caroline Islands | Federated States of Micronesia, Palau | 7 30 N | 148 00 E |
| Carpatho-Ukraine (region; former name for Zakarpattya oblast') | Ukraine | 48 22 N | 23 32 E |

| NAME | ENTRY IN THE WORLD FACTBOOK | LATITUDE (DEG MIN) | LONGITUDE (DEG MIN) |
|---|---|---|---|
| Carpentaria, Gulf of | Pacific Ocean | 14 00 S | 139 00 E |
| Casablanca (city) | Morocco | 33 35 N | 7 34 W |
| Castries (capital) | Saint Lucia | 14 01 N | 61 00 W |
| Catalonia (region) | Spain | 42 00 N | 2 00 E |
| Cato Island | Australia | 23 15 S | 155 32 E |
| Caucasus (region) | Russia | 42 00 N | 45 00 E |
| Cayenne (regional capital) | France (Guyane) | 4 56 N | 52 20 W |
| Celebes (island) | Indonesia | 2 00 S | 121 00 E |
| Celebes Sea | Pacific Ocean | 3 00 N | 122 00 E |
| Celtic Sea | Atlantic Ocean | 51 00 N | 6 30 W |
| Central African Empire (former name for Central African Republic) | Central African Republic | 7 00 N | 21 00 E |
| Ceram (Seram) Sea | Pacific Ocean | 2 30 S | 129 30 E |
| Ceska Republika (local name for Czech Republic) | Czech Republic | 49 45 N | 15 30 E |
| Ceskoslovensko (former local name for Czechoslovakia) | Czech Republic, Slovakia | 49 00 N | 17 30 E |
| Cetinje (capital city) | Montenegro | 42 24 N | 18 55 E |
| Ceuta (city) | Spain | 35 53 N | 5 19 W |
| Ceylon (former name for Sri Lanka) | Sri Lanka | 7 00 N | 81 00 E |
| Chafarinas, Islas (island) | Spain | 35 12 N | 2 26 W |
| Chagos Archipelago (Oil Islands) | British Indian Ocean Territory | 6 00 S | 71 30 E |
| Challenger Deep (Mariana Trench) | Pacific Ocean | 11 22 N | 142 36 E |
| Channel Islands | Guernsey, Jersey | 49 20 N | 2 20 W |
| Charlotte Amalie (capital) | Virgin Islands | 18 21 N | 64 56 W |
| Chatham Islands | New Zealand | 44 00 S | 176 30 W |
| Chechnya (region; also Chechnia) | Russia | 43 15 N | 45 40 E |
| Cheju Strait | Pacific Ocean | 34 00 N | 126 30 E |
| Cheju-do (island) | Korea, South | 33 20 N | 126 30 E |
| Chengdu (city) | China | 30 43 N | 104 04 E |
| Chennai (city; also Madras) | India | 13 04 N | 80 16 E |
| Chesterfield Islands (Iles Chesterfield) | New Caledonia | 19 52 S | 158 15 E |
| Chihli, Gulf of (see Bo Hai) | Pacific Ocean | 38 30 N | 120 00 E |
| Chiloe (island) | Chile | 42 50 S | 74 00 W |
| China, People's Republic of | China | 35 00 N | 105 00 E |

| NAME | ENTRY IN THE WORLD FACTBOOK | LATITUDE (DEG MIN) | LONGITUDE (DEG MIN) |
| --- | --- | --- | --- |
| China, Republic of | Taiwan | 23 30 N | 121 00 E |
| Chisinau (capital; also Kishinev) | Moldova | 47 00 N | 28 50 E |
| Choiseul (island) | Solomon Islands | 7 05 S | 121 00 E |
| Choson (local name for North Korea) | North Korea | 40 00 N | 127 00 E |
| Christmas Island (Indian Ocean) | Australia | 10 25 S | 105 39 E |
| Christmas Island (Pacific Ocean; also Kiritimati) | Kiribati | 1 52 N | 157 20 W |
| Chukchi Sea | Arctic Ocean | 69 00 N | 171 00 W |
| Chuuk Islands (Truk Islands) | Federated States of Micronesia | 7 25 N | 151 47 W |
| Cilicia (region) | Turkey | 36 50 N | 34 30 E |
| Ciskei (enclave) | South Africa | 33 00 S | 27 00 E |
| Citta del Vaticano (local name for Vatican City) | Holy See | 41 54 N | 12 27 E |
| Cochin China (region) | Vietnam | 11 00 N | 107 00 E |
| Coco, Isla del (island) | Costa Rica | 5 32 N | 87 04 W |
| Cocos Islands | Cocos (Keeling) Islands | 12 30 S | 96 50 E |
| Colombo (capital) | Sri Lanka | 6 56 N | 79 51 E |
| Colon, Archipielago de (Galapagos Islands) | Ecuador | 0 00 N | 90 30 W |
| Commander Islands (Komandorskiye Ostrova) | Russia | 55 00 N | 167 00 E |
| Comores (local name for Comoros) | Comoros | 12 10 S | 44 15 E |
| Con Son (islands) | Vietnam | 8 43 N | 106 36 E |
| Conakry (capital) | Guinea | 9 31 N | 13 43 W |
| Confederatio Helvetica (local name for Switzerland) | Switzerland | 47 00 N | 8 00 E |
| Congo (Brazzaville) (former name for Republic of the Congo) | Republic of the Congo | 1 00 S | 15 00 E |
| Congo (Leopoldville) (former name for the Democratic Republic of the Congo) | Democratic Republic of the Congo | 0 00 N | 25 00 E |
| Constantinople (city; former name for Istanbul) | Turkey | 41 01 N | 28 58 E |
| Cook Strait | Pacific Ocean | 41 15 S | 174 30 E |
| Copenhagen (capital) | Denmark | 55 40 N | 12 35 E |
| Coral Sea | Pacific Ocean | 15 00 S | 150 00 E |
| Corfu (island) | Greece | 39 40 N | 19 45 E |
| Corinth (region) | Greece | 37 56 N | 22 56 E |
| Corisco (island) | Equatorial Guinea | 0 55 N | 9 19 E |

| NAME | ENTRY IN THE WORLD FACTBOOK | LATITUDE (DEG MIN) | LONGITUDE (DEG MIN) |
|---|---|---|---|
| Corn Islands (Islas del Maiz) | Nicaragua | 12 15 N | 83 00 W |
| Corocoro Island | Guyana, Venezuela | 3 38 N | 66 50 W |
| Corsica (island; also Corse) | France | 42 00 N | 9 00 E |
| Cosmoledo Group (island group; also Atoll de Cosmoledo) | Seychelles | 9 43 S | 47 35 E |
| Cotonou (former capital) | Benin | 6 21 N | 2 26 E |
| Cotopaxi (volcano) | Ecuador | 0 39 S | 78 26 W |
| Courantyne River | Guyana, Suriname | 5 57 N | 57 06 W |
| Cozumel (island) | Mexico | 20 30 N | 86 55 W |
| Crete (island) | Greece | 35 15 N | 24 45 E |
| Crimea (region) | Ukraine | 45 00 N | 34 00 E |
| Crimean Peninsula | Ukraine | 45 00 N | 34 00 E |
| Crooked Island Passage | Atlantic Ocean | 22 55 N | 74 35 W |
| Crozet Islands (Iles Crozet) | French Southern and Antarctic Lands | 46 30 S | 51 00 E |
| Cyclades (island group) | Greece | 37 00 N | 25 10 E |
| Cyrenaica (region) | Libya | 31 00 N | 22 00 E |
| Czechoslovakia (former name for the entity that subsequently split into Czechia and Slovakia) | Czechia, Slovakia | 49 00 N | 18 00 E |
| D'Entrecasteaux Islands | Papua New Guinea | 9 30 S | 150 40 E |
| Dagestan (region) | Russia | 43 00 N | 47 00 E |
| Dahomey (former name for Benin) | Benin | 9 30 N | 2 15 E |
| Daito Islands | Japan | 43 00 N | 17 00 E |
| Dakar (capital) | Senegal | 14 40 N | 17 26 W |
| Dalmatia (region) | Croatia | 43 00 N | 17 00 E |
| Daman (city; also Damao) | India | 20 10 N | 73 00 E |
| Damascus (capital) | Syria | 33 30 N | 36 18 E |
| Danger Islands (see Pukapuka Atoll) | Cook Islands | 10 53 S | 165 49 W |
| Danish Straits | Atlantic Ocean | 58 00 N | 11 00 E |
| Danish West Indies (former name for the Virgin Islands) | Virgin Islands | 18 20 N | 64 50 W |
| Danmark (local name) | Denmark | 56 00 N | 10 00 E |
| Danzig (city; former name for Gdansk) | Poland | 54 23 N | 18 40 E |
| Dao Bach Long Vi (island) | Vietnam | 20 08 N | 107 44 E |
| Dar es Salaam (capital) | Tanzania | 6 48 S | 39 17 E |

| NAME | ENTRY IN THE WORLD FACTBOOK | LATITUDE (DEG MIN) | LONGITUDE (DEG MIN) |
|---|---|---|---|
| Dardanelles (strait) | Atlantic Ocean | 40 15 N | 26 25 E |
| Davis Strait | Atlantic Ocean | 67 00 N | 57 00 W |
| Dead Sea | Israel, Jordan, West Bank | 32 30 N | 35 30 E |
| Deception Island | Antarctica | 62 56 S | 60 34 W |
| Denmark Strait | Atlantic Ocean | 67 00 N | 24 00 W |
| Desolation Islands (Isles Kerguelen) | French Southern and Antarctic Lands | 49 30 S | 69 30 E |
| Deutschland (local name for Germany) | Germany | 51 00 N | 9 00 E |
| Devils Island (Ile du Diable) | French Guiana | 5 17 N | 52 35 W |
| Devon Island | Canada | 76 00 N | 87 00 W |
| Dhaka (capital) | Bangladesh | 23 43 N | 90 25 E |
| Dhivehi Raajje (local name for Maldives) | Maldives | 3 15 N | 73 00 E |
| Dhofar (region) | Oman | 17 00 N | 54 10 E |
| Diego Garcia (island) | British Indian Ocean Territory | 7 20 S | 72 25 E |
| Diego Ramirez (islands) | Chile | 56 30 S | 68 43 W |
| Dili (capital) | Timor-Leste | 8 35 S | 125 36 E |
| Dilmun (former name for Bahrain) | Bahrain | 7 00 N | 81 00 E |
| Diomede Islands | Russia (Big Diomede), United States (Little Diomede) | 65 47 N | 169 00 W |
| Diu (region) | India | 20 42 N | 70 59 E |
| Djibouti (capital) | Djibouti | 11 30 N | 43 15 E |
| Dnieper (river) | Belarus, Russia, Ukraine (Dnyapro, Dnepr, Dnipro) | 46 30 N | 32 18 E |
| Dniester (river) | Moldova, Ukraine (Nistru, Dnister) | 46 18 N | 30 17 E |
| Dobruja (region) | Bulgaria, Romania | 43 30 N | 28 00 E |
| Dodecanese (island group) | Greece | 36 00 N | 27 05 E |
| Dodoma (city) | Tanzania | 6 11 S | 35 45 E |
| Doha (capital) | Qatar | 25 17 N | 51 32 E |
| Donets Basin | Russia, Ukraine | 48 15 N | 38 30 E |
| Douala (city) | Cameroon | 4 03 N | 9 42 E |
| Douglas (capital) | Man, Isle of | 54 09 N | 4 28 W |
| Dover, Strait of | Atlantic Ocean | 51 00 N | 1 30 E |
| Drake Passage | Atlantic Ocean, Southern Ocean | 60 00 S | 60 00 W |
| Druk Yul (local name for Bhutan) | Bhutan | 27 30 N | 90 30 E |

| NAME | ENTRY IN THE WORLD FACTBOOK | LATITUDE (DEG MIN) | LONGITUDE (DEG MIN) |
|---|---|---|---|
| Dubai, Dubayy (city) | United Arab Emirates | 25 18 N | 55 18 E |
| Dublin (capital) | Ireland | 53 20 N | 6 15 W |
| Duesseldorf (city) | Germany | 51 13 N | 6 47 E |
| Durban (city) | South Africa | 29 51 S | 31 02 E |
| Dushanbe (capital) | Tajikistan | 38 35 N | 68 48 E |
| Dutch Antilles (former name for the Netherlands Antilles) | Aruba, Curacao, Sint Maarten | 12 10 N | 68 30 W |
| Dutch East Indies (former name for Indonesia) | Indonesia | 5 00 S | 120 00 E |
| Dutch Guiana (former name for Suriname) | Suriname | 4 00 N | 56 00 W |
| Dutch West Indies (former name for the Netherlands Antilles) | Aruba, Curacao, Sint Maarten | 12 10 N | 68 30 W |
| Dzungarian Gate (valley) | China, Kazakhstan | 45 25 N | 82 25 E |
| East China Sea | Pacific Ocean | 30 00 N | 126 00 E |
| East Frisian Islands | Germany | 53 44 N | 7 25 E |
| East Germany (German Democratic Republic; former name for eastern portion of Germany) | Germany | 52 00 N | 13 00 E |
| East Korea Strait (Eastern Channel or Tsushima Strait) | Pacific Ocean | 34 00 N | 129 00 E |
| East Pakistan (former name for Bangladesh) | Bangladesh | 24 00 N | 90 00 E |
| East Siberian Sea | Arctic Ocean | 74 00 N | 166 00 E |
| Easter Island (Isla de Pascua) | Chile | 27 07 S | 109 22 W |
| Eastern Channel (East Korea Strait or Tsushima Strait) | Pacific Ocean | 34 00 N | 129 00 E |
| Eastern Samoa (former name for American Samoa) | American Samoa | 14 20 S | 170 00 W |
| Edinburgh (city) | United Kingdom | 55 57 N | 3 11 W |
| Eesti (local name for Estonia) | Estonia | 59 00 N | 26 00 E |
| Eire (local name for Ireland) | Ireland | 53 00 N | 8 00 W |
| Elba (island) | Italy | 42 46 N | 10 17 E |
| Elemi Triangle (region) | Ethiopia (claimed), Kenya (de facto), Sudan (claimed) | 5 00 N | 35 30 E |
| Ellada, Ellas (local name for Greece) | Greece | 39 00 N | 22 00 E |
| Ellef Ringnes Island | Canada | 78 00 N | 103 00 W |
| Ellesmere Island | Canada | 81 00 N | 80 00 W |
| Ellice Islands | Tuvalu | 8 00 S | 178 00 E |
| Ellsworth Land (region) | Antarctica | 75 00 S | 92 00 W |

| NAME | ENTRY IN THE WORLD FACTBOOK | LATITUDE (DEG MIN) | LONGITUDE (DEG MIN) |
|---|---|---|---|
| Elobey, Islas de (island group) | Equatorial Guinea | 0 59 N | 9 33 E |
| Enderbury Island | Kiribati | 3 08 S | 171 05 W |
| Enewetak Atoll (Eniwetok Atoll) | Marshall Islands | 11 30 N | 162 15 E |
| England (region) | United Kingdom | 52 30 N | 1 30 W |
| English Channel | Atlantic Ocean | 50 20 N | 1 00 W |
| Eniwetok Atoll (see Enewetak Atoll) | Marshall Islands | 11 30 N | 162 15 E |
| Eolie, Isole (island group) | Italy | 38 30 N | 15 00 E |
| Epirus, Northern (region) | Albania, Greece | 40 00 N | 20 30 E |
| Episkopi Cantonment (capital) | Akrotiri, Dhekelia | 34 40 N | 32 51 E |
| Ertra (local name for Eritrea) | Eritrea | 15 00 N | 39 00 E |
| Espana | Spain | 40 00 N | 4 00 W |
| Essequibo (region; claimed by Venezuela) | Guyana | 6 59 N | 58 23 W |
| Etorofu (island; also Iturup) | Russia (de facto) | 44 55 N | 147 40 E |
| Europa Island | Indian Ocean | 22 20 S | 40 22 E |
| Farquhar Group (island group; also Atoll de Farquhar) | Seychelles | 10 10 S | 51 10 E |
| Fashoda (town; also Kodok) | South Sudan | 9 53 N | 32 7 E |
| Fergana Valley | Kyrgyzstan, Tajikistan, Uzbekistan | 41 00 N | 72 00 E |
| Fernando de Noronha (island group) | Brazil | 3 51 S | 32 25 W |
| Fernando Po (island; see Bioko) | Equatorial Guinea | 3 30 N | 8 42 E |
| Filipinas (local name for the Philippines; also Pilipinas) | Philippines | 13 00 N | 122 00 E |
| Finland, Gulf of | Atlantic Ocean (Baltic Sea) | 60 00 N | 27 00 E |
| Fiume (city; former name for Rijeka) | Croatia | 45 19 N | 14 25 E |
| Florence (city) | Italy | 43 46 N | 11 16 E |
| Flores (island) | Indonesia | 8 45 S | 121 00 E |
| Flores Sea | Pacific Ocean | 7 40 S | 119 45 E |
| Florida, Straits of | Atlantic Ocean | 25 00 N | 79 45 W |
| Fongafale (largest island of Funafuti) | Tuvalu | 8 30 S | 179 12 E |
| Former Soviet Union (FSU) | Armenia, Azerbaijan, Belarus, Estonia, Georgia, Kazakhstan, Kyrgyzstan, Latvia, Lithuania, Moldova, Russia, Tajikistan, Turkmenistan, Ukraine, Uzbekistan | | |
| Formosa (island) | Taiwan | 23 30 N | 121 00 E |

| NAME | ENTRY IN THE WORLD FACTBOOK | LATITUDE (DEG MIN) | LONGITUDE (DEG MIN) |
|---|---|---|---|
| Formosa Strait (see Taiwan Strait) | Pacific Ocean | 24 00 N | 119 00 E |
| Foroyar (local name for Faroe Islands) | Faroe Islands | 62 00 N | 7 00 W |
| Fort-de-France (regional capital) | France (Martinique) | 14 36 N | 61 04 W |
| Frankfurt am Main (city) | Germany | 50 07 N | 8 41 E |
| Franz Josef Land (island group) | Russia | 81 00 N | 55 00 E |
| Freetown (capital) | Sierra Leone | 8 30 N | 13 15 W |
| French Cameroon (former name for Cameroon) | Cameroon | 6 00 N | 12 00 E |
| French Guinea (former name for Guinea) | Guinea | 11 00 N | 10 00 W |
| French Indochina (former name for French possessions in southeast Asia) | Cambodia, Laos, Vietnam | 15 00 N | 107 00 E |
| French Morocco (former name for Morocco) | Morocco | 32 00 N | 5 00 W |
| French Somaliland (former name for Djibouti) | Djibouti | 11 30 N | 43 00 E |
| French Sudan (former name for Mali) | Mali | 17 00 N | 4 00 W |
| French Territory of the Afars and Issas (or FTAI; former name for Djibouti) | Djibouti | 11 30 N | 43 00 E |
| French Togoland (former name for Togo) | Togo | 8 00 N | 1 10 E |
| French West Indies (former name for French possessions in the West Indies) | Guadeloupe, Martinique | 16 30 N | 62 00 W |
| Friendly Islands | Tonga | 20 00 S | 175 00 W |
| Frisian Islands | Denmark, Germany, Netherlands | 53 35 N | 6 40 E |
| Frunze (city; former name for Bishkek) | Kyrgyzstan | 42 54 N | 74 36 E |
| Funafuti (capital, atoll) | Tuvalu | 8 30 S | 179 12 E |
| Fundy, Bay of | Atlantic Ocean | 45 00 N | 66 00 W |
| Futuna Islands (Hoorn Islands/Iles de Horne) | Wallis and Futuna | 14 19 S | 178 05 W |
| Fyn (island) | Denmark | 55 20 N | 10 25 E |
| Gaborone (capital) | Botswana | 24 45 S | 25 55 E |
| Galapagos Islands (Archipielago de Colon) | Ecuador | 0 00 N | 90 30 W |
| Galicia (region) | Poland, Ukraine | 49 30 N | 23 00 E |
| Galilee (region) | Israel | 32 54 N | 35 20 E |
| Galleons Passage | Atlantic Ocean | 11 00 N | 60 55 W |
| Gambier Islands (Iles Gambier) | French Polynesia | 23 09 S | 134 58 W |
| Gaspar Strait | Pacific Ocean | 3 00 S | 107 00 E |

| NAME | ENTRY IN THE WORLD FACTBOOK | LATITUDE (DEG MIN) | LONGITUDE (DEG MIN) |
| --- | --- | --- | --- |
| Gdansk (city; formerly Danzig) | Poland | 54 23 N | 18 40 E |
| Geneva (city) | Switzerland | 46 12 N | 6 10 E |
| Genoa (city) | Italy | 44 25 N | 8 57 E |
| George Town (capital) | Cayman Islands | 19 20 N | 81 23 W |
| George Town (city) | Malaysia | 5 26 N | 100 16 E |
| Georgetown (capital) | Guyana | 6 48 N | 58 10 W |
| Georgetown (city) | The Gambia | 13 30 N | 14 47 W |
| German Democratic Republic (East Germany; former name for eastern portion of Germany) | Germany | 52 00 N | 13 00 E |
| German Southwest Africa (former name for Namibia) | Namibia | 22 00 S | 17 00 E |
| Germany, Federal Republic of | Germany | 51 00 N | 9 00 E |
| Gibraltar (city, peninsula) | Gibraltar | 36 11 N | 5 22 W |
| Gibraltar, Strait of | Atlantic Ocean | 35 57 N | 5 36 W |
| Gidi Pass | Egypt | 30 13 N | 33 09 E |
| Gilbert Islands | Kiribati | 1 25 N | 173 00 E |
| Glorioso Islands | Indian Ocean | 11 30 S | 47 20 E |
| Goa (state) | India | 15 20 N | 74 00 E |
| Gobi (desert) | China, Mongolia | 42 30 N | 107 00 E |
| Godthab (capital; also Nuuk) | Greenland | 64 11 N | 51 44 W |
| Golan Heights (region) | Syria | 33 00 N | 35 45 E |
| Gold Coast (former name for Ghana) | Ghana | 8 00 N | 2 00 W |
| Golfo San Jorge (gulf) | Atlantic Ocean | 46 00 S | 66 00 W |
| Golfo San Matias (gulf) | Atlantic Ocean | 41 30 S | 64 00 W |
| Good Hope, Cape of | South Africa | 34 24 S | 18 30 E |
| Goteborg (city) | Sweden | 57 43 N | 11 58 E |
| Gotland (island) | Sweden | 57 30 N | 18 33 E |
| Gough Island | Saint Helena, Ascension, and Tristan da Cunha | 40 20 S | 9 55 W |
| Graham Land (region) | Antarctica | 65 00 S | 64 00 W |
| Gran Chaco (region) | Argentina, Paraguay | 24 00 S | 60 00 W |
| Grand Bahama (island) | The Bahamas | 26 40 N | 78 35 W |
| Grand Banks (fishing ground) | Atlantic Ocean | 47 06 N | 55 48 W |
| Grand Cayman (island) | Cayman Islands | 19 20 N | 81 20 W |
| Grand Turk (capital; also Cockburn Town) | Turks and Caicos Islands | 21 28 N | 71 08 W |

| NAME | ENTRY IN THE WORLD FACTBOOK | LATITUDE (DEG MIN) | LONGITUDE (DEG MIN) |
|---|---|---|---|
| Great Australian Bight | Indian Ocean | 35 00 S | 130 00 E |
| Great Belt (strait; also Store Baelt) | Atlantic Ocean | 55 30 N | 11 00 E |
| Great Bitter Lake | Egypt | 30 20 N | 32 23 E |
| Great Britain (island) | United Kingdom | 54 00 N | 2 00 W |
| Great Channel | Indian Ocean | 6 25 N | 94 20 E |
| Great Inagua (island) | The Bahamas | 21 00 N | 73 20 W |
| Great Rift Valley | Ethiopia, Kenya | 0 30 N | 36 00 E |
| Greater Sunda Islands | Brunei, Indonesia, Malaysia | 2 00 S | 110 00 E |
| Green Islands | Papua New Guinea | 4 30 S | 154 10 E |
| Greenland Sea | Arctic Ocean | 79 00 N | 5 00 W |
| Grenadines, Northern (island group) | Saint Vincent and the Grenadines | 13 15 N | 61 12 W |
| Grenadines, Southern (island group) | Grenada | 12 07 N | 61 40 W |
| Grytviken (town; on South Georgia) | South Georgia and the South Sandwich Islands | 54 15 S | 36 45 W |
| Guadalahara (city) | Mexico | 20 40 N | 103 24 W |
| Guadalcanal (island) | Solomon Islands | 9 32 S | 160 12 E |
| Guadaloupe (islands) | France | 16 15 N | 61 33 W |
| Guadalupe, Isla de (island) | Mexico | 29 11 N | 118 17 W |
| Guangzhou (city; also Canton) | China | 23 09 N | 113 21 E |
| Guantanamo Bay (US Naval Base) | Cuba | 20 00 N | 75 08 W |
| Guatemala (capital) | Guatemala | 14 38 N | 90 31 W |
| Guine-Bissau (local name for Guinea-Bissau) | Guinea-Bissau | 12 00 N | 15 00 W |
| Guinea Ecuatorial (local name for Equatorial Guinea) | Equatorial Guinea | 2 00 N | 10 00 E |
| Guinea, Gulf of | Atlantic Ocean | 3 00 N | 2 30 E |
| Guinee (local name for Guinea) | Guinea | 11 00 N | 10 00 W |
| Gustavia (capital) | Saint Barthelemy | 17 53 N | 62 51 W |
| Guyane (local name for French Guiana) | France | 4 00 N | 53 00 W |
| Ha'apai Group (island group) | Tonga | 19 42 S | 174 29 W |
| Habomai Islands | Russia (de facto) | 43 30 N | 146 10 E |
| Hadhramaut (region) | Yemen | 15 00 N | 50 00 E |
| Hagatna (capital; formerly Agana) | Guam | 13 28 N | 144 45 E |
| Hague, The (seat of government) | Netherlands | 52 05 N | 4 18 E |
| Haifa (city) | Israel | 32 50 N | 35 00 E |

| NAME | ENTRY IN THE WORLD FACTBOOK | LATITUDE (DEG MIN) | LONGITUDE (DEG MIN) |
|---|---|---|---|
| Hainan Dao (island) | China | 19 00 N | 109 30 E |
| Haiphong (city) | Vietnam | 20 52 N | 106 41 E |
| Hala'ib Triangle (region) | Egypt (claimed), Sudan (de facto) | 22 30 N | 35 00 E |
| Halifax (city) | Canada | 44 39 N | 63 36 W |
| Halmahera (island) | Indonesia | 1 00 N | 128 00 E |
| Halmahera Sea | Pacific Ocean | 0 30 S | 129 00 E |
| Hamburg (city) | Germany | 53 34 N | 9 59 E |
| Hamilton (capital) | Bermuda | 32 17 N | 64 46 W |
| Han-guk (local name for South Korea | South Korea | 37 00 N | 127 30 E |
| Hanoi (capital) | Vietnam | 21 02 N | 105 51 E |
| Harare (capital) | Zimbabwe | 17 50 S | 31 03 E |
| Hatay (province) | Turkey | 36 30 N | 36 15 E |
| Havana (capital) | Cuba | 23 08 N | 82 22 W |
| Hawaii (island) | United States | 19 45 N | 155 45 W |
| Hawaiian Islands | United States | 21 00 N | 157 45 W |
| Hawar (island) | Bahrain | 25 40 N | 50 47 E |
| Hayastan (local name for Armenia) | Armenia | 40 00 N | 45 00 E |
| Heard Island | Heard Island and McDonald Islands | 53 06 S | 73 30 E |
| Hejaz (region) | Saudi Arabia | 24 30 N | 38 30 E |
| Helsinki (capital) | Finland | 60 10 N | 24 58 E |
| Hervey Islands (former name for Cook Islands) | Cook Islands | 21 14 S | 159 46 W |
| Herzegovina (political region) | Bosnia and Herzegovina | 44 00 N | 18 00 E |
| Hiiumaa (island) | Estonia | 58 50 N | 22 30 E |
| Hispaniola (island) | Dominican Republic, Haiti | 18 45 N | 71 00 W |
| Ho Chi Minh City (formerly Saigon) | Vietnam | 10 45 N | 106 40 E |
| Hokkaido (island) | Japan | 44 00 N | 143 00 E |
| Holland (region) | Netherlands | 52 30 N | 5 45 E |
| Hong Kong (special administrative region) | Hong Kong | 22 15 N | 114 10 E |
| Honiara (capital) | Solomon Islands | 9 26 S | 159 57 E |
| Honshu (island) | Japan | 36 00 N | 138 00 E |
| Hormuz, Strait of | Indian Ocean | 26 34 N | 56 15 E |
| Horn of Africa (region) | Djibouti, Eritrea, Ethiopia, Somalia | 8 00 N | 48 00 E |

| NAME | ENTRY IN THE WORLD FACTBOOK | LATITUDE (DEG MIN) | LONGITUDE (DEG MIN) |
|---|---|---|---|
| Horn, Cape (Cabo de Hornos) | Chile | 55 59 S | 67 16 W |
| Horne, Iles de (island group) | Wallis and Futuna | 14 19 S | 178 05 W |
| Hrvatska (local name for Croatia) | Croatia | 45 10 N | 15 30 E |
| Hudson Bay | Arctic Ocean | 60 00 N | 86 00 W |
| Hudson Strait | Arctic Ocean | 62 00 N | 71 00 W |
| Hunter Island | New Caledonia, Vanuatu | 22 24 S | 172 06 E |
| Iberian Peninsula | Portugal, Spain | 40 00 N | 5 00 W |
| Iceland Sea | Arctic Ocean | 68 00 N | 20 00 W |
| Ifni (region; former name of part of Spanish West Africa) | Morocco | 29 22 N | 10 09 W |
| Inaccessible Island | Saint Helena, Ascension, and Tristan da Cunha | 37 17 S | 12 40 W |
| Indochina (region) | Cambodia, Laos, Vietnam | 15 00 N | 107 00 E |
| Ingushetia (region) | Russia | 43 15 N | 45 00 E |
| Inhambane (region) | Mozambique | 22 30 S | 34 30 E |
| Inini (former name for French Guiana) | French Guiana | 4 00 N | 53 00 W |
| Inland Sea | Japan | 34 20 N | 133 30 E |
| Inner Hebrides (islands) | United Kingdom | 56 30 N | 6 20 W |
| Inner Mongolia (region; also Nei Mongol) | China | 42 00 N | 113 00 E |
| Ionian Islands | Greece | 38 30 N | 20 30 E |
| Ionian Sea | Atlantic Ocean | 38 30 N | 18 00 E |
| Irian Jaya (province) | Indonesia | 5 00 S | 138 00 E |
| Irish Sea | Atlantic Ocean | 53 30 N | 5 20 W |
| Iron Gate (river gorge) | Romania, Serbia | 44 41 N | 22 31 E |
| Iskenderun (region; formerly Alexandretta) | Turkey | 36 34 N | 36 08 E |
| Islamabad (capital) | Pakistan | 33 42 N | 73 10 E |
| Island (local name for Iceland) | Iceland | 65 00 N | 18 00 W |
| Islas Malvinas (island group) | Falkland Islands (Islas Malvinas) | 51 45 S | 59 00 W |
| Istanbul (city) | Turkey | 41 01 N | 28 58 E |
| Istrian Peninsula | Croatia, Slovenia | 45 00 N | 14 00 E |
| Italia (local name for Italy) | Italy | 42 50 N | 12 50 E |
| Italian East Africa (former name for Italian possessions in eastern Africa) | Eritrea, Ethiopia, Somalia | 8 00 N | 38 00 E |
| Italian Somaliland (former name for southern Somalia) | Somalia | 10 00 N | 49 00 E |

| NAME | ENTRY IN THE WORLD FACTBOOK | LATITUDE (DEG MIN) | LONGITUDE (DEG MIN) |
|---|---|---|---|
| Ittihad al-Imarat al-Arabiyah (local name for the United Arab Emirates) | United Arab Emirates | 24 00 N | 54 00 E |
| Iturup (island; see Etorofu) | Russia (de facto) | 44 55 N | 147 40 E |
| Ityop'iya (local name for Ethiopia) | Ethiopia | 8 00 N | 38 00 E |
| Ivory Coast (former name for Cote d'Ivoire) | Cote d'Ivoire | 8 00 N | 5 00 W |
| Iwo Jima (island) | Japan | 24 47 N | 141 20 E |
| Izmir (region) | Turkey | 38 25 N | 27 10 E |
| Jakarta (capital) | Indonesia | 6 10 S | 106 48 E |
| James Bay | Arctic Ocean | 54 00 N | 80 00 W |
| Jamestown (capital) | Saint Helena, Ascension, and Tristan da Cunha | 15 56 S | 5 44 W |
| Jammu (city) | India | 32 42 N | 74 52 E |
| Jammu and Kashmir (region) | India, Pakistan | 34 00 N | 76 00 E |
| Japan, Sea of | Pacific Ocean | 40 00 N | 135 00 E |
| Jars, Plain of | Laos | 19 27 N | 103 10 E |
| Java (island) | Indonesia | 7 30 S | 110 00 E |
| Java Sea | Pacific Ocean | 5 00 S | 110 00 E |
| Jerusalem (capital, proclaimed) | Israel, West Bank | 31 47 N | 35 14 E |
| Jiddah, Jeddah (city) | Saudi Arabia | 21 30 N | 39 12 E |
| Johannesburg (city) | South Africa | 26 15 S | 28 00 E |
| Joseph Bonaparte Gulf | Pacific Ocean | 14 00 S | 128 45 E |
| Juan de Fuca, Strait of | Pacific Ocean | 48 18 N | 124 00 W |
| Juan de Nova Island | Indian Ocean | 17 03 S | 42 45 E |
| Juan Fernandez, Islas de (island group) | Chile | 33 00 S | 80 00 W |
| Juba (capital) | South Sudan | 04 51 N | 31 37 E |
| Jubal, Strait of | Indian Ocean | 27 40 N | 33 55 E |
| Judaea (region) | Israel, West Bank | 31 35 N | 35 00 E |
| Jugoslavia, Jugoslavija (local names for Yugoslavia, a former Balkan federation) | Bosnia and Herzegovina, Croatia, Macedonia, Montenegro, Serbia, Slovenia | 43 00 N | 21 00 E |
| Jutland (region) | Denmark | 56 00 N | 9 15 E |
| Juventud, Isla de la (Isle of Youth) | Cuba | 21 40 N | 82 50 W |
| Kabardino-Balkaria (region) | Russia | 43 30 N | 43 30 E |
| Kabul (capital) | Afghanistan | 34 31 N | 69 12 E |
| Kaduna (city) | Nigeria | 10 33 N | 7 27 E |
| Kailas Range | China, India | 30 00 N | 82 00 E |

| NAME | ENTRY IN THE WORLD FACTBOOK | LATITUDE (DEG MIN) | LONGITUDE (DEG MIN) |
|---|---|---|---|
| Kalaallit Nunaat (local name for Greenland) | Greenland | 72 00 N | 40 00 W |
| Kalahari (desert) | Botswana, Namibia | 24 30 S | 21 00 E |
| Kalimantan (region) | Indonesia | 0 00 N | 115 00 E |
| Kaliningrad (region; formerly part of East Prussia) | Russia | 54 30 N | 21 00 E |
| Kamaran (island) | Yemen | 15 21 N | 42 34 E |
| Kamchatka Peninsula (Poluostrov Kamchatka) | Russia | 56 00 N | 160 00 E |
| Kampala (capital) | Uganda | 0 19 N | 32 25 E |
| Kampuchea (former name for Cambodia) | Cambodia | 13 00 N | 105 00 E |
| Kane Basin (portion of channel) | Arctic Ocean | 79 30 N | 68 00 W |
| Kanton Island | Kiribati | 2 49 S | 171 40 W |
| Kara Sea | Arctic Ocean | 76 00 N | 80 00 E |
| Karachevo-Cherkessia (region) | Russia | 43 40 N | 41 50 E |
| Karachi (city) | Pakistan | 24 51 N | 67 03 E |
| Karafuto (island; former name for southern Sakhalin Island) | Russia | 50 00 N | 143 00 E |
| Karakoram Pass | China, India | 35 30 N | 77 50 E |
| Karelia, Kareliya (region) | Finland, Russia | 63 15 N | 30 48 E |
| Karelian Isthmus | Russia | 60 25 N | 30 00 E |
| Karimata Strait | Pacific Ocean | 2 05 S | 108 40 E |
| Kashmir (region) | India, Pakistan | 34 00 N | 76 00 E |
| Katanga (region) | Democratic Republic of the Congo | 10 00 S | 26 00 E |
| Kathmandu (capital) | Nepal | 27 43 N | 85 19 E |
| Kattegat (strait) | Atlantic Ocean | 57 00 N | 11 00 E |
| Kauai Channel | Pacific Ocean | 21 45 N | 158 50 W |
| Kazakstan (former name for Kazakhstan) | Kazakhstan | 48 00 N | 68 00 E |
| Keeling Islands | Cocos (Keeling) Islands | 12 30 S | 96 50 E |
| Kerguelen, Iles (island group) | French Southern and Antarctic Lands | 49 30 S | 69 30 E |
| Kermadec Islands | New Zealand | 29 50 S | 178 15 W |
| Kerulen River | China, Mongolia | 48 48 N | 117 00 E |
| Khabarovsk (city) | Russia | 48 27 N | 135 06 E |
| Khanka, Lake | China, Russia | 45 00 N | 132 24 E |
| Khartoum (capital) | Sudan | 15 36 N | 32 32 E |

| NAME | ENTRY IN THE WORLD FACTBOOK | LATITUDE (DEG MIN) | LONGITUDE (DEG MIN) |
|---|---|---|---|
| Khios (island) | Greece | 38 22 N | 26 04 E |
| Khmer Republic (former name for Cambodia) | Cambodia | 13 00 N | 105 00 E |
| Khuriya Muriya Islands (Kuria Muria Islands) | Oman | 17 30 N | 56 00 E |
| Khyber Pass | Afghanistan, Pakistan | 34 05 N | 71 10 E |
| Kibris (Turkish local name for Cyprus) | Cyprus | 35 00 N | 33 00 E |
| Kiel Canal (Nord-Ostsee Kanal) | Atlantic Ocean | 53 53 N | 9 08 E |
| Kiev (city; former name for Kyiv) | Ukraine | 50 26 N | 30 31 E |
| Kigali (capital) | Rwanda | 1 57 S | 30 04 E |
| Kingston (capital) | Jamaica | 18 00 N | 76 48 W |
| Kingstown (capital) | Saint Vincent and the Grenadines | 13 09 N | 61 14 W |
| Kinshasa (capital) | Democratic Republic of the Congo | 4 18 S | 15 18 E |
| Kipros (Greek local name for Cyprus) | Cyprus | 35 00 N | 33 00 E |
| Kirghiziya, Kirgizia (former name for Kyrgyzstan) | Kyrgyzstan | 41 00 N | 75 00 E |
| Kirguizstan (local name for Kyrgyzstan) | Kyrgyzstan | 41 00 N | 75 00 E |
| Kiritimati (Christmas Island) | Kiribati | 1 52 N | 157 20 W |
| Kishinev (see Chisinau) | Moldova | 47 00 N | 28 50 E |
| Kithira Strait | Atlantic Ocean | 36 00 N | 23 00 E |
| Kobe (city) | Japan | 34 41 N | 135 10 E |
| Kodiak Island | United States | 57 49 N | 152 23 W |
| Kodok (town; also Fashoda) | South Sudan | 9 53 N | 32 7 E |
| Kola Peninsula (Kol'skiy Poluostrov) | Russia | 67 20 N | 37 00 E |
| Kolonia (town; former capital; changed to Palikir) | Federated States of Micronesia | 6 58 N | 158 13 E |
| Korea Bay | Pacific Ocean | 39 00 N | 124 00 E |
| Korea Strait | Pacific Ocean | 34 00 N | 129 00 E |
| Korea, Democratic People's Republic of | North Korea | 40 00 N | 127 00 E |
| Korea, Republic of | South Korea | 37 00 N | 127 30 E |
| Koror (capital) | Palau | 7 20 N | 134 29 E |
| Kosovo (region) | Kosovo | 42 30 N | 21 00 E |
| Kosrae (island) | Federated States of Micronesia | 5 20 N | 163 00 E |
| Kowloon (city) | Hong Kong | 22 18 N | 114 10 E |

| NAME | ENTRY IN THE WORLD FACTBOOK | LATITUDE (DEG MIN) | LONGITUDE (DEG MIN) |
|---|---|---|---|
| Kra, Isthmus of | Burma, Thailand | 10 20 N | 99 00 E |
| Krakatoa (volcano) | Indonesia | 6 07 S | 105 24 E |
| Krakow (city) | Poland | 50 03 N | 19 56 E |
| Kuala Lumpur (capital) | Malaysia | 3 10 N | 101 42 E |
| Kunashiri (island; also Kunashir) | Russia (de facto) | 44 20 N | 146 00 E |
| Kunlun Mountains | China | 36 00 N | 84 00 E |
| Kuril Islands | Russia (de facto) | 46 10 N | 152 00 E |
| Kuwait (capital) | Kuwait | 29 20 N | 47 59 E |
| Kuznetsk Basin | Russia | 54 00 N | 86 00 E |
| Kwajalein Atoll | Marshall Islands | 9 05 N | 167 20 E |
| Kyiv (capital) | Ukraine | 50 26 N | 30 31 E |
| Kyushu (island) | Japan | 33 00 N | 131 00 E |
| La Paz (administrative capital) | Bolivia | 16 30 S | 68 09 W |
| La Perouse Strait | Pacific Ocean | 45 45 N | 142 00 E |
| Labrador (peninsula, region) | Canada | 54 00 N | 62 00 W |
| Labrador Sea | Atlantic Ocean | 60 00 N | 55 00 W |
| Laccadive Islands | India | 10 00 N | 73 00 E |
| Laccadive Sea | Indian Ocean | 7 00 N | 76 00 E |
| Lagos (former capital) | Nigeria | 6 27 N | 3 24 E |
| Lahore (city) | Pakistan | 31 33 N | 74 23 E |
| Lake Erie | Atlantic Ocean | 42 30 N | 81 00 W |
| Lake Huron | Atlantic Ocean | 45 00 N | 83 00 W |
| Lake Michigan | Atlantic Ocean | 43 30 N | 87 30 W |
| Lake Ontario | Atlantic Ocean | 43 30 N | 78 00 W |
| Lake Superior | Atlantic Ocean | 48 00 N | 88 00 W |
| Lakshadweep (Laccadive Islands) | India | 10 00 N | 73 00 E |
| Lantau Island | Hong Kong | 22 15 N | 113 55 E |
| Lao (local name for Laos) | Laos | 18 00 N | 105 00 E |
| Laptev Sea | Arctic Ocean | 76 00 N | 126 00 E |
| Las Palmas (city) | Spain (Canary Islands) | 28 06 N | 15 24 W |
| Latakia (region) | Syria | 36 00 N | 35 50 E |
| Latvija (local name for Latvia) | Latvia | 57 00 N | 25 00 E |
| Lau Group (island group) | Fiji | 18 20 S | 178 30 E |
| Lefkosa (see Nicosia) | Cyprus | 35 10 N | 33 22 E |

| NAME | ENTRY IN THE WORLD FACTBOOK | LATITUDE (DEG MIN) | LONGITUDE (DEG MIN) |
|---|---|---|---|
| Leipzig (city) | Germany | 51 21 N | 12 23 E |
| Lemnos (island) | Greece | 39 54 N | 25 21 E |
| Leningrad (city; former name for Saint Petersburg) | Russia | 59 55 N | 30 15 E |
| Lesser Sunda Islands | Indonesia | 9 00 S | 120 00 E |
| Lesvos (island) | Greece | 39 15 N | 26 15 E |
| Leyte (island) | Philippines | 10 50 N | 124 50 E |
| Liancourt Rocks (claimed by Japan) | South Korea | 37 15 N | 131 50 E |
| Liaodong Wan (gulf) | Pacific Ocean | 40 30 N | 121 20 E |
| Liban (local name for Lebanon) | Lebanon | 33 50 N | 36 50 E |
| Libreville (capital) | Gabon | 0 23 N | 9 27 E |
| Lietuva (local name for Lithuania) | Lithuania | 56 00 N | 24 00 E |
| Ligurian Sea | Atlantic Ocean | 43 30 N | 9 00 E |
| Lilongwe (capital) | Malawi | 13 59 S | 33 44 E |
| Lima (capital) | Peru | 12 03 S | 77 03 W |
| Lincoln Sea | Arctic Ocean | 83 00 N | 56 00 W |
| Line Islands | Jarvis Island, Kingman Reef, Kiribati, Palmyra Atoll | 0 05 N | 157 00 W |
| Lion, Gulf of | Atlantic Ocean | 43 20 N | 4 00 E |
| Lisbon (capital) | Portugal | 38 43 N | 9 08 W |
| Little Belt (strait; also Lille Baelt) | Atlantic Ocean | 55 05 N | 9 55 E |
| Ljubljana (capital) | Slovenia | 46 03 N | 14 31 E |
| Llanos (region) | Venezuela | 8 00 N | 68 00 W |
| Lobamba (city) | Swaziland | 26 27 S | 31 12 E |
| Lombok (island) | Indonesia | 8 28 S | 116 40 E |
| Lombok Strait | Indian Ocean | 8 30 S | 115 50 E |
| Lome (capital) | Togo | 6 08 N | 1 13 E |
| London (capital) | United Kingdom | 51 30 N | 0 10 W |
| Longyearbyen (capital) | Svalbard | 78 13 N | 15 33 E |
| Lord Howe Island | Australia | 31 30 S | 159 00 E |
| Lorraine (region) | France | 48 42 N | 6 11 E |
| Louisiade Archipelago | Papua New Guinea | 11 00 S | 153 00 E |
| Lourenco Marques (city; former name for Maputo) | Mozambique | 25 56 S | 32 34 E |
| Loyalty Islands (Iles Loyaute) | New Caledonia | 21 00 S | 167 00 E |

| NAME | ENTRY IN THE WORLD FACTBOOK | LATITUDE (DEG MIN) | LONGITUDE (DEG MIN) |
|---|---|---|---|
| Luanda (capital) | Angola | 8 48 S | 13 14 E |
| Lubnan (local name for Lebanon) | Lebanon | 33 50 N | 36 50 E |
| Lubumbashi (city) | Democratic Republic of the Congo | 11 40 S | 27 28 E |
| Lusaka (capital) | Zambia | 15 25 S | 28 17 E |
| Luxembourg (capital) | Luxembourg | 49 45 N | 6 10 E |
| Luzon (island) | Philippines | 16 00 N | 121 00 E |
| Luzon Strait | Pacific Ocean | 20 30 N | 121 00 E |
| Lyakhov Islands | Russia | 73 45 N | 138 00 E |
| Macao | Macau | 22 10 N | 113 33 E |
| Macau (special administrative region) | China | 22 10 N | 113 33 E |
| Macquarie Island | Australia | 54 36 S | 158 54 E |
| Madagasikara (local name for Madagascar) | Madagascar | 20 00 S | 47 00 E |
| Maddalena, Isola | Italy | 41 13 N | 09 24 E |
| Madeira Islands | Portugal | 32 40 N | 16 45 W |
| Madras (city; see Chennai) | India | 13 04 N | 80 16 E |
| Madrid (capital) | Spain | 40 24 N | 3 41 W |
| Magellan, Strait of | Atlantic Ocean | 54 00 S | 71 00 W |
| Maghreb (region) | Algeria, Libya, Mauritania, Morocco, Tunisia | 34 00 N | 3 00 E |
| Magreb (local name for Morocco) | Morocco | 32 00 N | 5 00 W |
| Magyarorszag (local name for Hungary) | Hungary | 47 00 N | 20 00 E |
| Mahe Island | Seychelles | 4 41 S | 55 30 E |
| Maiz, Islas del (Corn Islands) | Nicaragua | 12 15 N | 83 00 W |
| Majorca Island (Isla de Mallorca) | Spain | 39 30 N | 3 00 E |
| Majuro (capital) | Marshall Islands | 7 05 N | 171 08 E |
| Makassar Strait | Pacific Ocean | 2 00 S | 117 30 E |
| Makedonija (local name for Macedonia) | Macedonia | 41 50 N | 22 00 E |
| Malabo (capital) | Equatorial Guinea | 3 45 N | 8 47 E |
| Malacca, Strait of | Indian Ocean | 2 30 N | 101 20 E |
| Malagasy Republic | Madagascar | 20 00 S | 47 00 E |
| Malay Archipelago | Brunei, Indonesia, Malaysia, Papua New Guinea, Philippines | 2 30 N | 120 00 E |
| Malay Peninsula | Malaysia, Thailand | 7 10 N | 100 35 E |
| Male (capital) | Maldives | 4 10 N | 73 31 E |

| NAME | ENTRY IN THE WORLD FACTBOOK | LATITUDE (DEG MIN) | LONGITUDE (DEG MIN) |
|---|---|---|---|
| Mallorca, Isla de (island; also Majorca) | Spain | 39 30 N | 3 00 E |
| Malmady (region) | Belgium | 50 26 N | 6 02 E |
| Malpelo, Isla de (island) | Colombia | 4 00 N | 90 30 W |
| Malta Channel | Atlantic Ocean | 56 44 N | 26 53 E |
| Malvinas, Islas (island group) | Falkland Islands (Islas Malvinas) | 51 45 S | 59 00 W |
| Mamoutzou (regional capital) | France (Mayotte) | 12 46 S | 45 13 E |
| Managua (capital) | Nicaragua | 12 09 N | 86 17 W |
| Manama (capital) | Bahrain | 26 13 N | 50 35 E |
| Manchukuo (former state) | China | 44 00 N | 124 00 E |
| Manchuria (region) | China | 44 00 N | 124 00 E |
| Manila (capital) | Philippines | 14 35 N | 121 00 E |
| Manipa Strait | Pacific Ocean | 3 20 S | 127 23 E |
| Mannar, Gulf of | Indian Ocean | 8 30 N | 79 00 E |
| Manua Islands | American Samoa | 14 13 S | 169 35 W |
| Maputo (capital) | Mozambique | 25 58 S | 32 35 E |
| Marcus Island (Minami-tori-shima) | Japan | 24 16 N | 154 00 E |
| Margarita, Isla (island) | Venezuela | 10 00 N | 64 00 W |
| Mariana Islands | Guam, Northern Mariana Islands | 16 00 N | 145 30 E |
| Marie Byrd Land (region) | Antarctica | 77 00 S | 130 00 W |
| Marigot (capital) | Saint Martin | 18 04 N | 63 05 W |
| Marion Island | South Africa | 46 51 S | 37 52 E |
| Marmara, Sea of | Atlantic Ocean | 40 40 N | 28 15 E |
| Marquesas Islands (Iles Marquises) | French Polynesia | 9 00 S | 139 30 W |
| Marseille (city) | France | 43 18 N | 5 23 E |
| Martin Vaz, Ilhas (island group) | Brazil | 20 30 S | 28 51 W |
| Martinique (island) | France | 14 40 N | 61 00 W |
| Mas a Tierra (Robinson Crusoe Island) | Chile | 33 38 S | 78 52 W |
| Mascarene Islands | Mauritius, Reunion | 21 00 S | 57 00 E |
| Maseru (capital) | Lesotho | 29 28 S | 27 30 E |
| Mata-Utu (capital) | Wallis and Futuna | 13 57 S | 171 56 W |
| Matsu (island) | Taiwan | 26 13 N | 119 56 E |
| Matthew Island | New Caledonia, Vanuatu | 22 20 S | 171 20 E |
| Mauritanie (local name for Mauritania) | Mauritania | 20 00 N | 12 00 W |

| NAME | ENTRY IN THE WORLD FACTBOOK | LATITUDE (DEG MIN) | LONGITUDE (DEG MIN) |
|---|---|---|---|
| Mayotte (islands) | France | 12 50 S | 45 10 E |
| Mazatlan (city) | Mexico | 23 13 N | 106 25 W |
| Mbabane (capital) | Swaziland | 26 18 S | 31 06 E |
| McDonald Islands | Heard Island and McDonald Islands | 53 06 S | 73 30 E |
| Mecca (city) | Saudi Arabia | 21 27 N | 39 49 E |
| Mediterranean Sea | Atlantic Ocean | 36 00 N | 15 00 E |
| Melbourne (city) | Australia | 37 49 S | 144 58 E |
| Melilla (exclave) | Spain | 35 19 N | 2 58 W |
| Memel (region) | Lithuania | 55 43 N | 21 30 E |
| Mesopotamia (region) | Iraq | 33 00 N | 44 00 E |
| Messina, Strait of | Atlantic Ocean | 38 15 N | 15 35 E |
| Mexico City (capital) | Mexico | 19 24 N | 99 09 W |
| Mexico, Gulf of | Atlantic Ocean | 25 00 N | 90 00 W |
| Middle Congo (former name for Republic of the Congo) | Republic of the Congo | 1 00 S | 15 00 E |
| Milan (city) | Italy | 45 28 N | 9 11 E |
| Milwaukee Deep (Puerto Rico Trench) | Atlantic Ocean | 19 55 N | 65 27 W |
| Minami-tori-shima (Marcus Island) | Japan | 24 16 N | 154 00 E |
| Mindanao (island) | Philippines | 8 00 N | 125 00 E |
| Mindanao Sea | Pacific Ocean | 9 15 N | 124 30 E |
| Mindoro (island) | Philippines | 12 50 N | 121 05 E |
| Mindoro Strait | Pacific Ocean | 12 20 N | 120 40 E |
| Mingrelia (region) | Georgia | 42 30 N | 41 52 E |
| Minicoy Island | India | 8 17 N | 73 02 E |
| Minorca Island (Isla de Menorca) | Spain | 40 00 N | 4 00 E |
| Minsk (capital) | Belarus | 53 54 N | 27 34 E |
| Misr (local name for Egypt) | Egypt | 27 00 N | 30 00 E |
| Mitla Pass | Egypt | 30 02 N | 32 54 E |
| Mocambique (local name for Mozambique) | Mozambique | 18 15 S | 35 00 E |
| Mogadishu (capital) | Somalia | 2 04 N | 45 22 E |
| Moldavia (region) | Moldova, Romania | 47 00 N | 29 00 E |
| Molucca Sea | Pacific Ocean | 2 00 N | 127 00 E |
| Moluccas (Spice Islands) | Indonesia | 2 00 S | 128 00 E |
| Mombasa (city) | Kenya | 4 03 S | 39 40 E |

| NAME | ENTRY IN THE WORLD FACTBOOK | LATITUDE (DEG MIN) | LONGITUDE (DEG MIN) |
|---|---|---|---|
| Mona Passage | Atlantic Ocean | 18 30 N | 67 45 W |
| Monaco (capital) | Monaco | 43 44 N | 7 25 E |
| Mongol Uls (local name for Mongolia) | Mongolia | 46 00 N | 105 00 E |
| Monrovia (capital) | Liberia | 6 18 N | 10 47 W |
| Monterrey (city) | Mexico | 25 40 N | 100 19 W |
| Montevideo (capital) | Uruguay | 34 53 S | 56 11 W |
| Montreal (city) | Canada | 45 31 N | 73 34 W |
| Moravia (region) | Czech Republic | 49 30 N | 17 00 E |
| Moravian Gate (pass) | Czech Republic | 49 35 N | 17 50 E |
| Moroni (capital) | Comoros | 11 41 S | 43 16 E |
| Mortlock Islands (Nomoi Islands) | Federated States of Micronesia | 5 30 N | 153 40 E |
| Moscow (capital) | Russia | 55 45 N | 37 35 E |
| Mount Pinatubo (volcano) | Philippines | 15 08 N | 120 21 E |
| Mozambique Channel | Indian Ocean | 19 00 S | 41 00 E |
| Mumbai (city; also Bombay) | India | 18 58 N | 72 50 E |
| Munich, Muenchen (city) | Germany | 48 08 N | 11 35 E |
| Muritaniyah (local name for Mauritania) | Mauritania | 20 00 N | 12 00 W |
| Musandam Peninsula | Oman, United Arab Emirates | 26 18 N | 56 24 E |
| Muscat (capital) | Oman | 23 37 N | 58 35 E |
| Muscat and Oman (former name for Oman) | Oman | 21 00 N | 57 00 E |
| Myanma, Myanmar | Burma | 22 00 N | 98 00 E |
| N'Djamena (capital) | Chad | 12 07 N | 15 03 E |
| Nagorno-Karabakh (region) | Azerbaijan | 40 00 N | 46 40 E |
| Nairobi (capital) | Kenya | 1 17 S | 36 49 E |
| Namib (desert) | Namibia | 24 00 S | 15 00 E |
| Nampo-shoto (island group) | Japan | 30 00 N | 140 00 E |
| Nan Madol (ruins) | Federated States of Micronesia | 6 85 N | 158 35 E |
| Naples (city) | Italy | 40 51 N | 14 15 E |
| Nassau (capital) | The Bahamas | 25 05 N | 77 21 W |
| Natal (region) | South Africa | 29 00 S | 30 25 E |
| Natuna Besar Islands | Indonesia | 3 30 N | 102 30 E |
| Natuna Sea | Pacific Ocean | 3 30 N | 108 00 E |
| Naxcivan (region) | Azerbaijan | 39 20 N | 45 20 E |
| Naxos (island) | Greece | 37 05 N | 25 30 E |

| NAME | ENTRY IN THE WORLD FACTBOOK | LATITUDE (DEG MIN) | LONGITUDE (DEG MIN) |
|---|---|---|---|
| Nederland (local name for the Netherlands) | Netherlands | 52 30 N | 5 45 E |
| Nederlandse Antillen (local name for the former Netherlands Antilles) | Curacao, Sint Maarten | 12 15 N | 68 45 W |
| Negev (region) | Israel | 30 30 N | 34 55 E |
| Negros (island) | Philippines | 10 00 N | 123 00 E |
| Nejd (region) | Saudi Arabia | 24 05 N | 45 15 E |
| Netherlands Antilles (former name of Dutch Caribbean dependencies) | Curacao, Sint Maarten | 12 15 N | 68 45 W |
| Netherlands East Indies (former name for Indonesia) | Indonesia | 5 00 S | 120 00 E |
| Netherlands Guiana (former name for Suriname) | Suriname | 4 00 N | 56 00 W |
| Nevis (island) | Saint Kitts and Nevis | 17 09 N | 62 35 W |
| New Britain (island) | Papua New Guinea | 6 00 S | 150 00 E |
| New Delhi (capital) | India | 28 36 N | 77 12 E |
| New Guinea (island) | Indonesia, Papua New Guinea | 5 00 S | 140 00 E |
| New Hebrides (island group) | Vanuatu | 16 00 S | 167 00 E |
| New Ireland (island) | Papua New Guinea | 3 20 N | 152 00 E |
| New Siberian Islands | Russia | 75 00 N | 142 00 E |
| New Territories (mainland region) | Hong Kong | 22 24 N | 114 10 E |
| Newfoundland (island, with mainland area, and a province) | Canada | 52 00 N | 56 00 W |
| Niamey (capital) | Niger | 13 31 N | 2 07 E |
| Nicobar Islands | India | 8 00 N | 93 30 E |
| Nicosia (capital; also Lefkosia) | Cyprus | 35 10 N | 33 22 E |
| Nightingale Island | Saint Helena, Ascension, and Tristan da Cunha | 37 25 S | 12 30 W |
| Nihon, Nippon (local name for Japan) | Japan | 36 00 N | 138 00 E |
| Nomoi Islands (Mortlock Islands) | Federated States of Micronesia | 5 30 N | 153 40 E |
| Norge (local name for Norway) | Norway | 62 00 N | 10 00 E |
| Norman Isles (Channel Islands) | Guernsey, Jersey | 49 20 N | 2 20 W |
| North Atlantic Ocean | Atlantic Ocean | 30 00 N | 45 00 W |
| North Channel | Atlantic Ocean | 55 10 N | 5 40 W |
| North Frisian Islands | Denmark, Germany | 54 50 N | 8 12 E |
| North Greenland Sea | Arctic Ocean | 78 00 N | 5 00 W |
| North Island | New Zealand | 39 00 S | 176 00 E |

| NAME | ENTRY IN THE WORLD FACTBOOK | LATITUDE (DEG MIN) | LONGITUDE (DEG MIN) |
| --- | --- | --- | --- |
| North Ossetia (region) | Russia | 43 00 N | 44 10 E |
| North Pacific Ocean | Pacific Ocean | 30 00 N | 165 00 W |
| North Sea | Atlantic Ocean | 56 00 N | 4 00 E |
| North Vietnam (former name for northern portion of Vietnam) | Vietnam | 23 00 N | 106 00 E |
| North Yemen (Yemen Arab Republic; now part of Yemen) | Yemen | 15 00 N | 44 00 E |
| Northeast Providence Channel | Atlantic Ocean | 25 40 N | 77 09 W |
| Northern Areas | Pakistan | 36 0 N | 75 0 E |
| Northern Cyprus (region) | Cyprus | 35 15 N | 33 44 E |
| Northern Epirus (region) | Albania, Greece | 40 00 N | 20 30 E |
| Northern Grenadines (political region) | Saint Vincent and the Grenadines | 12 45 N | 61 15 W |
| Northern Ireland | United Kingdom | 54 40 N | 6 45 W |
| Northern Rhodesia (former name for Zambia) | Zambia | 15 00 S | 30 00 E |
| Northwest Passages | Arctic Ocean | 74 40 N | 100 00 W |
| Norwegian Sea | Atlantic Ocean | 66 00 N | 6 00 E |
| Nouakchott (capital) | Mauritania | 18 06 N | 15 57 W |
| Noumea (capital) | New Caledonia | 22 16 S | 166 27 E |
| Nouvelle-Caledonie (local name for New Caledonia) | New Caledonia | 21 30 S | 165 30 E |
| Nouvelles Hebrides (former name for Vanuatu) | Vanuatu | 16 00 S | 167 00 E |
| Novaya Zemlya (islands) | Russia | 74 00 N | 57 00 E |
| Nubia (region) | Egypt, Sudan | 20 30 N | 33 00 E |
| Nuku'alofa (capital) | Tonga | 21 08 S | 175 12 W |
| Nunavut (region) | Canada | 72 00 N | 90 00 W |
| Nuuk (capital; also Godthab) | Greenland | 64 11 N | 51 44 W |
| Nyasaland (former name for Malawi) | Malawi | 13 30 S | 34 00 E |
| Nyassa (region) | Mozambique | 13 30 S | 37 00 E |
| Oahu (island) | United States (Hawaii) | 21 30 N | 158 00 W |
| Ocean Island (Banaba) | Kiribati | 0 52 S | 169 35 E |
| Ocean Island (Kure Island) | United States | 28 25 N | 178 20 W |
| Oesterreich (local name for Austria) | Austria | 47 20 N | 13 20 E |
| Ogaden (region) | Ethiopia, Somalia | 7 00 N | 46 00 E |

| NAME | ENTRY IN THE WORLD FACTBOOK | LATITUDE (DEG MIN) | LONGITUDE (DEG MIN) |
|---|---|---|---|
| Oil Islands (Chagos Archipelago) | British Indian Ocean Territory | 6 00 S | 71 30 E |
| Okhotsk, Sea of | Pacific Ocean | 53 00 N | 150 00 E |
| Okinawa (island group) | Japan | 26 30 N | 128 00 E |
| Oland (island) | Sweden | 56 45 N | 16 40 E |
| Oman, Gulf of | Indian Ocean | 24 30 N | 58 30 E |
| Ombai Strait | Pacific Ocean | 8 30 S | 125 00 E |
| Oran (city) | Algeria | 35 43 N | 0 43 W |
| Orange River Colony (region; former name of Free State Province of South Africa) | South Africa | 28 20 S | 26 40 E |
| Oranjestad (capital) | Aruba | 12 33 N | 70 06 W |
| Oresund (The Sound) (strait) | Atlantic Ocean | 55 50 N | 12 40 E |
| Orkney Islands | United Kingdom | 59 00 N | 3 00 W |
| Osaka (city) | Japan | 34 42 N | 135 30 E |
| Oslo (capital) | Norway | 59 55 N | 10 45 E |
| Osumi Strait (Van Diemen Strait) | Pacific Ocean | 31 00 N | 131 00 E |
| Otranto, Strait of | Atlantic Ocean | 40 00 N | 19 00 E |
| Ottawa (capital) | Canada | 45 25 N | 75 40 W |
| Ouagadougou (capital) | Burkina Faso | 12 22 N | 1 31 W |
| Outer Hebrides (islands) | United Kingdom | 57 45 N | 7 00 W |
| Outer Mongolia (region) | Mongolia | 46 00 N | 105 00 E |
| P'yongyang (capital) | North Korea | 39 01 N | 125 45 E |
| Pacific Islands, Trust Territory of the (former name of a large area of the western North Pacific Ocean) | Marshall Islands, Federated States of Micronesia, Northern Mariana Islands, Palau | 10 00 N | 155 00 E |
| Pagan (island) | Northern Mariana Islands | 18 08 N | 145 47 E |
| Pago Pago (capital) | American Samoa | 14 16 S | 170 42 W |
| Palawan (island) | Philippines | 9 30 N | 118 30 E |
| Palermo (city) | Italy | 38 07 N | 13 21 E |
| Palestine (region) | Israel, West Bank | 32 00 N | 35 15 E |
| Palikir (capital) | Federated States of Micronesia | 6 55 N | 158 08 E |
| Palk Strait | Indian Ocean | 10 00 N | 79 45 E |
| Pamirs (mountains) | China, Tajikistan | 38 00 N | 73 00 E |
| Pampas (region) | Argentina | 35 00 S | 63 00 W |
| Panama (capital) | Panama | 8 58 N | 79 32 W |
| Panama Canal | Panama | 9 00 N | 79 45 W |

| NAME | ENTRY IN THE WORLD FACTBOOK | LATITUDE (DEG MIN) | LONGITUDE (DEG MIN) |
|---|---|---|---|
| Panama, Gulf of | Pacific Ocean | 8 00 N | 79 30 W |
| Panay (island) | Philippines | 11 15 N | 122 30 E |
| Pantelleria, Isola di (island) | Italy | 36 47 N | 12 00 E |
| Papeete (capital) | French Polynesia | 17 32 S | 149 34 W |
| Paramaribo (capital) | Suriname | 5 50 N | 55 10 W |
| Parece Vela (island) | Japan | 20 20 N | 136 00 E |
| Paris (capital) | France | 48 52 N | 2 20 E |
| Pascua, Isla de (Easter Island) | Chile | 27 07 S | 109 22 W |
| Pashtunistan (region) | Afghanistan, Pakistan | 32 00 N | 69 00 E |
| Passion, Ile de la (island) | Clipperton Island | 10 17 N | 109 13 W |
| Patagonia (region) | Argentina | 48 00 S | 61 00 W |
| Peking (see Beijing) | China | 39 56 N | 116 24 E |
| Pelagian Islands (Isole Pelagie) | Italy | 35 40 N | 12 40 E |
| Peleliu (Beliliou) (island) | Palau | 7 01 N | 134 15 E |
| Peloponnese (peninsula) | Greece | 37 30 N | 22 25 E |
| Pemba Island | Tanzania | 5 20 S | 39 45 E |
| Penang Island | Malaysia | 5 23 N | 100 15 E |
| Pentland Firth (channel) | Atlantic Ocean | 58 44 N | 3 13 W |
| Perim (island) | Yemen | 12 39 N | 43 25 E |
| Perouse Strait, La | Pacific Ocean | 44 45 N | 142 00 E |
| Persia (former name for Iran) | Iran | 32 00 N | 53 00 E |
| Persian Gulf | Indian Ocean | 27 00 N | 51 00 E |
| Perth (city) | Australia | 31 56 S | 115 50 E |
| Pescadores (islands) | Taiwan | 23 30 N | 119 30 E |
| Peshawar (city) | Pakistan | 34 01 N | 71 40 E |
| Peter I Island | Antarctica | 68 48 S | 90 35 W |
| Petrograd (city; former name for Saint Petersburg) | Russia | 59 55 N | 30 15 E |
| Philip Island | Norfolk Island | 29 08 S | 167 57 E |
| Philippine Sea | Pacific Ocean | 20 00 N | 134 00 E |
| Philipsburg (capital) | Sint Maarten | 18 1 N | 63 2 W |
| Phnom Penh (capital) | Cambodia | 11 33 N | 104 55 E |
| Phoenix Islands | Kiribati | 3 30 S | 172 00 W |
| Pinatubo, Mount (volcano) | Philippines | 15 08 N | 120 21 E |

| NAME | ENTRY IN THE WORLD FACTBOOK | LATITUDE (DEG MIN) | LONGITUDE (DEG MIN) |
|---|---|---|---|
| Pines, Isle of (island; former name for Isla de la Juventud) | Cuba | 21 40 N | 82 50 W |
| Pleasant Island | Nauru | 0 32 S | 166 55 E |
| Plymouth (capital) | Montserrat | 16 44 N | 62 14 W |
| Podgorica (administrative capital) | Montenegro | 42 26 N | 19 16 E |
| Polska (local name) | Poland | 52 00 N | 20 00 E |
| Polynesie Francaise (local name for French Polynesia) | French Polynesia | 15 00 S | 140 00 W |
| Pomerania (region) | Germany, Poland | 53 40 N | 15 35 E |
| Ponape (Pohnpei) (island) | Federated States of Micronesia | 6 55 N | 158 15 E |
| Port Louis (capital) | Mauritius | 20 10 S | 57 30 E |
| Port Moresby (capital) | Papua New Guinea | 9 30 S | 147 10 E |
| Port-au-Prince (capital) | Haiti | 18 32 N | 72 20 W |
| Port-of-Spain (capital) | Trinidad and Tobago | 10 39 N | 61 31 W |
| Port-Vila (capital) | Vanuatu | 17 44 S | 168 19 E |
| Porto-Novo (capital) | Benin | 6 29 N | 2 37 E |
| Portuguese East Africa (former name for Mozambique) | Mozambique | 18 15 S | 35 00 E |
| Portuguese Guinea (former name for Guinea-Bissau) | Guinea-Bissau | 12 00 N | 15 00 W |
| Portuguese Timor (former name for Timor-Leste) | Timor-Leste | 9 00 S | 126 00 E |
| Poznan (city) | Poland | 52 25 N | 16 55 E |
| Prague (capital) | Czech Republic | 50 05 N | 14 28 E |
| Praia (capital) | Cabo Verde | 14 55 N | 23 31 W |
| Prathet Thai (local name for Thailand) | Thailand | 15 00 N | 100 00 E |
| Pretoria (administrative capital) | South Africa | 25 42 S | 28 13 E |
| Prevlaka peninsula | Croatia | 42 24 N | 18 31 E |
| Pribilof Islands | United States | 57 00 N | 170 00 W |
| Prince Edward Island | Canada | 46 20 N | 63 20 W |
| Prince Edward Islands | South Africa | 46 35 S | 38 00 E |
| Prince Patrick Island | Canada | 76 30 N | 119 00 W |
| Principe (island) | Sao Tome and Principe | 1 38 N | 7 25 E |
| Pristina, Prishtina, Prishtine (capital) | Kosovo | 42 40 N | 21 10 E |
| Prussia (region) | Germany, Poland, Russia | 53 00 N | 14 00 E |
| Pukapuka Atoll | Cook Islands | 10 53 S | 165 49 W |

| NAME | ENTRY IN THE WORLD FACTBOOK | LATITUDE (DEG MIN) | LONGITUDE (DEG MIN) |
|---|---|---|---|
| Punjab (region) | India, Pakistan | 30 50 N | 73 30 E |
| Puntland (region) | Somalia | 8 21 N | 49 08 E |
| Qazaqstan (local name for Kazakhstan) | Kazakhstan | 48 00 N | 68 00 E |
| Qita Ghazzah (local name Gaza Strip) | Gaza Strip | 31 25 N | 34 20 E |
| Quebec (city) | Canada | 46 48 N | 71 15 W |
| Queen Charlotte Islands | Canada | 53 00 N | 132 00 W |
| Queen Elizabeth Islands | Canada | 78 00 N | 95 00 W |
| Queen Maud Land (claimed by Norway) | Antarctica | 73 30 S | 12 00 E |
| Quemoy (island) | Taiwan | 24 27 N | 118 23 E |
| Quito (capital) | Ecuador | 0 13 S | 78 30 W |
| Rabat (capital) | Morocco | 34 02 N | 6 51 W |
| Ralik Chain (island group) | Marshall Islands | 8 00 N | 167 00 E |
| Rangoon (capital; also Yangon) | Burma | 16 47 N | 96 10 E |
| Rapa Nui (Easter Island) | Chile | 27 07 S | 109 22 W |
| Ratak Chain (island group) | Marshall Islands | 9 00 N | 171 00 E |
| Red Sea | Indian Ocean | 20 00 N | 38 00 E |
| Redonda (island) | Antigua and Barbuda | 16 55 N | 62 19 W |
| Republica Dominicana (local name for Dominican Republic) | Dominican Republic | 19 00 N | 70 40 W |
| Republique Centrafricain (local name for Central African Republic) | Central African Republic | 7 00 N | 21 00 E |
| Republique Francaise (local name for France) | France | 46 00 N | 2 00 E |
| Republique Gabonaise (local name for Gabon) | Gabon | 1 00 S | 11 45 E |
| Republique Rwandaise (local name for Rwanda) | Rwanda | 2 00 S | 30 00 E |
| Republique Togolaise (local name for Togo) | Togo | 8 00 N | 1 10 E |
| Reunion (island) | France | 21 06 S | 55 36 E |
| Revillagigedo Island | United States (Alaska) | 55 35 N | 131 06 W |
| Revillagigedo Islands | Mexico | 19 00 N | 112 45 W |
| Reykjavik (capital) | Iceland | 64 09 N | 21 57 W |
| Rhodes (island) | Greece | 36 10 N | 28 00 E |
| Rhodesia, Northern (former name for Zambia) | Zambia | 15 00 S | 30 00 E |
| Rhodesia, Southern (former name for Zimbabwe) | Zimbabwe | 20 00 S | 30 00 E |

| NAME | ENTRY IN THE WORLD FACTBOOK | LATITUDE (DEG MIN) | LONGITUDE (DEG MIN) |
| --- | --- | --- | --- |
| Riga (capital) | Latvia | 56 57 N | 24 06 E |
| Riga, Gulf of | Atlantic Ocean | 57 30 N | 23 30 E |
| Rio de Janiero (city) | Brazil | 22 55 S | 43 17 W |
| Rio de la Plata (gulf) | Atlantic Ocean | 35 00 S | 59 00 W |
| Rio de Oro (region) | Western Sahara | 23 45 N | 15 45 W |
| Rio Muni (mainland region) | Equatorial Guinea | 1 30 N | 10 00 E |
| Riyadh (capital) | Saudi Arabia | 24 38 N | 46 43 E |
| Road Town (capital) | British Virgin Islands | 18 27 N | 64 37 W |
| Robinson Crusoe Island (Mas a Tierra) | Chile | 33 38 S | 78 52 W |
| Rocas, Atol das (island) | Brazil | 3 51 S | 33 49 W |
| Rockall (island) | United Kingdom | 57 35 N | 13 48 W |
| Rodrigues (island) | Mauritius | 19 42 S | 63 25 E |
| Rome (capital) | Italy | 41 54 N | 12 29 E |
| Roncador Cay (island) | Colombia | 13 32 N | 80 03 W |
| Roosevelt Island | Antarctica | 79 30 S | 162 00 W |
| Roseau (capital) | Dominica | 15 18 N | 61 24 W |
| Ross Dependency (claimed by New Zealand) | Antarctica | 80 00 S | 180 00 E |
| Ross Island | Antarctica | 81 30 S | 175 00 W |
| Ross Sea | Antarctica, Southern Ocean | 76 00 S | 175 00 W |
| Rossiya (local name for Russia) | Russia | 60 00 N | 100 00 E |
| Rota (island) | Northern Mariana Islands | 14 10 N | 145 12 E |
| Rotuma (island) | Fiji | 12 30 S | 177 05 E |
| Ruanda (former name for Rwanda) | Rwanda | 2 00 S | 30 00 E |
| Rub al Khali (desert) | Saudi Arabia | 19 30 N | 49 00 E |
| Rumelia (region) | Albania, Bulgaria, Macedonia | 42 00 N | 22 30 E |
| Ruthenia (region; former name for Carpatho-Ukraine) | Ukraine | 48 22 N | 23 32 E |
| Ryukyu Islands | Japan | 26 30 N | 128 00 E |
| Saar (region) | Germany | 49 25 N | 7 00 E |
| Saaremaa (island) | Estonia | 58 25 N | 22 30 E |
| Saba (island) | Netherlands | 17 38 N | 63 10 W |
| Sabah (state) | Malaysia | 5 20 N | 117 10 E |
| Sable Island | Canada | 43 55 N | 59 50 W |
| Safety Islands (Iles du Salut) | French Guiana | 5 20 N | 52 37 W |

| NAME | ENTRY IN THE WORLD FACTBOOK | LATITUDE (DEG MIN) | LONGITUDE (DEG MIN) |
|---|---|---|---|
| Sahara Occidental (former name for Western Sahara) | Western Sahara | 24 30 N | 13 00 W |
| Sahel (region) | Burkina Faso, Chad, The Gambia, Guinea- Bissau, Mali, Mauritania, Niger, Senegal | 15 00 N | 8 00 W |
| Saigon (city; former name for Ho Chi Minh City) | Vietnam | 10 45 N | 106 40 E |
| Saint Brandon (Cargados Carajos Shoals) | Mauritius | 16 25 S | 59 38 E |
| Saint Christopher (island) | Saint Kitts and Nevis | 17 20 N | 62 45 W |
| Saint Christopher and Nevis | Saint Kitts and Nevis | 17 20 N | 62 45 W |
| Saint Eustatius (island) | Netherlands | 17 30 N | 63 00 W |
| Saint George's (capital) | Grenada | 12 03 N | 61 45 W |
| Saint George's Channel | Atlantic Ocean | 52 00 N | 6 00 W |
| Saint Helena Island | Saint Helena, Ascension, and Tristan da Cunha | 15 57 S | 5 42 W |
| Saint Helens, Mount (volcano) | United States | 46 15 N | 122 12 W |
| Saint Helier (capital) | Jersey | 49 12 N | 2 07 W |
| Saint John (city) | Canada (New Brunswick) | 45 16 N | 66 04 W |
| Saint John's (capital) | Antigua and Barbuda | 17 06 N | 61 51 W |
| Saint Lawrence Island | United States | 49 30 N | 67 00 W |
| Saint Lawrence Seaway | Atlantic Ocean | 49 15 N | 67 00 W |
| Saint Lawrence, Gulf of | Atlantic Ocean | 48 00 N | 62 00 W |
| Saint Paul Island | Canada | 47 12 N | 60 09 W |
| Saint Paul Island (Ile Saint-Paul) | French Southern and Antarctic Lands | 38 43 S | 77 29 E |
| Saint Peter and Saint Paul Rocks (Penedos de Sao Pedro e Sao Paulo) | Brazil | 0 23 N | 29 23 W |
| Saint Peter Port (capital) | Guernsey | 49 27 N | 2 32 W |
| Saint Petersburg (city; former capital) | Russia | 59 55 N | 30 15 E |
| Saint Thomas (island) | Virgin Islands | 18 21 N | 64 55 W |
| Saint Vincent Passage | Atlantic Ocean | 13 30 N | 61 00 W |
| Saint-Denis (regional capital) | France (Reunion) | 20 52 S | 55 28 E |
| Saint-Pierre (capital) | Saint Pierre and Miquelon | 46 46 N | 56 11 W |
| Saipan (island) | Northern Mariana Islands | 15 12 N | 145 45 E |
| Sak'art'velo (local name for Georgia) | Georgia | 42 00 N | 43 30 E |
| Sakhalin Island (Ostrov Sakhalin) | Russia | 51 00 N | 143 00 E |
| Sakishima Islands | Japan | 24 30 N | 124 00 E |

| NAME | ENTRY IN THE WORLD FACTBOOK | LATITUDE (DEG MIN) | LONGITUDE (DEG MIN) |
|---|---|---|---|
| Sala y Gomez, Isla (island) | Chile | 26 28 S | 105 00 W |
| Salisbury (city; former name for Harare) | Zimbabwe | 17 50 S | 105 00 W |
| Salzburg (city) | Austria | 47 48 N | 13 02 E |
| Samar (island) | Philippines | 12 00 N | 125 00 E |
| Samaria (region) | West Bank | 32 15 N | 35 10 E |
| Samoa Islands | American Samoa, Samoa | 14 00 S | 171 00 W |
| Samos (island) | Greece | 37 48 N | 26 44 E |
| San Ambrosio, Isla (island) | Chile | 26 21 S | 79 52 W |
| San Andres y Providencia, Archipielago (island group) | Colombia | 13 00 N | 81 30 W |
| San Bernardino Strait | Pacific Ocean | 12 32 N | 124 10 E |
| San Felix, Isla (island) | Chile | 26 17 S | 80 05 W |
| San Jose (capital) | Costa Rica | 9 56 N | 84 05 W |
| San Juan (capital) | Puerto Rico | 18 28 N | 66 07 W |
| San Marino (capital) | San Marino | 43 56 N | 12 25 E |
| San Salvador (capital) | El Salvador | 13 42 N | 89 12 W |
| Sanaa (capital) | Yemen | 15 21 N | 44 12 E |
| Sandzak (region) | Montenegro, Serbia | 43 05 N | 19 45 E |
| Santa Cruz (city) | Bolivia | 17 48 S | 63 10 W |
| Santa Cruz Islands | Solomon Islands | 11 00 S | 166 15 E |
| Santa Sede (local name for the Holy See) | Holy See | 41 54 N | 12 27 E |
| Santiago (capital) | Chile | 33 27 S | 70 40 W |
| Santo Antao (island) | Cabo Verde | 17 05 N | 25 10 W |
| Santo Domingo (capital) | Dominican Republic | 18 28 N | 69 54 W |
| Sao Paulo (city) | Brazil | 23 35 S | 46 43 W |
| Sao Pedro e Sao Paulo, Penedos de (rocks) | Brazil | 0 23 N | 29 23 W |
| Sao Tiago (island) | Cabo Verde | 15 05 N | 23 40 W |
| Sao Tome (island) | Sao Tome and Principe | 0 12 N | 6 39 E |
| Sapporo (city) | Japan | 43 04 N | 141 20 E |
| Sapudi Strait | Pacific Ocean | 7 05 S | 114 10 E |
| Sarajevo (capital) | Bosnia and Herzegovina | 43 52 N | 18 25 E |
| Sarawak (state) | Malaysia | 2 30 N | 113 30 E |
| Sardinia (island) | Italy | 40 00 N | 9 00 E |
| Sargasso Sea (region) | Atlantic Ocean | 30 00 N | 55 00 W |

| NAME | ENTRY IN THE WORLD FACTBOOK | LATITUDE (DEG MIN) | LONGITUDE (DEG MIN) |
|---|---|---|---|
| Sark (island) | Guernsey | 49 26 N | 2 21 W |
| Savage Island (former name for Niue) | Niue | 19 02 S | 169 52 W |
| Savu Sea | Pacific Ocean | 9 30 S | 122 00 E |
| Saxony (region) | Germany | 51 00 N | 13 00 E |
| Schleswig-Holstein (region) | Germany | 54 31 N | 9 33 E |
| Schweiz (local German name for Switzerland) | Switzerland | 47 00 N | 8 00 E |
| Scopus, Mount | Israel, West Bank | 31 48 N | 35 14 E |
| Scotia Sea | Atlantic Ocean, Southern Ocean | 56 00 S | 40 00 W |
| Scotland (region) | United Kingdom | 57 00 N | 4 00 W |
| Scott Island | Antarctica | 67 24 S | 179 55 W |
| Senegambia (region; former name of confederation of Senegal and The Gambia) | The Gambia, Senegal | 13 50 N | 15 25 W |
| Senyavin Islands | Federated States of Micronesia | 6 55 N | 158 00 E |
| Seoul (capital) | South Korea | 37 34 N | 127 00 E |
| Serendib (former name for Sri Lanka) | Sri Lanka | 7 00 N | 81 00 E |
| Serrana Bank (shoal) | Colombia | 14 25 N | 80 16 W |
| Serranilla Bank (shoal) | Colombia | 15 51 N | 79 46 W |
| Settlement, The (capital) | Christmas Island | 10 25 S | 105 43 E |
| Severnaya Zemlya (island group; also Northland) | Russia | 79 30 N | 98 00 E |
| Shaba (region) | Democratic Republic of the Congo | 8 00 S | 27 00 E |
| Shag Island | Heard Island and McDonald Islands | 53 00 S | 72 30 E |
| Shag Rocks | South Georgia and the South Sandwich Islands | 53 33 S | 42 02 W |
| Shanghai (city) | China | 31 14 N | 121 30 E |
| Shenyang (city; also Mukden) | China | 41 46 N | 123 24 E |
| Shetland Islands | United Kingdom | 60 30 N | 1 30 W |
| Shikoku (island) | Japan | 33 45 N | 133 30 E |
| Shikotan (island) | Russia (de facto) | 43 47 N | 146 45 E |
| Shqiperia (local name for Albania) | Albania | 41 00 N | 20 00 E |
| Siam (former name for Thailand) | Thailand | 15 00 N | 100 00 E |
| Siberia (region) | Russia | 60 00 N | 100 00 E |
| Sibutu Passage | Pacific Ocean | 4 50 N | 119 35 E |

| NAME | ENTRY IN THE WORLD FACTBOOK | LATITUDE (DEG MIN) | LONGITUDE (DEG MIN) |
|---|---|---|---|
| Sicily (island) | Italy | 37 30 N | 14 00 E |
| Sicily, Strait of | Atlantic Ocean | 37 20 N | 11 20 E |
| Sidra, Gulf of | Atlantic Ocean | 31 30 N | 18 00 E |
| Sikkim (state) | India | 27 50 N | 88 30 E |
| Silesia (region) | Czech Republic, Germany, Poland | 51 00 N | 17 00 E |
| Sinai Peninsula | Egypt | 29 30 N | 34 00 E |
| Singapore (capital) | Singapore | 1 17 N | 103 51 E |
| Singapore Strait | Pacific Ocean | 1 15 N | 104 00 E |
| Sinkiang (autonomous region; also Xinjiang) | China | 42 00 N | 86 00 E |
| Sint Eustatius (island) | Netherlands | 17 29 N | 62 58 W |
| Sint Maarten (island; also Saint-Martin) | Sint Maarten, Saint Martin | 18 04 N | 63 04 W |
| Sjaelland (island) | Denmark | 55 30 N | 12 00 E |
| Skagerrak (strait) | Atlantic Ocean | 57 45 N | 9 00 E |
| Skopje (capital) | Macedonia | 41 59 N | 21 26 E |
| Slavonia (region) | Croatia | 45 27 N | 18 00 E |
| Slovenija (local name for Slovenia) | Slovenia | 46 00 N | 15 00 E |
| Slovensko (local name for Slovakia) | Slovakia | 48 40 N | 19 30 E |
| Smyrna (region; former name for Izmir) | Turkey | 38 25 N | 27 10 E |
| Society Islands (Iles de la Societe) | French Polynesia | 17 00 S | 150 00 W |
| Socotra (island) | Yemen | 12 30 N | 54 00 E |
| Sofia (capital) | Bulgaria | 42 41 N | 23 19 E |
| Solomon Islands, northern | Papua New Guinea | 6 00 S | 155 00 E |
| Solomon Islands, southern | Solomon Islands | 8 00 S | 159 00 E |
| Solomon Sea | Pacific Ocean | 8 00 S | 153 00 E |
| Somaliland (region) | Somalia | 9 30 N | 46 00 E |
| Somers Islands (former name for Bermuda) | Bermuda | 32 20 N | 64 45 W |
| Songkhla (city) | Thailand | 7 12 N | 100 36 E |
| Sound, The (strait; also Oresund) | Atlantic Ocean | 55 50 N | 12 40 E |
| South Atlantic Ocean | Atlantic Ocean | 30 00 S | 15 00 W |
| South China Sea | Pacific Ocean | 10 00 N | 113 00 E |
| South Georgia (island) | South Georgia and the South Sandwich Islands | 54 15 S | 36 45 W |
| South Island | New Zealand | 43 00 S | 171 00 E |

| NAME | ENTRY IN THE WORLD FACTBOOK | LATITUDE (DEG MIN) | LONGITUDE (DEG MIN) |
| --- | --- | --- | --- |
| South Korea | South Korea | 37 00 N | 127 30 E |
| South Orkney Islands | Antarctica | 61 00 S | 45 00 W |
| South Ossetia (region) | Georgia | 42 20 N | 44 00 E |
| South Pacific Ocean | Pacific Ocean | 30 00 S | 130 00 W |
| South Sandwich Islands | South Georgia and the South Sandwich Islands | 57 45 S | 26 30 W |
| South Shetland Islands | Antarctica | 62 00 S | 59 00 W |
| South Tyrol (region) | Italy | 46 30 N | 10 30 E |
| South Vietnam (former name for the southern portion of Vietnam) | Vietnam | 12 00 N | 108 00 E |
| South Yemen (People's Democratic Republic of Yemen; now part of Yemen) | Yemen | 14 00 N | 48 00 E |
| South-West Africa (former name for Namibia) | Namibia | 22 00 S | 17 00 E |
| Southern Grenadines (island group) | Grenada | 12 20 N | 61 30 W |
| Southern Rhodesia (former name for Zimbabwe) | Zimbabwe | 20 00 S | 30 00 E |
| Soviet Union (former name of a large Eurasian empire, roughly coequal with the former Russian Empire) | Armenia, Azerbaijan, Belarus, Estonia, Georgia, Kazakhstan, Kyrgyzstan, Latvia, Lithuania, Moldova, Russia, Tajikistan, Turkmenistan, Ukraine, Uzbekistan | | |
| Spanish Guinea (former name for Equatorial Guinea) | Equatorial Guinea | 2 00 N | 10 00 E |
| Spanish Morocco (former name for northern Morocco) | Morocco | 32 00 N | 7 00 W |
| Spanish North Africa (exclaves) | Spain (Ceuta, Islas Chafarinas, Melilla, Penon de Alhucemas, Penon de Velez de la Gomera) | 35 15 N | 4 00 W |
| Spanish Sahara (former name) | Western Sahara | 24 30 N | 13 00 W |
| Spanish West Africa (former name for Ifni and Spanish Sahara) | Morocco, Western Sahara | 25 00 N | 13 00 W |
| Spice Islands (Moluccas) | Indonesia | 2 00 S | 28 00 E |
| Spitsbergen (island) | Svalbard | 78 00 N | 20 00 E |
| Srbija (local name for Serbia) | Serbia | 44 00 N | 21 00 E |
| St. John's (city) | Canada (Newfoundland) | 47 34 N | 52 43 W |
| Stanley (capital) | Falkland Islands (Islas Malvinas) | 51 42 S | 57 41 W |
| Stockholm (capital) | Sweden | 59 20 N | 18 03 E |

| NAME | ENTRY IN THE WORLD FACTBOOK | LATITUDE (DEG MIN) | LONGITUDE (DEG MIN) |
|---|---|---|---|
| Strasbourg (city) | France | 48 35 N | 7 44 E |
| Stuttgart (city) | Germany | 48 46 N | 9 11 E |
| Sucre (constitutional capital) | Bolivia | 19 02 S | 65 17 W |
| Suez Canal | Egypt | 29 55 N | 32 33 E |
| Suez, Gulf of | Indian Ocean | 28 10 N | 33 27 E |
| Suisse (local French name for Switzerland) | Switzerland | 47 00 N | 8 00 E |
| Sulawesi (island; Celebes) | Indonesia | 2 00 S | 121 00 E |
| Sulawesi Sea | Pacific Ocean | 3 00 N | 122 00 E |
| Sulu Archipelago (island group) | Philippines | 6 00 N | 121 00 E |
| Sulu Sea | Pacific Ocean | 8 00 N | 120 00 E |
| Sumatra (island) | Indonesia | 0 00 N | 102 00 E |
| Sumba (island) | Indonesia | 10 00 S | 120 00 E |
| Sumba Strait | Pacific Ocean | 9 10 S | 120 00 E |
| Sumbawa (island) | Indonesia | 8 30 S | 118 00 E |
| Sunda Islands (Soenda Isles) | Indonesia, Malaysia | 2 00 S | 110 00 E |
| Sunda Strait | Indian Ocean | 6 00 S | 105 45 E |
| Suomi (local name for Finland) | Finland | 64 00 N | 26 00 E |
| Surabaya (city) | Indonesia | 7 13 S | 112 45 E |
| Surigao Strait | Pacific Ocean | 10 15 N | 125 23 E |
| Surinam (former name for Suriname) | Suriname | 4 00 N | 56 00 W |
| Suriyah (local name for Syria) | Syria | 35 00 N | 38 00 E |
| Surtsey (volcanic island) | Iceland | 63 17 N | 20 40 W |
| Suva (capital) | Fiji | 18 08 S | 178 25 E |
| Sverdlovsk (city; also Yekaterinburg) | Russia | 56 50 N | 60 39 E |
| Sverige (local name for Sweden) | Sweden | 62 00 N | 15 00 E |
| Svizzera (local Italian name for Switzerland) | Switzerland | 47 00 N | 8 00 E |
| Swains Island | American Samoa | 11 03 S | 171 15 W |
| Swan Islands | Honduras | 17 25 S | 83 56 W |
| Sydney (city) | Australia | 33 53 S | 151 13 E |
| T'bilisi (capital) | Georgia | 41 43 N | 44 49 E |
| Tadzhikistan (former name for Tajikistan) | Tajikistan | 39 00 N | 71 00 E |
| Tahiti (island) | French Polynesia | 17 37 S | 149 27 W |
| Taipei (capital) | Taiwan | 25 03 N | 121 30 E |
| Taiwan Strait | Pacific Ocean | 24 00 N | 119 00 E |

| NAME | ENTRY IN THE WORLD FACTBOOK | LATITUDE (DEG MIN) | LONGITUDE (DEG MIN) |
|---|---|---|---|
| Tallinn (capital) | Estonia | 59 25 N | 24 45 E |
| Tanganyika (former name for the mainland portion of Tanzania) | Tanzania | 6 00 S | 35 00 E |
| Tangier (city) | Morocco | 35 48 N | 5 45 W |
| Tannu-Tuva (region) | Russia | 51 25 N | 94 45 E |
| Tarawa (island) | Kiribati | 1 25 N | 173 00 E |
| Tartary, Gulf of | Pacific Ocean | 50 00 N | 141 00 E |
| Tashkent (capital) | Uzbekistan | 41 20 N | 69 18 E |
| Tasman Sea | Pacific Ocean | 4 30 S | 168 00 E |
| Tasmania (island) | Australia | 43 00 S | 147 00 E |
| Tatar Strait | Pacific Ocean | 50 00 N | 141 00 E |
| Taymyr Peninsula (Poluostrov Taymyr) | Russia | 76 00 N | 104 00 E |
| Tchad (local name for Chad) | Chad | 15 00 N | 19 00 E |
| Tegucigalpa (capital) | Honduras | 14 06 N | 87 13 W |
| Tehran (capital) | Iran | 35 40 N | 51 26 E |
| Tel Aviv (capital, de facto) | Israel | 32 05 N | 34 48 E |
| Teluk Bone (gulf) | Pacific Ocean | 4 00 S | 120 45 E |
| Teluk Tomini (gulf) | Pacific Ocean | 0 30 S | 121 00 E |
| Terre Adelie (claimed by France; also Adelie Land) | Antarctica | 66 30 S | 139 00 E |
| Terres Australes et Antarctiques Francaises (local name for the French Southern and Antarctic Lands) | French Southern and Antarctic Lands | 43 00 S | 67 00 E |
| Thailand, Gulf of | Pacific Ocean | 10 00 N | 101 00 E |
| The Former Yugoslav Republic of Macedonia | Macedonia | 41 50 N | 22 00 E |
| Thessaloniki (city; also Salonika) | Greece | 40 38 N | 22 57 E |
| Thimphu (capital) | Bhutan | 27 28 N | 89 39 E |
| Thuringia (region) | Germany | 51 00 N | 11 00 E |
| Thurston Island | Antarctica | 72 20 S | 99 00 W |
| Tiberias, Lake | Israel | 32 48 N | 35 35 E |
| Tibet (autonomous region; also Xizang) | China | 32 00 N | 90 00 E |
| Tibilisi (see T'bilisi) | Georgia | 41 43 N | 44 49 E |
| Tien Shan (mountains) | China, Kyrgyzstan | 42 00 N | 80 00 E |
| Tierra del Fuego (island, island group) | Argentina, Chile | 54 00 S | 69 00 W |
| Timor (island) | Timor-Leste, Indonesia | 9 00 S | 125 00 E |

| NAME | ENTRY IN THE WORLD FACTBOOK | LATITUDE (DEG MIN) | LONGITUDE (DEG MIN) |
|---|---|---|---|
| Timor Lorosa'e (local name for Timor-Leste) | Timor-Leste | 9 00 N | 126 00 E |
| Timor Sea | Pacific Ocean | 11 00 S | 128 00 E |
| Tinian (island) | Northern Mariana Islands | 15 00 N | 145 38 E |
| Tiran, Strait of | Indian Ocean | 28 00 N | 34 27 E |
| Tirana, Tirane (capital) | Albania | 41 20 N | 19 50 E |
| Tirol, Tyrol (region) | Austria, Italy | 47 00 N | 11 00 E |
| Tobago (island) | Trinidad and Tobago | 11 15 N | 60 40 W |
| Tokyo (capital) | Japan | 35 42 N | 139 46 E |
| Tonkin, Gulf of | Pacific Ocean | 20 00 N | 108 00 E |
| Toronto (city) | Canada | 43 40 N | 79 23 W |
| Torres Strait | Pacific Ocean | 10 25 S | 142 10 E |
| Torshavn (capital) | Faroe Islands | 62 01 N | 6 46 W |
| Toshkent (see Tashkent) | Uzbekistan | 41 20 N | 69 18 E |
| Transcarpathia (region; alternate name for Carpatho-Ukraine) | Ukraine | 48 22 N | 23 32 E |
| Transjordan (former name for Jordan) | Jordan | 31 00 N | 36 00 E |
| Transkei (enclave) | South Africa | 32 15 S | 28 15 E |
| Transvaal (region; former name for northeastern South Africa) | South Africa | 25 10 S | 29 25 E |
| Transylvania (region) | Romania | 46 30 N | 24 00 E |
| Trindade, Ilha de (island) | Brazil | 20 31 S | 29 20 W |
| Trinidad (island) | Trinidad and Tobago | 10 22 N | 61 15 W |
| Tripoli (capital) | Libya | 32 54 N | 13 11 E |
| Tripoli (city) | Lebanon | 34 26 N | 35 51 E |
| Tripolitania (region) | Libya | 31 00 N | 14 00 E |
| Tristan da Cunha Group (island group) | Saint Helena, Ascension, and Tristan da Cunha | 37 15 S | 12 30 W |
| Trobriand Islands | Papua New Guinea | 8 38 S | 151 04 E |
| Tromelin Island | Indian Ocean | 15 52 S | 54 25 E |
| Trucial Coast (former name for the United Arab Emirates) | United Arab Emirates | 24 00 N | 54 00 E |
| Trucial Oman (former name for the United Arab Emirates) | United Arab Emirates | 24 00 N | 54 00 E |
| Trucial States (former name for the United Arab Emirates) | United Arab Emirates | 24 00 N | 54 00 E |

| NAME | ENTRY IN THE WORLD FACTBOOK | LATITUDE (DEG MIN) | LONGITUDE (DEG MIN) |
|---|---|---|---|
| Truk Islands (former name for the Chuuk Islands) | Federated States of Micronesia | 7 25 N | 151 47 E |
| Tsugaru Strait | Pacific Ocean | 41 35 N | 141 00 E |
| Tuamotu Islands (Iles Tuamotu) | French Polynesia | 19 00 S | 142 00 W |
| Tubuai Islands (Iles Tubuai) | French Polynesia | 23 00 S | 150 00 W |
| Tunb al Kubra (island) | Iran | 26 14 N | 55 19 E |
| Tunb as Sughra (island) | Iran | 26 14 N | 55 09 E |
| Tunis (capital) | Tunisia | 36 48 N | 10 11 E |
| Turin (city) | Italy | 45 04 N | 7 40 E |
| Turkish Straits (see Bosporus and Dardenelles) | Atlantic Ocean | 40 40 N | 28 00 E |
| Turkiye (local name for Turkey) | Turkey | 39 00 N | 35 00 E |
| Turkmenia, Turkmeniya (former name for Turkmenistan) | Turkmenistan | 40 00 N | 60 00 E |
| Turks Island Passage | Atlantic Ocean | 21 40 N | 71 00 W |
| Tuscany (region) | Italy | 43 25 N | 11 00 E |
| Tutuila (island) | American Samoa | 14 18 S | 170 42 W |
| Tyrrhenian Sea | Atlantic Ocean | 40 00 N | 12 00 E |
| Ubangi-Shari (former name for the Central African Republic | Central African Republic | 6 38 N | 20 33 E |
| Ukrayina (local name for Ukraine) | Ukraine | 49 00 N | 32 00 E |
| Ulaanbaatar (capital) | Mongolia | 47 55 N | 106 53 E |
| Ullung-do (island) | South Korea | 37 29 N | 130 52 E |
| Ulster (region) | Ireland, United Kingdom | 54 35 N | 7 00 W |
| Uman (local name for Oman) | Oman | 21 00 N | 57 00 E |
| Unimak Pass (strait) | Pacific Ocean | 54 20 N | 164 50 W |
| Union of Soviet Socialist Republics or USSR (former name of a large Eurasian empire, roughly coequal with the former Russian Empire) | Armenia, Azerbaijan, Belarus, Estonia, Georgia, Kazakhstan, Kyrgyzstan, Latvia, Lithuania, Moldova, Russia, Tajikistan, Turkmenistan, Ukraine, Uzbekistan | | |
| United Arab Republic or UAR (former name for a federation between Egypt and Syria) | Egypt, Syria | | |
| Upper Volta (former name for Burkina Faso) | Burkina Faso | 13 00 N | 2 00 W |
| Ural Mountains | Kazakhstan, Russia | 60 00 N | 60 00 E |
| Urdunn (local name for Jordan) | Jordan | 31 00 N | 36 00 E |

| NAME | ENTRY IN THE WORLD FACTBOOK | LATITUDE (DEG MIN) | LONGITUDE (DEG MIN) |
| --- | --- | --- | --- |
| Urundi (former name for Burundi) | Burundi | 3 30 S | 30 00 E |
| Ussuri River | China, Russia | 48 28 N | 135 02 E |
| Vaduz (capital) | Liechtenstein | 47 09 N | 9 31 E |
| Vakhan (Wakhan Corridor) | Afghanistan | 37 00 N | 73 00 E |
| Valletta (capital) | Malta | 35 54 N | 14 31 E |
| Valley, The (capital) | Anguilla | 18 13 N | 63 04 W |
| Van Diemen Strait (Osumi Strait) | Pacific Ocean | 31 00 N | 131 00 E |
| Vancouver (city) | Canada | 49 16 N | 123 08 W |
| Vancouver Island | Canada | 49 45 N | 126 00 W |
| Vatican City (capital) | Holy See | 41 54 N | 12 27 E |
| Velez de la Gomera, Penon de (island) | Spain | 35 11 N | 4 18 W |
| Venda (enclave) | South Africa | 23 00 S | 31 00 E |
| Verde Island Passage | Pacific Ocean | 13 34 N | 120 51 E |
| Victoria (capital) | Seychelles | 4 38 S | 55 27 E |
| Victoria (island) | Canada | 71 00 N | 110 00 W |
| Victoria Land (region) | Antarctica | 72 00 S | 155 00 E |
| Vienna (capital) | Austria | 48 12 N | 16 22 E |
| Vientiane (capital) | Laos | 17 58 N | 102 36 E |
| Vilnius (capital) | Lithuania | 54 41 N | 25 19 E |
| Viti Levu (island) | Fiji | 18 00 S | 178 00 E |
| Vladivostok (city) | Russia | 43 10 N | 131 56 E |
| Vojvodina (region) | Serbia | 45 35 N | 20 00 E |
| Volcano Islands | Japan | 25 00 N | 141 00 E |
| Vostok Island | Kiribati | 10 06 S | 152 23 W |
| Wake Atoll | Wake Island | 19 17 N | 166 39 E |
| Wakhan Corridor (see Vakhan) | Afghanistan | 37 00 N | 73 00 E |
| Walachia (region) | Romania | 44 45 N | 26 05 E |
| Wales (region) | United Kingdom | 52 30 N | 3 30 W |
| Wallis Islands | Wallis and Futuna | 13 17 S | 176 10 W |
| Walvis Bay (city; former exclave) | Namibia | 22 59 S | 14 31 E |
| Warsaw (capital) | Poland | 52 15 N | 21 00 E |
| Washington, DC (capital) | United States | 38 53 N | 77 02 W |
| Weddell Sea | Southern Ocean | 72 00 S | 45 00 W |
| Wellington (capital) | New Zealand | 41 28 S | 174 51 E |

| NAME | ENTRY IN THE WORLD FACTBOOK | LATITUDE (DEG MIN) | LONGITUDE (DEG MIN) |
|---|---|---|---|
| West Frisian Islands | Netherlands | 53 26 N | 5 30 E |
| West Germany (Federal Republic of Germany; former name for western portion of Germany) | Germany | 53 22 N | 5 20 E |
| West Island (capital) | Cocos (Keeling) Islands | 12 10 S | 96 55 E |
| West Korea Strait (Western Channel) | Pacific Ocean | 34 40 N | 129 00 E |
| West Pakistan (former name for present-day Pakistan) | Pakistan | 30 00 N | 70 00 E |
| West Siberian Plain | Russia | 60 00 N | 75 00 E |
| Western Channel (West Korea Strait) | Pacific Ocean | 34 40 N | 129 00 E |
| Western Samoa (former name for Samoa) | Samoa | 13 35 S | 172 20 W |
| Wetar Strait | Pacific Ocean | 8 20 S | 126 30 E |
| White Sea | Arctic Ocean | 65 30 N | 38 00 E |
| Wilkes Land (region) | Antarctica | 71 00 S | 120 00 E |
| Willemstad (capital) | Curacao | 12 06 N | 68 56 W |
| Windhoek (capital) | Namibia | 22 34 S | 17 06 E |
| Windward Passage | Atlantic Ocean | 20 00 N | 73 50 W |
| Winnipeg (city) | Canada | 49 53 N | 97 10 W |
| Wrangel Island (Ostrov Vrangelya) | Russia | 71 14 N | 179 36 W |
| Xianggang (local name for Hong Kong) | Hong Kong | 22 15 N | 114 10 E |
| Y'israel (local name for Israel) | Israel | 31 30 N | 34 45 E |
| Yaitopya (local name for Ethiopia) | Ethiopia | 8 00 N | 38 00 E |
| Yalu River | China, North Korea | 39 55 N | 124 20 E |
| Yamoussoukro (capital) | Cote d'Ivoire | 6 49 N | 5 17 W |
| Yangon (see Rangoon) | Burma | 16 47 N | 96 10 E |
| Yaounde (capital) | Cameroon | 3 52 N | 11 31 E |
| Yap Islands | Federated States of Micronesia | 9 30 N | 138 00 E |
| Yaren (governmental center) | Nauru | 0 32 S | 166 55 E |
| Yekaterinburg (city; formerly Sverdlovsk) | Russia | 56 50 N | 60 39 E |
| Yellow Sea | Pacific Ocean | 36 00 N | 123 00 E |
| Yemen Arab Republic (also Yemen (Sanaa); former name for northern portion of Yemen) | Yemen | 15 00 N | 44 00 E |
| Yemen, People's Democratic Republic of (also Yemen (Aden); former name for southern portion of Yemen) | Yemen | 14 00 N | 46 00 E |
| Yerevan (capital) | Armenia | 40 11 N | 44 30 E |

| NAME | ENTRY IN THE WORLD FACTBOOK | LATITUDE (DEG MIN) | LONGITUDE (DEG MIN) |
|---|---|---|---|
| Yokohama (city) | Japan | 35 26 N | 139 37 E |
| Youth, Isle of (Isla de la Juventud) | Cuba | 21 40 N | 82 50 W |
| Yucatan Channel | Atlantic Ocean | 21 45 N | 85 45 W |
| Yucatan Peninsula | Mexico | 19 30 N | 89 00 W |
| Yugoslavia (former name for a federation of Serbia and Montenegro) | Montenegro, Serbia | 43 00 N | 21 00 E |
| Yugoslavia, Kingdom of (former name for a Balkan federation) | Bosnia and Herzegovina, Croatia, Macedonia, Montenegro, Serbia, Slovenia | 43 00 N | 19 00 E |
| Yugoslavia, Socialist Federal Republic of (former name for a Balkan federation) | Bosnia and Herzegovina, Croatia, Macedonia, Montenegro, Serbia, Slovenia | 43 00 N | 19 00 E |
| Zagreb (capital) | Croatia | 45 48 N | 15 58 E |
| Zaire (former name for the Democratic Republic of the Congo) | Democratic Republic of the Congo | 15 00 S | 30 00 E |
| Zakhalinskiy Zaliv (bay) | Pacific Ocean | 54 00 N | 142 00 E |
| Zaliv Shelikhova (bay) | Pacific Ocean | 60 00 N | 157 30 E |
| Zambezia (region) | Mozambique | 16 00 S | 37 00 E |
| Zanzibar (island) | Tanzania | 6 10 S | 39 11 E |
| Zhong Guo, Zhonghua (local name for China) | China | 35 00 N | 105 00 E |
| Zion, Mount (locale in Jerusalem) | Israel, West Bank | 31 46 N | 35 14 E |
| Zurich (city) | Switzerland | 47 23 N | 8 32 E |

# APPENDIX G :: WEIGHTS AND MEASURES

**Note:** At this time, only three countries - Burma, Liberia, and the US - have not adopted the International System of Units (SI, or metric system) as their official system of weights and measures. Although use of the metric system has been sanctioned by law in the US since 1866, it has been slow in displacing the American adaptation of the British Imperial System known as the US Customary System. The US is the only industrialized nation that does not mainly use the metric system in its commercial and standards activities, but there is increasing acceptance in science, medicine, government, and many sectors of industry.

## Mathematical Notation

| MATHEMATICAL POWER | NAME |
|---|---|
| $10^{18}$ or 1,000,000,000,000,000,000 | one quintillion |
| $10^{15}$ or 1,000,000,000,000,000 | one quadrillion |
| $10^{12}$ or 1,000,000,000,000 | one trillion |
| $10^{9}$ or 1,000,000,000 | one billion |
| $10^{6}$ or 1,000,000 | one million |
| $10^{3}$ or 1,000 | one thousand |
| $10^{2}$ or 100 | one hundred |
| $10^{1}$ or 10 | ten |
| $10^{0}$ or 1 | one |
| $10^{-1}$ or 0.1 | one-tenth |
| $10^{-2}$ or 0.01 | one-hundredth |
| $10^{-3}$ or 0.001 | one-thousandth |
| $10^{-6}$ or 0.000 001 | one-millionth |
| $10^{-9}$ or 0.000 000 001 | one-billionth |
| $10^{-12}$ or 0.000 000 000 001 | one-trillionth |
| $10^{-15}$ or 0.000 000 000 000 001 | one-quadrillionth |
| $10^{-18}$ or 0.000 000 000 000 000 001 | one-quintillionth |

## Metric Interrelationships

| PREFIX | SYMBOL | LENGTH, WEIGHT, OR CAPACITY |
|---|---|---|
| yotta | Y | $10^{24}$ |
| zetta | Z | $10^{21}$ |
| exa | E | $10^{18}$ |
| peta | P | $10^{15}$ |
| tera | T | $10^{12}$ |
| giga | G | $10^{9}$ |
| mega | M | $10^{6}$ |

| PREFIX | SYMBOL | LENGTH, WEIGHT, OR CAPACITY |
|---|---|---|
| kilo | k | $10^3$ |
| hecto | h | $10^2$ |
| deka | da | $10^1$ |
| basic unit | - | 1 meter, 1 gram, 1 liter |
| deci | d | $10^{-1}$ |
| centi | c | $10^{-2}$ |
| milli | m | $10^{-3}$ |
| micro | u | $10^{-6}$ |
| nano | n | $10^{-9}$ |
| pico | p | $10^{-12}$ |
| femto | f | $10^{-15}$ |
| atto | a | $10^{-18}$ |
| zepto | z | $10^{-21}$ |
| yocto | y | $10^{-24}$ |

**Conversion Factors**

| TO CONVERT FROM | TO | MULTIPLY BY |
|---|---|---|
| acres | ares | 40.468 564 224 |
| acres | hectares | 0.404 685 642 24 |
| acres | square feet | 43,560 |
| acres | square kilometers | 0.004 046 856 422 4 |
| acres | square meters | 4,046.856 422 4 |
| acres | square miles (statute) | 0.001 562 50 |
| acres | square yards | 4,840 |
| ares | square meters | 100 |
| ares | square yards | 119.599 |
| barrels, US beer | gallons | 31 |
| barrels, US beer | liters | 117.347 77 |
| barrels, US petroleum | gallons (British) | 34.97 |
| barrels, US petroleum | gallons (US) | 42 |
| barrels, US petroleum | liters | 158.987 29 |
| barrels, US proof spirits | gallons | 40 |
| barrels, US proof spirits | liters | 151.416 47 |
| bushels (US) | bushels (British) | 0.968 9 |
| bushels (US) | cubic feet | 1.244 456 |

| TO CONVERT FROM | TO | MULTIPLY BY |
|---|---|---|
| bushels (US) | cubic inches | 2,150.42 |
| bushels (US) | cubic meters | 0.035 239 07 |
| bushels (US) | cubic yards | 0.046 090 96 |
| bushels (US) | dekaliters | 3.523 907 |
| bushels (US) | dry pints | 64 |
| bushels (US) | dry quarts | 32 |
| bushels (US) | liters | 35.239 070 17 |
| bushels (US) | pecks | 4 |
| cables | fathoms | 120 |
| cables | meters | 219.456 |
| cables | yards | 240 |
| carat | milligrams | 200 |
| centimeters | feet | 0.032 808 40 |
| centimeters | inches | 0.393 700 8 |
| centimeters | meters | 0.01 |
| centimeters | yards | 0.010 936 13 |
| centimeters, cubic | cubic inches | 0.061 023 744 |
| centimeters, square | square feet | 0.001 076 39 |
| centimeters, square | square inches | 0.155 000 31 |
| centimeters, square | square meters | 0.000 1 |
| centimeters, square | square yards | 0.000 119 599 |
| chains, square surveyor's | ares | 4.046 86 |
| chains, square surveyor's | square feet | 4,356 |
| chains, surveyor's | feet | 66 |
| chains, surveyor's | meters | 20.116 8 |
| chains, surveyor's | rods | 4 |
| cords of wood | cubic feet | 128 |
| cords of wood | cubic meters | 3.624 556 |
| cords of wood | cubic yards | 4.740 7 |
| cups | liquid ounces (US) | 8 |
| cups | liters | 0.236 588 2 |
| degrees Celsius | degrees Fahrenheit | multiply by 1.8 and add 32 |
| degrees Fahrenheit | degrees Celsius | subtract 32 and divide by 1.8 |
| dekaliters | bushels | 0.283 775 9 |

| TO CONVERT FROM | TO | MULTIPLY BY |
|---|---|---|
| dekaliters | cubic feet | 0.353 146 7 |
| dekaliters | cubic inches | 610.237 4 |
| dekaliters | dry pints | 18.161 66 |
| dekaliters | dry quarts | 9.080 829 8 |
| dekaliters | liters | 10 |
| dekaliters | pecks | 1.135 104 |
| drams, avoirdupois | avoirdupois ounces | 0.062 55 |
| drams, avoirdupois | grains | 27.344 |
| drams, avoirdupois | grams | 1.771 845 2 |
| drams, troy | grains | 60 |
| drams, troy | grams | 3.887 934 6 |
| drams, troy | scruples | 3 |
| drams, troy | troy ounces | 0.125 |
| drams, liquid (US) | cubic inches | 0.226 |
| drams, liquid (US) | liquid drams (British) | 1.041 |
| drams, liquid (US) | liquid ounces | 0.125 |
| drams, liquid (US) | milliliters | 3.696 69 |
| drams, liquid (US) | minims | 60 |
| fathoms | feet | 6 |
| fathoms | meters | 1.828 8 |
| feet | centimeters | 30.48 |
| feet | inches | 12 |
| feet | kilometers | 0.000 304 8 |
| feet | meters | 0.304 8 |
| feet | statute miles | 0.000 189 39 |
| feet | yards | 0.333 333 3 |
| feet, cubic | bushels | 0.803 563 95 |
| feet, cubic | cubic decimeters | 28.316 847 |
| feet, cubic | cubic inches | 1,728 |
| feet, cubic | cubic meters | 0.028 316 846 592 |
| feet, cubic | cubic yards | 0.037 037 04 |
| feet, cubic | dry pints | 51.428 09 |
| feet, cubic | dry quarts | 25.714 05 |
| feet, cubic | gallons | 7.480 519 |

| TO CONVERT FROM | TO | MULTIPLY BY |
| --- | --- | --- |
| feet, cubic | gills | 239.376 6 |
| feet, cubic | liquid ounces | 957.506 5 |
| feet, cubic | liquid pints | 59.844 16 |
| feet, cubic | liquid quarts | 29.922 08 |
| feet, cubic | liters | 28.316 846 592 |
| feet, cubic | pecks | 3.214 256 |
| feet, square | acres | 0.000 022 956 8 |
| feet, square | square centimeters | 929.030 4 |
| feet, square | square decimeters | 9.290 304 |
| feet, square | square inches | 144 |
| feet, square | square meters | 0.092 903 04 |
| feet, square | square yards | 0.111 111 1 |
| furlongs | feet | 660 |
| furlongs | inches | 7,920 |
| furlongs | meters | 201.168 |
| furlongs | statute miles | 0.125 |
| furlongs | yards | 220 |
| gallons, liquid (US) | cubic feet | 0.133 680 6 |
| gallons, liquid (US) | cubic inches | 231 |
| gallons, liquid (US) | cubic meters | 0.003 785 411 784 |
| gallons, liquid (US) | cubic yards | 0.004 951 13 |
| gallons, liquid (US) | gills (US) | 32 |
| gallons, liquid (US) | liquid gallons (British) | 0.832 67 |
| gallons, liquid (US) | liquid ounces | 128 |
| gallons, liquid (US) | liquid pints | 8 |
| gallons, liquid (US) | liquid quarts | 4 |
| gallons, liquid (US) | liters | 3.785 411 784 |
| gallons, liquid (US) | milliliters | 3,785.411 784 |
| gallons, liquid (US) | minims | 61,440 |
| gills (US) | centiliters | 11.829 4 |
| gills (US) | cubic feet | 0.004 177 517 |
| gills (US) | cubic inches | 7.218 75 |
| gills (US) | gallons | 0.031 25 |
| gills (US) | gills (British) | 0.832 67 |

| TO CONVERT FROM | TO | MULTIPLY BY |
| --- | --- | --- |
| gills (US) | liquid ounces | 4 |
| gills (US) | liquid pints | 0.25 |
| gills (US) | liquid quarts | 0.125 |
| gills (US) | liters | 0.118 294 118 25 |
| gills (US) | milliliters | 118.294 118 25 |
| gills (US) | minims | 1,920 |
| grains | avoirdupois drams | 0.036 571 43 |
| grains | avoirdupois ounces | 0.002 285 71 |
| grains | avoirdupois pounds | 0.000 142 86 |
| grains | grams | 0.064 798 91 |
| grains | kilograms | 0.000 064 798 91 |
| grains | milligrams | 64.798 910 |
| grains | pennyweights | 0.042 |
| grains | scruples | 0.05 |
| grains | troy drams | 0.016 6 |
| grains | troy ounces | 0.002 083 33 |
| grains | troy pounds | 0.000 200 61 |
| grams | avoirdupois drams | 0.564 383 39 |
| grams | avoirdupois ounces | 0.035 273 961 |
| grams | avoirdupois pounds | 0.002 204 622 6 |
| grams | grains | 15.432 361 |
| grams | kilograms | 0.001 |
| grams | milligrams | 1,000 |
| grams | troy ounces | 0.032 150 746 6 |
| grams | troy pounds | 0.002 679 23 |
| hands (height of horse) | centimeters | 10.16 |
| hands (height of horse) | inches | 4 |
| hectares | acres | 2.471 053 8 |
| hectares | square feet | 107,639.1 |
| hectares | square kilometers | 0.01 |
| hectares | square meters | 10,000 |
| hectares | square miles | 0.003 861 02 |
| hectares | square yards | 11,959.90 |
| hundredweights, long | avoirdupois pounds | 112 |

| TO CONVERT FROM | TO | MULTIPLY BY |
| --- | --- | --- |
| hundredweights, long | kilograms | 50.802 345 |
| hundredweights, long | long tons | 0.05 |
| hundredweights, long | metric tons | 0.050 802 345 |
| hundredweights, long | short tons | 0.056 |
| hundredweights, short | avoirdupois pounds | 100 |
| hundredweights, short | kilograms | 45.359 237 |
| hundredweights, short | long tons | 0.044 642 86 |
| hundredweights, short | metric tons | 0.045 359 237 |
| hundredweights, short | short tons | 0.05 |
| inches | centimeters | 2.54 |
| inches | feet | 0.083 333 33 |
| inches | meters | 0.025 4 |
| inches | millimeters | 25.4 |
| inches | yards | 0.027 777 78 |
| inches, cubic | bushels | 0.000 465 025 |
| inches, cubic | cubic centimeters | 16.387 064 |
| inches, cubic | cubic feet | 0.000 578 703 7 |
| inches, cubic | cubic meters | 0.000 016 387 064 |
| inches, cubic | cubic yards | 0.000 021 433 47 |
| inches, cubic | dry pints | 0.029 761 6 |
| inches, cubic | dry quarts | 0.014 880 8 |
| inches, cubic | gallons | 0.004 329 0 |
| inches, cubic | gills | 0.138 528 1 |
| inches, cubic | liquid ounces | 0.554 112 6 |
| inches, cubic | liquid pints | 0.034 632 03 |
| inches, cubic | liquid quarts | 0.017 316 02 |
| inches, cubic | liters | 0.016 387 064 |
| inches, cubic | milliliters | 16.387 064 |
| inches, cubic | minims (US) | 265.974 0 |
| inches, cubic | pecks | 0.001 860 10 |
| inches, square | square centimeters | 6.451 600 |
| inches, square | square feet | 0.006 944 44 |
| inches, square | square meters | 0.000 645 16 |
| inches, square | square yards | 0.000 771 605 |

| TO CONVERT FROM | TO | MULTIPLY BY |
|---|---|---|
| kilograms | avoirdupois drams | 564.383 4 |
| kilograms | avoirdupois ounces | 35.273 962 |
| kilograms | avoirdupois pounds | 2.204 622 622 |
| kilograms | grains | 15,432.36 |
| kilograms | grams | 1,000 |
| kilograms | long tons | 0.000 984 2 |
| kilograms | metric tons | 0.001 |
| kilograms | short hundredweights | 0.022 046 23 |
| kilograms | short tons | 0.001 102 31 |
| kilograms | troy ounces | 32.150 75 |
| kilograms | troy pounds | 2.679 229 |
| kilometers | meters | 1,000 |
| kilometers | statute miles | 0.621 371 192 |
| kilometers, square | acres | 247.105 38 |
| kilometers, square | hectares | 100 |
| kilometers, square | square meters | 1,000,000 |
| kilometers, square | statute miles | 0.386 102 16 |
| knots (nautical mi/hr) | kilometers/hour | 1.852 |
| knots (nautical mi/hr) | statute miles/hour | 1.151 |
| leagues, nautical | kilometers | 5.556 |
| leagues, nautical | nautical miles | 3 |
| leagues, statute | kilometers | 4.828 032 |
| leagues, statute | statute miles | 3 |
| links, square surveyor's | square centimeters | 404.686 |
| links, square surveyor's | square inches | 62.726 4 |
| links, surveyor's | centimeters | 20.116 8 |
| links, surveyor's | chains | 0.01 |
| links, surveyor's | inches | 7.92 |
| liters | bushels | 0.028 377 59 |
| liters | cubic feet | 0.035 314 67 |
| liters | cubic inches | 61.023 74 |
| liters | cubic meters | 0.001 |
| liters | cubic yards | 0.001 307 95 |
| liters | dekaliters | 0.1 |

| TO CONVERT FROM | TO | MULTIPLY BY |
|---|---|---|
| liters | dry pints | 1.816 166 |
| liters | dry quarts | 0.908 082 98 |
| liters | gallons | 0.264 172 052 |
| liters | gills (US) | 8.453 506 |
| liters | liquid ounces | 33.814 02 |
| liters | liquid pints | 2.113 376 |
| liters | liquid quarts | 1.056 688 2 |
| liters | milliliters | 1,000 |
| liters | pecks | 0.113 510 4 |
| meters | centimeters | 100 |
| meters | feet | 3.280 839 895 |
| meters | inches | 39.370 079 |
| meters | kilometers | 0.001 |
| meters | millimeters | 1,000 |
| meters | statute miles | 0.000 621 371 |
| meters | yards | 1.093 613 298 |
| meters, cubic | bushels | 28.377 59 |
| meters, cubic | cubic feet | 35.314 666 7 |
| meters, cubic | cubic inches | 61,023.744 |
| meters, cubic | cubic yards | 1.307 950 619 |
| meters, cubic | gallons | 264.172 05 |
| meters, cubic | liters | 1,000 |
| meters, cubic | pecks | 113.510 4 |
| meters, square | acres | 0.000 247 105 38 |
| meters, square | hectares | 0.000 1 |
| meters, square | square centimeters | 10,000 |
| meters, square | square feet | 10.763 910 4 |
| meters, square | square inches | 1,550.003 1 |
| meters, square | square yards | 1.195 990 046 |
| microns | meters | 0.000 001 |
| microns | inches | 0.000 039 4 |
| mils | inches | 0.001 |
| mils | millimeters | 0.025 4 |
| miles, nautical | kilometers | 1.852 0 |

| TO CONVERT FROM | TO | MULTIPLY BY |
|---|---|---|
| miles, nautical | statute miles | 1.150 779 4 |
| miles, statute | centimeters | 160,934.4 |
| miles, statute | feet | 5,280 |
| miles, statute | furlongs | 8 |
| miles, statute | inches | 63,360 |
| miles, statute | kilometers | 1.609 344 |
| miles, statute | meters | 1,609.344 |
| miles, statute | rods | 320 |
| miles, statute | yards | 1,760 |
| miles, square nautical | square kilometers | 3.429 904 |
| miles, square nautical | square statute miles | 1.325 |
| miles, square statute | acres | 640 |
| miles, square statute | hectares | 258.998 811 033 6 |
| miles, square statute | sections | 1 |
| miles, square statute | square feet | 27,878,400 |
| miles, square statute | square kilometers | 2.589 988 110 336 |
| miles, square statute | square meters | 2,589,988.110 336 |
| miles, square statute | square nautical miles | 0.755 miles |
| miles, square statute | square rods | 102,400 |
| miles, square statute | square yards | 3,097,600 |
| milligrams | grains | 0.015 432 358 35 |
| milliliters | cubic inches | 0.061 023 744 |
| milliliters | gallons | 0.000 264 17 |
| milliliters | gills (US) | 0.008 453 5 |
| milliliters | liquid ounces | 0.033 814 02 |
| milliliters | liquid pints | 0.002 113 4 |
| milliliters | liquid quarts | 0.001 056 7 |
| milliliters | liters | 0.001 |
| milliliters | minims | 16.230 73 |
| millimeters | inches | 0.039 370 078 7 |
| minims (US) | cubic inches | 0.003 759 77 |
| minims (US) | gills (US) | 0.000 520 83 |
| minims (US) | liquid ounces | 0.002 083 33 |
| minims (US) | milliliters | 0.061 611 52 |

| TO CONVERT FROM | TO | MULTIPLY BY |
| --- | --- | --- |
| minims (US) | minims (British) | 1.041 |
| ounces, avoirdupois | avoirdupois drams | 16 |
| ounces, avoirdupois | avoirdupois pounds | 0.062 5 |
| ounces, avoirdupois | grains | 437.5 |
| ounces, avoirdupois | grams | 28.349 523 125 |
| ounces, avoirdupois | kilograms | 0.028 349 523 125 |
| ounces, avoirdupois | troy ounces | 0.911 458 3 |
| ounces, avoirdupois | troy pounds | 0.075 954 86 |
| ounces, liquid (US) | cubic feet | 0.001 044 38 |
| ounces, liquid (US) | centiliters | 2.957 35 |
| ounces, liquid (US) | cubic inches | 1.804 687 5 |
| ounces, liquid (US) | gallons | 0.007 812 5 |
| ounces, liquid (US) | gills (US) | 0.25 |
| ounces, liquid (US) | liquid drams | 8 |
| ounces, liquid (US) | liquid ounces (British) | 1.041 |
| ounces, liquid (US) | liquid pints | 0.062 5 |
| ounces, liquid (US) | liquid quarts | 0.031 25 |
| ounces, liquid (US) | liters | 0.029 573 53 |
| ounces, liquid (US) | milliliters | 29.573 529 6 |
| ounces, liquid (US) | minims | 480 |
| ounces, troy | avoirdupois drams | 17.554 29 |
| ounces, troy | avoirdupois ounces | 1.097 143 |
| ounces, troy | avoirdupois pounds | 0.068 571 43 |
| ounces, troy | grains | 480 |
| ounces, troy | grams | 31.103 476 8 |
| ounces, troy | pennyweights | 20 |
| ounces, troy | troy drams | 8 |
| ounces, troy | troy pounds | 0.083 333 3 |
| paces (US) | centimeters | 76.2 |
| paces (US) | inches | 30 |
| pecks (US) | bushels | 0.25 |
| pecks (US) | cubic feet | 0.311 114 |
| pecks (US) | cubic inches | 537.605 |
| pecks (US) | cubic meters | 0.008 809 77 |

| TO CONVERT FROM | TO | MULTIPLY BY |
| --- | --- | --- |
| pecks (US) | cubic yards | 0.011 522 74 |
| pecks (US) | dekaliters | 0.880 976 75 |
| pecks (US) | dry pints | 16 |
| pecks (US) | dry quarts | 8 |
| pecks (US) | liters | 8.809 767 5 |
| pecks (US) | pecks (British) | 0.968 9 |
| pennyweights | grains | 24 |
| pennyweights | grams | 1.555 200 84 |
| pennyweights | troy ounces | 0.05 |
| pints, dry (US) | bushels | 0.015 625 |
| pints, dry (US) | cubic feet | 0.019 444 63 |
| pints, dry (US) | cubic inches | 33.600 312 5 |
| pints, dry (US) | dekaliters | 0.055 061 05 |
| pints, dry (US) | dry pints (British) | 0.968 9 |
| pints, dry (US) | dry quarts | 0.5 |
| pints, dry (US) | liters | 0.550 610 47 |
| pints, liquid (US) | cubic feet | 0.016 710 07 |
| pints, liquid (US) | cubic inches | 28.875 |
| pints, liquid (US) | deciliters | 4.731 76 |
| pints, liquid (US) | gallons | 0.125 |
| pints, liquid (US) | gills (US) | 4 |
| pints, liquid (US) | liquid ounces | 16 |
| pints, liquid (US) | liquid pints (British) | 0.832 67 |
| pints, liquid (US) | liquid quarts | 0.5 |
| pints, liquid (US) | liters | 0.473 176 473 |
| pints, liquid (US) | milliliters | 473.176 473 |
| pints, liquid (US) | minims | 7,680 |
| points (typographical) | inches | 0.013 837 |
| points (typographical) | millimeters | 0.351 459 8 |
| pounds, avoirdupois | avoirdupois drams | 256 |
| pounds, avoirdupois | avoirdupois ounces | 16 |
| pounds, avoirdupois | grains | 7,000 |
| pounds, avoirdupois | grams | 453.592 37 |
| pounds, avoirdupois | kilograms | 0.453 592 37 |

| TO CONVERT FROM | TO | MULTIPLY BY |
|---|---|---|
| pounds, avoirdupois | long tons | 0.000 446 428 6 |
| pounds, avoirdupois | metric tons | 0.000 453 592 37 |
| pounds, avoirdupois | quintals | 0.004 535 92 |
| pounds, avoirdupois | short tons | 0.000 5 |
| pounds, avoirdupois | troy ounces | 14.583 33 |
| pounds, avoirdupois | troy pounds | 1.215 278 |
| pounds, troy | avoirdupois drams | 210.651 4 |
| pounds, troy | avoirdupois ounces | 13.165 71 |
| pounds, troy | avoirdupois pounds | 0.822 857 1 |
| pounds, troy | grains | 5,760 |
| pounds, troy | grams | 373.241 721 6 |
| pounds, troy | kilograms | 0.373 241 721 6 |
| pounds, troy | pennyweights | 240 |
| pounds, troy | troy ounces | 12 |
| quarts, dry (US) | bushels | 0.031 25 |
| quarts, dry (US) | cubic feet | 0.038 889 25 |
| quarts, dry (US) | cubic inches | 67.200 625 |
| quarts, dry (US) | dekaliters | 0.110 122 1 |
| quarts, dry (US) | dry pints | 2 |
| quarts, dry (US) | dry quarts (British) | 0.968 9 |
| quarts, dry (US) | liters | 1.101 221 |
| quarts, dry (US) | pecks | 0.125 |
| quarts, dry (US) | pints, dry (US) | 2 |
| quarts, liquid (US) | cubic feet | 0.033 420 14 |
| quarts, liquid (US) | cubic inches | 57.75 |
| quarts, liquid (US) | deciliters | 9.463 53 |
| quarts, liquid (US) | gallons | 0.25 |
| quarts, liquid (US) | gills (US) | 8 |
| quarts, liquid (US) | liquid ounces | 32 |
| quarts, liquid (US) | liquid pints (US) | 2 |
| quarts, liquid (US) | liquid quarts (British) | 0.832 67 |
| quarts, liquid (US) | liters | 0.946 352 946 |
| quarts, liquid (US) | milliliters | 946.352 946 |
| quarts, liquid (US) | minims | 15,360 |

| TO CONVERT FROM | TO | MULTIPLY BY |
|---|---|---|
| quintals | avoirdupois pounds | 220.462 26 |
| quintals | kilograms | 100 |
| quintals | metric tons | 0.1 |
| rods | feet | 16.5 |
| rods | meters | 5.029 2 |
| rods | yards | 5.5 |
| rods, square | acres | 0.006 25 |
| rods, square | square meters | 25.292 85 |
| rods, square | square yards | 30.25 |
| scruples | grains | 20 |
| scruples | grams | 1.295 978 2 |
| scruples | troy drams | 0.333 |
| sections (US) | square kilometers | 2.589 988 1 |
| sections (US) | square statute miles | 1 |
| spans | centimeters | 22.86 |
| spans | inches | 9 |
| steres | cubic meters | 1 |
| steres | cubic yards | 1.307 95 |
| tablespoons | milliliters | 14.786 76 |
| tablespoons | teaspoons | 3 |
| teaspoons | milliliters | 4.928 922 |
| teaspoons | tablespoons | 0.333 333 |
| ton-miles, long | metric ton-kilometers | 1.635 169 |
| ton-miles, short | metric ton-kilometers | 1.459 972 |
| tons, gross register | cubic feet of permanently enclosed space | 100 |
| tons, gross register | cubic meters of permanently enclosed space | 2.831 684 7 |
| tons, long (deadweight) | avoirdupois ounces | 35,840 |
| tons, long (deadweight) | avoirdupois pounds | 2,240 |
| tons, long (deadweight) | kilograms | 1,016.046 909 8 |
| tons, long (deadweight) | long hundredweights | 20 |
| tons, long (deadweight) | metric tons | 1.016 046 908 8 |
| tons, long (deadweight) | short hundredweights | 22.4 |
| tons, long (deadweight) | short tons | 1.12 |
| tons, metric | avoirdupois pounds | 2,204.623 |

| TO CONVERT FROM | TO | MULTIPLY BY |
| --- | --- | --- |
| tons, metric | kilograms | 1,000 |
| tons, metric | long hundredweights | 19.684 130 3 |
| tons, metric | long tons | 0.984 206 5 |
| tons, metric | quintals | 10 |
| tons, metric | short hundredweights | 22.046 23 |
| tons, metric | short tons | 1.102 311 3 |
| tons, metric | troy ounces | 32,150.75 |
| tons, net register | cubic feet of permanently enclosed space for cargo and passengers | 100 |
| tons, net register | cubic meters of permanently enclosed space for cargo and passengers | 2.831 684 7 |
| tons, shipping | cubic feet of permanently enclosed cargo space | 42 |
| tons, shipping | cubic meters of permanently enclosed cargo space | 1.189 307 574 |
| tons, short | avoirdupois pounds | 2,000 |
| tons, short | kilograms | 907.184 74 |
| tons, short | long hundredweights | 17.857 14 |
| tons, short | long tons | 0.892 857 1 |
| tons, short | metric tons | 0.907 184 74 |
| tons, short | short hundredweights | 20 |
| townships (US) | sections | 36 |
| townships (US) | square kilometers | 93.239 572 |
| townships (US) | square statute miles | 36 |
| yards | centimeters | 91.44 |
| yards | feet | 3 |
| yards | inches | 36 |
| yards | meters | 0.914 4 |
| yards | miles | 0.000 568 18 |
| yards, cubic | bushels | 21.696 227 |
| yards, cubic | cubic feet | 27 |
| yards, cubic | cubic inches | 46,656 |
| yards, cubic | cubic meters | 0.764 554 857 984 |
| yards, cubic | gallons | 201.974 0 |
| yards, cubic | liters | 764.554 857 984 |
| yards, cubic | pecks | 86.784 91 |
| yards, square | acres | 0.000 206 611 6 |

| TO CONVERT FROM | TO | MULTIPLY BY |
|---|---|---|
| yards, square | hectares | 0.000 083 612 736 |
| yards, square | square centimeters | 8,361.273 6 |
| yards, square | square feet | 9 |
| yards, square | square inches | 1,296 |
| yards, square | square meters | 0.836 127 36 |
| yards, square | square miles | 0.000 000 322 830 6 |

**Note:** At this time, only three countries - Burma, Liberia, and the US - have not adopted the International System of Units (SI, or metric system) as their official system of weights and measures. Although use of the metric system has been sanctioned by law in the US since 1866, it has been slow in displacing the American adaptation of the British Imperial System known as the US Customary System. The US is the only industrialized nation that does not mainly use the metric system in its commercial and standards activities, but there is increasing acceptance in science, medicine, government, and many sectors of industry.

## Mathematical Notation

| MATHEMATICAL POWER | NAME |
|---|---|
| $10^{18}$ or 1,000,000,000,000,000,000 | one quintillion |
| $10^{15}$ or 1,000,000,000,000,000 | one quadrillion |
| $10^{12}$ or 1,000,000,000,000 | one trillion |
| $10^{9}$ or 1,000,000,000 | one billion |
| $10^{6}$ or 1,000,000 | one million |
| $10^{3}$ or 1,000 | one thousand |
| $10^{2}$ or 100 | one hundred |
| $10^{1}$ or 10 | ten |
| $10^{0}$ or 1 | one |
| $10^{-1}$ or 0.1 | one-tenth |
| $10^{-2}$ or 0.01 | one-hundredth |
| $10^{-3}$ or 0.001 | one-thousandth |
| $10^{-6}$ or 0.000 001 | one-millionth |
| $10^{-9}$ or 0.000 000 001 | one-billionth |
| $10^{-12}$ or 0.000 000 000 001 | one-trillionth |
| $10^{-15}$ or 0.000 000 000 000 001 | one-quadrillionth |
| $10^{-18}$ or 0.000 000 000 000 000 001 | one-quintillionth |

## Metric Interrelationships

| PREFIX | SYMBOL | LENGTH, WEIGHT, OR CAPACITY |
|---|---|---|
| yotta | Y | $10^{24}$ |
| zetta | Z | $10^{21}$ |
| exa | E | $10^{18}$ |
| peta | P | $10^{15}$ |
| tera | T | $10^{12}$ |

| PREFIX | SYMBOL | LENGTH, WEIGHT, OR CAPACITY |
|---|---|---|
| giga | G | $10^9$ |
| mega | M | $10^6$ |
| kilo | k | $10^3$ |
| hecto | h | $10^2$ |
| deka | da | $10^1$ |
| basic unit | - | 1 meter, 1 gram, 1 liter |
| deci | d | $10^{-1}$ |
| centi | c | $10^{-2}$ |
| milli | m | $10^{-3}$ |
| micro | u | $10^{-6}$ |
| nano | n | $10^{-9}$ |
| pico | p | $10^{-12}$ |
| femto | f | $10^{-15}$ |
| atto | a | $10^{-18}$ |
| zepto | z | $10^{-21}$ |
| yocto | y | $10^{-24}$ |

**Conversion Factors**

| TO CONVERT FROM | TO | MULTIPLY BY |
|---|---|---|
| acres | ares | 40.468 564 224 |
| acres | hectares | 0.404 685 642 24 |
| acres | square feet | 43,560 |
| acres | square kilometers | 0.004 046 856 422 4 |
| acres | square meters | 4,046.856 422 4 |
| acres | square miles (statute) | 0.001 562 50 |
| acres | square yards | 4,840 |
| ares | square meters | 100 |
| ares | square yards | 119.599 |
| barrels, US beer | gallons | 31 |
| barrels, US beer | liters | 117.347 77 |
| barrels, US petroleum | gallons (British) | 34.97 |
| barrels, US petroleum | gallons (US) | 42 |
| barrels, US petroleum | liters | 158.987 29 |
| barrels, US proof spirits | gallons | 40 |
| barrels, US proof spirits | liters | 151.416 47 |
| bushels (US) | bushels (British) | 0.968 9 |
| bushels (US) | cubic feet | 1.244 456 |
| bushels (US) | cubic inches | 2,150.42 |
| bushels (US) | cubic meters | 0.035 239 07 |
| bushels (US) | cubic yards | 0.046 090 96 |

| TO CONVERT FROM | TO | MULTIPLY BY |
|---|---|---|
| bushels (US) | dekaliters | 3.523 907 |
| bushels (US) | dry pints | 64 |
| bushels (US) | dry quarts | 32 |
| bushels (US) | liters | 35.239 070 17 |
| bushels (US) | pecks | 4 |
| cables | fathoms | 120 |
| cables | meters | 219.456 |
| cables | yards | 240 |
| carat | milligrams | 200 |
| centimeters | feet | 0.032 808 40 |
| centimeters | inches | 0.393 700 8 |
| centimeters | meters | 0.01 |
| centimeters | yards | 0.010 936 13 |
| centimeters, cubic | cubic inches | 0.061 023 744 |
| centimeters, square | square feet | 0.001 076 39 |
| centimeters, square | square inches | 0.155 000 31 |
| centimeters, square | square meters | 0.000 1 |
| centimeters, square | square yards | 0.000 119 599 |
| chains, square surveyor's | ares | 4.046 86 |
| chains, square surveyor's | square feet | 4,356 |
| chains, surveyor's | feet | 66 |
| chains, surveyor's | meters | 20.116 8 |
| chains, surveyor's | rods | 4 |
| cords of wood | cubic feet | 128 |
| cords of wood | cubic meters | 3.624 556 |
| cords of wood | cubic yards | 4.740 7 |
| cups | liquid ounces (US) | 8 |
| cups | liters | 0.236 588 2 |
| degrees Celsius | degrees Fahrenheit | multiply by 1.8 and add 32 |
| degrees Fahrenheit | degrees Celsius | subtract 32 and divide by 1.8 |
| dekaliters | bushels | 0.283 775 9 |
| dekaliters | cubic feet | 0.353 146 7 |
| dekaliters | cubic inches | 610.237 4 |
| dekaliters | dry pints | 18.161 66 |
| dekaliters | dry quarts | 9.080 829 8 |
| dekaliters | liters | 10 |
| dekaliters | pecks | 1.135 104 |
| drams, avoirdupois | avoirdupois ounces | 0.062 55 |
| drams, avoirdupois | grains | 27.344 |

| TO CONVERT FROM | TO | MULTIPLY BY |
|---|---|---|
| drams, avoirdupois | grams | 1.771 845 2 |
| drams, troy | grains | 60 |
| drams, troy | grams | 3.887 934 6 |
| drams, troy | scruples | 3 |
| drams, troy | troy ounces | 0.125 |
| drams, liquid (US) | cubic inches | 0.226 |
| drams, liquid (US) | liquid drams (British) | 1.041 |
| drams, liquid (US) | liquid ounces | 0.125 |
| drams, liquid (US) | milliliters | 3.696 69 |
| drams, liquid (US) | minims | 60 |
| fathoms | feet | 6 |
| fathoms | meters | 1.828 8 |
| feet | centimeters | 30.48 |
| feet | inches | 12 |
| feet | kilometers | 0.000 304 8 |
| feet | meters | 0.304 8 |
| feet | statute miles | 0.000 189 39 |
| feet | yards | 0.333 333 3 |
| feet, cubic | bushels | 0.803 563 95 |
| feet, cubic | cubic decimeters | 28.316 847 |
| feet, cubic | cubic inches | 1,728 |
| feet, cubic | cubic meters | 0.028 316 846 592 |
| feet, cubic | cubic yards | 0.037 037 04 |
| feet, cubic | dry pints | 51.428 09 |
| feet, cubic | dry quarts | 25.714 05 |
| feet, cubic | gallons | 7.480 519 |
| feet, cubic | gills | 239.376 6 |
| feet, cubic | liquid ounces | 957.506 5 |
| feet, cubic | liquid pints | 59.844 16 |
| feet, cubic | liquid quarts | 29.922 08 |
| feet, cubic | liters | 28.316 846 592 |
| feet, cubic | pecks | 3.214 256 |
| feet, square | acres | 0.000 022 956 8 |
| feet, square | square centimeters | 929.030 4 |
| feet, square | square decimeters | 9.290 304 |
| feet, square | square inches | 144 |
| feet, square | square meters | 0.092 903 04 |
| feet, square | square yards | 0.111 111 1 |
| furlongs | feet | 660 |

| TO CONVERT FROM | TO | MULTIPLY BY |
| --- | --- | --- |
| furlongs | inches | 7,920 |
| furlongs | meters | 201.168 |
| furlongs | statute miles | 0.125 |
| furlongs | yards | 220 |
| gallons, liquid (US) | cubic feet | 0.133 680 6 |
| gallons, liquid (US) | cubic inches | 231 |
| gallons, liquid (US) | cubic meters | 0.003 785 411 784 |
| gallons, liquid (US) | cubic yards | 0.004 951 13 |
| gallons, liquid (US) | gills (US) | 32 |
| gallons, liquid (US) | liquid gallons (British) | 0.832 67 |
| gallons, liquid (US) | liquid ounces | 128 |
| gallons, liquid (US) | liquid pints | 8 |
| gallons, liquid (US) | liquid quarts | 4 |
| gallons, liquid (US) | liters | 3.785 411 784 |
| gallons, liquid (US) | milliliters | 3,785.411 784 |
| gallons, liquid (US) | minims | 61,440 |
| gills (US) | centiliters | 11.829 4 |
| gills (US) | cubic feet | 0.004 177 517 |
| gills (US) | cubic inches | 7.218 75 |
| gills (US) | gallons | 0.031 25 |
| gills (US) | gills (British) | 0.832 67 |
| gills (US) | liquid ounces | 4 |
| gills (US) | liquid pints | 0.25 |
| gills (US) | liquid quarts | 0.125 |
| gills (US) | liters | 0.118 294 118 25 |
| gills (US) | milliliters | 118.294 118 25 |
| gills (US) | minims | 1,920 |
| grains | avoirdupois drams | 0.036 571 43 |
| grains | avoirdupois ounces | 0.002 285 71 |
| grains | avoirdupois pounds | 0.000 142 86 |
| grains | grams | 0.064 798 91 |
| grains | kilograms | 0.000 064 798 91 |
| grains | milligrams | 64.798 910 |
| grains | pennyweights | 0.042 |
| grains | scruples | 0.05 |
| grains | troy drams | 0.016 6 |
| grains | troy ounces | 0.002 083 33 |
| grains | troy pounds | 0.000 200 61 |
| grams | avoirdupois drams | 0.564 383 39 |

| TO CONVERT FROM | TO | MULTIPLY BY |
| --- | --- | --- |
| grams | avoirdupois ounces | 0.035 273 961 |
| grams | avoirdupois pounds | 0.002 204 622 6 |
| grams | grains | 15.432 361 |
| grams | kilograms | 0.001 |
| grams | milligrams | 1,000 |
| grams | troy ounces | 0.032 150 746 6 |
| grams | troy pounds | 0.002 679 23 |
| hands (height of horse) | centimeters | 10.16 |
| hands (height of horse) | inches | 4 |
| hectares | acres | 2.471 053 8 |
| hectares | square feet | 107,639.1 |
| hectares | square kilometers | 0.01 |
| hectares | square meters | 10,000 |
| hectares | square miles | 0.003 861 02 |
| hectares | square yards | 11,959.90 |
| hundredweights, long | avoirdupois pounds | 112 |
| hundredweights, long | kilograms | 50.802 345 |
| hundredweights, long | long tons | 0.05 |
| hundredweights, long | metric tons | 0.050 802 345 |
| hundredweights, long | short tons | 0.056 |
| hundredweights, short | avoirdupois pounds | 100 |
| hundredweights, short | kilograms | 45.359 237 |
| hundredweights, short | long tons | 0.044 642 86 |
| hundredweights, short | metric tons | 0.045 359 237 |
| hundredweights, short | short tons | 0.05 |
| inches | centimeters | 2.54 |
| inches | feet | 0.083 333 33 |
| inches | meters | 0.025 4 |
| inches | millimeters | 25.4 |
| inches | yards | 0.027 777 78 |
| inches, cubic | bushels | 0.000 465 025 |
| inches, cubic | cubic centimeters | 16.387 064 |
| inches, cubic | cubic feet | 0.000 578 703 7 |
| inches, cubic | cubic meters | 0.000 016 387 064 |
| inches, cubic | cubic yards | 0.000 021 433 47 |
| inches, cubic | dry pints | 0.029 761 6 |
| inches, cubic | dry quarts | 0.014 880 8 |
| inches, cubic | gallons | 0.004 329 0 |
| inches, cubic | gills | 0.138 528 1 |

| TO CONVERT FROM | TO | MULTIPLY BY |
| --- | --- | --- |
| inches, cubic | liquid ounces | 0.554 112 6 |
| inches, cubic | liquid pints | 0.034 632 03 |
| inches, cubic | liquid quarts | 0.017 316 02 |
| inches, cubic | liters | 0.016 387 064 |
| inches, cubic | milliliters | 16.387 064 |
| inches, cubic | minims (US) | 265.974 0 |
| inches, cubic | pecks | 0.001 860 10 |
| inches, square | square centimeters | 6.451 600 |
| inches, square | square feet | 0.006 944 44 |
| inches, square | square meters | 0.000 645 16 |
| inches, square | square yards | 0.000 771 605 |
| kilograms | avoirdupois drams | 564.383 4 |
| kilograms | avoirdupois ounces | 35.273 962 |
| kilograms | avoirdupois pounds | 2.204 622 622 |
| kilograms | grains | 15,432.36 |
| kilograms | grams | 1,000 |
| kilograms | long tons | 0.000 984 2 |
| kilograms | metric tons | 0.001 |
| kilograms | short hundredweights | 0.022 046 23 |
| kilograms | short tons | 0.001 102 31 |
| kilograms | troy ounces | 32.150 75 |
| kilograms | troy pounds | 2.679 229 |
| kilometers | meters | 1,000 |
| kilometers | statute miles | 0.621 371 192 |
| kilometers, square | acres | 247.105 38 |
| kilometers, square | hectares | 100 |
| kilometers, square | square meters | 1,000,000 |
| kilometers, square | statute miles | 0.386 102 16 |
| knots (nautical mi/hr) | kilometers/hour | 1.852 |
| knots (nautical mi/hr) | statute miles/hour | 1.151 |
| leagues, nautical | kilometers | 5.556 |
| leagues, nautical | nautical miles | 3 |
| leagues, statute | kilometers | 4.828 032 |
| leagues, statute | statute miles | 3 |
| links, square surveyor's | square centimeters | 404.686 |
| links, square surveyor's | square inches | 62.726 4 |
| links, surveyor's | centimeters | 20.116 8 |
| links, surveyor's | chains | 0.01 |
| links, surveyor's | inches | 7.92 |

| TO CONVERT FROM | TO | MULTIPLY BY |
| --- | --- | --- |
| liters | bushels | 0.028 377 59 |
| liters | cubic feet | 0.035 314 67 |
| liters | cubic inches | 61.023 74 |
| liters | cubic meters | 0.001 |
| liters | cubic yards | 0.001 307 95 |
| liters | dekaliters | 0.1 |
| liters | dry pints | 1.816 166 |
| liters | dry quarts | 0.908 082 98 |
| liters | gallons | 0.264 172 052 |
| liters | gills (US) | 8.453 506 |
| liters | liquid ounces | 33.814 02 |
| liters | liquid pints | 2.113 376 |
| liters | liquid quarts | 1.056 688 2 |
| liters | milliliters | 1,000 |
| liters | pecks | 0.113 510 4 |
| meters | centimeters | 100 |
| meters | feet | 3.280 839 895 |
| meters | inches | 39.370 079 |
| meters | kilometers | 0.001 |
| meters | millimeters | 1,000 |
| meters | statute miles | 0.000 621 371 |
| meters | yards | 1.093 613 298 |
| meters, cubic | bushels | 28.377 59 |
| meters, cubic | cubic feet | 35.314 666 7 |
| meters, cubic | cubic inches | 61,023.744 |
| meters, cubic | cubic yards | 1.307 950 619 |
| meters, cubic | gallons | 264.172 05 |
| meters, cubic | liters | 1,000 |
| meters, cubic | pecks | 113.510 4 |
| meters, square | acres | 0.000 247 105 38 |
| meters, square | hectares | 0.000 1 |
| meters, square | square centimeters | 10,000 |
| meters, square | square feet | 10.763 910 4 |
| meters, square | square inches | 1,550.003 1 |
| meters, square | square yards | 1.195 990 046 |
| microns | meters | 0.000 001 |
| microns | inches | 0.000 039 4 |
| mils | inches | 0.001 |
| mils | millimeters | 0.025 4 |

| TO CONVERT FROM | TO | MULTIPLY BY |
|---|---|---|
| miles, nautical | kilometers | 1.852 0 |
| miles, nautical | statute miles | 1.150 779 4 |
| miles, statute | centimeters | 160,934.4 |
| miles, statute | feet | 5,280 |
| miles, statute | furlongs | 8 |
| miles, statute | inches | 63,360 |
| miles, statute | kilometers | 1.609 344 |
| miles, statute | meters | 1,609.344 |
| miles, statute | rods | 320 |
| miles, statute | yards | 1,760 |
| miles, square nautical | square kilometers | 3.429 904 |
| miles, square nautical | square statute miles | 1.325 |
| miles, square statute | acres | 640 |
| miles, square statute | hectares | 258.998 811 033 6 |
| miles, square statute | sections | 1 |
| miles, square statute | square feet | 27,878,400 |
| miles, square statute | square kilometers | 2.589 988 110 336 |
| miles, square statute | square meters | 2,589,988.110 336 |
| miles, square statute | square nautical miles | 0.755 miles |
| miles, square statute | square rods | 102,400 |
| miles, square statute | square yards | 3,097,600 |
| milligrams | grains | 0.015 432 358 35 |
| milliliters | cubic inches | 0.061 023 744 |
| milliliters | gallons | 0.000 264 17 |
| milliliters | gills (US) | 0.008 453 5 |
| milliliters | liquid ounces | 0.033 814 02 |
| milliliters | liquid pints | 0.002 113 4 |
| milliliters | liquid quarts | 0.001 056 7 |
| milliliters | liters | 0.001 |
| milliliters | minims | 16.230 73 |
| millimeters | inches | 0.039 370 078 7 |
| minims (US) | cubic inches | 0.003 759 77 |
| minims (US) | gills (US) | 0.000 520 83 |
| minims (US) | liquid ounces | 0.002 083 33 |
| minims (US) | milliliters | 0.061 611 52 |
| minims (US) | minims (British) | 1.041 |
| ounces, avoirdupois | avoirdupois drams | 16 |
| ounces, avoirdupois | avoirdupois pounds | 0.062 5 |
| ounces, avoirdupois | grains | 437.5 |

| TO CONVERT FROM | TO | MULTIPLY BY |
|---|---|---|
| ounces, avoirdupois | grams | 28.349 523 125 |
| ounces, avoirdupois | kilograms | 0.028 349 523 125 |
| ounces, avoirdupois | troy ounces | 0.911 458 3 |
| ounces, avoirdupois | troy pounds | 0.075 954 86 |
| ounces, liquid (US) | cubic feet | 0.001 044 38 |
| ounces, liquid (US) | centiliters | 2.957 35 |
| ounces, liquid (US) | cubic inches | 1.804 687 5 |
| ounces, liquid (US) | gallons | 0.007 812 5 |
| ounces, liquid (US) | gills (US) | 0.25 |
| ounces, liquid (US) | liquid drams | 8 |
| ounces, liquid (US) | liquid ounces (British) | 1.041 |
| ounces, liquid (US) | liquid pints | 0.062 5 |
| ounces, liquid (US) | liquid quarts | 0.031 25 |
| ounces, liquid (US) | liters | 0.029 573 53 |
| ounces, liquid (US) | milliliters | 29.573 529 6 |
| ounces, liquid (US) | minims | 480 |
| ounces, troy | avoirdupois drams | 17.554 29 |
| ounces, troy | avoirdupois ounces | 1.097 143 |
| ounces, troy | avoirdupois pounds | 0.068 571 43 |
| ounces, troy | grains | 480 |
| ounces, troy | grams | 31.103 476 8 |
| ounces, troy | pennyweights | 20 |
| ounces, troy | troy drams | 8 |
| ounces, troy | troy pounds | 0.083 333 3 |
| paces (US) | centimeters | 76.2 |
| paces (US) | inches | 30 |
| pecks (US) | bushels | 0.25 |
| pecks (US) | cubic feet | 0.311 114 |
| pecks (US) | cubic inches | 537.605 |
| pecks (US) | cubic meters | 0.008 809 77 |
| pecks (US) | cubic yards | 0.011 522 74 |
| pecks (US) | dekaliters | 0.880 976 75 |
| pecks (US) | dry pints | 16 |
| pecks (US) | dry quarts | 8 |
| pecks (US) | liters | 8.809 767 5 |
| pecks (US) | pecks (British) | 0.968 9 |
| pennyweights | grains | 24 |
| pennyweights | grams | 1.555 200 84 |
| pennyweights | troy ounces | 0.05 |

| TO CONVERT FROM | TO | MULTIPLY BY |
|---|---|---|
| pints, dry (US) | bushels | 0.015 625 |
| pints, dry (US) | cubic feet | 0.019 444 63 |
| pints, dry (US) | cubic inches | 33.600 312 5 |
| pints, dry (US) | dekaliters | 0.055 061 05 |
| pints, dry (US) | dry pints (British) | 0.968 9 |
| pints, dry (US) | dry quarts | 0.5 |
| pints, dry (US) | liters | 0.550 610 47 |
| pints, liquid (US) | cubic feet | 0.016 710 07 |
| pints, liquid (US) | cubic inches | 28.875 |
| pints, liquid (US) | deciliters | 4.731 76 |
| pints, liquid (US) | gallons | 0.125 |
| pints, liquid (US) | gills (US) | 4 |
| pints, liquid (US) | liquid ounces | 16 |
| pints, liquid (US) | liquid pints (British) | 0.832 67 |
| pints, liquid (US) | liquid quarts | 0.5 |
| pints, liquid (US) | liters | 0.473 176 473 |
| pints, liquid (US) | milliliters | 473.176 473 |
| pints, liquid (US) | minims | 7,680 |
| points (typographical) | inches | 0.013 837 |
| points (typographical) | millimeters | 0.351 459 8 |
| pounds, avoirdupois | avoirdupois drams | 256 |
| pounds, avoirdupois | avoirdupois ounces | 16 |
| pounds, avoirdupois | grains | 7,000 |
| pounds, avoirdupois | grams | 453.592 37 |
| pounds, avoirdupois | kilograms | 0.453 592 37 |
| pounds, avoirdupois | long tons | 0.000 446 428 6 |
| pounds, avoirdupois | metric tons | 0.000 453 592 37 |
| pounds, avoirdupois | quintals | 0.004 535 92 |
| pounds, avoirdupois | short tons | 0.000 5 |
| pounds, avoirdupois | troy ounces | 14.583 33 |
| pounds, avoirdupois | troy pounds | 1.215 278 |
| pounds, troy | avoirdupois drams | 210.651 4 |
| pounds, troy | avoirdupois ounces | 13.165 71 |
| pounds, troy | avoirdupois pounds | 0.822 857 1 |
| pounds, troy | grains | 5,760 |
| pounds, troy | grams | 373.241 721 6 |
| pounds, troy | kilograms | 0.373 241 721 6 |
| pounds, troy | pennyweights | 240 |
| pounds, troy | troy ounces | 12 |

| TO CONVERT FROM | TO | MULTIPLY BY |
| --- | --- | --- |
| quarts, dry (US) | bushels | 0.031 25 |
| quarts, dry (US) | cubic feet | 0.038 889 25 |
| quarts, dry (US) | cubic inches | 67.200 625 |
| quarts, dry (US) | dekaliters | 0.110 122 1 |
| quarts, dry (US) | dry pints | 2 |
| quarts, dry (US) | dry quarts (British) | 0.968 9 |
| quarts, dry (US) | liters | 1.101 221 |
| quarts, dry (US) | pecks | 0.125 |
| quarts, dry (US) | pints, dry (US) | 2 |
| quarts, liquid (US) | cubic feet | 0.033 420 14 |
| quarts, liquid (US) | cubic inches | 57.75 |
| quarts, liquid (US) | deciliters | 9.463 53 |
| quarts, liquid (US) | gallons | 0.25 |
| quarts, liquid (US) | gills (US) | 8 |
| quarts, liquid (US) | liquid ounces | 32 |
| quarts, liquid (US) | liquid pints (US) | 2 |
| quarts, liquid (US) | liquid quarts (British) | 0.832 67 |
| quarts, liquid (US) | liters | 0.946 352 946 |
| quarts, liquid (US) | milliliters | 946.352 946 |
| quarts, liquid (US) | minims | 15,360 |
| quintals | avoirdupois pounds | 220.462 26 |
| quintals | kilograms | 100 |
| quintals | metric tons | 0.1 |
| rods | feet | 16.5 |
| rods | meters | 5.029 2 |
| rods | yards | 5.5 |
| rods, square | acres | 0.006 25 |
| rods, square | square meters | 25.292 85 |
| rods, square | square yards | 30.25 |
| scruples | grains | 20 |
| scruples | grams | 1.295 978 2 |
| scruples | troy drams | 0.333 |
| sections (US) | square kilometers | 2.589 988 1 |
| sections (US) | square statute miles | 1 |
| spans | centimeters | 22.86 |
| spans | inches | 9 |
| steres | cubic meters | 1 |
| steres | cubic yards | 1.307 95 |
| tablespoons | milliliters | 14.786 76 |

| TO CONVERT FROM | TO | MULTIPLY BY |
| --- | --- | --- |
| tablespoons | teaspoons | 3 |
| teaspoons | milliliters | 4.928 922 |
| teaspoons | tablespoons | 0.333 333 |
| ton-miles, long | metric ton-kilometers | 1.635 169 |
| ton-miles, short | metric ton-kilometers | 1.459 972 |
| tons, gross register | cubic feet of permanently enclosed space | 100 |
| tons, gross register | cubic meters of permanently enclosed space | 2.831 684 7 |
| tons, long (deadweight) | avoirdupois ounces | 35,840 |
| tons, long (deadweight) | avoirdupois pounds | 2,240 |
| tons, long (deadweight) | kilograms | 1,016.046 909 8 |
| tons, long (deadweight) | long hundredweights | 20 |
| tons, long (deadweight) | metric tons | 1.016 046 908 8 |
| tons, long (deadweight) | short hundredweights | 22.4 |
| tons, long (deadweight) | short tons | 1.12 |
| tons, metric | avoirdupois pounds | 2,204.623 |
| tons, metric | kilograms | 1,000 |
| tons, metric | long hundredweights | 19.684 130 3 |
| tons, metric | long tons | 0.984 206 5 |
| tons, metric | quintals | 10 |
| tons, metric | short hundredweights | 22.046 23 |
| tons, metric | short tons | 1.102 311 3 |
| tons, metric | troy ounces | 32,150.75 |
| tons, net register | cubic feet of permanently enclosed space for cargo and passengers | 100 |
| tons, net register | cubic meters of permanently enclosed space for cargo and passengers | 2.831 684 7 |
| tons, shipping | cubic feet of permanently enclosed cargo space | 42 |
| tons, shipping | cubic meters of permanently enclosed cargo space | 1.189 307 574 |
| tons, short | avoirdupois pounds | 2,000 |
| tons, short | kilograms | 907.184 74 |
| tons, short | long hundredweights | 17.857 14 |
| tons, short | long tons | 0.892 857 1 |
| tons, short | metric tons | 0.907 184 74 |
| tons, short | short hundredweights | 20 |
| townships (US) | sections | 36 |
| townships (US) | square kilometers | 93.239 572 |
| townships (US) | square statute miles | 36 |
| yards | centimeters | 91.44 |
| yards | feet | 3 |
| yards | inches | 36 |

| TO CONVERT FROM | TO | MULTIPLY BY |
|---|---|---|
| yards | meters | 0.914 4 |
| yards | miles | 0.000 568 18 |
| yards, cubic | bushels | 21.696 227 |
| yards, cubic | cubic feet | 27 |
| yards, cubic | cubic inches | 46,656 |
| yards, cubic | cubic meters | 0.764 554 857 984 |
| yards, cubic | gallons | 201.974 0 |
| yards, cubic | liters | 764.554 857 984 |
| yards, cubic | pecks | 86.784 91 |
| yards, square | acres | 0.000 206 611 6 |
| yards, square | hectares | 0.000 083 612 736 |
| yards, square | square centimeters | 8,361.273 6 |
| yards, square | square feet | 9 |
| yards, square | square inches | 1,296 |
| yards, square | square meters | 0.836 127 36 |
| yards, square | square miles | 0.000 000 322 830 6 |

Made in the USA
San Bernardino, CA
26 March 2019